THE BLOOD ROYAL
OF BRITAIN

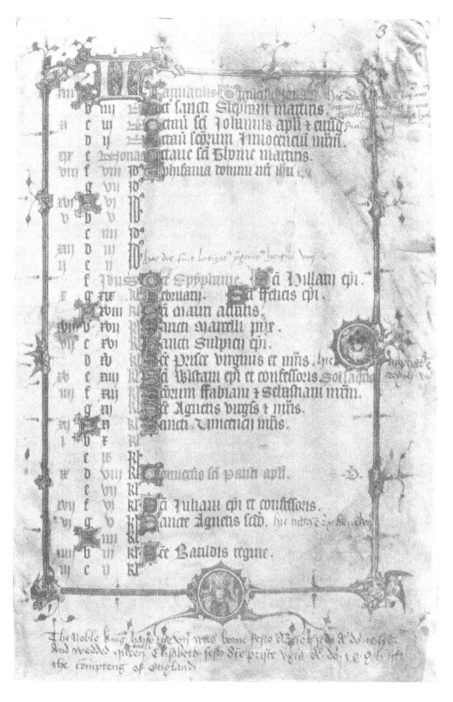

FACSIMILE PAGE OF THE COUNTESS OF RICHMOND'S MISSAL,

CONTAINING THE ENTRY OF THE BIRTH OF KING HENRY VII.

Reproduced by permission from the Original in the Library of Exeter College, Oxford.

THE
BLOOD ROYAL
OF
BRITAIN

BEING A ROLL OF THE LIVING DESCENDANTS
OF
Edward IV and Henry VII,
Kings of England, and
James III, King of Scotland

by

The Marquis of Ruvigny and Raineval

— Tudor Roll —

WITH A SERIES OF PORTRAITS

HERITAGE BOOKS
2011

HERITAGE BOOKS

AN IMPRINT OF HERITAGE BOOKS, INC.

Books, CDs, and more—Worldwide

For our listing of thousands of titles see our website
at
www.HeritageBooks.com

A Facsimile Reprint
Published 2011 by
HERITAGE BOOKS, INC.
Publishing Division
100 Railroad Ave. #104
Westminster, Maryland 21157

Originally published
London, 1903

International Standard Book Numbers
Paperbound: 978-0-7884-1693-4
Clothbound: 978-0-7884-8833-7

PREFACE

THE BLOOD ROYAL OF BRITAIN is the first attempt ever made to trace out all the descendants of the Sovereigns of these realms, and to show the number of descents which each descendant has; and the present volume aims at being exhaustive as regards the living descendants of Edward IV. (1441–1483) and Henry VII. (1455–1509), Kings of England, and James III. (1451–1488), King of Scotland.

Unlike previous works on Royal Descents which have been principally, if not wholly, confined to setting out the specific descents of those persons who have paid for that purpose, every attempt has been made in the present work to trace out *all* the descendants of the above-named kings, and no fee or charge or condition has been made for the insertion of any name or descent in this book.

The plan adopted has been to trace out the lines of descent in Tables to about the middle of the nineteenth century, and then in the body of the work to set out the living descendants of the persons last named in the Tables.

Thus, to take an instance which will be familiar to most readers, in the case of the reigning house, the line in the Chart is carried down to Queen Victoria, 1819–1901. Then in the body of the work we find King Edward VII. (No. 6040), eldest son (of Queen Victoria, the head of the line), followed by George, Prince of Wales (No. 6041), grandson (of the head of the line), only son of No. 6040 (King Edward VII.), and so on.

The names are arranged strictly as they come in the order of primogeniture, *i.e.* of succession to the throne; the number in the first column being that of the descent, and that in the second of the order in which they stand as regards living persons.

The distinction is important, for whereas it will be seen that the Roll contains the names of some 11,723 living (or very lately living) persons, the number of descents which they have among them is 36,735, an average of a little over three descents each. That this is only an average, however, must be remembered, for while the greater number have only one descent each, others have over fifty and sixty; the children of the Duke and Duchess of Calabria and of the Prince of the Asturias having seventy-eight each, those of the Archduke Leopold Salvator of Tuscany eighty each, and the daughter of the Duke and Duchess of Guise eighty-eight.

In the Tables the dates of birth, marriage, and death are given whenever possible, but as the object of the writer has been merely to trace out the living descendants of the monarchs whose names appear on the titlepage, and in order to keep the work within bounds, he has been obliged to omit (except in some few cases, where it has been thought desirable to show the descent of a title) the names of persons who died without issue, or whose issue subsequently failed, and also the parentage of the wives.

In the case of a person having been married more than once, only the name of the wife or wives (or husband or husbands) by whom he (or she) had issue are given, the figure in round brackets immediately following the marriage mark = signifying whether she (or he) is first, second, or third wife (or husband). Similarly, if the figure precedes the marriage mark, it signifies that he (or she) married as first or second wife (or husband), as the case may be. Wherever the compiler has been able to give the dates of birth and marriage, he has considered this sufficient indication of whether the children are by the first or second marriage; but where these dates have not been obtainable, the figure before the names shows of which marriage they are the issue.

In the Roll itself considerations of space have again rendered it necessary to adopt the briefest possible description, and the use of the term "Esquire" has been discarded, although it has been allowed to stand in the headings of some of the sections.

The dates following the names are those of birth. In the case of widows the dates of the birth and death of the husband are given where the writer has been able to discover them, and in these cases they immediately follow the husband's name and precede the date of birth of the wife.

In the case of British Peers their chief titles in the different peerages of England, Scotland, Ireland, Great Britain, and the United Kingdom are given, the letters E., S., I., G.B., and U.K. in square brackets indicating the peerage to which the title belongs. Similarly with foreign noblemen the name of the country to which the title belongs has been added. Also in the cases of those princes who but for wars and revolutions would now be reigning, their hereditary titles have been inserted within square brackets, so:—

> "Ernest Augustus [III. King of Hanover], Duke of Brunswick and Luneburg, Duke of Cumberland."

The work naturally divides itself into two parts, the first comprising the descendants of the Princess Margaret Tudor, Henry VII.th's elder daughter; and the second those of the Princess Mary Tudor, his younger daughter. All are descended from Henry VII. and Edward IV., but only those in the first part, Nos. 1 to 19,572, are descended from James III.

In the first part will be found the names of every Christian crowned head, with the exception of the Kings of Sweden and Norway, and Servia, and the Princes of Monaco and Montenegro; also the names of the Crown Princes of Sweden and Norway, and of Monaco, and the Crown Princess of Montenegro, and of the members of all the royal and princely houses of Europe, and of many of the higher nobility of France, Germany, Austria, Hungary, Poland, Bohemia, Italy, Spain, Portugal, Russia, &c.

The second part, which is almost wholly confined to persons of British nationality, contains the names of many British Peers and Baronets, and the heads of many of the old county families.

We have thus here one single pedigree embracing all the crowned heads of Europe, the representatives of a large number of the chief British and continental families, and some 10,000 other Britons in all ranks of life, and the writer thinks that he may fairly claim that this is the largest pedigree ever published.

It is a somewhat remarkable fact that, so far as the writer can ascertain, only three intermarriages have occurred between the descendants of the two daughters of Henry VII. during a period of over 350 years, the first being that of the Duke of Sussex in 1793 with the Lady Augusta Murray; the second that of the present Duke of Argyll in 1871 with the Princess Louise; and the third that of the Duke of Teck in 1894 with the Lady Margaret Grosvenor—and the three children of the last-named are the only persons now living who can show a legitimate descent from both daughters.

Nos. 1 to 6039 and 9787 to 15,825 (858 living persons, commencing with the Princess Louis of Bavaria, the hereditary and senior representative of all our sovereigns before 1714) are the descendants of King Charles I. and of the sons of his sister Elizabeth, Queen of Bohemia, who were excluded from the throne by the Act of Settlement in 1701; Nos. 6040 to 9786 and 15,826 to 19,572 (582 living persons, commencing with King Edward VII.) are those of the Electress Sophia of Hanover, the Queen of Bohemia's daughter, on whom, being

Protestants, the crown was entailed by the above-named Act of Settlement; Nos. 19,573 to 27,542 (5243 living persons, commencing with Lady Kinloss, the senior representative of the Princess Mary Tudor) are the descendants of the Lady Frances Brandon, elder daughter and co-heiress of the Princess Mary Tudor, on which line the crown would have devolved had the provisions of the will of King Henry VIII. (made in accordance with Act of Parliament) been carried out; while Nos. 27,543 to (the end) 36,735 (5040 living persons, commencing with the Earl of Jersey, probably the representative of the Lady Eleanor Brandon, younger daughter and co-heir of the Princess Mary Tudor) are the descendants of the aforesaid Lady Eleanor Brandon, on whose line the crown would have devolved under the aforesaid will of Henry VIII., " if Edward Seymour, Lord Beauchamp (son of Lady Katherine Grey [the daughter of Lady Frances Brandon], by Edward, Earl of Hertford), be considered (which he frequently was) illegitimate." [1]

King Henry VII. is the last English sovereign from whom any British subjects outside Royalty (with the exception of the daughters of the Duke and Duchess of Fife) can trace a legitimate descent, consequently the royal descents here set forth are the best that can be shown.

To find other descents from a King of England, it is necessary to go back over a hundred years to King Edward III., 1312–1377. Of the seven intervening sovereigns, Kings Richard II. and Edward V. died *s.p.* The issue of Kings Henry IV., Henry V., Henry VI., and Richard III. failed, while that of King Edward IV. merged, through his daughter and (in her issue) heiress Elizabeth, in that of her husband King Henry VII.

It will be observed that the above-named children of the Duke and Duchess of Fife are also the only living descendants of King James III. of British race and nationality. For others, to find a legitimate descent from a Scottish sovereign it is necessary to revert to King James II., 1430–1460.

In addition to the English and Scottish kings named the present work contains the names of all the living descendants of, among many others: Victor Amadeus II. of Savoy, 1st King of Sardinia, 1666–1732; Louis XV., King of France and Navarre, 1710–1774; Philip, 1st Duke of Parma, 1720–1765; Charles III., King of Spain, 1716–1788; Ferdinand I., 1st King of the Two Sicilies, 1751–1825; John VI., King of Portugal and Brazil, 1767–1826; Philip, 1st Duke of Orleans, 1640–1701; Leopold, Duke of Lorraine, 1679–1729; Rinaldo III., Duke of Modena, 1655–1737; the Empress Maria Theresa, 1717–1780, and her husband the Emperor Francis I., 1708–1765; Ferdinand III., Grandduke of Tuscany, 1769–1824; the Emperors Joseph I., 1678–1711, and Charles VII., 1697–1745; Frederick Christian, Elector of Saxony, 1722–1763; Frederick Augustus III., King of Poland, 1696–1763; Frederick I., 1st King of Prussia, 1657–1713; William IV. of Orange, Stadtholder of Holland, 1711–1751; Frederick V., King of Denmark and Norway, 1723–1766; Adolphus Frederick, King of Sweden, 1710–1771; Frederick Eugene, Duke of Würtemberg, 1732–1797; Nicholas I., Emperor of Russia, 1796–1855; William (Seymour), 2nd Duke of Somerset, 1588–1660; Henry (Scott), 2nd Duke of Buccleuch, K.T., 1694–1751; James (Stopford), 2nd Earl of Courtown, 1731–1810; Thomas (Brudenell-Bruce), 1st Earl of Ailesbury, K.T., 1739–1814; Thomas (Thynne), 1st Viscount Weymouth, 1640–1714; Hugh (Percy), 1st Duke of Northumberland, K.G., 1714–1786; George (Ashburnham), 3rd Earl of Ashburnham, K.G., 1760–1830; Francis (Greville), 1st Earl of Warwick, K.T., 1719–1773; John (Carteret), Earl Granville, K.G., 1690–1763; Thomas (Thynne), 1st Marquis of Bath, K.G., 1734–1796; John (Spencer), 1st Earl Spencer, 1734–1783; William (Cavendish), 4th Duke of Devonshire, K.G., 1720–1764; George (Howard), 6th Earl of Carlisle, K.G., 1773–1848; Granville (Leveson-Gower), 1st Earl Granville, 1773–1846; George (Leveson-Gower), 2nd Duke of Sutherland, K.G., 1786–1861; Hugh

[1] See *Complete Peerage*, iii. p. 72.

Preface

(Grosvenor), 1st Duke of Westminster, K.G., 1825–1899; William Henry (Bentinck), 3rd Duke of Portland, K.G., 1738–1809; Henry (Boyle), 1st Earl Shannon, 1686–1764, Somerset (Butler), 1st Earl of Carrick, 1718–1794; Armar (Lowry-Corry), 1st Earl of Belmore, 1740–1802; John (Manners), titular Marquis of Granby (father of the 4th Duke of Rutland), 1721–1770; Charles (Marsham), 1st Earl of Romney, 1744–1811; Henry (Herbert), 1st Earl of Carnarvon, 1741–1811; the Rt. Hon. Sir George Grenville, M.P., Chancellor of the Exchequer, 1712–1770; John (Egerton), 1st Earl of Bridgewater, 1579–1649; David (Cecil), 3rd Earl of Exeter, 1600–1643; William (Villiers), 3rd Earl of Jersey, –1769; Anthony (Ashley Cooper), 1st Earl of Shaftesbury, 1621–1683; Henry (Hastings), 5th Earl of Huntingdon, 1586–1643; John (Murray), 1st Marquis of Atholl, K.T., 1635–1703; Cosmo George (Gordon), 3rd Duke of Gordon, K.T., 1720–1752; Charles (Lennox), 4th Duke of Richmond and Lennox, K.G., 1764–1819; John (Russell), 6th Duke of Bedford, K.G., 1766–1839; William (Montagu), 5th Duke of Manchester, 1771–1843; Charles (Murray), 1st Earl of Dunmore, 1661–1710; John (Cochrane), 4th Earl of Dundonald, –1720; James (Hamilton), 5th Duke of Hamilton, 1702–1743; Alexander (Stewart), 6th Earl of Galloway, 1694–1773; William (Murray), 2nd Baron Nairne, 1665–1726; William (Drummond), 4th Viscount Strathallan, 1690–1747; Hugh (Fraser), 10th Lord Lovat, –1696. Norman, 18th Chief of Macleod, –1706; Robert Graham, 11th of Fintry, *temp.* 1735; Dudley (Ryder), 1st Earl of Harrowby, 1762–1847; George (Hay), 8th Marquis of Tweeddale, K.T., 1787–1876, &c. When it is remembered that the descendants of daughters are traced equally with those of sons, the scope of the work may be better realised.

It may also not be uninteresting to note that a descent from Henry VII. gives descents from (among various others) William the Conqueror, King of England, 1027–1087; Alfred the Great, King of England, 849–901; St. Louis IX., King of France, 1215–1270; Charlemagne, Emperor and King of France and Italy, 742–814; the Emperor Frederick I. (of Hohenstauffen), surnamed Barbarossa, 1123–1190; Rodrigo Diaz de Bivar, called the Cid Ruy Diaz, 1030/40–1099; Ferdinand III., the Saint, King of Castille and Leon, 1200–1252; Alfonso VIII., Emperor of Spain, 1107–1157; the Greek Emperors Isaac II.-Angelos, –1204; and Alexius I., Comnenus, 1048–1118; Rudolph of Hapsburg, King of the Romans, founder of the Imperial House of Hapsburg, 1218–1291, &c.

A small shield has been placed before the names of those entitled to quarter the Royal Arms. It will be observed that the Duke of Atholl, his children, and his cousin, Miss Caroline F. Murray, enjoy the unique distinction of three such shields.

In conclusion, although the writer is aware that many affect to despise royal descents, in consequence of the number who claim them, yet he ventures to think that his work cannot fail to prove of some little interest, as showing the descent of so many from one common ancestor, living only some three hundred and fifty years ago, and who are thus united in the inheritance of the glorious traditions of the Plantagenet kings.

Every effort has been made to render the Roll as complete as possible, but the writer is only too fully aware of the number of errors and imperfections which must, almost of necessity, occur in a first attempt of this kind, but he asks for the kind indulgence of his readers, and while thanking all those numerous correspondents who have so kindly revised the entries relating to their own families or supplied him with other information, he will be most grateful to all those who will point out to him omissions or other errors which may come under their notice.

CHERTSEY, *August* 1903.

REFERENCES TO NUMBERS

LIST OF ILLUSTRATIONS

TABLE I

THE HOUSE OF PLANTAGENET.

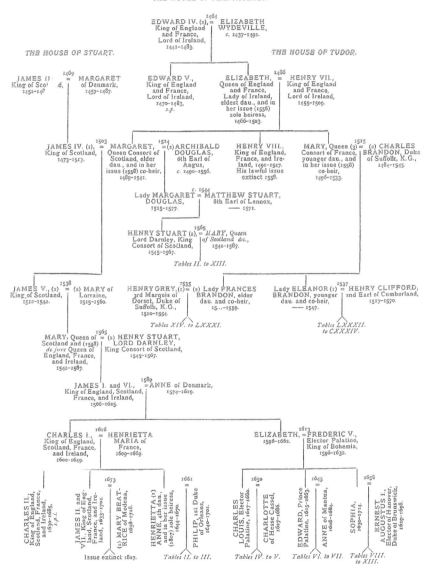

THE HOUSE OF STUART.

THE HOUSE OF TUDOR.

EDWARD IV. (2), = ELIZABETH
1464
King of England
and France,
Lord of England,
1441-1483.
WYDEVILLE,
c. 1437-1492.

JAMES II = MARGARET
1469
King of Scotland, 1451-14..,
of Denmark,
1457-1487.

EDWARD V.,
King of England
and France,
Lord of Ireland,
1470-1483,
s.p.

ELIZABETH, = HENRY VII.,
1486
Queen of England
and France,
Lady of Ireland,
eldest dau., and in
her issue (1556)
sole heiress,
1466-1503.
King of England
and France,
Lord of Ireland,
1455-1509.

JAMES IV. (1), = MARGARET,
1503
King of Scotland,
1473-1513.
Queen Consort of
Scotland, elder
dau., and in her
issue (1558) co-heir,
1489-1541.
= (2) ARCHIBALD
1514
DOUGLAS,
6th Earl of
Angus,
c. 1490-1556.

HENRY VIII.,
King of England,
France, and Ire-
land, 1491-1547.
His lawful issue
extinct 1558.

MARY, Queen (3) = (2) CHARLES
1515
Consort of France,
younger dau., and
in her issue (1558)
co-heir,
1496-1533.
BRANDON, Duke
of Suffolk, K.G.,
1484-1545.

c. 1544
Lady MARGARET = MATTHEW STUART,
DOUGLAS,
1515-1577.
8th Earl of Lennox,
—— 1571.

1565
HENRY STUART (2), = MARY, Queen
Lord Darnley, King
Consort of Scotland,
1545-1567.
of Scotland &c.,
1542-1587.

Tables II. to XIII.

JAMES V., (2) = (2) MARY of
1538
King of Scotland,
1512-1542.
Lorraine,
1515-1560.

HENRY GREY, (1) = (1) Lady FRANCES
1535
3rd Marquis of
Dorset, Duke of
Suffolk, K.G.,
1510-1554.
BRANDON, elder
dau. and co-heir,
15...-1559.

Lady ELEANOR (1) = HENRY CLIFFORD,
1537
BRANDON, younger
dau. and co-heir,
—— 1547.
and Earl of Cumberland,
1517-1570.

Tables XIV. to LXXXI.

*Tables LXXXII.
to CXXXIV.*

1565
MARY, Queen of = (2) HENRY STUART,
Scotland and (1558)
de jure Queen of
England, France,
and Ireland,
1542-1587.
LORD DARNLEY,
King Consort of Scotland,
1545-1567.

JAMES I. and VI., = ANNE of Denmark,
1589
King of England, Scotland,
France, and Ireland,
1566-1625.
1574-1619.

1626
CHARLES I., = HENRIETTA
King of England,
Scotland, France,
and Ireland,
1600-1649.
MARIA of
France,
1609-1669.

ELIZABETH, = FREDERIC V.,
1613
1596-1662.
Elector Palatine,
King of Bohemia,
1596-1632.

CHARLES II.,
King of England,
Scotland, France,
and Ireland,
1630-1685,
s.p.l.

1673
JAMES II. and
VII., King of Eng-
land, Scotland,
France, and Ire-
land, 1633-1701.
= (2) MARY BEAT-
RICE of Modena,
1658-1718.

1661
HENRIETTA (2)
ANNE, 4th dau.,
and in her issue
(1807) sole heiress,
1644-1670.
= PHILIP, 1st Duke
of Orleans,
1640-1701.

1650
CHARLES
LOUIS, Elector
Palatine, 1617-1680.

CHARLOTTE
of Hesse Cassel,
1617-1686.

1645
EDWARD, Prince
Palatine, 1615-1663.
= ANNE of Mantua,
1606-1684.

1658
SOPHIA,
1630-1714.
= ERNEST
AUGUSTUS I.,
Elector of Hanover,
Duke of Brunswick,
1629-1698.

Issue extinct 1807.

Tables II. to III.

Tables IV. to V.

Tables VI. to VII.

*Tables VIII.
to XIII.*

I

A

TABLE II

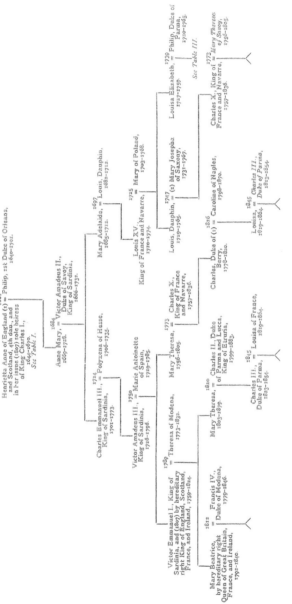

Henrietta Anne of England (†) = Philip, 1st Duke of Orleans,
and Scotland, 4th dau., and   1640-1701.
in her issue (1807) sole heiress
of King Charles I.,
1644-1670.
See Table I.

Anne Mary, = Victor Amadeus II.,
1669-1728.   Duke of Savoy,
             King of Sardinia.
             1666-1732.

Mary Adelaide, = Louis, Dauphin,
1685-1712.   1682-1712.

Charles Emmanuel III., = Polyxena of Hesse,
King of Sardinia,   1706-1735.
1701-1773.

Louis XV.
King of France and Navarre, = Mary of Poland,
1710-1774.   1703-1768.

Louisa Elizabeth, = Philip, Duke of
1727-1759.   Parma,
                    1720-1765.
                    See Table III.

Victor Amadeus III. = Marie Antoinette
King of Sardinia,   of Spain,
1726-1796.   1729-1785.

Louis, Dauphin, = (2) Mary Josepha
1729-1765.   of Saxony,
                   1731-1767.

Charles X., = Mary Theresa
King of France of Savoy,
and Navarre,   1756-1805.
1757-1836.

Mary Theresa, = Charles II., Duke
1756-1805.   of Parma and Lucca,
                King of Etruria,
                1799-1883.

Charles, Duke of (1) = Caroline of Naples,
Berry,   1798-1870.
1778-1820.

Charles X.,
King of France and Navarre,
1757-1836.

Charles III., = Louisa of France,
Duke of Parma, 1819-1864.
1823-1854.

Mary Theresa, = Charles II., Duke
1803-1879.   of Parma and Lucca,
                King of Etruria,
                1799-1883.

Louisa, = Charles III.,
1819-1864. Duke of Parma,
            1823-1854.

Victor Emmanuel I., King of   = Theresa of Modena,
Sardinia, and (1807) by hereditary 1773-1832.
right King of England, Scotland,
France, and Ireland, 1759-1824.

Francis IV.,
Duke of Modena,
1779-1846.

Mary Beatrice,
by hereditary right
Queen of Great Britain,
France, and Ireland,
1792-1840.

2

TABLE III

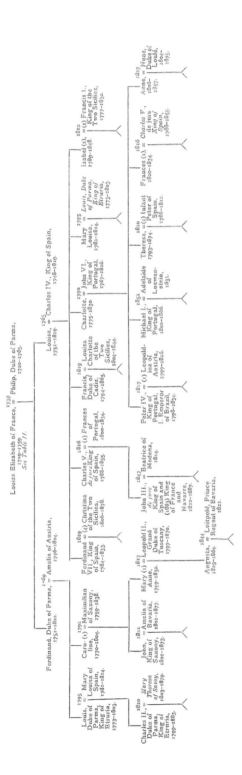

TABLE IV

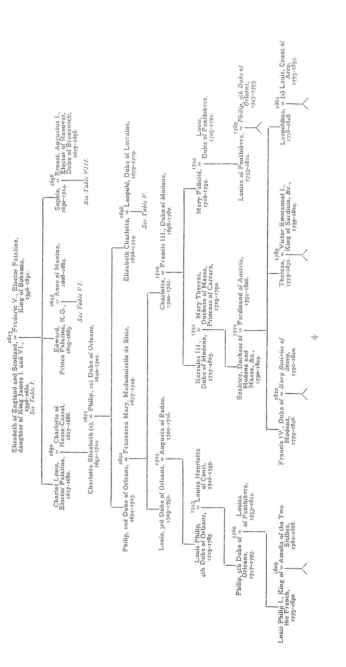

Elizabeth of England and Scotland, = Frederic V., Elector Palatine,
daughter of King James I. and VI., | King of Bohemia,
1596-1662. | 1596-1632.
See Table I.

Charles Louis, | Edward, | Sophia, = Ernest, Augustus I.,
Elector Palatine, | Prince Palatine, K.G., | 1630-1714. | Elector of Hanover,
1617-1680. | 1625-1663. | | Duke of Brunswick,
| = Anne of Mantua, | | 1629-1698.
= Charlotte of | 1608-1684. |
Hesse-Cassel, | *See Table VI.* | *See Table VIII.*
1627-1686. |

Charlotte Elizabeth (2), = Philip, 1st Duke of Orleans,
1652-1722. | 1640-1701.

Philip, 2nd Duke of Orleans, = Francesca Mary, Mademoiselle de Blois,
1674-1723. | 1677-1749.

Louis, 3rd Duke of Orleans, = Augusta of Baden,
1703-1752. | 1704-1726.

Louis Philip, = Louisa Henrietta
4th Duke of Orleans, | of Conti,
1725-1785. | 1726-1759.

Philip, 5th Duke of = Louisa
Orleans, | of Penthièvre,
1747-1793. | 1753-1821.

Louis Philip I., King of = Amelia of the Two
the French, | Sicilies,
1773-1850. | 1782-1866.

Elizabeth Charlotte, = Leopold, Duke of Lorraine,
1676-1744. | 1679-1729.
See Table V.

Charlotte, = Francis III., Duke of Modena,
1700-1761. | 1698-1780.

Hercules III., | Mary Theresa, | Mary Félicité, | Louis,
Duke of Modena, | Duchess of Massa, | 1726-1754. | Duke of Penthièvre,
1727-1803. | Princess of Carrara, | | 1725-1791.
| 1725-1790.

Beatrice, Duchess of = Ferdinand of Austria, | Louisa of Penthièvre, = Philip, 5th Duke of
Modena and | 1754-1806. | 1753-1821. | Orleans,
Massa, &c., | | | 1747-1793.
1750-1829. |

Francis IV., Duke of = Mary Beatrice of | Theresa, = Victor Emmanuel I., | Leopoldina, = (2) Louis, Count of
Modena, | Savoy, | 1773-1832. | King of Sardinia, &c., | 1776-1848. | Arco,
1779-1846. | 1792-1840. | | 1759-1824. | | 1773-1854.

TABLE V

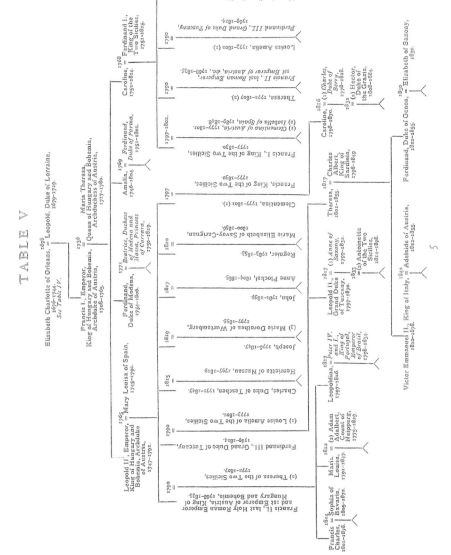

TABLE VI

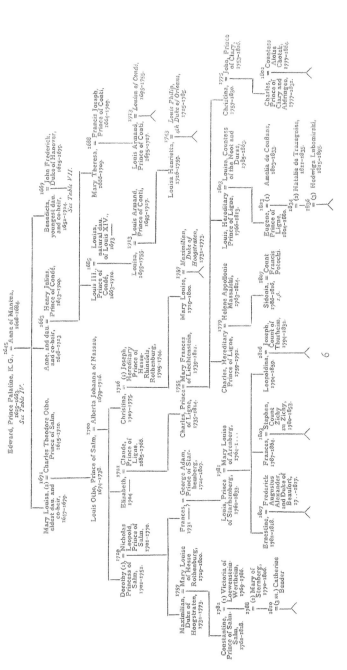

TABLE VII

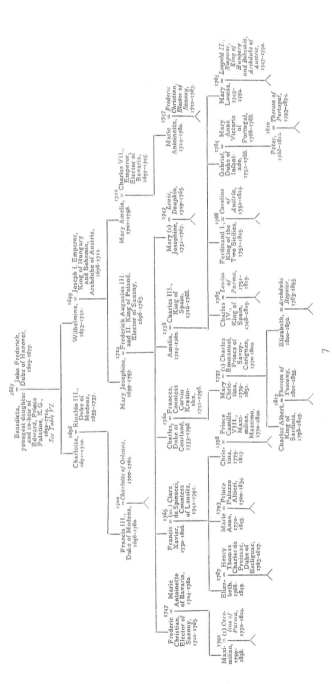

TABLE VIII

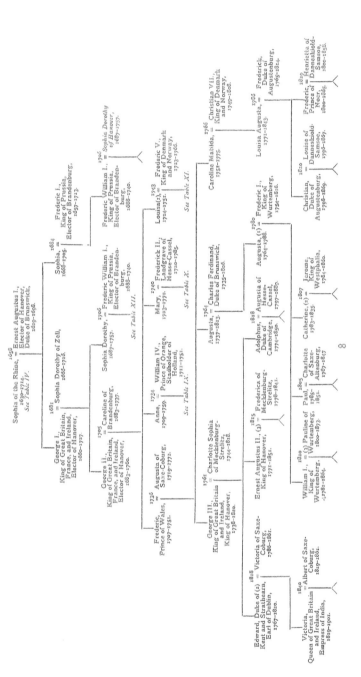

8

TABLE IX

Anne of Great Britain and Ireland and Hanover, 1709-1759. ^{1734} William IV., Prince of Orange, Stadholder of Holland, 1711-1751.
See Table VIII.

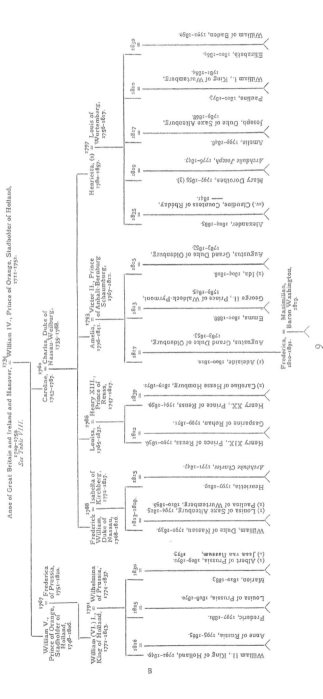

TABLE X

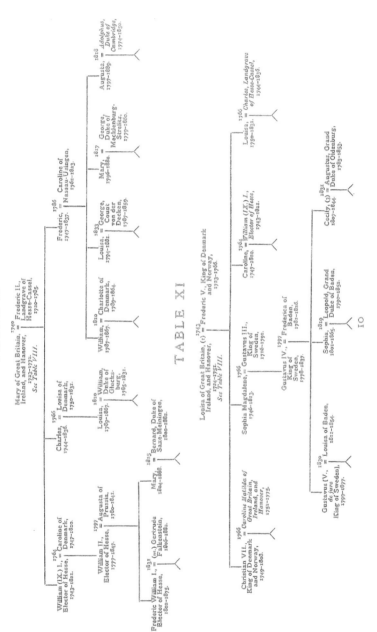

Mary of Great Britain, Ireland, and Hanover, 1723-1772. = 1740 Frederic II., Landgrave of Hesse-Cassel, 1720-1785. *See Table VIII.*

Charles, 1744-1836. = 1766 Louisa of Denmark, 1750-1831.

Frederic, 1747-1837. = 1786 Caroline of Nassau-Usingen, 1762-1823.

William II., Elector of Hesse, 1777-1847. = 1797 Augusta of Prussia, 1780-1841.

Louisa, 1789-1867. = 1800 William, Duke of Ghucksburg, 1785-1831.

Mary, 1804-1888. = 1825 Bernard, Duke of Saxe-Meiningen, 1800-1882.

William, 1787-1867. = 1810 Charlotte of Denmark, 1789-1864.

Louisa, 1794-1881. = 1833 George, Count von der Decken, 1787-1859.

Mary, 1796-1880. = 1817 George, Duke of Mecklenburg-Strelitz, 1779-1860.

Augusta, 1797-1889. = 1818 Adolphus, Duke of Cambridge, 1774-1850.

William (IX.) I., Elector of Hesse, 1743-1821. = 1764 Caroline of Denmark, 1747-1820.

Frederic William I., Elector of Hesse, 1802-1875. = 1831 (m.) Gertrude of Falkenstein, 1806-1882.

TABLE XI

Louisa of Great Britain, Ireland, and Hanover, 1724-1751. = 1743 Frederic V., King of Denmark and Norway, 1723-1766. *See Table VIII.*

Sophia Magdalene, 1746-1813. = 1766 Gustavus III., King of Sweden, 1746-1792.

Caroline, 1747-1820. = 1766 William (IX.) I., Elector of Hesse, 1743-1821.

Louisa, 1750-1831. = 1766 Charles, Landgrave of Hesse-Cassel, 1744-1836.

Gustavus IV., King of Sweden, 1778-1837. = 1797 Frederica of Baden, 1781-1826.

Sophia, 1801-1865. = 1819 Leopold, Grand Duke of Baden, 1790-1852.

Cecily, (2) 1807-1844. = 1831 Augustus, Grand Duke of Oldenburg, 1783-1853.

Christian VII., King of Denmark and Norway, 1749-1808. = 1766 Caroline Matilda of Great Britain, Ireland, and Hanover, 1751-1775.

Gustavus (V.,) de jure King of Sweden, 1799-1877. = 1830 Louisa of Baden, 1811-1854.

TABLE XII

Sophia Dorothy of Great Britain, Ireland, and Hanover, 1687-1757, = Frederic William I., King of Prussia, Elector of Brandenburg, 1688-1740. *See Table VIII.*

William, = Louisa of Brunswick, 1722-1780. 1742

Frederic William II., King of Prussia, 1744-1797. = (a) Louisa of Hesse Darmstadt, 1751-1805. 1769

Frederica, 1751-1800.

Ferdinand, 1730-1813. = Louisa of Schwedt, 1738-1820. 1755

William V., Prince of Orange, 1748-1806. 1767

Charlotte, 1716-1801. = Charles, Duke of Brunswick, 1713-1780. 1733

Sophia, 1719-1765. = Frederic William, Margrave of Brandenburg-Schwedt, 1700-1771. 1734

Ulrica of Prussia, 1720-1782. = Adolphus Frederic, King of Sweden, 1710-1771. 1744

Ferdinand of Prussia, 1730-1813. = Louisa, 1738-1820. 1755

Gusta-vus III., King of Sweden, 1746-1792. = Sophia of Denmark, 1746-1813.

Frederic Louis, Hereditary Grand Duke of Mecklenburg-Schwerin, 1778-1819.

Louisa of Hesse, 1757-1830. = Charles Augustus, Grand Duke of Saxe-Weimar, 1757-1828. 1775

Frederica, 1736-1798. = Frederic Eugene, Duke of Wurtemberg. *See Table XIII.*

Anne Amelia, 1739-1807. = Ernest Augustus II., Duke of Saxe-Weimar, 1737-1758. 1756

Augusta of Great Britain, Ireland, and Hanover, 1737-1813. = Charles Ferdinand, Duke of Brunswick, 1735-1806. 1764

Louisa, 1770-1836. = Anthony, Prince Radziwill, 1775-1833.

Frederica of Mecklenburg-Strelitz, 1778-1841. = Louis (1), 1773-1796. 1793

Louisa of Mecklenburg-Strelitz, 1776-1810. = Frederic William III., King of Prussia, 1770-1840. 1793

Wilhelmina, 1774-1837. = William I., King of Holland, 1772-1843. 1791

Mary Anne of Hesse-Homburg, 1785-1846. = William, 1783-1851. 1804

Augusta, 1780-1841. = William II., Elector of Hesse-Cassel, 1777-1847. 1797

Bogislaus of Radivill, 1809-1873. = Leontine of Clary, 1811-1890.

Matilda of Clary, 1805-1897. = William, Prince Radziwill, 1797-1870.

Caroline, 1786-1816 (=).

Ida of Saxe-Meiningen, 1794-1852. =

Bernard, 1792-1862. =

Mary of Russia, 1786-1864. =

Charles Frederic, Grand Duke of Saxe-Weimar, 1783-1853. 1804

Maximilian II., King of Bavaria, 1811-1864. = Mary, 1825-1889. 1842

Charles of Hesse-Darmstadt, 1809-1877. = Elizabeth, 1815-1885. 1836

Leopold, Duke of Anhalt, 1794-1871. = Frederica, 1796-1850. 1818

Frederic of the Netherlands, 1797-1881. = Louisa, 1808-1870. 1825

Paul Frederic, Grand Duke of Mecklenburg-Schwerin, 1800-1842. = Alexandrina, 1803-1892. 1822

Nicholas I., Emperor of Russia, 1796-1855. = Charlotte (afterwards Alexandra), 1798-1860. 1817

(1) Marion of Holland, 1810-1883. (2 m.) Rosalie de Rauch, 1810-1879. = Albert, 1809-1872. 1830-1883

Mary of Saxe-Weimar, 1808-1877. = Charles, 1801-1883. 1827

Augusta of Saxe-Weimar, 1811-1890. = William I., King of Prussia, German Emperor, 1797-1888. 1829

Helen, 1814-1858. = Ferdinand, Duke of Orleans, 1810-1842. 1837

11

TABLE XIII

Frederica of Brandenburg-Schwedt, 1736-1798. = Frederic Eugene, Duke of Wurtemberg, 1753, 1732-1797.
See Table XII.

Frederica, 1765-1785. = Peter, Grand Duke of Oldenburg, 1755-1829.
- 1809 = Catharine of Russia, 1788-1819.
- 1804 George (2), 1784-1812.
- 1817-1825-1831 = Augustus, Grand Duke of Oldenburg, 1783-1853.
  - (1) Adelaide of Anhalt-Bernburg, 1800-1820.
  - (2) Ida of Anhalt-Bernburg, 1804-1828.
  - (3) Cecily of Sweden, 1807-1844.

Sophia (Mary), 1759-1828. = Paul, Emperor of Russia, 1756-1801. 1776
- 1816 William II, King of Holland, 1792-1849.
- = Anne, 1795-1865.
- 1809-1816 (1) George of Oldenburg, 1784-1812. (2) William I., King of Wurtemberg, 1781-1864.
- = Catherine, 1788-1819.
- 1804 Charles Frederick, Grand Duke of Saxe-Weimar, 1783-1853.
- = Mary, 1786-1859.
- 1804 Frederic Louis, Grand Duke of Mecklenburg-Schwerin, 1778-1819.
- = Helen, 1784-1803.
- 1824 Charlotte (afterwards Helen) of Wurtemberg, 1807-1873.
- = Michael, 1798-1849.
- 1817 Charlotte (afterwards Alexandra) of Prussia, 1798-1860.
- = Nicholas I., Emperor of Russia, 1796-1855.

Alexander, 1771-1833. = Antoinette of Saxe-Coburg, 1779-1824. 1798
- 1860 (m.) Natalie Eschborn, Madame de Grunhof.
- = Ernest, 1807-1868.
- 1837 Mary of Orleans, 1813-1839.
- = Alexander, 1804-1881.

William, 1761-1830. = (m.) Wilhelmina, Rhodis de Tunderfeld, 1777-1822. 1800
- 1842 William, Count of Taubenheim, 1805-1894.
- = Mary, 1815-1866.
- 1841-1863 (1) Theodelinde of Leuchtenberg, 1814-1857. (2) Florestine of Monaco, 1833.
- = William, Duke of Urach, 1810-1869.

Eugene, 1758-1822. = Louisa of Stolberg-Gedern, 1764-1824. 1787
- 1831 Helen Festetics de Tolna, 1812-1886.
- = Alexander, 1801-1844 (2).

Louis, 1756-1817. = Henrietta of Nassau, 1780-1857. 1797

Frederick I., King of Wurtemberg, 1754-1816. = (1) Augusta of Brunswick, 1764-1788. 1780
- 1811 Augustus, Prince of Hohenlohe-Oehringen, 1784-1853.
- = Frederica Louisa, 1789-1851.
- 1817-1847 (1) Matilda of Waldeck, 1801-1825. (2) Helen of Hohenlohe-Langenburg, 1807-1880.
- = Eugene, 1788-1857.

12

TABLE XIV

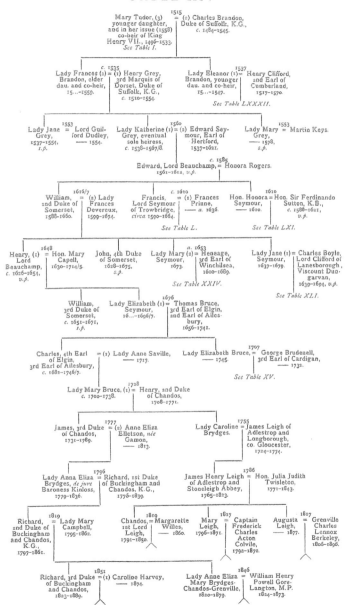

Mary Tudor, (3) = (2) Charles Brandon, younger daughter, and in her issue (1558) co-heir of King Henry VII., 1496-1533. Duke of Suffolk, K.G., c. 1484-1545. 1515 *See Table I.*

Lady Frances (2) = (1) Henry Grey, Brandon, elder dau. and co-heir, 15...-1559. 3rd Marquis of Dorset, Duke of Suffolk, K.G., c. 1510-1554. c. 1535

Lady Eleanor (1) = Henry Clifford, Brandon, younger dau. and co-heir, 15...-1547. 2nd Earl of Cumberland, 1517-1570. 1537 *See Table LXXXII.*

Lady Jane = Lord Guilford Dudley, Grey, 1537-1554, s.p. — 1554. 1553

Lady Katherine (1) = (2) Edward Seymour, Earl of Hertford, 1537-1621. Grey, eventual sole heiress, c. 1538-1567/8. 1560

Lady Mary = Martin Keys. Grey, — 1578, s.p. 1553

Edward, Lord Beauchamp, = Honora Rogers. 1561-1612, v.p. c. 1585

William, = (2) Lady 2nd Duke of Somerset, 1588-1660. Frances Devereux, 1599-1674. 1616/7

Francis, = (1) Frances Lord Seymour of Trowbridge, circa 1590-1664. Prinne, — a. 1636. c. 1620

Hon. Honora = Hon. Sir Ferdinando Seymour, — 1620. Sutton, K.B., c. 1588-1621, v.p. 1620 *See Table LXI.*

See Table L.

Henry, (1) = Hon. Mary Lord Beauchamp, c. 1626-1654, v.p. Capell, 1630-1714/5. 1648

John, 4th Duke of Somerset, 1648-1675, s.p.

Lady Mary (2) = Heneage, Seymour, 1673. 3rd Earl of Winchilsea, 1620-1689. a. 1653 *See Table XXIV.*

Lady Jane (1) = Charles Boyle, Seymour, 1637-1679. Lord Clifford of Lanesborough, Viscount Dungarvan, 1639-1694, v.p. 1620 *See Table XLI.*

William, 3rd Duke of Somerset, c. 1651-1671, s.p.

Lady Elizabeth (1) = Thomas Bruce, Seymour, 16...-1696/7. 3rd Earl of Elgin, and Earl of Ailesbury, 1656-1741. 1676

Charles, 4th Earl of Elgin, 3rd Earl of Ailesbury, c. 1682-1746/9. = (1) Lady Anne Saville, — 1717.

Lady Elizabeth Bruce, = George Brudenell, — 1745. 3rd Earl of Cardigan, — 1732. 1707 *See Table XV.*

Lady Mary Bruce, (1) = Henry, 2nd Duke c. 1700-1738. of Chandos, 1708-1771. 1728

James, 3rd Duke of Chandos, 1731-1789. = (2) Anne Eliza Elletson, née Gamon, — 1813. 1777

Lady Caroline = James Leigh of Brydges. Adlestrop and Longborough, co. Gloucester, 1724-1774. 1755

Lady Anna Eliza Brydges, de jure Baroness Kinloss, 1779-1836. = Richard, 1st Duke of Buckingham and Chandos, K.G., 1776-1839. 1796

James Henry Leigh = Hon. Julia Judith of Adlestrop and Stoneleigh Abbey, 1765-1823. Twisleton, 1771-1843. 1786

Richard, 2nd Duke of Buckingham and Chandos, K.G., 1797-1861. = Lady Mary Campbell, 1795-1862. 1819

Chandos, = Margarette 1st Lord Leigh, 1791-1850. Willes, — 1860. 1819

Mary = Captain Leigh, 1796-1871. Frederick Charles Acton Colvile, 1792-1872. 1817

Augusta Leigh, — 1877. 1827

= Grenville Charles Lennox Berkeley, 1806-1896.

Richard, 3rd Duke of Buckingham and Chandos, 1823-1889. = (1) Caroline Harvey, — 1874. 1851

Lady Anne Eliza Mary Brydges-Chandos-Grenville, 1820-1879. = William Henry Powell Gore-Langton, M.P., 1824-1873. 1846

13

TABLE XV

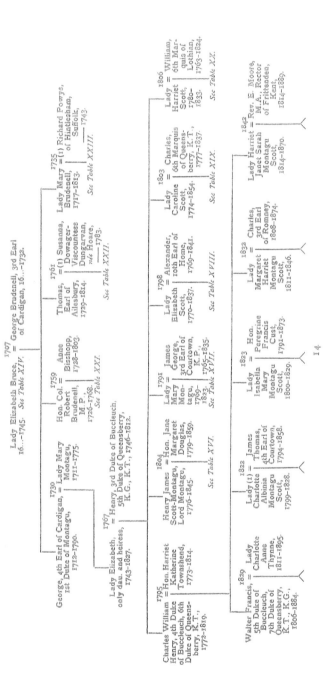

14

TABLE XVI

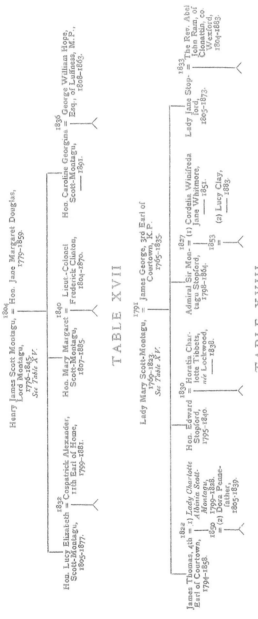

Henry James Scott Montagu, Lord Montagu, 1776-1845, *See Table XV.* =1804 Hon. Jane Margaret Douglas, 1775-1859.

Hon. Lucy Elizabeth Scott-Montagu, 1805-1877. =1832 Cospatrick Alexander, 11th Earl of Home, 1799-1881.

Hon. Mary Margaret Scott-Montagu, 1807-1885. =1840 Lieut.-Colonel Frederick Clinton, 1804-1870.

Hon. Caroline Georgina Scott-Montagu, —1891. =1836 George William Hope, Esq., of Luffness, M.P., 1808-1863.

TABLE XVII

Lady Mary Scott-Montagu, 1769-1823, *See Table XV.* =1791 James George, 3rd Earl of Courtown, K.P. 1765-1835.

James Thomas, 4th Earl of Courtown, 1794-1858. =1) 1822 *Lady Charlotte Albinia Scott-Montagu,* 1799-1828. =(2) 1850 Dora Penne-father, 1805-1839.

Hon. Edward Stopford, 1795-1840. =1830 Horatia Charlotte Tibbets, *née Lockwood,* —1838.

Admiral Sir Montagu Stopford, 1798-1864. =(1) 1827 Cordelia Winifreda Jane Whitmore, —1851. =(2) 1853 Lucy Clay, —1883.

Lady Jane Stopford, 1805-1873. =1833 The Rev. Abel John Ram, of Clonattin, co. Wexford, 1804-1883.

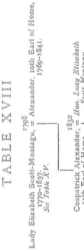

TABLE XVIII

Lady Elizabeth Scott-Montagu, 1770-1837, *See Table XV.* =1798 Alexander, 10th Earl of Home, 1769-1841.

Cospatrick Alexander, 11th Earl of Home, 1799-1881. =1832 Hon. Lucy Elizabeth Scott-Montagu, 1805-1877.

15

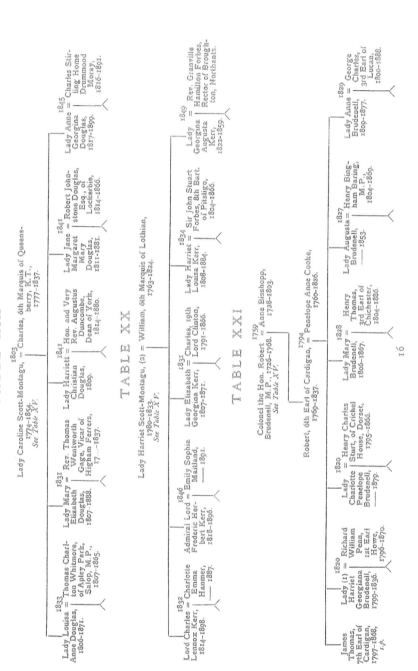

TABLE XIX

Lady Caroline Scott-Montagu, = [1803] Charles, 6th Marquis of Queensberry, K.T.,
1774-1854. 1777-1837.
See Table XV.

- [1833] Thomas Charlton Whitmore, of Apley Park, Salop, M.P., 1807-1865. = Lady Louisa Anne Douglas, 1806-1871.
- [1831] Rev. Thomas Wentworth Gage, Vicar of Higham Ferrers, 17...-1837. = Lady Mary Elizabeth Douglas, 1807-1888.
- Lady Harriett Christian Douglas, 1809.
- [1841] Hon. and Very Rev. Augustus Duncombe, Dean of York, 1814-1880. = Lady Jane Margaret Mary Douglas, 1811-1881.
- [1841] Robert Johnstone Douglas, Esq., of Lockerbie, 1814-1866.
- [1845] Charles Stirling Home Drummond Moray, 1816-1891. = Lady Anne Georgina Douglas, 1817-1899.

TABLE XX

Lady Harriet Scott-Montagu, (2) = William, 6th Marquis of Lothian,
1780-1833. 1763-1824.
See Table XV.

- [1832] Lord Charles Lennox Kerr, 1814-1898. = Charlotte Emma Hanmer, ——1887.
- [1846] Admiral Lord Frederic Herbert Kerr, 1818-1896. = Emily Sophia Maitland, ——1901.
- [1831] Charles, 19th Lord Clinton, 1791-1866. = Lady Elizabeth Georgina Kerr, 1807-1871.
- [1834] Sir John Stuart Forbes, 8th Bart. of Pitsligo, 1804-1866. = Lady Harriet Louisa Kerr, 1808-1884.
- [1849] Rev. Granville Hamilton Forbes, Rector of Broughton, Northants. = Lady Georgina Augusta Kerr, 1822-1859.

TABLE XXI

Colonel the Hon. Robert Brudenell, M.P., 1726-1768. = [1759] Anne Bisshopp, 1728-1803.
See Table XV.

Robert, 6th Earl of Cardigan, = [1794] Penelope Anne Cooke,
1769-1837. 1760-1826.

- James Thomas, 7th Earl of Cardigan, 1797-1866, *s.p.*
- [1820] Richard William Penn, 1st Earl Howe, 1796-1870. = Lady (1) Harriet Georgiana Brudenell, 1799-1836.
- [1820] Henry Charles Sturt, of Crichel House, Dorset, 1795-1866. = Lady Charlotte Penelope Brudenell, ——1879.
- [1828] Henry Thomas, 3rd Earl of Chichester, 1804-1886. = Lady Mary Brudenell, 1806-1867.
- [1827] Henry Bingham Baring, M.P., 1804-1869. = Lady Augusta Brudenell, ——1853.
- [1829] George Charles, 3rd Earl of Lucan, 1800-1888. = Lady Anne Brudenell, 1809-1877.

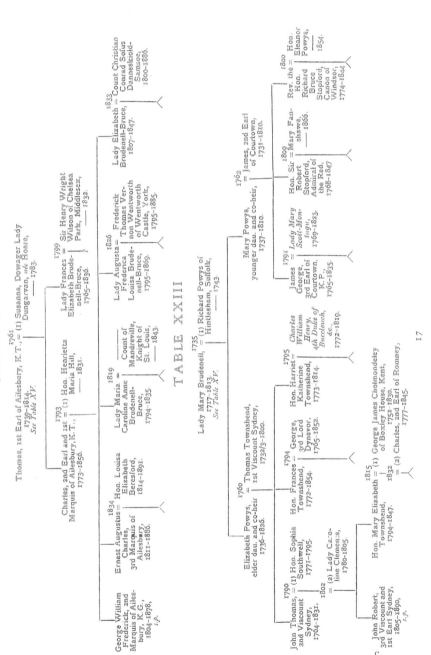

TABLE XXII

Thomas, 1st Earl of Ailesbury, K.T., = (1) Susanna, Dowager Lady [1761]
1729-1814. Dungarvan, née Hoare,
See Table XV. —— 1783.

Charles, 2nd Earl and 1st = (1) Hon. Henrietta [1793]
Marquis of Ailesbury, K.T., Maria Hill,
1773-1856. —— 1831.

Lady Frances = Sir Henry Wright [1799]
Elizabeth Brude- Wilson of Chelsea
nell-Bruce, Park, Middlesex,
1785-1830. —— 1832.

Lady Elizabeth = Count Christian [1833]
Brudenell-Bruce, Conrad Sofus
1807-1847. Danneskiold-
Samsoe,
1800-1886.

George William Ernest Augustus = Hon. Louisa [1834]
Frederick, 2nd Charles, Elizabeth
Marquis of Ailes- 3rd Marquis of Beresford,
bury, K.G., Ailesbury, 1814-1891.
1804-1878, 1811-1886.
s.p.

Lady Maria = Count of [1819]
Caroline Anne Mandreville,
Brudenell- Knight of
Bruce, St. Louis,
1794-1835. —— 1843.

Lady Augusta = Frederick [1826]
Frederica Thomas Ver-
Louisa Brude- non Wentworth
nell-Bruce, of Wentworth
1795-1869. Castle, York,
1795-1885.

TABLE XXIII

Lady Mary Brudenell, = (1) Richard Powys of [1735]
1717-1813. Hinlesham, Suffolk,
See Table XV. —— 1743.

Elizabeth Powys, = Thomas Townshend, [1760]
elder dau. and co-heir 1st Viscount Sydney,
1736-1825. 1732/3-1800.

Mary Powys, = James, 2nd Earl [1762]
younger dau. and co-heir of Courtown,
1737-1810. 1731-1810.

Charles = [1795]
William
Henry,
4th Duke of
Buccleuch,
&c.,
1772-1819.

Hon. Harriet = Katherine
Townshend,
1773-1814.

James = Lady Mary [1791]
George, Scott-Mon-
3rd Earl of tagu,
Courtown, 1769-1823.
K.P.,
1765-1835.

Hon. Sir = Mary Fan- [1809]
Robert shawe,
Stopford, —— 1866.
Admiral of
the Red,
1768-1847.

Rev. the = Hon. [1800]
Hon. Eleanor
Richard Powys,
Bruce —— 1854.
Stopford,
Canon of
Windsor,
1774-1844.

John Thomas, = (1) Hon. Sophia [1790]
2nd Viscount Southwell,
Sydney, 1771-1795.
1764-1831. = (2) Lady Caro- [1802]
line Clements,
1780-1805.

Hon. Frances George, = [1794]
Townshend, 3rd Lord
1772-1854. Dynevor,
1765-1852.

John Robert,
3rd Viscount and
1st Earl Sydney,
1805-1890,
s.p.

Hon. Mary Elizabeth = (1) George James Cholmondeley [1815]
Townshend, of Boxley House, Kent,
1794-1847. 1752-1830.
= (2) Charles, 2nd Earl of Romney, [1832]
1777-1845.

C

17

TABLE XXIV

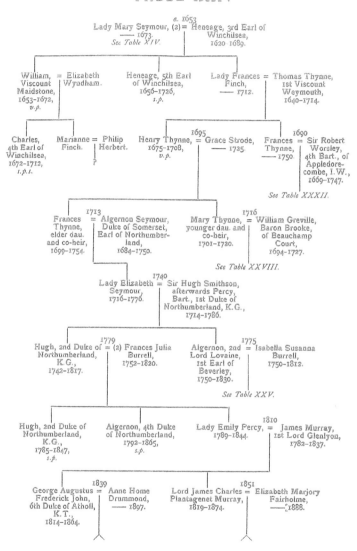

a. 1653
Lady Mary Seymour, (2) = Heneage, 3rd Earl of
—— 1673. Winchilsea,
See Table XIV. 1620–1689.

William, = Elizabeth | Heneage, 5th Earl | Lady Frances = Thomas Thynne,
Viscount | Wyndham. | of Winchilsea, | Finch, | 1st Viscount
Maidstone, | | 1656–1726, | —— 1712. | Weymouth,
1653–1672, | | *s.p.* | | 1640–1714.
v.p.

Charles, | Marianne = Philip | 1695 | 1690
4th Earl of | Finch. | Herbert. | Henry Thynne, = Grace Strode, | Frances = Sir Robert
Winchilsea, | | | 1675–1708, —— 1725. | Thynne, | Worsley,
1672–1712, | | ? | *v.p.* | —— 1750. | 4th Bart., of
s.p.s. | | | | | Appledore-
| | | | | combe, I.W.,
| | | | | 1669–1747.

See Table XXXII.

1713 | 1716
Frances = Algernon Seymour, | Mary Thynne, = William Greville,
Thynne, | Duke of Somerset, | younger dau. and | Baron Brooke,
elder dau. | Earl of Northumber- | co-heir, | of Beauchamp
and co-heir, | land, | 1701–1720. | Court,
1699–1754. | 1684–1750. | | 1694–1727.

See Table XXVIII.

1740
Lady Elizabeth = Sir Hugh Smithson,
Seymour, | afterwards Percy,
1716–1776. | Bart., 1st Duke of
| Northumberland, K.G.,
| 1714–1786.

1779 | 1775
Hugh, 2nd Duke of = (2) Frances Julia | Algernon, 2nd = Isabella Susanna
Northumberland, | Burrell, | Lord Lovaine, | Burrell,
K.G., | 1752–1820. | 1st Earl of | 1750–1812.
1742–1817. | | Beverley, |
| | 1750–1830. |

See Table XXV.

Hugh, 2nd Duke of | Algernon, 4th Duke | 1810
Northumberland, | of Northumberland, | Lady Emily Percy, = James Murray,
K.G., | 1792–1865, | 1789–1844. | 1st Lord Glenlyon,
1785–1847, | *s.p.* | | 1782–1837.
s.p.

1839 | 1851
George Augustus = Anne Home | Lord James Charles = Elizabeth Marjory
Frederick John, | Drummond, | Plantagenet Murray, | Fairholme,
6th Duke of Atholl, | —— 1897. | 1819–1874. | —— 1888.
K.T., | |
1814–1864. | |

18

TABLE XXV

Algernon, 1st Earl of Beverley, 2nd Lord Loraine, =1775 Isabella Susanah Burrell,
1750-1830.
See Table XXIV.

George, 2nd Earl = 1801 Louisa Harcourt
of Beverley, Stuart-Wortley,
5th Duke of 1781-1848.
Northumberland,
1778-1867.

Hon. Hugh = 1805 Mary Sutton,
Percy, Bishop 1831.
of Carlisle,
1784-1856.
See Table XXVI.

Hon. Josceline = 1810 Sophia
Percy, Elizabeth
Rear-Admiral, Walhouse,
R.N., C.B., 1875.
1784-1856.

Lady Mary = 1808 Andrew Mortimer
Emily Charlotte Drummond, of
Percy, Charing Cross and
1897. Doulham, Middlesex,
1785-1864.

Lady (2) = 1795 George, 3rd Earl
Charlotte of Ashburnham,
Percy, 1760-1830.
1776-1862. *See Table XXVII.*

Algernon George, 6th Duke = 1845 Louisa Drummond,
of Northumberland, K.G., 1813-1890.
1810-1899.

Lord Josceline = 1818 Margaret
William Percy, Davidson.
1811-1881.

Lady Margaret Percy, = 1841 Edward Richard,
1813-1897. 2nd Lord Hatherton,
1815-1880.

TABLE XXVI

Hon. Hugh Percy, Bishop of Carlisle, = 1856 Mary Sutton,
1784-1856. 1831.
See Table XXV.

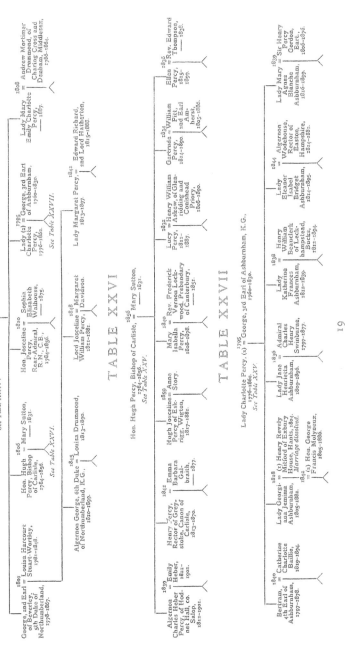

Algernon = 1830 Emily
Charles Heber Heber,
Percy, of Hod- 1902.
net Hall, co.
Salop,
1812-1901.

Henry Percy, = 1842 Emma
Rector of Grey- Barbara
stoke, Canon of Gil-
Carlisle, braith,
1815-1870. 1877.

Hugh Josceline = 1859 Anne
Percy, of Esk- Story.
rigg, Wigton,
1817-1888.

Mary = 1840 Rev. Frederick
Isabella Vernon Lock-
Percy, wood, Prebendary
1808-1878. of Canterbury,
1851.

Lucy = 1851 Henry William
Percy, Astew, of Glen-
1811- riding and
1887. Conishead
Priory,
1806-1890.

Gertrude = 1844 William
Percy, Pitt,
1814-1890. 3rd Earl Am-
herst,
1805-1886.

Ellen = Rev. Edward
Percy, Thompson,
1890. 1836.

TABLE XXVII

Lady Charlotte Percy, (2) = 1795 George, 3rd Earl of Ashburnham, K.G.,
1776-1862. 1760-1830.
See Table XXV.

Bertram, = 1840 Catherine
4th Earl of Charlotte
Ashburnham, Baillie,
1797-1878. 1819-1894.

Lady Georgi- = 1838 (1) Henry Revely
ana Jemima Mitford of Exbury
Ashburnham, House, Hants, 1804.
1805-1882. *Marriage dissolved.*
= (2) Hon. George
Francis Molyneux,
1805-1886.

Lady Jane = 1856 Admiral
Henrietta Charles
Ashburnham, Henry
1809-1896. Swinburne,
1797-1877.

Lady = 1838 Henry
Katherine William
Frances Beauclerk
Ashburnham, of Leck-
1811-1839. hampstead,
Bucks,
1811-1890.

Lady = 1844 Algernon
Eleanor Wodehouse,
Isabel Rector of
Bridget Easton,
Ashburnham, Hampshire,
1814-1895. 1814-1882.

Lady Mary = 1839 Sir Henry
Agnes Percy
Blanche Gordon,
Ashburnham, Bart.,
1816-1899. 1806-1876.

TABLE XXVIII

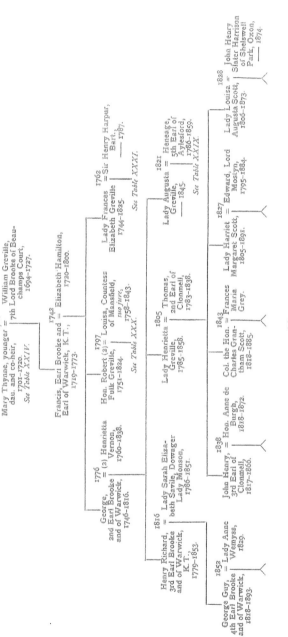

Mary Thynne, younger $=$ William Greville,
dau. and co-heir, 1716 7th Lord Brooke of Beau-
1701-1720. champs Court,
See Table XXIV. 1694-1727.

Francis, Earl Brooke and $=$ Elizabeth Hamilton,
Earl of Warwick, K.T., 1742 1720-1800.
1719-1773.

George, 1776 $=$ (2) Henrietta
2nd Earl Brooke Vernon,
and of Warwick, 1760-1838.
1746-1816.

Hon. Robert (2) $=$ Louisa, Countess
Fulk Greville, 1797 of Mansfield,
1751-1824. *suo jure,*
1758-1843.
See Table XXX.

Lady Frances 1762 $=$ Sir Henry Harpur,
Elizabeth Greville Bart.,
1744-1825. —— 1787.
See Table XXXI.

Henry Richard, $=$ Lady Sarah Eliza-
3rd Earl Brooke 1816 beth Savile, Dowager
and of Warwick, Lady Monson,
K.T., 1786-1851.
1779-1853.

Lady Henrietta $=$ Thomas,
Greville, 1805 2nd Earl of
1785-1858. Clonmell,
1783-1838.

Lady Augusta $=$ Heneage,
Greville, 1821 5th Earl of
1845. Aylesford,
1786-1859.
See Table XXIX.

George Guy, $=$ Lady Anne
4th Earl Brooke 1852 Wemyss,
and of Warwick, 1829.
1818-1893.

John Henry, $=$ Hon. Anne de
3rd Earl of 1838 Burgh,
Clonmell, 1818-1872.
1817-1866.

Col. the Hon. $=$ Frances
Charles Gran- 1843 Marie
tham Scott, Grey.
1818-1885.

Lady Harriet $=$ Edward, Lord
Margaret Scott, 1827 Moslyn,
1805-1891. 1795-1884.

Lady Louisa $=$ John Henry
Augusta Scott, 1828 Slater Harrison
1806-1873. of Shelswell
Park, Oxon,
—— 1874.

20

TABLE XXIX

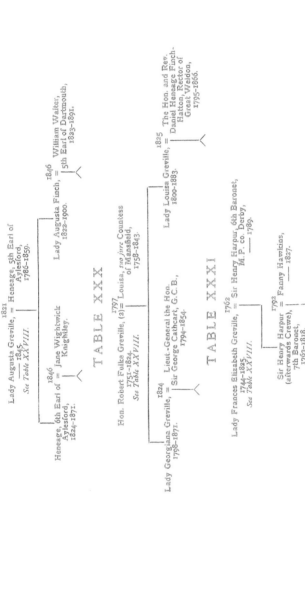

Lady Augusta Greville, = Heneage, 5th Earl of Aylesford, 1786-1859.
1821
1845
See Table XXVIII.

Heneage, 6th Earl of Aylesford, 1824-1871.

Lady Augusta Finch, 1822-1900.
1846 = William Walter, 5th Earl of Dartmouth, 1823-1891.

1846 = Jane Wightwick Knightley.

TABLE XXX

Hon. Robert Fulke Greville, 1751-1824, (2)= Louisa, *suo jure* Countess of Mansfield, 1758-1843.
1797
See Table XXVIII.

Lady Georgiana Greville, 1798-1871.
1824 = Lieut.-General the Hon. Sir George Cathcart, G.C.B., 1794-1854.

Lady Louisa Greville, 1800-1883.
1825 = The Hon. and Rev. Daniel Heneage Finch-Hatton, Rector of Great Weldon, 1795-1866.

TABLE XXXI

Lady Frances Elizabeth Greville, 1744-1825, = Sir Henry Harpur 6th Baronet, M.P. co. Derby, 1789.
1762
See Table XXVIII.

Sir Henry Harpur (afterwards Crewe), 7th Baronet, 1763-1818.
1792 = Fanny Hawkins, 1827.

Sir George Crewe, 8th Baronet, 1795.
1819 = Jane Whittaker, 1880.

Henry Robert Crewe, Rector of Breadsale, co. Derby, 1801-1865.
1827 = Frances Caroline Jenney, 1886.

Edmund Lewis Crewe of Repton Park, co. Derby, 1803-1874.
1832 = Caroline Anna Need, 1887.

Selina Crewe, 1838.
1822 = William Stanhope Lovell, Vice-Admiral, R.N., 1859.

2 I

TABLE XXXII

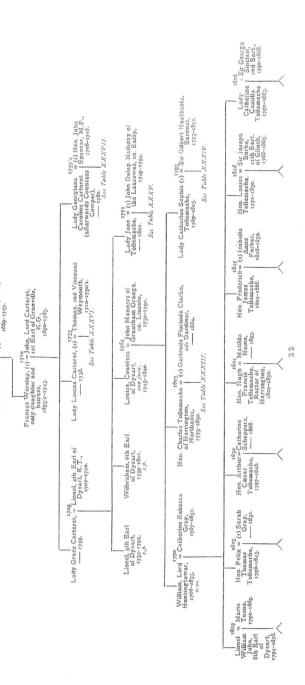

TABLE XXXIII

Hon. Charles Tollemache $=^{1803}$ Gertrude Florinda Clarke
of Harrington, Northants, né Gardiner,
1775-1850. —1864.
See Table XXXII.

William Tollemache, $=^{1838}$ (1) Lady Anna Maria Seymour,
1810-1806. 1807-1873.

TABLE XXXIV

Lady Catherine Sophia Tollemache, (1) $=^{1793}$ Sir Gilbert Heathcote, Bart.
1769-1825. 1773-1851.
See Table XXXII.

Sir Gilbert John Heathcote, $=^{1827}$ Clementina Elizabeth Drummond,
1st Lord Aveland, Baroness Willoughby de Eresby,
1795-1867. 1809-1888.

TABLE XXXV

Lady Jane Tollemache, $=^{1771}$ (1) Major John Delap Halliday,
1802. of the Leasowes, co. Salop,
See Table XXXVII. and Castlemains, Kirkcudbright,
1749-1794.

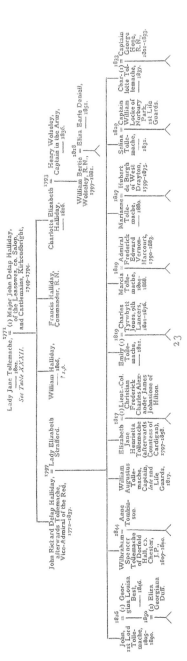

John Richard Delap Halliday, $=^{1797}$ Lady Elizabeth Strafford.
afterwards Tollemache,
Vice-Admiral of the Red,
1772-1837.

Francis Halliday, Commander, R.N., 1749-1794.

William Halliday, —1806.

Charlotte Elizabeth Halliday, —1826. $=^{1793}$ Henry Wolseley, Captain in the Army, 1826.

William Bertie de Burgh Wolseley, R.N., 1797-1881. $=^{1818}$ Eliza Earle Daniell, —1851.

Wilbraham Spencer Tollemache of Dorfold Hall, co. Chester, J.P., 1807-1890. $=^{1844}$ Anne Tomkinson.

Elizabeth Jane Henrietta Tollemache (afterwards Countess of Cardigan), 1797-1858. $=^{1817}$ (1) Lieut.-Col. Christian Frederick Charles Alexander James Johnstone of Hilton.

Emily (1) Tollemache, —1811. $=^{1809}$ Charles Tyrwhitt Jones, 9th Lancers, 1801-1676.

Marcia Tollemache, 1864-1868. $=^{1809}$ Admiral Frederick Edward Vernon-Harcourt, 1790-1883.

Marianne Tollemache, —1880. $=^{1827}$ Hubert de Burgh of West Drayton, 1799-1875.

Selina Tollemache, 1831. $=^{1850}$ Captain William Locke of Norbury Park, 1st Life Guards.

Char-(1) lotte Tollemache, 1837. $=^{1853}$ Captain George Hope, R.N., 1801-1893.

John, 1st Lord Tollemache, 1805-1890. $=^{1825}$ (1) Georgina Louisa Best, —1846.
$=^{1850}$ (2) Eliza Georgiana Duff.

23

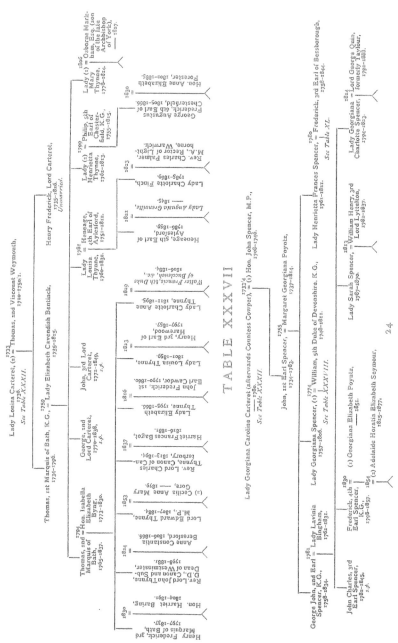

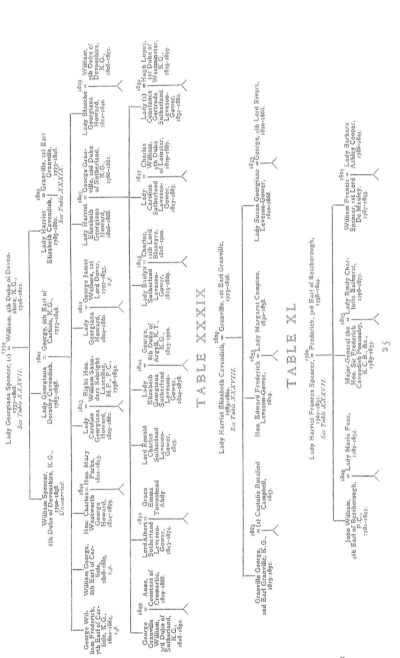

TABLE XXXVIII

TABLE XXXIX

TABLE XL

TABLE XLI

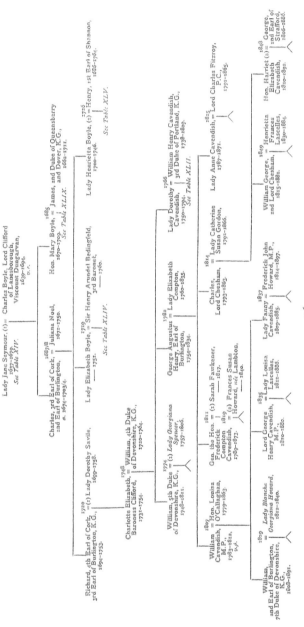

Lady Jane Seymour, (1)= Charles Boyle, Lord Clifford
1637–1679, Viscount Dungarvan,
See Table XLIV. 1639–1694,
v. r.

Charles, 3rd Earl of Cork, = Juliana Noel, Lady Elizabeth Boyle, = Sir Henry Arundel Bedingfeld, Hon. Mary Boyle, = James, 2nd Duke of Queensberry Lady Henrietta Boyle, (1) = Henry, 1st Earl of Shannon,
2nd Earl of Burlington, 1672–1750. 3rd Baronet, 1670–1750. and Dover, K.G., 1700–1746. 1686–1764.
v. 1674–1703/4. *See Table XLIV.* ——1760. 1662–1711. *See Table XLV.*
See Table XLIX.

Richard, 4th Earl of Cork, =(1) Lady Dorothy Savile,
3rd Earl of Burlington, K.G., 1699–1758.
1695–1753.

Charlotte Elizabeth, = William, 4th Duke George Augustus = Lady Elizabeth Lady Dorothy = William Henry Cavendish,
Baroness Clifford, of Devonshire, K.G., Henry, Earl of Compton, Cavendish, 3rd Duke of Portland, K.G.,
1731–1754. 1720–1764. Burlington, 1760–1835. 1750–1794. 1738–1809.
1754–1834. *See Table XLII.*

William, 5th Duke = (1) Lady Georgiana Charles, = Lady Catherine Lady Anne Cavendish, = Lord Charles Fitzroy,
of Devonshire, K.G., Spencer, Lord Chesham, Susan Gordon, 1787–1871. P.C.,
1748–1811. 1757–1806. 1793–1863. 1791–1866. 1791–1865.

William = Hon. Louisa Gen. the Hon. = (1) Sarah Fawkener, Lady Louisa = Lady Fanny Frederick John William George, = Henrietta Hon. Harriet (2) = George,
Cavendish, O'Callaghan, Frederick 1817. Lascelles, Cavendish, Howard, M.P., 2nd Lord Chesham, Frances Cavendish, and Earl of
M.P., 1779–1863. Compton = (2) Frances Susan 1811–1816. 1809–1885. 1814–1897. 1815–1882. Lascelles, 1800–1892. Strafford,
1783–1812, Cavendish, Howard, *née* Lambton, 1830–1864. 1806–1886.
v.f. 1769–1873. 1840.

William, = Lady Blanche Lord George = Lady Louisa
and Earl of Burlington, Georgiana Howard, Henry Cavendish, Lascelles,
7th Duke of Devonshire, 1812–1840. M.P., 1811–1816.
K.G., 1810–1880.
1808–1891.

26

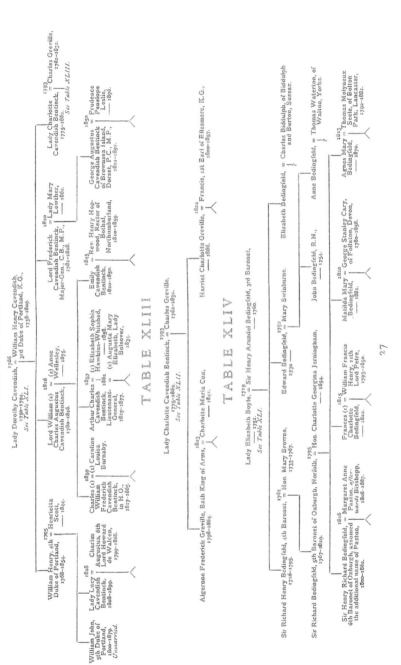

TABLE XLIII

1766
Lady Dorothy Cavendish, = William Henry Cavendish,
1750-1794. | 3rd Duke of Portland, K.G.,
See Table XLI. | 1738-1809.

William Henry, 4th 1795 = Henrietta Scott, —1844.
Duke of Portland, 1768-1854.

 William John, 5th Duke of Portland, 1800-1879, *Unmarried.*

Lady Lucy 1828 = Charles Augustus, 6th Lord Howard de Walden, 1799-1868.
Cavendish Bentinck, 1808-1890.

Lord William (2) 1816 = (2) Anne Wellesley, —1875.
Charles Augustus Cavendish Bentinck, 1780-1826.

 Charles (1) = (1) Caroline Louisa Burnaby.
William Frederick Cavendish Bentinck, in H.O., 1817-1865.

 Arthur Charles 1859 = (2) Elizabeth Sophia Hawkins-Whitshed, —1858.
Cavendish Bentinck, Lieutenant-General, 1819-1877.
= (1) Augusta Mary Elizabeth, Lady Bolsover, 1824.

Lord Frederick 1820 = Lady Mary Lowther, —1861.
Cavendish Bentinck, Major-Gen. C.B., M.P., 1781-1828.

 Emily 1845 = Rev Henry Hopwood, Rector of Bothal, Northumberland, 1840-1859.
Cavendish Bentinck, 1820-1850.

 George Augustus 1850 = Prudence Penelope Leslie, —1896.
Cavendish Bentinck of Brownsea Island, Dorset, P.C., M.P., 1821-1891.

Lady Charlotte 1793 = Charles Greville, 1762-1832.
Cavendish Bentinck, 1775-1862.
See Table XLIII.

TABLE XLIII

Lady Charlotte Cavendish Bentinck, 1793 = Charles Greville, 1762-1832.
1775-1862.
See Table XLII.

Algernon Frederick Greville, Bath King of Arms, 1802 = Charlotte Maria Cox, —1864.
1798-1864.

Harriet Charlotte Greville, 1822 = Francis, 1st Earl of Ellesmere, K.G., 1800-1857.
—1866.

TABLE XLIV

Lady Elizabeth Boyle, 1719 = Sir Henry Arundel Bedingfeld, 3rd Baronet,
1760.
See Table XLI.

Sir Richard Henry Bedingfeld, 4th Baronet, 1761 = Hon. Mary Browne, 1733-1767.
1716-1795.

Edward Bedingfeld, 1752 = Mary Swinburne.
1730.

 Sir Richard Bedingfeld, 5th Baronet of Oxburgh, Norfolk, 1795 = Hon. Charlotte Georgina Jerningham, —1854.
1767-1850.

 Frances (1) 1815 = William Francis Henry 11th Lord Petre, 1793-1850.
Charlotte Bedingfeld, —1822.

 Sir Henry Richard Bedingfeld, 1826 = Margaret Anne Paston, afterwards Bishopp, 1800-1862.
6th Baronet of Oxburgh, assumed the additional name of Paston, 1800-1862.

Elizabeth Bedingfeld, = Charles Biddulph, of Biddulph and Burton, Sussex.

John Bedingfeld, R.N., —1754.

 Matilda Mary 1820 = George Stanley Cary, of Follaton, Devon, 1780-1848.
Bedingfeld, —1881.

Anne Bedingfeld, = Thomas Waterton, of Walton, Yorks.

 Agnes Mary 1823 = Thomas Molyneux Steele, of Bolton Park, Lancaster, 1792-1881.
Bedingfeld, —1870.

27

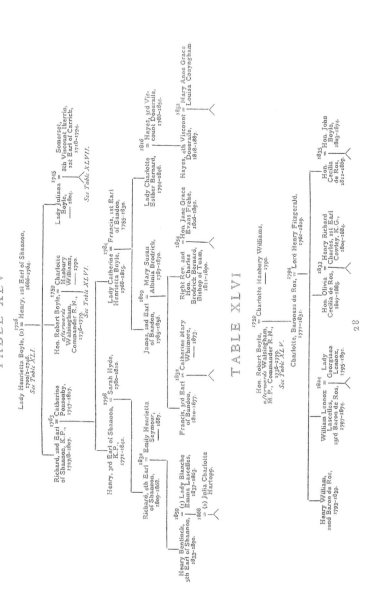

TABLE XLV

Lady Henrietta Boyle, (2) = Henry, 1st Earl of Shannon,
1700/1-1746.   1686-1764.
See Table XLI.

Richard, 2nd Earl = Catherine Ponsonby, Hon. Robert Boyle, = Charlotte Hanbury   Lady Juliana = Somerset, 8th Viscount Ikerrin,
of Shannon, K.P.,   1747-1827.   afterwards Walsingham Williams,   Boyle,   1st Earl of Carrick,
1727/8-1807.   Commander R.N.,   —1790.   1804-.   1718-1794.
                                          1736-1779.
                                          See Table XLVI.   See Table XLVI.

Henry, 3rd Earl of Shannon, = Sarah Hyde,   Lady Catherine = Francis, 1st Earl   Lady Charlotte = Hayes, 3rd Vis-
1771-1842.   1760-1810.   Henrietta Boyle,   of Bandon,   Esther Bernard,   count Doneraile,
                                                 1760-1815.   1755-1830.   1794-1846.   1766-1854.

Richard, 4th Earl = Emily Henrietta   Francis, 3rd Earl = Catherine Mary   James, 2nd Earl = Mary Susan   Right Rev. and = Hon. Jane Grace   Hayes, 4th Viscount = Mary Anne Grace
of Shannon,   Seymour,   of Bandon,   Whitmore,   of Bandon,   Albinia Brodrick, Hon. Charles   Evans Freke,   Doneraile,   Louisa Conyngham
1809-1868.   —1887.   1810-1877.   —1873.   1785-1856.   1787-1870.   Brodrick Bernard, 1806-1892.   1818-1887.
                                                                                                             Bishop of Tuam,
                                                                                                             1811-1890.

Henry Bentinck, = (1) Lady Blanche
5th Earl of Shannon,   Emma Lascelles,
1833-1890.   1827-1863.
                   = (2) Julia Charlotte
                       Hartopp.

TABLE XLVI

Hon. Robert Boyle, = Charlotte Hanbury Williams,
afterwards Walsingham,   —1790.
M.P., Commander R.N.,
1736-1779.
See Table XLV.

Charlotte, Baroness de Ros, = Lord Henry Fitzgerald,
1771-1831.   1761-1829.

Henry William, = Lady   William Lennox = Georgiana   Hon. Olivia = Henry Richard   Hon. John
2nd Baron de Ros,   Georgiana   Lascelles,   Lennox,   Cecilia de Ros, Charles, 1st Earl   Cecilia   Boyle,
1793-1839.   Lennox,   3rd Baron de Ros, 1795-1891.   1807-1885. Cowley, K.G.,   de Ros,   1803-1874.
                    1795-1891. 1797-1874.   1804-1884.   1811-1869.

28

TABLE XLVII

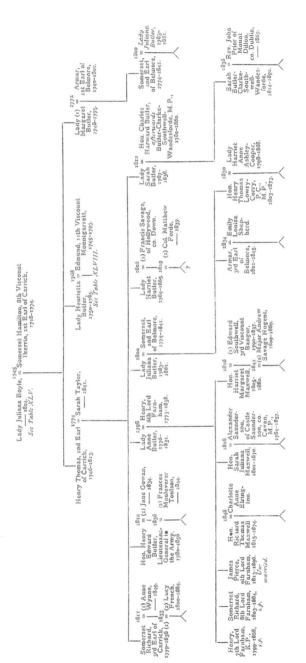

Lady Juliana Boyle, = [1745] Somerset Hamilton, 8th Viscount
[1804,]   Ikerrin, 1st Earl of Carrick,
See Table XLV.   1718-1774.

Henry Thomas, 2nd Earl = [1774] Sarah Taylor,
of Carrick,   —— 1841.
1746-1813.

Lady Henrietta = [1768] Edmund, 11th Viscount
Butler,   Mountgarrett,
1750-1783.   1745-1793.
See Table XLVIII.

Lady (?) = [1775] Armar,
Margaret Butler,   1st Earl of
1718-1775.   Belmore,
                      1740-1802.

Somerset = [1811] Anne
Richard,   Wynne,
3rd Earl of   —— 1849.
Carrick, [1833] (2) Lucy
1779-1838 (1).   French,
                  1800-1884.

Hon. Henry = [1812] (1) Jane Gowran,
Edward   —— 1836.
Butler,   (2) Frances
Lieutenant-   Mauleverer
General in   Toulson,
the Army,   —— 1844.
1788-1856.

Lady = [1798] Henry,
Anne   6th Lord
Butler,   Farn-
1776-   ham,
1831.   1773-1838.

Lady = [1800] Somerset,
Juliana   and Earl
Butler,   of Belmore,
1783-   1774-1841.
1861.

Lady = [1812] Hon. Charles
Sarah   Harward Butler,
Butler,   *afterwards*
1787-   Butler-Clarke-
1836.   Southwell-
              Wandesforde, M.P.,
              1780-1860.

Lady = [1805] (1) Francis Savage,
Harriet   of Hollywood,
Butler,   co. Down.
1784-1865.   —— 1837.
          [1819] (2) Col. Matthew
               Forde,
               —— 1837.

Armar, = [1797] Lady
and Earl   Juliana
of Belmore,   Butler,
1740-1802.   1783-
                1851.

Henry, = [1820] Charlotte
7th Lord   Anne
Farnham,   Elring-
1799-1858,   ton.
s.p.

James = [1848] Somerset
Pierce,   Richard,
6th Lord   5th Lord
Farnham,   Farnham,
1813-1896.   1803-1884,
Un-   *s.p.*
married.

Hon. = Charlotte
Richard   Anne
Thomas   Elring-
Maxwell,   ton.
1815-1874.

Hon. = [1848] Alexander
Sarah   Saunder-
Juliana   son,
Maxwell,   of Castle
1801-1890.   Saunder-
              son, co.
              Cavan,
              M.P.,
              1784-1857.

Hon. = [1806] (1) Edward
Harriet   Southwell,
Margaret   3rd Viscount
Maxwell,   Bangor,
1805-   1790-1837,
1880.   [1841] (2) Major Andrew
               Savage Nugent,
               1805-1889.

Armar, = [1824] Emily
3rd Earl   Louisa
of   Shep-
Belmore,   herd.
1801-1845.

Hon. = [1830] Harriet
Henry   Anne
Thomas   Ashley-
Lowry-   Cooper,
Corry,   1798-1808.
P.C.,
M.P.,
1803-1873.

Sarah = [1836] Rev. John
Butler-   Prior of
Clarke-   Mount
South-   Dillon,
well-   co. Dublin,
Wandes-   1807.
forde,
1812-1892.

= [1800] *Lady*
Juliana
Butler,
1783-
1851.

TABLE XLVIII

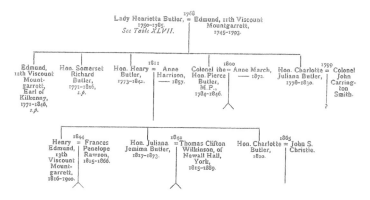

1768
Lady Henrietta Butler, = Edmund, 11th Viscount
1750-1785, Mountgarrett,
See Table XLVII. 1745-1793.

| Edmund, 12th Viscount Mountgarrett, Earl of Kilkenny, 1771-1846, *s.p.* | Hon. Somerset Richard Butler, 1771-1826, *s.p.* | 1811 Hon. Henry = Anne Butler, Harrison, 1773-1842. — 1857. | 1800 Colonel the = Anne March, Hon. Pierce — 1872. Butler, M.P., 1764-1846. | Hon. Charlotte 1799 Juliana Butler, = Colonel 1778-1830. John Carrington Smith. |

1844
Henry = Frances
Edmund, | Penelope
13th | Rawson,
Viscount | 1825-1866.
Mount-
garrett,
1816-1900.

1842
Hon. Juliana = Thomas Clifton
Jemima Butler, | Wilkinson, of
1817-1873. | Newall Hall,
York,
1815-1889.

1865
Hon. Charlotte = John S.
Butler, | Christie.
1820.

TABLE XLIX

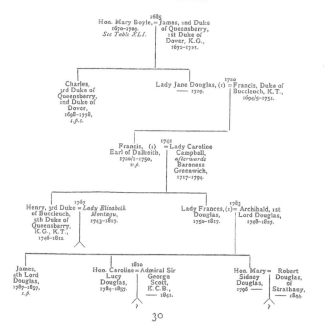

1685
Hon. Mary Boyle, = James, 2nd Duke
1670-1709. of Queensberry,
See Table XLI. 1st Duke of
Dover, K.G.,
1672-1711.

Charles,
3rd Duke of
Queensberry,
2nd Duke of
Dover,
1698-1778,
s.p.s.

1720
Lady Jane Douglas, (1) = Francis, Duke of
— 1729. | Buccleuch, K.T.,
1694/5-1751.

1742
Francis, (1) = Lady Caroline
Earl of Dalkeith, | Campbell,
1720/1-1750, | *afterwards*
v.p. | Baroness
Greenwich,
1717-1794.

1767
Henry, 3rd Duke = Lady Elizabeth
of Buccleuch, | Montagu,
5th Duke of | 1743-1827.
Queensberry,
K.C., K.T.,
1746-1812.

1783
Lady Frances, (1) = Archibald, 1st
Douglas, | Lord Douglas,
1750-1817. | 1748-1827.

James,
4th Lord
Douglas,
1787-1857,
s.p.

1810
Hon. Caroline = Admiral Sir
Lucy | George
Douglas, | Scott,
1784-1857. | K.C.B.,
— 1841.

Hon. Mary = Robert
Sidney | Douglas,
Douglas, | of
1796 — | Strathany,
— 1844.

30

TABLE L

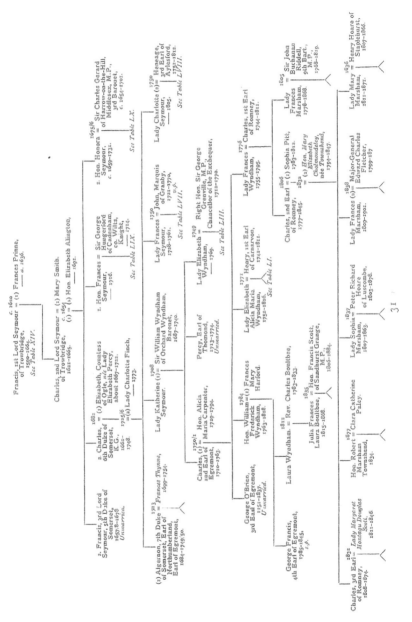

31

TABLE LI

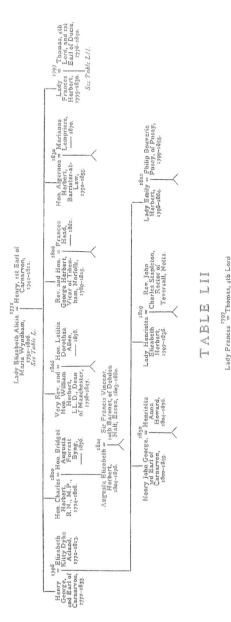
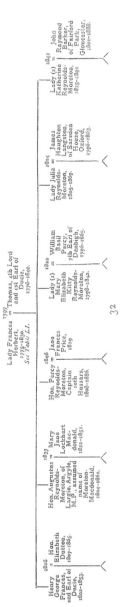

TABLE LII

32

TABLE LIII

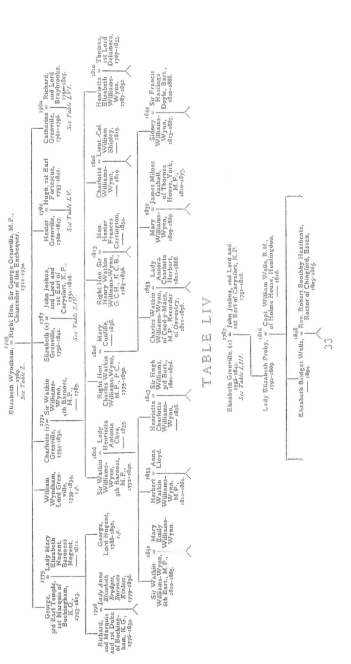

Elizabeth Wyndham, = Right Hon. Sir George Grenville, M.P.,
1749.
1769.
See Table L.
Chancellor of the Exchequer,
1712–1770.

George, = Lady Mary
3rd Earl Temple, 1775, Elizabeth
1st Marquis of Nugent,
Buckingham, Baroness
K.G., Nugent,
1753–1813. 1812.

William = Lady Mary
Wyndham, Elizabeth
Lord Gren- Nugent,
ville, Baroness
1759–1834. Nugent,
s.p. 1812.

Charlotte (2) = Sir Watkin
Grenville, 1771. Williams-
1754–1831. Wynn,
4th Baronet,
M.P.,
—1789.

Elizabeth (2) = John Joshua,
Grenville, 1787. 1st Lord and
1756–1842. 1st Earl of
Carysfort, K.P.,
1751–1828.
See Table LIV.

Hester = Hugh, 1st Earl
Grenville, 1782. Fortescue,
1760–1847. 1753–1841.
See Table LV.

Catherine = Richard,
Grenville, 1780. 2nd Lord
1761–1796. Braybrooke,
1750–1825.
See Table LVI.

Richard, = Lady Anne
2nd Marquis 1796. Elizabeth
and 1st Duke Bridges,
of Bucking- Baroness
ham, K.G., Kinloss,
1776–1839. 1779–1836.

George, Lord Nugent,
1788–1850,
s.p.

Sir Watkin = Lady
Williams- 1806. Henrietta
Wynn, Antonia
5th Baronet, Clive,
M.P., —1835.
1772–1840.

Right Hon. = Mary
Charles Watkin 1806. Cunliffe,
Williams-Wynn, —1838.
M.P., P.C.,
1775–1850.

Right Hon. Sir = Hon.
Henry Watkin 1813. Hester
Williams-Wynn, Frances
G.C.H., K.C.B., Carrington,
1783–1856. —1854.

Charlotte = Lieut.-Col.
Williams- 1805. William
Wynn, Shipley,
—. 1819.

Henrietta = Thomas,
Elizabeth 1820. 1st Lord
Williams- Delamere,
Wynn, 1767–1855.
1787–1852.

Sir Watkin = Mary
Williams-Wynn, 1852. Emily
6th Bart., M.P., Williams-
1820–1885. Wynn.

Herbert = Anna
Watkin 1865. Lloyd.
Williams-
Wynn,
M.P.,
1822–1862.

Henrietta = Sir Hugh
Charlotte 1842. Williams,
Williams- 3rd Bart.,
Wynn, 1802–1876.
—1878.

Charles Watkin
Williams-Wynn,
of Coed-y-Maen,
M.P., Recorder
of Oswestry,
1822–1896.

Lady = Sir Hugh
Annora 1853. Williams,
Charlotte 3rd Bart.,
Herbert, 1802–1876.
1822–1868.

Mary = James Milnes
Williams- 1832. Gaskell,
Wynn, of Thornes
1809–1869. House, York,
M.P.,
1810–1873.

Sidney = Sir Francis
Williams- 1844. Hastings
Wynn, Doyle, Bart.,
1815–1867. 1810–1888.

TABLE LIV

Elizabeth Grenville, (2) = John Joshua, 2nd Lord and
1756–1842. 1787. 1st Earl of Carysfort, K.P.,
See Table LIII. 1751–1828.

Lady Elizabeth Proby, = Capt. William Wells, R.N.,
1790–1869. 1816. of Holme House, Huntingdon,
—1806.

Elizabeth Bridget Wells, = Rev. Robert Boothby Heathcote,
—1894. 1848. Rector of Chingford, Essex,
1805–1865.

33

TABLE LV

Hester Grenville, 1782 = Hugh, 1st Earl Fortescue,
1760–1847. | 1753–1841.
See Table LIII.

TABLE LVI

Catherine Grenville, 1780 = Richard Aldworth,
1761–1796. | 2nd Lord Braybrooke,
See Table LIII. | 1750–1825.

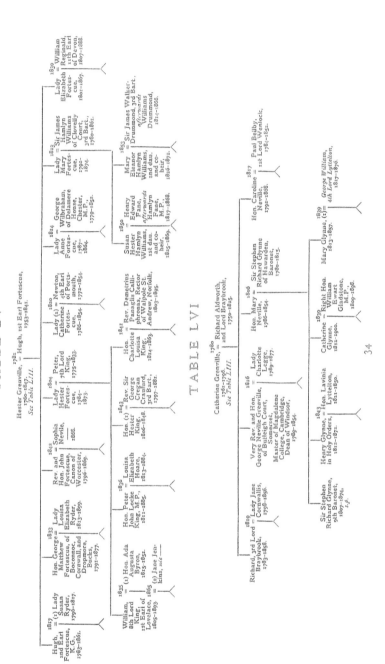

34

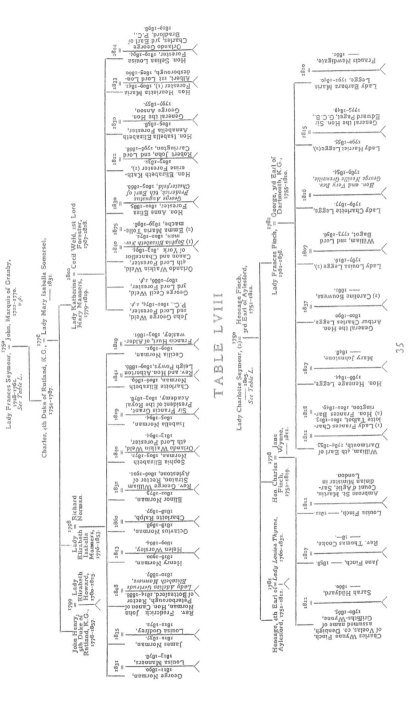

TABLE LIX

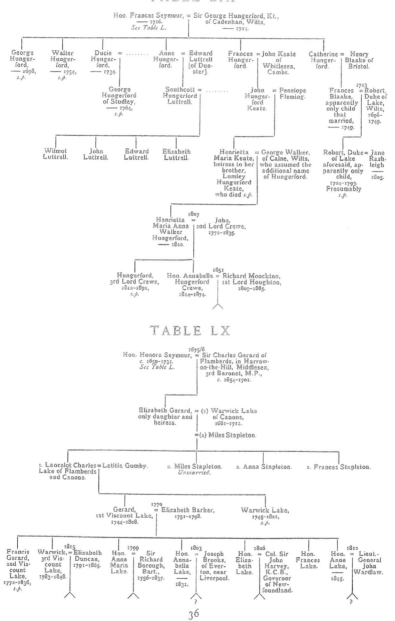

Hon. Frances Seymour, = Sir George Hungerford, Kt.,
——— 1716.
See Table L.
of Cadenham, Wilts,
——— 1714.

| George Hungerford, ——— 1698, *s.p.* | Walter Hungerford, ——— 1754, *s.p.* | Ducie Hungerford, ——— 1734. = ... | Anne Hungerford. = Edward Luttrell [of Dunster]. | Frances Hungerford = John Keate of Whitlesea, Cambs. | Catherine Hungerford. = Henry Blaake of Bristol. |

George Hungerford of Studley, ——— 1764, *s.p.*

Southcott Hungerford Luttrell. = ...

John Hungerford Keate. = Penelope Fleming.

1723
Frances Blaake, apparently only child that married, ——— 1749. = Robert, Duke of Lake, Wilts, 1696–1749.

| Wilmot Luttrell. | John Luttrell. | Edward Luttrell. | Elizabeth Luttrell. |

Henrietta Maria Keate, heiress to her brother, Lumley Hungerford Keate, who died *s.p.* = George Walker, of Calne, Wilts, who assumed the additional name of Hungerford.

Robert, Duke of Lake aforesaid, apparently only child, 1724–1793. Presumably *s.p.* = Jane Rashleigh ——— 1805.

1807
Henrietta Maria Anna Walker Hungerford, ——— 1820. = John, 2nd Lord Crewe, 1772–1835.

Hungerford, 3rd Lord Crewe, 1812–1890, *s.p.*

1851
Hon. Annabella Hungerford Crewe, 1814–1874. = Richard Monckton, 1st Lord Houghton, 1809–1885.

TABLE LX

1675/6
Hon. Honora Seymour, = Sir Charles Gerard of
c. 1659–1731.
See Table L.
Flamberds, in Harrow-on-the-Hill, Middlesex,
3rd Baronet, M.P.,
c. 1654–1701.

Elizabeth Gerard, only daughter and heiress. = (1) Warwick Lake of Canons, 1661–1712.

= (2) Miles Stapleton.

| 1. Lancelot Charles Lake of Flamberds and Canons. = Letitia Gumby. | 2. Miles Stapleton. *Unmarried.* | 1. Anna Stapleton. | 2. Frances Stapleton. |

1770
Gerard, 1st Viscount Lake, 1744–1808. = Elizabeth Barker, 1751–1798.

Warwick Lake, 1745–1821, *s.p.*

| Francis Gerard, 2nd Viscount Lake, 1772–1836, *s.p.* | 1815 Warwick, 3rd Viscount Lake, 1783–1848. = Elizabeth Duncan, 1791–1865. | 1799 Hon. Anna Maria Lake. = Sir Richard Borough, Bart., 1756–1837. | 1803 Hon. Anna-bella Lake. ——— 1831. = Joseph Brooks, of Ever-ton, near Liverpool. | 1806 Hon. Eliza-beth Lake. = Col. Sir John Harvey, K.C.B., Governor of New-foundland. | Hon. Frances Lake. | 1812 Hon. Anne Lake. ——— 1845. = Lieut.-General John Wardlaw. |

36

TABLE LXI

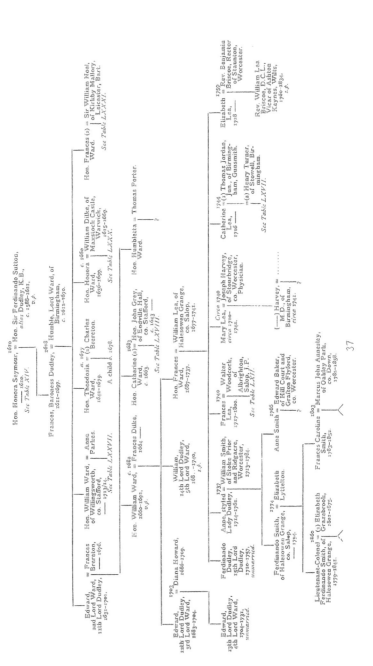

TABLE LXII

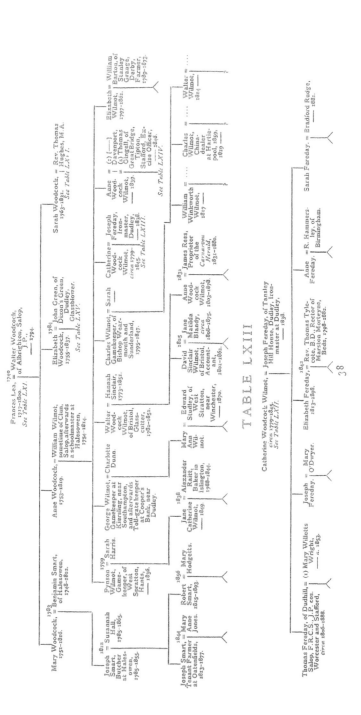

Frances Lea, = Walter Woodcock,
1717-1800. | of Albrighton, Salop,
See Table LXI. | J.P.,
—— 1794.

Mary Woodcock, 1783 = Benjamin Smart,
1751-1816. | of Halesowen,
| 1748-1822.

Anne Woodcock, = William Wilmot,
1753-1819. | sometime of Clun,
| Salop, afterwards
| a schoolmaster at
| Halesowen.
| 1754-1814.

Elizabeth = John Green, of
Woodcock, | Dixon's Green,
1755-1837. | Dudley,
| Glassblower.
See Table LXV.

Sarah Woodcock, = Rev. Thomas
1763-1831. | Hughes, M.A.
See Table LXVI.

Elizabeth = William
Wilmot, | Barton, of
1797-1861. | Stanley
| Grange,
| Derby,
| Farmer,
| 1789-1873.

Joseph = Susannah
Smart, | Hall,
Butcher | 1785-1865.
at Hales- |
owen. |
1785-1855. |

Pynson 1799 = Sarah
Wilmot, | Harris.
Game- |
keeper of |
West |
Spratton, |
Hants, |
—— 1836. |

George Wilmot, = Charlotte
Gamekeeper at | Dunn.
Kiersling, near |
Southampton, |
and afterwards |
Toll-gate keeper |
at Cooper's |
Bank, near |
Dudley. |

Walter = Hannah
Wood- | Sinclair,
cock, | 1773-1851.
of Bristol, |
Glass- |
cutter, |
1782-1851. |

Charles Wilmot, = Sarah
Gamekeeper, of | ——
Bishop Wear- |
mouth and |
Sunderland, |
1795-1847. |

Catherine = Joseph
Wood- | Fereday,
cock | Iron-
Wilmot, | master,
circa 1779- | Dudley,
1845. | —— 1878.
See Table LXIII.

Anne = (1) [——]
Wood- | Davenport,
cock | (2) Thomas
Wilmot, | Gingell, of
—— 1839. | Great Bridge,
| Tipton,
| Stafford, Ex-
| cise Officer,
| —— 1846.
See Table LXIV.

Joseph 1844 = Mary
Smart, | Anne
Tenant Farmer | Jones.
at Oatfields, |
1813-1877. |

Robert 1856 = Mary
Smart, | Hodgetts.
1815-1893. |

Jane = Alexander
Catherine | Raitt,
Wilmot, | Baker in
—— 1849. | Islington,
| 1788-1844.

Mary = Edward
Ann | Studley, of
Wil- | West
mot. | Stratton,
| near
| Winchester,
| 1870.

David 1845 = Jane
Sinclair | Matilda
Wilmot, | Blandy,
of Bristol, | circa
Account- | 1808-1865.
ant |
1801-1862. |

Anne = James Rees,
Wood- | Proprietor
cock | of the
Wilmot, | Carnarvon
1803-1898. | Herald,
| 1831-1880.

William
Winkworth
Wilmot,
1817 ——

Charles = ——
Wilmot, |
China- |
dealer |
at Hartle- |
pool, 1839. |
1819 —— |

Walter = ——
Wilmot, |
1814 ——

TABLE LXIII

Catherine Woodcock Wilmot, = Joseph Fereday, of Tansley
circa 1779-1845. | Hill House, Dudley, Iron-
See Table LXII. | master at Dudley,
| —— 1838.

Thomas Fereday, of Dudhill, = (1) Mary Willetts
Salop, F.R.C.S., J.P. for | Wright,
Worcester and Stafford, | —— c. 1853.
circa 1806-1888. |

Joseph = Mary
Fereday. | O'Dwyer.

Elizabeth Fereday, 1842 = Rev. Thomas Tyle-
1813-1898. | cote, B.D., Rector of
| Marston Morteyne,
| Beds, 1798-1881.

Anne = R. Hammers-
Fereday. | ley, of
| Birmingham.

Sarah Fereday. = Bradford Rudge,
| —— 1882.

38

TABLE LXIV

Anne Woodcock Wilmot, = (1) [——] Davenport.
—— 1839. | (2) Thomas Gingell, of Great Bridge,
See Table LXII. | Tipton, co. Stafford, Excise Officer,
  —— 1846.

- William Woodcock Davenport.
- Thomas Gingell, of Bilston, living 1846.
- Charles Gingell, 35th Foot, living 1846.
- Alexander Gingell, of Bilston, living 1846.
- Emma Gingell, of Dudley, living 1846.

TABLE LXV

Elizabeth Woodcock, [1784] = John Green, of Dixon's Green, Dudley, Glassblower.
1755-1831.
See Table LXVII.

- John Green, of Halesowen, J.P., 1789-1869, s.p.
- Elizabeth Green, [1843] = Edward Butler Walker, of Edgbaston, Birmingham, 1788-1836.
  1785 ——
- Frances Green. [1836] = Alexander Seymour Wills.
- Maria Green, [1834] = John Masson, of Albrighton, Salop, 1790-1852. —— 1840.

TABLE LXVI

Sarah Woodcock, [1784] = Rev. Thomas Hughes, M.A., of Colwall Green, Hereford,
1763-1831.   d. 1824.
See Table LXII.

- Thomas Hughes, Solicitor, of Abergavenny, 1797-1865, s.p.
- Frances Hughes, = James Tolley, of Dudley, Tailor, —— 1845.
  1791-1851.
  - Elizabeth Tolley. [d. 1848] = Henry Morgan, of Dudley, Painter.

TABLE LXVII

Catherine Lea, [1764] = (1) Thomas Jordan, Jun., of Birmingham, Gunsmith.
1726 ——   = (2) Henry Turner, of Stowall, Stafford.
See Table LXI.

- Daniel Turner of the Brown = Sarah Hanbury.
  Hills, co. Stafford.
  - Catherine Turner, [1802] = George Jones, of Dounington, Salop, .781-1857.
    1775-1858.
  - Phoebe Turner, = John Barker, 17.. -1860.
    1790-18..
- Catherine = Captain Lancelot Jordan.   Rutter.
- Frances Jordan. [1773] = Hugh Edwards.
- Anne Jordan = Thomas Smith.
  - Nathaniel Smith.
  - Anne Smith.
  - Mary Smith.

39

TABLE LXVIII

TABLE LXIX

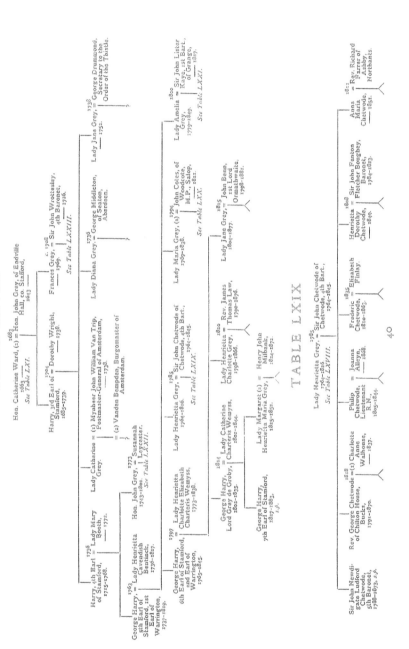

Hon. Catherine Ward, (1) = Hon. John Grey, of Enville Hall, co. Stafford, 1683. 1663. 1603.
See Table LXVI.

Harry, 3rd Earl of = Dorothy Wright, Stamford, 1730. 1685-1739. 1704.

Frances Grey, = Sir John Wrottesley, 1769. 4th Baronet, 1716. c. 1708. See Table LXXVII.

Lady Diana Grey. = George Middleton, 1736. of Seaton, Aberdeen.

Lady Jane Grey. = George Drummond, 1752. Secretary to the Order of the Thistle. 1738.

Harry, 4th Earl = Lady Mary Booth, of Stamford, 1771. 1715-1768. 1736.

Lady Catherine = (1) Mynheer John William Van Trip, Grey. Postmaster-General of Amsterdam, 1738. 1704. = (2) Vanden Bempden, Burgomaster of Amsterdam.

Hon. John Grey, = Susannah Leicester. 1743-1817. 1773. See Table LXXVII.

Lady Henrietta Grey, = Sir John Chetwode of Chetwode, 4th Bart. 1764-1846. 1764-1845. See Table LXXIX. 1785.

Lady Maria Grey, = John Coles, of 1769-1830. Woodcote, M.P., Salop. 1811. 1794. See Table LXX.

Lady Amelia = Sir John Lister Grey. Kaye, 1st Earl, 1773-1849. of Grange, 1857. 1800.

George Harry, = Lady Henrietta 5th Earl of Cavendish Stamford, 1st Bentinck, Earl of 1736-1827. Warrington, 1737-1819. 1763.

Lady Henrietta Charlotte Elizabeth Charteris Wemyss, 1773-1830.

George Harry, = Lady Catherine 6th Earl of Charteris Wemyss, Stamford, 1802-1835. and Earl of Warrington, 1765-1845. 1797.

Lady Henrietta Charlotte Grey, 1798-1866. See Table LXXIX.

Rev. James Thomas Law, 1790-1876. 1810.

Lady Jane Grey, = John Baua, 1801-1877. 1st Lord Ormathwaite. 1798-1881. 1805.

George Harry, Lord Grey de Groby, 1802-1835.

Lady Margaret (1) = Henry John Henrietta Maria Grey, Milbank, 1835-1852. 1824-1872.

George Harry, 7th Earl of Stamford, 1827-1883. s.p.

TABLE LXIX

Lady Henrietta Grey, = Sir John Chetwode of Chetwode, 4th Bart. 1764-1846. 1764-1845. See Table LXVIII.

Rev. George Chetwode = (1) Charlotte of Chilton House, Anne Walhouse, Bucks. 1837. 1791-1870. 1818.

Philip Chetwode, Lieutenant R.N., 1805-1844.

Joanna Allwyn, — 1868.

Frederic Chetwode, 1810-1865.

Elizabeth Finlay. 1835.

Henrietta Dorothy Chetwode, 1840.

Sir John Fenton Fletcher Boughey, Baronet, 1784-1823. 1808.

Anna Maria Chetwode, 1831.

Rev. Richard Ferrer, of Ashby Northants. 1813.

Sir John Newdigate Ludford Chetwode, 5th Baronet, 1788-1873. s.p.

40

TABLE LXX

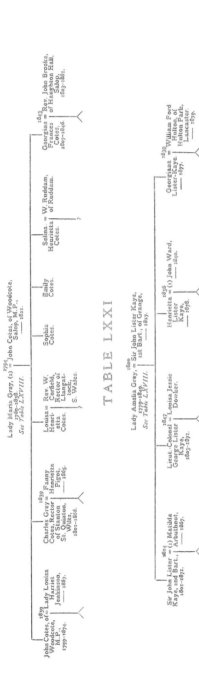

Lady Maria Grey, (2) = John Cotes, of Woodcote, Salop, M.P., 1821.
1766-1838.
See Table LXVIII.

- John Cotes, of Woodcote, M.P., 1799-1874. = Lady Louisa Harriet Jenkinson, —1887.
- Charles Grey Cotes, Rector of Stanton St. Quinton, Wilts., 1801-1866. = Fanny Henrietta Pigot, —1865.
- Louisa Henrietta Cotes. = Rev. W. Corfield, Rector of Llangattock, S. Wales.
- Sophia Cotes.
- Emily Cotes.
- Selina Henrietta Cotes. = W. Ruddam, of Ruddam.
- Georgiana Frances Cotes, 1807-1846. = Rev. John Brooke, of Haughton Hall, Salop, 1803-1881.

TABLE LXXI

Lady Amelia Grey, = Sir John Lister Kaye, 1st Bart., of Grange, 1847.
1779-1849.
See Table LXVIII.

- Sir John Lister Kaye, 2nd Bart., 1801-1871. = Matilda Arbuthnot, —1867.
- Lieut.-Colonel George Lister Kaye, 1809-1871. = Louisa Jessie Dowker.
- Henrietta Lister Kaye, —1878. = (1) John Ward, —1840.
- Georgiana Lister-Kaye, 1897. = William Ford Hulton, of Hulton Park, Lancaster, 1879.

TABLE LXXII

Hon. John Grey, 1763-1802. = Susanna Leycester.
See Table LXVIII.

- Rev. Harry Grey, 1798-1860. = (1) Frances Elizabeth Ellis.
- Henrietta (2) Grey, 1775-1811. = Rev. Charles Mytton, afterwards Thornycroft, 1810.
- Emma Grey, 1782-1851. = Thomas William Egerton Tatton, of Withenshawe, 1785-1817.
- Anne Maria Grey, 1791-1857. = Rev. Thomas Clarke, —1870.

41

TABLE LXXIII

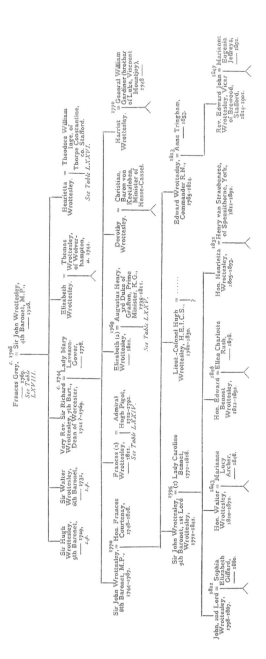

Frances Grey, = Sir John Wrottesley, M.P.,
—— 1769.   4th Baronet,
See Table   —— 1726.
LXVIII.

Sir Hugh Wrottesley, 5th Baronet, —— 1799, s.p.

Sir Walter Wrottesley, 6th Baronet, —— 1734, s.p.

Very Rev. Sir Richard Wrottesley, 7th Bart., Dean of Worcester, 1721?-1769. = c. 1744 Lady Mary Gower, —— 1778.

Elizabeth Wrottesley = Thomas Wrottesley, of Wolverhampton, u. 1741.

Henrietta Wrottesley. = Theodore William Inge, of Thorpe Constantine, co. Stafford. See Table LXXVI.

Sir John Wrottesley, 8th Baronet, M.P., 1744-1787. = 1770 Hon. Frances Courtenay, 1748-1828.

Frances (2) Wrottesley, —— 1811. = Admiral Hugh Pigot, 1722-1792. See Table LXXIII.

Elizabeth (1) Wrottesley, —— 1822. = 1769 Augustus Henry, 3rd Duke of Grafton, Prime Minister, K.G., 1735-1811. See Table LXXVI.

Dorothy Wrottesley. = Christian, Baron von Keselleben, Minister of Hesse-Cassel.

Harriet Wrottesley. = 1770 General William Gardiner (brother of Luke, Viscount Mountjoy), 1748- ——.

Sir John Wrottesley, 9th Baronet, 1st Lord Wrottesley, 1771-1841. = 1795 Lady Caroline Bennet, 1771-1818.

Lieut.-Colonel Hugh Wrottesley, H.E.I.C.S., 1780-1830. = ...?

Edward Wrottesley, Commander R.N., 1765-1814. = 1813 Anne Tringham, —— 1853.

John, 2nd Lord Wrottesley, 1798-1867. = 1821 Sophia Elizabeth Giffard, —— 1860.

Hon. Walter Wrottesley, 1810-1873. = 1843 Marianne Lucy Archer, —— 1808.

Hon. Edward Bennet Wrottesley, 1811-1892. = 1806 Ellen Charlotte Rush, —— 1878.

Hon. Henrietta Wrottesley, 1805-1893. = 1832 Henry van Straubenzee, of Spennithorne, York, 1811-1892.

Rev. Edward John Wrottesley, Vicar of Brewood, Stafford, 1814-1901. = 1847 Marianne Eugenia Jeffreys, —— 1892.

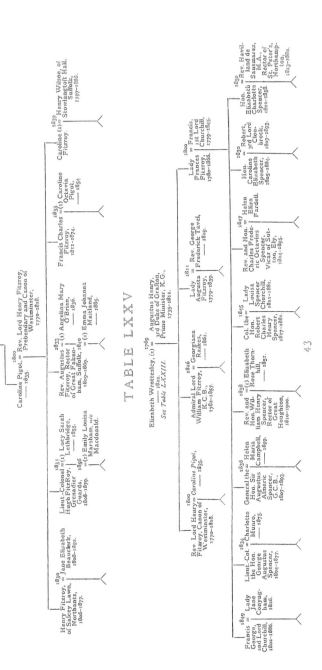

TABLE LXXIV

Frances Wrottesley, (=) = Admiral Hugh Pigot, 1722-1792.
1811.
See Table LXXIII.

1800
Caroline Pigot, = Rev. Lord Henry Fitzroy, Prebendary and Canon of Westminster, 1770-1828.
1835.

1850
Henry Fitzroy, = Jane Elizabeth Beauclerk, of Salcey Lawn, Northants, 1806-1877. 1808-1892.

1811
Lieut.-Colonel = (1) Lucy Sarah Lethbridge, Hugh FitzRoy, 1855. Grenadier Guards, 1808-1870.
1856 = (2) Emily Louisa Marsham, *née* Macdonald.

1823
Rev. Augustus = (1) Angelina Mary O'Brien, Fitzroy, Rector 1856. of Great Faken-ham, Suffolk, 1809-1869.
1840 = (2) Emma Johanna Maitland, 1865.

1825
Francis Charles = (1) Caroline Fitzroy, Octavia 1811-1874. Pigot, 1854.

1839
Caroline (=) = Henry Wilson, of Fitzroy. Stowlangtoft Hall, Suffolk, 1797-1866.

TABLE LXXV

Elizabeth Wrottesley, (=) = Augustus Henry, 3rd Duke of Grafton, Prime Minister, K.G., 1735-1811.
1811.
See Table LXXIII.

1800
Rev. Lord Henry = Caroline Pigot, Fitzroy, Canon of 1835. Westminster, 1770-1828.

1846
Admiral Lord = Georgiana William Fitzroy, Raikes, K.C.B., 1861. 1782-1857.

1838
Rev. and Hon. Wil- = (1) Elizabeth liam Henry Rose Thorn-Spencer, Rector of hill, Great 1831. Houghton, 1810-1900.

1811
Lady = Rev. George Augusta Frederick Tavel, Fitzroy, 1849. 1779-1839.

1800
Lady = Francis, Frances 1st Lord Fitzroy, Churchill, 1780-1866. 1779-1845.

1849
Francis = Lady George, Jane and Lord Conyng-Churchill, ham, 1802-1886. 1806.

1834
Lieut.-Col. = Charlotte the Hon. Munro, George 1875. Augustus Spencer, 1801-1877.

1856
General the = Helen Hon. Sir Maria Augustus Campbell, Almeric 1869. Spencer, G.C.B., 1807-1893.

1845
Col. the = Lady Hon. Louisa Robert Spencer Charles Churchill, Henry 1811-1881. Spencer, 1817-1881.

1847
Rev. and Hon. = Helen Charles Frede- Eliza ric Octavius Fardell. Spencer, Vicar of Sut-ton, Ely, 1824-1895.

1839
Hon. = Robert, Caroline 3rd Lord Elizabeth Clon-Spencer, brock, 1805-1864. 1807-1893.

1850
Hon. = Rev. Havri-Elizabeth land de Charlotte Sausmarez, Spencer, M.A., 1801-1858. Rector of St. Peter's, Northamp-ton, 1813-1882.

43

TABLE LXXVI

Henrietta Wrottesley. = Theodore William Inge,
See Table LXXIII. of Thorpe Constantine,
co. Stafford.

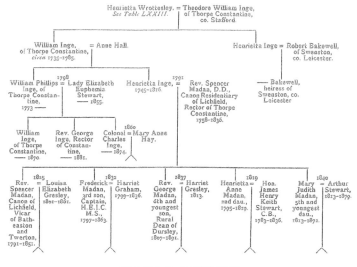

William Inge, = Anne Hall.
of Thorpe Constantine,
circa 1735–1785.

Henrietta Inge = Robert Bakewell,
of Swenston,
co. Leicester.

1798
William Phillips = Lady Elizabeth
Inge, of | Euphemia
Thorpe Constan- | Stewart,
tine, | —— 1855.
1773 ——

1791
Henrietta Inge, = Rev. Spencer
1745–1816. | Madan, D.D.,
| Canon Residentiary
| of Lichfield,
| Rector of Thorpe
| Constantine,
| 1758–1836.

—— Bakewell,
heiress of
Swenston, co.
Leicester

William
Inge,
of Thorpe
Constantine,
—— 1870.

Rev. George
Inge, Rector
of Constan-
tine,
—— 1881.

1860
Colonel = Mary Anne
Charles | Hay.
Inge,
—— 1874.

1825
Rev. = Louisa
Spencer | Elizabeth
Madan, | Gresley,
Canon of | 1801–1861.
Lichfield,
Vicar
of Bath-
easton
and
Twerton,
1791–1851.

1832
Frederick = Harriet
Madan, | Graham,
3rd son, | 1799–1836.
Captain,
H.E.I.C.
M.S.,
1797–1863.

1837
Rev. = Harriet
George | Gresley,
Madan, | 1813.
6th and
youngest
son,
Rural
Dean of
Dursley,
1807–1891.

1819
Henrietta = Hon.
Anne | James
Madan, | Henry
2nd dau., | Keith
1795–1829. | Stewart,
| C.B.,
| 1783–1836.

1840
Mary = Arthur
Judith | Stewart,
Madan, | 1813–1879.
5th and
youngest
dau.,
1813–1872.

TABLE LXXVII

Hon. William Ward, = Anne Parkes.
of Willingsworth,
co. Stafford,
—— 1713/14.
See Table LXI.

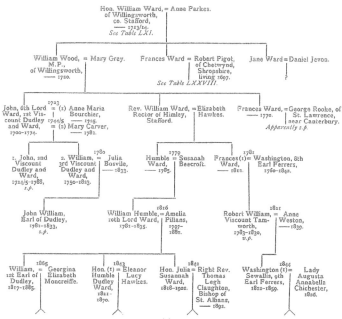

William Wood, = Mary Grey.
M.P.,
of Willingsworth,
—— 1750.

Frances Ward = Robert Pigot,
of Chetwynd,
Shropshire,
living 1697.
See Table LXXVIII.

Jane Ward = Daniel Jevon.
|
?

1723
John, 6th Lord = (1) Anne Maria
Ward, 1st Vis- | Bourchier,
count Dudley 1744/5 | —— 1725.
and Ward, = (2) Mary Carver,
1700–1774. | —— 1782.

Rev. William Ward, = Elizabeth
Rector of Himley, | Hawkes.
Stafford.

Frances Ward, = George Rooke, of
—— 1770. | St. Lawrence,
| near Canterbury.
Apparently s.p.

1. John, 2nd
Viscount
Dudley and
Ward,
1724/5–1788,
s.p.

1780
2. William, = Julia
3rd Viscount | Bosvile,
Dudley and | —— 1833.
Ward,
1750–1823.

1779
Humble = Susanah
Ward, | Beecroft.
—— 1785.

1781
Frances(1) = Washington, 8th
Ward, | Earl Ferrers,
—— 1811. | 1760–1842.

John William,
Earl of Dudley,
1781–1833,
s.p.

1816
William Humble, = Amelia
10th Lord Ward, | Pillans,
1781–1835. | 1797–
| 1881.

1821
Robert William, = Anne
Viscount Tam- | Weston,
worth, | —— 1839.
1783–1830,
v.p.

1865
William, = Georgina
1st Earl of | Elizabeth
Dudley, | Moncreiffe.
1817–1885.

1843
Hon. (1) = Eleanor
Humble | Lucy
Dudley | Hawkes.
Ward,
1811–
1870.

1842
Hon. Julia = Right Rev.
Susannah | Thomas
Ward, | Legh
1818–1902. | Claughton,
| Bishop of
| St. Albans,
| —— 1892.

1844
Washington (1) = Lady
Sewallis, 9th | Augusta
Earl Ferrers, | Annabella
1822–1859. | Chichester,
| 182d.

44

TABLE LXXVIII

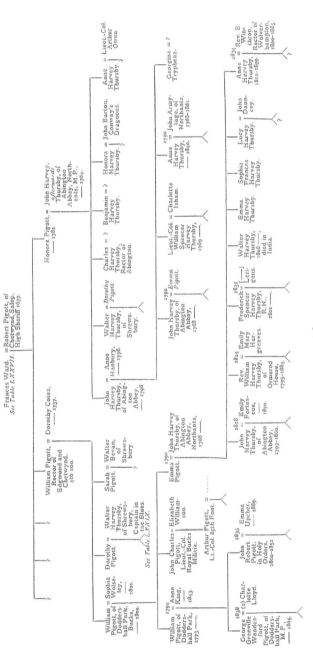

Frances Ward, = Robert Pigott, of
See Table LXXVII. | Chetwynd, Salop.
High Sheriff 1697.

Honora Pigott, = John Harvey,
1781. | afterwards
Thursby, of
Abingdon
Abbey, North-
ants, M.P.,
1764.

William Pigott, = Dorothy Coles,
Rector of 1757.
Edgmond and
Chetwynd,
4th son.

Anne = Lieut.-Col.
Harvey Arthur
Thursby. Owen.

Anne = John Burton,
Harvey Conway's
Thursby. Dragoons.

Honora = ?
Harvey
Thursby.

Benjamin = ?
Harvey
Thursby.

Charles = ?
Harvey
Thursby,
Rector of
Abington.

Walter = Dorothy
Harvey Pigott.
Thursby,
of
Shrews-
bury.

Anne = John Hanbury,
1778.

John
Harvey
Thursby,
of Abing-
ton
Abbey,
1798.

Georgiana = ?
Tryphena.

Anne 1790 = John Army-
Harvey tage, of
Thursby, Northants,
1840. 1766-1861.

Lieut.-Col. = Charlotte
William Isham.
Spencer
Harvey
Thursby,
1769.

John Harvey 1794 = Emma
Thursby, of Pigott.
Abington
Abbey,
1768.

William = Sophia
Pigott, of Wolse-
Dodders- ley,
hall Park, 1801.
Bucks,
1802.

Dorothy = Walter
Pigott. Harvey
Thursby,
of Shrews-
bury,
Captain in
the Blues.
See Table LXXIX.

Sarah = Walter
Pigott. Bevan,
of
Shrews-
bury.

Emma 1794 = John Harvey
Pigott. Thursby, of
Abington
Abbey,
Northants,
1768.

John Charles = Elizabeth
Pigott, William-
Lieut.-Col. son.
Royal Bucks
Militia.

Arthur Pigott, = ...
Lt.-Col. 85th Foot.

Anne = Rev. B
Harvey Win-
Thursby, throp,
1811-1896. Rector of
Wolver-
hampton,
1800-1865.
1804

Lucy = John
Harvey Daun-
Thursby. cey.

Sophia
Frances
Harvey
Thursby.

Emma
Harvey
Thursby.

Walter
Harvey
Thursby,
1806
died in
India.

Frederick = Leti-
Harvey tia.
Thursby,
R.N.,
1801.
1831

Rev. = Emily
William Mar-
Harvey greaves.
Thursby,
of
Ormerod
House,
1795-1884.
1824

Emily = Mary
Fortes-
cue,
1870.

John = Emily
Harvey
Thursby,
of
Abington
Abbey,
1793-1860.
1816

William 1794 = Anne
Pigott, of King,
Dodders- 1843.
hall Park,
1773.

John = Emma
Robert Upcher,
Pigott, 1889.
in Holy
Orders,
1800-1852.
1835

George = (2) Char-
Grenville lotte
Wandes- Lloyd.
ford
Pigott, of
Dodders-
hall Park,
M.P.,
1865.
1838

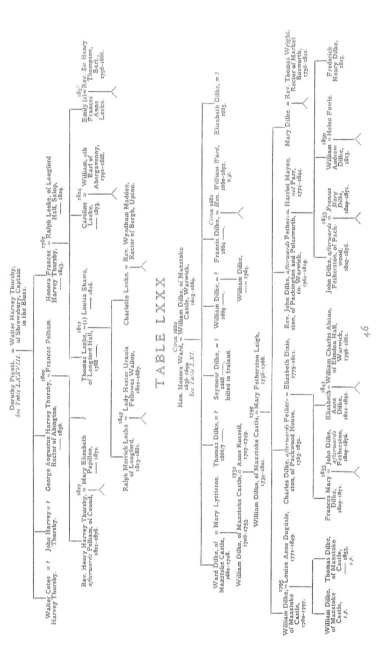

TABLE LXXIX

Dorothy Pigott. = Walter Harvey Thursby, of Shrewsbury, Captain in the Blues.
See Table LXXVIII.

Walter Cotes = ? Harvey Thursby. — John Harvey = ? Thursby. — George Augustus Harvey Thursby, Rector of Abington, —1836. = Frances Pelham. — Honora Frances Harvey Thursby, —1843. = Ralph Leeke, of Longford Hall, Salop, 1809.

Rev. Henry Harvey Thursby, *afterwards* Pelham, of Cound, 1801-1878. = Mary Elizabeth Papillon, —1872.

Thomas Leeke, of Longford Hall, 1788. = (1) Louisa Shawe, 1816.

Caroline Leeke, —1873. = William, 4th Earl of Abergavenny, 1792-1868.

Emily (2) = Rev. Sir Henry Frances Thompson, Anne Bart., Leeke. 1796-1868.

Ralph Merrick Leeke of Longford, 1813-1883. = Lady Hester Urania Fellowes Wallop, 1821-1887.

Charlotte Leeke. = Rev. Wyndham Madden, Rector of Bergh, Upton.

TABLE LXXX

Circa 1660
Hon. Honora Ward, 1656-1609. = William Dilke, of Maxstoke Castle, Warwick, 1615-1669.
See Table LXI.

Ward Dilke, of Maxstoke Castle, 1662-1728. = Mary Lyttleton. — Thomas Dilke, = ? 1666/7 —. — Seymour Dilke, = ? 1668 —, killed in Ireland. — William Dilke, = ? 1669 —. — Francis Dilke, = Hon. William Ward, 1660-1692. 1664 —. *v.p.* — Elizabeth Dilke, = ? 1665.

William Dilke, of Maxstoke Castle, 1706-1753. = Anne Russell, 1707-1749.

William Dilke, 1764.

William Dilke, of Maxstoke Castle, 1724-1801. = Mary Fetherston Leigh, 1736-1788.

William Dilke, of Maxstoke Castle, 1760-1797. = Louisa Anne Dugdale, 1771-1849. — Charles Dilke, *afterwards* Fetherston, of Packwood House, 1763-1832. — Rev. John Dilke, *afterwards* Fetherston, of Packington and Polesworth, co. Warwick, 1760-1819. = Elizabeth Dixie, 1775-1811. — Mary Dilke. = Rev. Thomas Wright, Rector of Market Bosworth, 1756-1810. — Harriet Mayou, née Parr, 1774-1844.

William Dilke, of Maxstoke Castle, —1853. *s.p.* — Thomas Dilke, of Maxstoke Castle, *s.p.* — Frances Mary Dilke, 1809-1871. — John Dilke, *afterwards* Fetherston, 1809-1870. — Elizabeth Anne Dilke, 1811-1891. = William Charles Alston, of Elmdon Hall, Warwick, 1796-1861. — John Dilke, *afterwards* of Packwood, 1809-1896. = Frances Mary Dilke, 1809-1871. — William Andrew Dilke, 1813. = Helen Fowle. — Frederick Henry Dilke, 1815.

46

TABLE LXXXI

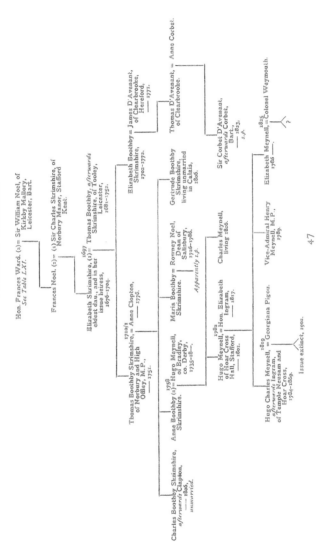

Hon. Frances Ward, (2) = Sir William Noel, of Kirkby Mallory, Leicester, Bart. *See Table LXI.*

Frances Noel, (2) = (1) Sir Charles Skrimshire, of Norbury Manor, Stafford Kent.

Elizabeth Skrimshire, (1) = Thomas Boothby, *afterwards* Skrimshire, of Tooley, Leicester, 1681–1752. — eldest dau., and in her issue heiress, 1676–1704. — 1697

Elizabeth Boothby = James D'Avenant, Skrimshire, of Clearbrooke, 1702–1772. Hereford, —1771.

Thomas D'Avenant, = Anne Corbet. of Clearbrooke.

Thomas Boothby Skrimshire, = Anne Clopton, of Norbury and High —1776. Offley, M.P., 1729/1 —1752.

Anne Boothby (2) = Hugo Meynell, Skrimshire. — of Bradley, co. Derby, 1758 — 1735–18—.

Maria Boothby = Rowney Noel, Skrimshire. Dean of Salisbury, 1726–1766. *Apparently s.p.*

Gertrude Boothby Skrimshire, living unmarried in Calais, 1806.

Charles Meynell, living 1806.

Sir Corbet D'Avenant, *afterwards* Corbet, Bart., —1823. *s.p.*

Hugo Meynell, = Hon. Elizabeth of Hoar Cross Ingram, Hall, Stafford, 1817. 1803 —1801.

Vice-Admiral Henry Meynell, M.P., 1789.

Elizabeth Meynell, = Colonel Weymouth. 1788. 1825

Charles Boothby Skrimshire, *afterwards* Clapton, —1805, *unmarried.*

Hugo Charles Meynell, = Georgiana Pigou. *afterwards* Ingram, 1819 of Temple Newsam and Hoar Cross, 1784–1869.

Issue extinct, 1902.

47

TABLE LXXXII

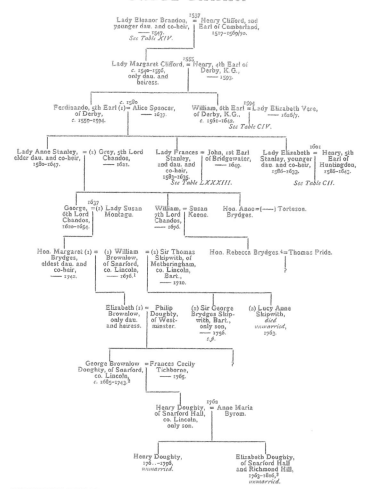

Lady Eleanor Brandon, = Henry Clifford, 2nd Earl of Cumberland, 1517-1569/70. younger dau. and co-heir, —— 1547. *See Table XIV.* 1537

Lady Margaret Clifford, = Henry, 4th Earl of Derby, K.G., —— 1593. c. 1540-1596, only dau. and heiress. 1555

Ferdinando, 5th Earl (1) = Alice Spencer, of Derby, —— 1637. c. 1559-1594. c. 1580 | William, 6th Earl = Lady Elizabeth Vere, of Derby, K.G., —— 1626/7. c. 1561-1642. *See Table CIV.* 1594

Lady Anne Stanley, = (1) Grey, 5th Lord elder dau. and co-heir, Chandos, 1580-1647. —— 1621. | Lady Frances = John, 1st Earl Stanley, of Bridgewater, 2nd dau. and —— 1649. co-heir, 1583-1635. *See Table LXXXIII.* | Lady Elizabeth = Henry, 5th Stanley, younger Earl of dau. and co-heir, Huntingdon, 1586-1633. 1586-1643. *See Table CII.* 1601

George, = (1) Lady Susan 6th Lord Montagu. Chandos, 1620-1654. 1637 | William, = Susan 7th Lord Keene. Chandos, —— 1676. | Hon. Anne = (——) Torteson. Brydges.

Hon. Margaret (1) = (1) William = (2) Sir Thomas Brydges, Brownlow, Skipwith, of eldest dau. and of Snarford, Metheringham, co-heir, co. Lincoln, co. Lincoln, —— 1742. —— 1676.[1] Bart., —— 1710. | Hon. Rebecca Brydges.[4] = Thomas Pride.

Elizabeth (1) = Philip Brownlow, Doughty, only dau. of West- and heiress. minster. | (2) Sir George Brydges Skip- with, Bart., only son, —— 1756. s.p. | (2) Lucy Anne Skipwith, died unmarried, 1763.

George Brownlow = Frances Cecily Doughty, of Snarford, Tichborne, co. Lincoln, —— 1765. c. 1685-1743.[2]

Henry Doughty, = Anne Maria of Snarford Hall, Byrom. co. Lincoln, only son. 1762

Henry Doughty, 176.-1796, unmarried. | Elizabeth Doughty, of Snarford Hall and Richmond Hill, 1763-1806,[3] unmarried.

---

[1] An attempt was made by certain writers to prove that Sir John Brownlow, of Humby, 3rd Baronet, was son, instead of nephew, of this William Brownlow. This claim, however, was fully disposed of by the editor of "Debrett's Peerage" in a correspondence in the *Gentleman's Magazine*, 1826.

[2] Administration of George Brownlow Doughty, late of Beenham, Berks, was granted to his son Henry, 10th April 1744.

[3] She left her estates to her maternal cousin, Sir Edward Tichborne, from which it may be inferred that she had no Doughty relations. Sir Edward Tichborne assumed the additional name of "Doughty."

[4] According to Sandford, Rebecca, daughter and heiress of William, 7th Lord Chandos, left by her husband, Thomas Pride, a daughter and heiress, Elizabeth, who was wife of William Sherwin; but a pedigree relating to the claim of Elizabeth Sherwin as heir to Monk, Duke of Albemarle, states her to have been *sister* and *not daughter* of Thomas Pride, and the relict of John Gibbs before her marriage with Sherwin, which is the fact. The statement of Sandford is therefore erroneous. See C. E. Long's *Royal Descents.*

TABLE LXXXIII

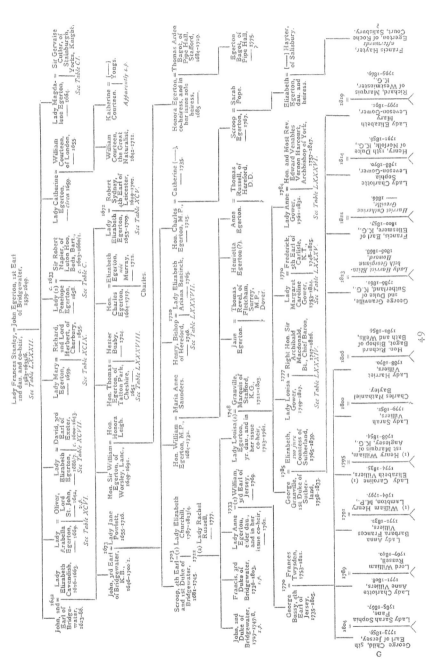

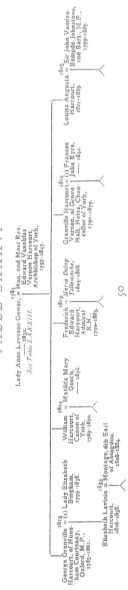

TABLE LXXXIV

Lady Louisa Gower, = The Right Hon. Sir Archibald Macdonald, Bart. Chief Baron, 1747-1826.
1749-1827.
See Table LXXXVIII.

1819

Sir James Macdonald, = (2) Lady Sophia Keppel, 1797-1844.
2nd Bart. M.P., 1784-1832.

Caroline Diana = Rev. Thomas Randolph, Prebendary of St. Paul's, Chaplain to the Queen, Rector of Hadham, Herts.
Macdonald, 1867, 1 d.

TABLE LXXXV

Lady Margaret Caroline Gower, = Frederick, 5th Earl of Carlisle, K.T., 1748-1825.
1753-1824.
See Table LXXXVIII.

George, 6th Earl of Carlisle, K.G., 1773-1848. = Lady Georgiana Cavendish, 1783-1858. 1804

Hon. Frede-(1) = Frances Susan Lambton, ——1840. 1841
rick Howard, 1785-1815.

Very Rev. Henry = Henrietta Elizabeth Wright, 1891. 1804
Edward John Howard, Prebendary of York, Dean of Lichfield, 1795-1868.

Lady Isabella = John, 1st Lord Cawdor, c. 1753-1821. 1780
Caroline Howard, 1771-1848.

Lady Elizabeth Howard, 1780-1825. = John Henry, 5th Duke of Rutland, K.G., 1778-1857. 1799

Lady Gertrude Howard, 1784-1870. = William Sloane Stanley, of Paulon's, Hants, ——1860. 1865

Frederick John Howard, M.P., 1814-1867. = Lady Fanny Cavendish, 1809-1885. 1837

John Frederick, 1st Earl Cawdor, 1790-1860. = Lady Elizabeth Thynne, 1795-1865. 1816

TABLE LXXXVI

Lady Anne Leveson-Gower, = Hon. and Most Rev. Edward Venables Vernon Harcourt, Archbishop of York, 1757-1847.
1761-
See Table LXXXVIII.

1784

George Granville = (1) Lady Elizabeth Bingham, 1795-1838. 1815
Harcourt, of Nune-ham Courtenay, Oxford, M.P., 1785-1861.

Frederick Edward Harcourt, Admiral R.N., 1790-1883. = Maria Delap Tollemache, 1804-1868. 1809

William Harcourt, Canon of York, 1789-1870. = Matilda Mary Gooch, ——1876. 1824

Granville Harcourt, Vernon, of Grove Hall, Notts, Chancellor of York, 1785-1879. = (1) Frances Julia Eyre, 1844. 1814

Louisa Augusta Harcourt, 1801-1869. = Sir John Vanden-Bempde-Johnstone, 2nd Bart. M.P., 1799-1869. 1825

Elizabeth Lavinia Harcourt, 1816-1838. = Montagu, 6th Earl of Abingdon, 1808-1884. 1835

50

TABLE LXXXVII

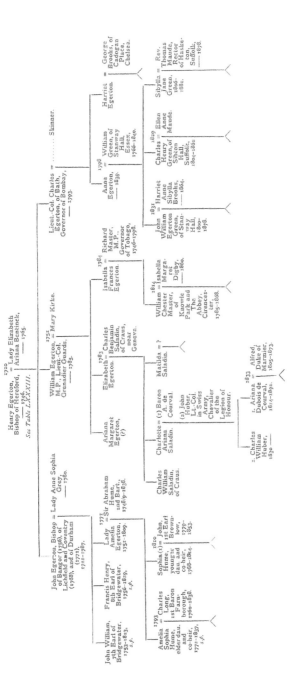

Henry Egerton, ¹⁷¹⁰ = Lady Elizabeth
Bishop of Hereford, 1746. | Ariana Bentinck,
——— 1765.
See Table LXXXVIII.

John Egerton, Bishop = Lady Anne Sophia
of Bangor (1756), of | Grey,
Lichfield and Coventry | ——— 1780.
(1768), and of Durham
(1771), (1771),
1721–1787.

William Egerton, ¹⁷⁵¹ = Mary Kirke.
M.P. Lieut.-Col. |
Grenadier Guards,
——— 1783.

Lieut.-Col. Charles = ... Skinner.
Egerton, of Bath, |
Governor of Bombay,
——— 1793.

Francis Henry, | Lady ¹⁷⁷¹ = Sir Abraham
8th Earl of | Amelia | Hume,
Bridgewater, | Egerton, | 2nd Bart.,
1756–1819, | 1751–1809. | 1748/9–1838.
s.p.

Ariana | Elizabeth = Charles
Margaret | Egerton. ¹⁷⁸² | Benjamin
Egerton, | | Saladin,
(?) | | of Craus,
| | near
| | Geneva.

Isabella = ¹⁷⁸⁴ Richard
Frances | Master,
Egerton. | M.P.
| Governor
| of Tobago,
| 1746–1798.

Anne ¹⁷⁹⁸ = William
Egerton, | Green, of
——— 1830. | Stanway
| Hall,
| Essex,
| 1766–1840.

Harriet = George
Egerton. | Brooks, of
| Cadogan
| Place,
| Chelsea.

John William, | Charles | Sophia (1) = John,
7th Earl of | Long, | Hume, | 1st Earl
Bridgewater, | 1st Baron | younger | Brown-
1753–1823, | Farn- | dau. and | low,
s.p. | borough, | co-heir, | 1779–
| 1766–1838. | 1768–1814. | 1853.

Charles | Matilda = ?
William | Saladin.
Saladin, |
of Craus. |

William = ¹⁸¹⁴ Isabella
Chester | Marga-
Master, | ret Digby,
of | ——— 1860.
Knowle |
Park and |
The |
Abbey, |
Cirences- |
ter, |
1785–1868. |

John ¹⁸³¹ = Harriet
William | Anne
Egerton | Sibylla
Green, | Brooks,
of Stan- | ——— 1864.
way |
Hall, |
1800– |
1898. |

Charles ¹⁸²⁹ = Ellen
Henry | Anne
Green, of | Maude.
Sibton |
Hall, |
Suffolk, |
1804–1862. |

Sibylla = Rev.
Jane | Thomas
Green, | Maude,
1806– | Rector
1881. | of Haske-
| ton,
| Suffolk,
| ——— 1878.

Amelia = ¹⁷⁹³ Charles
Sophia | Long,
Hume, | 1st Baron
elder dau. | Farn-
and | borough,
co-heir, | 1766–1838.
1772–1837, |
s.p. |

Charlotte = (1) Baron
Ariana | A. de
Saladin. | Courval.
| (2) John
| Huber,
| Lt.-Col.
| in Swiss
| Army,
| Chevalier
| of the
| Legion of
| Honour.

Charles | Alfred, ¹⁸³³
William | Duke of
Huber, | Marnier,
1820. | 1805–1873.
| 1. Ariana =
| Dubois de
| Courval,
| 1814–1890.
| 2. Charles =
| William
| Huber,
| 1820.

51

TABLE LXXXVIII

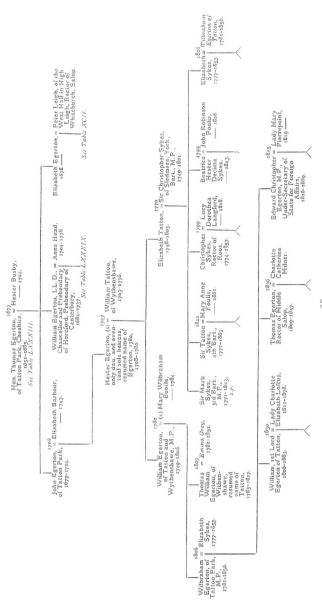

Hon. Thomas Egerton, = Hester Busby, 1677
of Tatton Park, Cheshire. ———— 1724.
1651-1685.
See Table LXXXVIII.

John Egerton, = Elizabeth Barbour, 1705
of Tatton Park, ———— 1743.
1679-1724.

William Egerton, LL.D., = Anne Head,
Chancellor and Prebendary 1701-1778.
of Hereford, Prebendary of
Canterbury,
1680-1737. *See Table LXXXIX.*

Elizabeth Egerton, = Peter Leigh, of the 1678
West Hallin High
Leigh, Rector of
Whitchurch, Salop.
See Table XCII.

Hester Egerton, (1) = William Tatton, 1747
only dau. and even- of Wythenshawe,
tual sole heiress, 1703-1776.
resumed name of
Egerton, 1780,
1708-1760.

William Egerton, 1780
of Tatton and = (2) Mary Wilbraham
Wythenshawe, M.P., Bootle,
1749-1806. ———— 1764.

Elizabeth Tatton, = Sir Christopher Sykes, 1770
1748-1803. of Sledmere, York,
Bart., M.P.,
1749-1801.

Wilbraham 1806
Egerton, of = Elizabeth
Tatton Park, Sykes,
M.P., 1777-1853.
1781-1856.

Thomas 1807
William = Emma Grey,
Egerton, of 1783-1851.
Wythen-
shawe,
resumed
name of
Tatton,
1783-1847.

Sir Mark
Sykes,
3rd Bart.,
M.P.,
1771-1823,
s.p.

Sir Tatton 1822
Sykes, = Mary Anne
4th Bart., Foulis,
1771-1863. ———— 1861.

Christopher = Lucy 1799
Sykes, Dorothea
Rector of Langford,
Roos, ———— 1828.
1774-1857.

Beatrice = John Robinson 1795
Hester Foulis,
Decima ———— 1806.
Sykes,
———— 1843.

Elizabeth = Wilbraham 1806
Sykes, Egerton of
1777-1852. Tatton,
1781-1856.

William, 1st Lord = Lady Charlotte 1830
Egerton of Tatton, Elizabeth Loftus,
1806-1883. 1811-1878.

Thomas Egerton, = Charlotte 1806
Rector of Middle Catherine
Salop, Milner.
1809-1847.

Edward Christopher = Lady Mary 1845
Egerton, M.P., Pierrepoint,
Under-Secretary of ———— 1819.
State for Foreign
Affairs,
1816-1869.

TABLE LXXXIX

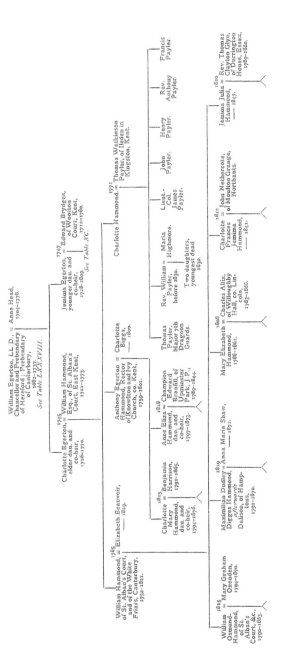

William Egerton, LL.D., = Anne Head,
Chancellor and Prebendary   1704-1776.
of Hereford; Prebendary
of Canterbury,
1682-1737.
See Table LXXXVIII.

Charlotte Egerton, = William Hammond,   Jemima Egerton, = Edward Brydges,
elder dau. and   Esq., of St. Alban's   younger dau. and   of Wootton
co-heir,   Court, East Kent,   co-heir,   Court, Kent,
1726-1770.   1721-1773.   1728-1809.   1712-1780.
                                                               See Table XC.

                   Anthony Egerton = Charlotte   Charlotte Hammond. = Thomas Watkinson
                   Hammond, Rector   Biggs,   Payler, of Ileden in
                   of Knowlton and Ivy — 1800.   Kingston, Kent.
                   Church, co. Kent,
                   1721-1773.

William Hammond, = Elizabeth Beauvoir,
of St. Alban's Court,   1829.
and of the White
Friars, Canterbury,
1752-1821.

Charlotte = Benjamin   Anne Eliza = Champion   Thomas   Rev. William = Maria   Lieut.-   John   Henry   Rev.   Francis
Mary   Harrison,   Hammond,   Edward   Payler,   Payler,   Highmore. Col.   Payler. Payler. Anthony   Payler.
Hammond,   1799-1865.   dau. and   Branfill, of Major 7th   before 1830.   James   Payler.
dau. and   co-heir,   Upminster   Dragoon   Two daughters,   Payler.
co-heir,   1797-1873.   Park, J.P.,   Guards.   youngest dead
1794-1876.   1789-1844.   1830.

Maximilian Dudley = Anna Maria Shaw,   Mary Elizabeth = Charles Allix,   Charlotte = John Nethercote,   Jemima Julia = Rev. Thomas
Digres Hammond,   1871.   Hammond,   of Willoughby   Frances   of Moulton Grange,   Hammond,   Clayton Glyn,
afterwards   1788-1861.   Hall, co. Lin-   Jemima,   Northants.   — 1847.   of Durrington
Dalison, of Hamp-   coln,   Hammond,   House, Essex,
tons,   1783-1865.   — 1841.   1789-1860.
1799-1870.

William = Mary Graham
Osmund-   Oxenden,
Hammond, 1794-1890.
of St.
Alban's
Court, &c.,
1790-1863.

53

TABLE XC

TABLE XCI

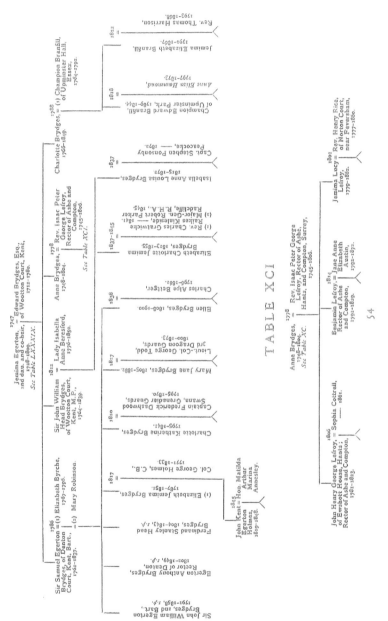

TABLE XCII

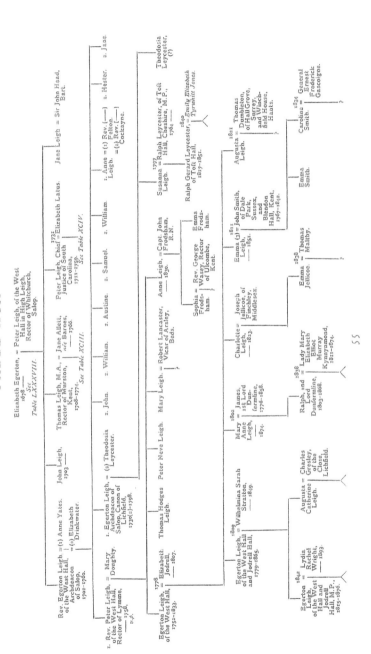

Elizabeth Egerton, = Peter Leigh, of the West
1678. Hall in High Leigh,
See Rector of Whitchurch,
Table LXXXVIII. Salop.

Rev. Egerton Leigh, = (1) Anne Yates.   John Leigh,   Thomas Leigh, M.A., = Jane Allett,   Peter Leigh, Chief = Elizabeth Latus.   Jane Leigh = Sir John Head,
of the West Hall,   = (2) Elizabeth   1793 ——   Rector of Murston,   *née* Barnes,   Justice of South   1731.   Bart.
Archdeacon   Drinkwater.   Kent,   —— 1766.   Carolina,
of Salop,   1708-1774.   1711-1759.
1702-1760.   *See Table XCIII.*   *See Table XCIV.*

1. Rev. Peter Leigh, = Mary   1. Egerton Leigh, = (2) Theodosia   1. Anne = (1) Rev. ——   2. Hester.   2. Jane.
of the West Hall,   Doughty.   Archdeacon of   Leycester.   Leigh.   Felton.
Rector of Lymme,   Salop, Canon of   = (2) Rev. ——
—— *v.p.*   Lichfield,   Cockayne.
1730(?)-1798.

Egerton Leigh, = Elizabeth   Thomas Hodges   Peter Neve Leigh.   1. John.   2. Austine.   2. Samuel.   2. William.   Susanna = Ralph Leycester, of Toft   Theodosia
of the West Hall,   Jodrell,   Leigh.   1797.   Hall, Cheshire, M.P.,   Leycester,
1753-1823.   —— 1807.   Leigh.   1764. ——   (?)

1778.   2. William.   Mary Leigh = Robert Lancaster,   Anne Leigh, = Capt. John   1840   Ralph Gerard Leycester, = *Emily Elizabeth*
    Vicar of Arsley,   —— 1830.   Frodsham,   of Toft Hall.   *Tyrwhitt Jones.*
    Beds.   R.N.   1817-1851.

Egerton Leigh = Wilhelmina Sarah   ?   Sophia = Rev. George   Emma = Capt. John Frods-   Augusta = Thomas
of the West Hall   Straiton,   Frods-   Wasey, Rector   Frods-   ham.   Leigh.   Dumbleton,
and Jodrell Hall,   —— 1849.   ham.   of Ulcombe,   ham.   1821   of Hall Grove,
1779-1865.   ?   Kent.   ?   Surrey,
    and Winch-
    field House,
    Hants.

1809   1801   Charlotte =   Joseph   1811   ?
    Mary James, = 1st Lord   Leigh,   Jellicoe, of   Emma (3) = John Smith,
    Anne Dun-   —— 1823.   Finchley,   Leigh,   of Dale
    Leigh, fermline,   Middlesex.   —— 1851.   Park,
    1874. 1776-1848.   Sussex,
    and
    Blendon
    Hall, Kent,
    1767-1842.

Augusta = Charles   1838   Emma   1838   Emma
Catherine   Gresley,   Ralph, and = Lady Mary   Jellicoe.   Thomas   Smith.
Leigh.   of the   Lord   Elizabeth   Maltby.
  Close,   Dunfermline,   Elliot
  Lichfield.   1803-1868.   Murray   ?   1834
    Kynnynmond,   Caroline   General
    1811-1874.   Smith.   Ernest
    Frederick
    Gascoigne.

1842   ?   ?
Egerton = Lydia
Leigh,   Rachel
of the West   Wright,
Hall and   —— 1803.
Jodrell
Hall, M.P.,
1815-1876.

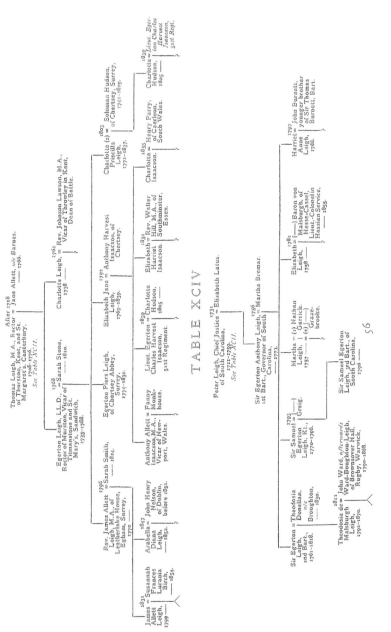

TABLE XCIII

Thomas Leigh, M.A., Rector of Thurston, Kent, and St. Margaret's, Canterbury. 1708-1776. *See Table XCII.* = Jane Allett, *née* Barnes. After 1718. —1766.

- Egerton Leigh, LL.D., Rector of Murston, Vicar of Titmanstone and St. Mary's, Sandwich. 1725-1788. = Sarah Stone. 1768. —1810.
- Charlotte Leigh. 1738. = Rev. Johnson Lawson, M.A., Vicar of Throwley in Kent, Dean of Battle. 1762.

- Rev. James Allett Leigh, M.A., of Leatherhead House, Egham, Surrey. 1770. = Sarah Smith. 1796. —1824.
- Egerton Piers Leigh, of Chertsey Abbey. 1771-1832.
- Anthony Allett Isaacson, M.A., Vicar of Newport, Wales. = Fanny Monkhouse.
- Elizabeth Jane Leigh. 1766-1839. = Anthony Harvest Isaacson, of Chertsey. 1793.
- Charlotte (2) Priscilla Leigh. 1771-1837. = Solomon Hudson, of Chertsey, Surrey. 1761-1849. 1803.

- Arabella Diana Leigh. 1832. = John Henry Neston, *née* Dublin, before 1832. 1807.
- Lieut. Egerton Charles Harvest Isaacson, 51st Regiment.
- Charlotte Hudson. 1805. 1830.
- Elizabeth Harriet Isaacson. = Rev. Walter Hill, M.A., of Southminster, Essex. 1831.
- Charlotte Isaacson. = Henry Parry, of Caerleon, South Wales. 1835.
- Charlotte Hudson. 1865. = Lieut. Egerton Charles Harvest Isaacson, 51st Regt. 1839.

- James Allett Leigh. 1799. = Susannah Frances Lurania Birch. —1854. 1831.

TABLE XCIV

Peter Leigh, Chief Justice, of South Carolina. 1711-1759. *See Table XCII.* = Elizabeth Latus. 1731.

- Sir Egerton Anthony Leigh, 1st Bart., Governor of South Carolina. 1773. = Martha Bremar. 1756.

- Sir Samuel Egerton Leigh, Kt. 1770-1796. 1793. = — Greig.
- Martha Leigh. 1757. = (1) Nathan Leigh. = (2) — Garrick. = — Grazebrooke.
- Sir Samuel Egerton Leigh, 3rd Bart., of South Carolina. 1796.
- Elizabeth Leigh. 1758. = — Baron von Malsburgh, of Hesse-Cassel, Lieut.-Colonel in Hessian Service. 1781. —1855.
- Harriet Leigh. = John Burnett, younger brother of Sir Thomas Burnett, Bart. 1797.
- Anne Leigh. 1766.

- Sir Egerton Leigh, 2nd Bart. 1761-1818. = Theodosia Donellan, *née* Broughton. —1830.
- Theodosia *née* Leigh. = John Ward, *afterwards* Ward-Boughton-Leigh, of Brownsover Hall, Rugby, Warwick. 1811. Malsburgh Leigh. 1792-1869.
- Theodosia Malsburgh Leigh. 1790-1860.

56

TABLE XCV

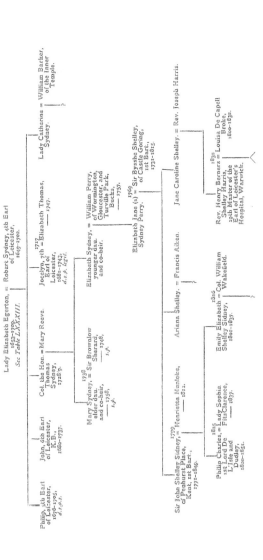

Lady Elizabeth Egerton, = Robert Sydney, 4th Earl
1653-1709.   of Leicester,
See Table LXXXVIII.   1649-1702.

Philip, 5th Earl
of Leicester,
1676-1705,
d.s.p.s.

John, 6th Earl
of Leicester,
K.B.,
1680-1737.

Col. the Hon. = Mary Reeve.
Thomas
Sydney,
1718-39.

Jocelyn, 7th = Elizabeth Thomas,
Earl of   — 1747.
Leicester,
1682-1743,
d.s.p. legit.

Lady Catharine = William Barker,
Sydney.   of the Inner
                                   Temple.
                                        ?

1738
Mary Sydney, = Sir Brownlow
elder dau.   Sherard,
and co-heir,   — 1748,
                        s.p.

Elizabeth Sydney, = William Perry,
younger dau.   of Wormington,
and co-heir.   Gloucester, and
                              Turville Park,
                              Bucks,
                              — 1757.

1766
Elizabeth Jane (a) = Sir Bysshe Shelley,
Sydney Perry.   of Castle Goring,
                              1st Bart.,
                              1731-1815.

Sir John Shelley Sidney, = Henrietta Hunloke,
of Penshurst Place,   — 1811.
Kent, 1st Bart.,
1771-1849.

Ariana Shelley. = Francis Aitken.

Jane Caroline Shelley. = Rev. Joseph Harris.

1805
Philip Charles, = Lady Sophia
1st Lord De   FitzClarence,
L'Isle and   — 1837.
Dudley,
1800-1851.

1826
Emily Elizabeth = Col. William
Shelley Sidney,   Wakefield.
1802-1877.
?

1835
Rev. Henry Berners = Louisa De Capell
Shelley Harris,   Broke,
19th Master of the   1800-1831.
Earl of Leicester's
Hospital, Warwick.

TABLE XCVI

Lady Arabella Egerton, = Oliver, Lord St. John, K.B.,
1660.   1642,
See Table LXXXVIII.   *v.p.*

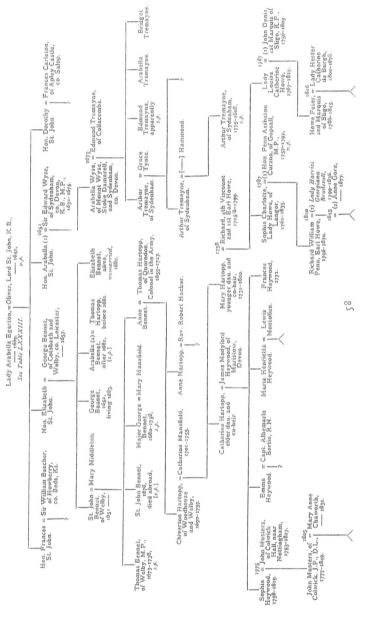

Hon. Frances = Sir William Beecher,
St. John.   of Howbarry,
co. Beds, Kt.
~?

Hon. Elizabeth = George Bennet,
St. John.   of Colsbach and
Welby, co. Leicester,
—— 1657.

Hon. Arabella (1) = Sir Edward Wyse,
St. John.   1651.   of Sydenham,
co. Devon,
K.B., M.P.,
1632–1675.

Hon. Dorothy = Frances Carleton,
St. John.   of Apley Castle,
co. Salop.
~?

St. John = Mary Middleton.
Bennet,
of Welby,
1651.

George
Bennet,
1651,
living 1663.

Arabella (2) = Thomas
Bennet,   Hartopp,
after 1682.   before 1682.
[s.p.]

Elizabeth
Bennet,
alive,
unmarried,
1682.

Arabella Wyse, = Edmund Tremayne,
of Mount Wyse,   of Collacombe.
Stoke Damarell,   1673.
and Sydenham,
co. Devon.

Bridget
Tremayne.

Thomas Bennet,
of Welby, M.P.,
1673–1738,
s.p.

St. John Bennet,
1660,
died abroad,
[s.p.]

Major George = Mary Mansfield.
Bennet,
1680–1739,
s.p.

Anne = Thomas Hartopp,
Bennet.   of Quorndon,
Colonel in the Army,
1655–1737.

Arthur, = Grace
Tremayne,   Tynte.
of Sydenham.

Edmund
Tremayne,
apparently
s.p.

Arabella
Tremayne.

Chiverton Hartopp, = Catherine Mansfield,
of Woodhouse   1701–1755.
and Welby,
1690–1759.

Anne Hartopp. = Rev. Robert Hacker.

Mary Hartopp,
younger dau. and
co-heir,
1731–1800.

Arthur Tremayne, = [——] Hammond.
of Sydenham.

Catherine Hartopp,
elder dau. and
co-heir.

James Modyford
Heywood, of
Maristow,
Devon.

Frances
Heywood,
1771.

Arthur Tremayne,
of Sydenham,
1725–1608,
s.p.

Arthur Tremayne.

Sophia
Heywood,
1758–1819.

Emma = Capt. Albemarle
Heywood.   Bertie, R.N.
~?

Maria Henrietta = Lewis
Heywood.   Montolieu.

Sophia Charlotte, = (1) Hon. Penn Assheton
Lady Howe, of   1787.
Langar,   Curzon, of Gopsall,
1762–1835.   M.P.,
1757–1797,
v.p.

Richard, 4th Viscount
and 1st Earl Howe,
1726–1799.   1758.

Lady
Louisa
Catherine
Howe,
1767–1817.

Lady = (1) John Denis,
1787.   1st Marquis of
Sligo, K.P.,
1756–1809.

Sophia = John Musters,
1775.   of Colwick
Heywood,   Hall, near
1758–1819.   Nottingham,
1753–1827.

John Musters, J.P., D.L., = Mary Anne
of Colwick, J.P., D.L.,...   Chaworth,
1777–1849.   —— 1832.

Richard William = (1) *Lady Harriet
Penn, Earl Howe,   1820.   Georgiana,*
1796–1870.   (2) Anne Gore,   *Brudenell,*
    1845.   —— 1877.   *1799–1836.*

Lady = (1) John Denis,
= (1) John Denis,
1787.

Howe Peter, = Lady Hester
2nd Marquis   1816.   Catherine
of Sligo,   de Burgh,
1788–1845.   1800–1876.

58

TABLE XCVII

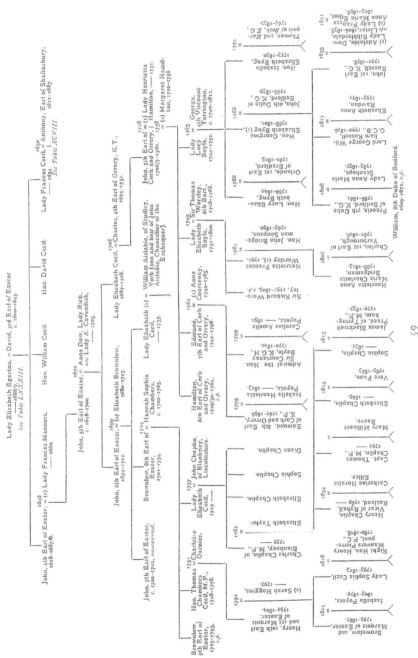

59

TABLE XCVIII

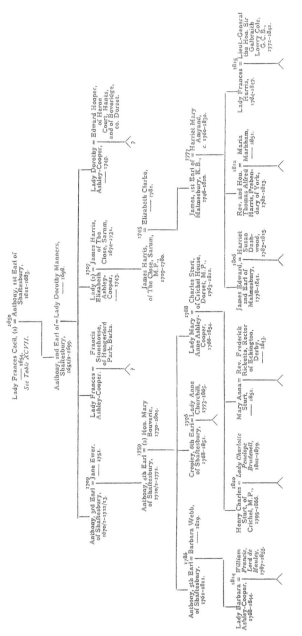

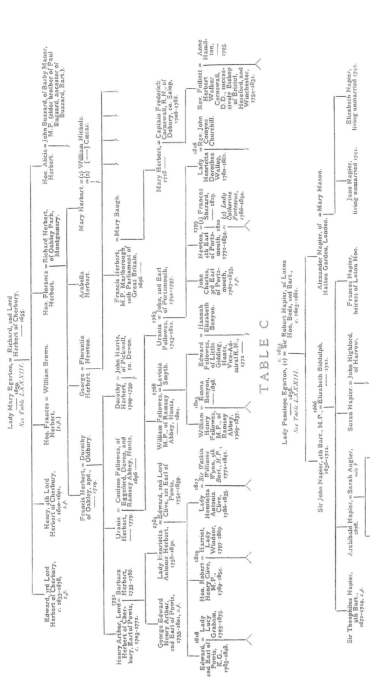

TABLE XCIX

Lady Mary Egerton, = Richard, 2nd Lord Herbert of Cherbury, 1659.
See Table LXXXVIII. 1655.

- Edward, 3rd Lord Herbert of Cherbury, c. 1633-1678, s.p.
- Henry, 4th Lord Herbert of Cherbury, c. 1640-1691, s.p.
- Hon. Frances = William Brown. Herbert, [s.p.]
- Hon. Florence = Richard Herbert, Herbert. of Oakley Park, Montgomery.
- Hon. Alicia = John Buzzard, of Barby Manor, Herbert. M.P. (elder brother of Paul Buzzard, ancestor of Buzzard, Bart.).

- Francis Herbert, = Dorothy of Oakley, apd., Oldbury. 1719.
- George = Florentia Herbert. Newton.
- Arabella Herbert.
- Francis Herbert, M.P. Marlborough, 10th Parliament of Great Britain, 1695
- Mary Herbert = (1) William Nichols. = (2) [—] Caesar.

- Henry Arthur, Lord = 1751 Barbara Herbert of Cher- Herbert, bury, Earl of Powis, 1725-1786. c. 1703-1772.
- Urania = Coulson Fellowes, of Herbert, Eggesford, Devon, and —1779. Ramsey Abbey, Hunts, 1696
- Dorothy = John Harris, Herbert, of Pickwell, 1699-1759. co. Devon.
- = Mary Baugh.
- Urania 1763 John, and Earl Fellowes, of Powis, 1743-1812. 1742-1797.
- Mary Herbert, = Captain Frederick 1710 Cornewall, R.N. of Debury, co. Salop, 1706-1783.

- George Edward Henry Arthur, 2nd Earl of Powis, 1755-1801, s.p.
- Lady Henrietta Antonia Herbert, 1758-1830.
- Edward, 1754 2nd Lord Clive, 1st Earl of Powis, 1754-1839.
- William Fellowes = 1758 Lavinia M.P. of Ramsey Smyth. Abbey, Hunts, 1804.
- John Charles, 3rd Earl of Portsmouth, 1769-1853, s.p.
- Newton, 1795 (1) Frances 4th Earl Sherard, of Ports- —1810. mouth, 1772-1854 = (2) Lady Catherine Portsmouth, 1786-1854.
- Edward Fellowes, of Little Gidding, Hunts, Vice-Ad- miral R.N., 1771
- Lady Henrietta Dorothea Wallop, 1780-1861.
- Rev. John Comyns Churchill.
- Rev. Folliott = Anne Herbert Hamil- Walker ton. Cornewall, 1795 D.D., succes- sive Bishop of Bristol, Hereford, and Winchester, 1756-1831.

- Edward, 1818 = Lady and Earl of Lucy Powis, Graham, K.G., 1793-1875. 1785-1848.
- Hon. Robert = Harriet Henry Clive, Lady M.P. Windsor, 1789-1854. 1797-1869.
- Lady 1819 = Sir Watkin Henrietta Williams Antonia Wynn, 5th Clive, Bart., M.P. 1786-1835. 1772-1841.
- Emma = 1848 Benyon.
- Hannah Elizabeth Benyon.
- William Henry Fellowes, M.P., of Ramsey Abbey, 1769-1837.

TABLE C

Lady Penelope Egerton, c. 1653 (1) = Sir Robert Napier, of Luton Hoo, Beds, and Bart., 1658. c. 1603-1661.
See Table LXXXVIII.

- Sir John Napier, 4th Bart, M.P., = Elizabeth Biddulph, 1635-1711. —1711.
- Alexander Napier, of Luton Hoo Garden, London. = Mary Mason.

- Sir Theophilus Napier, 5th Bart., 1675-1719, s.p.
- Archibald Napier = Sarah Angier, 1698. née ?
- Susan Napier, = John Highlord, of Harrow. ?
- Frances Napier, heiress of Luton Hoo.
- Jane Napier, living unmarried 1761.
- Elizabeth Napier, living unmarried 1761.

- Sir John Napier, Bart., 1748, s.p.
- Elizabeth Napier, died unmarried.

TABLE CI

Lady Magdalen Egerton, = Sir Gervase Cutler, of
1664.   Stainburgh, York, Kt.,
See Table LXXXIII.   1591–1645.

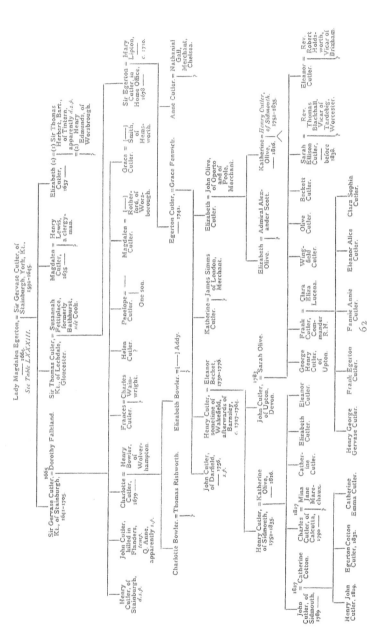

62

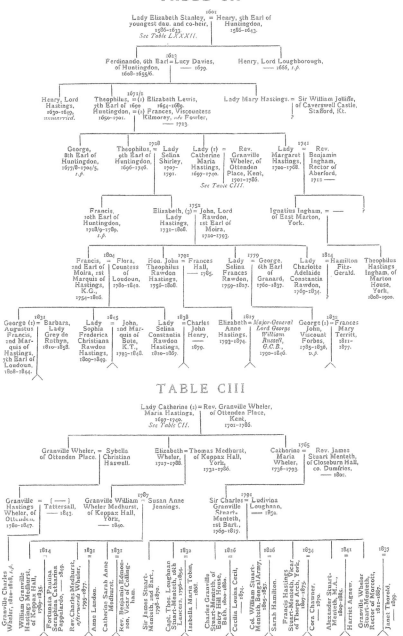

TABLE CII

1601
Lady Elizabeth Stanley, = Henry, 5th Earl of
youngest dau. and co-heir, | Huntingdon,
1586-1633. | 1586-1643.
See Table LXXXII.

1622
Ferdinando, 6th Earl = Lucy Davies,   Henry, Lord Loughborough,
of Huntingdon, | —— 1679.   —— 1666, s.p.
1608-1655/6.

Henry, Lord   Theophilus, = (1) Elizabeth Lewis,   Lady Mary Hastings. = Sir William Jolliffe,
Hastings,   7th Earl of 1600   1654-1689. | of Caverswell Castle,
1630-1649,   Huntingdon, = (2) Frances, Viscountess   ? Stafford, Kt.
unmarried.   1650-1701. | Kilmorey, née Fowler,
                           —— 1723.

George,   Theophilus, = Lady   Lady (1) =   Rev.   Lady   1741 = Rev.
8th Earl of   9th Earl of   Selina   Catherine   Granville   Margaret   Benjamin
Huntingdon,   Huntingdon,   Shirley, Maria   Wheler, of   Hastings,   Ingham,
1677/8-1704/5, 1696-1746.   1707-   Hastings,   Ottenden   1700-1768.   Rector of
s.p.   1791.   1697-1740.   Place, Kent,   Aberford,
                                                  1701-1786.   1712 ——
                                                  See Table CIII.

               Francis,   Elizabeth, (3) = John, Lord   Ignatius Ingham, = ——
               10th Earl of   Lady | Rawdon,   of East Marton,   ?
               Huntingdon,   Hastings,| 1st Earl of   York.
               1728/9-1789,   1731-1808.| Moira,
               s.p. | 1720-1793.

Francis,   = Flora,   Hon. John = Frances   Lady   = George,   Lady   = Hamilton Theophilus
2nd Earl of | Countess   Theophilus Hall,   Selina | 6th Earl Charlotte | Fitz-   Hastings
Moira, 1st | of   Rawdon   —— 1785.   Frances | of   Adelaide | Gerald.   Ingham, of
Marquis of | Loudoun,   Hastings,   Rawdon, | Granard, Constantia   Marton
Hastings, | 1780-1840. 1756-1808.   1759-1827. | 1760-1837.Rawdon,   House,
K.G.,   1769-1834.   York,
1754-1826.   1808-1900.

George (1) = Barbara,   Lady   = John,   Lady   = Charles   Elizabeth = Major-General George (1) = Frances
Augustus | Lady   Sophia | 2nd Mar-   Selina | John   Anne   Lord George   John, | Mary
Francis, | Grey de   Frederica| quis of   Constantia| Henry,   Hastings, William   Viscount | Territt,
2nd Mar- | Ruthyn,   Christiana| Bute,   Rawdon | —— 1879. 1793-1874. Russell,   Forbes, | 1811-
quis of | 1810-1858. Rawdon | K.T.,   Hastings,   G.C.B.,   1785-1836,   1877.
Hastings,   Hastings,| 1793-1848. 1810-1867.   1790-1846. v.p.
7th Earl of   1809-1849.|
Loudoun,
1808-1844.

TABLE CIII

Lady Catherine (1) = Rev. Granville Wheler,
Maria Hastings, | of Ottenden Place,
1697-1740. | Kent,
See Table CII. | 1701-1786.

Granville Wheler, = Sybella   Elizabeth = Thomas Medhurst,   Catherine = Rev. James
of Ottenden Place.| Christian   Wheler, | of Keppax Hall,   Maria | Stuart Menteth,
                  | Haswell.   1727-1788.| York,   Wheler, | of Closeburn Hall,
                                         | 1731-1786.   1736-1793.| co. Dumfries,
                                                                          | —— 1802.

Granville = [——]   Granville William = Susan Anne   Sir Charles = Ludivina
Hastings | Tattersall,| Wheler Medhurst,| Jennings.   Granville | Loughnan,
Wheler, of| —— 1843. | of Keppax Hall,   Stuart, | 1792.
Ottenden, | | York,   Menteth,
1780-1847.| | —— 1840.   1st Bart.,
                                                       1769-1817.

1814	1831	1831		1832	1826	1826	1824	1841	1837
Granville Charles Wheler, 1810-1818, s.p.	William Granville Hastings Medhurst, of Keppax Hall, 1769-1835.	Fortunata Paulina Seraphina Catharina Pappelardo, —— 1849.	Rev. Charles Medhurst, afterwards Wheler, 1795-1871.	Anne Landon.	Catherine Sarah Anne Medhurst.	Rev. Benjamin Edmonson, Vicar of Collingham.	Sir James Stuart-Menteth, 2nd Bart., 1798-1870.	Capt. Thos. Loughnan Stuart-Menteth, 16th Lancers, 1796-1854.	Isabella Maria Tobin, —— 1868.	Charles Granville Stuart-Menteth, of Entry Hill House, Bath, 1800-1880.	Cecilia Louisa Cecil, —— 1874.	Col. William Stuart-Menteth, Bengal Army, 1805-1867.	Sarah Hamilton.	Francis Hastings Stuart-Menteth, Vicar of Thorpe Arch, York, 1807-1875.	Cora Chawner, —— 1870.	Alexander Stuart-Menteth, M.A., 1809-1885.	Harriet Agnew.	Granville Wheler Stuart-Menteth, Rector of Morcott, 1811-1887.	Janet Thorold, —— 1899.

63

TABLE CIV

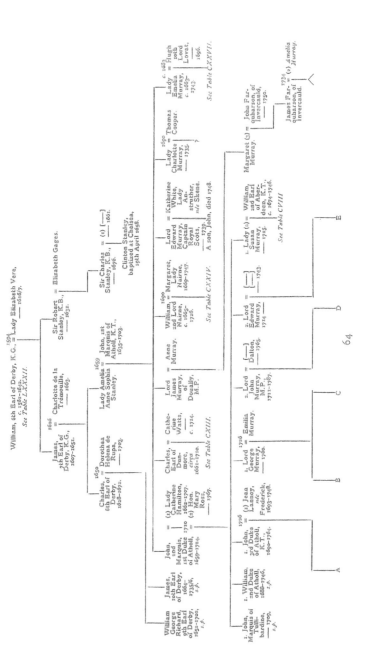

64

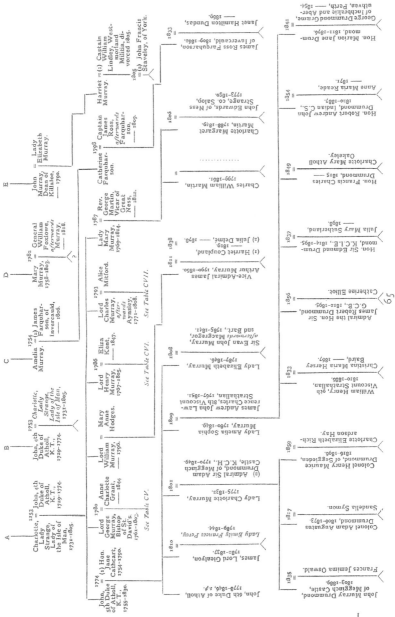

A — Charlotte, Lady Strange, Lady of the Isle of Man, 1731-1805. = 1753

B — John, 4th Duke of Athol, K.T., 1729-1774.

C — Amelia Murray. = 1754 (2) James Farquharson, of Invercauld, 1806.

D — Mary Murray, 1758-1863. = 1782 General William Foxlowe, afterwards Murray, —— 1818.

E — John Murray, Dean of Killaloe, —— 1790. = Lady Elizabeth Murray.

Catherine Farquharson. = 1798 Captain James Ross, afterwards Farquharson, —— 1809.

Harriet Murray. = (1) Captain William Lindley, Westmoreland Militia, divorced 1805. = (2) 1805 John Francis Staveley, of York.

John, 5th Duke of Athol, K.T., 1755-1830. = 1774 (1) Hon. Jane Cathcart, 1754-1790.

Lord George Murray, Bishop of St. David's, 1761-1803. = 1780 Anne Charlotte Grant, —— 1844.

Lord William Murray, 1796. = Mary Anne Hodges.

Lord Henry Murray, 1767-1805. = 1786 Eliza Kent, 1847.

Lord Charles Murray, afterwards Aynsley, 1771-1808. = 1793 Alice Mitford.

Lady Mary Murray, 1769-1814. = 1787 Rev. George Martin, Vicar of Great Ness, —— 1822.

John, 6th Duke of Athol, 1778-1846, s.p.

James, Lord Glenlyon, 1782-1837.

Lady Emily Frances Percy, 1789-1884. = 1811

Lady Charlotte Murray, 1775-1832. = 1801 Admiral Sir Adam Drummond, of Megginch Castle, K.C.H., 1770-1849.

Lady Amelia Sophia Murray, 1760-1849. = 1809 James Andrew John Lawrence Charles, 8th Viscount Strathallan, 1767-1851.

Lady Elizabeth Murray, 1787-1846. = 1808 Sir Evan John Murray, afterwards MacGregor, 1st Bart., 1785-1841.

Vice-Admiral James Arthur Murray, 1790-1850.

Charles William Martin, 1799-1861.

Charlotte Margaret Martin, 1788-1849. = 1805 John Edwards, of Ness Strange, co. Salop, 1773-1850.

James Ross Farquharson, of Invercauld, 1809-1862. = 1833 Janet Hamilton Dundas, —— 1869.

See Table CV.   *See Table CVI.*   *See Table CVII.*

John Murray Drummond, of Megginch Castle, 1863-1889. = 1891 Frances Jemima Oswald.

Colonel Adam Augustus Drummond, 1806-1873. = 1827 Sandelia Symon.

Colonel Henry Maurice Drummond, of Megginch Castle, 1816-1896. = 1859 Charlotte Elizabeth Richardson Hay.

William Henry, 9th Viscount Strathallan, 1810-1886. = 1834 Christina Maria Hersey Baird, —— 1867.

Admiral the Hon. Sir James Robert Drummond, G.C.B., 1812-1895. = 1866 Catherine Elliot.

Hon. Sir Edmund Drummond, K.C.I.E., 1814-1895. = 1842 Julia Mary Sutherland, —— 1898.

Hon. Francis Charles Drummond, 1815. = 1848 Charlotte Mary Athol Oakeley.

Hon. Robert Andrew John Drummond, Indian C.S., 1820-1887. = 1856 Anne Maria Reade, 1871.

Hon. Marion Jane Drummond, 1811-1876. = 1851 George Drummond Graeme, of Inchbrakie and Aberuthven, Perth, —— 1884.

65

I

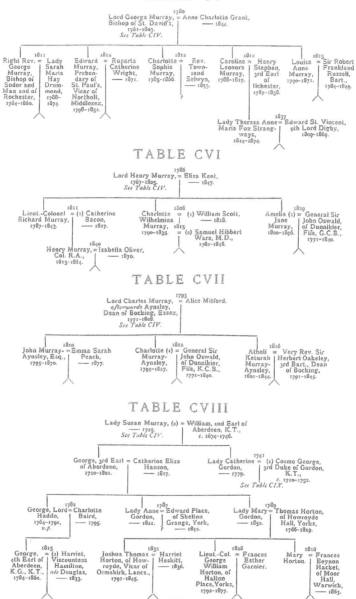

TABLE CV

1780
Lord George Murray, = Anne Charlotte Grant,
Bishop of St. David's, — 1844.
1761-1803.
See Table CIV.

| 1811 | | 1822 | | 1812 | | 1812 | | 1815 |
| Right Rev. = Lady
George
Murray,
Bishop of
Sodor and
Man and of
Rochester,
1784-1860. | Sarah
Maria
Hay
Drum-
mond,
1788-
1874. | Edward = Ruperta
Murray,
Preben-
dary of
St. Paul's,
Vicar of
Northolt,
Middlesex,
1798-1852. | Catherine
Wright,
— 1871. | Charlotte = Rev.
Sophia
Murray,
1785-1866. | Town-
send
Selwyn,
— 1853. | Caroline = Henry
Leonora
Murray,
1788-1819. | Stephen,
3rd Earl
of
Ilchester,
1787-1858. | Louisa = Sir Robert
Anne
Murray,
1790-1871. | Frankland
Russell,
Bart.,
1784-1849. |

1837
Lady Theresa Anne = Edward St. Vincent,
Maria Fox Strang- | 9th Lord Digby,
ways, | 1809-1889.
1814-1874.

TABLE CVI

1786
Lord Henry Murray, = Eliza Kent,
1767-1805. | — 1847.
See Table CIV.

| 1811 | | 1808 | | 1829 |
| Lieut.-Colonel = (1) Catherine
Richard Murray,
1787-1843. | Bacon,
— 1817. | Charlotte
Wilhelmina |
Murray,
1790-1835. | (1) William Scott,
— 1818.
= (2) Samuel Hibbert
Ware, M.D.,
1782-1848. | Amelia (2) = General Sir
Jane
Murray,
1800-1896. | John Oswald,
of Dunnikier,
Fife, G.C.B.,
1771-1840. |

1840
Henry Murray, = Isabella Oliver,
Col. R.A., | — 1870.
1815-1854.

TABLE CVII

1793
Lord Charles Murray, = Alice Mitford.
afterwards Aynsley,
Dean of Bocking, Essex,
1771-1808.
See Table CIV.

| 1820 | | 1812 | | 1826 |
| John Murray- = Emma Sarah
Aynsley, Esq.,
1795-1870. | Peach,
— 1877. | Charlotte (1) = General Sir
Murray-
Aynsley,
1794-1827. | John Oswald,
of Dunnikier,
Fife, K.C.B.,
1771-1840. | Atholl = Very Rev. Sir
Keturah
Murray-
Aynsley,
1801-1844. | Herbert Oakeley,
3rd Bart., Dean
of Bocking,
1791-1845. |

TABLE CVIII

Lady Susan Murray, (2) = William, 2nd Earl of
— 1725. | Aberdeen, K.T.,
See Table CIV. | c. 1674-1746.

| | 1741 |
| George, 3rd Earl = Catherine Eliza
of Aberdeen,
1720-1801. | Hanson,
— 1817. | Lady Catherine = (1) Cosmo George,
Gordon,
— 1779. | 3rd Duke of Gordon,
K.T.,
c. 1720-1752.
See Table CIX. |

| 1782 | | 1787 | | 1789 |
| George, Lord = Charlotte
Haddo,
1764-1791,
v.p. | Baird,
— 1795. | Lady Anne = Edward Place,
Gordon,
— 1821. | of Skelton
Grange, York,
— 1842. | Lady Mary = Thomas Horton,
Gordon,
— 1852. | of Howroyde
Hall, Yorks,
1766-1829. |

| 1815 | | 1832 | | 1826 | | 1816 |
| George, = (2) Harriet,
4th Earl of
Aberdeen,
K.G., K.T.,
1784-1860. | Viscountess
Hamilton,
née Douglas,
— 1833. | Joshua Thomas = Harriet
Horton, of How-
royde, Vicar of
Ormskirk, Lancs.,
1791-1845. | Heskitt,
— 1836. | Lieut.-Col. = Frances
George
William
Horton, of
Halton
Place, Yorks,
1792-1877. | Esther
Garnier. | Mary = Frances
Horton. | Beynon
Hacket,
of Moor
Hall,
Warwick,
— 1863. |

TABLE CIX

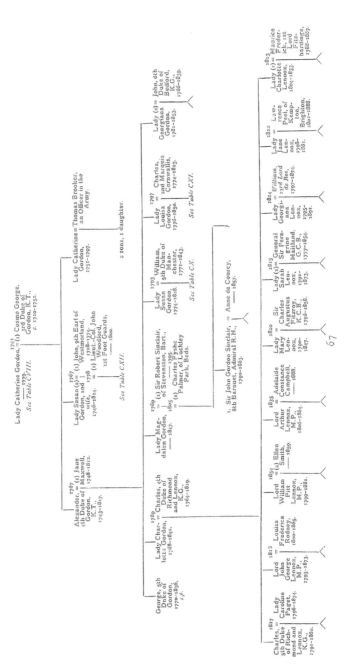

Lady Catherine Gordon, = (1) Cosmo George, 3rd Duke of Gordon, K.T., c. 1720-1752.
1741
See Table CVIII.

Alexander, = (1) Jane Maxwell, 4th Duke of Gordon, 1748-1812. Gordon, K.T., 1743-1827.
1767

Lady Susan (2) = (1) John, 9th Earl of Gordon, and wife, 1776-1814. = (2) Lieut.-Col. John Woodford, 1st Foot Guards, — 1800.
1767
1778 Westmorland,
See Table CXII.

Lady Catherine = Thomas Brooker, Gordon, an Officer in the 1751-1797. Army.

2 sons, 1 daughter.

Lady Mar- = Sir Robert Sinclair, Bart., daica Gordon, 1847. of Stevenston, 1795. = (2) Charles Fyshe Palmer, of Luckley Park, Beds.
1789
1805

Lady = William, Susan 5th Duke of Man- Gordon, chester, 1774-1828. 1777-1843.
1793
See Table CX.

Lady = Charles, Louisa 2nd Marquis Gordon, Cornwallis, 1776-1850. 1774-1823.
1797
See Table CXI.

Lady (2) = John, 6th Georgiana Duke of Gordon, Bedford, 1781-1853. K.G., 1766-1839.

Lady Char- = Charles, 4th lotte Gordon, Duke of 1768-1842. Richmond and Lennox, K.G., 1764-1819.
1789

? Sir John Gordon Sinclair, = Anne de Courcy, 1857.
8th Baronet, Admiral R.N., 1790-1863.

George, 5th Duke of Gordon, 1770-1836. s.p.

Charles, = 5th Duke of Rich- mond and Lennox, K.G., 1791-1860.
1817
Lady Caroline Paget, 1796-1874.

Lord John George Lennox, M.P., 1793-1873.
1813
Louisa Frederica Rodney, 1800-1865.

Lord William Pitt Lennox, 1799-1881.
1851(4) Ellen Smith, — 1850.

Lord Arthur Lennox, M.P., 1806-1864.
1835
Adelaide Constance Campbell, 1888.

Lady Mary Len- nox, 1790-1847.
1810
Sir Charles Augustus Fitzroy, K.C.B., 1796-1858.

Lady (2) = General Sarah Sir Pere- Len- grine nox, Maitland, 1792- G.C.B., 1873. 1777-1854.
1815

Lady = William, Georgi- 23rd Lord ana de Ros, Len- 1797-1874. nox, 1795- 1891.
1844

Lady = Law- Jane rence Len- Peel, of nox, Kemp- 1798- ton, 1861. Brighton, 1801-1888.
1822

Lady (2) = Maurice Charlotte Freder- Lennox, ick, 1st 1804-1833. Lord Fitz- hardinge, 1788-1867.
1823

67

TABLE CX

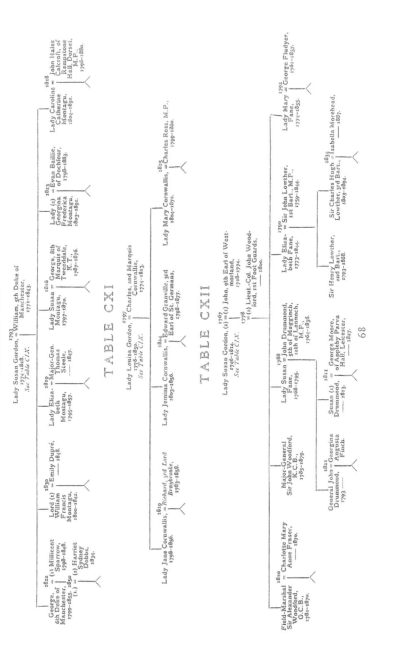

TABLE CX

Lady Susan Gordon, 1793 = William, 5th Duke of Manchester, 1774-1828. *See Table CIX.* 1771-1843.

- George, 1821 = (1) Millicent Sparrow, 6th Duke of Manchester, 1798-1848. 1799-1855. 1860 (1.) = (2) Harriet Sydney Dobbs, 1830.
  - Lord (1) 1830 = Emily Dupré, William Francis Montagu, —1848. 1800-1842.
- Lady Eliza-beth Montagu, 1795-1857. 1810 = Major-Gen. Thomas Steele, —1847.
- Lady Susan Montagu, 1797-1870. 1816 = George, 8th Marquis of Tweeddale, K.T., 1787-1876.
- Lady (2) 1823 = Evan Baillie, Georgina Frederica Montagu, 1803-1892. of Dochfour, 1798-1883.
- Lady Caroline 1828 = John Hales Catherine Montagu, 1804-1891. Calcroft, of Rempstone Hall, Dorset, M.P., 1796-1880.

TABLE CXI

Lady Louisa Gordon, 1797 = Charles, 2nd Marquis 1776-1850. Cornwallis, *See Table CIX.* 1774-1823.

- Lady Jane Cornwallis, 1810 = Richard, 3rd Lord 1798-1856. Braybrooke, 1783-1858.
- Lady Jemima Cornwallis, 1804 = Edward Grenville, 3rd 1803-1856. Earl of St. Germans, 1798-1877.
- Lady Mary Cornwallis, 1825 = Charles Ross, M.P., 1804-1872. 1799-1860.

TABLE CXII

Lady Susan Gordon, (2) 1767 = (1) John, 9th Earl of West-1766-1814. morland, 1728-1774. *See Table CIX.* 1798 = (2) Lieut.-Col. John Wood-ford, 1st Foot Guards, —1800.

- Field-Marshal Sir Alexander Woodford, G.C.B., 1782-1870. 1800 = Charlotte Mary Anne Fraser, —1870.
- Major-General Sir John Woodford, K.C.B., 1785-1879.
- Lady Susan 1788 = John Drummond, Fane, 1768-1795. 11th of Lennoch, M.P., 1764-1856.
  - Susan (1) 1811 = George Moore, Drummond, of Appleby Parva Hall, Leicester, —1813. —1827.
  - General John 1821 = Georgina Drummond, Augusta Finch. 1793 —
- Lady Eliza-beth Fane, 1773-1844. 1790 = Sir John Lowther, 1st Bart., M.P., 1759-1844.
  - Sir Henry Lowther, 2nd Bart., 1793-1868.
  - Sir Charles Hugh 1834 = Isabella Morehead, Lowther, 3rd Bart., 1803-1864. —1887.
- Lady Mary 1791 = George Fludyer, Fane, 1774-1855. Fane, 1761-1837.

TABLE CXIII.

Charles, 1st Earl of Dunmore, = Catherine Watts
circa 1660–1710.
See Table CV.
c. —— 1714.

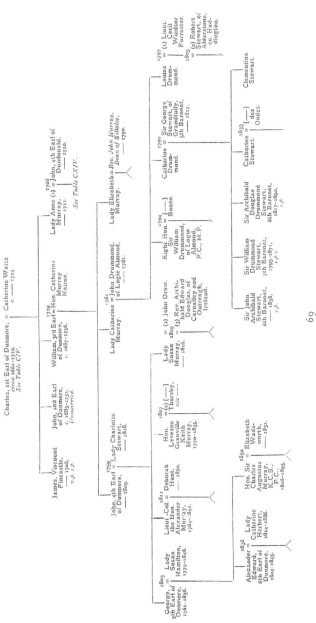

James, Viscount
Fincastle,
—— 1706,
v.p. s.p.

John, 2nd Earl
of Dunmore,
c. 1685–1752,
Unmarried.

William, 3rd Earl = Hon. Catherine
of Dunmore,
c. 1689–1756.
Murray
Nairne.
1710

Lady Anne (1) = John, 4th Earl of
Murray,
—— 1711.
Dundonald,
—— 1720.
1705

See Table CXIV.

John, 4th Earl = Lady Charlotte
of Dunmore,
—— 1809.
Stewart,
—— 1818.
1759

Lady Catherine = John Drummond,
Murray.
of Logie Almond,
—— 1781.
1761

Lady Elizabeth = *Rev. John Murray,*
Murray.
Dean. of Killaloe,
—— 1790.

George, = Lady
5th Earl of
Dunmore,
1762–1836.
Susan
Hamilton,
1774–1846.
1803

Lieut.-Col. = Deborah
the Hon.
Alexander
Murray,
1764–1842.
Hunt,
—— 1870.
1811

Hon. = (2) [——]
Leveson
Grenville
Keith
Murray,
1770–1835.
Thursby,
—— *née*
1809

Lady = (1) John Drew.
Susan
Murray,
—— 1866.
1809

= (3) Rev. Archi-
bald Edward
Douglas, of
Carnalley and
Outreagh,
Ireland.

Right Hon. = [——]
Sir
William
Drummond,
of Logie
Almond,
P.C., M.P.
Boone.
1794

Catherine = Sir George
Drum-
mond.
Stewart, of
Grandtully,
5th Baronet,
—— 1827.
1793

Louisa
Drum-
mond.
= (1) Lieut.
Cecil
Windsor
Forrester.
1797
= (2) Robert
Stewart, of
Alderstone,
co. Had-
dington.
1805

Alexander = Lady
Edward,
6th Earl of
Dunmore,
1804–1845.
Catherine
Herbert,
1814–1866.
1836

Hon. Sir = Elizabeth
Charles
Augustus
Murray,
K.C.B.,
1806–1895.
K.C.B.,
Wads-
worth,
—— 1851.
1850

Sir John
Archibald
Stewart,
6th Baronet,
—— 1836.
s.p.s.

Sir William
Drummond
Stewart,
7th Baronet,
1795–1871,
s.p.s.

Sir Archibald
Douglas
Drummond
Stewart,
8th Baronet,
1817–1890,
s.p.

Catherine = [——]
Stewart.
des
Ondes.
1833

Clementina
Stewart.

69

TABLE CXIV

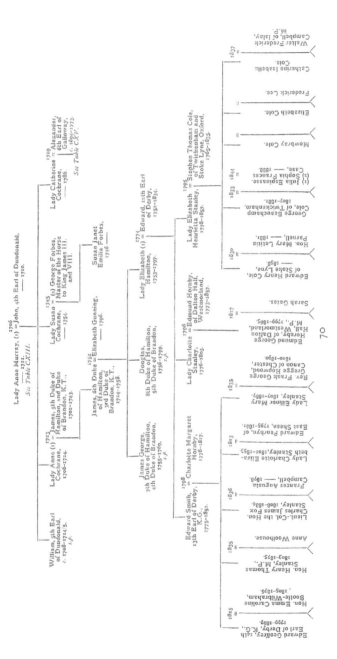

TABLE CXV

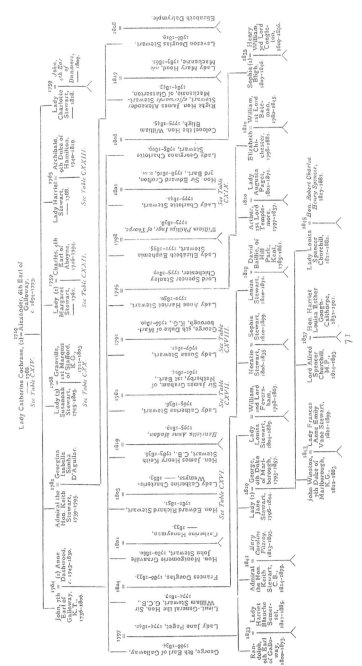

TABLE CXVI

Hon. Edward Richard Stewart, = Lady Catherine Charteris-Wemyss,
1782–1851.   1805   ——1863.
See Table CXV.

Rev. Edward Stewart, = Louisa Anne Herbert,   Algernon Stewart, = Charlotte Clement,   Arthur Stewart, = Mary Judith   Jane Frances (1) = George, 6th Duke
Rector of Lainston,   1838   ——1892.   1811–1875.   1833   ——1851.   1813–1879.   1840   Madan,   Clinton Stewart,   1851   of Marlborough,
Vicar of Sparsholt,   1813–1871.   1817–1897.   1793–1857.
Hants,
1806–1875.

TABLE CXVII

Lady Catherine Stewart, = Sir James Graham, of
1783.   Netherby, 1st Bart.,
See Table CXV.   1761–1824.

George Graham, = Maria Hassell,   Elizabeth = Rev. William   Caroline = Sir Wilfrid   Harriet = Capt. Fred   Charlotte = Sir George
Registrar-   1836   ——1855.   Anne   1816   James Durley   Graham,   1811   Lawson,   Anne   1823   Madan,   Graham,   1828   Musgrave,
General,   Graham,   Waddilove,   1793–1870.   1st Bart.,   Graham,   E.I.S.,   ——1873.   10th Bart.,
1821–1888.   1791–1874.   1786–1859.   1795–1867.   1799–1836.   1797–1863.   of Edenhall,
                                                                         1799–1872.

Right Hon. Sir = Fanny Callender,
James Robert   1857.
George Graham,
of Netherby,
2nd Bart., P.C.,
G.C.B.,
1791–1861.

TABLE CXVIII

Lady Susan Stewart, = George, 5th Duke of
1767–1841.   1791   Marlborough, K.G.,
See Table CXV.   1766–1840.

George, 6th Duke = (1) *Lady Jane Stewart,*   (2) Hon. Charlotte = (1) *Jane Frances*   Lord Charles = Ethelred Catherine
of Marlborough,   1819   1798–1844.   1846   Augusta Flower,   1851   *Clinton Stewart,*   Spencer Churchill,   1827   Bennet,
1793–1857.   1818–1850.   1847–1897.   1794–1840.   1839.

TABLE CXIX

Lady Charlotte Stewart, = Hon. Sir Edward Crofton,
1777–1842.   1801   3rd Bart.,
See Table CXV.   1778–1816, *v. m.*

Edward, 2nd = Lady   Hon. Susannah = St. George   Hon. Charlotte = Gibbs Crawford   Hon. Frances = Daniel Tighe,   Hon. Sophia = Eyre Evans,   Hon. Frede- = Rev. Hubert
Lord Crofton,   1833   Georgiana   Anne Crofton,   1830   Francis   Crofton,   1831   Antrobus, of   Crofton,   1825   of Rossana,   Crofton,   1827   of Ash Hill   rica Crofton,   1835   M'Laughlin,
1806–1869.   Paget,   1802–1890.   Caulfield,   1803–1839.   Eaton Hall,   1805–1881.   co. Wicklow,   1811–1884.   Towers,   1810–1881.   M.A., Preb.
          1800–1875.   of Donamon   co. Chester,   1796–1874.   Limerick,   of Hereford,
                                Castle,   1794–1861.   1865–1853.   Rector of
                           Roscommon,   Burford,
                           1806–1896.   Salop,
                                                                                                   ——1883.

TABLE CXX

Lady Susannah Stewart, (3) = Granville, 1st Marquis of Stafford, K.G., 1721–1803.
1768
1865.
See Table CXXV.

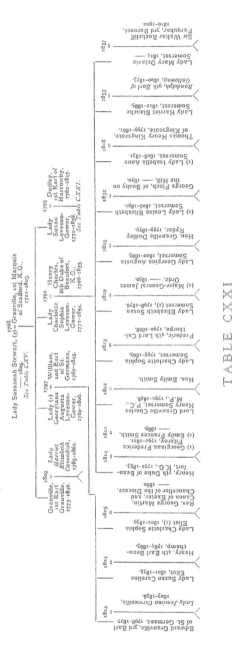

TABLE CXXI

Lady Susan Leveson-Gower = Dudley, 1st Earl of Harrowby, 1772–1838. 1762–1847.
See Table CXX.

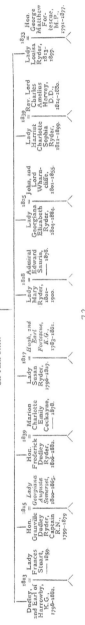

K

TABLE CXXII

Lady Margaret Stewart, (1) = Charles, 4th Earl of Aboyne,
1736–1794.
1759
1762.
See Table CXV.

George, 5th Earl of Aboyne, = Catherine Cope,
9th Marquis of Huntley, K.T., 1761–1832.
1791
1761–1853.

Lady Margaret Gordon, = William Beckford, of
c. 1760–1786. | Fonthill Gifford, Wilts,
1762 1760–1844.
1783

Charles, = (2) Maria
10th | Antoinette
Marquis | Pegus,
of | ——1893.
Huntley,
1792–1863.
1844

Lord = Louisa
Henry | Payne,
Gordon, | 1867.
1802–1865.
1827

Lord Cecil = Emily
James | Moore.
Gordon,
afterwards
Gordon-
Moore,
1806–1878.
1841

Lieut.-Col. = Isabel
Lord Fran- | Grant,
cis Arthur | 1890.
Gordon,
1st Life
Guards,
1808–1857.
1835

Lady = Charles
Susan | Compton,
Catherine | 1st Lord
Gordon, | Cheltham,
1790–1866. | 1796–1863.
1814

Lady (1) = Frederick
Mary | C. W.
Gordon, | Seymour,
1790– | 1797–1856.
1825.
1812

Margaret = Lieut.-Gen.
Mina | James Orde,
Elizabeth | 1850.
Beckford,
c. 1794–1818.
1811

Susanna =
Euphemia | Alexander,
Beckford, | 10th Duke of
1786–1859. | Hamilton,
| 7th Duke of
| Brandon, K.G.,
| 1767–1852.

William Alexander = Princess Mary
Anthony Archibald, | of Baden,
11th Duke of Hamil- | 1818–1888.
ton, 8th Duke of
Brandon,
1811–1863.
1843

Lady Susan = (1) Henry, Earl of Lincoln
Harriet | (afterwards 5th Duke of
Catherine | Newcastle), divorced 1850.
Hamilton, | 1811–1864.
1814–1889.

TABLE CXXIII

Lady Harriet Stewart, = Archibald, 9th Duke
1780. | of Hamilton, 6th Duke
See Table CXV. | of Brandon, Duke of
| Chatelherault,
| 1740–1819.
1765

Alexander, 10th Duke = Susanna Euphemia
of Hamilton, | Beckford,
7th Duke of | 1786–1859.
Brandon, &c., K.G.,
1767–1852.
1810

Lady Charlotte (1) = Edward Adolphus,
Hamilton, | 11th Duke of
1775–1847. | Somerset, K.C.,
| 1775–1855.
1800

Lady Susan = George,
Hamilton, | 5th Earl of
1774–1846. | Dunmore,
| 1762–1836.
1803

Lady (2) = William Blount,
Charlotte | of Orleton,
Jane Sey- | Hereford,
mour, | 1885.
1803–1889.
1835

Lady Anna (1) = William
Maria Jane | Tollemache,
Seymour, | 1810–1885.
1807–1873.
1838

Edward Adolphus, = Jane Georgiana
12th Duke of | Sheridan,
Somerset, K.G., | 1809–1884.
1804–1885.
1830

Archibald Henry
Algernon,
13th Duke of
Somerset,
1810–1891.

Algernon Percy = Horatia Isabel
Banks, 11th Duke | Harriet Morier.
of Somerset,
1813–1890.
1845

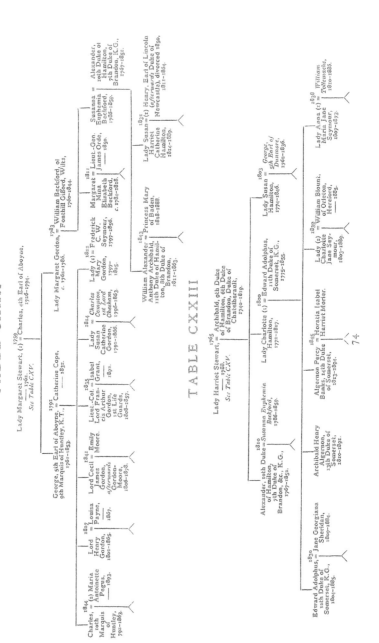

74

TABLE CXXIV

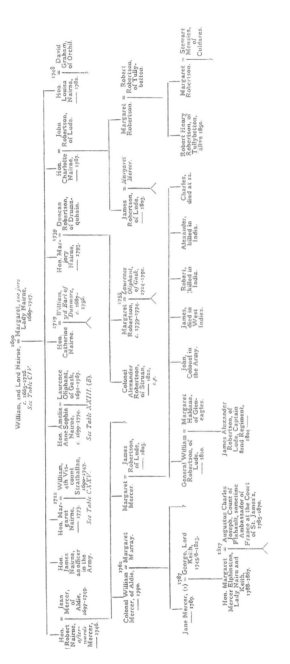

William, and Lord Nairne, = Margaret, *sui jurs*
c. 1665–1726.   Lady Nairne,
See Table CIV.   1669–1747.

TABLE CXXV

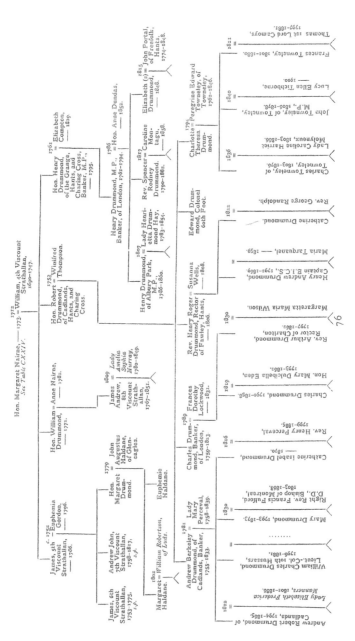

TABLE CXXVI

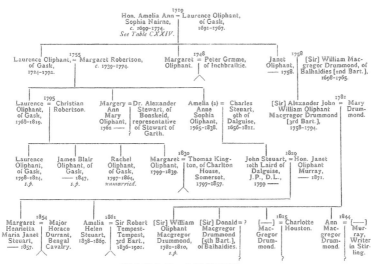

1719
Hon. Amelia Ann = Laurence Oliphant,
Sophia Nairne, | of Gask,
c. 1699-1774. | 1691-1767.
See Table CXXIV.

1755
Laurence Oliphant, = Margaret Robertson,
of Gask, | c. 1739-1774.
1724-1792.

1748
Margaret = Peter Græme,
Oliphant. | of Inchbraikie.

1758
Janet | [Sir] William Mac-
Oliphant, | gregor Drummond, of
— 1758. | Balhaldies [2nd Bart.],
1698-1765.

1795
Laurence = Christian
Oliphant, | Robertson.
of Gask,
1769-1819.

Margery = Dr. Alexander
Ann | Stewart, of
Mary | Bonskeid,
Oliphant, | representative
1762 — | of Stewart of
? | Garth.

Amelia (2) = Charles
Anne | Stewart,
Sophia | 9th of
Oliphant, | Dalguise,
1765-1838. | 1656-1821.

1781
[Sir] Alexander John = Mary
William Oliphant | Drum-
Macgregor Drummond | mond.
[3rd Bart.],
1758-1794.

Laurence | James Blair | Rachel
Oliphant, | Oliphant, of | Oliphant,
of Gask, | Gask, | of Gask,
1798-1824, | — 1847, | 1797-1864,
s.p. | s.p. | unmarried.

1830
Margaret = Thomas King-
Oliphant, | ton, of Charlton
1799-1839. | House,
Somerset,
1797-1857.

1859
John Steuart, = Hon. Janet
10th Laird of | Oliphant
Dalguise, | Murray,
J.P., D.L., | — 1871.
1799 —

1854
Margaret = Major
Henrietta | Horace
Maria Janet | Durrant,
Steuart, | Bengal
— 1857. | Cavalry.

1861
Amelia = Sir Robert
Helen | Tempest-
Steuart, | Tempest,
1838-1869. | 3rd Bart.,
1836-1901.

[Sir] William
Oliphant
Macgregor
Drummond,
1782-1810,
s.p.

[Sir] Donald = ?
Macgregor
Drummond
[5th Bart.],
of Balhaldies.

1815
[—] = Charlotte
Mac- | Houston.
Gregor
Drum-
mond.

1844
Ann = [—]
Mac- | Mur-
gregor | ray,
Drum- | Writer
mond. | in Stir-
ling.

TABLE CXXVII

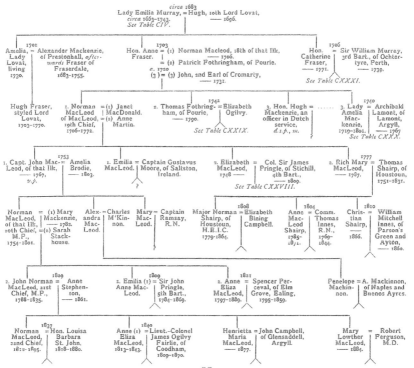

circa 1683
Lady Emilia Murray, = Hugh, 10th Lord Lovat,
circa 1663-1743. | — 1696.
See Table CIV.

1702
Amelia, = Alexander Mackenzie,
Lady | of Prestonhall, after-
Lovat, | wards Fraser of
living | Fraserdale,
1730. | 1683-1755.

1703
Hon. Anne = (1) Norman Macleod, 18th of that Ilk,
Fraser. | — 1706.
= (2) Patrick Fothringham, of Pourie.
c. 1720
(3) = (3) John, 2nd Earl of Cromarty,
— 1731.

1706
Hon. = Sir William Murray,
Catherine | 3rd Bart., of Ochter-
Fraser, | tyre, Perth,
— 1771. | — 1739.
See Table CXXXI.

Hugh Fraser,
styled Lord
Lovat,
1703-1770.

1. Norman = (1) Janet
MacLeod, | MacDonald.
of MacLeod, = (2) Anne
19th Chief, | Martin.
1706-1772.

1742
2. Thomas Fothring- = Elizabeth
ham, of Pourie, | Ogilvy.
— 1790.
See Table CXXIX.

3. Hon. Hugh = ...
Mackenzie, an
officer in Dutch
service,
d.s.p., m.

1740
3. Lady = Archibald
Amelia | Lamont, of
Mac- | Lamont,
kenzie, | Argyll.
1710-1801. | — 1767
See Table CXXX.

1753
1. Capt. John Mac- = Amelia
Leod, of that Ilk, | Brodie,
— 1767, | — 1803.
v.p.

1. Emilia = Captain Gustavus
MacLeod. | Moore, of Salkston,
Ireland.

2. Elizabeth = Col. Sir James
MacLeod, | Pringle, of Stichill,
1748 — | 4th Bart.,
— 1809.
See Table CXXVIII.

1777
2. Rich Mary = Thomas
MacLeod, | Shairp, of
— 1787. | Houstoun,
1751-1831.

Norman = (1) Mary
MacLeod, | Mackenzie,
of that Ilk, | — 1782.
20th Chief, = (2) Sarah
M.P., | Stack-
1754-1801. | house.

Alex- = Charles
andra | M'Kin-
Mac- | non.
Leod.

Mary = Captain
Mac- | Ramsay,
Leod. | R.N.

1808
Major Norman = Elizabeth
Shairp, of | Bining
Houstoun, | Campbell.
H.E.I.C.
1779-1864.

1804
Anne = Comm.
Mac- | Thomas
Leod | Innes,
Shairp, | R.N.,
1785- | 1769-
1871. | 1844.

1810
Chris- = William
tian | Mitchell
Shairp, | Innes, of
1866. | Parson's
Green and
Ayton,
— 1860.

1809
2. John Norman = Anne
MacLeod, 21st | Stephen-
Chief, M.P., | son,
1788-1835. | — 1861.

1809
2. Emilia (1) = Sir John
Anne Mac- | Pringle,
Leod. | 5th Bart.,
1784-1869.

1821
2. Anne = Spencer Per-
Eliza | ceval, of Elm
MacLeod, | Grove, Ealing,
1797-1889. | 1795-1859.

Penelope = A. Mackinnon,
Mackin- | of Naples and
non. | Buenos Ayres.

1837
Norman = Hon. Louisa
MacLeod, | Barbara
22nd Chief, | St. John,
1812-1895. | 1818-1880.

1840
Anne (1) = Lieut.-Colonel
Eliza | James Ogilvy
MacLeod, | Fairlie, of
1813-1843. | Coodham,
1809-1870.

Henrietta = John Campbell,
Maria | of Glensaddell,
MacLeod, | Argyll.
— 1877.

Mary = Robert
Lowther | Ferguson,
MacLeod, | M.D.
— 1884.

77

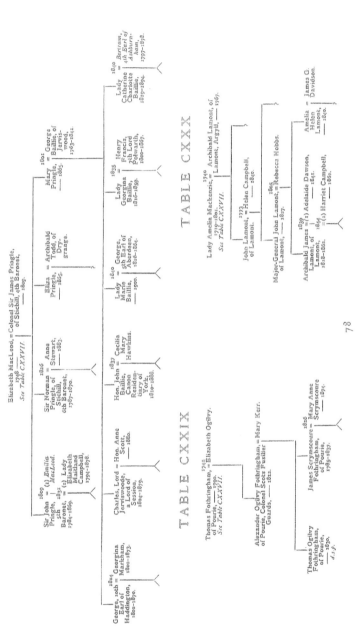

TABLE CXXVIII

Elizabeth MacLeod, = Colonel Sir James Pringle,
1748 | of Stichill, 4th Baronet,
See Table CXXVII. | 1809.

1809 Sir John = (1) *Emilia*
Pringle, | *MacLeod.*
5th |
Baronet,   = (2) Lady
1784-1869.   Elizabeth
Maitland
Campbell,
1794-1878.

Charles, Lord = Hon. Anne
Jerviswoode,   Scott,
a Lord of   1880.
Session,
1804-1879.

Sir Norman = **1826**
Pringle, of   Anne
Stichill,   Stewart,
6th Baronet,   1863.
1787-1870.

Mary = **1801** George
Pringle, | Baillie, of
1865.   Jervis-
wood,
1763-1841.

Eliza = Archibald
Pringle,   Todd, of
1855.   Dry-
grange.

Hon. John = **1839**
Baillie,   Cecilia
Canon   Mary
Residen-   Hawkins.
tiary of
York,
1810-1888.

Lady = **1840** George,
Marie   5th Earl of
Baillie,   Aberdeen,
1900.   1816-1864.

Lady   = Henry **1825**
Georgina   Francis,
Baillie,   7th Lord
1816-1850.   Polwarth,
1800-1867.

Lady = **1840** *Berisson,*
Catherine   *4th Earl of*
Charlotte   *Ashburn-*
Baillie,   *ham,*
1819-1894.   *1797-1878.*

George, 10th = **1844**
Earl of   Georgina
Haddington,   Markham,
1802-1870.   1802-1873.

TABLE CXXIX

Thomas Fothringham, = **1745**
of Pourie,   Elizabeth Ogilvy.
1790.
See Table CXXVII.

Alexander Ogilvy Fothringham, = Mary Kerr.
of Pourie, Colonel Scots Fusilier
Guards,   1811.

Thomas Ogilvy
Fothringham,
of Pourie,
1830,
d.s.p.

James Scrymgeour = **1826**
Fothringham,   Mary Anne
1785-1837.   Scrymgeour,
1874.

TABLE CXXX

Lady Amelia Mackenzie, = **1740** Archibald Lamont, of
1719-1801. | Lamont, Argyll,   1767.
See Table CXXVII.

John Lamont, = **1773**
of Lamont.   Helen Campbell,
1840.

Major-General John Lamont, = **1805**
of Lamont,   1807.   Rebecca Hobbs.

Archibald James = (1) Adelaide Dawson,
Lamont, of | 1841.
Lamont,   = (2) Harriet Campbell,
1818-1862. | **1844** 1869.
1839

Amelia = James G.
Helen   Davidson.
Lamont,
1840.

TABLE CXXXI

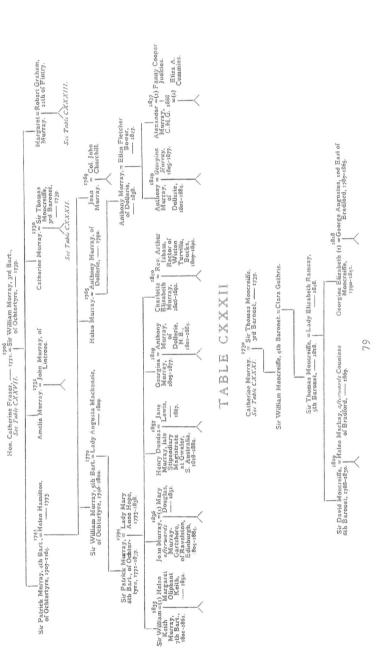

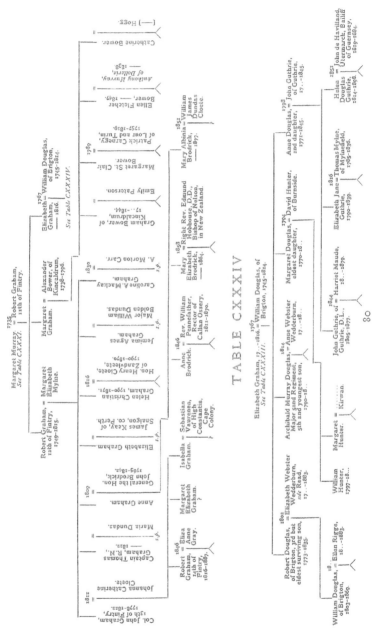

TABLE CXXXIII

TABLE CXXXIV

MARY OF MODENA, PRINCESS LOUIS OF BAVARIA

THE HEIR OF LINE AND SENIOR LINEAL REPRESENTATIVE OF THE ROYAL HOUSES
OF STUART, TUDOR, PLANTAGENET, ETC.

From a Photograph

A.—Descendants of Margaret (Tudor), Queen Consort of Scotland, 1489–1541, elder daughter, and in her issue (1558), co-heir of Henry VII., King of England. (See Table I.)

1. Descendants of King Charles I., 1600–1649. (See Table I.)

1. Descendants of Mary Beatrice of Savoy, who but for the Act of Settlement (1701) would have been *de jure hereditario* Queen of England, Scotland, France, and Ireland, 1792–1840, wife of Francis IV., Duke of Modena, 1779–1846. (See Table II.)

1	1	⛉ Mary Theresa Henrietta Dorothea, Princess Louis of Bavaria, Heiress of the Royal Houses of Stuart, Tudor, Plantagenet, Bruce, and Savoy, and of the Princely House of Este, who but for the Act of Settlement (1701) would now be *de jure hereditario* Queen of England, Scotland, France, and Ireland, 1849. *Wittelsbach Palace, Munich.*	Granddaughter. Only child of the Archduke Ferdinand of Modena, 1821–1849.
2	2	⛉ Prince Robert of Bavaria, 1869. *Bamberg.*	Great-grandchild. Son of No. 1.
3	3	⛉ Prince Luitpold Charles of Bavaria, 1901.	Great-great-grandchildren. Children of No. 2.
4	4	⛉ Princess Irmengard Mary of Bavaria, 1902.	
5	5	⛉ Prince Charles of Bavaria, 1874.	
6	6	⛉ Prince Francis of Bavaria, 1875.	Great-grandchildren. Children of No. 1.
7	7	⛉ Princess Adelgonda of Bavaria, 1870.	
8	8	⛉ Mary [Crown Princess of the Two Sicilies], Duchess of Calabria, 1872. *Madrid.*	
9	9	Roger, Duke of Noto, 1901.	
10	10	Princess Mary [of the Two Sicilies], 1898.	Great-great-grandchildren. Children of No. 8.
11	11	Princess Mary Christina [of the Two Sicilies], 1899.	
12	12	⛉ Matilda, Princess Louis of Saxe-Coburg-Gotha, 1877. *Innsbruck.*	Great-grandchild. 3rd daughter of No. 1.
13	13	Prince Antony of Saxe-Coburg-Gotha, 1901.	Great-great-grandchild. Son of No. 12.
14	14	⛉ Princess Hildegarda of Bavaria, 1881.	Great-grandchildren. Younger daughters of No. 1.
15	15	⛉ Princess Weltruda of Bavaria, 1884.	
16	16	⛉ Princess Helmtruda of Bavaria, 1886.	
17	17	⛉ Princess Gondelinda of Bavaria, 1891.	
18	18	⛉ Mary Beatrice [*de jure* Queen Dowager of France and Spain], 1824.	Daughter.

19	19	Don Carlos [de jure His Most Christian and Catholic Majesty Charles XI. and VII., King of France and Navarre—King of Spain, Castille, Leon, Aragon, the Two Sicilies, Jerusalem, Navarre, Grenada, Toledo, Valencia, Galicia, Majorca, Minorca, Seville, Sardinia, Cordova, Corsica, Murcia, Jaen, Algarves, Algeciras, Gibraltar, of the Canary Isles, of the East and West Indies, of India and the Oceanic Continent, Archduke of Austria, Duke of Burgundy, Brabant, and Milan, Count of Hapsburg, Flanders, Tyrol, and Barcelona, Lord of Biscay and Molina, &c., &c., &c.], 1848. *Palais Loredan, Venice.*	Grandson. Elder son of No. 18.
20	20	James [Dauphin and Prince of the Asturias], 1870.	Great-grandchildren. Elder children of No. 19.
21	21	Blanche, Archduchess Leopold Salvator of Tuscany, 1868. *Vienna.*	
22	22	Archduke Réné of Tuscany, 1895.	Great-great-grandchildren. Children of No. 21.
23	23	Archduke Leopold of Tuscany, 1897.	
24	24	Archduke Antony of Tuscany, 1901.	
25	25	Archduchess Maria de las Dolores of Tuscany, 1891.	
26	26	Archduchess Maria Immaculata of Tuscany, 1892.	
27	27	Archduchess Margaret of Tuscany, 1894.	
28	28	Archduchess Assunta of Tuscany, 1902.	
29	29	Infanta Elvira, 1871. *Milan.*	Great-grandchildren. Children of No. 19.
30	30	Infanta Beatrice, Princess of Roviano, 1874. *Rome.*	
31	31	Princess Margaret Massimo, 1898.	Great-great-grandchildren. Children of No. 30.
32	32	Princess Fabiola Massimo, 1900.	
33	33	Infanta Alice, Princess Frederic of Schönburg-Waldenburg, 1876. *Gauernitz.*	Great-grandchildren. Youngest daughter of No. 19.
34	34	Prince Charles Leopold of Schönburg-Waldenburg, 1902.	Great-great-grandchild. Son of No. 33.
35	35	Don Alfonso, Infant of Spain, 1849. *Château d'Ebenzweier, Upper Austria.*	Grandson. Younger son of No. 18.

2. Descendants of Charles III., Duke of Parma, 1823–1854. (See Table II.)

36	36	▽ Robert I., Duke of Parma, 1848. *Schwarzau-am-Steinfelde, Lower Austria.*	Son.
37	37	▽ Henry, Hereditary Prince of Parma, 1873.	Grandchildren. Children of No. 36.
38	38	▽ Prince Joseph of Parma, 1875.	
39	39	▽ Prince Elie Robert of Parma, 1880.	
40	40	▽ Prince Sextus of Parma, 1886.	
41	41	▽ Prince Xavier of Parma, 1889.	
42	42	▽ Prince Felix of Parma, 1893.	
43	43	▽ Prince Réné of Parma, 1894.	
44	44	▽ Prince Louis of Parma, 1899.	

1903.

DON CARLOS, DUKE OF MADRID

HEAD OF THE ROYAL HOUSE OF BOURBON, AND LINEAL REPRESENTATIVE OF
THE KINGS OF FRANCE AND NAVARRE AND OF SPAIN

From a Photograph

45	45	Boris, Crown Prince of Bulgaria, Prince of Tirnova, 1894.	Great-grandchildren. Children of Marie Louise, 1870–1899 (eldest daughter of No. 36), and her husband, Ferdinand, Prince of Bulgaria.
46	46	Cyril, Prince of Preslav, 1895.	
47	47	Princess Eudoxia of Bulgaria, 1898.	
48	48	Princess Nadejda of Bulgaria, 1899.	
49	49	▽ Princess Louise of Parma, 1872.	
50	50	▽ Princess Marie Immaculée of Parma, 1874.	
51	51	▽ Princess Maria Theresa of Parma, 1876.	
52	52	▽ Princess Pia of Parma, 1877.	Grandchildren. Children of No. 36.
53	53	▽ Princess Beatrice of Parma, 1879.	
54	54	▽ Princess Adelaide of Parma, 1885.	
55	55	▽ Princess Frances of Parma, 1890.	
56	56	▽ Princess Zitā of Parma, 1892.	
57	57	▽ Princess Maria Antonia of Parma, 1895.	
58	58	▽ Princess Isabel of Parma, 1898.	
59	59	▽ Henry, Count of Bardi, 1851. *Schwarzau-am-Steinfelde, Lower Austria.*	Son.
60 –75	}	Nos. 20–35.	Grandchildren and great-grandchildren. Descendants of Margaret, 1847–1893, 1st wife of Don Carlos. Elder daughter.
76	60	▽ Alice, Grand Duchess of Tuscany, 1849. *Salzburg, Austria.*	Younger daughter.
77	61	Archduke Leopold Ferdinand of Tuscany, 1868.	Grandchildren. Children of No. 76.
78	62	Archduke Joseph Ferdinand of Tuscany, 1872.	
79	63	Archduke Peter Ferdinand of Tuscany, 1874.	
80	64	Archduke Henry Ferdinand of Tuscany, 1878.	
81	65	Louisa Antoinette, Crown Princess of Saxony, 1870. *Dresden.*	
82	66	Prince George of Saxony, 1893.	Great-grandchildren. Children of No. 81.
83	67	Prince Frederic Christian of Saxony, 1893.	
84	68	Prince Ernest Henry of Saxony, 1896.	
85	69	Princess Margaret of Saxony, 1900.	
86	70	Princess Mary Alice of Saxony, 1901.	
87	71	Anne Maria Theresa, Princess of Hohenlohe-Bartenstein-Jagsberg, 1879. *Bartenstein, Wurtemberg.*	Grandchildren. Children of No. 76.
88	72	Archduchess Margaret Maria of Tuscany, 1881.	
89	73	Archduchess Germana Marie Theresa of Tuscany, 1884.	
90	74	Archduchess Agnes Maria Theresa of Tuscany, 1891.	

3. **Descendants of Louisa of France, 1819–1864, wife of Charles III., Duke of Parma, 1823–1854.** (See Table II.)

91 –145	}	Same as Nos. 36–90.

4. **Descendants of Charles X., King of France and Navarre, 1757–1836.** (See Table II.)

146 –200	}	Same as Nos. 36–90.

5. Descendants of Charles II., Duke of Parma, King of Etruria, 1799–1883. (See Table III.)

201 –255	}	Same as Nos. 36–90.	

6. Descendants of John, King of Saxony, 1801–1873. (See Table III.)

256	75	George, King of Saxony, 1832.	Son.
257	76	Frederic Augustus, Crown Prince of Saxony, 1865. *Dresden.*	} Grandson. Son of No. 256.
258 –62	}	Same as Nos. 82–86. Great-grandchildren.	Children of No. 257.
263	77	Prince John George of Saxony, 1869. *Dresden.*	
264	78	Prince Maximilian of Saxony, 1870.	} Grandchildren. Children of No. 256.
265	79	Princess Matilda of Saxony, 1863.	
266	80	Maria, Archduchess Otho of Austria [Duchess of Modena], 1869.	
267	81	Archduke Charles Francis Joseph of Austria, 1887.	} Great-grandchildren. Children of No. 266.
268	82	Archduke Maximilian Eugene Louis of Austria, 1895.	
269	83	Elizabeth, Dowager Duchess of Genoa, 1830. *Stresa, prov. de Novare, Italy.*	} Daughter.
270	84	Thomas, Duke of Genoa, 1854. *Turin.*	} Grandson. Son of No. 269.
271	85	Prince Ferdinand of Savoy-Genoa, 1884.	} Great-grandchildren. Children of No. 270.
272	86	Prince Philip Louis of Savoy-Genoa, 1895.	
273	87	Prince Adalbert of Savoy-Genoa, 1898.	
274	88	Princess Bona Margaret of Savoy-Genoa, 1896.	
275	89	Margaret, Queen Dowager of Italy, 1851. *Turin.*	} Granddaughter. Daughter of No. 269.
276	90	Victor Emmanuel III., King of Italy [King of Sardinia, Duke of Savoy, &c.], 1869.	} Great-grandson. Son of No. 275.
277	91	Princess Yolande of Savoy, 1901.	} Great-great-granddaughters. Children of No. 276.
278	92	Princess Mafalda of Savoy, 1902.	
279	93	Amelia, Duchess of Urach, 1865. *Stuttgart.*	{ Granddaughter. Daughter of Sophia of Saxony, 1845–1867, 1st wife of Charles Theodore, Duke in Bavaria, 1839.
280	94	Prince William of Urach, 1897.	} Great-grandchildren. Children of No. 278.
281	95	Prince Charles of Urach, 1899.	
282	96	Princess Gabrielle of Urach, 1893.	
283	97	Princess Elizabeth of Urach, 1894.	
284	98	Princess Carola of Urach, 1896.	
285	99	Princess . . . . of Urach, 1901.	

7. Descendants of Augusta of Tuscany, 1825–1864, late wife of Luitpold, Prince Regent of Bavaria, 1821. (See Table III.)

286	100	Prince Louis of Bavaria, 1845. *Munich.*	} Eldest son.
287 –302	}	Same as Nos. 2–17. Grandchildren.	Children of No. 286.

303	101	Prince Leopold of Bavaria, 1846. *Munich.*	} 2nd son.
304	102	Prince George of Bavaria, 1880.	
305	103	Prince Conrad of Bavaria, 1883.	Grandchildren.
306	104	Princess Elizabeth, Baroness Otho von Seefried auf Buttenheim, 1874. *Znaim, Mahren.*	Children of No. 303.
307	105	*Baroness Elizabeth von Seefried auf Buttenheim, 1897.	Great-grandchildren. Children of No. 306.
308	106	*Baroness Augusta von Seefried auf Buttenheim, 1899.	
309	107	Augustine, Archduchess Joseph Augustus of Austria, 1875. *Brünn.*	Grandchildren. Younger daughter of No. 303.
310	108	Archduke Joseph Francis of Austria, 1895.	Great-grandchildren. Children of No. 309.
311	109	Archduke Ladislaus of Austria, 1901.	
312	110	Archduchess Sophia of Austria, 1899.	
313	111	Prince Arnulph of Bavaria, 1852. *Munich.*	} 3rd son.
314	112	Prince Henry of Bavaria, 1884.	Grandson. Son of No. 313.
315	113	Princess Theresa of Bavaria, Abbess of St. Anne of Munich, 1850. *Munich.*	Daughter.

8. Descendants of Ferdinand VII., King of Spain, 1784–1833. (See Table III.)

316	114	Isabella II., ex-Queen of Spain, 1830. *19 Avenue Kléber, Paris.*	} Daughter.
317	115	Alfonso XIII., King of Spain, 1886.	Great-grandchildren. Children of Alfonso XII., 1857–1885, son of No. 316.
318	116	Infanta Maria de las Mercedes, Princess of the Asturias, 1880. *Madrid.*	
319	117	Infant Alfonso, 1902.	Great-great-grandson. Son of No. 318.
320	118	Infanta Maria Theresa, 1882.	Great-grandchild. Younger sister of No. 317.
321	119	Infanta Isabella, Countess Girgenti, 1851. *Madrid.*	Granddaughters. Daughters of No. 316.
322	120	Maria della Paz, Princess Louis Ferdinand of Bavaria, 1862. *Château de Nymphenbourg, Bavaria.*	
323	121	Prince Ferdinand of Bavaria, 1884.	Great-grandchildren. Children of No. 322.
324	122	Prince Adalbert of Bavaria, 1886.	
325	123	Princess Maria dell Pilar of Bavaria, 1891.	
326	124	Infanta Eulalie, Duchess of Galliera, 1864. *28 Boulevard des Invalides, Paris.*	Granddaughter. Younger daughter of No. 316.
327	125	Prince Alfonso of Montpensier, 1886.	Great-grandchildren. Children of No. 326.
328	126	Prince Louis Ferdinand of Montpensier, 1888.	
329	127	Anthony, Duke of Galliera [Italy], 1866. *28 Boulevard des Invalides, Paris.*	Grandson. Son of the Infanta Louisa, 1832–1897 (younger daughter), and her husband, Anthony, Duke of Montpensier, 1824–1890.
330 –31	}	Same as Nos. 327–328.	Great-grandchildren. Children of No. 329.

332	128	Isabella, Countess of Paris, 1848. *Villamanrique, near Seville.*	Granddaughter. Daughter of the Infanta Louisa, Duchess of Montpensier, 1832–1897.
333	129	Philip, Duke of Orleans, 1869. *Twickenham.*	Great-grandchildren. Children of No. 332.
334	130	Ferdinand, Duke of Montpensier, 1884.	
335	131	Amelia, Queen of Portugal, 1865.	
336	132	Louis Philip, Duke of Braganza, 1887.	Great-great-grandchildren. Children of No. 335.
337	133	Manuel, Duke of Beja, 1889.	
338	134	Helen, Duchess of Aosta, 1871. *Château de Mandria, near Turin.*	Great-granddaughter. 2nd daughter of No. 332.
339	135	Prince Amadeus of Aosta, 1898.	Great-great-grandsons. Children of No. 338.
340	136	Prince Aynon of Aosta, 1900.	
341	137	Isabella, Duchess of Guise, 1878. *Château du Nouvion, Aisne.*	Great-granddaughter. 3rd daughter of No. 332.
342	138	Princess Isabella of Guise, 1900.	Great-great-granddaughter. Daughter of No. 341.
343	139	Princess Louisa of Orleans, 1882.	Great-granddaughter. Youngest daughter of No. 332.

9. Descendants of Don Juan de Bourbon [John III., King of France and Navarre, King of Spain], 1822–1887. (See Table III.)

344 -60	}	Same as Nos. 19–35.

10. Descendants of Francis, Duke of Cadiz, 1794–1865. (See Table III.)

361 -72	}	Same as Nos. 317–328.	Grandchildren, &c. Children of Don Francis de Bourbon, King Consort of Spain, 1822–1902.
373	140	*Marie Louise, Duchess of Seville, 1868. *Real Sitio de Aranjúez, Madrid.*	Great-granddaughters. Daughters of Henry, Duke of Seville, 1848–1894, eldest son of the Infant Henry, Duke of Seville, 1823–1870.
374	141	*Princess Marta Maria Elena of Bourbon y Parade, 1880. *Madrid.*	
375	142	*Princess Henrietta of Bourbon y Parade, 1885.	
376	143	*Prince Francis of Bourbon y Castellvi, 1853. *Saragossa.*	Grandson. 2nd son of the Infant Henry, Duke of Seville, 1823–1870.
377	144	*Prince Francis de Paula of Bourbon y de la Torre, 1882.	Great-grandchildren. Children of No. 376.
378	145	*Prince Joseph of Bourbon y de la Torre, 1883.	
379	146	*Prince Henry of Bourbon y Leon, 1891.	
380	147	*Prince Alfonso of Bourbon y Leon, 1893.	
381	148	*Princess Elena of Bourbon y de la Torre, 1878.	
382	149	*Princess Maria of Bourbon y de la Torre, 1880.	
383	150	*Princess Maria de las Dolores of Bourbon y de la Torre, 1887.	
384	151	*Albert, Marquis of Santa Elena, 1854. *Barcelona.*	Grandson. 3rd son of the Infant Henry, Duke of Seville, 1823–1870.

385	152	*Prince Albert of Bourbon y d'Ast, 1883.	⎫
386	153	*Princess Ysabel of Bourbon y d'Ast, 1879.	Great-grandchildren.
387	154	*Princess Maria Immaculata of Bourbon y d'Ast, 1880.	Children of No. 384.
388	155	*Princess Maria, wife of Charles Fernandez Magnieira y Oyangureu, Captain of Cavalry, 1858. *Madrid.*	Granddaughter. Daughter of the Infant Henry, Duke of Seville, 1823–1870.
389	156	*Donna Maria Isabella de Bourbon y Gurowski, 1847.	Grandchild. Only surviving child of the Infanta Isabella, 1821–1897, and her husband, Count Ignatius Gurowski, 1812–1887.
390	157	*Francis, Duke of Sessa and Montemar, 1847.	Grandson. Son of the Infanta Louisa of Spain, 1824–1900, and her husband, Don Joseph Osorio de Moscoso y Carvajal, Duke of Sessa and Montemar, –1881.
391	158	*Francis, Marquis of Astorga, 1874.	Great-grandchildren.
392	159	*Don Louis Gonzagna Osorio de Moscoso y Borbon, 1875.	Sons of No. 390.
393	160	*Louis, Count of Cabra, 1849.	Grandchildren.
394	161	*Marie Christine, Princess of Bauffremont, 1850. *Paris, 87 Rue de Grenelle ; Brienne le Château, Aube ; Bauffremont, Vosges.*	Brother and sister to No. 390.
395	162	*Prince Theodore of Bauffremont, 1879.	Great-grandchildren.
396	163	*Maria Louisa, Countess John de Merode, 1874. *Brussels, 21 Rue aux Laines ; Château d'Everbergh, Brabant.*	Children of No. 394.
397	164	*Countess Louisa Eugenia de Merode, 1900.	Great-great-grandchild. Child of No. 396.
398	165	*Princess Helen of Bauffremont, 1878.	Great-grandchild. Child of No. 394.
399	166	Infanta Josephine of Spain, 1827. *Madrid.*	Eldest surviving daughter.
400	167	*Don Raymond Güell y Borbon, Marquis of Valcarios.	Grandsons. Sons of No. 399, and her husband, Don José Güell y Rente, Senator, 1822–1884.
401	168	*Don Ferdinand Güell y Borbon, Marquis of Güell.	
402	169	Francis, Duke of Marchena, 1861.	Grandson. Son of Christine, Infanta Sebastian of Spain, 1833–1902.
403	170	*Donna Marie Christine de Bourbon y Muguiro, 1889.	Great-granddaughters. Daughters of No. 402.
404	171	*Donna Elena de Bourbon y Muguiro, 1890.	
405	172	*Donna Angela de Bourbon y Muguiro.	
406	173	*Donna Maria Christina de Bourbon y Madan, 1886. *Paris.*	Great-grandchildren. Children of Peter, Duke of Durcal, 1862–1892, brother of No. 402.
407	174	*Donna Maria Pia de Bourbon y Madan, 1888. *Paris.*	
408	175	*Don Louis de Bourbon y Bernaldo de Quiros, 1887.	Great-grandsons. Sons of Louis, Duke of Ansola, 1864–1889, brother of No. 402.
409	176	*Don Manfred de Bourbon y Bernaldo de Quiros, 1889.	
410	177	Infant Alfonso of Spain, 1866. *Madrid.*	Grandson. Brother of No. 402.
411	178	Amelia, Princess Adalbert of Bavaria, 1834. *Château de Nymphenburg, Bavaria.*	3rd surviving daughter.

412	179	Prince Louis Ferdinand of Bavaria, 1859. *Château de Nymphenburg, Bavaria.*	Grandson. Son of No. 401.
413 -15	}	Same as Nos. 323-325.	Great-grandchildren. Children of No. 412.
416	180	Prince Alphonso of Bavaria, 1862. *Munich.*	Grandson. Son of No. 401.
417	181	Prince of Bavaria, 1902.	Great-grandson. Son of No. 416.
418	182	Isabella, Duchess of Genoa, 1863. *Turin.*	Granddaughter. Daughter of No. 401.
419 -22	}	Same as Nos. 271-274.	Great-grandchildren. Children of No. 418.
423	183	Elvira, Countess of Wrbna und Freudenthal, 1868.	Granddaughter. 2nd daughter of No. 401.
424	184	Count Rudolph von Wrbna und Freudenthal, 1892.	
425	185	Count Alphonso von Wrbna und Freudenthal, 1896.	Great-grandchildren. Children of No. 423.
426	186	Countess Isabella von Wrbna und Freudenthal, 1894.	
427	187	Princess Clara of Bavaria, Abbess of the Royal Convent aux Dames de St. Anne, 1874. *Wurzburg.*	Granddaughter. 3rd daughter of No. 401.

11. Descendants of Peter IV. and I., King of Portugal and the Algarves, Emperor of the Brazils, 1798-1834. (See Table III.)

428	188	Isabella [Empress of the Brazils], Countess of Eu, 1846. *Boulogne sur Seine, 7 Boulevard de Boulogne.*	Granddaughter. Daughter of Peter II., Emperor of the Brazils, 1825-1891.
429	189	Peter d'Alcantara [Prince Imperial of the Brazils], 1875. *Zolkiew.*	
430	190	Prince Louis [of Brazil], 1878. *Gratz.*	Great-grandsons. Sons of No. 428.
431	191	Prince Anthony [of Brazil], 1881.	
432	192	Prince Peter of Saxe-Coburg-Gotha, 1866.	Great-grandsons. Sons of the Princess Leopoldina, 1847-1871, wife of Prince Augustus of Saxe-Coburg-Gotha, 1845, 2nd daughter of the Emperor Peter II.
433	193	Prince Augustus Leopold of Saxe-Coburg-Gotha, 1867. *Pola.*	
434	194	Prince Augustus of Saxe-Coburg-Gotha, 1895.	
435	195	Prince Rainer of Saxe-Coburg-Gotha, 1900.	
436	196	Prince Philip of Saxe-Coburg-Gotha, 1901.	Great-great-grandchildren. Children of No. 433.
437	197	Princess Clementina of Saxe-Coburg-Gotha, 1897.	
438	198	Princess Marie of Saxe-Coburg-Gotha, 1899.	
439	199	Prince Louis of Saxe-Coburg-Gotha, 1870. *Innsbruck.*	Great-grandson. Younger son of the Princess Leopoldina, 1847-1871. *See above.*
440		Same as No. 13.	Great-great-grandson. Son of No. 439.

441	200	Charles I., King of Portugal and the Algarves, 1863.	Great-grandson. Son of Louis I., King of Portugal, 1838–1889, grandson of Maria II., Queen of Portugal, 1819–1853.
442–43	}	Same as Nos. 336–337.	Great-great-grandsons. Sons of No. 441.
444	201	Dom Alfonso, Duke of Oporto, 1865. *Lisbon.*	Great-grandson. Younger brother of No. 441.
445	202	Antoinette, Princess of Hohenzollern, 1845. *Château de Sigmaringen.*	Granddaughter. Daughter of Donna Maria II., 1819–1853.
446	203	William, Hereditary Prince of Hohenzollern, 1864. *Potsdam.*	Great-grandson. Son of No. 445.
447	204	Prince Frederick Victor of Hohenzollern, 1891.	
448	205	Prince Francis Joseph of Hohenzollern, 1891.	Great-great-grandchildren. Children of No. 446.
449	206	Princess Augustine Victoria of Hohenzollern, 1890.	
450	207	Ferdinand, Crown Prince of Roumania, 1865. *Bucharest.*	Great-grandson. 2nd son of No. 445.
451	208	Prince Carol of Roumania, 1893.	Great-great-grandchildren. Children of No. 450.
452	209	Princess Elizabeth of Roumania, 1894.	
453	210	Princess Marie of Roumania, 1899.	
454	211	Prince Charles Anthony of Hohenzollern, 1868. *Berlin.*	Great-grandson. 3rd son of No. 445.
455	212	Prince Albert of Hohenzollern, 1898.	Great-great-grandchildren. Children of No. 454.
456	213	Princess Stephanie of Hohenzollern, 1895.	
457	214	Princess Marie of Hohenzollern, 1896.	
458	215	Louis Marie, 2nd Count of Aquila, 1845.	Grandson. Son of the Infanta Donna Januaria of Brazil, 1822–1901, and her husband, Louis, Count of Aquila, 1824–1897
459	216	*Louis, Count of Rocca-Guiglielmo, 1873.	Great-grandchildren. Children of No. 458.
460	217	*Countess Marie of Rocca-Guiglielmo, 1870.	
461	218	Prince Philip of Aquila, 1847.	Grandson. Younger brother of No. 458.
462	219	Peter, Duke of Penthievre, 1845. *Paris, 65 Avenue d'Antin; Château d'Arc, Barrois.*	Grandchildren. Children of the Infanta Donna Frances of Brazil, 1824–1898, and her husband, Francis, Prince of Joinville, 1818–1900.
463	220	Frances, Duchess of Chartres, 1844. *Paris, 27 Rue Jean Goujon; St. Firmin, near Chantilly.*	
464	221	John, Duke of Guise, 1874. *Château du Nouvion, Ardennes.*	Great-grandson. Son of No. 463.
465		Same as No. 342.	Great-great-grandchild. Child of No. 464.
466	222	Marie, Princess Waldemar of Denmark, 1865. *Copenhagen and Château de Bernstorff.*	Great-granddaughter. Elder daughter of No. 463.
467	223	Prince Aage of Denmark, 1887.	Great-great-grandchildren. Children of No. 466.
468	224	Prince Axel of Denmark, 1888.	
469	225	Prince Eric of Denmark, 1890.	
470	226	Prince Viggo of Denmark, 1893.	
471	227	Princess Margaret of Denmark, 1895.	

472	228	Margaret, Duchess of Magenta, 1869. *Luneville ; Paris, 70 Rue de Bellechasse.*	{ Great-granddaughter. Younger daughter of No. 463.
473	229	Marie Elizabeth MacMahon, 1899.	{ Great-great-granddaughter. Daughter of No. 472.

12. Descendants of Michael I., King of Portugal and the Algarves, 1802–1866. (See Table III.)

474	230	Dom Miguel [His Most Faithful Majesty, Michael II., King of Portugal and the Algarves], 1853. *Château de Seebenstein, Lower Austria.*	} Only son.
475	231	Michael [Crown Prince of Portugal], Duke of Braganza, 1878.	
476	232	Infant Dom Francis Joseph of Portugal, 1879.	
477	233	Maria Theresa Princess Louis of Thurn and Taxis, 1881. *Château de Haus, près Ratisbonne.*	Grandchildren. Children of No. 474.
478	234	Infanta Donna Elizabeth of Portugal, 1894.	
479	235	Infanta Donna Maria Benedicta of Portugal, 1895.	
480	236	Infanta Donna Mafalda of Portugal, 1898.	
481	237	Infanta Donna Maria Anne of Portugal, 1899.	
482	238	Maria de las Neves, Infanta Alfonso of Spain, 1852.	
483	239	Maria Theresa, Archduchess Charles Louis of Austria, 1855.	Elder daughters.
484	240	Archduchess Maria Annonciada of Austria, 1876, Abbess of the Convent of the Noble Dames du Hradschin, Prague.	Granddaughters. Daughters of No. 483.
485	241	Archduchess Elizabeth of Austria, 1878.	
486	242	Maria Josepha, Duchess Charles Theodore in Bavaria, 1857. *Munich and Château de Tegernsee.*	3rd daughter.
487	243	Duke Louis William in Bavaria, 1884.	
488	244	Duke Francis Joseph in Bavaria, 1888.	
489	245	Duchess Sophia Adelaide in Bavaria, wife of Hans Vert, Count of Torring-Jettenbach, 1875.	Grandchildren. Children of No. 486.
490	246	Elizabeth Valerie, Princess Albert of Belgium, 1876.	
491	247	Prince Leopold of Belgium, 1901.	{ Great-grandchildren. Children of No. 490.
492	248	Mary Gabrielle, Princess Rupert of Bavaria, 1878.	} Grandchild. Youngest daughter of No. 486.
493 –94	}	Same as Nos. 3–4.	{ Great-grandchildren. Children of No. 492.
495	249	Adelgonda, Countess of Bardi, 1858. *Schwarzau-am-Steinfelde.*	
496	250	Maria Anne, Hereditary Grandduchess of Luxemburg, 1861. *Luxemburg.*	Younger daughters.
497	251	Princess Mary of Luxemburg, 1894.	
498	252	Princess Charlotte of Luxemburg, 1896.	
499	253	Princess Hilda of Luxemburg, 1897.	Granddaughters. Daughters of No. 496.
500	254	Princess Antoinette of Luxemburg, 1897.	
501	255	Princess Elizabeth of Luxemburg, 1901.	
502	256	Maria Antonia, Duchess of Parma, 1862.	Youngest daughter.
503 –12	}	Same as Nos. 40–44 and 54–58.	{ Grandchildren. Children of No. 502.

The Blood Royal of Britain

13. Descendants of the Infanta Theresa of Portugal, 1793–1874, wife of the Infant Peter of Spain, 1786–1812. (See Table III.)

513 -21	}	Same as Nos. 402–410.	{	Grandchildren, &c. Children of the Infant Sebastian, 1811–1875.

14. Descendants of the Infanta Frances of Portugal, 1800–1834 [Queen Consort of Charles V., King of Spain], 1788–1855. (See Table III.)

522 -38	}	Same as Nos. 19–35.	{	Grandchildren, &c. Children of Don John [III. King of France and Spain], 1822–1887.

15. Descendants of the Infanta Anne de Jesus Mary of Portugal, 1806–1857, wife of Dom Nuno Joseph Severo de Mendonça Rolin de Moura Barreto, 1st Duke and 2nd Marquis of Loulé, 9th Count of Valle de Reis, 24th Lord of Azambuja, 14th Lord of Morgado da Quarteira, 12th Lord of Povoa and Meada, Peer of Portugal, &c., &c., 1804–1875. (See Table III.)

539	257	Peter, 2nd Duke of Loulé [Portugal], 1830. *Lisbon.*	}	Elder son.
540	258	Dom Marie Dominic de Mendonça, 1853.		Grandchildren. Children of No. 539.
541	259	Donna Anne de Jesus Marie de Mendonça, 1854.	}	
542	260	Augustus, Count of Azambuja [Portugal], 1835. *Lisbon.*	}	2nd son.
543	261	Dom Nuno de Mendonça, 1861.		
544	262	Dom Anthony de Mendonça, 1862.		
545	263	Dom Peter de Mendonça, 1864.		
546	264	Dom Joseph de Mendonça, 1871.		Grandchildren. Children of No. 542.
547	265	Donna Antoinette de Mendonça, 1861.		
548	266	Donna Anne de Mendonça, 1863.		
549	267	Donna Margaret de Mendonça, 1865.		
550	268	Donna Marie de Carma, Countess Henry Zileri dal Verme degli Oblizi, 1866. *Vicenza, Italy.*		
551	269	Count George Zileri dal Verme, 1886.		
552	270	Countess Maria Antonia Zileri dal Verme, 1889.		Great-grandchildren. Children of No. 550.
553	271	Countess Anna Zileri dal Verme, 1890.		
554	272	Countess Mary Caroline Zileri dal Verme, 1890.		
555	273	Countess Adelgonda Zileri dal Verme, 1893.		
556	274	Donna Anne Charlotte, wife of Dom Roderic de Souza-Continho, Count of Linhares [Portugal], 1827.	}	Eldest daughter.
557 -65	275 -83	} Counts and Countesses of Linhares.	{	Grandchildren. Children of No. 556.
566	284	Donna Maria, widow of Dom Vasco de Figueiredo Cabral de Camara, Count of Belmonte, 1829–1870, 1829.	}	2nd daughter.
567 -72	285 -90	} Counts and Countesses of Belmonte.	{	Grandchildren. Children of No. 566.
573	291	Donna Amelia de Mendonça.		3rd daughter.

91

16. Descendants of the Infanta Mary Louisa of Spain, 1782–1824, and her husband, Louis, Duke of Parma, King of Etruria, 1773–1803. (See Table III.)

574 –628	}	Same as Nos. 36–90.

17. Descendants of the Infanta Isabella of Spain, 1789–1848, 2nd wife of Francis I., King of the Two Sicilies, 1777–1830. (See Table III.)

629	292	Maria Theresa, Hereditary Princess of Hohenzollern, 1867.	Great-granddaughter. Daughter of Louis, Count of Trani, 1838–1886, son of Ferdinand II., 1810–1859.
630 –32	}	Same as Nos. 447–449.	Great-great-grandchildren. Children of No. 629.
633	293	Alphonso [King of the Two Sicilies], Count of Caserta, 1841. *Cannes.*	Grandson. Son of Ferdinand II., King of the Two Sicilies, 1810–1859.
634	294	Ferdinand [Crown Prince], Duke of Calabria, 1869. *Madrid.*	Great-grandson. Son of No. 633.
635 –37	}	Same as Nos. 9–11. Great-grandchildren. Children of No. 634.	
638	295	Charles, Prince of the Asturias, 1870. *Madrid.*	Great-grandson. 2nd son of No. 633.
639		Same as No. 319. Great-great-grandson. Son of No. 638.	
640	296	Prince Januario of the Two Sicilies, 1882.	
641	297	Prince René of the Two Sicilies, 1883.	
642	298	Prince Philip of the Two Sicilies, 1885.	
643	299	Prince Francis of the Two Sicilies, 1888.	
644	300	Prince Gabriel of the Two Sicilies, 1897.	
645	301	Princess Marie Immaculée of the Two Sicilies, 1874.	Great-grandchildren. Children of No. 633.
646	302	Mary Christina, Archduchess Peter Ferdinand of Austria, 1877. *Linz.*	
647	303	Princess Mary of the Two Sicilies, 1878.	
648	304	Princess Mary Josephine of the Two Sicilies, 1880.	
649	305	Pascal, Count of Bari, 1852. *Paris, 8 Rue Martignon.*	Grandson. Youngest son of Ferdinand II., 1810–1859.
650	306	Archduke Francis Ferdinand of Austria, 1863.	Great-grandson. Son of Marie Annonciada, 1843–1871, 2nd wife of the Archduke Charles Louis, 1810–1859, eldest daughter of Ferdinand II.
651	307	*Prince Maximilian of Hohenberg, 1902.	Great-great-grandchildren. Children of No. 650.
652	308	*Princess Sophia of Hohenberg, 1901.	
653	309	Archduke Otto of Austria [Duke of Modena], 1901. *Vienna.*	Great-grandson. Brother to No. 650.
654 –55	}	Same as Nos. 267–268.	Great-great-grandsons. Children of No. 653.
656	310	Archduke Ferdinand Charles Louis of Austria, 1868. *Vienna.*	Great-grandson. Younger son of Princess Maria Annonciada, 1843–1871. *See above.*

657	311	Duke Philip Albert of Würtemberg, 1893. *Stuttgart.*	
658	312	Duke Albert Eugene of Würtemberg, 1895.	Great-great-grandchildren. Children of the Archduchess Margaret Sophia, 1870–1902 (daughter of the Princess Maria Annonciada, *see above*), wife of Duke Albert of Würtemberg.
659	313	Duke Charles Alexander of Würtemberg, 1896.	
660	314	Duchess Maria Amelia of Würtemberg, 1897.	
661	315	Duchess Maria Theresa of Würtemberg, 1898.	
662	316	Archduke Leopold Salvator of Tuscany, 1863. *Vienna.*	Great-grandson. Eldest son of the Princess Maria Immaculée, Archduchess Charles Salvator of Tuscany, 1844–1899, 2nd daughter of Ferdinand II.
663 –69		Same as Nos. 22–28.	Great-great-grandchildren. Children of No. 662.
670	317	Archduke Francis Salvator of Tuscany, 1866. *Château de Wallsee, sur-le-Danube, Lower Austria.*	Great-grandson. Next brother to No. 662.
671	318	Archduke Francis Charles Salvator of Tuscany, 1893.	
672	319	Archduke Hubert Salvator of Tuscany, 1894.	
673	320	Archduke Theodore Salvator of Tuscany, 1899.	Great-great-grandchildren. Children of No. 670.
674	321	Archduchess Elizabeth Frances of Tuscany, 1892.	
675	322	Archduchess Hedwiga of Tuscany, 1896.	
676	323	Archduchess Gertrude of Tuscany, 1900.	
677	324	Maria Theresa, Archduchess Charles Stephen of Austria, 1862. *Pola.*	Great-granddaughter. Elder sister of No. 662.
678	325	Archduke Charles of Austria, 1888.	Great-great-grandchildren. Children of No. 677.
679	326	Archduke Leo of Austria, 1893.	
680	327	Archduke William of Austria, 1895.	
681	328	Archduchess Eleanor of Austria, 1886.	
682	329	Archduchess Rennée of Austria, 1888.	
683	330	Archduchess Mechtilda of Austria, 1891.	
684	331	Caroline Maria Immaculée, Princess Augustus Leopold of Saxe-Coburg-Gotha, 1869. *Pola.*	Great-granddaughter. 2nd sister of No. 662.
685 –89		Same as Nos. 434–438.	Great-great-grandchildren. Children of No. 684.
690	332	Maria Immaculée Rennée, Duchess Robert of Würtemberg, 1878.	Great-granddaughter. Youngest sister of No. 662.
691	333	*Francis, Count of Mascali, 1837.	Grandchildren. Morganatic children of Charles Ferdinand, Prince of Capua, 1811–1862.
692	334	*Countess Penelope Victoria of Mascali, 1838.	
693 –96		Same as Nos. 458–461.	Grandchildren. Children of Louis, Count of Aquila, 1824–1897.
697	335	Antoinette [Queen of the Two Sicilies], Countess of Caserta, 1851.	Granddaughter. Eldest daughter of Francis de Paula, Count of Trapani, 1827–1892.
698 –712		Same as Nos. 634–648.	Great-grandchildren. Children of No. 697.

713	336	Caroline, Countess Andrew Zamoyski, 1856. *Varsovia and Château de Labowla, Hungary.*	Granddaughter. 2nd daughter of Francis de Paula, Count of Trapani, 1827–1892.
714	337	Count Francis de Paula Zamoyski, 1888.	
715	338	Count Stanislaus Zamoyski, 1889.	
716	339	Countess Maria Josepha Zamoyski, 1887.	Great-grandchildren.
717	340	Countess Isabella Rose Zamoyski, 1891.	Children of No. 713.
718	341	Countess Theresa Zamoyski, 1894.	
719	342	Countess Caroline Zamoyski, 1896.	
720 -86	}	Same as Nos. 361–427.	Grandchildren, &c. Descendants of Louisa, 1804–1844, wife of Francis, Duke of Cadiz, 1794–1865, eldest daughter.
787 -814	}	Same as Nos. 316–343.	Grandchildren, &c. Descendants of Christina, 1806–1878, 4th wife of Ferdinand VII., King of Spain, 2nd daughter.
815	343	Ferdinand IV., Grandduke of Tuscany, 1835 *Salzburg.*	Grandson. Eldest son of Maria Antoinette, 1814–1898, 2nd wife of Leopold II., Grandduke of Tuscany, 1797–1870, 3rd daughter.
816 -29	}	Same as Nos. 77–90.	Great-grandchildren. Children, &c., of No. 815.
830 -58	}	Same as Nos. 662–690.	Great-grandchildren, &c. Children of the Archduke Charles Salvator, 1839–1892, 2nd son of Maria Antoinette, Grandduchess of Tuscany, 1814–1898.
859 -81	}	Same as Nos. 697–719.	Great-grandchildren. Children of Maria Isabella, Countess of Trapani, 1834–1901, eldest daughter of Maria Antoinette, Grandduchess of Tuscany, 1814–1898.
882	344	Maria Louisa Annonciada, Dowager Princess of Isemburg-Birstein, 1845. *Birstein.*	Granddaughter. Younger daughter of Maria Antoinette, Grandduchess of Tuscany, 1814–1898.
883	345	Prince Leopold of Isemburg-Birstein, 1866. (Renounced the succession.) *Birstein.*	Great-grandsons. Elder sons of No. 882.
884	346	Francis Joseph, Prince of Isemburg-Birstein, 1869.	
885	347	Francis Ferdinand, Hereditary Prince of Isemburg-Birstein, 1900.	Great-great-grandchildren. Children of No. 884.
886	348	Princess Marie of Isemburg-Birstein, 1897.	
887	349	Princess Alexandra Johanna of Isemburg-Birstein, 1899.	
888	350	Prince Charles of Isemburg-Birstein, 1871. *Paris.*	
889	351	Prince Victor of Isemburg-Birstein, 1872.	
890	352	Prince Alphonso of Isemburg-Birstein, 1875.	
891	353	Princess Antoinette of Isemburg-Birstein, 1867.	Great-grandchildren. Younger sons and daughters of No. 882.
892	354	Princess Marie of Isemburg-Birstein, 1868, a nun in the Convent of St. Joseph at Treves.	
893	355	Princess Elizabeth, "Sister Augustine," in the Convent of St. Joseph at Treves, 1877.	
894	356	Princess Adelaide of Isemburg-Birstein, 1878.	
895 -907	}	Same as Nos. 428–440.	Grandchildren, &c. Descendants of Theresa, 1822–1889, Consort of Peter II., Emperor of the Brazils, younger daughter.

II. Descendants of the Princess Elizabeth, Queen Consort of Bohemia, Electress Palatine, 1596–1662. Sister of King Charles I. (See Table I.)

A.—Descendants of Charles Louis, Elector Palatine, 1617–1680, second son of Elizabeth, Queen of Bohemia. (See Table IV.

18. Descendants of Louis-Philippe, Duke of Orleans, King of the French, 1773–1850. (See Table IV.)

908 -18	}	Same as Nos. 333–343.	Great-grandchildren. Descendants of Louis Philippe, Duke of Orleans (Count of Paris), 1838–1894, elder son of Ferdinand, Duke of Orleans, 1810–1842.
919	357	Robert, Duke of Chartres, 1840. *Paris, 27 Rue Jean Goujon.*	Grandson. Younger son of Ferdinand, Duke of Orleans, 1810–1842.
920 -29	}	Same as Nos. 464–473.	Great-grandchildren. Children of No. 919.
930	358	Gaston, Count of Eu, 1842. *Boulogne sur Seine, 7 Boulevard de Boulogne.*	Grandson. Elder son of Louis, Duke of Nemours, 1814–1896.
931 -33	}	Same as Nos. 429–431.	Great-grandchildren. Children of No. 930.
934	359	Ferdinand, Duke of Nemours and Alençon, 1844. *Château de Mentelberg, Tyrol ; Paris, 11 Rue Beaujon.*	Grandson. Younger son of Louis, Duke of Nemours, 1814–1896.
935	360	Emmanuel, Duke of Vendôme, 1872. *Neuilly-s-Seine, 10 Rue Borghèse.*	Great-grandson. Son of No. 934.
936	361	Princess Marie Louisa of Orleans, 1896.	Great-great-granddaughters. Daughters of No. 935.
937	362	Princess Sophia of Orleans, 1898.	
938	363	Princess Geneviève of Orleans, 1901.	
939	364	Louisa, Princess Alfonso of Bavaria, 1869.	Great-granddaughter. Daughter of No. 934.
940	365	Adam, Prince Czartoryski, 1872. *Cracow, Château de Sieniawa, Galicia.*	Great-grandsons. Sons of the Princess Margaret, 1846–1893, wife of Ladislaus, Prince Czartoryski, 1828–1894, eldest daughter of Louis, Duke of Nemours, 1814–1896.
941	366	Prince Witold Czartoryski, 1876. *Paris, Hotel Lambert.*	
942	367	Princess Blanche of Nemours, 1857. *Paris, 9 Avenue Kleber.*	Granddaughter. Younger daughter of Louis, Duke of Nemours, 1814–1896.
943 -54	}	Same as Nos. 462–473.	Grandchildren, &c. Children of Francis, Prince of Joinville, 1818–1900.
955 -69	}	Same as Nos. 329–343.	Grandchildren. Children of Anthony, Duke of Montpensier, 1824–1890.

970	368	Leopold II., King of the Belgians, 1835.	Grandson. Elder son of Louisa of Orleans, 1812–1850, Queen Consort of Leopold I., King of the Belgians, 1790–1865.
971	369	Louisa, Princess Philip of Saxe-Coburg-Gotha, 1858.	Great-granddaughter. Elder daughter of No. 970.
972	370	Prince Leopold of Saxe-Coburg-Gotha, 1878.	Great-great-grandchildren. Children of No. 971.
973	371	Dorothy, Duchess of Sleswig and Holstein, 1881. *Primkenau, Silesia.*	
974	372	Stephanie, Countess Lonyay (*late Crown Princess of Austria, Hungary, and Bohemia*), 1864. *Château de Lonyay, Kalksburg, near Vienna, and Château de Bodroy, Olaszi.*	Great-granddaughter. 2nd daughter of No. 970.
975	373	Archduchess Elizabeth, Princess Otto of Windisch-Graetz, 1883. *Vienna.*	Great-great-granddaughter. Only child of No. 974.
976	374	Princess Clementina of Belgium, 1872.	Great-granddaughter. Youngest daughter of No. 970.
977	375	Philip, Count of Flanders, 1837. *Brussels.*	Grandson. Youngest son of Louisa of Orleans, 1812–1850. *See above.*
978	376	Prince Albert of Flanders, 1875.	Great-grandchildren. Children of No. 977.
979		Same as No. 491. Great-great-grandchild. Child of No. 978.	
980	377	Henrietta, Duchess of Vendome, 1870.	Great-grandchild. Daughter of No. 977.
981 –83		Same as Nos. 936–938.	Great-great-grandchildren. Children of No. 980.
984	378	Josephine, Princess Charles Anthony of Hohenzollern, 1872.	Great-granddaughter. Daughter of No. 977.
985 –87		Same as Nos. 455–457. Great-grandchildren. Children of No. 984.	
988	379	Charlotte, Empress of Mexico, 1840.	Granddaughter. Elder daughter of Louisa of Orleans, 1812–1850. *See above.*
989	380	Duke Philip of Würtemberg, 1838. *Stuttgart.*	Grandson. Son of Mary of Orleans, 1813–1839, wife of Duke Alexander of Würtemberg, 1804–1881.
990	381	Duke Albert of Würtemberg, 1865. *Stuttgart.*	Great-grandson. Son of No. 989.
991 –95		Same as Nos. 657–661.	Great-great-grandchildren. Children of No. 990.
996	382	Duke Robert of Würtemberg, 1873.	Great-grandchildren. Younger children of No. 989.
997	383	Duke Ulrick of Würtemberg, 1877.	
998	384	Marie Isabella, Princess John George of Saxony, 1871. *Dresden.*	
999	385	Clementina, Princess Augustus of Saxe-Coburg-Gotha, 1817. *Château de Ebenthal, Austria,* 1817.	Youngest daughter.
1000	386	Prince Philip of Saxe-Coburg-Gotha, 1844.	Grandson. Elder son of No. 999.
1001 –02		Same as Nos. 972–973. Great-grandchildren. Children of No. 1000.	
1003	387	Prince Augustus of Saxe-Coburg-Gotha, 1845.	Grandson. 2nd son of No. 999.

1004 -12	}	Same as Nos. 432-440. Great-grandchildren. Children of No. 1003.
1013	388	Ferdinand, Prince of Bulgaria, 1861. { Grandson. Youngest son of No. 999.
1014 -17	}	Same as Nos. 45-48. Great-grandchildren. Children of No. 1013.
1018	389	Clotilda, Archduchess Joseph of Austria, 1846. } Granddaughter. Elder *Alesuth.* } daughter of No. 999.
1019	390	Archduke Joseph Augustus of Austria, 1872. } Great-grandson. Son *Brünn.* } of No. 1018.
1020 -22	}	Same as Nos. 310-312. { Great-great-grandchildren. Children of No. 1019.
1023	391	Mary Dorothy, Duchess of Orleans, 1867. *Twickenham.*
1024	392	Margaret Clementina, Princess of Thurn and Taxis, 1870. *Ratisbon.*
1025	393	Francis Joseph, Hereditary Prince of Thurn and Taxis, 1893.
1026	394	Prince Charles Augustus of Thurn and Taxis, 1898.
1027	395	Prince Louis Philip of Thurn and Taxis.
1028	396	Archduchess Elizabeth of Austria, 1883.
1029	397	Archduchess Clotilda of Austria, 1884.
1030	398	Duke Sigefred in Bavaria, 1876. *Munich.*
1031	399	Duke Christopher in Bavaria, 1879.
1032	400	Duke Luitpold in Bavaria, 1890.

(Right-hand bracketed notes, grouped:)

Great-grandchildren. Elder daughter of No. 1018. (for 1023, 1024)

Great-great-grandsons. Sons of No. 1024. (for 1025, 1026)

Great-granddaughters. Younger daughters of No. 1018. (for 1027, 1028, 1029)

Great-grandsons. Sons of Amelia, Duchess Maximilian in Bavaria, 1848-1894, younger daughter of No. 999. (for 1030, 1031, 1032)

19. Descendants of Francis IV., Duke of Modena, 1779-1846. (See Table IV.)

1033 -67	}	Same as Nos. 1-35.

20. Descendants of the Archduchess Theresa of Modena, 1773-1832, and her husband, Victor Emmanuel I., King of Sardinia, &c., &c., 1759-1824. (See Table IV.)

1068 to 1156	}	Same as Nos. 1-90.

21. Descendants of the Archduchess Leopoldina of Modena, 1776-1848, and her 2nd husband, Louis, Count of Arco, 1773-1854. (See Table IV.)

1157	401	*Sophia, Countess of Arco-Stepperg, 1868. { Granddaughter. Daughter of Aloysius, Count of Arco-Stepperg, 1808-1891.
1158	402	*Count Joseph von Arco-Zinneberg, 1881.
1159	403	*Count Ferdinand von Arco-Zinneberg, 1882.
1160	404	*Walburga, Countess Otto von und zu Lerchenfeld, 1873.

Great-grandchildren. Children of Count Louis, 1840-1882, eldest son of Maximilian, Count von und zu Arco-Zinneberg, 1811-1885. (for 1158, 1159, 1160)

1161	405	*Count Louis von und zu Lerchenfeld, 1894.	
1162	406	*Count Joseph von und zu Lerchenfeld, 1895.	Great-great-grandchildren.
1163	407	*Count Hugo von und zu Lerchenfeld, 1896.	Children of No. 1160.
1164	408	*Count Henry von und zu Lerchenfeld, 1897.	
1165	409	*Countess Marie Sidonia von Arco-Zinneberg, 1880.	Great-grandchild. Youngest daughter of Count Louis, 1840–1882, 2nd son of Maximilian. *See above.*
1166	410	*Countess Matilda Leopoldina Irène von Arco-Zinneberg, 1869.	Great-grandchild. Only child of Count Charles, 1841–1873, 2nd son of Maximilian. *See above.*
1167	411	*Count Maximilian von Arco-Zinneberg, 1850.	Grandson. 3rd but eldest surviving son of Maximilian. *See above.*
1168	412	*Count Nicholas von Arco-Zinneberg, 1881.	
1169	413	*Count Aloysius von Arco-Zinneberg, 1886.	
1170	414	*Countess Leopoldina von Arco-Zinneberg,1876.	
1171	415	*Countess Helen von Arco-Zinneberg, 1877.	
1172	416	*Countess Mechtilda von Arco-Zinneberg, 1879.	Great-grandchildren.
1173	417	*Countess Marie Sophia von Arco-Zinneberg, 1882.	Children of No. 1167.
1174	418	*Countess Irène von Arco-Zinneberg, 1884.	
1175	419	*Countess Anna von Arco-Zinneberg, 1890.	
1176	420	*Countess Elizabeth von Arco-Zinneberg, 1891.	
1177	421	*Count Francis von Arco-Zinneberg, 1851.	Grandson. 4th but 2nd surviving son of Maximilian. *See above.*
1178	422	*Charles Policarpe, Count of Leiningen-Billiegheim, 1860. *Munich, 5 Neue Wittelsbacherstrasse.*	Great-grandchildren. Children of Countess Marie, 1834–1894, 2nd wife of Charles, Count of Leiningen-Billiegheim, 1823–1900, eldest daughter of Maximilian. *See above.*
1179	423	*Leopoldina, Baroness Godefroy von Vegue-Westernach, 1857. *Hohenkammer, near Petershausen, Bavaria.*	
1180	424	*Baron Charles von Vegue-Westernach, 1886.	
1181	425	*Baroness Theresa von Vegue-Westernach, 1888.	Great-great-grandchildren.
1182	426	*Baroness Maria von Vegue-Westernach, 1889.	Children of No. 1179.
1183	427	*Baroness Mechtilde von Vegue-Westernach, 1894.	
1184	428	*Mechtilda, Baroness Maximilian von Cetto, 1870. *Ober-Lauterbach, Lower Bavaria.*	Great-grandchild. Younger daughter of Countess Marie, 1834–1894, 2nd wife of Charles, Count of Leiningen-Billiegheim, 1823–1900. *See above.*
1185	429	*Baron Ernest von Cetto, 1897.	Great-great-grandchildren. Children of No. 1184.
1186	430	*Baroness Maria Augusta von Cetto, 1894.	
1187	431	*Baroness Leopoldina von Cetto, 1895.	
1188	432	*Theresa, Countess of Loë-Wissen, 1835. *Schloss Adendorf.*	Granddaughter. 2nd daughter of Maximilian. *See above.*

1189	433	*Degenhard Bertram, 5th Count of Loë, 1889.	} Great-great-grandchildren. Children of Frederic Leopold, 4th Count of Loë, 1861–1899, son of No. 1188.
1190	434	*Count Clement von Loë, 1893.	
1191	435	*Count Felix von Loë, 1896.	
1192	436	*Countess Maria Matilda von Loë, 1895.	
1193	437	*Count Louis von Loë, 1866. Priest of the Dominican Order in Oüffeldorf.	} Great-grandchildren. Children of No. 1188.
1194	438	*Count George von Loë, 1868.	
1195	439	*Countess Louise von Loë, 1863. A sister in the Dominican convent at Torquay.	
1196	440	*Countess Matilda, 1865, wife of Hans Freiherr von Gumppenburg.	
1197	441	*John Henry von Gumppenburg, 1891.	} Great-great-grandchildren. Children of No. 1196.
1198	442	*Maria Theresa von Gumppenburg, 1888.	
1199	443	*Elizabeth von Gumppenburg, 1889.	
1200	444	*Hildegarde von Gumppenburg, 1894.	
1201	445	*Sophia, Princess of Waldburg-Wolffegg-Waldsee, 1836. *Waldsee.*	} Granddaughter. 3rd daughter of Maximilian. See above.
1202	446	*Maximilian, Hereditary Count of Waldburg, 1863. *Waldsee.*	} Great-grandson. Son of No. 1201.
1203	447	*Count Francis of Waldburg, 1892.	} Great-great-grandchildren. Children of No. 1202.
1204	448	*Count George of Waldburg, 1893.	
1205	449	*Count Frederic of Waldburg, 1895.	
1206	450	*Countess Anne of Waldburg, 1896.	
1207	451	*Countess Sophia of Waldburg, 1899.	
1208	452	*Count Joseph of Waldburg, 1864.	} Great-grandchildren. Children of No. 1201.
1209	453	*Count Louis of Waldburg, 1871.	
1210	454	*Count Henry of Waldburg, 1874.	
1211	455	*Countess Marie of Waldburg, 1866.	
1212	456	*Elizabeth Bona, Countess of Stolberg-Wernigerode, 1867. *Wernigerode in the Harz.*	
1213	457	*Francis Xavier, Hereditary Count of Stolberg-Wernigerode, 1894.	} Great-great-grandchildren. Children of No. 1212.
1214	458	*Count Joseph of Stolberg-Wernigerode, 1900.	
1215	459	*Countess Marie Anne of Stolberg-Wernigerode, 1895.	
1216	460	*Baron Conrad von Franckenstein, 1875.	} Great-grandchildren. Children of Countess Helen, 1837–1897, wife of Baron Henry von Franckenstein, 1826–1883, 4th daughter of Maximilian. See above.
1217	461	*Baron Francis von Franckenstein, 1879.	
1218	462	*Margaret, wife of Augustin, Count von und zu Elk-Herrschaft, 1869.	
1219	463	*Count Francis von Elk-Herrschaft, 1893.	} Great-great-grandchildren. Children of No. 1218.
1220	464	*Count Henry von Elk-Herrschaft, 1896.	
1221	465	*Count Charles von Elk-Herrschaft, 1897.	
1222	466	*Countess Helen von Elk-Herrschaft, 1892.	
1223	467	*Countess Mary Ida von Elk-Herrschaft, 1898.	
1224	468	*Irene, Countess of Oberndoff, 1842.	} Granddaughter. 5th daughter of Maximilian. See above.

1225	469	*Count Francis von Oberndoff, 1862.	Great-grandson. Son of No. 1224.
1226	470	*Count Frederick von Oberndoff, 1891.	
1227	471	*Countess Hedwiga von Oberndoff, 1890.	Great-great-grandchildren. Children of No. 1225.
1228	472	*Count Maximilian von Oberndoff, 1867	Great-grandchildren.
1229	473	*Count Wolfgang von Oberndoff, 1871.	Children of No.
1230	474	*Countess Antonia von Oberndoff, 1863.	1224.
1231	475	*Anne, Countess of Stolberg-Stolberg, 1844. *Brauna.*	Granddaughter. 6th daughter of Maximilian. *See above.*
1232	476	*Frederic Leopold, Count of Stolberg-Stolberg, 1868.	Great-grandchildren.
1233	477	*Mary Pia, Baroness Maurice von Franckenstein, 1870. *Nördlingen.*	Children of No. 1231.
1234	478	*Baron George von Franckenstein, 1898.	Great-great-grandchildren. Children of No. 1233.
1235	479	*Baroness Sophia von Franckenstein, 1896.	
1236	480	*Countess Leopoldina von Stolberg-Stolberg, 1872.	Great-grandchildren. Youngest daughters of No. 1231.
1237	481	*Countess Sophia von Stolberg-Stolberg, 1874.	
1238	482	*Countess Maria von Bissingen und Nippenburg, 1869.	Great-grandchildren. Children of Countess Mechtilda, 1845–1875, wife of Count Ferdinand von Bissingen und Nippenburg, 7th daughter of Maximilian. *See above.*
1239	483	*Countess Gajetan von Bissingen und Nippenburg, 1870.	
1240	484	*Countess Elizabeth von Bissingen und Nippenburg, 1873.	
1241	485	*Christina, Countess Conrad von Preysing-Lichtenegg-Moos, 1852.	Grandchild. 8th daughter of Maximilian. *See above.*
1242	486	*Count Emmanuel von Preysing-Lichtenegg-Moos, 1879.	
1243	487	*Count Jaspar von Preysing-Lichtenegg-Moos, 1880.	
1244	488	*Count George von Preysing-Lichtenegg-Moos, 1887.	
1245	489	*Count John von Preysing-Lichtenegg-Moos, 1889.	
1246	490	*Count Christopher von Preysing-Lichtenegg-Moos, 1891.	Great-grandchildren. Children of No. 1241.
1247	491	*Countess Maria Immaculée von Preysing-Lichtenegg-Moos, 1881.	
1248	492	*Countess Anna von Preysing-Lichtenegg-Moos, 1882.	
1249	493	*Countess Elizabeth von Preysing-Lichtenegg-Moos, 1883.	
1250	494	*Countess Josepha von Preysing-Lichtenegg-Moos, 1884.	
1251	495	*Countess Mechtilda von Preysing-Lichtenegg-Moos, 1886.	

22. Descendants of Louisa of Penthièvre, 1753–1821, and her husband, Philip, 5th Duke of Orleans, 1747–1793. (See Table IV.)

1252 to 1376	Same as Nos. 908–1032.

The Blood Royal of Britain

23. Descendants of the Archduke Francis Charles of Austria, 1802–1878. (See Table V.)

1377	496	Francis Joseph, Emperor of Austria, Apostolic King of Hungary, King of Bohemia, King of Dalmatia, Croatia, Slavonia, Galicia, Lodomeria, and Illyria, King of Jerusalem, &c., Archduke of Austria, Grandduke of Tuscany and Cracow, Duke of Lorraine, Salzburg, Styria, Carinthia, Carniola, and Bukowina, Grand Prince of Transylvania, Margrave of Moravia, Duke of Upper and of Lower Silesia, Modena, Parma, Placentia and Guastalla, Auschwitz and Zator, Teschen, Friuli, Ragusa and Zara, Princely Count of Hapsburg and the Tyrol, Kyburg, Görz, and Gradiska, Prince of Trent and Brixen, Margrave of Upper and Lower Lusatia and in Istria, Count of Hohenembs, Feldkirch, Brigance, Sonnenberg, &c., Lord of Trieste, Cattaro, and of the Wendish Mark, Grand-voyvode of the Voyvodia of Servia, &c., &c., 1830.	Son.
1378		Same as No. 975 { Great-granddaughter. Daughter of the Crown Prince Rudolph, 1858–1889, son of No. 1377.
1379	497	Archduchess Gisele, Princess Leopold of Bavaria, 1856. *Munich.*	Granddaughter. Eldest daughter of No. 1377.
1380 –88	}	Same as Nos. 304–312. Great-grandchildren. Children of No. 1379.
1389	498	Marie Valerie, Archduchess Frances Salvator of Tuscany, 1868. *Château de Wallsee s/le Danube, Lower Austria.*	Granddaughter. 2nd daughter of No. 1377.
1390 –95	}	Same as Nos. 671–676. Great-grandchildren. Children of No. 1389.
1396 –409	}	Same as Nos. 650–661, and 484–485. { Grandchildren, &c. Children, &c., of the Archduke Charles Louis, 1833–1896.
1410	499	Archduke Louis Victor of Austria, 1842. *Vienna.*	3rd son.

24. Descendants of the Archduchess Marie Louise, 1791–1847, wife 1st of the Emperor Napoleon I., and her 2nd husband, Adam, Count of Niepperg, 1775–1829. (See Table V.)

1411	500	*Alfred, 2nd Prince of Montenuovo [Austria], 1854. *Vienna, 6 Löwelstrasse. Margarethen-sur-Moos, Lower Austria.*	Grandson. Son of William, 1st Prince of Montenuovo, 1821 1897.
1412	501	*Prince Ferdinand of Montenuovo, 1888.	
1413	502	*Princess Julia of Montenuovo, 1880.	Great-grandchildren. Children of No. 1411.
1414	503	*Princess Mary of Montenuovo, 1881.	
1415	504	*Princess Frances of Montenuovo, 1893.	
1416	505	*Count Alexander Wielopolski, 1875.	Great-grandchildren. Children of Princess Albertine, 1853–1895, wife of Sigismond, Count Wielopolski, Marquis Gonzaga, 1833, elder daughter of Prince William, 1821–1897.
1417	506	*Count Alfred Wielopolski, 1879.	
1418	507	*Count Albert Wielopolski, 1884.	
1419	508	*Countess Margaret, wife of Josaphat, Count von dem Broele-Plater, 1876.	

1420	509	*Marie, Countess Anthony Apponyi, 1859.	}	Granddaughter. Younger daughter of Prince William, 1821–1897.
1421	510	*Count Anthony Apponyi, 1883.	}	Great-grandchildren. Children
1422	511	*Countess Julia Apponyi, 1879.		of No. 1420.
		*Children, if any, of Marie, Countess of San Vitali, 1819–185 ? (daughter).		

25. Descendants of the Archduchess Leopoldina, 1797–1826, wife of Peter IV. and I., King of Portugal, Emperor of Brazil, 1798–1834. (See Table V.)

1423 to 1468	}	Same as Nos. 428–473.

26. Descendants of Leopold II., Grand Duke of Tuscany, 1797–1870. (See Table V.)

1469 to 1578	}	Same as Nos. 815–858, 286–315, and 859–894.

27. Descendants of Victor Emmanuel II., King of Italy [King of Sardinia], 1820–1878. (See Table V.)

1579 -81	}	Same as Nos. 276–278.	{	Grandchildren, &c. Descendants of Humbert, King of Italy, 1844–1901.
1582	512	Emmanuel, 2nd Duke of Aosta, 1869. Château de Mandria, near Turin.	{	Grandson. Son of Amadeus, 1st Duke of Aosta, 1845–1890.
1583 -84	}	Same as Nos. 339–340.		Great-grandchildren. Children of No. 1582.
1585	513	Victor, Count of Turin, 1870. Florence.		Grandchildren. Youngest sons of Amadeus, 1st Duke of Aosta, 1845–1890.
1586	514	Louis, Duke of the Abruzzi, 1873.	}	
1587	515	Humbert, Count of Salemi, 1889.		
1588	516	Clotilda, Princess Bonaparte, 1843.		Elder daughter.
1589	517	Prince Napoleon Bonaparte, 1862. Brussels, 241 Avenue Louise.		Grandchildren. Children of No. 1588.
1590	518	Prince Louis Bonaparte, 1864. Peterhof.		
1591	519	Letitia, Duchess of Aosta, 1866.		
1592		Same as No. 1587.		Great-grandchild. Son of No. 1591.
1593	520	Maria Pia, Queen-Dowager of Portugal, 1847.	}	2nd daughter.
1594 -97	}	Same as Nos. 441–444.	{	Grandchildren, &c. Children, &c., of No. 1593.

28. Descendants of Ferdinand, Duke of Genoa, 1822–1855. (See Table V.)

1598 -06	}	Same as Nos. 270–278.

The Blood Royal of Britain

29. Descendants of the Archduke Charles of Austria, 1771–1847. (See Table V.)

1607	521	Archduchess Maria Theresa, Duchess Philip of Würtemberg, 1845. *Stuttgart.*	Granddaughter. Daughter of the Archduke Albert, Duke of Teschen, 1817–1895.
1608 –16	}	Same as Nos. 990–998.	Great-grandchildren. Children of No. 1607.
1617	522	Archduke Frederic, 3rd Duke of Teschen, 1856. *Presburg.*	Grandson. Son of the Archduke Charles Ferdinand, 1818–1874.
1618	523	Archduke Albert of Austria, 1897.	
1619	524	Archduchess Mary Christine of Austria, 1879.	
1620	525	Archduchess Mary Anne of Austria, 1882.	Great-grandchildren.
1621	526	Archduchess Mary Henrietta of Austria, 1883.	Children of No.
1622	527	Archduchess Gabrielle of Austria, 1887.	1617.
1623	528	Archduchess Isabella of Austria, 1888.	
1624	529	Archduchess Mary Alice of Austria, 1893.	
1625	530	Archduke Charles Stephen of Austria, 1860. *Pola.*	Grandson. Brother to No. 1617.
1626 –31	}	Same as Nos. 678–683.	Great-grandchildren. Children of No. 1625.
1632	531	Archduke Eugene of Austria, 1863.	Grandchildren. Brother
1633	532	Christina, Queen-Dowager of Spain, 1858.	and sister to No. 1617.
1634 –37	}	Same as Nos. 317–320.	Great-grandchildren. Children of No. 1633.
1638 to 1699	}	Same as Nos. 629–690.	Grandchildren, &c. Children of the Archduchess Maria Theresa, 1816–1867, 2nd wife of Ferdinand II., King of the Two Sicilies, 1810–1859.
1700	533	Marie Caroline, Archduchess Renier of Austria, 1825.	Daughter.

30. Descendants of the Archduke Joseph of Austria, Palatine of Hungary, 1776–1847. (See Table V.)

1701	534	Archduke Joseph of Austria, 1833. *Alcsuth.*	Son.
1702 –12	}	Same as Nos. 1019–1029.	Grandchildren, &c. Children, &c., of No. 1701.
1713	535	Elizabeth, Archduchess Charles Ferdinand of Austria, 1831. *Vienna.*	Elder daughter.
1714 –29	}	Same as Nos. 1617–1632.	Grandchildren. Sons of No. 1651, by her 2nd husband, the Archduke Charles Ferdinand of Austria, 1818–1874.
1730 –46	}	Same as Nos. 1–17.	Grandchildren, &c. Daughter (and her children) of No. 1651, by 1st husband, the Archduke Ferdinand of Modena, 1821–1849.
1747 –51	}	Same as Nos. 1633–1637.	Grandchildren. Daughter (and her children) of No. 1651, by 2nd husband. *See above.*
1752 –57	}	Same as Nos. 971–976.	Grandchildren. Children of the Archduchess Maria Henrietta, Queen Consort of Leopold II. of Belgium, 1836–1902.

31. Descendants of the Archduke John of Austria, 1782–1859. (See Table V.)

1758	536	*John, 2nd Count of Meran, 1867. *Graz.*	Grandson. Elder son of Francis, 1st Count of Meran,1839–1891 ; morganatic son.
1759	537	*Count Francis of Meran, 1891.	
1760	538	*Count Philip of Meran, 1894.	Great-grandchildren.
1761	539	*Count John of Meran, 1896.	Children of No.
1762	540	*Countess Maria Theresa of Meran, 1893.	1758.
1763	541	*Countess Maria Anne of Meran, 1897.	
1764	542	*Count Francis of Meran, 1868.	
1765	543	*Count Rudolph of Meran, 1872.	
1766	544	*Count Albert of Meran, 1874.	
1767	545	*Countess Anne, wife 1st of Alphonso Stefenelli di Prenterhof et Hohenmaur, Lieutenant in the Austrian Army, and 2ndly of John Raden, 1864.	Grandchildren. Brothers and sisters to No. 1758.
		*Children, if any, of No. 1767.	
1768	546	*Countess Mary of Meran, 1865.	
1769	547	*Caroline, Baroness Doblhoff-Dier, 1870.	
1770	548	*Baron Henry Doblhoff-Dier, 1894.	
1771	549	*Baron Francis Doblhoff-Dier, 1897.	Great-grandchildren. Children of No. 1769.
1772	550	*Baroness Maria Theresa Doblhoff-Dier, 1896.	

32. Descendants of the Archduke Regnier of Austria, 1783–1853. (See Table V.)

1773	551	Archduke Regnier of Austria, 1827. *Vienna.*	Son.
1774	552	*Marie Renière, Countess of Waideck, wife of Henry, Count Lucchesi-Palli di Campo et Pignatelli, Prince of Campofranco, 1872. *Bozen.*	Granddaughter. Morganatic daughter of the Archduke Henry, 1828–1891.
1775	553	Maria Renata Lucchesi-Palli, 1895.	Great-granddaughter. Daughter of No. 1774.
1776 -94	}	Same as Nos. 1579–1597.	Grandchildren. Children, &c., of the Archduchess Adelaide, 1822–1855, wife of Victor Emmanuel II. of Italy, 1820–1878.

33. Descendants of Caroline of Naples, 1798–1870, wife 1st of Charles, Duke of Berry, 1778–1820, and 2ndly of Hector, Count Lucchesi-Palli, Duke della Grazia, 1808–1864. (See Table V.)

1795	554	*Adinolphe, Count Lucchesi-Palli, Duke della Grazia [Sicily and Spain], 1840. . *Palazzo Vendramini, Venice.*	Son by 2nd husband.
1796	555	*Henry, Count Lucchesi-Palli di Campo et Pignatelli, Prince of Campofranco [Sicily and Spain], 1861. *Bozen.*	Grandson. Eldest son of No. 1795.
1797		*Same as No. 1775.	Great-grandchild. Child of No. 1796.

1798	556	*Charles, Count Lucchesi-Palli, 1868.	Grandson. 2nd son

1798 556 *Charles, Count Lucchesi-Palli, 1868.   }   Grandson. 2nd son
     Brunnsee.   }   of No. 1795.

1799 557 *Robert, Count Lucchesi-Palli, 1897.   }   Great-grandchildren.

1800 558 *Frances Lucchesi-Palli, 1894.   }   Children of No.

1801 559 *Antoinette Lucchesi-Palli, 1899.   }   1798.

1802 560 *Peter, Count Lucchesi-Palli, 1870.
     Palermo.

1803 561 *Maria, wife of Edward Moora, 1862.   Grandchildren.

1804 562 *Blanche, Altgravine George of Salm-Reifferscheid-   Children of
     Krautheim, 1865.   No. 1795.
     Neucilli, Styria.

1805 563 *Altgravine Josa of Salm-Reifferscheid-Krau-
     theim, 1893.

1806 564 *Altgravine Rose of Salm-Reifferscheid-Krau-   Great-grandchildren.
     theim, 1895.   Children of No.

1807 565 *Altgravine Eleanor of Salm-Reifferscheid-Krau-   1804.
     theim, 1901.

1808 566 *Caroline, wife of Rudolph, Count of Euzenberg
     zum Freyen und Jöchelsthurm, 1872.
     Schwaz, Tyrol.   Grandchild. Younger

1809 567 *Gabrielle, wife of Girolamo, Count Brandolin-   daughter of No.
     Rota, 1875.   1795.
     Cison di Valmarino.

1810 }   Same as Nos. 36–90.   { Grandchildren, &c. Descendants of Louisa,
-64 }   Duchess of Parma, 1819–1864, daughter
      by 1st husband.

1865 568 *Clementina, widow of Camillo, Count Zileri dal   Elder daughter by
     Verme,   -1896, 1835.   2nd husband.
     Vicenza.

1866 569 *Henry, Count Zileri dal Verme-degli-Obbizi,   Grandson. Elder son
     1857.   of No. 1865.
     Vicenza.

1867 }   *Same as Nos. 551–555.   { Great-grandchildren. Children
-71 }   of No. 1866.

1872 570 *Count Robert Zileri dal Verme, 1858.   Grandson. 2nd son
     Parma.   of No. 1865.

1873 571 *Count Guilio Zileri dal Verme, 1895.   Great-grandchildren. Chil-

1874 572 *Countess Berica Isabella Zileri dal   dren of No. 1872.
     Verme, 1893.

1875 573 *Count Luchino Zileri dal Verme, 1861.

1876 574 *Count Alexander Zileri dal Verme, 1863.

1877 575 *Countess Grazcella, wife of Don Jayme
     Alvarez-Pereira de Melo, Duke of   Grandchildren. Younger
     Cadaval [Spain].   sons and elder daugh-
     Children, if any, of No. 1877.   ters of No. 1865.

1878 576 *Countess Maria Frances, wife of George,
     Count Emolapodilista, 1869.
     Padua.

1879 577 *Count Alvise Emolapodilista, 1898.   Great-grandson. Son
        of No. 1878.

1880 578 *Frances, Princess Massimo and Arsoli, 1836.   Younger daughter by
     Rome, Palazzo Massimo alle Colonne.   2nd husband.

1881 579 *Francis, Prince of Arsoli, 1865.   Grandson. Elder son
     Rome.   of No. 1880.

1882 580 *Prince Leon Massimo, 1896.   Great-grandson. Son of No. 1881.

1883 581 *Fabrizio, Prince of Roviano, Duke of Anticoli-   Grandson. 2nd son
     Corrado, 1868.   of No. 1880.
     Rome.

1884 }   *Same as Nos. 31–32.   Great-grandchildren. Children of No. 1883·
-85 }

The Blood Royal of Britain

1886	582	*Gabrielle, Countess Robert Zileri dal Verme, 1861. *Parma.*	Granddaughter Elder daughter of No. 1880.
1887 -88	}	*Same as Nos. 1873-1874.	Great-grandchildren. Children of No. 1886.
1889	583	*Princess Caroline Massimo, 1871. *Rome.*	Granddaughter. Younger daughter of No. 1880.

34. Descendants of Ferdinand, Duke of Modena, 1754-1806. (See Table V.)

1890 to 2109	}	Same as Nos. 1033-1251.

35. Descendants of the Archduchess Amelia of Austria, 1746-1804, wife of Ferdinand, Duke of Parma, 1751-1802. (See Table V.)

2110 -224	}	Same as Nos. 201-315.

36. Descendants of Francis I., King of the Two Sicilies, 1777-1830. (See Table V.)

2225 -598	}	Same as Nos. 629-719, 1795-1889, and 720-907.

37. Descendants of Theresa of Naples, 1772-1807, 2nd wife of Francis II., Roman Emperor, King of Hungary and Bohemia, afterwards (1804) Francis I., Emperor of Austria, 1768-1835. (See Table V.)

2599 -690	}	Same as Nos. 1377-1468.

38. Descendants of Louisa Amelia of Naples, 1773-1802, 1st wife of Ferdinand III., Grandduke of Tuscany, 1769-1824. (See Table V.)

2691 -819	}	Same as Nos. 1469-1606.

39. Descendants of Mary Amelia of Naples, 1782-1866, wife of Louis Philip, King of the French, 1773-1850. (See Table V.)

2820 -944	}	Same as Nos. 908-1032.

The Blood Royal of Britain

B.—Descendants of Edward, Prince Palatine of the Rhine, K.G., 1625–1663, fifth son of Elizabeth, Queen of Bohemia, 1596–1662. (See Table IV.)

40. Descendants of Constantine, Prince of Salm-Salm, 1762–1828. (See Table VI.)

2945	584	Leopold, Prince of Salm-Salm, 1838. *Château d'Anholt, près Bocholt, Westphalia.*	Great-grandsons. Sons of Prince Alfred, 1814–1886, and grandsons of Prince Florentine, 1786–1846, eldest son by 1st marriage.
2946	585	Prince Charles of Salm-Salm, 1845.	
2947	586	Prince Alfred of Salm-Salm, 1846. *Haus Rede, Westphalia.*	
2948	587	Prince Emmanuel of Salm-Salm, 1871. *Berlin.*	
2949	588	Prince Francis of Salm-Salm, 1878. *Gross-Lichterfelde.*	
2950	589	Prince Alfred of Salm-Salm, 1879.	
2951	590	Princess Mary of Salm-Salm, a nun, 1874. *Riedenburg, near Bregenz.*	Great-great-grandchildren. Children of No. 2947.
2952	591	Princess Henrietta of Salm-Salm, 1875.	
2953	592	Princess Rose of Salm-Salm, 1878.	
2954	593	Princess Augusta of Salm-Salm, 1881.	
2955	594	Princess Eleanor of Salm-Salm, 1887.	
2956	595	Adelaide, Princess Philip of Cröy-Dülmen, 1840. *Dusseldorf.*	Great-granddaughter. Sister to No. 2945, &c.
2957	596	Prince Emmanuel of Cröy-Dülmen, 1874.	Great-great-grandchildren. Children of No. 2956.
2958	597	Princess Mary of Cröy-Dülmen, 1876.	
2959	598	Princess Mary of Salm-Salm, 1843.	
2960	599	Princess Constance of Salm-Salm, 1851. *Munster.*	Great-grandchildren. Sisters to No. 2945, &c.
2961	600	Flaminia, Countess Ferdinand Wolff-Metternich-zur-Gracht, 1853. *Château de Gracht, near Lieblar, Rhenish Prussia.*	
2962	601	Count Alfred Wolff-Metternich-zur-Gracht, 1872.	
2963	602	Count Paul Wolff-Metternich-zur-Gracht, 1873.	
2964	603	Count Fritz Wolff-Metternich-zur-Gracht, 1874.	
2965	604	Count Louis Anthony Wolff-Metternich-zur-Gracht, 1877.	
2966	605	Count Ferdinand Wolff-Metternich-zur-Gracht, 1881.	Great-great-grandchildren. Children of No. 2961.
2967	606	Count Joseph Wolff-Metternich-zur-Gracht, 1884.	
2968	607	Count Francis Wolff-Metternich-zur-Gracht, 1893.	
2969	608	Countess Marie Josephine Wolff-Metternich-zur-Gracht, 1876.	
2970	609	Countess Josephine Hedwiga Wolff-Metternich-zur-Gracht, 1879.	
2971	610	Countess Eleanor Wolff-Metternich-zur-Gracht, 1888.	

2972	611	Princess Olga of Salm-Salm, wife of Alexander de Padberg, 1854. *Hildesheim.* Children, if any, of No. 2972.	Great-granddaughter. Daughter of Prince Emile, 1820–1858, 2nd son of Prince Florentine. *See above.*
2973	612	Frances, Princess Alexis of Cröy-Dülmen, 1833. *Slabetz, Bohemia.*	Granddaughter. Daughter of Prince Maximilian, 1793–1836, son by 2nd marriage.
2974	613	Prince Max of Cröy-Dülmen, 1864.	Great-grandchildren. Children of No. 2973.
2975	614	Eleanor, Princess of Salm-Salm, 1855. *Château d'Anholt, near Bocholt, Westphalia.*	
2976	615	*Count Manfred of Salm-Hoogstraten, 1843.	Grandson. Son of Count Rudolph, 1817–1869, son by 3rd and morganatic marriage.
2977	616	*Count Rudolph of Salm-Hoogstraten, 1877.	Great-grandson. Son of No. 2976.
2978	617	*Count Armand of Salm-Hoogstraten, 1844.	
2979	618	*Count Constantine of Salm-Hoogstraten, 1846.	
2980	619	*Count Conrad of Salm-Hoogstraten, 1855.	
2981	620	*Countess Mary, wife of Amely Louis Theodore de Petersen, Lieut.-Col. in the Danish Army, 1840. Children, if any, of No. 2981.	Grandchildren. Brothers and sisters of No. 2976.
2982	621	*Countess Pauline, widow of Francis Stotten, Captain in the Prussian Army, -1879, 1849. Children, if any, of No. 2982.	
2983	622	*Count Albert of Salm-Hoogstraten, 1819.	4th son by 3rd and morganatic marriage.
2984	623	*Count Hermann of Salm-Hoogstraten, Colonel in the Austrian Army, 1844.	Grandchildren. Children of No. 2983.
2985	624	*Count Otho of Salm-Hoogstraten, 1848.	
2986	625	*Count William of Salm-Hoogstraten, 1887.	Great-grandchildren. Children of No. 2985.
2987	626	*Count Hermann of Salm-Hoogstraten, 1888.	
2988	627	*Count Alfred of Salm-Hoogstraten, 1851.	Grandson. 2nd son of No. 2983.
2989	628	*Count Louis of Salm-Hoogstraten, 1885.	Great-grandchildren. Children of No. 2988.
2990	629	*Count Otho of Salm-Hoogstraten, 1886.	
2991	630	*Count Alfred of Salm-Hoogstraten, 1888.	
2992	631	*Countess Augusta of Salm-Hoogstraten, 1845.	Granddaughter. Daughter of No. 2983.
2993	632	*Count Hermann of Salm-Hoogstraten, 1821.	5th son by 3rd and morganatic marriage.
2994	633	Charles, Duke of Cröy, 1859. *Dülmen, Cercle de Coesfeld, Westphalia.*	Great-grandson. Son of Rudolph, Duke of Cröy, 1823–1902, and grandson of the Princess Eleanor of Salm-Salm, 1794–1871, wife of Alfred, Duke of Cröy, 1789–1861.
2995	634	Charles, Hereditary Prince of Cröy, 1889.	Great-great-grandchildren. Children of No. 2994.
2996	635	Prince Englebert, of Cröy, 1891.	
2997	636	Prince Anthony of Cröy, 1893.	
2998	637	Princess Isabella of Cröy, 1890.	
2999	638	Isabella, Archduchess Frederic of Austria, 1856. *Presburg.*	Great-grandchild. Eldest sister of No. 2994.
3000 -006	}	Same as Nos. 1618–1624.	Great-great-grandchildren. Children of No. 2999.

The Blood Royal of Britain

		Children, if any, of Clementina, 1857–1893, wife of Adhémar Louis Francis Ghislan, Count of Oultremont, 1845. 2nd sister of No. 2994.		
3007	639	Natalie, Princess of Grimberghe and Rubempré, wife of Henry, 5th Prince of Grimberghe, 8th Prince of Rubempré [Belgium], 1863. *Brussels, 23 Rue aux Laines.*	}	Great-grandchild. Youngest sister of No. 2994.
3008	640	Charles, Prince of Rubempré, 1887.	}	Great-great-grandchildren. Children of No. 3007.
3009	641	Countess Mary de Merode, 1884.		
3010	642	Countess Henrietta de Merode, 1885.		
3011 –12	}	Same as Nos. 2974–2975.	{	Great-grandchildren. Children of Prince Alexis of Cröy, 1825–1899, and grandchildren of the Princess Eleanor of Salm-Salm, 1794–1871. *See above.*
3013	643	Prince Louis of Cröy, 1862. *Paris, 54 Avenue du Bois de Boulogne.*		
3014	644	Prince Francis of Cröy, Lieutenant 147th Regiment of Infantry, 1873. *Verdun.*		
3015	645	Princess Eleanor, widow of Marie Louis René, Viscount de Chévigné, –1899, 1864. *Paris, 13 Rue Las Cases.* Children, if any, of No. 3015.		Great-grandchildren. Children of Prince George of Cröy, 1828–1879, and grandchildren of the Princess Eleanor of Salm-Salm, 1794–1871. *See above.*
3016	646	Princess Elizabeth, wife of Charles, Count de Bruce, 1865. *Paris, 30 Rue St. Dominique.* Children, if any, of No. 3016.		
3017	647	Princess Jane, wife of Herbert d'Espagne, Marquis of Venevelles, 1870. *Paris, 40 Avenue d'Iéna.* Children, if any, of No. 3017.		
3018	648	Leopoldina, Princess Emmanuel of Cröy, 1821. *Florence.*	}	Granddaughter. Eldest daughter of the Princess Eleanor of Salm-Salm. *See above.*
3019	649	Prince Edward of Cröy, 1843. *Rœulx.*	}	Great-grandson. Son of No. 3018.
3020	650	Prince Stephen of Cröy, 1872. *Rœulx.*	{	Great-great-grandson. Son of Prince Gustavus, 1845–1889, brother to No. 3019.
3021	651	Prince Stephen of Cröy, 1898.	}	Great-great-great-grandchildren. Children of No. 3020.
3022	652	Princess Eleanor Dorothea of Cröy, 1897.		
3023	653	Princess Margaret, wife of Théodule, Count of Grammont, 1869. *Paris.* Children, if any, of No. 3023.		Great-great granddaughters. Daughters of Prince Gustavus, 1845–1889, brother to No. 3019.
3024	654	Princess Constance of Cröy, 1876.		
3025	655	Princess Alice of Cröy, 1884.		
3026	656	Princess Pauline of Cröy, 1887.		
3027	657	Princess Emma of Cröy, 1858.	{	Great-grandchild. Daughter of No. 3018.
3028	658	Princess Emma Augusta of Cröy, 1826. *Paris.*	}	Granddaughters. Sisters to No. 3018.
3029	659	Princess Bertha, wife of Ignatius, Baron von Landsburg-Velen, 1833. *Drensteinfurt, Westphalia.*		

109

3030	660	Baron Engelbert von Landsburg-Velen, 1866.	Great-grandchildren. Children of No. 3029.
3031	661	Baron Alfred von Landsburg-Velen, 1872.	
3032	662	Baron Emmanuel von Landsburg-Velen, 1876.	
3033	663	Baron Hermann Joseph von Landsburg-Velen, 1879.	
3034	664	Baroness Marie, wife of John, Count Prasehma, 1865.	
3035	665	Count Joseph Ferdinand Prasehma, 1893.	Great-great-grandchildren. Children of No. 3034.
3036	666	Count Engelbert Prasehma, 1898.	
3037	667	Count Leopold Prasehma, 1900.	
3038	668	Countess Elizabeth Prasehma, 1895.	
3039	669	Baroness Emma, wife of Arthur, Count von Strachwitz auf Reichenau, 1868.	Great-grandchild. 2nd daughter of No. 3029.
3040	670	Count Alexander von Strachwitz, 1894.	Great-great-grandchildren. Children of No. 3039.
3041	671	Count Rudolph von Strachwitz, 1896.	
3042	672	Count Stanislaus von Strachwitz, 1899.	
3043	673	Countess Helen von Strachwitz, 1899.	
3044	674	Countess Mary Agnes von Strachwitz, 1900.	
3045	675	Baroness Gabrielle von Landsburg-Velen, 1874.	Great-grandchildren. Youngest daughters of No. 3029.
3046	676	Baroness Antoinette von Landsburg-Velen, 1877.	
3047	677	Gabrielle, Princess Louis of Polignac, 1835. *Paris, 28 Boulevard Flandrin.*	Granddaughter. Youngest sister to No. 3018.
3048	678	Prince Charles of Cröy, 1866.	Great-grandchildren. Children of Prince Alexander, 1828–1887, and grandchildren of the Princess Jane of Salm-Salm, 1796–1868, wife of Prince Philip, of Cröy, 1801 – 1871, 2nd daughter.
3049	679	Prince William of Cröy, 1869.	
3050	680	Prince Leopold of Cröy, 1871.	
3051	681	Prince Clement of Cröy, 1873.	
3052	682	Prince Alexander of Cröy, 1873.	
3053	683	Princess Cunegonda of Cröy, 1864.	
3054	684	Princess Elise of Cröy, 1868.	

Buchburg, Lower Austria. (for 3048–3052)

| 3055 | 685 | Prince Philip of Cröy, 1849. *Dusseldorf.* | Grandson. Son of the Princess Jane of Salm-Salm, 1796–1868. *See above.* |
| 3056–57 | } | Same as Nos. 2957–2958. | Great-grandchildren. Children of No. 3055. |

Children, if any, of Princess Louise of Cröy (eldest daughter of the Princess Jane of Salm-Salm, 1796–1868), 1825–1890, and her husband Constantine, Count Benckendorff, Major-General in the Russian Army, 1786–1858.

3058	686	Princess Stephanie of Cröy, 1831.	Grandchildren. 2nd and 3rd surviving daughters of the Princess Jane of Salm-Salm, 1796–1868.
3059	687	Mary, Princess of Lichnowsky, &c., wife of Charles, 5th Prince of Lichnowsky [Prussia], Count of Wardenburg [Bohemia], Peer of Prussia, &c., 1837. *Kuchelna und Kreuzenort, Prussian Silesia.*	
3060	688	Prince Charles Max of of Lichnowsky, 1860.	Great-grandchildren. Children of No. 3059.
3061	689	Mary Caroline, Countess of Redern, 1861. *Berlin.*	
3062	690	Count William von Redern, 1888.	Great-great-grandchildren. Children of No. 3061.
3063	691	Countess Victoria von Redern, 1889.	
3064	692	Countess Mary von Redern, 1890.	
3065	693	Countess Margaret von Redern, 1893.	
3066	694	Countess Hermione von Redern, 1899.	

3067	695	Margaret, Countess of Brzezie-Lancko-rónski, 1863. *Vienna.*	Great-grandchild. Youngest daughter of No. 3059.
3068	696	Countess Caroline von Brzezie-Lanckorónski, 1898.	Great-great-grandchild. Child of No. 3067.

41. Descendants of the Princess Ernestine of Starhemberg, 1782–1818, and her husband, Frederick Augustus Alexander, 3rd Duke of Beaufort, 17 –1817. (See Table VI.)

3069	697	Frederic, 5th Duke of Beaufort-Sponten, 1843. *Vienna ; Petschau, Bohemia.*	Grandson. Son of Alfred, 4th Duke of Beaufort, 1816–1888.
3070	698	Count Henry de Beaufort, 1880.	
3071	699	Pauline, Princess Alphonso of Isemberg, 1876. *Langensebold.*	Great-grandchildren. Children of No. 3069.
3072	700	Countess Mary de Beaufort.	
3073	701	Countess Eleanor de Beaufort.	
		Children, if any, of Valerie, Countess of Straten (daughter), 1811– Children, if any, of Hermengilda, Countess of Laubespin (daughter), 1813.	

42. Descendants of the Princess Frances of Starhemberg, 1787–1864, wife of Stephen, Count Zicky zu Zicky, 1780–1853. (See Table VI.)

3074	702	Anna, Countess Kinsth, 1824.	Daughter.

43. Descendants of Princess Leopoldina of Starhemberg, 1793–1859, wife of Joseph, Count of Thürheim, 1794–1832. (See Table VI.)

3075	703	Andrew, Count of Thürheim, 1827. *Weinberg bei Kasermarkt.*	Son.
3076	704	Count Louis of Thürheim, 1874.	Grandchildren. Children of No. 3075.
3077	705	Countess Marie, wife of Richard, Baron von Gablenz, 1868.	
3078	706	Theresa, Countess Joseph von Platz, 1871. *Brunn.*	
3079	707	Theresa, Baroness von Schwiter, 1831. *Paris.*	Daughter.
		Children, if any, of No. 3079.	

44. Descendants of Eugene, 9th Prince of Ligne, 1804–1880. (See Table VI.)

3080	708	Louis, 10th Prince of Ligne, 1854. *Château de Belœil, near Mons, Belgium.*	Grandson. Son of Prince Henry of Ligne, 1824–1871.
3081	709	Princess Susan of Ligne, 1885.	Great-granddau. Dau. of No. 3080.
3082	710	Prince Ernest of Ligne, 1857. *Paris, 14 Place Vendôme. Brussels, Rue Montoyer.*	Grandson. Brother of No. 3080.

3083	711	Prince Eugene of Ligne, 1893.	Great-grandchildren. Children of No. 3082.
3084	712	Prince Baldwin of Ligne, 1896.	
3085	713	Princess Jane of Ligne, 1887.	
3086	714	Princess Isabella of Ligne, 1889.	
3087	715	Princess Henrietta of Ligne, 1893.	
3088	716	Princess Mary of Ligne, 1898.	
3089	717	Mary, Duchess of Beaufort-Spontin, 1855. *Vienna.*	Granddaughter. Sister to No. 3080.
3090 –93	}	Same as Nos. 3070–3073.	Great-grandchildren. Children of No. 3089.
3094	718	Prince Charles of Ligne, 1837. *Brussels, 55 Avenue des Arts.*	2nd but eldest surviving son.
3095	719	Prince Florent of Ligne, 1881.	Grandchildren. Children of No. 3094.
3096	720	Hedwiga, Duchess of Arenberg. *Recklinghausen and Brussels.*	
3097	721	Engelbert Charles, Hereditary Prince of Arenberg, 1899.	Great-grandchild. Child of No. 3096.
3098	722	Prince Edward of Ligne, 1839. *La Neuville.*	3rd but 2nd surviving son.
3099	723	Prince Albert of Ligne, 1874.	Grandchildren. Children of No. 3098.
3100	724	Prince George of Ligne, 1879.	
3101	725	Princess Eleanor of Ligne, 1877.	
3102	726	Princess Helen of Ligne, 1887.	
3103 –119	}	Same as Nos. 2994–3010.	Grandchildren, &c. Children of Princess Natalie of Ligne, 1835–1863, wife of Rudolph, Duke of Cröy, 1823–1902.
3120	727	Charles, Duke of Estrees [Spain], 1863. *Paris, 47 Rue de Varenne.*	Grandson. Son of the Princess Marie of Ligne, 1843–1898, wife of Sosthènes, 4th Duke of Doudeauvile.
3121	728	Margaret de La Rochefoucauld, 1886.	Great-grandchild. Daughter of No. 3120.
3122	729	Armand, 2nd Duke of Bisaccia [Naples and Bavaria], 1870. *Paris, 18 Rue Vaneau.*	Grandson. Brother to No. 3120.
3123	730	Sosthènes de La Rochefoucauld, 1897.	Great-grandchildren. Children of No. 3122.
3124	731	Hedwiga de La Rochefoucauld, 1896.	
3125	732	Marie de La Rochefoucauld, 1901.	
3126	733	Count Edward de La Rochefoucauld, 1874.	Grandchildren. Brother and sister to No. 3120, &c.
3127	734	Elizabeth, Princess of Ligne, 1865.	
3128		Same as No. 3081.	Great-grandchild. Child of No. 3127.
3129	735	Marie, Duchess of Harcourt, 1871, wife of Henry, Duke of Harcourt [France]. *Paris, 47 Rue de Varenne.*	Grandchild. Sister to No. 3120, &c.
3130	736	Countess Lydia de Harcourt, 1898.	Great-grandchildren. Children of No. 3129.
3131	737	Countess Elizabeth de Harcourt, 1901.	

45. Descendants of Charles, 2nd Prince of Clary and Aldringen, 1777–1831. (See Table VI.)

3132	738	Carlos, 4th Prince Clary and Aldringen [Holy Roman Empire], Count of Teplitz [Bohemia], 1844. *Teplitz, Bohemia.* *Vienna, 9 Herrengasse.*	Grandson. Son of Edmund, 3rd Prince Clary and Aldringen, 1813–1894.
3133	739	Count John Baptist of Clary, 1878.	Great-grandchildren. Children of No. 3132.
3134	740	Countess Mary of Clary, 1874.	
3135	741	Count Sigefroi of Clary, 1848.	Grandson. Brother to No. 3132.

3136	742	Count Alphonso of Clary, 1887.	Great-grandchildren·
3137	743	Countess Elizabeth Alexandrina of Clary, 1885.	Children of No.
3138	744	Countess Sophia of Clary, 1891.	3135.
3139	745	Edmée, Countess of Robilant and Cereaglio, widow of Charles Nicholas, Count of Robilant and Cereaglio, *late* Italian Ambassador in London, –1888, 1842.	Granddaughter. Sister to No. 3132.

Turin.

Children, if any, of No. 3139.

3140	746	Anthony, Prince Radziwill [Holy Roman Empire and Poland], 1833.	Grandson. Son of Matilda of Clary, 1806–1896, and her husband, William, Prince Radziwill, 1797–1870.

Berlin, W., 3 Pariser Platz.
Nieswiez-Minsk, Russia.

3141	747	Prince George Radziwill, 1860.	Great-grandchild. Son of No. 3140.
3142	748	Prince Albert Radziwill, 1885.	
3143	749	Prince Charles Radziwill, 1886.	
3144	750	Prince Leon Radziwill, 1888.	Great-great-grandchildren.
3145	751	Princess Rose Radziwill, 1884.	Children of No. 3141.
3146	752	Princess Theresa Radziwill, 1889.	
3147	753	Princess Elizabeth Radziwill, 1894.	
3148	754	Prince Stanislaus Radziwill, 1880.	

Hanover.

3149	755	Princess Elizabeth, Countess Roman Potocki, 1861.	Great-grandchildren. Children of No. 3140.

Lancut, Galicia.
Vienna, 22 Franzensring.

Children, if any, of No. 3149.

3150	756	Princess Helen, Countess Joseph Potocki, 1874.	

Antoniny, Gouv. de Volhynie.

Children, if any, of No. 3150.

3151	757	Prince Janusz Radziwill, 1843.	Grandchildren. Brothers of No. 3140.

Cerkliszki, près de Vilna.

3152	758	Prince William Radziwill, 1845.	

Varsovia.

3153	759	Prince Waclaw Radziwill, 1880.	

Le Cap.

3154	760	Prince Casimir Radziwill, 1888.	

Varsovia.

3155	761	Princess Louise Radziwill, 1876.	Great-grandchildren. Children of No. 3152.

Hasburg, Carniola.

3156	762	Wanda, Princess Blücher de Wahlstatt [Prussia], 1877.	

Château de Radun, Austrian Silesia.

3157	763	Princess Gabrielle Radziwill, 1879.	

Hasburg, Carniola.

3158	764	Matilda, Princess of Windisch-Grætz, 1836.	Granddaughter. Sister to No. 3140.

Vienna, 8 Wullnerstrasse.

3159	765	Ferdinand, Prince Radziwill, Duke of Olyka, 1834.	Grandchild. Son of the Princess Leontine of Clary,1811–1890, wife of Bogislaus, Prince Radziwill, 1809–1873.

Berlin W., 66 Wilhelmstr.

3160	766	Prince Michael Radziwill, 1870.	Great-grandchild. Eldest son of No. 3159.

Belgrave Square, London.

3161	767	Prince Anthony Radziwill, 1899.	Great-great-grandchild. Son of No. 3160.
3162	768	Prince Charles Radziwill, 1874.	Great-grandchildren. Children of No. 3159.
3163	769	Prince Janusz Radziwill, 1880.	
3164	770	Princess Margaret Radziwill, 1875.	

3165	771	Prince Wladislaus Radziwill, in Holy Orders, of the Society of Jesus, 1836. *Wynandsrade, Holland.*	} Grandchildren. Brothers to No. 3159.
3166	772	Prince Charles Radziwill, 1839. *Château de Bagatela, near Ostrowo.*	
3167	773	Prince Wladislaus Radziwill, 1881.	{ Great-grandchild. Son of No. 3166.
3168	774	Prince Bogislaus Radziwill, 1844. *Berlin.*	} Grandchildren. Brother and sister to No. 3159.
3169	775	Felice, Princess of Clary and Aldringen, 1849. *Vienna, 9 Herringasse.*	
3170 −71	} 776	Same as Nos. 3133–3134.	{ Great-grandchildren. Children to No. 3169.
3172	776	Princess Elizabeth Radziwill, 1850. *Berlin.*	} Grandchild. Youngest sister to No. 3159.
3173	777	Felice, Altgravine Robert of Salm-Reifferscheid-Reitz, 1815.	} 3rd but only surviving daughter.

46. Descendants of Mary Louisa of Hesse-Rhinefels-Rothenburg, 1729–1800, and her husband, Maximilian, Duke of Hoogstraten, 1732–1773. (See Table VI.)

| 3174 −297 | } | Same as Nos. 2945–3068. |

47. Descendants of Louisa Henrietta of Conti, 1726–1759, and her husband, Louis Philip, 4th Duke of Orleans, 1725–1785. (See Table VI.)

| 3298 −422 | } | Same as Nos. 908–1032. |

48. Descendants of Louis Armand, Prince of Conti, 1695–1727. (See Table VI.)

| 3423 −547 | } | Same as Nos. 3298–3422. |

49. Descendants of Francis III., Duke of Modena, 1698–1780. (See Table VII.)

| 3548 −891 | } | Same as Nos. 1033–1376. |

50. Descendants of Prince Maximilian of Saxony, 1759–1838. (See Table VII.)

| 3892 −951 | } | Same as Nos. 256–315. |

51. Descendants, if any, of *Elizabeth of Saxony, 1768–1849, and her husband, Henry Thomas Charles de Preissac, Duke of Esclignac, 1763–1827. (See Table VII.)

52. Descendants of *Mary Anne of Saxony, 1770–1845, and her husband, Prince Paluzzo Altieri, 1760–1834. (See Table VII.)

3952	778	*Louis, Prince Altieri [Rome], 1878. *Rome, Piazza del Gesu.*	Great-great-grandchildren. Children of Prince Paul, 1849–1901, grandchildren of Prince Emile, 1819–1900, and great-grandchildren of Prince Clement, 1795–1873.
3953	779	*Mark Antony Altieri, 1891.	
3954	780	Theodolinda, wife of Francis Paul di Napoli, Duke of Campobello, 1876. *Rome.*	
		Children, if any, of No. 3954.	
3955	781	*Maria Augusta Altieri, 1880.	
3956	782	*Camilla Altieri, 1889.	
3957	783	*Victoria, wife of John, Count Revedin di Ferrara, 1844. *Bologna.*	Great-grandchildren. Daughters of Prince Emile, 1819–1900. *See above.*
		Children, if any, of No. 3957.	
3958	784	*Christina, wife of Jerome, Count of Siciliano Nobile dei Marchesi Theodoli, 1852. *Rome.*	
3959	785	*Alberto dei Marchesi Theodoli, 1870.	Great-great-grandchildren. Children of No. 3958.
3960	786	*Clement dei Marchesi Theodoli, 1878.	
3961	787	*Theodolo dei Marchesi Theodoli, 1882.	
3962	788	*Hugo dei Marchesi Theodoli, 1886.	
3963	789	*Laura dei Marchesi Theodoli, 1875.	
3964	790	*Maria dei Marchesi Theodoli, 1876.	
3965	791	*Beatrice dei Marchesi Theodoli, 1880.	
3966	792	*Louisa dei Marchesi Theodoli, 1881.	
3967	793	*Mary Anne, wife of Alexander, Count Rocca-Saporiti, 1856. *Reggio, Emilia.*	Great-grandchild. 3rd daughter of Prince Emile, 1819–1900.
		Children, if any, of No. 3967.	
3968	794	*Prince Francis Boncompagni-Ludovisi, 1886.	Great-great-grandchildren. Children of Laura Altieri, 1858–1892, 2nd wife of Hugo, Duke of Sora, youngest daughter of Prince Emile, 1819–1900.
3969	795	*Princess Eleanor Boncompagni-Ludovisi, 1885.	
3970	796	*Princess Theresa Boncompagni-Ludovisi, 1889.	
3971	797	*Louisa Altieri (formerly wife of Jerome, Count of Codroipo, marriage annulled 1897), 1877.	Great-grandchildren. Daughter of Lorenzo Altieri, 1829–1899, 2nd son of Prince Clement, 1795–1873.
3972	798	*Paul, Marquis Colloredo, 1850.	Great-grandchild. Son of Livia Altieri, 1820–1886, and her husband, Marquis Jerome Colloredo di Udine, 1809–1882.
3973	799	*Countess Livia Colloredo, 1888.	Great-great-grandchildren. Children of No. 3972.
3974	800	*Countess Eurelia Colloredo, 1892.	
3975	801	*Countess Paola Colloredo, 1894.	
3976	802	*Count Henry Colloredo, 1853.	Great-grandchild. Brother to No. 3972.

3977	803	*Count Rudolph Colloredo, 1879.	Great-great-grandchildren.
3978	804	*Count Emmanuel Colloredo, 1883.	Children of No. 3976.
3979	805	*Countess Maria Pia Colloredo, 1888.	
3980	806	*Countess Guilia, wife of Anthony Cerasi, Count of Monterado, 1841. Children, if any, of No. 3980.	Great-grandchildren.
3981	807	*Countess Victoria, widow of Count Jerome Codroipo, -1865, 1843. Children, if any, of No. 3981.	Sisters to No. 3972, &c.
3982	808	*Thomas, Prince Antici-Mattei, 1846. *Rome.*	Great-grandchild. Son of Clara Altieri, 1824-1888, wife of Matthew, Marquis Antici-Mattei, 1807-1883, 2nd daughter of Prince Clement, 1795-1873.
3983	809	*Marquis Louis Antici-Mattei, 1870.	
3984	810	*Marquis Guy Antici-Mattei, 1889.	Great-great-grandchildren.
3985	811	*Johanna Antici-Mattei, 1883.	Children of No. 3982.
3986	812	*Clotilda Antici-Mattei, 1886.	
3987	813	*Chiara Antici-Mattei, 1892.	
3988	814	*Marquis Philip Patrizi, 1859.	Great-grandchildren. Sons of Theresa Altieri, 1835- , wife of Marquis Francis Patrizi, , youngest daughter of Prince Clement, 1795-1873.
3989	815	*Marquis Joseph Patrizi, 1872.	
3990	816	*Guendolina Boncompagni-Ludovisi, 1878.	Great-great-grandchildren. Daughters of Victoria Patrizi, 1867-1883, 1st wife of Hugo, Duke of Sora, daughter of Theresa Altieri, 1835, and Marquis Francis Patrizi. *See above.*
3991	817	*Guglielmina Boncompagni-Ludovisi, 1881.	

53. Descendants of Christina of Saxony, 1775-1827, and her husband, Prince Camille VIII. Maximilian Massimo, 1770-1840. (See Table VII.)

3992	818	*Camille Charles Albert, Prince Massimo [Rome], 1836. *Rome, Palazzo Massimo alle Colonne.*	Grandson. Son of Prince Camille IX , Victor Emmanuel, 1803-1893.
3993 to 4001		Same as Nos. 1881-1889.	Great-grandchildren. Children of No. 3992.
4002	819	*Prince Philip Massimo, Prince Lancellotti, 1843. *Rome.*	Grandson. Brother to No. 3992.
4003	820	*Prince Joseph Lancellotti, 1865. *Rome.*	Great-grandchild. Son of No. 4002.
4004	821	*Prince Philip Lancellotti, 1892.	
4005	822	*Prince Maximilian Lancellotti, 1895.	Great-great-grandchildren. Children of No. 4003.
4006	823	*Princess Anna Lancellotti, 1890.	
4007	824	*Princess Maria Lancellotti, 1890.	
4008	825	*Princess Frances Lancellotti, 1893.	
4009	826	*Princess Caroline Lancellotti, 1896.	
4010	827	*Prince Louis Lancellotti, 1881.	
4011	828	*Prince Lawrence Lancellotti, 1883.	Great-grandchildren. Children of No. 4002.
4012	829	*Prince Peter Lancellotti, 1888.	
4013	830	*Princess Maria Pia Lancellotti, 1875.	
4014	831	*Princess Rufina Lancellotti, 1886.	

4015	832	*Prince Maximilian Massimo, a Jesuit Priest, 1849. Rome.	Grandson. Brother to No. 3992.

Children, if any, of Princess Frances Massimo, 1846– (sister to No. 3992, &c), and her husband, Ragnier, Duke Bourbon del Monte Saint Maria, Prince of S. Faustino.

Children, if any, of Princess Josephine Massimo, 1799– (daughter), and her husband, Prince Octavius Lancellotti, –1852.

4016	833	*Philip, Prince del Drago [Rome], 1824. Rome.	Grandson. Son of Theresa Massimo, 1801–1858, wife of Urban, Prince del Drago, 1773–1851.
4017	834	*Ferdinand, Prince of Antuni, 1857. Rome.	Great-grandson. Son of No. 4016.
4018	835	*Alfonso del Drago, 1882.	
4019	836	*John del Drago, 1884.	Great-great-grandchildren. Children of No. 4017.
4020	837	*Rudolph del Drago, 1900.	
4021	838	*Maria Christina del Drago, 1895.	
4022	839	*Ortensia del Drago, 1897.	
4023	840	*Francis d'Assisi del Drago, Count of Ascrea, 1858. Rome.	Great-grandsons. Sons of No. 4016.
4024	841	*Louis del Drago, 1859. Rome, Villino del Drago, 7 Via Vicenza.	
4025	842	*Clement del Drago, 1897.	Great-great-grandsons. Sons of No. 4024.
4026	843	*Mario del Drago, 1899.	

Descendants, if any, of Theresa del Drago, 1826 (sister of No. 3929), wife of Louis, Count Mastai-Ferretti, nephew of Pope Pius IX.

4027	844	Francis, Prince Ruspoli [Rome], 1839. Rome, Palais Ruspoli.	Grandson. Son of Barbara Massimo, 1813–1849, and her husband, John, Prince Ruspoli, 1807–1876.
4028	845	Alexander, Prince of Cerveteri, 1869. Rome.	Great-grandchildren. Son of No. 4027.
4029	846	Frances Ruspoli, 1899.	Great-great-grandchildren. Children of No. 4028.
4030	847	Giacinta Ruspoli, 1898.	
4031	848	John Ruspoli, 1871.	
4032	849	Maria Ruspoli, 1874.	Great-grandchildren. Children of No. 4027.
4033	850	Laura, wife of Alexander, Count Martini Marescotti, 1878. Rome.	
4034	851	Giacinta Ruspoli, 1883.	
4035	852	Alexander, Marquis of Riano, 1844. Lucca.	Grandson. Brother of No. 4027.
4036	853	Fabrizio Ruspoli, 1878.	Great-grandchildren. Children of No. 4035.
4037	854	Sforza Ruspoli, 1882.	
4038	855	Napoleon Ruspoli, 1885.	
4039	856	Christina, Princess Napoleon Charles Bonaparte, 1842. Rome.	Granddaughter. Sister to No. 4027.
4040	857	Princess Maria, wife of Enrico Gotti, Lieutenant 5th Regiment of Infantry in the Italian Army. Rome.	Great-grand-children. Children of No. 4039.
4041	858	Princess Eugenia, wife of Napoleon Ney d'Elchingen, 4th Prince de la Moskowa [France], 1872. Paris, 10 Rue Jean-Goujon.	

54. Descendants of Charles Albert, King of Sardinia, Duke of Savoy, 1798–1849. (See Table VII.)

4042 –69		Same as Nos. 1579–1606.

55. Descendants of the Princess Mary Elizabeth of Savoy-Carignan, 1800–1856, and her husband, the Archduke Regnier of Austria, 1783–1853. (See Table VII.)

| 4070 –089 | } | Same as Nos. 1773–1794. |

56. Descendants of Charles IV., King of Spain, 1748–1819. (See Table VII.)

| 4090 –681 | } | Same as Nos. 316–907. |

57. Descendants of Ferdinand I., King of the Two Sicilies, 1751–1825. (See Table VII.)

| 4682 to 5392 | } | Same as Nos. 2234–2944. |

58. Descendants of the Infant Peter of Spain, 1786–1812. (See Table VII.)

| 5393 –401 | } | Same as Nos. 513–521. |

59. Descendants of the Infanta Mary Louise of Spain, 1745–1792, and her husband, Leopold II., Roman Emperor, King of Hungary and Bohemia, Archduke of Austria, 1747–1792. (See Table VII.)

| 5402 –924 | } | Same as Nos. 1377–1899. |

60. Descendants of the Princess Mary Josephine of Saxony, 1731–1767, and her husband, the Dauphin Louis, 1729–1765. (See Table VII.)

| 5925 –979 | } | Same as Nos. 146–200. |

61. Descendants of the Princess Marie Antoinette of Bavaria, 1724–1780, and her husband, Frederic Christian, Elector of Saxony, 1722–1763. (See Table VII.)

| 5980 to 6039 | } | Same as Nos. 256–315. |

EDWARD VII. OF THE UNITED KINGDOM OF GREAT BRITAIN
AND IRELAND AND OF THE BRITISH DOMINIONS BEYOND
THE SEAS, KING, EMPEROR OF INDIA

Photo, W. & D. Downey, London

C.—Descendants of Sophia, Electress of Hanover, 1630–1714, wife of Ernest Augustus I., Elector of Hanover, 1629–1698, eleventh and youngest child of Elizabeth, Queen of Bohemia, 1596–1662. (See Table V.)

62. Descendants of VICTORIA, Queen of the United Kingdom of Great Britain and Ireland, Empress of India, 1819–1901. (See Table VIII.)

6040	859	⋃ Edward VII., of the United Kingdom of Great Britain and Ireland, and of the British Dominions beyond the Seas, King, Defender of the Faith, Emperor of India, 1841.	Eldest son.
6041	860	⋃ George, Prince of Wales, 1865. *York Lodge, St. James's Palace.*	Grandson. Only son of No. 6040.
6042	861	⋃ Prince Edward of Wales, 1894.	
6043	862	⋃ Prince Albert of Wales, 1895.	Great-grandchildren.
6044	863	⋃ Prince Henry of Wales, 1900.	Children of No.
6045	864	⋃ Prince George of Wales, 1902.	6041.
6046	865	⋃ Princess Victoria Alexandra of Wales, 1897.	
6047	866	⋃ Louise, Princess Royal, Duchess of Fife, 1867. *15 Portman Square, W.*	Granddaughter. Eldest daughter of No. 6040.
6048	867	Lady Alexandra Duff, 1891.	Great-granddaughters. Children of No. 6047.
6049	868	Lady Maud Duff, 1893.	
6050	869	⋃ Princess Victoria of Great Britain and Ireland, 1868.	Granddaughters. Daughters of No. 6040.
6051	870	⋃ Maud, Princess Charles of Denmark, 1869.	
6052	871	⋃ Marie, Crown Princess of Roumania, 1875. *Bucharest.*	Granddaughter. Eldest daughter of Alfred, Duke of Saxe-Coburg and Gotha, Duke of Edinburgh, 1844–1900.
6053–055		Same as Nos. 451–453.	Great-grandchildren. Children of No. 6052.
6056	872	⋃ Victoria Melita, Grand Duchess of Hesse, 1876. *The New Palace, Darmstadt.*	Granddaughter. 2nd sister of No. 6052.
6057	873	Princess Elizabeth of Hesse, 1895.	Great-granddaughter. Only child of No. 6056.
6058	874	⋃ Alexandra, Hereditary Princess of Hohenlohe-Langenburg, 1878. *Ehrenburg Castle, Coburg. Castle of Langenburg, Würtemberg.*	Granddaughter. 3rd sister of No. 6052.
6059	875	Prince Gottfried of Hohenlohe-Langenburg, 1897.	Great-grandchildren. Children of No. 6058.
6060	876	Princess Marie Melita of Hohenlohe-Langenburg, 1899.	
6061	877	Princess Alexandra of Hohenlohe-Langenburg, 1901.	
6062	878	⋃ Princess Beatrice of Saxe-Coburg and Gotha, 1884.	Granddaughter. Youngest sister of No. 6052.

6063	879	◻ Arthur, Duke of Connaught and Strathearn, 1850. *Bagshot Park, Surrey.*	} 3rd son.
6064	880	◻ Prince Arthur of Connaught, 1883.	
6065	881	◻ Princess Margaret of Connaught, 1882.	Grandchildren. Children of No. 6063.
6066	882	◻ Princess Victoria of Connaught, 1886.	
6067	883	◻ Leopold Charles Edward, Duke of Saxe-Coburg and Gotha, 2nd Duke of Albany, 1884.	Grandchildren. Children of Leopold, 1st Duke of Albany, 1853-1884,
6068	884	◻ Princess Alice of Albany, 1883.	4th son.
6069	885	William II., German Emperor, King of Prussia, Elector and Margrave of Brandenburg, Burgrave of Nuremberg, Count of Hohenzollern, Premier Duke and Sovereign of Silesia and of the County of Glatz, Grandduke of the Lower Rhine and of Posnania, Duke of Saxony, Westphalia and Engern, of Pomerania, Luneburg, Holstein, and Schleswig, of Magdeburg, Bremen, Guelders, Cleves, Juliers and Berg, of the Wendes and the Kassoubes, of Krossen, Lauenburg, Mecklenburg, Landgrave of Hesse and of Thuringia, Margrave of Upper and of Lower Lusatia, Prince of Orange, Lord of Rügen, East Friesland, Paderborn and Pyrmont, of Halberstadt, Munster,Minden,Osnaburg,Hildesheim, Verden, Kammin, Fulda, Nassau and Mœrs, Princely Count of Henneburg, Count of the Marches and of Ravensberg, of Hohenstein, Tecklenburg, and Lingen, of Mansfeld, Sigmaringen, and Veringen, Lord of Frankfort, &c., &c., 1859.	Grandchild. Elder son of the Princess Victoria of Great Britain and Ireland, 1840-1901, and her husband, Frederick III., German Emperor, King of Prussia, 1831-1888.
6070	886	William, German Crown Prince, and Crown Prince of Prussia, 1882.	
6071	887	Prince Eitel Frederick of Prussia, 1883.	Great-grandchildren. Children of No. 6069.
6072	888	Prince Adalbert of Prussia, 1884.	
6073	889	Prince Augustus William of Prussia, 1887.	
6074	890	Prince Oscar of Prussia, 1888.	
6075	891	Prince Joachim of Prussia, 1890.	
6076	892	Princess Victoria Louise of Prussia, 1892.	
6077	893	Prince Henry of Prussia, 1862. *Royal Palace, Kiel.*	Grandchild. Brother to No. 6069.
6078	894	Prince Waldemar of Prussia, 1889.	Great-grandchildren. Children of No. 6077.
6079	895	Prince Sigismund of Prussia, 1896.	
6080	896	Prince Henry of Prussia, 1900.	
6081	897	Charlotte, Hereditary Prince of Saxe-Meiningen, 1860. *Breslau.*	Grandchild. Elder sister to No. 6069.
6082	898	Feodor, Princess Henry XXX. of Reuss, 1879. *Frankfort on the Oder.*	Great-grandchild. Daughter of No. 6081.
6083	899	Victoria, Princess Adolphus of Schaumburg-Lippe, 1866. *Bonn.*	Grandchildren. 2nd and 3rd sisters to No. 6069.
6084	900	Sophia, Crown Princess of Greece, Duchess of Sparta, 1870. *Château de Dekéleia, near Athens.*	

6085	901	Prince George of Greece, 1890.	Great-grandchildren. Children of No. 6084.
6086	902	Prince Alexander of Greece, 1893.	
6087	903	Prince Paul of Greece, 1902.	
6088	904	Princess Helen of Greece, 1896.	
6089	905	Margaret, Princess Frederick Charles of Hesse-Cassel, 1872. *Frankfort on the Main. Château de Friedrichshof.*	Grandchild. Youngest sister to No. 6069.
6090	906	Prince Frederick William of Hesse-Cassel, 1893.	Great-grandchildren. Children of No. 6089.
6091	907	Prince Maximilian of Hesse-Cassel, 1894.	
6092	908	Prince Philip of Hesse-Cassel, } twins, 1896.	
6093	909	Prince Wolfgang of Hesse-Cassel,	
6094	910	Prince Richard of Hesse-Cassel, } twins, 1901.	
6095	911	Prince Christopher of Hesse-Cassel,	
6096	912	Ernest Louis, Grandduke of Hesse and of the Rhine, 1868. *Darmstadt.*	Grandson. Son of the Princess Alice, 1843–1878, and her husband, Louis IV., Grandduke of Hesse-Darmstadt.
6097		Same as No. 6057. Great-grandchild. Daughter of No. 6096.	
6098	913	Victoria, Princess of Battenberg, 1863, wife of Louis, 2nd Prince of Battenberg [Hesse].	Granddaughter. Eldest sister to No. 6096.
6099	914	Prince George of Battenberg, 1892.	Great-grandchildren. Children of No. 6098.
6100	915	Prince Louis of Battenberg, 1900.	
6101	916	Princess Alice of Battenberg, 1885.	
6102	917	Princess Louisa of Battenberg, 1889.	
6103	918	Elizabeth, Grandduchess Sergius of Russia, 1864. *Moscow.*	Granddaughters. 2nd and 3rd sisters to No. 6096.
6104	919	Irene, Princess Henry of Prussia, 1866.	
6105 –07	}	Same as Nos. 6078–6080.	Great-grandchildren. Children of No. 6104.
6108	920	Alexandra, Empress of Russia, 1872.	Granddaughter. 4th sister to No. 6096.
6109	921	Granduchess Olga of Russia, 1895.	Great-grandchildren. Children of No. 6108.
6110	922	Granduchess Tatiana of Russia, 1897.	
6111	923	Granduchess Marie of Russia, 1899.	
6112	924	Granduchess Anastasia of Russia, 1901.	
6113	925	▽ Helena, Princess Christian of Schleswig-Holstein, 1846. *Cumberland Lodge, Windsor Park.*	3rd but eldest surviving daughter.
6114	926	Prince Albert of Schleswig-Holstein, 1869.	Grandchildren. Children of No. 6113.
6115	927	Princess Victoria of Schleswig-Holstein, 1870.	
6116	928	Princess Louise of Schleswig-Holstein, 1872.	
6117	929	▽ Princess Louise, Duchess of Argyll, 1848. *Kensington Palace, London. Inveraray Castle, Argyllshire.*	4th and 5th but 2nd and 3rd surviving daughters.
6118	930	▽ Beatrice, Princess Henry of Battenberg, 1857. *Kensington Palace, London. Osborne Cottage, Isle of Wight.*	
6119	931	Prince Alexander of Battenberg, 1886.	Grandchildren. Children of No. 6118.
6120	932	Prince Leopold of Battenberg, 1889.	
6121	933	Prince Maurice of Battenberg, 1891.	
6122	934	Princess Victoria Eugénie of Battenberg, 1887.	

The Blood Royal of Britain

63. Descendants of Ernest Augustus II., King of Hanover, 1771–1851. (See Table VIII.)

6123	935	⛒ Ernest Augustus [III. King of Hanover], Duke of Brunswick and Luneburg, Duke of Cumberland, 1845. *Penzing, near Vienna.* *Gmunden, Upper Austria.*	Grandson. Son of King George V., 1819–1878.
6124	936	⛒ Prince George William [of Hanover], 1880.	
6125	937	⛒ Prince Ernest Augustus [of Hanover], 1887.	
6126	938	⛒ Mary Louise, Princess Maximilian of Baden, 1879. *Carlsruhe.*	Great-grandchildren. Children of No. 6123.
6127	939	⛒ Princess Alexandra [of Hanover], 1882.	
6128	940	⛒ Princess Olga [of Hanover], 1884.	
6129	941	⛒ Princess Frederica, wife of Alphonso, Baron von Pawel-Rammingen, 1848. *Mouris·ot, Bois de Boulogne, Biarritz.*	Grandchildren. Sisters to No. 6123.
6130	942	⛒ Princess Mary of Hanover, 1849. *Gmunden, Upper Austria.*	

64. Descendants of Adolphus, Duke of Cambridge, 1774–1850. (See Table VIII.)

6131	943	⛒ George, 2nd Duke of Cambridge, 1879. *Gloucester House, Piccadilly, W.*	Children.
6132	944	⛒ Augusta Caroline, Grandduchess of Mecklenburg-Strelitz, 1822.	
6133	945	Adolphus Frederic, Hereditary Grandduke of Mecklenburg-Strelitz, 1848. *Neustrelitz.*	Grandchild. Child of No. 6132.
6134	946	Duke Adolphus Frederic of Mecklenburg-Strelitz, 1882.	
6135	947	Duke Charles Borwin of Mecklenburg-Strelitz, 1888.	
6136	948	Duchess Mary, wife of George, Count Jametel, 1878. *Paris.*	Great-grandchildren. Children of No. 6133.
		Children, if any, of No. 6136.	
6137	949	[Jutta] Militza, Crown Princess of Montenegro, 1888.	
6138	950	Adolphus, 2nd Duke of Teck [Würtemberg], 1868. *4 Devonshire Place, London, W.*	Grandson. Elder son of the Princess Mary of Cambridge, 1833–1897, and her husband, Francis, 1st Duke of Teck, 1887–1900.
6139	951	Prince George of Teck, 1895.	
6140	952	Princess Victoria of Teck, 1897.	Great-grandchildren. Children of No. 6138.
6141	953	Princess Helen Augusta of Teck, 1899.	
6142	954	Prince Francis of Teck, 1870. *Dublin.*	
6143	955	Prince Alexander of Teck, 1874. *Aldershot.*	Grandchildren. Brothers and sister of No. 6138.
6144	956	Mary Victoria, Princess of Wales, 1867.	
6145 –49		Same as Nos. 6042–6046.	Great-grandchildren. Children of No. 6144.

65. Descendants of William I., King of Würtemberg, 1781–1864. (See Table VIII.)

6150	957	William II., King of Würtemberg, 1848.	Grandson. Son of the Princess Catherine of Würtemberg, 1821–1898, and her husband, Prince Frederic, 1808–1870.
6151	958	Pauline, Hereditary Princess of Wied, 1877. *Potsdam.*	Great-granddaughter. Daughter of No. 6150.
6152	959	Prince Hermann of Wied, 1899.	Great-great-grandson. Son of No. 6151.
6153	960	Prince William of Saxe-Weimar, 1853. *Heidelberg.*	Grandson. Son of Princess Augusta of Würtemberg, 1826–1898, and her husband, Prince Hermann of Saxe-Weimar, 1825–1901.
6154	961	Prince Hermann of Saxe-Weimar, 1886.	Great-grandchildren. Children of No. 6153.
6155	962	Prince Albert of Saxe-Weimar, 1886.	
6156	963	Princess Sophia of Saxe-Weimar, 1888.	
6157	964	Bernard, Count of Crayenburg, 1855.	
6158	965	Prince Ernest of Saxe-Weimar, 1859. *Ludwigsburg.*	Grandchildren. Brothers and elder sister to No. 6153.
6159	966	Pauline, Dowager Hereditary Grandduchess of Saxe-Weimar, 1852. *Weimar.*	
6160	967	William Ernest, Grandduke of Saxe-Weimar, 1876.	Great-grandchild. Son of No. 6159.
6161	968	Princess Olga of Saxe-Weimar, 1869.	Grandchild. Younger sister to No. 6153.

66. Descendants of Prince Paul of Würtemberg, 1785–1852. (See Table VIII.)

6162 -64		Same as Nos. 6150–6152.	Grandchildren, &c. Descendants of Prince Frederic, 1808–1870.
6165	969	Duke George Alexander of Mecklenburg-Strelitz, 1859. *St. Petersburg.*	Great-grandchildren. Children of the Grandduchess Catherine of Russia, 1827–1894, wife of Duke George of Mecklenburg-Strelitz, 1824–1876, and grandchildren of Princess Charlotte of Würtemberg, 1807–1873, wife of the Grandduke Michael of Russia, 1798–1849.
6166	970	Duke Michael of Mecklenburg-Strelitz, 1863. *St. Petersburg.*	
6167	971	Helen, Princess Albert of Saxe-Altenburg, 1857. *Château de Serrahn, Mecklenburg-Schwerin.*	
6168	972	Prince Nicholas of Nassau, 1832. *Wiesbaden.*	Grandson. Son of the Princess Pauline of Würtemberg, 1810–1856, 2nd wife of William, Duke of Nassau, 1792–1839.
6169	973	*George, Count of Merenberg, 1871. Children, if any, of No. 6169.	Great-grandchildren. Children of No. 6168 by morganatic marriage.
6170	974	*Sophia, Countess Torby [Luxemburg], wife of the Grandduke Michael of Russia, 1868.	

6171	975	*Michael, Count Torby, 1898.	Great-great-grandchildren. Children of No. 6170.
6172	976	*Countess Anastasia Torby, 1892	
6173	977	*Countess Nadejda Torby, 1896.	
6174	978	*Countess Alexandra of Merenberg, 1869.	Great-grandchildren. Younger sister to No. 6169, &c.
6175	979	Frederic, Prince of Waldeck and Pyrmont, 1865.	Great-grandson. Son of the Princess Helen of Nassau, 1831–1888, 1st wife of George Victor, Prince of Waldeck and Pyrmont, 1831–1893, elder daughter of the Princess Pauline of Würtemberg, 1810–1856. *See above.*
6176	980	Josias, Hereditary Prince of Waldeck and Pyrmont, 1896.	Great-great-grandchildren. Children of No. 6175.
6177	981	Prince Maximilian of Waldeck-Pyrmont, 1898.	
6178	982	Princess Helen of Waldeck-Pyrmont, 1899.	
6179	983	Pauline, Princess of Bentheim-Steinfurt, 1855. *Château de Steinfurt, Westphalia.*	Great-granddaughter. Eldest sister to No. 6175.
6180	984	Eberwyn, Hereditary Prince of Bentheim-Steinfurt, 1882.	Great-great-grandchildren. Children of No. 6179.
6181	985	Prince Victor Adolphus of Bentheim-Steinfurt, 1883.	
6182	986	Prince Charles of Bentheim-Steinfurt, 1884.	
6183	987	Prince Alexius of Bentheim-Steinfurt, 1891.	
6184	988	Prince Frederic of Bentheim-Steinfurt, 1894.	
6185	989	Princess Elizabeth of Bentheim-Steinfurt, 1886.	
6186	990	Princess Victoria of Bentheim-Steinfurt, 1887.	
6187	991	Princess Emma of Bentheim-Steinfurt, 1889.	
6188	992	Emma, Queen Dowager of the Netherlands, 1858.	Great-granddaughter. 2nd sister to No. 6175.
6189	993	Wilhelmina, Queen of the Netherlands, 1880.	Great-great-granddaughter. Daughter of No. 6188.
6190	994	Helen, Duchess of Albany, 1861. *Claremont.*	Great-granddaughter. 3rd sister to No. 6175.
6191 –92		Same as Nos. 6067–6068.	Great-great-grandchildren. Children of No. 6190.
6193	995	Princess Elizabeth, wife of Alexander, Hereditary Count of Erbach-Schönburg, 1873. *Schönburg, Hesse.*	Great-granddaughter. 4th sister of No. 6175.
6194	996	Countess Imma of Erbach-Schönburg, 1901.	Great-great-granddaughter. Daughter of No. 6193.
6195	997	Sophia, Queen of Sweden and Norway, 1836.	Granddaughter. Younger daughter of the Princess Pauline of Würtemberg, 1810–1856.
6196	998	Gustavus, Crown Prince of Sweden and Norway, Duke of Wermeland, 1858.	Great-grandson. Son of No. 6195.
6197	999	Gustavus Adolphus, Duke of Scania, 1882.	Great-great-grandchildren. Children of No. 6196.
6198	1000	William, Duke of Sudermania, 1884.	
6199	1001	Eric, Duke of Westmanland, 1889.	

6200	1002	Oscar, Prince Bernadotte, 1859. *Stockholm.*	Great-grandson. 2nd son of No. 6195.
6201	1003	*Count Charles de Wisberg, 1890.	Great-great-grandchildren. Children of No. 6200 by morganatic marriage.
6202	1004	*Count Folke de Wisberg, 1895.	
6203	1005	*Countess Mary de Wisberg, 1889.	
6204	1006	*Countess Sophia de Wisberg, 1892.	
6205	1007	*Countess Victoria de Wisberg, 1893.	
6206	1008	Charles, Duke of Westrogothia, 1861. *Stockholm.*	Great-grandson. 3rd son of No. 6195.
6207	1009	Princess Margaret of Sweden and Norway, 1899.	Great-great-grandchildren. Children of No. 6206.
6208	1010	Princess Martha of Sweden and Norway, 1901.	
6209	1011	Eugene, Duke of Nericia, 1865. *Stockholm.*	Great-grandson. Younger son of No. 6195

67. Descendants of the Princess Catherine of Würtemberg, 1783–1835, 2nd wife of Jerome Bonaparte, King of Westphalia, 1784-1860. (See Table VIII.)

6210 -13		Same as Nos. 1589–1592.	Grandchildren. Children of Prince Napoleon Bonaparte, 1822–1891.
6214	1012	Princess Matilda, widow of Anatole, Count Demidow, Prince of San Donato, -1870, 1820. *Paris, 20 Rue de Berri.*	Daughter.

68. Descendants of Christian, Duke of Schleswig-Holstein Augustenburg, 1798-1869. (See Table VIII.)

6215	1013	Ernest Gunther, Duke of Schleswig and Holstein, 1863. *Primkenau, Sprottau, Silesia.*	Grandchildren. Children of Frederick VIII., Duke of Schleswig and Holstein, 1829–1880.
6216	1014	Augusta Victoria, German Empress, Queen of Prussia, 1858.	
6217 -23		Same as Nos. 6070–6076.	Great-grandchildren, &c. Children of No. 6216.
6224	1015	Caroline Matilda, Duchess of Schleswig-Holstein-Sonderburg-Glucksburg, 1860. *Château de Glucksburg.*	Granddaughter. 2nd sister to No. 6215.
6225	1016	Prince Frederick of Glucksburg, 1891.	Great-grandchildren. Children of No. 6224.
6226	1017	Princess Victoria Adelaide of Glucksburg, 1885.	
6227	1018	Princess Alexandra Victoria of Glucksburg, 1887.	
6228	1019	Princess Helen of Glucksburg, 1888.	
6229	1020	Princess Adelaide of Glucksburg, 1889.	
6230	1021	Princess Caroline Matilda of Glucksburg, 1894.	
6231	1022	Louisa Sophia, Princess Frederic Leopold of Prussia, 1866. *Klein-Glienicke, near Potsdam.*	Granddaughter. 3rd sister to No. 6215.
6232	1023	Prince Frederick Sigismund of Prussia, 1891.	Great-grandchildren. Children of No. 6231.
6233	1024	Prince Frederick Charles of Prussia, 1893.	
6234	1025	Prince Frederick Leopold of Prussia, 1895.	
6235	1026	Princess Victoria Margaret of Prussia, 1890.	
6236	1027	Princess Feodora of Glucksburg, 1874. *Primkenau, Sprottau.*	Granddaughter. 4th sister to No. 6215.

6237	1028	Prince Christian of Schleswig-Holstein, 1831.	}	Son.
		Cumberland Lodge, Windsor Park.		
6238	}			
-40	}	Same as Nos. 6114-6116. Grandchildren. Children of No. 6237.		
6241	1029	Princess Henrietta, wife of John Frederick Augustus	}	
		d'Esmarch, M.D., 1833.	}	Daughter.
		Kiel.	}	

69. Descendants of Frederick, Prince of Noer, 1800–1865. (See Table VIII.)

6242	1030	*Carmelite, wife of Ernest, Count of	}	Grandchildren. Children of
		Rantzu, 1871.		Prince Frederick, Count of
		Children, if any, of No. 6242.	}	Noer, 1830-1881, by mor-
6243	1031	*Countess Louise de Noer, 1873.	}	ganatic marriage.
		Children, if any, of *Princess Louise (daughter), 1836-1866, wife of		
		Michael, Prince Vlangali-Handjéri, 1836.		

70. Descendants of William II., King of the Netherlands, 1792–1849. (See Table IX.)

6244		Same as No. 6189.	{	Granddaughter. Only child of William III., 1817-1890.
6245		Same as No. 6160.	(...)	Great-grandson. Son of Charles Augustus, Hereditary Grandduke of Saxe-Weimar, 1844-1894, and grandson of Sophia of Holland, 1824-1897, wife of Charles Alexander, Grandduke of Saxe-Weimar, 1818-1901.
6246	1032	Mary, Princess Henry VII. of Reuss, 1849.	}	Granddaughter. Daughter of the Princess Sophia of Holland, 1824-1897. *See above.*
		Trebschen, near Züllichau.	}	
6247	1033	Prince Henry XXXII. of Reuss, 1878.	}	Great-grandchildren.
6248	1034	Prince Henry XXXIII. of Reuss, 1879.	}	Children of No.
6249	1035	Prince Henry XXXV. of Reuss, 1887.	}	6246.
6250	1036	Princess Sophia of Reuss, 1884.	}	
6251	1037	Elizabeth, Duchess John Albert of Mecklenburg-Schwerin, 1854.	}	Granddaughter. Younger sister to No. 6246.
		Schwerin.	}	

71. Descendants of Prince Frederick of the Netherlands, 1797–1881. (See Table IX.)

6252	1038	Louisa, Crown Princess of Denmark, 1851.	{	Granddaughter. Daughter of the Princess Louisa of Holland, 1828-1871, wife of Charles XV., King of Sweden and Norway, 1826-1872.
		Château de Charlottenlund.		
6253	1039	Prince Christian of Denmark, 1870.	}	Great-grandchild. Child
		Château de Sorgenfri, Lyngby.	}	of No. 6252.
6254	1040	Prince Frederick of Denmark, 1899.	}	Great-great-grandchildren.
6255	1041	Prince Knud of Denmark, 1900.	}	Children of No. 6253.
6256	1042	Prince Charles of Denmark, 1872.		
		Copenhagen.		
6257	1043	Prince Harold of Denmark, 1876.	}	Great-grandchildren.
6258	1044	Prince Gustavus of Denmark, 1887.	}	Children of No.
6259	1045	Louise, Princess Frederic of Schaumburg-Lippe, 1875.	}	6252.
		Oldenburg.		

6260	1046	Princess Christian of Schaumburg-Lippe, 1898.	Great-great-grand-children. Children of No.6259.
6261	1047	Princess Marie Louise of Schaumburg-Lippe, 1897.	
6262	1048	Princess Stephanie of Schaumburg-Lippe, 1899.	
6263	1049	Ingeburg, Duchess of Westrogothia, 1878.	
6264 –65	}	Same as Nos. 6207–8.	Great-great-grand-children. Children of No. 6263. / Great-grandchildren. Children of No. 6252.
6266	1050	Princess Thyra of Denmark, 1880.	
6267	1051	Princess Dagmar of Denmark, 1890.	
6268	1052	Marie, Princess of Wied, 1845. *Neuwied, Rhenish Prussia.*	Daughter.
6269	1053	Frederic, Hereditary Prince of Wied, 1872. *Potsdam.*	Grandson. Son of No. 6268.
6270		Same as No. 6152. Great-grandchild. Son of No. 6269.	
6271	1054	Prince William of Wied, 1876.	Grandchildren. Children of No. 6268.
6272	1055	Prince Victor of Wied, 1877.	
6273	1056	Princess Louise of Wied, 1880.	
6274	1057	Princess Elizabeth of Wied, 1883.	

72. Descendants of the Princess Marion of the Netherlands, 1810–1883, 1st wife of Prince Albert of Prussia, 1809–1872. (See Table IX.)

6275	1058	Prince Albert of Prussia, Regent of Brunswick, 1837. *Brunswick.*	Son.
6276	1059	Prince Frederick Henry of Prussia, 1874. *Berlin.*	Grandsons. Sons of No. 6275.
6277	1060	Prince Joachim Albert of Prussia, 1876. *Berlin.*	
6278	1061	Prince Frederick William of Prussia, 1880. *Potsdam.*	
6279	1062	Bernard, Hereditary Prince of Saxe-Meiningen, 1851. *Breslau.*	Grandson. Son of the Princess Charlotte of Prussia, 1831–1855, 1st wife of George II., Duke of Saxe-Meiningen.
6280	1063	Feodora, Princess Henry XXX. of Reuss, 1879. *Frankfort on the Oder.*	Great-granddaughter. Daughter of No. 6279.
6281	1064	Princess Mary of Saxe-Meiningen.	Granddaughter. Sister of No. 6279.
6282	1065	Alexandra, Duchess William of Mecklenburg-Schwerin, 1842. *Marly, near Potsdam.*	2nd daughter.
6283	1066	Charlotte, Princess Henry XVIII. of Reuss, 1868. *Ludwigslust.*	Granddaughter. Daughter of No. 6282.
6284	1067	Prince Henry XXXVII. of Reuss, 1888.	Great-grandchildren, &c. Children of No. 6283.
6285	1068	Prince Henry XXXVIII. of Reuss, 1889.	
6286	1069	Prince Henry XLII. of Reuss, 1892.	

73. Descendants of William, Duke of Nassau, 1792–1839. (See Table IX.)

6287	1070	Adolphus, Grandduke of Luxemburg, Duke of Nassau, 1817.	Son.
6288	1071	William, Hereditary Grandduke of Luxemburg, 1852.	Grandchild. Child of No. 6287.

6289 -93	}	Same as Nos. 497–501. {	Great-grandchildren. Children of No. 6288.
6294	1072	Hilda, Grandduchess of Baden, 1864. {	Granddaughter. Daughter of No. 6287.
6295 -301	}	Same as Nos. 6168–6174.	2nd son and his children.
6302	1073	*Countess Vera of Osternburg, 1871. {	Great-granddaughter. Daughter of Duke Nicholas of Oldenburg, 1840 – 1886, by morganatic marriage, and granddaughter of Theresa of Nassau, 1815–1871, wife of Duke Peter of Oldenburg, 1812–1881.
6303	1074	Duke Alexander of Oldenburg, 1844. *St. Petersburg.*	Grandson. Son of Theresa of Nassau, 1815–1871. See above.
6304	1075	Duke Peter of Oldenburg, 1868. *St. Petersburg.*	Great-grandson. Son of No. 6303.
6305	1076	Duke Constantine of Oldenburg, 1850. *St. Petersburg.*	Grandson. Brother to No. 6303.
6306	1077	Grandduke Nicholas Nicholovitch, 1856. *St. Petersburg.*	Great-grandchildren. Children of the Duchess Alexandra, 1838–1900 (sister to No. 6303), wife of the Grandduke Nicholas of Russia, 1831–1891.
6307	1078	Grandduke Peter Nicholovitch, 1864. *St. Petersburg.*	
6308	1079	Prince Roman of Russia.	Great-great-grandchildren. Children of No. 6307.
6309	1080	Princess Marina of Russia.	
6310	1081	Princess Nadeshda of Russia.	
6311	1082	Prince Alexander Romanowski [de Beauharnais], 1881. *St. Petersburg.*	Great-grandchild. Son of Duchess Theresa of Oldenburg, 1852–1883 (sister to No. 6303), wife of George, 5th Duke of Leuchtenburg.
6312	1083	Marie, Princess Dowager of Wied, 1825. *Segenhaus, near Neuwied.*	Daughter.
6313	1084	William, Prince of Wied, 1845. *Neuwied, Rhenish Prussia.*	Grandson. Son of No. 6312.
6314 -19	}	Same as Nos. 6269–6274. {	Great-grandchildren. Children, &c., of No. 6313.
6320	1085	Elizabeth, Queen of Roumania. {	Granddaughter. Daughter of No. 6312.
6321 -55	}	Same as Nos. 6175–6209. {	Descendants of daughters of 2nd marriage.

74. Descendants of the Princess Henrietta of Nassau, 1797–1829, and her husband, the Archduke Charles of Austria, 1771–1847. (See Table IX.)

6356 -449	}	Same as Nos. 1607–1700.

75. Descendants of Henry XIX., Prince of Reuss-Greiz, 1790–1836. (See Table IX.)

6450	1086	Prince Albert of Saxe-Altenburg, 1843. *Château de Serrahn, Mecklenburg-Schwerin.*	Grandson. Son of Louisa of Reuss, 1822–1875, and her 1st husband, Prince Edward of Saxe-Altenburg, 1804–1852.

6451	1087	Princess Olga of Saxe-Altenburg, 1886.	} Great-grandchildren.
6452	1088	Princess Mary of Saxe-Altenburg, 1888.	Children of No. 6450.
6453	1089	Henry XXIV., Prince of Reuss-Kœstritz, 1855. *Ernstbrunn, Lower Austria.*	Grandson. Son of Louisa of Reuss, 1822–1875, and her 2nd husband, Prince Henry IV. of Reuss, 1821–1894.
6454	1090	Prince Henry XXXIX. of Reuss, 1891.	
6455	1091	Prince Henry XLI. of Reuss, 1892.	Great-grandchildren.
6456	1092	Princess Régine of Reuss, 1886.	Children of No.
6457	1093	Princess Sybella of Reuss, 1888.	6453.
6458	1094	Princess Viola of Reuss, 1898.	
6459	1095	Marie, Princess of Schwarzburg-Sondershausen, 1845. *Sondershausen.*	Granddaughter. Daughter of Louisa of Reuss, 1822–1875, by 1st husband. *See above.*
6460	1096	Princess Eleanor of Reuss. 1860.	Granddaughters. Daughters of Louisa of Reuss,
6461	1097	Princess Elizabeth of Reuss. 1865. *Ernstbrunn, Lower Austria.*	1822–1875, by 2nd husband. *See above.*
6462	1098	Princess Amelia of Fürstenburg, 1848. *Baden.*	Granddaughter. Daughter of Elizabeth of Reuss, 1824–1861, wife of Prince Charles Egon of Fürstenburg, 1820–1892.

76. Descendants of Henry XX., Prince of Reuss-Greiz, 1794–1859. (See Table IX.)

6463	1099	Henry XXIV., Prince of Reuss-Greiz, 1878. *Greiz.*	
6464	1100	Princess Emma of Reuss, 1881.	Grandchildren. Children of Henry
6465	1101	Princess Mary of Reuss, 1882.	XXII., Prince of
6466	1102	Princess Caroline of Reuss, 1884.	Reuss-Greiz, 1846–
6467	1103	Princess Hermine of Reuss, 1887.	1902.
6468	1104	Princess Ida of Reuss, 1891.	
6469	1105	Prince Henry of Schönburg-Waldenburg, 1863. *Potsdam.*	Grandchild. Daughter of Hermine of Reuss, 1840–1890, wife of Prince Hugh of Schönburg, 1822–1897.
6470	1106	Princess Hermine of Schönburg-Waldenburg, 1899.	Great-grandchild. Child of No. 6469.
6471	1107	Margaret, Princess Henry of Schönaich-Carolath-Beuthen, 1864.	Grandchildren.
6472	1108	Princess Elizabeth of Schönburg-Waldenburg, 1867. *Droyssig.*	Sisters to No. 6460.
6473	1109	Princess Mary, Dowager Hereditary Countess of Ysemburg-Budingen, 1855.	} Daughter.

77. Descendants of Frederica of Oldenburg, 1820–1891, and her husband, Maximilian Emmanuel Wilibald Jean Gebhard, Baron Washington, 1829. (See Table IX.)

6474	1110	George Washington, 1856.	} Sons.
6475	1111	Stephen Washington, 1858.	

78. Descendants of the Princess Emma of Anhalt-Bernburg-Schaumburg, 1802–1888, and her husband, George II., Prince of Waldeck-Pyrmont, 1789–1845. (See Table IX.)

6476 -79	}	Same as Nos. 6175–6178.	Grandson, &c. Son, &c., of George Victor, Prince of Waldeck-Pyrmont, 1831–1893, by his 1st wife, Helen of Nassau, 1831–1888.
6480	1112	Prince Wolrad Frederick of Waldeck-Pyrmont, 1892.	Grandson. Son of Prince George Victor, 1831–1893, by 2nd marriage.
6481 -96	}	Same as Nos. 6179–6194.	Granddaughter, &c. Daughter, &c., of Prince George Victor, 1831–1893, by 1st wife.
6497	1113	Waffgang, Hereditary Prince of Stolberg-Stolberg, 1849. *Stolberg.*	Grandson. Son of the Princess Augusta of Waldeck-Pyrmont, 1824–1893, wife of Alfred, Prince of Stolberg-Stolberg.
6498	1114	Princess Imagina of Stolberg, 1901.	Great-grandchild. Child of No. 6497.
6499	1115	Prince Vollrath of Stolberg, 1852. *Stolberg.*	
6500	1116	Prince Henry of Stolberg, 1854. *Goslar, in the Harz.*	
6501	1117	Prince Albert of Stolberg, 1861. *Stolberg.*	Grandchildren. Brothers and Sister to No. 6497.
6502	1118	Prince Volkwin of Stolberg, 1865. *Halberstadt.*	
6503	1119	Erika, Countess of Erbach-Erbach, 1856. *Erbach in the Odenwald.*	
6504	1120	Erasmus, Hereditary Count of Erbach-Erbach, 1883.	Great-grandchild. Child of No. 6503.
6505	1121	Hermine, Dowager Princess of Schaumburg-Lippe, 1827.	Daughter.
6506	1122	George, Prince of Schaumburg-Lippe, 1846. *Bucheburg.*	Grandson. Son of No. 6505.
6507	1123	Adolphus, Hereditary Prince of Schaumburg-Lippe, 1883.	
6508	1124	Prince Maurice of Schaumburg-Lippe, 1884.	Great-grandchildren. Sons of No. 6506.
6509	1125	Prince Volrad of Schaumburg-Lippe, 1887.	
6510	1126	Prince Stephen of Schaumburg-Lippe, 1891.	
6511	1127	Prince Henry of Schaumburg-Lippe, 1894.	
6512	1128	Prince Hermann of Schaumburg-Lippe, 1848.	Grandchildren. Sons of No. 6505.
6513	1129	Prince Otho of Schaumburg-Lippe, 1854. *Longeville, Metz.*	
6514	1130	*. . . . . . . Count of Hagenburg, 1895.	Great-grandchildren. Children of No. 6513, by morganatic marriage.
6515	1131	*Countess . . . . of Hagenburg.	
6516	1132	Prince Adolphus of Schaumburg-Lippe, 1859.	Grandchildren. Children of No. 6505.
6517	1133	Hermine, Duchess Maximilian of Würtemberg, 1845.	
6518 -23	}	Same as Nos. 6463–6468.	Grandchildren. Children, &c., of Ida of Schaumburg-Lippe, 1852–1891, wife of Henry XXII. of Reuss, 1846–1902.

79. Descendants of Ida of Anhalt Bernburg-Schaumburg, 1804–1828, 2nd wife of Augustus, Grandduke of Oldenburg, 1783–1853. (See Table IX.)

6524	1134	Augustus, Grandduke of Oldenburg, 1852.	Grandson. Son of Peter, Grandduke of Oldenburg, 1827–1900.	
6525	1135	Nicholas, Hereditary Grandduke of Oldenburg, 1897.	Great-grandchildren. Children of No. 6524.	
6526	1136	Duchess Sophia Charlotte of Oldenburg, 1879.		
6527	1137	Duchess Alice of Oldenburg, 1901.		
6528	1138	Duke George of Oldenburg, 1855.	Grandson.	Brother to No. 6524.

80. Descendants of Alexander of Würtemberg, 1804–1885. (See Table IX.)

6529 -40	}	*Same as Nos. 6138–6149.	Descendants by morganatic marriage.

81. Descendants of Mary Dorothea of Würtemberg, 1797–1855, 3rd wife of the Archduke Joseph of Austria, 1776–1847. (See Table IX.)

6541 -99	}	Same as Nos. 1701–1757.

82. Descendants of Amelia of Würtemberg, 1799–1848, wife of Joseph, Duke of Saxe-Altenburg, 1789–1868. (See Table IX.)

6600	1139	Marie, Queen Dowager of Hanover, 1818.		Eldest daughter.
6601 -8	}	Same as Nos. 6123–6130.	Children and grandchildren of No. 6600.	
6609	1140	Princess Theresa of Saxe-Altenburg, 1823.		2nd daughter.
6610 -14	}	Same as Nos. 6524–6528.	Grandchildren. Children of Elizabeth of Saxe-Altenburg, 1826–1896, wife of Peter, Grandduke of Oldenburg, 1827–1900.	
6615	1141	Alexandra, Grandduchess Constantine of Russia, 1830.		4th daughter.
6616	1142	Grandduke Nicholas Constantinovitch, 1850.	Grandchildren. Children of No. 6615.	
6617	1143	Grandduke Constantine Constantinovitch, 1858.		
6618	1144	Prince John of Russia, 1886.		
6619	1145	Prince Gabriel of Russia, 1887.		
6620	1146	Prince Constantine of Russia, 1890.	Great-grandchildren. Children of No. 6617.	
6621	1147	Prince Oleg of Russia, 1892.		
6622	1148	Prince Igor of Russia, 1894.		
6623	1149	Princess Tatiana of Russia, 1890.		
6624	1150	Grandduke Demetrius Constantinovitch, 1860.	Grandchildren. Youngest son and eldest daughter of No. 6615.	
6625	1151	Olga, Queen of the Hellenes, 1851.		
6626	1152	Constantine, Crown Prince of Greece, Duke of Sparta, 1868. *Château de Dekéleia, near Athens.*	Great-grandson. Son of No. 6625.	
6627 -30	}	Same as Nos. 6085–6088.	Great-great-grandchildren. Children of No. 6626.	

6631	1153	Prince George, Governor of Crete, 1869.	⎫ Great-grandchildren.
6632	1154	Prince Nicholas of Greece, 1872	⎬ Children of No.
6633	1155	Prince Andrew of Greece, 1882.	6625.
6634	1156	Prince Christopher of Greece, 1888.	⎭
6635	1157	Grandduke Demetrius Pavlovitch, 1891.	⎧ Great-great-grandchildren. Children of the Princess Alexandra, Grandduchess Paul Alexandrovitch, 1870–1891, elder daughter of No. 6625.
6636	1158	Grandduchess Mary Pavlovna, 1890.	
6637	1159	Mary, Grandduchess George Michaelovitch, 1878. *St. Petersburg.*	⎫ Great-grandchild. Younger ⎬ daughter of No. 6625.
6638	1160	Vera, Duchess Eugene of Würtemberg, 1854. *Stuttgart.*	⎫ Granddaughter. Younger ⎬ daughter of No. 6615.
6639	1161	Elsa, Princess Albert of Schaumburg-Lippe, 1876. *Wels.*	⎫ Great-grandchild. Elder ⎬ twin daughter of No. 6638.
6640	1162	Prince Maximilian of Schaumburg-Lippe, 1898.	
6641	1163	Prince Francis Joseph of Schaumburg-Lippe, 1899.	⎫ Great-great-grandchildren. ⎬ Children of No. 6639.
6642	1164	Prince Alexander of Schaumburg-Lippe, 1901.	
6643	1165	Olga, Princess Maximilian of Schaumburg-Lippe, 1876. *Ludwigsburg.*	⎫ Great-grandchild. Younger ⎬ twin daughter of No. 6638.
6644	1166	Prince Eugene of Schaumburg-Lippe, 1899.	⎫ Great-great-grandchildren.
6645	1167	Prince Albert of Schaumburg-Lippe, 1900.	⎬ Children of No. 6643.

83. Descendants of Pauline of Würtemberg, 1800–1873, and her husband, William I., King of Würtemberg, 1781–1864. (See Table IX.)

6646 –57	⎱	Same as Nos. 6150–6161.

84. Descendants of Elizabeth of Würtemberg, 1802–1864, wife of Prince William of Baden, 1792–1859. (See Table IX.)

6658	1168	Sophia, Princess of Lippe, 1834. *Carlsruhe.*	⎫
6659	1169	Leopoldina, Princess of Hohenlohe-Langenburg, 1837. *Strasburg.*	⎬ Daughters.
6660	1170	Ernest, Hereditary Prince of Hohenlohe-Langenburg, Regent of Coburg and Gotha, 1863.	⎫ Grandson. Eldest son ⎬ of No. 6659.
6661 –63	⎱	Same as Nos. 6059–6061.	⎰ Great-grandchildren. Children ⎱ of No. 6660.
6664	1171	Elise, Princess Henry XXVII. of Reuss, 1864.	⎫ Granddaughter. Elder ⎬ daughter of No. 6659.
6665	1172	Prince Henry XLIII. of Reuss, 1893.	⎫ Great-grandchildren.
6666	1173	Prince Henry XLV. of Reuss, 1895.	⎬ Children of No. 6664.
6667	1174	Princess Victoria of Reuss, 1889.	
6668	1175	Princess Louisa Adelaide of Reuss, 1890.	⎭

6669	1176	Feodora, Hereditary Princess of Lein- ingen, 1866. *Amorbach, Lower Franconia.*	} Granddaughter. Younger daughter of No. 6659.
6670	1177	Prince Ernich Ernest of Leiningen, 1896.	} Great-grandchildren.
6671	1178	Prince Frederic Charles of Leiningen, 1898.	Children of No.
6672	1179	Prince Hermann of Leiningen, 1901.	6669.
6673	1180	Princess Victoria of Leiningen, 1895.	

85. Descendants of Frederic William I., Elector of Hesse-Cassel, 1802–1875, by his morganatic marriage. (See Table X.)

6674	1181	*Frederick Augustus, Count of Schaum- burg [Hesse], 1864.	} Grandchildren. Children of Prince Frederick William
6675	1182	*Count Louis of Schaumburg, 1872.	of Hanau, 1832–1889.
6676	1183	*William, 3rd Prince of Hanau [Austria and Hesse], 1836. *Horzowitz, Bohemia.*	
6677	1184	*Prince Charles of Hanau, 1840. *Cassel.*	
6678	1185	*Prince Henry of Hanau, 1842. *Berlin.*	} Sons.
6679	1186	*Prince Philip of Hanau, 1844. *Oberurf, Hesse-Nassau.*	
6680	1187	*Frederic, Count of Schaumburg, 1875.	} Grandchildren. Children
6681	1188	*Charles Augustus, Count of Schaumburg, 1878.	of No. 6679.
6682	1189	*Frederick William, Hereditary Prince of Ysemburg-Büdingen à Wächtersbach, 1850.	{ Grandson. Son of Augusta of Hanau, 1829 – 1887, wife of Ferdinand, Prince of Ysemburg, &c.
6683	1190	*Prince Ferdinand Maximilian of Ysemburg, 1880.	
6684	1191	*Princess Mary of Ysemburg, 1881.	
6685	1192	*Princess Elizabeth, wife of Ange-Louis- Alphonso Edward, Count Desrous- seaux de Vandières, 1883. *Vandières, Marne.*	} Great-grandchildren. Children of No. 6682.
6686	1193	*Princess Ida of Ysemburg, 1885.	
6687	1194	*Princess Anne of Ysemburg, 1887.	
6688	1195	*Princess Theresa of Ysemburg, 1888.	
6689	1196	*Prince Maximilian of Ysemburg, 1867.	} Grandchildren. Brother
6690	1197	*Prince Alexandra, wife of Robert, Baron von Pagenhardt, 1855. *Wächtersbach.*	and sister to No. 6682.
6691	1198	*Augustus von Pagenhardt, 1879.	
6692	1199	*Ferdinand von Pagenhardt, 1881.	} Great-grandchildren.
6693	1200	*Robert von Pagenhardt, 1882.	Children of No.
6694	1201	*Maximilian von Pagenhardt, 1884.	6690.
6695	1202	*Kraft von Pagenhardt, 1889.	
6696	1203	*Anna von Pagenhardt, 1890.	
6697	1204	*Gerta, Princess William of Saxe-Weimar, 1863. *Heidelberg.*	} Grandchild. Younger sister to No. 6682, &c.
6698	1205	*Prince Hermann of Saxe-Weimar, 1886.	} Great-grandchildren.
6699	1206	*Prince Albert of Saxe-Weimar, 1886.	Children of No.
6700	1207	*Princess Sophia of Saxe-Weimar, 1888.	6697.

6701	1208	*Prince Kraft of Hohenlohe-Oehringen, 1861.	
6702	1209	*Alexander, Baron von Gabelstein, 1871.	Grandchildren. Children of Alexandra of Hanau, 1830– 1871, wife of Prince Felix of Hohenlohe-Oehringen, 1818–1900.
6703	1210	*Princess Judwiga, wife of Francis Eric, Count of Benzel zu Sternau und Hobenau, 1857. *Château de Jägersburg, Upper Franconia.*	
6704	1211	*Count Hugo Alexander von Benzel zu Sternau, 1881.	Great-grandchildren. Children of No. 6703.
6705	1212	*Count Maurice von Benzel zu Sternau, 1882.	
6706	1213	*Olga, Princess John of Hohenlohe-Oehringen, 1862.	Grandchild. Sister of No. 6701, &c.
6707	1214	*Prince Augustus of Hohenlohe-Oehringen, 1890.	Great-grandchildren. Children of No. 6706.
6708	1215	*Prince Kraft of Hohenlohe-Oehringen, 1892.	
6709	1216	*Princess Alexandrina of Hohenlohe-Oehringen, 1891	
6710	1217	*Princess Dorothy of Hohenlohe-Oehringen, 1892.	
6711	1218	*Louise, Princess Albert of Waldeck and Pyrmont, 1867. *Arolsen.*	Grandchild. Younger sister to No. 6701, &c.
6712	1219	*Prince Charles Alexander of Waldeck and Pyrmont, 1891.	Great-grandchild. Child of No. 6711.
6713	1220	*Mary, Princess of Ardeck, 1839. *Bonn.*	Daughter.
6714	1221	*Frederic William, Prince of Ardeck [Prussia], 1858.	Grandchildren. Children of No. 6713.
6715	1222	*Prince Charles of Ardeck, 1861.	
6716	1223	*Elizabeth, Countess of Ysemburg-Budingen-Philippseich, 1864.	
6717	1224	*Countess Mary Bertha of Ysemburg, 1890.	Great-grandchildren. Children of No. 6716.
6718	1225	*Countess Irmgard of Ysemburg, 1894.	
6719	1226	*Countess Elizabeth of Ysemburg, 1898.	
6720	1227	*Louise, Countess Rudolph of Lippe-Biesterfeld, 1868. *Drogelwitz, near Weissholz, Glogau.*	Grandchild. Younger daughter of No. 6713.
6721	1228	*Count Frederick William of Lippe-Biesterfeld, 1890.	Great-grandchildren. Children of No. 6720.
6722	1229	*Count Ernest of Lippe-Biesterfeld, 1892.	
6723	1230	*Countess Marie of Lippe-Biesterfeld, 1895.	

86. Descendants of Mary of Hesse-Cassel, 1804–1888, wife of Bernard, Duke of Saxe-Meiningen, 1800 – 1882. (See Table X.)

6724	1231	George II., Duke of Saxe-Meiningen, 1826.	Son.
6725 –26		Same as Nos. 6279–6280.	Grandchildren, &c. Son, &c., by 1st wife of No. 6724.
6727	1232	Prince Ernest of Saxe-Meiningen, 1859. *Frankfort-on-the-Main.*	Grandson. Elder son of No. 6724 by 2nd wife.
6728	1233	*George William, Baron of Saalfeld, 1893.	Great-grandchildren. Children of No. 6727.
6729	1234	*Baron . . . . of Saalfeld, 1900.	
6730	1235	*Baroness Elizabeth Helen of Saalfeld, 1895.	
6731	1236	Prince Frederick of Saxe-Meiningen, 1861. *Cologne.*	Grandson. 2nd son of No. 6724 by 2nd wife.

6732	1237	Prince George of Saxe-Meiningen, 1892.	
6733	1238	Prince Ernest of Saxe-Meiningen, 1895.	Great-grandchildren.
6734	1239	Prince Bernard of Saxe-Meiningen, 1901.	Children of No.
6735	1240	Princess Carola of Saxe-Meiningen, 1890.	6731.
6736	1241	Princess Adelaide of Saxe-Meiningen, 1901.	
6737	1242	Princess Louise of Saxe-Meiningen, 1899.	
6738		Same as No. 6281.	Granddaughter. Daughter of No. 6724.
6739	1243	Augustine, Princess Maurice of Saxe-Altenburg, 1843. *Altenburg.*	Daughter.
6740	1244	Prince Ernest of Saxe-Altenburg, 1871. *Potsdam.*	Grandson. Son of No. 6739.
6741	1245	Prince George Maurice of Saxe-Altenburg, 1900.	Great-grandchildren. Children of No. 6740.
6742	1246	Princess Charlotte of Saxe-Altenburg, 1899.	
6743	1247	Mary Anne, Princess of Schaumburg-Lippe, 1864. *Buckeburg.*	Granddaughter. Eldest daughter of No. 6739.
6744 –48		Same as Nos. 6507–6511.	Great-grandchildren. Children of No. 6743.
6749	1248	Elizabeth, Grandduchess Constantine of Russia, 1865.	Granddaughter. 2nd daughter of No. 6739.
6750 –55		Same as Nos. 6618–6623.	Great-grandchildren. Children of No. 6749.
6756	1249	Louise, Princess Edward of Anhalt, 1873. *Dessau.*	Granddaughter. 3rd daughter of No. 6739.
6757	1250	Prince Joachim Ernest of Anhalt, 1901.	Great-grandchildren. Children of No. 6756.
6758	1251	Princess Mary Augustine of Anhalt, 1898.	

87. Descendants of Louisa of Hesse-Cassel, 1789–1867, and her husband, William, Duke of Schleswig-Holstein-Sonderburg-Glucksburg, 1785–1831. (See Table X.)

6759	1252	Frederick Ferdinand, Duke of Schleswig-Holstein-Sonderburg-Glucksburg, 1855. *Château de Glucksburg.*	Grandson. Son of Duke Frederick, 1814–1885.
6760 –65		Same as Nos. 6225–6230.	Great-grandchildren. Children of No. 6759.
6766	1253	Prince Albert of Glucksburg, 1863.	Grandchildren. Brother and sister to No. 6759.
6767	1254	Augusta, Princess William of Hesse-Philippsthal-Barchfeld, 1844. *Rothenburg-on-the-Fulda.*	
6768	1255	Prince Christian of Hesse-Philippsthal-Barchfeld, 1887.	Great-grandchild. Child of No. 6767.
6769	1256	Louisa, Princess of Waldeck and Pyrmont, 1858.	Grandchild. 2nd sister to No. 6759.
6770		Same as No. 6480	Great-grandchild. Son of No. 6769.
6771	1257	Princess Mary, Abbess of a convent at Itzehoe, 1859.	Grandchild. 3rd sister to No. 6759.
6772	1258	Christian IX., King of Denmark, 1818.	4th son.
6773	1259	Frederick, Prince Royal of Denmark, 1843.	Grandson. Eldest son of No. 6772.
6774 –88		Same as Nos. 6253–6267.	Great-grandchildren. Children of No. 6773.
6789	1260	George I., King of the Hellenes, 1845.	Grandson. 2nd son of No. 6772.

6790 –801	}	Same as Nos. 6626–6637.	{ Great-grandchildren. Children of No. 6789.
6802	1261	Prince Waldemar of Denmark, 1858.	{ Grandson. 3rd son of No. 6772.
6803 –7	}	Same as Nos. 467–471.	{ Great-grandchildren. Children of No. 6802.
6808	1262	Alexandra, Queen of the United Kingdom of Great Britain and Ireland, and of the British Dominions beyond the Seas, Empress of India, 1844.	} Granddaughter. Elder daughter of No. 6772.
6809 –19	}	Same as Nos. 6041–6051.	{ Great-grandchildren, &c. Children of No. 6808.
6820	1263	Mary [Dagmar], Dowager-Empress of all the Russias, 1847.	} Granddaughter. 2nd daughter of No. 6772.
6821	1264	Nicholas II., Emperor and Autocrat of all the Russias; Czar at Moscovy, Kief, Vladimir Novgorod, and Astrakhan; Czar of Poland, Siberia, and the Chersonesus; Lord of Pskof; Grandduke of Smolensk, Lithuania, Volhynie, Podolsk, and Finland; Prince of Esthonia, Livonia, Courland, &c., &c., 1868.	} Great-grandson. Son of No. 6820.
6822 –25	}	Same as Nos. 6109–6112.	{ Great-great-grandchildren. Children of No. 6821.
6826	1265	Grandduke Michael of Russia, 1878.	} Great-grandchildren. Younger son and elder daughter of No. 6820.
6827	1266	Xenia, Grandduchess Alexander Michaelovitch, 1866.	
6828	1267	Prince Andrew of Russia, 1897.	} Great-great-grandchildren. Children of No. 6827.
6829	1268	Prince Feodor of Russia, 1898.	
6830	1269	Prince Nicholas of Russia, 1900.	
6831	1270	Prince Demetrius of Russia, 1901.	
6832	1271	Prince . . . . of Russia, 1902.	
6833	1272	Princess Irene of Russia, 1895.	
6834	1273	Olga, Duchess Peter of Oldenburg, 1882. St. Petersburg.	{ Great-grandchild. Younger daughter of No. 6820.
6835	1274	Thyra [Queen of Hanover], Duchess of Brunswick and Luneburg, Duchess of Cumberland, 1853. Gmunden, Upper Austria.	} Grandchild. Youngest daughter of No. 6772.
6836 –40	}	Same as Nos. 6124–6128.	{ Great-grandchildren. Children of No. 6835.
6841	1275	Prince Jules of Glucksburg, 1824.	} Younger sons and daughter.
6842	1276	Prince John of Glucksburg, 1825.	
6843	1277	Frederica, Dowager-Duchess of Anhalt-Bernburg, 1811.	

88. Descendants of the Landgrave William of Hesse-Cassel, 1787–1867. (See Table X.)

6844	1278	Alexander Frederick, Landgrave [and Elector] of Hesse-Cassel, 1863. Philippsruhe, near Hanau.	} Grandsons. Sons of Frederic [Elector] of Hesse, 1826–1884.
6845	1279	Prince Frederick Charles of Hesse, 1868. Frankfort-on-the-Main.	
6846 –51	}	Same as Nos 6090–6095.	{ Great-grandchildren. Children of No. 6845.
6852	1280	Elizabeth, Dowager Hereditary Princess of Anhalt, 1861. Dessau.	} Granddaughter. Eldest sister to Nos. 6844, &c.

The Blood Royal of Britain

6853	1281	Princess Antoinette Anne of Anhalt, 1885.	Great-grandchild. Daughter to No. 6852.
6854	1282	Princess Sybella, wife of Frederic, Baron Vincke, 1877. *Metz.*	Granddaughter. Younger sister to Nos. 6844, &c.
6855	1283	Adelaide, Grandduchess of Luxemburg, 1833.	Granddaughter. Daughter of Mary of Hesse-Cassel, 1814–1895, wife of Frederick of Anhalt, 1799–1864.
6856 -62	}	Same as Nos. 6288–6294.	Great-grandchildren. Children of No. 6855.
6863	1284	Battilda, Princess William of Schaumburg-Lippe, 1837.	Granddaughter. Sister to No. 6855.
6864	1285	Prince Frederic of Schaumburg-Lippe, 1868. *Oldenburg.*	Great-grandchild. Son of No. 6863.
6865 -67	}	Same as Nos. 6260–6262.	Great-great-grandchildren. Children of No. 6864.
6868	1286	Prince Albert of Schaumburg-Lippe. *Wels.*	Great-grandchild. 2nd son of No. 6863.
6869 -71	}	Same as Nos. 6640–6642.	Great-great-grandchildren. Children of No. 6868.
6872	1287	Prince Maximilian of Schaumburg-Lippe, 1871. *Ludwigsburg.*	Great-grandchild. 3rd son of No. 6863.
6873 -74	}	Same as Nos. 6644–6645.	Great-great-grandchildren. Children of No. 6872.
6875	1288	Charlotte, Queen of Würtemberg, 1864.	Great-grandchildren. Elder daughters of No. 6863.
6876	1289	Bathilda, Princess of Waldeck and Pyrmont, 1873.	
6877 -79	}	Same as Nos. 6176–6178.	Great-great-grandchildren. Children of No. 6876.
6880	1290	Adelaide, Princess Ernest of Saxe-Altenburg, 1875. *Potsdam.*	Great-grandchild. 3rd daughter of No. 6863.
6881 -82	}	Same as Nos. 6741–6742.	Great-great-grandchildren. Children of No. 6880.
6883	1291	Princess Alexandra of Schaumburg-Lippe.	Great-grandchild. Child of No. 6883.
6884	1292	Princess Hilda of Anhalt, 1839. *Dessau.*	Granddaughter. Youngest sister of No. 6855, &c.
6885 -952	}	Same as Nos. 6773–6840.	Grandchildren. Descendants of Louisa of Hesse-Cassel, Queen of Denmark, 1817–1898.
6953	1293	*Baron Charles Gustavus de Blixen-Finecke, 1857.	Grandchildren. Children of Augustus of Hesse-Cassel, 1823–1889, and her husband, Charles Frederic Axel Bror, Baron de Blixen-Finecke, 1822–1873.
6954	1294	*Baron Axel de Blixen-Finecke, 1863.	

s

89. Descendants, if any, of Louisa of Hesse-Cassel, 1794–1881, wife of George, Count von der Decken, 1787–1859. (See Table X.)

90. Descendants of Mary of Hesse-Cassel, 1796–1880, wife of George, Grandduke of Mecklenburg-Strelitz, 1779–1860. (See Table X.)

6955	1295	Frederick William, Grandduke of Mecklenburg-Strelitz, 1819.	} Elder son.
6956 -60	}	Same as Nos. 6133-6137. { Grandchildren, &c. of No. 6955.	Children, &c.,
6961	1296	Duke George Alexander of Mecklenburg-Strelitz, 1859. *St. Petersburg and Oranienbaum.* Children, if any, of No. 6961 by morganatic marriage.	
6962	1297	Duke Michael of Mecklenburg-Strelitz, 1863. *St. Petersburg.*	Grandchildren. Children of Duke George, 1824–1876.
6963	1298	Helen, Princess Albert of Saxe-Altenburg, 1857. *Château de Serrahn, Mecklenburg-Schwerin.*	

91. Descendants of Augusta of Hesse-Cassel, 1797–1889, wife of Adolphus, Duke of Cambridge, 1774–1850. (See Table X.)

6964 -82	}	Same as Nos. 6131-6149.

92. Descendants of Christian VII., King of Denmark and Norway, 1749–1808. (See Table XI.)

6983 to 7011	}	Same as Nos. 6215-6243.

93. Descendants of Gustavus [V.], Vasa [King of Sweden], 1799–1877. (See Table XI.)

7012	1299	Caroline [Queen of Sweden], Queen-Dowager of Saxony.	Only child.

94. Descendants of the Princess Sophia of Sweden, 1801–1865, wife of Leopold, Grandduke of Baden, 1790–1852. (See Table XI.)

7013	1300	Frederick, Grandduke of Baden, 1826.	Son.
7014	1301	Frederick, Hereditary Grandduke of Baden, 1857.	Grandchildren.
7015	1302	Victoria, Crown Princess of Sweden and Norway, 1862.	Children of No. 7013.
7016 -18	}	Same as Nos. 6197-6199. {	Great-grandchildren. Children of No. 7015.
7019	1303	Prince Maximilian of Baden, 1867. *Carlsruhe.*	
7020	1304	Mary, Hereditary Princess of Anhalt, 1865. *Dessau.*	Grandchildren. Children of Prince William of Baden, 1829–1897.

7021	1305	Prince Charles of Baden, 1832.	2nd surviving son.
7022	1306	*Frederic, Count of Rhena [Baden], 1877.	Grandson. Son of No. 7021 by morganatic marriage.
7023	1307	Alexandra, Dowager-Duchess of Saxe-Coburg-Gotha, 1820. *Coburg.*	Daughter.
7024	1308	Ernich, Hereditary Prince of Leiningen, 1866. *Amorbach, Lower Franconia.*	Grandson. Son of Mary of Baden, 1834-1899, and her husband, Ernest, Prince of Leiningen.
7025 -28	}	Same as Nos. 6670–6673.	Great-grandchildren. Children of No. 7024.
7029	1309	Grandduke Nicholas Michaelovitch, 1859. *Tiflis.*	Grandsons. Sons of Cecily [Olga] of Baden, 1839–1891, wife of the Grandduke Michael Nicholovitch, 1832.
7030	1310	Grandduke Michael Michaelovitch, 1861.	
7031 -33	}	*Same as Nos. 6171–6173.	Great-grandchildren. Children of No. 7030 by morganatic marriage.
7034	1311	Grandduke George Michaelovitch, 1863. *St. Petersburg.*	Grandsons. Younger brothers to No. 7029, &c.
7035	1312	Grandduke Alexander Michaelovitch, 1866. *St. Petersburg.*	
7036 -41	}	Same as Nos. 6828–6833.	Great-grandchildren. Children of No. 7035.
7042	1313	Grandduke Sergius Michaelovitch, 1869. *St. Petersburg.*	Grandchildren. Youngest brother and sister of No. 7029, &c.
7043	1314	Anastasia, Grandduchess of Mecklenburg-Schwerin, 1860.	
7044	1315	Frederick Francis IV., Grandduke of Mecklenburg-Schwerin, 1882.	Great-grandchildren. Children of No. 7043.
7045	1316	Alexandrina, Princess Christian of Denmark, 1879. *Château de Sorgenfri, near Lyngby.*	
7046 -47	}	Same as Nos. 6254–6255.	Great-great-grandchildren. Children of No. 7045.
7048	1317	Duchess Cecily of Mecklenburg-Schwerin, 1886.	Great-grandchildren. Younger daughter of No. 7043.

95. Descendants of the Princess Cecily of Sweden, 1807–1844, 3rd wife of Augustus, Grandduke of Oldenburg, 1783–1853. (See Table XI.)

7049	1318	*Alexander, Count of Welsburg [Oldenburg], 1878.	Grandchildren. Children of Duke Elimar, 1844–1895, by morganatic marriage.
7050	1319	*Countess Frederica of Welsburg, 1877. *Château de Brogyan, Neutra.*	

96. Descendants of the Princess Caroline of Denmark, 1747–1820, wife of William [IX.] I., Elector of Hesse, 1743–1821. (See Table XI.)

7051 -135	}	Same as Nos. 6674–6758.

97. Descendants of the Princess Louisa of Denmark, 1750–1831, wife of Charles, Landgrave of Hesse-Cassel, 1744–1386. (See Table XI.)

| 7136 –220 | } | Same as Nos. 6759–6843. | |

98. Descendants of William I., King of Prussia, German Emperor, 1797–1881. (See Table XII.)

7221 –47	}	Same as Nos. 6069–6095.	{ Descendants of the Emperor King Frederick III., 1831–1888.
7248	1320	Louisa, Grandduchess of Baden, 1838.	Daughter.
7249 –53	}	Same as Nos. 7014–7018.	Grandchildren. Children of No. 7248.

99. Descendants of Prince Charles of Prussia, 1801–1883. (See Table XII.)

7254	1321	Prince Frederick Leopold of Prussia, 1865. *Klein-Glienicke, near Potsdam.*	}	Grandson. Son of Prince Frederick Charles, 1828– 1885.
7255 –58	}	Same as No. 6232–6235.	{	Great-grandchildren. Children of No. 7254.
7259 –60	}	Same as Nos. 6451–6452.	{	Great-grandchildren. Daughters of Mary of Prussia, 1855–1888, 1st wife of Prince Albert of Saxe-Altenburg, and eldest sister to No. 7254.
7261		Same as No. 6526.	{	Great-grandchild. Daughter of Elizabeth of Prussia, 1857–1895, 1st wife of Augustus, Grandduke of Oldenburg, and 2nd sister to No. 7254.
7262	1322	Louisa Margaret, Duchess of Connaught and Strathearn. *Bagshot Park, Surrey.*	}	Granddaughter. Only surviving sister to No. 7254.
7263 –65	}	Same as Nos. 6064–6066.	{	Great-grandchildren. Children of No. 7262.
7266	1323	Anne, Landgravine of Hesse-Cassel, 1836. *Frankfort-on-the-Main.*	}	Daughter.
7267 –77	}	Same as Nos. 6844–6854.	{	Grandchildren, &c. Children, &c., of No. 7266.

100. Descendants of Prince Albert of Prussia, 1809–1872. (See Table XII.)

7278 –81	}	Same as Nos. 6275–6278.	Son by 1st wife and his children.
7282	1324	*William, Count of Hohenau, 1854.	{ Son by 2nd and morganatic marriage.
7283	1325	*Count Frederick of Hohenau, 1890.	
7284	1326	*Countess Elizabeth of Hohenau, 1879.	} Grandchildren. Children of No. 7282.
7285	1327	*Countess Rosalie of Hohenau, 1880.	
7286	1328	*Countess Mary Victoria of Hohenau, 1889.	
7287	1329	*Count Frederick of Hohenau, 1857.	{ Younger son by 2nd and morganatic marriage.

7288	1330	*Count Albert of Hohenau, 1882.	⎫ Grandchildren. Children
7289	1331	*Count William of Hohenau, 1884.	⎬ of No. 7287.
7290 -97	⎱	Same as Nos. 6279–6286.	⎰ Daughters by 1st wife and their children.

101. Descendants of the Princess Charlotte (afterwards Alexandra) of Prussia, 1798–1860, wife of Nicholas I., Emperor of all the Russias, 1796–1855. (See Table XII.)

7298 -311	⎱	Same as Nos. 6821–6834.	Great-grandchildren. Children of the Czar Alexander III., 1845–1894, and grandchildren of the Czar Alexander II., 1818–1881.
7312	1332	Grandduke Vladimir Alexandrovitch, 1847. *St. Petersburg.*	Grandson. 2nd son of the Czar Alexander II., 1818–1881.
7313	1333	Grandduke Cyril Vladimirovitch, 1876.	⎫ Great-grandchildren.
7314	1334	Grandduke Boris Vladimirovitch, 1877.	⎬ Children of No.
7315	1335	Grandduke Andrew Vladimirovitch, 1879.	⎬ 7312.
7316	1336	Grandduchess Helen Vladimirovna, 1882.	⎭
7317	1337	Grandduke Alexis Alexandrovitch, 1850. *St. Petersburg.*	⎫ Grandsons. Younger
7318	1338	Grandduke Sergius Alexandrovitch, 1857. *Moscow.*	⎬ sons of the Czar Alexander II., 1818–
7319	1339	Grandduke Paul Alexandrovitch, 1860. *St. Petersburg.*	⎭ 1881.
7320 -21	⎱	Same as Nos. 6635–6636.	⎰ Great-grandchildren. Children of No. 7319.
7322	1340	Marie, Duchess of Saxe-Coburg-Gotha, 1853. *Coburg.*	⎱ Daughter.
7323 -33	⎱	Same as Nos. 6052–6062.	⎰ Grandchildren, &c. Children of No. 7322.
7334 -63	⎱	Same as Nos. 6616–6645.	Grandchildren, &c. Children, &c., of the Grandduke Constantine, 1827–1892, 2nd son.
7364 -68	⎱	Same as Nos. 6306–6310.	Grandchildren. Children of the Grandduke Nicholas, 1831–1891, 3rd son.
7369	1341	Grandduke Michael Nicholovitch, 1832. *St. Petersburg.*	⎱ 4th but only surviving son.
7370 -89	⎱	Same as Nos. 7029–7048.	⎰ Grandchildren, &c. Children of No. 7369.
7390	1342	*Nicholas, Duke of Leuchtenberg [Russia], 1868. *St. Petersburg.*	Great-grandson. Son of Nicholas, 3rd Duke of Leuchtenberg, 1843–1890, 1891, by morganatic marriage, and grandson of the Grandduchess Marie of Russia, 1819–1876, and her 1st husband, Maximilian, 2nd Duke of Leuchtenberg, 1817–1852.
7391	1343	*Duke Nicholas of Leuchtenberg, 1896.	⎫
7392	1344	*Duke Maximilian of Leuchtenberg, 1900.	⎬ Great-great-grandchildren.
7393	1345	*Duchess Alexandra of Leuchtenberg, 1895.	⎬ Children of No. 7390.
7394	1346	*Duchess Nadejda of Leuchtenberg, 1898.	⎭
7395	1347	*Duke George of Leuchtenberg, 1872.	⎰ Great-grandson. Younger brother to No. 7390.

7396	1348	*Duke Demetrius of Leuchtenberg, 1898.	Great-great-grandchildren. Children of No. 7395.
7397	1349	*Duchess Helen of Leuchtenberg, 1896.	
7398	1350	*Duchess Natalie of Leuchtenberg, 1900.	
7399	1351	*Daria, Countess of Beauharnais [Russia], wife of Leon, Prince Kotchoubey.	Great-granddaughter. Only child of Eugene, 4th Duke of Leuchtenberg, 1847-1901, by morganatic marriage.
7400	1352	George, Prince Romanowsky, 5th Duke of Leuchtenberg [Russia], 1852. *St. Petersburg.*	Grandson. Son of the Grandduchess Maria of Russia, 1819-1876. See above.
7401	1353	Prince Alexander Romanowsky, 1881.	Great-grandchildren. Children of No. 7400.
7402	1354	Prince Sergej Romanowsky, 1890.	
7403	1355	Princess Helen Romanowsky, 1892.	
7404	1356	Mary, Princess William of Baden, 1841.	Grandchildren. Sisters to No. 7400.
7405	1357	Eugenia, Duchess Alexander of Oldenburg, 1845.	
7406	1358	*Marie Strogonow, wife of Colonel Cheremetiew, 1856.	Grandchild. Daughter of the Grandduchess Marie of Russia, 1819-1876, by her 2nd husband, Gregory Alexandrovitch, Count Strogonow, 1824-1879.

102. Descendants of the Princess Alexandrina of Prussia, 1803–1892, wife of Paul Frederick, Grandduke of Mecklenburg-Schwerin, 1800–1842. (See Table XII.)

7407 -11	}	Same as Nos. 7044-7048.	Great-grandchildren. Children of Frederick Francis III., 1851-1897, and grandchildren of Frederick Francis II., 1823-1883.
7412	1359	Duke Paul Frederick of Mecklenburg-Schwerin, 1852.	Grandson. Son of Duke Frederick Francis II., 1823-1883.
7413	1360	Duke Paul Frederick of Mecklenburg-Schwerin, 1882.	Great-grandchildren. Children of No. 7412.
7414	1361	Duke Henry of Mecklenburg-Schwerin, 1885.	
7415	1362	Duchess Marie Antoinette of Mecklenburg-Schwerin, 1884.	
7416	1363	Duke John Albert of Mecklenburg-Schwerin, 1857.	Grandchildren. Brothers and sister to No. 7412.
7417	1364	Duke Adolphus Frederick of Mecklenburg-Schwerin, 1873.	
7418	1365	Duke Henry of Mecklenburg-Schwerin, 1876.	
7419	1366	Marie, Grandduchess Vladimir Alexandrovitch, 1854.	
7420 -23	}	Same as Nos. 7313-7316.	Great-grandchildren. Children of No. 7419.
7424	1367	Elizabeth, Grandduchess of Oldenburg, 1869.	Grandchild. Younger sister to No. 7412.
7425 -26	}	Same as Nos. 6525 and 6527.	Great-grandchildren. Children of No. 7424.
7427 -30	}	Same as Nos. 6283-6286.	Grandchildren, &c. Daughter, &c., of Duke William of Mecklenburg-Schwerin, 1827-1879.
7431	1368	Prince Hugh of Windisch-Graetz, 1854. *Vienna, 21 Strohgasse.*	Grandson. Son of Louise of Mecklenburg-Schwerin, 1824-1859, 1st wife of Hugh, Prince of Windisch-Graetz.

7432	1369	Prince Hugh of Windisch-Graetz, 1887.	
7433	1370	Prince Alfred of Windisch-Graetz, 1890.	
7434	1371	Prince Edward of Windisch-Graetz, 1891.	
7435	1372	Prince Nicholas of Windisch-Graetz, 1896.	
7436	1373	Prince Gottlieb of Windisch-Graetz, 1899.	Great-grandchildren.
7437	1374	Princess Louise of Windisch-Graetz, 1886.	Children of No.
7438	1375	Princess Elizabeth Matilda of Windisch-Graetz, 1889.	7431.
7439	1376	Princess Olga of Windisch-Graetz, 1893.	
7440	1377	Princess Wilhelmina of Windisch-Graetz, 1894.	
7441	1378	Princess Gabrielle of Windisch-Graetz, 1898.	
7442	1379	Princess Alexandrina of Windisch-Graetz, 1850. *Vienna and Haasberg.*	Grandchildren.
7443	1380	Princess Olga, widow of Andrew, Count Mocenigo, Patrician of Venice, -1878, 1853. *Venice.*	Sisters to No. 7431.
7444	1381	Countess Valentine, wife of Edmund Nicholas, Count Robilant, Baron Cereaglio. *Turin, Via Göeto, 3.*	Great-grandchild. Daughter of No. 7443.
7445	1382	Mary, Duchess Paul Frederick of Mecklenburg-Schwerin, 1856.	Grandchild. Youngest sister to No. 7431.
7446 -48	}	Same as Nos. 7413–7415.	Great-grandchildren. Children of No. 7445.

103. Descendants of the Princess Louisa of Prussia, 1808–1870, and her husband, Prince Frederick of the Netherlands, 1797–1881. (See Table XII.)

7449 -71	}	Same as Nos. 6252–6274.

104. Descendants of the Princess Frederica of Prussia, 1796–1850, and her husband, Leopold, Duke of Anhalt, 1794–1871. (See Table XII.)

7472	1383	Frederick, Duke of Anhalt, 1831.	Son.
7473		Same as No. 6853.	Great-granddaughter. Daughter of the Hereditary Prince Leopold, 1855–1886, son of No. 7472.
7474	1384	Prince Frederick of Anhalt, 1856. *Dessau.*	Grandchildren. Sons of No. 7472.
7475	1385	Prince Edward of Anhalt, 1861. *Dessau.*	
7476 -77	}	Same as Nos. 6757–6758.	Great-grandchildren. Children of No. 7475.
7478	1386	Prince Aribert of Anhalt, 1864. *Dessau.*	Grandchildren. Children of No. 7472.
7479	1387	Elizabeth, Hereditary Grandduchess of Mecklenburg-Strelitz, 1857.	
7480 -83	}	Same as Nos. 6134–6137.	Great-grandchildren. Children of No. 7479.
7484 -86	}	Same as Nos. 6276–6278.	Great-grandchildren, &c. Children, &c., of Marie of Saxe-Altenburg, 1854–1898, wife of Prince Albert of Prussia, and grandchildren of Agnes of Anhalt, 1824–1897, and her husband, Ernest, Duke of Saxe-Altenburg.

| 7487 | 1388 | Mary Anne, Princess Frederic Charles of Prussia, 1837. | } | Younger daughter. |
| 7488 -99 | } | Same as Nos. 7254–7265. | { Grandchildren, &c. Children, &c., of No. 7487. |

105. Descendants of Princess Elizabeth of Prussia, 1815–1815, wife of Prince Charles of Hesse-Darmstadt, 1809–1877. (See Table XII.)

7500 -16	}	Same as Nos. 6096–6112.	{ Grandchildren. Children, &c., of the Grandduke Louis IV. of Hesse, 1837–1892.
7517	1389	*Charles, Count of Nidda [Hesse], 1879.	} Grandchildren. Children of Prince Henry of Hesse, 1838–1900, by his morganatic marriages.
7518	1390	*Eleniar, Baron of Dornberg [Hesse], 1893.	
7519	1391	*Godefroy de Lichtenberg.	{ Grandchild. Son of Prince William of Hesse, 1845–1900, by morganatic marriage.
7520 -40	}	Same as Nos. 7407–7427.	{ Grandchildren. Children of Anne of Hesse, 1843–1865, wife of Frederick Francis II., Grandduke of Mecklenburg-Schwerin.

106. Descendant of Princess Mary of Prussia, 1825–1889, wife of Maximilian II., King of Bavaria, 1811–1864. (See Table XII.)

| 7541 | 1392 | Otho, King of Bavaria. | Son. |

107. Descendants of Princess Wilhelmina of Prussia, 1774–1837, wife of William I., King of the Netherlands, 1772–1843. (See Table XII.)

| 7542 -84 | } | Same as Nos. 6244–6286. |

108. Descendants of the Princess Augusta of Prussia, 1780–1841, and her husband, William II., Elector of Hesse-Cassel, 1777–1847. (See Table XII.)

| 7585 -669 | } | Same as Nos. 6674–6758. |

109. Descendants of the Princess Frederica of Prussia, 1751–1820, wife of William V., Prince of Orange, Stadholder of Holland, 1748–1806. (See Table XII.)

| 7670 -712 | } | Same as Nos. 6244–6286. |

110. Descendants of William, Prince Radziwill, 1797–1870. (See Table XII.)

7713 -31	}	Same as Nos. 3140–3158.

111. Descendants of Prince Bogislaus Radziwill, 1809–1873. (See Table XII.)

7732 -45	}	Same as Nos. 3159–3172.

112. Descendants of Charles Ferdinand, Duke of Brunswick, 1735–1806. (See Table XII.)

7746 -810	}	Same as Nos. 6150–6214.

113. Descendants of Charles Frederick, Grandduke of Saxe-Weimar, 1783–1853. (See Table XII.)

7811		Same as No. 6160.	{ Great-grandchild. Son of the Hereditary Grandduke Charles Augustus, 1844–1894, and grandchild of the Grandduke Charles Alexander, 1818–1901.
7812 -35	}	Same as Nos. 7254–7277.	{ Grandchildren, &c. Descendants of the Princess Mary of Saxe-Weimar, 1808–1877, wife of Prince Charles of Prussia, 1801–1853.
7836 -68	}	Same as Nos. 7221–7253.	{ Grandchildren, &c. Descendants of the Prince Augusta of Saxe-Weimar, 1811–1890, wife of William I., German Emperor, King of Prussia.

114. Descendants of Duke Bernard of Saxe-Weimar, 1792–1862. (See Table XII.)

7869 -77	}	Same as Nos. 6153–6161.	{ Grandchildren. Children of Prince Hermann of Saxe-Weimar, 1825–1901.

115. Descendants of Princess Helen of Mecklenburg-Schwerin, 1814–1858, wife of Ferdinand, Duke of Orleans, 1810–1842. (See Table XII.)

7878 -99	}	Same as Nos. 908–929.

116. Descendants of Frederick I., King of Würtemberg, 1754–1816. (See Table XIII.)

7900 -64	}	Same as Nos. 6150–6214.

117. Descendants of Duke Louis of Würtemberg, 1756–1817. (See Table XIII.)

7965 to 8109	}	Same as Nos. 6529–6673.

118. Descendants of Duke Eugene of Würtemberg, 1788–1857. (See Table XIII.)

8110 -16	}	Same as Nos. 6639–6645.	Great-granddaughters, &c. Daughters of Duke Eugene, 1846–1877, and granddaughters of Duke Eugene, 1820–1875.
8117	1393	Pauline, Madame de Kirbach, 1854, wife of Melchior John Ottocar Willim, M.D. *Breslau.*	Granddaughter. Daughter of Duke Eugene, 1820–1875.
8118	1394	Children, if any, of No. 8117. Nicholas, Duke of Würtemberg, 1833. *Carlsruhe, Silesia.*	Son.
8119	1395	Ernest II., Landgrave of Hesse-Philippsthal, 1846. *Philippsthal, Cassel.*	Grandsons. Sons of Duchess Mary of Würtemberg, 1818–1888, and her husband, Landgrave Charles II., 1803–1868.
8120	1396	Prince Charles of Hesse-Philippsthal, 1853.	
8121	1397	Duchess Alexandrina Matilda of Würtemberg, Abbess of the Noble House of Oberstenfeld, 1829.	Daughter.
8122	1398	Prince Henry XXVII. of Reuss, 1858. *Gera.*	Grandson. Son of Duchess Agnes of Würtemberg, 1835–1886, wife of Henry XIV., Prince of Reuss.
8123 -26	}	Same as Nos. 6665–6668.	Great-grandchildren. Children of No. 8122.
8127	1399	Elizabeth, Princess Hermann of Solms-Braunfels, 1859.	Granddaughter. Sister of No. 8122.
8128	1400	Prince Ernest-Augustus of Solms-Braunfels, 1892.	Great-grandchildren. Children of No. 8127.
8129	1401	Prince Frederick of Solms-Braunfels, 1893.	
8130	1402	Princess Mary Agnes of Solms-Braunfels, 1888.	
8131	1403	Princess Helen of Solms-Braunfels, 1890.	

119. Descendants of Duchess Frederica Louisa of Würtemberg, 1789–1851, wife of Augustus, Prince of Hohenlohe-Oehringen, 1784–1853. (See Table XIII.)

8132	1404	Christian Kraft, Prince of Hohenlohe-Oehringen, 1848. *Oehringen, Würtemberg.*	Grandsons. Sons of Prince Hugh, 1816–1897.
8133	1405	Prince Frederic of Hohenlohe-Oehringen, 1855.	
8134	1406	Princess Erica of Hohenlohe-Oehringen, 1893.	Great-grandchildren. Children of No. 8133.
8135	1407	Princess Elizabeth of Hohenlohe-Oehringen, 1896.	
8136	1408	Prince John of Hohenlohe-Oehringen, 1858.	Grandson. Brother to No. 8133, &c.

8137 -40	}	Same as Nos. 6707–6710.	{	Great-grandchildren. Children of No. 8136.
8141	1409	Prince Max of Hohenlohe-Oehringen, 1860.	{	Grandson. Brother to No. 8133, &c.
8142	1410	Prince Vladimir of Hohenlohe-Oehringen, 1890.		
8143	1411	Prince Max Hugh of Hohenlohe-Oehringen, 1893.		Great-grandchildren. Children of No. 8141.
8144	1412	Princess Margaret of Hohenlohe-Oehringen, 1894.		
8145	1413	Prince Hugh of Hohenlohe-Oehringen, 1864.		
8146	1414	Mary, Princess Henry XIX. of Reuss, 1849. *Metz.*		
8147	1415	Princess Louise, wife of Frederick Louis Ernest, Count of Frankenburg and Ludwigsdorff, Baron Schellindorf, 1851. *Tillowitz.* Children, if any, of No. 8147.		Grandchildren. Youngest brother and sisters to No. 8133, &c.
8148	1416	Princess Margaret, wife of William, Count of Hohenau, 1865. *Potsdam.*		
8149 -52	}	Same as Nos. 7283–7286.	{	Great-grandchildren. Children of No. 8148.
8153 -64	}	Same as Nos. 6701–6712.	{	Grandchildren. Children of Prince Felix, 1818–1900.
8165	1417	Princess Mary of Schwarzburg Sondershaussen, 1837. *Arnstadt and Reichenhall.*		Granddaughter. Daughter of Matilda of Hohenlohe-Oehringen, 1814–1888, 2nd wife of Gonthier Frederick, Charles II., Prince of Schwarzburg, 1801–1889.

120. Descendants of *Alexander, Count of Würtemberg, 1801–1844. (See Table XIII.)

8166	1418	*Countess Wilhelmina of Würtemberg, 1834.	}	Daughters.
8167	1419	*Countess Pauline, wife of Maximilian Henry Adam de Wuthenau, 1836. Children, if any, of No. 8167.		

121. Descendants of *William, 1st Duke of Urach, 1810–1869. (See Table XIII.)

8168	1420	William, 2nd Duke of Urach [Würtemberg], 1864. *Stuttgart.*	}	Son.
8169	1421	*Prince William of Urach, 1897.		
8170	1422	*Prince Charles of Urach, 1899.		
8171	1423	*Princess Gabrielle of Urach, 1893.		Grandchildren. Children of No. 8168.
8172	1424	*Princess Elizabeth of Urach, 1894.		
8173	1425	*Princess Carola of Urach, 1896.		
8174	1426	*Princess . . . . of Urach, 1901.		
8175	1427	*Prince Charles of Urach, 1865. *Stuttgart.*		
8176	1428	*Princess Augustine Eugenia, widow of Francis, Count of Thun and Hohenstein, –1888, 1842. *Gratz.*	}	Children.

8177	1429	*Rudolph, Count of Enzenburg, 1868.	}	Grandchildren. Children of No. 8176 by 1st husband, Rudolph, Count of Enzenburg, 1835–1874
8178	1430	*Count Edward of Enzenburg, 1872.		
8179	1431	*Constantine, Count of Thun and Hohenstein, 1878.	}	Grandchild. Son of No. 8176 by 2nd husband.
8180	1432	*Theodolinda, Countess Velter von der Lilie, 1866.	}	Grandchild. Daughter of No. 8176 by 1st husband.
8181	1433	*Countess Maria of Thun and Hohenstein, 1879.	}	Grandchild. Daughter of No. 8176 by 2nd husband.
8182	1434	*Matilda, Dowager Princess Altieri, 1854. *Rome.*	}	2nd daughter.
8183 -87	}	*Same as Nos. 3952–3956.		Grandchildren. Children of No. 8182.

122. Descendants of Countess Mary of Würtemberg, 1815–1866, wife of William, Count of Taubenheim, 1805–1894. (See Table XIII.)

8188	1435	*Countess Maria of Taubenheim, 1843.	}	Children.
8189	1436	*Olga, Frau von Wollworth-Lauterberg, 1850. Children, if any, of No. 8189.		
8190	1437	*Sophia, Frau Ernest Gayer von Ehrenburg, 1852. *Frankfort-on-Main.*		

123. Descendants of Duke Alexander of Würtemberg, 1804–1881. (See Table XIII.)

8191 -200	}	Same as Nos. 989–998.

124. Descendants of Duke Ernest of Würtemberg, 1807–1868. (See Table XIII.)

8201	1438	*Alexandra de Grunhof, wife of Robert Felix Max Leopold de Kendell, *late* German Ambassador, 1861. Children, if any, of No. 8201.	}	Daughter.

125. Descendants of Nicholas I., Emperor of Russia, 1796–1855. (See Table XIII.)

8202 -310	}	Same as Nos. 7298–7406.

126. Descendants of the Grandduke Michael of Russia, 1798–1849. (See Table XIII.)

8311 -13	}	Same as Nos. 6165–6167.

127. Descendants of the Grandduchess Helen of Russia, 1784–1803, wife of Frederic Louis, Grandduke of Mecklenburg-Schwerin, 1778–1819. (See Table XIII.)

8314	1439	Ernest, Duke of Saxe-Altenburg, 1826.	Grandson. Son of Mary of Mecklenburg-Schwerin, 1803–1862, wife of George, Duke of Saxe-Altenburg, 1796–1853.
8315 –17	}	Same as Nos. 7485–7487.	Great-great-grandchildren. Grandchildren of No. 8314.
8318	1440	Prince Maurice of Saxe-Altenburg, 1829.	Grandson. Brother of No. 8314.
8319 –37	}	Same as Nos. 6740–6758.	Great-grandchildren. Children of No. 8318.

128. Descendants of the Grandduchess Mary of Russia, 1786–1859, wife of Charles Frederic, Grandduke of Saxe-Weimar, 1783–1853. (See Table XIII.)

8338 –95	}	Same as Nos. 7812–7869.

129. Descendants of the Grandduchess Catherine of Russia, 1788–1819, and her 1st husband, Duke George of Oldenburg, 1784–1812. (See Table XIII.)

8396 –405	}	Same as Nos. 6302–6311.

130. Descendants of the Grandduchess Anne of Russia, 1795–1865, wife of William II., King of the Netherlands, 1792–1849. (See Table XIII.)

8406 –13	}	Same as Nos. 6244–6251.

131. Descendants of Augustus, Grandduke of Oldenburg, 1783–1853. (See Table XIII.)

8414 –18	}	Same as Nos. 6524–6528.	Grandsons. Sons of the Grandduke Peter, 1827–1900, son by 2nd wife.
8419 –20	}	*Same as Nos. 7049–7050.	Grandsons. Morganatic sons of Duke Elimar, 1844–1895, son by 3rd wife.
8421 –22	}	*Same as Nos. 6474–6475.	Grandsons. Morganatic sons of Duchess Frederica, 1820– (wife of Baron Washington), daughter by 1st wife.

132. Descendants of Duke George of Oldenburg, 1784–1812. (See Table XIII.)

8423 –32	}	Same as Nos. 6302–6311.

133. Descendants of Louisa of Brandenburg, 1738–1820, wife of Prince Ferdinand of Prussia, 1730–1813. (See Table XII.)

| 8433 –65 | } | Same as Nos. 7713–7745. |

134. Descendants of Gustavus III., King of Sweden, 1746–1792. (See Table XII.)

| 8466 –503 | } | Same as Nos. 7013–7050. |

135. Descendants of Frederic William I., King of Prussia, 1688–1740. (See Table VIII.)

| 8504 to 9786 | } | Same as Nos. 7221–8503. |

136. [3] Descendants of Henry Stuart, Lord Darnley, King Consort of Scotland, 1545–1567. (See Table I.)

| 9787 to 19572 | } | Same as Nos. 1–9786. |

MARY, QUEEN CONSORT OF FRANCE, DUCHESS OF SUFFOLK,
DAUGHTER OF HENRY VII., WITH HER SECOND HUSBAND,
CHARLES (BRANDON), DUKE OF SUFFOLK, K.G.

THE COMMON ANCESTRESS OF NOS. 19573-36735.

*By kind permission of the Earl of Yarborough, from the Portrait in his lordship's
possession. Photo, W. E. Gray.*

The Blood Royal of Britain

B.—Descendants of Mary (Tudor), Queen Consort of France, Duchess of Suffolk, 1496–1533, younger daughter, and in her issue (1558) co-heir of Henry VII., King of England. (See Table I.)

I. Descendants of the Lady Frances Brandon, 15…–1559 (elder daughter and co-heir of Mary Tudor, Queen Consort of France, Duchess of Suffolk), and her husband, Henry Grey, Marquis of Dorset, Duke of Suffolk, K.G., 1510–1554. (See Table XIV.)

137. Descendants of Richard Plantagenet Campbell Temple-Nugent-Brydges-Chandos-Grenville, 3rd and last Duke of Buckingham and Chandos, 10th Lord Kinloss, 1823–1889. (See Table XIV.)

19573	1441	▽ Mary, Baroness Kinloss [S.], 1852. *Stowe, Buckingham.*	Elder daughter.
19574	1442	▽ Hon. Richard George Grenville Morgan-Grenville, 1887.	
19575	1443	▽ Hon. Luis Chandos Francis Temple Morgan-Grenville, 1889.	
19576	1444	▽ Hon. Thomas George Breadalbane Morgan-Grenville, 1891.	Grandchildren. Children of No. 19573.
19577	1445	▽ Hon. Robert William Morgan-Grenville, 1892.	
19578	1446	▽ Hon. Harry Nugent Morgan-Grenville, 1896.	
19579	1447	▽ Hon. Caroline Mary Elizabeth Morgan-Grenville, 1886.	
19580	1448	▽ Caroline Adelaide Hadaway, 1884.	Granddaughters. Daughters of Lady Anne Grenville, 1853–1890 (2nd daughter), and her husband, Lieut.-Colonel George Rowley Hadaway, R.A.
19581	1449	▽ Alice Eva Hadaway, 1888.	
19582	1450	▽ Lady Caroline Jemima Elizabeth Chandos-Grenville, 1856. *Grenville, Godalming.*	3rd daughter.

138. Descendants of the Lady Anne Eliza Mary Grenville, 1820-1879, and her husband, William Henry Powell Gore-Langton, of Newton Park and Hatch Beauchamp, co. Somerset, M.P., 1824-1873. (See Table XIV.)

19583	1451	Algernon William Stephen, 5th Earl Temple [U.K.], 1871. *Chandos House, Cavendish Square, W.*	
19584	1452	Hon. Chandos Graham Gore-Langton, 1873.	
19585	1453	Hon. Evelyn Arthur Grenville Gore-Langton, 1884.	Grandchildren. Children of William Stephen, 4th Earl Temple, 1847-1902.
19586	1454	Lady Gertrude Alice Gore-Langton, 1874.	
19587	1455	Lady Mabel Evelyn Gore-Langton, ⎱ twins,	
19588	1456	Lady Alice Mary Gore-Langton, ⎰ 1876.	
19589	1457	Lady Frances Aline Gore-Langton, 1877.	
19590	1458	Lady Clare Violet, wife of Thomas Francis Egerton, 1880. *The Mount, York.*	
19591	1459	Hon. Henry Powell Gore-Langton, 1854. *Hatch Park, Hatch Beauchamp, Taunton.*	2nd son.
19592	1460	Hubert Edwin Gore-Langton, 1883.	
19593	1461	Robert Lancelot Gore-Langton, 1885.	Grandchildren. Children of No. 19591.
19594	1462	Norman Eric Gore-Langton, 1886.	
19595	1463	Richard Gerald Gore-Langton, 1892.	
19596	1464	Hon. Edward Grenville Gore-Langton, 1858. *La Cava, Bordighera, Italy. Tower Hill, Ascot.*	3rd son.
19597	1465	Grenville Edward Murray Gore-Langton, 1891.	Grandchildren. Children of No. 19576.
19598	1466	Anna Dorothea Florence Gore-Langton, 1894.	
19599	1467	Lady Mary Jane, wife of Colonel Henry Mills Skrine, J.P. *Warleigh Manor, near Bath.*	Elder daughter.
19600	1468	Henry Langton Skrine, 1880.	
19601	1469	Anna Dorothea Mary Skrine.	Grandchildren. Children of No. 19599.
19602	1470	Mary Alice Caroline Skrine.	
19603	1471	Margaret Cicely Skrine.	
19604	1472	Frances Ethel Rosamond Skrine.	
19605	1473	Lady Frances Anne, wife of Henry Gribble Turner, M.C.S. *19 Sloane Gardens, S.W.*	Younger daughter.

139. Descendants of Chandos, 1st Lord Leigh, 1791-1850. (See Table XIV.)

19606	1474	William Henry, 2nd Lord Leigh [U.K.], 1824. *Stoneleigh Abbey, Kenilworth, Warwick.*	Son
19607	1475	Hon. Francis Dudley Leigh, 1855. *27 Hertford St., S.W.*	
19608	1476	Major the Hon. Rupert Leigh, 4th Dragoon Guards, 1856. *Naval and Military; Bachelors'.*	Grandchildren Children of No. 19606.
19609	1477	Hon. Rowland Charles Frederick Leigh, 1859. *St. James'.*	
19610	1478	Margaret Elizabeth, Countess of Jersey [E.], Viscountess Grandison [I.], 1849. *Middleton Park, Bicester. Osterley Park, Isleworth.*	

FRANCES, DUCHESS OF SUFFOLK, ELDER DAUGHTER OF THE PRINCESS MARY (TUDOR) BY CHARLES (BRANDON) DUKE OF SUFFOLK. (WITH HER SECOND HUSBAND, ADRIAN STOKES)

THE COMMON ANCESTRESS OF NOS. 19573–27542

Painted by Lucas de Heere.   From the Portrait Collection at South Kensington, 1866

19611	1479	⋃ George Henry Robert Child, Viscount Villiers, 1873. *Bachelors'; Turf; White's.*	Great-grandchildren. Children of No. 19610.
19612	1480	⋃ Hon. Arthur George Child Villiers, 1883.	
19613	1481	⋃ Lady Margaret, wife of the Hon. Walter Fitz-Uryan Rice, 1875. *24 Chapel Street, S.W.*	
19614	1482	Charles Arthur Uryan Rice, 1899.	Great-great-grandsons. Sons of No. 19613.
19615	1483	Elwyn Villiers Rice, 1900.	
19616	1484	⋃ Mary Julia, Countess of Longford [I.], 1877. *Pakenham Hall, Castle Pollard, Ireland.*	Great-granddaughters. 2nd and 3rd daughters of No. 19610.
19617	1485	⋃ Lady Beatrice Child Villiers, 1880.	
19618	1486	Hon. Agnes Eleanor Leigh, 1853.	Granddaughters. Daughters of No. 19606.
19619	1487	Hon. Mary Cordelia Emily Leigh, 1866.	
19620	1488	Hon. Sir Edward Chandos Leigh, K.C.B., K.C., Recorder of Nottingham, 1832. *45 Upper Grosvenor Street, S.W.*	2nd son.
19621	1489	Chandos Leigh, Captain 1st Battalion King's Own Scottish Borderers, D.S.O., 1873.	Grandchildren. Children of No. 19620.
19622	1490	Edward Henry Leigh, 1888.	
19623	1491	Violet Agnes Evelyn, wife of Bertram Hardy, 1875. *30 Grosvenor Square, W.*	
19624	1492	Audrey Cecilia Leigh, 1880.	
19625	1493	Very Rev. the Hon. James Wentworth Leigh, D.D., 1838, Dean of Hereford. *The Deanery, Hereford.*	3rd son.
19626	1494	Alice Dudley Leigh, 1874.	Grandchild. Daughter of No. 19625.
19627	1495	Hon. Charles Leigh Adderley, J.P., D.L., 1846. *Walton House, Tewkesbury.*	Grandson. Son of the Hon. Julia Anne Eliza Leigh, 1820–1887 and her husband, Charles, 1st Lord Norton.
19628	1496	Ralph Bowyer Adderley, 1872.	
19629	1497	Charles Arthur Reginald Kenelm Adderley, 1881.	
19630	1498	Humphrey James Arden Adderley, 1882.	Great-grandchildren. Children of No. 19627.
19631	1499	Randolph Adderley, 1884.	
19632	1500	Ronald Wolstan Fleetwood Adderley, 1885.	
19633	1501	Sybil Maud, wife of Captain John Charles Digby Pinney, Central India Horse, 1871.	
19634	1502	John Charles William Adderley Pinney, 1896.	Great-great-grandson. Son of No. 19633.
19635	1503	Julia Caroline Margaret Adderley, 1875.	Great-grandchildren. Children of No. 19627.
19636	1504	Dorothy Evelyn Adderley, 1878.	
19637	1505	Gladys Isabel Annette Adderley, 1881.	
19638	1506	Hon. Henry Arden Adderley, J.P., D.L., 1854. *Fillongley Hall, Coventry.*	Grandson. Son of the Hon. Julia Anne Eliza Leigh, 1820–1887, and her husband, Charles, Lord Norton.
19639	1507	Hubert Bowyer Arden Adderley, 1886.	Great-grandchildren. Children of No. 19638.
19640	1508	Muriel Grace Adderley, 1882.	
19641	1509	Ruth Margaret Adderley, 1884.	
19642	1510	Isabel Julia Adderley, 1887.	
19643	1511	Joan Adderley, 1889.	
19644	1512	Lettice Mary Adderley, 1894.	

19645	1513	Rev. and Hon. Reginald Edmund Adderley, 1857. *St. Augustine's Vicarage, Victoria Park, E.*	
19646	1514	Rev. and Hon. James Granville Adderley, 1861. *St. Mark's Vicarage, Marylebone Road, N.W.*	Grandchildren. Younger sons and daughters of
19647	1515	Hon. Anna Margarette Adderley, 1843.	the Hon. Julia Anne
19648	1516	Hon. Caroline Jane Adderley, 1847.	Eliza Leigh, 1820 –
19649	1517	Hon. Frances Georgina Mary Adderley, 1849.	1887, and her husband, Charles, Lord Norton.
19650	1518	Hon. Evelyn Augusta Adderley, 1851.	
19651	1519	Hon. Isabel, Lady Crewe, wife of Sir Vauncey Harpur Crewe, 10th Bart., 1852. *Calke Abbey, Derby.* *Warslow Hall, Ashbourne.*	
19652	1520	Richard Fynderne Harpur Crewe, 1880.	Great-grandchildren.
19653	1521	Hilda Ethelfreda Harpur Crewe, 1877.	Children of No.
19654	1522	Winifred Isabella Harpur Crewe, 1879.	19651.
19655	1523	Airmyne Catherine Harpur Crewe, 1882.	
19656	1524	Frances Caroline Julia Harpur Crewe, 1887.	
19657	1525	Caroline, Dowager Lady Saye and Sele [E.], 1825. 16 *Bridge Street, Hereford.*	Eldest surviving daughter.
19658	1526	Hon. Mary, wife of the Rev. Hon. Henry Pitt Cholmondeley, 1827. *Adlestrop Rectory, near Chipping Norton.*	2nd surviving daughter.
19659	1527	Rev. Francis Grenville Cholmondeley, MA., 1850. *Leek Wootton Vicarage, Warwick.*	
19660	1528	Rev. Lionel Berners Cholmondeley, M.A., 1858. *St. Barnabas, Ushigome, Tokio.*	Grandchildren. Children of
19661	1529	Edward Chandos Cholmondeley, 1860. *Principal, Holkar College, Indore, Central India.*	No. 19658.
19662	1530	Hugh Grenville Cholmondeley, 1897.	Great-grandson. Son of No. 19661.
19663	1531	Henry Reginald Cholmondeley, *late* Captain 2nd Battalion Cheshire. Regiment, D.S.O., 1862.	
19664	1532	Rev. Charles Fiennes Cholmondeley, 1863. *Rectory, Little Sampford, Braintree.*	Grandchildren. Children of
19665	1533	Alice Margarette, wife of the Rev. Harrison Goodenough Hayter, 1849. *The Rectory, Elmdon, Birmingham.*	No. 19658.
19666	1534	George Hayter, 1886.	Great-grandchildren.
19667	1535	John Grenville Hayter, 1890.	Children of No.
19668	1536	Mark Cholmondeley Hayter, 1891.	19665.
19669	1537	James Benedict Arden Hayter, 1893.	
19670	1538	Mary Louisa, Lady Mordaunt, 1851. *Walton Hall, Warwick.*	Granddaughter. Daughter of No. 19658.
19671	1539	Sir Osbert L'Estrange Mordaunt, 11th Bart., 1884. *Walton Hall, Warwick.*	
19672	1540	Adela Mordaunt, 1879.	Great-grandchildren.
19673	1541	Irene Mordaunt, 1880.	Children of No.
19674	1542	Lilian Mordaunt, 1882.	19670.
19675	1543	Cecily Mordaunt, 1889.	
19676	1544	Winifred Mordaunt, 1891.	
19677	1545	Rose Evelyn Cholmondeley, 1856.	Granddaughters. Younger
19678	1546	Eleanor Caroline Cholmondeley, 1858.	daughters of No. 19658.

HENRY (GREY), DUKE OF SUFFOLK, K.G., MARQUIS OF DORSET.

THE COMMON ANCESTOR OF NOS. 19573-27542.

From the Painting by Joannes Corvus in the National Portrait Gallery.

19679	1547	Hon. Louisa Georgina, wife of Lieut.-Col. Francis William Newdigate, *late* Coldstream Guards, 1829. 26 *Seymour Street, W.*	} 3rd and 4th surviving daughters.
19680	1548	Hon. Sophia, wife of Granville William Gresham Leveson-Gower, 1838. *Hookwood, Limpsfield, Surrey.*	
19681	1549	Granville Charles Gresham Leveson-Gower, J.P., 1865. *Titsey Place, Limpsfield.*	} Grandson. Son of No. 19680.
19682	1550	Richard Henry Gresham Leveson-Gower, 1894.	} Great-grandchildren. Children of No. 19681.
19683	1551	Ronald Charles Granville Leveson-Gower, 1896.	
19684	1552	Rev. Frederick Archibald Gresham Leveson-Gower, 1871. *Linton Vicarage, Maidstone.*	} Grandson. Son of No. 19680.
19685	1553	Freda Sophia Gresham Leveson-Gower, 1899.	} Great-granddaughter. Daughter of No. 19684.
19686	1554	Evelyn Marmaduke Gresham Leveson-Gower, 1872. *Langley Lodge, Sutton Valence, Kent.*	} Grandchildren. Children of No. 19680.
19687	1555	Henry Dudley Gresham Leveson-Gower, 1873. *Hookwood, Limpsfield, Surrey.*	
19688	1556	Cecil Octavius Gresham Leveson-Gower, 1875. *Java Lodge, Craignure, Isle of Mull.*	
19689	1557	Granville Howard Roderick Gresham Leveson-Gower, 1900.	} Great-grandson. Son of No. 19688.
19690	1558	Clement Edward Gresham Leveson-Gower, Lieutenant Prince Albert's (Somerset) Light Infantry, 1876.	} Grandchildren. Children of No. 19680.
19691	1559	Margaret Emily, wife of Charles Lyon Liddell, 1862. *The Place, Peasemarch, Sussex.*	
19692	1560	Audrey Margaret Liddell.	} Great-granddaughters. Daughters of No. 19691.
19693	1561	Mary Sophia Liddell.	
19694	1562	Ethel Sophia Gresham Leveson-Gower, 1866.	} Grandchildren. Children of No. 19680.
19695	1563	Katharine Ursula Gresham Leveson-Gower, 1878.	

140. Descendants of Mary Leigh, 1796–1871, and her husband, Captain Frederick Charles Acton Colvile, 1792–1872. (See Table XIV.)

19696	1564	Edward Leigh Mansel Colvile, 1856.	} Grandsons. Sons of the Rev. Frederick Leigh Colvile, 1818–1886.
19697	1565	Spencer Twisleton Colvile, 1856.	
19698	1566	Rev. Gerald Henry Colvile, 1859. *Weston Shifnal Rectory.*	
19699	1567	Mansel Brabazon Fiennes Colvile, 1887.	} Great-grandchildren. Children of No. 19698.
19700	1568	Margaret Elinor Colvile.	
19701	1569	Evelyn May Colvile, 1899.	
19702	1570	Harriet Emily Colvile.	} Granddaughter. Daughter of the Rev. Frederick Leigh Colvile, 1818–1886.
19703	1571	Lieut.-Gen. Fiennes Middleton Colvile, C.B., 1832. *St. Mildred's, Guildford, Surrey.*	} Eldest surviving son.

19704	1572	Captain George Northcote Colvile, Captain 1st Battalion Oxfordshire Light Infantry, D.S.O., 1867.	
19705	1573	Fiennes Maurice Colvile, Lieutenant 1st Battalion Stafford Regiment, 1872.	Grandchildren. Children of No. 19703.
19706	1574	Agnes, wife of G. Hamilton, Barrister-at-Law. 14 Lincoln's Inn, W.C.	
19707	1575	Mary Hilen, wife of Herbert Knollys Bather.	
19708	1576	Isabel, wife of John Clavell Mansell-Pleydell, J.P., D.L.	Elder daughter.
		Whatcombe, Longthorns, Milborne, Dorset.	
19709	1577	Edmund Morton Mansel-Pleydell, Colonel late 12th Royal Lancers, J.P., D.L., 1850. Longthorns, Blandford.	Grandson. Son of No. 19708.
19710	1578	Edmund Morton Mansel-Pleydell, 1886.	
19711	1579	Harry Grove Morton Mansel-Pleydell, 1895.	Great-grandchildren.
19712	1580	Vivien Mansel-Pleydell, 1889.	Children of No. 19709.
19713	1581	Daphne Mansel-Pleydell, 1893.	
19714	1582	Rev. John Colvile Morton Mansel-Pleydell, R.A., 1851. Vicarage, Sturminster Newton, Dorset.	Grandson. 2nd son of No. 19708.
19715	1583	John Morton Mansel-Pleydell, } 1884.	
19716	1584	Evan Morton Mansel-Pleydell, }	
19717	1585	Harry Percy Morton Mansel-Pleydell, 1891.	Great-grandchildren.
19718	1586	Ralph Morton Mansel-Pleydell, 1895.	Children of No. 19714.
19719	1587	Dorothy Isabel Morton Mansel-Pleydell, 1881.	
19720	1588	Cicely Morton Mansel-Pleydell, 1882.	
19721	1589	Caroline Mary Colvile.	Younger daughter.

141. Descendants of Augusta Leigh, –1877, and her husband, Grenville Charles Lennox Berkeley, Esq., 1806–1896. (See Table XIV.)

19722	1590	Alice Berkeley, 1829.	
19723	1591	Georgina Louisa, widow of Sydney Kerr Buller Atherley, –1878, 1831. 17 Chapel Street, S.W.	Daughters.

142. Descendants of Walter Francis, 5th Duke of Buccleuch and 7th Duke of Queensberry, K.G., P.C., 1806–1884. (See Table XV.)

19724	1592	William Henry Walter, 6th Duke of Buccleuch and 8th Duke of Queensberry [S.], 6th Earl of Doncaster [E.], K.G., K.T., 1831. Montagu House, Whitehall, S.W. Dalkeith House, Edinburgh.	Son.
19725	1593	John Charles, Earl of Dalkeith, M.P., 1864. Eildon Hall, St. Boswells, N.B.	Grandson. Son of No. 19724.
19726	1594	Walter John, Lord Whitchester, 1894.	
19727	1595	Hon. William Walter Montagu Douglas Scott, 1896.	
19728	1596	Lady Margaret Ida Montagu Douglas Scott, 1893.	Great-grandchildren. Children of No. 19725.
19729	1597	Lady Sybil Anne Montagu Douglas Scott, 1899.	
19730	1598	Lady Alice Christina Montagu Douglas Scott, 1901.	

MARY, *SUO JURE* BARONESS KINLOSS

THE HEIR OF LINE AND SENIOR CO-HEIR OF THE PRINCESS MARY TUDOR

Photo, L. Varney, Buckingham

19731	1599	Lord George William Montagu Douglas Scott, 1866.	⎫
19732	1600	Lord Henry Francis Montagu Douglas Scott, 1868.	⎪ Grandchildren.
19733	1601	Lord Herbert Andrew Montagu Douglas Scott, 1872.	⎪ Younger sons
19734	1602	Lord Francis George Montagu Douglas Scott, 1879.	⎬ and daughters
19735	1603	Lady Katharine Mary, wife of Major the Hon.	⎪ of No. 19724.
		Thomas Walter Brand, 10th Hussars, 1875.	⎭
		The Hoo, Welwyn, Herts.	
19736	1604	Thomas Henry Brand, 1900. ⎰	Great-grandsons. Sons of
19737	1605	David Francis Brand, 1902. ⎱	No. 19735.
19738	1606	Lady Constance Anne Montagu Douglas ⎱	Grandchild. Youngest
		Scott, 1877. ⎰	daughter of No.19724.
19739	1607	Henry John, 1st Lord Montagu [U.K.], 1832. ⎫	
		Palace House, Beaulieu, Hants. ⎬	2nd son.
		3 *Tilney Street, W.* ⎭	
19740	1608	Hon. John Walter Edward Douglas Scott ⎱	Grandson. Elder son
		Montagu, M.P., 1866. ⎰	of No. 19739.
		3 *Tilney Street, W.*	
19741	1609	Helen Cecil Douglas Scott Montagu, ⎱	Great-grandchild. Only child
		1890. ⎰	of No. 19740.
19742	1610	Hon. Robert Henry Douglas Scott Montagu, ⎫	
		1867. ⎪	Grandchildren. Youn-
19743	1611	Hon. Rachel Cecily, wife of Henry William ⎬	ger son and only
		Forster, M.P., 1868. ⎪	daughter of No.
		Exbury, Southampton. ⎪	19739.
		Southend Hall, Catford, S.E. ⎭	
19744	1612	John Forster, 1893. ⎫	
19745	1613	Alfred Henry Forster, 1898. ⎪	Great-grandchildren. Chil-
19746	1614	Dorothy Charlotte Forster, 1891. ⎬	dren of No. 19743.
19747	1615	Emily Rachel Forster, 1896. ⎭	
19748	1616	Francis Walter Montagu Douglas Scott, ⎫	
		1870. ⎪	
19749	1617	Charles Henry Montagu Douglas Scott, ⎪	Grandchildren. Children
		1862. ⎪	of Lord Walter Charles
19750	1618	Walter George Leon Montagu Douglas ⎬	Montagu Douglas Scott,
		Scott, 1860. ⎪	1834–1895, 3rd son.
19751	1619	Evelyn Mary Montagu Douglas Scott, ⎪	
		1865. ⎭	
19752	1620	Admiral Lord Charles Thomas Montagu Douglas Scott, ⎱	
		K.C.B., 1839. ⎬	4th son.
		Devonport. ⎭	
19753	1621	Charles William Montagu Douglas Scott, ⎱	Grandchildren. Chil-
		1884. ⎰	dren of No. 19752.
19754	1622	David John Montagu Douglas Scott, 1887.	
19755	1623	Victoria Alexandrina, Marchioness of Lothian ⎫	
		[S.], Baroness Ker [U.K.], 1844. ⎬	Eldest daughter.
		Monteviot, Jedburgh, N.B. ⎭	
19756	1624	Robert Schomberg, 10th Marquis of Lothian [S.], ⎫	
		5th Baron Ker [U.K.], 1874. ⎪	
		Newbattle Abbey, Dalkeith, Mid-Lothian. ⎪	Grandchildren.
19757	1625	Lady Cecil Victoria Constance, wife of the Hon. ⎬	Children of
		John Walter Edward Douglas Scott Montagu, ⎪	No. 19755.
		M.P., 1866. ⎪	
		The Lodge, Beaulieu, Hants. ⎭	
19758		Same as No. 19741. ⎰	Great-grandchild. Only
		⎱	child of No. 19757.
19759	1626	Lady Margaret Isobel Kerr, 1868. ⎫	Grandchildren.
19760	1627	Lady Mary, wife of Henry Kidd, 1870. ⎬	Children of
		Lowood House, Melrose, N.B. ⎭	No. 19755.
19761	1628	Robert Charles Henry Kidd, 1899. ⎱	Great-grandchildren. Chil
19762	1629	Mary Cecil Kidd, 1902. ⎰	dren of No. 19760.

19763	1630	Lady Helen Victoria Lilian, wife of Major F. W. Kerr, D.S.O., 1872.	Grandchildren. Children of No. 19755.
19764	1631	Lady Victoria Alexandrina Alberta Kerr, 1876.	
19765	1632	Lady Isobel Alice Adelaide Kerr, 1881.	
19766	1633	Lady Margaret Elizabeth Cameron of Lochiel, 1846. *Achnacarry, Spean Bridge, Inverness.*	2nd daughter.
19767	1634	Donald Walter Cameron, younger, of Lochiel, 1876.	Grandsons. Sons of No. 19766.
19768	1635	Ewen Charles Cameron, 1878.	
19769	1636	Allan George Cameron, 1880.	
19770	1637	Archibald Cameron, 1886.	
19771	1638	Lady Mary Charlotte, widow of Colonel the Hon. Walter Rodolph Trefusis, C.B., 1838–1885, 1851. *45 Princes Gate, S.W.*	Youngest daughter.
19772	1639	Adela Mary Charlotte Trefusis, 1879.	Grandchildren. Children of No. 19771.
19773	1640	Eva Mary Louisa Trefusis, 1880.	
19774	1641	Katherine Helen Elizabeth Trefusis, 1881.	
19775	1642	Marion Gertrude Trefusis, 1882.	
19776	1643	Margaret Harriet Trefusis, 1885.	

143. Descendants of Lady Charlotte Albinia Montagu Douglas Scott, 1799–1828, and her husband, James Thomas, 4th Earl of Courtown, 1794–1858. (See Table XV.)

19777	1644	James George Henry, 5th Earl of Courtown [I.], 4th Baron Saltersford [G.B.], 1823. *Courtown House, Gorey, Ireland.*	Eldest son.
19778	1645	James Walter Milles, Viscount Stopford, 1853. *Marlfield, Gorey, Ireland.*	Grandson. Eldest son of No. 19777.
19779	1646	Hon. James Richard Neville Stopford, 1877.	Great-grandchildren. Children of No. 19778.
19780	1647	Hon. Arthur Stopford, R.N., 1879.	
19781	1648	Hon. Guy Stopford, R.N., 1884.	
19782	1649	Hon. Charles William Stopford, 1892.	
19783	1650	Hon. Sybil Stopford, 1882.	
19784	1651	Hon. Eileen Stopford, 1887.	
19785	1652	Hon. Alma Stopford, 1889.	
19786	1653	Hon. Edith Mary Stopford, 1890.	
19787	1654	Captain the Hon. Edward Barrington Lewis Henry Stopford, 1858. *Norlands, Thomastown, Kilkenny.*	Grandson. 2nd son of No. 19777.
19788	1655	Barrington George Dashwood Stopford, 1889.	Great-grandchildren. Children of No. 19787.
19789	1656	Patricia Eileen Stopford, 1896.	
19790	1657	Hon. George Frederick William Stopford, 1859.	Grandson. Youngest son of No. 19777.
19791	1658	George Christian Noel Stopford, 1891.	Great-grandchildren. Children of No. 19790.
19792	1659	Montagu Henry Aubrey Stopford, 1894.	
19793	1660	Sydney Vivian James Stopford.	
19794	1661	Cynthia Mareli Mabel Stopford, 1899.	
19795	1662	Lady Charlotte Elizabeth Stopford, 1847.	Granddaughters. Daughters of No. 19777.
19796	1663	Lady Eleanor Margaret Stopford, 1849.	
19797	1664	Lady Mary Jane Jemima, wife of Lieut.-Col. Sir Charles Shelley, 5th Bart., 1851. *Avington, Alresford, Hants.*	

19798	1665	John Courtown Edward Shelley, 1871.	
19799	1666	Percy Bysshe Shelley, 1872.	
19800	1667	Cecil William Charles Shelley, 1873.	Great-grandchildren.
19801	1668	Sydney Patrick Shelley, 1880.	Children of No.
19802	1669	Hubert Shelley, 1881.	19797.
19803	1670	Ernestine Elizabeth Shelley.	
19804	1671	Maud Shelley.	
19805	1672	Nora Kathleen Shelley.	
19806	1673	Lady Grace Harriet, wife of Captain J. Strachan Bridges, 1854. *Woodcote, Fleet, Hants.*	Granddaughter. 4th daughter of No. 19777.
19807	1674	Mary Frances Conway Bridges, 1880.	Great-grandchildren.
19808	1675	Muriel Grace Bridges, 1883.	Children of No.
19809	1676	Monica Bridges, 1888.	19806.
19810	1677	Lady Lily Frances, wife of Sir William Conyngham Greene, K.C.B., 1862. *Glencarrig House, Glenealy, Wicklow.*	Granddaughter. 5th daughter of No. 19777.
19811	1678	Barrington Stopford Conyngham Greene, 1888.	Great-grandchildren.
19812	1679	Geoffrey Plunket Conyngham Greene, 1893.	Children of No.
19813	1680	Kathleen Conyngham Greene, 1885.	dren of No.
19814	1681	Norah Conyngham Greene, 1889.	19810.

144. Descendants of Lady Isabella Mary Montagu Douglas Scott, 1800–1829, and her husband, Lieut.-Col. the Hon. Peregrine Francis Cust, 1791–1873. (See Table XV.)

19815	1682	Lieut.-Col. John Francis Cust, 1825. *Harewood Bridge, Leeds.*	
19816	1683	Charlotte Isabella, wife of Colonel John Clark-Kennedy, C.B., 1828. 6 *West Eaton Place, S.W.* *Knockgray, N.B.*	Son and daughter.
19817	1684	Minnie Frances, Lady Hampson, wife of Sir George Francis Hampson, 10th Bart. 62 *Stanhope Gardens, S.W.* *Thurnham Court, Maidstone.*	Granddaughter. Eldest daughter of No. 19816.
19818	1685	Dennys Francis Hampson, 1897.	Great-grandchildren.
19819	1686	Marjorie Eleanor Hampson, 1895.	Children of No.
19820	1687	Honoria Mary Hampson, 1900.	19817.
19821	1688	Isabella Charlotte Clark-Kennedy.	Granddaughters. Younger
19822	1689	Harriet Sophia, wife of Captain Stewart Lygon Murray.	daughters of No. 19816.
19823	1690	Elsie Dorothea Isabel Murray, 1897.	Great-granddaughter. Daughter of No. 19822.

145. Descendants of Lady Margaret Harriet Montagu Douglas Scott, 1811–1846, and her husband, Charles, 3rd Earl of Romney, 1808–1874. (See Table XV.)

19824	1691	Charles, 4th Earl of Romney [G.B.], 1841. 4 *Upper Belgrave Street, S.W.*	Eldest son.
19825	1692	▽ Charles, Viscount Marsham, 1864. 2 *Herbert Crescent, S.W.*	Grandson. Eldest son of No. 19824.

19826	1693	▽ Hon. Charles Marsham, 1892.	Great-grandson. Son of No. 19825.
19827	1694	▽ Captain the Hon. Reginald Hastings Marsham, 7th Hussars, 1865.	
19828	1695	▽ Hon. Sydney Edward Marsham, 1879.	Grandchildren.
19829	1696	▽ Lady Florence Mary Constance Hare, wife of Sir George Ralph Leigh Hare, 3rd Bart., 1868. *Gressenhall House, East Dereham, Norfolk.*	Children of No. 19824.
19830	1697	Grace Constance Leigh Hare, 1893.	Great-grandchildren.
19831	1698	Mary Leigh Hare, 1896.	Children of No.
19832	1699	Marjorie Florence Rhoda Leigh Hare, 1897.	19829.
19833	1700	Rev. and Hon. John Marsham, Rector of Barton Segrave, 1842. *Barton Segrave Rectory, near Kettering.*	2nd son.
19834	1701	Keith Henry Marsham, 1868.	
19835	1702	Walter John Marsham, 1869.	
19836	1703	Cyril Montagu Charles Marsham, 1871.	
19837	1704	Hubert Wheler Marsham, 1876.	
19838	1705	John Ralph Theodore Marsham, 1885.	Grandchildren.
19839	1706	Mabel Pensie Marsham, 1867.	Children of
19840	1707	Violet Mary Marsham, 1872.	No. 19833.
19841	1708	Evelyn Florence Marsham, 1874.	
19842	1709	Grace Margaret Marsham, 1877.	
19843	1710	Mary Verena Marsham, 1878.	
19844	1711	Olive Home Marsham, 1881.	
19845	1712	Hon. Henry Marsham, 1845. *28 Bury Street, St. James's, S.W.*	3rd son and eldest daughter.
19846	1713	Lady Margaret Marsham, 1834. *Weavering House, Maidstone.*	
19847	1714	Arthur Fletcher, 1868.	
19848	1715	Herbert Fletcher, 1871.	Grandchildren. Children of
19849	1716	Wilfred Fletcher, 1875.	the Lady Harriet Mars-
19850	1717	Harold John Fletcher, 1876.	ham, 1838–1886, and her
19851	1718	Maud Ellen, wife of the Rev. Hugh Cairns Alexander Back, 1865. *Rostherne Vicarage, Knutsford, Cheshire.*	husband, Colonel Henry Charles Fletcher, C.M.G., –1879.
19852	1719	Terence Hugh Back, 1895.	Great-grandchildren. Chil-
19853	1720	Cecily Maud Back, 1893.	dren of No. 19851.
19854	1721	Edith Margaret Fletcher, 1870.	Grandchildren. Younger
19855	1722	Muriel Harriet, wife of Henry Fitzherbert Wright, 1873. *3 Kensington Court, W.*	daughters of Colonel and Lady Harriet Fletcher.
19856	1723	Helen Hermione Wright, 1897.	Great-grandchildren. Chil-
19857	1724	Margaret Stella Wright, 1899.	dren of No. 19855.
19858	1725	Evelyn Wright, 1901.	
19859	1726	Agnes Stella Mary Fletcher, 1879.	Granddaughter. Youngest daughter of Colonel and Lady Harriet Fletcher
19860	1727	Lady Mary Marsham, 1840. *Weavering House,*	Daughters.
19861	1728	Lady Anne Marsham, 1846. *Maidstone.*	

The Blood Royal of Britain

146. Descendants of Lady Harriet Janet Sarah Montagu Douglas Scott, 1814–1870, and her husband, the Rev. Edward Moore, of Frittenden House, co. Kent, M.A., Hon. Canon of Canterbury Cathedral, Rural Dean, 1814–1889. (See Table XV.)

19862	1729	Rev. Edward Marsham Moore, M.A., Hon. Canon of Peterborough Cathedral, Rural Dean, 1844. } Son. *Benefield Rectory, Oundle.*
19863	1730	Aubrey Edward Duncombe Moore, Lieutenant R.N., 1879. } Grandchildren. Children of No. 19862.
19864	1731	Noel Arthur Moore, 1889.
19865	1732	Constance Evelyn Harriet Moore, 1886.
19866	1733	Charles Henry Moore, *formerly* Member of the Bengal Legislative Council, 1846. *22 Ryder Street, S.W.*
19867	1734	Sir Arthur William Moore, Rear-Admiral R.N., K.C.B., C.M.G., Commander-in-chief of the Cape of Good Hope and West Africa Station, 1847. } Sons. *Admiralty House, Simon's Bay.*
19868	1735	Henry Walter Moore, 1849. *Geraldine, Canterbury, New Zealand.*
19869	1736	Francis Henry Moore, 1881. Grandson. Son of No. 19868.
19870	1737	William Francis Moore, 1850. } 5th son. *1 Fulwood Park, Liverpool.*
19871	1738	William Arthur Montagu Moore, 1884. } Grandchildren. Children of No. 19870.
19872	1739	Evelyn Marjorie Moore, 1882.
19873	1740	Gwendolen Mary Harriet Moore, 1883.
19874	1741	Elinor Alice Moore, 1887.
19875	1742	Kathleen Victoria Moore, 1888.
19876	1743	Elfreda Helen Moore, 1892.
19877	1744	Lieut.-Col. Walter Montagu Moore, New Zealand Volunteers, 1851. } 6th son. *Geraldine, Canterbury, New Zealand.*
19878	1745	Walter Hugh Moore, 1881. Grandson. Son of No. 19877.
19879	1746	Francis Edward Moore, 1853. } 7th son. *Adbury, Hawera, New Zealand.*
19880	1747	John Moore, 1897. } Grandchildren. Children of No. 19879.
19881	1748	Phyllis Marion Moore, 1885.
19882	1749	Dorothy Evelyn Moore, 1886.
19883	1750	Marjorie Frances Moore, 1891.
19884	1751	Evelyn Moore, 1892.
19885	1752	Rev. Herbert Octavius Moore, M.A., Domestic Chaplain to the Lord Bishop of Calcutta, 1854. } 8th son. *The Palace, Calcutta.*
19886	1753	Alice Margaret, wife of the Rev. Sidney Phillips, Vicar of Kidderminster, 1845. } Elder daughter. *Kidderminster.*
19887	1754	Rev. Basil Sidney Phillips, 1875. *Dorking.* } Grandchildren. Children of No. 19886.
19888	1755	Francis Edward Phillips, 1880.
19889	1756	Sidney Piers Victor Phillips, 1887.
19890	1757	Mary Alice Phillips, 1869.
19891	1758	Hilda Fanny Harriet Phillips, 1871.
19892	1759	Monica Evelyn Juliet, wife of the Rev. George Philip Trevelyan, 1872. *10 Kemerton Road, Beckenham.*
19893	1760	Mary Trevelyan, 1897. } Great-grandchildren. Children of No. 19892.
19894	1761	Avice Trevelyan, 1898.
19895	1762	Beryl Trevelyan, 1899.

19896	1763	Florence Montagu, wife of the Rev. Oswald Allen Moore, 1873. *Lower Mitton Vicarage, Stourport, Worcs.*	Grandchild. 4th daughter of No. 19886.
19897	1764	Stephen Sidney Moore, 1902.	Great-grandchild. Son of No. 19896.
19898	1765	Dorothy Margaret Phillips, 1877.	Grandchild. 5th daughter of No. 19886.
19899	1766	Hon. Evelyn Isabella Moore, *formerly* Maid of Honour to Queen Victoria, 1856. *Admiralty House, Simon's Bay.*	Daughter.

147. Descendants of the Hon. Lucy Elizabeth Scott Montagu, 1805–1877, and her husband, Cospatrick Alexander, 11th Earl of Home, 1799–1881. (See Table XVI.)

19900	1767	Charles Alexander, 12th Earl of Home [S.], 2nd Baron Douglas [U.K.], 1834. *The Hirsel, Coldstream.* 6 *Grosvenor Square, W.*	Son.
19901	1768	Charles Cospatrick Archibald, Lord Dunglass, 1873.	Grandchildren. Only son and eldest daughter of No. 19900.
19902	1769	Mary Elizabeth Margaret, Lady Gillford, 1871. 32 *Belgrave Square, S.W.*	
19903	1770	Hon. Theodosia Beatrix Catherine Mary Meade, 1898.	Great-granddaughter. Daughter of No. 19902.
19904	1771	Lady Beatrix Lucy, wife of Captain Henry Herbert Philip Dundas, 1876.	Granddaughter. 2nd daughter of No. 19900.
19905	1772	Philip Dundas, 1899.	Great-grandson. Only child of No. 19904.
19906	1773	Lady Margaret Jane Douglas Home, 1880.	Granddaughters. 3rd and 4th daughters of No. 19900.
19907	1774	Lady Isobel Charlotte Douglas Home, 1882.	
19908	1775	Hon. James Archibald Home, 1837. 66 *Curzon Street, Mayfair, W.*	
19909	1776	Major-General the Hon. William Sholto Home, 1842. *Cliveden Chambers, Mount Street, W.*	
19910	1777	Lieut.-Col. the Hon. Cospatrick Home, 1848. *Naval and Military ; Carlton.*	Sons and daughters.
19911	1778	Hon. George Douglas Home, 1853. *Bonkyl Lodge, Duns, N.B.*	
19912	1779	Lady Elizabeth Eleanora Home, 1844. *Bonkyl Lodge, Duns, N.B.*	
19913	1780	Lady Ada, wife of the Hon. Henry Robert Hepburne-Scott, 1846. *Knipton Lodge, Grantham.*	
19914	1781	James Cospatrick Hepburne Scott, 1882.	Grandchildren. Children of No. 19913.
19915	1782	Francis William Hepburne Scott, 1886.	
19916	1783	Lucy Georgina Hepburne Scott, 1881.	
19917	1784	Mary Helen Charlotte Hepburne Scott, 1885.	
19918	1785	Lady Charlotte Lucy Home, 1850. *Bonkyl Lodge, Duns, N.B.*	Youngest daughter.

148. Descendants of the Hon. Mary Margaret Scott Montagu, 1807–1885, and her husband, Colonel Frederick Clinton, Grenadier Guards, 1804–1870. (See Table XVI.)

19919	1786	Lieut.-Col. Henry Renebald Clinton, *late* Grenadier Guards, 1841.	
		Ashley Clinton, Lymington.	Sons.
19920	1787	Rev. William Osbert Clinton, 1850.	
		The Rectory, Padworth, Berks.	
19921	1788	Walter Laurence Clinton, 1883.	Grandchildren. Children of No. 19920.
19922	1789	Frances Eleanor Clinton, 1881.	
19923	1790	Lucy Dorothea Marryat, wife of George Selwyn Marryat, 1843.	Daughter.
19924	1791	Mary Margaret Jephson, wife of the Rev. William Vincent Jephson.	Grandchildren. Children of No. 19923.
		Chilworth Vicarage, Romsey.	
19925	1792	Dorothea Charlotte Edith Marryat	

149. Descendants of the Hon. Caroline Georgina Scott Montagu, –1891, and her husband, George William Hope, Esq., of Luffness, M.P., 1808–1863. (See Table XVI.)

19926	1793	Henry Walter Hope.	Son.
		Luffness, Aberlady, Haddington.	
19927	1794	George Everard Hope, 1886.	Grandchild. Son of No. 19926.
19928	1795	Caroline Violet Mary Hope, 1878.	Granddaughter. Only daughter of Colonel Montagu Hope, 1844–1870.
19929	1796	Edward Stanley Hope, C.B., 1846.	3rd son.
		102 *Gloucester Place, Portman Square, W.*	
19930	1797	John Alexander Henry Hope, 1882.	Grandchildren. Children of No. 19929.
19931	1798	Elizabeth Caroline Hope, 1885.	
19932	1799	Herbert James Hope, 1851.	
		23 *Down Street, W.*	
19933	1800	Caroline Jane Hope.	4th son and daughters.
19934	1801	Lucy Georgina Hope.	
		North Berwick, N.B.	

150. Descendants of James Thomas, 4th Earl of Courtown, 1794–1858. (See Table XVII.)

19935 –72		Same as Nos. 19777–19814.	
19973	1802	Dora Claire Stopford, 1883.	Granddaughter. Only daughter of the Hon. John Montagu Stopford, 1853–1885.
19974	1803	Colonel the Hon. Frederick William Stopford, C.B., 1854.	2nd surviving son.
		Guards'; Travellers'.	
19975	1804	Captain the Hon. Walter George Stopford, R.N., 1855, Naval Adviser and Inspector-General of Fortifications.	3rd surviving son.
		10 *Courtfield Road, S.W.*	

19976	1805	Walter John Stopford, 1897.	⎫ Grandchildren.
19977	1806	Frederick Stopford, 1900.	⎬ Children of
19978	1807	Dora Mary Loraine Stopford, 1894.	⎭ No. 19975.

151. Descendants of Lieut.-Col. the Hon. Edward Stopford, 1795–1840. (See Table XVII.)

19979	1808	The Rev. Frederick Manners Stopford, M.A., 1831. *Tichmarsh Rectory, Thrapston.*	⎱ Son.
19980	1809	Algernon Edward Stopford, 1858. *Australia.*	Grandson. Son of No. 19979.
19981	1810	Grosvenor Francis Stopford, 1889.	Great-grandchildren. Children of No. 19980.
19982	1811	Eveleen Emma Stopford, 1891.	
19983	1812	Albert Henry Stopford, 1860.	Grandsons. Sons
19984	1813	Francis Powys Stopford, 1861.	of No. 19979.
19985	1814	Mary Horatia Stopford, 1896.	Great-grandchildren. Children of No. 19984.
19986	1815	Eveleen Emily Stopford, 1897.	
19987	1816	Kathleen Stewart Stopford, ⎱ 1900.	
19988	1817	Eleanor Montagu Stopford, ⎰	
19989	1818	Charles Alexander Stopford, 1864.	
19990	1819	Wilfrid Sydney Stopford, 1868. *9 Brook Street, Grosvenor Square, W.*	Grandchildren. Children of No. 19979.
19991	1820	Gerald Frederick Stopford, 1870.	
19992	1821	Walter Montagu Stopford, 1874.	
19993	1822	Mary Kathleen, wife of the Rev. William Percy Powys, 1863.	
19994	1823	Eveleen Frances Stopford, 1871.	
19995	1824	Walter James Stopford, C.B., 1833. *107 St. George's Square, S.W.*	Youngest son.
19996	1825	Edward Montagu Stopford, 1872.	Grandchildren. Sons and eldest daughter of No. 19995.
19997	1826	Cyril Montagu Stopford, 1874.	
19998	1827	Horatia Winifred, wife of Edward Constable Curtis, 1864. *The Old Rectory House, North Petherton, nr. Bridgewater.*	
19999	1828	Walter Stopford Constable Curtis, 1899.	Great-grandchildren. Son and daughter of No. 19998.
20000	1829	Mabel Rose Constable Curtis, 1900.	
20001	1830	Louise Stopford, 1865.	Granddaughters. Younger daughters of No. 19995.
20002	1831	Nina Stopford, 1868.	
20003	1832	Annette Hilda Stopford.	
20004	1833	Hon. Horatia Charlotte Frances Stopford, V.A., one of the Bedchamber Women in Ordinary to the late Queen. *6 St. Katharine's, Regent's Park, N.W.*	Daughter.

152. Descendants of the Hon. Sir Montagu Stopford, 1798–1864. (See Table XVII.)

20005	1834	Charlotte Mary Leycester, widow of John Arden Birch, 1855. *15 Ennismore Gardens, S.W.*	Granddaughter. Eldest daughter of Major George Montagu Stopford, R.E., 1828–1860.

20006	1835	John Henry Stopford Birch, 1883.	
20007	1836	George Charles Birch, 1887.	Great-grandchildren.
20008	1837	Francis Lyall Birch, 1889.	Children of No.
20009	1838	Dorothy Julia Charlotte Birch, 1882.	20005.
20010	1839	Cecily Mary Birch, 1885.	
20011	1840	Caroline Anne Kate, wife of W. Morton Philips, 1856. *Heybridge, Staffordshire.*	Granddaughter. Younger daughter of Major George Montagu Stopford, 1828–1860.
20012	1841	Mark Hibbert Philips, 1886.	
20013	1842	Humphrey Burgoyne Philips, 1894.	Great-grandchildren.
20014	1843	Mary Adelaide Philips, 1884.	Children of No.
20015	1844	Christobel Selina Philips, 1888.	20011.
20016	1845	Rosamond Winifred Philips, 1889.	
20017	1846	Montagu Charles Henry Stopford, 1837.	
20018	1847	Captain Lionel Arthur Montagu Stopford, 1860. *Naval and Military.*	Sons.
20019	1848	Montagu George North Stopford, 1892.	Grandsons. Sons
20020	1849	Lionel Montagu Phipps Stopford.	of No. 20018.
20021	1850	Mary Cordelia, Lady Adye, widow of General Sir John Millar Adye, G.C.B., 1831. *92 St. George's Square, S.W.*	Daughter.
20022	1851	Lieut.-Col. John Adye, R.A., C.B., 1857. *Junior United Service*	Grandchild. Son of No. 20021.
20023	1852	John Frederick Adye, 1900.	Great-grandchild. Son of No. 20022.
20024	1853	Captain Mortimer Stopford Adye, 1867. *Junior United Service.*	Grandchildren.
20025	1854	Winifreda Jane, wife of William Armstrong Watson-Armstrong, J.P., D.L., 1860. *Cragside, Rothbury, Northumberland.*	Children of No. 20021.
20026	1855	William John Montagu Watson-Armstrong, 1892.	Great-grandchildren.
20027	1856	Winifreda Margaret Watson-Armstrong, 1894.	Children of No. 20025.
20028	1857	Mary Caroline, wife of Lieut.-Col. Apsley Smith, R.A., C.B., 1861.	Granddaughter. 2nd daughter of No. 20021.
20029	1858	Winifreda Emily Mary Smith, 1887.	Great-granddaughter. Daughter of No. 20028.
20030	1859	Ethel Montagu Adye, 1865.	Granddaughters. 3rd and 4th daughters of No. 20021.
20031	1860	Evelyn Violet, wife of John Meade Falkner, 1869. *The Divinity House, Durham.*	
20032	1861	Annette Jane, wife of Captain Walter James Stopford, C.B., 1842. *107 St. George's Square, S.W.*	2nd daughter.
20033 –40		Same as Nos. 19996–20003.	Grandchildren. Descendants of No. 20032.
20041	1862	Emily Evelyn Lucy, Lady Markham, 1854, wife of Lieut.-Gen. Sir Edwin Markham, K.C.B. *Royal Military College, Camberley, Surrey.*	4th but 3rd surviving daughter.
20042	1863	Edwyn Guy Markham, 1877.	Grandchildren.
20043	1864	Montagu Wilfred Markham, 1884.	Children of
20044	1865	Muriel Markham, 1879.	No. 20041.
20045	1866	Dora, wife of Lieut.-Col. Richard Henry Atkinson, 1858. *48 St. George's Square, S.W.*	5th but 4th surviving daughter.
20046	1867	Marjorie Stopford Atkinson, 1886.	Granddaughters. Daughters
20047	1868	Lucy Mary Montagu Atkinson, 1890.	of No. 20045.

153. Descendants of Lady Jane Stopford, 1805–1873, and her husband, the Rev. Abel John Ram, of Clonattin. (See Table XVII.)

20048	1869	Rev. Edward Digby Stopford Ram, M.A., 1868. *Oxtead Rectory, Surrey.*	Grandson. Son of the Rev. George Stopford Ram, 1838–1889.
20049	1870	Mabel Charlotte Ram, ⎫ twins, 1897.	Great-grandchildren.
20050	1871	Eileen Isabel Ram, ⎭	Children of No.
20051	1872	. . . . Ram, 1902.	20048.
20052	1873	George Montagu Ram, 1881.	
20053	1874	Mary Frances Jane Ram.	
20054	1875	Evelyn Charlotte, wife of Archibald Aitchison.	Grandchildren. Younger son
20055	1876	Geraldine Louisa Ram.	and daughters of the Rev.
20056	1877	Kathleen Lucy Ram.	George Stopford Ram.
20057	1878	Winifred Ram.	
20058	1879	Dorothy Ram.	
20059	1880	Marjorie Freda Ram.	
20060	1881	Abel John Ram, K.C., M.A., Recorder of Wolverhampton, 1842. 31 *Eaton Square, S.W.*	Eldest surviving son.
20061	1882	Lucius Abel John Granville Ram, 1885.	Grandchildren.
20062	1883	Elen Augusta Ram, 1882.	Children of
20063	1884	Irene Mary Montagu Ram, 1888.	No. 20060.
20064	1885	The Rev. Robert Digby Ram, M.A., 1844. *The Vicarage, Hampton, Middlesex.*	2nd surviving son.
20065	1886	George Edward Ram, 1879.	Grandchildren.
20066	1887	Frederic Montagu Anson Ram, 1885.	Children of
20067	1888	Emily Jane, wife of Sir John Home Purves Hume Campbell, Bart. *Marchmont, N.B.*	No. 20064.
20068	1889	Frances Anne Jane, widow of John Robert Miller, M.D., Surgeon-General and *late* Inspector-General of Hospitals in the Punjab.	Daughter.

154. Descendants of Cospatrick Alexander, 11th Earl of Home, 1799–1881. (See Table XVIII.)

20069 -87	⎬	Same as Nos. 19900–19918.

155. Descendants of Lady Louisa Anne Douglas, 1806–1871, and her husband, Thomas Charlton Whitmore, of Apley Park, Salop, M.P., 1807–1865. (See Table XIX.)

20088	1890	Thomas Charles Douglas Whitmore, of Orsett Hall, Essex, J.P., D.L., 1839. 2 *Lowndes Square.*	Son.
20089	1891	Francis Henry Douglas Charlton Whitmore, J.P., 1872. *Orsett Hall, Essex.*	Grandchildren.
20090	1892	Mildred Louisa, wife of Hugh B. Craven. *Chaddesden Moor, Derby.*	Children of No. 20088.
20091	1893	Ethel Mary Alberta, wife of William Thomas Reginald Houldsworth. *Orsett House, Essex.*	

20092	1894	Caroline Louisa, wife of John William Scott. *Delgany, co. Wicklow.*	}	Eldest daughter.
20093	1895	James Whitmore Scott.	}	Grandchildren. Chil-
20094	1896	Albinia Louisa Scott.		dren of No. 20092.
20095	1897	Emily Harriet, wife of Major-General Tweedie, C.S.I., Bengal Staff Corps.		
20096	1898	Lucy Albinia Whitmore.		
20097	1899	Cecil Elizabeth, wife of Lieut.-Col. Duncan Stewart, *late* 92nd Gordon Highlanders. 89 *Eaton Place, S.W.*	}	Daughters.
20098	1900	Evelyn Octavia Whitmore.		

156. Descendants of Lady Mary Elizabeth Douglas, 1807–1888, and her husband, the Rev. Thomas Wentworth Gage, Vicar of Higham Ferrers, 17 –1837. (See Table XIX.)

20099	1901	Charles Wentworth Gage, 1868.	{	Grandchildren. Children of Charles Wentworth Gage, 1832–1868.
20100	1902	Mary Clarissa Gage, 1869.		
20101	1903	Fanny Gage, 1833.	}	Daughters.
20102	1904	Lucy Gage, 1835.		

20103	1905	Lady Harriet Christian Duncombe, 1809. 49 *Berkeley Square, W.*	}	See Table XIX.

157. Descendants of No. 8069, and her husband, the Very Rev. and Hon. Augustus Duncombe, Dean of York, 1814–1880. (See Table XIX.)

20104	1906	Captain Alfred Charles Duncombe, *late* 1st Life Guards. *Calwich Abbey, Staffordshire,* J.P., 1843.	}	Children.
20105	1907	Augustus Gerald Duncombe, *of Rockborough, Yorks,* 1849.		
20106	1908	Adolphus Montagu Duncombe, J.P., 1852. *The Manor House, N. Deighton, Wetherby, Yorks.*		
20107	1909	Evelyn Duncombe, 1842.		
20108	1910	Eleanor Harriet Duncombe, 1845.		

158. Descendants of Lady Jane Margaret Mary Douglas, 1811–1881, and her husband, Robert Johnstone Douglas, Esq., of Lockerbie, 1814–1866. (See Table XIX.)

20109	1911	Arthur Henry Johnstone Douglas, D.L., 1846, *of Lockerbie. Comlongon Castle, Ruthwell, Dumfries.*	}	Son.
20110	1912	Robert Sholto Johnstone Douglas, 1871.	}	Grandchildren. Children of No. 20109.
20111	1913	Walter Henry George Johnstone Douglas, 1886.		
20112	1914	Sybil Johnstone Douglas.		
20113	1915	Margaret Jean, wife of the Hon. Douglas George Carnegie. *Rosehill Cottage, Longwood, Winchester.*		
20114	1916	John Douglas Carnegie, 1895.	}	Great-grandchildren. Children of No. 20113.
20115	1917	David Alexander Carnegie, 1897.		
20116	1918	Jean Douglas Carnegie, 1899.		

20117	1919	Muriel Grace Johnstone Douglas.	
20118	1920	Bryde Helen Johnstone Douglas.	
20119	1921	Olive Christian Johnstone Douglas.	Grandchildren. Children
20120	1922	Caroline Elsie Johnstone Douglas.	of No. 20109.
20121	1923	Octavia Johnstone Douglas, } twins.	
20122	1924	Nina Johnstone Douglas,	
20123	1925	Grace Elizabeth, Lady Kensington [U.K. and I.].	Daughter.
		St. Brides, Little Haven, R.S.O., S. Wales.	
20124	1926	Hugh, 6th [I.] and 3rd [U.K.] Lord Kensington, 1873.	
		St. Brides, Little Haven, R.S.O., S. Wales.	
20125	1927	Hon. Cecil Edwardes, 1876.	Grandchildren.
20126	1928	Hon. George Henry Edwardes, 1877.	Children of
20127	1929	Hon. Gwendoline, wife of Captain William Augustus	No. 20123.
		Home Drummond Moray.	
		Abercairney, Crieff, co. Perth.	
20128	1930	James William Home Drummond Moray, 1900.	Great-grandchildren.
20129	1931	Anne Grace Christina Home Drummond Moray, 1902.	Children of No. 20127.
20130	1932	Hon. Sybil Laura Edwardes, 1871.	
20131	1933	Hon. Grace Louisa, wife of J.H. V. Lane.	Grandchildren. Younger
		King's Bromley Manor, Lichfield.	daughters of No. 20123.
20132	1934	Hon. Winifred Edwardes, 1875.	
20133	1935	Hon. Isobel Caroline Edwardes, 1879.	
20134	1936	Alice Louisa, wife of Charles Stewart.	Younger daughter.
		38 *Eaton Place, S.W.*	

159. Descendants of Lady Anne Georgina Douglas, 1817–1899, and her husband, Charles Stirling Home Drummond Moray, Esq., of Blair Drummond and Abercairney, co. Perth, J.P., D.L., 1816–1891. (See Table XIX.)

20135	1937	Henry Edward Stirling Home Drummond, Lieut.-Col. *late* Scots Guards, J.P., D.L., 1846.	Children.
		Blair Drummond, co. Perth.	
20136	1938	William Augustus Home Drummond Moray, Captain *late* Scots Guards, J.P., D.L., 1852.	
		Abercairney, co. Perth.	
20137 -38	}	Same as Nos. 20128–20129.	Grandchildren. Children of No. 20136.
20139	1939	Caroline Frances, wife of Arthur Edward Whitmore Drummond Forbes.	Child.
20140	1940	Charles William Arthur Drummond Forbes, 1885.	Grandchildren. Children of No. 20139.
20141	1941	Mary Christian Drummond Forbes, 1882.	

160. Descendants of Lord Charles Lennox Kerr, 1814–1898. (See Table XX.)

20142	1942	Charles Ian Kerr, 1874.	
20143	1943	Walter William Kerr, 1875.	Grandchildren. Children of
20144	1944	Basil Kerr, 1879.	Charles Wyndham Rudolph
20145	1945	Violet Kerr, 1877.	Kerr, 1849–1894.
20146	1946	Olive Kerr, 1878.	
20147	1947	Helen Cecily Kerr, 1884.	

20148	1948	Harriet Georgina Edith, wife of William Warcop Peter Consett, *of Brawith Hall, Yorks*, 1840. 39 *Bryanston Square, W*.	} Eldest daughter.
20149	1949	D'Arcy Preston Consett, *late* 20th Hussars, 1870.	} Grandchildren.
20150	1950	Montagu William Consett, Lieutenant R.A., 1871.	Children of
20151	1951	Violet Elizabeth, wife of M. Charles Nicaise.	No. 20148.
20152	1952	Marguerite Nicaise, 1898.	{ Great-granddaughter. Only daughter of No. 20151.
20153	1953	Victoria Florence Consett.	} Grandchildren. Chil-
20154	1954	Winifred Edith, Countess Louis de Boisgelin.	dren of No. 20148.
20155	1955	Alexandre de Boisgelin, 1893.	} Great-grandchildren. Children
20156	1956	Henri de Boisgelin, 1897.	of No. 20154.
20157	1957	Edith de Boisgelin, 1890.	
20158	1958	Mildred Sophia Consett.	} Grandchildren. Younger
20159	1959	Vera Margaret Consett.	daughters of No.
20160	1960	Cordelia Mary, Marchioness of Lambert [France].	20148.
20161	1961	Florence Elizabeth, Countess of Dunraven and Mountearl [I.], Baroness Kenry [U.K.], 1841. *Adare Manor, Ireland. Dunraven Castle, Wales.*	} 2nd daughter.
20162	1962	Lady Aileen May Wyndham Quin, 1873.	{ Granddaughter. Daughter of No. 20161.
20163	1963	Amy Frances, wife of Henley Eden, 1847. *Woodstock, Ascot, Berks.*	} 3rd daughter.
20164	1964	Lieutenant Schomberg Henley Eden, Black Watch, 1873.	} Grandsons. Sons of No. 20163.
20165	1965	Charles William Guy Eden, 1874.	

161. Descendants of Admiral Lord Frederic Herbert Kerr, 1818–1896. (See Table XX.)

20166	1966	Arthur Herbert Kerr, 1862. 2 *Driffield Terrace, York*.	} Eldest son.
20167	1967	Mark Peregrine Charles Kerr, 1891.	} Grandchildren. Children
20168	1968	Margaret Vere Kerr, 1890.	of No. 20166.
20169	1969	Irene Mildred Kerr, 1896.	
20170	1970	Commander Mark Edward Frederic Kerr, R.N., 1864. *White's.*	} 2nd and 3rd sons and eldest daughter.
20171	1971	Major Frederic Walter Kerr, D.S.O., 1867. *Naval and Military.*	
20172	1972	Emily Georgina, Countess of Strafford [U.K.], 1847. 5 *St. James' Square, S.W.*	
20173	1973	Hon. Ivo Francis Byng, 1874.	} Grandchildren.
20174	1974	Hon. Anthony Schomberg Byng, 1876.	Children of
20175	1975	Lady Rachel Theodora Byng, 1869.	No. 20172.
20176	1976	Lady Irene Hilare Byng, 1870.	
20177	1977	Lady Anne Dorothy Frederica Byng, 1881.	
20178	1978	Lady Hester Joan Byng, 1888.	
20179	1979	Sidney Katherine, wife of the Rev. Gordon Bolles Wickham, 1849. *The Vicarage, Bradford Abbas, near Sherborne, Dorset.*	} 2nd, 3rd, and 4th daughters.
20180	1980	Edith Harriet Kerr, 1852.	
20181	1981	Mary Frances, wife of George Henry Longman, 1856. *West Hill House, Epsom.*	

20182	1982	Henry Kerr Longman.	⎫ Grandchildren. Children
20183	1983	Robert Guy Longman.	⎬ of No. 20181.
20184	1984	Margaret Frances Longman.	⎭
20185	1985	Hon. Constance Honora Kerr, sometime extra Maid of Honour to Queen Victoria, 1859.	⎫
20186	1986	Cecil Nona Kerr, 1875. *Kensington Palace, W.*	⎬ Younger daughters. ⎭

162. Descendants of Lady Elizabeth Georgina Kerr, 1807–1871, and her husband, Charles Rudolph, 19th Lord Clinton, 1791–1866. (See Table XX.)

20187	1987	Charles Henry Rolle, 20th Lord Clinton [E.], 1834. *41 Portland Place, W.*	⎱ Eldest son.
20188	1988	Major the Hon. Charles John Robert Trefusis, 1863. *Fettercairn House, N.B.*	⎱ Grandson. Son ⎰ of No. 20187.
20189	1989	Harriet Trefusis, 1887.	⎱ Great-granddaughters. Daughters
20190	1990	Fenella Trefusis, 1889.	⎰ of No. 20188.
20191	1991	Captain the Hon. Walter Henry Trefusis, 1864. *Guard's; Wellington.*	
20192	1992	Hon. John Frederick Trefusis, 1878.	
20193	1993	Lieutenant the Hon. Walter Alexander Trefusis, Scots Guards, 1879. *Guards'.*	
20194	1994	Hon. Schomberg Charles Trefusis, 1882.	
20195	1995	Hon. Robert Henry Trefusis, 1888.	Grandchildren.
20196	1996	Hon. Ada Harriet Trefusis, 1860.	Children of
20197	1997	Hon. Mary Elizabeth Trefusis, 1861.	No. 20187.
20198	1998	Hon. Margaret Adela, wife of the Rev. Leonard Jauncey White Thomson, 1866. *The Vicarage, Ramsgate.*	
20199	1999	Hon. Edith Trefusis, 1876.	
20200	2000	Hon. Evelyn Mary Trefusis, 1883.	
20201	2001	Hon. Harriet Margaret Trefusis, 1891.	
20202	2002	Hon. Mark George Kerr Rolle Trefusis, D.L., 1835. *Stevenstone, near Torrington, Devon.* *Bicton, near Budleigh, Salterton.*	⎱ 2nd son.
20203	2003	Gertrude Emily, wife of Hugh Henry John Williams-Drummond, 1865.	⎱ Granddaughters.
20204	2004	Mary Frances, wife of Arthur Scott Browne. *Buckland Filleigh, North Devon.*	⎰ Daughters of No. 20202.
20205 –09	⎱	Same as Nos. 19772–19776.	⎰ Grandchildren. Children of Lieut.-Col. the Hon. Walter Rudolph Trefusis, 1838–1885.
20210	2005	Colonel the Hon. John Schomberg Trefusis, 1852. *Rockbeare Grange, Exeter.*	⎱ 3rd surviving son.
20211	2006	Schomberg Kerr Trefusis, 1888.	⎱
20212	2007	Denys Robert Trefusis, 1890.	Grandchildren.
20213	2008	Beatrice Morwenna Trefusis, 1884.	Children of
20214	2009	Elizabeth Katherine Mary Trefusis, 1887.	No. 20210.
20215	2010	Hon. Emily Harriet Trefusis, 1832. *Torquay.*	⎱
20216	2011	Hon. Mary Louisa, wife of John Carpenter Garnier, D.L., *of Mount Tavy, Devon,* 1836. *Rookesbury Park, Fareham.*	⎬ 1st and 2nd daughters.

20217	2012	John Trefusis Carpenter Garnier, Captain 2nd Battalion Scots Guards, 1874.	
20218	2013	George William Carpenter Garnier, 1877.	Grandchildren.
20219	2014	Mark Rodolph Carpenter Garnier, 1881.	Children of
20220	2015	Mary Lucy Carpenter Garnier, 1869.	No. 20216.
20221	2016	Evelyn Carpenter Garnier, 1871.	
20222	2017	Adela Elizabeth Carpenter Garnier, 1873.	
20223	2018	Hon. Evelyn Anne, wife of the Hon. Edward William Douglas, 1841. *Heatherlea, Christchurch.*	3rd daughter.
20224	2019	Gertrude Evelyn Augusta Douglas, 1883.	Granddaughter. Daughter of No. 20233.
20225	2020	Hon. Helen Georgina Trefusis, 1843. *Torquay.*	4th daughter.
20226	2021	Lieutenant George Windsor-Clive, Coldstream Guards, 1878. 12 *Stratford Place, W.*	Grandson. Son of the late Hon. Gertrude Albertina Trefusis, 1845–1878, and her husband, Lieut.-Col. the Hon. George Herbert Windsor-Clive.
20227	2022	Hon. Alice Morwenna Trefusis, 1849. *Torquay.*	Youngest daughter.

163. Descendants of Lady Harriet Louisa Kerr, 1808–1884, and her husband, Sir John Stuart Hepburn Forbes, 8th Bart., 1804–1866. (See Table XX.)

20228 –34	}	Same as Nos. 20188–20191 and 20196–20198.	Descendants of Harriet Wilhelmina Hepburn Forbes, 1835–1869, only child, 1st wife of Charles, 20th Lord Clinton.

164. Descendants of Lady Georgina Augusta Kerr, 1822–1859, and her husband, the Rev. Granville Hamilton Forbes, Rector of Broughton, Northants. (See Table XX.)

20235	2023	Henry Francis Gordon Forbes, Lieutenant Rifle Brigade, 1850.	Son.
20236	2024	Sydney Forbes.	Granddaughter. Daughter of No. 20235.

165. Descendants of Lady Harriet Georgiana Brudenell, 1799–1836, 1st wife of Richard William Penn, 1st Earl Howe, 1796–1870. (See Table XXI.)

20237	2025	Penn Curzon Sherbrooke, 1871.		Great-grandchildren. Children of Lady Harriet Alice Curzon Howe, 1848–1875, and her husband, the Rev. Henry Nevile Sherbrooke, and granddaughter of George A. F. L., 2nd Earl Howe, 1821–1876.
20238	2026	Sybil Mary Curzon Sherbrooke.	*Clifton Vicarage, Bristol.*	
20239	2027	Eveleen Alice Curzon Sherbrooke.		

20240	2028	Richard George Penn, 4th Earl Howe [U.K.], 6th Baron Curzon and Howe [G.B.], 1861. *Curzon House, Curzon Street, W.* *Penn House, Amersham, Bucks.*	Grandson. Son of Richard William, 3rd Earl Howe, 1822–1900.
20241	2029	Francis Richard Henry Penn, Viscount Curzon, 1884.	Great-grandson. Son of No. 20240.
20242	2030	Hon. Frederick Graham Curzon Howe, 1868. *7 Devonport Street, Hyde Park, W.*	Grandson. 2nd son of Richard William, 3rd Earl Howe, 1822–1900.
20243	2031	Chambré George William Penn Curzon Howe, 1898.	Great-grandchildren. Children of No. 20242.
20244	2032	Evelyn Ellis Isabella Curzon Howe, 1897.	
20245	2033	Lady Evelyn Alice, wife of John Eyre, 1862. *Curzon House, Mayfair.* *Great Enton, Godalming.*	Granddaughters. Sisters of No. 20240.
20246	2034	Lady Edith Cecilia, wife of Harry W. Franklin, 1864. *27 Emperor's Gate, S.W.*	
20247	2035	Charles Peter Damian Franklin, 1900.	Great-grandchildren. Son and daughter of No. 20246.
20248	2036	Violet Catherine Cecilia Mary Franklin, 1897.	
20249	2037	Hon. Henry Dugdale Curzon, J.P., D.L., 1824. *East Dean, Salisbury.*	Eldest surviving son.
20250	2038	Henry Curzon, 1865.	Grandchildren. Children of No. 20249.
20251	2039	Assheton Curzon, 1876.	
20252	2040	Nina Curzon, 1859.	
20253	2041	Millicent, wife of John Henry Jacob, 1860. *The Close, Salisbury.*	
20254	2042	John Henry Jacob, 1893.	Great-grandchildren. Children of No. 20253.
20255	2043	Mary Jacob, 1891.	
20256	2044	Sybil Curzon, 1869.	Granddaughter. 3rd daughter of No. 20249.
20257	2045	Major the Hon. William Henry Curzon, *late* 17th Light Dragoons, 1827. *10 Chester Square, S.W.*	2nd surviving son.
20258	2046	Hilda Georgina Susan Curzon, 1879.	Granddaughter. Only child of No. 20257.
20259	2047	Captain Ernest Charles Penn Curzon, *late* 18th Hussars, 1856.	Grandson. Eldest son of Colonel the Hon. Ernest George Curzon, 1828–1885.
20260	2048	Charles Ernest Basset Lothian Curzon, 1885.	Great-grandchildren. Children of No. 20259.
20261	2049	Lorna Katherine Curzon, 1887.	
20262	2050	Captain Fitzroy Edmund Penn Curzon, Royal Irish Rifles, 1859.	Grandchildren. Children of Colonel the Hon. Ernest George Curzon, 1828–1885.
20263	2051	Arthur Wardlaw Curzon, 1861. *Goderich, Ontario, Canada.*	
20264	2052	Harriet Augusta, wife of Thomas George Lithgow, Esq., F.R.C.S., L.R.C.P., D.P.H. Lond., 1862. *Blackwell House, Farnborough, Hants.*	
20265	2053	Ernest George Robert Lithgow, 1883.	Great-grandchildren. Children of No. 20264.
20266	2054	Thomas Richardson Penn Curzon Lithgow, 1884.	
20267	2055	Arthur Fitzroy Lithgow, 1888.	
20268	2056	Elizabeth Nie Constance Mary Lithgow, 1885.	

20269	2057	Mary Ellen, wife of the Rev. Arthur Lewis Whitfeld, M.A., 1866. *Little Easton Rectory, Essex.*	Granddaughter. Sister to No. 20262, &c.
20270	2058	Arthur Noel Whitfeld, 1890.	Great-grandsons.
20271	2059	Ernest Hamilton Whitfeld, 1894.	Sons of No
20272	2060	Gerald Herbert Penn Whitfeld, 1896.	20269.
20273	2061	Georgiana Charlotte, Duchess Dowager of Beaufort [E.], 1825. *Stoke Park, Stapleton, near Bristol.*	Eldest daughter.
20274	2062	Henry Adelbert Wellington Fitzroy, 9th Duke of Beaufort [E.], 1847. *Badminton House, Chippenham.*	Grandson. Eldest son of No. 20273.
20275	2063	Henry Hugh Arthur Fitzroy, Marquis of Worcester, 1900.	Great-grandchildren. Children of No. 20274.
20276	2064	Lady Blanche Linnie Somerset, 1897.	
20277	2065	Lady Diana Maud Nina Somerset, 1898.	
20278	2066	Right Hon. Lord Henry Richard Charles Somerset, P.C., 1849. *1 Via Guido Monaco, Firenze, Italy.*	Grandson. 2nd son of No. 20273.
20279	2067	Henry Charles Somers Augustus Somerset, 1874. *The Priory, Reigate.*	Great-grandson. Son of No. 20278.
20280	2068	Henry Robert Somers Fitzroy de Vere Somerset, 1898.	Great-great-grandson. Son of No. 20279.
20281	2069	Lord Henry Arthur George Somerset, 1851.	Grandson. 3rd son of No. 20273.
20282	2070	Henry Fitzroy Edward Somerset, 1886.	Great-grandson. Only child of Lord Henry Edward Brudenell Somerset, 1853–1897, and grandson of No. 20273.
20283	2071	Henry, 6th Marquis of Waterford [I.], 6th Baron Tyrone [G.B.], 1875. *Curraghmore, Portlaw, co. Waterford.*	Great-grandson. Son of the Lady Blanche Elizabeth Adelaide Somerset, 1856–1897, 2nd wife of John Henry, 5th Marquis of Waterford, 1844–1895, and grandson of No. 20273.
20284	2072	John Charles, Earl of Tyrone, 1900.	Great-great-grandchildren. Children of No. 20283.
20285	2073	Lady Blanche Maud De la Poer Beresford, 1898.	
20286	2074	Lady Katherine Nora De la Poer Beresford, 1899.	
20287	2075	Lady . . . . De la Poer Beresford, 1902.	
20288	2076	Lady Susan De la Poer Beresford, 1877.	Granddaughters. Sisters of No. 20283.
20289	2077	Lady Clodagh De la Poer, wife of the Hon. Claud Anson, 1879.	
20290	2078	Adelaide Ida, Countess Dowager of Westmorland [E.]. *13 Queen Square, Mayfair, W.*	2nd daughter.
20291	2079	Anthony Mildmay Julian, 13th Earl of Westmorland [E.], 1859. *Apethorpe Hall, Wansford, Northants.*	Grandson. Son of No. 20290.
20292	2080	Vere Anthony Francis St. Clair, Lord Burghersh, 1893.	Great-grandchildren. Children of No. 20291.
20293	2081	Hon. Mountjoy John Charles Wedderburn Fane, 1900.	
20294	2082	Lady Enid Victoria Rachel Fane, 1894.	
20295	2083	Grace Augusta, Countess of Londesborough [U.K.], 1860. *Londesborough Park, Market Weighton.*	Granddaughter. Elder daughter of No. 20290.

20296	2084	George Francis William Henry, Viscount Raincliffe, 1892.	Great-grandchildren. Children of No. 20295.
20297	2085	Hon. Hugo William Cecil Denison, 1894.	
20298	2086	Hon. Irene Frances Adza Denison, 1890.	
20299	2087	Lady Margaret Mary, wife of Captain John Edmund P. Spicer, *late* 1st Life Guards, 1870. *Spye Park, Chippenham.*	Granddaughter. Younger daughter of No. 20290.
20300	2088	John Francis Julian Fane Spicer, 1890.	Great-grandchildren. Children of No. 20299.
20301	2089	Anthony Napier Fane Spicer, 1891.	
20302	2090	Frank Fitzroy Fane Spicer, 1893.	
20303	2091	Simon Ralph Fane Spicer, 1894.	
20304	2092	Julian Fane Spicer, 1900.	
20305	2093	Joan Adelaide Fane Spicer, 1896.	
20306	2094	Lady Emily Marie, wife of Colonel Sir Robert Nigel Fitzhardinge Kingscote, K.C.B., 1836. *Kingscote, Wotton-under-Edge.* *19 South Audley Street, S.W.*	3rd daughter.
20307	2095	Nigel Richard Fitzhardinge Kingscote, 1857.	Grandchildren. Children of No. 20306.
20308	2096	Harriet Maud Isabella, wife of Arthur Maitland Wilson. *Stowlangtoft, Suffolk.*	
20309	2097	Winifred Ida, Marchioness [U.K.], Countess [E.], and Viscountess [I.] of Cholmondeley, Baroness Newburgh [G.B.]. *Cholmondeley Castle, Malpas, Cheshire.* *Houghton Hall, King's Lynn, Norfolk.*	
20310	2098	George Horatio Charles, Earl of Rocksavage, 1883.	Great-grandchildren. Children of No. 20309.
20311	2099	Lord George Hugo Cholmondeley, 1887.	
20312	2100	Lady Lettice Joan Cholmondeley, 1882.	

166. Descendants of Lady Charlotte Penelope Brudenell, 1802–1879, and her husband, Henry Charles Sturt, Esq., of Crichel, Dorset, 1795–1866. (See Table XXI.)

20313	2101	Henry Gerard, 1st Lord Alington [U.K.], 1825. *Alington House, South Audley Street, W.* *Crichel, Wimborne.*	Eldest son.
20314	2102	Hon. Humphrey Napier Sturt, M.P., 1859. *38 Portman Square, W.*	Grandson. Only son of No. 20313.
20315	2103	Gerard Philip Montagu Napier Sturt, 1893.	Great-grandchildren. Children of No. 20314.
20316	2104	Napier George Henry Sturt, 1896.	
20317	2105	Diana Isabel Sturt, 1884.	
20318	2106	Lois Ina Sturt, 1900.	
20319	2107	Hon. Hilda Mary, wife of the Rev. Frederic Wilson Cooper, 1863. *Prestwich Rectory, Manchester.*	Granddaughters. 1st and 2nd daughters of No. 20313.
20320	2108	Hon. Winifred Selina, wife of the Hon. Charles Hardinge, C.B. *The British Embassy, St. Petersburg.*	
20321	2109	Edward Charles Hardinge, 1892.	Great-grandchildren. Children of No. 20320.
20322	2110	Alexander Henry Louis Hardinge, 1894.	
20323	2111	Diamond Evelyn Violet Hardinge, 1900.	
20324	2112	Mildred Cecilia Harriet, Viscountess Chelsea, 1869. *31a Green Street, W.*	Granddaughter. 3rd daughter of No. 20313.

20325	2113	Hon. Sibyl Louise Beatrix Cadogan, 1893.	⎫
20326	2114	Hon. Edith Mary Winifred Cadogan, 1895.	Great-grandchildren.
20327	2115	Hon. Cynthia Cadogan, 1896.	Daughters of No.
20328	2116	Hon. . . . . Cadogan, 1900.	20324.
20329	2117	Hon. . . . . Cadogan, 1901.	⎭

20330
-32 } Same as Nos. 20237-20239.

Great-grandchildren. Grandchildren of Harriet Mary Sturt, 1822–1877 (2nd daughter), and her husband, George A. F. L., 2nd Earl Howe, 1821–1876.

20333	2118	Francis George, Viscount Baring, 1850. 10 *Belgrave Square, S.W.*	Grandchildren. Children of Elizabeth Harriet Sturt, 1824–1867 (3rd
20334	2119	Lady Jane Emma, wife of Colonel the Hon. Henry George Lewis Crichton. *Netley Castle, Netley Abbey, Hants.*	daughter), and her husband, Thomas George, 1st Earl of Northbrook, 1826.

20335	2120	Henry St. George Foley, Private Secretary to the Secretary of State for Foreign Affairs, 1866. 10 *Curzon Street, W.*	Grandson. Elder son of Augusta Selina Sturt, 1828–1901, wife of General the Hon. Sir St. George Gerard Foley, K.C.B.

20336	2121	Gerald Henry Foley, 1898.	⎱ Great-grandchildren. Children of
20337	2122	Mildred Caroline Foley, 1895.	⎰ No. 20335.
20338	2123	Cyril Foley, 1868. 10 *Curzon Street, W.*	⎱ Grandson. Younger brother ⎰ of No. 20335.

167. Descendants of Lady Mary Brudenell, 1806–1867, and her husband, Henry Thomas, 3rd Earl of Chichester, 1804–1886. (See Table XXI.)

20339	2124	Francis Godolphin, 5th Earl of Chichester [U.K.], 6th Baron Pelham [G.B.], Hon. Canon of Bangor, 1844. *Great Yarmouth Vicarage, Norfolk. Stanmer, Lewes.*	⎫ Son. ⎭
20340	2125	Jocelyn Brudenell, Lord Pelham, 1871. 9 *Tite Street, Chelsea, S.W.*	⎱ Grandson. Son of ⎰ No. 20339.
20341	2126	Elizabeth Jocelyn Pelham, 1899.	Great-granddaughter. Daughter of No. 20340.
20342	2127	Henry George Godolphin Pelham, 1875.	⎫ Grandchildren.
20343	2128	Anthony Ashley Ivo Pelham, 1879.	Children of
20344	2129	Herbert Lyttelton Pelham, 1884.	No. 20339.
20345	2130	Ruth Mary Pelham, 1873.	⎭
20346	2131	Hon. Thomas Henry William Pelham, M.A., 1847. *Deene House, Putney Hill, S.W.*	2nd surviving son.
20347	2132	Walter Henry Pelham, 1886.	⎫ Grandchildren. Children
20348	2133	Mary Louisa Pelham, 1885.	of No. 20346.
20349	2134	Maud Katherine Pelham, 1887.	⎭
20350	2135	Hon. Arthur Lowther Pelham, 1850. *Moorcroft, Monmouth.* 15 *Duke Street, Manchester Square, W.*	⎫ 3rd surviving son and eldest daughter.
20351	2136	Harriet Mary, Countess of Darnley [I.], 1829. 21 *Hill Street, Berkeley Square, S.W.*	⎭

20352	2137	Elizabeth Adeline Mary, Baroness Clifton of Leighton Bromswold [E.], 1900.	Great-granddaughter. Daughter of Edward Henry, 7th Earl of Darnley, 1851–1900, elder son of No. 20351.
20353	2138	Ivo Francis Walter, 8th Earl of Darnley [I.], 1859. *Cobham Hall, Gravesend.*	Grandson. Son of No. 20351.
20354	2139	Esmé Ivo, Lord Clifton of Rathmore, 1886.	Great-grandchildren. Children of No. 20353.
20355	2140	Hon. Noel Gervase Bligh, 1888.	
20356	2141	Lady Dorothy Violet Bligh, 1893.	
20357	2142	Hon. Arthur Frederick Pelham Bligh, 1865.	Grandchildren. Children of No. 20351.
20358	2143	Lady Edith Louisa Mary, wife of George Burvill Rashleigh, 1853. *Riseley, Horton Kirby, Kent.*	
20359	2144	Henry Pelham Rashleigh, 1883.	Great-grandchildren. Children of No. 20358.
20360	2145	Isabel Mary Rashleigh, 1884.	
20361	2146	Beatrice Mary Rashleigh, 1885.	
20362	2147	Mary Elizabeth Joan Rashleigh, 1887.	
20363	2148	Katherine Maria Theodosia Rashleigh, 1888.	
20364	2149	Lady Kathleen Susan Emma Bligh, 1854.	Granddaughters. Younger daughters of No. 20351.
20365	2150	Lady Alice Isabella Harriet Bligh, 1860.	
20366	2151	Lady Constance Violet Lucy, wife of William Shakespear Childe-Pemberton, 1869. *Sunny Hill, Crawley Down, Sussex.* *12 Portman Street, W.*	
20367	2152	Edmund William Baldwyn Childe-Pemberton, 1895.	Great-grandsons. Sons of No. 20366.
20368	2153	Roland Ivo Lacon Childe-Pemberton, 1898.	
20369	2154	Abel Henry Smith, 1862. *Woodhall Park, Herts.*	Grandson. Son of Lady Susan Pelham, 1831–1875, and her husband, Abel Smith, of Woodhall, M.P., 1829–1898.
20370	2155	Winifred Susan Smith.	Great-granddaughters. Daughters of No. 20369.
20371	2156	Gladys Evelyn Smith.	
20372	2157	Violet Frances Gertrude Smith.	
20373	2158	Edward Pelham Smith, Captain R.A., 1868.	Grandchildren. Younger son and daughter of the aforesaid Lady Susan Pelham, 1831–1875.
20374	2159	Evelyn Mary Smith.	
20375	2160	Lady Isabella Charlotte, wife of Samuel Whitbread, 1836. *16 Grosvenor Crescent, S.W.*	Youngest daughter.
20376	2161	Samuel Howard Whitbread, J.P., 1858.	Grandchildren. Sons of No. 20375.
20377	2162	Henry William Whitbread, 1861. *13 Buckingham Gate, S.W.*	
20378	2163	William Henry Whitbread, 1900.	Great-grandchildren. Children of No. 20377.
20379	2164	Judith Joan Mary Whitbread, 1898.	
20380	2165	Francis Pelham Whitbread, 1867. *12 Hans Place, S.W.*	Grandchild. Son of No. 20375.
20381	2166	Peter Whitbread, 1897.	Great-grandchildren. Children of No. 20380.
20382	2167	Beatrice Whitbread, 1894.	

168. Descendants of Lady Augusta Brudenell, 1808–1853, and her husband, Henry Bingham Baring, Esq., M.P., 1804–1869. (See Table XXI.)

20383	2168	Godfrey Baring, D.L., J.P., 1871. *Nubia House, West Cowes, I.W.*	Grandson. Only son of Lieut.-General Charles Baring, 1829–1890.

ELIZABETH WYDEVILLE, QUEEN CONSORT OF EDWARD IV.

THE COMMON ANCESTRESS OF NOS. 1–36735.

From the Painting at Queen's College, Canterbury, by permission of the President of the College.

20384	2169	Charles Christian Baring, 1898.	Great-grandchildren. Children of No. 28383.
20385	2170	Helen Azalia Baring, 1901.	
20386	2171	Mabel, wife of Richard Grant, 1861. *Staffa, West Cowes, I.W.*	Granddaughter. Only surviving daughter of Lieut.-Gen. Charles Baring, 1829–1870.
20387	2172	Henry Baring, *late* Captain 17th Lancers, 1831. *Tunbridge Wells.*	Only surviving son.
20388	2173	Henry Baring, 1893.	Grandchildren. Children of No. 20387.
20389	2174	Francis Guy Baring,	
20390	2175	Augusta Baring, 1889.	
20391	2176	Sir Richard Henry Williams-Bulkeley, 12th Baronet. *Baron Hill, Beaumaris.*	Grandson. Only son of the late Mary Emily Baring, and her 1st husband, Sir Richard Lewis Mostyn Williams-Bulkeley, 1833–1889.
20392	2177	Richard Gerard Wellesley Williams-Bulkeley, 1887.	Great-grandchildren. Children of No. 20391.
20393	2178	Generis Alma Windham Williams-Bulkeley, 1889.	
20394	2179	Æira Helen Williams-Bulkeley, 1891.	

169. Descendants of Lady Anne Brudenell, 1809–1877, and her husband, Field-Marshal George Charles, 3rd Earl of Lucan, 1800–1888. (See Table XXI.)

20395	2180	George, 4th Earl of Lucan, K.P. [I.], 1830. *Castlebar, co. Mayo.* *Laleham House, Staines.*	Eldest son.
20396	2181	George Charles, Lord Bingham, 1860. 38 *Bryanston Square, W.*	Grandson. Son of No. 20395.
20397	2182	Hon. George Charles Patrick Bingham, 1898.	Great-grandson. Only child of No. 20396.
20398	2183	Hon. Cecil Edward Bingham, C.B., Lieut.-Col. 1st Life Guards, 1861. 25 *Charles Street, Berkeley Square, W.*	Grandson. 2nd son of No. 20395.
20399	2184	Ralph Charles Bingham, 1885.	Great-grandchildren. Children of No. 20398.
20400	2185	David Cecil Bingham, 1887.	
20401	2186	Cecilia Mary Lavinia Bingham, 1893.	
20402	2187	Hon. Francis Richard Bingham, Major R.A., 1863. *White's.*	Grandson. 3rd son of No. 20395.
20403	2188	Francis Humphrey Bingham, 1899.	Great-grandson. Only son of No. 20402.
20404	2189	Hon. Alexander Frederic Bingham, 1864.	Grandchildren. Younger sons and daughter of No. 20395
20405	2190	Hon. Albert Edward Bingham, 1866. *White's.*	
20406	2191	Hon. Lionel Ernest Bingham, 1876.	
20407	2192	Rosalind Cecilia Caroline, Marchioness of Hamilton, 1869. 15 *Montagu Square, W.*	
20408	2193	Lady Mary Cecilia Rhodesia Hamilton, 1896.	Great-granddaughters. Daughters of No. 20407.
20409	2194	Lady Cynthia Elinor Beatrice Hamilton, 1897.	
20410	2195	Lady Katherine Hamilton, 1900.	
20411	2196	Captain the Hon. Richard Bingham, R.N., 1847. 8 *Denmark Terrace, Brighton.*	2nd son.

20412	2197	Violet Mary Bingham, 1880.	} Granddaughters. Daughters of No. 20411.
20413	2198	Edith Lavinia Bingham, 1881.	
20414 –29	}	Same as Nos. 20314–20329.	Grandchildren. Descendants of the Lady Augusta Bingham, 1832–1888, and her husband, Henry Gerard, 1st Lord Alington.
20430	2199	Henry Charles, 3rd Viscount Hardinge [U.K.], 1857. *South Park, Penshurst, Tonbridge.*	Grandson. Eldest son of the Lady Lavinia Bingham, 1835–1864, and her husband, Charles, 2nd Viscount Hardinge, 1822–1894.
20431	2200	Hon. Ralph Henry Hardinge, 1895.	Great-grandchildren.
20432	2201	Hon. Ruby Hardinge, 1897.	Children of No.
20433	2202	Hon. Sybil Hardinge, 1898.	20430.
20434	2203	Hon. Charles Hardinge, C.B., 1858. *British Embassy, St. Petersburg.*	Grandson. Brother of No. 20430.
20435 –37	}	Same as Nos. 20321–20323.	Great-grandsons. Sons of No. 20434.
20438	2204	Hon. Robert Nicholas Hardinge, 1863. *White's.*	Grandson. Brother of No. 20430, &c.
20439	2205	Patrick Robert Hardinge, 1893.	Great-grandson. Only son of No. 20438.
20440	2206	Hon. George Arthur Hardinge, Commander R.N., 1864. *Naval and Military.*	Grandchildren. Brother and sisters of Nos. 20430, &c.
20441	2207	Hon. Lavinia Hardinge, 1860.	
20442	2208	Hon. Emily Maude, widow of George Hanbury Field, of Ashurst Place, Kent, 1861. *97 Eaton Square, S.W.*	
20443	2209	Reginald George Field, 1895.	Great-grandson. Son of No. 20442.
20444	2210	Hon. Mary Hilda Madelina, wife of the Rev. Ernest John Wild, 1862. *Rattlesden Rectory, Bury St. Edmunds.*	Granddaughter. Sister of Nos. 20430, &c.
20445	2211	Gladys Lavinia Mary Wild, 1897.	Great-granddaughters. Daughters of No. 20444.
20446	2212	Monica Hilda Mary Wild, 1898.	
20447	2213	Joan Mary Wild, 1900.	

170. Descendants of Ernest Augustus Charles, 3rd Marquis of Ailesbury, 1811–1886. (See Table XXII.)

20448	2214	Lady Mabel Emily Louisa, wife of Robert Standish Sievier, 1866.	Granddaughter. Daughter of George John Brudenell Bruce, 1839–1868.
20449	2215	Robert Brudenell Bruce Sievier, 1894.	Great-grandchildren. Children of No. 20448.
20450	2216	Mabel Henrietta Louisa Sievier, 1893.	
20451	2217	Barbara Bruce Sievier, 1898.	
20452	2218	Henry Augustus, 5th Marquis [U.K.], and 6th Earl [G.B.] of Ailesbury, 11th Earl of Cardigan [E.], 1842. *Savernake, Marlborough.*	Eldest surviving son.
20453	2219	George William James Chandos, Earl of Cardigan, D.S.O., 1873.	Grandchildren. Children of No. 20452.
20454	2220	Lady Ernestine Mary Alma Georgiana, wife of Harry Brady Hunt, 1871.	
20455	2221	Lady Violet Louisa Marjorie Brudenell Bruce, 1880.	

20456	2222	Lord Robert Thomas Brudenell Bruce, Commander R.N., 1845. *Stamford Lodge, Hayling Island.*	2nd surviving son.
20457	2223	James Ernest John Brudenell Bruce, 1879.	
20458	2224	George Lionel Thomas Brudenell Bruce, 1880.	
20459	2225	Robert Hanbury Brudenell Bruce, Lieutenant 4th Battalion Norfolk Regiment, 1881.	Grandchildren. Children of No. 20456.
20460	2226	John Charles Brudenell Bruce, 1885.	
20461	2227	Frances Edith Agnes Brudenell Bruce, 1883.	
20462	2228	Gwyneth Marjorie Brudenell Bruce, 1890.	
20463	2229	Lord Charles Frederick Brudenell Bruce, 1849. *Everton Grange, Lymington.* 11 *Gloucester Terrace, Regent's Park, N.W.*	
20464	2230	Ernestine Mary, Countess of Listowel [I.], Baroness Hare [U.K.], 1847. *Convamore, Ballyhooly, co. Cork. Kingston House, Prince's Gate, S.W.*	3rd surviving son and only surviving daughter.
20465	2231	Richard Granville, Viscount Ennismore, 1866.	
20466	2232	Lady Margaret Ernestine Augusta, wife of Reginald Bemhard Loder, 1869. *Maidwell Hall, Northants.*	Grandchildren. Children of No. 20464.
20467	2233	Marjorie Kathleen Loder, 1897.	Great-grandchild. Daughter of No. 20466.
20468	2234	Lady Beatrice Mary, wife of the Hon. Edward Donough O'Brien, 1870. *Moyriesk, Quin, co. Clare.*	Granddaughter. Younger daughter of No. 20464.
20469	2235	Terence O'Brien, 1899.	Great-grandchild. Son of No. 20468.

171. Descendants, if any, of Lady Maria Caroline Anne Brudenell-Bruce, 1794-1835, and her husband, Count of Mondreville, Knight of St. Louis, and Colonel of the late Royal Garde-du-Corps, -1843. (See Table XXII.)

172. Descendants of Lady Augusta Frederica Louisa Brudenell-Bruce, 1795-1869, and her husband, Thomas Frederick Vernon Wentworth, Esq., of Wentworth Castle, Yorks, 1795-1885. (See Table XXII.)

20470	2236	Captain Bruce Canning Vernon Wentworth, M.P., Grenadier Guards, 1862. *Wentworth Castle, Yorks.* 2 *First Avenue, Brighton.*	Grandchildren. Children of Thomas Frederick Charles Vernon Wentworth, of Wentworth Castle, 1831-1902.
20471	2237	Frederick Charles Ulick Vernon Wentworth, Captain R.N., 1866. *Black Heath, Saxemundham, Suffolk.*	
20472	2238	John Charles Vernon Wentworth, 1900.	Great-grandchildren. Children of No. 20471.
20473	2239	Mary Guise Vernon Wentworth, 1902.	
20474	2240	Mary Joan, wife of Francis Huntsman. *West Retford Hall, Notts.*	Grandchild. Sister to No. 20471.
20475	2241	Benjamin Canning Huntsman, 1895.	Great-grandchildren. Children of No. 20474.
20476	2242	Joan Alice Huntsman.	
20477	2243	Sylvia Mary Huntsman.	
20478	2244	Muriel Hester, wife of William Evelyn Long. *Hurts Hall, Suffolk.*	Grandchild. 2nd sister of No. 20471.

20479	2245	William George Long, 1899.	Great-grandson. Son of No. 20478.
20480	2246	Louisa Mary Henrietta Vernon Wentworth.	Only surviving daughter.
20481	2247	Fredericka Charlotte Louisa, wife of Mortimer Rooke, 1861. 54 Eccleston Square, S.W.	Grandchild. Daughter of Henrietta Frances Elizabeth Vernon Wentworth, -1873, and her husband, Lieut.-Col. Arthur John Bethell Thellusson of Aldeburgh, Suffolk.
20482	2248	John Wentworth Rooke, 1887.	
20483	2249	Wallace Mortimer Rooke, 1890.	
20484	2250	George Alexander Rooke, 1892.	Great-grandchildren.
20485	2251	Gladys Mina Henrietta Rooke, 1885.	Children of No.
20486	2252	Phyllis Mabel Rooke, 1888.	20481.
20487	2253	Ellen Marjory Rooke, 1898.	
20488	2254	Doris Mary Frederika Rooke, 1901.	
20489	2255	Katherine Emily Wilhelmina, wife of Augustus F. Manns, 1865. Gleadale, Harold Road, Norwood, S.E.	Granddaughters. Sisters of No. 20481.
20490	2256	Selina Mabel Henrietta, wife of Herbert Longe, 1871. Thellusson Lodge, Aldeburgh, Suffolk.	

173. Descendants of Lady Elizabeth Brudenell-Bruce, 1807–1847, and her husband, His Excellency Count Christian Conrad Sofus Danneskiold Samsoe, 1800–1886. (See Table XXII.)

20491	2257	Count Christian Frederick Danneskiold Samsoe [Denmark], 1838. Copenhagen.	Elder son.
20492	2258	Count Aage Conrad Danneskiold Samsoe, 1886.	Grandchildren. Son and two elder daughters of No. 20491.
20493	2259	Elizabeth Thyra, Countess Aage Moltke, 1869.	
20494	2260	Ingeborg Agnes, Countess Adam Moltke, 1871.	
20495	2261	Count Otto Moltke, 1893.	Great-grandson. Son of No. 20494.
20496	2262	Dagmar Louisa, Countess Francis Brockenhuus-Schack, 1875.	Grandchild. 3rd daughter of No. 20491.
20497	2263	Count Knud Bille Christian Piler Brockenhuus-Schack, 1896.	Great-grandson. Son of No. 20496.
20498	2264	Countess Magdalene Danneskiold Samsoe, 1876.	Granddaughters. Younger daughters of No. 20491.
20499	2265	Countess Karen Amy Danneskiold Samsoe, 1877.	
20500	2266	Countess Clara Danneskiold Samsoe, 1878.	
20501	2267	Countess Mary Danneskiold Samsoe, 1880.	
20502	2268	Countess Ragnhild Danneskiold Samsoe, 1882.	
20503	2269	Count Christian August Frederick Sofus Charles George Ernest Danneskiold Samsoe, 1840.	Younger son.

20504	2270	Mary Elizabeth Agnes, Countess of Mauny Talvande [France]. *Domaine du Bourg, Pontvallain, Sarthe.*	Granddaughters. Only children of the Countess Henrietta Danneskiold Samsoe, – 1880 (eldest daughter), and her husband, Henry William John, 4th Earl of Strafford, 1831–1899.
20505	2271	Amy Frederica Alice, Countess of Normanton [I.], Baroness Somerton [U.K.]. *Somerley, Ringwood, Hants.*	
20506	2272	Lady Georgina Mary Elizabeth Fanny Agar, 1896.	Great-grandchildren. Children of No. 20505.
20507	2273	Lady Alexandra Henrietta Alice Agar, 1897.	
20508	2274	Lady Caroline Amy Cora Agar, 1899.	
20509	2275	Lady Karen Mary Agar, 1901.	

174. Descendants, if any, of Lady Frances Elizabeth Brudenell-Bruce, 1765–1836, and her husband, Sir Henry Wright Wilson, of Chelsea Park, Middlesex, –1832. (See Table XXII.)

---

175. Descendants of the Hon. Mary Elizabeth Townshend, 1794–1847, wife 1st of George James Cholmondeley of Boxley House, Kent, 1752–1830, and 2ndly of Charles, 2nd Earl of Romney, 1777–1845. (See Table XXIII.)

20510	2276	Hon. Robert Marsham-Townshend, J.P., D.L., 1834. *Frognal, Foot's Cray, Kent.* *5 Chesterfield Street, W.*	Son by 2nd husband.
20511	2277	Hugh Sydney Marsham-Townshend, Lieutenant 4th Battalion Gloucestershire Regiment, 1878.	Grandsons. Sons of No. 20510.
20512	2278	Ferdinand Marsham-Townshend, 1880.	
20513	2279	Sir John Walter Buchanan-Riddell, 11th Bart., 1849. *Hepple, Rothbury, Northumberland.* *46 Beaufort Gardens, S.W.*	Grandson. Son of Frances Sophia Cholmondeley, 1826–1887 (daughter by 1st husband), wife of the Rev. John Charles Buchanan-Riddell, 1814–1879.
20514	2280	Walter Robert Buchanan-Riddell, 1879.	Great-grandchildren. Children of No. 20513.
20515	2281	Katherine Margaret Buchanan-Riddell, 1875.	
20516	2282	Olive Frances Buchanan-Riddell, 1877.	
20517	2283	Dorothy Isabel Buchanan-Riddell, 1885.	
20518	2284	Margaret Frances Buchanan-Riddell, 1896.	Great-granddaughters. Daughters of Colonel Robert George Buchanan Riddell, 1854–1900 (Spion Kop). Brother to No. 20513.
20519	2285	Elizabeth Agnes Buchanan-Riddell, 1898.	
20520	2286	Frances Mary Buchanan-Riddell, 1847.	Granddaughters. Sisters to No. 20513.
20521	2287	Mary Amelia Buchanan-Riddell, 1850.	
20522	2288	Sophia Anne Buchanan-Riddell, 1852. *9 Sloane Gardens, S.W.*	

The Blood Royal of Britain

176. Descendants of the Hon. Frances Townshend, 1772–1854, and her husband, George, 3rd Lord Dynevor, 1765–1852. (See Table XXIII.)

20523	2289	Mervyn Edward George Rhys Wingfield, Captain 4th Battalion Gloucestershire Regiment, 1872. *Barrington Park, Burford.*	Great-great-grandchildren. Children of Edward Rhys Wingfield, of Barrington Park, 1849–1901, grandchildren of Captain Edward Ffolliott Wingfield, 1823–1865, and his wife, the Hon. Frances Emily Rice, 1826–1863, eldest daughter and co-heir of George, 4th Lord Dynevor, 1795–1869.
20524	2290	William Jocelyn Rhys Wingfield, Lieutenant 19th Hussars, 1873.	
20525	2291	Charles John Fitzroy Wingfield, Captain 7th Battalion Royal Fusiliers, 1877.	
20526	2292	Maurice Ffolliott Wingfield, 1879.	
20527	2293	Cecil John Talbot Wingfield, 1881.	
20528	2294	Muriel Frances Wingfield, 1878.	
20529	2295	Gwenllian Wingfield, 1882.	
20530	2296	Charles Trevor Wingfield, 1889.	Great-great-grandson. Only child of Major Charles George Lewis Wingfield, 1850–1890, 2nd son of Capt. E. F. Wingfield, 1823–1865. *See above.*
20531	2297	George Talbot Wingfield, *late* Commander R.N., 1853.	Great-grandson. 3rd son of Captain Edward Ffolliott Wingfield, 1823–1865. *See above.*
20532	2298	Ela Mary Wingfield, 1883.	Great-great-granddaughters. Daughters of No. 20531.
20533	2299	Joan Ffolliott Wingfield, 1885.	
20534	2300	Rhona Frances Wingfield, 1886.	
20535	2301	Elianore Maud Rhys Wingfield, 1887.	
20536	2302	Henry Jocelyn Wingfield, 1863. *Wolverton House, Stony Stratford, Bucks.*	Great-grandson. Brother of No. 20531.
20537	2303	Henry Granville Wingfield, 1892.	Great-great-grandchildren. Children of No. 20536.
20538	2304	Brian Ffolliott Wingfield, 1894.	
20539	2305	Dorothy Maud Wingfield, 1889.	
20540	2306	Sybil Joceline Wingfield, 1891.	
20541	2307	Selina Emily Wingfield, 1856.	Great-granddaughters. Sisters of No. 20531.
20542	2308	Frances Louisa Wingfield, 1857.	
20543	2309	Maud Isabel Wingfield, 1859.	
20544	2310	Hon. Eva Frances Caroline, widow of Alfred David Ker, *of Montalto, co. Down,* 1850. *12 Grosvenor Place, S.W.*	Great-granddaughter. Elder daughter and co-heir of Thomas, 1st Lord Deramore, 1819–1890, and his wife, Caroline Elizabeth Anne Rice, 1827–1887, 2nd daughter and co-heir of George, 4th Lord Dynevor, 1795–1869.
20545	2311	Sybil Anna Ker.	Great-great-granddaughters. Daughters of No. 20544.
20546	2312	Eva Winifred Selina, wife of Wilmot Inglis-Jones. *Derry Ormond, R.S.O., Cardiganshire.*	
20547	2313	John Alfred Inglis-Jones, 1898.	Great-great-great-grandchildren. Children of No. 20546.
20548	2314	Elizabeth Winifred Inglis-Jones, 1900.	
20549	2315	Kathleen Elianore Mary Ker.	Great-great-granddaughters. 3rd and 4th daughters of No. 20544.
20550	2316	Eva Cecil Violet Ker.	

20551	2317	Hon. Kathleen Mary, widow of Walter Randolph Farquhar, 1852. *78 Eaton Square, S.W.*	Great-granddaughter. Younger sister of No. 20544.
20552	2318	Walter Randolph Fitzroy Farquhar, 1878.	Great-great-grandson. Child of No. 20551.
20553	2319	Selina, Countess Dowager of Longford [I.], Baroness Silchester [U.K.], 1836. *24 Bruton Street, W.*	Granddaughter. 3rd daughter and co-heir of George, 4th Lord Dynevor, 1795–1869.
20554	2320	Thomas, 5th Earl of Longford [I.], 4th Baron Silchester [U.K.], K.P., 1864. *Pakenham Hall, Castle Pollard, Westmeath.* *24 Bruton Street, W.*	Great-grandchildren. Children of No. 20553.
20555	2321	Captain the Hon. Edward Michael Pakenham, 1866.	
20556	2322	Georgiana Frances Henrietta, Viscountess Gough [U.K.], 1863. *Lough Cutra Castle, Gort.* *British Embassy, Berlin.*	
20557	2323	Hon. Hugh William Gough, 1892.	Great-great-grandchildren. Children of No. 20556.
20558	2324	Hon. Katharine Nora Gough, 1890.	
20559	2325	Lady Katharine Louisa Pakenham, 1868.	Great-granddaughter. Younger daughter of No. 20553.
20560	2326	Hon. Maria Elizabeth Rice, 1815. *Matson House, near Gloucester.*	Only surviving daughter.

177. Descendants of the Hon. Harriet Katherine Townshend, 1773–1814, and her husband, Charles William, 4th Duke of Buccleuch and 6th Duke of Queensberry, K.T., 1772–1819. (See Table XXIII.)

| 20561 –736 | } | Same as Nos. 19724–19899. |

178. Descendants of James George, 3rd Earl of Courtown, K.P., 1765–1835. (See Table XXIII.)

| 20737 –870 | } | Same as Nos. 19935–20068. |

179. Descendants of the Hon. Sir Robert Stopford, Admiral of the Red, 1768–1847. (See Table XXIII.)

20871	2327	Rear-Admiral Robert Wilbraham Stopford, 1844. *Shroton House, Blandford.*	Grandson. Son of Admiral Robert Fanshawe Stopford, 1811–1891.
20872	2328	Robert Neville Stopford, 1888.	Great-grandchildren. Children of No. 20871.
20873	2329	Audrey Stopford, 1887.	
20874	2330	William Edward Stopford, 1848.	Grandsons. Brothers of No. 20871.
20875	2331	Captain Frederick George Stopford, R.A., 1852.	

20876	2332	Robert Edward Wilbraham Stopford, 1897.	} Great-grandchildren. Children of No. 20875.
20877	2333	Emily Wilbraham Stopford, 1894.	
20878	2334	Francis James Stopford, Barrister-at-Law, 1857.	
20879	2335	Mary Louisa, wife of the Rev. William Ulyat, 1854. *The Vicarage, Freeland, Oxford.*	Grandchildren. Younger brothers and sisters of No. 20871.
20880	2336	Henrietta Julia Stopford, 1859.	
20881	2337	Eleanor Anna, wife of Leonard Malet, 1862. *Lismore, Canterbury, New Zealand.*	
20882	2338	Louisa Catherine Stopford, 1820.	
20883	2339	Charlotte Anne, wife of the Very Rev. Robert Gregory, Dean of St. Paul's, 1823. *The Deanery, St. Paul's, E.C.*	Daughters.
20884	2340	Eleanor Charlotte Gregory.	Grandchildren. Children of No. 20883.
20885	2341	Christiana Stopford Gregory.	
20886	2342	Alice Sophia Gregory.	

180. Descendants of the Rev. and Hon. Richard Bruce Stopford, Canon of Windsor, 1774-1844. (See Table XXIII.)

20887	2343	Hilda Frances Marguerite, wife of Arthur Alison Barnard, Barrister-at-Law, 1874. *14 Kensington Mansions, Earl's Court, S.W.*	Great-granddaughter. Daughter of Arthur Chas. Stopford, 1846–1895, and granddaughter of the Rev. Charles Stopford, 1805–1864.
20888	2344	Alice Mary Stopford, 1848. *31 Brunswick Place, Hove, Brighton.*	Granddaughter. Only daughter of the Rev. Charles Stopford, 1805–1864.
20889	2345	Sackville George Stopford Sackville, M.P., Hon. Col. 3rd Battalion Northampton Regiment, 1840. *Drayton House, Thrapston.*	Grandsons. Sons of William Bruce Stopford, of Drayton House, Thrapston, who assumed the additional name of Sackville, 1806–1872.
20890	2346	Lionel Richard Stopford Sackville, Colonel *late* Rifle Brigade, 1845. *Army and Navy; Travellers'.*	
20891	2347	Lionel Charles Stopford Sackville, 1891.	Great-grandchildren. Children of No. 20890.
20892	2348	Geoffrey William Stopford Sackville, 1893.	
20893	2349	Nigel Victor Stopford-Sackville, 1901.	
20894	2350	Elinor Beryl Stopford Sackville, 1888.	
20895	2351	Diana Mary Stopford Sackville, 1889.	
20896	2352	Alexander William Stopford Sackville, 1846. *Carlton; Junior Carlton.*	Grandson. Brother of Nos. 20889, &c.
20897	2353	Edward Rupert Sydney Stopford Sackville.	Great-grandson. Only son of Sydney Robert Stopford Sackville, 1850–1888, brother of Nos. 20889, &c.
20898	2354	Harriet Caroline Stopford Sackville, 1838.	Granddaughters. Sisters of Nos. 20889, &c.
20899	2355	Fanny Louisa, wife of the Hon. and Right Rev. Augustus Legge, Bishop of Lichfield, 1841. *The Palace, Lichfield.*	
20900	2356	Francis Augustus Legge, 1880.	Great-grandchildren. Children of No. 20899.
20901	2357	George Stopford Legge, 1882.	
20902	2358	Beatrice Mary Caroline Legge, 1883.	
20903	2359	Rhoda Stefanie Legge, 1887.	

20904	2360	Georgina Mary, wife of the Hon. Edward Peirson Thesiger, C.B., 1842. *142 Sloane Street, S.W.*	Granddaughter. 3rd sister of Nos. 20889, &c.
20905	2361	Arthur Lionel Bruce Thesiger, 1872.	Great-grandchildren. Children of No. 20904.
20906	2362	Bertram Sackville Thesiger, Lieut. R.N., 1875.	
20907	2363	Ernest Frederick Graham Thesiger, 1879.	
20908	2364	Sibyl Adeline Thesiger, 1883.	
20909	2365	Margaret Elizabeth, wife of William Edmund Wood Collins, 1847. *Langley Place, Slough.*	Granddaughter. 4th sister of Nos. 20889, &c.
20910	2366	Edith Stella Collins, 1887.	Great-granddaughter. Daughter of No. 20909.
20911	2367	Eleanor Mary Agnes, wife of Lionel John William Fletcher, 1851. *Ewell Manor, West Farleigh, Maidstone.*	Granddaughter. 5th sister of Nos. 20889, &c.
20912	2368	Lancelot Sackville Fletcher, 1881.	Great-grandsons. Sons of No. 20911.
20913	2369	Roland Sackville Fletcher, Lieutenant 5th Fusiliers, 1882.	
20914	2370	Walter John Fletcher, Lieutenant R.N., 1883.	
20915	2371	Horace William Fletcher, 1889.	
20916	2372	Beatrice Evelyn, wife of Harry Samuel Cumming Clark Jervoise, 1853. *Chelwood Beacon, Uckfield, Sussex.*	Granddaughter. 6th sister of Nos. 20889, &c.
20917	2373	Kathleen Margaret Clarke Jervoise.	Great-grandchild. Daughter of No. 20916.
20918	2374	Grace, wife of the Hon. Henry Arden Adderley, 1854. *Fillongley Hall, Coventry.*	Granddaughter. 7th sister of Nos. 20889, &c.
20919 -24		Same as Nos. 19639–19644.	Great-grandchildren. Children of No. 20918.
20925	2375	George Walter Stopford, 1870.	Grandchildren. Children of James Sydney Stopford, 1808–1885.
20926	2376	Philip James Stopford, Lieutenant R.N., 1872.	
20927	2377	Reginald Arthur Stopford, 1873.	
20928	2378	Heneage Frank Stopford, Captain R.A., 1877.	
20929	2379	Wyndham Horace Stopford, Lieut. R.M.L.I., 1878.	
20930	2380	Mabel Catherine Stopford, 1869.	
20931	2381	Eleanor Frances Stopford, 1874.	
20932	2382	Edith Louisa, wife of Vice-Admiral Sir William Robert Kennedy, K.C.B., 1843. *Falconers Hill, Daventry.*	Granddaughter. Daughter of Captain Edward Stopford, R.N., 1809–1895.
20933	2383	Alice Emily Kennedy, 1870.	Great-granddaughter. Daughter of No. 20932.
20934	2384	Robert Maurice Stopford, 1890. *Gleneden,*	Great-grandchildren. Children of Lieut.-Col. Horace Robert Stopford, 1855–1899 (Modder River), son of Robert Stopford, 1813–1878.
20935	2385	Nora Grace Eden Stopford, 1889. *Sheringham, Norfolk.*	
20936	2386	Evelyn Emma, wife of Walter Copland Perry, M.A., Ph.D., Barrister-at-Law. *5 Manchester Square, W.*	Granddaughter. Daughter of Robert Stopford, 1813–1878.
20937	2387	Evelyn Walter Copland Perry, 1890.	Great-grandson. Son of No. 20936.

20938	2388	Ambrose Bartholomew Tunnard, 1851.	Grandson. Eldest son of Harriet Jane Stopford, 1816–1902, and her husband, Captain Bartholomew Tunnard.
20939	2389	Michael Victor Tunnard, 1901.	Great-grandchildren. Children of No. 20938.
20940	2390	Bridget Lucy Tunnard, 1900.	
20941	2391	William Francis Tunnard, Captain R.N., 1854.	Grandsons. 2nd and 3rd brothers of No. 20938.
20942	2392	Henry Stopford Tunnard, *late* Captain Royal Inniskilling Fusiliers, 1856.	
20943	2393	Henry Bartholomew Tunnard, 1892.	Great-grandchildren. Children of No. 20942.
20944	2394	Dorothy Evelyn Tunnard, 1883.	
20945	2395	Eleanor Lucy Tunnard, 1859.	Granddaughter. Sister of Nos. 20942, &c.

181. Descendants of George Augustus Frederick John, 7th Duke of Atholl, K.T., 1814–1864. (See Table XXIV.)

20946	2396	▽ ▽ ▽ John James Hugh Henry, 8th Duke of Atholl [S.], 4th Earl Strange [G.B.], 11th Baron Strange [E.], 3rd Baron Glenlyon [U.K.], K.T., 1840. *Blair Castle, Blair Atholl.* 84 *Eaton Place, S.W.*	Son.
20947	2397	▽ ▽ ▽ John George, Marquis of Tullibardine, D.S.O., 1871. *Turf ; Marlborough.*	Grandchildren. Children of No. 20946.
20948	2398	▽ ▽ ▽ Lord George Murray, 1873.	
20949	2399	▽ ▽ ▽ Lord James Thomas Murray, 1879.	
20950	2400	▽ ▽ ▽ Lady Dorothea Louisa, wife of Captain Harold G. Ruggles-Brise, 1866.	
20951	2401	▽ ▽ ▽ Lady Helen Murray, 1867.	
20952	2402	▽ ▽ ▽ Lady Evelyn Murray, 1868.	

182. Descendants of Lord James Charles Plantagenet Murray, 1819–1874. (See Table XXIV.)

| 20953 | 2403 | ▽ ▽ ▽ Caroline Frances Murray, 1858. 8 *Royal Crescent, Bath.* | Only surviving child. |

183. Descendants of Algernon George, 6th Duke of Northumberland, K.G., 1810–1899. (See Table XXV.)

20954	2404	▽ Henry George, 7th Duke of Northumberland [E.], K.G., P.C., 1846. *Alnwick Castle, Northumberland.* 2 *Grosvenor Place, S.W.*	Son.
20955	2405	▽ Henry Algernon George, Earl Percy, M.P., 1871. 64 *Curzon Street, S.W.*	Grandchildren. Children of No. 20954.
20956	2406	▽ Lord Alan Ian Percy, 1880.	
20957	2407	▽ Lord William Richard Percy, 1882.	
20958	2408	▽ Lord James Percy, 1885.	
20959	2409	▽ Lord Eustace Sutherland Campbell Percy, 1887.	
20960	2410	▽ Lady Edith Eleanor Percy, 1869.	
20961	2411	▽ Lady Margaret Percy, 1873.	
20962	2412	▽ Lady Victoria Alexandrina Percy, 1875.	
20963	2413	▽ Lady Mary Percy, 1878.	
20964	2414	▽ Lady Muriel Evelyn Nora Percy, 1890.	

Atholl

JOHN JAMES HUGH HENRY, DUKE OF ATHOLL, K.T.

From a Photograph

20965	2415	⛉ Lord Algernon Malcolm Arthur Percy, 1851. *Guy's Cliffe, Warwick.*	} 2nd son.
20966	2416	⛉ Algernon William Percy, 1884.	} Grandchildren. Chil-
20967	2417	⛉ Katharine Louisa Victoria Percy, 1882.	dren of No. 20965.

184. Descendants of Lord Josceline William Percy, 1811–1881. (See Table XXV.)

| 20968 | 2418 | ⛉ Lieut.-Col. George Algernon Percy, *late* Grenadier Guards, 1849. | } Son. |

185. Descendants of Lady Margaret Percy, 1813–1897, and her husband, Edward Richard, 2nd Lord Hatherton, 1815–1888. (See Table XXV.)

20969	2419	Edward George Percy, 3rd Lord Hatherton [U.K.], C.M.G., 1842. *Teddesley Park, near Penkridge.*	} Son.
20970	2420	Hon. Edward Charles Rowley Littleton, 1868.	{ Grandson. Son of No. 20969.
20971	2421	Edward Thomas Walhouse Littleton, 1900.	} Great-grandchildren.
20972	2422	Joyce Marie Littleton, 1898.	Children of No.
20973	2423	Nora Hyacinthe Littleton, 1899.	20970.
20974	2424	Hon. Algernon Joshua Percy Littleton, *late* Lieutenant South African M.I., 1871.	
20975	2425	Hon. Charles Christopher Josceline Littleton, 1872.	Grandchildren.
20976	2426	Hon. William Hugh Littleton, Lieutenant 5th Battalion Northumberland Fusiliers, 1882.	Children of No. 20969.
20977	2427	Hon. Margaret Louisa, wife of Major Bertram Percy Portal, D.S.O., 17th Lancers, 1869 [*Naval and Military*].	
20978	2428	Melville Edward Portal.	{ Great-grandchild. Child of No. 20977.
20979	2429	Hon. Hyacinthe Frances Littleton, 1874.	
20980	2430	Hon. Susan Helen, wife of the Rev. Owen F. Jacson. *The Rectory, Moreton Saye, co. Salop.*	Grandchildren. Younger children of No. 20969.
20981	2431	Hon. Mary Cecilia Littleton, 1884.	
20982	2432	Hon. Edith Modwena Littleton, 1888.	
20983	2433	Hon. Algernon Charles Littleton, Rear-Admiral R.N., 1843. *59 Warwick Square, S.W.*	} 2nd son.
20984	2434	Algernon Edward Percy Littleton, 1881.	
20985	2435	Josceline William Littleton, 1886.	
20986	2436	Richard Charles Arthur Littleton, 1888.	Grandchildren. Children of No. 20983.
20987	2437	Cecil Francis Henry Littleton, 1890.	
20988	2438	Louisa Lucy, wife of Captain Henry Arthur Clowes, 1876. *Norbury Hall, Derby.*	
20989	2439	Henry Samuel Littleton Clowes, 1900.	} Great-grandchildren. Chil-
20990	2440	Leigh Algernon Clowes, 1901.	dren of No. 20988.
20991	2441	Hyacinthe Mary Henrietta Littleton, 1877.	} Grandchildren. Youn-
20992	2442	Isabel Littleton, 1879.	ger daughters of No.
20993	2443	Blanche Littleton, 1880.	20983.
20994	2444	Eleanor Littleton, 1884.	

20995	2445	Hon. Henry Stuart Littleton, 1844. *Travellers'; Athenæum.*	3rd and 4th sons.
20996	2446	Hon. and Rev. Cecil James Littleton, Hon. Canon of Southwell, 1850. *St. Mary's Rectory, Stafford.*	

186. Descendants of Algernon Charles Percy, afterwards Heber-Percy, of Hodnet Hall, co. Salop, and Airmine Hall, York, J.P., D.L., 1812–1901. (See Table XXVI.)

20997	2447	▽ Algernon Heber-Percy, J.P., Major Shropshire Yeomanry, 1845. *Hodnet Hall, Salop. Airmine Hall, York.*	Son.
20998	2448	▽ Algernon Hugh Heber-Percy, 1869.	Grandsons. Sons of No. 20997.
20999	2449	▽ Josceline Reginald Heber-Percy, 2nd Lieutenant Northumberland Fusiliers, 1880.	
21000	2450	▽ Reginald Josceline Heber-Percy, 1849, Lieut.-Col. *late* Rifle Brigade. *Hinstock, Market Drayton.*	2nd, 3rd, and 4th sons.
21001	2451	▽ Hugh Louis Heber-Percy, 1853. *St. James'.*	
21002	2452	▽ Rev. Henry Vernon Heber-Percy, 1858. *The Rectory, Hodnet, Market Drayton, co. Salop.*	
21003	2453	▽ Charles Rowland Heber-Percy, 1887.	Grandchildren. Children of No. 21002.
21004	2454	▽ Neville Henry Heber-Percy, 1891.	
21005	2455	▽ Hermione Constance Heber-Percy, 1888.	
21006	2456	▽ Aileen Judith Heber-Percy, 1889.	
21007	2457	▽ Rachel Joan Heber-Percy, 1893.	
21008	2458	▽ Hilda Bridget Heber-Percy, 1897.	
21009	2459	▽ Alan William Heber-Percy, 1865. *Durweston, Blandford.*	5th son.
21010	2460	▽ Hugh Alan Heber-Percy, 1897.	Grandchildren. Children of No. 21009.
21011	2461	▽ Margaret Eleanor Heber-Percy, 1894.	
21012	2462	▽ Ida Mary Heber-Percy, 1899.	
21013	2463	▽ Constance Emily Heber-Percy, 1901.	
21014	2464	▽ Edith Cecilia, wife of the Hon. Alexander Frederic Hood, 1851. *Airmyn Hall, Goole, Yorks.*	1st daughter.
21015	2465	Alexander Nelson Hood, Lieutenant I.S.C., 1873.	Grandchildren. Children of No. 21014.
21016	2466	Charles Hugh Hood, Lieutenant R.M.L.I., 1877.	
21017	2467	Grosvenor Percy Hood, 1882.	
21018	2468	Sibell Ethel Hood, 1875.	
21019	2469	Gertrude Margaret Hood, 1879.	
21020	2470	▽ Agnes Katherine Heber-Percy, 1857.	2nd and 3rd daughters.
21021	2471	▽ Maud Ellen, wife of Colonel Sir Edward Law Durand, 1st Bart., C.B., 1859. *Ruckley Grange, Shifnal, Salop.*	
21022	2472	Edward Percy Marion Durand, 1884.	Grandchildren. Children of No. 21021.
21023	2473	Reginald Heber Marion Durand, 1892.	
21024	2474	Alan Algernon Marion Durand 1893.	
21025	2475	Mortimer Henry Marion Durand, 1898.	
21026	2476	Isabel Marion Durand.	
21027	2477	Everild Blanche Marion Durand.	
21028	2478	Beryl Marion Durand.	
21029	2479	▽ Gertrude Amelia, wife of J. J. Hardy Eustace, 1861. *Castlemore, co. Carlow.*	4th daughter.

21030	2480	Oliver Hardy Eustace, 1890.	
21031	2481	Rowland Hugh Eustace, 1902.	Grandchildren. Children
21032	2482	Elizabeth Gertrude Eustace, 1897.	of No. 21029.
21033	2483	Doris Anna Eustace, 1901.	
21034	2484	Ⓥ Evelyn Mary, wife of Francis Monckton, 1863. *Stretton Hall, co. Stafford.*	5th daughter.
21035	2485	Francis Algernon Monckton, 1890.	
21036	2486	Geoffrey Valentine Francis Monckton, 1895.	Grandchildren.
21037	2487	Reginald Francis Percy Monckton, 1896.	Children of
21038	2488	Evelyn Frances Monckton, 1891.	No. 21034.
21039	2489	Constance Frances Monckton, 1892.	
21040	2490	Violet Maude Frances Monckton, 1894.	
21041	2491	Ⓥ Isabel Harriet, wife of Andrew Greville Rouse-Boughton-Knight, 1867. *Wormesley Grange, Hereford.*	6th daughter.
21042	2492	Thomas Andrew Rouse-Boughton-Knight, 1897.	Grandchildren.
21043	2493	Dorothy Emily Rouse-Boughton-Knight, 1892.	Children of
21044	2494	Isabel Bridget Rouse-Boughton-Knight, 1899.	No. 21041.

187. Descendants of Henry Percy, Rector of Greystoke and Canon of Carlisle, 1813–1870. (See Table XXVI.)

21045	2495	Ⓥ Alfred Percy, 1850.	Son.
21046	2496	Ⓥ Henry Percy, 1901.	Grandson. Son of No. 21045.
21047	2497	Ⓥ Edward Galbraith Henry Percy, 1854.	
21048	2498	Ⓥ Josceline Hugh Percy, 1856. *49 Talbot Road, Highgate, N.*	Sons.
21049	2499	Ⓥ Henry Edward Percy, 1893.	Grandchildren. Children
21050	2500	Ⓥ Josceline Richard Percy, 1894.	of No. 21048.
21051	2501	Ⓥ Margaret Percy, 1898.	
21052	2502	Ⓥ Elizabeth Mary, wife of the Rev. John Adams, 1845. *Offchurch Vicarage, near Leamington.*	1st daughter.
21053	2503	Henry Theophilus Adams, 1872.	
21054	2504	John Cadwallader Adams, 1873.	
21055	2505	Hugh Geoffrey Coker Adams, 1880.	Grandchildren.
21056	2506	Edward Josceline Percy Adams, 1888.	Children of
21057	2507	Elsie Emma Mary, wife of Thomas Owen Lloyd, 1876.	No. 21052.
21058	2508	Kathleen Alice Georgina Adams, 1882.	
21059	2509	Ⓥ Charlotte Florentia Frances Percy, 1848.	
21060	2510	Ⓥ Emma Annie Isabel, wife of Lieut.-Col. Herbert Cranstoun Adams, 1858. *Exmouth.*	2nd and 3rd daughters.
21061	2511	Henry Launcelot Elford Adams, 1885.	
21062	2512	John Percy Fitzherbert Adams, 1891.	
21063	2513	William Herbert Adams, 1893.	Grandchildren.
21064	2514	Alan St. George Adams, 1894.	Children of
21065	2515	Alice Barbara Adams, 1886.	No. 21060.
21066	2516	Margaret Hyale Adams, 1887.	
21067	2517	Norah Roberta Adams, 1889.	

188. Descendants of Hugh Josceline Percy, Esq., of Eskrigg, Wigton, 1817–1882. (See Table XVI.)

21068	2518	Ⓥ Edward Josceline Percy, 1864. *Eskrigg, Wigton.*	Children.
21069	2519	Ⓥ Agnes Ellen, wife of Frederic George Mather, 1869. *Huntley Hall, Cheadle, Staffordshire.*	

21070	2520	Marjorie Helen Mather, 1892.	⎫	Grandchildren. Children
21071	2521	Phyllis Mather, 1898.	⎬	of No. 21069.
21072	2522	Sylvia Mather, 1900.	⎭	

189. Descendants of Mary Isabella Percy, 1808–1878, wife of the Rev. Frederic Vernon Lockwood, Prebendary of Canterbury, –1851. (See Table XXVI.)

| 21073 | 2523 | Alice Charlotte Mary, wife of Major Algernon Heber-Percy. ⎫
 Hodnet Hall, Salop. Airmine Hall, York. ⎬ | Only child. |
| 21074 -75 | ⎱⎰ | Same as Nos. 20998–20999. { | Grandchildren. Children of
 No. 21073. |

190. Descendants of Lucy Percy, 1811–1887, wife of Henry William Askew, Esq., of Glenridding, Cumberland and Conishead Priory, 1808–1890. (See Table XXVI.)

21076	2524	Henry Hugh Askew, *late* 6th Dragoon Guards, 1847. ⎫ *Thatcham House, Newbury.* ⎬	Elder son.
21077	2525	Caroline, wife of Major Hill, D.S.O. ⎫	
21078	2526	Lucy, wife of the Rev. J. Hill.	Granddaughters. Daughters
21079	2527	Anne Askew.	of No. 21076.
21080	2528	Louisa Askew. ⎭	
21081	2529	Rev. Edmund Adam Askew, 1849. ⎫ *The Rectory, Greystoke.* ⎬	2nd son.
21082	2530	Henry Adam Askew, Lieutenant Border Regiment, 1881. ⎫	
21083	2531	Edmund Joscelyn Percy Askew, 1887.	Grandchildren. Children
21084	2532	Elsie Lucy Victoire, wife of the Rev. Frederick St. John Corbett, M.A., F.R.S.L., 1876. *Long Marton Rectory, Carlisle.*	of No. 21081.
21085	2533	Elsie Mabel Corbett, 1901. {	Great-grandchild. Daughter of No. 21084.
21086	2534	Lilian Julia Charlotte Askew, 1878. ⎫	
21087	2535	Eleanor Louisa Cecily Askew, 1879.	Grandchildren. Sisters
21088	2536	Mary Evelyn Marjorie Askew, 1880.	to No. 21082.
21089	2537	Constance Frances Ann Askew, 1883.	
21090	2538	Ida Stephanie Askew, 1885. ⎭	
21091	2539	Charlotte Elizabeth Askew. ⎫	
21092	2540	Emily Mary Askew. ⎬	Daughters.
21093	2541	Frances Louisa Askew. ⎭	

191. Descendants of Gertrude Percy, 1814–1890, and her husband, William Pitt, 2nd Earl Amherst, 1805–1886. (See Table XXVI.)

21094	2542	William Archer, 3rd Earl [U.K.] and 4th Baron [G.B.] Amherst, 1836. ⎫ *Montreal, Sevenoaks.* 3 *Wilton Terrace, S.W.*	
21095	2543	Hon. and Rev. Percy Arthur Amherst, 1839. ⎬	Sons.
21096	2544	Hon. Hugh Amherst, *late* Captain Coldstream Guards, 1856. *Covelley, Weymouth.* ⎭	

21097	2545	Jeffrey John Archer Amherst, 1896.	Grandchildren.
21098	2546	Joan Gertrude Elizabeth Amherst, 1899.	Children of
21099	2547	Mary Evelyn Amherst, 1902.	No. 21096.
21100	2548	Gertrude Lucia, Countess of Albemarle [E.]. *Quidenham Park, Attleborough, Norfolk.*	Granddaughter. Only child of Lady Mary Sarah Amherst (eldest daughter), 1837–1892, 1st wife of Wilbraham, 1st Earl of Egerton, 1832.
21101	2549	Walter Egerton George Lucian, Viscount Bury, 1882.	
21102	2550	Hon. Arnold Joost William Keppel, 1884.	Great-grandchildren.
21103	2551	Hon. Rupert Oswald Derek Keppel, 1886.	Children of No.
21104	2552	Hon. Albert Edward George Arnold Keppel, 1898.	21100.
21105	2553	Lady Elizabeth Mary Gertrude Keppel, 1890.	
21106	2554	Charles Arthur Middleton, 1873. *Belsay Castle, Newcastle-on-Tyne.*	Grandchildren. Children of Lady Constance Harriet Amherst (3rd daughter),
21107	2555	Hugh Jeffery Middleton, Midshipman R.N., 1874.	–1879, and her husband, Sir Arthur Edward Middleton, 7th Bart.
21108	2556	Gertrude Mary Middleton, 1875.	
21109	2557	Elinor Isabel Middleton, 1876.	
21110	2558	Lady Margaret Catherine Amherst, 1848. *5 Upper Berkeley Street, W.*	
21111	2559	Lady Elinor, wife of Captain William Evelyn Denison, 1850. *Ossington, Newark.*	4th and 5th daughters.
21112	2560	William Frank Evelyn Denison, 1878.	Grandson. Only child of No. 21111.
21113	2561	Lady Charlotte Florentia Amherst, 1851. *5 Upper Berkeley Street, W.*	6th and youngest daughter.

192. Descendants of Ellen Percy, 1815–1899, and her husband, the Rev. Edward Thompson, 18 –1838. (See Table XXVI.)

21114	2562	▽ Henry Thompson, Lieutenant R.N., 1864.	Grandchildren. Only surviving sons and eldest daughter of Edward Percy Thompson, 7th Hussars, 1837–1879.
21115	2563	▽ Alexander Maurice Thompson, 1869.	
21116	2564	▽ Grace Anne, wife of Josceline Hugh Percy. *49 Talbot Road, Highgate, N.*	
21117 –19	}	Same as Nos. 21049–21051.	Great-grandchildren. Children of No. 21116.
21120	2565	▽ Gertrude Thompson, Sister of Mercy.	Granddaughters. Sisters of No. 21114.
21121	2566	▽ Constance Thompson.	

193. Descendants of the Hon. Josceline Percy, Rear-Admiral R.N., C.B., 1784–1856. (See Table XXV.)

21122	2567	▽ Sophia Louisa, widow of the *late* Colonel Charles Bagot, Grenadier Guards, 1808–1880, 1821. *42 Lowndes Street, S.W.*	Eldest daughter.
21123	2568	▽ Josceline Fitzroy Bagot, J.P., D.L., 1854. *Levens Hall, Westmorland.*	Grandson. Son of No. 21122.

21124	2569	Alan Desmond Bagot, 1896.	Great-grandchildren. Children of No. 21123.
21125	2570	Dorothy Bagot, 1886.	
21126	2571	Marjory Constance Bagot, 1888.	
21127	2572	Mary Bagot, 189 .	
21128	2573	Richard Bagot, 1860. *42 Lowndes Street, S.W.* *1 Via Somma Campagna, Rome.*	Grandchildren. Children of No. 21122.
21129	2574	Alice Mary Bagot, 1853.	
21130	2575	Emily Lady D'Aguilar, wife of General Sir Charles D'Aguilar, G.C.B., 1826. *4 Clifton Crescent, Folkestone.*	2nd daughter.
21131	2576	Emily Gertrude D'Aguilar.	Granddaughter. Daughter of No. 21130.
21132	2577	Charlotte Alice, widow of Edward Percy Thompson, 1837–1879, 1831. *The Haven, Victoria Grove, Southsea.*	3rd daughter.
21133 -40		Same as Nos. 21114–21121.	

194. Descendants of Bertram, 4th Earl of Ashburnham, 1797–1878. (See Table XXVII.)

21141	2578	Bertram, 5th Earl of [G.B.] and 7th Baron [E.] Ashburnham, 1840. *Ashburnham Place, Battle, Sussex.*	Son.
21142	2579	Lady Mary Catherine Charlotte Ashburnham, 1890.	Granddaughter. Only child of No. 21141.
21143	2580	Hon. John Ashburnham, 1845. *Shernfold Park, Frant.*	
21144	2581	Hon. Thomas Ashburnham, *late* Captain 7th Hussars, 1855. *Naval and Military.*	
21145	2582	Hon. George Ashburnham, 1863. *Wellington.*	Children.
21146	2583	Lady Margaret, wife of John Joseph Bickersteth, Barrister-at-Law, 1851. *Beechwood, Driffield, Yorks.*	
21147	2584	Edward Robert Bickersteth, 1889.	Grandchildren. Children of No. 21146.
21148	2585	John Richard Bickersteth, 1897.	
21149	2586	Ruth Bickersteth, 1885.	
21150	2587	Lady Mary, wife of the Hon. Sydney George Holland, 1859. *44 Bryanston Square, W.*	Younger daughter.
21151	2588	Lucy Katherine Holland, 1886.	Granddaughters. Daughters of No. 21150.
21152	2589	Rachel Mary Holland, 1891.	

195. Descendants of Lady Georgiana Jemima Ashburnham, 1805–1882, wife 1st of Henry Revely Mitford, of Exbury House, 1804–1883, and 2ndly of the Hon. Francis George Molyneux, 1805–1886. (See Table XXVII.)

21153	2590	Henry Mitford, 1833. Children of No. 21153, if any.	Sons by 1st husband.
21154	2591	Algernon Bertram, 1st Baron Redesdale [U.K.], C.B., C.V.O., 1837. *Batsford Park, co. Gloucester.* *Birdhope Craig, Northumberland.*	

21155	2592	Hon. Clement Bertram Ogilvy Freeman-Mitford, 2nd Lieutenant 10th Royal Hussars, 1876.	
21156	2593	Hon. David Bertram Ogilvy Freeman-Mitford, Imperial Yeomanry, 1878.	
21157	2594	Hon. Bertram Thomas Carlyle Ogilvy Freeman-Mitford, Midshipman R.N., 180.	Grandchildren. Children of No. 21154.
21158	2595	Hon. John Power Bertram Ogilvy Freeman-Mitford, 1884.	
21159	2596	Hon. Ernest Rupert Bertram Ogilvy Freeman-Mitford, 1895.	
21160	2597	Hon. Frances Georgina Freeman-Mitford, 1875.	
21161	2598	Hon. Iris Elizabeth Freeman-Mitford, 1879.	
21162	2599	Hon. Joan Freeman-Mitford, 1887.	
21163	2600	Hon. Daphne Freeman-Mitford, 1895.	
21164	2601	Constance Philipina Georgina, wife of William Melville, 1848.	Daughter by 2nd husband.

196. Descendants of Lady Jane Henrietta Ashburnham, 1809–1896, and her husband, Admiral Henry Charles Swinburne, 1797–1877. (See Table XXVII.)

21165	2602	Algernon Charles Swinburne, the poet, 1837. The Pines, Putney.	Children.
21166	2603	Alice Swinburne.	
21167	2604	Isabel Swinburne.	

197. Descendants of Lady Katherine Frances Ashburnham, 1812–1839, wife of Henry William Beauclerk, of Leckhampstead, Bucks, 1812–1894. (See Table XXVII.)

21168	2605	Kathleen Isabel Boyd, 1865. Manor House, Ballycastle, co. Antrim.	Granddaughter. Only child of Katherine Mary Beauclerk, 1839–1867, 1st wife of the Rev. Sir Frederick Boyd, 1820–1889.

198. Descendants of Lady Eleanor Isabel Bridget Ashburnham, 1814–1895, and her husband, Algernon Wodehouse, Rector of Easton, Hampshire, 1814–1882. (See Table XXVII.)

21169	2606	Arthur Hugh Wodehouse, 1879.	Grandchildren. Children of the Rev. William Wentworth Wodehouse, 1846–1888.
21170	2607	Alice Mary Wodehouse, 1864.	
21171	2608	Francis John Wodehouse,	twins, 1855. Children.
21172	2609	Thomas Frederick Wodehouse, Hunstrete, Pensford, Bristol.	
21173	2610	Elinor Alice Hilda Wodehouse, 1897.	Granddaughter. Daughter of No. 21172.
21174	2611	Mary Elizabeth, wife of J. J. Ransome, 1852. San Francisco, U.S.A.	Daughter.
21175	2612	Algernon Lee Ransome, 1883.	Grandchildren. Children of No. 21174.
21176	2613	Reginald Hugh Ransome, 1886.	

The Blood Royal of Britain

199. Descendants of Lady Mary Agnes Blanch Ashburnham, 1816–1899, and her husband, Sir Henry Percy Gordon, Bart., 1806–1876. (See Table XXVII.)

21177	2614	Mary Charlotte Julia, widow of General Robert William Disney Leith, C.B., 1819–1892. *Westhall, Oyne, Aberdeen. Northcourt, Isle of Wight.*	Daughter.
21178	2615	Alexander Henry Leith, Captain 3rd Gordon Highlanders, 1866. *Glenkindie, Inverkindie, Aberdeenshire.*	Grandson. Son of No. 21177.
21179	2616	Mildred Katherine Leith, 1894.	Great-grandchild. Daughter of No. 21178.
21180	2617	Mary Levina Leith.	Grandchildren.
21181	2618	Maria Alice, wife of Captain Maynard Francis Colchester-Wemyss, Cameronians.	Daughters of No. 21177.
21182	2619	Francis Disney Colchester-Wemyss, 1899.	Great-grandchild. Son of No. 21181.
21183	2620	Edith, wife of Major Thomas Algernon Earle. *Hartford, Cheshire.*	Grandchildren. Younger daughters of No. 21177.
21184	2621	Elizabeth Charlotte Leith.	

200. Descendants of Lady Mary Emily Charlotte Percy,   –1887, and her husband, Andrew Mortimer Drummond, Esq., of Charing Cross and Denham, Middlesex, 1786–1864. (See Table XXV.)

21185	2622	Mortimer Percy George Douglas Drummond, 1860.	Grandchildren. Children of Mortimer Percy Drummond, 1816–1893.
21186	2623	Mary Frances Drummond, 1863.	
21187	2624	Louisa Emmeline, wife of Breedon Newland Everard. *Bardon Lodge, Leicester,* 1865.	
21188	2625	Major-General Josceline Heneage Wodehouse, C.B., C.M.G., 1852. *Lahore.*	Grandchildren. Children of Eleanor Charlotte Drummond, 1810–1888, and her husband, Rear-Admiral George Wodehouse, 1810.
21189	2626	Evelyn Georgina Susan Wodehouse, 1849. 10 *Palace Mansions, Addison Bridge, Kensington, W.*	
21190	2627	Algernon Heneage Drummond, Captain, *late* Rifle Brigade, 1844. 73 *Cornwall Gardens, S.W.*	Grandson. Son of Cecil Elizabeth Drummond, 1814–1897, and her husband, the Rev. Heneage Drummond, of Leckamstead, Bucks, 1810–1881.
21191	2628	Algernon Cecil Heneage Drummond, 1880.	Great-grandchildren. Children of No. 21190.
21192	2629	Spencer Heneage Drummond, 1884.	
21193	2630	Geoffrey Heneage Drummond, 1886.	
21194	2631	Jocelyn Heneage Drummond, 1888.	
21195	2632	Frederick Boyd Heneage Drummond, 1890.	
21196	2633	Mortimer Heneage Drummond, 1892.	
21197	2634	Maurice John Heneage Drummond, 1894.	
21198	2635	Barbara Drummond, 1881.	
21199	2636	Isobel Drummond, 1887.	

21200	2637	John Edward Compton-Brace-bridge, 1859. *Feldholm, Barnes.*	{ Grandson. Son of Agnes Priscilla Drummond, 1815–1902, wife of the Rev. Prebendary Berdmore Compton.
21201	2638	Charles Compton-Bracebridge, 1883.	} Great-grandchildren. Children of No. 21200.
21202	2639	James Compton-Bracebridge, 1888.	
21203	2640	Margaret Compton-Bracebridge, 1885.	
21204	2641	Mary Compton-Bracebridge, 1887.	
21205	2642	Emily Agnes, widow of the Rev. Frederic Ball.	} Granddaughters. Sisters of No. 21200.
21206	2643	Frances Compton.	
21207	2644	Susan Caroline, widow of Harvey Drummond, 1875–1820. *Sherborne House, Warwick.*	} Only surviving daughter.
21208	2645	Allan Harvey Drummond, Major retd., 1845. *7 Ennismore Gardens, S.W.*	} Grandson. Son of No. 21207.
21209	2646	Frederick Harvey John Drummond, 1892.	} Great-grandchildren. Children of No. 21208.
21210	2647	Margaret Hester Drummond, 1888.	
21211	2648	Alice Mary Drummond, 1890.	
21212	2649	Constance Adine Maude Drummond, 1895.	
21213	2650	Malcolm Hugh Drummond, Commander R.N., 1848, H.B.M.'s Consul. *Oporto, Portugal.*	} Grandson. 2nd son of No. 21207.
21214	2651	Malcolm David George Drummond, 1895.	} Great-grandchildren. Children of No. 21213.
21215	2652	Susin Iris Harriet Drummond, 1892.	
21216	2653	Archibald Spencer Drummond, Major, *late* Scots Guards, 1853. *Guards'.*	} Grandson. 3rd son of No. 21207.
21217	2654	Harvey Gerald Burns Drummond, 1898.	} Great-grandchildren. Children of No. 21216.
21218	2655	Helen Susan Drummond, 1896.	
21219	2656	William Percy Drummond, *late* Rifle Brigade, 1855. *Marlborough ; Naval and Military.*	} Grandchildren. 4th son and eldest surviving daughter of No. 21207.
21220	2657	Susan Horatia, wife of Richard Cecil Corbett, *late* R.H.A., 1851.	
21221	2658	Cecil Uvedale Corbett, 1880.	{ Great-grandchild. Child of No. 21220.
21222	2659	Katherine Georgina, wife of Charles Aloysius Leslie, 1859. *Balquhain, Aberdeen.*	} Granddaughter. 2nd daughter of No. 21207.
21223	2660	Allan Charles Malcolm Leslie, 1881.	{ Great-grandson. Son of No. 21222.
21224	2661	Issobel Hester, widow of the Hon. Ernest Bowes-Lyon, 1858–1891, 1860. *22 Ovington Square, S.W.*	} Granddaughter. 3rd surviving daughter of No. 21207.
21225	2662	Ernest Hubert Bowes-Lyon, 1883.	} Great-grandchildren. Children of No. 21224.
21226	2663	Joan Issobel Margaret Bowes-Lyon, 1888.	
21227	2664	Marjorie Effie Bowes-Lyon, 1889.	
21228	2665	Ernestine Hester Maud Bowes-Lyon, 1891.	
21229	2666	Marion Blanche Drummond, 1861.	{ Granddaughter. 4th surviving daughter of No. 21207.

201. Descendants of George Guy, 4th Earl of Warwick and Brooke, 1818–1893. (See Table XXVIII.)

21230	2667	Francis Richard Charles Guy, 5th Earl of Warwick and Brooke [G.B.], 12th Baron Brooke [E.], 1853. *Warwick Castle, Warwick.*	Son.
21231	2668	Leopold Guy Francis Maynard, Lord Brooke, 1882.	Grandchildren.
21232	2669	Hon. Maynard Greville, 1898.	Children of
21233	2670	Lady Marjorie Blanch Eva Greville, 1884.	No. 21230.
21234	2671	Hon. Alwyn Henry Fulke Greville, *late* Captain King's Royal Rifle Corps, 1854. *Bachelors'.*	2nd son.
21235	2672	Charles Henry Greville, 1889.	Grandchildren. Son and daughter
21236	2673	. . . . Greville, 1900.	of No. 21234.
21237	2674	Hon. Louis George Greville, 1856. *35 Berkeley Square, W.*	3rd son.
21238	2675	George Gordon Francis Greville, 1890.	Grandson. Son of No. 21237.
21239	2676	Hon. Sydney Robert Greville, C.V.O., C.B., 1866. *106 Mount Street, W.*	4th son.
21240	2677	Lady Eva Sarah Louisa, wife of Frank Dugdale, 1860. *95 Mount Street, W.*	Daughter.
21241	2678	James George Greville Dugdale, 1898.	Grandchildren. Children
21242	2679	Victoria Mary Enid Anne Dugdale, 1896.	of No. 21240.

202. Descendants of John Henry, 3rd Earl of Clonmell, 1817–1866. (See Table XXVIII.)

21243	2680	Lady Mary Henrietta, widow of Captain the Hon. George Fitz-Clarence, 1836–1894, 1841. *32 Beaufort Gardens, S.W.*	Daughter.
21244	2681	Charles Fitz-Clarence, V.C., Major Irish Guards, 1865.	Grandson. Son of No. 21243.
21245	2682	Edward Charles Fitz-Clarence, 1899.	Great-grandchildren. Children
21246	2683	Joan Harriet Fitz-Clarence, 1901.	of No. 21244.
21247	2684	William Henry Fitz-Clarence, Lieutenant R.N., 1868. *Travellers'.*	
21248	2685	Lionel Ashley Arthur Fitz-Clarence, Lieutenant Border Regiment, 1870. *Travellers'.*	Grandchildren. Children of No. 21243.
21249	2686	Annette Mary Fitz-Clarence, 1873.	
21250	2687	Mary Fitz-Clarence, 1877.	
21251	2688	Lady Annette Louisa, wife of Percy Robert O'Connor La Touche, 1844. *Newberry, Kilcullen, co. Kildare.*	
21252	2689	Lady Rachel Mary, wife of Llewellyn Traherne Basset Saunderson, 1846. *Dremkeen House, co. Cavan.* 10 *De Vesci Terrace, Kingstown, Dublin.*	2nd and 3rd daughters.
21253	2690	Reginald Traherne Saunderson, 1873.	
21254	2691	Maurice Traherne Saunderson, 1875.	Grandchildren.
21255	2692	Samuel Traherne Saunderson, 1884.	Children of
21256	2693	Mabel Charlotte, wife of the Hon. Alfred John Mulholland, 1867. *Worlingham Hall, Beccles, Suffolk.*	No. 21252.

21257	2694	Daphne Rachel Mulholland, 1890.	{ Great-grandchild. Child of No. 21256.
21258	2695	Ethel Rose Saunderson, 1872.	⎫ Grandchildren. Daughters
21259	2696	Rachel Cecilia, wife of Captain Robert Clements Gore, 1877.	⎬ of No. 21252.
21260	2697	Adrian Clements Gore, 1900.	Great-grandson. Child of No. 21259.
21261	2698	Esther Eliza Saunderson, 1881.	⎫ Granddaughters. Younger
21262	2699	Olive Julia Saunderson, 1886.	⎬ daughters of No. 21252.
21263	2700	Cresta Jeannette Saunderson, 1892.	⎭
21264	2701	Edith Caroline Sophia, Viscountess [I.], and Baroness [U.K.] Monck, 1852. *Charteville, Enniskerry, co. Wicklow.*	⎫ 4th daughter.
21265	2702	Hon. Charles Henry Stanley Monck, Lieutenant Coldstream Guards, 1876.	⎫ Grandchildren.
21266	2703	Hon. George Scott Stanley Monck, 1888.	⎬ Children of
21267	2704	Hon. Annette Louisa, wife of the Hon. Arthur Foljambe, 1875.	⎭ No. 21264.

203. Descendants of Colonel the Hon. Charles Grantham Scott, 1818–1885. (See Table XXVIII.)

21268	2705	Rupert Charles, 7th Earl of Clonmell [I.], 1877. *Bishop's Court, Straffan, co. Kildare.*	⎫ Grandson. Son of Beauchamp Henry John, 6th Earl of Clonmell, 1847–1898.
21269	2706	Inna Vera Evelyn Scott, 1886.	{ Granddaughter. Only child of the Hon. Louis Guy Scott, 1856–1900.
21270	2707	Hon. Dudley Alexander Charles Scott, 1853. *45 Eaton Square, S.W.*	
21271	2708	Lady Evelyn Mary Scott, 1845.	
21272	2709	Lady Jessie Louisa Scott, 1857.	⎬ Children.
21273	2710	Lady Annie Henrietta, wife of Frederick William Fane, 1859. *42 Chester Square, S.W.*	

204. Descendants of Lady Harriet Margaret Scott, 1805–1891, and her husband Edward, 2nd Lord Mostyn, 1795–1884. (See Table XXVIII.)

21274	2711	Llewelyn Nevill Vaughan, 3rd Lord Mostyn [U.K.], 1856. *Mostyn Hall, Holywell, Flintshire.*	⎫ Grandson. Son of the Hon. Thomas Edward Lloyd-Mostyn, M.P., 1830–1861.
21275	2712	Hon. Edward Llewelyn Roger Lloyd-Mostyn, 1885.	⎫ Great grandchildren. Children of No. 21274.
21276	2713	Hon. Roderick Clements Lloyd-Mostyn, 1887.	
21277	2714	Hon. Gwynedd Mary Lloyd-Mostyn, 1889.	⎭
21278	2715	Henry Richard Howel Lloyd-Mostyn, 1857. *Bodysgallen, Llandudno.*	⎫ Grandson. Brother of No. 21274.
21279	2716	Ievan Lloyd-Mostyn, 1884.	⎫ Great-grandsons. Sons
21280	2717	Morys Lancelot Lloyd-Mostyn, 1887.	⎬ of No. 21278.
21281	2718	Major-General the Hon. Savage Lloyd-Mostyn, C.B., 1835. *Maes-y-nant, Wrexham.*	⎫ Eldest surviving son.
21282	2719	Rhona Felicia Bridget Lloyd-Mostyn, 1893.	{ Granddaughter. Daughter of No. 21281.

21283	2720	Rev. the Hon. Hugh Wynne Lloyd-Mostyn, 1838. *The Rectory, Buckworth, near Huntingdon.*	2nd surviving son.
21284	2721	Edward Hugh Lloyd-Mostyn, 1871.	
21285	2722	James Price Lloyd Lloyd-Mostyn, 1879.	Grandchildren.
21286	2723	Maria Bridget, wife of Anthony Alfred Bowlby, C.M.G., 1867. *24 Manchester Square, W.*	Children of No. 21283.
21287	2724	Frances Winifred Mostyn Bowlby, 1899.	Great-grandchild. Daughter of No. 21286.
21288	2725	Essex Lloyd Lloyd-Mostyn, 1869.	
21289	2726	Katherine Ellen Grey Lloyd-Mostyn, 1873.	Grandchildren. Youn-
21290	2727	Harriot Emily Lloyd-Mostyn, 1875.	ger daughters of No.
21291	2728	Elizabeth Margaret Wynne Lloyd-Mostyn, 1888.	21283.
21292	2729	Hon. Harriot Margaret Lloyd-Mostyn, 1828.	*7 Chester Place,*
21293	2730	Hon. Essex Lloyd-Mostyn, 1833.	*Hyde Park Square, W.* Daughters.
21294	2731	Hon. Katherine Lloyd-Mostyn, 1846.	

205. Descendants of Lady Louisa Augusta Scott, 1806–1873, and her husband, John Harrison Slater Harrison, Esq., of Shellswell Park, Oxon., –1874. (See Table XXVIII.)

21295	2732	Edward Slater Harrison, J.P., 1832. *Shellswell Park, near Bicester.*	Son.
21296	2733	Arthur Dewar, Captain Lincolnshire Regiment, 18 .	Grandson. Son of Harrison, 18 –18 , and her husband, Dewar.
21297	2734	John Dewar, 1900.	Great-grandson. Only child of No. 21296.
21298	2735	Colonel James Dewar.	Grandchildren. Younger
21299	2736	Charles Dewar.	brothers and only sister
21300	2737	Florence Dewar.	of No. 21296.

206. Descendants of Heneage, 6th Earl of Aylesford, 1824–1871. (See Table XXIX.)

21301	2738	Lady Hilda Joanna Gwendolin, wife of Captain Malcolm Donald Murray, Seaforth Highlanders, 1872.	Granddaughters. Daugh-
21302	2739	Lady Alexandra Louisa Minna, wife of Philip Danby, 1875.	ters of Heneage, 7th Earl of Aylesford, 1849–1885.
21303	2740	Charles Wightwick, 8th Earl of Aylesford [G.B.], 1851. *Packington Hall, Coventry.*	Only surviv- ing son.
21304	2741	Heneage Greville, Lord Guernsey, 1883.	
21305	2742	Hon. Charles Daniel Finch, 1886.	
21306	2743	Hon. Ronald William Edward Finch, 1889.	Grandchildren. Sons
21307	2744	Lady Violet Ella Finch, 1880.	and daughters of
21308	2745	Lady Muriel Gladwys, wife of William Worthington Worthington, J.P., 1881. *Netherseale Old Hall, Ashby-de-la-Zouche.*	No. 21303.
21309	2746	Lady Anne Francesca Wilhelmina, wife of Charles James Murray, M.P., 1853. *Lochcarron, Ross.* 41 *Belgrave Square, S.W.*	Daughter.
21310	2747	▽ Charles Wadsworth Murray, 1894.	Grandchildren. Children of
21311	2748	▽ Sybil Louisa Murray, 1876.	No. 21309.

The Blood Royal of Britain

207. Descendants of Lady Augusta Finch, 1822-1900, and her husband, William Walter, 5th Earl of Dartmouth, 1823-1891. (See Table XIX.)

21312	2749	William Heneage, 6th Earl of [G.B.] and 7th Baron [E.] Dartmouth, P.C., 1851. *Patshull House, Wolverhampton.* 37 *Charles Street, Berkeley Square.*	} Son.
21313	2750	William, Viscount Lewisham, 1881.	
21314	2751	Hon. Gerald Legge, 1882.	} Grandchildren. Children of No. 21312.
21315	2752	Hon. Humphrey Legge, 1888.	
21316	2753	Lady Dorothy Legge, 1883.	
21317	2754	Lady Joan Margaret Legge, 1885.	
21318	2755	Lieut.-Col. the Hon. Henry Charles Legge, C.V.O., 1852. *Fulmer Gardens, Slough.*	} 2nd son.
21319	2756	Nigel Walter Henry Legge, 1889.	} Grandchildren. Children of No. 21318.
21320	2757	Victoria Alexandra Stella Legge, 1885.	
21321	2758	Lady Frances Charlotte Legge, 1848.	
21322	2759	Lady Elizabeth Sarah Legge, 1850.	} Daughters.
21323	2760	Lady Augusta Georgina Legge, 1854.	

208. Descendants of Lady Georgiana Greville, 1798-1871, and her husband, Lieutenant-General the Hon. Sir George Cathcart, G.C.B., 1794-1854. (See Table XXX.)

21324	2761	Jane Cathcart, 1825.	
21325	2762	Hon. Emily Sarah Cathcart, 1834. *Ascot Lodge, Ascot, Berks.*	} Daughters.
21326	2763	Anne Cathcart, 1840. *Ascot Lodge, Sunninghill.*	

209. Descendants of Lady Louisa Greville, 1800-1883, and her husband, Rev. the Hon. Daniel Heneage Finch-Hatton, Rector of Great Weldon and Chaplain to Queen Victoria, 1795-1866. (See Table XXX.)

21327	2764	Rev. William Robert Finch-Hatton, 1827. *Weldon Rectory, Kettering, Northants.*	} Son.
21328	2765	George Daniel Finch-Hatton, 1856. *Junior Carlton.*	
21329	2766	William David Finch-Hatton-Besley, 1857.	
21330	2767	Nigel Montagu Finch-Hatton, 1859.	
21331	2768	Edward Heneage Finch-Hatton, D.S.O., Captain 2nd Battalion The Buffs, 1868.	} Grandchildren. Children of No. 21327.
21332	2769	Flora Elizabeth Louisa Finch-Hatton, 1855.	
21333	2770	Agnes Edith Finch-Hatton, 1860.	
21334	2771	Ethel Beatrice, wife of Captain Charles Vere Gunning, *late* Durham Light Infantry, 1862. *Weldon, Kettering.*	
21335	2772	Essex Vere Gunning.	{ Great-grandchild. Daughter of No. 21334.
21336	2773	Elizabeth Anna, wife of Captain Davison Bruce Stewart, R.F.A., 1864.	{ Granddaughter. Youngest daughter of No. 21327.

199

21337	2774	Isabella, wife of Sir Percy Dixwell Nowell Dixwell-Oxenden, 10th Bart., 1845.	} Daughter.
21338	2775	Basil Heneage Dixwell Dixwell-Oxenden, 1871. *St. James'.*	
21339	2776	Muriel Elizabeth Anna Louisa, wife of Edward Henry Capel Cure. *Isola S. Giovanni, Lago Maggiore, Italy.*	Grandchildren. Children of No. 21337.
21340	2777	Bettina Zoë Capel Cure, 1898.	{ Great-granddaughter. Daughter of No. 21339.
21341	2778	Guendolen Isabel Dixwell-Oxenden.	{ Granddaughter. Youngest daughter of No. 21337.

210. Descendants of Sir George Crewe, 8th Bart., 1795–1844. (See Table XXXI.)

21342	2779	Sir Vauncey Harpur Crewe, 10th Bart. *Calke Abbey, Derby.*	{ Grandson. Son of Sir John Harpur Crewe, 9th Bart., 1824–1886.
21343 -47	{	Same as Nos. 19652–19656.	{ Great-grandchildren. Children of No. 21342.
21348	2780	Hugo Harpur Crewe, D.L., 1858. *Derby.*	Grandchildren. Brother and sister of No. 21342.
21349	2781	Alice Georgiana Harpur Crewe.	
21350	2782	Isabel Jane Crewe.	
21351	2783	Mary Adeline Crewe. *36 Stanhope Gardens, S.W.*	} Daughters.

211. Descendants of the Rev. Henry Robert Crewe, of Breadsale, co. Derby, 1801–1865. (See Table XXXI.)

21352	2784	Frances Jane Crewe.	{ Granddaughter. Only child of Alfred Godley Crewe, M.D., 18 –1894.
21353	2785	Willoughby Harpur Crewe	
21354	2786	Henrietta Frances Crewe.	
21355	2787	Charlotte Elizabeth Selina Crewe.	*Etwall Lawn, Derby.* Children.
21356	2788	Caroline Lucy Crewe.	
21357	2789	Frances Louisa Crewe.	
21358	2790	Ellen Barbara Crewe.	

212. Descendants of Edmund Lewis Crewe, of Repton Park, co. Derby, 1803–1874. (See Table XXXI.)

21359	2791	John Edmund Crewe, *late* 64th Foot. *The Grange, Milton, Burton-on-Trent.*	} Son.
			{ Grandchildren. Children (3 sons and 3 daughters) of Louisa Crewe, –1880, wife (1861) of Ion Turner, 16th Lancers.

213. Descendants of Selina Crewe, -1838, wife of Vice-Admiral William Stanhope Lovell, formerly Badcock, R.N., -1859. (See Table XXXI.)

21360	2792	Lovell Stanhope Richard Lovell, *late* Captain 13th Regiment, 1826.	} Son.
21361	2793	William Stanhope Lovell, 1848.	
21362	2794	George Herbert Salathiel Lovell, 1859.	Grandchildren. Children of No. 21360.
21363	2795	Edith Laura Matilda, wife of Percy Duke Coleridge.	
21364	2796	Emily Georgina Lovell.	
21365	2797	Amy Isabel Jane Lovell.	
21366	2798	Mary Winnie Katherine Selina Lovell.	
21367	2799	Selina Frances Nannette Louisa Lovell.	Eldest daughter.
21368	2800	Georgina Jane Henrietta Dowager Lady Crewe.	2nd daughter.
21369 -76	}	Same as Nos. 21342–21349.	{ Grandchildren. Children of No. 21368.
21377	2801	Matilda Sophia Lovell.	Youngest daughter.

214. Descendants of Lionel William John, 8th Earl of Dysart, 1794–1878. (See Table XXXII.)

21378	2802	William John Manners, 9th Earl of Dysart [S.], 1859. *Buckminster Park, Grantham.*	Grandchildren. Children of William Lionel Felix, Lord Huntingtower,1820–1872.
21379	2803	Lady Agnes Mary Manners, wife of Charles Norman Lindsay Scott, 1855. *Bosworth Park, Market Bosworth, Leicestershire.*	
21380	2804	Wenefryde Agatha Tollemache Scott, 1889.	} Great-grandchild. Daughter of No. 21379.
21381	2805	Agatha Manners, Lady Westbury [U.K.], 1857. *30 Hill Street, Berkeley Square, W.*	} Granddaughter. Sister of Nos. 21379, &c.
21382	2806	Hon. Richard Bethell, 1883.	{ Great-grandson. Child of No. 21381.

215. Descendants of the Hon. Felix Thomas Tollemache, 1796–1843. (See Table XXXII.)

21383	2807	Lyonel Felix Carteret Eugene Tollemache, 1854. *24 Selwyn Road, Eastbourne.*	Grandson. Son of Caroline Tollemache, 1828–1867, 1st wife of the Rev. R. W. L. T. Tollemache, 1826–1895.
21384	2808	Cecil Lyonel Newcomen Tollemache, 1886.	Great-grandchildren. Children of No. 21383.
21385	2809	John Eadred Tollemache, 1892.	
21386	2810	Humphrey Thomas Tollemache, 1897.	
21387	2811	Beryl Hersilia Tollemache, 1887.	
21388	2812	Cynthia Joan Caroline Tollemache, 1890.	
21389	2813	Sibell Agnes Tollemache, 1895.	
21390	2814	Florence Caroline Artemisia, wife of Colonel Thomas Hall, *late* Connaught Rangers, 1855.	Granddaughters. Sisters to No. 21383.
21391	2815	Evelyne Clementina Wentworth Cornelia Maude Tollemache, 1856.	

The Blood Royal of Britain

216. Descendants of the Hon. Arthur Cæsar Tollemache, 1797–1848. (See Table XXXII.)

21392	2816	Arthur Frederick Churchill Tollemache, J.P., 1860. *Ballincor, King's County.*	Grandson. Son of Arthur Lionel Tollemache, 1825–1874.
21393	2817	Arthur Henry William Tollemache, 1894.	Great-grandchildren.
21394	2818	Eleanor Louisa Cornelia Tollemache.	Children of No.
21395	2819	Hermione Edith Agnes Tollemache.	21392.
21396	2820	Emily Katherine, wife of George R. FitzRoy Cole, 1858. *98 Gloucester Place, Portman Square.*	Granddaughter. Sister to No. 21392.
21397	2821	Ronald Lionel FitzRoy Cole, 1890.	Great-grandchildren.
21398	2822	Nigel Edwin FitzRoy Cole, 1892.	Children of No.
21399	2823	Derck Arthur Stephen FitzRoy Cole, 1895.	21396.
21400	2824	Mary Rowena Tollemache, 1868. *Combe Grange, Ascot.*	Granddaughter. Younger sister of No. 21392.
21401	2825	Catherine Eliza Tollemache, 1823.	
21402	2826	Laura, Countess of Lastic St. Jal [France], wife of Albert, Count of Lastic St. Jal, 1830. *Montauban, France.*	Daughters.

217. Descendants of Rev. the Hon. Hugh Francis Tollemache, Rector of Harrington, 1802–1890. (See Table XXXII.)

21403–09	}	Same as Nos. 21383–21389.	Grandchildren, &c. Descendants of the Rev. Ralph William Lyonel Tollemache Tollemache, rector of South Wytham, co. Lincoln, 1826–1895.
21410	2827	Lyulph Ydwallo Odin Nestor Egbert Lyonel Toedmag Hugh Erchenwyne Saxon Esa Cromwell Orma Nevill Dysart Plantagenet Tollemache Tollemache, 1876. *Welcome Bay, Tauranga, New Zealand.*	Grandson. Eldest son of the above Rev. Ralph William Lyonel Tollemache Tollemache, 1826–1895, by 2nd wife.
21411	2828	Lyulph Thomas Tollemache Tollemache, 1890.	
21412	2829	Winifred Dora Tollemache Tollemache, 1898.	Great-grandchildren. Children of No. 21410.
21413	2830	Celia Kathrine Mabel Tollemache Tollemache, 1901.	
21414	2831	Leo Quintus de Orellana Plantagenet Tollemache Tollemache, 1879.	
21415	2832	Leonè Sextus Denys Oswolf Fraudati filius Tollemache Tollemache de Orellana Plantagenet Tollemache Tollemache, 1884.	Grandsons. Brothers of No. 21410.
21416	2833	Lyonulph Cospatrick Bruce Berkeley Jermyn Tullibardine Petersham de Orellana Dysart Plantagenet Tollemache Tollemache, 1892.	
21417–18	}	Same as Nos. 21390–21391.	Granddaughters. Daughters of the above Rev. Ralph William Lyonel Tollemache Tollemache by 1st wife, 1826–1895.

21419	2834	Mabel Helmingham Ethel Huntingtower Beatrice Blazonberrie Evangeline Vise de Lou de Orellana Plantagenet Toedmag Saxon, wife of Rev. William Bryant, 1872. *Holcombe House, Deddington, Oxford.*	Granddaughters. Elder daughters of the above Rev. R. W. L. Tollemache Tollemache by 2nd wife.
21420	2835	Lyonesse Matilda Dora Ida Agnes Ernestine Curson Paulet Wilbraham Joyce Eugenie Bentley Saxonia Dysart Plantagenet, wife of Francis William Astley Cooper, 1874. *Ham Lodge, Richmond, Surrey.*	
21421	2836	Theodora Mary Astley Cooper, 1899.	Great-granddaughter. Daughter of No. 21420.
21422	2837	Lyona Decima Veronica Esyth Undine Cyssa Hylda Rowena Adela Thyra Ursula Ysabel Blanche Lelias Dysart Plantagenet Tollemache Tollemache, 1878.	Granddaughters. Younger daughters of the above Rev. R. W. L. Tollemache Tollemache by 2nd wife.
21423	2838	Lyonella Fredegunda Cuthberga Ethelswytha Ideth Ysabel Grace Moncia de Orellana Plantagenet Tollemache Tollemache, 1882.	
21424	2839	Lyonetta Edith Regina Valentine Myra Polwarth Avelina Philippá Violantha de Orellana Plantagenet Tollemache Tollemache, 1887.	
21425	2840	Mary Tollemache, 1869. } *Batheaston*	Granddaughters. Daughters of the Rev. Clement Reginald Tollemache, 1835–1895.
21426	2841	Grace Tollemache, 1871. } *Villa,*	
21427	2842	Ethel Tollemache, 1874. } *near Bath.*	
21428	2843	Hugh Ernest Tollemache, 1871. *Kennia Mallai Estate, Munaar, P.O.S., India.*	Grandson. Son of the Rev. Ernest Celestine Tollemache, 1838–1880.
21429	2844	John Ernest Tollemache, 1892. Great-grandson. Son of No. 21428.	
21430	2845	Henry Gilbert Tollemache, 1874. *Lomas de Zamora, Buenos Ayres, Argentine.*	Grandson. Brother of No. 21428.
21431	2846	Douglas Hugh Tollemache, 1898. } Great-grandchildren. Children of No. 21430.	
21432	2847	Dorothy Clare Tollemache, 1895. }	
21433	2848	Ralph Charles Tollemache, 1875. *Sungei Rambei Kuala, Selangor, Straits Settlements.*	Grandchildren. Brothers and sister of Nos. 21428, &c
21434	2849	Reginald Douglas Tollemache, 1877.	
21435	2850	Gwendoline Anna Tollemache, 1872.	
21436	2851	Rev. Augustus Francis Tollemache, *late* Vicar of Whitwick, Leicester, 1839. *Northampton.*	Sons.
21437	2852	Anastasius Eugene Tollemache, *late* Captain 22nd Regiment, 1842. *Laystone House, Buntingford, Herts.*	
21438	2853	Eugene Saxon Curzon Hengist Stewart Tollemache, 1875.	Grandchildren. Children of No. 21437.
21439	2854	Harold Egbert Wilbraham Molyneux Tollemache, 1881.	
21440	2855	Lyonel Alexander Arthur Tollemache, 1887.	
21441	2856	Alice Dysart Evelyn Stewart Tollemache, 1871.	
21442	2857	Matilda Amy Jane Ellen Louisa Manners Tollemache, 1874.	
21443	2858	Eugenia Saxonia Tollemache, 1877.	
21444	2859	Louisa Ethelgun Rowena Tollemache, 1878.	
21445	2860	Dorothy Agnes Catherine Tollemache, 1885.	

21446	2861	Louisa Harrington, widow of Colonel the Right Hon. Thomas Edward Taylor, of Ardgillan Casile, co. Dublin, M.P., 1811–1883, 1833. *Bowden Place, Wargrave, Henley-on-Thames.*	Daughter.
21447	2862	Edward Richard Taylor, J.P., 1863. *Ardgillan Castle, co. Dublin.*	Grandchildren. Children of No. 21446.
21448	2863	Basil Reginald Hamilton Taylor, 1865.	
21449	2864	Wilfred Doneraile Stanhope Taylor, 1868.	
21450	2865	. . . . Taylor.	Great-granddaughters. Daughters of No. 21449.
21451	2866	. . . . Taylor.	
21452	2867	. . . . Taylor.	
21453	2868	Cecil Cornelia Marianne St. Leger, wife of Major Frederick Stanley Maude, C.M.G., D.S.O., Coldstream Guards, 1866. *Government House, Ottawa, Canada.*	Granddaughter. Daughter of No. 21446.
21454	2869	Edward Frederick Maude, 1897.	Great-granddaughters. Daughters of No. 21453.
21455	2870	Stella Evelyn Maude, 1894.	
21456	2871	Beryl Mary Maude, 1896.	
21457	2872	Beatrice Virginia Louisa, wife of Captain Randal Skeffington Smyth, Coldstream Guards, 1866.	Granddaughter. Younger daughter of No. 21446.
21458	2873	Cornelia Katharine Tollemache, 1836.	*Benteleigh, Burnham, Maidenhead.* Daughters.
21459	2874	Cecilia Eleanor Tollemache, 1840.	

218. Descendants of the Hon. Frederick James Tollemache, 1804–1888. (See Table XXXII.)

21460	2875	Ada Maria Katharine, Baroness Sudeley [U.K.], 1848. *Ormeley Lodge, Ham Common, Surrey.*	Daughter.
21461	2876	Hon. William Charles Frederick Hanbury-Tracy, *late* Lieutenant 3rd Battalion Royal Scots, 1870. *Bachelors'.*	Grandchildren. Children of No. 21460.
21462	2877	Hon. Algernon Henry Charles Hanbury-Tracy, Captain and Brevet-Major Royal Horse Guards, 1871. *Bachelors'.*	
21463	2878	Hon. Felix Charles Hubert Hanbury-Tracy, Lieutenant Scots Guards, 1882.	
21464	2879	Hon. Eva Isabella Henrietta, wife of Henry Torrens Anstruther, M.P., 1869. *6 Chester Street, S.W.*	
21465	2880	Douglas Tollemache Anstruther, 1893.	Great-grandchildren. Children of No. 21464.
21466	2881	Joyce Anstruther, 1901.	
21467	2882	Hon. Florence Emma Louisa, wife of Captain Charles Warden Sergison, 1873. *Cuckfield Park, Sussex.*	Granddaughter. 2nd daughter of No. 21460.
21468	2883	Prudence Ida Evelyn Sergison, 1892.	Great-granddaughters. Daughters of No. 21467.
21469	2884	. . . . Sergison, 1897.	
21470	2885	Hon. Ida Madeleine Agnes, wife of Frances Pelham Whitbread, 1875. *12 Hans Place, S.W.*	Granddaughter. 3rd daughter of No. 21460.
21471 –72	}	Same as Nos. 20381–20382.	Great-grandchildren. Children of No. 21470.

21473	2886	Hon. Alice Evelyn Agatha, wife of Bertram William Arnold Keppel, 1877. *Lexham Hall, Swaffham, Norfolk.*	} Granddaughter. 4th daughter of No. 21460.
21474	2887	Marguerite Evelyn Keppel, 1899.	} Great-grandchildren. Children of No. 21473.
21475	2888	Judith Iris Keppel, 1900.	
21476	2889	Hon. Rhona Margaret Ada Hanbury-Tracy, 1879.	} Granddaughter. Youngest daughter of No. 21460.

219. Descendants of the Hon. Louisa Tollemache, 1791–1830, wife of Sir Joseph Burke of Glinsk, 11th Bart., 1786–1865. (See Table XXXII.)

21477 -81	}	Same as Nos. 21378–21382.	(Grandchildren, &c. Children of Katherine Elizabeth Camilia Burke, –1896, wife of William Lionel Felix, Lord Huntingtower, 1820–1872.

220. Descendants of Lady Catherine Camilla Tollemache, 1792–1863, wife of Sir George Sinclair, 2nd Bart., 1790–1868. (See Table XXXII.)

21482	2890	Sir John George Tollemache Sinclair, 3rd Bart. of Ulbster, 1825. *14 King Street, St. James', S.W.* *Thurso Castle, Caithness.*	} Son.
21483	2891	Archibald Henry Macdonald Sinclair, 1890.	(Great-grandson. Only child of Lieut.-Col. Clarence Granville Sinclair, 1858–1895. Eldest son of No. 21482.
21484	2892	Captain George Felix Standish Sinclair, 1861. *Thurso Castle, Thurso, N.B.*	(Grandson. Only surviving son of No. 21482.
21485	2893	Algernon Ronald Tollemache Sinclair, 1886.	} Great-grandchildren. Children of No. 21484.
21486	2894	Dorothy Emma Olivia Sinclair, 1885.	
21487	2895	Olive Mary Camilla Sinclair, 1892.	
21488	2896	Amy Camilla, wife of John Henry Fullarton Udny. *Udny Castle, co. Aberdeen.*	
21489	2897	Nina Mary Adelaide, wife of Lieut.-Gen. Owen Lewis Cope Williams, *late* M.P. for Great Marlow. *Temple House, Bucks.*	} Granddaughters. Daughters of No. 21482.
21490	2898	Godfrey Power.	(Grandchildren. Son and daughters of Emilia Magdalin Louisa Sinclair, –1864, and her 2nd husband, Major John Power, –1855.
21491	2899	Olive, wife of Colonel Frederick Elton.	
21492	2900	Mary Power.	
21493	2901	Charles Cecil Gordon Hope-Johnstone, 1846. *Fane Valley, Dundalk.*	(Grandson. Elder son of Adelaide Mary Wentworth Sinclair, 1873, and George Gordon Hope-Johnstone, 1820–1866.

21494	2902	George Wentworth Hope-Johnstone, 1872.	
21495	2903	Edmund William Gordon Hope-Johnstone, 1873.	Great-grandchildren. Children of No. 21493.
21496	2904	David Percy Hope-Johnstone, 1876.	
21497	2905	Francis Ellinor Hope-Johnstone.	
21498	2906	William James Hope-Johnstone, 1855.	Grandson. Brother of No. 21493.
21499	2907	. . . . Hope-Johnstone, 1880.	Great-grandchildren. Sons and daughters of No. 21498.
21500	2908	. . . . Hope-Johnstone, 1887.	
21501	2909	. . . . Hope-Johnstone, 1879.	
21502	2910	. . . . Hope-Johnstone, 1882.	
21503	2911	Evelyn Anne, widow of Captain Percy Alexander Hope-Johnstone, 1845-1899, 1849. *Ardsallagh, Navan, co. Meath.*	Granddaughter. Sister of No. 21493.
21504	2912	Evelyn Wentworth Hope-Johnstone, 1879.	Great-grandchildren. Children of No. 21503.
21505	2913	Constance Hope-Johnstone, 1880.	
21506	2914	Alice Hope-Johnstone, 1883.	

221. Descendants of William Tollemache, 1810–1886. (See Table XXXIII.)

21507	2915	Algernon Seymour Tollemache, *late* Major 108th Foot, 1842.	Son.
21508	2916	Algernon Montriou Tollemache, 1884.	Grandson. Son of No. 21507.
21509	2917	Hon. Orlando St. Maur Forester, 1877.	Grandson. Son of Emma Maria Tollemache, 1839-1898, 2nd wife of Orlando, 4th Lord Forester, 1813-1894.
21510	2918	Matilda Jane, widow of Captain Marcus Augustus Stanley Hare, R.N., 1836-1878, 1840. *Court Grange, Newton Abbot.*	Daughter.
21511	2919	Ethel Lucy, wife of Sir Herbert Charles Perrott, Bart., *late* Lieut.-Col. Commanding and Hon. Col. 3rd Battalion The Buffs, 1875. *Brook Hill House, Plumstead.*	Grandchildren. Children of No. 21510.
21512	2920	Hilda Maud Hare, 1877.	
21513	2921	Caroline Elizabeth, wife of Jerome Moriz Neuburger, 1852. *55a Gloucester Place, Portman Square, W.*	Daughter.

222. Descendants of Gilbert John, 1st Lord Aveland, 1795–1867. (See Table XXXIV.)

21514	2922	Gilbert Henry, 1st Earl of Ancaster [U.K.], 24th Lord Willoughby de Eresby [E.], 2nd Lord Aveland [U.K.], P.C., 1830. *Normanton Park, Stamford.* *12 Belgrave Square, S.W.*	Son.

21515	2923	Gilbert, Lord Willoughby de Eresby, M.P., 1867. 12 *Belgrave Square, S.W.*	
21516	2924	Hon. Charles Strathavon Heathcote-Drummond-Willoughby, Captain Scots Guards, 1870. *Guards'; White's.*	
21517	2925	Hon. Claud Heathcote-Drummond-Willoughby, Captain Coldstream Guards, 1872. *Guards'; White's.*	Grandchildren. Children of No. 21514.
21518	2926	Hon. Peter Robert Heathcote-Drummond-Willoughby, Midshipman R.N., 1885.	
21519	2927	Lady Evelyn Clementina, wife of Major-General Sir Henry Peter Ewart, K.C.B., K.C.V.O., 1865. *Felix Hall, Kelvedon.* *Royal Mews, Buckingham Palace, S.W.*	
21520	2928	Victor Alexander Ewart, 1891.	Great-grandson. Son of No. 21519.
21521	2929	Lady Margaret Mary Heathcote-Drummond-Willoughby, 1866.	
21522	2930	Lady Nina Heathcote-Drummond-Willoughby, 1869.	Grandchildren. Children of No. 21514.
21523	2931	Lady Cecilia, wife of Thomas Clarence Edward Goff, 1874. *Carrowroe Park, Roscommon.* 46 *Pont Street, S.W.*	
21524	2932	Thomas Robert Charles Goff, 1898.	Great-grandchildren. Children of No. 21523.
21525	2933	Elizabeth Moyra Goff, 1897.	
21526	2934	Lady Alice Heathcote-Drummond-Willoughby, 1876.	Grandchildren. Younger daughters of No. 21514.
21527	2935	Lady Mary Adelaide Heathcote-Drummond-Willoughby, 1878.	
21528	2936	Clementina Charlotte, Lady Tryon, widow of the *late* Vice-Admiral Sir George Tryon, K.C.B., 1833. 45 *Eaton Place, S.W.*	Elder daughter.
21529	2937	George Clement Tryon, Captain Grenadier Guards, 1871. *Guards'.*	Grandson. Only son of No. 21528.
21530	2938	Hon. Elizabeth Sophia Heathcote-Drummond-Willoughby, 1838. 4 *Belgrave Square, S.W.*	Younger daughter.

223. Descendants of John, 1st Lord Tollemache, 1805–1890. (See Table XXXV.)

21531	2939	Wilbraham Frederic, 2nd Lord Tollemache [U.K.], 1832. *Peckforton Castle, Tarporley, Cheshire.* 61 *Cadogan Gardens, S.W.*	Eldest son.
21532	2940	Hon. Lyonel Plantagenet Tollemache, 1860. *Manton, Oakham.*	Grandson. Son of No. 21531.
21533	2941	Bentley Lyonel John Tollemache, 1883.	Great-grandson. Son of No. 21532.
21534	2942	Denis Plantagenet Tollemache, 1884.	
21535	2943	Hon. Wilbraham John Tollemache, 1865.	Grandchildren. Children of No. 21531.
21536	2944	Hon. Randolph Stewart Tollemache, *late* Lieutenant R.N., 1866.	
21537	2945	Hon. Arthur Wilbraham Tollemache, 1867.	
21538	2946	Hon. Emma Georgina Blanche Tollemache.	
21539	2947	Hon. Grace Emma Tollemache.	

21540	2948	Hon. Lionel Arthur Tollemache, 1838. *Athenæum.*	
21541	2949	Hon. John Richard Delap Tollemache, 1850. *Arthur's.*	} Sons.
21542	2950	Edward Devereux Tollemache, 1885.	
21543	2951	Henry Robert Tollemache, 1888.	Grandchildren. Children
21544	2952	Marguerite Emily Tollemache, 1880.	of the Hon. Hamilton
21545	2953	Winifred Gertrude Tollemache, 1882. *Waterford House, Hertford.*	Jas. Tollemache, 1852–1893.
21546	2954	Hon. Murray Tollemache, 1853. *Junior Carlton.*	
21547	2955	Hon. Stanhope Tollemache, 1855. *Junior Carlton.*	
21548	2956	Hon. Duff Tollemache, 1859.	} Sons.
21549	2957	Hon. Douglas Alfred Tollemache, Captain Suffolk Yeomanry Cavalry, 1862. *South Beach, Felixstowe.*	
21550	2958	Bevil Douglas Tollemache, 1889.	
21551	2959	Humphrey Douglas Tollemache, 1893.	Grandchildren. Children
21552	2960	Mary Cynthia Tollemache, 1890.	of No. 21549.
21553	2961	Angela Mariota Tollemache, 1900.	
21554	2962	Hon. Stratford Halliday Robert Louis Tollemache, 1864.	
21555	2963	Hon. Ranulph Tollemache, 1865. *Hillside, Baetonsborough, Somerset.*	} Sons.
21556	2964	Cyril Tollemache, 1889.	
21557	2965	Murray Tollemache, 1890.	
21558	2966	Devereux Tollemache, 1891.	Grandchildren. Children of
21559	2967	Eric Tollemache, 1892.	No. 21555.
21560	2968	Lawrence Tollemache, 1894.	
21561	2969	Harold Tollemache, 1896.	
21562	2970	Hilda Tollemache, 1895.	
21563	2971	Hon. Mortimer Granville Tollemache, 1872. *Bury St. Edmunds.*	} Youngest son.
21564	2972	Dorothy Margaret Tollemache, 1895.	Grandchildren. Children
21565	2973	Leila Mary Tollemache, 1896.	of No. 21563.
21566	2974	Hon. Rhona Cecilia Emily, wife of Thomas Wood, late of the Grenadier Guards, 1857. *Gwernyfed Park, Three Cocks, Breconshire.*	} Daughter.
21567	2975	Thomas David Wood, 1885.	
21568	2976	Einon Alexander Wood, 1886.	Grandchildren. Children of
21569	2977	Elyned Rhona Wood, 1884.	No. 21566.
21570	2978	Marslie Joyce Wood, 1895.	

224. Descendants of Wilbraham Spencer Tollemache, of Dorfold Hall, Cheshire, J.P., D.L., 1807–1890. (See Table XXXV.)

21571	2979	Henry James Tollemache, M.P., 1846. *Dorfold Hall, Cheshire.*	
21572	2980	Rev. Algernon Edward Tollemache, 1851. *The Vicarage, Weston. near Crewe.*	Children.
21573	2981	Julia Elizabeth Anne, wife of Charles Savile Roundell, M.P. *Dorfold Hall, Cheshire.*	
21574	2982	Christopher Roundell.	Grandson. Son of No. 21573.
21575	2983	Alice Georgina Tollemache.	Daughter.

| 21576 | 2984 | William Augustus Tollemache, *late* Captain 2nd Life Guards, 1817. *Risby, Bury St. Edmunds.* | See Table XXXV. |

225. Descendants of Elizabeth Jane Henrietta Tollemache (afterwards Countess of Cardigan), 1797–1858, and her 1st husband, Lieut.-Col. Christian Frederick Charles Alexander James Johnstone, of Hilton. (See Table XXXV.)

226. Descendants of Emily Tollemache, –1821, 1st wife of Charles Tyrwhitt, Esq., 1801–1876. (See Table XXXV.)

21577	2985	Emily Elizabeth, widow of Ralph Gerard Leycester, *of Toft Hall,* 1817–1851.	Only daughter.
21578	2986	Rafe Oswald Leycester, 1844. *Toft Hall, near Knutsford,* 6 *Cheyne Walk, S.W.*	Grandchildren.
21579	2987	Ernest Gerard Leycester, J.P., 1849. *Mobberley Old Hall, Knutsford.*	Children of No. 21577.
21580	2988	Amy Theodosia, wife of the Rev. John Storr. *The Rectory, Great Horkesley, near Colchester.*	

227. Descendants of Marcia Tollemache, 1804–1868, and her husband, Admiral Frederick Edward Vernon-Harcourt, 1790–1883. (See Table XXXV.)

21581	2989	Augustus George Vernon-Harcourt, F.R.S., 1834. *Cowley Grange, Oxford.*	Eldest son.
21582	2990	Bernard Francis Vernon-Harcourt, Lieutenant Welsh Regiment, 1877.	
21583	2991	Simon Evelyn Vernon-Harcourt, 1882.	
21584	2992	Mildred Edith Vernon-Harcourt, } twins, 1874.	
21585	2993	Mabel Frances Vernon-Harcourt, }	Grandchildren.
21586	2994	Cecil Violet Vernon-Harcourt, 1875.	Children of
21587	2995	Helen Dorothea, wife of William Beach Thomas, 1876.	No. 21581.
21588	2996	Janet Isabel Vernon-Harcourt, 1879.	
21589	2997	Doris Margaret Vernon-Harcourt, 1883.	
21590	2998	Winifred Rachel Vernon-Harcourt, 1886.	
21591	2999	Isabel Marcia Vernon-Harcourt, 1887.	
21592	3000	Leveson Francis Vernon-Harcourt, M.I.C.E., 1830. 6 *Queen Anne's Gate, S.W. Haddon House, Weybridge.*	2nd son.
21593	3001	Leveson William Vernon-Harcourt, Barrister-at-Law, 1871. 222 *Cromwell Road, S.W.* 7 *New Square, Lincoln's Inn.*	Grandson. Son of No. 21592.
21594	3002	Rose Mary Dorothy Vernon-Harcourt, 1900.	Great-granddaughter. Child of No. 21593.
21595	3003	Evelyn Alice Vernon-Harcourt, 1876.	Grandchildren. Daughters
21596	3004	Violet Mary Vernon-Harcourt, 1883.	of No. 21592.
21597	3005	Emily Anne Vernon-Harcourt, 1836. 61 *Cadogan Square, S.W.*	Daughter.

2 D

| 21598 | 3006 | D'Arcy Legard, Captain 17th Lancers, 1873. | Grandchildren. Children of Jane Vernon - Harcourt, 1846–1875, and her husband, the Rev. Francis Digby Legard. |
| 21599 | 3007 | Marcia, wife of the Rev. Arthur Blunt, 1875. | |

228. Descendants of Marianne Tollemache,   –1880, and her husband, Hubert de Burgh, Esq., of West Drayton, 1799–1875. (See Table XXXV.)

| 21600 | 3008 | Edith, wife of Rafe Oswald Leycester. *Toft Hall, co. Chester. West Drayton Manor, Uxbridge.* | Only surviving children. |
| 21601 | 3009 | Eva de Burgh. *61 Eccleston Square, S.W.* | |

229. Descendants of Selina Tollemache,   –1832, wife of Captain William Locke, of Norbury Park, 1st Life Guards. (See Table XXXV.)

21602	3010	Augusta Selina Elizabeth, Lady Walsingham [G.B.] *Merton Hall, Thetford, Norfolk. Eaton House, Eaton Square, S.W.*	Only child.
21603	3011	Teresa Caraccola, Princess Colonna [Rome], 1855. *Rome, Palais Colonna, 66 Piazza S.S. Apostoli.*	Granddaughter. Only child of No. 21602 by her second husband, Duke of San Teodoro.
21604	3012	Isabella, Marchioness Chigi-Zondadari, 1879. *Rome.*	Great-grandchildren. Daughters of No. 21603.
21605	3013	Vittoria, Princess of Teano, 1880. *Rome.*	

230. Descendants of Charlotte Tollemache,   –1837, 1st wife of Captain George Hope, R.N., 1801–1893. (See Table XXXV.)

21606	3014	Selina Eliza, widow of the Rev. Thomas Edmund Franklyn, M.A., Vicar of Old Dalby, 1833.	Daughter.
21607	3015	William Edmund Franklyn, Lieut.-Col. and Chief Staff Officer Scottish District, 1856.	Grandchildren. Children of No. 21606.
21608	3016	Lionel Dudley Franklyn, 1865.	
21609	3017	Arthur Herbert Hope Franklyn, 1868.	
21610	3018	Edith Mary Selina, wife of John Munton Jaffray. *The Stydd House, Lyndhurst.*	
21611	3019	Edith Mabel Jaffray, 1878.	Great-grandchildren. Children of No. 21610.
21612	3020	Gladys Hope Jaffray, 1882.	
21613	3021	Evelyn Mildred Tollemache Franklyn.	Grandchildren. Children of No. 21606.

231. Descendants of William Bertie Wolseley, R.N., 1797–1881. (See Table XXXV.)

| 21614 | 3022 | Henry John Wolseley, 1846. *Barbados.* | Grandson. Eldest son of William Augustus Wolseley, M.D., 1819–1839. |

21615	3023	Ellen Graham Wolseley.	
21616	3024	Emily Bertie Wolseley.	Great-granddaughters.
21617	3025	Alice Hamilton Wolseley.	Daughters of No.
21618	3026	Minnie Bathurst Wolseley.	21614.
21619	3027	Janet Porter Wolseley.	
21620	3028	William Augustus Daniel Wolseley, Member of the Executive Council of Guiana. *Lusignan, British Guiana.* *29 Bramham Gardens, S.W.*	Grandson. Brother of No. 21614.
21621	3029	William Bertie Wolseley, 1896.	Great-grandchild. Son of No. 21620.
21622	3030	Francis Vivian Wolseley, 1855.	Grandchildren. Brothers and sister of No. 21614, &c.
21623	3031	Robert Flockhart Wolseley, 1857.	
21624	3032	Eliza Porter, wife of Thomas Lynch, M.D.	
21625	3033	Mary Rosa Matilda Lynch.	Great-grandchildren. Children of No. 21624.
21626	3034	Cecilia Wolseley Lynch.	
21627	3035	Mary Jane Bourne, widow of John Shine Wilson, −1900. *Woodford Street, Trinidad.*	Grandchild. 2nd sister of No. 21614.
21628	3036	John Wolseley Wilson.	
21629	3037	George Shine Wilson.	
21630	3038	Mary Cecilia Wilson.	Great-grandchildren. Children of No. 21627.
21631	3039	May Wilson.	
21632	3040	Grace Ethel Wilson.	
21633	3041	Louise Wilson.	
21634	3042	Edith Clothilde Wilson.	
21635	3043	Charlotte Elizabeth, wife of Thomas Porter.	Daughters.
21636	3044	Frances Anne, wife of J. F. Hills.	
21637	3045	Francis Frederick Hills.	Grandchildren. Children of No. 21636.
21638	3046	Thomas Hills.	
21639	3047	Fanny Eliza Hills.	
21640	3048	Catherine Louisa Henrietta Hills.	
21641	3049	Eliza Jane Hills.	
21642	3050	Cecilia Lewis Pauline, wife of Dr. Hutson.	3rd daughter.
21643	3051	John Richard Farre Hutson, 1863.	Grandchildren. Children of No. 21642.
21644	3052	Henry Wolseley Hutson, 1866.	
21645	3053	Eliza Anne Hutson.	
21646	3054	John Henry Wolseley Bourne, 1845.	Grandchildren. Children of Eliza Jane Wolseley, −1848, and her husband, the Rev. John Frederick Bourne.
21647	3055	William Wykeham Frederick Bourne.	
21648	3056	Richard Bertie Butts, 1855.	Grandchildren. Children of Catherine Norval Magdalene Dysart Wolseley, and her husband, Harry Grosvenor Butts, M.D.
21649	3057	Sarah Eliza Earle Ada, wife of Walter Meyrick North, son of the Archdeacon of Cardigan.	
21650	3058	Gladys Ada Constance North. Great-grandchild. Daughter of No. 21649.	
21651	3059	Catherine Grosvenor Butts.	
21652	3060	Henrietta Augusta Meade, wife of Edward Poulton Wells.	4th surviving daughter.
21653	3061	Allison Seymour Laird Wells, 1857.	Grandson. Child of No. 21652.

232. Descendants of Henry Frederick, 3rd Marquis of Bath, 1797–1837. (See Table XXXVI.)

21654	3062	Thomas Henry, 5th Marquis of Bath [G.B.], 7th Viscount Weymouth [E.], 1862. *Longleat, Warminster.*	Grandson. Son of John Alexander, 4th Marquis of Bath, 1831–1896.
21655	3063	John Alexander, Viscount Weymouth, 1895.	Great-grandchildren. Children of No. 21654.
21656	3064	Lady Alice Kathleen Violet Thynne, 1891.	
21657	3065	Lady Emma Marjory Thynne, 1893.	
21658	3066	Lord Alexander George Thynne, 1873.	
21659	3067	Lady Alice Emma, wife of Michael Hugh Shaw Stewart, M.P. *Carnock, Larbert, N.B.* 20 *Mansfield Street, W.*	
21660	3068	Katherine Georgina Louisa, Countess of Cromer [U.K.], 1865. *British Consulate General, Cairo.*	Grandchildren. Brother and sisters of No. 21654.
21661	3069	Lady Beatrice Thynne, 1867.	
21662	3070	Right Hon. Lord Henry Frederick Thynne, P.C., 1832. *Muntham Court, Worthing.*	Son.
21663	3071	Thomas Ulric Thynne, Captain and Hon. Major 4th Battalion Highland L.I., 1861. *Army and Navy.*	Grandchildren. Children of No. 21662.
21664	3072	John Alexander Roger Thynne, 1864.	
21665	3073	Ulric Oliver Thynne, D.S.O., Captain Royal Wilts. Yeomanry Cavalry, 1871. 21 *Hans Place, S.W.*	
21666	3074	Oliver St. Maur Thynne, 1901.	Great-grandchild. Son of No. 21665.
21667	3075	Alice Rachel Thynne.	Grandchildren. Children of No. 21662.
21668	3076	Alice Ruth Hermione, wife of Alexander Edward Lane Fox-Pitt-Rivers. *Rushmore, Salisbury.*	
21669	3077	George Henry Fox-Pitt-Rivers, 1890.	Great-grandchildren. Children of No. 21668.
21670	3078	Marcia Ruth Georgina Fox-Pitt-Rivers, 1891.	
21671	3079	Lady Louisa Isabella Harriet, wife of General the Hon. Sir Percy Robert Basil Feilding, K.C.B., 1834. *Broome Park, Betchworth, Surrey.*	Daughter.
21672	3080	Geoffrey Percy Thynne Feilding, D.S.O., Captain Coldstream Guards, 1866.	Grandchildren. Children of No. 21671.
21673	3081	Percy Henry Feilding, 1867.	
21674	3082	Alice Augusta Feilding, 1863.	
21675	3083	Louisa Mary Feilding, 1864.	
21676	3084	Grace Darling, wife of Frederick Keppel North, 1865. *Bryanston Street, W.*	
		Roger North, 1901.	Great-grandchild. Son of No. 21676.
21677	3085	Margaret Agnes Feilding, 1871.	Grandchild. Daughter of No. 21671.
21678	3086		

233. Descendants of the Rev. Lord John Thynne, D.D., Canon and Sub-Dean of Westminster, 1798–1881. (See Table XXXVI.)

21679	3087	Francis John Thynne, J.P., D.L., 1830. *Haynes Park, Beds.* 67 *Eaton Place, S.W.*	Son.

21680	3088	Bevil Granville Carteret Thynne, *late* Lieutenant 3rd Battalion Beds. Regiment, 1867.	
21681	3089	Algernon Carteret Thynne, Captain North Somerset Yeomanry Cavalry, 1868.	Grandchildren.
21682	3090	George Augustus Carteret Thynne, 1869.	Children of No. 21679.
21683	3091	Marcia Selina Helena Thynne.	
21684	3092	Margaret Carteret Thynne.	
21685	3093	Isabel Carteret Thynne.	
21686	3094	Rev. Arthur Christopher Thynne, Hon. Canon of Truro, Rector of Kirlhampton, 1832. *Penstowe, Kirlhampton, N. Cornwall.*	2nd son.
21687	3095	William Francis Granville Thynne, 1862. *Vancouver, B.C.*	Grandchildren. Children of No. 21686.
21688	3096	John Granville Thynne, 1865.	
21689	3097	Mary Ethel Thynne. Great-grandchild.	Child of No. 21688.
21690	3098	Arthur Granville Thynne, 1867.	
21691	3099	Denis Granville Thynne, Lieutenant R.N., 1875.	
21692	3100	Richard Granville Thynne, 1878. *36 Chelsea Gardens, S.W.*	Grandchildren.
21693	3101	Hugh Edward Granville Thynne, 1881.	Children of No. 21686.
21694	3102	Sophie Gwenllian Granville Thynne, 1861.	
21695	3103	Mary Granville Thynne, 1863.	
21696	3104	Anne Constantia Granville Thynne, 1870.	
21697	3105	Grace Granville Thynne, 1873.	
21698	3106	Margaret Ethel Granville Thynne, 1883.	
21699	3107	Alfred Walter Thynne, Lieut.-Col. *late* Grenadier Guards, J.P. Beds., 1836. *50 Cadogan Square, S.W.*	3rd and 4th sons.
21700	3108	John Charles Thynne, M.A., Barrister, D.L., 1838. *17B Great Cumberland Place, W.*	
21701	3109	Joan Emily Mary, Viscountess Emlyn, 1872. *Fernacres Cottage, Fulmer, Bucks.*	Granddaughter. Daughter of No. 21700.
21702	3110	Hon. John Duncan Vaughan Campbell, 1900.	Great-grandchildren. Children of No. 21701.
21703	3111	Hon. Janet Helena Campbell, 1899.	
21704	3112	Agatha Lilian Thynne, 1879.	Granddaughters. Younger
21705	3113	Mary Beryl Thynne, 1890.	daughters of No. 21700.
21706	3114	Reginald Thomas Thynne, Major-General, C.B., 1843. *Travellers'; Guards'.*	5th surviving son.
21707	3115	Katharine Angela Thynne, 1893.	Grandchildren. Children
21708	3116	Beatrix Elaine Thynne, 1895.	of No. 21706.
21709	3117	Emily Constantia, Marchioness of Headfort [I.], Baroness Kenlis [U.K.], 1840. *32 Wilton Place, S.W.*	Daughter.
21710	3118	Geoffrey Thomas, 4th Marquis of Headfort [I], 3rd Baron Kenlis [U.K.], 1878. *Headfort House, Kells, co. Meath.*	Grandson. Son of No. 21709.
21711	3119	John Thomas Geoffrey, Earl of Bective, 1902.	Great-grandchild. Son of No. 21710.
21712	3120	Constance Ellinor, wife of Lieut.-Col. the Hon. Osbert Victor George Atheling Lumley, 11th Hussars, 1864. *62 Pont Street, S.W.*	Granddaughter. Daughter of No. 21709, by 1st husband, Captain the Hon. Eustace John Wilson-Patten, 1836–1873, *v.p.*
21713	3121	Richard John Lumley, 1894.	Great-grandchildren.
21714	3122	Lawrence Roger Lumley, 1896.	Children of No.
21715	3123	Lilian Mary Theodora Lumley, 1900.	21712.

The Blood Royal of Britain

21716	3124	Evelyn Louisa, wife of Lieut.-Col. the Hon. Charles Harbord, C.B., 1870. *47 Pont Street, S.W.*	} Granddaughter. Sister to No. 21712.
21717	3125	Victor Alexander Charles Harbord, 1897.	{ Great-grandchildren. Children of No.
21718	3126	Doris Cecilia Harbord, 1900.	21716.
21719	3127	Lady Beatrice Taylour, 1877.	{ Grandchild. Daughter of No. 21709 by 2nd husband.
21720	3128	Selina Charlotte Thynne, 1842. *50 Cadogan Square, S.W.*	} Younger daughter.

234. Descendants of Lord Edward Thynne, M.P., 1807–1884. (See Table XXXVI.)

| 21721 | 3129 | Mary Isabella Emma, *formerly* wife of Stephen Ormston Eaton. | } Only child. |
| 21722 | 3130 | Charles Edward Thynne Eaton, 1891. *Tolethorpe Hall, Stamford.* | { Grandson. Son of No. 21721. |

235. Descendants of the Rev. Lord Charles Thynne, Canon of Canterbury, 1813–1894. (See Table XXXVI.)

21723	3131	Charles Ernest Thynne, Barrister-at-Law, 1849. *104 Queen's Gate, S.W.*	} Son.
21724	3132	Roger Charles Seymour Thynne, 1885.	} Grandchildren. Children
21725	3133	Mary Harriet Thynne, 1881.	} of No 21723.
21726	3134	Gertrude Harriet, Countess of [I.] and Baroness [U.K.] Kenmare, 1840. *Killarney House, Killarney.* *40 Egerton Gardens, S.W.*	} Daughter.
21727	3135	Valentine Charles, Viscount Castlerosse, 1860. *Killarney House, Killarney.*	} Grandson. Son of No. 21726.
21728	3136	Hon. Valentine Edward Charles Browne, 1891.	
21729	3137	Hon. Maurice Henry Dermot Browne, 1894.	Great-grandchildren. Children of No.
21730	3138	Hon. Gerald Ralph Desmond Browne, 1896.	21727.
21731	3139	Hon. Dorothy Margaret Browne, 1888.	
21732	3140	Hon. Cicely Kathleen Browne, 1888.	
21733	3141	Lady Margaret Theodora Mary Catherine, wife of Greville Douglas. *27 Wilton Crescent, S.W.*	} Granddaughter. Daughter of No. 21726.

236. Descendants of Lady Elizabeth Thynne, 1795–1866, and her husband, John Frederick, 1st Earl Cawdor, 1790–1860. (See Table XXXVI.)

| 21734 | 3142 | Frederick Archibald Vaughan, 3rd Earl [U.K.] and 4th Baron [G.B.] Cawdor, 1847. *Cawdor Castle, Nairn.* *7 Prince's Gardens, S.W.* | } Grandson. Eldest son of John Frederick Vaughan, 2nd Earl Cawdor, 1817–1898. |
| 21735 | 3143 | Hugh Frederick Vaughan, Viscount Emlyn, 1870. *Fernacres Cottage, Fulmer, Bucks.* | } Great-grandson. Son of No. 21734. |

214

21736 –37	}	Same as Nos. 21702–21703.	{ Great-great-grandchildren. Children of No. 21735.
21738	3144	Rev. and Hon. Nigel Campbell, Curate of All Souls, 1873. *21 Blenheim Square, Leeds.*	
21739	3145	Hon. Ralph Alexander Campbell, Captain Cameron Highlanders, 1877.	
21740	3146	Hon. Elidor Ronald Campbell, 1881.	Great-grandchildren. Children of No. 21734.
21741	3147	Hon. Ian Malcolm Campbell, 1883.	
21742	3148	Hon. Eric Octavius Campbell, 1885.	
21743	3149	Lady Edith Aline Caroline Campbell, 1869.	
21744	3150	Lady Mabel Marjorie Campbell, 1876.	
21745	3151	Lady Lilian Katharine Campbell, 1879.	
21746	3152	Lady Muriel Dorothy Campbell, 1887.	
21747	3153	Rev. Guy Ronald Campbell, 1874. *34 Onslow Gardens, S.W.*	Great-grandchildren. Children of the late Captain the Hon. Ronald George Elidor Campbell, 1848–1879, brother to No. 21734.
21748	3154	John Vaughan Campbell, Captain Coldstream Guards, 1876.	
21749	3155	Robert Campbell, Lieutenant Cameron Highlanders, 1878.	
21750	3156	Hon. Alexander Francis Henry Campbell, *late* Captain 3rd Battalion Royal Scots, 1855. *Cavalry.*	Grandson. Only surviving brother of No. 21734.
21751	3157	Duncan Elidor Campbell, 1880.	Great-grandsons. Sons of No. 21750.
21752	3158	Niel Alister Henry Campbell, Lieutenant 13th Somerset Light Infantry, 1881.	
21753	3159	Lady Victoria Alexandrina Elizabeth, wife of Lieut.-Col. Francis William Lambton, Scots Guards, 1843. *Brownslade, Pembroke.*	Granddaughter. Eldest sister to No. 21734.
21754	3160	Cuthbert Archibald Lambton, 1871.	Great-grandchildren. Children of No. 21753.
21755	3161	George Charles Lambton, Captain 2nd Battalion Worcestershire Regiment, D.S.O., 1872.	
21756	3162	Edward Lambton, 1877. *Public Works Department, Egypt.*	
21757	3163	Philip Octavius Lambton, 1880.	
21758	3164	Aline Lambton, 1870.	
21759	3165	Lady Muriel Sarah, widow of Sir Courtenay Edmund Boyle, K.C.B., 1845. *86 Beulah Hill, Upper Norwood.*	Granddaughters. Younger surviving sisters to No. 21734.
21760	3166	Lady Evelyn Caroline Louisa Campbell, 1851.	
21761	3167	Lady Rachel Anne Georgiana, 1853, wife of Edward Stafford Howard, C.B. *Thornbury Castle, Gloucestershire.* *9 Egerton Place, S.W.*	
21762	3168	Algar Henry Stafford Howard, Lieutenant Carmarthen Artillery, 1880.	Great-grandchildren. Children of No. 21761.
21763	3169	Ruth Evelyn, wife of Gardner Sebastian Bazley, 1877. *Hatherop Castle, Fairford.*	
21764	3170	Alianore Rachel Howard, 1886.	
21765	3171	Donald George Campbell, 1860. *Grosvenor.*	Grandson. Son of the Rev. and Hon. Archibald George Campbell, 1827–1902.
21766	3172	Mary Charlotte Campbell, 1889.	Great-grandchildren. Children of No. 21765.
21767	3173	Evelyn Hope Campbell, 1894.	
21768	3174	Margaret Mary Campbell, 1856.	Grandchildren. Sisters of No. 21765.
21769	3175	Elizabeth Harriet Campbell, 1858.	

21770	3176	Hon. Henry Walter Campbell, *late* Lieut.-Col. Coldstream Guards, 1835. 44 *Charles Street, Berkeley Square, W.*	Only surviving son.
21771	3177	Alice Mary, wife of Seymour Pleydell-Bouverie, 1860. 36 *Park Street, W.*	Granddaughter. Eldest daughter of No. 21770.
21772	3178	Philip Hales Pleydell-Bouverie, 1900.	Great-grandchildren.
21773	3179	Joan Pleydell-Bouverie, 1881.	Children of No.
21774	3180	Winifred Pleydell-Bouverie, 1883.	21771.
21775	3181	Edith Caroline, wife of Horace George Devas, 1862. *Hartfield Hayes, Kent.*	Granddaughter. Younger daughter of No. 21770.
21776	3182	Geoffrey Charles Devas, 1887.	Great-grandchildren.
21777	3183	Marjorie Edith Devas, 1890.	Children of No.
21778	3184	Nancy Marion Devas, 1894.	21775.
21779	3185	Lady Emily Caroline, widow of the Hon. Octavius Duncombe, 1817-1879, 1819. 84 *Eaton Square, S.W.*	Eldest daughter.
21780	3186	Walter Henry Octavius Duncombe, 1846. *Waresley Park, Sandy, Bedfordshire.*	
21781	3187	Henry Charles Duncombe, 1848.	Grandchildren.
21782	3188	Emily Charlotte Duncombe, 1843.	Children of
21783	3189	Blanche Elizabeth Caroline Duncombe, 1845.	No. 21779
21784	3190	Maud Augusta Louisa, Lady Calthorpe [G.B.], 1850. *Elvetham Park, Winchfield.* 38 *Grosvenor Square, W.*	
21785	3191	Hon. Walter Gough-Calthorpe, 1873.	
21786	3192	Hon. Rachel, wife of Fitzroy Hamilton Lloyd-Anstruther, 1871.	Great-grandchildren. Children of No. 21784.
21787	3193	Hon. Constance Gough-Calthorpe, 1877.	
21788	3194	Hon. Hilda Gough-Calthorpe, 1880.	
21789	3195	Hon. Dorothy Gough-Calthorpe, 1885.	
21790	3196	Edward Balfour, J.P., D.L., 1849. *Balbirnie, co. Fife.* 43 *Grosvenor Square, W.*	Grandson. Elder surviving son of Lady Georgiana Isabella Campbell, 1826-1884, and her husband, Colonel John Balfour of Balbirnie, 1811-1895.
21791	3197	Robert Frederick Balfour, 1883.	
21792	3198	Edward William Sturgis Balfour, 1885.	Great-grandchildren.
21793	3199	John Balfour, 1895.	Children of No.
21794	3200	Alice Georgiana Balfour, 1880.	21790.
21795	3201	Eva Catherine Balfour, 1888.	
21796	3202	Alfred Granville Balfour, Captain H.L. Infantry, 1858.	Grandson. Younger brother of No. 21790.
21797	3203	James Balfour, 1889.	Great-grandchild. Son of No. 21796.
21798	3204	Alan George Finch, 1863.	Great-grandchildren. Children of Emily Eglantine Balfour, -1865, and her husband, G. H. Finch, M.P.
21799	3205	Magdalen Louisa Finch, 1861.	*Burley-on-Hill, Oakham.*
21800	3206	Gwendoline Harriet, wife of Evan Hanbury, 1864.	
21801	3207	Georgiana Elizabeth, Marchioness of Downshire [I.], Countess of Hillsborough [G.B.]. 36 *Wilton Crescent, S.W.*	Granddaughter. Elder surviving sister of No. 21790.
21802	3208	Arthur Wills John Willington Blundell Trumbull, 6th Marquis of Downshire [I.], Earl of Hillsborough [G.B.], 1871. *Easthampstead Park, Wokingham, Berks.*	Great-grandchild. Only child of No. 21801.

JAMES III of Scotland.
AND HIS SON AFTERWARDS JAMES IV.
THE TRINITY COLLEGE ALTAR-PIECE.

21803	3209	Arthur Wills Percy Wellington Blundell, Earl of Hillsborough, 1894.	Great-great-grand-children. Children of No. 21802.
21804	3210	Lord Arthur Francis Henry Hill, 1895.	
21805	3211	Lady Kathleen Nina Hill, 1898.	
21806	3212	Mary Louisa Balfour.	Granddaughter. Younger sister to No. 21790.
21807	3213	Lady Kathleen Mary Alexina, wife of Colonel Sir Thomas Edward Milborne-Swinnerton-Pilkington, 12th Bart., 1872. *2 Upper Berkeley Street, S.W. Chevet Park, Wakefield.*	Great-grandchild. Only child of William Ulick O'Connor, 4th Earl of Desart, 1845 – 1898, eldest son of Lady Elizabeth Lucy Campbell, 1822–1898, and her husband, Otway, 3rd Earl of Desart, 1818–1865.
21808	3214	▽ Arthur William Milborne-Swinnerton-Pilkington, 1898.	Great-great-grand-children. Children of No. 21807.
21809	3215	▽ Phyllis Milborne-Swinnerton-Pilkington, 1896.	
21810	3216	Hamilton John Agmondesham, 5th Earl of Desart [I.], 1848. *Desart Court, Kilkenny. 2 Rutland Gardens, S.W.*	Grandson. Elder surviving son of Lady Elizabeth Lucy Campbell, 1822–1878. *See above.*
21811	3217	Lady Joan Elizabeth Mary, wife of Harry Lloyd Lloyd-Verney, 1877. *10 Ovington Gardens, W.*	Great-granddaughter. Daughter of No. 21810.
21812	3218	Gerald Harry George Lloyd-Verney, 1900.	Great-great-grandchild. Child of No. 21811.
21813	3219	Lady Sybil Marjorie, wife of William Bayard Cutting. *Westbrook, Long Island, New York.*	Great-granddaughter. 2nd daughter of No. 21810.
21814	3220	Hon. Otway Frederick Seymour Cuffe, *late* Captain Rifle Brigade, 1853. *2 Upper Berkeley Street, W.*	Grandson. Younger brother of No. 21810.
21815	3221	Hon. Charles Henry Chandos Henniker-Major, 1872.	Great-grandchildren. Children of Lady Alice Mary Cuffe, 1844–1893, and her husband, John Major, 5th and present Lord Henniker.
21816	3222	Hon. Gerald Arthur George Henniker-Major, 1872.	
21817	3223	Hon. Victor Alexander Henniker-Major, 1878.	
21818	3224	Hon. John Ernest De Grey Henniker-Major, 1883.	
21819	3225	Hon. Alice Margaret Mary Henniker-Major, 1870.	
21820	3226	Hon. Ethel Elizabeth Emily Henniker-Major, 1874.	
21821	3227	Hon. Lilian Bertha Aline Henniker-Major, 1880.	
21822	3228	Hon. Dorothy Florence Stella Henniker-Major, 1885.	
21823	3229	Mary Louisa, Dowager Countess of Ellesmere [U.K.], 1825. *Burwood House, Cobham, Surrey.*	Younger surviving daughter.
21824	3230	▽ Francis Charles Granville, 3rd Earl of Ellesmere [U.K.], 1847. *Worsley Hall, Manchester. Bridgewater House, Cleveland Square, S.W.*	Grandson. Son of No. 21823.

21825	3231	▽ John Francis Granville Scrope, Viscount Brackley, 1872.	Great-grandchildren. Children of No. 21824.
21826	3232	▽ Hon. Francis William George Egerton, 1874. 1 *Onslow Crescent, S.W.*	
21827	3233	▽ Roger Francis Egerton, 1899.	Great-great-grandchildren.
21828	3234	▽ Phyllis Mary Egerton, 1900.	Children of No. 21826.
21829	3235	▽ Hon. Thomas Henry Frederick Egerton, 1876.	
21830	3236	▽ Hon. Wilfred Charles William Egerton, Lieutenant 1st Dragoons, 1879.	
21831	3237	▽ Hon. Reginald Arthur Egerton, 1886.	Great-grandchildren. Children of No. 21824.
21832	3238	▽ Lady Mabel Laura Egerton, 1869.	
21833	3239	▽ Lady Alice Constance Egerton, 1870.	
21834	3240	▽ Lady Beatrice Mary, wife of Lieutenant-Colonel George Kemp, M.P. 71 *Portland Place, W. Lingholme, Kiswick.*	
21835	3241	Patience Kemp, 1898.	Great-great-grandchild. Daughter of No. 21834.
21836	3242	▽ Lady Katharine Augusta Victoria Egerton, 1877.	Great-grandchildren. Granddaughters of No. 21824.
21837	3243	▽ Lady Leila Georgina Egerton, 1881.	

237. Descendants of Lady Louisa Thynne, 1801–1859, and her husband, Henry, 3rd Earl of Harewood, 1797–1859. (See Table XXXVI.)

21838	3244	Henry Ulick, 5th Earl of [U.K.] and Baron [G.B.] Harewood, 1846. *Harewood House, Leeds.* 13 *Upper Belgrave Street, S.W.*	Grandson. Son of Henry Thynne, 4th Earl of Harewood, 1824–1892.
21839	3245	Henry George Charles, Viscount Lascelles, 1882.	Great-grandchildren. Children of No. 21838.
21840	3246	Hon. Edward Cecil Lascelles, 1887.	
21841	3247	Lady Margaret Selina Lascelles, 1883.	
21842	3248	Hon. Frederick Canning Lascelles, Commander R.N., 1848. *Sutton Waldron House, Blandford.*	Grandson. Brother of No. 21838.
21843	3249	Alan Frederick Lascelles, 1887.	Great-grandchildren. Children of No. 21842.
21844	3250	Helen Elizabeth Lascelles, 1879.	
21845	3251	Blanche Isabella Lascelles, 1880.	
21846	3252	Maud Frederica Lascelles, 1882.	
21847	3253	Margaret Mary Lascelles, 1883.	
21848	3254	Hon. Gerald William Lascelles, 1849. *The King's House, Lyndhurst, Hants.*	Grandson. Brother of No. 21838.
21849	3255	Gerald Hubert Lascelles, 1876.	Great-grandchildren. Children of No. 21848.
21850	3256	John Beilby Lascelles, 1884.	
21851	3257	Cynthia Rachel Lascelles, 1885.	
21852	3258	Hon. Edwin Harry Lascelles, Captain, *late* 7th Hussars, 1861.	
21853	3259	Hon. Daniel Henry Lascelles, 1862.	
21854	3260	Hon. George Algernon Lascelles, Captain 3rd Battalion Princess of Wales' Own Yorkshire Regiment, 1865.	Grandsons. Brothers of No. 21838.
21855	3261	Hon. William Horace Lascelles, 1868. *Annandale, Grenada, West Indies.*	

The Blood Royal of Britain

21856	3262	Mary Madge Lascelles, 1900.	Great-granddaughter. Child of No. 21855.
21857	3263	Hon. Francis John Lascelles, 1871.	
21858	3264	Constance Mary, Lady Wenlock [U.K.], 1852. *Escrick Park, York.* 26 *Portland Place, W.*	Grandchildren. Youngest brother and eldest sister of No. 21838.
21859	3265	Hon. Irene Constance Lawley, 1889.	Great-grandchild. Child of No. 21858.
21860	3266	Margaret Joan, Countess of Desart [I.], 1853. *Desart Court, Kilkenny.* 2 *Rutland Gardens, S.W.*	Granddaughter. 2nd sister of No. 21838.
21861 –63		Same as Nos. 21811–21813.	Great-grandchildren, &c. Children and grandchildren of No. 21860.
21864	3267	Lady Susan Elizabeth, wife of Francis Richard Hugh Seymour Sutton, 1860. 18 *Curzon Street, W.*	Granddaughter. 3rd sister to No. 21838.
21865	3268	Francis Henry Sutton, 1882.	
21866	3269	Lionel Tatton Sutton, 1894.	Great-grandchildren. Children of No. 21864.
21867	3270	Violet Eveleen Sutton.	
21868	3271	Angela Desirée Sutton.	
21869	3272	Lady Mary Diana, wife of Robert Wentworth Doyne, 1877. *Ashton, Gorey, co. Wexford.*	Granddaughter. Youngest sister to No. 21838.
21870	3273	Robert Harry Doyne, 1899.	Great-grandson. Son of No. 21869.
21871	3274	Marion, wife of Captain Henry Dent Brocklehurst, *late* 2nd Life Guards, 1858. *Middlethorpe Manor, York.*	Granddaughter. Only surviving child of the Hon. Egremont William Lascelles, 1825–1892.
21872	3275	Hon. George Edwin Lascelles, 1826. *Sion Hill, Thirsk.*	Eldest surviving son.
21873	3276	David Arthur George Lascelles, Captain, *late* 47th Regiment, 1852. *Leeming Garth, Bedale.*	Grandson. Son of No. 21872.
21874	3277	Gladys Maud Lascelles, 1886.	Great-grandchild. Child of No. 21873.
21875	3278	Alfred George Lascelles, Attorney-General, Ceylon, 1857. *Colombo, Ceylon.*	Grandsons. Sons of No. 21872.
21876	3279	Edward George Lascelles, 1859. *Mount Pleasant, Bowen, Queensland.*	
21877	3280	Evelyn Herbert Lascelles, 1894.	Great-grandchildren. Children of No. 21876.
21878	3281	Geoffrey Edward Lascelles, 1895.	
21879	3282	Rev. Maurice George Lascelles, 1860. *Vicarage, Harewood, Leeds.*	
21880	3283	Arthur George Lascelles, 1869. *Broseley, Salop.*	
21881	3284	Ernest George Lascelles, 1874.	
21882	3285	Evelyn Louisa Lascelles, 1853.	Grandchildren. Children of No. 21872.
21883	3286	Alice Margaret, wife of the Rev. J. Thorneycroft Hartley, M.A., 1855. *Burneston Vicarage, near Bedale.*	
21884	3287	Blanche, Lady Smith-Dodsworth, 1864. *Thornton Watlass, near Bedale, York.*	
21885	3288	Agnes Nina Lascelles, 1868.	
21886	3289	Margaret Emily Lascelles, 1876.	

21887	3290	William James Lascelles, *late* Lieutenant Rifle Brigade, 1858.	Grandson. Son of the Rev. and Hon. James Walter Lascelles, Hon. Canon of Ripon, 1831–1901.
21888	3291	Cecil Elizabeth Lascelles, 1894.	Great-grandchildren. Children of Cecil Henry Lascelles, 1865–1899, brother of No. 21887.
21889	3292	Ruth Carr Lascelles, 1895.	
21890	3293	Walter Charles Lascelles, Captain Durham Light Infantry, D.S.O., 1867.	Grandchildren. Brothers and sister of No. 21887.
21891	3294	Reginald Francis Lascelles, 1868.	
21892	3295	Edith Katherine, widow of Walter Pleydell-Bouverie, 1848–1893, 1857.	
21893	3296	Humphrey Pleydell-Bouverie, 1883.	Great-grandchildren. Children of No. 21892.
21894	3297	Nancy Pleydell-Bouverie, 1885.	
21895	3298	Mary Pleydell-Bouverie, 1887.	
21896	3299	Elizabeth Pleydell-Bouverie, 1888.	
21897	3300	Rachel Blanche, wife of Hugh Francis Seymour, 1859. 25 *Lennox Garden, S.W.*	Grandchild. Sister of No. 21887.
21898	3301	Horace James Seymour, 1885.	Great-grandchildren. Children of No. 21897.
21899	3302	Frances Seymour, 1886.	
21900	3303	Mabel Seymour, 1888.	
21901	3304	Kathleen Georgiana Seymour, 1892.	
21902	3305	Katharine Maria, widow of Major Charles Bateson Harvey, 10th Hussars, 1859–1900, 1860.	Grandchild. Sister of No. 21887.
21903	3306	Norah Harvey, 1892.	Great-grandchildren. Children of No. 21902.
21904	3307	Sylvia Harvey, 1899.	
21905	3308	Emma, wife of the Rev. William Travis Travis, 1861. *The Rectory, Ripley, Yorks.*	Grandchildren. Sisters of No. 21887.
21906	3309	Mabel Louisa, widow of Albert Childers Meysey-Thompson, Q.C., 1848–1894, 1862.	
21907	3310	Hubert Charles Meysey-Thompson, 1883.	Great-grandchild. Son of No. 21906.
21908	3311	Louisa Isabella, Dowager Lady Hillingdon [U.K.], 1830. *Wildernesse, Sevenoaks. Vernon House, Park Place, S.W.*	Eldest daughter.
21909	3312	Charles William, 2nd Baron Hillingdon [U.K.], 1855. *Hillington Court, Uxbridge. Camelford House, Park Lane, W.*	Grandson. Son of No. 21908.
21910	3313	Hon. Charles Thomas Mills, 1887.	Great-grandchildren. Children of No. 21909.
21911	3314	Hon. Arthur Robert Mills, 1891.	
21912	3315	Hon. Algernon Henry Mills, 1856. *Calcot Park, Reading.*	Grandson. 2nd son of No. 21908.
21913	3316	Henry Christian George Mills, 1886.	Great-grandson. Son of No. 21912.
21914	3317	Hon. Egremont John Mills, Captain West Kent Yeomanry Cavalry, D.S.O., 1866.	Grandchildren. Children of No. 21908.
21915	3318	Hon. Geoffrey Edward Mills, Lieutenant West Kent Yeomanry Cavalry, 1875.	
21916	3319	Elizabeth Louisa Mills.	Great-grandchild. Daughter of No. 21915.
21917	3320	Hon. Isabel Mary, wife of Captain the Hon. Herbert Alexander Lawrence, 17th Lancers, D.A.A.G. Headquarters. 10 *Sloane Gardens, S.W.*	Grandchild. Daughter of No. 21908.

21918	3321	Oliver John Lawrence, 1893.	Great-grandchildren. Children of No. 21917.
21919	3322	Michael Charles Lawrence, 1894.	
21920	3323	Hon. Mabel Blanche, wife of Charles Molyneux Grenfell. 8 *Chester Square, S.W.*	Granddaughter. Daughter of No. 21908.
21921	3324	Sylvia Caroline Grenfell, 1887.	Great-granddaughter. Daughter of No. 21920.
21922	3325	Hon. Violet Louisa Mills.	Granddaughter. Youngest daughter of No. 21908.
21923	3326	Susan Charlotte, Countess of Wharncliffe [U.K.], 1834. *Woodhill, Send, Surrey.*	2nd daughter.
21924	3327	Richard Henry, 6th Earl of Shannon [I.], 5th Baron Carleton [G.B.], 1860. *Castle Martyr, co. Cork.*	Grandson. Eldest son of the late Lady Blanche Emma Lascelles, 1837–1863, 1st wife of Henry Bentinck, 5th Earl of Shannon, 1833–1890.
21925	3328	Richard Bernard, Viscount Boyle, 1897.	Great-grandchildren. Children of No. 21924.
21926	3329	Hon. Robert Henry Boyle, 1900.	
21927	3330	Lady Helen Boyle, 1898.	
21928	3331	Hon. Henry George Boyle, 1862. *White's.*	Grandchildren. Younger brothers of No. 21924.
21929	3332	Hon. Robert Francis Boyle, Commander R.N., 1863. *Naval and Military.*	
21930	3333	Lady Maud Caroline, wife of the Right Hon. Lord George Francis Hamilton, P.C., M.P., 1846. 17 *Montagu Street, W. Deal Castle, Kent.*	Youngest surviving daughter.
21931	3334	Ronald James Hamilton, 1872.	Grandsons. Sons of No. 21930.
21932	3335	Anthony George Hamilton, 1874.	
21933	3336	Robert Cecil Hamilton, Lieutenant R.N., 1882.	

238. Descendants of Lady Charlotte Anne Thynne, 1811–1895, and her husband, Walter Francis, 5th Duke of Buccleuch, K.G., 1806–1884. (See Table XXXVI.)

| 21934 –86 | | Same as Nos. 19724-19776. |

239. Descendants of Heneage, 5th Earl of Aylesford, 1786–1859. (See Table XXXVI.)

| 21987 –2009 | | Same as Nos. 21301-21323. |

240. Descendants of Lady Charlotte Finch, 1785–1869, and her husband, the Rev. Charles Palmer, M.A., Rector of Lighthorne, Warwick. (See Table XXXVI.)

22010	3337	Henry Charles Palmer, 1826 [1]	Children.
22011	3338	Louisa Palmer [1]	
22012	3339	Mary Isabella Palmer [1]	
22013	3340	Frances Palmer [1]	
22014	3341	Charlotte Ellen Palmer [1]	

[1] If living.

The Blood Royal of Britain

241. Descendants of George Augustus, 6th Earl of Chesterfield, 1805-1866. (See Table XXXVI.)

22015	3342	George Edward Stanhope Molyneux, 5th Earl of Carnarvon [G.B.], 1866. *Highclere Castle, Newbury.* 13 *Berkeley Square, W.*	Grandson. Only son of Lady Evelyn Stanhope, 1834-1875, 1st wife of Henry H. M., 4th Earl of Carnarvon, 1831-1890.
22016	3343	Henry George Alfred Marius Victor Francis, Lord Porchester, 1898.	Great-grandson. Son of No. 22015.
22017	3344	Winifred Anne Henrietta Christina, Baroness Burghclere [U.K.], 1864. 48 *Charles Street, Berkeley Square, W.*	Granddaughter. Elder sister of No. 22015.
22018	3345	Hon. Juliet Mary Evelyn Stanhope Gardner, 1892.	Great-grandchildren. Children of No. 22017.
22019	3346	Hon. Alethea Margaret Gwendolen Valentine Gardner, 1893.	
22020	3347	Hon. Mary Sydney Katharine Almina Gardner, 1896.	
22021	3348	Lady Margaret Leonora Evelyn Selina Herbert, 1870.	Granddaughters. Younger sisters to No. 22015.
22022	3349	Lady Victoria Alexandrina Mary Cecil Herbert, 1874.	

242. Descendants of Lady Mary Thynne, 1778-1814, and her husband, Osborne Markham, Esq., M.P., 1769-1827. (See Table XXXVI.)

		Children, if any, of Mary Markham (daughter), W. Sheppard of Hampton Manor, Bath.	-1885, wife of

243. Descendants of Frederick, 4th Earl Spencer, K.G., 1798-1857. (See Table XXXVII.)

22023	3350	John Poyntz, 5th Earl Spencer, K.G., P.C., 1835. *Althorp Park, Northampton;* 27 *St. James' Place, S.W.*	Sons.
22024	3351	Right Hon. Charles Robert Spencer, P.C., M.P., 1857. *Dallington House, Northampton.* 28 *St. James' Place, S.W.*	
22025	3352	Albert Edward John Spencer, 1892.	Grandchildren. Children of No. 22024.
22026	3353	Cecil Edward Robert Spencer, 1894.	
22027	3354	Adelaide Margaret Spencer, 1889.	
22028	3355	Lavinia Emily Spencer, 1899.	
22029	3356	Lady Sarah Isabella Spencer, 1838.	Daughters.
22030	3357	Victoria Alexandrina, Baroness Sandhurst [U.K.], 1855. 60 *Eaton Square, S.W.*	

244. Descendants of Lady Sarah Spencer, 1787-1870, wife of William Henry, 3rd Lord Lyttelton, 1782-1837. (See Table XXXVII.)

22031	3358	Charles George, 8th Viscount Cobham, 5th Lord Lyttelton [G.B.], 5th Baron Westcote [I.], 1842. *Hagley Hall, Stourbridge.*	Grandson. Son of George William, 4th Lord Lyttelton, P.C., 1817-1876.

22032	3359	Hon. John Cavendish Lyttelton, Lieutenant 1st Battalion Rifle Brigade, 1881.	
22033	3360	Hon. George William Lyttelton, 1883.	
22034	3361	Hon. Charles Frederick Lyttelton, 1883.	Great-grandchildren. Children of No. 22031.
22035	3362	Hon. Richard Glynne Lyttelton, 1893.	
22036	3363	Hon. Maud Mary Lyttelton, 1880.	
22037	3364	Hon. Frances Henrietta Lyttelton, 1885.	
22038	3365	Hon. Rachel Beatrice Lyttelton, 1891.	
22039	3366	Rev. and Hon. Albert Victor Lyttelton, Curate of St. Michael's, Southwark, 1844. *Collegiate House, Southwark.*	Grandchildren. Brothers of No. 22031.
22040	3367	Hon. Sir Neville Gerald Lyttelton, Lieutenant-General commanding all the Forces in South Africa, K.C.B., 1845. *Pretoria, South Africa.* *28 Grosvenor Road, S.W.*	
22041	3368	Lucy Blanche Lyttelton, 1884.	Great-grandchildren. Children of No. 22040.
22042	3369	Hilda Margaret Lyttelton, 1886.	
22043	3370	Mary Hermione Lyttelton, 1894.	
22044	3371	Hon. George William Spencer Lyttelton, C.B., 1847. *49 Hill Street, Berkeley Square, W.* *The Castle House, Petersfield.*	Grandchild. Brother of No. 22031.
22045	3372	Archer Geoffrey Lyttelton, 1884.	Great-grandchildren. Children of Hon. Arthur Temple, Bishop of Southampton, 1852–1903.
22046	3373	Stephen Clive Lyttelton, 1887.	
22047	3374	Margaret Lucy Lyttelton, 1882.	
22048	3375	Hon. Robert Henry Lyttelton, Solicitor, of the firm of Stow, Preston & Lyttelton, 1854. *9 Barton Street, Westminster.*	Grandchildren. Brothers of No. 22031.
22049	3376	Rev. and Hon. Edward Lyttelton, Head-Master Haileybury College, Hertford, and Hon. Canon of St. Albans, 1855. *Haileybury College, Hertford.*	
22050	3377	Nora Joan Lyttelton, 1890.	Great-grandchildren. Children of No. 22049.
22051	3378	Delia Lyttelton, 1892.	
22052	3379	Hon. Alfred Lyttelton, K.C., M.P., Recorder of Oxford, 1857. *16 Great College Street, S.W.*	Grandchild. Brother of No. 22031.
22053	3380	Oliver Lyttelton, 1893.	Great-grandchildren. Children of No. 22052.
22054	3381	Mary Frances Lyttelton, 1895.	
22055	3382	Meriel Sarah, wife of the Right Hon. John Gilbert Talbot, P.C., M.P., 1840. *10 Great George Street, S.W.* *Falconhurst, Eden Bridge, Kent.*	Grandchild. Sister of No. 22031.
22056	3383	George John Talbot, Chancellor of the dioceses of Lincoln, Ely, and Lichfield, 1861. *3 Eaton Terrace, S.W.*	Great-grandson. Son of No. 22055.
22057	3384	John Bertram Talbot, 1900.	Great-great-grandchild. Son of No. 22056.
22058	3385	Bertram Talbot, 1865. *Travellers'.*	Great-grandchild. Sons of No. 22055.
22059	3386	John Edward Talbot, 1870.	
22060	3387	Anne Meriel Talbot, 1899.	Great-great-grandchildren. Children of No. 22059.
22061	3388	Joan Ankaret Talbot, 1901.	
22062	3389	Eustace Talbot, 1873.	Great-grandchild. Youngest son of No. 22055.
22063	3390	Hilda Mary Burrows, 1897.	Great-great-grandchild. Child of Mary Talbot, 1862–1897 (daughter of No. 22055), and her husband, the Rev. Winfrid Oldfield Burrows, Vicar of Holy Trinity, Leeds.

22064	3391	Caroline Agnes, wife of Talbot Baines, 1863.	Great-grandchild. Eldest surviving daughter of No. 22055.
22065	3392	Frederick John Talbot Baines, 1892.	Great-great-grandchildren. Children of No. 22064.
22066	3393	Edward Russell Baines, 1899.	
22067	3394	Susan Meriel Talbot Baines, 1894.	
22068	3395	Meriel Lucy Talbot, 1866.	Great-grandchildren. Granddaughters of No. 22055.
22069	3396	Evelyn Talbot (twin), 1873.	
22070	3397	Gwendolen Talbot, 1877.	
22071	3398	Margaret Isabel Talbot, 1878.	
22072	3399	Lucy Caroline, Lady Frederick Cavendish, 1841. 21 *Carlton House Terrace, S.W.*	Grandchildren. 2nd and 3rd sisters to No. 22031.
22073	3400	Hon. Lavinia, wife of the Right Rev. Edward Stuart Talbot, D.D., Lord Bishop of Rochester, 1849. *Bishop's House, Kennington Park, S.E.*	
22074	3401	Edward Keble Talbot, 1877.	Great-grandchildren. Children of No. 22073.
22075	3402	Neville Stuart Talbot, Lieutenant Rifle Brigade, 1879.	
22076	3403	Gilbert Walter Lyttelton Talbot, 1891.	
22077	3404	Mary Catherine Talbot, 1875.	
22078	3405	Lavinia Caroline Talbot, 1882.	
22079	3406	Hon. Sarah Kathleen, wife of John C. Bailey, 1870. 20 *Egerton Gardens, S.W.*	Grandchild. 4th sister to No. 22031.
22080	3407	Sybella Jane Bailey, 1901.	Great-grandchildren. Children of No. 22079.
22081	3408	Rachel Bailey, } twins, 1902.	
22082	3409	Ruth Bailey,	
22083	3410	Hon. Sybil, wife of Lionel Henry Cust, M.V.O., Surveyor of His Majesty's Pictures and Works of Art, &c., 1873. *Oliphant House, Windsor.*	Grandchild. 5th sister to No. 22031.
22084	3411	Lionel George Archer Cust, 1896.	Great-grandchild. Child of No. 22083.
22085	3412	Hon. Hester Margaret Lyttelton, 1874. *The Chantry, Ross-upon-Wye.*	Grandchild. 6th and youngest sister to No. 22031.
22086	3413	Mary Glynne.	Grandchildren. Daughters of the Hon. Lavinia Lyttelton, 1821–1850, and her husband, the Rev. Henry Glynne, Rector of Hawarden, 1812–1872.
22087	3414	Gertrude, Baroness Penrhyn [U.K.]. *Penrhyn Castle, Bangor. Mortimer House, Halkin Street, S.W.*	
22088	3415	Hon. George Henry Douglas-Pennant, Grenadier Guards, 1876.	Great-grandchildren. Children of No. 22087.
22089	3416	Hon. Charles Douglas-Pennant, Coldstream Guards, 1877.	
22090	3417	Hon. Gwynedd, wife of William Eley Cuthbert-Quilter, 1879. *Bawdsey Manor, Woodbridge.*	
22091	3418	George Eley Cuthbert-Quilter, 1900.	Great-great-grandchildren. Children of No. 22090.
22092	3419	John Raymond Cuthbert-Quilter, 1902.	
22093	3420	Hon. Lilian Douglas-Pennant, 1881.	Great-grandchildren. Younger daughters of No. 22087.
22094	3421	Hon. Winifred Douglas-Pennant, 1882.	
22095	3422	Hon. Margaret Douglas-Pennant, 1886.	
22096	3423	Hon. Nesta Douglas-Pennant, 1888.	
22097	3424	Hon. Elin Douglas-Pennant, 1889.	

245. Descendants of Lady Georgiana Charlotte Spencer, 1794–1823, and her husband, Lord George Quin, formerly Taylour, 1792–1888. (See Table XXXVII.)

22098	3425	Catherine Selina Sarah Quin, 1853. *Ewelme Manor, Wallingford.*	}	Granddaughters. Children of the late Rear-Admiral Richard Robert Quin, 1820–1870.
22099	3426	Georgiana Lavinia, wife of George Francis Stewart, D.L., 1859. *Summerhill, Killiney.*	
22100	3427	Clements George Stewart, 1882.	}	Great-grandchildren. Children of No. 22099.
22101	3428	Robert Henry Rynn Stewart, 1883.	
22102	3429	Mary Selina Stewart, 1887.	
22103	3430	Ethel Georgiana Stewart, 1890.	
22104	3431	Selina Gertrude Quin, 1862.	{	Granddaughter. Younger sister to Nos. 22098, &c.
22105	3432	Christabel Sarah Lavinia Watson, 1874.		Great-grandchildren. Daughters of the late Edward Spencer Watson, 1843–1889, son of Lavinia Jane Quin, 1816–1888, and her husband, the Hon. Richard Watson, M.P., 1800–1852.
22106	3433	Grace Mary Watson, 1876.	
22107	3434	Margaret Isabella Watson, 1877.	*Cransby Hall, near Kettering.*
22108	3435	Meriel Georgiana Watson, 1879.	
22109	3436	Frederica Katherine Watson, 1880.	
22110	3437	Anne Caroline Watson, 1882.	
22111	3438	Evelyn Horatia Watson, 1884.	
22112	3439	Selina Charlotte Watson, 1885.	
22113	3440	Cecily Eleanor Watson, 1887.	
22114	3441	Gwendolen Olivia Watson, 1888.	
22115	3442	Rev. Wentworth Watson, 1848. *Rockingham Castle, Northamptonshire.*	
22116	3443	Mary Georgiana, Lady Culme-Seymour, wife of Admiral Sir Michael Culme-Seymour, G.C.B., G.C.V.O., Vice-Admiral of the United Kingdom, 3rd Bart. *1 Egerton Gardens, S.W.*		Grandchildren. Children of the above-named Lavinia Jane Quin, 1816–1888.
22117	3444	Michael Culme-Seymour, Com. R.N., 1867. *Naval and Military.*	}	Great-grandchildren. Children of No. 22116.
22118	3445	John Wentworth Culme-Seymour, 1876.	
22119	3446	George Culme-Seymour, Lieutenant 2nd Battalion King's Royal Rifle Corps, 1878.	
22120	3447	Mary Elizabeth, wife of Com. Treveylan Dacres Willes Napier, R.N.	
22121	3448	Treveylan Michael Napier, 1901.	}	Great-great-grandchild. Child of No 22120.
22122	3449	Lavinia Grace, Baroness Eugene von Roeder, 1853. *Villa Roeder, Interlaken, Switzerland.*	}	Granddaughter. Sister of Nos. 22115, &c.
22123	3450	. . . . von Roeder.	}	Great-grandchildren. Children of No. 22122.
22124	3451	. . . . von Roeder.	

246. Descendants of the Hon. Charles Wentworth George Howard, 1814–1879. (See Table XXXVIII.)

22125	3452	George James, 9th Earl of Carlisle [E.], 1843. *Naworth Castle, Carlisle.* *1 Palace Green, Kensington, W.*	}	Son.

22126	3453	Charles James Stanley, Viscount Morpeth, 1867. *41 Devonshire Place, W.*	Grandson. Son of No. 22125.
22127	3454	Hon. George Josslyn L'Estrange Howard, 1895.	Great-grandson.
22128	3455	Hon. Constance Ankaret Howard, 1897.	Children of
22129	3456	Hon. Ankaret Cecilia Caroline Howard, 1900.	No. 22126.
22130	3457	Hon. Oliver Howard, 1875. *Brooks'.*	Grandchild. 2nd son of No. 22125.
22131	3458	Hubert Arthur George Howard, 1901.	Great-grandchild. Son of No. 22130.
22132	3459	Hon. Geoffrey Howard, 1877. *Brooks'.*	
22133	3460	Hon. Michael Francis Stafford Howard, Lieutenant 8th Hussars, 1880.	Grandchildren. Children of No. 22125.
22134	3461	Lady Mary Henrietta, wife of George Gilbert Aimé Murray, LL.D., Professor of Greek, *Glasgow University.* *Barford, Churt, Farnham.*	
22135	3462	Denis George Murray, 1892.	Great-grandchildren. Children of No. 22134.
22136	3463	Basil Andrew Murray, 1902.	
22137	3464	Rosalind Murray, 1890.	
22138	3465	Agnes Elizabeth Murray, 1894.	
22139	3466	Lady Cecilia Maude, wife of Charles Henry Roberts, Fellow of Exeter College, Oxford, 1868. *Bracklands, Shottermill, Surrey.*	Grandchildren. 2nd daughter of No. 22125.
22140	3467	Wilfrid Herbert Wace Roberts, 1900.	Great-grandchildren. Children of No. 22139.
22141	3468	Rosa Winifred Roberts, 1893.	
22142	3469	Christina Henrietta Roberts, 1895.	
22143	3470	Lady Dorothy Georgiana Howard, 1881.	Grandchildren. Younger daughters of No. 22125.
22144	3471	Lady Aurea Fredeswyde Howard, 1884.	

247. Descendants of Lady Caroline Georgiana Howard, 1803–1881, and her husband, the Right Hon. William Saunders Sebright Lascelles, M.P., P.C., 1798–1851. (See Table XXXVIII.)

22145	3472	Claude George William Lascelles, Major *late* R.A., 1831.	Elder sons.
22146	3473	Right Hon. Sir Frank Cavendish Lascelles, P.C., G.C.B., H.B.M.'s Ambassador to Germany, 1841. *British Embassy, Berlin.*	
22147	3474	William Frank Lascelles, Captain Scots Guards, A.D.C. to Governor-General of Canada, 1868. *15 West Eaton Place, S.W.*	Grandson. Son of No. 22146.
22148	3475	Vrede Esther Mary Lascelles, 1900.	Great-granddaughter. Daughter of No. 22147.
22149	3476	Gerald Claude Lascelles, H.B.M.'s Consul, Tunis, 1869.	Grandchildren. Children of No. 22146.
22150	3477	Florence Caroline Lascelles.	
22151	3478	Henry Arthur Lascelles, Lieut.-Col. *late* Rifle Brigade, 1842. *Woolbeding, Midhurst, Sussex.*	3rd son.
22152	3479	Edward Lascelles, 1884.	Grandchildren. Children of No. 22151.
22153	3480	Henry Lascelles, 1886.	
22154	3481	Francis Lascelles, 1890.	
22155	3482	John Lascelles, 1895.	

22156	3483	Georgiana Caroline, widow of the late Charles William Grenfell, M.P., 1826. *Taplow Court, Maidenhead.*	Daughter.
22157	3484	William Henry Grenfell, M.P., 1855. *Taplow Court, Maidenhead,* 4 *St. James' Square, S.W.*	Grandson. Son of No. 22156.
22158	3485	Julian Henry Francis Grenfell, 1888.	Great-grandchildren. Children of No. 22157.
22159	3486	Gerald William Grenfell, 1890.	
22160	3487	Ivo George Winfred Grenfell, 1898.	
22161	3488	Monica Margaret Grenfell, 1893.	
22162	3489	Charles Molyneux Grenfell, *late* Lieutenant 10th Hussars, 1857. 8 *Chester Square, S.W.*	Grandson. 2nd son of No. 22156.
22163	}	Same as No. 21921.	Great-granddaughter. Daughter of No. 22162.
22164	3490	Algernon Granville Grenfell, 1859. 29 *Chester Square, S.W.*	Grandson. 3rd son of No. 22156.
22165	3491	Charles Francis Meade, 1881.	Great-grandson. Son of Caroline Georgiana Grenfell, -1881 (daughter of No. 22156), and her husband, the Hon. Sir Robert Meade, G.C.B., 1835-1898.
22166	3492	Constance Isabella, wife of Lieut.-Col. Frederick Arthur Aylmer, R.A.	Granddaughter. Daughter of No. 22156.
22167	3493	Christopher Aylmer, 1890.	Great-grandchildren. Children of No. 22166.
22168	3494	Edward Arthur Aylmer, 1892.	
22169	3495	Henry Gerald Aylmer, 1896.	
22170	3496	Claud Aylmer, 1900.	
22171	3497	Rose Caroline Georgiana Aylmer, 1893.	
22172	3498	Charles Compton William, 3rd Lord Chesham, P.C. [U.K.], 1850. *Latimer, Chesham, Bucks.*	Grandson. Son of Henrietta Frances Lascelles, 1830-1884, and William George, 2nd Lord Chesham, 1815-1882.
22173	3499	Hon. John Compton Cavendish, 1894.	Great-grandchildren. Children of No. 22172.
22174	3500	Hon. Lilah Constance Cavendish, 1884.	
22175	3501	Hon. William Edwin Cavendish, Captain Grenadier Guards, 1862.	Grandson. Brother of No. 22172.
22176	3502	Evan George Charles Cavendish, 1891.	Great-grandchildren. Children of No. 22175.
22177	3503	Elizabeth Compton Cavendish, 1887.	
22178	3504	Hon. Edwin William Cavendish, 1865.	Grandchildren. Brother and sister of Nos. 22172, &c.
22179	3505	Georgiana Caroline, Countess of Leicester [U.K.], 1852. *Holkham, Norfolk.*	
22180	3506	Hon. Richard Coke, Lieutenant Scots Guards, 1876.	Great-grandchildren. Children of No. 22179.
22181	3507	Hon. Edward Coke, Lieutenant Rifle Brigade, 1879.	
22182	3508	Hon. John Spencer Coke, Lieutenant Scots Guards, 1880.	
22183	3509	Hon. Reginald Coke, 1883.	
22184	3510	Hon. Lovell William Coke, 1893.	
22185	3511	Lady Mabel Coke, 1878.	
22186	3512	Mary Susan Caroline, Viscountess Cobham [G.B.], Baroness Westcote [I.], 1853. *Hagley Hall, Stourbridge.*	Granddaughter. Sister to Nos. 22172, &c.
22187 -93	}	Same as Nos. 22032-22038.	Great-grandchildren. Children of No. 22186.

22194	3513	Katharine Caroline, Duchess Dowager of Westminster [U.K.], Countess Grosvenor [G.B.], 1857. *Combermere Abbey, Whitchurch, Salop.*	Granddaughter. Sister of Nos. 22172, &c.
22195	3514	Lord Hugh William Grosvenor, 1884.	Great-grandchildren. Children of No. 22194.
22196	3515	Lord Edward Arthur Grosvenor, 1892.	
22197	3516	Lady Mary Cavendish Grosvenor, 1883.	
22198	3517	Lady Helen Frances Grosvenor, 1888.	
22199	3518	Hon. Mary Louisa Lascelles, 1835. *87 Chester Square, S.W.*	Daughters.
22200	3519	Emma Elizabeth, Lady Edward Cavendish, 1838. *6 Carlos Place, S.W.*	
22201	3520	Victor Christian William Cavendish, M.P., 1868. *37 Park Lane, W.*	Grandson. Son of No. 22200.
22202	3521	Edward William Spencer Cavendish, 1895.	Great-grandchildren. Children of No. 22201.
22203	3522	Maud Louisa Emma Cavendish, 1896.	
22204	3523	Blanche Katherine Cavendish, 1898.	
22205	3524	Dorothy Evelyn Cavendish, 1900.	
22206	3525	Richard Frederick Cavendish, M.P., 1871. *7 Culford Gardens, S.W.*	Grandson. 2nd son of No. 22200.
22207	3526	Elizabeth Cavendish, 1897.	Great-granddaughters. Children of No. 22206.
22208	3527	Alix Cavendish, 1901.	
22209	3528	John Spencer Cavendish, D.S.O., Lieutenant 1st Life Guards, 1875.	Grandson. 3rd son of No. 22200.
22210	3529	Beatrice Blanche, widow of the Most Rev. Frederick Temple, D.D., Archbishop of Canterbury, 1821–1902, 1844. *The Palace, Lambeth, S.E. Old Palace, Canterbury.*	Daughter.
22211	3530	Frederick Charles Temple, 1879.	Grandchildren. Children of No. 22210.
22212	3531	William Temple, 1881.	

248. Descendants of Lady Georgiana Howard, 1804–1860, and her husband, George James Welbore, 1st Lord Dover, 1797–1833, v.p. (See Table XXXVIII.)

22213	3532	Lilah Georgiana Augusta Constance, Baroness Annaly [U.K.], 1862. *43 Berkeley Square, W. Luttrellstown, Consilla, co. Dublin.*	Granddaughter. Daughter of Henry, 2nd Lord Dover, 3rd Viscount Clifden, 1825–1866.
22214	3533	Hon. Luke Henry White, 1885.	Great-grandchildren. Children of No. 22223.
22215	3534	Hon. Lilah Charlotte Sarah White, 1889.	
22216	3535	Hon. Lucia Emily Margaret White, 1890.	
22217	3536	Leopold Fawcett.	Great-grandchild. Child of the Hon. Caroline Agar-Ellis, 1865–1891, daughter of Leopold George Frederick, 5th Viscount Clifden, 1829–1899, and her husband, Major James Farish Malcolm Fawcett, of Scalesby Castle, Cumberland.
22218	3537	Hon. Harriet, wife of Thomas Granville Knox, 1867. *White Rose Grange, Woking.*	Granddaughter. Daughter of Leopold George Frederick, 5th Viscount Clifden, 1829–1899.
22219	3538	Constance Georgiana Knox.	Great-granddaughter. Daughter of No. 22218.

22220	3539	Hon. Evelyn Mary, wife of the Hon. Edward Harry Vanden-Bemphe-Johnstone, 1869. *6 Lower Sloane Street, S.W.*	Granddaughter. Sister to No. 22218.
22221	3540	Leopold Edward Vanden-Bemphe-Johnstone, 1897.	Great-grandchildren. Children of No. 10120.
22222	3541	George Harcourt Vanden-Bemphe-Johnstone, 1899.	
22223	3542	William, 4th Lord Bagot [G.B.], 1857. *Blithfield, Rugeley.*	Grandchildren. Sons of the late Hon. Lucia Caroline Elizabeth Agar-Ellis, 1827–1895, and her husband, William, 3rd Lord Bagot, 1811–1887.
22224	3543	Hon. Walter Lewis Bagot, D.S.O., Captain *late* Grenadier Guards, 1864. *43 Rutland Gate, S.W.*	
22225	3544	Edward Bagot, 1896.	Great-grandchildren. Children of No. 22224.
22226	3545	Marjorie Olive Bagot, 1893.	
22227	3546	Hon. Louisa, wife of the Rev. Bernard Day Douglas-Shaw, 1853. *48 Cadogan, Place, S.W.*	Granddaughter. Sister to No. 22223.
22228	3547	William Arthur Hamar Bass, Lieutenant 10th Hussars, 1879.	Great-grandchildren. Children of No. 22227 and her 1st husband, Hamar Alfred Bass, M.P., 1842–1898.
22229	3548	Sibell Lucia, wife of Captain John Talbot Berkeley Levett, Scots Guards, 1881. *Wychnor Park, Staffordshire.*	
22230	3549	Hon. Katherine Jane, wife of Colonel David Murray Smythe of Methven, 1859. *Methven Castle, Perth.* 30 *Green Street, W.*	Granddaughter. Sister to No. 22223.
22231	3550	Barbara Emily Smythe, 1899.	Great-granddaughter. Daughter of No. 22230.
22232	3551	Hon. Elizabeth Sophia Lucia, wife of Francis Alexander Newdigate-Newdegate, M.P., *of Weston-in-Arden, co. Warwick,* 1861. 1 *Tilney Street, Park Lane, W.*	Granddaughter. Sister to No. 22223.
22233	3552	Lucia Charlotte Susan Newdigate, 1896.	Great-granddaughters. Daughters of No. 22232.
22234	3553	Susan Theodora Newdigate, 1900.	

249. Descendants of George Granville William, 3rd Duke of Sutherland, K.G., 1828-1892. (See Table XXXVIII.)

22235	3554	▽ Cromartie, 4th Duke [U.K.] and 21st Earl [S.] of Sutherland, 5th Marquis of Stafford [G.B.], 7th Baron Gower [E.], 1851. *Dunrobin Castle, Sutherland. Stafford House, St. James', S.W.*	Son.
22236	3555	▽ George, Marquis of Stafford, 1888.	Grandchildren. Children of No. 22235.
22237	3556	▽ Lord Alister St. Clair Sutherland-Leveson-Gower, 1890.	
22238	3557	▽ Lady Rosemary Millicent Sutherland-Leveson-Gower, 1893.	
22239	3558	▽ Sibell Lilian, Countess of Cromartie [U.K.], 1878. *Tarbat House, Ross.*	Granddaughters. Daughters of Francis, Earl of Cromartie, 1852–1893.
22240	3559	▽ Lady Constance Mackenzie, 1882.	

22241	3560	Eric Chaplin, 1877.	Grandchildren. Children of the late Lady Florence Sutherland Gower, 1855–1881, and her husband, the Right Hon. Henry Chaplin, P.C., M.P., of Blankney House, Lincolnshire.
22242	3561	Edith Viscountess Castlereagh, 1878. *Londonderry House, Park Lane, W.*	
22243	3562	Edward Charles Stewart Robert, Lord Stewart, 1902.	Great-grandchild. Son of No. 22242.
22244	3563	Florence Chaplin, 1881.	Grandchild. Younger sister to No. 22241.

250. Descendants of Lord Albert Sutherland-Leveson-Gower, 1843–1874. (See Table XXXVIII.)

22245	3564	▽ Frederick Neville Leveson-Gower, M.P., 1874. *Berkeley House, Hay Hill, Berkeley Square.*	Son.

22246	3565	▽ Lord Ronald Charles Sutherland-Gower, 1845. *Hammerfield, Penshurst, Kent.*	See Table XXXVIII.

251. Descendants of Lady Elizabeth Georgiana Sutherland-Leveson-Gower, 1824–1878, and her husband, George, 8th Duke of Argyll, K.G., K.T., 1823–1900. (See Table XXXVIII.)

22247	3566	John Douglas Sutherland, 9th Duke [S.] and 2nd Duke [U.K.] of Argyll, 5th Baron Sundridge and Hamilton [G.B.], P.C., K.T., 1845. *Inverary Castle, Argyllshire. Kensington Palace, W.*	Sons.
22248	3567	Lord Archibald Campbell, 1846. *Coombe Hill Farm, Norbiton, Kingston-on-Thames.*	
22249	3568	Niall Diarmaid Campbell, 1872.	Grandchildren. Children of No. 22248.
22250	3569	Espeth Angela Campbell, 1873.	
22251	3570	Douglas Walter Campbell, 1877.	Grandchildren. Children of Lord Walter Campbell, 1848–1889.
22252	3571	Lilah Olive Campbell, 1875.	
22253	3572	Lord George Granville Campbell, 1850. *2 Bryanston Square, W.*	3rd son.
22254	3573	Ivar Campbell, 1890.	Grandchildren. Children of No. 22253.
22255	3574	Joan Campbell, 1887.	
22256	3575	Enid Campbell, 1892.	
22257	3576	Edith, Duchess of Northumberland [G.B.], 1849. *Alnwick Castle, Northumberland. 2 Grosvenor Place, S.W.*	Eldest daughter.
22258 –67		Same as Nos. 20955–20964.	Grandchildren. Children of No. 22257.
22268	3577	Edward Lorne Frederic Clough-Taylor, 1881.	Grandchildren. Children of the late Lady Elizabeth Campbell, 1852–1896, and her husband, Major Edward Harrison Clough-Taylor, of Firby Hall, Yorkshire, 1849.
22269	3578	Lesley Venetia Clough-Taylor, 1886.	

22270	3579	Lady Victoria Campbell, 1854.		
		The Lodge, Tiree, Argyllshire.		
22271	3580	Lady Evelyn, wife of James Baillie-Hamilton, 1855.	Daughters.	
22272	3581	Lady Frances, wife of Eustace James Anthony Balfour, 1858.		
		32 Addison Road, W.		
22273	3582	Francis Cecil Campbell Balfour, 1884.		
22274	3583	Oswald Herbert Campbell Balfour, 1894.		
22275	3584	Blanche Elizabeth Campbell Balfour, 1880.	Grandchildren.	Children of No. 22272.
22276	3585	Joan Eleanor Campbell Balfour, 1889.		
22277	3586	Alison Catherine Campbell Balfour, 1891.		
22278	3587	Lady Mary Emma, wife of the Right Rev. the Hon. Edward Carr Glyn, D.D., Bishop of Peterborough, 1859.	5th surviving daughter.	
		The Palace, Peterborough.		
22279	3588	Ralph George Campbell Glyn, 1884.	Grandchildren.	Children of No. 22278.
22280	3589	Margaret Isabel Frances Glyn, 1888.		
22281	3590	Alice Sybil Glyn, 1889.		
22282	3591	Lady Constance Harriet, wife of Charles Emmott, 1864.	7th daughter.	
		Snow Hall, Gainford, Darlington.		
22283	3592	Charles Ernest George Campbell Emmott, 1898.	Grandchildren. Children of No. 22282.	
22284	3593	Constance Hilda Campbell Emmott, 1897.		

252. Descendants of Lady Evelyn Sutherland-Leveson-Gower, 1825–1869, and her husband, Charles, 12th Lord Blantyre, 1818–1900. (See Table XXXVIII.)

22285	3594	Hon. Mary Stuart, 1845.		
		Torquay, Devon.	Children.	
22286	3595	Hon. Ellen, Lady Baird, 1846.		
		Newbyth House, Prestonkirk, N.B.		
22287	3596	David Baird, Captain 2nd Battalion Black Watch, 1865.	Grandchildren. Children of No. 22286.	
22288	3597	William Arthur Baird, 1879.		
22289	3598	Evelyn Baird, 1871.		
22290	3599	Hilda Baird, 1875.		
22291	3600	Mabel Baird, 1880.		
22292	3601	Archibald, Earl of Cassillis, 1872.		
		Culzean Castle, Ayrshire.	Grandchildren. Children of the late Hon. Evelyn Stuart, 1848–1888, 1st wife of Archibald, 3rd Marquis of Ailsa, 1847.	
22293	3602	Lord Charles Kennedy, 1875.		
		White's.		
22294	3603	Lord Angus Kennedy, 1882.		
22295	3604	Lady Aline, wife of the Hon. John Edward Deane Browne, 1877.		
		Gaulston Park, Killucan.		
22296	3605	Hon. Gertrude, widow of the late William Henry Gladstone, M.P., 1840–1891, 1849.	Daughter.	
		Hawarden Castle, Chester.		
22297	3606	William Glynne Charles Gladstone, 1885.		
		Hawarden Castle, co. Chester.	Grandchildren. Children of No. 22296.	
22298	3607	Evelyn Catherine Gladstone, 1882.		
22299	3608	Constance Gertrude Gladstone, 1883.		

253. Descendants of Lady Caroline Sutherland-Leveson-Gower, 1827-1887, and her husband, Charles William, 4th Duke of Leinster, 1819-1887. (See Table XXXVIII.)

22300	3609	Maurice, 6th Duke of [I.] and Viscount [G.B.] Leinster, 1887. *Carton, Maynooth, co. Kildare.*	Grandchildren. Children of Gerald, 5th Duke of Leinster, 1851-1893.	
22301	3610	Lord Desmond FitzGerald, 1888.		
22302	3611	Lord Edward FitzGerald, 1892.		
22303	3612	Gerald Hugh FitzGerald, 1886.		Grandchildren. Children of Lord Maurice FitzGerald, 1852-1901.
22304	3613	Geraldine Mary FitzGerald, 1881.	*Johnstown Castle, co. Wexford.*	
22305	3614	Kathleen FitzGerald, 1892.		
22306	3615	Lord Frederick FitzGerald, 1857. *Carton, Maynooth, co. Kildare.*		
22307	3616	Lord Walter FitzGerald, 1858. *Kilkea Castle, Mageney, co. Kildare.*	Sons.	
22308	3617	Lord Charles FitzGerald, 1859. *Fernlea Villa, Riddell's Creek, Victoria, Australia.*		
22309	3618	George FitzGerald, 1890.		
22310	3619	Charles Otho FitzGerald, 1895.	Grandchildren. Children of No. 22308.	
22311	3620	Rupert Augustus FitzGerald, 1900.		
22312	3621	Nesta Sidonia FitzGerald, 1888.		
22313	3622	Mabel Geraldine FitzGerald, 1891.		
22314	3623	Lord George FitzGerald, 1862. *Kilkea Castle, Mageney, co. Kildare.*	Sons.	
22315	3624	Lord Henry FitzGerald, 1863. 1 *Sloane Court, S.W.*		
22316	3625	Dermot FitzGerald, 1891. Grandson. Son of No. 22315.		
22317	3626	Lady Alice, wife of Colonel Charles John Oswald FitzGerald, C.B., 1853. *Dunmore, Carlisle Road, Eastbourne.*	Daughter.	
22318	3627	Arthur FitzGerald, 1891.		
22319	3628	Terence George FitzGerald, 1895.	Grandchildren. Children of No. 22317.	
22320	3629	Mabel FitzGerald, 1884.		
22321	3630	Leila FitzGerald, 1889.		
22322	3631	Lady Eva FitzGerald, 1855.	*Kilkea Castle, Mageney, co. Kildare.*	Daughters.
22323	3632	Lady Mabel FitzGerald, 1855.		
22324	3633	Lady Nesta FitzGerald, 1865.		

254. Descendants of Lady Constance Gertrude Sutherland-Leveson-Gower, 1834-1880, 1st wife of Hugh Lupus, 1st Duke of Westminster, K.G., 1825-1899. (See Table XXXVIII.)

22325	3634	Hugh Richard Arthur, 2nd Duke of Westminster [U.K.], 5th Earl Grosvenor [G.B.], 1879. *Eaton Hall, Chester.* *Grosvenor House, 33 Upper Grosvenor Street, W.*	Grandchildren. Children of Victor Alexander, Earl Grosvenor, 1853-1884.
22326	3635	Constance Sibell, Countess of Shaftesbury [E.], 1875. *St. Giles' House, Salisbury.*	

22327	3636	Anthony Lord Ashley, 1900.	Great-grandchildren.
22328	3637	Lady Victoria Mary Ashley-Cooper, 1902.	Children of No. 22326.
22329	3638	Lady Lettice Mary Elizabeth Grosvenor, 1876.	Grandchild. Sister of Nos. 22325, &c.
22330	3639	Lord Arthur Hugh Grosvenor, 1860. Broxton, Chester.	Son.
22331	3640	Robert Arthur Grosvenor, 1895.	Grandchildren. Children of No. 22330.
22332	3641	Constance Isolde Grosvenor, 1900.	
22333	3642	Barbara Grosvenor, 1901.	
22334	3643	Lord Henry George Grosvenor, 1861. Tittensor, Stoke-upon-Trent.	2nd surviving son.
22335	3644	William Grosvenor, 1894.	Grandchildren. Children of No. 22334.
22336	3645	Millicent Constance Grosvenor, 1889.	
22337	3646	Dorothy Alice Margaret Augusta Grosvenor, 1890.	
22338	3647	Lord Gerald Richard Grosvenor, 1874.	Eldest son and daughter.
22339	3648	Elizabeth Harriet, Marchioness of [I.] and Baroness Ormonde [U.K.], 1856. Kilkenny Castle, Kilkenny. 32 Upper Brook Street, W.	
22340	3649	Lady Beatrice Frances Elizabeth, wife of Major-General Sir Reginald Pole-Carew, K.C.B., C.V.O., 1876. Antony, Devonport.	Granddaughter. Daughter of No. 22339.
22341	3650	John Gawen Pole-Carew, 1902.	Great-grandchild. Son of No. 22340.
22342	3651	Lady Constance Mary Butler, 1879.	Granddaughter. Younger child of No. 22339.
22343	3652	Beatrice Constance, Lady Chesham [U.K.], 1858. Latimer, near Chesham, Bucks.	2nd daughter.
22344-45		Same as Nos. 22173–22174.	Grandchildren. Children of No. 22343.
22346	3653	Margaret Evelyn, Duchess of Teck [Würtemberg], 1873. 4 Devonshire Place, W.	3rd surviving daughter.
22347-49		Same as Nos. 6139–6141.	Grandchildren. Children of No. 22346.

255. Descendants of Lady Blanche Georgiana Howard, 1812–1840, and her husband, William, 7th Duke of Devonshire, K.G., 1808–1891. (See Table XXXVIII.)

22350	3654	Spencer Compton, 8th Duke of Devonshire [E.], 3rd Earl of Burlington [U.K.], P.C., K.G., 1833. Chatsworth, Chesterfield. Devonshire House, Piccadilly, W.	Son.
22351-59		Same as Nos. 22201–22209.	Grandchildren. Children of Lord Edward Cavendish, 1828–1891.
22360	3655	Lady Louisa Caroline, widow of Admiral the Hon. Francis Egerton, 1824–1895, 1835. St. George's Hill, Weybridge.	Daughter.
22361	3656	▽ William Francis Egerton, late Lieutenant 17th Lancers, 1868. Gawithfield, Arrad Foot, Ulverston.	Grandson. Son of No. 22360.
22362	3657	▽ Francis Egerton, 1896. Great-grandson. Son of No. 22361.	
22363	3658	▽ Blanche Harriet Egerton, 1871.	Grandchildren. Daughters of No. 22360.
22364	3659	▽ Dorothy Charlotte Egerton, 1874.	
22365	3660	▽ Christian Mary Egerton, 1876.	

256. Descendants of Granville George, 2nd Earl Granville, K.G., 1815–1891. (See Table XXXIX.)

22366	3661	Granville George, 3rd Earl Granville, 1872. *British Legation, The Hague.*	
22367	3662	Hon. William Spencer Leveson-Gower, Midshipman R.N., 1880.	Children.
22368	3663	Lady Victoria Alberta, wife of Harold John Hastings Russell, 1867. 16 *Beaufort Gardens, S.W.*	
22369	3664	☿ Elizabeth Frances Russell, 1899.	Granddaughter. Daughter of No. 22368.
22370	3665	Lady Sophia Castalia Mary, wife of Hugh Morrison, 1870. 34 *Cadogan Place, S.W.*	Younger daughter.

22371	3666	Hon. Edward Frederick Leveson-Gower, 1819. 14 *South Audley Street, W.*	See Table XXXIX.

257. Descendants of No. 22371.

22372	3667	George Granville Leveson-Gower, 1858. 13 *Seymour Street, Portman Square, W.*	Son.
22373	3668	Iris Irma Leveson-Gower, 1899.	Granddaughter. Daughter of No. 22372.

258. Descendants of Lady Susan Georgiana Leveson-Gower, 1810–1866, and her husband, George, 4th Lord Rivers, 1810–1866. (See Table XXXIX.)

22374	3669	Hon. Susan Harriet, widow of Edmund Oldfield, Barrister-at-Law, 1835. *Rushmore, Torquay.*	Eldest daughter.
22375	3670	George Godolphin, 10th Duke of Leeds [E.], 9th Viscount Dunblane [S.], 4th Baron Godolphin [U.K.], 1862. 11 *Grosvenor Crescent, S.W.*	Grandson. Son of the late Hon. Fanny Georgiana Pitt, 1836–1896, and her husband, George, 9th Duke of Leeds, 1828–1895.
22376	3671	John Francis Godolphin, Marquis of Carmarthen, 1901.	Great-grandchildren. Children of No. 22375.
22377	3672	Lady Guendolen Fanny Godolphin Osborne, 1885.	
22378	3673	Lady Olga Katherine Godolphin Osborne, 1886.	
22379	3674	Lady Dorothy Beatrix Osborne, 1888.	
22380	3675	Lady Moira Godolphin Osborne, 1892.	

22381	3676	Lord Francis Granville Godolphin Osborne, 1864. *Naval and Military.*	⎫ Grandchildren. Brothers and sister to No. 22375.
22382	3677	Lord Albert Edward Godolphin Osborne, 1866. 20 *De Vere Gardens, W.*	
22383	3678	Lady Harriet Castalia, wife of Henry Frederick Compton Cavendish, 1867. *Cromford, Matlock, Derbyshire.*	⎭
22384	3679	Henry James Francis Cavendish, 1893.	⎫ Great-grandchildren. Children of No. 22383.
22385	3680	George Sydney Godolphin Cavendish, 1895.	
22386	3681	Emily Georgiana Harriet Cavendish, 1890.	
22387	3682	Evelyn Alice Beatrix Cavendish, 1892.	⎭
22388	3683	Lady Alice Susan, wife of William Francis Egerton, Lieutenant 17th Hussars, 1869. *Gawithfield, Arrad Foot, Ulverston.*	Granddaughter. Sister of No. 22375.
22389		Same as No. 22362.	Great-grandson. Son of No. 22388.
22390	3684	Lady Ada Charlotte, wife of the Hon. William Hugh Spencer Wentworth-Fitzwilliam, 1870.	⎫ Granddaughters. Younger sisters of No. 22375.
22391	3685	Lady Alexandra Louisa Godolphin Osborne, 1872. 1 *Queensberry Place, S.W.*	
22392	3686	Lady Constance Blanche Godolphin, wife of Ernest Frederick George Hatch, M.P., 1875. 11 *Mount Street, Grosvenor Square, W.*	⎭
22393	3687	Hon. Blanche Caroline Pitt, 1840. *Stepleton, Blandford.*	2nd surviving daughter.
22394	3688	Victor Alexander George Eliot.	Grandson. Son of the Hon. Mary Emma Pitt, 1843–1900, and her husband, the Very Rev. Philip Frank Eliot, D.D., Dean of Windsor.
22395	3689	Hon. Margaret Grace, wife of the Rev. William Page Roberts, Minister of St. Peter's, Vere Street, and Canon Residentiary of Canterbury, 1847. *The Precincts, Canterbury.*	3rd surviving daughter.
22396	3690	George Rivers Page-Roberts, 1880.	⎫ Grandchildren. Children of No. 22395.
22397	3691	Mary Margaret Page-Roberts, 1881.	
22398	3692	Constance Susan Page-Roberts, 1882.	
22399	3693	Alice Marcia Page-Roberts, 1888.	⎭
22400	3694	Hon. Gertrude Emily Pitt, 1852. *Stepleton, Blandford.*	4th surviving daughter.

259. Descendants of John William, 4th Earl of Bessborough, P.C., 1781–1847. (See Table XL.)

22401	3695	Walter William Brabazon, 7th Earl of Bessborough [I.] and Baron Ponsonby of Sysonby [G.B.], 4th Baron Duncannon [U K.], 1821. *Bessborough, Piltown, co. Kilkenny.* 38 *Eccleston Square, S.W.*	Eldest surviving son.
22402	3696	Edward Viscount Duncannon, C.B., 1851. 17 *Cavendish Square, W.*	Grandson. Eldest son of No. 22401.

22403	3697	Hon. Vere Brabazon Ponsonby, 1880.	⎫
22404	3698	Hon. Cyril Myles Brabazon Ponsonby, M.V.O.,	
		Lieutenant Grenadier Guards, 1881.	Great-grandchildren.
22405	3699	Hon. Bertie Brabazon Ponsonby, 1885.	Children of No.
22406	3700	Olwen Verena, Baroness Oranmore and Browne	22402.
		[I.], 1876.	
		Castle Macgarrett, Claremorris, co. Mayo.	⎭
22407	3701	Hon. Geoffrey Dominick Edward Browne-	Great-great-grandchild.
		Guthrie, 1901.	Son of No. 22406.
22408	3702	Hon. Helena Blanche Irene Ponsonby,	Great-grandchildren.
		1878.	Children of No.
22409	3703	Hon. Gweneth Frida Ponsonby, 1888.	22402.
22410	3704	Hon. Cyril Walter Ponsonby, a Lieutenant for	Grandson. 2nd
		the City of London, 1853.	son of No.
		31 *Grosvenor Road, S.W.*	22401.
22411	3705	Cyril Thomas Ponsonby, 1894.	Great-grandchildren. Sons of
22412	3706	Michael Henry Ponsonby, 1896.	No. 22410.
22413	3707	Hon. Granville Ponsonby, Chief of the	
		Police, St. Lucia, M.L.C., 1854.	
		Castries, St. Lucia, West Indies.	
22414	3708	Hon. Arthur Cornwallis Ponsonby,	
		1856.	
22415	3709	Hon. Gerald Walter Ponsonby, Bar.	Grandchildren. Younger
		Inner Temple, 1859.	sons and elder daughters
22416	3710	Lady Maria Ponsonby, 1852.	of No. 22401.
22417	3711	Ethel Jemima, Baroness Raglan	
		[U.K.], 1857.	
		Cefntilla Court, Usk, Mon-	
		mouthshire.	
		27 *Half Moon Street, W.*	
22418	3712	Hon. FitzRoy Richard Somerset, 1885.	
22419	3713	Hon. Wellesley FitzRoy Somerset, 1887.	Great-grandchil-
22420	3714	Hon. Nigel FitzRoy Somerset, 1893.	dren. Chil-
22421	3715	Hon. Ethel Georgiana Frances Somerset, 1889.	dren of No.
22422	3716	Hon. Frederica Susan Katherine Somerset,	22417.
		1891.	
22423	3717	Hon. Ivy Felicia Somerset, 1897.	
22424	3718	Lady Sara Kathleen, wife of Charles Lancelot	Granddaughter.
		Andrewes Skinner, *late* 4th Hussars,	3rd daughter
		1861.	of No. 22401.
		57 *Eccleston Square, S.W.*	
22425	3719	Edgar Louis Skinner, 1884.	
22426	3720	Philip John Lancelot Skinner, 1894.	Great-grandchildren.
22427	3721	Marjorie Isabel Skinner, 1885.	Children of No.
22428	3722	Faith Mary Wordsworth Skinner, 1887.	22424.
22429	3723	Lilian Frances Skinner, 1891.	
22430	3724	Right Hon. Sir Spencer Cecil Brabazon Ponsonby-	
		Fane, P.C., G.C.B., 1824.	2nd surviving
		Brympton, Yeovil.	son.
		19 *Bryanston Street, W.*	
22431	3725	John Henry Ponsonby, 1848.	Grandson. Eldest son
		15 *Chesham Place, S.W.*	of No. 22430.
22432	3726	Richard Arthur Brabazon Ponsonby, 1878.	Great-grandchildren.
22433	3727	Violet Louisa Ponsonby, 1876.	Children of No. 22431.
22434	3728	Robert Charles Ponsonby, 1854.	Grandson. 2nd sur-
		73 *Egerton Gardens, S.W.*	viving son of No.
		4 *Clement's Inn, W.C.*	22430.
22435	3729	George Arthur Ponsonby, 1878.	Great-grandson. Son of No. 22434.

22436	3730	Sydney Alexander Ponsonby, 1863. *Elm Field, Potter's Bar.*	} Grandson. 3rd surviving son of No. 22430.
22437	3731	Patrick Spencer John Ponsonby, 1894.	} Great-grandchildren. Children of No. 22436.
22438	3732	James Michael Ponsonby, 1901.	
22439	3733	Eleanor Elizabeth Anne Ponsonby, 1899.	
22440	3734	Hugh Spencer Ponsonby, 1865. *Carreros, Oporto.*	} Grandson. 4th surviving son of No. 22430.
22441	3735	Spencer Lawrence Ponsonby, 1896.	} Great-grandsons. Sons of No. 22440.
22442	3736	David Brabazon Ponsonby, 1901.	
22443	3737	Theobald Brabazon Ponsonby, 1868.	} Grandchildren. Children of No. 22430.
22444	3738	Constance Louisa, wife of William Robert Phelips. *Montacute House, Montacute, Somerset.*	
22445	3739	Edward Frederick Phelips, 1882.	} Great-grandchildren. Children of No. 22444.
22446	3740	Gerard Amanes Phelips, 1884.	
22447	3741	Clare Louisa Phelips, 1883.	
22448	3742	Margaret Maria, widow of the Hon. and Rev. Arnald de Grey, 1856–1889, 1857. *Brympton, Yeovil.*	} Grandchild. Daughter of No. 22430.
22449	3743	Nigel de Grey, 1886. {	Great-grandson. Son of No. 22448.
22450	3744	Clementina Sarah, wife of Edmund Russborough Turton. *Upsall Castle, Thirsk, York.*	} Granddaughter. Youngest daughter of No. 22430.
22451	3745	Edmund Spencer Turton, 1889. {	Great-grandson. Son of No. 22450.
22452	3746	Hon. Gerald Henry Brabazon Ponsonby, 1829. 3 *Stratford Place, W.*	} 3rd surviving son.
22453	3747	Mabel Elizabeth Ponsonby, 1883.	Great-grandchildren. Children of Louis George de Hale Ponsonby, 1858–1887, son of No. 22452.
22454	3748	Eileen Cecilia Ponsonby, 1885.	
22455	3749	Joan Ponsonby, 1887.	
22456	3750	Geraldine Sarah, Countess of Mayo [I.], 1863. 3 *Stratford Place, W.* *Palmerstown, Straffan, co. Kildare.*	} Grandchild. Child of No. 22452.
22457	3751	Ven. Cecil Frederick Joseph Bourke, Archdeacon of Buckingham, 1841. *Hill House, Taplow.*	Grandchildren. Children of Lady Georgiana Sarah Ponsonby, 1807–1861, and her husband, the Rev. Sackville Gardiner Bourke, 1805–1860.
22458	3752	Lucy Josepha Maria Bourke, 1845. *Hill House, Taplow.*	
22459	3753	Augusta Lavinia, Countess of Kerry, 1814. *West Side, Wimbledon Common, S.W.*	} Eldest surviving daughter.
22460	3754	Francis Charles Gore, Solicitor to the Inland Revenue, 1846. 46 *Egerton Gardens, S.W.*	Grandson. Eldest son of No. 22459, and her 2nd husband, the Hon. Charles Alexander Gore, 1811–1897.
22461	3755	Arthur Charles Gore, 1880.	} Great-grandchildren. Children of No. 22460.
22462	3756	Charles Henry Gore, 1881.	
22463	3757	John Francis Gore, 1885.	
22464	3758	Evelyn Mary Gore, 1883.	
22465	3759	Spencer William Gore, 1850. *Holywell Park, Wrotham, Kent.*	} Grandson. Brother of No. 22460.
22466	3760	George Pym Gore, 1875.	} Great-grandchildren. Children of No. 22465.
22467	3761	Spencer Frederick Gore, 1878.	
22468	3762	Kathleen Amy Gore, 1877.	
22469	3763	Florence Gore, 1883.	

22470	3764	Right Rev. Charles Gore, Lord Bishop of Worcester. *Hartlebury Castle, Kidderminster. Bishop's House, Worcester.*	Grandson. Brother of No. 22460.
22471	3765	Lady Mary Herbert, widow of General the Right Hon. Sir Percy Egerton Herbert, P.C., M.P., K.C.B., 1822–1876, 1835. *Styche, Market Drayton, Salop.*	Granddaughter. Daughter of No. 22459 by 1st husband, William Thomas, Earl of Kerry, 1811–1836.
22472	3766	George Charles, 4th Earl of Powis [U.K.], Baron Clive of Walcot [G.B.], and 5th Baron Clive of Plassey [I.], 1862. *Powis Castle, Welshpool. 45 Berkeley Square, W.*	Great-grandson. Son of No. 22471.
22473	3767	Percy Robert, Viscount Clive, 1892.	Great-great-grandchildren. Children of No. 22472.
22474	3768	Lady Hermione Glwadys Herbert, 1900.	
22475	3769	Lady Magdalen Lucy Herbert, 1864.	Great-granddaughters. Daughters of No. 22471.
22476	3770	Lady Margaret Augusta, wife of Thomas Richard Cholmondeley, 1868. *Council House Court, Shrewsbury.*	
22477	3771	Richard Hugh Cholmondeley, 1900.	Great-great-grandchildren. Children of No. 22476.
22478	3772	Margaret Mary Cholmondeley, 1898.	
22479	3773	Emily Caroline Augusta Gore.	Grandchildren. Daughters of No. 22459 by 2nd husband.
22480	3774	Caroline Maria, wife of Lieut.-Col. Henry Arthur Lascelles. *Woolbeding, Midhurst, Sussex.*	
22481	3775	Edward Lascelles, 1884.	Great-grandchildren. Sons of No. 22480.
22482	3776	Henry Lascelles, 1886.	
22483	3777	Francis Lascelles, 1890.	
22484	3778	John Lascelles, 1895.	
22485	3779	William Ashley Webb, 3rd Lord De Mauley [U.K.], 1843. *Langford House, Lechlade.*	Grandchildren. Children of Lady Maria Jane Elizabeth Ponsonby, 1819–1897, and her husband, Charles Frederick Ashley Cooper, 2nd Lord De Mauley, 1815–1896.
22486	3780	Rev. and Hon. Maurice John George Charles Ponsonby, Hon. Canon of Bristol and Rural Dean of Cricklade, 1846. *New Swindon Vicarage, Wilts.*	
22487	3781	Gerald Maurice Ponsonby, Lieutenant 3rd Battalion Royal Warwickshire Regiment, 1876.	Great-grandsons. Sons of No. 22486.
22488	3782	Hubert William Ponsonby, 1878.	
22489	3783	Hon. Frederick John William Ponsonby, 1847. *14 Chapel Street, Belgrave Square, S.W.*	Grandson. Brother of Nos. 22485, &c.
22490	3784	Mary Fanny Louisa Ponsonby, 1879.	Great-granddaughters. Daughters of No. 22489.
22491	3785	Evelyn Margaret Ponsonby, 1887.	
22492	3786	Hon. Edwin Charles William Ponsonby, J.P., D.L., 1851. *Woodleys, Woodstock.*	Grandson. Brother of Nos. 22485, &c.
22493	3787	Charles Edward Ponsonby, 1879.	Great-grandchildren. Children of No. 22492.
22494	3788	Maurice George Jesser Ponsonby, 1880.	
22495	3789	Ashley William Neville Ponsonby, 1882.	
22496	3790	Victor Coope Ponsonby, 1887.	
22497	3791	Diana Helen Ponsonby, 1891.	
22498	3792	Hon. Emily Priscilla Maria, wife of the Rev. Charles William Norman Ogilvy, 1841. *The Vicarage, Oswestry.*	Granddaughter. Sister of Nos. 22485, &c.

22499	3793	Alice Jane Marion Ogilvy.	Great-granddaughters. Daughters of No. 22498.
22500	3794	Diana Maria Elizabeth Ogilvy.	
22501	3795	Helen Geraldine Maria, Countess of Morton [S.], 1852. *Conaglen, Ardgour, Argyleshire. Loddington Hall, Leicester.*	Granddaughter. Sister of Nos. 22485, &c.
22502	3796	Sholto Charles, Lord Aberdour, 1878.	
22503	3797	Hon. Charles William Sholto Douglas, Lieut. 4th Battalion Oxfordshire Light Infantry, 1881.	Great-grandchildren. Children of No. 22501.
22504	3798	Hon. Archibald Roderick Sholto Douglas, 1883.	
22505	3799	Hon. William Sholto Douglas, 1886.	
22506	3800	Hon. Ronald John Sholto Douglas, 1890.	
22507	3801	Edward Kenrick Bunbury-Tighe, 1862. *Woodstock Park, co. Kilkenny.*	Grandson. Son of Lady Kathleen Louisa Georgina Ponsonby, 1826–1863, and her husband, Colonel Frederick Edward Bunbury-Tighe, 1826–1891.
22508	3802	Kathleen Augusta Louisa Tighe, 1897.	Great-granddaughter. Daughter of No. 22507.

260. Descendants of Major-General the Hon. Sir Frederick Cavendish Ponsonby, K.C.B., G.C.M.G., K.C.H., K.M.T., K.S.G., 1783–1837. (See Table XL.)

22509	3803	John Ponsonby, D.S.O., Captain Coldstream Guards, 1866. *Guards'.*	Grandsons. Sons of General the Right Hon. Sir Henry Frederick Ponsonby, P.C., G.C.B., 1825–1895.
22510	3804	Frederick Edward Grey Ponsonby, C.V.O., Captain Grenadier Guards, Equerry-in-Ordinary and Assistant Private Secretary to the King, 1867. *Ambassadors' Court, St. James' Palace.*	
22511	3805	Arthur Augustus William Henry Ponsonby, 1871.	
22512	3806	Elizabeth Ponsonby, 1900.	Great-granddaughter. Child of No. 22511.
22513	3807	Alberta Victoria, wife of Major-General William Edward Montgomery, *late* Scots Guards, 1862. *Grey Abbey, co. Down.*	Grandchildren. Children of General the Right Hon. Sir Henry Frederick Ponsonby, P.C., G.C.B., 1825–1895.
22514	3808	Magdalen Ponsonby, 1864.	
22515	3809	Harriet Julia Frances Ponsonby, 1830. *4 Wilton Crescent, S.W.*	Daughters.
22516	3810	Selina Barbara, widow of the *late* William Windham Baring, 1876, 1835. *4 Wilton Crescent, S.W.*	

261. Descendants of William Francis Spencer, 1st Lord De Mauley, 1787–1855. (See Table XL.)

| 22517 –38 | | Same as Nos. 22485–22506. | Descendants of Charles Frederick Ashley Cooper, 2nd Lord De Mauley, 1815–1896. |
| 22539 | 3811 | Claude Ashley Charles Ponsonby, 1859. *33 Queen's Gate Terrace, W.* | Grandson. Eldest son of Captain the Hon. Ashley George John Ponsonby, 1831–1898. |

22540	3812	Harold Ashley Curzon Ponsonby, 1891.	Great-grandchildren.
22541	3813	Moira Blanche May Diana Ponsonby, 1901.	Children of No. 22539.
22542	3814	Eustace Ashley William Ponsonby, 1863.	Grandson. Brother of No. 22539.
22543	3815	Frances Anne Georgiana, Baroness Kinnaird [S.], and Rossie and Kinnaird [U.K.], 1817. *The Knapp, Inchture, Scotland.*	Daughter.
22544	3816	Angus Howard Reginald Ogilvy, Major D.S.O., *late* 13th Hussars, 1860. *Baldoven House, Strathmartine, Forfarshire.*	Great-grandson. Eldest son of the Hon. Olivia Barbara Kinnaird, 1839–1871, and her husband, Sir Reginald Howard Alexander Ogilvy, 10th Bart., 1832.
22545	3817	Gilchrist Nevill Ogilvy, 1892.	Great-great-grandchildren.
22546	3818	Olivia Frances Isabel Ogilvy, 1891.	Children of No. 22544.
22547	3819	Herbert Kinnaird Ogilvy, W.S., 1865. *Wellington, New.*	Great-grandchildren. Children of the Hon. Olivia Barbara Kinnaird, 1839 – 1871, and her husband, Sir Reginald Howard Alexander Ogilvy, 10th Bart.
22548	3820	Commandant Frederick Charles Ashley Ogilvy, R.N., 1866. *Naval and Military.*	
22549	3821	Gilbert Frances Molyneux Ogilvy, 1868. *Brooks'.*	
22550	3822	Violet Olivia Juliana Ogilvy.	

262. Descendants of William, 5th Duke of Devonshire, K.G., 1748–1811. (See Table XLI.)

22551 –825	}	Same as Nos. 22125–22400.

263. Descendants of William, 2nd Earl of Burlington and 7th Duke of Devonshire, K.G., 1808–1891. (See Table XLI.)

22826 –41	}	Same as Nos. 22350–22365.

264. Descendants of Lord George Henry Cavendish, M.P., 1810–1880. (See Table XLI.)

22842	3823	James Charles Cavendish, Colonel *late* Captain R.A., 1838. *3 Belgrave Place, S.W.*	Children.
22843	3824	Alice Louisa, widow of the late Hon. Algernon Fulke Egerton, 1825–1891, 1837. *3 Belgrave Place, S.W.*	
22844	3825	▽ George Algernon Egerton, Captain and Brevet-Major 19th Hussars, 1870.	Grandchildren. Children of No. 22843.
22845	3826	▽ Margaret Louisa, wife of George Chichester May, 1864. *13 Fitzwilliam Square, Dublin.*	
22846	3827	Margaret Olivia May, 1902.	Great-grandchild. Daughter of No. 22845.

22847	3828	⛉ Blanche Susan Egerton, 1865.	
22848	3829	⛉ Katherine Alice Egerton, 1867.	Grandchildren. Children
22849	3830	⛉ Violet Ellinor Egerton, 1872.	of No. 22843.
22850	3831	⛉ Mary Florence Egerton, 1874.	
22851	3832	⛉ Evelyn Harriet Egerton, 1879.	
22852	3833	Susan Henrietta, Viscountess Hampden [U.K.], and Baroness Dacre [E.], 1846. *The Hoo, Welwyn, Herts.*	Youngest daughter.
22853	3834	Hon. Thomas Walter Brand, Captain 10th Hussars, 1869. *The Hoo, Welwyn, Herts.*	Grandson. Son of No. 22852.
22854 -55		Same as Nos. 19736-19737.	Great-grandsons. Sons of No. 22853.
22856	3835	Hon. Hubert George Brand, Commander R.N., 1870.	
22857	3836	Hon. Robert Brand, 1878.	Grandchildren.
22858	3837	Hon. Roger Brand, 1880.	Children of
22859	3838	Hon. Margaret, wife of Major Algernon Francis Holford Ferguson, 2nd Life Guards, 1873. *Polebrooke Hall, Oundle.*	No. 22852.
22860	3839	Victor John Ferguson, 1898.	Great-grandsons. Sons
22861	3840	Andrew Henry Ferguson, 1899.	of No. 22859.
22862	3841	Hon. Alice Brand, 1875.	Grand-daughters.
22863	3842	Hon. Dorothy, wife of Percy Henry Guy Feilden, 1877.	Daughters of No. 22852.

265. Descendants of Lady Fanny Cavendish, 1809–1885, and her husband, Frederick John Howard, Esq., M.P., 1814–1897. (See Table XLI.)

22864	3843	William Frederick Howard, 1838.	
22865	3844	George Francis Howard, 1840.	Children.
22866	3845	Lieut.-Col. Frederick Compton Howard, J.P., 1847. *66 Esplanade, Scarborough, York.*	
22867	3846	Richard Fitzroy Howard, Lieutenant 3rd Battalion Yorks Regiment, 1879.	Grandchildren.
22868	3847	George Frederick Howard, 1894.	Children of
22869	3848	Grace Mary, wife of Alder Anderson-Smith, 1878.	No. 22866.
22870	3849	Frederick George Anderson-Smith, 1902.	Great-grandson. Son of No. 22869.
22871	3850	Evelyn Fanny Louisa Howard, 1883.	Grandchildren. Children
22872	3851	Helen Emma Edith Howard, 1887.	of No. 22866.
22873	3852	Dorothy Ann Howard, 1889.	
22874	3853	Alfred John Howard, 1848. *Worton Hall, Isleworth.*	4th son.
22875	3854	William Gilbert Howard, Lieutenant R.A., 1877.	Grandchildren.
22876	3855	Ronald Howard, Lieutenant R.N., 1878.	Children of
22877	3856	Frederick Charles Howard, 1882.	No. 22874.
22878	3857	Margaret Howard, 1880.	
22879	3858	Gerald Richard Howard, *late* Lieutenant R.N., 1853.	5th son.
22880	3859	Alfred Howard, 1888.	
22881	3860	Bertram Marcus Howard, 1891.	Grandchildren. Children
22882	3861	Mildred Rachel Howard, 1896.	of No. 22879.
22883	3862	Joan Edith Barbara Howard, 1898.	

22884	3863	Hon. Arthur William de Brito Savile Foljambe, Captain Rifle Brigade, M.V.O., 1870.	} 2 *Carlton House Terrace, S.W.*	Grandchild. Son of Louisa Blanche Howard, 1842–1871, 1st wife of Cecil G. S., 1st Lord Hawkesbury.
22885	3864	Margaret Fanny, wife of the Hon. Frederick John William Ponsonby, 1844. 14 *Chapel Street, Belgrave Square, S.W.*	}	Elder surviving daughter.
22886 –87	}	Same as Nos. 22490–22491.	{	Granddaughters. Daughters of No. 22885.
22888	3865	Edith Susan Louisa Howard.		Younger daughter.

266. Descendants of General the Hon. Frederick Compton Cavendish, 1789–1873. (See Table XLI.)

22889	3866	Henry Frederick Compton Cavendish, J.P., D.L., 1854. *Cromford, Matlock, Derbyshire.*	Grandson. Son of Lieut.-Col. William Henry Frederick Cavendish, 1789–1873.
22890	3867	Henry James Francis Cavendish, 1893.	Great-grandchildren.
22891	3868	George Sidney Godolphin Cavendish, 1895.	Children of No. 22889.
22892	3869	Emily Georgiana Harriet Cavendish, 1890.	
22893	3870	Evelyn Alice Beatrix Cavendish, 1892.	
22894	3871	Cecil Charles Cavendish, Major Royal Garrison Regiment, 1885.	Grandson. Brother to No. 22889.
22895	3872	Frederick George Cavendish, 1891.	
22896	3873	Ronald Valentine Cecil Cavendish, 1896.	Great-grandchildren. Children of No. 22894.
22897	3874	. . . . Cavendish, 1902.	
22898	3875	Spencer Frederick George Cavendish, *late* Captain 1st Battalion The King's (Shropshire Light Infantry).	Grandchildren. Brother and sister to No. 22889.
22899	3876	Susan Louisa, Lady Hawkesbury [U.K.], 1848. 2 *Carlton House Terrace, S.W. Kirkham Abbey, York.*	
22900	3877	Hon. Gerald William Frederick Savile Foljambe, Lieutenant 43rd Oxfordshire Light Infantry, 1878.	
22901	3878	Hon. Josceline Charles William Savile Foljambe, Lieutenant Northumberland Fusiliers, 1882.	
22902	3879	Hon. Robert Anthony Edward St. Andrew Savile Foljambe, 1887.	
22903	3880	Hon. Bertram Marmaduke Osbert Savile Foljambe, 1891.	
22904	3881	Hon. Victor Alexander Cecil Savile Foljambe, 1895.	Great-grandchildren. Children of No. 22899.
22905	3882	Hon. Edith Margaret Mary Emily Foljambe, 1879.	
22906	3883	Hon. Alice Etheldreda Georgiana Mary Foljambe, 1880.	
22907	3884	Hon. Mabel Evelyn Selina Mary Foljambe, 1881.	
22908	3885	Hon. Constance Blanche Alethea Mary Foljambe, 1885.	
22909	3886	Hon. Rosamond Sylvia Diana Mary Foljambe, 1893.	

22910	3887	Reginald Richard Frederick Cavendish, 1857.	Grandchild. Eldest son of Francis William Henry Cavendish, 1820-1893.
22911	3888	Godfrey Lionel John Cavendish, 1884.	
22912	3889	Richard Charles Alexander Cavendish, 1885.	
22913	3890	Rachel Muriel Evelyn Constance Cavendish, 1882.	Great-grandchildren. Children of No. 22910.
22914	3891	Diana Violet Gladys Cavendish, 1887.	
22915	3892	Beatrice Francis Dupuis Cavendish, 1888.	
22916	3893	Dorothy Alice Georgina Cavendish, 1891.	
22917	3894	Alfred Edward John Cavendish, C.M.G., Major Princess Louise's (Argyll and Sutherland Highlanders), 1859. *Naval and Military.*	Grandson. Brother to No. 22910.
22918	3895	Ralph Henry Voltelin Cavendish, 1887.	Great-grandson. Son of No. 22917.
22919	3896	Ernest Lionel Francis Cavendish, Deputy-Governor H.M.'s Prison, Wormwood Scrubs, 1863. *Deputy-Governor's House, Wormwood Scrubs.*	Grandson. Brother to No. 22910.
22920	3897	Alwyn Lionel Compton Cavendish, 1890.	Great-grandson. Son of No. 22919.
22921	3898	Nigel Frederick Rupert Cavendish, 1879.	Grandson. Brother to No. 22910.
22922	3899	Charles George Cavendish, 1874. 71 *Via Cavour, Rome.*	Grandson. Son of Charles William Cavendish, 1822-1890.
22923	3900	William Henry Alexander George Delmar Cavendish, 1849.	Grandson. Son of George Henry Cavendish, Captain 1st Life Guards, 1824-1889.
22924	3901	Charles Alfred William Delmar Cavendish, 1878.	
22925	3902	Georgiana Edith Bessie, wife of Winsloe Hall, 1875.	Great-grandchildren. Children of No. 22923.
22926	3903	Edith Emily Ida Cavendish, 1881.	
22927	3904	Louisa Anna Grace Cavendish, 1882.	
22928	3905	Emily Frances Ida, Princess Luigi Pignatelli d'Aragon, 1852.	Granddaughter. Sister to No. 22923.
22929	3906	Prince Lodovico Pignatelli d'Aragon, 1878.	Great-grandchildren. Children of No. 22928.
22930	3907	Princess Cristina Pignatelli d'Aragon, 1881.	
22931	3908	Sarah Mary Sophia, widow of William Deedes, M.P., -1887. *Sandling Park, Kent.*	Granddaughters. Elder daughters, and co-heirs of Elizabeth Georgiana Harriet Cavendish, 1892, by 1st husband, William Bernard, Marquis of Harcourt, - 1846.
22932	3909	Elizabeth Mary, widow of Henry Ralph Lambton, 1824-1896. *Winslow Hall, Bucks.*	

22933	3910	William Henry Lambton, Captain *late* Coldstream Guards, 1867. *Redfield, Winslow, Bucks.*	
22934	3911	Ralph Edward Lambton, 1871. *5 St. Thomas' Street, Newcastle-on-Tyne.*	Great-grandchildren. Children of No. 22932.
22935	3912	Bertha Mary, wife of Thomas Henry Bernard.	
22936	3913	Margaret Beatrix, wife of Major J. F. Erskine, Scots Guards.	
22937	3914	Dorothy Lambton.	
22938	3915	Alice Anne Caroline, wife of Bertrand, Baron de Langsdorff [France]. *Chateau de Pumel, Lot et Garonne.*	Granddaughter. Sister to No. 22931.
22939	3916	Baron Roger de Langsdorff.	
22940	3917	Baron Alain de Langsdorff.	Great-grandchildren. Children of No. 22938.
22941	3918	Victorine, wife of the Baron Vuillet.	
22942	3919	Baroness Helen de Langsdorff.	
22943	3920	Sarah Florence Elizabeth Craufurd. *44 Lowndes Street, London.*	Granddaughter. Only daughter of Elizabeth Georgiana Harriet Cavendish, – 1892, by 2nd husband, Lieut.-Gen. James R. Craufurd, –1888.
22944 -74		Same as Nos. 21734–21764.	Grandchildren, &c. Children, &c., of Sarah Mary Cavendish, 1813–1881, and her husband, John Frederick Vaughan, 2nd Earl Cawdor, 1817–1898.
22975	3921	Hon. Caroline Fanny Cavendish, V.A., 1826. *Berry Brook House, Sedge Hill, Shaftesbury.*	Daughter.

267. Descendants of William George, 2nd Lord Chesham, 1815–1822. (See Table XLI.)

22976 to 23002		Same as Nos. 22172–22198.

268. Descendants of the Hon. Harriet Elizabeth Cavendish, 1820–1892, 2nd wife of George Stevens, 2nd Earl of Strafford, 1806–1886. (See Table XLI.)

23003	3922	Hon. Charles Cavendish George Byng, *late* Colonel commanding 1st Life Guards, 1849. *Edymead House, Launceston.*	
23004	3923	Hon. Lionel Francis George Byng, *late* Major Royal Horse Guards, 1858. *15 Chester Square, S.W.*	
23005	3924	Hon. Julian Hedworth George Byng, M.V.O., Lieut.-Col. 10th Hussars, 1862.	Children.
23006	3925	Lady Susan Catherine Harriet Byng, 1854. *Bayman Manor, Chesham.*	
23007	3926	Lady Elizabeth Henrietta Alice Byng, 1855. *15 Chester Square, S.W.*	
23008	3927	Lady Margaret Florence Lucy, wife of the Hon. John John Richard de Clare Boscawen, 1860. *Tregye, Perranwell, Cornwall.*	
23009	3928	Catherine Margaret Boscawen, 1891.	Grandchild. Daughter of No. 23008.

269. Descendants of Lady Lucy Cavendish Bentinck, 1808–1899, and her husband, Charles Augustus, 6th Lord Howard de Walden, 1799–1868. (See Table XLII.)

23010	3929	Thomas Evelyn, 8th Lord Howard de Walden [E.], 4th Baron Seaford [U.K.], 1880. *Seaford House, Belgrave Square, S.W.*	Grandson. Only child of Frederick George, 7th Lord Howard de Walden, 1830–1899.
23011	3930	Rev. and Hon. William Charles Ellis, 1835. *Bothalhaugh, Morpeth.*	Eldest surviving son.
23012	3931	Henry Guysulf Bertram Ellis, 1875.	
23013	3932	Humphrey Cadogan Ellis, 1879.	Grandchildren.
23014	3933	Francis Bevis Ellis, 1883.	Children of
23015	3934	Roland Arthur Ellis, 1884.	No. 23011.
23016	3935	Lucy Henrietta Katharine Ellis, 1876.	
23017	3936	Henrietta Christobel Ellis, 1886.	
23018	3937	Hon. Charles Arthur Ellis, Barrister-at-Law, 1839. *36 Piccadilly, W. Frensham Hall, Shottermill.*	2nd and 3rd surviving sons.
23019	3938	Hon. Evelyn Henry Ellis, 1843. *35 Portland Place, W.*	
23020	3939	Arthur Ellis, 1894.	Grandchildren. Children
23021	3940	Mary Ellis, 1888.	of No. 23019.
23022	3941	Harriet Georgina, Duchess of Sermoneta [Italy], 1831. *39 Grosvenor Place, S.W. Florence, Palazzo Guadagni.*	Daughter.

270. Descendants of the Rev. Charles William Frederick Cavendish Bentinck, 1817–1865. (See Table XLII.)

23023	3942	Cecilia Nina, Lady Glamis, 1862. *St. Paul's Walden Bury, Welwyn, Herts.*	Eldest daughter.
23024	3943	Patrick, Master of Glamis, 1884.	
23025	3944	Hon. John Herbert Bowes-Lyon, 1886.	
23026	3945	Hon. Alexander Francis Bowes-Lyon, 1887.	
23027	3946	Hon. Fergus Bowes-Lyon, 1889.	Grandchildren.
23028	3947	Hon. Michael Claude Hamilton Bowes-Lyon, 1893.	Children of
23029	3948	Hon. Mary Frances Bowes-Lyon, 1883.	No. 23023.
23030	3949	Hon. Rose Constance Bowes-Lyon, 1890.	
23031	3950	Hon. Elizabeth Angela Marguerite Bowes-Lyon, 1900.	
23032	3951	Anne Violet Bentinck,	
23033	3952	Hyacinthe Mary, wife of Augustus twins, 1864. Edward Jessup. *Philadelphia, U.S.A.*	Younger daughters.

271. Descendants of Lieutenant - General Arthur Cavendish Bentinck, 1819–1877. (See Table XLII.)

23034	3953	William John Arthur Charles James, 6th Duke of Portland [G.B.], 7th Earl of Portland [E.], 2nd Baron Bolsover [U.K.], K.G. *Welbeck Abbey, Worksop. 3 Grosvenor Square, W.*	Eldest son.

23035	3954	William Arthur Henry, Marquis of Titchfield, 1893.	
23036	3955	Lord Francis Dallas Morven Cavendish Bentinck, 1900.	Grandchildren. Children of No. 23034.
23037	3956	Lady Victoria Alexandrina Violet Cavendish Bentinck, 1890.	
23038	3957	Lord Henry Cavendish Bentinck, M.P., 1863. 13 *Grosvenor Place, S.W.*	
23039	3958	Lord William Augustus Cavendish Bentinck, D.S.O., 1865.	
23040	3959	Lord Charles Cavendish Bentinck, 1868. 13 *Grosvenor Place.*	Younger sons and daughter.
23041	3960	Lady Ottoline Violet Anne Cavendish, wife of Philip Morrell, 1873. 32 *Grosvenor Road, S.W.*	

272. Descendants of Emily Cavendish Bentinck, 1820–1850, and her husband, the Rev. Henry Hopwood, Rector of Bothal, Northumberland, 1810–1859. (See Table XLII.)

23042	3961	John Bentinck Hopwood, 1846.	Sons.
23043	3962	Arthur Hopwood, 1848.	

273. Descendants of the Right Hon. George Augustus Cavendish Bentinck, of Brownsea Island, Dorset, P.C., M.P., 1821–1891. (See Table XLII.)

23044	3963	William George Cavendish Bentinck, J.P., 1854. 4 *Richmond Terrace, Whitehall, S.W.*	Eldest son.
23045	3964	Mary Augusta Cavendish Bentinck, 1881.	Grandchildren. Children of No. 23044.
23046	3965	Ruth Evelyn Cavendish Bentinck, 1883.	
23047	3966	William George Frederick Cavendish Bentinck, J.P., 1856. 16 *Mansfield Street, Cavendish Square, W.*	2nd son.
23048	3967	Ferdinand William Cavendish Bentinck, 1888.	
23049	3968	Victor Frederick William Cavendish Bentinck, 1897.	Grandchildren. Children of No. 23047.
23050	3969	Lucy Joan Cavendish Bentinck, 1889.	
23051	3970	Venetia Barbara Bentinck, 1902.	
23052	3971	Christina Anne Jessica, wife of Sir Tatton Sykes, Bart. 2 *Chesterfield St., W.*	Eldest daughter.
23053	3972	Mark Sykes, Lieutenant 3rd Battalion Yorks Regiment, 1879. *Marlborough Club.*	Grandson. Son of No. 23052.
23054	3973	Mary Venetia, wife of John Arthur James, 1861. *Coton House, Rugby.*	2nd daughter.

274. Descendants of Algernon Frederick Greville, Bath King of Arms, 1798–1864. (See Table XLIII.)

23055	3974	Charles Henry, Earl of March and Darnley, 1845. *Molecomb, Chichester.*	Grandson. Son of the late Frances Harriet Greville, 1824–1887, wife of Charles Henry, 6th Duke of Richmond, Gordon, and Lennox, K.G.

The Blood Royal of Britain

23056	3975	Charles Henry, Lord Settrington, D.S.O., 1870. *Turf ; Bachelors'.*	Great-grandson. Son of No. 23055.
23057	3976	Hon. Charles Henry Gordon-Lennox, 1899.	Great-great-grandchildren. Children of No. 23056.
23058	3977	Hon. Amy Gwendoline Gordon-Lennox, 1894.	
23059	3978	Hon. Doris Hilda Gordon-Lennox, 1896.	
23060	3979	Hon. Esmé Charles Gordon-Lennox, Captain Scots Guards, 1875. *Bachelors' ; Guards'.*	Great-grandchildren. Children of No. 23055.
23061	3980	Hon. Bernard Charles Gordon-Lennox, Lieutenant Grenadier Guards, 1878. *Bachelors' ; Guards'.*	
23062	3981	Lady Evelyn Amy, wife of Sir John Richard Geers Cotterell, 4th Bart. 10 *Hertford Street, Mayfair, W.*	
23063	3982	Sylvia Evelyn Cotterell, 1896.	Great-great-grandchildren. Children of No. 23062.
23064	3983	Cecily Violet Cotterell, 1899.	
23065	3984	Mildred Katharine Cotterell, 1902.	
23066	3985	Lady Violet Mary, wife of Henry Leonard Campbell Brassey, 1874. 40 *Upper Grosvenor Street, W.*	Great-grandchildren. 2nd daughter of No. 23055.
23067	3986	Cecil Henry Brassey, 1896.	Great-great-grandchildren. Children of No. 23066.
23068	3987	Gerard Charles Brassey, 1898.	
23069	3988	Lady Muriel Beatrice Gordon-Lennox, 1884.	Great-grandchildren. Younger daughters of No. 23055.
23070	3989	Lady Helen Magdalen Gordon-Lennox, 1886.	
23071	3990	Lord Algernon Charles Gordon-Lennox, *late* Colonel Grenadier Guards, 1847. *Broughton Castle, Banbury, Oxfordshire.*	Grandson. Next brother to No. 23055.
23072	3991	Ivy Gordon-Lennox, 1887.	Great-grandchild. Child of No. 23071.
23073	3992	Right Hon. Lord Walter Charles Gordon-Lennox, P.C., 1865. 12 *Princes Gardens, S.W.*	Grandson. 3rd brother of No. 23055.
23074	3993	Victor Charles Hugh Gordon Lennox, 1897.	Great-grandson. Son of No. 23073.
23075	3994	Lady Caroline Elizabeth Gordon-Lennox, 1844.	Granddaughter. Sister of No. 23055.
23076	3995	Augusta Mary, widow of George Montagu Warren Sandford, formerly Peacocke, M.P., 1821–1879, 1831. 33 *Hertford Street, W.*	Daughter.
23077	3996	Francis Marmaduke Henry Sandford, 1860. 30 *Rutland Gate, S.W.*	Grandchildren. Children of No. 23076.
23078	3997	Charlotte Mary Sandford.	
23079	3998	Alice Rose Sandford.	
23080	3999	Blanche Caroline Sandford.	
23081	4000	Caroline Amabel Sandford.	

275. Descendants of Harriet Catherine Greville, –1866, and her husband, Francis, 1st Earl of Ellesmere, K.G., 1800–1857. (See Table XLIII.)

23082 –95	Same as Nos. 21824–21837.	Descendants of George Granville Francis, 2nd Earl of Ellesmere, 1823–1862.

The Blood Royal of Britain

23096 -100	}	Same as Nos. 22361– 22365.	} Grandchildren. Children, &c., of Admiral the Hon. Francis Egerton, 1824–1895.
23101 -08	}	Same as Nos. 22844– 22851.	} Grandchildren. Children of the Hon. Algernon Fulke Egerton, 1825–1891.
23109	4001	▽ Granville George Algernon Egerton, Lieut.-Col. 1st Battalion Seaforth Highlanders, 1859. *Travellers' ; Naval and Military.*	Grandchildren. Children of Lieut.-Col. the Hon. Arthur Frederick Egerton, 1829–1866.
23110	4002	▽ Cecil Martin Egerton, 1860. 13 *South Street, Park Lane, W.*	
23111	4003	▽ Claude Francis Arthur Egerton, M.I.C.E., 1864. *Blythburgh, Suffolk.*	
23112	4004	▽ Serope Arthur Francis Sutherland Egerton.	} Great-grandchild. Child of No. 23111.
23113	4005	▽ Arthur Frederick Egerton, D.S.O., *late* Captain 1st Battalion Cameron Highlanders, 1866. *Naval and Military.*	Grandchildren. Brother and sister to Nos. 23109, &c.
23114	4006	▽ Louisa Blanche, wife of John Jameson. *Glen Lodge, Sligo.*	
23115	4007	Clare Helen Jameson, 1899.	{ Great-granddaughter. Child of No. 23114.

276. Descendants of Sir Henry Bedingfeld, afterwards Paston-Bedingfeld, 6th Bart., 1800–1862. (See Table XLIV.)

23116	4008	Sir Henry George Paston-Bedingfeld, 7th Bart. *Oxburgh, near Stoke Ferry, Norfolk.*	} Son.
23117	4009	Henry Edward Paston-Bedingfeld, Captain 3rd Battalion Liverpool Regiment, 1860.	Grandchildren. Children of No. 23116.
23118	4010	Richard Henry Clavering Paston-Bedingfeld, 1862.	
23119	4011	Charles Paston-Bedingfeld, 1864.	
23120	4012	William Paston-Bedingfeld, 1873.	
23121	4013	Frank Paston-Bedingfeld, 1874.	
23122	4014	Herbert Paston-Bedingfeld, 1877.	
23123	4015	Alice, wife of Rear-Admiral James Lacon Hammet, R.N.	
23124	4016	Cecil Ferdinand James Hammet, 1892.	} Great-grandchildren. Children of No. 23123.
23125	4017	Violet Irene May Hammet, 1894.	
23126	4018	Mary Maud Paston-Bedingfeld.	} Grandchildren. Younger daughters of No. 23116.
23127	4019	Edith Mary Paston-Bedingfeld.	
23128	4020	Raoul-Stephen Bisshopp, *formerly* Paston-Bedingfeld, 1835. *Brailes, co. Warwick.*	2nd son and elder daughter.
23129	4021	Matilda Charlotte, wife of Captain George Nevill. *Nevill Holt, co. Leicester.*	
23130	4022	Henry William Nevill, 1857. Grandson. Son of No. 23129.	
23131	4023	Mary Gabrielle, wife of Ferdinand John Eyre. 51 *Berkeley Square, W.*	} Younger daughter.

277. Descendants of Frances Charlotte Bedingfeld, –1822, 1st wife of William Francis Henry, 11th Lord Petre, 1793–1850. (See Table XLIV.)

23132	4024	Bernard Henry Philip, 14th Lord Petre [E.], 1858. *Thorndon Hall, Brentwood.*	} Grandson. Son of William Bernard, 12th Lord Petre, 1817–1884.

MARGARET OF DENMARK
QUEEN OF JAMES III OF SCOTLAND
THE TRINITY COLLEGE ALTAR-PIECE

23133	4025	Hon. Mary Frances Katherine Petre, 1900.	}	Great-granddaughter. Child of No. 23132.
23134	4026	Hon. Philip Benedict Joseph Petre, 1864.	}	Grandson. Next brother to No. 23132.
23135	4027	Lionel George Carroll Petre, 1890.	}	Great-grandchildren.
23136	4028	Barbara Louisa Mary Petre, 1889.		Children of No.
23137	4029	Clare Stella Mary Petre, 1893.		23134.
23138	4030	Frances Mary, Countess of Granard [I.], Baroness Granard [U.K.]. *Castle-Forbes, Newtown Forbes, co. Longford.*	}	Granddaughter. Daughter of William Bernard, 12th Lord Petre, 1817–1884.
23139	4031	Bernard Arthur William Patrick Hastings, 8th Earl of Granard [I.], and 3rd Baron Granard [U.K.], 1874. *Castle-Forbes, Newtown Forbes, co. Longford.*		
23140	4032	Hon. Reginald George Benedict Forbes, Captain 2nd Battalion Gordon Highlanders, 1877.	}	Great-grandchildren. Children of No. 23138.
23141	4033	Hon. Donald Alexander Forbes, 2nd Lieutenant R.A., 1880.		
23142	4034	Hon. Bertram Aloysius Forbes, Lieutenant Royal Irish Rifles, } twins, 1882.		
23143	4035	Hon. Fergus George Arthur Forbes, }		
23144	4036	Lady Eva Mary Margaret Forbes, 1877.		
23145	4037	Lady Margaret Mary Theresa Forbes, 1879.		
23146	4038	Hon. Isabella Mary, wife of Frederick Stapleton-Bretherton, J.P. *The Hall, Rainhill, Lancashire. Heathfield House, Fareham.*	}	Granddaughter. 2nd daughter of William Bernard, 12th Lord Petre, 1817–1884.
23147	4039	Frederick Bartholomew Stapleton-Bretherton, 1873. *Wheler Lodge, Husbands Bosworth, Rugby.*	}	Great-grandson. Son of No. 23146.
23148	4040	Osmund Frederick Stapleton-Bretherton, 1898.	}	Great-great-grandchildren. Children of No. 23147.
23149	4041	Ruth Mary Elizabeth Stapleton-Bretherton, 1897.		
23150	4042	Edmund Joseph Stapleton-Bretherton, 1881.	}	Great-grandchildren. Children of No. 23146.
23151	4043	Evelyn Mary Stapleton Bretherton.		
23152	4044	Agnes Mary Stapleton-Bretherton.		
23153	4045	Edith Mary Stapleton-Bretherton.		
23154	4046	Winifred Mary Stapleton-Bretherton.		
23155	4047	Ethel Mary Stapleton-Bretherton.		
23156	4048	Hon. Margaret Mary Petre, a Nun of the Order of the Good Shepherd. *Dalbeth, Glasgow,* 1850.	}	Grandchildren. Children of William Bernard, 12th Lord Petre, 1817–1884.
23157	4049	Hon. Katharine Mary Lucy Petre, 1851.		
23158	4050	Hon. Theresa Mary Louisa Petre, a Nun of the Order of the Good Shepherd. *Ashford, Middlesex.*		
23159	4051	Hon. Mary Winifride Petre, a Sister of Charity, 1855. *Carlisle Place, Westminster, S.W.*		
23160	4052	Hon. Eleanor Mary Petre, wife of Edward Southwell Trafford, 1856. *Wroxham Hall, Norwich.*		

The Blood Royal of Britain

23161	4053	Sigismund William Joseph Trafford, 1883.	
23162	4054	Cecil Edward Trafford, 1884.	
23163	4055	Edward Bernard Trafford, 1885.	
23164	4056	Raphael Henry Trafford, 1886.	
23165	4057	Joseph Louis Trafford, 1888.	
23166	4058	Harold Henry Trafford, 1891.	Great-grandchildren.
23167	4059	Geoffrey Michael Trafford, 1893.	Children of No.
23168	4060	Eleanor Mary Josephine Southwell Trafford, 1882.	23160.
23169	4061	Dorothy Mary Trafford (twin), 1884.	
23170	4062	Sibylla Mary Trafford, 1889.	
23171	4863	Rosamond Mary Isabel Trafford, 1895.	
23172	4064	Imelda Mary Agnes Trafford, 1897.	
23173	4065	Hon. Monica Mary, wife of John Erdeswick Butler-Bowdon, Lieut.-Col. and Hon. Colonel 3rd Battalion South Lancashire Regiment, 1860. *Pleasington Hall, Blackburn. Southgate House, Clown, Derbyshire.*	Grandchild. Youngest daughter of William Bernard, 12th Lord Petre, 1817-1884.
23174	4066	William Butler-Bowdon, Lieutenant Duke of Cornwall's Light Infantry, 1880.	
23175	4067	Leonard Butler-Bowdon, 1881.	
23176	4068	Basil Butler-Bowdon, 1898.	
23177	4069	Theresa Mary Sophie Butler - Bowdon, 1882.	Great-grandchildren. Children of No. 23173.
23178	4070	Angela Mary Josephine Butler-Bowdon, 1884.	
23179	4071	Monica Mary Rose Butler-Bowdon, 1885.	
23180	4072	Gladys Mary Ella Butler-Bowdon, 1886.	
23181	4073	Ursula Mary Cora Butler-Bowdon, 1889.	
23182	4074	Isabel Mary Helena Butler-Bowdon, 1892.	
23183	4075	Francis William Petre, 1847.	Grandson. Elder son of Hon. Henry William Petre, 1820-1889.
23184	4076	Edward Henry Petre, 1881.	Great-grandchildren.
23185	4077	Bernard Francis Petre, 1884.	Children of No.
23186	4078	Rosamond Margaret Petre, 1883.	23183.
23187	4079	Oswald Arthur Petre, 1848.	Grandsons. 2nd and 3rd sons of Hon. Henry William Petre, 1820-1889.
23188	4080	Sebastian Henry Petre, Solicitor, 1856. *Heybridge House, Ingatestone, Essex.*	
23189	4081	Henry Aloysius Petre, 1884.	
23190	4082	Edward Petre, 1886.	
23191	4083	William Petre, 1888.	Great-grandchildren.
23192	4084	Bernard Francis Petre, 1891.	Children of No.
23193	4085	John Joseph Petre, 1894.	23188.
23194	4086	Mary Josephine Laura Petre, 1882.	
23195	4087	Sybil May Petre, 1899.	
23196	4088	Gerald Petre, 1859.	
23197	4089	Robert George Petre, 1861.	Grandchildren. Younger sons and elder daughter of Hon. Henry William Petre, 1820-1889.
23198	4090	John Petre, 1866.	
23199	4091	Lucy Agnes, wife of Philip Wellesley-Colley, J.P., 1846. *Shinglestreet, Woodbridge.* 31 *Montagu Square, W.*	
23200	4092	Reginald Wellesley Colley, 1873.	Great-grandson. Son of No. 23199.
23201	4093	Lucy Colley, 1901.	Great-great-grandchild. Daughter of No. 23200.

23202	4094	Francis Wellesley Colley, 1877.	
23203	4095	John Wellesley Colley.	
23204	4096	Edward Wellesley Colley.	
23205	4097	Joseph Wellesley Colley.	Great-grandchildren.
23206	4098	Robert Wellesley Colley.	Children of No.
23207	4099	Philip Wellesley Colley.	23199.
23208	4100	William Wellesley Colley.	
23209	4101	Mary Wellesley Colley.	
23210	4102	Elizabeth Wellesley Colley.	
23211	4103	Mary Julia, wife of Edward Carington Wright, J.P., 1850. *Kelvedon Hall, Essex.*	Grandchild. 2nd daughter of Hon. Henry William Petre, 1820–1889.
23212	4104	Beatrice Mary, wife of Lieut.-Col. Edgar Edwin Bernard, Army Service Corps and Financial Secretary to the Soudan Government, 1874.	Great-granddaughter. Child of No. 23211.
23213	4105	Bernard Frederick Paul Bernard, 1894.	Great-great-grandchildren.
23214	4106	Evelyn Edith Mary Bernard, 1895.	Children of No. 23212.
23215	4107	Emma Mary Petre.	
23216	4108	Alice Mary Petre.	
23217	4109	Dorothea Mary, wife of Theodore Sibeth, 1860.	Grandchildren. Younger daughters of Hon. Henry William Petre, 1820–1889.
23218	4110	Mabel Mary, wife of Frank Chadwick, 1862.	
23219	4111	Sybil Mary Petre, a Nun, 1864.	
23220	4112	Florence Mary, wife of Surgeon-Major Charles Randolph Kilkelly, C.M.G., Grenadier Guards, 1865. *Lyndhurst, Caterham.*	
23221	4113	Edward Charles Randolph Kilkelly, 1895.	Great-grandchildren.
23222	4114	Gerald Francis Kilkelly, 1900.	Sons of No. 23220.
23223	4115	Helena Mary, wife of Sir William Laurence Young, 8th Bart., 1868. *35 Lower Seymour Street, Portman Square, W.*	Grandchild. Youngest daughter of Hon. Henry William Petre, 1820–1889.

278. Descendants of Matilda Mary Bedingfeld, –1881, and her husband, George Stanley Cary, Esq., of Follaton, Devon, J.P., 1780–1858. (See Table XLIV.)

23224	4116	Francis Joseph Cary, 1878. *Follaton, near Totnes, Devon.*	Grandchildren. Children of Stanley Edward George Cary, of Follaton, J.P., 1825–1902.
23225	4117	Cecilia Mary, wife of Thomas Boylan. *Hilltown, co. Meath.*	
23226	4118	George Boylan.	Great-grandchildren.
23227	4119	Edward Thomas Boylan.	Children of No.
23228	4120	Francis Michael Boylan.	23225.
23229	4121	Bertha Cary.	Grandchild. Sister to No. 23224.
23230	4122	Carnilla Annabella Cary.	
23231	4123	Helen Cary.	Daughters.
23232	4124	Bertha Cary.	

279. Descendants of Mary Agnes Bedingfeld, –1870, and her husband, Thomas Molyneux-Seel, Esq., of Boston Park, Lancaster, 1792–1881. (See Table XLIV.)

23233	4125	Edmund Richard Thomas Molyneux-Seel, 1824. *Huyton Hey, Lancashire.* 1 *Bolton Road, Birkdale, Southport.*	Eldest son.

23234	4126	Edmund Harrington Molyneux-Seel, Major King's Liverpool Regiment, 1857.	Grandson. Son of No. 23233.
23235	4127	Theresa Mary Antoinette Clare Molyneux-Seel.	Great-granddaughter. Daughter of No. 23231.
23236	4128	Edward Honoré Molyneux-Seel, Captain Royal Scots, 1862.	Grandchildren. Children of No. 23233.
23237	4129	Agnes Mary Matilda, wife of Sir John Lawson, 2nd Bart. *Brough Hall, Yorks.*	
23238	4130	Henry Joseph Lawson, 1877.	Great-grandchildren. Children of No. 23237.
23239	4131	Charlotte Mary Lawson, 1871.	
23240	4132	Teresa, wife of Francis William Macdonnell. *Dunfierth, Enfield, co. Kildare.*	
23241	4133	Francis Edward Anthony Macdonnell, 1899.	Great-great-grandchildren. Children of No. 23240.
23242	4134	Edward Henry Patrick Macdonnell 1901.	
23243	4135	Joan Agnes Mary Macdonnell, 1900.	
23244	4136	Edith, wife of John Herbert Riley. *Ewood Hall, Mytholmroyd, co. York.*	Great-grandchildren. Children of No. 23237.
23245	4137	Herbert Lawson Riley, 1899.	Great-great-grandchildren. Children of No. 23244.
23246	4138	Eileen Edith Riley, 1897.	
23247	4139	Mabel Mary Lawson.	Great-grandchildren. Younger daughters of No. 23237.
23248	4140	Beatrice Mary Lawson.	
23249	4141	Margaret Mary Lawson.	
23250	4142	Charlotte Amelia Molyneux-Seel.	Granddaughter. Younger daughter of No. 23233.
23251	4143	. . . . Molyneux-Seel.	Grandchildren. Son and daughter of Charles William Molyneux Seel, 1830–1857.
23252	4144	. . . . Molyneux-Seel.	
23253	4145	. . . . Molyneux-Seel.	Grandsons. Sons of Henry Harrington Molyneux Seel, Richmond Herald, 1839–1882.
23254	4146	. . . . Molyneux-Seel.	

280. Descendants, if any, of John Bedingfeld, R.N.,   –1754, Anne Bedingfeld, 1   –17 , wife of Thomas Waterton of Walton, Yorks, and of Elizabeth Bedingfeld, 1720–   , wife of Charles Biddulph, of Biddulph and Burton, Sussex. (See Table XLIV.)

281. Descendants of Henry Bentinck, 5th Earl of Shannon, 1833–1890. (See Table XLV.)

23255 –60	}	Same as Nos. 21924–21929.	
23261	4147	Hon. Walter John Harry Boyle, 1869. *The Bath.*	Younger sons.
23262	4148	Hon. Edward Spencer Harry Boyle, Commander R.N., 1870.	
23263	4149	Hon. Algernon Douglas Edward Harry Boyle, Commander R.N., 1871. *The United Service.*	

The Blood Royal of Britain

282. Descendants of Francis, 3rd Earl of Bandon, 1810–1877. (See Table XLV.)

23264	4150	James Francis, 4th Earl of Bandon [I.], 1850. *Castle Bernard, Bandon, co. Cork.*	
23265	4151	Lady Mary Catherine Henrietta, widow of Colonel Richard William Aldworth, D.L., 1837 *Newmarket Court, Cork.*	Children.
23266	4152	Lady Louisa Albinia Bernard, 1841.	
23267	4153	Lady Charlotte Esther Emily Bernard, 1843.	78 *Chester Square, S.W.*
23268	4154	Lady Emma Harriet Bernard, 1844.	
23269	4155	Henry Bernard De la Poer Beresford-Peirse, Lieutenant Yorkshire Hussars Yeomanry Cavalry, D.S.O., 1875. *The Hall, Bedale.*	Grandchildren. Children of the Lady Adelaide Mary
23270	4156	Rev. Richard Windham De la Poer Beresford-Peirse, 1876. *Leeds.*	Lucy Bernard, 1846–1884, wife of Sir Henry Monson
23271	4157	Evelyn Frances De la Poer Beresford-Peirse, 1877.	De la Poer Beresford-Peirse, Bart.
23272	4158	Ernest Arthur De la Poer Beresford-Peirse, 1879.	
23273	4159	John William De la Poer Beresford-Peirse, 1883.	
23274	4160	Lady Kathleen Frances, wife of Alfred William William George Gaussen, 1853. *3 Walpole Street, Chelsea, S.W.*	Youngest daughter.
23275	4161	Mary Frances Letitia Gaussen, 1886.	Grandchild. Daughter of No. 23274.

283. Descendants of the Right Rev. and Hon. Charles Brodrick Bernard, Bishop of Tuam, 1811–1890. (See Table XLV.)

23276	4162	Percy Brodrick Bernard, J.P., D.L. *Castle Hackett, Tuam.*	Eldest son.
23277	4163	Ronald Percy Hamilton Bernard, 1875.	
23278	4164	Denis John Charles Kirwan Bernard, 1882.	
23279	4165	Percy Arthur Ernald Bernard, 1889.	Grandchildren.
23280	4166	Morogh Wyndham Percy Bernard, 1902.	Children of No. 23276.
23281	4167	Frances Mary, wife of George Arthur Paley, 1880. *Ampton Hall, Bury St. Edmunds.*	
23282	4168	Mary Winifred Bernard, 1886.	
23283	4169	Albert Charles Fenton Gascoyne Bernard, Lieutenant 3rd Battalion Norfolk Regiment, 1878.	Grandchildren. Children of James Boyle Bernard, 1847–1884.
23284	4170	Beatrice Mary Georgina Louisa, wife of Ernest Hutton, 1877. *Solberge, Northallerton.*	

284. Descendants of Hayes, 4th Viscount Doneraile, 1818–1887. (See Table XLV.)

23285	4171	Ursula Clara Emily, Lady Castletown [U.K.], 1853. *Granston Manor, Abbey Leix, Queen's Co.*	Only child.

285. Descendants of William Lennox Lascelles, 23rd Baron de Ros, P.C., 1797–1874. (See Table XLVI.)

23286	4172	Dudley Charles, 24th Lord de Ros [E.], Premier Baron of England, K.P., K.C.V.O., 1827. *Old Court, Strangford, co. Down.* 28 *Wilton Crescent, S.W.*	Son.
23287	4173	Hon. Mary Frances, wife of the Hon. Anthony Lucius Dawson, 1854. *Forberry Grove, Kintbury, Berks.*	Granddaughter. Only child of No. 23286.
23288	4174	Una Mary Dawson, 1879.	Great-granddaughters. Children of No. 23287.
23289	4175	Maude Elizabeth Dawson, 1882.	
23290	4176	Eleanor Charlotte Augusta Dawson, 1885.	

286. Descendants of the Hon. Olivia Cecilia de Ros, 1807–1885, and her husband, Henry Richard Charles, 1st Earl Cowley, K.G., 1804–1884. (See Table XLVI.)

23291	4177	Henry Arthur Mornington, 3rd Earl Cowley [U.K.], 1866. 11 *South Audley Street, S.W.*	Grandson. Son of William Henry, 2nd Earl Cowley, 1834–1895.
23292	4178	Christian Arthur, Viscount Dangan, 1890.	Great-grandson. Son of No. 23291.
23293	4179	Lady Eva Cecilia Margaret, wife of Randolph Gordon Erskine Wemyss. *Wemyss Castle, Kirkcaldy, N.B.*	Granddaughter. Sister to No. 23291.
23294	4180	Hon. Cecil Charles Foley Wellesley, 1842.	Sons.
23295	4181	Hon. Frederick Arthur Wellesley, formerly Colonel Coldstream Guards, 1844.	
23296	4182	Victor Wellesley, 1876. Page of Honour to Queen Victoria, 1887–1892.	Grandson. Son of No. 23295.
23297	4183	Lady Feodorowna Cecilia, wife of the Hon. Sir Francis Leveson Bertie, K.C.B., 1840. *British Embassy, Rome.*	Daughter.
23298	4184	Vere Frederick Bertie, 1878.	Grandson. Child of No. 23297.
23299	4185	Sophia Georgiana Robertina, Countess of Hardwicke [G.B.], 1841. 8 *York Terrace, Regent's Park.*	Younger daughter.
23300	4186	Albert Edward Philip Henry, 6th Earl of Hardwicke [G.B.], 1867. 9 *Cavendish Square, W.*	Grandchildren. Children of No. 23299.
23301	4187	Lady Feodorowna, wife of the Hon. Humphrey Napier Stuart, 1864. 38 *Portman Square, W.*	
23302 –05	}	Same as Nos. 20315–20318.	Great-grandchildren. Children. of No. 23301.
23306	4188	Lady Magdalen, wife of Sir Richard Henry Williams-Bulkeley, 12th Bart., 1865. *Baron Hill, Beaumaris.*	Granddaughter. Daughter of No. 23299.
23307 –09	}	Same as Nos. 20392–20394.	Great-grandchildren. Children of No. 23306.

The Blood Royal of Britain

287. Descendants of the Hon. Cecilia de Ros, 1811–1869, and her husband, the Hon. John Boyle, 1803–1874. (See Table XLVI.)

23310	4189	Gerald Edmund Boyle, Colonel (retired) *late* Rifle Brigade, 1840. *48 Queen's Gate Terrace, S.W.*	Son.
23311	4190	Arthur Gerald Boyle, Captain Prince Albert's Somersetshire Light Infantry, 1865. *Naval and Military.*	
23312	4191	William Henry Dudley Boyle, Lieutenant R.N., 1873.	Grandchildren. Children of No. 23310.
23313	4192	Frederick John Boyle, 1875. *Wellington.*	
23314	4193	Reginald Courtenay Boyle, 1877.	
23315	4194	Caroline Elizabeth, wife of Charles Drummond, 1868. *6 Great Cumberland Place, S.W.*	
23316	4195	Robert Charles Crosbie Drummond, 1896.	Great-grandchildren. Children of No. 23315.
23317	4196	Angela Cecilia Mary Drummond, 1893.	
23318	4197	Cecilia Georgiana Boyle, 1870.	Grandchildren. Children of No. 23310.
23319	4198	Theresa Selina, wife of Arthur Stewart Herbert, 1871. *Cahirnane, Killarney, Kerry.*	
23320	4199	Geoffrey Richard Arthur Herbert, 1902.	Great-grandchild. Child of No. 23319.
23321	4200	Evelyn Blanche Boyle, 1873.	Grandchildren. Children of No. 23310.
23322	4201	Geraldine Lilian Boyle, 1899.	
23323	4202	Georgina Olivia, widow of Rear-Admiral Richard Robert Quin, 1820–1870, 1843. *14 Hill Street, Berkeley Square, W.*	Daughter.

288. Descendants of Somerset Richard, 3rd Earl of Carrick, 1779–1838. (See Table XLVII.)

23324	4203	Sarah Juliana, Countess of Clancarty [I.], Viscountess Clancarty [U.K.], and Marchioness of Heusden [Netherlands]. *Coorheen House, Loughrea, co. Galway.*	Daughter.
23325	4204	William Frederick, 5th Earl of Clancarty [I.], 4th Viscount Clancarty [U.K.], and 4th Marquis of Heusden [Netherlands]. *Garbally, Ballinasloe, co. Galway.*	Great-grandson. Son of Richard Somerset, 4th Earl of Clancarty, 1834–1891, eldest son of No. 23324.
23326	4205	Richard Frederick John Donough, Lord Kilconnel, 1891.	Great-great-grandchildren. Children of No. 23325.
23327	4206	Hon. Roderic Charles Berkeley Le Poer Trench, 1895.	
23328	4207	Hon. . . . . Le Poer Trench.	
23329	4208	Lady Beryl Franzeska Kathleen Bianca Le Poer Trench, 1893.	
23330	4209	Hon. Richard John Le Poer Trench, 1877.	Great-grandchildren. Brother and sister of No. 23325.
23331	4210	Lady Katharine Anne Le Poer Trench, 1871.	

23332	4211	Hon. Frederick Le Poer Trench, 1835. *Earlie Bank, Craigie, Perthshire.*	
23333	4212	Hon. William Le Poer Trench, 1837. *St. Hubert's, Gerrard's Cross, Bucks.* 3 *Hyde Park Gardens, W.*	Grandsons. Sons of No. 23324.
23334	4213	William Martins Le Poer Trench, 1866.	Great-grandchildren.
23335	4214	Power Mash Le Poer Trench, 1869. 10 *King's Bench Walk, Temple, E.C.*	Children of No. 23333.
23336	4215	Gladys Marjorie Le Poer Trench, 1899.	Great-great-granddaughter. Child of No. 23335.
23337	4216	Lady Anne, widow of the Hon. Frederick Sydney Charles Trench, 1839–1879, 1839.	Granddaughter. Daughter of No. 23324.
23338	4217	Frederick Oliver, 3rd Lord Ashtown [I.], 1868. *Woodlawn, co. Galway.*	Great-grandson. Son of No. 23337.
23339	4218	Hon. Frederick Sydney Trench, 1894.	
23340	4219	Hon. Robert Power Trench, 1897.	Great-great-grandchildren.
23341	4220	Hon. Arthur Cosby Trench, 1899.	Children of No. 23338.
23342	4221	Hon. Grace Mary Trench, 1896.	
23343	4222	Hon. William Cosby Trench, J.P., 1869. *Clonodfoy Castle, co. Limerick.*	Great-grandson. Grandson of No. 23337.
23344	4223	Percy Richard Oliver Trench, 1894.	Great-great-grandchildren.
23345	4224	Walter Frederick Oliver Trench, 1899.	Children of No. 23343.
23346	4225	Algernon Oliver Trench, 1900.	
23347	4226	Hon. Sydney Trench, 1877.	Great-grandchildren.
23348	4227	Hon. Charlotte Anne Trench, 1871.	Children of No. 23337.
23349	4228	Hon. Sarah May Trench, 1873.	
23350	4229	Hon. Hugh Somerset John Massy, 1864. *Hermitage Castle, Connell.*	Grandson. Son of the Lady Lucy Maria Butler, 1837–1896, and her husband, John Thomas William, 6th Lord Massy.
23351	4230	Hugh Hamon Charles George Massy, 1894.	
23352	4231	Francis John Ingoldsby Tristram Massy, 1895.	Great-grandchildren.
23353	4232	Ida Lucy Massy, 1887.	Children of No. 23350.
23354	4233	Muriel Olive Massy, 1892.	
23355	4234	Lilian Irene Susan Massy, 1897.	
23356	4235	Hon. Lucy Matilda Anne, wife of Major Charles Davis Guinness, R.A., 1865.	Granddaughter. Elder sister of No. 23350.
23357	4236	Hugh Spencer Guinness, 1890.	Great-grandchildren. Children
23358	4237	Owen Charles Guinness, 1894.	of No. 23356.
23359	4238	Hon. Matilda Isabella, wife of Spencer Charles Vansittart, J.P. *Coolbawn House, Castleconnel, co. Limerick.*	Granddaughter. Younger sister of No. 23350.
23360	4239	Everina Lucy Vansittart, } twins, 1890.	Great-grandchildren.
23361	4240	Slaney Theresa Vansittart, }	Daughters of No.
23362	4241	Marjorie Vansittart, 1892.	23359.

289. Descendants of Lieutenant-General the Hon. Henry Edward Butler, 1780–1856. (See Table XLVII.)

23363	4242	Charles Henry Somerset, 6th Earl of Carrick [I.], 1851. *Mount Juliet, Thomastown, Kilkenny.*	Grandson. Son of Captain Charles George Butler, 86th Foot, 1823–1854.

23364	4243	Charles Ernest Alfred French Somerset, Viscount Ikerrin, 1873. *Glasnevin, Dublin.*	} Great-grandson. Son of No. 23363.
23365	4244	Hon. Rosamond Kathleen Margaret Butler, 1899.	} Great-great-granddaughters. Children of No. 23364.
23366	4245	Hon. Irene Jane Beatrice Butler, 1901.	
23367	4246	Kathleen, wife of Walter Charles Lindsay, 1876.	} Great-granddaughter. Daughter of No. 23363.
23368	4247	Doreen Lindsay, 1899.	{ Great-great-granddaughter. Daughter of No. 23367.
23369	4248	Emily Mary, wife of the Rev. George Platt Dew, 1852. *Shire Newton Rectory, Monmouthshire.*	} Granddaughter. Sister to No. 23363.
23370	4249	Violet Annie Janet, wife of John Charles Trevelyan Adam.	} Great-grandchild. Daughter of No. 23369.
23371	4250	Pierce Armar Butler, 1863.	{ Grandson. Son of the Rev. Pierce Butler, 1825–1868.
23372	4251	Pierce Rollo Butler, 1885.	Great-grandson. Son of No. 23371.
23373	4252	Harriet Frances Butler.	Granddaughter. Sister to No. 23371.
23374	4253	Edward John Butler, *late* Captain 21st Fusiliers, 1842.	} Children.
23375	4254	Fanny Hester Butler, 1840.	

290. Descendants of the Hon. Richard Thomas Maxwell, 1815–1874. (See Table XLVII.)

23376	4255	Arthur Kenlis, 11th Lord Farnham [I.], 1879. *Farnham, co. Cavan.*	} Grandchildren. Children of Somerset Henry, 10th Lord Farnham, 1849–1900.
23377	4256	Hon. Edward Saunderson John Maxwell, 1889.	
23378	4257	Hon. Denis Crichton Maxwell, 1892.	
23379	4258	Hon. Zoë Emma Maxwell, 1881.	
23380	4259	Hon. Stella Frances Maxwell, 1886.	
23381	4260	Hon. Henry Edward Maxwell, Major 2nd Battalion Black Watch, D.S.O., 1857. *Portland, Mount Nugent, co. Cavan.*	} Son.
23382	4261	Richard Sydney Somerset Maxwell, 1893.	} Grandchildren. Children of No. 23381.
23383	4262	Ismay Alice Maxwell, 1888.	
23384	4263	Hon. Anna Frances, wife of Thomas Cosby Burrowes. *Lismore, Cavan.*	} Daughter.
23385	4264	Eleanor Mary Cosby Burrowes.	} Granddaughters. Children of No. 23384.
23386	4265	Rosamond Charlotte Cosby Burrowes.	

291. Descendants of the Hon. Sarah Juliana Maxwell, 1801–1870, and her husband, Colonel Alexander Saunderson, of Castle Saunderson, co. Cavan, M.P., 1784–1857. (See Table XLVII.)

23387	4266	Henry Saunderson.	} Grandchildren. Children of Somerset Bassett Saunderson, 11th Hussars, A.D.C., 1834–1892.
23388	4267	Richard Saunderson.	
23389	4268	Charles Saunderson.	
23390	4269	Maud, wife of Llewellyn Thomas Llewellyn.	
23391	4270	Colonel the Right Hon. Edward James Saunderson, M.P., P.C., 1837. *Castle Saunderson, co. Cavan.*	} Elder surviving son.

23392	4271	Somerset Francis Saunderson, Lieutenant Rifle Brigade, 1867.	
23393	4272	Edward Saunderson.	Grandchildren.
23394	4273	Armar Saunderson.	Children of
23395	4274	John Vernon Saunderson.	No. 23391.
23396	4275	Rosa, wife of Henry Nugent Head, Major 28th Cameronian Rifles.	
23397	4276	Henry William Head, 1898.	Great-grandchildren.
23398	4277	Helen Constance Head, 1893.	Children of No.
23399	4278	Angela Nita Head, 1895.	23396.
23400	4279	Llewellyn Traherne Bassett Saunderson, J.P., 1841. *Dromkeen House, co. Cavan. St. Hilary, co. Glamorgan.*	2nd surviving son.
23401 -11		Same as Nos. 21253-21263.	Grandchildren, &c. Children, &c., of No. 23400.

292. Descendants of the Hon. Harriette Margaret Maxwell, 1805–1880, wife 1st of Edward Southwell, 3rd Viscount Bangor, 1790–1837, and 2ndly of Major Andrew Savage Nugent, of Strangford, co. Down, J.P., D.L., 1809–1889. (See Table XLVII.)

23412	4280	Henry William Crosbie, 5th Viscount Bangor [I.], 1828. *Castle Ward, Downpatrick, co. Down.*	Son.
23413	4281	Hon. Maxwell Richard Crosbie Ward, Captain Royal Artillery, 1868. *Army and Navy.*	
23414	4282	Hon. Harriette Mary, wife of Major-Gen. John Edmund Waller, 1856. *Aughnacloy, Killiney, co. Dublin.*	Grandchildren. Children of
23415	4283	Hon. Kathleen Annette Norah Ward, 1859.	No. 23412.
23416	4284	Hon. Bertha Jane, wife of Robert John Kennedy, C.M.G., 1860. *British Legation, Cettinjé. Cultra, Holywood, co. Down.*	
23417	4285	Mary Grace Enid Kennedy, 1884.	Great-grandchildren.
23418	4286	Bertha Catharine Maud Kennedy, 1885.	Children of No.
23419	4287	Matilda Kathleen Kennedy, 1888.	23416.
23420	4288	Lucy Emily Harriette Kennedy, 1893.	
23421	4289	Hon. Emily Georgiana Ward, 1865.	Granddaughter. Youngest daughter of No. 23412.
23422	4290	Lieut.-Gen. the Hon. Bernard Matthew Ward, 1831. *Staplecross Lodge, Christchurch, Hants.*	2nd surviving son.
23423	4291	Ernest Otway Ward, 1867. *The Kildare Street Club, Dublin.*	
23424	4292	Herbert Bernard Ward, Lieutenant Royal Irish Fusiliers, 1876.	Grandchildren.
23425	4293	Evan Bernard Ward, Lieutenant Duke of Cornwall's Light Infantry, 1878.	Children of No. 23422.
23426	4294	Maxwell William Bernard Ward, 1889.	
23427	4295	Rose Florence, wife of Lieut.-Col. John Hotham, Royal Horse Artillery, 1866.	
23428	4296	Charles Ernest Hotham, 1891.	Great-grandchildren. Chil-
23429	4297	Angela Rose Emily Hotham, 1902.	dren of No. 23427.

23430	4298	Evelyn Margaret Ward, 1873.	
23431	4299	Hildred Laura Ward, 1877.	
23432	4300	Edith Marion Ward, 1882.	Grandchildren. Younger daughters of No. 23422.
23433	4301	Doreen Harriette Ward, 1884.	
23434	4302	Constance Katharine Ward, 1891.	
23435	4303	Captain the Hon. Somerset Richard Hamilton Augusta Ward, 1833. *Isle o' Valla House, Strangford, co. Down.*	3rd surviving son.
23436	4304	George Augustus Crosbie Ward, Commander R.N., 1865.	Grandchildren.
23437	4305	Crosbie Charles Ward, 1868.	Children of
23438	4306	Norah Louisa Fanny, Lady Dunleath [U.K.], 1861. *Ballywalter Park, Ballywalter, co. Down.*	No. 23435.
23439	4307	Hon. Andrew Edward Somerset Mulholland, 1882.	
23440	4308	Hon. Charles Henry George Mulholland, 1886.	Great-grandchil-
23441	4309	Hon. Henry George Hill Mulholland, 1888.	dren. Children
23442	4310	Hon. Godfrey John Arthur Murray Lyle Mulholland, 1892.	of No. 23438.
23443	4311	Hon. Eva Norah Helen Mulholland, 1884.	
23444	4312	Harriette Annette Catherine, wife of Henry Haswell Head, M.D. *Thornhill, Bray, co. Wicklow.*	Daughter by 2nd husband.
23445	4313	Henry Nugent Head, Major 26th Cameronian Rifles, 1864.	Grandson. Son of No. 23444.
23446 -48		Same as Nos. 23397–23399.	Great-grandchildren. Children of No. 23445.
23449	4314	Arthur Maxwell Head, Captain R.A., 1876.	
23450	4315	Gertrude Harriette Head, 1865.	Grandchildren.
23451	4316	Annette Norah, wife of Robert Lister Bower, C.M.G., Major 60th Rifles, 1868. *Welham, Yorks.*	Children of No. 23444.
23452	4317	Robert Tatton Bower, 1894.	Great-grandchildren. Chil-
23453	4318	Constance Marcia Bower, 1896.	dren of No. 23451.
23454	4319	Christian Meriel Bower, 1901.	
23455	4320	Louisa Meriel Head, 1869.	Grandchildren. Daughters
23456	4321	Edith Grace, wife of R. Perceval Maxwell, 1871.	of No. 23444.
23457	4322	John Robert Maxwell, 1896.	Great-grandchildren. Chil-
23458	4323	Richard Henry Maxwell, 1897.	dren of No. 23456.
23459	4324	Patrick Edward Maxwell, 1901.	

293. Descendants of Armar, 3rd Earl of Belmore, 1801–1845. (See Table XLVII.)

23460	4325	Somerset Richard, 4th Earl of Belmore [I.], P.C., G.C.M.G. *Castle Coole, Enniskillen, co. Fermanagh.*	Eldest son.
23461	4326	Armar, Viscount Corry, 1870.	
23462	4327	Hon. Cecil Lowry Corry, 1873.	
23463	4328	Hon. Ernest Lowry Corry, 1874.	Grandchildren.
23464	4329	Lady Theresa Lowry Corry, 1862.	Children of
23465	4330	Lady Florence, wife of Lieut.-Col. John Henry Eden. *Bishopton Grange, Ripon.*	No. 23460.
23466	4331	Robert John Patrick Eden, 1896.	Great-grandchildren.
23467	4332	Christian Florence Eden, 1894.	Children of No.
23468	4333	Norah Madeline Eden, 1895.	23465.

23469	4334	Lady Mary Lowry Corry, 1867.	
23470	4335	Lady Winifred Lowry Corry, 1876.	
23471	4336	Lady Edith Lowry Corry, 1878.	Grandchildren.
23472	4337	Lady Violet Lowry Corry, 1881.	Children of
23473	4338	Lady Margaret Lowry Corry, 1883.	No. 22460.
23474	4339	Lady Dorothy Lowry Corry, 1885.	
23475	4340	Lady Kathleen Lowry Corry, 1887.	
23476	4341	Admiral the Hon. Armar Lowry Corry, 1836. *15 Warwick Square, S.W.*	2nd son.
23477	4342	Arthur Lowry Corry, 1869.	
23478	4343	Rev. Gerald Lowry Corry, 1871. *The Oratory, Brompton, S.W.*	
23479	4344	Adrian Lowry Corry, 2nd Lieutenant Royal West Kent Regiment, 1876.	Grandchildren. Children of No. 23476.
23480	4345	Hubert Armar Lowry Corry, 1881.	
23481	4346	Walter Lowry Corry, 1885.	
23482	4347	Rosamond Florence Lowry Corry, 1873.	
23483	4348	Muriel Lowry Corry, 1877.	
23484	4349	Evelyn Lowry Corry, 1879.	
23485	4350	Colonel the Hon. Henry William Lowry Corry, 1845. *Edwardstone Hall, Boxford, Suffolk.*	3rd son.
23486	4351	Henry Charles Lowry Corry, 1887.	Grandchildren.
23487	4352	Frederick Richard Henry Lowry Corry, 1890.	Children of
23488	4353	Emily Mary Lowry Corry, 1882.	No. 23485.
23489	4354	Alice Frances Louisa Lowry Corry, 1885.	
23490	4355	Lady Louisa Ann, widow of Major Richard Henry Magenis, 1837. *Iveagh, co. Down.* *34 Lennox Gardens, S.W.*	Daughters.
23491	4356	Lady Florence Elizabeth, wife of William Edward King-King, 1842. *Staunton Court, Staunton-on-Arrow.* *Bodenham Manor, Herefordshire.*	
23492	4357	Eustace King-King, Lieutenant Queen's Royal West Surrey Regiment, 1880.	Grandchildren. Children of No. 23491.
23493	4358	Alice Marion King-King, 1877.	
23494	4359	Blanche Mary Cochrane King-King, 1883.	

294. Descendants of the Right Hon. Henry Thomas Lowry Corry, P.C., M.P., 1803–1873. (See Table XLVII.)

23495	4360	Noel Armar Lowry Corry, Captain Grenadier Guards, D.S.O., 1867. *8 Eaton Square, S.W.*	Grandson. Son of Armar Henry Lowry Corry, 1836–1893.
23496	4361	Armar Valentine Lowry Corry, 1896.	Great-grandchildren. Children of No. 23495.
23497	4362	Rosemary Victoria Lowry Corry, 1897.	
23498	4363	Oscar Henry Lowry Corry, 1869.	
23499	4364	Reginald Charles Lowry Corry, 1875.	Grandchildren.
23500	4365	Berta Mary, wife of Maurice Wilhelm Ernest de Bunsen, C.B. *H.M. Embassy, Paris.* *Abbey Lodge, Regent's Park, N.W.*	Brothers and elder sister of No. 23495.
23501	4366	Hilda Violet Helena de Bunsen, 1900.	Great-granddaughters. Children of No. 23500.
23502	4367	Elizabeth Cicely de Bunsen, 1902.	
23503	4368	Violet Edith Lowry Corry, 1880.	Granddaughter. Younger sister to No. 23495.

23504	4369	Montagu William, 1st Lord Rowton [U.K.], P.C., 1838. *Rowton Castle, Shrewsbury.* *17 Berkeley Square, W.*	Only surviving son.
23505	4370	Stanlake Henry Batson, 1863. *New Zealand.*	Grandchildren. Children of Gertrude Juliana Lowry Corry, 1831–1874, wife of Stanlake Ricketts Batson, of Horsheath, –1871.
23506	4371	Gertrude Isabel, wife of Sir Arthur Douglas Brooke, Bart. *Colebrooke Park, co. Fermanagh.*	
23507	4372	Basil Stanlake Brooke, 1888.	Great-grandchildren. Children of No. 23506.
23508	4373	Victor Mervyn Brooke, 1893.	
23509	4374	Arthur Francis Brooke, 1896.	
23510	4375	Sylvia Henrietta Brooke, 1890.	
23511	4376	Sheelah Brooke, 1895.	

295. Descendants, if any, of Lady Harriet Butler, 1784–1865, wife 1st of Francis Savage of Hollywood, co. Down, 2ndly of Colonel Matthew Forde, –1837. (See Table XLVII.)

296. Descendants of Sarah Butler-Clarke-Southwell-Wandesforde, of Castlecomer and Kirklington, 1814–1892, and her husband, the Rev. John Prior, of Mount Dillon, co. Dublin, Rector of Kirklington, Yorks., –1867. (See Table XLVII.)

23512	4377	Richard Henry Prior-Wandesforde, of Castlecomer, co. Kilkenny, and Kirklington, Hipswell, and Hudswell, co. York, J.P., D.L., 1870. *Castlecomer House, co. Kilkenny.*	Grandson. Eldest son of Charles Butler Prior, 1840–1875.
23513	4378	Christopher Butler Prior-Wandesforde, 1896.	Great-grandchildren. Children of No. 23512.
23514	4379	Ferdinand Charles Richard Prior-Wandesforde, 1897.	
23515	4380	Richard Cambridge Prior-Wandesforde, 1902.	
23516	4381	Vera Prior-Wandesforde.	
23517	4382	Charles Butler Prior, 1872.	Grandchildren. Brothers and sisters of No. 23512.
23518	4383	Harold Astley Somerset Prior, 1874.	
23519	4384	Mary Caroline Wandesforde Prior.	
23520	4385	Sarah Emily Edith Prior.	
23521	4386	Henry Wallis Prior-Wandesforde, J.P., 1844. *Lechlade Manor, Lechlade, co. Gloucester.*	Eldest surviving son.
23522	4387	Sarah Maude Butler Prior-Wandesforde, 1884.	Grandchildren. Children of No. 23521.
23523	4388	Gertrude Anne Ormonde Prior-Wandesforde, 1889.	
23524	4389	Sophia Elizabeth, wife of Major-General Henry Frederick Winchilsea Ely. *18 Sussex Square, Brighton.* *Heather Brae, Hindhead, Haslemere.*	Daughter.
23525	4390	Sarah Prior Ely.	Grandchildren. Children of No. 23524.
23526	4391	Florence Wandesforde, wife of the Rev. J. Tongue. *Mundford Rectory, Norfolk.*	
23527	4392	Elinor Victoria Ely.	

297. Descendants of Henry Edmund, 13th Viscount Mountgarrett, 1816–1900. (See Table XLVIII.)

23528	4393	Henry Edmund, 14th Viscount Mountgarrett [I.], 1844. *Ballyconra, co. Kilkenny. Nidd Hall, Ripley.*	Son.
23529	4394	Hon. Edmund Somerset Butler, 1875.	Grandchildren. Children of No. 23528.
23530	4395	Hon. Elinor Frances, wife of Andrew S. Lawson. *Aldborough Manor, Boroughbridge, Yorkshire.*	
23531	4396	Margery Elinor Lawson, 1889.	Great-grandchildren. Children of No. 23530.
23532	4397	Mary Doreen Lawson, 1892.	
23533	4398	Hon. Ethel Mary, wife of Henry Rimington-Wilson. *Broomhead Hall, near Sheffield.*	Grandchild. Younger daughter of No. 23528.
23534	4399	Henry Edmund Rimington-Wilson, 1899.	Great-grandchildren. Son and daughters of No. 23533.
23535	4400	Pamela Rimington-Wilson, } 1900.	
23536	4401	Lettice Rimington-Wilson, }	
23537	4402	Hon. Frances Sarah, wife of Edward Arthur Whittuck. *77 South Audley Street, W.*	Daughter.

298. Descendants of the Hon. Juliana Jemima Butler, 1817–1873, and her husband, Thomas Clifton Wilkinson, Esq., of Newall Hall, Yorks, 1815–1889. (See Table XLVIII.)

23538	4403	Thomas Clifton Wilkinson, 1844. *Newall Hall, Otley, Yorks.*	Children.
23539	4404	Francis Ernest Wilkinson, 1856.	
23540	4405	Charlotte Mary Wilkinson.	

299. Descendants of Colonel the Hon. Pierce Butler, M.P., 1784–1846. (See Table XLVIII.)

23541	4406	Anne, wife of John Hewson, 1834. *Dunelm, Hartington Grove, Rock Estate, Cambridge.*	Granddaughter. Daughter of the Rev. Edmund John Butler, 1804–1873.
23542	4407	Lieutenant-Colonel Somerset James Butler, 1849. *Kilmurry, Thomastown, co. Kilkenny.*	Grandchildren. Children of Capt. Henry Butler, 1805–1881.
23543	4408	Major Walter Theobald Butler, 1853.	
23544	4409	Isabel Harriet Butler, 185–.	
23545	4410	Mildred Anne Butler, 185–.	
23546	4411	Walter Butler, 1842.	Grandson. Son of Lieut. William Butler, R.N., 1814–1847.
23547	4412	Theobald Butler, 1853.	Grandson. Son of Walter Butler, 1821–1900.
23548	4413	Theobald Stuart Butler, 1884.	Great-grandchildren. Children of No. 23547.
23549	4414	Kathleen Dorothea Butler.	
23550	4415	Walter Butler, 1855. *Shortlands, Eastbourne.*	Grandson. Children of Walter Butler, 1821–1900.
23551	4416	Beatrice Amelia Butler.	
23552	4417	Isabella Butler. *17 Rue Jean-Binet, Colombes, Paris.*	

300. Descendants, if any, of the Hon. Charlotte Juliana Butler, 1778–1830, and her husband, Colonel John Carrington Smith. (See Table XLVIII.)

---

301. Descendants of Somerset, 2nd Earl of Belmore, 1774–1841. (See Table XLVII.)

23553 −604	}	Same as Nos. 23460–23511.

302. Descendants of Henry, 3rd Duke of Buccleuch, 5th Duke of Queensberry, 1746–1812. (See Table XLIX.)

23605 −4117	}	Same as Nos. 19724–20236.

303. Descendants, if any, of the Hon. Catherine Lucy Douglas, 1784–1857, and her husband, Admiral Sir George Scott, K.C.B., –1841. (See Table XLIX.)

---

304. Descendants, if any, of the Hon. Mary Sidney Douglas, 1796– , and her husband, Robert Douglas, of Strathany, –1844. (See Table XLIX.)

---

305. Descendants of Algernon, 7th Duke of Somerset, 1684–1749–50. (See Table L.)

24118 −401	}	Same as Nos. 20946–21229.

306. Descendants of Julia Frances Laura Boultbee, 1815–1868, wife of the Hon. Francis Scott, of Sandhurst Grange, Surrey, M.P., 1806–1884. (See Table L.)

24402	4418	Frances Margaret Julia, wife of Joseph William Baxendale. 78 *Brook Street, W.*	Only surviving children.
24403	4419	Joseph Francis Noel Baxendale, 1877.	Grandchildren. Children of No. 24402.
24404	4420	Laura Mary, wife of Leonard Rodwell Wilkinson, Barrister-at-Law, 1875. 62 *Chester Square, S.W.*	
24405	4421	Harold Francis Wilkinson, 1899.	Great-grandchildren. Children of No. 24404.
24406	4422	Arthur Vernon Wilkinson, 1902.	
24407	4423	Dorothy Margaret Baxendale, 1885.	Grandchild. Younger daughter of No. 24402.

The Blood Royal of Britain

307. Descendants of Henry John George, 3rd Earl of Carnarvon, 1800–1849. (See Table LI.)

24408 -09	}	Same as Nos. 22015–22016.	Grandchildren. Children of Henry Howard Molyneux, 4th Earl of Carnarvon, P.C., 1831–1890, by 1st wife.
24410	4424	Hon. Aubrey Nigel Henry Molyneux Herbert, 1880.	Grandchildren. Sons of Henry Howard Molyneux, 4th Earl of Carnarvon, 1831–1890, by 2nd wife.
24411	4425	Hon. Mervyn Robert Howard Molyneux Herbert, 1882.	
24412 -17	}	Same as Nos. 22017–22022.	Grandchildren. Daughters of Henry Howard Molyneux, 4th Earl of Carnarvon, 1831–1890, by 1st wife.
24418	4426	Hon. Alan Percy Harty Molyneux Herbert, M.D., 1836. 18 *Rue Duplot, Paris.*	Sons.
24419	4427	Hon. Auberon Edward William Molyneux Herbert, 1838. *The Old House, Berrywood, Ringwood, Hants.*	
24420	4428	Auberon Thomas Herbert, 1876.	Grandchildren. Children of No. 24419.
24421	4429	Nan Ino Herbert, 1880.	
24422	4430	Eveline Alicia Juliana, Countess of Portsmouth [G.B.], 1834. *Over Wallop, Stockbridge, Hants.*	Elder daughter.
24423	4431	Newton, 6th Earl of Portsmouth [G.B.], 1856. *Harstbourne Park, Whitchurch.* 2 *Abbey Gardens, Westminster, S.W.*	Grandchildren. Children of No. 24422.
24424	4432	Hon. John Fellowes Wallop, 1859. *Barton House, Morchard-Bishop.*	
24425	4433	Hon. Oliver Henry Wallop, 1861. *Big Horn, Sheridan co., Wyoming, U.S.A.*	
24426	4434	Gerard Vernon Wallop, 1898.	Great-grandchildren. Children of No. 24425.
24427	4435	Hon. Robert Gerard Valoynes Wallop, 1864. 30 *South Audley Street, W.*	Grandchildren. Youngest sons and eldest daughter of No. 24422.
24428	4436	Hon. Frederick Henry Arthur Wallop, 1870. *Brooks' ; St. James'.*	
24429	4437	Lady Catherine Henrietta, wife of Charles George Milnes Gaskell, 1856. *Thornes House, Wakefield.* *Wenlock Abbey, Salop.*	
24430	4438	Evelyn Milnes Gaskell, 1877.	Great-grandchildren. Children of No. 24429.
24431	4439	Mary Milnes Gaskell, 1881.	
24432	4440	Lady Rosamond Alicia, wife of Augustus Langham Christie, 1861. *Tapeley Park, Bideford, Instow, North Devon.*	Grandchild. 2nd daughter of No. 24422.
24433	4441	John Christie, 1882.	Great-grandchild. Child of No. 24432.
24434	4442	Lady Dorothea Hester Bluet, wife of Sir Richard Nelson Rycroft, 5th Bart., 1863. *Dummer House, Basingstoke.*	Grandchild. 3rd daughter of No. 24422.
24435	4443	Nelson Edward Oliver Rycroft, 1886.	Great-grandchildren. Children of No. 24434.
24436	4444	Richard Michael Rycroft, 1897.	
24437	4445	Lady Gwendolen Margaret, wife of Vernon James Watney, 1866. 11 *Berkeley Square, W.*	Granddaughter. 4th daughter of No. 24422.

24438	4446	Oliver Vernon Watney, 1902.	Great-grandchildren.
24439	4447	Rosalind Margaret Watney, 1891.	Children of No.
24440	4448	Silvia Katharine Watney, 1896.	24437.
24441	4449	Lady Henrietta Anna, wife of John Carbery Evans, Barrister-at-Law, 1872.	Grandchild. 5th daughter of No. 24422.
24442	4450	Margaret Alice Carbery Evans, 1891.	Great-grandchildren.
24443	4451	Henrietta Joan Camilla Evans, 1895.	Children of No. 24441.
24444	4452	Lady Gwendolen Ondine Herbert, 1842. *Fair Croft, Upper Richmond Road, Putney.*	Younger daughter.

308. Descendants of Lady Henrietta Elizabeth Herbert, 1797–1836, and her husband, the Rev. John Charles Stapleton, Rector of Teversall, Notts. (See Table LI.)

309. Descendants of Lady Emily Herbert, 1798–1864, and her husband, Philip Bouverie-Pusey, Esq., of Pusey, 1799–1855. (See Table LI.)

24445	4453	Sidney Edward Bouverie Pusey, *of Pusey*, 1839. *Pusey, Farringdon.*	
24446	4454	Edith Lucy Pusey, 1831.	Children.
24447	4455	Clara, wife of Captain Francis Charteris Fletcher, *late* 60th Rifles, 1834.	
24448	4456	Philip Fletcher.	Grandchild. Child of No. 24447.

310. Descendants of Augusta Elizabeth Herbert, 1804–1876, wife of Sir Francis Vincent of Debden Hall, Essex, 10th Bart., 1803–1880. (See Table LI.)

24449	4457	Blanche, widow of John Raymond Cely-Trevilian, 1884. *10 Tite Street, Chelsea Embankment, S.W.*	Only child.

311. Descendants of the Very Rev. and Hon. William Herbert, LL.D., Dean of Manchester, 1778–1847. (See Table LI.)

24450	4458	William George Herbert, J.P., 1841. *10 West Cliff Gardens, Folkestone.*	Grandson. Only child of Henry William Herbert of The Cedars, Newark, New Jersey, U.S.A., 1807–1859.
24451	4459	George Frederick Herbert, Major R.F.A., 1862.	Grandson. Son of Charles Frederick Herbert, Commander R.N., 1819–1868.
		Children of Louisa Emily Julia Herbert, 1849–1889 (daughter), and her husband, Robert Hervey Monro Elwes, *of Stoke College, Suffolk*.	
24452	4460	Hilda Augusta, wife of the Rev. Frederick Philip Greene de Freville, 1858. *Horsepools, Stroud, Gloucester.*	Grandchild. Elder surviving sister of No. 24451.

24453	4461	Geoffrey Philip Herbert de Freville, 1883.	Great-grandchildren.
24454	4462	Cecily Hilda de Freville, 1884.	Children of No.
24455	4463	Audrey Sylvia Herbert de Freville, 1887.	24452.
24456	4464	Beatrice Mary Herbert, 1860. Grandchild. *Chesterford, Saffron Walden.*	Younger surviving sister of No. 24451.
24457	4465	Louisa Catherine Georgina, widow of Major-General Godfrey Charles Mundy, Lieutenant-Governor of Jersey, −1860, 1809.	Daughter.
24458	4466	Robert Mundy.	Great-grandchildren. Children of the *late*
24459	4467	Sybil Mundy.	Herbert Godfrey Mundy, 1849–1876, and grandchildren of No. 24457.
24460	4468	Cyril Percy Mundy, Barrister Inner Temple, 1854.	Godson. Son of No. 24457.
24461	4469	Percy Charles Dryden Mundy, 1879.	Great-grandchildren.
24462	4470	Hugh Algernon Godfrey Mundy, 1883.	Children of No. 24460.
24463	4471	Beatrice Louisa Florence, wife of John Tryon.	Granddaughters. Daughters of Cecilia Augusta Henrietta Herbert, 1828– ,
24464	4472	Francesca Ferguson.	and her husband, Colonel A. T. Ferguson, of Lennox Hill, Kentucky, −1863.

312. Descendants of the Rev. and Hon. George Herbert, Vicar of Tibenham, Norfolk, 1789–1825. (See Table LI.)

| 24465 | 4473 | Agnes Katinka Herbert, 1820. 135 *Avenue Victor Hugo, Paris.* | Daughter. |

313. Descendants of the Hon. Algernon Herbert, Barrister-at-Law, 1792–1855. (See Table LI.)

24466	4474	Sir Robert George Wyndham Herbert, G.C.B., 1831. *Icleton, Great Chesterford, Essex.*	Children.
24467	4475	Elizabeth Alicia Maria, widow of the Rev. William Lempriere Lewis, −1872. 10 *Lower Sloane Street, S.W.*	
24468	4476	Alicia Maria Lempriere, wife of William Francis Beddoes, Barrister-at-Law. 53 *Drayton Gardens, S.W.*	Grandchild. Child of No. 24467.
24469	4477	Jane Caroline Herbert, 1837. 103 *Oakley Street, Chelsea, S.W.*	Younger daughter.

314. Descendants of Henry George Francis, 2nd Earl of Ducie, 1802–1853. (See Table LII.)

24470	4478	Henry John, 3rd Earl of Ducie [U.K.], 6th Baron Ducie [G.B.], P.C., 1827. 16 *Portman Square, W.*	Son.
24471	4479	Henry Haughton Reynolds, Lord Moreton, 1857. *Sarsden House, Chipping Norton.*	Grandchildren. Children of No. 24470.
24472	4480	Lady Constance Emily, wife of the Right Hon. George John Shaw-Lefèvre, P.C., 1850. 18 *Bryanston Square, W.*	

24473	4481	Hon. Berkeley Basil Moreton, 1834. *Waratah, Maryborough, Queensland.*	2nd surviving son.
24474	4482	Capel Henry Berkeley Moreton, 1875.	
24475	4483	Algernon Howard Moreton, 1880.	
24476	4484	Eleanor Alice Moreton, 1863.	
24477	4485	Evelyn Beatrice Moreton, 1865.	Grandchildren. Children of No. 24473.
24478	4486	Constance Ethel Moreton, 1866.	
24479	4487	May Isabel Moreton, 1868.	
24480	4488	Beatrice Lilian Moreton, 1873.	
24481	4489	Ada Georgina Moreton, 1877.	
24482	4490	Irmengarde Moreton, 1879.	
24483	4491	Hon. Reynolds Moreton, 1835. *Woodham Walter House, Maldon, Essex.*	3rd surviving son.
24484	4492	Henry John Moreton, 1862.	Grandchild. Son of No. 24483.
24485	4493	Theodore Reynolds Moreton, 1890.	Great-grandchildren. Children of No. 24484.
24486	4494	Hugh Berkeley Moreton, 1891.	
24487	4495	Francis James Moreton, 1863. *Le Mars, Iowa, U.S.A.*	Grandchild. 2nd son of No. 24483.
24488	4496	Constance Moreton, 1895.	Great-grandchildren. Children of No. 24487.
24489	4497	Evelyn Jane Moreton, 1898.	
24490	4498	Reginald Moreton, 1869.	Grandchildren. Younger children of No. 24483.
24491	4499	Florence Lilian Moreton, 1871.	
24492	4500	Mabel Evelyn, wife of Arthur Cortlandt Macgregor, 1874.	
24493	4501	Hon. Seymour Moreton, 1841. *Macdonnell Street, Toowong, Brisbane.*	4th surviving son.
24494	4502	Albert Eliott Kingscote Moreton, 1875.	Grandchildren. Children of No. 24493.
24495	4503	Douglas Seymour Herbert Moreton, 1878.	
24496	4504	Elizabeth Emily Moreton, 1880.	
24497	4505	Ida Jeanette Moreton, 1883.	
24498	4506	Hon. Richard Charles Moreton, 1846. *Crookham House, Winchfield, Hants.*	5th surviving son.
24499	4507	Marie Evelyn, wife of Colonel the Hon. Julian Hedworth George Byng, M.V.O., 1870.	Granddaughter. Daughter of No. 24498.
24500	4508	Hon. Matthew Henry Moreton, 1847. *New Guinea.*	6th surviving son.
		(4 sons and 3 daughters, if living.)	Grandchildren. Children of Lady Georgina Mary Louisa Moreton, 1831–1867, and her husband, the Rev. Charles Edward Oakley, rector of St. Paul's, Covent Garden, –1865.
24501	4509	Lady Alice, widow of Lieutenant-General Sir Henry Marshman Havelock-Allan, G.C.B., V.C., M.P., 1st Bart., 1830–1897; 1843. *Blackwell Grange, Darlington.*	Daughter.
24502	4510	Sir Henry Spencer Moreton Havelock-Allan, 2nd Bart., 1872. *Blackwell Grange, Darlington.*	Grandchildren. Children of No. 24501.
24503	4511	Allan Havelock-Allan, 1874. *Blackwell Manor, Darlington.*	
24504	4512	Henry Ralph Moreton Havelock-Allan, 1899.	Great-grandchildren. Children of No. 24503.
24505	4513	. . . . Havelock-Allan, 1901.	
24506	4514	Hope Aline Havelock-Allan, 1898.	
24507	4515	Ethel, wife of Joseph Albert Pease, M.P. *Munthorpe Hall, Yorks.*	Granddaughter. Daughter of No. 24501.
24508	4516	Joseph Pease, 1889.	Great-grandchildren. Children of No. 24507.
24509	4517	Miriam Blanche Pease, 1887.	

24510	4518	Lady Eleanor, widow of Hugh Ashley Fife Brodie, 1840–1889, 1844. *Brodie Castle, Forres, Moray.*	} 2nd daughter.
24511	4519	Ian Brodie, 1868.	
24512	4520	Ronald Brodie, 1872.	
24513	4521	Douglas Brodie, 1873.	
24514	4522	Duncan Reynett Brodie, 1877.	Grandchildren. Children
24515	4523	Elizabeth Gertrude Brodie, 1869.	of No. 24510.
24516	4524	Eleanor Mary Brodie, 1879.	
24517	4525	Margaret Frances Vere Brodie, 1881.	
24518	4526	Evelyn Sydney Brodie, 1882.	
24519	4527	Lady Evelyn Moreton, 1849. *7 Barkston Gardens.*	} 3rd daughter.

315. Descendants of the Hon. Augustus Henry Reynolds-Moreton, afterward Moreton-Macdonald, of Largie, M.P., 1804–1862. (See Table LII.)

24520	4528	John Ronald Moreton-Macdonald, 1873. *Largie, Argyll.*	Grandchildren. Children
24521	4529	Esther, wife of Thomas William Westropp-Bennett, 1871. *Ballytigue, Limerick.*	of Charles Moreton-Macdonald, of Largie, 1840–1879.
24522	4530	Augustus Henry Macdonald-Moreton, Lieut.-Col. *late* Coldstream Guards, 1848. *Hill Grove, Bembridge, I.W.*	} Son.
24523	4531	Norman Charles Henry Macdonald-Moreton, 1888.	
24524	4532	Cara Mary Amelia, wife of Keith Ronald Mackenzie, 1875. *Gillotts, Henley-on-Thames.*	
24525	4533	Hilda Maud, Lady Lockhart, wife of Sir Simon Macdonald Lockhart, 5th Bart., M.V.O., 1878. *Carnwath House, Lanark.*	Grandchildren. Children of No. 24522.
24526	4534	Evelyn Geraldine Macdonald-Moreton, 1879.	
24527	4535	Muriel Harriet Charles Macdonald-Moreton, 1880.	
24528	4536	Margaret Aline Macdonald-Moreton, 1881.	
24529	4537	Audrey Beatrice Macdonald-Moreton, 1887.	
24530	4538	Islay Mary Cecil Macdonald-Moreton, 1891.	
24531	4539	John Hampden Nicholson, 1871. *Balrath-Burry, Kells.*	{ Grandchild. Son of Frances Augusta Moreton-Macdonald, 1839–1902, wife of Christopher Armytage Nicholson, 1 –1887.
24532	4540	Joyce Frances Nicholson, 1902.	{ Great-grandchild. Daughter of No. 24531.
24533	4541	Mary Jane, wife of Edward Sclater.	
24534	4542	Elizabeth Katherine Nicholson.	Grandchildren. Sisters
24535	4543	Emilia Olivia, wife of R. Arthur Alexander.	of No. 24531.
24536	4544	Emelia Olivia, widow of the Hon. Algernon Reynolds-Moreton, 1829–1880. *23 Tedworth Square, Chelsea, S.W.*	
24537	4545	Mary Macdonald-Moreton.	
24538	4546	Julia, wife of Thomas Digby Pigott, C.B., Comptroller of H.M.'s Stationery Office, 1844. *5 Ovington Gardens, S.W.*	} Daughters.

24539	4547	Charles Moreton Digby Pigott, 1879.	
24540	4548	Morag Digby Pigott, 1881.	
24541	4549	Emma Julia Digby Pigott, 1882.	Grandchildren. Children of No. 24538.
24542	4550	Harriet Mary Digby Pigott, 1883.	
24543	4551	Winifride Digby Pigott, 1887.	
24544	4552	Jane Geraldine, wife of the Rev. Edmund Vincent Pigott. *Trentham Vicarage, Staffordshire.*	Daughter.

316. Descendants of the Hon. Percy Reynolds-Moreton, Captain 10th Hussars, 1808–1886. (See Table LII.)

24545	4553	Maurice Fitzhardinge Reynolds Moreton, 1884. *St. Paul's Square, Burton-on-Trent.*	Grandson. Son of the late Robert Moreton, 1850–1884.
24546	4554	Rev. Percy Dundas Moreton, 1855. *Compton Dundon Vicarage, Somerton, Somerset.*	Son.
24547	4555	Percy Clifford Reynolds Moreton, 1885.	
24548	4556	Claude Anthony Moreton, 1897.	Grandchildren. Children of No. 24546.
24549	4557	Gwendolen Alti Moreton, 1884.	
24550	4558	Muriel Evelyn Moreton, 1887.	
24551	4559	Edith Moreton, 1848.	
24552	4560	Florence Moreton, 1853.	Daughters.
24553	4561	Rose Moreton, 1856.	

317. Descendants of Lady Mary Elizabeth Kitty Moreton, 1798–1842, wife of William Basil Percy, 7th Earl of Denbigh, 1796–1865. (See Table LII.)

24554	4562	Rudolph Robert Basil Aloysius Augustine, 9th Earl of Denbigh [E.], 8th Earl of Desmond [I.], 1859. *Newnham Paddox, near Lutterworth.*	Grandson. Son of Rudolph William Basil, 8th Earl of Denbigh, 1823–1892.
24555	4563	Rudolph Edmund Aloysius, Viscount Feilding, 1885.	
24556	4564	Hon. Hugh Cecil Robert Feilding, 1886.	
24557	4565	Hon. Henry Simon Feilding, 1894.	Great-grandchildren. Children of No. 24554.
24558	4566	Lady Mary Alice Clare Feilding, 1888.	
24559	4567	Lady Dorothie Mary Evelyn Feilding, 1889.	
24560	4568	Lady Agnes Mary Mabel Feilding, 1891.	
24561	4569	Lady Marjorie Mary Winifrede Feilding, 1892.	
24562	4570	Lady Clare Mary Cecilia Feilding, 1896.	
24563	4571	Lady Betty Mary Feilding, 1899.	
24564	4572	Lady Victoria Mary Dolores Feilding, 1900.	
24565	4573	Hon. Francis Henry Everard Joseph Feilding, 1867. *5 John Street, Mayfair, W.*	
24566	4574	Rev. and Hon. Basil George Edward Vincent Feilding, 1873. *The Presbytery, Snow Hill, Wolverhampton.*	Grandchildren. Brothers and sisters to No. 24554.
24567	4575	Lady Edith Mary Frances Feilding, a Sister of Charity, 1862. *Convent of the Sisters of Charity, Dover.*	
24568	4576	Lady Mary Winefride Elizabeth, wife of Gervase Henry Cary-Elwes, 1868. *The Manor House, Brigg, Lincolnshire.*	

24569	4577	Robert Geoffrey Gervase John Cary-Elwes, 1890.	Great-grandchildren. Children of No. 24568.
24570	4578	Rudolph Philip Cary-Elwes, 1892.	
24571	4579	Francis Guy Robert Cary-Elwes, 1895.	
24572	4580	Aubrey Valentine Denis Cary-Elwes, 1898.	
24573	4581	Richard Everard Cary-Elwes, 1901.	
24574	4582	Simon Vincent Edmund Paul Cary-Elwes, 1902.	
24575	4583	Lady Agnes Mary Pia, wife of Charles Edmund de Trafford, 1870. *Hothorpe, Theddingworth, Rugby.*	Granddaughter. Younger sister to No. 24554.
24576	4584	Hubert Edmund Francis de Trafford, 1893.	Great-grandchildren. Children of No. 24575.
24577	4585	Clare Mary Annette de Trafford, 1895.	
24578	4586	Hilda Mary Clare de Trafford, 1898.	
24579	4587	Hon. Sir Percy Robert Basil Feilding, K.C.B., 1827. *Broome Park, Betchworth, Surrey.*	Son.
24580 –86	}	Same as Nos. 21672-21678.	Grandchildren. Children of No. 24579.
24587	4588	John Basil Feilding, J.P., 1868. *Upper Downing, Holywell, North Wales.*	Grandchild. Son of the Rev. and Hon. Charles William Alexander Feilding, 1833-1893.
24588	4589	Charles Rudolph Feilding, 1902.	Great-grandchild. Son of No. 24587.
24589	4590	Rowland Charles Feilding, Captain 6th Battalion Lancashire Fusiliers, 1871. *White's.*	Grandchildren. Brother and sisters of No. 24587.
24590	4591	Adelaide Mary Feilding, } 8 *Tite St., Chelsea.*	
24591	4592	Lucy Constance Feilding,	
24592	4593	Lady Jane Lissey Harriet, widow of Theophilus John Levett, J.P., D.L., 1829-1899, 1829. *Oldfield Lodge, Maidenhead.*	Elder daughter.
24593	4594	Theophilus Basil Percy Levett. *Wychnor Park, Burton-on-Trent.* 39 *Wilton Crescent, S.W.*	Grandchildren. Children of No. 24592.
24594	4595	Berkeley John Talbot Levett, Captain 3rd Battalion Scots Guards, 1863.	
24595	4596	Mary Louisa Margaret Levett.	
24596	4597	Ronald William Murray, 1866.	Grandchildren. Children of the Lady Adelaide Emily Feilding, 1836-1870, 1st wife of Charles Archibald Murray, 1836.
24597	4598	Archibald John Percy Murray, 1867.	
24598	4599	Margaret Frances, wife of Arthur Holford. *Taymount, Stanley, Perthshire.* 4A *Bickenhall Mansions, Gloucester Place, W.*	
24599	4600	Lady Ida Matilda Alice, wife of Malcolm Low, of Clatto, J.P., D.L., 1840. 22 *Roland Gardens, S.W.*	Younger surviving daughter.
24600	4601	Ida Mary Ursula Low.	Grandchildren. Children of No. 24599.
24601	4602	Hilda Lucy Adelaide, wife of William Arthur Mount, M.P. *Wasing Place, near Reading.*	
24602	4603	Percy Archer Clive, J.P., D.L., Captain Grenadier Guards, 1873. *Whitfield, co. Hereford.*	Grandchildren. Children of the Lady Katherine Elizabeth Mary Julia Feilding, 1842-1882, by her husband, Charles Meysey Bolton Clive.
24603	4604	Robert Henry Clive, 1877.	
24604	4605	Mabel Adelaide Clive, 1871.	
24605	4606	Marjory Katherine Clive, 1881.	

318. Descendants of Lady Julia Reynolds-Moreton, 1805–1869, and her husband, James Haughton Langston, Esq., of Sarsden House, Oxford, 1796–1863. (See Table LII.)

24606 -07	}	Same as Nos. 24471–24472.	Grandchildren. Children of Julia Langston, –1895, and her husband, Henry John, 3rd Earl of Ducie.

319. Descendants of Lady Katherine Moreton, 1815–1892, 2nd wife of John Raymond Raymond-Barker, Esq., of Fairford Park, Gloucester, 1801–1888. (See Table LII.)

24608	4607	Reginald Henry Raymond-Barker, 1875. *Fairford Park, Gloucester.* *The Ferns, Telbury, Gloucester.*	Grandsons. Sons of Percy FitzHardinge Raymond - Barker, J.P., 1843–1895.
24609	4608	Hugh William Heneage Raymond-Barker, 1876.	

320. Descendants of Charles, 3rd Earl of Romney, 1808–1874. (See Table L.)

24610 -47	}	Same as Nos. 19824–19861.

24648		Same as No. 20510. (See Table L.)

321. Descendants of above, No. 24648.

24649 -50	}	Same as Nos. 20511–20512.	Children.

322. Descendants of Lady Sophia Marsham, 1807–1863, and her husband, Peter Richard Hoare, of Clayton Hall, Lancashire, and Luscombe House, Devon, 1803–1878. (See Table L.)

24651	4609	Peter Arthur Marsham Hoare, 1869. *Luscombe Castle, Dawlish, Devon.*	Grandson. Son of Peter Merrik Hoare, of Luscombe, M.P., 1843–1894.
24652	4610	Peter William Hoare, 1898.	Great-grandchildren. Children of No. 24651.
24653	4611	Joyce Hoare, 1902.	
24654	4612	Lennox Merrick Noel Colt Hoare, 1871.	Grandson. Brother of No. 24651.
24655	4613	Dorothy Augusta Edith Hoare, 1897.	Great-granddaughter. Daughter of No. 24654.
24656	4614	Norah Lillian Augusta Hoare, 1868.	Granddaughter. Sister to No. 24651.
24657	4615	Charles Arthur Richard Hoare, 1847. *Kelsey Manor, Beckenham, Kent.*	Son.

The Blood Royal of Britain

24658	4616	Wilfred Arthur Richard Hoare, 1876.	Grandchildren. Children of No. 24657.
24659	4617	Reginald Arthur Hoare, 1878.	
24660	4618	Ralph Francis Hoare, 1881.	
24661	4619	Agatha Margaret Sophia Hoare, 1869.	
24662	4620	Isabella Mary Hoare, 1839.	Daughter.
24663	4621	Algernon Henry Peter Strickland, 1863. 22 *Lower Sloane Street, S.W.*	Grandson. Son of Charlotte Anne Hoare, 1841–1890, and her husband, Algernon Augustine de Lille Strickland, of Apperley Court, 1837.
24664	4622	Algernon Walter Strickland, 1891.	Great-grandchildren. Children of No. 24663.
24665	4623	Barbara Mary Strickland, 1894.	
24666	4624	Augustine Cecil Strickland, 1864.	Grandchildren. Brothers to No. 24663.
24667	4625	Hubert Arthur Strickland, 1867. *5 Hans Mansions, S.W.*	
24668	4626	Claud Hugh Strickland, 1871. *Forthampton House, Tewkesbury.*	
24669	4627	Walter Claud Strickland, 1896.	Great-grandsons. Sons of No. 24668.
24670	4628	Hugh Baring Strickland, 1899.	
24671	4629	Hilda Rachel, wife of Arthur Charles Stanley Clarke, Captain West Surrey Regiment, 1869.	Grandchildren. Sisters to No. 24663.
24672	4630	Gwendolen Mary Strickland, 1878.	

323. Descendants of Lady Frances Marsham, 1809–1901, 2nd wife of Major-General Edward Charles Fletcher, 1799–1877. (See Table L.)

24673	4631	Charles Edward Fletcher, 1844. *Yalding, Maidstone.*	Sons.
24674	4632	Lionel John William Fletcher, 1845. *Ewell Manor, West Farleigh, Maidstone.*	
24675 –78		Same as Nos. 20912–20915.	Grandchildren. Children of No. 24674.
24679	4633	Isabella Margaret Fletcher, 1839.	Daughters.
24680	4634	Mary Catherine Fletcher, 1848.	

324. Descendants of Lady Mary Marsham, 1811–1871, and her husband, Henry Hoare, Esq., of Staplehurst Place, Kent, 1807–1866. (See Table L.)

24681	4635	Henry Hoare, Captain Loyal Suffolk Hussars, 1866. *Barking Hall, Needham, Suffolk.*	Grandson. Son of Henry Hoare, 1838–1898.
24682	4636	Hugh Peregrine Hoare, 1901.	Great-grandchild. Son of No. 24681.
24683	4637	Frederick Henry Hoare, 1871.	Grandchildren. Brothers and sister of No. 24681.
24684	4638	Edward Henry Hoare, 2nd Lieutenant Buffs, 1872.	
24685	4639	Robert Henry Hoare, 1873.	
24686	4640	Eric Henry Hoare, 1878.	
24687	4641	Beatrice Mary, wife of Arthur Edward Hollond, 1865. *Great Ashfield House, Bury St. Edmunds, Suffolk.*	

24688	4642	Henry Arthur Hollond, 1884.	
24689	4643	Victor Andrew Hollond, 1894.	
24690	4644	Gladys Margaret Beatrice Hollond, 1887.	Great-grandchildren.
24691	4645	Phyllis Caroline Pansy Hollond, 1893.	Children of No.
24692	4646	Muriel Matilda Hollond, 1896.	24687.
24693	4647	Ivy Iseult Hollond, 1897.	
24694	4648	Elspeth Enid Hollond, 1898.	
24695	4649	Evangeline, wife of Percy Brodrick Bernard, J.P., D.L., 1867. *Castle Hackett, Tuam.* *Vevay House, Bray, Wicklow.*	Grandchild. Sister to No. 24681.
24696		Same as No. 23280.	Great-grandchild. Son of No. 24695.
24697	4650	Linda, wife of the Rev. Sydney Rhodes James, Headmaster of Malvern College, 1869. *The Schoolhouse, Malvern College.*	Grandchild. Sister to No. 24681.
24698	4651	Sydney Herbert Rhodes James, 1901.	Great-grandchildren.
24699	4652	Evelyn Zoë Rhodes James, 1898.	Children of No.
24700	4653	Linda Margery Rhodes James, 1900.	24697.
24701	4654	Violet Hoare, 1872.	Grandchild. Youngest sister to No. 24681.
24702	4655	Rev. Walter Marsham Hoare, 1840. *Colkirk Rectory, Norfolk.*	Son.
24703	4656	Walter Robertson Hoare, 1867. *Daneshill, Basingstoke.*	Grandson. Son of No. 24702.
24704	4657	Michael Walter Hoare, 1900.	Great-grandchildren. Children
24705	4658	Veronica Constance Hoare, 1898.	of No. 24703.
24706	4659	Rev. Arthur Robertson Hoare, 1871.	Grandchildren.
24707	4660	Vincent Robertson Hoare, Lieutenant Suffolk Yeomanry Cavalry, 1873.	Sons of No. 24702.
24708	4661	Margaret Elspeth Hoare, 1902.	Great-grandchild. Daughter of No. 24707.
24709	4662	Alice Mary Hoare, 1869.	
24710	4663	Mary Hoare, 1870.	Grandchildren. Children of No. 24702.
24711	4664	Jessie Katherine Hoare, 1875.	
24712	4665	Winifred Ina Hoare, 1879.	
24713	4666	Charles Hervey Hoare, Captain Glamorganshire Imperial Yeomanry Cavalry, 1875.	
24714	4667	Arthur Hervey Hoare, 1877.	Grandchildren. Children of Charles Hoare, 1844–1898.
24715	4668	Guy Sydenham Hoare, 1879.	
24716	4669	Reginald Hervey Hoare, 1882.	
24717	4670	Patience Mary Hoare, 1883.	
24718	4671	Constance Sarah Hoare, 1885.	
24719	4672	Katherine Angelina Adeliza Hoare, 1887.	
24720	4673	William Hoare, 1847. *Iden Manor, Staplehurst, Kent.*	2nd surviving son.
24721	4674	Geoffrey Lennard Hoare, Lieutenant Kent Artillery, 1879.	Grandchildren. Children of No. 24720.
24722	4675	Lionel Lennard Hoare, 2nd Lieutenant Royal Field Artillery, 1881.	
24723	4676	Richard Lennard Hoare, 1883.	
24724	4677	Mary Laura Hoare, 1886.	
24725	4678	Alfred Hoare, 1850.	3rd surviving son.
24726	4679	John Edward Alford Hoare, 1895.	
24727	4680	Joanna Beatrice Hoare, 1882.	Grandchildren. Children of No. 24725.
24728	4681	Olive Mary Hoare, 1884.	
24729	4682	Helen Lucy Hoare, 1885.	
24730	4683	Sybil Frances Hoare, 1887.	

The Blood Royal of Britain

24731	4684	Hugh Edward Hoare, 1854. *Danbury Palace, Chelmsford; Hurley House, Marlow.*	4th surviving son.
24732	4685	Percival Hugh Trench Hoare, 1888.	Grandchildren. Children
24733	4686	Evelyn Melville Shovel Hoare, 1889.	of No. 24731.
24734	4687	Mary Sophia, widow of the Rev. Thomas William Onslow Hallward, Rector of Frittenden, Kent, 1827–1899, 1837. *Maplehurst Farm, Staplehurst, Kent.*	Eldest surviving daughter.
24735	4688	Rev. John Hallward, 1870.	
24736	4689	Henry Hallward, 1872.	
24737	4690	Herbert Charles Hallward, 1873.	
24738	4691	Walter Toke Hallward, 1878.	
24739	4692	Bernard Marsham Hallward, 1882.	Grandchildren. Children
24740	4693	Mary Gertrude Hallward, 1867.	of No. 24734.
24741	4694	Margaret Emily Hallward, 1868.	
24742	4695	Kathleen Leslie Hallward, 1875.	
24743	4696	Dorothy Hallward, 1888.	
24744	4697	Caroline Charlotte Hoare, 1841.	
24745	4698	Sophia Louisa Hoare, 1846.	Daughters.
24746	4699	Katherine Hoare, 1852.	

325. Descendants of Lady Frances Marsham, 1778–1868, and her husband, Sir John Buchanan-Riddell, 9th Bart., M.P., 1768–1819. (See Table L.)

24747 –56	}	Same as Nos. 20513–20522.	Descendants of the Rev. John Charles Buchanan-Riddell, 1814–1879.
24757	4700	Charles James Buchanan-Riddell, C.B., Major-General Royal Artillery, 1817. *Oaklands, Chudleigh, South Devon.*	3rd, but only surviving son.
24758	4701	Mary Frances Buchanan-Riddell, 1854.	Granddaughter. Daughter of No. 24757.
24759	4702	John Walter Rowlands, 1889.	Great-grandson. Only child of Emily Elizabeth Charlotte Adams, 1848–1889, wife of the Rev. William Edward Rowlands, Vicar of Bonchurch, Isle of Wight, 1837, and grandchild of Emily Buchanan-Riddell, 1808–1881, and her husband, John Adams, Barrister-at-Law, 1813–1848.

326. Descendants of Richard, 2nd Marquis and 1st Duke of Buckingham, K.G., 1776–1839. (See Table LIII.)

24760 –92	}	Same as Nos. 19573–19605.

327. Descendants of Sir Watkin Williams-Wynn, 6th Bart., M.P., 1820–1885. (See Table LIII.)

24793	4703	Louisa Alexandra, *late* wife of Sir Herbert Lloyd Watkin Williams-Wynn, 7th Bart.	Only surviving child.
24794	4704	Watkin Williams-Wynn, 1891.	Grandchildren.
24795	4705	Gwladys Elin Williams-Wynn, 1885.	Children of
24796	4706	Constance Mary Williams-Wynn, 1895.	No. 24793.

The Blood Royal of Britain

328. Descendants of Herbert Watkin Williams-Wynn, M.P., 1822 1862. (See Table LIII.)

24797	4707	Sir Herbert Lloyd Watkin Williams-Wynn, 7th Bart., C.B., 1860. *Wynnstay, Rhuabon, North Wales.*	Son.
24798 –800	}	Same as Nos. 24794–24796.	Grandchildren. Children of No. 24797.
24801	4708	Robert William Herbert Watkin Williams-Wynn, Major Montgomeryshire Yeomanry Cavalry, D.S.O., J.P., 1862. *Plas-yn-Cefn, St. Asaph.*	Children.
24802	4709	Helen Florentia Williams-Wynn.	

329. Descendants of Henrietta Charlotte Williams-Wynn, – 1878, and her husband, Sir Hugh Williams, 3rd Bart., 1802-1876. (See Table LIII.)

24803	4710	Sir William Grenville Williams, 4th Bart. of Bodelwyddan, 1844. *Bodelwyddan, Rhuddlan, R.S.O.*	Eldest son.
24804	4711	William Willoughby Williams, 1888.	Grandchildren. Children of No. 24803.
24805	4712	Hugh Grenville Williams, 1889.	
24806	4713	Francis Edris Williams, 1891.	
24807	4714	Ellinor Henrietta Williams, 1886.	
24808	4715	The Right Rev. Watkin Herbert, Lord Bishop of Bangor, 1845. *Glyngarth Palace, Menai Bridge.*	
24809	4716	Owen John Williams, J.P., *late* Captain Denbigh Yeomanry Cavalry, 1850. *Junior Carlton.*	Sons.
24810	4717	Charles Henry Bennett Williams, J.P., *late* Captain and Hon. Major 4th Battalion Oxfordshire Light Infantry. *Dolben, St. Asaph.*	
24811	4718	Evelyn Hugh Watkin Williams, 1884.	Grandchildren. Children of No. 24810.
24812	4719	Mary Nesta Harriet Williams, 1883.	
24813	4720	Hugh Edmund Ethelston Peel, J.P., 1871. *Bryn-y-pys, Salop.*	Grandchild. Son of Henrietta Margaret Williams, – 1885, 2nd wife of Edmund Peel, of Bryn-y-pys, 1826–
24814	4721	Edmund Owen Ethelston Peel, 1893.	Great-grandchild. Child of No. 24813.
24815	4722	Herbert Wicksted Ethelston (formerly Peel).	Grandchildren. Brothers and sisters of No. 24813.
24816	4723	Ernest Ethelston Peel.	
24817	4724	Margaret Anne Peel.	
24818	4725	Ethel Mary Peel.	
24819	4726	Edith Sarah, widow of Salusbury Kynaston Mainwaring, J.P., 1844– 1895. *Bryn Bella, St. Asaph.*	Eldest surviving daughter.

24820	4727	Charles Francis Kynaston Mainwaring, Captain 3rd Battalion Oxfordshire Light Infantry, 1871. *Oteley, Ellesmere, Salop.*	Grandsons. Sons of No. 24819.
24821	4728	Watkin Randle Kynaston Mainwaring, Captain Denbighshire Hussars Yeomanry Cavalry, 1875.	
24822	4729	Mary Charlotte Lucy Williams. } 6 *Sloane Gar-*	Younger surviving
24823	4730	Arabella Antonia Williams. } *dens, S.W.*	daughters.

330. Descendants of Charles Watkin Williams-Wynn, of Coed-y-maen, M.P., Recorder of Oswestry, 1822–1896. (See Table LIII.)

24824	4731	Arthur Watkin Williams-Wynn, *late* Major and Hon. Lieut.-Col. Montgomeryshire Y.C., 1856. *Coed-y-maen, Welshpool.* 71 *Eccleston Square, S.W.*	2nd but only surviving son.
24825	4732	Charles Watkin Williams-Wynn, 1896.	Grandchildren.
24826	4733	Maud Annora Williams-Wynn, 1893.	Children of
24827	4734	Alice Nesta Margaret Williams-Wynn, 1894.	No. 24824.
24828	4735	Henry Cunliffe Williams-Wynn, Major R.F.A.	
24829	4736	Frederick Rowland Williams-Wynn, *late* Captain Montgomeryshire Yeomanry Cavalry, 1865. 54 *Seymour Street, W.*	Children.
24830	4737	Mary, wife of Henry Goulburn Chetwynd-Stapylton. *Hilliers, Petworth.*	
24831	4738	Henry Miles Chetwynd-Stapylton, 1887.	Grandchildren. Children
24832	4739	Annora Esther Chetwynd-Stapylton, 1889.	of No. 24830.
24833	4740	Agnes Sophia Williams-Wynn. 54 *Seymour Street, Portman Square.*	
24834	4741	Annora Margaret, wife of William Douglas Watson Smyth. *Wadhurst Castle, Sussex.*	Younger daughters.
24835	4742	Annora Violet Watson Smyth, 1901.	Grandchild. Daughter of No. 24834.
24836	4743	Constance Harriet Williams-Wynn. 54 *Seymour Street, Portman Square, W.*	Youngest daughter.

331. Descendants of Mary Williams-Wynn, 1809–1869, and her husband, James Milnes Gaskell, of Thornes House, Yorks, M.P., 1810–1873. (See Table LIII.)

24837	4744	Charles George Milnes Gaskell, *late* M.P., 1842. *Thornes House, Yorks. Wenlock Abbey, Salop.*	Elder and only surviving son.
24838 -39	}	Same as Nos. 24430–24431.	Grandchildren. Only children of No. 24837.
24840	4745	Rev. Francis Milnes Temple Palgrave, 1865. *Little Park, Lyme Regis, Dorset.*	Grandchildren. Children of Cecil Grenville Milnes Gaskell, 1833–1890, wife of Francis Turner Palgrave.
24841	4746	Cecil Ursula, widow of the Rev. James Duncan. *The Close, Canterbury.*	
24842	4747	Gwenllian Florence Palgrave.	
24843	4748	Annora Georgina Palgrave.	
24844	4749	Margaret Irene Palgrave.	

24845	4750	Isabel Milnes, widow of the Rev. Fitzgerald Thomas Wintour. *High Hoyland, Barnsley, Yorks.*	Younger but only surviving daughter.
24846	4751	FitzGerald Wintour, Lieut.-Col. West Kent Regiment.	
24847	4752	Francis Wintour.	
24848	4753	Evelyn Wintour, Captain 3rd Madras Lancers.	
24849	4754	Charles John Wintour, Lieutenant R.N.	Grandchildren.
24850	4755	Ulick FitzGerald Wintour.	Children of
24851	4756	Mildred, wife of the Rev. James Cross.	No. 24845.
24852	4757	Mary Wintour.	
24853	4758	Isabel Wintour.	
24854	4759	Anna Mabel Wintour.	
24855	4760	Kathleen Wintour.	

332. Descendants of Sidney Williams-Wynn, 1813–1867, wife of Sir Francis Hastings Doyle, 2nd Bart., 1810–1888. (See Table LIII.)

24856	4761	Sir Everard Hastings Doyle, 3rd Bart., 1852. *7 Grosvenor Gardens, S.W.*	
24857	4762	Arthur Havelock James Doyle, Lieut.-Col. commanding 2nd Battalion King's (Shropshire) Light Infantry, 1858.	Surviving children.
24858	4763	Mary Annabel, wife of Charles Carmichael Lacaita, *late* M.P., Dundee. *Selham House, Petworth.* *65 Eaton Square, S.W.*	
24859	4764	Francis Charles Lacaita, 1887.	Grandchildren. Children
24860	4765	Sidney Guendolen Lacaita, 1886.	of No. 24858.

333. Descendants of the Right Hon. Sir Henry Watkin Williams-Wynn, G.C.H., K.C.B., P.C., 1783–1856. (See Table LIII.)

24861	4766	Jessie Marie, widow of Stanley Leighton, M.P., 1837–1901. *70 Chester Square, S.W.*	Grandchild. 2nd but eldest surviving daughter, and co-heir of Henry Bertie Watkin Williams-Wynn, 1820–1895.
24862	4767	Bertie Edward Parker Leighton, Captain 1st Dragoons, 1875.	Great-grandchildren. Children of No.
24863	4768	Rachel Frances Marion Leighton.	24861.
24864	4769	Frances Caroline, widow of Samuel Richard Brewis, 1843–1897. *Ibstone House, Tetsworth.*	Grandchild. Sister to No. 24861.
24865	4770	Robert Henry Watkin Brewis, Captain Royal Warwickshire Regiment, 1873.	
24866	4771	Charles Richard Wynn Brewis, Lieutenant R.N., 1874.	
24867	4772	Percy Jasper Brewis, 1879.	
24868	4773	Francis Bertie Brewis, Lieutenant King's Own Yorkshire Light Infantry, 1881.	Great-grandchildren. Children of No. 4864.
24869	4774	Humphrey Brewis, 1886.	
24870	4775	Geoffrey Sydney Brewis, 1891.	
24871	4776	Hester Constance, wife of Charles P. Piers, 1875.	
24872	4777	Violet Marie Brewis, 1877.	
24873	4778	Margherita Janet Brewis, 1878.	
24874	4779	Nesta Joan Brewis, 1883.	
24875	4780	Kathleen Mary Brewis, 1893.	

24876	4781	Bertha Marion, widow of Joseph Godman, J.P., 1831–1896. 55 *Lowndes Square, S.W.*	Grandchild. Sister to No. 24861.
24877	4782	Walter Williams Wynn Godman, 1895.	Great-grandchildren. Children of No. 24876.
24878	4783	Joyce Williams Wynn Godman, 1889.	
24879	4784	Marjorie Williams Wynn Godman, 1892.	
24880	4785	Henrietta Katharine Letitia, wife of the Hon. Robert William Henry Rodney. *The Parks, Thornbury, Gloucester.*	Grandchild. Sister to No. 24861.
24881	4786	Mervyn Harley Rodney, 1890.	Great-grandchildren. Children of No. 24880.
24882	4787	Robert Henry Basil Rodney, 1893.	
24883	4788	Ivor Morgan Rodney, 1896.	
24884	4789	Patience Bertha Sarah Rodney, 1883.	
24885	4790	Grace Marion Rodney, 1887.	
24886	4791	Hester Pearl Rodney, 1888.	
24887	4792	Efah Katherine Rodney, 1894.	
24888	4793	Otto Franz Karl, Count von Bismark-Schierstein [Prussia], 1854. *Schierstein, Hessen-Nassau, Prussia.*	Grandchildren. Children of Charlotte Henrietta Williams-Wynn, 1814–1873, and her husband, Friedrich August Ludwig, Count von Bismark - Schierstein, 1809–1893.
24889	4794	Marie Henriette Katharine, Countess von Bismark, 1848. *Wiesbaden.*	
24890	4795	Helen Auguste Wilhelmine, Countess von Bismark, wife of Wilfred Joseph Cripps, C.B., 1850. *Cripps Mead, Cirencester.*	
24891	4796	The Rev. John Studholme Brownrigg, Canon of Bangor, 1841. 127 *St. George's Road, S.W.*	Grandson. Eldest son of Katharine Williams-Wynn, 1817–1881, 1st wife of Gen. John Studholme Brownrigg, C.B., 1814–1889.
24892	4797	Katharine Laura Verena Studholme, wife of John Matthew Knapp, J.P., 1873. *Linford Hall, Bucks.*	Great-granddaughter. Only child of No. 24891.
24893	4798	Henry Studholme Brownrigg, Colonel *late* Rifle Brigade, 1843	Grandson. Brother to No. 24891.
24894	4799	Henry John Studholme Brownrigg, R.N., 1882.	Great-grandchildren. Children of No. 24893.
24895	4800	Bertha Madeline Alice Studholme Brownrigg, 1885.	
24896	4801	Beatrice Rye Studholme Brownrigg, 1887.	
24897	4802	Metcalfe Studholme Brownrigg, Brigadier-General *late* Oxford Light Infantry, 1845.	Grandson. Youngest brother to No. 24891.
24898	4803	Constance Elizabeth, wife of Charles Dundas Hohler. 26 *Chesham Place, S.W.*	Great-granddaughters. Only surviving children of No. 24897.
24899	4804	Viva Augusta Studholme Brownrigg, 1871.	
24900	4805	Marie Emily Lady Williams-Wynn, widow of Sir Watkin Williams-Wynn, M.P., 6th Bart., 1820–1885, 1827. 20 *St. James' Square, S.W.*	Daughter.
24901 -04	}	Same as Nos. 24793–24796.	Children and grandchildren of No. 24900.

334. Descendants of Charlotte Williams-Wynn, 18 –1819, and her husband, Lieut.-Col. William Shipley, –1819. (See Table LIII.)

24905	4806	Maurice William Glyn Rowley-Conwy, J.P., *late* Captain 4th Battalion Oxfordshire Light Infantry, 1874. *Bodrhyddan, Rhuddlan, Rhyl.*	Great-grandchildren. Children of Conwy Grenville Hercules Rowley-Conwy, of Bodrhyddan, J.P., D.L., 1841–1900, and grandchildren of Charlotte Shipley, 18 –1871, 1st wife of the Hon. Richard Thomas Rowley, 1812–1887.
24906	4807	Rafe Grenville Rowley-Conwy, Lieutenant R.N., 1875.	
24907	4808	Geoffrey Seymour Rowley-Cowny, 1877.	
24908	4809	Ivor Harford Rowley-Conwy, 1884.	
24909	4810	Gwladys Freda, wife of Hugh Edmund Ethelston Peel, J.P., D.L. *Bryn-y-pys, Salop.*	
24910		Same as No. 24814.	Great-great-grandchild. Son of No. 24909.
24911	4811	Gwenydd Frances, wife of Hugh Henry Erskine. *Torquay.*	Granddaughters. Daughters of Charlotte Shipley, 18 – 1871, 1st wife of the Hon. Richard Thomas Rowley, 1812–1887.
24912	4812	Efah Penelope, widow of Admiral Leveson Eliot Henry Somerset, 1829–1900.	

335. Descendants of Henrietta Elizabeth Williams-Wynn, 1787–1852, and her husband, Thomas, 1st Lord Delamere, 1767–1855. (See Table LIII.)

24913	4813	Hugh, 3rd Lord Delamere [U.K.], 1870. *Vale Royal, Northwich.*	Grandson. Only son of Hugh, 2nd Lord Delamere, 1811–1887.
24914	4814	Hon. Thomas Pitt Hamilton Cholmondeley, 1900	Great-grandson. Son of No. 24913.
24915	4815	Hon. Sybil, wife of Algernon Edwyn Burnaby, 1871. *Baggrave Hall, Leicester.*	Granddaughter. Only sister of No. 24913.
24916	4816	Hugh Edwyn Burnaby, 1897.	Great-grandson. Only child of No. 24915.
24917	4817	Hugh Cecil Cholmondeley, *late* Captain 4th Battalion Rifle Brigade, Lieut.-Col. commanding 1st City of London Rifle Volunteer Brigade, 1852. *Edstaston, Wem, Salop.*	Grandson. Eldest son of Colonel the Hon. Thomas Grenville Cholmondeley, 1818–1883.
24918	4818	Cecily Charlotte Cholmondeley, 1886.	Great-grandchild. Child of No. 24917.
24919	4819	Henry Arthur Cholmondeley, 1855.	Grandchildren. Brothers and sisters to No. 24917.
24920	4820	Randel Berners Cholmondeley, 1860.	
24921	4821	Thomas Tatton Reginald Cholmondeley, 1865.	
24922	4822	Beatrice Sarah, wife of Major Francis Hibbert, –1882, 1851.	
24923	4823	Essex Mary, wife of Thomas Egerton Tatton, 1854. *Wythenshawe, Northenden, Cheshire.*	

24924	4824	⋃ Robert Henry Grenville Tatton, 1883.	}	Great-grandchildren.
24925	4825	⋃ Alice Tatton.		Children of No.
24926	4826	⋃ Eva Beatrice Tatton.		24923.
24927	4827	Emily Katherine Cholmondeley, 1861.		
24928	4828	Mildred Henrietta, wife of Edward Lee Townshend, 1868. *Wincham Hall, Knutsford, Cheshire.*		Grandchildren. Younger sisters to No. 24917.
24929	4829	Rev. and Hon. Henry Pitt Cholmondeley, Hon. Canon of Gloucester and Rural Dean of Stow, 1820. *Adlestrop Rectory, near Chipping Norton.*		3rd but only surviving son.
24930 -49	}	Same as Nos. 19659–19678.		Descendants of No. 24929.

336. **Descendants of Elizabeth Bridget Wells,** –1894, 2nd wife of the Rev. Robert Boothby Heathcote, Rector of Chingford, Essex, 1805–1865. (See Table LIV.)

24950	4830	William Edward Heathcote, 1853. *Friday Hill, Chingford.*		
24951	4831	Frederick Granville Sinclair, formerly Heathcote, J.P., D.L., 1857. *Barrogill Castle, Thurso.*	}	Children.
24952	4832	Emily Frances, Lady Cranworth [U.K.], 1850. *5 Portman Square, W.*		
24953	4833	Hon. Bertram Francis Gurdon, 1877.		Grandchildren. Children of No. 24952.
24954	4834	Hon. Muriel Charlotte Gurdon, 1876.		
24955	4835	Louisa Gertrude Heathcote. *Round Coppice, Uxbridge.*	}	Youngest daughter.

337. **Descendants of Hugh, 2nd Earl Fortescue, K.G.,** 1783–1861. (See Table LV.)

24956	4836	Hugh, 3rd Earl Fortescue [G.B.], 1818. *Castle Hill, South Molton.*	}	Elder son.
24957	4837	Hugh, Viscount Ebrington, 1854. *Exmoor, South Molton, Devon.*		Grandson. Eldest son of No. 24956.
24958	4838	Hon. Hugh William Fortescue, 1888.		Great-grandchildren. Children of No. 24957.
24959	4839	Hon. Denzil George Fortescue, 1893.		
24960	4840	Hon. Seymour John Fortescue, *late* Captain R.N., C.V.O., C.M.G., 1856. *St. James' Palace, S.W.*		Grandson. 2nd son of No. 24956.
24961	4841	Grenville Fortescue, 1887.		Great-grandchildren. Children of Captain the Hon. Arthur Grenville Fortescue, 1858–1895.
24962	4842	Joyce Margaret Fortescue, 1892.		

HENRY THE SEVENTH, KING OF ENGLAND AND FRANCE,
LORD OF IRELAND.

THE COMMON ANCESTOR OF NOS. 1-36735.

Painted in 1505 by an unknown Flemish artist. In the National Portrait Gallery.

24963	4843	Hon. John William Fortescue, *late* Major Royal North Devon Yeomanry, 1859. *59A Brook Street, W.*	
24964	4844	Hon. Charles Granville Fortescue, C.M.G., D.S.O., Major and Brevet Lieut.-Col. Rifle Brigade, 1861. *Naval and Military; Travellers'.*	Grandchildren. Children of No. 24956.
24965	4845	Lady Susan Elizabeth Fortescue, 1848.	
24966	4846	Lady Mary Eleanor, wife of George Arthur Bridgeman Bridgeman, formerly Simpson, 1849. *Darrington Hall, Pontefract.*	
24967	4847	Lady Lucy Charlotte, wife of the Right Hon. Sir Michael Hicks-Beach, P.C., M.P., 9th Bart., 1851. *Coln St. Aldwyns, Fairford.*	
24968	4848	Michael Hugh Hicks-Beach, Lieutenant 4th Battalion Gloucestershire Regiment, 1877.	Great-grandchildren. Children of No. 24967.
24969	4849	Eleanor Lucy Hicks-Beach, 1875.	
24970	4850	Susan Evelyn Hicks-Beach, 1878.	
24971	4851	Victoria Alexandrina Hicks-Beach, 1879.	
24972	4852	Lady Georgiana Seymour, wife of Lord Ernest Seymour, 1852. *The Birches, Hagley, Stourbridge.*	Granddaughter. 4th daughter of No. 24956.
24973	4853	Francis Ernest Seymour, Lieutenant R.N., 1878.	
24974	4854	Reginald Guy Seymour, 1880.	Great-grandchildren. Children of No. 24972.
24975	4855	Arthur George Seymour, 1884.	
24976	4856	Ruth Seymour, 1881.	
24977	4857	Eleanor Alice Seymour, 1883.	
24978	4858	Constance Emily Mary Seymour, 1887.	
24979	4859	Lady Frances Blanche, wife of Archibald Hay Gordon-Duff, 1865. *Ebrington, Chipping Campden, Gloucestershire.*	Granddaughter. 7th but 5th surviving daughter of No. 24956.
24980	4860	John Beauchamp Gordon-Duff, 1899.	Great-grandchildren. Children of No. 24979.
24981	4861	Helen Alice Gordon-Duff, 1897.	
24982	4862	Hon. Dudley Francis Fortescue, 1820. *9 Hertford Street, W.*	Youngest surviving son.

338. Descendants of the Hon. George Matthew Fortescue, of Boconnoc, Cornwall, and Dropmore, Bucks, 1791–1877. (See Table LV.)

24983	4863	John Bevill Fortescue, J.P., 1850. *Boconnoc, Cornwall.* *48 Berkeley Square, W.*	Eldest surviving son.
24984	4864	George Grenville Fortescue, 1892.	Grandsons. Sons of No. 24983.
24985	4865	John Grenville Fortescue, 1896.	
24986	4866	Anne Constance Louisa, widow of Captain W. G. Wyld, Hampshire Regiment, 1864.	Granddaughter. Only child of Louisa Susan Anne Fortescue, 1833–1864, 1st wife of William Westby Moore, of Higham, Hants, 1826–

24987	4867	Harriet Eleanor, Lady Phillimore, widow of Admiral Sir Augustus Phillimore, K.C.B., 1836. *Shedfield House, Botley, Hants.*	2nd and eldest surviving daughter.
24988	4868	Richard Fortescue Phillimore, Commander R..N., 1864.	Grandsons. Elder sons of No. 24987.
24989	4869	George Grenville Phillimore, 1867. 6 *Culford Gardens, S.W.* 1 *Mitre Court Buildings, Temple.*	
24990	4870	Henry Augustus Grenville Phillimore, 1894.	Great-grandchildren. Children of No. 24989.
24991	4871	Matthew Arden Phillimore, 1896.	
24992	4872	Hester Mary Melba Phillimore, 1900.	
24993	4873	Charles Augustus Phillimore, 1871. *Oxford and Cambridge.*	Grandchildren. Children of No. 24987.
24994	4874	John Swinnerton Phillimore, Professor of Greek, Glasgow University, 1873. 5 *The College, Glasgow.*	
24995	4875	Cynthia Mary Louisa Phillimore, 1901.	Great-grandchild. Daughter of No. 24994.
24996	4876	Valentine Egerton Bagot Phillimore, Lieutenant R.N., D.S.O., 1875.	Grandchildren. Children of No. 24987.
24997	4877	Rev. Edward Granville Phillimore, 1876. *St. Deney's, Southampton.*	
24998	4878	Violet Elizabeth Annie, wife of John E. A. Willis-Fleming, 1869. *Chilworth Manor, North Stoneham Park, Hants.*	
24999	4879	John Baynes Phillimore Willis-Fleming, 1895.	Great-grandchildren. Children of No. 24998.
25000	4880	Richard Thomas Cyril Willis-Fleming, 1896.	
25001	4881	Ida Harriet Willis-Fleming, 1894.	
25002	4882	Elizabeth Katherine Willis-Fleming, 1899.	
25003	4883	Mary, wife of the Rev. Vernon Harcourt Aldham, Hon. Canon of Truro, 1840. *Braddock Rectory. Lostwithiel, Cornwall.*	Daughters.
25004	4884	Elizabeth Frances Fortescue, 1843. *Chilworth Tower, Romsey, Hants.*	

339. Descendants of the Rev. and Hon. John Fortescue, Canon of Worcester, 1796–1869. (See Table LV.)

25005	4885	Rev. Hugh John Fortescue, 1844. *The Rectory, Honiton, Devon.*	Children.
25006	4886	Hester Emily, wife of the Ven. Albert Eden Seymour, Archdeacon of Barnstaple, 1843. *Chittlehampton Vicarage, Devon.*	
25007	4887	Rev. Richard Seymour, 1877.	Grandchildren. Children of No. 25006.
25008	4888	Hugh Seymour, Lieutenant R.N., 1879.	
25009	4889	Michael Richard Seymour, 1880.	
25010	4890	Edward Albert Seymour, 1884.	
25011	4891	Algernon Giles Seymour, 1886	
25012	4892	Arthur Seymour, 1888.	
25013	4893	Eleanor Frances Seymour.	
25014	4894	Hester Sophia Seymour.	
25015	4895	Alice Mary Seymour.	

25016	4896	Sophia Elizabeth, wife of the Rev. Leigh Thomas Rendell, 1846. *Timsbury Rectory, Bath.*	Daughter.
25017	4897	Mary Emily Rendell, 1880.	Grandchildren. Children of No. 25016.
25018	4898	Edith Sophia Rendell, 1881.	
25019	4899	Eleanor Fortescue, 1847. *The Rectory, Honiton, Devon.*	Daughter.

340. Descendants of William, 1st Earl of Lovelace, 1805–1893. (See Table LV.)

25020	4900	Ralph Gordon Noel, 2nd Earl of Lovelace [U.K.], 9th Baron King and Oakham [G.B.], 13th Baron Wentworth [E.], 1839. *Ockham Park, Ripley.* *Wentworth House, Chelsea Embankment, S.W.*	Son.
25021	4901	Lady Ada Mary Milbanke, 1871.	Granddaughter. Daughter. of No. 25020.
25022	4902	Hon. Lionel Fortescue King-Noel, 1865. *Horsley Towers, Leatherhead.*	Younger son.
25023	4903	Evelyn Catherine King, 1896.	Grandchildren. Children of No. 25022.
25024	4904	Phyllis Edith King, 1897.	
25025	4905	Rosemary Diana King, 1902.	
25026	4906	Lady Anne Isabella, wife of Wilfrid Scawen Blunt, 1837. *Crabbet Park, Three Bridges, Sussex.*	Daughter.
25027	4907	Judith Anne Dorothea, wife of the Hon. Neville Stephen Bulwer Lytton. *Rake Mill, Milford, Surrey.*	Granddaughter. Only child of No. 25026.
25028	4908	Noel Anthony Scawen Bulwer Lytton, 1900.	Great-grandchildren. Son and daughter of No. 25027.
25029	4909	Anne Bulwer Lytton, 1901.	

341. Descendants of the Hon. Peter John Locke King, M.P., 1811–1885. (See Table LV.)

25030	4910	Hugh Fortescue Locke King, J.P., 1848. *Brooklands, Weybridge.* *4 Mount Street, W.*	Surviving children.
25031	4911	Hester Fortescue King, 1837.	Shere Lodge, Guildford; 16 Gloucester Place, W.
25032	4912	Anna Clementina King, 1846.	
25033	4913	Eleanor Elizabeth King, 1850.	

342. Descendants of the Hon. Hester King, 1806–1848, 1st wife of the Rev. Sir George William Craufurd, 3rd Bart., 1797–1881. (See Table LV.)

| 25034 | 4914 | Sir Charles William Frederick Craufurd, 4th Bart., 1847. *10 Warwick Square, S.W.* | Son. |

25035	4915	George Standish Gage Craufurd, Captain Gordon Highlanders, D.S.O., 1872.	
25036	4916	Quentin Charles Alexander Craufurd, Lieutenant R.N., 1875.	
25037	4917	Alexander John Fortescue Craufurd, 1876.	Grandchildren.
25038	4918	Charles Edward Vereker Craufurd, R.N., 1885.	Children of
25039	4919	Hester Jane Laline Craufurd.	No. 25034.
25040	4920	Laline Isolda Craufurd.	
25041	4921	Isolda Mabel Cecil Craufurd	
25042	4922	Eleanor Mary Dorothea Craufurd.	
25043	4923	Margaret Elizabeth Maria Craufurd.	

343. Descendants of the Hon. Charlotte Louisa King, 1814–1863, wife of the Rev. Demetrius Panaglis Calliphronas, Rector of Walpole St. Andrew, Norfolk, and afterwards of Melton, Woodbridge, Suffolk, 1803–1895. (See Table LV.)

25044	4924	Rev. Theodore Calliphronas, 1846. *The Rectory, Nedging, Ipswich.*	Eldest son.
25045	4925	Constantine Calliphronas, 1877.	
25046	4926	Irene Chariclea Dora Calliphronas.	Grandchildren. Children
25047	4927	Dora Calliphronas.	of No. 25044.
25048	4928	Helen Mary Calliphronas.	
25049	4929	Christine Athene Calliphronas.	
25050	4930	Cyril Locke Calliphronas Locke, 1848. *St. Neots, Eversley, Winchfield.*	2nd son.
25051	4931	Ivo King Hervey Locke, 1882.	Grandchildren. Children
25052	4932	Lilah Theodora Hervey Locke, 1887.	of No. 25050.
25053	4933	George Constantine Calliphronas, 1852.	
25054	4934	Louisa Iréné Hester, widow of the Rev. Charles Cecil Sumner.	Children
25055	4935	Piers Sumner, 1877.	
25056	4936	Chawney Hugh Sumner, 1881.	Grandchildren. Children
25057	4937	Charlotte Iréné King Sumner.	of No. 25054.

344. Descendants of Lady Catherine Fortescue, 1786–1854, 2nd wife of Newton, 4th Earl of Portsmouth, 1772–1854. (See Table LV.)

25058 –78		Same as Nos. 24423–24443.	Descendants of Isaac Newton, 5th Earl of Portsmouth, 1825–1891.
25079	4938	Henry Seymour Allen, J.P., 1847. *Cresselly House, co. Pembroke.*	Grandchildren. Children of the Lady Catherine Fellowes, 1821–1900,
25080	4939	Frederick Seymour Allen, Colonel commanding 5th Regimental District, 1849. *Cliddesden Rectory, Basingstoke.*	by her husband, Seymour Phillips Allen, of Cresselly, J.P., 1814–1861.
25081	4940	Catherine Seymour Allen, 1897.	Great-grandchild. Child of No. 25080.

25082	4941	Frances Seymour Allen, Lieut.-Col. 2nd Battalion Worcester Regiment, 1853. *74 Redcliffe Gardens, S.W.*	Grandchildren. Brothers of No. 25080.
25083	4942	Rev. John Seymour Allen, 1855. *Cliddesden Rectory, Basingstoke, Hants.*	
25084	4943	Newton Seymour Allen, Lieut.-Col. South Stafford Regiment. *Cliddesden Rectory, Basingstoke.*	
25085	4944	Ralph Leeke, J.P., Colonel *late* Grenadier Guards, 1849. *Longford Hall, near Newport, Salop.*	Grandson. Elder son of the Lady Hester Urania Fellowes, 1822-1887, and her husband, Ralph Merrick Leeke, of Longford, 1813-1882.
25086	4945	Ralph Henry Leeke, 1883.	Great-grandsons. Sons of No. 25085.
25087	4946	Charles Leeke, 1887.	
25088	4947	Rev. Thomas Newton Leeke, 1854. *Bideford Rectory, North Devon.*	Grandson. 2nd brother of No. 25085.
25089	4948	Edwin Hugh Leeke, 1884.	Great-grandchildren. Children of No. 25088.
25090	4949	Walter Henry Leeke, 1885.	
25091	4950	Mary Eleanor Leeke, 1887.	
25092	4951	Hester Marion Leeke, 1893.	
25093	4952	Margaret Leeke, 1896.	
25094	4953	Rev. William Leeke, Vicar of The Abbey, Shrewsbury, 1862. *Shrewsbury.*	Grandchild. 3rd brother of No. 25085.
25095	4954	Honor Frances Leeke, 1894.	Great-grandchild. Daughter of No. 25094.
25096	4955	Hester Catherine Leeke.	Grandchildren. Sisters to No. 25085.
25097	4956	Charlotte Urania, wife of the Rev. William Booth Corfield. *Llangattoc Rectory, Abergavenny.*	
25098	4957	Emily Dorothy Leeke.	
25099	4958	Eveline Frances Leeke.	
25100	4959	Caroline Louisa, widow of the Rev. Henry Mather.	
25101	4960	Harry Ralph Mather.	Great-grandchildren. Children of No. 25100.
25102	4961	George Rupert Mather.	
25103	4962	Lady Camilla Eleanor, wife of the Hon. Dudley Fortescue, 1830. *9 Hertford Street, W.*	Daughter.

345. Descendants of Lady Anne Fortescue, 1787-1864, and her husband, George Wilbraham, Esq., of Delamere, M.P., 1779-1852. (See Table LV.)

25104	4963	Hugh Edward Wilbraham, J.P., 1857. *Delamere House, Northwich.*	Grandson. Son of Roger William Wilbraham, of Delamere, 1817-1897.
25105	4964	George Hugh de Vernon Wilbraham, 1890.	Great-grandchildren. Children of No. 25104.
25106	4965	Ralph Venables Wilbraham.	
25107	4966	Vere May Wilbraham.	
25108	4967	Rhoda Joan Wilbraham.	
25109	4968	Barbara Francesca Wilbraham.	

25110	4969	Herbert Vere Wilbraham, Captain Shropshire Light Infantry, 1858.	
25111	4970	Henry Dudley Wilbraham, 1862.	Grandchildren.
25112	4971	Frederick William Wilbraham, 1864.	Brothers and
25113	4972	William Robartes Wilbraham, 1871.	sisters of No.
25114	4973	Alice Mary Wilbraham.	25104.
25115	4974	Beatrice Augusta Wilbraham.	
25116	4975	Ada Louisa Wilbraham.	
25117	4976	Ralph James Wilbraham, Major Duke of Cornwall's Light Infantry, 1858.	Grandchildren. Children of Colonel Thomas
25118	4977	Edward Sydney Wilbraham, 1860.	Edward Wilbraham,
25119	4978	Henry George Wilbraham, 1863.	1820–1884.
25120	4979	Mary Catherine Wilbraham.	
25121	4980	Donald Fortescue Wilbraham, 1865.	
25122	4981	Cecil Grenville Wilbraham, 1866.	Grandchildren. Children
25123	4982	Roger Wilbraham, 1871.	of Henry Wilbraham,
25124	4983	Charles Thackeray Wilbraham, 1875.	1825–1883.
25125	4984	Maurice Wilbraham, 1878.	
25126	4985	Hester Mary Wilbraham.	
25127	4986	Bernard Hugh Wilbraham, 1880.	Grandchildren. Children
25128	4987	Augusta Julia Wilbraham.	of Hugh Wilbraham,
25129	4988	Ethnea Catherine Wilbraham.	1827–1890.

345. Descendants of Susan Hester Hamlyn Williams, 1825–1869, and her husband, Henry Edward Fane, afterwards Hamlyn-Fane, of Clovelly Court, Devon, M.P., 1817–1868. (See Table LV.)

25130	4989	Marion Elizabeth, wife of Sir William Lewis Stucley, 2nd Bart., 1851. *Affeton Castle, West Worlington, Devon.*	
25131	4990	Eveline Harriet Hamlyn-Fane, 1854. 65 *Cadogan Gardens, S.W.*	
25132	4991	Christine Louisa, wife of Frederick Hamlyn, formerly Gosling, 1855. *Clovelly Court, North Devon.*	Daughters.
25133	4992	Constance Edwina, Lady Manners [U.K.], 1861. 18 *New Cavendish, S.W.*	
25134	4993	Hon. John Nevile Manners, 1892.	
25135	4994	Hon. Francis Henry Manners, 1897.	Grandchildren. Children
25136	4995	Hon. Mary Christine Manners, 1886.	of No. 25133.
25137	4996	Hon. Betty Constance Manners, 1889.	
25138	4997	Hon. Angela Margaret Manners, 1889.	

346. Descendants of Mary Eleanor Hamlyn Williams, 1826–1872, and her husband, Sir James Walker Drummond, afterwards Williams-Drummond, 3rd Bart., 1814–1866. (See Table LV.)

| 25139 | 4998 | Sir James Hamlyn Williams Williams-Drummond, 4th Bart., 1857. *Edwinsford, Llandilo, Carmarthenshire. Hawthornden, Midlothian.* | Son. |
| 25140 | 4999 | James Hamlyn Williams Williams-Drummond, 1891. | Grandson. Son of No. 25139. |

25141	5000	Hugh Henry John Williams-Drummond, Captain Royal North Devon Y.C., 1859.	Children
25142	5001	Frances Dudley Williams-Drummond, J.P., 1863. *Portiscliff, Ferryside, South Wales.*	
25143	5002	William Hugh Dudley Williams-Drummond, 1901.	Grandchildren. Children of No. 25142.
25144	5003	Eleanor Mary Williams-Drummond, 1891.	
25145	5004	Constance Marie Katherine Williams-Drummond, 1893.	
25146	5005	Annabella Mary, wife of the Rev. Thomas Newton Leeke. *Bideford Rectory, North Devon.*	Daughter.
25147 –51	}	Same as Nos. 25089–25093. {	Grandchildren. Children of No. 25146

347. Descendants of Lady Elizabeth Fortescue, 1801–1867, and her husband, Reginald, 11th Earl of Devon, 1807–1888. (See Table LV.)

25152	5006	Agnes Elizabeth, Viscountess Halifax [U.K.], 1838. *Hickleton Hall, Doncaster.* *79 Eaton Square, S.W.*	Daughter.
25153	5007	Hon. Edward Frederick Lindley Wood, 1881.	Grandchildren. Children of No. 25152.
25154	5008	Hon. Alexandra Mary Elizabeth, wife of Captain Hugh Clement Sutton, Coldstream Guards, 1871.	
25155	5009	Margaret Agnes Sutton, 1899. {	Great-grandchild. Child of No. 25154.
25156	5010	Hon. Mary Agnes Emily Wood, 1877. {	Granddaughter. Younger daughter of No. 25152.

348. Descendants of Richard, 3rd Lord Braybrooke, 1783–1858. (See Table LVI.)

25157	5011	Hon. Augusta, wife of the Hon. Richard Strutt, 1860. *Rayleigh House, 2 Chelsea Embankment, S.W.*	Grandchild. Only child of Charles Cornwallis, 5th Lord Braybrooke, 1823–1902.
25158	5012	Richard Neville Strutt, 1886.	Great-grandchildren. Children of No. 25157.
25159	5013	Geoffrey St. John Strutt, 1888.	
25160	5014	Olivia Maud Strutt, 1890.	
25161	5015	Latimer, 6th Baron Braybrooke [G.B.], Master of Magdalene College, Cambridge, Rural Dean and Hon. Canon of St. Albans, 1827. *Magdalene College, Cambridge.* *Heydon Rectory, Royston.*	Son.
25162	5016	Hon. Henry Neville, J.P., D.L., 1855. *Royston, Herts.*	Grandchildren. Sons of No. 25161.
25163	5017	Rev. and Hon. Grey Neville, 1857. *Waltham St. Lawrence Vicarage, Twyford.*	
25164	5018	Henry Seymour Neville, 1897.	Great-grandchildren. Children of No 25163.
25165	5019	Grey Aldworth Neville, 1900.	
25166	5020	Magdalene Grace Neville, 1890.	
25167	5021	Evelyn Neville, 1891.	
25168	5022	Mirabel Mary Neville, 1893.	
25169	5023	Audrey Neville, 1895.	
25170	5024	Cicely Neville, 1898.	

25171	5025	Hon. Alice Mirabel Cornwallis Neville, 1869.	Grandchild. Daughter of No. 25161.
25172	5026	Constance, wife of the Rev. Alfred Hobart-Hampden. *Langley Vicarage, Bishop's Stortford.*	Granddaughter. Only surviving child of the Hon. Louisa Anne Neville, 1822–1889, and her husband, Sir Henry M. Vavasour, 3rd Bart.
25173	5027	Hon. Lucy Georgina, widow of the Rev. and Hon. Arthur Savile, 1819–1870, 1828. *Heydon House, Royston.*	Daughter.
25174	5028	Arthur Cornwallis Savile, 1865. 79 *Davies Street, W.* *Travellers'.*	
25175	5029	Latimer Savile, 1868. *Isthmian.*	Grandchildren. Children of No. 25173.
25176	5030	Elizabeth Jane Savile, 1853.	
25177	5031	Mirabel Anne, wife of William Marsland Francis Schneider. 1 *Sydney Terrace, Ryde, S.W.*	
25178	5032	Ulrica Schneider, 1878.	Great-grandchildren. Children of No. 25177.
25179	5033	Ione Schneider, 1885.	
25180	5034	Alethea Savile, 1856.	
25181	5035	Georgina Lucy Savile, 1859.	
25182	5036	Vere Philippa, wife of William Blackburn, Barrister-at-Law, 1861. *Roshven, Lochailort, Fort William.*	Grandchildren. Children of No. 25173.
25183	5037	Blanche Audley Savile, 1862.	
25184	5038	Florence Augusta Savile, 1863.	
25185	5039	Octavia Louisa Savile, 1864.	

349. Descendants of the Very Rev. and Hon. George Neville Grenville, of Butleigh Court, Somerset, Master of Magdalene College, Cambridge, Dean of Windsor, 1789–1854. (See Table LVI.)

25186	5040	Robert Neville Grenville, J.P., D.L., 1846. *Butleigh Court, Somerset.*	Grandsons. Sons of Ralph Neville Grenville, M.P., 1817–1886.
25187	5041	George Neville, Captain R.N., M.V.O., 1850. *United Service ; Naval and Military.*	
25188	5042	Ralph Neville, 1887.	Great-grandsons. Children of No. 25187.
25189	5043	Philip Lloyd Neville, 1888.	
25190	5044	Alfred Geoffrey Neville, 1891.	
25191	5045	Hugh Neville, Barrister-at-Law, 1851. 1 *Essex Court, Temple, E.C.*	Grandsons. Brothers to No. 25186.
25192	5046	Louis Neville, 1852.	
25193	5047	Bertram Neville, 1880.	Great-grandchildren. Children of No. 25192.
25194	5048	Margaret Neville, 1881	
25195	5049	Claud Neville, 1858.	Grandchildren. Brothers and elder sister to No. 25186.
25196	5050	Percy Neville, 1868.	
25197	5051	Agnes Magdalene, wife of William James Maitland, C.I.E., 1848. 18 *Lennox Gardens, S.W.*	

The Blood Royal of Britain

25198	5052	Marjorie Maitland, 1884.	Great-grandchild. Daughter of No. 25197.
25199	5053	Beatrice Neville, 1853.	Grandchildren. Sisters to No. 25186.
25200	5054	Etheldreda, wife of Rear-Admiral Robert Wilbraham Stopford, 1856. *Shroton House, Blandford.*	
25201 -02		Same as Nos. 20872–20873.	Great-grandchildren. Children of No. 25200.
25203	5055	Rev. William Neville, 1850. *St. Mary's Rectory, Reading.*	Grandchildren. Children of the Rev. William Frederick Neville, 1818–1882.
25204	5056	Mary, wife of the Ven. Frederick Augustus Brymer, Archdeacon of Wells, 1847. *Charlton Mackrell Rectory, Somerton.*	
25205	5057	Wilfred John Brymer, 1883.	Great-grandchildren. Children of No. 25204.
25206	5058	Constance Mary Brymer, 1885.	
25207	5059	Constance, wife of Lieut.-Col. Sir Arthur John Bigge, G.C.V.O., K.C.B., K.C.M.G., *late* Equerry and Private Secretary to Queen Victoria, 1849. *Colour Court, St. James's Palace.*	Grandchild. Sister to No. 25203.
25208	5060	John Neville Bigge, 1887.	Great-grandchildren. Children of No. 25207.
25209	5061	Victoria Eugénie Bigge, 1881.	
25210	5062	Margaret Bigge, 1885.	
25211	5063	Grace Neville, 1853. 22 *Wilton Place, S.W.*	Grandchild. Younger sister to No. 25204.
25212	5064	Rev. Seymour Neville, *late* Rector of Ockham, 1823.	Children.
25213	5065	Edward Neville, Lieut.-Col. *late* Scots Fusilier Guards. *Thurgoland, Sheffield.*	
25214	5066	Francis Catherine, widow of the Rev. Edmund Peel, 1817–1877, 1820. *Coombe Lodge, Bruton, Somerset.*	
25215	5067	George Neville Peel, 1854. 26 *Elm Park Gardens, S.W.*	Grandchild. Son of No. 25214.
25216	5068	Vyvyan Neville Peel, 1892.	Great-grandchildren. Children of No. 25215.
25217	5069	Phyllis Eveline Neville Peel, 1895.	
25218	5070	Harriet Louisa, wife of the Rev. Charles Arundell St.-John-Mildmay, 1828. *Hazlegrove, Somerset.* 72 *Chester Square, S.W.*	Younger daughter.
25219	5071	Wyndham Paulet St.-John-Mildmay, 1855. *Wales House, Queen Camel, Bath.*	
25220	5072	George St.-John-Mildmay, Barrister-at-Law, 1856. 16 *Bolton Street, Piccadilly.* *Rand Club, Johannesburg.*	Grandsons. Sons of No. 25218.
25221	5073	Rev. Arundell Glastonbury St.-John-Mildmay, Rural Dean of Burnham, 1859. *Old Wolverton Vicarage, Bucks.*	
25222	5074	Bouverie Walter St.-John-Mildmay, 1899.	Great-grandchild. Son of No. 25221.
25223	5075	Walter Hervey St.-John-Mildmay, Captain Assam Valley Light Horse, 1860. *Luckwah, Nazira, Assam.*	
25224	5076	Paulet Bertram St.-John-Mildmay, 1862. *Eden Lodge, Tilford, Surrey.*	Grandchildren. Children of No. 25218.
25225	5077	Aubrey Neville St.-John-Mildmay, 1865. *New Oxford and Cambridge.*	
25226	5078	Isabel Emily, wife of Gerald Anthony Shaw-Lefevre-St.-John-Mildmay. *Trewsbury, Cirencester.*	

25227	5079	Anthony Shaw-Lefevre-St.-John-Mildmay, 1894.	}	Great-grandchildren. Children of No. 25226.
25228	5080	Helena Shaw-Lefevre-St.-John-Mildmay, 1897.	}	
25229	5081	Meriel Harriet Caroline St.-John-Mildmay.	}	Grandchild. Younger daughter of No. 25218.

350. Descendants of the Rev. Henry Glynne, 1812–1872. (See Table LVI.)

| 25230 -41 | } | Same as Nos. 22086–22097. |

351. Descendants of Catherine Glynne, 1812–1900, wife of the Right Hon. William Ewart Gladstone, M.P., P.C., &c., 1809–1898. (See Table LVI.)

25242 -44		Same as Nos. 22308–22310.	{	Grandchildren. Children of William Henry Gladstone, of Hawarden, M.P., 1840–1891.
25245	5082	The Rev. Stephen Edward Gladstone, 1844. *Hawarden Rectory, Chester.*	}	Eldest surviving son.
25246	5083	Albert Charles Gladstone, 1886.		
25247	5084	Charles Andrew Gladstone, 1888.		
25248	5085	Stephen Deiniol Gladstone, 1891.		Grandchildren. Children of No. 25245.
25249	5086	William Herbert Gladstone, 1898.		
25250	5087	Catherine Gladstone.		
25251	5088	Edith Gladstone.		
25252	5089	Henry Neville Gladstone, 1852. *4 Whitehall Court, S.W.*		Sons.
25253	5090	Right Hon. Herbert John Gladstone, M.P., P.C., 1854. *2 Cowley Street, Westminster.*		
25254	5091	Agnes, wife of the Very Rev. Edward Charles Wickham, D.D., Dean of Lincoln. *The Deanery, Lincoln.*	}	Daughter.
25255	5092	William Gladstone Wickham, 1877.		
25256	5093	Edward Stephen Wickham, 1882.		Grandchildren. Children of No. 25254.
25257	5094	Catherine Mary Lavinia Wickham.		
25258	5095	Lucy Christian Wickham.		
25259	5096	Margaret Agnes Wickham.		
25260	5097	Mary, wife of the Rev. Harry Drew. *Buckley Vicarage, Chester.*	}	2nd surviving daughter.
25261	5098	Dorothy Mary Catherine Drew, 1890.	{	Grandchild. Child of No. 25260.
25262	5099	Helen Gladstone, formerly Vice-Principal of Newnham College, Cambridge. *Hawarden Castle, Flintshire.*	}	Youngest surviving daughter.

352. Descendants of Mary Glynne, 1813–1857, wife of George William, 4th Lord Lyttelton, 1817–1876. (See Table LVI.)

| 25263 -317 | } | Same as Nos. 22031–22085. |

353. Descendants of the Hon. Caroline Neville, 1792–1868, and her husband, Paul Beilby, 1st Lord Wenlock, 1784–1852. (See Table LVI.)

25318	5100	Beilby, 3rd Lord Wenlock [U.K.], 1849, P.C., G.C.S.I., G.C.I.E., K.C.B. 26 *Portland Place, W.*	Grandson. Eldest son of Beilby Richard, 2nd Lord Wenlock, 1818–1880.
25319	5101	Same as No. 21859.	Great-grandchild. Daughter of No. 25318.
25320	5102	Hon. Richard Thompson Lawley, Lieut.-Col. 7th Hussars, C.B., 1856. *Turf; Army and Navy.*	
25321	5103	Rev. and Hon. Algernon George Lawley. *The Rectory, Hackney, N.E.*	Grandsons. Brothers of No. 25318.
25322	5104	Hon. Sir Arthur Lawley, *late* Captain 10th Hussars, K.C.M.G., 1860. *Pretoria.*	
25323	5105	Richard Edward Lawley, 1887.	Great-grandchildren.
25324	5106	Ursula Mary Lawley, 1888.	Children of No.
25325	5107	Margaret Cecilia Lawley, 1889.	25322.
25326	5108	Hon. Robert Lawley, 1863. 3 *Down Street, W.*	Grandson. Brother of No. 25318.
25327	5109	Hon. Caroline Elizabeth, wife of the Hon. Caryl Craven Molyneux, 1848. *The Red House, Bodicote, Banbury.*	Granddaughter. Sister to No. 25318.
25328	5110	Caryl Richard Molyneux, *late* Lieutenant 10th Hussars, 1871.	Grandchild. Son of No. 25327.
25329	5111	Hon. Alethea Jane, wife of the Nobile Cavaliere Professore Taddeo Wiel, formerly of the Marciana Library, Venice. *Palazzo Soranzo, San Polo, Venice.*	Granddaughters. Sisters to No. 25318.
25330	5112	Hon. Constance Mary, wife of the Hon. Edward William Berkeley Portman, 1854. 33 *Great Cumberland Place, S.W.*	
25331	5113	Ivo Richard Vesey, Lieutenant Irish Guards, 1881.	Great-grandchildren. Children of No. 25330 by her 1st husband, Captain the Hon. Eustace Vesey, 1851–1886.
25332	5114	Osbert Eustace Vesey, 1884.	
25333	5115	Thomas Eustace Vesey, 1885.	
25334	5116	Hon. Katherine, wife of Walter Forbes, 1859. 64 *Belgrave Road, S.W.*	Granddaughter. Youngest sister to No. 25318.
25335	5117	Rev. and Hon. Stephen Willoughby Lawley. *Spurfield, Exminster, Exeter.*	Only surviving child.
25336	5118	Archibald John Stuart-Wortley, 1849. *Turf; Marlborough; Carlton.*	Grandchildren. Children of the Hon. Jane Lawley, 1820–1900, and her husband, the Right Hon. James Stuart-Wortley, P.C., M.P., Q.C., 1805–1881.
25337	5119	Right Hon. Charles Beilby Stuart-Wortley, P.C., M.P. 7 *Cheyne Walk, Chelsea, S.W.*	
25338	5120	Beatrice Susan Theodosia Stuart-Wortley, 1881.	Great-grandchildren Children of No. 25337.
25339	5121	Clare Euphemia Stuart-Wortley, 1889.	

25340	5122	Mary Caroline, Countess of Lovelace [U.K.], Baroness King and Oakham [G.B.], Baroness Wentworth [E.], 1848. *Oakham Park, Ripley. Wentworth House, Chelsea Embankment, S.W.*	
25341	5123	Margaret Jane, wife of Major-General the Hon. Sir Reginald Arthur James Chetwynd Talbot, K.C.B. *12 Manchester Square, W.*	Granddaughters. Sisters to No. 25336.
25342	5124	Blanche Georgiana, wife of Colonel Frederick Firebrace, R.E., 1856. *28 Old Queen Street, Westminster, S.W.*	
25343	5125	Caroline Susan Theodora, widow of the Hon. Norman de l'Aigle Grosvenor, 1845–1898, 1858. *30 Upper Grosvenor Street, S.W.*	
25344	5126	Susan Charlotte Grosvenor, 1882.	Great-granddaughters. Daughters of No. 25343.
25345	5127	Margaret Sophie Katherine Grosvenor, 1886.	
25346	5128	Katherine Sarah, wife of Lieut.-Gen. the Hon. Sir Neville Gerald Lyttelton, K.C.B., 1860. *28 Grosvenor Road, S.W. Pretoria.*	Granddaughter. Youngest sister to No. 25336.
25347 –49	}	Same as Nos. 22045–22047.	Great-grandchildren. Children of No. 25346.

354. Descendants of John Henry, 5th Duke of Rutland, K.G., 1778–1857. (See Table LVII.)

25350	5129	John James Robert, 7th Duke of Rutland [E.], 1st Baron Roos of Belvoir [U.K.], K.G., G.C.B., P.C., 1818. *3 Cambridge Gate, Regent's Park, N.W. Belvoir Castle, Grantham.*	Son.
25351	5130	Henry John Brinsley, Marquis of Granby, 1852. *16 Arlington Street, S.W.*	Grandson. Son of No. 25350.
25352	5131	John Henry Montagu, Lord Roos of Belvoir, 1886.	Great-grandchildren. Children of No. 25351.
25353	5132	Lady Victoria Marjorie Harriet Manners, 1883.	
25354	5133	Lady Violet Katherine Manners, 1888.	
25355	5134	Lady Diana Olivia Winifred Maud Manners, 1892.	
25356	5135	Lord Cecil Reginald John Manners, M.P., 1868. *Wellington ; Bachelors'.*	Grandchildren. Children of No. 25350.
25357	5136	Lord Robert William Orlando Manners, Captain 1st Battalion King's Royal Rifle Corps, D.S.O., 1870.	
25358	5137	Lady Victoria Alexandrina Elizabeth Dorothy Manners, 1876.	
25359	5138	Lady Elizabeth Emily Manners, 1878.	
25360	5139	Charles George Edmund John Manners, *late* Captain Grenadier Guards, 1858. *Guards' ; White's ; Wellington.*	Grandchildren. Children of Colonel Lord George John Manners, M.P., 1820–1874.
25361	5140	George Espec John Manners, J.P., *late* Captain and Hon. Major 2nd Battalion Leicestershire Regiment, 1860. *Fornham Park, Bury St. Edmunds.*	
25362	5141	Cecily Elizabeth Adeliza Manners, 1856.	

25363	5142	Andrew John Drummond, 1823.	Grandson. Son of the Lady Elizabeth Frederica Manners, 1801–1886, and her husband, Andrew Robert Drummond, of Cadland, 1794–1865.
25364	5143	Andrew Cecil Drummond, J.P., D.L. *Cadland, Southampton.* *8 Princes Gardens, W.*	
25365	5144	Maldwin Drummond, *late* Lieutenant 7th Battalion King's Royal Rifle Corps, 1872. *4 Down Street, W.*	Great-grandchildren. Children of Edgar Atheling Drummond, of Cadland, J.P., D.L., 1826–1893, brother to No. 25363.
25366	5145	Cyril Augustus Drummond, *late* Lieutenant 3rd Battalion Northumberland Fusiliers, 1873.	
25367	5146	Lilias Elizabeth, widow of the Rev. Robert Manners Norman, 1854–1895, 1859.	
25368	5147	Edith Mary Frances Drummond, 1861.	
25369	5148	Winifred Louisa, wife of John Allan Maconochie Welwood, 1869. *Meadowbank, Kirknewton, N.B.*	
25370	5149	Laurence Robert Welwood, 1902.	Great-great-grandchildren. Children of No. 25369.
25371	5150	Cynthia Louisa Winifred Welwood, 1900.	
25372	5151	Constance Louisa, wife of Francis Algernon Fulford, J.P., 1870. *Great Fulford, Dunsford.*	Great-grandchild. Sister to No. 25364, &c.
25373	5152	Francis Edgar Anthony Fulford, 1898.	Great-great-grandsons. Sons of No. 25372.
25374	5153	Humphrey Pennington Fulford, 1902.	
25375	5154	Mary Louisa, wife of Captain Edward John Russell Peel, 1876.	Great-grandchildren. Sisters to No. 25364, &c.
25376	5155	Jean Cicely Drummond, 1877.	
25377	5156	Alfred Manners Drummond, *late* Captain Rifle Brigade, 1829. *54 Fitzjohn's Avenue, N.W.*	
25378	5157	Victor Arthur Wellington Drummond, C.B., Minister to the Courts of Bavaria and Würtemberg, 1833. *British Legation, Munich.*	Grandchildren. Brothers to No. 25363.
25379	5158	Cecil George Assheton Drummond, J.P., D.L., *late* Captain Rifle Brigade, 1839. *Enderby Hall, Leicester.*	
25380	5159	Eric Roderick Brook Drummond, 1884.	Great-grandchildren. Children of No. 25379.
25381	5160	Elizabeth Cecil Drummond, 1872.	
25382	5161	Muriel Constance, wife of Cecil H. Haig, 1874. *7 Eaton Terrace, S.W.*	
25383	5162	Rodolf Cecil Drummond Haig, 1901.	Great-great-grandchildren. Children of No. 25382.,
25384	5163	Lily Drummond, 1875.	Great-grandchildren. Younger daughters of No. 25379.
25385	5164	Grace Janet Drummond, 1877.	
25386	5165	Margaret Annabella Drummond, 1878.	
25387	5166	Dorothy Charlotte Drummond, 1885.	
25388	5167	Violet Emily Drummond, 1888.	
25389	5168	Annabella Mary Elizabeth, Baroness Lamington [U.K.], 1824. *26 Wilton Crescent, S.W.*	Granddaughter. Elder sister to No. 25363.
25390	5169	Charles Wallace Alexander Napier Ross, 2nd Baron Lamington [U.K.], 1860. *Lamington, Lanarkshire.* *26 Wilton Crescent, S.W.*	Great-grandson. Son of No. 25389.

25391	5170	Hon. Victor Alexander Brisbane William Cochrane-Baillie, 1896.	Great-great-grandchildren. Children of No. 25390.
25392	5171	Hon. Grisell Annabella Gem Cochrane-Baillie, 1898.	
25393	5172	Constance Mary Elizabeth, Countess De La Warr [G.B.], Baroness De La Warr [E.], Baroness Buckhurst [U.K.], 1846. *25 Chesham Street, S.W.*	Great-grandchild. Daughter of No. 25389.
25394	5173	Gilbert George Reginald, 8th Earl De La Warr [G.B.], 14th Baron De La Warr [E.], 3rd Baron Buckhurst [U.K.], 1869. *Buckhurst, Sussex.* *The Manor House, Bexhill-on-Sea.*	Great-great-grandson. Son of No. 25393.
25395	5174	Herbrand Edward Dundonald Brassey, Lord Buckhurst, 1900.	Great-great-great-grandchildren. Children of No. 25394.
25396	5175	Lady Myra Idina Sackville, 1893.	
25397	5176	Lady Avice Ela Muriel Sackville, 1897.	
25398	5177	Lady Edeline, wife of Sir Gerald Bologna Strickland, 6th Count della Catena [Malta], K.C.M.G., 1870. *Villa Bologna, Malta.* *Sizergh Castle, Westmorland.*	Great-great-grandchild. Daughter of No. 25393.
25399	5178	Walter James Sackville, Contino della Catena, 1901.	Great-great-great-grandchildren. Children of No. 25398.
25400	5179	Mary Christina Strickland, dei Conti della Catena, 1896.	
25401	5180	Cecilia Strickland, dei Conti della Catena, 1897.	
25402	5181	Mabel Strickland, dei Conti della Catena, 1899.	
25403	5182	Margaret Strickland, dei Conti della Catena, 1900.	
25404	5183	Lady Leonore Mary Sackville, 1872.	Great-great-grandchildren. Younger daughters of No. 25393.
25405	5184	Lady Margaret Sackville, 1881.	
25406	5185	Amy Augusta Frederica Annabella, Marchioness Francesco Nobili Vitelleschi [Italy], 1852. *Rome.*	Great-grandchildren. Younger daughters of No. 25389.
25407	5186	Violet Marie Louise, Viscountess Melville [U.K.], 1856. *Melville Castle, Lasswade, Midlothian.*	
25408	5187	Hon. Maisie Violet Annabella Dundas, 1892.	Great-great-grandchildren. Children of No. 25407.
25409	5188	Hon. Montagu Lilias Nina Dundas, 1893.	
25410	5189	Frederica Mary Adeliza, Countess of Scarbrough [E.], Viscountess Lumley [I.], 1826. *Lumley Castle, Chester-le-Street, Durham.* *The Solent Cottage, Fawley, Southampton.*	Granddaughter. Younger sister to No. 25363.
25411	5190	Aldred Frederick George Beresford, 10th Earl of Scarbrough [E.], 11th Viscount Lumley [I.], 1857. *Lumley Castle, Durham.* *21 Park Lane, W.*	Great-grandchild. Son of No. 25410.
25412	5191	Lady Serena Mary Barbara Lumley, 1901.	Great-great-grandchild. Daughter of No. 25411.

25413	5192	Hon. Osbert Victor George Atheling Lumley, Lieut.-Col. Commanding 11th Hussars, 1862. 62 *Pont Street, S.W.*	Great-grandchild. 2nd son of No. 25410.
25414 -16	}	Same as Nos. 21713–21715.	Great-great-grandchildren. Children of No. 25413.
25417	5193	Algitha Frederica Mary, Baroness Bolton [G.B.], 1847. *Bolton Hall, Leyburn, R.S.O., Yorkshire.*	Great-grandchild. Eldest daughter of No. 25410.
25418	5194	Hon. William George Algar Orde-Powlett, Major 1st Volunteer Battalion Yorkshire Regiment, 1869. *Wensley Hall, Leyburn, R.S.O., Yorkshire.*	Great-great-grandchild. Son of No. 25417.
25419 25420 25421	5195 5196 5197	William Percy Orde-Powlett, 1894. Nigel Amyas Orde-Powlett, 1900. Elaine Letitia Algitha Orde-Powlett, 1895.	Great-great-great-grandchildren. Children of No. 25418.
25422	5198	Myra Rowena Sibell, Marchioness [U.K.] and Countess [E.] of Exeter, 1879. *Burghley House, near Stamford.* 114 *Ashley Gardens, S.W.*	Great-great-grandchild. Daughter of No. 25417.
25423	5199	Ida Frances Annabella, Countess of [U.K.] and Baroness [G.B.] Bradford, 1848. *Weston Park, Shifnal.* 44 *Lowndes Square, S.W.*	Great-grandchild. 2nd daughter of No. 25410.
25424	5200	Orlando, Viscount Newport, Assistant Private Secretary to Prime Minister, 1873.	
25425	5201	Hon. Richard Orlando Beaconsfield Bridgeman, Lieutenant R.N., 1879.	Great-great-grandchildren. Children of No. 25423.
25426	5202	Hon. Henry George Orlando Bridgeman, Lieutenant R.A., 1882.	
25427	5203	Lady Beatrice Adine, wife of Captain Ernest George Pretyman, D.L., M.P., *late* R.A., 1870. 2 *Belgrave Square, S.W.*	
25428 25429 25430 25431 25432	5204 5205 5206 5207 5208	George Marcus Tomline Pretyman, 1895. Herbert Ernest Pretyman, 1900. Walter Frederic Pretyman, 1901. Ida Beatrice Pretyman, 1896. Marjorie Elizabeth Pretyman, 1897.	Great-great-great-grand children. Children of No. 25427.
25433	5209	Margaret Alice, Countess of Dalkeith, 1872. *Eildon Hall, St. Boswells, N.B.*	Great-great-grandchild. 2nd daughter of No. 25423.
25434 -38	}	Same as Nos. 19726–19730.	Great-great-great-grandchildren. Children of No. 25433.
25439	5210	Helena Mary, Countess of [I.] and Baroness [U.K.] Sefton, 1875. *Croxteth Hall, Liverpool.*	Great-great-grandchild. 3rd daughter of No. 25423.
25440	5211	Hugh William Osbert, Viscount Molyneux, 1898.	Great-great-great-grandchildren. Sons of No. 25439.
25441	5212	Hon. Cecil Richard Molyneux, 1899.	
25442	5213	Lady Florence Sibell Bridgeman, 1877.	Great-great-grandchild. 4th daughter of No. 25423.
25443	5214	Lilian Selina Elizabeth, Marchioness of Zetland [U.K.], Baroness Dundas [G.B.], 1851. *Aske, Richmond.* 19 *Arlington Street, S.W.*	Great-grandchild. 3rd daughter of No. 25410.

25444	5215	Lawrence John Lumley, Earl of Ronaldshay, 1876.	Great-great-grandchildren. Children of No. 25443.
25445	5216	Lord George Heneage Lawrence Dundas, 2nd Lieutenant 2nd Battalion Argyll and Sutherland Highlanders, 1882.	
25446	5217	Hilda Mary, Baroness Southampton [G.B.], 1872. *Idlicote, Shipston-on-Stour.*	
25447	5218	Hon. Dorothy Fitzroy, 1895.	Great-great-great-grandchildren. Children of No. 25446.
25448	5219	Hon. Victoria Alexandrina Sybil Fitzroy, 1898.	
25449	5220	Maud Frederica Elizabeth, Countess Fitzwilliam [I. & G.B.], 1877. *Wentworth Woodhouse, Rotherham.* 4 *Grosvenor Square, W.*	Great-great-grandchild. Younger daughter of No. 25443.
25450	5221	Lady Maud Lilian Elfrida Mary Wentworth-Fitzwilliam, 1898.	Great-great-great-grandchildren. Daughters of No. 25449.
25451	5222	Lady Marjorie Joan Mary Wentworth-Fitzwilliam, 1900.	
25452	5223	Sibell Mary, Countess Grosvenor, 1855. 35 *Park Lane, W.*	Great-grandchild. 4th and youngest daughter of No. 25410.
25453		Same as No. 22325.	Great-great-grandchild. Son of No. 25452.
25454	5224	Percy Lyulph Wyndham, 1887.	Great-great-grandchild. Son of No. 25452 by 2nd husband, the Right Hon. George Wyndham, P.C., M.P.
25455 -58		Same as Nos. 22326–22329.	Great-great-grandchildren. Daughters of No. 25452.
25459	5225	Hon. Victoria Alexandrina, Lady Welby-Gregory, 1837, wife of Sir William Earle Welby-Gregory, 4th Bart. *Duneaves, Harrow.*	Granddaughter. Only surviving child of Lady Emmiline Charlotte Elizabeth Manners, 1806–1855, and her husband, the Hon. Charles Stuart-Wortley, M.P., 1802–1844.
25460	5226	Frederick William John, 3rd Marquis of Bristol [U.K.], 7th Earl of Bristol [G.B.], and Baron Hervey [E.], 1834. *Ickworth Park, Bury St. Edmunds.*	Grandson. Son of the Lady Katherine Isabella Manners, 1809–1848, and her husband, Frederick William, 2nd Marquis of Bristol, 1800–1864.
25461	5227	Lady Katherine Adine Geraldine, wife of Allan Harvey Drummond, 1864. 7 *Ennismore Gardens, S.W.*	Great-granddaughter. Daughter of No. 25460.
25462 -65		Same as Nos. 21209–21212.	Great-great-grandchildren. Children of No. 25461.
25466	5228	Alice Adeliza, Lady Hylton [U.K.], 1874. *Ammerdown Park, Radstock, Bath.*	Great-granddaughter. Daughter of No. 25460.
25467	5229	Hon. William George Hervey Jolliffe, 1898.	Great-great-grandchildren. Children of No. 25466.
25468	5230	Hon. Thomas Hedworth Jolliffe, 1900.	
25469	5231	Hon. Mary Lepel Jolliffe, 1897.	

25470	5232	Lord Francis Hervey, 1846. 34 *Buckingham Palace Mansions,* *S. W.*	
25471	5233	Adeliza Georgiana, Countess of [I.], and Viscountess [U.K.], Clan- carty, Marchioness of Heusden [Netherlands]. 30 *Pont Street, S. W.*	Grandchildren. Brother and sister to No. 25460.
25472 -78	}	Same as Nos. 23325–23331.	Great-grandchildren. Children of No. 25471.
25479	5234	Lady Mary Katherine Isabella Hervey, 1845. *Ickworth, Bury St. Edmunds.*	Grandchild. Youngest sister to No. 25460.
25480	5235	John Frederick Charles Norman, 1850.	Grandchildren. Children of the Lady Adeliza Ger- trude Elizabeth Man- ners, 1810–1887, and her husband, Canon Frederick John Nor- man, 1814–1888.
25481	5236	Robert Manners Norman, 1854.	
25482	5237	Elizabeth Cecilia Sophia, wife of George James Drummond. *Swaylands, Kent.* 14 *Belgrave Square, S. W.*	
25483	5238	George Henry Drummond, 1883.	
25484	5239	David Robert Drummond, 1884.	
25485	5240	Alexander Victor Drummond, 1888.	Great-grandchildren. Children of No. 25482.
25486	5241	Cecile Elizabeth Drummond, 1878.	
25487	5242	Adeliza Beatrix Drummond, 1879.	
25488	5243	Ida Mary Drummond, 1880.	
25489	5244	Euphemia Mabel Drummond, 1881.	

355. Descendants of George Norman, 1811–1890. (See Table LVII.)

		Children of Cecil Manners Norman, 18 –1894 (son).	
25490	5245	George Osborn Norman.	Grandchildren. Chil- dren of Cecil George Norman,1837–1880.
25491	5246	Evelyn Mary, wife of Ranulph C. de R. Norman.	
25492	5247	Cecilia Florence, wife of Dr. Mason.	
25493	5248	Ranulph Conrad de Roos Norman.	Grandchildren. Children of Richard Ernest Nor- man, 1843–1894.
25494	5249	Marmaduke Manners Norman.	
25495	5250	Harold Rhode Norman.	
25496	5251	Mabel Ida, wife of Harley.	
25497	5252	Rosamund, wife of Conway.	
25498	5253	Edward James Norman, 1844.	Son.
25499	5254	Otho Norman.	Grandchildren. Children of No. 25498.
25500	5255	Phillipa Ida Norman.	
25501	5256	Winifred Norman.	
25502	5257	Dorothy Norman.	
25503	5258	Emilius Ralph Norman, 1846. *Syston, Leicester.*	Son.
25504	5259	Henry Norman, aged 25.	Grandchildren. Children of No. 25503.
25505	5260	Frederick Norman, aged 22.	
25506	5261	Elizabeth Norman.	
25507	5262	Florence Elizabeth, widow of the Rev. Stevenson Gilbert Bellairs, –1882, 1839.	Daughter.
25508	5263	Stevenson Gilbert Bellairs.	Grandchildren. Children of No. 25507.
25509	5264	Laura Florence Bellairs.	
25510	5265	Rachel Elizabeth Bellairs.	
25511	5266	Julia Cecilia, widow of the Rev. James Skewring Swift, –1893, 1841.	Daughter.
25512	5267	Francis Manners Swift.	Grandson. Son of No. 25511.

356. Descendants of James Norman, 1812-1837. (See Table LVII.)

25513	5268	Louisa Emma, wife of Theodore Octavius Hurt. *Holly Bank, Rocester, Stafford.*	Daughter.

357. Descendants of the Rev. Frederick John Norman, Canon of Peterborough, Rector of Bottesford, 1814-1888. (See Table LVII.)

25514 -23	}	Same as Nos. 25480-25489.	

358. Descendants of Henry Anne Norman, 1816-1900. (See Table LVII.)

25524	5269	Helen Isabella, wife of Childers Henry Thompson, *late Captain 7th Dragoons, 1844. Winster, Matlock.*	Daughter.

359. Descendants of Manners Octavius Norman, 1818-1898. (See Table LVII.)

25525	5270	James Richard Norman, 1868.	Son.

360. Descendants of Elinor Katharine Norman, 1802-1873, wife of the Rev. George William Straton, Rector of Aylestone, 1806-1901. (See Table LVII.)

25526	5271	Right Rev. Norman Dumenil John, Lord Bishop of Sodor and Man, 1840. *Bishop's Court, Isle of Man.*	Children.
25527	5272	Edith Mary Elinor, wife of the Rev. N. Bergheim, 1844. *Swillington Rectory, co. York.*	
25528	5273	Arthur Cecil Bergheim, 1881.	Grandchildren. Children of No. 25527.
25529	5274	Elinor Katharine Margaret Bergheim, 1877.	
25530	5275	George Ralph Norman Ward Jackson.	Great-grandchild. Son of Elizabeth Georgina Bergheim, 1878-1900, wife of R. Ward Jackson and grandson of No. 25527.

361. Descendants of Sophia Elizabeth Norman, 1803-1872, 1st wife of Orlando Watkin Weld, 4th Lord Forester, 1813-1894. (See Table LVII.)

25531	5276	Cecil Theodore, 5th Lord Forester [U.K.], 1842. *Willey Park, Broseley, Shropshire. Dothill Park, Wellington.*	Only child.

The Blood Royal of Britain

25532	5277	Hon. George Cecil Beaumont Weld Forester, Captain Royal Horse Guards, 1867. *Barrow, Broseley, Shropshire.*	Grandson. Son of No. 25531.
25533	5278	Cecil George Wilfrid Weld Forester, 1899.	Great-grandchild. Child of No. 25532.
25534	5279	Hon. Charles Cecil Orlando Weld Forester, 1869. *The Crossways, Sunninghill, Ascot.*	Grandson. 2nd son of No. 25531.
25535	5280	Wolstan Beaumont Charles Weld Forester, 1899.	Great-grandchildren. Sons of No. 25534.
25536	5281	Raymond Cecil Forester, 1900.	
25537	7282	Hon. Francis Henry Cecil Weld Forester, 1871.	
25538	5283	Hon. Edgar Cecil Wolstan Weld Forester, 1871.	Grandchildren. Children of No. 25531.
25539	5284	Hon. Arthur Orlando Wolstan Cecil Weld Forester, 1877.	
25540	5285	Hon. Edric Alfred Cecil Weld Forester, 1880.	
25541	5286	Hon. Mary Isabella Sophia Louisa Weld Forester, 1873.	

362. Descendants of Isabella Elizabeth Norman, 1805–1894, wife of Sir Francis Grant, President of the Royal Academy, 1803–1878. (See Table LVII.)

25542	5287	Ronald Antony Markham, Lieutenant Coldstream Guards, 1870. *Becca Hall, Yorks.*		Grandchildren. Children of Anne Emily Sophia Grant, 1835–1880, wife of Colonel William Thomas Markham, J.P., of Becca Hall, 1830–188 .
25543	5288	Nigel Ivan Markham, 1872. *New Zealand.*		
25544	5289	Francis, Viscount Glerawly, 1884.	*Castlewellan, co. Down; Annesley Lodge, Regent's Park.*	Great-grandchildren. Children of Mabel Wilhelmina Frances Markham, 1858–1891, 1st wife of Hugh, 5th Earl Annesley, and grandchildren of Anne Emily Sophia Grant. *See above.*
25545	5290	Lady Mabel Marguerite Annesley, 1881.		
25546	5291	Cécile Mary Isabella, wife of Cecil d'Aguilar Samuda. *Bruern Abbey, Oxford.*		Grandchild. Sister to No. 25542.
25547	5292	Richard Samuda.	Great-great-grandchild. Child of No. 25546.	
25548	5293	Hermione Violet Cyril, wife of Major Malcolm Patton.		Grandchildren. Sisters to No. 25542.
25549	5294	Ethel Winifred Victoria Markham.		
25550	5295	Averil Constance Antoinette Jeanette Markham.		
25551	5296	Gwendolen Beatrice Sanchia May Markham.		
25552	5297	Sybil Annesley Giana, wife of William Jocelyn Rhys Wingfield, Lieutenant 19th Hussars.		
25553	5298	Frederic Dudley North, C.M.G., Clerk of the Executive Council and Under-Secretary of West Australia, 1866. *Catlidge, Coltesloe, W. Australia.*		Grandchild. Son of Rachel Elizabeth Grant, 1842–1871, wife of Charles Augustus North, 1829–1893.

25554	5299	Charles Frederic John North, 1887.	Great-grandchildren. Children of No. 25553.
25555	5300	George Eustace Dudley North, 1893.	
25556	5301	Margaret Frances Emily Muriel North, 1889.	
25557	5302	Wilhelmina Mary Isabel Flora North, 1891.	
25558	5303	Brownlow Francis Gordon North, 1869.	Grandchildren. Brother and sister to No. 25553.
25559	5304	Mary Isabella, *late* wife of Sir William Edmund Garstein, K.C.M.G.	
25560	5305	William Charles North Garstein, 1894.	Great-grandchild. Son of No. 25559.
25561	5306	Rachel Elizabeth, widow of Captain Henry Montagu Clifton Hawkes, -1896, 1871.	Grandchild. Younger sister to No. 25553.
25562	5307	Elizabeth Catherine Grant, 1847. *The Lodge, Melton Mowbray.*	Daughter.

363. Descendants of Charlotte Elizabeth Norman, 1806–1869, wife of the Rev. and Hon. Atherton Legh Powys, Rector of Titchmarsh, 1809–1886. (See Table LVII.)

25563	5308	Richard Atherton Norman Powys, 1844. *9 Burnaby Gardens, Chiswick.*	Son.
25564	5309	Atherton Richard Norman Powys, 1888.	Grandchild. Son of No. 25563.
25565	5310	. . . . Powys.	Grandchildren. Daughters of Walter Norman Powys, 1849–1892.
25566	5311	. . . . Powys.	
25567	5312	Evelyn Mary, wife of Edward Pennefather Wade Browne, 1846.	Daughters.
25568	5313	Alice Elizabeth Juliana, wife of the Rev. Frederic Armine Wodehouse, 1848. *Gotham Rectory, Kegworth, Derby.*	
25569	5314	Arthur Wodehouse, Lieutenant York and Lancaster Regiment, 1881.	Grandchildren. Children of No. 25568.
25570	5315	Frederic Armine Wodehouse, 1884.	
25571	5316	Norman Atherton Wodehouse, 1887.	
25572	5317	Mabel Evelyn Wodehouse, 1882.	

364. Descendants of Cecilia Emily Norman, 1809–1891, wife of Francis Hurt, of Alderwasley, J.P., D.L., 1803–1861. (See Table LVII.)

25573	5318	Albert Frederic Hurt, J.P., D.L., Major and Hon. Lieut.-Col. (retired), Derbyshire Regiment. *Alderwasley, Matlock, Derby.*	Son.
25574	5319	Francis Cecil Albert Hurt, Lieutenant Royal Welsh Fusiliers, 1878.	Grandchildren. Children of No. 25573.
25575	5320	Seymour Frederic Auckland Albert Hurt, Lieutenant Royal Scots Fusiliers, 1879.	
25576	5321	Henry Albert le Fowne Hurt, 1881.	
25577	5322	Ralph Anthony Lowe Ponsonby Hurt, 1885.	
25578	5323	Grace Emma Julia Hurt.	

25579	5324	Theodore Octavius Hurt, 1839.	
25580	5325	George Edward Hurt, 1843.	
25581	5326	Louis Charles Hurt, 1845.	Children.
25582	5327	Rev. Richard Norman Hurt, 1847.	
		Sandal Magna Vicarage, Wakefield.	
25583	5328	Francis William Richard Hurt, 1873.	
25584	5329	Edward Norman Richard Hurt, 1880.	Grandchildren.
25585	5330	Lilias Alice, wife of the Rev. Louis Busch.	Children of
		Chapelthorpe Vicarage.	No. 25582.
25586	5331	Dorothy Alice, wife of Sydney Harold Garnett.	
25587	5332	Walter James Hurt.	Grandchildren. Children of James
25588	5333	Constance Cecilia Hurt.	Nicholas Hurt, R.N., 1849–1886.
25589	5334	Grace Selina Frances Hurt.	Grandchild. Daughter of Cecilia Isabella Hurt, –1884, wife of the Rev. John Francis Hurt, –1868.
25590	5335	Henrietta Maria, wife of Arthur Radford, J.P. *Smalley Hall, co. Derby.*	Daughter.
25591	5336	John Radford, Lieutenant 3rd Sherwood Forest Regiment, 1877.	Grandchildren.
25592	5337	Eveleyne Vaughan, Baroness Foley [G.B.]. *Ruxley Lodge, Esher.* 7 *Audley Square, W.*	Children of No. 25590.

365. Descendants of Orlando Watkin Weld, 4th Lord Forester, 1813–1894. (See Table LVII.)

25593 –603	}	Same as Nos. 25531–25541.
25604		Same as No. 21509.

366. Descendants of the Hon. Anne Eliza Forester, 1802–1885, and her husband, George Augustus Frederick, 6th Earl Chesterfield, 1805–1866. (See Table LVII.)

25605 –12	}	Same as Nos. 22015–22022.

367. Descendants of the Hon. Elizabeth Katherine Forester, 1803–1832, 1st wife of Robert John, 2nd Lord Carrington, 1796–1868. (See Table LVII.)

25613	5338	Cecile Katherine Mary, Viscountess [U.K.] and Baroness [S.] Colville of Culross, 1829. 42 *Eaton Place, S.W.*	Daughter.
25614	5339	Charles Robert William, Master of Colville, 1854. *Guards'; Carlton.*	Grandson. Son of No. 25613.
25615	5340	Charles Alexander Colville, 1888.	Great-grandchildren.
25616	5341	John Gilbert Colville, 1892.	Children of No.
25617	5342	Margaret Colville, 1886.	25614.
25618	5343	Sybil Marion Colville, 1897.	

25619	5344	Hon. Stanley Cecil James Colville, C.V.O., C.B., Captain R.N., 1861. *Naval and Military; United Service.*	
25620	5345	Hon. George Charles Colville, 1867. *Carlton.*	Grandchildren. Children of No. 25613.
25621	5346	Hon. Blanche Cecile, wife of Admiral Richard Frederick Britten, D.L., Worcestershire, 1857. *Kenswick, Worcester.*	
25622	5347	Forester Cecil Robin Britten, 1893.	Great-grandchildren. Children of No. 25621.
25623	5348	Charles Richard Britten, 1894.	
25624	5349	Violet Emma Britten, 1897.	

368. Descendants of the Hon. Isabella Elizabeth Annabella Forester, 1805–1858, and her husband, Major-General the Hon. George Anson, 1797–1857. (See Table LVII.)

25625	5350	Isabella Katherine, Countess Howe [U.K.], Baroness Curzon and Howe [G.B.], 1832. 20 *Curzon Street, W.*	Eldest daughter and co-heir.
25626 –34	}	Same as Nos. 20240–20248.	Grandchildren. Children of No. 25625.
25635	5351	George Charles Wentworth-Fitzwilliam, J.P., D.L., 1866. *Milton Park, near Peterborough.*	Grandchild. Child of Alice Louisa Anson, –1879, and her husband, the Hon. George Wentworth-Fitzwilliam, of Milton, M.P., 1817–1874.
25636	5352	George James Charles Wentworth-Fitzwilliam, 1889.	Great-grandchild. Son of No. 25635.
25637	5353	Alice Mary, wife of Arthur Watkin Williams-Wynn, 1869. 71 *Eccleston Square, S.W.*	Grandchild. Sister of No. 25635.
25638 –40	}	Same as Nos. 24825–24827.	Great-grandchildren. Children of No. 25637.
25641	5354	Maud, wife of the Hon. Cospatrick Thomas Dundas, 1871. *Ainderby Hall, Northallerton.*	Granddaughter. Sister to Nos. 25635.
25642	5355	John George Lawrence Dundas, 1893.	Great-grandchildren. Children of No. 25641.
25643	5356	Winifred Maud Dundas, 1895.	
25644	5357	Elgiva Margaret Dundas, 1897.	
25645	5358	Geraldine Georgiana Mary, Marchioness [U.K.] and Countess [G.B.] of Bristol, Baroness Hervey [E.], 1843. *Ickworth Park, Bury St. Edmunds.* 19 *Sussex Square, Brighton.*	Youngest daughter and co-heir.
25646 –54	}	Same as Nos. 25461–25469.	Grandchildren. Children of No. 25645.

369. Descendants of the Hon. Henrietta Maria Forester, 1809–1841, 1st wife of Albert, 1st Lord Londesborough, 1805–1860. (See Table LVII.)

25655	5359	William Francis Henry, 2nd Earl of Londesborough [U.K.], 1864. *Londesborough Park, Market Weighton.*	Grandson. Son of William Henry Forester, 1st Earl of Londesborough, 1834–1900.

25656	5360	George Francis William Henry, Viscount Raincliffe, 1892.	Great-grandchildren. Children of No. 25655.
25657	5361	Hon. Hugo William Cecil Denison, 1894.	
25658	5362	Lady Irene Francis Adza Denison.	
25659	5363	Lady Edith Henrietta Sybil, wife of Sir Gerald William Henry Codrington, 1st Bart., 1866. *Dodington Park, Chipping Sodbury, Gloucestershire.*	Granddaughter. Sister to No. 25655.
25660	5364	Christopher William Gerald Henry Codrington, 1894.	Great-grandchildren. Children of No. 25659.
25661	5365	Edith Georgiana Veronica Codrington, 1888.	
25662	5366	John Francis Chaloner Ogle, 1898. *59 Green Street, Grosvenor Square, W.*	Great-grandchild. Child of Lady Lilian Katherine Selina Denison, 1867–1899, sister to No. 25655, wife of Newton Charles Ogle, of Kirkley Hall.
25663	5367	Lady Ida Emily Augusta, wife of Sir George Reresby Sitwell, 4th Bart., 1869. *Belvoir Terrace, Scarborough.*	Granddaughter. Sister to No. 25655.
25664	5368	Francis Osbert Sacheverell Sitwell, 1892.	Great-grandchildren. Children of No. 25663.
25665	5369	Sacheverell Sitwell, 1897.	
25666	5370	Edith Louisa Sitwell, 1887.	
25667	5371	Lady Mildred Adelaide Cecilia, wife of Sir William Henry Charles Wemyss Cooke, 10th Bart., 1872. *Wheatley Park, Doncaster.*	Granddaughter. Youngest sister to No. 25655.
25668	5372	Hon. Albert Denison Somerville Denison, Rear-Admiral R.N., 1835. *Woodside, Wootten, I.W.* *United Service; Army and Navy.*	Eldest surviving son.
25669	5373	Ernest William Denison, Lieutenant R.N., 1876.	Grandchildren. Children of No. 25668.
25670	5374	Daisy, wife of Robert Lockhart Hobson, 1875.	
25671	5375	Robert Denison Hobson, 1902. Great-grandson. Son of No. 25670.	
25672	5376	Ivy Denison, 1878.	Grandchildren. Children of No. 25668.
25673	5377	Lily Denison, 1882.	
25674	5378	Hon. Henrietta Sophia Elizabeth, widow of Sir Philip le Belward Grey-Egerton, 11th Bart., 1833–1891. *51 Mount Street, W.*	Daughter.
25675	5379	Sir Philip Henry Brian Grey-Egerton, 12th Bart., 1864. *Oulton Park, Tarporley, Cheshire.* *5 Carlos Place, Grosvenor Square, W.*	Grandson. Son of No. 25674.
25676	5380	Philip de Malpas Wayne Grey-Egerton, 1895.	Great-grandchildren. Children of No 25675.
25677	5381	Rowland le Belward Grey-Egerton, 1895.	
25678	5382	Cecily Alice Grey Grey-Egerton, 1893.	
25679	5383	Violet Edith Grey, Lady Romilly [U.K.]. *Porthkerry, Barry, Glamorganshire.*	Granddaughter. Daughter of No. 25674.
25680	5384	Hon. William Gaspard Guy Romilly, 1899.	Great-grandchild. Child of No. 25679.
25681	5385	Hon. Victor Alexander Wrottesley, 1873.	Grandchildren. Children of the Hon. Augusta Elizabeth Denison, 1841–1887, and her husband, Arthur, 3rd Lord Wrottesley, 1824.
25682	5386	Hon. Walter Bennet Wrottesley, 1877.	*Wrottesley, Wolverhampton, Staffordshire.*
25683	5387	Hon Evelyn Henrietta Wrottesley, 1866.	

370. Descendants of the Hon. Selina Louisa Forester, 1819–1894, and her husband, Orlando George Charles, 3rd Earl of Bradford, P.C., 1819–1898. (See Table LVII.)

25684	5388	George Cecil Orlando, 4th Earl of Bradford [U.K.], 5th Baron Bradford [G.B.]. *Weston Park, Shifnal.* 44 *Lowndes Square, S.W.*	Son.
25685 –703	}	Same as Nos. 25424–25442.	Descendants of No. 25684.
25704	5389	Hon. Francis Charles Bridgeman, *late* Colonel 1st Battalion Scots Guards, 1846. 59 *Ennismore Gardens, S.W.*	2nd son.
25705	5390	Reginald Francis Orlando Bridgeman, 1884.	Grandchildren. Children of No. 25704.
25706	5391	Francis Paul Orlando Bridgeman, 1888.	
25707	5392	Humphrey Herbert Orlando Bridgeman, 1891.	
25708	5393	Orlando Clive Bridgeman, 1898	
25709	5394	Selina Adine Bridgeman, 1886.	
25710	5395	Lady Mabel Selina, wife of Colonel William Slaney Kenyon-Slaney, M.P., 1855. *Hatton Grange, Shifnal, Salop.*	Eldest daughter.
25711	5396	Robert Orlando Rodolph Kenyon-Slaney, 1892.	Grandchildren. Children of No. 25710.
25712	5397	Sybil Agnes Kenyon-Slaney, 1888.	
25713	5398	Florence Katherine, Countess of [U.K.] and Baroness [G.B.] Harewood, 1859. *Harewood House, Leeds.* 13 *Upper Belgrave Street, S.W.*	2nd daughter.
25714 –16	}	Same as Nos. 21839–21841.	Grandchildren. Children of No. 25713.

371. Descendants of Heneage, 4th Earl of Aylesford, 1751–1812. (See Table LVIII.)

25717 –39	}	Same as Nos. 21987–22009.	

372. Descendants of Charles Wynne Finch, afterwards Griffith-Wynne, of Voelas, co. Denbigh, 1780-1865. (See Table LVIII.)

25740	5399	Charles Arthur Wynne-Finch, *of Voelas*, J.P., D.L., Lieut.-Col. Scots Guards, 1841. 11 *Bruton Street, W.*	Grandson. Son of Charles Wynne-Finch, M.P., 1815–1874.
25741	5400	John Charles Wynne-Finch, 1891.	Great-grandchildren. Children of No. 25740.
25742	5401	William Heneage Wynne-Finch, 1893.	
25743	5402	Edward Heneage Wynne-Finch, J.P., 1842 *Stokesley, Yorkshire.*	Grandson. Brother of No. 25740.
25744	5403	Heneage Wynne-Finch, 1871. *New University.*	Great-grandchildren. Children of No. 25743.
25745	5404	Arthur Wynne-Finch, 1878.	
25746	5405	Griffith Wynne-Finch, Lieutenant 4th Battalion King's Royal Rifle Corps, 1880.	
25747	5406	Helen Wynne-Finch, 1877.	

25748	5407	John Seymour Wynne-Finch, *late* Captain Royal Horse Guards, 1845. 105 *Mount Street, W.*	Grandson. Brother of No. 25740.
25749	5408	Thomas Somers Vernon Cocks, 1850. *Uplands, Hughenden, Bucks.* 13 *Montagu Place, W.*	Grandchild. Son of Sarah Louisa Griffith Wynne, 1817–1895, and her husband, Thomas Somers Cocks, M.P., 1815–1899.
25750	5409	Charles Vernon Somers Cocks, 1895.	Great-grandchildren. Children of No. 25749.
25751	5410	Margaret Agneta Cocks, 1889.	
25752	5411	Jane Ethel Mary Cocks, 1891.	
25753	5412	Muriel Emily Cocks, 1892.	
25754	5413	Alfred Heneage Cocks, 1851.	Grandchild. Brother of No. 25740.
25755	5414	Charlotte, widow of John Robert Godley, –1861. *Killigar, Belturbet.* 11 *Gloucester Place, Portman Square, W.*	Daughter.
25756	5415	Sir Arthur Godley, K.C.B., 1847. 13 *Ennismore Gardens, S.W.*	Grandson. Son of No. 25755.
25757	5416	Hugh John Godley, 1877.	Great-grandchildren. Children of No. 25756.
25758	5417	Helen Sarah, wife of Henry Rice, 1872. *Dane Court, Dover.*	
25759	5418	Edward Denis Rice, 1899.	Great-great-grandsons. Children of No. 25758.
25760	5419	Patrick Arthur Rice, 1902.	
25761	5420	Eveline Godley, 1874.	Great-grandchildren. Children of No. 25756.
25762	5421	Katharine Godley, 1880.	
25763	5422	Rose Godley.	Granddaughters. Daughters of No. 25755.
25764	5423	Eleanor Godley.	
25765	5424	Margaret Godley.	
25766	5425	Frances Elizabeth Griffith-Wynne, 1835.	*Craig Lledr, Bettws-y-Coed, North Wales.* 62 *Park Street, W.* — Daughter.

373. Descendants, if any, of Jane Finch, 17 –1858, wife of the Rev. Thomas Cooke. (See Table LVIII.)

374. Descendants, if any, of Louisa Finch, 17 –1822, wife (1822) of Ambrose St. Martin, Count of Aglié, Sardinian Minister to St James'. (See Table LVIII.)

375. Descendants of William, 4th Earl of Dartmouth, 1784–1853. (See Table LVIII.)

25767 –78	}	Same as Nos. 21312–21323.	Grandchildren, &c. Children of William Walter, 5th Earl of Dartmouth, 1823–1891.

25779	5426	Arthur Edward John Legge, Lieutenant 18th Middlesex Volunteer Rifles, 1863. *Wellington.*	Grandchildren. Children of the Rev. and Hon. George Barrington Legge, 1831–1900.
25780	5427	Robert George Legge, 1864. *Garrick.*	
25781	5428	Rev. Hugh Legge, 1870. 60 *Romford Road, Stratford.*	
25782	5429	Augusta Sophia Legge, 1861.	
25783	5430	Margaret Legge, 1872.	
25784	5431	Walter Traversari Legge, Clerk in the House of Commons, 1874. *Wellington.*	Grandchildren. Children of Lieut.-Col. the Hon. Edward Henry Legge, 1834–1900.
25785	5432	Montague George Bentinck Legge, R.N., 1883.	
25786	5433	John Douglas Legge, 1886.	
25787	5434	Heneage Cecil Legge, 1890.	
25788	5435	Hugo Molesworth Legge, 1891.	
25789	5436	Lois Marjorie Legge, 1881.	
25790	5437	Cecilia Katherine Legge, 1895.	
25791	5438	Anne Imogen Traversari Legge, 1896.	
25792	5439	The Right Rev. Augustus, Bishop of Lichfield, 1839. *The Palace, Lichfield.*	Son.
25793 –96		Same as Nos. 20900–20903.	Grandchildren. Children of No. 25792.
25797	5440	Hon. Charles Gounter Legge, 1842. 36 *Victoria St., S.W.*	2nd surviving son.
25798	5441	William Kaye Legge, Captain Essex Regiment, 1869. *Junior Army and Navy.*	Grandchildren. Children of No. 25797.
25799	5442	John Augustus Legge, P. & O. Company, Sub-Lieutenant R.N.R., 1871.	
25800	5443	Thomas Charles Legge, Lieutenant Imperial Yeomanry, 1872.	
25801	5444	Francis Cecil Legge, 1873.	
25802	5445	Ronald George Legge, Lieutenant Imperial Yeomanry, 1878.	
25803	5446	Helen Beatrice Legge, 1870.	
25804	5447	Hon. Heneage Legge, M.P., 1845. 90 *Piccadilly, W.*	3rd surviving son.
25805	5448	Lady Frances Elizabeth, widow of Major-Gen. George Bruce Michell, –1866.	Eldest daughter.
25806	5449	George Baily Michell, *late* Captain 24th Middlesex (Post Office) Volunteer Rifles, 1864.	Grandson. Son of No. 25805.
25807	5450	Lady Louisa Jane Cecil Legge, 1830.	2nd and 3rd surviving daughters.
25808	5451	Lady Katherine, widow of Colonel Robert J. Eustace-Eustace, formerly Robertson, *of Baltinglass,* –1889, 1837. *Montague House, Wokingham, Berks.*	
25809	5452	Captain Charles Legge Eustace, D.S.O., 1867. *Wellington.*	Grandchildren. Children of No. 25808.
25810	5453	Robert William Barrington Eustace, *late* Captain 4th Battalion South Staffordshire Regiment, 1870.	
25811	5454	Seton George Legge Eustace, 1871.	
25812	5455	Alicia Katherine Eustace.	
25813	5456	Adelaide Mary Eustace.	
25814	5457	Violet Theresa Eustace.	

The Blood Royal of Britain

25815	5458	Lady Florence, wife of Colonel Nathaniel Barnardiston, J.P., D.L., 1838. *The Rydes, near Sudbury, Suffolk.*	4th surviving daughter.
25816	5459	Nathaniel Walter Barnardiston, Major Duke of Cambridge's Own (Middlesex) Regiment, 1858. *Naval and Military.*	Grandson. Son of No. 25815.
25817	5460	Joan Barnardiston, 1897.	Great-grandchild. Child of No. 25816.
25818	5461	Thomas Legge Barnardiston, Commandant R.N., 1866. *Naval and Military.*	
25819	5462	Geoffrey Barnardiston, 1868.	
25820	5463	Ernald Barnardiston, Captain R.E., 1871. *Junior United Service.*	
25821	5464	Samuel John Barrington Barnardiston, D.S.O., Lieutenant Suffolk Regiment, 1875.	Grandchildren. Children of No. 25815.
25822	5465	Florence Maria Barnardiston.	
25823	5466	Maud Augusta Barnardiston.	
25824	5467	Gertrude Elizabeth Frances Barnardiston.	
25825	5468	Cecil Laura Barnardiston.	
25826	5469	Mary Barnardiston.	
25827	5470	Bertha Sophia Barnardiston.	
25828	5471	Lady Barbara Caroline, wife of the Right Rev. Huyshe Wolcott Yeatman-Biggs, D.D., Bishop of Southwark, 1841. *Dartmouth House, Blackheath Hill, S.E.*	5th surviving daughter.
25829	5472	William Huyshe Yeatman-Biggs, 1878.	Grandchildren. Children of No. 25828.
25830	5473	Lewys Legge Yeatman-Biggs, 1879.	
25831	5474	Barbara Margaret Yeatman-Biggs, 1876.	
25832	5475	Lady Charlotte Anne Georgiana Legge, 1843. *5 South Eaton Place, S.W.*	
25833	5476	Lady Harriet Octavia Legge, 1847. *5 South Eaton Place, S.W.*	Younger daughters.
25834	5477	Lady Wilhelmina, widow of John Townshend Brooke, 1844–1899, 1849. *Haughton Hall, Shifnal.*	
25835	5478	William John Brooke, 1876.	Grandchildren. Children of No. 25834.
25836	5479	George Townshend Brooke, 1878.	
25837	5480	Basil Richard Brooke, R.N., 1882.	
25838	5481	Madeline Harriet Brooke, 1879.	
25839	5482	Evelyn Georgiana Brooke, 1881.	
25840	5483	Bertha Mary Brooke, 1884.	

376. Descendants of the Hon. Heneage Legge, 1788–1844. (See Table LVIII.)

25841	5484	Mary, wife of F. W. Mackenzie, M.D.	Only child.

377. Descendants of General the Hon. Arthur Charles Legge, 1800–1890. (See Table LVIII.)

25842	5485	Rev. Alfred Arthur Kaye Legge, 1839. *37 Sloane Gardens, S.W.*	Children.
25843	5486	Alice Mary, wife of the Rev. Edward Samson, 1843. *Armitage Lodge, near Rugeley.*	

The Blood Royal of Britain

378. Descendants of Lady Louisa Legge, 1787–1816, 2nd wife of William, 2nd Lord Bagot, 1773–1856. (See Table LVIII.)

25844 -55	}	Same as Nos. 22223-22234.	{ Grandchildren. Children of William, 3rd Lord Bagot, 1811–1887.
25856	5487	John Henry Hervey Vincent Lane, *late* Captain 4th Battalion South Staffordshire Regiment, J.P., D.L., 1867. *King's Bromley Manor, near Lichfield.*	⎧ Great-grandchildren. Children of Colonel John Henry Bagot Lane, of King's Bromley, 1829–1886, son of Hon. Agnes Bagot, 1806–1885, and her husband, John Newton Lane, of King's Bromley, 1800–1869.
25857	5488	Arthur Edward Cecil Lane, J.P., 1871.	
25858	5489	George Alfred Osborne Lane, Lieutenant Coldstream Guards, 1875.	
25859	5490	Florence Louisa Jane, wife of the Hon. Frederic William Anson, J.P., 1865. *Cell Barnes, St. Albans.*	
25860	5491	Ernald Henry Anson, 1893.	⎫
25861	5492	Arthur Anson, } twins, 1896.	Great-great-grandchildren. Children of No. 25859.
25862	5493	Frederic Anson, }	
25863	5494	Helen Frances Anson, 1892.	
25864	5495	Sibyl Florence Anson, 1894.	
25865	5496	Constance Jane Lane, 1869.	⎫ Great-grandchildren. Sisters of No. 25856, &c.
25866	5497	Lilian Emily Isabel Jane, wife of Walter Bromley Davenport, 1878.	
25867	5498	Sidney Leveson Lane, J.P., D.L., 1831. *Manor House, Great Addington, Thrapston.*	Grandson. Son of the above Hon. Agnes Bagot, 1806–1885, and John Newton Lane, 1800–1869.
25868	5499	Sydney Ernald Ralph Lane, *late* Captain 3rd Battalion Princess of Wales' Own Yorkshire Regiment, 1863.	⎫ Great-grandchildren. Children of No. 25867.
25869	5500	Mary Beatrice Sydney, wife of Walter Richard Shaw Stewart. *Berwick House, Hindon, Salisbury.*	
25870	5501	Walter Guy Shaw Stewart, 1892.	⎫ Great-great-grandchildren. Children of No. 25869.
25871	5502	Niel Shaw Stewart, 1894.	
25872	5503	Mary Sibell Agnes Shaw Stewart, 1896.	
25873	5504	Irene Beatrice Shaw Stewart, 1901.	
25874	5505	Newton Frederic Seymour Lane, 1879.	⎧ Great-grandchildren. Children of Colonel Cecil Newton Lane, of Whiston Hall, Salop, J.P., C.M.G., 1833–1897, 3rd son of the above-named Hon. Agnes Bagot, &c.
25875	5506	Percy Ernald Lane, 1881.	
25876	5507	John Ronald Lane, 1884.	
25877	5508	Georgina Agnes Jane Lane, 1882.	
25878	5509	Ven. Ernald Lane, Archdeacon of Stoke-upon-Trent, 1836. *Leigh Rectory, co. Stafford.*	Grandson. Brother to No. 25867.
25879	5510	Geoffrey Ernald William Lane, 1881.	} Great-grandchildren. Children to No. 25878.
25880	5511	Marjorie Agnes Jane Lane.	
25881	5512	Ronald Bertram Lane, C.B., Major-General Commanding at Malta, 1847.	} Grandson. Brother to No. 25867, &c.
25882	5513	George Ronald Lane, 1894.	{ Great-grandson. Son of No. 25881.
25883	5514	Edith Emmeline Mary, Lady Northbourne [U.K.]. *Betteshanger, Sandwich, Kent.*	} Granddaughter. Sister to No. 25867.
25884	5515	Hon. Walter John James, 1869. 1 *Courtfield Road, S.W.*	} Great-grandson. Son of No. 25883.

25885	5516	Walter Ernest Christopher James, 1896.	Great-great-grandchildren. Children of No. 25884.
25886	5517	Dorothea Gwenllian James, 1897.	
25887	5518	Hon. Cuthbert James, Lieutenant East Surrey Regiment, 1872.	Great-grandchildren. Children of No. 25883.
25888	5519	Hon. Robert James, 1873. *St. Nicholas, Richmond, Yorkshire.*	
25889	5520	Hon. Wilfred James, 1874. 1 *Montagu Mansions, Portman Square, W.*	
25890	5521	John Wilfred James, 1900.	Great-great-grandson. Son of No. 25889.
25891	5522	Hon. Sarah Agnes, wife of the Rev. Adolphus Benjamin Parry Evans, 1870. *The Vicarage, Uttoxeter, Staffordshire.*	Great-grandchild. Child of No. 25883.
25892		Same as No. 23277.	Great-grandson. Son of Isabel Emma Beatrice Lane, –1876 (sister to No. 25867), wife of Percy Brodrick Bernard.

379. Descendants of Lady Charlotte Legge, 1789–1877, and her husband, the Very Rev. and Hon. George Neville Grenville, 1789–1854. (See Table LVIII.)

25893 –936	}	Same as Nos. 25186–25229.

380. Descendants of Lady Harriet Legge, 1790–1855, 2nd wife of General the Hon. Sir Edward Paget, G.C.B., 1775–1849. (See Table LVIII.)

25937	5523	Gertrude Florence, wife of Major Phelips Brooke Hanham, R.A., 1860.	Granddaughter. Daughter of Lieut.-Col. Patrick Lewis Cole Paget, 1820–1879.
25938	5524	Esmond Henry Paget Hanham, 1887.	Great-grandchildren. Children of No. 25937.
25939	5525	Patrick John Hanham, 1893.	
25940	5526	Florence Mary Emily Paget, 1862.	Granddaughters. Younger sisters to No. 25937.
25941	5527	Violet Evelyn Paget, 1864.	
25942	5528	Mildred Eileen May, wife of Captain Henry Lloyd Powell, R.A., 1865.	
25943	5529	Henry Edward Clarence Paget, J.P. and Deputy Commissioner of Police, Calcutta, 1860. *West Coker Manor, Yeovil.*	Grandchildren. Children of Rev. Edward Heneage Paget, 1828–1884.
25944	5530	Hugh Arthur Paget, 1862. *55 Cambridge Terrace, Hyde Park.*	
25945	5531	Eden Wilberforce Paget, 1865. *Castle Close, Wareham.*	
25946	5532	Eric Morton Paget, 1867. *Prestbury, Cheltenham.*	
25947	5533	Claude Edmund Paget, 1869. *Leaseland, Exmouth.*	
25948	5534	Frances Jane, Marchioness of [I.] and Baroness [U.K.] Ormonde, 1817. *Glenarun, Horsham.*	Daughter.

25949	5535	James Edward William Theobald, 3rd Marquis of Ormonde [I.] and Baron Ormonde of Llanthony [U.K.], K.P., 1844. 32 *Upper Brook Street, W.*	Grandson. Son of No. 25948.
25950 -52		Same as Nos. 22340-22342.	Great-grandchildren. Children of No. 25949.
25953	5536	Lord James Arthur Wellington Foley Butler, 1849. *Travellers'; Carlton.*	Grandson. 2nd son of No. 25948.
25954	5537	James George Anson Butler, 1890.	
25955	5538	James Arthur Norman Butler, 1893.	Great-grandchildren.
25956	5539	Evelyn Frances Butler, 1887.	Children of No.
25957	5540	Eleanor Rachel Butler, 1894.	25953.
25958	5541	Rev. Lord James Theobald Bagot John Butler, 1852. *Ulcombe Rectory, Kent.*	Grandson. 3rd son of No. 25948.
25959	5542	James Walter Theobald Gordon Butler, 1886.	
25960	5543	James Hubert Theobald Charles Butler, 1899.	Great-grandchildren. Children of No. 25958.
25961	5544	Violet Mary Emily Maud Butler, 1889.	
25962	5545	Sybil Frances Christina Lilah Butler, 1891.	
25963	5546	Victoria Blanche Constance Theodora Butler, 1897.	
25964	5547	Lady Mary Grace Louisa, wife of the Hon. William Henry Wentworth Fitzwilliam, 1846. *Wigganthorpe, York.*	Granddaughter. Elder daughter of No. 25948.
25965	5548	Marie Albreda Blanche Wentworth Fitzwilliam, 1878.	
25966	5549	Isabel Elizabeth Mary Wentworth Fitzwilliam, 1880.	Great-grandchildren. Children of No. 25964.
25967	5550	Irène Serga Alice Jane Mary Wentworth Fitzwilliam, 1883.	
25968	5551	Lady Blanche Henrietta Maria, wife of Lieut.-Col. the Hon. Cuthbert Ellison Edwardes, 1854. 39 *Lancaster Gate, W.*	Granddaughter. Younger daughter of No. 25948.
25969	5552	Hubert William John Edwardes, 1883.	
25970	5553	Arthur Henry Francis Edwardes, 1885.	Great-grandchildren.
25971	5554	Cuthbert Theobald Edwardes, 1887.	Children of No
25972	5555	Richard Edwardes, } twins, 1894.	25968.
55973	5556	Owen Edwardes,	
25974	5557	Harriet Mary Paget, 1819. *Glenarum, Horsham.*	
25975	5558	Charlotte Louisa Paget, 1821. *Hermitage, Horsham.*	Daughters.

381. Descendants of Lady Barbara María Legge, 1791–1840, and her husband, Francis Newdigate, Esq., of Kirk and West Hallam, 1774–1862. (See Table LVIII.)

25976	5559	Francis Alexander Newdigate-Newdegate, *of Weston-in-Arden, and Arbury, co. Warwick, and West Hallam, co. Derby,* M.P., J.P., D.L., 1862. 1 *Tilney Street, Park Lane, W.*	Grandson. Son of Lieut.-Col. Francis William Newdigate, of West Hallam, 1822–1893.

25977 -78	}	Same as Nos. 22233–22234.	{ Great-granddaughters. Children of No. 25976.	
25979	5560	Francis Henry Newdigate.		
25980	5561	William Newdigate.		
25981	5562	Arthur Patrick Newdigate.	_Forest Hall, Knysna, Cape Colony._	Grandchildren. Children of William Henry Newdigate, 1824–1885.
25982	5563	Caroline Barbara Newdigate.		
25983	5564	Constance Newdigate.		
25984	5565	Annie Harriet Newdigate.		
25985	5566	Mabel Charlotte Newdigate.		
25986	5567	Eleanor Gertrude Newdigate.		
25987	5568	George Newdigate, J.P., _late_ Lieut.-Col. 5th Battalion Derbyshire Regiment, 1826.		} Sons.
25988	5569	Alfred Newdigate, M.A., 1829. _27 Clarendon Square, Leamington Spa._		
25989	5570	Charles Alfred Newdigate, 1863.		Grandchildren. Children of No. 25988.
25990	5571	Bernard Henry Newdigate, 1869.		
25991	5572	Sebastian Francis Newdigate, 1880.		
25992	5573	Mary Newdigate, 1864.		
25993	5574	Agnes Newdigate, 1870.		
25994	5575	Edith Margaret Newdigate, 1872.		
25995	5576	Katherine Margaret Mary Newdigate, 1875.		
25996	5577	Barbara Maria Newdigate, 1878.		
25997	5578	Sir Henry Richard Legge Newdigate, K.C.B., Lieut.-Gen., _late_ Commanding Infantry Brigade, 1832. _Gable End, Allesley, near Coventry._		} Son.
25998	5579	Richard Francis Newdigate, 1894.		Grandchildren. Children of No. 25997.
25999	5580	Violet Phyllis Newdigate.		
26000	5581	Millicent Newdigate.		
26001	5582	Winifred Mary Augusta Newdigate.		
26002	5583	Frances Barbara, widow of General Sir Lynedoch Gardiner, C.B., K.C.V.O., R.A., Groom-in-Waiting to Queen Victoria, −1897. _Thatched House Lodge, Richmond Park._		} Daughter.
26003	5584	Evelyn Gardiner, 1861.		Grandchildren. Daughters of No. 26002.
26004	5585	Sidney, wife of Charles Orlando Bridgeman, 1864. _Thatched House Lodge, Richmond Park._		
26005	5586	Roger Orlando Bridgeman, 1889.		Great-grandchildren. Children of No. 26004.
26006	5587	Victoria Alexandrina Leopoldina Bridgeman, 1894.		

382. Descendants of Annabella Hungerford Crewe, 1814–1874, and her husband, Richard Monckton, 1st Lord Houghton, 1809–1885. (See Table LIX.)

26007	5588	Robert Offley Ashburton, 1st Earl of Crewe [U.K.], P.C., 1858. _Crewe Hall, Crewe._ _Crewe House, Curzon St., W._		} Son.
26008	5589	Lady Annabella Hungerford, wife of Capt. the Hon. Arthur O'Neill, 1881.		Grandchildren. Children of No. 26007.
26009	5590	Lady Celia Hermione Crewe-Milnes, } 1884.		
26010	5591	Lady Helen Cynthia Crewe-Milnes,		
26011	5592	Hon. Amicia Henrietta, wife of Sir Gerald FitzGerald, K.C.M.G., 1852. _18 Cadogan Gardens, S.W._		} Elder daughter.
26012	5593	Gerald Milnes FitzGerald, 1883.	{ Grandchild. Child of No. 26011.	

| 26013 | 5594 | Hon. Florence Ellen Hungerford, wife of Col. the Hon. Arthur Henry Henniker, C.B., 2nd Battalion Coldstream Guards. 13 *Stratford Place, W.* | Younger daughter. |

---

383. Descendants of Warwick, 3rd Viscount Lake, 1783–1848. (See Table LX.)

| | | Children, if any, of the Hon. Elizabeth Georgiana Lake, 1821–18 , wife (1866) of John Austin Gloag, 18 –1883. |

---

384. Descendants of the Hon. Anna Maria Lake, , and her husband, Sir Richard Borough, 1st Bart., 1756–1837. (See Table LX.)

26014	5595	Margaret Anna Maria, Lady Campbell, widow of Sir George Campbell, 4th Bart., 1829–1874. *Garscube, Dumbartonshire.* *Crarae, Inverary, N.B.*	
26015	5596	Elizabeth Borough.	Grandchildren. Surviving children of Sir Edward Richard Borough, 2nd Bart., 1800–1879.
26016	5597	Augusta Frances, Lady Fludyer, wife of Sir Arthur John Fludyer, 5th Bart. *Ayston Hall, Uppingham.*	
26017	5598	Emily Georgiana, wife of Brig.-Gen. Metcalfe Studholme Brownrigg, Commanding 30th and 47th Regimental Districts and Northern Counties Volunteer Infantry Brigade. *Preston.*	
26018 -19	}	Same as Nos. 24898–24899.	Great-grandchildren. Children of No. 26017.
26020	5599	Sir Thomas George Fermor-Hesketh, 7th Bart., 1849. *Rufford Hall, Ormskirk.*	Great-grandson. Son of Sir Thomas George Hesketh, 5th Bart., 1825–1872, by the Lady Anna Maria Arabella Fermor, 1828–1870, daughter of Thomas William, 4th Earl of Pomfret, 1770–1833, and his wife, Amabel Elizabeth Borough, 1802–1887.
26021	5600	Thomas Fermor-Hesketh, Lieutenant Royal Horse Guards, 1881.	Great-great-grandchildren. Children of No. 26020.
26022	5601	Frederick Fermor-Hesketh, 1883.	
26023	5602	Edith Elizabeth, wife of Lawrence Rawstorne. *Penwortham Priory, Preston.*	Great-granddaughter. Sister to No. 26020.
26024	5603	Lawrence Rawstorne, Captain 7th Hussars, 1874.	Great-great-grandchildren. Children of No. 26023.
26025	5604	Thomas Geoffrey Rawstorne, 1879.	
26026	5605	Marjory, wife of Charles Marson.	
26027	5606	Constance Maria Hesketh.	Great-granddaughter. Younger sister to No. 26020.

KING JAMES IV
1473 - 1513
PAINTED BY DANIEL MYTENS

385. Descendants, if any, of the Hon. Annabella Lake, 17 –1831, wife of Joseph Brooks, of Everton, near Liverpool; of the Hon. Elizabeth Lake, 17 –18 , wife of Colonel Sir John Harvey, K.C.B., Governor of Newfoundland; the Hon. Frances Lake, 17 –18 ; and the Hon. Anne Lake, 17 – 1845, wife of Lieut.-General John Wardlaw. (See Table LX.)

---

386. Descendants of Lieut.-Col. Ferdinando Smith, of Halesowen, Grange, co. Worcester, 1779–1841. (See Table LXI.)

26028	5607	Ferdinando Dudley Lea Smith, J.P., D.L., 1834. *Halesowen Grange, Worcester.*	Only surviving child.
26029	5608	Ferdinando Dudley William Lea Smith, 1872.	Grandchildren. Children of No. 26028.
26030	5609	Lilian Amy Lea Smith.	

387. Descendants of Frances Caroline Smith, 1783–1852, and her husband, Marcus John Annesley of Oakley Park, co. Down, 1782–1858. (See Table LXI.)

26031	5610	Harriet Annesley. *Nyewood, Bognor.*	Daughter.

388. Descendants, if any, of Anne Smith, and her husband, Edward Baker, of Hill Court and Grafton Flyford, co. Worcester. (See Table LXI.)

---

389. Descendants of Joseph Smart, Tenant Farmer at Oatenfields, 1813–1877. (See Table LXII.)

26032	5611	Robert Smart, Farmer, 1848. *Barnsley Hall, Bromsgrove.*	Eldest son.
26033	5612	Harry Smart, 1875.	
26034	5613	George Smart, 1884.	Grandchildren. Children of No. 26032.
26035	5614	Amy Smart, 1882.	
26036	5615	Gertrude Smart, 1889.	
26037	5616	Charlotte Smart, 1891.	
26038	5617	Joseph Smart, Auctioneer and Estate Agent, 1850. *Halesowen, co. Worcester.*	2nd and 3rd sons.
26039	5618	William Smart, Farmer, 1852. *Frankley, near Halesowen.*	
26040	5619	William Smart.	
26041	5620	Joseph Smart.	
26042	5621	Edward Smart.	
26043	5622	Harry Smart.	Grandchildren. Children of No. 26039.
26044	5623	Edith Smart.	
26045	5624	Lilian Smart.	
26046	5625	Annie Smart.	

26047	5626	John Green Smart, Butcher, 1855. *Belfast.*	} 4th son.	
26048	5627	Edward Smart.		Grandchildren. Children of No. 26047.
26049	5628	Walter Smart.		
26050	5629	Edith Smart.		
26051	5630	Susanna Jane, wife of Thomas Higgins, 1846. *Braffield-on-Green, Northampton.*	} Eldest daughter.	
26052	5631	Joseph Thomas Higgins, 1876.	} Grandchildren. Children of No. 26051.	
26053	5632	Emily Higgins, 1878.		
26054	5633	Emily, wife of Hugh Higgins, 1858. *Stoke Goldington Lodge, near Newport Pagnell, Bucks.*	} 2nd daughter.	
26055	5634	Hugh Higgins, 1889.		
26056	5635	Emily Higgins, 1880.		
26057	5636	Mary Higgins, 1881.		
26058	5637	Elizabeth Higgins, 1883.		Grandchildren. Children of No. 26054.
26059	5638	Gertrude Higgins, 1885.		
26060	5639	Constance Higgins, 1887.		
26061	5640	Alice Higgins, 1891.		
26062	5641	Ethel Higgins, 1895.		
26063	5642	Violet Higgins, 1898.		
26064	5643	Lizzie Maria, wife of Walter Henderson, 1860. *Sunnybank, Strandtown, Belfast.*	} 3rd daughter.	
26065	5644	Walter Henderson.		Grandchildren. Children of No. 26064.
26066	5645	Dorothy Henderson.		
26067	5646	Gladys Henderson.		
26068	5647	Edith Smart, 1866. *Halesowen.*	} Younger daughters	
26069	5648	Alice, wife of Richard Edmund, 1866. *Johannesburg, South Africa.*		
26070	5649	Lewie Edmund.	Grandchild. Son of No. 26069.	

390. Descendants of Robert Smart, 1815–1893. (See Table LXII.)

26071	5650	Frances, wife of John Page, 1858. *Hill Pool, Kidderminster.*	} Elder daughter.	
26072	5651	John Edward Page, 1884.		Grandchildren. Children of No. 26071.
26073	5652	Robert Page, 1887.		
26074	5653	Ethel Mary Page, 1885.		
26075	5654	Dorothy Frances Page, 1893.		
26076	5655	Elsie Oldnall Page, 1895.		
26077	5656	Nancy Hilda Page, 1897.		
26078	5657	Lucy, wife of Richard Thomas Pearson, 1862. *Brooklands, Halesowen, Worcester.*	} Younger daughter.	
26079	5658	Ruby Smart Pearson, 1887.		Grandchildren. Children of No. 26078.
26080	5659	Ada Pearson, 1888.		
26081	5660	Kathleen Edna Pearson, 1899.		

391. Descendants of Jane Catherine Wilmot, –1849, and her husband, Alexander Rait, Baker, of 12 Southampton Terrace, Islington, London, 1788–1844. (See Table LXII.)

| 26082 | 5661 | Alexander Francis William Rait, Sailor, 1842. Children of No. 13667. | Son. | |

392. Descendants of Mary Anne Wilmot, –18 , and her husband, Edward Studley, of West Stratton, near Winchester, –1870. (See Table LXII.)

26083	5662	Walter Studley.	
26084	5663	Edward Studley. Children, if any, of Charlotte Studley, wife of Edward Young, of Petersfield, Hants.	
26085	5664	Catherine, wife of . . . . Filford. Children, if any, of No. 26085.	Children.
26086	5665	Julia, wife of . . . . Yard. Children, if any, of No. 26086.	

393. Descendants of David Sinclair Wilmot, Accountant, of Bristol, 1801–1862. (See Table LXII.)

26087	5666	Frederick Lea Wilmot, 1861.	Grandchild. Eldest son of Walter Benjamin Wilmot, 1827–1897.
26088	5667	Francis Wilmot, 1894.	Great-grandchildren. Children of No. 26087.
26089	5668	Dudley Wilmot, 1901.	
26090	5669	Dorothy Wilmot, 1892.	
26091	5670	Edward Dudley Lea Wilmot, Solicitor, 1869. 220 *Brixton Road, S.W.*	Grandchildren. Brothers and sister to No. 26087.'
26092	5671	Henry Sinclair Wilmot, 1870.	
26093	5672	Frances Mary, wife of Robert Morton Ody, 1864.	
26094	5673	Robert Henry Morton Ody, 1902.	Great-grandchild. Son of No. 26093.
26095	5674	Caroline Dudley, wife of Victor Herbert Sanders, 1868.	Grandchild. Younger sister to No. 26087.
26096	5675	Katherine Frances Elizabeth Sanders, 1899.	Great-grandchild. Daughter of No. 26095.
26097	5676	George Lea Wilmot, 1833. *Cliff Terrace, Wigram Road, Forest Lodge, Sydney, N.S.W.*	Eldest surviving son.
26098	5677	George Ernest Dudley Wilmot, 1867. *Sydney Road, Parkville, Victoria.*	Grandson. Son of No. 26097.
26099	5678	Edith Wilmot.	Great-grandchild. Daughter of No. 26098.
26100	5679	Frederick Lea Dudley Wilmot, 1869. *Wigram Road, Forest Lodge, Sydney.*	Grandchildren. Children of No. 26097.
26101	5680	Nellie Blanche Dudley, wife of Alfred John Heskett, 1866. *Western Australia.*	
26102	5681	Herbert Heskett.	Great-grandchildren. Children of No. 26101.
26103	5682	Frank Heskett.	
26104	5683	Jane Kate, wife of Henry Lovell Woolacott, 1873. 112 *Annandale Street, Annandale, Sydney.*	Grandchildren. Children of No. 26097.
26105	5684	Edith Wingrove, wife of Benjamin Arthur Wells, 1875. "*Wingrove," Belgrave Street, Kogarah, Sydney, N.S.W.*	
26106	5685	Arthur Dudley Wells.	Great-grandchildren. Children of No. 26105.
26107	5686	Edith Amiè Wilmot Wells.	
21108	5687	Florence Rose, wife of Arthur H. Reuss, 1880. *Mosman's Bay, Sydney, N.S.W.*	Grandchildren. Daughters of No. 26097.
26109	5688	Millicent Alice Wilmot, } twins, 1882.	
26110	5689	Maud Ada Wilmot,	

26111	5690	William Henry Wilmot, 1839.	Zanesville, Ohio, U.S.A.	Younger surviving son and daughters.
26112	5691	Jane Sinclair Wilmot, 1828.		
26113	5692	Emma Woodcock Wilmot, 1837.		

394. Descendants of Anne Woodcock Wilmot, 1803–1878, wife of James Rees, Proprietor of the "Carnarvon Herald," 1801–1880. (See Table LXII.)

26114	5693	James Herbert Rees, late Captain 2nd Battalion V.B. Royal Welsh Fusiliers, 1866. *Bronseiriol, Carnarvon.*	Grandchildren. Children of Wilmot Rees, 1836–1869.
26115	5694	Ernest Wilmot Rees, 1867. *New Brighton, Cheshire.*	
26116	5695	Percy Llewellyn Rees, 1869. *Durban, Natal, South Africa.*	
26117	5696	Ethel Sinclair, wife of Harry Williamson Teed. 11 *Grove Hill Road, Denmark Hill, S.E.*	Grandchild. Daughter of Llewellyn Rees, 1842–1876.
26118	5697	Charles Herbert Rees, Solicitor, late Colonel Commanding 3rd Volunteer Battalion Royal Welsh Fusiliers, 1847. *Plas Llanwnda, Carnarvon.*	Son.
26119	5698	Lionel Rees, 1884. *Royal Military Academy, Woolwich.*	Grandchildren. Children of No. 26118.
26120	5699	Muriel Rees.	
26121	5700	Catherine Mary Rees. 40 *Bon Accord Terrace, Aberdeen.*	Daughters.
26122	5701	Frances Ellen, wife of the Rev. James Myers Danson, D.D. 19 *Bon Accord Terrace, Aberdeen.*	
26123	5702	Arthur Llewellyn Danson, B.A., Indian Civil Service, 1875.	Grandchildren. Children of No. 26122.
26124	5703	Edmund Wilmot Danson, R.I.M., 1877.	
26125	5704	Ernest Denny Logie Danson, 1880.	
26126	5705	James Gordon Danson, 1885.	
26127	5706	John Rhys Danson, 1887.	
26128	5707	Mary Christabel Danson.	
26129	5708	Theodora Danson, } twins.	
26130	5709	Frances Sybil Danson, }	
26131	5710	Emily Danson.	

395 Descendants, if any, of William Winkworth Wilmot, 1817–18 , of Charles Wilmot, China dealer at Hartlepool (1859), 1819–18 , or of Walter Wilmot, 1824–18 . (See Table LXII.)

396. Descendants of Thomas Fereday of Dudhill, Salop, J.P., F.R.C.S., 1806–1888. (See Table LXIII.)

26132	5711	Fanny Wright, wife of Edward Lloyd Gatacre, of Gatacre. *Dudhill, Bridgnorth, Salop.*	Only surviving child.

The Blood Royal of Britain

397. Descendants of Joseph Fereday, 7th Hussars. See Table LXIII.)

26133	5712	Joseph Bernard Fereday.	Elder son.
26134	5713	Gerald Andrew Fereday, aged 11.	Grandchildren. Children
26135	5714	Millicent Sheridan Fereday, aged 17.	of No. 26133.
26136	5715	(Patrick) Edward Fereday.	Younger son.
26137	5716	Joseph Beaufort Fereday, aged 18.	
26138	5717	Walter Dudley Fereday, aged 14.	Grandchildren. Children
26139	5718	Hilda Kathleen Fereday, aged 12.	of No. 26136.
26140	5719	Norah Olive Fereday, aged 7.	
26141	5720	Catherine, wife of J. P. Millerchip. *South Africa.*	Daughter.
26142	5721	William Millerchip.	
26143	5722	Olive Millerchip.	
26144	5723	Kathleen Millerchip.	Grandchildren. Children of No. 26141.
26145	5724	Elizabeth Millerchip.	
26146	5725	. . . . . . Millerchip.	

398. Descendants of Elizabeth Fereday, 1813–1898, wife of the Rev. Thomas Tylecote, B.D., Canon of Ely, and Rector of Marston - Morteyne, Bedfordshire, 1798 - 1882. (See Table LXIII.)

26147	5726	Rev. Thomas Beaufort Tylecote, Rector of Lowther. *Askham Hall, Penrith.*	
26148	5727	Charles Brandon Lea Tylecote. *Askham Hall, Penrith.*	
26149	5728	Edward Ferdinando Sutton Tylecote. *Durham House, Lansdowne Road, Bournemouth.*	Sons and daughter.
26150	5729	Henry Grey Tylecote. *The Golden Parsonage, Hemel Hempstead, Herts.*	
26151	5730	Elizabeth Margaret Beaufort Tylecote. *Askham Hall, Penrith.*	

399. Descendants of Anne Woodcock Fereday, –18 , wife of Robert Hammersley, of Birmingham, –18 . (See Table LXIII.)

26152	5731	Zanora Wilmot Hammersley. *Hayes, Beckenham, Kent.*	Daughter.

26153	5732	Sarah, widow of Bradford Rudge,	–1882.	Table LXIII.
		Leahurst, Bedford.		

400. Descendant of above, No. 26153.

26154	5733	Catherine Helen Frances Lea Rudge.	Daughter

401. Descendants, if any, of William Woodcock Davenport, Thomas Gingell of Bilston, 1846, Charles Gingell, 35th Foot, 1846, Alexander Gingell of Bilston, 1846, or Emma Gingell of Bilston, 1846. (See Table LXIV.)

---

402. Descendants of Elizabeth Wilmot, 1797–1862, wife of William Barton, of Stanley Grange, Derby, Farmer, 1789–1873. (See Table LXII.)

26155	5734	William Barton, 1869.	Arundel, Duffield Road, Derby.	Grandchildren. Children of William Barton, 1821–1890.
26156	5735	Mary Barton, 1862.		
26157	5736	Annie Barton, 1864.		
26158	5737	Catherine Barton, 1866.		
26159	5738	John Arthur Barton, 1872.		Grandchildren. Children of John Barton, 1827–1890.
26160	5739	William Barton, 1874.		
26161	5740	Edward Barton, 1876. 40 Gerard Street, Derby.		
26162	5741	Elizabeth Ann Barton, 1878.		
26163	5742	Kate Barton, 1880.		
26164	5743	Thomas Barton, 1833. London Road, Kegworth.		Son and daughter.
26165	5744	Elizabeth, wife of Samuel Tomlinson, 1830. Beech-Hurst, Thulston, Derby.		
26166	5745	Kate, wife of Richard Poyser, 1865. Onebarrow Lodge, Coalville.		Grandchild. Eldest daughter of No. 26165.
26167	5746	Richard Wilmot Poyser, 1901.		Great-grandchildren. Children of No. 26166.
26168	5747	Kathleen Poyser, 1892.		
26169	5748	Mary Wilmot Poyser, 1894.		
26170	5749	Jean Poyser, 1895.		
26171	5750	Mona Poyser, 1897.		
26172	5751	Mary, wife of William Riley, 1867. Thulston, Derby.		Grandchild. 2nd daughter of No. 26165.
26173	5752	Edith Mary Riley, 1895.		Great-grandchildren. Children of No. 26172.
26174	5753	Margaret Riley, 1898.		
26175	5754	Norah Tomlinson Riley, 1902.		
26176	5755	Elizabeth Anne Tomlinson, 1869.		Grandchildren. Younger daughters of No. 26165.
26177	5756	Edith Tomlinson, 1871.		

---

403. Descendants, if any, of Elizabeth Green, 1785–18 , wife of Edward Butler Walker, of Edgbaston, Birmingham, 1788–1836. (See Table LXV.)

---

404. Descendants, if any, of Frances Green, 18 , wife of Alexander Seymour Wills. (See Table LXV.)

---

405. Descendants, if any, of Maria Green, 1792–1852, wife of John Meeson, of Albrighton, Salop, –1840. (See Table LXV.)

406. Descendants, if any, of Elizabeth Tolley, wife of Henry Morgan of Dudley, Painter. (See Table LXVI.)

---

407. Descendants, if any, of Mary Lea, c. 1720-1742, wife of Joseph Harvey of Stourbridge, Worcester, Physician.* (See Table LXI.)

---

408. Descendants of Catherine Turner, 1775-1858, wife of George Jones of Donington, Salop, 1781-1857. (See Table LXVII.)

26178	5757	Henry Francis John Vaughan, Lord of the Manor of Humphreston, 1841. 30 *Edwardes Square, Kensington.*	Grandson. Son of John Jones, of Ruckley Grange, Salop, 1805-1882.
26179	5758	Henry Humphreston Scott Vaughan, 2nd Lieutenant Royal Field Artillery, 1877.	Great-grandchildren. Children of No. 26178.
26180	5759	John Courtenay Folliott Dudley Vaughan, of St. Thomas' Hospital, 1879.	
		Other children of John Jones of Ruckley (son).	
26181	5760	Theodosia, widow of John Barker, Sheriff of Staffordshire, -1851.	Daughters.
		Children of No. 26181.	
26182	5761	Eleanor Jones.	

409. Descendants, if any, of Phoebe Turner, 1790-18 , wife of John Barker, 17 -1860. (See Table LXVII.)

---

410. Descendants, if any, of Catherine Jordan, 17 -18 , wife of Captain Lancelot Rutter, 17 . (See Table LXVII.)

---

411. Descendants,† if any, of Frances Jordan, 17 -18 , wife (1773) of Hugh Edwards, 17 -18 . (See Table LXVII.)

---

412. Descendants of Anne Jordan, 17 - , wife of Thomas Smith, 17 - . (See Table LXVII.)

---

* Died on Thursday (22nd March 1821), Mrs. Venour, formerly an inhabitant of this town, and daughter of the *late* Dr. Hervey.—*Birmingham Gazette*, 26th March 1821.
† On 11th November 1802, Hugh Edwards and his wife were both living. See a letter of that date written from the War Office. He mentions his son, and Fanny, Kitty, and Anne, presumably his daughters.

413. Descendants of Lady Margaret Henrietta Maria Grey, 1825–1852, 1st wife of Henry John Milbank, of Newsham, Yorks, J.P., D.L., 1824–1872. (See Table LXVIII.)

26183	5762	Katharine Henrietta Venezia, wife of Arthur Duncombe, J.P., D.L., 1848. *Sutton Hall, Easingwold, Yorkshire.*	Daughter.
26184	5763	Cecily, wife of the Hon. Edmund Somerset Butler Rawson, 1877. *111 Park Street, W.*	Grandchildren. Children of No. 26183.
26185	5764	Muriel Katharine, wife of the Hon. George Nicholas de Yarburgh-Bateson, 1880. *The Danes, Little Berkhampstead, Hertford.*	
26186	5765	Margaret Louisa Arkwright. *Overton, Marton, Wanganee, N.Z.*	Grandchild. Daughter of Louisa Elizabeth Jane Milbank, 1849–1873, 1st wife of Francis Arkwright, of Overton Hall, Derby, and Marton, Wellington, N.Z.

414. Descendants of Lady Henrietta Charlotte Grey, 1798–1866, and her husband, the Rev. James Thomas Law, Chancellor of Lichfield and Coventry, Master of St. John's Hospital, Lichfield, 1790–1876. (See Table LXVIII.)

26187	5766	James Adeane Law, *late* Major 3rd Battalion Somerset A.V., J.P., Somerset, 1824.	Eldest surviving son.
26188	5767	James Henry Adeane Law, 1860.	Grandsons. Children of No. 26187.
26189	5768	Charles William Albert Law, 1861.	
26190	5769	Edmund Christian Law, Barrister-at-Law, *late* principal Surrogate at Lichfield, 1828.	2nd surviving son.
26191	5770	Francis Grey Cotgrave Law, 1876.	Grandchildren. Children of No. 26190.
26192	5771	Cyril Warrington Law, 1877.	
26193	5772	Eliza Henrietta Law.	
26194	5773	. . . . Law, 1879.	
26195	5774	Charlotte Jane Law.	Daughter.

415. Descendants of Lady Jane Grey, 1804–1877, and her husband, John Benn, 1st Lord Ormathwaite, 1798–1881. (See Table LXVIII.)

26196	5775	Arthur, 2nd Lord Ormathwaite [U.K.], 1827. *Strettington, Chichester.*	Son.

26197	5776	Hon. Arthur Henry John Walsh, D.L., 1859. *Warfield Park, Bracknell, Berks.*	
26198	5777	Hon. Charles Edward Walsh, Chief Constable of Radnor, Captain and Brevet-Major, *late* 3rd Battalion Rifle Brigade, 1862. *Penybont, Radnorshire.*	
26199	5778	Hon. George Harry William Walsh, Captain, Reserve of Officers, 1863. *Guards'.*	
26200	5779	Hon. Gerald Walsh, 1864. 6 *St James' Place, S.W.*	Grandchildren. Children of No. 26196.
26201	5780	Hon. Nigel Christopher Walsh, Inspector of Reformatories, 1867.	
26202	5781	Hon. Reginald Walsh, H.B.M.'s Consul at the Piræus. *British Consulate, Piræus, Greece.*	
26203	5782	Hon. Margaret Blanche Walsh, 1860.	
26204	5783	Hon Edith Katharine Walsh, 1861.	
26205	5784	Hon. Emily Gertrude Walsh, 1870.	
26206	5785	Rev. Arthur George Digby Walsh, 1856. *Carrington Vicarage, Cheshire.*	
26207	5786	Henry John Digby Walsh, 1859.	27 *Royal Crescent, Bath.*
26208	5787	Jane Grey Digby Walsh, 1861.	Grandchildren. Children of the Rev. and Hon. Digby Walsh, 1829–1869.
26209	5788	Hon. Maria Katherine, wife of Captain Horace Dormer Trelawny. *Shotwick Park, near Chester.*	Elder daughter.
26210	5789	Florence, wife of Francis Edward Rooper. *Bronydd, Glyn, Ruabon.*	Grandchild. Child of No. 26209.
26211	5790	Florence Isolda Rooper, 1899.	Great-grandchild. Daughter of No. 26210.
26212	5791	Maud Trelawny.	Grandchildren. Children of No. 26209.
26213	5792	Hilda, wife of John Herbert Upton-Cottrell-Dormer.	
26214	5793	John Trelawny Upton-Cottrell-Dormer, 1893.	Great-grandchildren. Children of No. 26213.
26215	5794	Joan Upton-Cottrell-Dormer, 1901.	
26216	5795	Lilian Trelawny.	Grandchildren. Children of No. 26209.
26217	5796	Miny Trelawny.	
26218	5797	Hon. Augusta Rosa, wife of Charles Edward Barnett, 1840. *Edge Grove, Watford.*	Younger daughter.
26219	5798	Walter Edward Barnett, 1873. *The Red Hall, Rickmansworth.*	Grandson. Son of No. 26218.
26220	5799	Charles Richard Barnett, 1900.	Great-grandson. Son of No. 26219.
26221	5800	Henry Granville Barnett, 1877.	
26222	5801	Geoffrey Arthur Barnett, 1880.	
26223	5802	Ralph Francis Barnett, 1882.	Grandchildren. Children of No. 26218.
26224	5803	Mabel Alice, wife of the Rev. and Hon. Kenneth Francis Gibbs, Hon. Canon of St. Albans, 1874. *Aldenham Vicarage, Herts.*	
26225	5804	Alan Christopher Henry Gibbs, 1895.	
26226	5805	Leonard Charles Michael Gibbs, 1806.	Great-grandchildren. Children of No. 26224.
26227	5806	Raymond Kenneth Gibbs, 1901.	
26228	5807	Dorothea Louisa Gibbs, 1897.	

416. Descendants of the Rev. George Chetwode, of Chilton House, Bucks, 1791–1870. (See Table LXIX.)

26229	5808	Sir George Chetwode, 6th Baronet, 1823. *Oakley, Market Drayton. Chetwode, Buckingham.*	Son.
26230	5809	Philip Walhouse Chetwode, D.S.O., Captain 19th Hussars, 1869.	
26231	5810	George Knightley Chetwode, Lieutenant R.N., 1877.	
26232	5811	Evelyn Hamar, wife of Percy Alfred Leyland Laming, 1870. *25 Pont Street, S.W.*	Grandchildren. Children of No. 26229.
26233	5812	Laura Grey, wife of Christian Edward Cornwallis Eliot, 1872. *114 Sloane Street, S.W.*	
26234	5813	Frederica Betty Cornwallis Eliot, 1900.	Great-grandchild. Child of No. 26233.
26235	5814	Florence Hyacinthe Chetwode, 1876.	Grandchild. Child of No. 26229.
26236	5815	Augustus Littleton Chetwode, 1833. *Berners Hall, Ongar.*	2nd son.
			Grandchildren. Children of Emily Hyacinthe Anne Chetwode, –1899, wife of Joseph Baily of Skenley House, Bucks.
26237	5816	Hyacinthe Laura, widow of the Rev. William Mundeford Bramston, 1892. *Ongar, Essex.*	Daughter.
26238	5817	Mabel Charlotte Bramston.	Grandchildren. Children of No. 26237.
26239	5818	Eleanor Hyacinthe Bramston.	

417. Descendants of Philip Chetwode, Lieutenant R.N., 1805–1844. (See Table LXIX.)

26240	5819	Henrietta Dorothy Boughey, wife of the Rev. John Thomas Vaudrey, M.A. *Wyke Regis, Dorset.*	Only child.

418. Descendants of Frederic Chetwode, 1810–1863. (See Table LXIX.)

26241	5820	John Frederic Saunders King, 1859.	
26242	5821	Richard King, 1860.	
26243	5822	Chetwode Henry Waters King, 1863.	
26244	5823	Philip Alexander King, 1864.	Grandchildren. Children of Elizabeth Louisa Chetwode, –1879, and her husband, Richard King, Staff Surgeon R.N.
26245	5824	George Chetwode King, 1865.	
26246	5825	Arthur Herbert King, 1867.	
26247	5826	William Charles Dumas King, 1869.	
26248	5827	Ernest Walter Andrew Stamford King, 1874.	
26249	5828	Reginald Herbert Chetwode King, 1876.	
26250	5829	Margaret Elizabeth Henrietta Sophia King.	
26251	5830	Rosalie Florence Mary Rebecca King.	

The Blood Royal of Britain

419. Descendants of Henrietta Dorothy Chetwode, —1849, and her husband, Sir John Fenton Fletcher Boughey, 2nd Bart., M.P., 1784–1823. (See Table LXIX.)

26252	5831	Sir Thomas Fletcher Boughey, 4th Bart., D.L., 1836. *Aqualate, Newport, Shropshire.*	Grandchildren. Children of the late Sir Thomas Fletcher Boughey, 3rd Bart., 1809–1880.
26253	5832	Rev. George Boughey, 1837. *Forton Rectory, Newport, Shropshire.*	
26254	5833	Ethel Boughey.	Great-grandchildren. Children of No. 26253.
26255	5834	Eva Paulina Boughey.	
26256	5835	Dorothy Boughey.	
26257	5836	Mary Boughey	
26258	5837	William Fletcher Boughey, Commander R.N. (retired), 1840.	Grandchildren. Brothers and sisters to No. 26252, &c.
26259	5838	Rev. Robert Boughey, 1843. *Betley Vicarage, Crewe.*	
26260	5839	Francis Boughey, 1848.	
26261	5840	Henry Boughey, Colonel, *late* York and Lancaster Regiment, 1850.	
26262	5841	Louisa Boughey.	
26263	5842	Lucy Harriet Boughey.	
26264	5843	Selina Henrietta Boughey.	
26265	5844	George Fletcher Ottley Boughey, C.S.I., *late* Colonel R.E., 1844.	Grandson. Son of Lieut.-Col. George Fenton Fletcher Boughey, 1813–1855.
26266	5845	George Menteth Boughey, 1879.	Great-grandchildren. Children of No 26265.
26267	5846	Amy Matilda, wife of William Arthur Briscoe.	
26268	5847	Elizabeth Mabws, wife of Captain Duncan Darroch, 2nd Battalion Princess Louise's (Argyll and Sutherland) Highlanders.	
26269	5848	. . . . Darroch, 1901.	Great-great-grandchild. Daughter of No. 26268.
26270	5849	John Boughey, Major-General, *late* Wiltshire Regiment, 1845.	Grandson. Brother to No. 26265.
26271	5850	Percy Fletcher Boughey, 1882.	Great-grandchildren. Children of No. 26270.
26272	5851	Ethel Boughey.	
26273	5852	Rev. Anchitel Harry Fletcher Boughey, Senior Dean and Fellow, Trinity College, Cambridge, 1849. *11 Harvey Road, Cambridge.*	Grandson. Brother to No. 26265.
26274	5853	Charles Lovell Fletcher Boughey, 1887.	Great-grandchildren. Children of No 26273.
26275	5854	Anchitel Edward Fletcher Boughey, 1891.	
26276	5855	Constance Evelyn Mary Boughey.	
26277	5856	Katharine Clara Boughey.	
26278	5857	William Charles Fletcher Boughey, 1874.	Grandchildren. Children of William Fenton Fletcher Boughey, Recorder of Shrewsbury, 1814–1890.
26279	5858	Edward Harry Fletcher Boughey, Lieutenant R.N., 1878. *Junior Naval and Military.*	
26280	5859	John Fletcher Boughey, } twins, 1882.	
26281	5860	George Fletcher Boughey, }	
26282	5861	Alfred Fletcher Boughey, R.N., 1883.	
26283	5862	Henrietta Emma Boughey.	

323

26284	5863	Walter Thomas Courtenay Giffard, J.P., D.L., 1839. *Chillingham, near Wolverhampton. Pendryl Hall, Codsall Wood.*	Grandchild. Child of Henrietta Dorothy Boughey, —1889, and her husband, Walter Peter Giffard of Chillington, 1796–1877.
26285	5864	Thomas Arthur Walter Giffard, 1882.	Great-grandchildren. Children of No. 26284.
26286	5865	Hugh Peter William Giffard, 1892.	
26287	5866	Winifred Mary Sophia Giffard.	
26288	5867	Barbara Constance Anne Giffard.	
26289	5868	Henrietta Charlotte, wife of Charles Henry Inge. *Broom Leasoe, Whittington, co. Stafford.*	Grandchildren. Sisters of No. 26284.
26290	5869	Selina Anne, wife of Augustus Leveson Vernon. *Hilton Park, co. Stafford.*	
26291	5870	Henry Arthur Leveson Vernon, D.L., 1868. *Culmleigh, Stoke Canon, Exeter.*	Great-grandchild. Son of No. 26290.
26292	5871	Dorothy Vernon, 1898.	Great-great-grandchild. Daughter of No. 26291.
26293	5872	Walter Bertie William Vernon, 1871.	Great-grandchildren. Children of No. 26290.
26294	5873	Henrietta Catherine Vernon, 1867.	
26295	5874	Selina Mary Vernon, 1870.	
26296	5875	Edward Joseph Mostyn, 1857. *Tower House, Arundel.*	Grandchild. Son of Anastasia Elizabeth Boughey, — 1893, and her 2nd husband, Captain Edward Henry Mostyn, 1813–1895.
26297	5876	Joseph Edward Mostyn, 1889.	Great-grandchildren. Children of No. 26296.
26298	5877	Joseph Cecil Mostyn, 1891.	
26299	5878	Joseph Philip Mostyn, 1894.	
26300	5879	Mary Filumina Mostyn, 1895.	
26301	5880	Mary Josephine Mostyn, a nun, 1849.	Grandchildren. Sisters to No. 26296.
26302	5881	Frances Barbara Mostyn, 1850.	
			Grandchildren. Children of Elizabeth Boughey, — 1876, and her husband, the Rev. Robert Dayrell.

420. Descendants, if any, of Anne Maria Chetwode,   —1851, wife of the Rev. Richard Farrer, of Ashley, co. Northampton. (See Table LXIX.)

421. Descendants of John Cotes, of Woodcote, co. Salop, M.P., 1799–1874. (See Table LXX.)

26303	5882	Charles James Cotes, *of Woodcote and Pitchford Hall, co. Salop,* J.P., *late* Lieut.-Col. Grenadier Guards, 1847. *Woodcote, Newport, Salop.*	Children.
26304	5883	Victoria Alexandrina, wife of Lieut.-Gen. Sir Robert Grant, G.C.B., R.E. *14 Granville Place, Portman Square, W.*	
26305	5884	Charles John Cecil Grant, 1877.	Grandchild. Son of No. 26304.
26306	5885	Catherine Maria, wife of Orlando John George Bridgeman-Simpson.	2nd daughter.

26307	5886	Lilian Frances Bridgeman-Simpson, 1874.	Grandchildren. Children of No. 26306.
26308	5887	Evelyn Mary Bridgeman-Simpson, 1877.	
26309	5888	Olga Florence Bridgeman-Simpson, 1878.	
26310	5889	Elizabeth Evelyn, wife of John Murray Mordaunt, 66 *Eccleston Square, W.*	3rd daughter.
26311	5890	Henry John Mordaunt, 1867.	Grandchildren. Children of No. 26310.
26312	5891	Eustace Mordaunt, 1870.	
26313	5892	Gerald John Mordaunt, 1873.	
26314	5893	Eustace John Mordaunt, 1901.	Great-grandchild. Son of No. 26313.
26315	5894	Mabel Louisa Mordaunt.	Grandchildren. Daughters of No. 26310.
26316	5895	Gertrude Mordaunt.	
26317	5896	Selina Charlotte Cotes.	Youngest daughters.
26318	5897	Louisa Harriet Cotes.	

422. Descendants of the Rev. Charles Grey Cotes, Rector of Stanton St. Quintin, Wilts, 1801–1866. (See Table LXX.)

26319	5898	Charles Cotes, *of Burcot, Leighton Buzzard*, 1846. 8A *Gloucester Place, W.*	Sons.
26320	5899	Arthur Cotes, *of Seagry, Chippenham*, C.C. and J.P., Major, *late* Suffolk Regiment, 1850. *Seagry House, Chippenham.*	
26321	5900	Lucy Cotes.	Daughter.

423. Descendants, if any, of Louisa Henrietta Cotes,   –   , wife of the Rev. W. Corfield, Rector of Llangattock, South Wales, Sophia Cotes, Emily Cotes, and Selina Henrietta Cotes,   –   , wife of W. Ruddam of Ruddam. (See Table LXX.)

424. Descendants of Georgina Frances Cotes, 1807–1846, and her husband, the Rev. John Brooke, of Haughton Hall, Salop, 1803–1881. (See Table LXX.)

26322	5901	William John Brooke, 1876. *Haughton Hall, Salop.*	Grandchildren. Children of John Townshend Brooke, of Haughton Hall, 1844–1899.
26323	5902	George Townshend Brooke, 1878.	
26324	5903	Basil Richard Brooke, 1882.	
26325	5904	Madeline Harriet Brooke, 1879.	
26326	5905	Evelyn Georgiana Brooke, 1881.	
26327	5906	Bertha Mary Brooke, 1884.	
26328	5907	Rev. Charles Brooke, 1846. *Grendon Vicarage, Northampton.*	Son.

425. Descendants of Sir John Lister-Kaye, 2nd Bart., 1801–1871. (See Table LXXI.)

| 26329 | 5908 | Sir John Pepys Lister-Kaye, 3rd Bart., 1853. 26 *Manchester Square, W.* | Grandsons. Sons of Lister Lister-Kaye, 1827–1855. |
| 26330 | 5909 | Cecil Edmund Lister-Kaye, J.P., D.L., 1854. *Denby Grange, Wakefield.* | |

26331	5910	Kenelm Arthur Lister-Kaye, 1892.	Great-grandchildren. Children of No. 26330.
26332	5911	Adeline Cecilia Lister-Kaye, 1881.	
26333	5912	Frances Lois Lister-Kaye, 1882.	
26334	5913	Florence Lister-Kaye, 1885.	
26335	5914	Lister Lister-Kaye, 1873.	Grandchildren. Children of Captain Arthur Lister-Kaye, 1834–1893.
26336	5915	Arthur Lister-Kaye, 1876.	
26337	5916	John Arthur Lister-Kaye, 1895.	Great-grandchildren. Children of No. 26336.
26338	5917	Reginald Aubrey Lister-Kaye, 1901.	
26339	5918	Helen Lister-Kaye, 1896	
26340	5919	Hermione, wife of William Howard Murphy Grimshaw. 109 *Cromwell Road, S. W.*	Grandchild. Sister to Nos. 26335, &c.
26341	5920	Hermione Eugenia Elizabeth Grimshaw, 1895.	Great-grandchild. Daughter of No. 26340.
26342	5921	Amelia Lister-Kaye.	Grandchildren. Younger sisters to No. 26335, &c.
26343	5922	Violet Eugenia, wife of Arthur Hyde Hulton. *Wood Bank, Macclesfield.*	
26344	5923	Emma Lister-Kaye. *Overton Lodge, Wakefield.*	Daughters.
26345	5924	Laura, Lady Paul, widow of Sir Aubrey John Dean Paul, 3rd Bart., 1829–1890. *Molino del Ponte, Alassio, Liguria.*	
26346	5925	Marcia, widow of Robert Hartley Bower, 1886. *Daresbury House, York.*	
26347	5926	Major Robert Lister Bower, C.M.G., 1860. *Naval and Military.*	Grandson. Son of No. 26346.
26348 -50	}	Same as Nos. 23452–23454.	Great-grandchildren. Children of No. 26347.
26351	5927	Tatton Henry Bower, 1867. *Nun Appleton, Bolton Percy.*	Grandson. Son of No. 26346.
26352	5928	Leonard Tatton Bower, 1898.	Great-grandsons. Sons of No. 26351.
26353	5929	Jasper Angus Tatton Bower, 1902.	
26354	5930	Helen Matilda Bower.	Grandchildren. Daughters of No. 26346.
26355	5931	Maud Amelia, wife of Alfred James Bethell. *Middlethorpe Lodge, Dringhouses, York.*	
26356	5932	Esmée Violet Helen Bethell.	Great-grandchildren. Children of No. 26355.
26357	5933	Enid Maud Bethell.	
26358	5934	Ruth Marcia Bethell.	
26359	5935	Ada Rosamond, wife of Lieut.-Col. Charles Rhoderick Robert McGrigor, King's Royal Rifle Corps.	Grandchild. 3rd daughter of No. 26346.
26360	5936	Rhoderick Robert McGrigor, 1893.	Great-grandchildren. Children of No. 26359.
26361	5937	Mary Ada Bower McGrigor, 1894.	
26362	5938	Marcia Blanche Florence, wife of Arthur Wykeham Cornwallis. *Twitton House, Sevenoaks.*	Grandchild. 4th daughter of No. 26346.
26363	5939	Iris Beryl Cornwallis. Great-grandchild. Child of No. 26362.	
26364	5940	Rosa, widow of Colonel James Crosbie, 1832–1897. *Ballyheigue Castle, co. Kerry.* 53 *Drayton Gardens, S. W.*	Daughter.
26365	5941	James Dayrolles Crosbie, J.P., D.L., 1865. *Ballyheigue Castle, co. Kerry.*	Grandson. Son of No. 26364.
26366	5942	Oonah Mary Crosbie.	Great-grandchild. Daughter of No. 26365.
26367	5943	Kathleen Matilda, wife of J. Hamlyn Borrer, J.P. *Angeston Grange, Dursley, Gloucestershire.*	Grandchildren. Children of No. 26364.
26368	5944	Rosa Margaret Anna, widow of John Alan George Bengough. *The Ridge, Wotton-under-Edge, Gloucestershire.*	

26369	5945	John Crosbie Bengough.		
26370	5946	Nigel James Bengough.		
26371	5947	Evelyn Rosa Bengough.	Great-grandchildren. Children	
26372	5948	Gwenda Kathleen Bengough.	of No. 26368.	
26373	5949	Madeline Lois Bengough.		
26374	5950	Marcia Ellen, wife of Ernest A. Kinnear.	Grandchild. Child of No. 26364.	
26375	5951	Ronald Crosbie Kinnear, 1887.	Great-grandchildren. Children	
26376	5952	Vera Harriet Kinnear.	of No. 26374.	

426. Descendants of Lieut.-Col. George Lister-Kaye, 1803–1871. (See Table LXXI.)

26377	5953	Charles Wilkinson Lister-Kaye, 1849. *Scofton, near Worksop, Notts.*	Son.	
26378	5954	George Lister Lister-Kaye, 1885.		
26379	5955	Russell Lister-Kaye, 1887.	Grandchildren. Children	
26380	5956	Charles Lister-Kaye, 1890.	of No. 26377.	
26381	5957	Kathleen Lister-Kaye.		
26382	5958	Alan Lister-Kaye, 1854. *Grappenhall, Warrington.*	2nd son.	
26383	5959	Dorothea Lister-Kaye, 1885.	Grandchildren. Children	
26384	5960	Rhoda Lister-Kaye, 1889.	of No. 26382.	
26385	5961	Jessie Maria, wife of Joseph Charlton Parr. *Grappenhall Heys, Warrington.*	Daughter.	
26386	5962	Roger Charlton Parr, 1874.		
26387	5963	Katherine Agnes Parr, 1878.	Grandchildren. Children	
26388	5964	Ellinor Jessie Parr, 1883.	of No. 26385.	
26389	5965	Margaret Alicia Parr, 1887.		
26390	5966	Louisa Lister-Kaye. *St. Leonard's Place, York.*	Younger daughter.	

427. Descendants of Henrietta Lister-Kaye, –1878, and her 1st husband, John Ward, –1840. (See Table LXXI.)

26391	5967	Amelia Susan, widow of Lieut.-Col. Henry Clement Swinnerton-Dyer, R.A., *of Westhope*, 1834–1898, 1838. *The Cottage, Westhope, Craven Arms, Salop.*	Only child.	
26392	5968	Leonard Whitworth Swinnerton-Dyer, 1875. *Westhope, Craven Arms, Salop.*	Grandchild. Son of No. 26391.	
26393	5969	Leonard Schroeder Swinnerton-Dyer, 1898.	Great-grandchild. Child of No. 26392.	
26394	5970	Evelyn Henrietta, wife of Colonel George Blake Napier Martin, C.B., *late* R.A.	Grandchild. Daughter of No. 26391.	

428. Descendants of Georgiana Lister-Kaye, 18 –1877, wife of William Ford Hulton, of Hulton Park, co. Lancaster, J.P., D.L., 18 –1879. (See Table LXXI.)

26395	5971	William Wilbraham Blethyn Hulton, Constable of Lancaster Castle, J.P., D.L., 1844. *Hulton Park, near Bolton-le-Moor.*	Son.	

26396	5972	William Ruthwell Hulton, J.P. *Leyland Lodge, near Preston.*	} Grandson. Son of No. 26395.
26397	5973	Roger Braddyll Hulton, 1891. }	Great-grandchildren. Chil-
26398	5974	Leslie Florence Hulton, 1892. }	dren of No. 26396.
26399	5975	Montagu Lister Hulton, Lieutenant R.N., 1871.	
26400	5976	Arthur Hyde Hulton, Barrister-at-Law, 1873. *Wood Bank, Macclesfield.*	Grandchildren. Children of No. 26395.
26401	5977	Caroline Maria, wife of Percy Tindal-Robertson, 1872.	
26402	5978	Edward Grey Hulton, Rear-Admiral R.N., 1845.	
26403	5979	Frances Amelia Jessie, wife 1st of John Dennison Hargreaves, –1886, and 2ndly of George Oakley Trower.	Children.
26404	5980	Georgiana Maria, wife of William Clough. *Newbald Hall, Yorkshire.*	

429. Descendants of the Rev. Harry Grey, 1783–1860. (See Table LXXII.)

26405	5981	Lady Mary Grey, 1881.	{ Granddaughter. Daughter of Harry, 8th Earl of Stamford, 1812–1890.
26406	5982	William, 9th Earl of Stamford [E.], 1850. 15 *St. James' Place, S.W.* *Llandaff House, Weybridge.*	Grandson. Son of the Rev. William Grey, 1819–1872.
26407	5983	Roger, Lord Grey of Groby, 1896.	{ Great-grandchildren. Children of No. 26406.
26408	5984	Lady Jane Grey, 1899.	
26409	5985	Lucius Anchitel William Erskine Lumsden.	Grandchildren. Children of the Lady Mary Grey, 1813–1885, and her husband, James Grant Lumsden, H.E.I.C.S., –1863.
26410	5986	Emma Edith Malet, widow of Colonel Charles Birch, J.P, 1838–1899. *Lympstone Grange, South Devon.*	
26411	5987	Agnes, wife of C. Hall.	
26412	5988	Gertrude, wife of George Charlesworth.	Great-grandchildren. Children of No. 26411.
26413	5989	Aline Hall.	
26414	5990	Ellen Mary, wife of Walter Bignold, Commander R.N. *Podds House, Brockhurst, Gosport.*	Grandchild. Sister to No. 26409.
26415	5991	Lady Frances Charlotte Elizabeth, wife of the Rev. Joseph Rhodes Charlesworth, 1828. *Elstead Rectory, Godalming.*	Daughter.
26416	5992	Joseph Grey Charlesworth, 1861.	Grandchildren. Children of No. 26415.
26417	5993	William Henry Charlesworth, 1862.	
26418	5994	Lady Anna, widow of John Watson, M.D., 1833. *Uplands, Sandown, I.W.*	Younger surviving daughter.
26419	5995	Ada Rose Tredger, 1870.	{ Granddaughter. Daughter of No. 26418 by 1st husband, William Rose Tredger, –1875.

430. Descendants of Henrietta Grey, 1775–1812, 1st wife of the Rev. Charles Mytton, afterwards Thornycroft, of Thornycroft Hall, –1840. (See Table LXXII.)

26420	5996	Charles Edward Thornycroft, J.P., 1849. *Thornycroft Hall, co. Chester.*	Grandson. Son of the Rev. John Thornycroft, of Thornycroft Hall, J.P., 1809–1884.
26421	5997	Charles Mytton Thornycroft, 1879.	
26422	5998	Francis John Mytton Thornycroft, 1886.	
26423	5999	Muriel Blanche, wife of John Black Atkins.	Great-grandchildren.
26424	6000	Ruth Edith Sophia Thornycroft.	Children of No.
26425	6001	Gwendolin Agnes Thornycroft.	26420.
26426	6002	Frederica Frances Thornycroft.	
26427	6003	John Ralph Thornycroft, 1884.	Great-grandson. Son of the Rev. John Mytton Thornycroft, 1856–1886, brother to No. 26420.
26428	6004	Henrietta Susanna Thornycroft.	Grandchildren. Sisters to No. 26420.
26429	6005	Agnes Thornycroft.	
26430	6006	Henrietta Beck Arkwright.	Grandchildren. Daughters of Henrietta Thornycroft, – 1884, 1st wife of the Rev. Henry Arkwright, Vicar of Bodenham, 1811–1889.
26431	6007	Sophia Mary Arkwright.	

431. Descendants of Emma Grey, 1782–1851, and her husband, Thomas William Egerton Tatton, of Wythenshawe, 1783–1827. (See Table LXXII.)

26432	6008	▽ Thomas Egerton Tatton, J.P., 1846. *Wythenshawe, near Northenden, Chester.*	Grandson. Son of Lieut.-Col. Thomas William Tatton, of Wythenshawe, J.P.,D.L., 1816–1885.
26433 –35		Same as Nos. 24924–24926.	Great-grandchildren. Children of No. 26432.
26436	6009	▽ Robert Grey Tatton, 1847.	Grandchildren. Brothers of No. 26432.
26437	6010	▽ Reginald Arthur Tatton, 1857. *Chelford Manor House, Cheshire.*	
26438	6011	▽ Thomas Arthur Tatton, 1893.	Great-grandchildren. Children of No. 26437.
26439	6012	▽ Harry Tatton, 1896.	
26440	6013	▽ Mary Emily Tatton.	Grandchild. Sister to No. 26432.
26441	6014	Sir Philip Tatton Mainwaring, 4th Bart., 1838. *Peover Hall, Knutsford, Cheshire.*	Grandchild. Son of Emma Tatton, 1809–1886, and her husband, Sir Henry Mainwaring, 2nd Bart., 1804–1875.
26442	6015	Harry Stapleton Mainwaring.	Great-grandchildren. Children of No. 26441.
26443	6016	Hester Marjorie Mainwaring.	
26444	6017	Violet Mainwaring.	
26445	6018	. . . . Mainwaring.	Great-granddaughter. Daughter of Randle Cotton Mainwaring, 1840–1875, brother to No. 26441.
26446	6019	Rowland Leycester Mainwaring, 1845. *New Zealand.*	Grandchild. Brother to No. 26441.
26447	6020	Eleanor Mainwaring.	Great-granddaughters. Daughters to No. 26446.
26448	6021	Maude Mainwaring.	

26449	6022	Emma Sophia Mainwaring. *Park Cottage, Hartford, Cheshire.*	⎫ Grandchildren.
26450	6023	Henrietta Elizabeth, Lady Brooke, widow of Sir Richard Brooke, 7th Bart., 1814–1888. *73 Eccleston Square, S.W.*	⎬ Sisters to No. 26441.
26451	6024	Constance Ida Brooke. ⎱ Great-grandchildren.	Children
26452	6025	Rosalind Hester Brooke. ⎰ of No. 26450.	
26453	6026	Susannah Maud Mainwaring.	⎫
26454	6027	Ellinor Caroline Louisa, wife of Henry Gaskell Close. *101 Eaton Square, S.W.*	⎬ Grandchildren. Younger sisters to No. 26441.
26455	6028	Thomas Close, *late* Rifle Brigade, 1873.	⎫ Great-grandchildren.
26456	6029	Frederick Close.	⎬ Children of No.
26457	6030	Henrietta Close.	26454.
26458	6031	. . . . Close.	⎭
26459	6032	Henry Francis Pelham, Camden Professor of Ancient History, and President of Trinity College, Oxford, 1846. *Trinity College, Oxford.*	Grandson. Son of Henrietta Tatton, 1811–1893, and her husband, the Rt. Rev. and Hon. John Thomas Pelham, Bishop of Norwich, 1811–1894.
26460	6033	Edward Henry Pelham, Junior Examiner to Board of Education, 1876.	⎫ Great-grandchildren.
26461	6034	Herbert Sidney Pelham, 1881.	⎬ Children of No. 26459.
26462	6035	Laura Grace Pelham, 1888.	⎭
26463	6036	Rev. John Barrington Pelham, 1848. *Higham Vicarage, Colchester.*	⎫ Grandchildren.
26464	6037	Ven. Sidney Pelham, Archdeacon of Norfolk,1849. *18 Chapel Field, Norwich.*	⎬ Brothers and sister to No. 26459.
26465	6038	Fanny Pelham, 1853. *Cathedral Close, Norwich.*	⎭
26466	6039	Frederick Mansel Turner, Colonel R.A., 1846. *Gun Wharf, Portsmouth.*	Grandson. Son of Louisa Tatton, 1815–1888, wife of the Rev. Canon Charles Turner.
26467	6040	George Turner.	⎫ Great-grandchildren. Children of No. 26466.
26468	6041	Charles Turner.	⎬
26469	6042	Dorothy Turner.	⎭
26470	6043	Charles Tatton Turner, Captain R.N., 1847. *Heathcote, Lymington.*	⎫ Grandchildren. Brothers of No. 26466.
26471	6044	Bingham Dixon Turner, 1857. *Loughborough.*	⎬
26472	6045	Roger Turner. ⎱ Great-grandchildren.	
26473	6046	James Turner. ⎰ of No. 26471. Sons	
26474	6047	Emma Harriet Turner. ⎰ *St. Andrew's* ⎱ Grandchildren. Sisters	
26475	6048	Sophia Frances Turner. ⎬ *Lodge,* ⎬ of No. 26466.	
26476	6049	Anna Maria Turner. ⎱ *Southampton.* ⎰	
26477	6050	George Dixon, J.P., 1842. *Astle Hall, Chelford, Cheshire.*	Grandson. Son of Sophia Tatton, 1817–1885, and her husband, Colonel John Dixon of Astle Hall, 1799–1873.
26478	6051	John Dixon, 1886. ⎱ Great-grandchildren. Children	
26479	6052	Sophia Evelyn Dixon, 1887. ⎰ of No. 26477.	
26480	6053	Charles Egerton Dixon, Lieut.-Col. *late* 18th Royal Irish, 1848. *Plas Trevor, Llandudno.*	⎫ Grandchildren. Brothers to No. 26477.
26481	6054	Sir Henry Grey Dixon, *late* Lieut.-Col. commanding King's Own Scottish Borderers, K.C.B., A.D.C., 1850. *Berogwell, Duns, N.B.*	⎬

26482	6055	Harold Dixon, 1901.	Great-grandson. Son of No. 26481.
26483	6056	Frederick Parker Dixon, 1852. *Westfield Park, Harold's Cross, Dublin.*	Grandchild. Brother to No. 26477.
26484	6057	Reginald Dixon.	Great-grandchildren. Children
26485	6058	Maurice Dixon.	of No. 26483.
26486	6059	William Arthur Tatton Dixon, 1854. *Bowmere, Tarporley, Cheshire.*	Grandchildren. Younger brothers to No. 26477.
26487	6060	Edward Wilbraham Dixon, 1860.	
26488	6061	Noel Dixon.	Great-grandchildren. Children
26489	6062	Katharine Dixon.	of No. 26487.
26490	6063	Wilbraham Harrie Arundell.	*Cheriton Fitzpaine Rectory, Devon.* — Great-grandchildren. Children of Anna Louisa Dixon, 1841–1901, eldest sister of No. 26477, wife of the Rev. W. H. Arundell.
26491	6064	Reinfred Tatton Arundell.	
26492	6065	Louisa Anne Arundell.	
26493	6066	Sophia Lydia, wife of Lieut.-Col. W. Lisle Blenkinsopp Coulson. *Newburgh, Forestones-on-Tyne, Northumberland.*	Grandchild. Second sister to No. 26477.
26494	6067	George Grahame, 2nd Secretary British Embassy, Berlin.	Great-grandson. Son of No. 26493 by 1st husband, Richard Grahame, –1874.
26495	6068	Lisle Coulson.	Great-grandchildren. Children of No. 26493 by 2nd husband.
26496	6069	Dorothy, wife of Charles Henry Copley Du Cane, J.P., D.L. *Braxted Park, Witham.*	
26497	6070	Jessie Maria, wife of H. G. Seaman. *Vines Gate, Brasted, Kent.*	Grandchildren. Younger sisters to No. 26477.
26498	6071	Eleanor Georgina, wife of the Rev. A. L. Royds. *Brereton Rectory, Cheshire.*	
26499	6072	⛒ Susanna Theodosia Tatton, 1820. *11 Belvedere Terrace, Tunbridge Wells.*	Daughter.

432. Descendants of Anne Maria Grey, 1791–1827, and her husband, the Rev. Thomas Clarke, Vicar of Micheldever, Hants, –1870. (See Table LXXII.)

26500	6073	Harry St. John Clarke, 1882.	Great-grandchildren. Children of Thomas St. John Grey Clarke, 1851–1890, and grandchildren of the Rev. Thomas Grey Clarke, 1817–1891.
26501	6074	Matilda Catherine Clarke, 1880.	
26502	6075	William Edmund Grey Clarke, 1864.	Grandchildren. Children of the Rev. Thomas Grey Clarke, 1817–1891.
26503	6076	Louisa Frances Agnes, wife of Dudley Buxton, M.D., 1857.	
26504	6077	Leonard Halford Dudley Buxton.	Great-grandchildren. Children of No. 26503.
26505	6078	Noel St. John Grey Dudley Buxton.	
26506	6079	John Leycester Dudley Buxton.	
26507	6080	Evelyn, wife of Count Lombardi, 1871.	Granddaughter. Sister to No. 26502.
26508	6081	Achille Lombardi, 1898.	Great-grandchild. Son of No. 26507.
26509	6082	Rev. William Clarke, 1823.	Son.

26510	6083	John Clarke.	
26511	6084	Winifred Clarke.	Grandchildren. Children of No. 26509.
26512	6085	Leycester Clarke.	
26513	6086	Dorothy Clarke.	

26514	6087	Rev. Theodore Townson Churton, 1853. *Bexhill Rectory.*	Grandson. Son of Anna Maria Clarke, – 1879, wife of the Rev. H. B. Whitaker Churton, Vicar of Icklesham, –1891.

26515	6088	Percy Theodore Churton, 1895.	Great-grandchildren. Children of No. 26514.
26516	6089	Ethel Dorothy Churton, 1896.	
26517	6090	Edith Mary Churton, 1900.	
26518	6091	Agnes Mary Esther Churton.	Grandchildren.
26519	6092	Alice Anna Grey Churton.	Sisters to No.
26520	6093	Susanna Elizabeth, wife of the Rev. Arthur Izard.	26514.
26521	6094	Theodore Arthur Izard.	
26522	6095	Whitaker Izard.	
26523	6096	Henry Izard.	Great-grandchildren. Children of No. 26520.
26524	6097	Lily Izard.	
26525	6098	Ann Margaret Izard.	
26526	6099	Constance Churton Izard.	
26527	6100	Mary Churton Izard.	
26528	6101	Mary Annette Churton.	Grandchild. Youngest sister to No. 26514.
26529	6102	Henry Stillington Stephenson. *Lympsham Manor, Weston-super-Mare.*	Grandson. Son of Susan Clarke, 1821–1902, wife of the Rev. Prebendary Joseph H. Stephenson.
26530	6103	Bertrand Stephenson.	Great-grandchildren. Children of No. 26529.
26531	6104	Chambré Stephenson.	
26532	6105	Alice Edith Stephenson.	
26533	6106	Gurdon Stephenson.	Grandson. Brother of No. 26529.
26534	6107	Irene Blanche Stephenson.	Great-grandchildren. Children of No. 26533.
26535	6108	Evelyn Mary Stephenson.	
26536	6109	Herbert Stephenson.	Grandchildren. Brother and sisters of No. 26529.
26537	6110	Anna Margaret Stephenson.	
26538	6111	Edith, wife of the Rev. Vincent Rorison.	
26539	6112	Henry Rorison.	Great-grandchildren. Children of No. 26538.
26540	6113	William Rorison.	
26541	6114	Edith Rorison.	
26542	6115	Rose Rorison.	
26543	6116	Blanche, wife of the Rev. Charles Manby Ashwin.	Grandchild. Youngest sister of No. 26529.

433. Descendants, if any, of Lady Catherine Grey,   – , wife 1st of Mynheer John William van Trip, Postmaster-General of Amsterdam,   –1738, and secondly of Vanden Bempden, Burgomaster of Amsterdam. (See Table LXVIII.)

434. Descendants, if any, of Lady Diana Grey,   – , wife of George Middleton, of Seaton, Aberdeen. (See Table LXVIII.)

The Blood Royal of Britain

435. Descendants, if any, of Lady Jane Grey, –1752, wife of George Drummond, Secretary to the Order of the Thistle. (See Table LXVIII.)

436. Descendants of John, 2nd Lord Wrottesley, 1798–1867. (See Table LXXIII.)

26544	6117	Arthur, 3rd Lord Wrottesley [U.K.], 1824. *Wrottesley, Wolverhampton.*	} Son.
26545	6118	Hon. Victor Alexander Wrottesley, 1873.	Grandchildren.
26546	6119	Hon. Walter Bennet Wrottesley, 1877.	Children of
26547	6120	Hon. Evelyn Henrietta Wrottesley, 1866.	No. 26544.
26548	6121	Hon. Charles Wrottesley, *late* Major 1st Stafford Militia, 1826. *Oaken House, Wolverhampton.*	
26549	6122	Hon. George Wrottesley, Major-Gen. *late* R.E., 1827. *75 Cadogan Gardens, S.W.*	Younger sons.

437. Descendants of the Hon. Walter Wrottesley, 1810–1872. (See Table LXXIII.)

26550	6123	Lucy Edith, wife of Charles Gilbert Heathcote. *5 Arlington Street, S.W.* *10 Palmeira Square, Brighton.*	Daughter.
26551	6124	Walter John Heathcote, 1870.	Grandchildren. Children
26552	6125	Isabel Lucy Heathcote.	of No. 26550.
26553	6126	Mabel Frances Heathcote.	

438. Descendants of the Hon. Edward Bennet Wrottesley, 1811–1892. (See Table LXXIII.)

26554	6127	Hugh Edward Wrottesley, Lieutenant Rifle Brigade, 1882.	Grandchildren. Children of Major Alfred Edward
26555	6128	Maud Ellen Wrottesley, 1884.	Wrottesley, 1855–1899.
26556	6129	Ellen Maria, wife of the Rev. Canon Charles Rowland Haydock Hill, 1852. *Holy Trinity Rectory, Dorchester.*	Daughter.
26557	6130	Walter Edward Hill, 1892.	Grandchild. Son of No. 26556

439. Descendants of the Hon. Henrietta Wrottesley, 1805–1893, and her husband, Henry van Straubenzee, of Spennithorne, York, 1811–1892. (See Table LXXIII.)

26558	6131	Major-General Turner van Straubenzee, C.B., 1838. *Spennithorne, Leyburn, Yorks.*	Elder surviving son.
26559	6132	Henry Turner van Straubenzee, 1878.	Grandchildren.
26560	6133	Percival van Straubenzee, 1880.	Children of
26561	6134	Alexander William van Straubenzee, 1884.	No. 26558.
26562	6135	Eileen Mary van Straubenzee.	

26563	6136	Emma Katie, wife of Horace Falls.	Grandchild. Daughter of Emma Jane van Straubenzee, 1837–1898, and her 1st husband, Harry Reginald Sykes, – 1866.
26564	6137	William Frederick Horace Falls, 1902.	Great-grandchildren. Children of No. 26563.
26565	6138	Alicia Emma Katie Falls.	
26566	6139	Mary, Lady Chaytor. *Croft Hall, Darlington.*	Daughter.
26567	6140	Sir William Henry Edward Chaytor, 4th Bart., 1867. *Croft Hall, Darlington.* *Clervaux Castle, Croft.*	Grandchildren. Children of No. 26566.
26568	6141	Walter Clervaux Chaytor, Lieutenant R.N., 1874. *Junior Naval and Military.*	
26569	6142	Edmund Hugh Chaytor, 1876.	
26570	6143	Clervaux Arthur Chaytor, Lieutenant 3rd Battalion York and Lancaster Regiment, 1879.	
26571	6144	Lilian Emma Chaytor, 1868.	
26572	6145	Marion Henrietta Chaytor, 1870.	
26573	6146	Annie Julia, wife of Allan Havelock-Allan, 1872.	
26574	6147	Henry Ralph Moreton Havelock-Allan, 1899.	Great-grandchildren. Children of No. 26573.
26575	6148	. . . . Havelock-Allan, 1901.	
26576	6149	Hope Aline Havelock-Allan, 1898.	

440. Descendants of Lieut.-Col. Hugh Wrottesley, H.E.I.C.S., 1782–1830. (See Table LXXIII.)

441. Descendants of the Rev. Edward John Wrottesley, Prebendary of Lichfield, Vicar of Brewood, Stafford, 1814–1901. (See Table LXXIII.)

26577	6150	Rev. Francis John Wrottesley, 1848 *Denstone Vicarage, Uttoxeter, Staffordshire.*	Son.
26578	6151	Francis Robert Wrottesley, Lieutenant R.N., 1877.	Grandchildren. Children of No. 26577.
26579	6152	Edward Algernon Wrottesley, 1879.	
26580	6153	Frederic John Wrottesley, 1880.	
26581	6154	Anna Caroline, wife of the Rev. Edward Salt. *Standon Rectory, Eccleshall, Stafford.*	Daughter.
26582	6155	Alexander Edward Wrottesley Salt, 1874.	Grandchildren. Children of No. 26581.
26583	6156	Charles Joseph Salt, 1877.	
26584	6157	Arthur Henry Salt, 1878.	
26585	6158	Cecil William Salt, 1880.	
26586	6159	Caroline Mary Salt, 1876.	
26587	6160	Sophia Frances Salt, 1881.	

442. Descendants of Henry FitzRoy, of Salcey Lawn, co. Northants, 1806–1877. (See Table LXXIV.)

26588	6161	Algernon Henry FitzRoy, 1834. *Salcey Lawn, Northants.*	Son.

The Blood Royal of Britain

26589	6162	Cecilia Dorothy Charlotte Sitwell, 1888.	Great-grandchild. Child of Lieut.-Col. Claude George Henry Sitwell, D.S.O., 1858–1900, eldest son of Cecilia Fanny FitzRoy, 1836–1873, and her husband, Captain George Frederick Sitwell, 1828–1884.
26590	6163	Herbert Wellington Sitwell, *late* Lieutenant 4th Battalion (Princess Louise's) Argyll and Sutherland Highlanders, 1861. *Bedford City, Bedford co., Virginia, U.S.A.*	Grandchild. Child of the above named Cecilia Fanny Fitz-Roy, 1836–1873, &c.
26591	6164	Herbert Cecil FitzRoy Sitwell, 1896.	Great-grandchildren. Children of No. 26590.
26592	6165	Evelyn Juliette Fay Sitwell, 1888.	
26593	6166	Blanche Adeliza, Countess of Rosslyn [U.K.], Baroness Loughborough [G.B.], 1839. *Lady Anne's House, Stamford.*	Daughter.
26594	6167	James Francis Harry, 5th Earl of Rosslyn [U.K.], Baron Loughborough [G.B.], 1869. *Dysart, Fife. Carlton.*	Grandson. Son of No. 26593.
26595	6168	Francis Edward Scudamore, Lord Loughborough, 1892.	Great-grandchildren. Children of No. 26594.
26596	6169	Lady Rosabelle Millicent St. Clair Erskine, 1891.	
26597	6170	Hon. Alexander FitzRoy St. Clair Erskine, 1870.	Grandchild. Child of No. 26593.
26598	6171	Frances Evelyn, Countess of Warwick and Brooke [G.B.], Baroness Brooke [E.], 1861. *Warwick Castle, Warwick.*	Grandchildren. Children of No. 26593 by her 1st husband, Colonel the Hon. Charles Henry Maynard, 1814–1865.
26599 -601		Same as Nos. 21231–21233. Great-grandchildren. Children of No. 26598.	
26602	6172	Blanche, Lady Algernon Charles Gordon-Lennox, 1864. *Broughton Castle, Banbury.*	
26603		Same as No. 23072. Great-grandchild. Child of No. 26602.	
26604	6173	Millicent Fanny, Duchess of Sutherland [U.K.], Marchioness of Stafford [G.B.], Countess of Sutherland [S.], Baroness Gower [E.], 1867. *Dunrobin Castle, Sutherland. Stafford House, St. James', S.W.*	Grandchild. Daughter of No. 26593 by 2nd husband.
26605 -07		Same as Nos. 22236–22238. Great-grandchildren. Children of No. 26604.	
26608	6174	Sybil Mary, Countess of Westmorland [E.], 1871. *Apethorpe Hall, Wansford, Northants.*	Grandchild. Daughter of No. 26593.
26609 -11		Same as Nos. 20292–20294. Great-grandchildren. Children of No. 26608.	
26612	6175	Lady Angela Selina Blanche, wife of James Stuart Forbes, 1876. *Kirby Hall, Melton Mowbray.*	Granddaughter. Daughter of No. 26593.
26613	6176	. . . . Forbes, 1897.	Great-granddaughter. Daughter of No. 26612.

26614	6177	Evelyn Matilda, wife of George Watson-Taylor, 1841. *Kingston Hill Place, Surrey.*	} Younger daughter.
26615	6178	Sidney de Vere Beauclerk, 1866.	{ Grandchild. Son of No. 26614 by her 1st husband, Aubrey de Vere Beauclerk.

443. Descendants of Lieut.-Col. Hugh FitzRoy, 1808–1879. (See Table LXXIV.)

26616	6179	Thomas Henry Hollis Bradford Atkinson, Captain Grenadier Guards. *Angerton, near Morpeth.*	} Grandchildren. Children of Amy Emily Sarah FitzRoy, 1833–18 , and her husband, Lieut.-Col. Ralph Bradford Atkinson, –1888.
26617	6180	. . . . Atkinson.	
26618	6181	. . . . Atkinson.	
26619	6182	. . . . Atkinson.	
26620	6183	Adela Louisa FitzRoy, 1857. *Budleigh Salterton, South Devon.*	} Daughters.
26621	6184	Augusta Caroline, wife of Robert William Rankine Wilson, Barrister-at-Law.	

444. Descendants of the Rev. Augustus FitzRoy, Rector of Great Fakenham, Suffolk, 1809–1869. (See Table LXXIV.)

26622	6185	Rev. Ernest James Augustus FitzRoy, formerly Vicar of St. Jude's, West Derby, Lancashire, 1834.	} Son.
26623	6186	Stafford Frances FitzRoy, 1863. *New Orleans, U.S.A.*	} Grandchildren. Children of No. 26622.
26624	6187	Constance Angelina Mary FitzRoy, 1856.	
26625	6188	Lilias Evelyn Elizabeth FitzRoy, 1868.	
26626	6189	Hugh Maitland FitzRoy, *late* Lieutenant Rifle Brigade, 1843.	} 2nd son.
26627	6190	Ronald Hugh FitzRoy, Lieutenant Scots Guards, 1878. *12 Park Lane, W. Benthall Hall, Salop.*	} Grandchildren. Children of No. 26626.
26628	6191	Victor Robert Charles FitzRoy, 1880. *Hill Croome, Earl's Croome, near Worcester.*	

445. Descendants of Francis Charles FitzRoy, 1811–1874. (See Table LXXIV.)

26629	6192	Lavinia, wife of Colonel Charles Clitherow Gore, 1837. *29 Wilton Crescent, Belgrave Square, S.W.*	} Daughter.

446. Descendants of Caroline FitzRoy, –18 , 2nd wife of Henry Wilson, of Stowlangtoft Hall, J.P., D.L., M.P., 1797–1866. (See Table LXXIV.)

26630	6193	FitzRoy Wilson, Rifle Brigade, 1840.	Son.
26631	6194	Reginald Francis Wilson, 1873. *Fleet House, Weymouth.*	} Grandson. Son of the Rev. Cyril FitzRoy Wilson, 1841–1898.
26632	6195	Nigel George FitzRoy Wilson, 1900.	{ Great-grandchild. Son of No. 26631.

26633	6196	Edmund Algernon Wilson, 1879.	⎫	
26634	6197	Fanny Gertrude Wilson, 1877.	⎬ Grandchildren. Brother	
26635	6198	Edith Caroline Wilson, 1879.	⎪ and sisters of No. 26631.	
26636	6199	Amy Mary Wilson, 1883.	⎭	
26637	6200	Caroline FitzRoy Wilson.	Daughter.	

447. Descendants of the Rev. Lord Henry FitzRoy, Canon of Westminster, 1770-1828. (See Table LXXV.)

26638 -87 }	Same as Nos. 26588-26637.

448. Descendants of Admiral Lord William FitzRoy, K.C.B., 1782–1857. (See Table LXXV.)

26688	6201	Almeric William FitzRoy, C.V.O., Clerk to the Privy Council, 1851. *55 Lower Belgrave Street, S.W.*	⎧ Grandson. Son of ⎪ Francis Horatio ⎨ FitzRoy, 1823– ⎩ 1900.
26689	6202	Nigel Horatio Trevor FitzRoy, 1889.	⎫ Great-grandchildren. Chil-
26690	6203	Yvonne Alice Gertrude FitzRoy, 1891.	⎬ dren of No. 26688.
26691	6204	Cyril Duncombe Fitzroy, H.M.'s Inspector of Schools, 1861. *43 Jermyn Street, S.W.*	⎫
26692	6205	Gertrude Louisa Georgiana, wife of Lieut.-Col. Robert Hamilton Lloyd-Anstruther, J.P., D.L., 1850. *Hintlesham Hall, Ipswich.*	⎬ Grandchildren. Bro- ther and sister to No. 26688.
26693	6206	FitzRoy Hamilton Lloyd-Anstruther, 1872. *Travellers.*	⎫ Great-grandchildren.
26694	6207	Rosalind Gertrude, wife of Captain Noel Armar Lowry-Corry, D.S.O., Grenadier Guards. *8 Eaton Square, S.W.*	⎬ Children of No. 26692.
26695 -96 }		Same as Nos. 23496-23497.	Great-great-grandchildren. Children of No. 26694.
26697	6208	Kathleen Horatia FitzRoy, 1854.	⎫
26698	6209	Helen Mary, wife of Charles Milnes Newton, 1857.	⎬ Grandchildren. Sisters to No. 26688, &c.
26699	6210	Esmé, wife of Colonel the Hon. Montagu Curzon, 1859. *Garatshay, Loughborough.*	⎭
26700	6211	William Montagu Curzon, 1891.	⎫ Great-grandchildren. Chil-
26701	6212	Mary Curzon, 1887.	⎬ dren of No. 26699.

Children, if any, of Harriet Elizabeth Fitzroy, 1817–1875 (daughter), wife (1862) of Colonel Michael Dawes, *late* H.M. Bengal Artillery,   –1871.

449. Descendants of Lady Augusta Fitzroy, 1779–1839, wife of the Rev. George Frederick Tavel,   –1829. (See Table LXXV.)

26702	6213	Augusta Louisa, widow of John Murray, 1804–1884. *Gartshore, Ravelston, Midlothian.*	⎫ ⎬ Only child. ⎭

450. Descendants of Francis George, 2nd Lord Churchill, 1802–1886. (See Table LXXV.)

26703	6214	Victor Albert Francis Charles, 1st Viscount Churchill [U.K.], K.C.V.O., 1864. *Rolleston, Leicester.*	Only child.
26704	6215	Hon. Victor Alexander Spencer, Page of Honour to King Edward VII., 1890.	Grandchildren. Children of No. 26703.
26705	6216	Hon. Victoria Ivy Louise Spencer, 1897.	
26706	6217	Hon. Ursula Spencer, 1901.	

451. Descendants of Lieut.-Col. the Hon. George Augustus Spencer, 1804–1877. (See Table LXXV.)

26707	6218	John Winston Thomas Spencer, Lieut.-Col. and Brevet-Col. late Royal Artillery, 1849. *Junior United Service.*	Son.
26708	6219	Almeric Stuart John Spencer, 1885.	Grandson. Son of No. 26707.
26709	6220	Charlotte Frances Bona, widow of Lieut.-Col. George FitzRoy, 1800–1883, 1834. *Yardley House, Yardley Gobion, Stony Stratford.*	Daughter.
26710	6221	George Vere Hugh Cholmondeley, 1871. *Hatton Lodge, Chester.*	Grandson. Son of Frances Isabella Catherine Spencer, 1837–1900, and Lord Henry Vere Cholmondeley, 1834–1882.
26711	6222	Hugh Henry Vere Cholmondeley, 1899.	Great-grandchildren. Children of No. 26710.
26712	6223	Irene Marcia Cholmondeley, 1902.	
26713	6224	Charles Almeric John Cholmondeley, Lieutenant Border Regiment, 1880.	Grandchildren. Brother and sisters to No. 26710.
26714	6225	Edith Charlotte Frances, wife of Captain Robert Edward Heaven, 4th Battalion Cheshire Regiment, 1867. *132 Ebury Street, S.W.*	
26715	6226	Caroline Marcia Cecily Cholmondeley, 1873.	
26716	6227	Georgiana Millicent Julia Spencer, 1846. *25 York Street, Portman Square, W.*	Younger daughter.

452. Descendants of General the Hon. Sir Augustus Almeric Spencer, G.C.B., 1807–1893. (See Table LXXV.)

26717	6228	Augustus Campbell Spencer, Lieut.-Col., *late* 5th Lancers and 1st Dragoon Guards, 1851. *Lascombe, Puttenham, Surrey.*	Son.
26718	6229	Richard Augustus Spencer, 1888.	Grandchildren. Children of No. 26717.
26719	6230	Edward Almeric Spencer, 1892.	
26720	6231	Helen Frances, wife of Colonel Robert Spencer Liddell, *late* 10th Hussars, 1843.	Daughter.
26721	6232	Evelyn Helen Liddell, 1872.	Granddaughter. Daughter of No. 26720.

26722	6233	Caroline Laura Spencer, 1844.	
26723	6234	Elizabeth Maria Spencer, 1845.	
26724	6235	Augusta Melita, widow of the Rev. Edward Mallet Young, *late* Headmaster of Sherborne School, 18 – 1900, 1848. *Allendale Rectory, Northumberland.*	Younger daughters.
26725	6236	Rev. Henry Spencer Stephenson, 1871. *Allendale Rectory, Northumberland.*	Grandson. Son of No. 26724 by her 1st husband, Colonel Sussex Vane Stephenson.

453. Descendants of the Rev. and Hon. William Henry Spencer, Rector of Great Houghton, 1810–1900. (See Table LXXV.)

26726	6237	William Francis Spencer, J.P., *late* Captain 46th Foot, 1838. *Eardisland, Pembridge, Herefordshire.*	Eldest son.
26727	6238	John Almeric Walter Spencer, Lieutenant Rifle Brigade, 1881.	Grandchildren. Children of No. 26726.
26728	6239	Sybil Frances Spencer, 1875.	
26729	6240	Almeric George Spencer, Colonel *late* commanding 33rd Regimental District, 1841.	2nd son.
26730	6241	Almeric Arthur William Spencer, Captain 2nd Battalion Prince of Wales' Own (W. Yorkshire Regiment), 1874.	Grandchildren. Children of No. 26729.
26731	6242	Rose Frances, wife of Lieut.-Col. Raymond Northland Revell Reade, Commandant Royal Military College, 1870. *Kingston, Canada.*	
26732	6243	Charles Spencer Greenway, 1891.	Great-grandson. Son of No. 26731 by 1st husband, Captain Charles Greenway, 1892.
26733	6244	Mary Spencer Revell Reade, 1897.	Great-grandchild. Child of No. 26731 by 2nd husband.
26734	6245	Alice Katharine, wife of Captain Francis Hugh Neish, Gordon Highlanders, 1872. *18 Lower Belgrave Street, W.*	Grandchild. 2nd daughter of No. 26729.
26735	6246	Frances Feodora Spencer Neish, 1900.	Great-grandchild. Child of No. 26734.
26736	6247	Dorothy Julia, wife of George Fraser, 1876.	Grandchild. 3rd daughter of No. 26729.
26737	6248	Frances Rose, Lady Gunning, widow of the Rev. Sir Henry John Gunning, 4th Bart., 1797–1885, 1840.	Daughters.
26738	6249	Isabella Elizabeth, wife of Marten Harcourt Griffin, J.P., 1843. *Colehurst Manor, Market Drayton.*	
26739	6250	Almeric Edward Spencer Griffin, *late* Lieutenant R.H.A., 1867. *Junior Carlton ; Naval and Military.*	Grandchildren. Children of No. 26738.
26740	6251	Francis William Latimer Griffin, 1869.	
26741	6252	Isabel Frances Griffin, 1896.	Great-grandchild. Daughter of No. 26740.

26742	6253	Noel Henry Rose Griffin, 1877.	
26743	6254	Reginald Herbert Griffin, 1879.	Grandchildren.
26744	6255	Fitzroy Nicholas Griffin, 1881.	Children of
26745	6256	Isabel Rose Helen Griffin, 1872.	No. 26738.
26746	6257	Evelyn Ida Griffin, 1885.	

454. Descendants of Colonel the Hon. Robert Charles Henry Spencer, 1817–1881. (See Table LXXV.)

26747	6258	Gerald Robert Spencer, *late* Captain R.A., 1853. *Delves House, Ringmer, Sussex.*	
26748	6259	Blanche Louisa, wife of Captain Henry George Fane, *late* 52nd Regiment, 1850. *Bicester House, Bicester.*	Children.
26749	6260	Hubert William Fane, Associate Royal School of Mines, 1878.	
26750	6261	Almeric Cecil Fane, 1880.	Grandchildren.
26751	6262	Arthur George Cecil Fane, 1880.	Children of
26752	6263	Robert Gerald Fane, Lieutenant R.N., 1882.	No. 26748.
26753	6264	Horatio Alfred Fane, 1884.	
26754	6265	Francis John Fane, 1885.	
26755	6266	Octavius Edward Fane, 1886.	

455. Descendants of the Rev. and Hon. Charles Frederic Octavius Spencer, M.A., Vicar of Sutton, Isle of Ely, 1824–1895. (See Table LXXV.)

26756	6267	Charles Francis Henry Spencer, Lieut.-Col., *late* Royal Inniskilling Fusiliers, 1848.	Eldest son.
26757	6268	Francis Elmhirst Spencer, Lieutenant R.G.A., 1881.	Grandson. Son of No. 26756.
26758	6269	Henry Montagu Spencer, Captain and Hon. Major 2nd Volunteer Battalion Gloucester Regiment, 1851. *Blockley, Worcestershire.*	2nd son.
26759	6270	Henry Beresford Spencer, Lieutenant 2nd Volunteer Battalion Gloucester Regiment, 1881.	Grandchildren. Children of No. 26758.
26760	6271	Hilda Agnes Spencer, 1882.	
26761	6272	Eleanor Cicely Spencer, 1883.	
26762	6273	Hereward George Edward Spencer, 1861. *Châlet Cumnor, Biarritz, France.*	Youngest son.

456. Descendants of the Hon. Caroline Elizabeth Spencer, 1805–1864, and her husband, Robert, 3rd Lord Clonbrock, 1807–1893. (See Table LXXV.)

26763	6274	Luke Gerald, 4th Lord Clonbrock [I.], P.C., K.P., 1834. *Clonbrock, Ahaseragh, co. Galway.*	Elder surviving son.
26764	6275	Hon. Robert Edward Dillon, 1869. *Bachelors', Kildare Street.*	Grandchildren. Children of No. 26763.
26765	6276	Hon. Georgiana Caroline Dillon, 1867.	
26766	6277	Hon. Edith Augusta Dillon, 1878.	
26767	6278	Hon. Ethel Louisa Dillon, 1880.	

26768	6279	Hon. Robert Villiers Dillon, Colonel (retired) R.A., 1838. *Wootton House, Wootton, Bedford.*	Younger surviving son.
26769	6280	Hilda May, wife of Roger Estcourt Bucknall, 1875. *Biddenham Manor, Bedford.*	Grandchildren. Children of No. 26768.
26770	6281	Stella Margaret Dillon, 1889.	
26771	6282	Hon. Frances Letitia Dillon, 1831. *Acton Lodge, Leamington.*	
26772	6283	Hon. Caroline Anastasia, widow of William Dealtry, C.M.G., –1900, 1837. *17 Cambridge Square, Hyde Park, W.*	Daughters.
26773	6284	Hon. Helen Isabella Dillon, 1840.	*Acton Lodge, Leamington.*
26774	6285	Hon. Louisa Emilia Dillon, 1841.	
26775	6286	John Congreve, 1872. *Mount Congreve, Waterford.*	Grandchildren. Children of the Hon. Alice Elizabeth Dillon, 1845–1878, and Ambrose Congreve, of Mount Congreve, Waterford, 1832–1901.
26776	6287	Ambrose Congreve, 1875.	
26777	6288	Leopold Congreve, 1877.	
26778	6289	Eleanor Augusta Congreve.	
26779	6290	Violet Jane Congreve.	
26780	6291	Hon. Katherine Charlotte Dillon, 1847. *Acton Lodge, Leamington.*	Younger daughters.
26781	6292	Elizabeth Octavia, Hon. Lady Ellis-Nanney, wife of Sir Hugh J. Ellis-Nanney, 1st Bart., 1848. *Gwynfryn, Criccieth, Carnarvonshire.*	
26782	6293	Mary Elizabeth Ellis-Nanney, 1877.	Grandchild. Daughter of No. 26781.

457. Descendants of the Hon. Elizabeth Charlotte Spencer, 1822–1858, and her husband, the Rev. Havilland de Sausmarez, M.A., Rector of St. Peter's, Northampton, 1813–1882. (See Table LXXV.)

26783	6294	Rev. George Spencer De Sausmarez, 1855. *The Rectory, Acton, W.*	Only child.
26784	6295	Havilland George Temple De Sausmarez, 1894.	Grandchildren. Children of No. 26783.
26785	6296	Elizabeth Fanny De Sausmarez, 1885.	
26786	6297	Madeline Amy De Sausmarez, 1887.	
26787	6298	Dorothy Louisa De Sausmarez, 1888.	
26788	6299	Rosamond Annie Carterette De Sausmarez, 1889.	
26789	6300	Maud Havilland De Sausmarez, 1891.	
26790	6301	Evelyn Mary De Sausmarez, 1891.	
26791	6302	Helen Isabel De Sausmarez, 1893.	
26792	6303	Agatha Katherine De Sausmarez, 1896.	
26793	6304	Cecily Florence De Sausmarez, 1898.	

458. Descendants, if any, of Dorothy Wrottesley, – , wife of Christian, Baron von Keetzleben, Minister of Hesse-Cassel, – . (See Table LXXIII.)

459. Descendants, if any, of Harriet Wrottesley, – , wife (1770) of General William Gardiner, 1748–1806. (See Table LXXIII.)

460. Descendants, if any, of Elizabeth Wrottesley, wife of Thomas Wrottesley, of Wolverhampton, –1741. (See Table LXXIII.)

461. Descendants of Colonel Charles Inge, of Thorpe Constantine, –1874. (See Table LXXVI.)

26794	6305	William Frederick Inge, *of Thorpe Constantine*, J.P., D.L., 1863. *Thorpe Hall, Thorpe Constantine, near Tamworth.*	} Son.	
26795	6306	Margaret Ethel Inge, 1894. }	Granddaughters.	Daughters
26796	6307	Hilda Mary Inge, 1898. }	of No. 26794.	
26797	6308	Ethel Harriet, wife of Duncan Davidson. *Inchmarlo, Banchory, co. Aberdeen.*	}	Daughter.
26798	6309	Mai Davidson. }	Granddaughters.	Daughters
26799	6310	Ethel Violet Davidson. }	of No. 26797.	

462. Descendants of the Rev. Spencer Madan, Canon Residentiary of Lichfield, Vicar of Batheaston and Tiverton, near Bath, 1791–1851. (See Table LXXVI.)

26800	6311	Spencer Madan, 1867. *Lichfield.*	} Grandchildren. Children of the Rev. Spencer Madan, Rector of Standon, 1832–1869.	
26801	6312	Louisa Fanny Madan, 1864. }	*Walford,*	
26802	6313	Charlotte Mary Madan, 1866. }	*Eccleshall,*	
26803	6314	Henrietta Leonora Madan, 1869. }	*Staffordshire.*	
26804	6315	William Spencer Madan, 1893.	{ Great-grandchildren. Children of Charles Spencer Madan, 1860–1903, and grandchildren of William Madan, 1834–1871.	
26805	6316	Charlotte Mary Madan, 1892.		
26806	6317	Honora Penelope Madan, 1894.		
26807	6318	Bertha Louisa Madan, 1896.		
26808	6319	Frederick Martin Madan, 1862.	{ Grandchild. Son of William Madan, 1834–1871.	
26809	6320	Rev. Nigel Madan, Canon of Lichfield, 1840. *Doveridge Vicarage, Derby.*	} Children.	
26810	6321	Charlotte Madan, 1831. *Preswylfa, Llanfairfechan, North Wales.*		
26811	6322	Penelope Maria Madan, 1844. *Preswylfa, Llanfairfechan, North Wales.*		

463. Descendants of Captain Frederick Madan, 1797–1863. (See Table LXXVI.)

26812	6323	Maria, widow of John Digby Wingfield-Digby, *of Sherborne Castle*, 1832–1888, 1833.	} Elder daughter.	
26813	6324	John Kenelm Digby Wingfield-Digby, M.P., J.P., 1859. *Sherborne Castle, Dorset.*	} Grandson. Son of No. 26812.	
26814	6325	Frederick James Bosworth Wingfield-Digby, 1885.	} Great-grandchild. Child of No. 26813.	

26815	6326	Everard George Wingfield-Digby.	Grandchildren.
26816	6327	Rev. Frederick Wyldbore Wingfield-Digby. Toller Vicarage, Dorset.	Sons of No. 26812.
26817	6328	Frederick John William Wingfield-Digby, 1899.	Great-grandchild. Child of No. 26816.
26818	6329	William Richard Wingfield-Digby, Lieutenant Rifle Brigade, 1869.	
26819	6330	Stephen Harold Wingfield-Digby	
26820	6331	Anne Eliza Wingfield-Digby.	
26821	6332	Caroline Frances Wingfield-Digby.	Grandchildren.
26822	6333	Rosamond Marion, wife of the Rev. J. Warrington Strong.	Children of No. 26812.
26823	6334	Henrietta Maria Wingfield-Digby.	
26824	6335	Kathleen Lydia Wingfield-Digby.	
26825	6336	Mildred Lettice Wingfield-Digby.	
26826	6337	Hilda Octavia Wingfield-Digby.	
26827	6338	Caroline, widow of the Rev. Henry Mayers, 1834. Jesus Lane, Cambridge.	Younger daughter.
26828	6339	Henry Montgomery Stewart Mayers, 1858.	
26829	6340	John Perkins Mayers, 1859.	
26830	6341	Francis Nigel Mayers, 1870.	Grandchildren. Children of No. 26827.
26831	6342	Clara Maria Mayers, 1862. Jesus Lane, Cambridge.	
26832	6343	Caroline Harriet Mayers, 1865. Jesus Lane, Cambridge.	

464. Descendants of the Rev. George Madan, Rural Dean of Dursley, 1807-1891. (See Table LXXVI.)

26833	6344	James Russell Madan, 1841.	
26834	6345	Arthur Cornwallis Madan, 1846. Bearland House, Gloucester.	Sons.
26835	6346	William Nigel Madan, 1848.	
26836	6347	George Nigel Madan.	Grandchildren. Children of No. 26834.
26837	6348	Angela Mary Madan.	
26838	6349	Arthur Gresley Madan.	
26839	6350	Falconer Madan, 1851. Bodleian Library, Oxford.	5th son.
26840	6351	Francis Falconer Madan, 1886.	
26841	6352	Nigel Cornwallis Madan, 1889.	Grandchildren. Children of No. 26839.
26842	6353	Geoffrey Spencer Madan, 1895.	
26843	6354	Ethel Wordsworth Madan, 1891.	
26844	6355	Mary Madan, 1844. Bearland House, Gloucester.	Daughters.
26845	6356	Edith Harriet, 1855.	

465. Descendants of Henrietta Anne Madan, 1795-1829, wife of the Hon. James Henry Keith Stewart, C.B., 1783-1836. (See Table LXXVI.)

| 26846 | 6357 | Charles Nigel Stewart, 1864. | Grandson. Son of Charles Patrick Stewart, 1823-1882. |
| 26847 | 6358 | Herbert Nigel Stewart, 1896. | Great-grandchild. Child of No. 26846. |

26848	6359	Arthur Courtenay Stewart, Lieutenant R.N., 1871.	
26849	6360	Charlotte Evelyn, wife of the Rev. Ernest George Beckwith, 1866. *Filleigh Rectory, South Moulton.*	Grandchildren. Brother and sister to No. 26846.
26850	6361	Charles Edward Beckwith, 1901.	
26851	6362	Evelyn Marjorie Beckwith, 1894.	Great-grandchildren. Children of No. 26849.
26852	6363	Helen Frances Beckwith, 1895.	
26853	6364	Rosamond Mary Beckwith, 1897.	
26854	6365	Penelope Blanche Stewart, 1868.	Grandchild. Sister to No. 26846.

466. Descendants of Mary Judith Madan, 1813–1872, wife of Arthur Stewart, 1813–1879. (See Table LXXVI.)

26855	6366	Alan Stewart, Barrister, 1844. 47 *Eardley Crescent, S.W.*	Son.
26856	6367	Arthur Charles Stewart, 1877. 6 *Cathcart Studios, 1 Cathcart Road, S.W.*	Grandchildren. Children of No. 26855.
26857	6368	Catherine Frances Stewart, 1878.	
26858	6369	Sophia Louisa, wife of Major-General George Fuller Walker, 1845. 1 *Avenue Elmers, Surbiton.*	Daughter.
26859	6370	Philip Stewart Walker, Lieutenant 1st Battalion Suffolk Regiment, 1881.	Grandchildren. Children of No. 26858.
26860	6371	Henry Stewart Walker, 1882.	
26861	6372	Georgina Frances Walker, 1878.	
26862	6373	Alice Louisa Walker, 1883.	
26863	6374	Adela Jane Stewart, 1848.	
26864	6375	Jessie Charteris, widow of Lieut.-Col. John Rimington Sharp, 1843–1898, 1849. *The Hill, Batheaston, Bath.*	Younger daughters.
26865	6376	Mary, wife of Colonel Henry Walter Phillips, Chief Paymaster, Egypt, 1852. 5 *The Crescent, Mount Radford, Exeter.*	
26866	6377	Herbert Stewart Phillips, 1886.	
26867	6378	Walter Seymour Phillips, 1889.	Grandchildren. Children of No. 26865.
26868	6379	Henry Walter Phillips, 1894.	
26869	6380	Vera Katharine Phillips, 1884.	
26870	6381	Gwendoline Phillips, 1887.	
26871	6382	Dorothy Mary Phillips, 1892.	
26872	6383	Mary Stewart Phillips, 1897.	

467. Descendants, if any, of Henrietta Inge,   –17 , and her husband, Robert Bakewell, of Swenston, co. Leicester, –17 . (See Table LXXVI.)

468. Descendants, if any, of the Hon. Humbletta Ward, 16 – , and her husband, Thomas Porter, 16 – . (See Table LXI.)

The Blood Royal of Britain

469. Descendants of William, 1st Earl of Dudley, 1817–1885. (See Table LXXVII.)

26873	6384	William Humble, 2nd Earl of Dudley [U.K.] and 12th Baron Ward [E.], P.C., Lord Lieutenant of Ireland, 1867. *Himley Hall, Dudley.* *7 Carlton Gardens, S.W.*	Son.
26874	6385	William Humble Eric, Viscount Ednam, 1894.	Grandchildren. Children of No. 26873.
26875	6386	Lady Gladys Honor Ward, 1892.	
26876	6387	Lady Morvyth Lillian Ward, 1896.	
26877	6388	Hon. John Hubert Ward, Assistant Private Secretary (unpaid) to Financial Secretary to War Office, 1870. *14 Chesterfield Street, W.*	
26878	6389	Hon. Robert Arthur Ward, Lieutenant Worcestershire I.Y., 1871. *Carlton; Marlborough.*	
26879	6390	Hon. Reginald Ward, Captain Royal Horse Guards, D.S.O., 1874.	Younger sons and daughter.
26880	6391	Hon. Cyril Augustus Ward, Lieutenant R.N., 1876.	
26881	6392	Hon. Gerald Ernest Francis Ward, Lieutenant 1st Life Guards, 1877. *15 Hyde Park Street, W.*	
26882	6393	Edith Amelia, Lady Wolverton [U.K.], 1872. *Iwerne Manor House, Blandford.* *26 St. James' Place, S.W.*	
26883	6394	Hon. George Edward Dudley Glyn, 1896.	Grandchildren. Children of No. 26882.
26884	6395	Hon. Marion Féoderowna Louise Glyn, 1900.	

470. Descendants of the Hon. Humble Dudley Ward, 1821–1870. (See Table LXXVII.)

26885	6396	William Humble Dudley Ward, Captain Herts Yeomanry Cavalry, 1849. *63 Cromwell Road, S.W.*	Son.
26886	6397	William Dudley Ward, 1877.	Grandchildren. Children of No. 26885.
26887	6398	Charles Humble Ward, 1879.	
26888	6399	Eugénie Sybil, wife of Captain Dermot Howard Blundell - Hollinshead - Blundell, M.V.O., King's Royal Rifle Corps, 1878.	
26889	6400	Georgie Viola Eleanor Ward, 1881.	
26890	6401	Eugénie Fanny Eveline Ward, 1884.	
26891	6402	Enid Violet Ada Ward, 1897.	
26892	6403	Amelia Alice Julia, widow of Lieut.-Gen. James Keith Fraser, C.M.G., *late* 1st Life Guards, –1895. *43 Lowndes Square, S.W.*	Daughter.
26893	6404	Sir Keith Alexander Fraser, 5th Bart. of Ledeclune and Morar, Inverness, 1867. *59 Sloane Street, S.W.*	Grandchildren. Children of No. 26892.
26894	6405	Hugh Craufurd Keith Fraser, Captain 1st Life Guards, 1869. *6A The Albany, Piccadilly, W.*	
26895	6406	Helena Violet Alice, Countess of Stradbroke [U.K.], Baroness Rous [G.B.]. *Henham Hall, Wangford, Suffolk.*	

345

2 x

26896	6407	Lady Pleasance Elizabeth Rous, 1899.	Great-grandchildren.
26897	6408	Lady Catherine Charlotte Rous, 1900.	Children of No.
26898	6409	Lady Betty Helena Joanna Rous, 1901.	26895.
26899	6410	Henrietta Maria, widow of George Stewart Forbes, 1844–1894, 1848. *23 Pont Street, S.W.*	Younger daughter.
26900	6411	James Stuart Forbes, 1872. *Kirby Hall, Melton Mowbray.*	Grandson. Son of No. 26899.
26901		Same as No. 26613. Great-grandchild. Daughter of No. 26900.	
26902	6412	Ida Agnes, wife of Sir Archibald Edmonstone, 5th Bart. *Duntreuth Castle, Strathblane, Stirlingshire.* 17 *Lowndes Square, S.W.*	Granddaughter. Daughter of No. 26899.
26903	6413	William George Edmonstone, 1896.	Great-grandchildren. Sons of No. 26902.
26904	6414	Archibald Charles Edmonstone, 1898.	
26905	6415	Edward St. John Edmonstone, 1901.	

471. Descendants of the Hon. Julia Susannah Ward, 1818–1902, wife of the Right Rev. Thomas Legh Claughton, D.D., Lord Bishop of St. Albans, –1892. (See Table LXXVII.)

26906	6416	Rev. Thomas Legh Claughton, Canon Residentiary of Worcester, 1847. *The College, Worcester.*	Eldest son.
26907	6417	William Thomas Alban Claughton, 1876.	Grandchildren.
26908	6418	Harold Claughton, 1882.	Children of
26909	6419	Susan Helena Claughton, 1890.	No. 26906.
26910	6420	Piers Leopold Claughton, 1850.	
26911	6421	Gilbert Henry Claughton, 1856.	
26912	6422	Katherine Susan, widow of the Hon. Ronald George Elidor Campbell, 1848–1879. 34 *Onslow Gardens, S.W.*	Children.
26913 –15		Same as Nos. 21747–21749.	Grandchildren. Children of No. 26912.
26916	6423	Lucy Elinor Claughton.	Younger daughter.

472. Descendants of Washington Sewallis, 9th Earl Ferrers, 1822–1859. (See Table LXXVII.)

| 26917 | 6424 | Sewallis Edward, 10th Earl Ferrers [G.B.], 1847. *Staunton Harold, Ashby-de-la-Zouch.* | Children. |
| 26918 | 6425 | Lady Augusta Amelia, wife of Sir Archdale Robert Palmer, 4th Bart., 1849. *Wanlip Hall, Leicester.* | |

473. Descendants, if any, of Frances Ward, –1770, and her husband, George Rooke, of St. Lawrence, near Canterbury. (See Table LXXVII.)

474. Descendants, if any, of the three elder sons of Frances Ward, – , and her husband, Robert Pigott, of Chetwynd, Salop, temp. 1697. (See Table LXXVIII.)

475. Descendants of George Grenville Wandesford Pigott, of Dod-
dershall Park, M.P.,   –1865.   (See Table LXXVIII.)

26919	6426	William Harvey Pigott, J.P., Captain R.N., 1848. *Doddershall Park, Bucks.*	} Son.	Children
26920	6427	Editha Ivy Pigott.	} Grandchildren.	
26921	6428	Lettice Harvey Pigott.	of No. 26919.	

476. Descendants of the Rev. John Robert Pigott, J.P., Rector of
Ashwellthorpe and Wreningham, 1800–1852. (See Table
LXXVIII.)

26922	6429	Vincent Randolphe Pigott, Captain Royal Warwickshire Regiment, J.P., 1866. *Grendon Underwood, Bucks.*	Grandchildren. Sons and elder daughters of the Rev. Randolphe Henry Pigott, Rector and Lord of the Manor of Grendon Underwood, J.P., 1837–1900.
26923	6430	Arthur Randolphe Pigott, 1873.	
26924	6431	Adeline Augusta Harriet Pigott, 1867.	
26925	6432	Lilian Emma, wife of Arnold Robinson Burrowes, Captain and Adjutant Royal Irish Fusiliers, 1869.	
26926	6433	Arnold Brian Burrowes, 1896.	Great-grandchild. Son of No. 26925.
26927	6434	Mabel Mary Pigott, 1870.	Grandchildren. Younger sisters of No. 26922.
26928	6435	Christobella Caroline Pigott, 1875.	
26929	6436	Marjory Jane Pigott, 1876.	
26930	6437	William Pigott, 1838.	
26931	6438	Thomas Digby Pigott, C.B., Comptroller of H.M.'s Stationery Office, 1840. *5 Ovington Gardens, S.W. The Lodge, Sheringham.*	2nd and 3rd sons.
26932 –36	}	Same as Nos. 24539–24543.	Grandchildren. Children of No. 26931.
26937	6439	Rev. Edmund Vincent Pigott, 1843. *Trentham Vicarage, Staffordshire.*	4th son.
26938	6440	Grenville Edmund Pigott, D.S.O., Captain Army Service Corps, 1870.	
26939	6441	Henry Lionel Pigott, Lieutenant (retired) R.N., 1877.	
26940	6442	William Godfrey Pigott, 1885.	
26941	6443	Katharine Gwendoline, wife of Francis Hamilton Wedgwood, 1868.	Grandchildren. Children of No. 26937.
26942	6444	Caroline Ethel Pigott, 1872.	
26943	6445	Isabel Ursula Pigott, 1873.	
26944	6446	Frances Sibyl Rose Pigott, 1876.	
26945	6447	Mary Winifred Pigott, 1880.	
26946	6448	Emma Nora Pigott, 1882.	
26947	6449	John Robert Wilson Pigott, H.B.M. Consul at Paramaribo, Surinam, 1850.	Youngest son and elder daughters.
26948	6450	Emma Charlotte Pigott, 1841.	
26949	6451	Edith Augusta, wife of the Rev. William Henry Draper, 1845. *Middleton Stoney Rectory, Oxford.*	

26950	6452	John Pigott George Draper, 1871.	
26951	6453	Christopher Robert Burroughes Draper, 1878.	
26952	6454	Eardly Harry Upcher Draper, 1879.	
26953	6455	Aubrey Marsham Draper, 1883.	
26954	6456	Noel Ponsonby Draper, 1884.	Grandchildren.
26955	6457	Harry Cecil Draper, 1886.	Children of
26956	6458	Ethelwyn Draper, 1872.	No. 26949.
26957	6459	Edith Rhoda Draper, 1874.	
26958	6460	Dorothy Mary Draper, 1881.	
26959	6461	Geraldine Eustace Draper, 1887.	
26960	6462	Rosaline Emma Marion Draper, 1889.	
26961	6463	Rev. Hugh Digby Birley.	Grandson. Only child of Mary Isabella Pigott, 1846–1877 (3rd daughter), and her husband, the Rev. Edward Hornby Birley, Vicar of Ellastone.
26962	6464	Blanche Anne Frances Pigott, 1848.	Youngest daughter.

477. Descendants of Arthur Pigott, Lieut.-Col. 89th Foot (Royal Irish), – . (See Table LXXVIII.)

26963	6465	Arthur Frederick Hamilton Pigott.	Grandchildren. Children of Major Arthur Romer Pigott, 1846–1875.
26964	6466	Hilda Mary Pigott, 1872.	
26965	6467	Theodora Catherine Pigott, 1874.	
26966	6468	John Charles Matthew Pigott, Major (retired) *late* Royal Berks Regiment, 1850.	Son.
26967	6469	Olive Winifred Hugolyne Pigott, 1874.	Granddaughter. Only surviving child of No. 26966.
26968	6470	Rev. Edward Caledon Pigott, 1855.	Son.
26969	6471	Godfrey Pigott, 1888.	Grandchildren. Children of No. 26968.
26970	6472	Elsie Pigott, 1882.	
26971	6473	Jane Marianne Pigott, 1852.	Daughter.

478. Descendants of John Harvey Thursby, of Abington Abbey, 1793–1860. (See Table LXXVIII.)

26972	6474	John Harvey Thursby, *late* Captain 38th and 41st Regiment, 1819. *Abington Abbey, Northampton.*	Son.
26973	6475	Frederick Charles Neville Gospatrick Thursby, 1895.	Great-grandson. Only child of Percy Thursby, 1851–1898, and grandson of the Rev. Matthew William Frederic Thursby, 1821–1869.
26974	6476	Neville Thursby, 1852. 16 *Queen Street, Mayfair.*	Grandson. Son of the Rev. Matthew William Frederic Thursby, 1821–1869.
26975	6477	Audley Delves Thursby, 1888.	Great-grandchildren. Children of No. 26974.
26976	6478	Honor Zoë Thursby, 1886.	
26977	6479	Fortescue Thursby, 1855. 22 *Queen's Gate, S.W.*	Grandchildren. Children of the Rev. Matthew William Frederic Thursby, 1821–1869.
26978	6480	Charles Radcliffe Thursby, 1857.	
26979	6481	Ralph Thursby, 1863.	
26980	6482	Emily, wife of Captain Ernest Henry Curtis, *late* Bengal Cavalry.	
26981	6483	Henry Piers Thursby Curtis, 1878.	Great-grandchildren. Children of No. 26980.
26982	6484	Charles Nevill Curtis, 1880.	
26983	6485	Edgar Ralph Curtis, 1883.	
26984	6486	Beatrice Curtis, 1877.	
26985	6487	Cecilia Constance Curtis, 1878.	

26986	6488	Sophia Sybil Thursby.	{ Grandchild. Youngest daughter of the Rev. M. W. F. Thursby, 1821-1869.
26987	6489	Sylvia Gladys Dorcas Thursby, 1891.	Great-grandchildren. Children of Harry Forster Thursby of Sydney Lodge, Leamington Spa, 1860-1899, and grandson of Captain Spencer George Augustus Thursby, 1823-1871.
26988	6490	Catherine Dorothy Thursby, 1893.	
26989	6491	Anna Maria Emma, wife of the Rev. Thomas Reginald Horley. *Eaton Socon Vicarage, St. Neots.*	Grandchild. Daughter of Captain Spencer George Augustus Thursby, 1823-1871.
26990	6492	Rev. Herbert Edward Thursby, 1858. *Castle Rising Rectory, King's Lynn.*	Grandson. Son of the Rev. Walter Thursby, 1830-1868.
26991	6493	Walter Thursby, 1890.	
26992	6494	Miles Herbert Thursby, 1893.	
26993	6495	Samuel James Thursby, 1902.	Great-grandchildren.
26994	6496	Katherine Gwenllian Thursby, 1891.	Children of No.
26995	6497	Dorothy Guenilda Thursby, 1895.	26990.
26996	6498	Mary Victoria Thursby, 1897.	
26997	6499	Marjorie Christina Thursby, 1901.	
26998	6500	Cecil Fiennes Thursby, C.B., Commander R.N., 1861.	Grandson. Son of the Rev. Walter Thursby, 1830-1868.
26999	6501	Irene Constance Adelaide Thursby, 1900.	Great-grandchild. Daughter of No. 26998.
27000	6502	Hugh Thursby, 1862.	Grandson. Brother of No. 26998.
27001	6503	Charles Pelham Thursby, 1890.	Great-grandchildren. Children of No. 27000.
27002	6504	Phyllis Cecil Thursby, 1889.	
27003	6505	Florence, wife of the Rev. William Drake Sargeaunt. *Stoke Abbott, Beaminster, Dorset.*	Grandchild. Daughter of the Rev. Walter Thursby, 1830-1868.
27004	6506	William Thursby Sergeaunt, 1893.	Great-grandchildren. Children of No. 27003.
27005	6507	Christopher Sergeaunt, 1898.	
27006	6508	Walter John Sergeaunt, 1900.	
27007	6509	Mary Katherine Sergeaunt, 1896.	
27008	6510	Francis Dehaney Thursby, 1858.	{ Grandson. Son of Francis Thursby, 1822-1863.

479. Descendants of the Rev. William Harvey Thursby, of Ormerod House, 1795-1884. (See Table LXXVIII.)

27009	6511	Sir John Ormerod Scarlett Thursby, 2nd Bart., 1861. *Ormerod House and Bank Hall, Burnley.*	Grandson. Son of Sir John Hardy Thursby, 1st Bart., 1826-1901.
27010	6512	Clara Thursby, 1889. Great-grandchild. Daughter of No. 27009.	
27011	6513	George James Thursby, 1869. *Boveridge, Cranborne, Salisbury.*	Grandchildren. Brother and sister to No. 27009.
27012	6514	Violet, wife of Willoughby Aston Littledale. *26 Cranley Gardens, S.W.*	
27013	6515	Willoughby John Littledale, 1896.	Great-grandchildren. Children of No. 27012.
27014	6516	Eleanor Violet Littledale, 1890.	
27015	6517	Mary Eleanor Thursby, 1871.	{ Grandchild. Younger sister to No. 27009.
27016	6518	William Legh Thursby, 1865.	Grandchildren. Children of Major James Legh Thursby, of Craig-le, co. Carnarvon, 1828-1886.
27017	6519	Hilda, wife of Captain Herbert Roberts, R.M.L.I., 1867.	
27018	6520	Winifred, wife of A. H. de Vreque-French, Count de Castel-d'Homond, 1868.	

27019	6521	Arthur Harvey Thursby, J.P., D.L., 1832. *Culverlands, Mortimer, Berks.*	} Son.
27020	6522	Piers Henry Thursby, 1894. ⎫ Great-grandchildren.	Children
27021	6523	Arthur William Charles Thursby, ⎪ of Colonel Arthur Edmund 1899. ⎪ Thursby, 1861–1902, and	
27022	6524	Diana Mary Thursby, 1891. ⎭ grandchildren of No. 27019.	
27023	6525	Rev. Harvey William Gustavus Thursby, 1867. ⎫	
27024	6526	Eleanor Mary Anne, wife of the Rev. Godfrey Armytage Littledale, 1862. *Chipping Norton Vicarage.*	
27025	6527	Fanny Charlotte, wife of the Rev. Charles Hubert Whitfield, 1864. *Grazeley Vicarage, Berks.*	Grandchildren. Children of No. 27019.
27026	6528	Emma Harriet, wife of the Rev. Hugh Langford Sainsbury, 1865. *Birkington Rectory, Somerset.*	
27027	6529	Piers Thursby, J.P., late Captain 9th Lancers, 1834. *Broadwell Hill, Stow-on-the-Wold, co. Gloucester.*	} Son.
27028	6530	Arthur Doncaster Thursby, 1860. ⎫	
27029	6531	Edmund Hasell Thursby, 1862. ⎪	
27030	6532	Charles Augustus Hathorne Thursby, 1872. ⎪	
27031	6533	Florence Emma Mabel Gwindoline, widow of Captain Walter Lascelles, 1862–1897.	Grandchildren. Children of Lieut.-Col. Richard Hasell Thursby, 1836–1885.
27032	6534	Violet Rachel Lascelles, 1892. ⎫ Great-grandchildren.	
27033	6535	Constance Gertrude ⎬ Children of No. Lascelles, 1894. ⎭ 27031.	
27034	6536	Ethel Constance Geraldine, widow of Lieut.-Col. Thomas Duncan, –1900.	

480. Descendants of Frederick Spencer Thursby, R.N., 1801– . (See Table LXXVIII.)

27035	6537	Lucie, wife of Julius Cremer.	Daughter.

481. Descendants, if any, of Emma Harvey Thursby, Sophia Frances Harvey Thursby, and Lucy Harvey Thursby, wife of John Dauncey. (See Table LXXVIII.)

482. Descendants of Anne Harvey Thursby, 1812–1899, wife of the Rev. Benjamin Winthrop, Rector of Wolverhampton, 1800–1885. (See Table LXXVIII.)

27036	6538	Benjamin Winthrop, 1838.	Son.
27037	6539	Walter Thursby Winthrop, 1875.	⎫
27038	6540	John Gerard Winthrop, 1877.	⎪
27039	6541	Harry Stephen Winthrop, 1878.	⎪
27040	6542	Neville Eveleigh Winthrop, 1880.	Grandchildren.
27041	6543	Beatrice Constance, wife of John Fox, 1870.	Children of
27042	6544	Maud Christian Ada Winthrop, 1871.	No. 27036.
27043	6545	Cecil Margaret Winthrop, 1872.	⎪
27044	6546	Monica Mary Winthrop, 1880.	⎪
27045	6547	Muriel Gertrude Winthrop, 1885.	⎭

27046	6548	Guy Everard Winthrop, 1868.	⎫ Grandchildren. Children
27047	6549	William Henry Winthrop, 1873.	⎬ of Stephen Winthrop,
27048	6550	Charles Frederick Winthrop, 1875.	⎭ 1839–1879.
27049	6551	Evelyn Vanda Louisa Winthrop, 1902.	⎰ Great-grandchildren. Daughter of No. 27048.
27050	6552	Arthur Thursby Winthrop, 1877.	⎱ Grandchildren. Brothers
27051	6553	Stephen Winthrop, 1879.	of No. 27046.
27052	6554	William Young Winthrop, 1852.	Son.
27053	6555	Evelyn Annie Welch, 1864.	⎱ Grandchildren. Daughters of Mary
27054	6556	Ethel Mary, wife of W. H. Warrington, 1866.	⎰ Anne Emma Winthrop, 1835–1899, wife of Dr. Welch.
27055	6557	Margaret Courtney, 1864.	⎰ Grandchildren. Daughters of
27056	6558	Alice Courtney, 1866.	⎱ Eleanor Winthrop, 1843–1871, wife of Henry Courtney.
27057	6559	Emily Frances Winthrop, 1845.	⎱ Daughters.
27058	6560	Florence Ellen, wife of J. F. Armstrong, 1848.	
27059	6561	Harry Armstrong, 1880.	Grandchild. Child of No. 27058.
27060	6562	Annie Gertrude Winthrop, 1850.	⎱ Daughters.
27061	6563	Constance Ella, wife of Francis N. Smith, 1854.	
27062	6564	Bernard Winthrop Smith, 1882.	⎱ Grandchildren. Children
27063	6565	Esmée Winthrop Smith, 1885.	of No. 27061.

483. Descendants, if any, of Walter Cotes Harvey Thursby, or John Harvey Thursby, temp. 1800? (See Table LXXIX.)

484. Descendants of the Rev. Henry Thursby, afterwards Pelham, of Cound Hall, co. Salop, 1801–1878. (See Table LXXIX.)

27064	6566	James Augustine Harvey Thursby-Pelham, 1869. *Manor House, Kineton, Warwickshire.*	⎰ Grandson. Son of Walter Harvey Thursby-Pelham, J.P., 1830–1874.
27065	6567	Mary Audley Nina Thursby-Pelham.	⎱ Great-granddaughter. Daughter of No. 27064.
27066	6568	Rev. Augustus Thursby-Pelham, 1832. *Cound Rectory, Salop.*	⎱ Son.
27067	6569	Arthur Harvey Thursby-Pelham.	⎰ Grandson. Son of No. 27066.
27068	6570	John Francis Thursby-Pelham, 1870.	⎰ Grandchildren. Children
27069	6571	Frances Mary Thursby-Pelham.	⎱ of Francis Thursby-Pelham, C.E., 1838–1889.
27070	6572	Eleanor Etua Audley Thursby-Pelham. *Abermarlaris Park, Carmarthenshire.*	⎰ Grandchild. Daughter of Capt. Pelham Thursby-Pelham, of Abermarlaris Park, 1840–1897.
27071	6573	Edward Cressett Thursby-Pelham, 1871.	
27072	6574	Henry Cressett Thursby-Pelham, 1881.	
27073	6575	Nevill Thursby-Pelham, 1883.	
27074	6576	Constance Ann, wife of Cecil Fiennes Thursby, C.B., Commander R.N.	Grandchildren. Children of Cressett Thursby-Pelham, 1843–1884.
27075		Same as No. 26999.	⎰ Great-grandchild. Daughter of No. 27074.
27076	6577	Dorothy Harriet Thursby-Pelham.	

485. Descendants of Ralph Merrick Leeke, of Longford Hall, co. Salop, 1813–1882. (See Table LXXIX.)

27077 –94	}	Same as Nos. 25085–25102.

486. Descendants of Charlotte Leeke, –, and her husband, the Rev. Wyndham Madden, Rector of Bergh Upton, –. (See Table LXXIX.)

27095	6578	Rev. Wyndham Madden, 1849. *Longford Rectory, Salop.*	}	Son.
27096	6579	Wyndham Ralph Carlyon Madden.		
27097	6580	Hestor Charlotte Madden.		
27098	6581	Rachel Madden.	Grandchildren. Children of No. 27095.	
27099	6582	Mary Evelyn Madden.		
27100	6583	Marjorie Constance Madden.		
27101	6584	Emily Charlotte, wife of L. H. Bland, 1847. *Abbeville, Belfast.*	}	Daughter.
27102	6585	Robert Wyndham Humphrey Bland.	Grandchildren. Children of No. 27101.	
27103	6586	Eva Charlotte Bland.		
27104	6587	Lilian Bland.		
27105	6588	Clara Louisa, wife of Ludlow Eustace Maude, 1848.	2nd daughter.	
27106	6589	Eustace Maude.		
27107	6590	Kathleen Maude.		
27108	6591	Norah Maude.	Grandchildren. Children of No. 27105.	
27109	6592	Dorothy Maude.		
27110	6593	Beatrice Maude.		
27111	6594	Caroline Madden, 1852.		
27112	6595	Amy Madden, 1853.	Daughters.	
27113	6596	Charlotte, wife of Pierpoint Mitchell, 1860.		
27114	6597	Winefred Mitchell.	Grandchild. Child of No. 27113.	

487. Descendants of Caroline Leeke, –1873, and her husband, William, 4th Earl of Abergavenny, 1792–1868. (See Table LXXIX.)

27115	6598	William, 1st Marquis [U.K.] and 5th Earl [G.B.] of, and 21st Baron [E.] of Abergavenny, K.G., 1826. *Eridge Castle, Sussex.* 64 *Eccleston Square, S.W.*	}	Son.
27116	6599	Reginald William Bransby, Earl of Lewes, 1853.	Grandchildren. Sons of No. 27115.	
27117	6600	Lord Henry Gilbert Ralph Nevill, 1854. *Eridge Castle, Sussex.*		
27118	6601	Joan Marion, Marchioness [U.K.] and Countess [G.B.] Camden, 1877. *Bayham Abbey, Lamberhurst.*	Great-grandchild. Daughter of No. 27117.	
27119	6602	John Charles Henry, Earl of Brecknock, 1899.	Great-great-grandchild. Child of No. 27118.	
27120	6603	Marguerite Helen Nevill, 1887.	Great-granddaughter. Daughter of No. 27117.	

27121	6604	Lord George Montacute Nevill, 1856. *Dane Gate House, Eridge, Sussex.*	Grandson. 3rd son of No. 27115.
27122	6605	Guy Temple Montacute Nevill, 1883.	Great-grandchildren.
27123	6606	Rupert William Nevill, 1884.	Children of No.
27124	6607	Marjorie Nevill, 1886.	27121.
27125	6608	Lord William Beauchamp Nevill, 1860.	
27126	6609	Lord Richard Plantagenet Nevill, 1862. *Carlton.*	Grandchildren. Children of No. 27115.
27127	6610	Lady Cicely Louisa, wife of Colonel the Hon. Charles Gathorne Gathorne-Hardy, 1851. *43 Lennox Gardens, S.W.*	
27128	6611	Violet Caroline, wife of Henry Ernest Crawley, 1873.	Great-grandchildren. Children of No. 27127.
27129	6612	Cicely Muriel Gathorne-Hardy, 1877.	
			Great-grandchildren. Children of the Lady Alice Maud Nevill, 1858–1898, wife of Major Henry Courtenay Morland.
27130	6613	Lady Idina Mary, wife of the Hon. Thomas Allnutt Brassey, 1865. *23 Park Lane, W.*	Grandchildren. Children of No. 27115.
27131	6614	Rose, Countess of Cottenham [U.K.], 1866. *Ridley Hall, Nantwich.*	
27132	6615	Kenelm Charles Francis, Viscount Crowhurst, 1901.	Great-grandchild. Son of No. 27131.
27133	6616	Honer Dorothy Leigh, 1892.	Great-grandchild. Daughter of No. 27131 by 1st husband, John Blundell Leigh.
27134	6617	Violet, Countess Cowley [G.B.], Baroness Lucas, Butler, and Cowper [E.], Baroness Dingwall [S.], wife of Robert Edward Myddelton, *formerly* Myddelton-Biddulph, J.P., 1866. *Church Leys, Rearsby, Leicester.*	Granddaughter. Youngest daughter of No. 27115.
27135	6618	Christian Arthur Viscount Dangan, 1890.	Great-grandchild. Son of No. 27134 by 1st husband.
27136	6619	Ririd Myddelton, 1902.	Great-grandchildren. Children of
27137	6620	Idina Joan Myddelton, 1899.	No. 27134 by 2nd husband.
27138	6621	Hon. Ralph Pelham Nevill, 1832. *38 Lowndes Square, S.W.*	Younger son.
27139	6622	Ralph William Plantagenet Nevill, J.P., 1865.	
27140	6623	Percy Llewelyn Nevill, 1877.	Grandchildren. Children of No. 27138.
27141	6624	Constance Emily Nevill, 1862.	
27142	6625	Isabel Louisa, wife of Major Angus Howard Reginald Ogilvy, D.S.O., 13th Hussars. *Naval and Military.*	
27143	6626	Gilchrist Nevill Ogilvy, 1892.	Great-grandchildren. Children of No. 27142.
27144	6627	Olivia Frances Isabel Ogilvy, 1891.	
27145	6628	Mary Frances, Viscountess Hardinge [U.K.], 1869. *South Park, Penshurst, Tonbridge.*	Grandchild. Child of No. 27138.
27146 –48		Same as Nos. 20431–20433.	Great-grandchildren. Children of No. 27145.
27149	6629	Cecily Augusta, wife of Philip Wyndham Cobbold, 1872.	Grandchildren. Children of No. 27138.
27150	6630	Eleanor Georgiana, wife of Rowland Francis Meyrick, 1873.	
27151	6631	Lady Henrietta Augusta, widow of the Hon. Thomas Mostyn Lloyd-Mostyn, M.P., 1830–1861, 1830. *6 Portman Square, W.*	Elder daughter.

27152 –58	}	Same as Nos. 21274-21280.	Grandchildren, &c. Children, &c., of No. 27151.
27159	6632	Lady Isabel Mary Frances, wife of the Rev. and Hon. Edward Vesey Bligh. 6 *Portman Square, W.*	} Younger daughter.
27160	6633	Lodovick Edward Bligh, Major *late* 3rd Battalion the Buffs, J.P., 1854. *Cambria House, Minehead, Somerset.*	} Grandson. Son of No. 27159.
27161 27162 27163	6634 6635 6636	Algernon Stuart Bligh, 1888. Jack Frederick Bligh, 1893. Rose Marion Bligh, 1896.	} Great-grandchildren. Children of No. 27160.
27164	6637	Rosalind Isabel, wife of Lieut.-Col. Cecil Vernon Wingfield-Stratford, R.E., 1857.	{ Granddaughter. Daughter of No. 27159.
27165 27166 27167	6638 6639 6640	Esmé Cecil Wingfield-Stratford, 1882. Geoffrey Edward Wingfield-Stratford, 1887. Rosalind Frances Cecily Wingfield-Stratford, 1893.	} Great-grandchildren. Children of No. 27164.

488. Descendants of Emily Frances Anne Leeke, 18 –18 , 2nd wife of the Rev. Sir Henry Thompson, 3rd Bart., 1796–1868. (See Table LXXIX.)

27168	6641	Caroline Eleanor Thompson (if alive).	Daughter.

489. Descendants, if any, of Sarah Pigott, temp. 1750? and her husband, Walter Bevan, of Shrewsbury, – . (See Table LXXVIII.)

490. Descendants of John Harvey Thursby, of Abington Abbey, Northants, 1768– . (See Table LXXVIII.)

27169 –232	}	Same as Nos. 26972-27035.

491. Descendants of Lieut.-Col. William Spencer Harvey Thursby, 1769– . (See Table LXXVIII.)

492. Descendants of Anne Harvey Thursby, –1840, wife of John Armitage, of Northants, Lieutenant in the Blues, 1768-1861. (See Table LXXVIII.)

27233	6642	John Godfrey Luard, 1862. *Blyborough Hall, co. Lincoln.*	{ Great-grandson. Son of John Godfrey Luard, 1829-1862, and grandson of Henriette Armytage, –1873, wife of Charles Bourryau, of Blyborough, 1785-1855.

27234	6643	Alfred Luard, 1832.	Grandchildren. Children
27235	6644	Rev. Arthur Charles Luard, 1832.	of Henriette Armytage.
27236	6645	Henriette Louisa, wife of the Rev. Thomas Booth Wright.	*See above.*

Children, if any, of Maria Catherine Armytage, –1871 (daughter), wife of the Rev. John Johnson, Vicar of Houghton, co. Northampton.

493. Descendants of Captain Walter Harvey Thursby, of Shrewsbury. (See Table LXXVIII.)

| 27237 –341 | } | Same as Nos. 27064–27168. |

494. Descendants, if any, of the Rev. Charles Harvey Thursby, Rector of Abington; Benjamin Harvey Thursby; Honora Harvey Thursby, wife of John Burton, of Conway's Dragoons; and Anne Harvey Thursby, wife of Lieut.-Col. Arthur Owen. (See Table LXXVIII.)

495. Descendants, if any, of Jane Ward, temp. 1710? wife of Daniel Jevon. (See Table LXXVII.)

496. Descendants, if any, of the Hon. Theodosea Ward, 1630? wife 1st of Sir Thomas Brereton, Bart., and 2ndly of Charles Brereton. (See Table LXI.)

497. Descendants of Frances Mary Dilke, 1809–1871, wife of John Dilke, afterwards Fetherston, of Packwood, 1809–1876. (See Table LXXX.)

27342	6646	Beaumont Thomas Fetherston, 1839. *Maxstoke Castle, Coleshill, Warwickshire.*	
27343	6647	Frances Elizabeth Fetherston.	Children.
27344	6648	Edith Isabella, wife of Theodore H. Perceval. *Pomona, Shanklin, I.W.*	
27345	6649	Beaumont Albany Perceval, 1875.	
27346	6650	Sydney Theodore Perceval, 1877.	Grandchildren. Children
27347	6651	Rose Edith Perceval, 1880.	of No. 27344.
27348	6652	Gladys Violet Perceval, 1882.	
27349	6653	Katherine Rosamond Fetherston.	Daughter.

498. Descendants of Elizabeth Anne Dilke, afterwards Fetherston, 1812–1891, wife of William Charles Alston, of Elmdon Hall, Warwick, 1796–1862. (See Table LXXX.)

| 27350 | 6654 | William Charles Alston, J.P., Major and Hon. Lieut.-Col. Warwickshire Yeomanry, 1842. *Elmdon Hall, near Birmingham.* | Children. |
| 27351 | 6655 | Elizabeth Louisa, wife of James Roberts-West, J.P., D.L. *Alscott Park, Gloucestershire.* | |

27352	6656	James Bowmont Roberts-West, 1871.	}	Grandchildren.
27353	6657	Harry Charles John Roberts-West, Lieutenant R.N., 1872.	}	Children of No. 27351.
27354	6658	William Reginald James Roberts-West, 1900.	}	Great-grandchildren. Children of No.
27355	6659	Gilian Mary Roberts-West, 1902.	}	27353.
27356	6660	Reginald Montagu Roberts-West, Lieutenant R.N., 1873.	}	Grandchildren. Children of
27357	6661	Algernon Claude Philip Roberts-West, 1878.	}	No. 27351.
27358	6662	Frances Emily, wife of Colonel Edmund Charles Cradock-Hartopp. *Copsewood, Walton-on-the-Hill, Epsom.*	}	2nd daughter.
27359	6663	William Edmund Cecil Cradock-Hartopp, 1872.	}	
27360	6664	Francis Gerald Cradock-Hartopp, 1877.	}	Grandchildren.
27361	6665	Ronald Arthur Charles Cradock-Hartopp, 1881.	}	Children of
27362	6666	Louis Montagu Cradock-Hartopp, 1884.	}	No. 27358.
27363	6667	Mildred Eveline Nora Cradock-Hartopp, 1889.	}	
27364	6668	Mary Anne, wife of William Mynors Smythe. *Newbold Beeches, Leamington.*	}	3rd daughter.

499. Descendants of John Dilke, afterwards Fetherston, of Pack-wood House, 1809–1876. (See Table LXXX.)

27365 -372	}	Same as Nos. 27342–27349.

500. Descendants of William Andrew Dilke, 1813–18 . (See Table LXXX.)

27373	6669	Charles Wentworth Dilke.	Son.
27374	6670	Thomas Dilke.	
27375	6671	Charles Dilke.	Grandchildren. Children
27376	6672	William Dilke.	of No. 27373.
27377	6673	Charles Dilke.	
27378	6674	Helen Dilke.	Daughter.

501. Descendants of Mary Dilke, – , wife of the Rev. Thomas Wright, Rector of Market Bosworth, 1756–1840. (See Table LXXX.)

27379	6675	Florence Hester Lavinia, wife of Frederick Henry Cotton.	Great-granddaughter. Daughter of Mary Jane Annabella Wright, wife of Charles Richard Banastre Legh, of Adlington Hall, 1821–1888, and granddaughter of the Rev. Henry Wright, of Mottram Hall, –1864.
27380	6676	Caroline Mary Florence, wife of Arthur Masterton Robertson Legh, *formerly Renny.* *Adlington Hall, Macclesfield, Cheshire.*	Great-great-granddaughter. Elder daughter of No. 27379.

27381	6677	Cynthia Combermere Legh, 1896.	}	Great-great-great-grandchild. Daughter of No. 27380.
27382	6678	Gwendolene Mabel Lucy, wife of Frank Thomas Wisden. *Henfield, Sussex.*	}	Great-great-granddaughter. Younger daughter of No. 27379.
27383	6679	Julia Catherine, widow of James Frederick D'Arley Wright, *formerly* Street, J.P., Captain R.A., 1827–1889. *Mottram Hall, Prestbury, Cheshire.*	}	Granddaughter. Daughter of the Rev. Henry Wright, of Mottram Hall, – 1864.
27384	6680	Julia Mary Catherine, wife of Edward Wetherden Curteis, *late* Captain 24th Regiment.	}	Great-granddaughter. Daughter of No. 27383.
27385	6681	Edward Laurence Frederick Curteis, 1885.	}	Great-great-grandchild. Son of No. 27384.
27386	6682	Thomas Wright.	}	Grandchildren. Sons of the
27387	6683	Charles Wright.	}	Rev. Charles Wright.
		Children, if any, of Jane Wright (daughter), wife of Captain Blakiston, 27th Regiment.		

502. Descendants, if any, of Thomas Dilke, 1666/7–   , or Seymour Dilke, 1668, killed in Ireland,   –   . (See Table LXXX.)

503. Descendants, if any, of William Dilke,   –1764. (See Table LXXX.)

504. Descendants of Frances Dilke, 1664–   , wife of the Hon. William Ward, 1660–1692. (See Table LXXX.)

| 27388 –542 | } | Same as Nos. 26028–26182. |

505. Descendants, if any, of Elizabeth Dilke, 1665–   . (See Table LXXX.)

506. Descendants, if any, of Vice-Admiral Henry Meynell, M.P., 1789–   , Elizabeth Meynell, 1786-18 , wife of Colonel Weymouth, 17 –   , or of Charles Meynell, of The Grove, near Ashbourne. (See Table LXXXI.)

II.—𝔇escenŭants of t𝔥e 𝔏aŭy 𝔈leanor 𝔅ranŭon, 15 -1547 (younger ŭaug𝔥ter anŭ co=𝔥eir of 𝔐ary 𝔗uŭor, 𝔔ucen 𝔆onsort of 𝔉rance, 𝔇uc𝔥ess of 𝔖uffol𝔨), 1st 𝔴ife of 𝔥enry 𝔆liffor𝔡, 2n𝔡 𝔈arl of 𝔆umberlan𝔡, 1517–1570. (See Tables XIV. and LXXXII.)

507. Descendants,[1] if any, of the Hon. Anne Bridges,   ,
wife of   Torteson. (See Table LXXXII.)

---

508. Descendants of George, 5th Earl of Jersey, 1773–1859. (See Table LXXXIII.)

27543	6684	▽ Victor Albert George, 7th Earl of Jersey [E.], 10th Viscount Grandison [I.], P.C., 1845. *Middleton Park, Bicester.*	Grandson. Son of George Augustus Frederic, 6th Earl of Jersey, 1808–1859.
27544 –50	}	Same as Nos. 19611–19617.	Great-grandchildren. Children of No. 27543.
27551	6685	▽ Hon. Robert Frederick Villiers, late Captain Scots Guards, 1847. *Turf; Travellers'.*	
27552	6686	▽ Hon. Edward Reginald Clement Villiers, 1849. 68 *Curzon Street, W.*	Grandchildren. Brothers and elder sister to No. 27543.
27553	6687	▽ Lady Julia Sarah Alice, wife of Sir George Orby Wombwell, 4th Bart., 1842. *Newburgh Priory, Easingwold.*	
27554	6688	Julia Georgiana Sarah, Countess of Dartrey [U.K.], Baroness Cremorne [I]. *Dartrey, co. Monaghan.* 10 *Upper Belgrave Street, S.W.*	Great-grandchild. Eldest daughter of No. 27553.
27555	6689	Lady Edith Anne Dawson, 1883.	Great-great-grandchildren. Children of No. 27554.
27556	6690	Lady Mary Augusta Dawson, 1887.	
27557	6691	Mabel Caroline, wife of Henry Robert Hohler. 43 *Upper Brook Street, W.*	Great-grandchildren. Younger daughters of No. 27553.
27558	6692	Cecilia Clementina, wife of William Dudgeon Graham Menzies. *Hallyburton, Coupar Angus.* 6 *Hereford Gardens, S.W.*	
27559	6693	Alaister Menzies, 1892.	Great-great-grandchildren. Children of No. 27558.
27560	6694	Victor Malcolm Menzies, 1893.	

[1] Would be entitled to quarter the royal arms failing surviving issue of the 6th and 7th Lords Chandos.

ELEANOR, COUNTESS OF CUMBERLAND, YOUNGER DAUGHTER OF
THE PRINCESS MARY (TUDOR) AND CHARLES (BRANDON),
DUKE OF SUFFOLK

THE COMMON ANCESTRESS OF NOS. 27543-36735

From the Collection at South Kensington

27561	6695	⊽ Lady Caroline, wife of William Henry Phillips Jenkins, 1843. *Frenchay Park, Bristol.*	Grandchild. Younger sister to No. 27543.
27562	6696	William Reginald Haldane Jenkins, Lieutenant 7th Dragoon Guards, 1877.	Great-grandchildren Children of No 27561.
27563	6697	Caroline Julia Georgiana Jenkins.	
27564	6698	Evelyn Anne Jenkins.	
27565	6699	Nicholas, Prince Esterházy de Galántha [H.R.E.], Princely Count of Edelstetten [Austria], Count of Forchtenslein [Hungary], 1869. *Vienna, 4 Wallnerstrasse.*	Great-grandchildren. Children of Paul, Prince Esterházy, 1843–1898, and grandchildren of Lady Sarah Villiers, 1822–1853, wife of Nicholas, Prince Esterházy, 1817–1890.
27566	6700	Prince Rudolph Esterházy, 1880. *Eisenstadt, Kismarton.*	
27567	6701	Prince Aloysius Esterházy, Military Attaché to the Austrian Embassy, London, 1844.	Grandchildren. Sons of Lady Sarah Villiers, 1822–1858. *See above.*
27568	6702	Prince Nicholas Esterházy, 1851. *Pottendorf.*	
			Grandchildren. Children of Lady Adela Corsanda Maria Villiers, 1828–1860, wife of Colonel C. P. Ibbetson.

509. Descendants of Lady Charlotte Anne Villiers, 1771–1808, wife of Lord William Russell, 1767–1840. (See Table LXXXIII.)

27569	6703	Jack Southwell, 25th Baron de Clifford [E.], 1884.	Great-great-grandchild. Son of Edward Southwell, 24th Baron de Clifford, 1855–1894, grandson of Edward Southwell, 23rd Baron de Clifford, 1824–1877, and great-grandson of Captain John Russell, R.N., 1796–1835.
27570	6704	Hon. Maud Clara Russell, 1853. *Twycross, Atherstone.*	Great-grandchildren Daughters of Edward Southwell, 23rd Baron de Clifford. *See above.*
27571	6705	Hon. Katharine, wife of Reginald Corbet, 1861. *Adderley, Market Drayton.*	
27572	6706	Sybil Corbet.	Great-great-grandchild. Daughter of No. 27571.
27573	6707	Hon. Katharine Sarah Georgiana, widow of Charles Robert Colvile, M.P., 1815–1886, 1827. *Lullington, Burton-on-Trent.*	Granddaughter. Daughter of Captain John Russell. *See above.*
27574	6708	Sir Henry Edward Colvile, K.C.M.G., C.B., Major-General, 1852. *Lullington, Burton-on-Trent.*	Great-grandchild. Son of No. 27573.
27575	6709	Gilbert de Préville Colvile, 1887.	Great-great-grandchild. Son of No. 27574.
27576	6710	Hon. Mary, wife of William Edward Oakeley, J.P., D.L. *The Plas, Tan-y-Bwlch, N. Wales.*	Granddaughter. Sister to No. 27573.
27577	6711	Edward de Clifford William Oakeley, 1864.	Great-grandchildren. Children of No. 27576.
27578	6712	Mary Caroline, wife of William Frederick Inge. *Thorpe Constantine, near Tamworth.*	

27579 -80	}	Same as Nos. 26795-26796.	{ Great-great-grandchildren. Children of No. 27578.
27581	6713	George Russell, 1830. *Westerhall, Dumfries.*	} Grandson. Son of William Russell, 1800-1884.
27582	6714	George William Henry Russell, 1864.	{ Great-grandchild. Son of No. 27581.
27583	6715	Odo George Henry Russell, 1899.	{ Great-great-grandchild. Son of No. 27582.
27584	6716	John Russell, 1869.	} Great-grandchildren. Children of No. 27581.
27585	6717	Lilian Emmeline, wife of Captain St. John Halford Coventry, 1874. 36 *Elvaston Place, S.W.*	
27586	6718	George St. John Coventry, 1896.	} Great-great-grandchildren. Children of No. 27585.
27587	6719	Laura Coventry, 1899.	
27588	6720	Muriel Elsie Augusta Russell, 1884.	{ Great-grandchild. Daughter of Reginald Russell, 1839-1897, and granddaughter of William Russell, 1800-1884.
27589	6721	Laura Caroline, Countess of Wilton [U.K.], wife of Sir Frederick John William Johnstone, Bart., 1842. *Westerhall, Dumfries.* 9 *Arlington Street, S.W.*	Granddaughter. Daughter of William Russell, 1800-1884.
27590	6722	Arthur George, 5th Earl of Wilton [U.K.], 1865. *Houghton Hall, Swaffham.*	{ Great-grandchild. Son of No. 27589 by 1st husband, Seymour John Grey, 4th Earl of Wilton, 1839-1898.
27591	6723	Seymour Edward Frederic, Viscount Grey de Wilton, 1896.	} Great-great-grandchildren. Children of No. 27590.
27592	6724	Hon. George Arthur Egerton, 1898.	
27593	6725	Lady Egerton, 1901.	
27594	6726	Lady Elizabeth Emma Geraldine, wife of George William Taylor, 1865. *Turvey House, Turvey, Bedford.*	} Great-grandchild. Sister to No. 27590.
27595	6727	Seymour George Frederick Taylor, 1892.	
27596	6728	Sylvia Olive Frances Taylor, 1890.	Great-great-grandchildren. Children of No. 27594.
27597	6729	Miriam Katharine Taylor, 1894	
27598	6730	Phyllis Evelyn Taylor, 1896.	
27599	6731	Charlotte Emma Georgiana, widow of the Right Hon. Patrick Fitz-Stephen French, M.P., 1801-1873, 1818.	{ Granddaughter. Daughter of Gertrude Frances Russell, 1771-1841, wife of the Hon. Henry Grey Bennet, 1777-1856.
27600	6732	Louisa Emma Corisande, wife of Captain George H. Bridges, A.D.C.	} Great-grandchildren. Children of No. 27599.
27601	6733	Augusta Sarah French.	
27602	6734	Gertrude Frances, widow of Hamilton Gorges of Kilbrew, -1860, 1822.	{ Granddaughter. Younger sister to No. 27599.
27603	6735	Algernon Wriothesley Russell, co-heir to the Baronies of Beauchamp of Bletsho, and Mordaunt of Turvey, 1835. *Chenies, Rickmansworth, Herts.*	Grandchildren, &c. Children of Elizabeth Laura Henrietta Russell, 1803-1886, wife of Lord Wriothesley Russell, 1804-1886.
27604	6736	Evelyn Mary Eliza Russell, 1837. *Chenies, Rickmansworth, Herts.*	

VICTOR ALBERT GEORGE CHILD, EARL OF JERSEY, P.C., G.C.B.

PROBABLY REPRESENTATIVE OF THE LADY ELEANOR BRANDON, YOUNGER DAUGHTER
AND CO-HEIR OF THE PRINCESS MARY TUDOR

Photo, Gillman & Co., Ltd., Oxford

The Blood Royal of Britain

510. Descendants of Lady Anna Barbara Frances Villiers, 1772–1832, wife of William Henry Lambton, of Lambton, M.P., 1764–1797. (See Table LXXXIII.)

27605	6737	John George, 3rd Earl of Durham [U.K.], 1855. *Lambton Castle, Fence Houses.* 39 *Grosvenor Square, W.*	Great-grandchildren. Children of George Frederick D'Arcy, 2nd Earl of Durham, 1828–1879, and grandchildren of John George, 1st Earl of Durham, 1792–1840.
27606	6738	Hon. Frederick William Lambton, M.P., 1855. *Fenton, Wooler, Northumberland.*	
27607	6739	John Frederick Lambton, 1884.	
27608	6740	Geoffrey Lambton, 1887.	
27609	6741	Claud Lambton, 1888.	Great-great-grandchildren. Children of No. 27606.
27610	6742	Violet Lambton, 1880.	
27611	6743	Lilian Lady Dunglass.	
27612	6744	Joan Lambton, 1893.	
27613	6745	Hon. Hedworth Lambton, O.V.O., C.B., Rear-Admiral R.N., 1856. *Naval and Military ; United Service.*	
27614	6746	Hon. Charles Lambton, D.S.O., Lieut.-Col. and Brevet-Colonel Commanding 2nd Battalion Northumberland Fusiliers, 1857. *Naval and Military.*	
27615	6747	Hon. George Lambton, 1860. *Bedford Lodge, Newmarket.*	Great-grandchildren. Brothers of Nos. 27605, &c.
27616	6748	Hon. William Lambton, D.S.O., Major Coldstream Guards and Military Secretary to High Commissioner for South Africa, 1863. *Government House, Johannesburg, Transvaal.*	
27617	6749	Hon. Claud Lambton, 1865. 15 *Bolton Street, Piccadilly, W.*	
27618	6750	Angela Marjory Lambton, 1902.	Great-great-grandchild. Daughter of No. 27617.
27619	6751	Hon. D'Arcy Lambton, Captain 3rd Battalion Duke of Cornwall's Light Infantry, 1866.	Great-grandchild. Brother of Nos. 27605, &c.
27620	6752	Eileen Lambton, 1891.	Great-great-grandchild. Child of No. 27619.
27621	6753	Hon. Francis Lambton, 1871.	Great-grandchildren. Youngest brother and eldest sister to Nos. 27605, &c.
27622	6754	Beatrix Louisa, Countess of Pembroke [E.], Baroness Herbert of Lea [U.K.], 1859. *Wilton House, Salisbury.*	
27623	6755	Reginald, Lord Herbert, M.V.O., Lieutenant Royal Horse Guards, 1880.	Great-great-grandchildren. Children of No. 27622.
27624	6756	Hon. George Sidney Herbert, 1886.	
27625	6757	Lady Beatrix Frances Gertrude Herbert, 1878.	
27626	6758	Lady Muriel Katherine Herbert, 1883.	
27627	6759	Katherine Frances, Duchess of Leeds [E.], Viscountess Dunblane [S.], and Baroness Godolphin [U.K.], 1862. 11 *Grosvenor Crescent, S.W.*	Great-grandchild. 2nd sister to Nos. 27605, &c.
27628 –32	}	Same as Nos. 22376–22380.	Great-great-grandchildren. Children of No. 27627.

27633	6760	Lady Eleanor, wife of Lord Edgar Algernon Robert Gascoyne-Cecil, 1868. *20 Manchester Square, W.*	Great-grandchildren. 3rd and 4th sisters to No. 27605.
27634	6761	Lady Anne Lambton, 1869. *Lambton Castle, Durham.*	
27635	6762	Victor Alexander, 9th Earl of Elgin and 13th Earl of Kincardine [S.], 2nd Baron Elgin [U.K.], K.G., P.C., 1849. *Broomhall, Dunfermline. 18 Ennismore Gardens, S.W.*	Great-grandchild. Son of Lady Mary Louisa Lambton,1819–1898, 2nd wife of James, 8th Earl of Elgin, &c., K.T., 1811–1863, and grandson of John George, 1st Earl of Durham.
27636	6763	Edward James, Lord Bruce, 1881.	
27637	6764	Hon. Robert Bruce, 1884.	
27638	6765	Hon. Alexander Bruce, 1884.	
27639	6766	Hon. David Bruce, 1888.	Great-great-grandchildren. Children of No. 27635.
27640	6767	Hon. John Bernard Bruce, 1892.	
27641	6768	Hon. Victor Alexander Bruce, 1897.	
27642	6769	Lady Elisabeth Mary, wife of Henry Babington Smith, C.S.I., 1877. *Constantinople.*	
27643	6770	Michael James Babington Smith, 1901.	Great-great-great-grandchildren. Sons of No. 27642.
27644	6771	Henry George Babington Smith, 1902.	
27645	6772	Lady Christian Augusta Bruce, 1879.	Great-great-grandchildren. Younger daughters of No. 27635.
27646	6773	Lady Constance Veronica Bruce, 1880.	
27647	6774	Lady Rachel Catherine Bruce, 1890.	
27648	6775	Hon. Frederick John Bruce, 1854. *Seaton House, Arbroath, N.B.*	Great-grandson. Brother to No. 27635.
27649	6776	Lewis Bruce, 1880.	
27650	6777	Charles Bruce, 1883.	
27651	6778	James Bruce, 1887.	
27652	6779	Richard Frederick Bruce, 1894.	Great-great-grandchildren. Children of No. 27648.
27653	6780	Margaret Bruce, 1881.	
27654	6781	Marion Bruce, 1884.	
27655	6782	Katharine Bruce, 1885.	
27656	6783	Janette Elizabeth Bruce, 1890.	
27657 -77	}	Same as Nos. 22889–22909.	Great-grandchildren, &c. Children, &c., of Lady Emily Lambton, 1823–1886, wife of Lieut.-Col. William Henry Frederick Cavendish, 1817–1881, and grandchildren of John George, 1st Earl of Durham.
27678	6784	Alice Anne Caroline, Countess of Morton [S.], Baroness Douglas [G.B.], 1831. *Dalmahoy, Kirknewton.*	Granddaughter. Daughter of John George, 1st Earl of Durham.
27679 -83	}	Same as Nos. 22933–22937.	Great-grandchildren. Children of Henry Ralph Lambton, 1824–1896, and grandchildren of William Henry Lambton, 1793–1866.
27684	6785	Frederick William Lambton, Lieut.-Col. *late* 71st L.I.	Grandchildren. Children of William Henry Lambton, 1793–1866.
27685	6786	Francis William Lambton, Lieut.-Col. *late* Scots Guards, 1834. *Brownslade, Pembroke.*	
27686 -90	}	Same as Nos. 21754–21758.	Great-grandchildren. Children of No. 27685.

27691	6787	Arthur Lambton, Lieut.-Col. *late* Coldstream Guards, 1836.	⎫ Grandchildren. Brother and sister to Nos. 27684, &c.
27692	6788	Louisa Caroline, widow of General Sir Charles Henry Ellice, G.C.B., 1821–1888. 87 *Eaton Place, S.W.*	
27693	6789	William Henry Ellice, and others. ⎫	⎬ Great-grandchildren. Children of No. 27692.
27694	6790	Gertrude Nina Lambton.	⎰ Grandchild. Eldest sister to Nos. 27684, &c.

Children, if any, of Hedworth Lambton, M.P., 1797–1876 (son).

27695 -717	⎱ ⎰	Same as Nos. 22864–22888.	⎧ Great-grandchildren, &c. Children of Frederick John Howard, M.P., 1814–1897, and grandchildren of Frances Susan Lambton, 1794–1840, and her 1st husband, Colonel the Hon. Frederick Howard, 1785–1815.
27718 -39	⎱ ⎰	Same as Nos. 22910–22930, and 22975.	⎧ Grandchildren, &c. Children and grandchildren of Frances Susan Lambton, 1794–1840, and her 2nd husband, General the Hon. Henry Frederick Compton Cavendish, 1789–1873.

511. Descendants of Lady Caroline Elizabeth Villiers, 1774–1835, 1st wife of Henry William, 1st Marquis of Anglesey, K.G., 1768–1854. (See Table LXXXIII.)

27740	6791	Henry Cyril, 5th Marquis of Anglesey [U.K.], 6th Earl of Uxbridge [G.B.], 14th Baron Paget [E.], 1875. *Plas Newydd, Anglesey.*	⎫ Great-grandson. Son of Henry, 4th Marquis of Anglesey, 1835–1898, and grandson of Henry, 2nd Marquis of Anglesey, 1797–1869.
27741	6792	Charles Henry Alexander Paget, 1885.	⎫ Great-grandchildren. Children of Lord Alexander Victor Paget, 1839–1896, son of the 2nd Marquis of Anglesey. *See above.*
27742	6793	Victor William Paget, 1889.	14 *Southwark Crescent, Hyde Park, W.*
27743	6794	Winifred Constance Hester Paget, 1881.	
27744	6795	Beatrice Eleanor Paget, 1883.	
27745	6796	Lord Berkeley Charles Sydney Paget, 1844. 11 *Upper Wimpole Street, W.*	⎫ Grandson. Son of 2nd Marquis of Anglesey. *See above.*
27746	6797	Rowland Edward Paget, Lieutenant Sussex Regiment, 1878.	⎫ Great-grandchildren. Children of No. 27745.
27747	6798	Muriel Helen Florence, wife of Rupert Evelyn Beckett, 1878. *The Lodge, Doncaster.*	
27748	6799	Gwladys Helen Beckett, 1897.	⎫ Great-great-grandchildren. Children of No. 27747.
27749	6800	Violet Consuelo Beckett, 1899.	
27750	6801	Marjorie Nell Beckett, 1900.	
27751	6802	Lady Constance Eleanora Caroline, widow of the Hon. Frederick Charles Howard, 1840–1893, 1847.	⎫ Grandchild. Daughter of the Lady Constance Henrietta Paget, 1823–1878, 1st wife of George James, 11th Earl of Winchilsea and Nottingham, 1815–1878.

27752	6803	Gordon Frederick Henry Charles Howard, 1873. *Junior Constitutional.*	Great-grandchildren. Children of No. 27751.
27753	6804	Algernon George Mowbray Frederick Howard, 1874. *Junior Constitutional.*	
27754	6805	. . . . Higgins, 1878, and others.	Great-grandchildren. Children of Lady Hilda Jane Sophia Finch, 1856–1893 (sister to No. 27751), wife of Henry Vincent Higgins.
27755	6806	Florence Cecilia, Marchioness of Hastings [U.K.], Countess of Loudoun [S.] and Moira [I.], Baroness Hastings, Hungerford, Botreaux, De Molyns, and Grey de Ruthyn [E.] and Rawdon [G.B.], wife of Sir George Chetwynd, 4th Bart. *7 Hans Mansions, S.W.*	Granddaughter. Daughter of the 2nd Marquis of Anglesey. *See above.*
27756	6807	Grey George Chetwynd, 1874.	Great-grandchildren. Children of No. 27755.
27757	6808	Lilian Florence Maud, Marchioness of Anglesey [U.K.], Countess of Uxbridge [G.B.], Baroness Paget [E.], 1876. *Plas Newydd, Anglesey.*	
27758	6809	Olive Nina Mary Chetwynd, 1877.	
27759	6810	William Henry Paget, Major-General (retired) Indian Army, 1829. *129 Victoria Street, S.W.*	Grandson. Son of Lord William Paget, 1803–1873.
27760	6811	Bertha Frances Paget.	Great-granddaughter. Daughter of No. 27759.
27761	6812	Anna Blanche Constance, wife of Colonel Ulick George Campbell de Burgh, C.B., 1859. *Scarva, Clones, co. Monaghan.*	Great-granddaughter. Daughter of Lieutenant Charles Augustus Paget, R.N., 1831–1864, brother to No. 27759.
27762	6813	Desmond Herlouin de Burgh, 1897.	Great-great-grandchild. Son of No. 27761.
27763	6814	Charles Henry, 6th Duke of Richmond [E.], 6th Duke of Lennox [S.], 1st Duke of Gordon [U.K.), and 6th Duke of Aubigny [France], K.G., P.C., 1818. *Goodwood, Chichester. Gordon Castle, Banff.*	Grandson. Son of Lady Caroline Paget, 1796–1874, wife of Charles, 5th Duke of Richmond and Lennox, K.G., 1791–1860.
27764 –84 }		Same as Nos. 23055–23075.	Great-grandchildren, &c. Children of No. 27763.
27785	6815	Cosmo Charles Gordon-Lennox, a member of the dramatic profession, 1868. *Turf.*	Great-grandchild. Son of Lord Alexander Francis Charles Gordon-Lennox, 1825–1892.
277 6	6816	Augusta Catherine, Princess Edward of Saxe-Weimar, 1827. *16 Portland Place, W.*	Granddaughters. Sisters to No. 27763.
27787	6817	Cecilia Catherine, Countess of Lucan [I.], 1838. *Laleham House, Staines.*	
27788 –802 }		Same as Nos. 20396–20410.	Great-grandchildren. Children of No. 27787
27803	6818	Victor George Henry Francis, 5th Marquis Conyngham [I.], and Baron Minster [U.K.], 1883. *Slane Castle, Meath.*	Great-great-grandchildren. Children of Henry Francis, 4th Marquis Conyngham, 1857–1897, and grandchildren of George Henry, 3rd Marquis Conyngham, 1825–1882, and great-grandchildren of Lady Jane Paget, 1798–1876, wife of Francis Nathaniel, 2nd Marquis Conyngham, K.P., 1797–1876.
27804	6819	Lord Frederick William Burton Conyngham, 1890.	
27805	6820	Lady Blanche Frances Conyngham, 1884.	
27806	6821	Lady Mildred Martha Conyngham, 1886.	
27807	6822	Lady Hersey Constance Evelyn Conyngham, 1887.	
27808	6823	Lady Edena Dorothy Conyngham, 1888.	
27809	6824	Lady Barbara Helen Conyngham, 1893.	

27810	6825	Lord Charles Arthur Conyngham, 1871.	⎫ Great-grandchildren.
27811	6826	Lady Blanche Conyngham, 1856.	⎬ Children of the 3rd
27812	6827	Lady Constance Augusta, wife of Richard Combe, 1859. 33 *Lennox Gardens, S.W.*	⎱ Marquis Conyngham. *See above.*
27813	6828	George Henry Richard Combe, 1889.	⎫
27814	6829	Blanche Esther Combe, 1886.	⎬ Great-great-grandchildren.
27815	6830	Constance Combe, 1887.	Children of No. 27812.
27816	6831	Marjorie Combe, 1894.	
27817	6832	Eileen Combe, 1900.	⎭
27818	6833	Lady Jane Seymour, wife of Captain Christian Combe, 1860. 63 *Cadogan Square, S.W. Strathconan, Muir of Ord, N.B.*	⎫ Great-grandchild. ⎬ Sister to No. ⎭ 27810, &c.
27819	6834	Henry Christian Seymour Combe, 1891.	⎫
27820	6835	John Frederick Boyce Combe, 1895.	⎬ Great-great-grandchildren.
27821	6836	Winifred Phyllis Combe, 1891.	Children of No. 27818.
27822	6837	Gladys Jean Combe, 1900.	⎭
27823	6838	Lady Elizabeth Maud, wife of Captain Frederick William Ramsden, 1862. 69 *Grosvenor Street, W.*	⎫ Great-grandchild. ⎬ Sister to No. ⎭ 27810.
27824	6839	Charles Frederick Ingram Ramsden, 1888.	⎫ Great-great-grandchildren.
27825	6840	Cynthia Maud Ramsden.	⎬ Children of No. 27823.
27826	6841	Moyra Gwendolin Ramsden.	⎭
27827	6842	Lady Florence, wife of Bertram Frankland Frankland-Russell-Astley, 1866. *Chequers Court, Bucks.*	⎫ Great-grandchild. ⎬ Sister to No. ⎭ 27810.
27828	6843	Henry Jacob Delaval Astley, 1888.	⎱ Great-great-grandchildren.
27829	6844	Olive Joan Astley, 1893.	⎰ Children of No. 27827.
27830 -33	⎱	Same as Nos. 26703–26706.	Great-grandchildren, &c. Son, &c., of Lady Jane Conyngham, 1826–1900, wife of Frances George, 2nd Baron Churchill, 1802–1886, and grandson of Lady Jane Paget, 1798–1876. *See above.*
27834	6845	Francis Gustavus William Lambart, Major (retired), Secretary to the Order of St. Patrick, 1848. *St. James'; Kildare Street, Dublin.*	Great - grandchildren. Children of Lady Frances Caroline Maria Conyngham, 1827–1898, wife of Gustavus William Lambart, of Beau Parc, co. Meath, 1814–
27835	6846	Cyril Henry Edward Lambart, 1866.	1886, and grandchildren of Lady Jane Paget. *See above.*
27836	6847	. . . . Lambart, 1900.	⎰ Great-great-grandchild. Son of ⎱ No. 27835.
27837	6848	George James Richard Lambart, 1867.	⎫ Great - grandchild.
27838	6849	Hon. Amy Gwendoline, wife of the Hon. Henry Charles Legge, 1852. *The Gardens, Fulmer, Slough.*	⎬ Brother and sister to No. 27834.
27839 -40	⎱	Same as Nos. 21319–21320.	⎰ Great-great-grandchildren. Children of No. 27838.
27841	6850	Cecil Jane Lambart, 1854.	⎫
27842	6851	Constance Una Elizabeth, wife of the Hon. Henry Bourke, 1856. *Millburn, Esher, Surrey.*	
27843	6852	Georgiana Rose, widow of John Macdonald, of Betmore, –1891, 1859. 12 *Cavendish Place, W.*	⎬ Great-grandchildren. Sisters to No. 27834.
27844	6853	Violet Anne Blanche, wife of John Dunville Dunville, 1861. 46 *Portland Place, W.*	⎭

·27845	6854	. . . . Dunville, 1900.	{ Great-great-grandchild. Son of No. 27844.
27846	6855	Lilian Fanny Ermangarde Lambart, 1864.	
27847	6856	Hon. Bertha Madeline Frances Lambart, 1869.	Beau Parc, Slane, co. Meath. Great-grandchildren. Younger sisters to No. 27834.
27848	6857	Adeline Octavia Lambart, 1871.	

27849 | 6858 | Elizabeth Georgiana, Countess of Winchilsea and Nottingham [E.], 1829. 19 *Elvaston Place, S.W.* } Granddaughter. Daughter of Lady Jane Paget. *See above.*

27850 | 6859 | Theodore Francis Brinckman, C.B., Lieut.-Col. and Hon. Col. 3rd Battalion the Buffs, 1862. 49 *St. James' Street.* } Great-grandchild. Son of Lady Cecilia Augusta Conyngham, 1831–1877 (sister to No. 27849), wife of Sir Theodore Henry Brinckman, 2nd Baronet.

27851	6860	Theodore Ernest Warren Brinckman, 1898.	Great-great-grandchildren.
27852	6861	Daphne Cecilia Brinckman, 1900.	Children of No. 27850.
27853	6862	Claude Brinckman, 1871. *Fetcham Grove, Leatherhead.*	Great-grandchild. Brother to No. 27850.

27854 | 6863 | Edward Henry Churchill, 3rd Baron Crofton [I.], 1834. 49 *Jermyn Street, S.W.* *Mote Park, Ballymurray, Roscommon.* } Grandson. Son of Lady Georgiana Paget, 1800–1875, wife of Edward, 2nd Baron Crofton, 1806–1869.

27855 | 6864 | Arthur Edward Lowther Crofton, Captain *late* Northumberland Fusiliers, 1866. *Mote Park, Ballymurray.* { Great-grandson. Son of the Hon. Charles St. George Crofton, 1836–1895.

27856	6865	Edward Charles Crofton, 1896.	
27857	6866	Arthur Marcus Lowther Crofton, 1898.	Great-great-grandchildren. Children of No. 27855.
27858	6867	Eileen Mabel Lowther Crofton, 1894.	
27859	6868	Mabel Georgiana Crofton, 1865.	*Mote Park, Ballymurray, co. Roscommon.* Great-granddaughters. Sisters to No. 27855.
27860	6869	Theresa Diana Crofton, 1867.	
27861	6870	Ernest Alfred Crofton, 1878.	
27862	6871	George Crofton, 1881.	Great-grandchildren. Children of the Hon. Frances George Crofton, Captain R.N., 1838–1900.
27863	6872	Alfred Gerald Crofton, 1882.	
27864	6873	Francis Lowther Crofton, 1883.	
27865	6874	Gertrude Catherine Georgiana Crofton, 1867.	

27866 | 6875 | Augusta Caroline, Baroness Clonbrock [I.], 1839. *Clonbrock, Ahaseragh, co. Galway.* { Granddaughter. Sister to No. 27854.

27867 –70 } | | Same as Nos. 26764–26767. | { Great-grandchildren. Children of No. 27866.

27871 | 6876 | Henry Spencer, 2nd Lord Templemore [U.K.], 1821. *Dunbrody Park, Wexford.* 11 *Upper Grosvenor Street, W.* } Grandson. Son of Lady Augusta Paget, 1802–1872, wife of Arthur, 1st Lord Templemore, 1797–1837.

27872 | 6877 | Hon. Arthur Henry Chichester, *late* Major 3rd Battalion Royal Irish Regiment, 1854. 4 *Portman Square, W.* } Great-grandson. Son of No. 27871.

27873	6878	Arthur Claud Spencer Chichester, 1880.	Great-great-grandchildren. Children of No. 27872.
27874	6879	Gerald Henry Crofton Chichester, 1886.	
27875	6880	Richard Cecil Frederick Chichester, 1889.	
27876	6881	Hon. Hilda Caroline Chichester, 1875.	Great-granddaughter. Daughter of No. 27871.

27877	6882	Spencer Frederick Chichester, *late* Major 1st Battalion Royal Scots Fusiliers, 1854. *Naval and Military.*	Great-grandson. Son of the Hon. Frederick Arthur Henry Chichester, 1824–1863.
27878	6883	Charles Frederick Spencer Chichester, 1893.	Great-great-grandchild. Son of No. 27877.
27879	6884	Alan George Chichester, *late* Lieut.-Col. 2nd Battalion Royal Irish Regiment, Chief Constable of Huntingdonshire, 1857. *Huntingdon.*	
27880	6885	Ernest William Chichester, 1858.	Great-grandchildren. Brothers and sister of No. 27877.
27881	6886	Athole Augustus Chichester, 1861.	
27882	6887	Reginald de Blaquiere Chichester, Captain 2nd Battalion Border Regiment, 1862. *Naval and Military.*	
27883	6888	Violet Amelia Chichester, 1860.	
27884	6889	Shane Randolph Chichester, 1883.	
27885	6890	Augusta Jane Chichester, 1862.	Great-grandchildren. Children of the Hon. Francis Algernon James Chichester, 1829–1885.
27886	6891	Evangeline Blanche, wife of Captain Hubert Alcock Nepean Fyers, M.V.O., 1876. *114 Park Street, W.*	
27887	6892	FitzRoy Hubert Fyers, 1899.	Great-great-grandchildren. Children of No. 27886.
27888	6893	Enid Elizabeth Blanche Fyers, 1902.	
27889	6894	Kathleen Mary Chichester, 1877.	Great-grandchildren. Sisters of No. 27884.
27890	6895	Sheelah Maud Emily, wife of Essex Edgeworth Reade, 1878.	
27891	6896	Arthur Essex Edgeworth Reade, 1902.	Great-great-grandchild. Child of No. 27890.
27892	6897	Morna Sybil Chichester, 1879.	Great-grandchildren. Sisters of No. 27884.
27893	6898	Margaret Rosa Chichester, 1880.	
27894	6899	George Arthur Peel, 1852.	Great-grandson. Son of the Hon. Caroline Georgiana Chichester, 1826–1892, wife of Sir Charles Lennox Peel, G.C.B., 1893–1899.
27895	6900	Frances Caroline Peel, 1896.	Great-great-grandchildren. Children of No. 27894.
27896	6901	Vera Jane Peel, 1898.	
27897	6902	Horace Peel, 1857. *2 Lennox Gardens, S.W.*	Great-grandson. Brother to No. 27894.
27898	6903	Pemela Georgiana Peel, 1900.	Great-great-grandchild. Child of No. 27897.
27899	6904	Edward Lawrence Peel, 1860. *12 Hans Road, S.W.*	Great-grandson. Brother to No. 27894.
27900	6905	Caroline Marian Peel, 1897.	Great-great-grandchildren. Children of No. 27899.
27901	6906	Joan May Cecilia Peel, 1899.	
27902	6907	Algernon Robert Peel, 1862.	
27903	6908	Florence Caroline, wife of Colonel Charles Seymour Corkran, *formerly* Commanding 1st Battalion Grenadier Guards. *72 Princes Gate, S.W.*	Great-grandchildren. Younger brother and sisters of No. 27894.
27904	6909	Augusta Jane, wife of Montagu Scott Turner. *Woodcroft, Cuckfield, Hayward's Heath.*	
27905	6910	Cecilia Georgiana Peel. *45 Cadogan Place, S.W.*	
27906	6911	Lady Blanche Sybil, wife of the Hon. Lyonel Plantagenet Tollemache, 1862. *Manton, Oakham.*	Great-granddaughter. Only child of the Hon. Augusta Chichester, 1831–1873, and her 1st husband, Robert, 7th Earl of Kingston, 1831–1871.

27907 -08	}	Same as Nos. 21533-21534.	Great-great-grandchildren. Children of No. 27906.
27909 -14	}	Same as Nos. 20504-20509.	Great-grandchildren. Daughters, &c., of Henry William John, 4th Earl of Strafford, 1831-1899, and granddaughters of the Lady Agnes Paget, 1804-1845, 1st wife of George Stevens, 2nd Earl of Strafford, P.C., 1806-1886.
27915	6912	Francis Edmund Cecil, 5th Earl of Strafford [U.K.], 1835. *Wrotham Park, Barnet.* 5 *St. James' Square, W.*	Grandson. Son of the 2nd Earl of Strafford. *See above.*
27916	6913	Edmund Henry, Viscount Enfield, 1862. *Dancers' Hill, Barnet.*	Great-grandson. Son of No. 27915.
27917 27918	6914 6915	Hon. Florence Elizabeth Alice Byng, 1897. Hon. Mary Millicent Rachel Byng, 1899.	Great-great-grandchildren. Children of No. 27916.
27919 -24	}	Same as Nos. 20173-20178.	Great-grandchildren. Younger children of No. 27915.
27925	6916	Hylton George Hylton, 3rd Baron Hylton [U.K.], 1862. *Ammerdown Park, Radstock, Bath.* *Heath House, Petersfield.*	Great-grandchild. Son of Lady Agnes Mary Byng, 1853-1878, 1st wife of Hedworth, 2nd Lord Hylton, 1829-1899, and grandson of the Lady Agnes Paget. *See above.*
27926 -29	}	Same as Nos. 25467-25469.	Great-great-grandchildren. Children of No. 27925.
27930	6917	Hon. Agatha Eleanor, wife of the Hon. Ailwyn Fellowes, M.P., 1863. *Honingham Hall, Norwich.*	Great-grandchild. Sister to No. 27925.
27931 27932 27933 27934	6918 6919 6920 6921	Ronald Townshend Fellowes, 1886. Eric William Edward Fellowes, 1887. Hedworth George Ailwyn Fellowes, 1891. Carol Arthur Fellowes, 1896.	Great-great-grandchildren. Children of No. 27930.
27935	6922	Lady Mary Caroline Charlotte, wife of Richard Arkwright, 1838. 55 *Chester Square, S.W.* *Tor Castle, Banavie, N.B.*	Granddaughter. Sister to No. 27915.

512. Descendants, if any, of Lady Sarah Villiers, 1779-1852, wife of Charles Nathaniel Bayley. (See Table LXXXIII.)

513. Descendants of Lady Harriet Villiers, 1788-1870, wife of the Rev. and Hon. Richard Bagot, Bishop of Bath and Wells, 1782-1854. (See Table LXXXIII.)

27936	6923	Ponsonby Bagot, Lieut.-Col. *late* Scots Guards, 1845. *Carlton.*	Grandchildren. Children of Major-General Edward Bagot, 1808-1874.
27937	6924	Villiers Spencer Bagot, Lieut.-Col. *late* Rifle Brigade, 1847. 26 *Charles Street, W.*	

27938	6925	. . . . Bernal.	Grandchildren. Children of
27939	6926	. . . . Bernal.	Evelyn Bagot, –1877,
27940	6927	. . . . Bernal.	wife (1869) of Augustus
27941	6928	. . . . Bernal.	Woodley Bernal.
27942	6929	Ian Valentine Paton, D.S.O., Lieutenant Royal Scots Fusiliers, 1875.	Grandchildren. Children of Ethel Bagot, 1844–1885, 1st wife of Major-General George Paton, C.M.G. (*Army and Navy.*)
27943	6930	Basil George Bagot, Lieutenant South Wales Borderers, 1876.	
27944	6931	Arthur Greville Bagot, 1849. *Army and Navy.*	Grandson. Son of Admiral Henry Bagot, 1810–1877.
27945	6932	Frederic Spencer Wellesley Bagot, 1888.	Great-grandchild. Son of No. 27944.
27946	6933	Henry Richard Reginald Bagot, 1860.	
27947	6934	Claud Leveson Bagot, 1865.	Grandchildren. Brothers and sisters to No. 27944.
27948	6935	Gerald William Bagot, 1866.	
27949	6936	Florence Eleanor, wife of Charles Frederick Heneage Bagot, 1859.	
27950	6937	Agnes Mary Bagot, 1867.	
27951	6938	Rev. Lewis Richard Charles Bagot, 1846. *Stanton Lacy Vicarage, Salop.*	Grandson. Son of the Rev. Charles Walter Bagot, 1812–1884.
27952	6939	Caryl Ernest Bagot, 1877.	Great-grandchildren. Children of No. 27951.
27953	6940	Ysolde Cicely, wife of R. Gordon Snell, 1874.	
27954	6941	Gladys Mary Beatrice Bagot, 1880.	
27955	6942	Enid Avice Bagot, 1883.	
27956	6943	Charles Frederick Heneage Bagot, 1858.	Grandchildren. Brothers and sister to No. 27951.
27957	6944	Hugh Villiers, 1860.	
27958	6945	Constance Mary, wife of William Algernon Cajetan Law. 45A *Chester Square, S.W.*	
27959	6946	Nigel Walter Law, 1890. Great-grandchild. Son of No. 27958.	
27960	6947	Adela Harriet Sophia, wife of the Right Hon. Edmond Robert Wodehouse, P.C., M.P., 1854. *Minley Grange, Farnborough, Hants.*	Grandchildren. Sisters of No. 27951.
27961	6948	Mildred Emily Barbara, wife of Charles Elphinstone Fleeming Cunninghame Graham, 1856. 60 *Warwick Square, S.W.*	
27962	6949	Angus Edward Malise Cunninghame Graham, 1893.	Great-grandchildren. Children of No. 27961.
27963	6950	Olave Barbara Clementina Cunninghame Graham, 1884.	
27964	6951	Cecil Villiers Bagot, 1865. 22 *Brechin Place, S.W.*	Grandchildren. Children of the Rev. Frederic Bagot, 1822–1892.
27965	6952	Rev. Sidney Charles Bagot, 1873. *Horningsham, Warminster, Wilts.*	
27966	6953	Mary Harriet Agnes Bagot, 1868.	
27967 –77	}	Same as Nos. 21723–21733.	Grandchildren, &c. Children of Harriet Frances Bagot, 1816–1881, wife of the Rev. Lord Charles Thynne, 1813–1894.
27978	6954	Rev. Ernest Richard Orlando Bridgeman, 1851. *Blymhill Rectory, Shifnal.*	Grandchildren. Children of Emily Mary Bagot, 1823–1853, wife of the Rev. and Hon. George Thomas Orlando Bridgeman, 1823–1895.
27979	6955	Charles George Orlando Bridgeman, 1852. *Thatched House Lodge, Richmond Park.*	
27980	6956	Roger Orlando Bridgeman, 1889.	Great-grandchildren. Children of No. 27979.
27981	6957	Victoria Alexandrina Leopoldine Bridgeman, 1894.	

27982	6958	Harriet Georgina Isabel, wife of the Rev. Douglas Stuart Murray, 1853. *Blithfield Rectory, Rugeley, Stafford.*	} Grandchild. Sister to No. 27978, &c.
27983	6959	Walter Murray, 1882.	
27984	6960	George Murray, 1884.	
27985	6961	Leonard Murray, 1896.	Great-grandchildren.
27986	6962	Edward Murray, 1899.	Children of No.
27987	6963	Emily Murray, 1886.	27982.
27988	6964	Mabel Murray, 1888.	
27989	6965	Margaret Murray, 1894.	
27990	6966	Hugh Richard, 8th Viscount Downe [I.], 1st Baron Dawnay [U.K.], C.B., C.I.E., 1844. *Danby Lodge, Grosmont, York.*	Grandson. Son of Mary Isabel Bagot, 1825-1900, and her 1st husband, William Henry, 7th Viscount Downe, 1812-1857.
27991	6967	Hon. John Dawnay, D.S.O., Captain 10th Hussars, 1872. *Bachelors'.*	
27992	6968	Hon. Hugh Dawnay, D.S.O., Captain Rifle Brigade, 1875. *Bachelors'.*	Great-grandchildren. Children of No.
27993	6969	Hon. Beryl Dawnay, 1873.	27990.
27994	6970	Hon. Norah Dawnay, 1874.	
27995	6971	Hon. Faith Dawnay, 1877.	
27996	6972	Hon. Lewis Payn Dawnay, Captain and Lieut.-Col. Coldstream Guards, J.P., 1846. *Beningbrough Hall, York.* 51 *Charles Street, Berkeley Square, W.*	Grandson. Brother to No. 27990.
27997	6973	Guy Payan Dawnay, D.S.O., Lieutenant Coldstream Guards, 1878.	Great-grandchildren.
27998	6974	Alan Geoffrey Charles Dawnay, 1888.	Children of No.
27999	6975	Margaret Dawnay, 1880.	27996.
28000	6976	Marion Vere Dawnay, 1884.	
28001	6977	Hon. Eustace Henry Dawnay, J.P., D.L., 1850. *West Heslerton Hall, York.*	Grandson. Brother to No. 27990.
28002	6978	Cuthbert Henry Dawnay, 1891.	Great-grandchildren.
28003	6979	Dorothy Maud Dawnay, 1884.	Children of No.
28004	6980	Leila Mary Dawnay, 1886.	28001.
28005	6981	Hon. William Frederick Dawnay, J.P., D.L., 1851. *Brampton House, Northampton.*	Grandson. Brother to No. 27990.
28006	6982	Nigel William Dawnay, 1878.	
28007	6983	Sybil Mary Dawnay, 1876.	
28008	6984	Helen Louise Dawnay, 1877.	Great-grandchildren. Children of No. 28005.
28009	6985	Hylda Dawnay, 1880.	
28010	6986	Olive Dawnay, 1886.	
28011	6987	Hon. Geoffrey Nicholas Dawnay, 1852. *The Lodge, Malton, York.*	Grandson. Brother to No. 27990.
28012	6988	Eric Geoffrey Dawnay, 1890.	Great-grandchildren.
28013	6989	Marjorie Clare Dawnay, 1888.	Children of No.
28014	6990	Kathleen Dawnay, } twins, 1892.	28011.
28015	6991	Eileen Dawnay, }	
28016	6992	Hon. Francis Herbert Dawnay, Captain and Honorary Major Yorkshire Hussars Yeomanry Cavalry, 1853. *Bachelors'; Wellington.*	Grandchild. Youngest brother to No. 27990.
28017		Same as No. 25868.	Grandson. Son of Mary Isabel Bagot, 1825-1900, and her 2nd husband, Sidney Leveson Lane, 1831.
28018	6993	Hon. Alice Isabel Dawnay.	Grandchildren.
28019	6994	Hon. Edith Mary, wife of Robert Grant-Suttie, 1856. *Balgone, North Berwick.*	Sisters to No. 27990.

28020	6995	Hubert Francis Grant-Suttie, 1884.	
28021	6996	Archibald Ronald Grant-Suttie, 1896.	Great-grandchildren.
28022	6997	Hilda Margaret Grant-Suttie.	Children of No.
28023	6998	Muriel Katherine Grant-Suttie.	28019.
28024	6999	Ethel Mary Grant-Suttie.	
28025 –29	}	Same as Nos. 25869–25873.	Grandchild, &c. Sister, &c., to No. 28017.

514. Descendants of George Granville, 2nd Duke of Sutherland, 1758–1833. (See Table LXXXIII.)

28030 –144	}	Same as Nos. 22235–22349.

515. Descendants of Francis, 1st Earl of Ellesmere, K.G., 1800–1857. (See Table LXXXIII.)

28145 –78	}	Same as Nos. 23082–23115.

516. Descendants of Lady Charlotte Sophia Leveson-Gower, 1788–1870, and her husband, Henry, 13th Duke of Norfolk, K.G., 1791–1856. (See Table LXXXIII.)

28179	7000	Henry, 15th Duke of Norfolk [E.], Earl Marshall, K.G., P.C., 1847. *Arundel Castle, Sussex.* *Norfolk House, St. James' Square, S.W.*	Grandchildren. Sons of Henry, 14th Duke of Norfolk, 1815–1860.
28180	7001	Lord Edmund Bernard Talbot, *formerly* Howard, D.S.O., M.P., 1855. *Carlton; Naval and Military; White's.*	
28181	7002	Henry Edmund Talbot, 1883.	Great-grandchildren. Chil-
28182	7003	Mary Caroline Magdalen Talbot, 1880.	dren of No. 28180.
28183	7004	James Fitzalan Hope, M.P., 1870. *Heron's Ghyll, Uckfield.*	Great-grandson. Son of Lady Victoria Alexandrina Howard, 1840–1870, 2nd wife of James Robert Hope-Scott, of Abbotsford, Q.C., 1812–1873, and sister to No. 28179.
28184	7005	Arthur Oswald James Hope, 1897.	Great-great-grandchildren.
28185	7006	Henry John Hope, 1899.	Children of No. 28183.
28186	7007	Richard Frederick Hope, 1901.	
28187	7008	Joan Mary Hope, 1900.	
28188	7009	Minna Margaret, wife of the Right Hon. Sir Nicholas O'Conor, P.C., G.C.B., G.C.M.G., H.B.M.'s Ambassador at Constantinople, 1862. *The British Embassy, Constantinople.*	Great-granddaughter. Sister to No. 28183.
28189	7010	Fearga Victoria Mary O'Conor, 1892.	Great-great-grandchil-
28190	7011	Muriel Margaret Minna O'Conor, 1894.	dren. Children of
28191	7012	Eileen Winifred Madeleine O'Conor, 1897.	No. 28188.
28192	7013	Josephine Mary, wife of Wilfred Ward, 1864. *Lotus, Dorking.*	Great-granddaughter. Sister to Nos. 28183, &c.

28193	7014	Wilfred Hope Ward, 1890.	Great-great-grandchildren. Children of No. 28192.
28194	7015	Herbert Joseph Ward, 1894.	
28195	7016	Leo Paul Ward, 1896.	
28196	7017	Mary Josephine Ward, 1889.	
28197	7018	Teresa Victoria Ward, 1891.	
28198	7019	Lady Minna Charlotte Howard, a Carmelite nun, 1843.	Granddaughters. Sisters to No. 28179, &c.
28199	7020	Lady Mary Adeliza Howard, 1845. *Norfolk House, St. James', S.W.*	
28200	7021	Lady Etheldreda Howard, a Sister of Charity, 1849.	
28201	7022	Lady Philippa, wife of Edward Stewart, M.D., 1852. *Brook House, East Grinstead.*	
28202	7023	Henry Edward Stewart, 1891.	Great-grandchildren. Children of No. 28201.
28203	7024	Minna Philippa Stewart, 1892.	
28204	7025	Dorothy Stewart, 1895.	
28205	7026	Clare Margaret Stewart, 1897.	
28206	7027	Lady Anne, wife of Major-General Lord Ralph Drury Kerr, 1857. *Woodburn, Dalkeith, N.B.*	Granddaughter. Youngest sister to No. 28179, &c.
28207	7028	Philip Henry Kerr, 1882.	Great-grandchildren. Children of No. 28206.
28208	7029	David Anselm Kerr, 1893.	
28309	7030	Anne Cecil Kerr, 1883.	
28210	7031	Margaret Mary Kerr, 1884.	
28211	7032	Gertrude Minna Kerr, 1887.	
28212	7033	Francis Edward, 2nd Lord Howard of Glossop [U.K.], 1859. *Glossop Hall, Derbyshire.* 19 *Rutland Gate, S.W.*	Grandson. Son of Edward George, 1st Lord Howard of Glossop, P.C., 1818–1883.
28213	7034	Hon. Bernard Edward Fitzalan-Howard, 1885.	Great-grandchildren. Children of No 28212.
28214	7035	Hon. Philip Granville James Fitzalan-Howard, 1895.	
28215	7036	Hon. Muriel Augusta Mary Fitzalan-Howard, 1884.	
28216	7037	Hon. Frances Alice Mary Fitzalan-Howard, 1892.	
28217	7038	Gwendoline Mary Anne, Marchioness of Bute [G.B.] and Countess of Dumfries [S.], 1854. *St. John's Lodge, Regent's Park, N.W.*	Granddaughter. Sister to No. 28212.
28218	7039	John, 4th Marquis of Bute [G.B.], and 8th Earl of Dumfries [S.], 1881. *Mount Stuart, Rothesay. St. John's Lodge, Regent's Park.*	Great-grandchildren. Children of No. 28217.
28219	7040	Lord Ninian Edward Crichton-Stuart, 1883. *Falkland House, Fife.*	
28220	7041	Lord Colum Edmund Crichton-Stuart, 1886.	
28221	7042	Lady Margaret Crichton-Stuart, 1875.	
28222	7043	Angela Mary Charlotte, Lady Herries [S. and U.K.], 1855. *Everingham Park, near York.*	Granddaughter. Sister to No. 28212.
28223	7044	Hon. Gwendolen Mary Constable-Maxwell, 1877.	Great-granddaughters. Daughters of No. 28222.
28224	7045	Hon. Angela Mary Constable-Maxwell, 1877.	
28225	7046	Alice Mary Elizabeth, Countess of Loudoun [S.], Baroness Botreaux, Hungerford, De Moleyns, and Hastings [E.], and Donington [U.K.], 1856. *Loudoun Castle, Galston, N.B.*	Granddaughters. Sisters to No. 28212.
28226	7047	Hon. Constance Mary Germana, wife of Lieut.-Col. Charles Lennox Tredcroft, J.P., *late* R.H.A., 1857. *Glen Ancrum, near Guildford.*	

28227	7048	John Lennox Tredcroft, 1889.	Great-grandchildren. Children of No. 28226.
28228	7049	Augusta Mary Gwendolen Tredcroft, 1891.	
28229	7050	Hon. Winifred Mary, wife of William W. Middleton, 1861. *Stuart Lodge, Malvern Wells.*	Granddaughter. Youngest sister to No. 28212.
28230	7051	Winifrede Mary Angela Middleton, 1891.	Great-grandchildren. Children of No. 28229.
28231	7052	Margaret Alice Mary Middleton, 1893.	
28232	7053	Mary Gertrude Agnes Middleton, 1896.	
28233	7054	Ida Agatha Mary Middleton, 1898.	
28234	7055	Henry Thomas, 5th Lord Foley [G.B.], 1850. *Ruxley Lodge, Esher.* *7 Audley Square, W.*	Grandchildren. Sons of Lady Mary Charlotte Howard, 1822–1897, and her husband, Thomas Henry, 4th Lord Foley, 1808–1869.
28235	7056	Hon. Fitzalan Charles John Foley, J.P., Major 3rd Battalion Sherwood Foresters. *Barnwell Court, Surrey.*	
28236	7057	Lady Adeliza Matilda, widow of Colonel Lord George John Manners, M.P., 1820–1874, 1829. *Belgrave Mansions, Grosvenor Gardens, S.W.*	Only surviving daughter.
28237 –39		Same as Nos. 25360–25362.	Grandchildren. Children of No. 28236.

517. Descendants of Lady Elizabeth Mary Leveson-Gower, 1797–1891, and her husband, Richard, 2nd Marquis of Westminster, K.G., 1795–1869. (See Table LXXXIII.)

28240 –68		Same as Nos. 22325–22338, 22195–22196, 22339–22349, 22198–22199.	Descendants of Hugh Lupus, 3rd Marquis and 1st Duke of Westminster, K.G., 1825–1899.
28269	7058	Richard de Aquila, 1st Lord Stalbridge [U.K.], P.C., 1837. *32 Queensborough Terrace, W.* *Motcombe House, Shaftesbury.*	Son.
28270	7059	Hon. Hugh Grosvenor, Lieutenant 14th Hussars, 1880.	Grandchildren. Children of No. 28269.
28271	7060	Hon. Gilbert Grosvenor, Lieutenant Rifle Brigade (Prince Consort's Own), 1881.	
28272	7061	Hon. Richard Eustace Grosvenor, 1883.	
28273	7062	Hon. Elizabeth Emma Beatrice, wife of Lieutenant Aubrey Clare Hugh Smith, R.N., 1875.	
28274	7063	Hon. Blanche, wife of Captain James Henry Edward Holford, D.S.O., 7th Hussars, 1880.	
28275	7064	Hon. Eleanor Lilian Grosvenor, 1885.	
28276	7065	Eleanor, Duchess of Northumberland [G.B.], 1820. *Stanwick Park, Darlington.* *10 Upper Grosvenor Street, W.*	Elder daughters.
28277	7066	Mary Frances, Countess of Macclesfield [G.B.], 1821. *Shirburn Castle, Wallingford.*	
28278	7067	George Loveden William Henry, 7th Earl of Macclesfield [G.B.], 1888. *Shirburn Castle, Wallingford.*	Great-grandson. Son of George Augustus Viscount Parker, 1843–1895, and grandson of No. 28277.
28279	7068	Hon. Cecil Thomas Parker, J.P., 1845. *The Paddocks, Eccleston, Chester.*	Grandchild. Son of No. 28277.

28280	7069	Gerald Longley Parker, 1871. *Australia.*	⎫
28281	7070	Arthur Cecil Parker, 1873. *The Bath.*	⎬ Great-grandchildren.
28282	7071	Geoffrey Parker, 1880.	⎬ Children of No.
28283	7072	Wilfrid Parker, 1883.	⎬ 28279.
28284	7073	Caroline Beatrix, wife of William Clive Bridge-man, 1872. 13 *Mansfield Street, W.*	⎭
28285	7074	Robert Clive Bridgeman, 1896.	⎫ Great-great-grandchildren.
28286	7075	Geoffrey John Orlando Bridgeman, 1898.	⎭ Children of No. 28284.
28287	7076	Cecily Mary Parker, 1875.	⎰ Great-grandchild. Youngest daughter of No. 28279.
28288	7077	Rev. and Hon. Algernon Robert Parker, 1849. *Malpas Rectory, Cheshire.*	⎱ Grandson. 2nd surviving son of No. 28277.
28289	7078	Robert Edward Parker, 1878.	⎫
28290	7079	Hugh Algernon Parker, 1879.	⎬
28291	7080	Thomas Frederick Parker, 1882.	⎬
28292	7081	Eustace Parker, 1884.	⎬ Great-grandchildren. Children of No. 28288.
28293	7082	Leonard Parker, 1886.	⎬
28294	7083	Eric Parker, 1892.	⎬
28295	7084	Algitha Parker, 1880.	⎬
28296	7085	Constance Jessie Parker, 1889.	⎭
28297	7086	Hon. Francis Parker, Barrister Inner Temple, 1851. *Wilton House, Hobart Place, S.W.*	⎱ Grandson. 3rd surviving son of No. 28277.
28298	7087	Ronald Francis Parker, 1883.	⎫
28299	7088	Oliver Ivan Parker, 1891.	⎬ Great-grandchildren. Children of No. 28297.
28300	7089	Ivo Murray Parker, 1899.	⎬
28301	7090	Norah Henrietta Parker, 1885.	⎬
28302	7091	Phyllis Blanche Parker, 1889.	⎭
28303	7092	Hon. Reginald Parker, 1854. *Clifton Lodge, York.*	⎱ Grandson. 4th surviving son of No. 28277.
28304	7093	Victor Parker, 1877.	⎫ Great-grandchildren.
28305	7094	Doreen Maude Parker, 1879.	⎬ Children of No.
28306	7095	Ethel Henrietta, wife of Wilfred Forbes Home Thomson, 1880.	⎭ 28303.
28307	7096	. . . . Thomson.	⎰ Great-great-grandchild. Child of No. 28306.
28308	7097	Winifred Mary Parker, 1883.	⎰ Great-grandchild. Child of No. 28303.
28309	7098	Hon. Edmund William Parker, 1857. *Boodle's.*	⎱ Grandson. 5th surviving son of No. 28277.
28310	7099	Cyril Edmund Parker, 1884.	⎫ Great-grandchildren.
28311	7100	Wilfred Henry Parker, 1888.	⎬ Children of No.
28312	7101	Gwendoline Mary Parker, 1886.	⎭ 28309.
28313	7102	Rev. and Hon. Archibald Parker, 1859. *Abbotsford, Wymondham, Norfolk.*	⎱ Grandson. 6th surviving son of No. 28277.
28314	7103	Charles Edward Parker, 1890.	⎫
28315	7104	Frederic Archibald Parker, 1894.	⎬ Great-grandchildren. Children of No. 28313.
28316	7105	Violet Maud Parker, 1892.	⎬
28317	7106	Evelyn Sylvia Parker, 1897.	⎭
28318	7107	Hon. Henry Parker, 1860. *Shirburn Castle, Wallingford.*	⎫ Grandchildren. 7th and 8th surviving sons of No. 28277.
28319	7108	Hon. Alexander Edward Parker, 1864. *Deeside, Bangor-on-Dee, Wrexham.*	⎭
28320	7109	Sydney Alexander Parker, 1899.	⎰ Great-grandchild. Son of No. 28319.
28321	7110	Lady Elizabeth Amelia Parker, 1846.	⎫ Grandchildren. Elder
28322	7111	Lady Adelaide Helen, wife of the Hon. William Frederick Dawnay, 1848. *Brampton House, Northampton.*	⎬ daughters of No. 28277.

28323 -27	}	Same as Nos. 28006–28010.	{ Great-grandchildren. Children of No. 28322.
28328	7112	Lady Mary Alice, wife of the Rev. Charles Fane De Salis, Prebendary of Wells, 1863. *The Rectory, Weston-super-Mare.*	Grandchild. 3rd daughter of No. 28277.
28329	7113	Sydney Charles De Salis, 1898.	Great-grandchildren.
28330	7114	Dorothy Mary De Salis, 1897.	Children of No.
28331	7115	Ruth De Salis, 1900.	28328.
28332	7116	Lady Evelyn Florence Parker, 1867.	{ Grandchild. Youngest daughter of No. 28277.
28333 -49	}	Same as Nos. 25318–25334.	{ Grandchildren, &c. Descendants of Lady Elizabeth Grosvenor, 1824–1899, and Beilby Richard, 2nd Lord Wenlock, 1818–1880.
28350	7117	Caroline Amelia, Lady Leigh [U.K.], 1828. *Stoneleigh Abbey, Kenilworth.*	3rd surviving daughter.
28351 -63	}	Same as Nos. 19607–19619.	{ Grandchildren, &c. Descendants of No. 28350.
28364	7118	Lady Octavia, wife of Sir Michael Robert Shaw-Stewart, 7th Bart., 1829. *11 Grosvenor Place, S.W.*	4th surviving daughter.
28365	7119	Michael Hugh Shaw-Stewart, M.P., 1854. *20 Mansfield Street, W.*	Grandchildren. Elder sons of No. 28364.
28366	7120	Rev. Charles Robert Shaw-Stewart, 1856. *Sanderstead Rectory, Croydon.*	
28367	7121	Una Mary Shaw-Stewart, 1890.	Great-grandchildren. Children of No. 28366.
28368	7122	Katharine Shaw-Stewart, 1893.	
28369	7123	Walter Richard Shaw-Stewart, J.P., C.C., late Captain 4th Battalion Princess Louise's (Argyll and Sutherland Highlanders), 1861. *Berwick House, Hindon, Salisbury.*	Grandson. 2nd son of No. 28364.
28370 -73	}	Same as Nos. 25870–25873.	Great-grandchildren. Children of No. 28369.
28374	7124	Archibald William Shaw-Stewart, *late* Lieutenant R.N., 1865.	Grandchildren. Children of No. 28364.
28375	7125	Helen, Countess Manvers [U.K.], Viscountess Newark [G.B.]. *Holme Pierrepont, Nottingham.*	
28376	7126	Evelyn Robert, Viscount Newark, 1888.	Great-grandchildren. Children of No. 28375.
28377	7127	Lady Cecily Mary Pierrepont, 1886.	
28378	7128	Lady Alice Helen Pierrepont, 1889.	
28379	7129	Lady Sibell Pierrepont, 1892.	
28380	7130	Agnes Caroline, wife of the Hon. Henry Stuart Littleton. *16 Lennox Gardens, Chelsea, S.W.*	Grandchild. Younger daughter of No. 28364.
28381	7131	Lady Agnes, wife of Philip Frank, M.D., F.R.C.P., Army Medical Staff, 1831. *3 Elvaston Place, S.W.*	5th surviving daughter.
28382	7132	Helen Constance Frank, 1872.	{ Grandchild. Daughter of No. 28381.
28383	7133	Jane Louisa Octavia, Lady Muncaster [I.], wife of Hugh Barlow Lindsay, 1834. *35 Eaton Terrace, S.W.*	6th surviving daughter.
28384	7134	Nigel Crawford Lindsay, 1870.	Grandchildren. Children of No. 28383.
28385	7135	Alan Grosvenor Lindsay, 1872.	
28386	7136	Evelyn Agnes, wife of Henry William Grant Gordon-Cumming, 1869. *Stoneyfield, Inverness.*	

28387	7137	Henry Ronald Gordon-Cumming, 1893.	Great-grandchildren. Children of No. 28386.
28388	7138	Evelyn Irene Katherine Gordon-Cumming, 1894.	
28389	7139	Lettice Elizabeth Gordon-Cumming, 1897.	
28390	7140	Rose Margaret Sandford Lindsay, 1876.	Grandchild. Child of No. 28383.
28391	7141	Lady Theodora, wife of Thomas Merthyr Guest, 1840. *Inwood, Henstridge, Blandford.*	7th and youngest surviving daughter.
28392	7142	Elizabeth Augusta Grosvenor Guest, 1879.	Granddaughter. Daughter of No. 28391.

518. Descendants of Sir James Macdonald, 2nd Bart., M.P., 1784–1832. (See Table LXXXIV.)

28393	7143	Sir Archibald John Macdonald, 4th Bart., 1871. *Woolmer Liphook, Hampshire.*	Grandchildren. Children of Sir Archibald Keppel Macdonald, 3rd Bart., 1820–1901.
28394	7144	Mary Catherine, wife of Leonard Labouchere Hillyer.	

519. Descendants of George, 6th Earl of Carlisle, K.G., 1773–1848. (See Table LXXXV.)

28395 –635	}	Same as Nos. 22125–22365.

520. Descendants of Frederick John Howard, M.P., 1814–1897. (See Table LXXXV.)

28636 –60	}	Same as Nos. 22864–22888.

521. Descendants of the Very Rev. and Hon. Henry Edward John Howard, Prebendary of York, Dean of Lichfield, 1795–1868. (See Table LXXXV.)

28661	7145	George Howard, Barrister-at-Law, *late* Librarian of the House of Commons, 1826. *Brighstone, Newport, I.W.*	Sons.
28662	7146	John Henry Howard, Captain R.N., 1827. *Rushett, Faversham.*	
28663	7147	Robert John Howard, Lieutenant R.N., 1878.	Grandchildren. Children of No. 28661.
28664	7148	Charles Wilbraham John Howard, Lieutenant R.N., 1880.	
28665	7149	Edmund John Howard, 1891.	
28666	7150	Gertrude Alathea Howard, 1876.	
28667	7151	Muriel Adelicia Howard, 1881.	
28668	7152	Algitha Fanny Howard, 1883.	
28669	7153	Winifrede Alice Howard, 1886.	
28670	7154	Edith Mary Howard, 1888.	

28671	7155	Harold Edward Howard. 1879.	16	Grandchildren. Children of Vice-Admiral Edward Henry Howard,1832–1900.
28672	7156	Eleanor Caroline Henrietta Howard, 1874.	Granville Park, Blackheath, S.E.	
28673	7157	Julia Margaret Lucille Howard, 1885.		
28674	7158	Charles John Henry Howard, *late* Captain 71st Regiment, 1834. *Middleton Cottage, Salwarpe, Droitwich.*		3rd and 4th surviving sons.
28675	7159	Rev. Henry Frederick Howard, 1844. *Brightwalton Rectory, Berks.*		
28676	7160	Bernard Henry Howard, Lieutenant I.S.C., 1879.		Grandchildren. Children of No. 28675.
28677	7161	Arthur Henry Howard, 1885.		
28678	7162	Henry Charles Mowbray Howard, 1895.		
28679	7163	Margaret Elizabeth Howard, 1880.		
28680	7164	Nevill Mary Howard, 1881.		
28681	7165	Evelyn Frances Howard, 1884.		
28682	7166	Maud Agnes Mima Howard, 1887.		
28683	7167	Henrietta Dorothea Howard, 1892.		
28684	7168	Julia Maria, widow of Peter S. King-Salter, *of Gorleston, Suffolk,* –1895, 1825.		Eldest daughter.
28685	7169	Henry Peter King-Salter, Major 3rd Battalion Rifle Brigade, 1861. *Naval and Military.*		Grandson. Son of No. 28684.
28686	7170	Nigel Henry King-Salter, 1888.		Great-grandson. Son of No. 28685.
28687	7171	Julian James King-Salter, Assistant Naval Constructor to the Admiralty.		Grandson. 2nd son of No. 28684.
28688	7172	Edward Julian Cowan King-Salter, 1899.		Great-grandchildren. Children of No. 28687.
28689	7173	Margaret Eva King-Salter, 1901.		
28690	7174	Margaret Howard King-Salter.		Grandchild. Daughter of No. 28684.
28691 –95	}	Same as Nos. 21765–21769.		Grandchildren, &c. Children of Charlotte Henrietta Howard, 1829–1896, and her husband the Rev. and Hon. Archibald George Campbell, 1827.
28696	7175	Emily Georgiana Howard, 1830. *Rosleigh, Meole Brace, Shrewsbury.*		Younger daughters.
28697	7176	Caroline Octavia, wife of Robert Bateman, J.P., 1839. *Benthall Hall, Broseley.*		
28698	7177	Elizabeth Henrietta, wife of the Rev. Nigel Madan, Hon. Canon of Southwell, 1842. *Doveridge Vicarage, Derby.*		

522. Descendants of John Frederick, 1st Earl Cawdor, 1790–1860. (See Table LXXXV.)

28699 –802	}	Same as Nos. 21734–21837.

523. Descendants of Lady Elizabeth Howard, 1780–1825, and her husband, John Henry, 5th Duke of Rutland, K.G., 1778–1857. (See Table LXXXV.)

28803 –942	}	Same as Nos. 25350–25489.

The Blood Royal of Britain

524. Descendants of Lady Gertrude Howard, 1784–1870, and her husband, William Sloane-Stanley, of Paultons, Hants, M.P., –1860. (See Table LXXXV.)

28943	7178	Roger Cyril Hans Sloane-Stanley, Captain 4th Battalion Hampshire Volunteers, 1875. *Paultons, near Romsey, Hants.*	Great-grandchildren. Children of Hans Sloane-Stanley, of Paultons, 1849–1888, and grand-children of William Hans Sloane-Stanley, of Paultons, –1879.
28944	7179	Lavender Elizabeth Sloane-Stanley, 1900. } Great-great-grandchild. Daughter of No. 28943.	
28945	7180	Gwendolen Irene Emily, wife of the Hon. Algernon Henry Bourke, 1870.	
28946	7181	Daphne Marjorie Bourke, 1895. {	Great-great-granddaughter. Child of No. 28945.
28947	7182	Frederick Sloane-Stanley.	Grandchildren. Sons of the Rev. George Sloane-Stanley, –1896.
28948	7183	Francis Sloane-Stanley, J.P., D.L., 1841. *The Bay House, Alverstoke, Hants.*	
28949	7184	Ronald Francis Assheton Sloane-Stanley, Captain 16th Lancers, 1867.	Great-grandchildren. Children of No. 28948.
28950	7185	Cecil Vivian Sloane-Stanley, 12th Lancers, 1869.	
28951	7186	William Felix Sloane-Stanley.	Grandchildren. Brothers and sisters to No. 28947.
28952	7187	Henry Charles Sloane-Stanley.	
28953	7188	Florence Laura, wife of the Rev. Walter Hugh Earle Welby, J.P. *St. George's Lodge, Ryde.*	
28954	7189	Blanche, wife of J. Murray.	
28955	7190	Grace Sloane-Stanley.	
28956	7191	Evelyn, wife of Henry George Sutton. *9 Elvaston Place, S.W.*	
28957	7192	John Stanley Mott, J.P., *late* Major Prince of Wales' Own Norfolk Artillery Militia, 1838. *Barningham Hall, Hanworth.*	Grandson. Son of Caroline Sloane-Stanley, 18 –19 , wife of John Thomas Mott, of Barningham Hall, 1809–1884.
28958	7193	Theresa Caroline, wife of Captain Charles Edward Radclyffe, 1868. *Little Park, Wickham, Hants.*	Great-grandchild. Only child of No. 28957.
28959	7194	Gertrude Sophia Mott, 1841.	Grandchildren. Sisters of No. 28957.
28960	7195	Harriett Elizabeth, widow of the Rev. Arthur Edward Robinson, Rector of Wootton, 1843.	
28961	7196	Fiennes Stanley Wykeham Cornwallis, M.P., J.P., D.L., 1864. *Linton Place, Maidstone.*	Great-grandchild. Child of No. 28960 by 1st husband, Major Fiennes Wykeham Cornwallis, 1832–1867.
28962	7197	Fiennes Wykeham Mann Cornwallis, 1890.	Great-great-grand-children. Children of No. 28961.
28963	7198	Stanley Wykeham Cornwallis, 1892.	
28964	7199	Oswald Wykeham Cornwallis, 1894.	
29965	7200	Julia Dorothy Cornwallis, 1887.	
28966	7201	Vere Mabel Cornwallis, 1889.	
28967	7202	Yvonne Cornwallis, 1896.	
28968	7203	Bridget Frances Kate Cornwallis, 1900.	
28969	7204	Arthur Wykeham Cornwallis. {	Great-grandchild. 2nd son of No. 28960.
28970	7205	Iris Beryl Cornwallis. {	Great-great-grandchild. Daughter of No. 28969.

28971	7206	Helen Florence Cornwallis. ⎱	Great-grandchildren. Daughters
28972	7207	Caroline Vere Cornwallis. ⎰	of No. 28960.
28973	7208	Frederica Lucy, wife of the Rev. Henry Berners Upcher, 1846. *Broom Hill, Saham, Norfolk.*	Granddaughter. 3rd sister of No. 28957.
28974	7209	Howard Berners Upcher, 1870.	
28975	7210	Ronald Berners Upcher, 1874.	
28976	7211	Gerald Frederick Upcher, 1877.	Great-grandchildren.
28977	7212	Constance Gertrude, wife of the Rev. Cecil Gallopine Hall, M.A., 1868. *Cramlington Vicarage, R.S.O., Northumberland.*	Children of No. 28973.
28978	7213	Ronald Owen Hall, 1895.	
28979	7214	Giles Arthur Michael Hall, 1896.	Great-great-grandchildren.
28980	7215	Cecil Berners Hall, 1898.	Children of No. 28977.
28981	7216	Philip Humphrey Hall, 1900.	
28982	7217	Gertrude Marion Hall, 1894.	

525. Descendants of Elizabeth Lavinia Vernon-Harcourt, 1816–1858, and her husband, Montagu, 6th Earl of Abingdon, 1808–1884. (See Table LXXXVI.)

28983	7218	Montagu Arthur, 7th Earl of Abingdon [E.], 1836. *Wytham Abbey, Oxford.*	Eldest son.
28984	7219	Montagu Charles Francis, Lord Norreys, 1860. *Turf ; Travellers' ; Brooks'.*	Grandson. Eldest son of No. 28983.
28985	7220	Hon. Montagu Henry Edmund Cecil Towneley-Bertie, 1887.	Great-grandchildren. Children of No. 28984.
28986	7221	Hon. Alexandra Rose Alice Towneley-Bertie, 1886.	
28987	7222	Hon. Arthur Michael Bertie, 1886.	
28988	7223	Hon. James Willoughby Bertie, 1901.	Grandchildren. Younger
28989	7224	Lady Mary Caroline, wife of Lieut.-Col. Lord Edmund Bernard Talbot, D.S.O., M.P., 1859.	sons and eldest daughter of No. 28983.
28990 –91	⎱⎰	Same as Nos. 28181–28182.	Great-grandchildren. Children of No. 28989.
28992	7225	Lady Alice Josephine, wife of Commandant Reyntiens, Belgian Artillery, 1865. *Chateau de Caster, Eben-Emael, Belgium.*	Grandchild. 2nd daughter of No. 28983.
28993	7226	Priscilla Reyntiens, 1899.	Great-grandchild. Daughter of No. 28992.
28994	7227	Lady Gwendeline Theresa Mary Bertie, 1885.	Grandchildren. Younger daughters of No. 28983.
28995	7228	Lady Betty Constance Bertie, 1895.	
28996	7229	Hon. Sir Francis Leveson Bertie, K.C.B., Ambassador to Italy, 1844. 21 *Hertford Street, W.* *British Embassy, Rome.*	2nd son.
28997		Same as No. 23298.	Grandson. Son of No. 28996.
28998	7230	Rev. and Hon. Alberic Edward Bertie, 1846. *Gedling Rectory, Nottingham.*	3rd son.
28999	7231	Aubrey Charles Bertie, 1882.	
29000	7232	Schomberg Montagu Bertie, 1888.	
29001	7233	Alberic Willoughby Bertie, 1891.	Grandchildren. Children
29002	7234	Ninian Mark Kerr Bertie, 1896.	of No. 28998.
29003	7235	Irene Elsie Bertie, 1883.	
29004	7236	Lavinia May Bertie, 1887.	
29005	7237	Olivia Bridget Bertie, 1900.	

29006	7238	Hon. George Aubrey Vere Bertie, late Major and Lieut.-Col. 1st Battalion Coldstream Guards, 1850. *Maresfield, East Cowes, I.W.*	4th son.
29007	7239	Claude Peregrine Bertie, 1890.	Grandchildren. Children of No. 29006.
29008	7240	Vere Mary Bertie, 1886.	
29009	7241	Margaret Adine Bertie, 1888.	
29010	7242	Hon. Charles Claude Bertie, 1851. *Boodle's.*	
29011	7243	Hon. Reginald Henry Bertie, C.B., Lieut.-Col. Commanding 2nd Battalion Royal Welsh Fusiliers, 1856. *Naval and Military ; Wellington.*	Younger sons and daughters.
29012	7244	Lady Elizabeth Emily Bertie, 1838.	
29013	7245	Lady Lavinia Louisa, wife of Robert Bickersteth, 1843. *70 Cromwell Road, S.W.*	
29014	7246	Lady Frances Evelyn Bertie, a nun, 1848. *Convent of the Visitation, Harrow-on-the-Hill.*	

526. Descendants of the Rev. William Harcourt, of Nuneham Courtenay, Canon of York, 1789–1871. (See Table LXXXVI.)

29015	7247	Aubrey Harcourt, J.P., D.L., 1852. *Nuneham Park, Abingdon. Stanton Harcourt, Eynsham.*	Grandchildren. Children of Edward William Harcourt, M.P., 1825–1891.
29016	7248	Edith, Countess of Winchilsea and Nottingham [E.]. *Haverholme Dower House, Sleaford.*	
29017	7249	Lady Muriel Evelyn Vernon, wife of Richard Arthur Surtees Paget, 1876. *The Dower House, North Cray, Kent.*	Great-grandchild. Daughter of No. 29016.
29018	7250	Sylvia Mary Paget, 1901.	Great-great-grandchild. Daughter of No. 29017.
29019	7251	Right Hon. Sir William George Granville Venables Vernon Harcourt, M.P., P.C., K.C., &c., &c., 1827. *Malwood, Lyndhurst, Hants.*	Son.
29020	7252	Lewis Vernon Harcourt, 1863. *14 Berkeley Square, W.*	Grandson. Son of No. 29019.
29021	7253	Doris Mary Thérèse Vernon Harcourt, 1900.	Great-grandchildren. Daughters of No. 29020.
29022	7254	Olivia Vernon Harcourt, 1902.	
29023	7255	Robert Vernon Harcourt, 1878.	Grandson. 2nd son of No. 29019.
29024	7256	Emily Julia Vernon Harcourt, 1829.	Daughters.
29025	7257	Cecilia Caroline, wife of Admiral Sir Edward Bridges Rice, R.N., K.C.B., 1831. *Dane Court, Kent.*	
29026	7258	Henry Edward Harcourt Rice, 1864.	Grandson. Son of No. 29025.
29027	7259	Edward Denis Rice, 1899.	Great-grandson. Son of No. 29026.
29028	7260	Mary Annabella, wife of George De La Poer Beresford, 1835. *Ovenden, Sevenoaks.*	Youngest daughter.
29029	7261	Edward De La Poer Beresford, 1863.	Grandchild. Son of No. 29028.
29030	7262	Mary De La Poer Beresford.	Great-grandchildren. Daughters of No. 29029.
29031	7263	Anne De La Poer Beresford.	
29032	7264	Kathleen De La Poer Beresford.	Grandchild. Daughter of No. 29028.

527. Descendants of Admiral Frederick Edward Vernon Harcourt, R.N., 1790–1883. (See Table LXXXVI.)

29033 –51	}	Same as Nos. 21581–21599.

528. Descendants of Granville Harcourt Vernon, of Grove Hall, Notts, Chancellor of the Diocese of York, 1792–1879. (See Table LXXXVI.)

29052	7265	Edward Evelyn Harcourt Vernon, J.P., D.L., 1853. *Grove Hall, Retford, Notts.*	Grandson. Son of the Rev. Evelyn Hardolph Harcourt Vernon, Prebendary of Lincoln, 1821–1890.
29053	7266	Granville Charles FitzHerbert Harcourt Vernon, 1891.	
29054	7267	Egerton Gervase Edward Harcourt Vernon, 1891.	Great-grandchildren. Children of No. 29052.
29055	7268	Sybil Ida Harcourt Vernon, 1884.	
29056	7269	Ida Beatrice Harcourt Vernon, 1885.	
29057	7270	Muriel Theresa Harcourt Vernon, 1887.	
29058	7271	Evelyn Hermione Harcourt Vernon, 1889.	
29059	7272	Rev. Algernon Hardolph Harcourt Vernon, 1858. *Clocolan Vicarage, Orange River Colony, South Africa.*	Grandson. Brother to No. 29052.
29060	7273	Granville Arthur Harcourt Vernon, 1888.	
29061	7274	Hardolph Evelyn Harcourt Vernon, 1889.	Great-grandchildren. Children of No. 29059.
29062	7275	Janet Kate Harcourt Vernon, 1883.	
29063	7276	Dorothy Margaret Harcourt Vernon, 1887.	
29064	7277	Marjorie Frances Harcourt Vernon, 1891.	
29065	7278	Walter Granville Harcourt Vernon, 1860.	Grandson. Brother to No. 29052.
29066	7279	Evelyn Maude Harcourt Vernon, 1886.	Great-grandchild. Child of No. 29065.
29067	7280	Herbert Evelyn Harcourt Vernon, 1863. *16 Spadina Road, Toronto, Canada.*	Grandson. Brother to No. 29052.
29068	7281	Humphrey Bingham Harcourt Vernon, 1889.	Great-grandchildren. Children of No. 29067.
29069	7282	Arthur Arundell Harcourt Vernon, 1895.	
29070	7283	Mary Frances, wife of the Rev. Algernon Frederick Ebsworth, 1850. *East Retford Vicarage, Notts.*	Granddaughters. Sisters to No. 29052.
29071	7284	Frances Jessie Harcourt Vernon, 1854.	
29072	7285	Selina Jane, wife of Paulet Bertram St. John-Mildmay, 1856. *Eden Lodge, Tilford, Surrey.*	
29073	7286	Lucy Frances Jane, wife of Captain James Thomas Richard Lane-Fox, J.P., D.L. *Bramham Park, co. York.*	Granddaughter. Eldest daughter of Marianne Frances Harcourt Vernon, 1814–1873, 2nd wife of Humphrey St. John Mildmay, M.P., 1794–1853.

29074	7287	George Richard Lane-Fox, 1870.	Great-grandchildren.
29075	7288	Edward Lane-Fox, 1874.	Children of No.
29076	7289	Maria Mary Lane-Fox.	29073.
29077	7290	Emily Mary St. John Mildmay.	
29078	7291	Alice Catherine, wife of Captain the Hon. Henry Hervey Molyneux, R.N. *Sanham House, Melton Mowbray.*	Granddaughters. Sisters to No. 29073.

529. Descendants of Louisa Augusta Harcourt, 1804–1869, and her husband, Sir John Vanden-Bempde-Johnstone, 2nd Bart., M.P., 1799–1869. (See Table LXXXVI.)

29079	7292	Harcourt, 1st Baron Derwent [U.K.], 1829. *Hackness Hall, near Scarborough.*	Eldest son.
29080	7293	Hon. Francis Vanden-Bempde-Johnstone, J.P., D.L., *late* Captain 2nd Life Guards, 1851. *Hackness Grange, Scarborough.*	Grandson. Son of No. 29079.
29081	7294	Sibell Vanden-Bempde-Johnstone, 1881.	Great-grandchildren. Chil-
29082	7295	Freda Vanden-Bempde-Johnstone, 1885.	dren of No. 29080.
29083	7296	Hon. Edward Henry Vanden-Bempde-Johnstone, 1854. *6 Lower Sloane Street, S.W.*	Grandson. 2nd son of No. 29079.
29084 –85		Same as Nos. 22221–22222.	Great-grandchildren. Children of No. 29083.
29086	7297	Hon. Cecil Vanden-Bempde-Johnstone, C.E., 1856. *Brooks'.*	
29087	7298	Hon. Alan Vanden-Bempde-Johnstone, C.V.O., 1st Secretary of Embassy and Chargé d'Affaires at Darmstadt and Carlsruhe, 1858. *St. James'; Turf.*	Grandchildren. 3rd and 4th sons of No. 29079.
29088	7299	Harcourt Vanden-Bempde-Johnstone, 1895.	Great-grandchild. Son of No. 29087.
29089	7300	Hon. Louis Vanden-Bempde-Johnstone, 1862. *Woolverstone House, Ipswich.*	Grandchild. 5th son of No. 29079.
29090	7301	Granville Henry Vanden-Bempde-Johnstone, 1891.	
29091	7302	Robin Talbot Vanden-Bempde-Johnstone, 1901.	Great-grandchildren. Children of No. 29089.
29092	7303	Dorothy Ethel Vanden-Bempde-Johnstone, 1892.	
29093	7304	Joan Gwendoline Vanden-Bempde-Johnstone, 1895.	
29094	7305	Hon. Gilbert Vanden-Bempde-Johnstone, Lieutenant Royal West Surrey Regiment, 1865. *Wilton Crescent, S.W.*	Grandchild. 6th son of No. 29079.
29095	7306	Mark Vanden-Bempde-Johnstone, 1900.	Great-grandchild. Son of No. 29094.
29096	7307	Hon. Edith Vanden-Bempde-Johnstone, 1860.	Grandchild. Daughter to No. 29079.
29097	7308	Henry Richard Johnstone-Scott, 1830. *Woodhall, Wetherby, Yorks.*	2nd son.
29098	7309	Henry Lister Johnstone-Scott, 1869.	
29099	7310	Charles Johnstone-Scott, 1870.	Grandchildren. Chil-
29100	7311	Egerton Johnstone-Scott, 1873.	dren of No. 29097.
29101	7312	Lucy Cressida Johnstone-Scott.	

29102 –23		Same as Nos. 27116-27137.	Grandchildren. Children of Caroline Vanden-Bempde-Johnstone, 1826–1892, wife of William, 1st Marquis of Abergavenny.
29124	7313	Elizabeth Margaret, Lady Perry, widow of the Right Hon. Sir Thomas Erskine Perry, –1882. 51 *Eaton Square, S.W.*	Daughter.
29125	7314	Edwin Charles Perry, 1858.	Grandchildren.
29126	7315	Hilda, wife of Alastair Grant, 1860.	Children of
29127	7316	Helen, wife of E. G. W. Phillips, 1865.	No. 29124.
29128	7317	Edward John Swann, 1863.	Grandchildren. Children of Blanche Maria Vanden-Bempde-Johnstone,
29129	7318	Mabel Georgiana Swann.	–1878, wife of Robert Swann, of *Askham Hall, co. York.*

530. Descendants,[1] if any, of Jane Egerton ∇, wife of Thomas Revel, of Fletcham, Surrey, M.P. for Dover,[2] Henrietta Egerton ∇, or Anne Egerton ∇, wife of Thomas Russell, D.D., Hereford. (See Table LXXXIII.)

531. Descendants of Sophia Hume, 1788-1814, 1st wife of John, 1st Earl Brownlow, 1779-1853. (See Table LXXXVII.)

29130	7319	∇ Adelbert Wellington Brownlow, 3rd Earl [U.K.], and 4th Baron [G.B.] Brownlow, P.C., 1844. *Belton House, Grantham.* 8 *Carlton House Terrace, S.W.*	Grandson. Son of John Hume, Viscount Alford, 1812–1851, *v.p.*
29131	7320	∇ Emma Augusta Charlotte Cust, 1844. 13 *Great Stanhope Street, W.*	Granddaughters. Daughters of the Hon. Charles Henry Cust, M.P., 1813–1875.
29132	7321	∇ Alice Marian, widow of Lieut.-Col. Allan Roger Charles Porcelli-Cust, formerly Porcelli, – 1897, 1845. 13 *Great Stanhope Street, W.*	
29133	7322	Margaret Mary Ernestine Dorothy, wife of Commander William Coldingham Masters Nicholson, R.N. *The Rookery, Emsworth.*	Great-granddaughter. Daughter of No. 29132.
29134	7323	Adelbert William Cust John Nicholson, 1901.	Great-great-grandsons. Sons of No. 29133.
29135	7324	Reginald Wodehouse James Nicholson, 1902.	
29136	7325	Adelaide Florence Caroline Porcelli-Cust.	Great-granddaughters. Daughters of No. 29132.
29137	7326	Ernestine Annie Cust, wife of George Frederick Thomas Tankerville Johnstone. *Cliff Side, West Cowes, I.W.*	
29138	7327	Laura Adeline Johnstone, 1902.	Great-great-grandchild. Child of No. 29137.
29139	7328	Christopher John Hume Tower, J.P., D.L., 1841. *Weald Hall, Brentwood.* *Huntsmoor Park, Ux-bridge.*	Grandson. Son of the Lady Sophia Frances Cust, 1811–1882, wife of Christopher Tower, of Huntsmoor Park, J.P., D.L., 1804–1884.

[1] Would be entitled to quarter the royal arms.
[2] Their heiress married the late (1821) Sir George Warren, K.B.

29140	7329	Christopher Cecil Tower, 1884.	Great-grandchildren. Children of No. 29139.
29141	7330	Hugh Christopher Tower, 1886.	
29142	7331	Brownlow Richard Christopher Tower, 1851. *Ellesmere House, co. Salop.*	Grandson. Brother to No. 29139.
29143	7332	Geoffrey Egerton Tower, 1891.	Great-grandchildren. Children of No. 29142.
29144	7333	Sylvia Sophia Tower, 1882.	
29145	7334	Averil Tower, 1884.	
29146	7335	Iris Tower, 1885.	
29147	7336	Egerton Augustus Tower, *late* Lieutenant 95th Foot, 1857.	Grandson. Youngest brother to No. 29139.
29148	7337	John Francis Charles, 7th Count of Salis [H.R.E.], J.P., D.L., 1864. *Loughgur, co. Limerick.*	Great-grandchild. Son of Amelia Frances Harriet Tower, – 1885 (sister to No. 29139), wife of John Francis William, 6th Count of Salis, 1825–1871.
29149	7338	Count John Eugène de Salis, 1891.	Great-great-grandchild. Son of No. 29148.
29150	7339	Henry Rodolph de Salis, J.P., C.C., 1866. *Ivy Lodge, Iver Heath, Bucks.*	Great-grandchildren. Brother and sister to No. 29148.
29151	7340	Catherine Sophia, wife of Thomas George Hare, 1863.	
29152	7341	Charlotte Marian, widow of David M'Intosh, –1881. *Havering Park, Essex.*	Grandchildren. Sisters to No. 29139.
29153	7342	Adelaide Caroline, wife of Lieut.-Col. Charles Meeking, J.P. 31 *Belgrave Square, W.* *Richings Park, Colnbrook, Bucks.*	
29154	7343	Viola Meeking.	Great-great-grandchildren. Daughters of Captain Bertram Charles Christopher Spencer Meeking, 1864–1900, son of No. 29153.
29155	7344	Finola Meeking.	
29156	7345	Hume Francis Meeking, 1874.	Great-grandchildren. Children of No. 29153.
29157	7346	Adelaide Maud Sophia Meeking.	
29158	7347	Sir Francis Ernest Waller, 4th Baronet, 1880. *Woodcote, Warwick.*	Great-grandchildren. Children of Beatrice Katherine Frances Tower, 1846–1898 (sister to No. 29139), wife of Major-General Sir George Henry Waller, 3rd Baronet, 1837–1892.
29159	7348	Wathen Arthur Waller, 1881.	
29160	7349	Margaret Beatrice, wife of Captain Dennis Granville, 1874, Chief Constable. *Dorsetshire.*	
29161	7350	Judith Margaret Granville, 1896.	Great-great-grandchild. Daughter of No. 29160.
29162	7351	Edith Sophia Waller, 1884.	Great-grandchild. Sister to No. 29158.
29163	7352	Arthur Algernon Dorrien-Smith, Lieutenant 4th Battalion Bedfordshire Regiment, 1876. *Tresco Abbey, Scilly Isles.*	Great-grandchildren. Children of Edith Anna Maria Tower, –1892 (youngest sister to No. 29139), wife of Thomas Algernon Smith-Dorrien-Smith, of Tresco Abbey, J.P., D.L.
29164	7353	Edward Pendarves Dorrien-Smith, 1879.	
29165	7354	Mary Sophia Dorrien-Smith, 1877.	
29166	7355	Edith Innes Dorrien-Smith, 1881.	
29167	7356	Cicely Frances Dorrien-Smith, 1882.	
29168	7357	Gwendolen Dorrien-Smith, 1883.	
29169	7358	Charlotte Dorrien-Smith, 1886.	

532. Descendants, if any, of Ariana Margaret Egerton (? 1783) ▽, of Charles William Saladin, of Craus ▽ (living 1845), or of Charles William Huber, 1830–   . (See Table LXXXVII.)

533. Descendants of Ariana Dubois de Courval, 1814–1892, wife of Alfred, 1st Duke of Marmier, 1805–1873. (See Table LXXXVII.)

29170	7359	¹ Raynald, 2nd Duke of Marmier [France], 1834. *Chateau de Ray-sur-Saône.*	} Son.
29171	7360	¹ Francis de Marmier, Lieutenant 138th Infantry Regiment, 1866.	Grandchildren.
29172	7361	¹ Stephen de Marmier, 1876.	Children of
29173	7362	¹ Anne de Marmier, 1871.	No. 29170.

534. Descendants of Matilda Saladin,[2] – wife of (See Table LXXXVII.)

535. Descendants of Lieut.-Col. William Chester Master, of Knolle Park and The Abbey, Cirencester, 1785–1868. (See Table LXXXVII.)

29174	7363	⋃ Thomas William Chester Master, Colonel *late* 4th Gloucester Regiment, J.P., 1841. *The Abbey, Cirencester. Knolle Park, near Bristol.*	Grandson. Son of Thomas William Chester Master, of The Abbey, &c., 1815–1899.
29175	7364	⋃ Richard Chester Master, Lieutenant King's Royal Rifle Corps, 1870.	
29176	7365	⋃ Cyril Chester Master, 1874.	
29177	7366	⋃ Charles Andrew Chester Master, 1876.	Great-grandchildren.
29178	7367	⋃ Jessy Catherine Master.	Children of No.
29179	7368	⋃ Isabel Mary Master.	29174.
29180	7369	⋃ Florence Master.	
29181	7370	⋃ Margaret Master.	
29182	7371	⋃ Alice Mary Jane, wife of William Aitchison, *late* Lieut.-Col. Scots Fusilier Guards. *Drummore, Musselburgh, N.B.*	Granddaughter. Elder sister to No. 29174.
29183	7372	William Aitchison, 1876.	Great-grandchildren. Children of No. 29182.
29184	7373	Katherine Anne Helen Aitchison.	
29185	7374	Anne Maud Aitchison.	
29186	7375	⋃ Isabel Catherine, wife of Cornwallis Henry Chichester, Colonel 5th Lancers.	Granddaughter. Younger sister to No. 29174.
29187	7376	Constance Chichester.	
29188	7377	Mildred C. A. Chichester.	Great-grandchildren. Children of No. 29186.
29189	7378	Mabel J. Chichester.	
29190	7379	Winifred Chichester.	
29191	7380	⋃ Francis Charles Master, 1846.	Grandchildren. Children of the Rev. George Francis Master, Rector of Stratton, 1816–1875.
29192	7381	⋃ Harry Chester Master, 1848.	
29193	7382	⋃ Algy William Chester Master, 1851.	

[1] Are entitled to quarter the royal arms failing surviving issue of the above-named Charles William Saladin and Charles William Huber. See Section 532.

[2] She is said to have been married with issue in 1844. Her children, if any survive, would be entitled to quarter the royal arms failing surviving issue of the above-named Charles William Saladin. See Section 532.

29194	7383	▽ William Charles Chester Master, C.B., *late* Colonel 5th Foot, 1821. *Hampton Park House, Leominster.*	} Son.
29195	7384	▽ Richard St. George Chester Master, 1866.	} Grandchildren. Children of No. 29194.
29196	7385	▽ Ariana Georgina Chester Master.	
29197	7386	▽ Helen Alexandra Chester Master.	
29198	7387	▽ Madeline Isabel Chester Master.	
29199	7388	▽ Godfrey Cornwall Chester Master, 1859.	{ Grandson. Son of the Rev. Augustus Chester Master, 1829–1887.
29200	7389	▽ Mary Augusta Grace Master.	} Great-grandchildren. Children of No. 29199.
29201	7390	▽ Joan Marion Herbert Master.	
29202	7391	▽ Digby Chester Master, 1867.	} Grandchildren. Brother and sister to No. 29199.
29203	7392	▽ Marion Frances, wife of John Adamthwaite.	
29204	7393	▽ Francis Robert Chester Master, *late* Lieutenant 58th Foot, 1833. (2 sons and 1 daughter.)	} Younger surviving son.

Grandchildren. Children of No. 29204.

29205	7394	▽ Isabella Mary Frances Charlotte, wife of Sir George William Gunning, 5th Bart., 1828. *Little Horton, Northampton.*	} Elder daughter.
29206	7395	Frederick Digby Gunning, 1853. *Junior Carlton Club.*	} Grandchildren. Elder sons of No. 29205.
29207	7396	Charles Vere Gunning, *late* Major Reserve of Officers, 1859. *Junior United Service.*	
29208		Same as No. 21335.	{ Great-grandchild. Daughter of No. 29207.
29209	7397	Rev. Henry William Maud Gunning, M.A., 1865. *Abingdon Rectory, Northants.*	} Grandchildren. Children of No. 29205.
29210	7398	Emma Louisa, wife of Christopher Smyth. *Little Houghton, Northampton.*	
29211	7399	Barbara Mary Smyth, 1894.	} Great-grandchildren. Children of No. 29210.
29212	7400	Ursula Catherine Smyth, 1898.	
29213	7401	Georgina Mary Gunning.	{ Grandchild. Younger daughter to No. 29205.
29214	7402	▽ Emily Ariana, wife of George Berney Charleton.	} Younger daughter.
29215	7403	Sir William Michael Curtis, 4th Bart., 1859. *Caynham Court, Ludlow, Salop.*	{ Grandson. Son of No. 29214 by 1st husband, William Edmund Curtis, 1833–1860.
29216	7404	Constance Mabel Curtis, 1888.	} Great-grandchildren. Children of No. 29215.
29217	7405	Victoria Margaret Curtis, 1897.	
29218	7406	Bettine Ariana Curtis, 1898.	
		Children, if any, of No. 29214 by 2nd husband.	

536. Descendants of John William Egerton Green, of Stanway Hall, Essex, 1800–1878. (See Table LXXXVII.)

29219	7407	▽ Claude Egerton Egerton-Green, of King's Ford, J.P., D.L. *East Hill House, Colchester.*	{ Grandson. Son of Henry Egerton Green, of King's Ford, 1832–1882.
29220	7408	▽ John William Egerton Egerton-Green, 1891.	} Great-grandchildren. Children of No. 29219.
29221	7409	▽ Charles Scroop Egerton Green, 1896.	
29222	7410	▽ Audrey Egerton Egerton-Green, 1888.	
29223	7411	▽ Mary Helen Egerton Green, 1890.	

29224	7412	⛉ Francis Egerton Green, Major 12th Lancers, 1864.	Grandchildren. Brother and sisters to No. 29219.
29225	7413	⛉ Harriet Sybil Egerton, wife of Edmund Deacon, *late* 1st Dragoon Guards.	
29226	7414	⛉ Mary Egerton, wife of Captain Frederick Edward Errington Brock, R.N.	
29227	7415	⛉ Horace George Egerton Green, J.P., D.L., 1838. *King's Ford, Essex.*	Sons.
29228	7416	⛉ Cecil Egerton Green, 1847. *Burgh Woodbridge, co. Suffolk.*	
29229	7417	⛉ Mary Sibylla Frances Green, 1880.	Grandchild. Daughter of No. 29228.

537. Descendant of Charles Henry Green, of Sibton Hall, Suffolk, 1804–1862. (See Table LXXXVII.)

| 29230 | 7418 | ⛉ Anne Green, 1831. | Daughter. |

538. Descendants of Sibylla Jane Green, 1806–1882, and her husband, the Rev. Thomas Maude, Rector of Hasketon, Suffolk, –1878. (See Table LXXXVII.)

29231	7419	Thomas William Maude. *Woodbridge, Suffolk.*	Son.
29232	7420	Thomas Maude.	
29233	7421	Charles Edward Maude.	
29234	7422	Arthur Maude.	
29235	7423	Edward Maude.	Grandchildren. Children of No. 29231.
29236	7424	Sibylla Emily Maude.	
29237	7425	Ellen Cordelia Maude.	
29238	7426	Mary Maude.	
29239	7427	Eva Eleanor Maude.	
29240	7428	Edmund Hussey Maude. *Cork.*	Son.
29241	7429	Mary Maude.	Grandchildren. Children of No. 29240.
29242	7430	Dorothy Agnes Maude.	
29243	7431	Rev. Arthur Maude. *Burgh Rectory, Woodbridge, Suffolk.*	Children.
29244	7432	Rev. Charles Frewin Maude. *Burwash Rectory, Sussex.*	
29245	7433	Cordelia, wife of Frederick Barlow. *Hasketon, Suffolk.*	
29246	7434	Eustace Barlow.	Grandchildren. Children of No. 29245.
29247	7435	Mark Masterton Barlow.	
29248	7436	Harriet Sibylla Barlow.	
29249	7437	Mary Cordelia Barlow.	
29250	7438	Rosamund Barlow.	

539. Descendants of Harriet Egerton, 17 –18 , wife of George Brooks, of Cadogan Place, Chelsea, 17 –18 . (See Table LXXXVII.)

29251	7439	⛉ Harriet, wife of the Rev. J. Brooks.	Granddaughter. Daughter of the Rev. George Brooks.
29252	7440	⛉ John Brooks.	Great-grandchildren. Children of No. 29251.
29253	7441	⛉ . . . . Brooks.	
29254	7442	⛉ . . . . Brooks.	
29255	7443	⛉ Georgiana, wife of Robertson.	Grandchildren. Sisters of No. 29251.
29256	7444	⛉ Alice, wife of	

29257	7445	▽ Ellen Maude.	Grandchildren. Daughters of Thomas Brooks.
29258	7446	▽ Lucy Harriet, wife of M. Ivanka.	
29259	7447	▽ Constance, wife of Colonel Voyle.	
29260	7448	▽ Thomas Voyle.	Great-grandchildren. Children of No. 29259.
29261	7449	▽ Vera Voyle.	
29262 -72	}	Same as Nos. 29219-29229.	Descendants of Harriet Anne Sibylla Brooks, -1864, wife of John William Egerton Green, of Stanway, 1800-1879.

540. Descendants,[1] if any, of Francis Hayter, afterwards Egerton ▽, of Roche Court, Salisbury [? 1800]. (See Table LXXXIII.)

541. Descendants,[1] if any, of Egerton Bagot ▽, of Pipe Hall, Stafford, -1775. (See Table LXXXVII.)

542. Descendants of William, 1st Lord Egerton of Tatton, 1806-1883. (See Table LXXXVIII.)

29273	7450	▽ Wilbraham, 1st Earl Egerton [U.K.], 1832. *Tatton Park, Knutsford.* *7 St. James' Square, S.W.*	Son.
29274	7451	▽ Gertrude Lucia, Countess of Albemarle [E.], 1861. *Quidenham Park, Attleborough, Norfolk.*	Granddaughter. Daughter of No. 29273.
29275	7452	Walter Egerton George Lucian, Viscount Bury, 1882.	Great-grandchildren. Children of No. 29274.
29276	7453	Hon. Arnold Joost William Keppel, 1884.	
29277	7454	Hon. Rupert Oswald Derek Keppel, 1886.	
29278	7455	Hon. Albert Edward George Arnold Keppel, 1898.	
29279	7456	Lady Elizabeth Mary Gertrude Keppel, 1890.	
29280	7457	▽ Hon. Alan de Tatton Egerton, M.P., 1845. *9 Seamore Place, Mayfair, W.*	2nd son.
29281	7458	▽ Maurice Egerton, 1874. Grandson.	Son of No. 29280.
29282	7459	▽ Hon. Emily Marion, widow of Percy Mitford, 1884, 1837. *Mitford House, Lennox Gardens, S.W.*	Daughters.
29283	7460	▽ Hon. Beatrix Lucia Catherine, wife of the Hon. Lionel Arthur Tollemache, 1840.	

543. Descendants of the Rev. Thomas Egerton, Rector of Middle, Salop, 1809-1847. (See Table LXXXVIII.)

29284	7461	▽ Thomas Francis Egerton, 1869.	*The Mount, York.*	Grandchildren. Children of Major George Mark Leycester Egerton, 1837-1898.
29285	7462	▽ Margaret Charlotte Egerton, 1867.		
29286	7463	▽ Helen Lucy Egerton, 1872.		
29287	7464	▽ Alice Mary, wife of Yarburgh Lloyd Graeme, 1875. *Sewerby House, Hull,*		
29288	7465	▽ Kathleen Alethea Egerton, 1883. *The Mount, York.*		

[1] Would be entitled to quarter the royal arms.

29289	7466	▢ Frederick Wilbraham Egerton, Rear-Admiral R.N., 1838.	Sons.
29290	7467	▢ Sir Edwin Henry Egerton, K.C.B., H.B.M.'s Envoy Extraordinary and Minister Plenipotentiary to the King of the Hellenes, 1841. *The British Embassy, Athens.*	
29291	7468	▢ John Frederick Egerton, 1896.	Grandchild. Child of No. 29290.
29292	7469	▢ Alfred Mordaunt Egerton, C.V.O., C.B., Colonel, *late* Royal Horse Guards, Comptroller of the Household of H.R.H. the Duke of Connaught, 1843.	3rd surviving son.
29293	7470	▢ Arthur George Edward Egerton, Lieutenant Coldstream Guards, 1879.	Grandchildren. Children of No. 29292.
29294	7471	▢ Louis Edwin William Egerton, 1880.	
29295	7472	▢ Joseph Seymour Egerton, *late* Page of Honour to Queen Victoria, 1883.	
29296	7473	▢ Alfred Charles Glyn Egerton, 1886.	
29297	7474	▢ Georgina Egerton.	Daughters.
29298	7475	▢ Mary Laura Egerton.	
29299	7476	▢ Lucy Constance, widow of the Right. Hon. Edward Stanhope, P.C., M.P., 1840–1893. *Revesby Abbey, Boston.*	

544. Descendants of Edward Christopher Egerton, M.P., Under Secretary of State for Foreign Affairs, 1816–1869. (See Table LXXXVIII.)

29300	7477	▢ Charles Augustus Egerton, J.P., D.L., 1846. *The Banks, Robertsbridge, Sussex.*	Eldest surviving son.
29301	7478	▢ Edward Brassey Egerton, 1889.	Grandchildren. Children of No. 29300.
29302	7479	▢ Hugh Sydney Egerton, 1890.	
29303	7480	▢ Henry Jack Egerton, 1892.	
29304	7481	▢ Cicely Annie Egerton.	
29305	7482	▢ Phyllis Mabel Egerton.	
29306	7483	▢ Hugh Edward Egerton, Barrister-at-Law, J.P., 1855. 11 *Tite Street, Chelsea.*	Younger surviving son.
29307	7484	▢ Guy William Egerton, 1892.	Grandchildren. Children of No. 29306.
29308	7485	▢ Arthur Edward Egerton, 1893.	
29309	7486	▢ Frances Lilias Noel Egerton, 1887.	
29310	7487	▢ Sibyl Alice Egerton, 1889.	
29311	7488	▢ Mary Alice, wife of Beauchamp Tower. *Brentwood, Essex.*	Daughters.
29312	7489	▢ Charlotte Egerton.	
29313	7490	▢ Georgina Renira Egerton.	

545. Descendants of Thomas William Egerton, afterwards Tatton, of Wythenshawe, Chester, 1783–1827. (See Table LXXXVIII.)

29314 –81	}	Same as Nos. 26432–26499.

546. Descendants of Sir Tatton Sykes, 4th Bart., 1772–1863. (See Table LXXXVIII.)

29382	7491	Sir Tatton Sykes, 5th Bart., 1826. *Sledmere, York.* 46 *Grosvenor Street, W.*	Son.

29383		Same as No. 23053.	Grandson. Son of No. 29382.
29384	7492	Katherine Lucy, widow of the Hon. Thomas Greville Cholmondeley, 1818–1883. *Abbotts Moss, Northwich, Cheshire.*	Elder surviving daughter.
29385 –96	}	Same as Nos. 24917–24928.	Grandchildren. Children of No. 29384.
29397	7493	Edward Tatton Pakenham, Captain and Hon. Major 3rd Battalion Royal Irish Rifles, 1859.	
29398	7494	William Christopher Pakenham, Commander R.N., 1861.	
29399	7495	Georgiana Mary, wife of the Rev. Thomas Geoffrey Wyatt, 1854. *St. Wilfrid's Vicarage, Hayward's Heath.*	Grandchildren. Children of Sophia Frances Sykes, 1826–1898, and her husband, Rear-Admiral the Hon. Thomas Alexander Pakenham, 1820–1889.
29400	7496	Selina Frances Pakenham, 1863.	
29401	7497	Katherine Louisa Pakenham, 1866.	
29402	7498	Margaret Elizabeth, wife of Captain Frederic Charles Strickland-Constable, 1873. *The Old Hall, Hornsea.*	
29403	7499	Mary Anne, wife of Major William Clive Hussey, 1864. *113 Park Street, W.*	Grandchild. Daughter of Elizabeth Beatrice Sykes, –1883, wife of the Very Rev. and Hon. George Herbert, 1825–1894.
29404	7500	Christopher Edward Hussey, 1899.	Great-grandchild. Son of No. 29403.
29405	7501	Winifred Lucy Elizabeth Herbert, 1872. *113 Park Street, W.*	Grandchild. Sister of No. 29403.
29406	7502	Emma Julia, wife of Philip Bryan Davies-Cooke. *Owston, Doncaster.* *Gwysaney, Mold.*	Younger surviving daughter.

547. Descendants of Christopher Sykes, Rector of Roos, 1774–1875. (See Table LXXXVIII.)

29407	7503	Edward York, Captain 1st Royal Dragoons, 1872. *Hutton Hall, Yorkshire.*	Great-grandchildren. Children of Edward Christopher York, of Hutton Hall, 1842–1885, and grandchildren of Penelope Beatrix Sykes, 1810–1873, wife of Edward York, of Wighill Park, 1802–1861.
29408	7504	Richard Lister York, 1880.	
29409	7505	Frances Stafford York, 1883.	
29410	7506	Edwin Arthur York, 1885.	
29411	7507	Beatrix Penelope Lucy York, 1874.	
29412	7508	Mabel Rose York, 1878.	
29413	7509	Sebell Marguerite York, 1881.	
29414	7510	Edward Clitherow Brooksbank, Major, *late* Yorks Artillery, J.P., 1858. *Healaugh Manor, Tadcaster.*	Great-grandchild. Child of Lucy Mary York, 1838–1893 (daughter of Penelope Beatrix Sykes, *see above*), 1st wife of Edward Brooksbank, of Healaugh.
29415	7511	Stamp Brooksbank, 1887.	
29416	7512	Edward York Brooksbank, 1889.	Great-great-grandchildren. Children of No. 29414.
29417	7513	Hugh Godfrey Brooksbank, 1893.	
29418	7514	Margaret Graham Brooksbank.	
29419	7515	Philip Brooksbank, 1869.	Great-grandchild. Brother to No. 29414.

29420	7516	Thomas Slingsby, 1886.	Great-great-grandchildren. Children of Laura Sophia Brooksbank, 1861–1887 (sister to No. 29414), wife of Frederick William Slingsby, of Red House, Monckton, York.
29421	7517	Hugh Slingsby, 1887.	
29422	7518	Lucy Hilda Brooksbank.	Great-grandchild. Sister to No. 29414.
29423	7519	Caroline Penelope, wife of the Rev. John Morland Rice, *Bramber Rectory, Sussex.*	Grandchildren. Daughters of Penelope Beatrix Sykes, 1810–1873, wife of Edward York, of Wighill Park, 1802–1861.
29424	7520	Laura Marianne, wife of Captain Ernest Rice, R.N. Children of No. 29424.	
29425	7521	Harriett, wife of R. Hewetson.	

548. Descendants, if any, of Beatrix Hester Decima Sykes, 1843, wife of John Robinson Foulis, –1826. (See Table LXXXVIII.)

549. Descendants of Elizabeth Sykes, 1777–1853, wife of Wilbraham Egerton, of Tatton, 1781–1856. (See Table LXXXVIII.)

29426 –66	}	Same as Nos. 29273–29313.

550. Descendants of William Osmund Hammond, of St. Albans Court, 1790–1863. (See Table LXXXIX.)

29467	7522	⛉ William Oxenden Hammond, J.P., D.L., 1817. *St. Albans Court, Kent.*	Son.
29468	7523	⛉ William Whitmore Hammond, Lieut.-Col. *late Rifle Brigade,* 1848.	Grandsons. Sons of the Rev. Egerton Douglas Hammond, 1822–1897.
29469	7524	⛉ Egerton Hammond, 1863.	
29470	7525	⛉ Douglas William Hammond, 1897.	Great-grandson. Son of No. 29469.
29471	7526	⛉ Minna Hammond.	Grandchildren. Sisters to No. 29468, &c.
29472	7527	⛉ Annie Hammond.	
29473	7528	⛉ Florence Hammond.	
29474	7529	⛉ Nina Charlotte Hammond.	Granddaughter. Daughter of Captain Maximilian Montagu Hammond, 1824–1855.
29475	7530	⛉ Rev. Henry Anthony Hammond, 1829.	Youngest surviving son.
29476	7531	⛉ John Maximilian Hammond.	Grandchildren. Children of No. 29475.
29477	7532	⛉ Dorothea Egerton Hammond.	
29478	7533	⛉ Charlotte Anne Maria Hammond.	Daughter.

551. Descendants of Maximilian Dudley Digges Hammond, afterwards Dalison, of Hamptons, 1792–1870. (See Table LXXXIX.)

29479	7534	⛉ Maximilian Dudley Peirse Dalison, 1881. *Hamptons, Kent.*	Great-grandchildren. Children of Captain Maximilian Dudley Digges Dalison, 1852–1885, and grandchildren of Maximilian Hammond Dalison, J.P., 1820–1902.
29480	7535	⛉ Joan Mary Dalison, 1878.	

29481	7536	⛉ Rev. Charles Edmund Waller Dalison, 1858. *Park House, Boxley, Maidstone.*	
29482	7537	⛉ Rev. Roger William Hammond Dalison, 1861. *Powerstok Vicarage, Dorsetshire.*	Grandchildren. Children of Maximilian Hammond Dalison, 1820–1902.
29483	7538	⛉ John Pelham Dalison, Major Royal West Kent Regiment, 1863. *5 Wilton Crescent, S.W.*	
29484	7539	⛉ Maude Theodosia Dalison.	
29485	7540	⛉ Dorothea Caroline, wife of Arthur Hardress Borrer. *6 Durham Place, Chelsea, S.W.*	
29486	7541	Arthur Cary Hampton Borrer.	Great-grandchildren. Children of No. 29485.
29487	7542	Clifford Dalison Borrer.	
29488	7543	John Maximilian Borrer.	
29489	7544	⛉ Anna Maria Louisa Dalison.	Grandchildren. Sisters of No. 29481.
29490	7545	⛉ Mary Sylvestre Charlotte, wife of Francis Broadwood. *Stanley Grange, Sevenoaks.*	
29491	7546	Maximilian Francis Broadwood, 1893.	Great-grandchildren. Children of No. 29490.
29492	7547	Daniel Broadwood, 1896.	
29493	7548	Mary Maud Broadwood, 1891.	
29494	7549	Dorothy Sylvia Broadwood, 1892.	
29495	7550	⛉ Rev. John Beauvoir Dalison, 1822. *Upwell St. Peter's Rectory, Wisbech.*	2nd son.
29496	7551	⛉ Charles Beauvoir Dalison.	Great-grandchild. Son of Charles G. H. Dalison, grandson of No. 29495.
29497	7552	⛉ Osmund Beauvoir Dalison.	Grandchildren. Sons of No. 29495.
29498	7553	⛉ Bernard Edward Dalison.	
29499	7554	⛉ John Bernard Dalison.	Great-grandchildren. Children of No. 29498.
29500	7555	⛉ Mary Eleanor Dalison.	
29501	7556	⛉ Georgiana, wife of the Rev. Alfred Burton.	Grandchild. Daughter of No. 29495.
29502	7557	Robert Francis Wolsley Burton.	Great-grandchildren. Children of No. 29501.
29503	7558	Gerald John Dalison Burton.	
29504	7559	Dudley Alfred Burton.	
29505	7560	Valentine Frederick Bindon Burton.	
29506	7561	Maximilian Hamilton Burton.	
29507	7562	Margaret Theodora Burton.	
29508	7563	Kathleen Mary Burton.	
29509	7564	Dorothy Eleanor Burton.	
29510	7565	Norah Georgina Burton.	
29511	7566	⛉ Harriet Grace Dalison.	Grandchildren. Daughters of No. 29495.
29512	7567	⛉ Katherine Frances, wife of Dudley Newman.	
29513	7568	⛉ Anna Maria Julia, wife of James Alexander. *Oak Bank, Sevenoaks.*	Eldest daughter.
29514	7569	James Dalison Alexander.	
29515	7570	Ulick Francis Canning Alexander, 1889.	Great-grandchildren. Children of No. 29514.
29516	7571	James Cedric Alexander, 1897.	Grandchildren. Children of No. 29513.
29517	7572	Evelyn Catherine Alexander, 1887.	
29518	7573	Jacqueline Harriet Alexander, 1892.	
29519	7574	Mabel Emma Alexander.	

29520	7575	Richard Maximilian Pulteney, *late* Captain 52nd Light Infantry.	
29521	7576	Frederick Evelyn Pulteney.	
29522	7577	Francis Basil Pulteney.	
29523	7578	Rev. Arthur Wykeham Pulteney. *Ashley Rectory, Market Harboro'.*	Grandchildren. Children of Emma
29524	7579	William Pulteney Pulteney, D.S.O., Lieut.-Col. Scots Guards, 1861.	Dalison, −1884, wife of the Rev.
29525	7580	Emma Margaret, wife of George Fellows. *Beeston Fields, Nottingham.*	Richard Pulteney, −1874.
29526	7581	Francis Pulteney.	
29527	7582	Alice, wife of Lieut.-Col. Lionel R. C. Boyle. *Spencer House, Stanstead, Essex.*	
29528	7583	Richard Courtenay Boyle, 1902.	Great-grandchildren.
29529	7584	Mary Agneta Frances Boyle, 1884.	Children of No.
29530	7585	Alice Leonora Zacyntha Boyle, 1886.	29527.
29531	7586	Audrey Janet Boyle, 1888.	
29532	7587	Elizabeth Evelyn, wife of Captain Arthur Gerald Boyle.	Grandchildren. Sisters of
29533	7588	Judith Sutton Pulteney.	No. 29520,
29534	7589	Beatrice, wife of Major George Lascelles.	&c.
29535	7590	Isabel Pulteney.	
29536	7591	⋃ Georgiana, widow of Charles Watson Townley, J.P., 1824–1893. *Fulbourne, Cambridge.*	2nd surviving daughter.
29537	7592	Rev. Charles Francis Townley, 1856. *Fulbourne, Cambridge.*	Grandson. Son of No. 29536.
29538	7593	Charles Evelyn Townley, 1888.	
29539	7594	Gladys Mary Townley.	Great-grandchildren. Children
29540	7595	Rosalind Cecil Townley.	of No. 29537.
29541	7596	Selina Georgiana Townley.	
29542	7597	Walter Beaupré Townley, Second Secretary Diplomatic Service, 1863. *British Legation, Pekin.*	
29543	7598	Maximilian Gowran Townley, 1864.	
29544	7599	Alexander Peregrine Townley, 1872.	Grandchildren.
29545	7600	Harriet Anna Townley.	Children of
29546	7601	Georgiana Caroline Townley.	No. 29536.
29547	7602	Louisa Cecil Townley.	
29548	7603	Margaret Evelyn, wife of Thomas Hugh Anderson Denman.	
29549	7604	Richard Charles Denman, 1896.	Great-grandchildren. Children of No. 29548.
29550	7605	John Evelyn Thomas Denman, 1901.	
29551	7606	Margaret Cecil Denman, 1898.	
29552	7607	Mabel Constance Townley.	Grandchild. Daughter of No. 29536.
29553	7608	⋃ Louisa Dalison.	3rd surviving daughter.

552. Descendants of Mary Hammond, 1788–1861, wife of Charles Allix, of Willoughby Hall, co. Lincoln, J.P., D.L., 1783–1866. (See Table LXXXIX.)

29554	7609	Noel Charles Noel Allix, J.P., D.L., 1846. *Willoughby Hall, Grantham.*	Grandson. Son of Frederick William Allix, of Willoughby Hall, 1816–1894.
29555	7610	Muriel Lilian Helen de Burgh Allix.	Great-granddaughter. Daughter of No. 29554.
29556	7611	Helen Harriet Elizabeth, wife of Abel Humphrey Ram. *Ramsfoot, co. Wexford.*	Granddaughter. Sister to No. 29554.

29557	7612	William Kent Allix, 1823.		Son.
29558	7613	Barbara Allix. } Tunbridge { Granddaughters. Daughters of Wager		
29559	7614	Margery Allix. } Wells. { Townley Allix, 1825–1878.		
29560	7615	Charles Peter Allix, J.P., D.L., } Grandson. Son of Mary Catherine 1842. Elizabeth Allix, –1842, wife Swaffham Prior House, of Colonel Charles Allix, of Swaffham, 1787–1862. Cambridge.		
29561	7616	Charles Israel Loraine Allix, J.P., 1872.		
29562	7617	John Peter Allix, 1879.		Great-grandchildren.
29563	7618	Laura Matilda Ethelwyn, wife of Arthur Frances Pease, 1867. Hummersknott, Darlington.		Children of No. 29560.
29564	7619	Richard Arthur Pease.		Great-great-grandchildren. Children of No. 29563.
29565	7620	Mary Ethelwyn Pease.		
29566	7621	Dorothy Laura Pease.		
29567	7622	Elizabeth Frances Pease.		
29568	7623	Isabella Maude, wife of Captain Edward Gordon Young, R.E., 1869.		Great-grandchildren. Children of No. 29560.
29569	7624	Mary Cecily Allix, 1890.		
29570	7625	Louisa Margaret, wife of the Rev. James Griffith, Rector of Flaxton.		Daughter.
		Children (6 sons, 4 daughters) of No. 29570.		
29571	7626	Alice, wife of General E. W. D. Bell, C.B., V.C., 23rd Regiment.	Granddaughter. Daughter of Juliana Jemima Allix, – 1840, 1st wife of Francis Capper Brooke, of Ufford Place, Suffolk, 1810–1886.	
29572	7627	Edward Bell, Captain Worcester Regiment, 1866.		Great-grandson. Son of No. 29571.
29573	7628	Emily Persis, wife of A. D. Vesey. Castle Hill House, co. Huntingdon.		2nd surviving daughter.
29574	7629	Eustace Allix Vesey.		Grandchildren. Children of No. 29573.
29575	7630	Cuthbert David Vesey.		
29576	7631	Florence Emily, wife of the Rev. Reginald Alfred Gatty. Hooton Roberts Rectory.		

553. Descendants of Charlotte Jemima Hammond, 17 –1841, wife of John Nethercote, of Moulton Grange, Northampton. (See Table LXXXIX.)

29577	7632	Ellen Mary, widow of Colonel Edward Baldwin Wake, 1832–1883.		Granddaughter. Daughter of Henry Osmund Nethercote, of Moulton Grange, 1819–1886.
29578	7633	Mary Charlotte Baldwin Wake, 1873.		Great-grandchildren. Children of No. 29577.
29579	7634	Henrietta Louisa Baldwin Wake, 1874.		
29580	7635	Dorothy Blanche Baldwin Wake, 1876.		
29581	7636	Chattie Baldwin Wake, 1877.		
29582	7637	Louisa Harriet Julia, widow of Drury Wake, 1827–1891. Pitsford House, Northampton.		Granddaughter. Sister to No. 29577.
29583	7638	Drury Wake, 1875. New Oxford and Cambridge.		Great-grandchildren. Children of No. 29582.
29584	7639	Emily Matilda Wake.		
29585	7640	Susan Ellen Wake.		
29586	7641	Mary Alice Wake.		
29587	7642	Charlotte Eliza Mary, widow of Captain John Rooper, Rifle Brigade.		Daughter.

29588	7643	Maximilian Rooper.	
29589	7644	Herbert Rooper.	
29590	7645	Walter Rooper.	
29591	7646	William Rooper.	Grandchildren. Children
29592	7647	Percy Rooper.	of No. 29587.
29593	7648	Mary Rooper.	
29594	7649	Constance Rooper.	
29595	7650	Blanche Rooper.	
29596	7651	Lucy Rooper.	

554. Descendants of Jemima Julia Hammond,   –1847, wife of the Rev. Thomas Clayton Glyn, of Durrington House, co. Essex, 1789–1860.   (See Table LXXXIX.)

29597	7652	Clayton Louis Glyn, *of Durrington,* J.P., 1857. *Sheering Hall, Harlow, Essex.*	Grandson. Son of Clayton William Feake Glyn, of Durrington, 1821–1887.
29598	7653	Margot Elinor Glyn, 1893.	Great-grandchildren. Children
29599	7654	Juliette Evangeline Glyn, 1898.	of No. 29597.
29600	7655	Egerton John Glyn, *late* Captain 4th Battalion Essex Regiment, 1863. *Newland Lodge, Ingatestone, Essex.*	Grandson. Brother to No. 29597.
29601	7656	John Murray Egerton Glyn, 1894.	Great-grandchild. Son of No. 29600.
29602	7657	Julia Mary, wife of William Griffith Richards. 26 *Queensberry Place, S.W.*	Granddaughter. Sister to No. 29597.
29603	7658	Dora Evelyn Mary Richards, 1892.	Great-grandchildren. Daughters of No. 29602.
29604	7659	Gwenllian Helen Riou Richards, 1895.	
29605	7660	Evelyn Margaret, wife of Colonel Henry Marsh Pratt, C.B., Indian Staff Corps. 43 *Courtfield Gardens, S.W.*	Granddaughter. 2nd sister to No. 29597.
29606	7661	Pleasance Millicent Mary Pratt, 1893.	Great-grandchildren. Daughters of No. 29605.
29607	7662	Evelyn Lucy Pratt, 1894.	
29608	7663	Emily Georgiana Glyn. 12 *Selwood Place, Onslow Gardens, S.W.*	Granddaughter. 3rd sister to No. 29597.
29609	7664	Charles Clayton Glyn, 1850. *Yenna, Limpsfield.*	Grandchildren. Sons of Canon Henry Thomas Glyn, 1823–1900.
29610	7665	Richard Montague Glyn, 1854. 134 *Worple Road, Wimbledon.*	
29611	7666	Sylvia Glyn, 1899.	Great-grandchildren. Children
29612	7667	Veronica Glyn, 1901.	of No. 29610.
29613	7668	Rev. Frederick Ware Glyn, J.P., 1857. *Brancepeth Rectory, Durham.*	Grandchild. Brother to No. 29609, &c.
29614	7669	Edith Frances Glyn, 1889.	Great-granddaughters. Daughters of No. 29613.
29615	7670	Eleanor Valentine Glyn, 1896.	
29616	7671	Angela Bayntun Glyn, 1897.	
29617	7672	Mary Isabel Glyn.	Grandchild. Sister to No. 29609, &c.
29618	7673	General Sir Julius Richard Glyn, K.C.B., 1824. *Sherborne House, Sherborne, Dorset.*	Son.
29619	7674	Ada (Hilda) Glyn.	Grandchildren. Children of No. 29618.
29620	7675	Marion, wife of Lieut.-Col. Wentworth Odiarne Cavenagh. *The Goodwyns, St. Margaret's Bay.*	

29621	7676	Wentworth Glyn Cavenagh. 1890.	} Great-grandchildren. Children of No. 29620.
29622	7677	Emma Doreen Cavenagh, 1893.	
29623	7678	Rachel, wife of Hugh Bertram Cox, C.B., B.C.L., Legal Assistant, Under Secretary at Colonial Office.	} Grandchild. 3rd daughter of No. 29618.
		25A *Sussex Place, South Kensington, S.W.*	
29624	7679	Henrietta Georgiana, widow of Gilbert John Ansley, –1875.	} Daughter.
		The How, St. Ives, Hants.	
29625	7680	John Henry Ansley, Major Loyal North Lancashire Regiment, 1863.	} Grandchildren. Children of No. 29624.
		Naval and Military.	
29626	7681	Agnes Georgiana, wife of the Rev. Charles Burroughs Darling.	
		St. Mary Magdalene's Rectory, Toronto, Canada.	
29627	7682	Basil Stewart Darling, 1885.	} Great-grandchildren. Children of No. 29626.
29628	7683	Gerald Glyn Darling, 1891.	
29629	7684	Oswald Gilbert Darling, 1893.	
29630	7685	Dorothy Mary Ansley Darling, 1886.	
29631	7686	Agnes Mary Darling, 1888.	
29632	7687	Hilda Darling, 1892.	
29633	7688	Florence Ansley.	} Grandchildren. Children of No. 29624.
29634	7689	Maud Ellen Ansley.	

555. Descendants of Charlotte Mary Hammond, 1794–1876, wife of Benjamin Harrison, M.C.S., 1792–1865. (See Table LXXXIX.)

29635	7690	▽ Thomas Branfill Harrison, Major-General, late Bengal Staff Corps, 1827.	} Son.
29636	7691	▽ Henry Benjamin Harrison, 1849.	} Grandchildren. Children of No. 29635.
29637	7692	▽ Amy Branfill Harrison, 1854.	
29638	7693	▽ Gertrude Eleanor, wife of Percy Kidd, M.D., 1855.	
29639	7694	Guy Egerton Kidd, 1882.	} Great-grandchildren. Children of No. 29638.
29640	7695	Alan Harrison Kidd, 1885.	
29641	7696	Eric Leslie Kidd, 1889.	
29642	7697	▽ Mary Beatrice Harrison, 1873.	{ Grandchild. Youngest daughter of No. 29635.
29643	7698	▽ Rev. Francis Lupton Harrison, 1831.	} 2nd surviving son.
		Braintfield, co. Herts.	
29644	7699	▽ Dora Mary Harrison, 1862.	} Grandchildren. Daughters of No. 29643.
29645	7700	▽ Florence Emily Harrison, 1863.	
29646	7701	▽ Henry Anthony Harrison, J.P., late Bengal Civil Service, 1834.	} 3rd surviving son.
29647	7702	▽ Keith Cockburn Harrison, 1859.	} Grandchildren. Children of No. 29646.
29648	7703	▽ Henry Francis Harrison, 1862.	
29649	7704	▽ Archibald William Harrison, 1875.	
29650	7705	▽ Kathleen Emma, wife of Thomas Campbell Donaldson, M.D.	
29651	7706	Dennis Harrison Donaldson, 1896.	{ Great-grandchild. Son of No. 29650.
29652	7707	▽ May Alice Harrison, 1877.	{ Grandchild. Youngest daughter of No. 29646.
29653	7708	▽ Egerton Bartlett Harrison, 1836.	4th surviving son.

The Blood Royal of Britain

556. Descendants of Anne Eliza Hammond, 1797–1873, wife of Champion Edward Branfill, of Upminster Park, co. Essex, 1789–1844. (See Table LXXXIX.)

29654	7709	▽ Champion Branfill Russell, J.P., 1860. *Stubbers, North Ockenden, co. Essex.*	Grandson. Son of Champion Branfill, afterwards Russell, of Stubbers, 1820–1887.
29655	7710	▽ Champion Maxwell Russell, 1890.	Great-grandchildren. Children of No. 29654.
29656	7711	▽ Henry Branfill Russell, 1894.	
29657	7712	▽ John Napier Russell, 1899.	
29658	7713	▽ Rachel Augusta Russell.	
29659	7714	▽ Isabel Marjorie Russell.	
29660	7715	▽ Pamela Russell, 1898.	
29661	7716	▽ Charles Russell.	
29662	7717	▽ Eva, wife of George H. Rew, 1856.	Grandchildren. Brother and sisters to No. 29654.
29663	7718	▽ Mary, wife of Major-Gen. Sir William Freeman Kelly, K.C.B., 1858. *Broadlands, Petersfield.*	
29664	7719	▽ Lilian Russell, 1867.	
29665	7720	▽ Violet Russell, 1874.	
29666	7721	▽ Champion Andrew Branfill, 1889. *Upminster Hall, Romford, Essex.*	Great-grandchildren. Children of Champion Edward Branfill, of Martyns, 1858–1890, and grandchildren of Lieut.-Col. Benjamin Aylett Branfill, of Upminster Hall, 1828–1899.
29667	7722	▽ Helena Edith Champion Branfill, 1885.	
29668	7723	▽ Capel Aylett Branfill, 1859.	Grandson. Son of Lieut.-Col. Benjamin Aylett Branfill. *As above.*
29669	7724	▽ Capel Lisle Aylett Branfill, 1884.	Great-grandchildren. Children of No. 29668.
29670	7725	▽ Geoffrey Dougles Aylett Branfill, 1895.	
29671	7726	▽ Galadys Murielle Aylett Branfill, 1886.	
29672	7727	▽ Enid Mary Aylett Branfill, 1888.	
29673	7728	▽ Iris Aylett Branfill, 1891.	
29674	7729	▽ Adeline Mawde Aylett Branfill, 1894.	
29675	7730	▽ Francis Lisle Branfill, 1865.	Grandchildren. Brothers and sisters to No. 29668.
29676	7731	▽ Benjamin Branfill, 1871.	
29677	7732	▽ Mary Leigh, wife of Charles Cusack, 1860.	
29678	7733	▽ Ethel, wife of Francis Seymour Haden, 1861.	
29679	7734	▽ Helen Hammond Branfill, 1863.	
29680	7735	▽ Major-Gen. Brydges Robinson Branfill, J.P., 1833. *Billericay, Brentwood, Essex.*	Son.
29681	7736	▽ May Leila Branfill, 1873.	Grandchildren. Children of No. 29680.
29682	7737	▽ Amy Blanche Brydges Branfill, 1880.	
29683	7738	▽ Damaris Shakespear Branfill.	
29684	7739	▽ John Arthur Capel Branfill, 1838.	Children.
29685	7740	▽ Eliza Jemima Mary, wife of the Rev. Edward Francis Gepp, 1822. *High Easter Vicarage, near Chelmsford.*	
29686	7741	▽ Charlotte Jane, wife of the Rev. Arthur Richard Godson, Vicar of All Saints, Gordon Square, 1831.	
29687	7742	▽ Agnes Josepha, wife of Captain Walter E. S. Battescombe, 1835. *Hill Side Worle, Weston-super-Mare.*	

557. Descendants, if any, of Major Thomas Payler, 7th Dragoon Guards, the Rev. William Payler, dead before 1830, Lieut.-Col. James Payler, John Payler, Henry Payler, the Rev. Anthony Payler, and Francis Payler. (See Table LXXXIX.)

---

558. Descendants of John Kent Egerton Holmes, Lieutenant R.I. Fusiliers, 1819–1848. (See Table XC.)

29688	7743	☐ Eleanor Elizabeth Georgiana, wife of Horace Stafford Stafford-O'Brien, J.P., D.L., 1846. *Blatherwycke Park, near Wansford.*	Only child.
29689	7744	☐ Egerton Augustus Stafford-O'Brien, 1872.	Grandchildren. Sons
29690	7745	☐ Horace Henry Stafford-O'Brien, 1883.	of No. 29688.

559. Descendants of Charlotte Katherine Brydges, 1795–1841, wife of Captain Frederick Dashwood Swann, 1st Grenadier Guards, 1795–1870. (See Table XC.)

29691	7746	☐ Charles Frederick Theodore Swann, 185 .	Grandchildren. Sons of the Rev. Frederick Egerton
29692	7747	☐ . . . . Swann, 1871.	Brydges Swann, 1821–1876.
29693	7748	☐ Edward Gibbon Swann.	Son.

560. Descendants of Mary Jane Brydges, 1805–1882, wife of Lieut.-Col. George Todd, 3rd Dragoon Guards, 1800–1873. (See Table XC.)

29694	7749	☐ Laura Emma Chamberlain, wife of Harry Craven Sneyd-Kynnersley, 1864. *Spillsill, Staplehurst, Kent.*	Granddaughters. Daughters of Colonel William Egerton Todd, 1831–1896.
29695	7750	☐ Ada Drummond Todd, 1866. *Hove, Brighton.*	
29696	7751	☐ John Spencer Brydges Todd, C.M.G., Secretary Cape of Good Hope Government Agency, London, 1840. *24 Cathcart Road, South Kensington, S.W.*	Son.
29697	7752	☐ Arthur Brydges Todd, 1870. *Battersea Park, London.*	Grandchild. Son of No. 29696.
29698	7753	☐ George Dudley Todd, 1898.	Great-grandchildren. Children of No. 29697.
29699	7754	☐ Noel Edward Todd, 1901.	
29700	7755	☐ Margaret Laura Todd, 1895.	
29701	7756	☐ Egerton Brydges Todd, 1874.	Grandchildren. Children of No. 29696.
29702	7757	☐ Mary Charlotte, wife of Walter Barrett Jacks, 1867. *22 Redcliffe Square, S.W.*	
29703	7758	Muriel Barrett Jacks, 1889.	Great-grandchild. Daughter of No. 29702.

29704	7759	⋃ Alice Eliza, wife of Desmond Forde, Chartered Accountant, 1878. *Epsom.*	Grandchildren. Younger daughters of No. 29696.
29705	7760	⋃ Vera Enid Todd, 1885.	
29706	7761	⋃ Mary Sophia Louisa Todd, 1835. *Torquay.*	Daughter.

561. Descendants of Ellen Brydges, 1808–1900, wife of Charles Alpe Bettger, 1796–1861. (See Table XC.)

29707	7762	⋃ Charles Henry Renn Stansfield, 1856. *The Hollies, Bromley Common, Kent.*	Grandson. Eldest son of Rosalie Gousant Bettger, 1839–1874, wife of Henry William Stansfield, 1827–1898.
29708	7763	⋃ Egerton Charles Henry Stansfield, 1884.	Great-grandchildren.
29709	7764	⋃ Alfred Hubert Brydges Stansfield, 1888.	Children of No.
29710	7765	⋃ Arthur Reginald Grey Stansfield, 1890.	29707.
29711	7766	⋃ Harry Egerton Stansfield, 1867.	
29712	7767	⋃ Percy Alpe Stansfield, 1871.	Grandchildren. Brothers and sisters to No. 29707.
29713	7768	⋃ Frank Bedo Stansfield, 1872.	
29714	7769	⋃ Spencer Stansfield, 1873.	
29715	7770	⋃ Florence Martha Stansfield, 1859.	
29716	7771	⋃ Grace Charlotte, wife of Evelyn Brindley.	
29717	7772	Dorothy Grace Brindley, 1894.	Great-grandchild. Daughter of No. 29716.

562. Descendants of Elizabeth Charlotte Jemima Brydges, 1813–1855, wife first of the Rev. Charles Gratwicke Raikes Kinleside, Vicar of Poling, Sussex, –1841, and secondly of Major‐General Robert Parker Radcliffe, Inspector‐General Royal Artillery, –1845. (See Table XC.)

29718	7773	⋃ Sir Thomas Edward Milborne-Swin-nerton-Pilkington, 12th Bart., 1857. *Chevet Park, Wakefield.* *2 Upper Berkeley Street, W.*	Grandson. Son of Isabella Elizabeth Georgina Kinleside, 1838–1894, wife of Sir Lionel Pilkington, 11th Bart., 1835–1901.
29719 -20	}	Same as Nos. 21808–21809.	Great-grandchildren. Children of No. 29718.
29721	7774	⋃ Ernest Milborne Milborne-Swinnerton-Pilkington, 1858. *20 Vincent Square, Westminster, S.W.*	Grandchildren. Brothers and sister to No. 29718.
29722	7775	⋃ Claude William Egerton Pilkington, Captain *late* 4th Battalion Princess Louise's (Argyll and Sutherland Highlanders), 1863. *Wollaton, Nottingham.*	
29723	7776	⋃ Renée Elizabeth, wife of William Frederick Lee. *Grove Hall, Knottingley.*	
29724	7777	Charles Frederick Lee, 1887.	Great-grandchildren. Children of No. 29723.
29725	7778	Michael Philip Edward Lee.	
29726	7779	Hilda Renée Lee.	
29727	7780	Diana Marian Lee.	
29728	7781	Doris Sophia Lee.	
29729	7782	Phyllis Aimée Lee.	
29730	7783	Joan Margaret Lee.	

29731	7784	⋃ Ida Mary, wife of John Montague Spencer-Stanhope, J.P. *Hill House, Cawthorne, Barnsley.*	Grandchildren. Sisters to No. 29718.
29732	7785	⋃ Aimée, wife of George Ayscough Armytage, Captain 4th Battalion King's Royal Rifle Corps. *Kirklees Park, Brighouse, Yorkshire.*	
29733	7786	⋃ Veronica Pilkington.	
29734	7787	⋃ Ada, widow of Edmund William Cripps, of Ampney Park, J.P., 1843–1899. *Ampney Park, Cirencester.*	Daughter and co-heir.
29735	7788	⋃ Frederick William Beresford Cripps, J.P., 1873. *Ampney Park, Cirencester.*	Grandson. Son of No. 29734.
29736	7789	⋃ Joseph William Wykeham Cripps, 1900.	Great-grandchildren. Children of No. 29735.
29737	7790	⋃ Philip Wilfred Cripps, 1902.	
29738	7791	⋃ Freda Constance Cripps, 1898.	
29739	7792	⋃ Egerton Timewell Cripps, 1874.	Grandchildren. Children of No. 29734.
29740	7793	⋃ Gwendolen Elizabeth Cripps.	
29741	7794	⋃ Eleanore Dorothea Cripps.	
29742	7795	⋃ Rose Madeline Radcliffe.	Younger daughters and co-heirs.
29743	7796	⋃ Florence Leila, wife of the Rev. Arthur Symonds.	

563. Descendants of Isabella Anne Louisa Brydges, 1815–1872, wife of Captain Stephen Ponsonby Peacocke, 25th Regiment, 18 –1872. (See Table XC.)

29744	7797	⋃ Ponsonby John Raleigh Peacocke.	Sons.
29745	7798	⋃ John FitzRoy Beresford Peacocke.	
29746	7799	⋃ Egerton Francis Peacocke, 1880.	Grandchildren. Children of No. 29745.
29747	7800	⋃ Cyril Peacocke.	
29748	7801	⋃ Noel Peacocke.	
29749	7802	⋃ . . . . Peacocke.	
29750	7803	⋃ Florence Blanche Mary Peacocke, 1876.	
29751	7804	⋃ Frederica Isabel Peacocke, 1878.	
29752	7805	⋃ Muriel Charlotte Anne Peacocke, 1881.	
29753	7806	⋃ Gerald Loftus Torin Peacocke.	Children.
29754	7807	⋃ Reginald Thomas Stephen Peacocke.	
29755	7808	⋃ Georgina Elizabeth Emma Peacocke.	
29756	7809	⋃ Inez Eva Isabel, wife of Thomas Lindesay. *Howick, New Zealand.*	

564. Descendants of the Rev. John Henry George Lefroy, of Ewsholt House, Hants, Rector of Aske, Hants, and Compton, Surrey, 1781–1823. (See Table XCI.)

29757	7810	Charles James Maxwell Lefroy, *late* Captain 14th Hussars, 1848. *Itchell Manor, Hants.*	Grandson. Son of Charles Edward Lefroy, of Ewsholt, 1810–1861.
29758	7811	Charles Alfred Henry Lefroy, 1873.	Great-grandchildren. Children of No. 29757.
29759	7812	George Langlois Lefroy, 1874.	
29760	7813	Cecil Lefroy, 1876.	
29761	7814	Harold Lefroy, 1877.	
29762	7815	Patrick Egerton Lefroy, 1888.	
29763	7816	Evelyn Lefroy, 1879.	
29764	7817	Kathleen Margaret Lefroy, 1882.	
29765	7818	Clement George Lefroy, 1850.	Grandson. Brother to No. 29757.
29766	7819	Hugh Lefroy.	Great-grandchildren. Children of No. 29765.
29767	7820	Janet Muriel Lefroy.	

MARGARET QUEEN OF JAMES IV.
1489 - 1541

PAINTED BY MABUSE

The Blood Royal of Britain

29768	7821	Rev. Anthony Cottrell Lefroy, 1812. *Crookham.*		Son.
29769	7822	Mary Sophia, wife of the Rev. G. Mead.		
29770	7823	Lucy Sophia Lefroy.	Grandchildren.	Daughters
29771	7824	Antonia, wife of Alexander Russell, I.C.S.	of No. 29768.	
29772	7825	Grace Lefroy.		
29773	7826	Henry George Lefroy, 44th Regiment, 1847.	Grandchildren. Children of	
29774	7827	Augustus Henry Frazer Lefroy, Professor of Roman Law, &c., at Toronto University, 1852. *Toronto, Canada.*	General Sir John Henry Lefroy, K.C.M.G., C.B., 1817–1892.	
29775	7828	Henry Chichell Lefroy, 1890.	Great-grandchildren.	
29776	7829	Langlois Dundas Lefroy, 1892.	Children of No.	
29777	7830	Frazer Keith Lefroy, 1895.	29774.	
29778	7831	Emily Mary, wife of Colonel Charles Chenevix-Trench, R.A., Chief Instructor of School of Gunnery. *Shoeburyness.*	Grandchild. Sister to No. 29773.	
29779	7832	Richard Henry Chenevix-Trench, I.S.C., 1876.		
29780	7833	Charles Godfrey Chenevix-Trench, 1877.		
29781	7834	Francis Maxwell Chenevix-Trench, 1879.	Great-grandchildren. Children of No. 29778.	
29782	7835	Christopher Chenevix-Trench, 1881.		
29783	7836	Lawrence Chenevix-Trench, 1883.		
29784	7837	Ralph Chenevix-Trench, 1885.		
29785	7838	Alfred Chenevix-Trench, 1887.		
29786	7839	Emily Maude Chenevix-Trench.		
29787	7840	Augusta Maude, wife of Commander Crofton, R.N.	Grandchild. Sister to No. 29773.	
29788	7841	George Anthony Cottrell Lefroy, 1860.	Grandchildren. Children of Henry Maxwell Lefroy, Director of Convict Prisons, West Australia, 1818–1879.	
29789	7842	Charles Edward Lefroy, 1862.		
29790	7843	John Henry Maxwell Lefroy, 1865.		
29791	7844	Frederick Ernest Langlois Lefroy, 1867.		
29792	7845	Annette Elizabeth Lefroy.		
29793	7846	Lucy Blatchford Sophia Lefroy.		
29794	7847	Anna Theodora Lefroy.		
29795	7848	Arthur George Rickards, 1848.		
29796	7849	Katharine Sophia, wife of the Rev. George Fell, D.D. *Worldham Rectory.*	Grandchildren. Children of Frances Phœbe Lefroy, 1811–1859, 1st wife of Sir George Kettelby Rickards, K.C.B.	
29797	7850	Helen Frances Rickards.		
29798	7851	Edith Cordelia Rickards.		
29799	7852	Emily Mabel Rickards.		
29800	7853	Laura Georgina, wife of the Rev. Francis Jervoise Causton.		
29801	7854	Charles Reid Seymour, 1855.	Grandchildren. Children of Isabella Elizabeth Lefroy, 1823–18 , wife of the Rev. Charles Frederick Seymour, of Winchfield.	
29802	7855	Mary Anne, wife of Captain Ross.		
29803	7856	Agnes Isabella, wife of Major Eyton.		

565. Descendants of the Rev. Benjamin Langlois Lefroy, Rector of Aske, 1791–1829. (See Table XCI.)

29804	7857	Franklin George Lefroy, 1861.	Grandchildren. Children of George Benjamin Austen Lefroy, 1818–18	
29805	7858	Florence Emma, wife of the Rev. A. Austin Leigh.		
29806	7859	Jessie Lefroy.		
29807	7860	Mary Isabella Lefroy.		
29808	7861	Louisa Langlois Lefroy.		

29809	7862	William Chambers Lefroy, 1849.	Grandchildren. Children of Anna Jemima Lefroy, 18 –18 , wife of Thomas E. Preston Lefroy, 18 –1855.
29810	7863	Jemima Anna Lefroy.	
29811	7864	Mary Georgiana Lefroy.	
29812	7865	Georgiana Brydges, wife of G. Alured Seymer Terry. 3rd daughter.	
29813	7866	Edward Seymer Terry, 1852	
29814	7867	Henry Alured Terry, 1855.	Grandchildren. Children of No. 29812.
29815	7868	Etheldred Georgiana Terry.	
29816	7869	Caroline Louisa Terry.	
29817	7870	Anna Jemima Terry.	
29818	7871	Louisa Langlois, wife of the Rev. Septimus Bellas. *Monk Sherborne Vicarage.*	5th daughter.
29819	7872	Margaret Bellas. Grandchild. Daughter of No. 29818.	
29820	7873	Elizabeth Lucy, wife of the Rev. Arthur P. Loveday. 6th daughter.	
29821	7874	Arthur Philip Loveday, 1860.	Grandchildren. Children of No. 29820.
29822	7875	Charles Edward Loveday.	
29823	7876	Frances Charlotte Loveday.	

566. Descendants of Jemima Lucy Lefroy, 1779–1862, wife of the Rev. Henry Rice, of Norton Court, near Feversham. (See Table XCI.)

29824	7877	Douglas Rice Hodgson, 1829.	Grandsons. Sons of Sarah Rice, 1804–1842, 1st wife of the Rev. T. Douglas Hodgson, 18 –1884.
29825	7878	Henry John Hodgson, Commander R.N., 1832.	
29826	7879	Lucy Eleanor Hodgson, 1868.	Great-grandchildren. Children of No. 29825.
29827	7880	Etheldred Mary Hodgson, 1870.	
29828	7881	Maud Alice Hodgson, 1872.	
29829	7882	Lilian Rose Hodgson, 1876.	
29830	7883	George Egerton Hodgson, Captain 44th Regiment, 1837.	Grandson. Brother of No. 29824.
29831	7884	Philip Egerton Hodgson, 1864.	Great-grandchildren. Children of No. 29830.
29832	7885	Edith Emily Hodgson, 1878.	
29833	7886	Christopher Albert Hodgson, 1841.	Grandson. Brother of No. 29824
29834	7887	John St. Barbe Hodgson, 1872.	Great-grandchildren. Children of No. 29833.
29835	7888	Christopher Lefroy Hodgson, 1879.	
29836	7889	Ruth Hodgson, 1874.	
29837	7890	Mabel Grace Hodgson, 1875.	
29838	7891	Dorothy Hodgson, 1876.	
29839	7892	Marjorie May Hodgson, 1887.	
29840	7893	Sarah Jemima, wife of the Rev. Canon W. Eycott Martin. *West Farleigh Vicarage.*	Granddaughter. Sister to No. 29824.
29841	7894	Douglas Eycott Martin, 1866.	Great-grandchildren. Children of No. 29840.
29842	7895	William Egerton Martin, 1869.	
29843	7896	Mary Sophia Martin, 1857.	
29844	7897	Etheldred Sophia Martin, 1861.	
29845	7898	Eleanor Frances Amy Martin, 1864.	
29846	7899	Eleanor Sarah Jordan, 1863.	Great-grandchild. Daughter of Eleanor Mary Rice, 1838–1864 (sister to No. 29824), wife of the Rev. Gibbs Jordan.

567. Descendants of Champion Edward Branfill, of Upminster Park, co. Essex, J.P., 1789–1844. (See Table XC.)

| 29847 –80 | } | Same as Nos. 29654–29687. |

568. Descendants of Jemima Elizabeth Branfill, 1792–1867, wife of the Rev. Thomas Harrison, Incumbent of Womenswold (Wymynyswold), Kent, 1793–1868. (See Table XC.)

29881	7900	Heneage Egerton Brydges Harrison, one of H.M.'s Inspectors of Schools, 1850.	Grandchildren. Children of the Rev. John Branfill Harrison, Rector of Great Mongeham, Kent, 1823–1893.
29882	7901	Cholmeley Edward Carl Branfill Harrison, Lieut.-Col. Royal West Kent Regiment, 1857.	
29883	7902	Thurlow Dering Walter Hill Harrison, 1863. *3 Devonshire Terrace, Hyde Park, W.*	
29884	7903	Dering Hill Arthur Capel Harrison, 1866.	
29885	7904	Edith Agnes Marian Dering Harrison, 1852.	
29886	7905	Ida Constance Maria Cholmeley, wife of Delamark Banks Roffey, 1854.	
29887	7906	Ianthe Mina Gertrude Lyon, wife of Capt. G. V. Robinson, R.M.L.I., 1868.	
29888	7907	Edward Branfill Harrison, *late* Royal Irish Fusiliers, 1861.	Grandchildren. Children of Edward Francis Harrison, C.S.I., Bengal Civil Service, 1829–1887.
29889	7908	Francis Capel Harrison, Bengal Civil Service, 1863.	
29890	7909	Thomas Aylett Harrison, Captain Indian Staff Corps, 1865. *Chew Magna, Somerset.*	
29891	7910	Lilian Theodora Harrison, 1893.	Great-grandchildren. Children of No. 29890.
29892	7911	Marjory Aylett Harrison, 1896.	
29893	7912	Dorothy May Harrison, 1898.	
29894	7913	Arthur Hugo Harrison, 1870.	Grandchildren. Brothers and sisters to No. 29888, &c.
29895	7914	Charles Holmes Harrison, Punjab Civil Service, 1872.	
29896	7915	Herbert Champion Harrison, 1876.	
29897	7916	Margaret Annie Harrison, 1856.	
29898	7917	Alice Jemima Harrison, 1859.	
29899	7918	Lilian Josepha, wife of Henry Hetley, M.D. *Beaufort House, Church Road, Upper Norwood, S.E.*	
29900	7919	Henry Edward Hetley, 1887.	Great-grandchildren. Children of No. 29899.
29901	7920	George Harrison Hetley, 1893.	
29902	7921	Hilda Margaret Hetley, 1889.	
29903	7922	Lilian Maude Hetley, 1895.	
29904	7923	Hilda Charlotte, wife of Edward Charles Long, 1873. *Basutoland.*	Grandchildren. Sisters to No. 29888, &c.
29905	7924	Dorothy Sarah Harrison, 1880.	
29906	7925	Ruth Mary Harrison, 1883.	
29907	7926	Mary Louisa, widow of the Rev. Alfred Matthew Preston, Vicar of Winslow, 18 –1882, 1834.	Daughter.
29908	7927	Francis Harrison Preston, 1857.	Grandchildren. Children of No. 29907.
29909	7928	Charlotte Isabella Preston, 1858.	
29910	7929	Mary Emily Preston, 1862.	
29911	7930	Mabel Amelia Jane Preston, 1866.	

569. Descendants of Lieut.-Col. Egerton Leigh, of the West Hall and Jodrell Hall, Chester, M.P., 1815–1875. (See Table XCII.)

29912	7931	Egerton Leigh, J.P., D.L., 1843. *West Hall, High Leigh, near Knutsford. Jodrell Hall, Holmes Chapel.*	Son.

29913	7932	Edward Egerton Leigh-White, 1876. *Bantry House, co. Cork.*	⎫
29914	7933	Cecil Egerton Leigh, 1890.	Grandchildren.
29915	7934	Margaret Elizabeth Egerton, wife of Richard Oliver Marton, Captain R.A. *Capernwray, Lancashire.*	Children of No. 29912.
29916	7935	Cynthia Egerton Leigh, 1898.	⎭
29917	7936	Edward Egerton Leigh, J.P., 1851. *Broadwell Manor House. Stow on the Wold, Gloucester.*	2nd surviving son.
29918	7937	John Egerton Leigh, Lieutenant 2nd Battalion Warwickshire Regiment, 1876.	Grandchildren. Children of
29919	7938	Henry Egerton Leigh, 1877.	No. 29917.
29920	7939	Rev. Neville Egerton Leigh, 1852. *Kirkstall Vicarage, Leeds.*	⎫
29921	7940	Arthur Egerton Leigh, J.P., 1853. *The Manor House, Sherborne, Dorset.*	Sons.
29922	7941	Gladwys Mary Egerton Leigh.	Grandchild. Daughter of No. 29921.
29923	7942	Foster Hugh Egerton Cunliffe, 1875.	Grandchildren. Children of Eleanor
29924	7943	Robert Neville Henry Cunliffe, 1884. *Acton Park, Wrexham.*	Sophia Egerton Leigh, −1898,
29925	7944	Mary Evelyn Cunliffe, 1878.	1st wife of Sir Robert Alfred Cun-
29926	7945	Kythe Cunliffe, 1881.	liffe, 5th Bart.

29927	7946	Augusta Catherine, widow of Charles Gresley. *The Close, Lichfield.*	See Table XCII.

570. Descendants of No. 29927.

29928	7947	Nigel Egerton Gresley, 1860.	⎫
29929	7948	Charles Vincent Gresley, 1865.	
29930	7949	Wilhelmina Mary Gresley.	
29931	7950	Isabel Beatrice Gresley.	
29932	7951	Augusta Penelope Gresley.	Children.
29933	7952	Eleanor Louisa Gresley.	
29934	7953	Rosamond Evelyn Gresley.	
29935	7954	Margaret Morewood Gresley.	⎭

571. Descendants of Ralph, 2nd Lord Dunfermline, 1803–1868. (See Table XCII.)

29936	7955	Hon. Mary Catherine Elizabeth, wife of Lieut.-Col. John Mowbray Trotter, *formerly* of B.S.C., 1849. *Colinton, Midlothian.*	Only child.
29937	7956	Archibald Macgregor Trotter, 1878.	⎫
29938	7957	Gilbert Ralph Abercromby John Trotter, 1880.	Grandchildren.
29939	7958	Alexander Lockhart Trotter, 1887.	Children of
29940	7959	Mary Elliott Trotter, 1877.	No. 29936.
29941	7960	Margaret Nina Trotter, 1882.	⎭

572. Descendants, if any, of Emma Jellicoe, — , wife (1836) of Thomas Maltby. (See Table XCII.)

573. Descendants, if any, of Emma Smith, and Caroline Smith, wife (1834) of General Ernest Frederick Gascoigne. (See Table XCII.)

574. Descendants, if any, of Augusta Leigh, – wife (1821) of Thomas Dumbleton, of Hall Grove, Surrey, and Winch-field House, Hants. (See Table XCII.)

575. Descendants, if any, of Thomas Hodges Leigh, Peter Neve Leigh, Mary Leigh, wife of the Rev. Robert Lancaster, Vicar of Arsley, Bedfordshire. (See Table XCII.)

576. Descendants, if any, of Sophia Frodsham, wife of George Wasey, Rector of Ulcombe, Kent, and Emma Frodsham (? 1840). (See Table XCII.)

577. Descendants of Ralph Gerard Leycester, of Toft Hall, Cheshire, 1817–1851. (See Table XCII.)

29942 –45	}	Same as Nos. 21577–21580.

578. Descendants, if any, of John Leigh, William Leigh, Austine Leigh, Samuel Leigh, William Leigh, Anne Leigh, wife 1st of the Rev.   Felton, and 2ndly of the Rev. Cockayne, Hester Leigh and Jane Leigh, ? temp. 1758. (See Table XCII.)

579. Descendants,[1] if any, of John Leigh, of Manchester, 1703–17   . (See Table XCII.)

580. Descendants, if any, of James Allett Leigh, 1799–   , and of Arabella Diana Leigh,   –1852, wife (1847) of John Harry Nelson, of Dublin,   –   , before 1852. (See Table XCIII.)

---

[1] He had issue Peter, John, Mary, and Elizabeth. Mary was living and married in 1771.

581. Descendants, if any, of the Rev. Anthony Allett Isaacson, Vicar of Newport, Monmouth, Lieutenant Egerton Charles Harvest Isaacson, 51st Regiment, Elizabeth Harvest Isaacson, wife (1832) of the Rev. Walter Hill of Southminster, Essex, and of Charlotte Isaacson, wife of (1835) Henry Parry of Caerleon, South Wales. (See Table XCIII.)

582. Descendants, if any, of Charlotte Hudson, 1805–   , wife (1839) of Lieutenant Egerton Charles Harvest Isaacson, 51st Regiment. (See Table XCIII.)

583. Descendants of Charlotte Leigh,[1] 1738–   , wife (1762) of the Rev. Johnson Lawson, M.A., Vicar of Throwley, Kent, Dean of Battle. (See Table XCIII.)

584. Descendants of Theodosia de Malsburgh Leigh, 1792–1870, wife of John Ward, afterwards Ward-Boughton-Leigh, of Brownsover Hall, near Rugby, 1790–1868. (See Table XCIV.)

29946	7961	Henry Allesley Ward-Boughton-Leigh, 2nd Lieutenant Warwickshire Yeomanry Cavalry, 1877. *Brownsover Hall, near Rugby.*	Grandchildren. Children of Edward Allesley Boughton Ward-Boughton-Leigh, of Brownsover Hall, 1822–1894.
29947	7962	Ellen Theodosia Ward-Boughton-Leigh.	
29948	7963	Maude Mary Ward-Boughton-Leigh.	
29949	7964	Ada Rose Ward-Boughton-Leigh.	
29950	7965	Edith Violet Ward-Boughton-Leigh.	
29951	7966	Mabel Constance Ward-Boughton-Leigh.	
29952	7967	Rev. Theodosius Ward-Boughton-Leigh. *Newbold-on-Avon Vicarage, Warwick.*	Son.
29953	7968	Rev. Theodosius Ward-Boughton-Leigh. *Bradfield Rectory, Suffolk.*	
29954	7969	Rev. Bridgeman Ward-Boughton-Leigh. *Harborough Magna Rectory, Warwick.*	Grandchildren. Children of No. 29952.
29955	7970	Cotterell Ward-Boughton-Leigh.	
29956	7971	John Hugh Ward Ward-Boughton-Leigh, *late* Honorary Major 4th Battalion Royal Warwickshire Regiment. *67 Albert Hall Mansions, S.W.*	
29957	7972	Egerton Ward-Boughton-Leigh, 1897.	Great-grandchildren. Children of No. 29956.
29958	7973	Mona de Malsburgh Ward-Boughton-Leigh.	
29959	7974	Percy Ward-Boughton-Leigh.	Grandchildren. Children of No. 29952.
29960	7975	Alice Ward-Boughton-Leigh.	
29961	7976	Ethel B. Ward-Boughton-Leigh.	
29962	7977	Lelia Annette, wife of William Edward Manley, R.A.	

---

[1] She was living in 1782, and had then a son, Sheffield James Lawson.

		(4 daughters.) { Grandchildren. Children of the Rev. Egerton Ward-Boughton-Leigh, –1870.	
29963	7978	Theodosia, wife of Thomas Fanshawe Parratt. *Effingham House, Surrey.* Children, if any, of No. 29963.	
29964	7979	Grace, widow of Captain Charles Rowley, R.N., –1879.	} Daughters.
29965	7980	Emma Adeline, wife of Julius Cæsar Levison. *Copenhagen.* Children, if any, of No. 29965.	

585. Descendants, if any, of Sir Samuel Egerton Leigh, 3rd Bart., of South Carolina, U.S.A., 1796– . (See Table XCIV.)

---

586. Descendants, if any, of Martha Leigh,[1] 1757– , wife 1st of Nathan Garrick, and 2ndly of Grazebrooke. (See Table XCIV.)

---

587. Descendants, if any, of Elizabeth Harry Leigh, 1758– , wife (1781) of Baron von Malsburgh, of Hesse Cassel, Lieut.-Col. in Hessian Service, 17 –1855.[2] (See Table XCIV.)

---

588. Descendants, if any, of Harriet Anne Leigh, 1716– , wife of John Burnett. (See Table XCIV.)

---

589. Descendants, if any, of the Hon. Charles Egerton, 1664–1717.[3] (See Table LXXXIII.)

---

590. Descendants of Philip Charles, 1st Lord de L'Isle and Dudley, 1800–1851. (See Table XCV.)

29966	7981	Philip, 3rd Lord de L'Isle and Dudley [U.K.], 1853. *Penshurst Place, Tonbridge, Kent.*	
29967	7982	Hon. Algernon Sidney, Lieut.-Col. R.A., 1854. *Marlborough ; Pratts' ; Naval and Military.*	Grandchildren. Children of Philip, 2nd Lord de L'Isle and Dudley, 1828–1898.
29968	7983	Hon. William Sidney, Barrister, Inner Temple, 1859. *8 Lennox Gardens, S.W.*	
29969	7984	Hon. Mary Sophia Sidney, 1851. *Ingleby Manor, Middlesborough.*	

---

[1] She had at least three sons by her first husband—N. D. Garrick, David Garrick, and Egerton Garrick—who were all alive in 1858, when they owned property at Roxeth near Harrow and a house at 1 Devonshire Terrace, Marylebone. N. D. Garrick was then married.

[2] He died in Vienna, and was succeeded at his seat, Eschberg, by his eldest son.

[3] Would be entitled to quarter the royal arms.

29970	7985	Hon. Adelaide Augusta Wilhelmina, widow of the Hon. Frederic Charles Hunloke, *formerly* Fitz-Clarence, 1826–1878, 1826. 8 *Lennox Gardens, Pont Street, S.W.*	} Daughters.
29971	7986	Hon. Ernestine Wellington, widow of Philip Perceval, 1813–1897, 1834. *Holmwood, West Cowes, I.W.*	
29972	7987	Philip Perceval, } twins, 1868.	Grandchildren. Children of No. 29971.
29973	7988	Kathleen Sophy Perceval,	
29974	7989	Sophia Philippa, Countess Kielmansegg, wife of Alexander, Count Kielmansegg, 1837. *Gülzow, Lauenburg-on-the-Elbe.*	} Youngest daughter.

591. Descendants, if any, of Ariana Shelley, wife of Francis Aiken. (See Table XCV.)

592. Descendants of Jane Caroline Shelley,   –1851, wife of the Rev. Joseph Harris,   –1834. (See Table XCV.)

29975	7990	Louisa Helen, widow of the Right Rev. Edward Trollope, D.D., Lord Bishop of Nottingham, 1817–1893. 99 *Sloane Street, S.W.*	Grandchild. Child of the Rev. Henry Berners Shelley Harris, 19th Master of the Earl of Leicester's Hospital, Warwick, 1800–1863.
29976	7991	Elizabeth Jane Caroline, wife of Edward Semmens.	Grandchildren.
29977	7992	Maria, wife of John Wagstaff. *Highbury Lodge, Highbury.*	Daughters of Sidney Harris.
29978	7993	Emily Harris.	

593. Descendants, if any, of Lady Catherine Sydney, wife of William Barker of the Inner Temple,[1] both living about 1720. (See Table XCV.)

594. Descendants, if any, of the Hon. Frances St. John, wife of Sir William Beecher, of Howberry, Beds, Knt., temp. 1642. (See Table XCVI.)

595. Descendants of John Musters, of Colwick Hall, near Nottingham, J.P., DL., 1777–1849. (See Table XCVI.)

| 29979 | 7994 | John Patricus Chaworth-Musters, J.P., 1860. *Annesley Park, Nottingham.* | Great-grandson. Son of John Chaworth-Musters, of Annesley, 1838–1887, grandson of John George Musters, of Wiverton, 1807–1842. |

[1] Admitted as William Barking, son and heir of Antony Barker, of Sonning, Berks, 1718.

29980	7995	George Patricus Chaworth-Musters, 1888.	
29981	7996	John Nevile Chaworth-Musters, 1890.	
29982	7997	Anthony Chaworth-Musters, 1892.	
29983	7998	Philip Mundy Chaworth-Musters, 1895.	Great-great-grandchildren. Children of No. 29979.
29984	7999	Robert Chaworth-Musters, 1896.	
29985	8000	Douglas Chaworth-Musters, 1898.	
29986	8001	Margarita Chaworth-Musters.	
29987	8002	Elsie Chaworth-Musters.	
29988	8003	Ruth Mary Chaworth-Musters.	
29989	8004	Catherine Lina Chaworth-Musters.	
29990	8005	Lancelot George Eden Michael Musters, 1868.	Great-grandchildren. Brother and sisters to No. 29979.
29991	8006	Mary Catherine Musters, 1863.	
29992	8007	Catherine Emily, wife of Penn Curzon Sherbrooke, Lieutenant Notts Yeomanry Cavalry, 1864.	
29993	8008	Rosita Chaworth-Musters.	Great-grandchild. Daughter of George Chaworth Musters, R.N., 1840–1879.
29994	8009	Annesley Horace Packe.	Great-grandchildren. Sons of Mary Anne Chaworth Musters, 1881, wife of Captain Horatio Packe, R.N.
29995	8010	George Anthony Packe.	
29996	8011	William Musters.	
29997	8012	Henry Musters.	Grandchildren. Children of the Rev. William Musters, –1874.
29998 to 30003		6 daughters.	
30004	8013	John George Musters, Commander R.N., J.P., 1841.	Grandchildren. Children of Lieut.-Colonel Henry Musters, J.P., D.L., –1896.
30005	8014	Caroline Alicia Victoria, wife of Annesley Horace Packe.	
30006	8015	Vice-Admiral Richard Horace Hamond, J.P., D.L., 1843. *The Abbey, Westacre.* *The Manor House, Swaffham.*	Grandchildren. Children of Mary Anne Musters, 1806–1900, wife of Anthony Hamond, of Westacre, 1805–1869.
30007	8016	Thomas Astley Horace Hamond, 1845.	
30008	8017	Mary Anne, wife of Henry Birkbeck. *Stoke Holy Cross, Norfolk.*	
30009	8018	Henry Birkbeck, 1857. *Westacre High House, Swaffham.*	Great-grandson. Son of No. 30008.
30010	8019	Henry Anthony Birkbeck, 1885.	
30011	8020	Gervase William Birkbeck, 1886.	
30012	8021	Christopher Robert Birkbeck, 1890.	Great-great-grandchildren. Children of No. 30009.
30013	8022	Gillian Mary Birkbeck.	
30014	8023	Judith Birkbeck.	
30015	8024	Isabel Birkbeck.	
30016	8025	Minna, wife of Samuel Gurney Buxton, J.P., D.L. *Catton Hall, Norwich.*	Great-grandchild. Child of No. 30008.
30017	8026	Richard Gurney Buxton, 1887.	Great-great-grandchildren. Children of No. 30016.
30018	8027	Minna Alice Buxton.	
30019	8028	Alice Birkbeck.	Great-grandchildren. Children of No. 30008.
30020	8029	Katharine Birkbeck.	
30021	8030	Frances Hamond.	Granddaughters. Sisters to No. 30006, &c.
30022	8031	Susan Maria, wife of William Birkbeck, J.P. *Thorpe, Norwich.*	
30023	8032	Antonia Birkbeck.	Great-granddaughter. Daughter of No. 30022.
30024	8033	Caroline Penelope, widow of the Rev. and Hon. John Harbord, 1832–1900. *Southrepps Rectory.*	Granddaughter. Sister to No. 30006, &c.

30025	8034	Ralph Assheton Harbord, 1859. *Salisbury, Rhodesia.*	Great-grandson. Son of No. 30024.
30026	8035	Judith Mary Harbord, 1900.	Great-great-grandchild. Child of No. 30025.
30027	8036	Philip Harbord, J.P., 1861. *Morden House, Cromer.*	Great-grandson. 2nd son of No. 30024.
30028	8037	John Harbord, 1893.	Great-great-grandsons. Sons of No. 30027.
30029	8038	Philip Anthony Assheton Harbord, 1897.	
30030	8039	Richard Morden Harbord, Commander R.N., 1865.	
30031	8040	Rev. Arthur Morden Harbord, 1866. *Ramleh, Egypt.*	Great-grandsons. Sons of No. 30024.
30032	8041	Lionel Anthony Harbord, *late* Lieutenant 4th Battalion Bedfordshire Regiment, 1870. *Cairo, Egypt.*	
30033	8042	Phyllis Mary Harbord, 1895.	Great-great-grandchildren. Daughters of No. 30032.
30034	8043	Patience Harbord, 1900.	
30035	8044	Maurice Assheton Harbord, 1874.	Great-grandchildren. Children of No. 30024.
30036	8045	Mary, wife of Lieut.-Col. Geoffrey Fowell Buxton, 1858. *Dunston Hall, Norwich.*	
30037	8046	Geoffrey Charles Buxton, Lieutenant Suffolk Yeomanry Cavalry, 1879.	
30038	8047	Bernard Buxton, R.N., 1882.	
30039	8048	Ivor Buxton, 1884.	
30040	8049	Guy Buxton, 1888.	
30041	8050	Joan, wife of John Frecheville Ramsden, D.L., 1881. *Longley Hall, Huddersfield.*	Great-great-grandchildren. Children of No. 30036.
30042	8051	Olive Buxton, 1886.	
30043	8052	Avery Buxton, 1889.	
30044	8053	Hazel Mary Buxton, 1893.	
30045	8054	Rose Buxton, 1898.	
30046	8055	Rachel Harbord, 1864.	Great-grandchildren. Children of No. 30024.
30047	8056	Dorothy Harbord, 1868.	
30048	8057	Katherine Harbord, 1869.	
30049	8058	Margaret Harbord, 1872.	
30050	8059	Maud, wife of Captain Alexander Graham Shortt, R.A., 1877.	
30051	8060	Ronald Shortt, 1901.	Great-great-grandchild. Son of No 30050.
30052	8061	Hilda Harbord, 1881.	Great-grandchild. Youngest daughter of No. 30024.
30053	8062	Katherine Sarah, wife of Somerville Arthur Gurney, J.P., D.L. *North Runcton Hall, Norfolk.*	Granddaughter. Sister to No. 30006, &c.
30054	8063	Walter Somerville Gurney, 1858.	Great-grandchild. Son of No. 30053.
30055	8064	Daniel Walter Thomas Gurney, 1898.	Great-great-grandchildren. Son and daughters of No. 30054.
30056	8065	Diana Katherine Gurney.	
30057	8066	Philippa Gurney.	
30058	8067	Anthony Francis Gurney, R.N., 1864.	Great-grandchildren. Children of No. 30053.
30059	8068	Hugh Gurney, 1867.	
30060	8069	Philip Hamond Gurney, 1876.	
30061	8070	Somerville Arthur Gurney.	Great-great-grandchild. Child of No. 30060.
30062	8071	Rose Catherine, wife of William John Birkbeck. *Stratton, Norwich.*	Great-grandchild. Daughter of No. 30053.
30063	8072	Benedict Birkbeck, 1886.	Great-great-grandchildren. Children of No. 30062.
30064	8073	Michael Birkbeck.	
30065	8074	Elizabeth Birkbeck.	

30066	8075	Lily Cecilia, wife of Adair Craigie.	{ Great-grandchild. Daughter of No. 30053.
30067	8076	Lily Sara Craigie. {	Great-great-grandchild. Child of No. 30066.
30068	8077	Ruth, wife of Joseph Fry Whitwell. }	Great-grandchild. Daughter of No. 30053.
30069	8078	David Gurney Whitwell. {	Great-great-grandchild. Child of No. 30068.
30070		Same as No. 29216. {	Great-great-grandchild. Daughter of Mabel Gurney, –1888, 1st wife of Sir William Michael Curtis, 4th Bart.
30071	8079	Audrey Florence, wife of Francis Champion.	Great-grandchildren. Younger daughters of No. 30053.
30072	8080	Muriel Constance Amy, wife of the Rev. Edmund Seymour Daubeney. *Southacre Rectory.*	
30073	8081	Emily, wife of Charles Wigley Wicksted, J.P. *Shakenhurst, Cleobury Mortimer, Salop.*	{ Granddaughter. Youngest sister to No. 30006.
30074	8082	Robert Nicholas Hamond, R.N., 1844.	Great-grandchildren. Children of Sophia Caroline Musters, –1894, wife of Commander Robert Nicholas Hamond, R.N., 1809– Daughter.
30075	8083	Nicholas Hamond, 1845.	
30076	8084	Sophy Hamond.	
30077	8085	Blanche Hamond.	
30078	8086	Alicia, wife of Gerald Upcher	

596. Descendants, if any, of Emma Heywood, wife of Captain Albemarle Bertie, ? temp. 1775. (See Table XCVI.)

597. Descendants, if any, of Maria Henrietta Heywood, wife of Louis Montelieu, ? temp. 1775. (See Table XCVI.)

598. Descendants, if any, of Frances Heywood, 1771. (See Table XCVI.)

599. Descendants of Richard William Penn, Earl Howe, 1796–1870. (See Table XCVI.)

30079 –114	}	Same as Nos. 20237–20272.	Sons, &c., of above by 1st wife.
30115	8087	Hon. Montagu Curzon-Howe, Colonel (retired) Rifle Brigade, 1846. *Garatshay, Loughborough.*	Elder son by 2nd wife.
30116 –17	}	Same as Nos. 26700–26701.	{ Grandchildren. Children of No. 30115.
30118	8088	Hon. Assheton Gore Curzon-Howe, C.B., C.M.G., C.V.O., Rear-Admiral R.N., 1850. *Hubborn, Christchurch, Hants.*	Younger son by 2nd wife.
30119	8089	Leicester Charles Assheton St. John Curzon-Howe, 1894.	Grandchildren. Children of No. 30118.
30120	8090	Assheton Penn Curzon-Howe, 1898.	
30121	8091	Victoria Alexandrina Alice Curzon-Howe, 1896.	

30122 –61	}	Same as Nos. 20273–20312.	Daughters, &c., by 1st wife.
30162	8092	Mary Anna, Duchess [I.], Marchioness [G.B.] and Countess [S.] of Abercorn, Duchess of Châtelherault [France], 1848. *Hampden House, 61 Green Street, W.*	Daughter by 2nd wife.
30163	8093	James Albert Edward, Marquis of Hamilton, M.P., 1869. 15 *Montagu Square, W.*	Grandson. Son of No. 30162.
30164 –66	}	Same as Nos. 20408–20410.	Great-grandchildren. Children of No. 30163.
30167	8094	Lord Arthur John Hamilton, Lieutenant 3rd Battalion Royal Scots, 1883.	Grandchildren. Children of No. 30162.
30168	8095	Lord Claud Hamilton, 1889.	
30169	8096	Lady Alexandra Phyllis Hamilton, 1876.	
30170	8097	Gladys Mary, Countess of Wicklow [I.], 1880. *Shelton Abbey, Arklow, co. Wicklow.*	
30171	8098	—— Lord Clonmore, 1902. Great-grandchild. Child of No. 30170.	

600. Descendants of Howe Peter, 2nd Marquis of Sligo, 1788–1845. (See Table XCVI.)

30172	8099	Lady Mary Isabel Peyronnet Browne, 1881, twins. { *Mount Browne, Guildford, Surrey.*	Grandchildren. Children of George John, 3rd Marquis of Sligo, 1820–1896.
30173	8100	Lady Isabel Mary Peyronnet Browne,	
30174	8101	John Thomas, 4th Marquis of Sligo [I.], Baron Monteagle [U.K.], 1824. *Westport House, Westport, co. Mayo.*	Sons.
30175	8102	Lord Henry Ulick Browne, 1831. 41 *Eccleston Square, S.W.*	
30176	8103	George Ulick Browne, *late* Captain B.S.C., 1856. *Highfield, Haslemere, Surrey.*	Grandchildren. Children of No. 30175.
30177	8104	Ulick de Burgh Browne, 1898.	Great-grandchildren. Children of No. 30176.
30178	8105	Eileen Agatha Browne, 1889.	
30179	8106	Moya Melisende Browne, 1892.	
30180	8107	Doreen Geraldine Browne, 1896.	
30181	8108	Arthur Howe Browne, Captain 1st Battalion Royal Munster Fusiliers, 1867. *Naval and Military.*	Grandchildren. Children of No. 30175.
30182	8109	Terence Morris Browne, Assistant Superintendent Bengal Police, 1873.	
30183	8110	Alfred Eden Browne, Lieutenant R.A., 1878.	
30184	8111	Edith Hester, wife of John George Charles, *late* B.C.S., 1860.	
30185	8112	Eric Edmonstone Charles, 1883.	Great-grandchildren. Children of No. 30184.
30186	8113	Ulick de Burgh Charles, 1884.	
30187	8114	Arthur Denis Charles, 1890.	
30188	8115	Evelyn Gladys Isabella Charles, 1888.	
30189	8116	Florence Marion, wife of Major William Randal Hamilton Beresford-Ash, 1863. *Ashbrook, co. Londonderry.*	Grandchild. Child of No. 30175.
30190	8117	Douglas Beresford-Ash, 1887.	Great-grandchild. Child of No. 30189.
30191	8118	Norah Browne, 1873.	Grandchildren. Younger daughters of No. 30175.
30192	8119	Alice Evelyn, wife of John FitzGerald Mahon, 1877. 16 *Regent Street, W.*	

30193	8120	Lord Richard Howe Browne, 1834. *Leith Villa, London Road, Reigate.*	} 3rd surviving son.
30194	8121	Arthur Richard Howe Browne, 1893.	Great-grandson. Son of Arthur Richard Browne, 1866–1900, eldest son of No. 30193.
30195	8122	Percy Howe Browne, 1868.	Grandson. Eldest surviving son of No. 30193.
30196	8123	Margaret Kathleen Browne, 1898.	Great-granddaughter. Daughter of No. 30195.
30197	8124	Cyril Edward Browne, 1873.	
30198	8125	Helen Augusta, wife of George Mitchell, 1867. *Buluwayo, Rhodesia, South Africa.*	Grandchildren. Children of No. 30193.
30199	8126	Marion Agnes Browne, 1871.	
30200	8127	Colonel Charles Howe Cuffe Knox. *Creagh, Ballinrole, co. Mayo.*	Grandchildren. Children of Lady Louisa Catherine Browne, wife of Charles Knox, *of Castle Lacken, co. Mayo.*
30201	8128	Colonel Howe Knox.	
30202	8129	Hubert Thomas Knox.	
30203	8130	Philippa Knox.	
30204	8131	Lady Harriet, widow of Sir Robert Lynch-Blosse, 10th Bart., 1825–1893. *Athavallie, Balla, co. Mayo.*	Eldest surviving daughter.
30205	8132	Sir Henry Lynch-Blosse, 11th Bart., 1857. *Athavallie, Balla, co. Mayo.*	
30206	8133	Robert Lynch-Blosse, Captain Reserve of Officers and Royal Scottish Reserve Regiment, 1861.	
30207	8134	Francis Lynch-Blosse, Captain 2nd West India Regiment, 1868.	Grandchildren. Children of No. 30204.
30208	8135	Harriet, wife of the Right Hon. Sir Henry Augustus Robinson, P.C., K.C.B., 1862. *12 Haddington Terrace, Kingstown.*	
30209	8136	Mary, wife of the Hon. Robert Nicholas Hardinge. *Southlawn House, Wychwood, R.S.O., Oxon.*	
30210		Same as No. 20439.	Great-grandchildren. Children of No. 30209.
30211	8137	Lady Emily Charlotte Browne, 1829. *34 Montagu Square, W.*	2nd and 3rd surviving daughters.
30212	8138	Lady Hester Georgiana, widow of the Hon. Shapland Francis Carew, 1826–1892, 1837. *9 Bryanston Street, Portman Square, W.*	
30213	8139	Gerald Shapland Carew, 1860. *White's.*	Grandchildren. Children of No. 30212.
30214	8140	Nesta Elizabeth Carew, 1861.	
30215	8141	Lady Augusta Browne, 1838. *Old Head House, Westport, co. Mayo.*	
30216	8142	Lady Marian, widow of Hugh Wilbraham, 1827–1890, 1839. *Old Head House, Westport, co. Mayo.*	Younger daughters.
30217 –19	}	Same as Nos. 25127–25129.	Grandchildren. Children of No. 30216.

601. Descendants, if any, of Anne Hartopp, born ? 1685–1695, wife of the Rev. Robert Hacker. (See Table XCVI.)

602. Descendants, if any, of George Bennet, 1652, living 1683, and Elizabeth Bennet, alive unmarried 1682. (See Table XCVI.)

603. Descendants, if any, of Arabella Wyse, of Mount Wyse, Stoke Damarell and Sydenham, co. Devon, wife (1673) of Edmund Tremayne, of Collacombe, co. Cornwall. (See Table XCVI.)

604. Descendants, if any, of the Hon. Dorothy St. John (living? 1651), wife of Francis Carleton, of Apley Castle, co. Salop. (See Table XCVI.)

605. Descendants of Brownlow, 2nd Marquis of Exeter, 1795–1867. (See Table XCVII.)

30220	8143	William Thomas Brownlow, 5th Marquis [U.K.] and 14th Earl [E.] of Exeter, 1876. 114 *Ashley Gardens, S.W. Burghley House, Stamford.*	Great-grandson. Son of Brownlow Henry George, 4th Marquis of Exeter, 1849–1898, eldest son of William Alleyne, 3rd Marquis of Exeter, 1825–1895.
30221	8144	Ean Francis Cecil, *late* Lieutenant Lincolnshire Regiment, 1880. *Moffatts, Hatfield, Herts. Craigendinnie, Aboyne.*	Great-grandchildren. Children of Lord Francis Horace Pierrepont Cecil, 1851–1889, 2nd son of the 3rd Marquis of Exeter. *See above.*
30222	8145	Richard William Francis Cecil, Lieutenant 4th Battalion Lincolnshire Regiment, 1882. *Stocken Hall, Oakam, Rutland.*	
30223	8146	Ethel Frances Sophia, wife of Major Edward Crichton Hawkshaw, R.A., J.P., 1875. *Plâs Gwyn, Hampton Park, Hereford.*	
30224	8147	Roderic Edward William Cecil Hawkshaw, 1900.	Great-great-grandchildren. Children of No. 30223.
30225	8148	Violet Dorothea, wife of Colonel Oswald Henry Ames, 2nd Life Guards, 1878. 15 *Cambridge Square, W.*	Great-grandchildren. Sisters of Nos. 30221, &c.
30226	8149	Edith Celandine Cecil, 1886.	
30227	8150	Lord William Cecil, M.V.O., *late* Captain Grenadier Guards, Lieut.-Col. and Hon. Colonel 4th Battalion Lincolnshire Regiment, Comptroller and Treasurer of the Household to H.R.H. Princess Henry of Battenberg, 1854. *Hunmanby Hall, Yorkshire.*	Grandson. Elder surviving son of 3rd Marquis. *See above.*
30228	8151	William Amherst Cecil, 1886.	Great-grandchildren. Children of No. 30227.
30229	8152	Thomas James Amherst Cecil, 1887.	
30230	8153	John Francis Amherst Cecil, 1890.	
30231	8154	Henry Mitford Amherst Cecil, 1893.	
30232	8155	Lord John Pakenham Joicey-Cecil, Lieut.-Col. 4th Battalion Lincolnshire Regiment, 1867. *Newton Hall, Stokesfield-on-Tyne.*	Grandson. Younger surviving son of the 3rd Marquis. *See above.*
30233	8156	John Francis James Joicey-Cecil, 1897.	Great-grandchildren. Children of No. 30232.
30234	8157	Isabella Rosamond Georgiana Cecil, 1901.	

30235	8158	Lady Isabella Georgiana Katherine, wife of William Henry Battie-Wrightson, formerly Thomas, 1853. *Cusworth Park, Doncaster.*	Granddaughter. Eldest daughter of 3rd Marquis. *See above.*
30236	8159	Robert Cecil Battie-Wrightson, 1888.	Great-grandchildren. Children of No. 30235.
30237	8160	Barbara Isabella Georgiana Battie-Wrightson, 1890.	
30238	8161	Lady Mary Louisa Wellesley, wife of the Hon. James Henry Cecil Hozier, M.P., 1857. *36 Grosvenor Square, W.*	Granddaughters. 2nd and 3rd surviving daughters of 3rd Marquis. *See above.*
30239	8162	Catherine Sarah, Baroness Barnard [E.], 1861. *Raby Castle, Darlington.*	
30240	8163	Hon. Henry Cecil Vane, Lieutenant 2nd Volunteer Battalion Durham Light Infantry, 1882.	Great-grandchildren. Children of No. 30239.
30241	8164	Hon. Christopher William Vane, 1888.	
30242	8165	Hon. Ralph Frederick Vane, 1891.	
30243	8166	Lady Frances Emily Cecil, 1862.	Granddaughters. Youngest daughters of 3rd Marquis. *See above.*
30244	8167	Lady Louisa Alexandrina Cecil, 1864.	
30245	8168	Lord Brownlow Thomas Montague Cecil, 1827. *Cowdray, Reigate.*	Surviving children.
30246	8169	Mary Frances, Countess of [U.K.], and Baroness [G.B.], Harrowby, 1832. *44 Grosvenor Square, W.*	
30247	8170	Victoria, Baroness Carbery [I.], 1843. *Bisbrook Hall, and Glaston House, near Uppingham.*	
30248	8171	John, 10th Baron Carbery [I.], 1892. *Castle Freke, co. Cork.*	Great-grandchildren. Sons of Algernon William George, 9th Lord Carbery, 1868–1898.
30249	8172	Hon. Ralfe Evans-Freke, 1897.	
30250	8173	Hon. Percy Cecil Evans-Freke, Lieutenant Leicestershire Imperial Yeomanry, 1871. *Glaston, near Uppingham.*	Grandchild. Son of No. 30247.
30251	8174	Maida Cecil Evans-Freke, 1897.	Great-grandchildren. Children of No. 30250.

606. Descendants of Lady Sophia Cecil, 1792–1823, and her husband, the Right Hon. Henry Manvers Pierrepont, P.C., 1780–1858. (See Table XCVII.)

30252	8175	Arthur Charles, 4th Duke of Wellington [U.K.], 8th Earl of Mornington [I.], 4th Duke of Ciudad Rodrigo and Grandee of the 1st Class [Spain], Duke of Vittoria [Portugal], and Prince of Waterloo [Netherlands], 1849. *Apsley House, Piccadilly, W.*	Grandson. Son of Augusta Sophia Anne Pierrepont, 1820 – 1893, and Lord Charles Wellesley, 1808–1858.
30253	8176	Arthur Charles, Marquis Douro, 1876.	Great-grandchildren. Children of No. 30252.
30254	8177	Lord Richard Wellesley, 1879.	
30255	8178	Lord Gerald Wellesley, 1885.	
30256	8179	Lord George Wellesley, 1889.	
30257	8180	Lady Evelyn Kathleen, wife of the Hon. Robert James, 1873. *St. Nicholas, Richmond, Yorks.*	
30258	8181	Lady Eileen Wellesley, 1887.	

30259	8182	Victoria Alexandrina, Baroness HolmPatrick [U.K.], 1847. *Abbotstown, Castleknock, co. Dublin.*	}	Granddaughter. Sister to No. 30252.
30260	8183	Hans Wellesley, 2nd Baron HolmPatrick [U.K.], 1886. *Abbotstown, Castleknock, co. Dubin.*		
30261	8184	Hon. Margaret Augusta Hamilton, 1879.		Great-grandchildren.
30262	8185	Hon. Georgina, wife of Cecil Anderson Pelham, 1880.	}	Children of No. 30259.
30263	8186	Hon. Sybil Evelyn Hamilton, 1882.		
30264	8187	Hon. Winifred Hamilton, 1884.		
30265	8188	Hon. Clare Hamilton, 1888.		
30266	8189	Lady Mary Angela, widow of George Arthur Jervoise Scott, 1833-1895, 1850. *22 Grafton Street, W.*	}	Granddaughter. Younger sister to No. 30252.
30267	8190	Ronald Malcolm, 1876.		Great-grandchildren. Children
30268	8191	Dougal Orme Malcolm, 1877.	*Walton Manor, Epsom.*	of Lady Georgina Wellesley, 1853-1880, 1st wife of William
30269	8192	Angela Malcolm.		Rolle Malcolm, of Walton Manor, Epsom.

607. Descendants of the Rev. Henry Chaplin, Vicar of Ryhall, Rutland, 1789–18 (See Table XCVII.)

30270	8193	The Right Hon. Henry Chaplin, P.C., M.P. *Blankney, near Sleaford. Stafford House, St. James', S.W.*	}	Son.
30271 -74	}	Same as Nos. 22241–22244.	{	Grandchildren. Children of No. 30270.
30275	8194	Muriel Theresa Chaplin. } Grandchildren. Children of Lieut.-Col.		
30276	8195	Sibell Evelyn Chaplin. } Edward Chaplin, M.P., 1842–1883.		
30277	8196	Cecil Chaplin, 1844. *Whissendine, Oakham.* *21 Grafton Street, W.*	}	2nd surviving son.
30278	8197	Frank Chaplin, 1870.		
30279	8198	Vere Chaplin, 1874.		Grandchildren. Children
30280	8199	Frederick Chaplin, 1876.		of No. 30277.
30281	8200	Bertha Cecilia Chaplin, 1878.		
30282	8201	Ernest Chaplin. 105 *Eaton Square, S.W.*		
30283	8202	Helen Matilda, Countess of Radnor [G.B.]. *12 Upper Brook Street, W.*	}	Children.
30284	8203	Jacob, 6th Earl of Radnor [G.B.], 1868. *The Manor House, Folkestone.*	}	Grandson. Son of No. 30283.
30285	8204	William, Viscount Folkestone, 1895.		
30286	8205	Hon. Edward Pleydell-Bouverie, 1899.		Great-grandchildren.
30287	8206	Hon. Bartholomew Pleydell-Bouverie, 1902.	}	Children of No.
30288	8207	Lady Jeane Pleydell-Bouverie, 1892.		30284.
30289	8208	Lady Katharine Pleydell-Bouverie, 1894.		
30290	8209	Lady Elizabeth Pleydell-Bouverie, 1897.		
30291	8210	Hon. Stuart Pleydell-Bouverie, 1877. *High Barn, Godalming.*	}	Grandson. Younger son of No. 30283.
30292	8211	Christopher Pleydell-Bouverie, 1901.	{	Great-grandson. Son of No. 30291.
30293	8212	Wilma, Countess of Lathom [U.K.], 1869. 1 *Bryanston Square, W. Lathom House, Ormskirk.*	}	Granddaughter. Daughter of No. 30283.
30294	8213	Edward William, Lord Skelmersdale, 1895.		Great-grandchildren.
30295	8214	Lady Helen Alice Bootle-Wilbraham, 1890.	}	Children of No.
30296	8215	Lady Barbara Ann Bootle-Wilbraham, 1893.		30293.
30297	8216	Lady Margaret Edith Bootle-Wilbraham, 1899.		

608. Descendants, if any, of Colonel Thomas Chaplin, M.P., 1794–   . (See Table XCVII.)

---

609. Descendants of Elizabeth Chaplin,   –1865, wife of Vere Fane, 1785-1863. (See Table XCVII.)

30298	8217	Vere Henry Birch-Reynardson, *late* Captain 3rd Battalion Hants Regiment, 1864. *Rushington Manor, Totton, Hants.*	Grandson. Son of Emily Fane, 1822–1893, wife of Colonel Edward Birch-Reynardson, C.B., 1812–1896.
30299	8218	Edward Vere Birch-Reynardson, 1894.	Great-grandchildren. Children of No. 30298.
30300	8219	Morgan Henry Birch-Reynardson, 1895.	
30301	8220	Geraldine Rosa Augusta Birch-Reynardson, 1893.	
30302	8221	Rose Catherine, widow of Rear-Admiral John Hugh Bainbridge, R.N., of Frankfield, Cork. *Elfordleigh, Plympton, South Devon.*	Granddaughter. Sister to No. 30298.
30303	8222	John Hugh Bainbridge, Lieutenant R.N., 1879.	Great-grandchildren. Children of No. 30302.
30304	8223	Kathleen Grace Fane Bainbridge.	
30305	8224	Gwendolen Eleanor, wife of Captain A. B. Fox.	
30306	8225	Dorothy Emily Bainbridge.	
30307	8226	Adela Augusta, wife of Sir Henry Bromley, 5th Bart., 1847. *Stoke, Newark, Notts.*	Grandchild. Only child of Emma Fane, 1823–1847, wife of Westley Richards, of Ashwell, Rutland, 1814–1897.
30308	8227	Robert Bromley, 1874.	Great-grandchild. Son of No. 30307.
30309	8228	Ruperta Sibyl Bromley, 1901.	Great-great-grandchild. Daughter of No. 30308.
30310	8229	Maurice Bromley-Wilson, J.P., 1875. *Dallam Tower, Milnthorpe.*	Great-grandchildren. Children of No. 30307.
30311	8230	Arthur Bromley, Lieutenant R.N., 1876.	
30312	8231	Herbert Assheton Bromley, 1879.	
30313	8232	Esther Bromley.	
30314	8233	Georgiana Ellen, Lady Bromley, widow of Sir Henry Bromley, 4th Bart., 1816–1895. *Stoke Hall, Newark, Notts.*	Daughter.

---

610. Descendants of Sophia Chaplin,   –1854, wife of James Blackwell Praed, M.P., of Tyringham, 1779–1837. (See Table XCVII.)

30315	8234	Roger William Gifford Tyringham, J.P., 1870. *Tyringham, Bucks.* *Trevethoe, Cornwall.*	Grandchildren. Children of William Blackwell Praed, *afterwards* Tyringham of Tyringham, &c., 1829–1870.
30316	8235	Mary Isabel, wife of Cookson, 1867.	
30317	8236	Louisa Agnes, wife of Edmund Chase Marriott. *Poltair, Cornwall.*	Daughters.
30318	8237	Charlotte, widow of Sidmouth Stowell Skipwith, Commander R.N., 1825–1872.	

30319	8238	Reginald Skipwith, 1866. 1 *Culford Gardens, Chelsea.*	Grandson. Son of No. 30318.
30320	8239	Geoffrey Reginald Skipwith, 1900.	Great-grandsons. Sons of
30321	8240	Arthur Grey Skipwith, 1902.	No. 30319.
30322	8241	Gerald Skipwith, 1869. *Wellington.*	Grandchildren. Chil-
30323	8242	Eva, wife of Edmund H. Whitmore. 28 *Milner Street, Lennox Gardens, S.W.*	dren of No. 30318.

611. Descendants of Lady Elizabeth Cecil, –1733, 1st wife of William Aislabie, of Studley, York. (See Table XCVII.)

612. Descendants of Edmund, 8th Earl of Cork and Orrery, K.P., 1767–1856. (See Table XCVII.)

30324	8243	Richard Edmund St. Lawrence, 9th Earl of Cork and Orrery [I.], 7th Baron Boyle of Marston [G.B.], 1829. 40 *Charles Street, Berkeley Square, W.* *Marston House, Frome.*	Grandson. Son of Charles, Viscount Dungarvan, 1800–1834.
30325	8244	Charles Spencer Canning, Viscount Dungarvan, 1861. *White's ; Bachelors' ; Turf.*	Great-grandchildren. Children of No. 30324.
30326	8245	Hon. Robert John Lascelles Boyle, 1864.	
30327	8246	Lady Emily Harriet Catherine, wife of James Dalison Alexander, 1854.	
30328 –31		Same as Nos. 29515–29518.	Great-great-grandchildren. Children of No. 30327.
30332	8247	Lady Grace Elizabeth, wife of the Hon. Francis Henry Baring, 1856. 34 *Great Cumberland Place, W.*	Great-grandchild. 2nd daughter of No. 30324.
30333	8248	Francis Arthur Baring, 1882.	Great-great-grandchildren. Chil-
30334	8249	John Henry Baring, 1885.	dren of No. 30332.
30335	8250	Lady Honora Janet, wife of Robert Kirkman Hodgson, 1857. *Ashgrove, Sevenoaks.*	Great-grandchild. 3rd daughter of No. 30324.
30336	8251	Francis Wentworth Kirkman Hodgson, 1876.	
30337	8252	Michael Reginald Kirkman Hodgson, 1879.	Great-great-grand-
30338	8253	Maurice Kirkman Hodgson, 1880.	children. Chil-
30339	8254	Patrick Kirkman Hodgson, 1884.	dren of No.
30340	8255	Denis Kirkman Hodgson, 1887.	30335.
30341	8256	Celia Emily Kirkman Hodgson, 1882.	
30342	8257	Lady Dorothy Blanche, wife of the Right Hon. Walter Hume Long, P.C., M.P., 1858. *Chittern Lodge, Codford.*	Great-grandchild. 4th daughter of No. 30324.
30343	8258	Walter Long, Capt. 2nd Dragoons, D.S.O., 1879.	Great-great-grand-
30344	8259	Richard Eric Onslow Long, 1892.	children. Chil-
30345	8260	Victoria Florence de Burgh, wife of George A. Gibbs, 1880.	dren of No. 30342.
30346	8261	Lettice Margaret Long, 1885.	
30347	8262	Lady Isabel Lettice Theodosia, wife of James Walker Larnach, 1860. 1 *Carlton Gardens, S.W.*	Great-grandchild. 5th daughter of No. 30324.
30348	8263	Isabel Nellie Larnach, 1890.	Great-great-grandchild. Daughter of No. 30347.

30349	8264	Lieut.-Col. the Hon. William George Boyle, J.P., 1830.	Grandson. Son of Charles, Viscount Dungarvan, 1800–1834.
30350	8265	Ida Frances Boyle, 1867.	Great-grandchild. Daughter of Major the Hon. Edmund John Boyle, 1831–1901, brother to No. 30349.
30351	8266	Hon. Arthur Algernon Capell, 1864. 23 Draycott Place, S.W.	Great-grandchild. Son of the Lady Louisa Caroline Elizabeth Boyle, 1833–1876, 2nd wife of Arthur Algernon, 6th Earl of Essex, 1803–1892.
30352	8267	Constance Audrey Capell, 1891.	Great-great-grandchildren. Children of No. 30351.
30353	8268	Rachel Julia Capell, 1894.	
30354	8269	Lady Beatrice Mary Capell, 1870. 26 Tedworth Square, Chelsea, S.W.	Great-grandchild. Sister to No. 30351.
30355	8270	Lady Mary Emily, wife of Lord David Kennedy, 1834. 93 Queen's Gate, S.W.	Granddaughter. Sister to No. 30349.
30356	8271	Major James Charles Hope-Vere, J.P., D.C., 1858. Craigie Hall, Midlothian.	Great-grandchild. Son of No. 30355 by 1st husband, William Edward Hope-Vere, of Craigie Hall, 1824–1872.
30357	8272	Edward James Hope-Vere, 1885.	Great-great-grandchildren. Children of No. 30356.
30358	8273	Ralph Jean James Hope-Vere, 1887.	
30359	8274	Rachel Magdeleine Mary Hope-Vere, 1886.	
30360	8275	Mary St. Lawrence, widow of Sir Everett Millais, 2nd Baronet, 1856–1897. 38 Lower Belgrave Street, S.W.	Great-grandchild. Daughter of No. 30355 by 1st husband.
30361	8276	Sir John Everett Millais, 3rd Baronet, 1888.	Great-great-grandchildren. Children of No. 30360.
30362	8277	Pérrine Millais, 1893.	
30363	8278	Mary Amice Millais, 1897.	
30364	8279	Evelyn Mary, wife of Charles Helbert Helbert. 93 Queen's Gate, S.W.	Great-granddaughter. Daughter of No. 30355 by 2nd husband.
30365 –78		Same as Nos. 23310–23323.	Grandchildren, &c. Children, &c., of the Hon. John Boyle, 1803–1874.
30379	8280	Edmund Robarts Boyle, late Lieutenant Coldstream Guards, and Page of Honour to Queen Victoria, 1846. Travellers'; Royal Yacht Squadron.	Grandchildren. Children of Lieut.-Col. the Hon. Robert Boyle, M.P., 1809–1854.
30380	8281	Emily Cecilia, wife of Cecil Chaplin, 1847. 21 Grafton Street, Bond Street, W.	
30381 –84		Same as Nos. 30278–30281.	Great-grandchildren. Children of No. 30380.
30385	8282	Charlotte Jane, widow of Major Mordaunt Charles Boyle, 1850–1885, 1851.	Grandchild. Sister to No. 30379, &c.
30386	8283	Robert Boyle, 1880.	Great-grandchild. Son of No. 30385.
30387	8284	Hamilton Richard Boyle, late Lieutenant 23rd Foot, 1848.	Grandchildren. Children of the Rev. and Hon. Richard Cavendish Boyle, 1812–1886.
30388	8285	Charles John Boyle, J.P., late Captain and Hon. Major 4th Battalion Oxfordshire Light Infantry, 1849. Ipsden House, Wallingford.	

30389	8286	Charles Roger Cavendish Boyle, 1886.	
30390	8287	Richard Frederick Robert Pochin Boyle, 1888.	Great-grandchildren. Children of No. 30388.
30391	8288	John Parke Boyle, 1893.	
30392	8289	Edmund Michael Gordon Laventhorpe Boyle, 1895.	
30393	8290	Lilian Joanna Vere Boyle.	
30394	8291	Algernon Edward Richard Boyle, J.P., 1864. *Elrick House, Aberdeenshire.*	Grandchildren. Brother and sister to No. 30387, &c.
30395	8292	Isabella Albinia, wife of Sir George Gough Arbuthnot, 1851. *4 Grosvenor Crescent, S.W.*	
30396	8293	Cecilia Albina Arbuthnot.	Great-grandchild. Daughter of No. 30395.

613. Descendants of Admiral the Hon. Sir Courtenay Boyle, K.G.H., 1770–1844. (See Table XCVII.)

30397		Same as No. 30386.	Great-grandson. Son of Major Mordaunt Charles Boyle, 1850–1885, and grandson of Charles John Boyle, 1806–1885.
30398	8294	Lieut.-Col. Lionel Richard Cavendish Boyle, 1851. *Spencer House, Stanstead, Essex.*	Grandson. Son of Charles John Boyle, 1806–1885.
30399 –402	}	Same as Nos. 29528–29531.	Great-grandchildren. Children of No. 30398.
30403	8295	Dorothy Cecil Boyle, 1879.	
30404	8296	Elizabeth Adeline Cecil Boyle, 1889. *Avon Dassett, Warwickshire.*	Great-grandchildren. Daughters of Captain Cecil William Boyle, 1853–1900, brother to No. 30398.
30405	8297	William Lewis Boyle, 1859. *Elsing Hall, East Dereham, Norfolk.*	Grandson. Brother to No. 30398.
30406	8298	Charles Norman Cavendish Boyle, 1890.	Great-grandchildren. Children of No. 30405.
30407	8299	Evelyn Vere Boyle.	
30408	8300	Ernest Charles Patrick Boyle, Captain Imperial Yeomanry, 1860. *134 Sloane Street, S.W.*	Grandchildren. Youngest brother and sister to No. 30398.
30409	8301	Audrey Georgiana Florence, Lady Tennyson [U.K.]. *Government House, Melbourne.* *Aldworth, near Haslemere.*	
30410	8302	Hon. Lionel Hallam Tennyson, 1889.	Great-grandchildren. Children of No. 30409.
30411	8303	Hon. Alfred Audrey Tennyson, 1891.	
30412	8304	Hon. Harold Courtenay Tennyson, 1896.	
30413	8305	Sir Charles Cavendish Boyle, K.C.M.G., Governor and Commander-in-Chief of Newfoundland, 1849. *Government House, St. John's.*	Grandson. Son of Captain Cavendish Spencer Boyle, 1814–1868.
30414	8306	Adelaide Margaret Rose Lane.	Great-granddaughter. Daughter of Caroline Louisa Boyle, 1847–1883 (sister to No. 30413), wife of the Rev. Charlton George Lane, rector of Little Gaddesden, Herts.

The Blood Royal of Britain

614. Descendants of Henrietta Anna Maria Charlotte Bridgeman, 1788–1813, wife of Charles, 1st Earl of Yarborough, 1781–1846. (See Table XCVII.)

30415	8307	Charles Alfred Worsley, 4th Earl of [U.K.], and 5th Baron [G.B.] Yarborough, P.C., 1859. *7 Arlington Street, S.W. Brocklesby Park, Lincolnshire.*	Great-grandson. Son of Charles, 3rd Earl of Yarborough, 1835–1875, and grandson of Charles, 2nd Earl of Yarborough, 1809–1862.
30416	8308	Charles Sackville, Lord Worsley, 1887.[1]	Great-great-grandchildren Children of No. 30415.
30417	8309	Hon. Sackville George Anderson-Pelham, 1888.[1]	
30418	8310	Hon. Marcus Herbert Anderson-Pelham, 1893.[1]	
30419	8311	Hon. Victor Ralph Anderson-Pelham, 1866. *Wellington; Naval and Military.*	Great-grandsons. Brothers to No. 30415.
30420	8312	Hon. Henry Cornwallis Anderson-Pelham, 1868. *White's.*	
30421	8313	Esmé Marcia Rose Anderson-Pelham, 1893.	Great-great-grandchildren. Daughters of No. 30420.
30422	8314	Marjorie Edith Anderson-Pelham, 1897.	
30423	8315	Hon. Dudley Roger Hugh Anderson-Pelham, Captain 10th Hussars, 1872. *Cavalry.*	Great-grandchildren. Brother and sister to No. 30415.
30424	8316	Lady Gertrude Augusta, wife of Sir Francis Edmund George Astley-Corbett, 4th Bart., 1861. *45 Cadogan Gardens, S.W.*	
30425	8317	John Dugdale Pelham Astley-Corbett, 1883.	Great-great-grandchildren. Children of No. 30424.
30426	8318	Marjorie Gertrude Marcia Astley-Corbett.	
30427	8319	Norah Sybil Astley-Corbett.	
30428	8320	Hon. Evelyn Cornwallis Anderson-Pelham, 1851. *29 Belgrave Square, S.W.*	Grandson. Son of Charles, 2nd Earl of Yarborough, 1809–1862.
30429	8321	Cecil Henry Anderson-Pelham, Lieutenant 12th Lancers, 1874. *Wellington.*	Great-grandchildren. Children of No. 30428.
30430	8322	Charles Cornwallis Anderson-Pelham, 1876. *Bisbrook Hall, Uppingham.*	
30431	8323	Reginald Evelyn Anderson-Pelham, 1884.	
30432	8324	Alfred Ronald Anderson-Pelham, 1888.	
30433	8325	Adelaide Muriel Anderson-Pelham, 1878.	
30434	8326	Florence Gwendoline Anderson-Pelham, 1882.	
30435	8327	Elena Blanche Anderson-Pelham, 1885.	
30436	8328	Lady Sophia Constance, wife of Samuel Hynman Montgomerie, *formerly* Allenby, J.P., D.L., 1863. *Southannan, Fairlie, N.B.*	Great-granddaughter. Eldest daughter of Lady Sophia Adelaide Theodosia Anderson-Pelham, 1840–1886 (daughter of 2nd Earl of Yarborough), wife of Archibald, 14th Earl of Eglinton and Winton, 1841–1892.

[1] They are also descended from James I. and VI. through their mother, Marcia Amelia Mary, Countess of Yarborough, *suo jure* Baroness Conyers, who descends from Caroline, Duchess of Schomberg, daughter of the Elector Palatine Charles Louis, 1617–1680, and Maria Susanna Louisa von Degenfeld, 1636–16—. The legitimacy of this descent, however, turns on (1) the legality of the alleged divorce between Charles Louis and his 1st wife, and (2) of his re-marriage in 1657 to the said Maria Susanna Louisa von Degenfeld.

30437	8329	Sophia Egidia Guendolen Montgomerie, 1886.	Great-great-grand-children. Children of No. 30436.
30438	8330	Eleanor Theresa Montgomerie, 1889	
30439	8331	Adelaide Margaret Constance Montgomerie, 1892.	
30440	8332	Lady Theresa, wife of John Cross, 1866. *Kibworth Grange, Leicester.*	Great-granddaughter. Sister to No. 30436.
30441	8333	Archibald David Cross, 1891.	Great-great-grandchildren. Children of No. 30440.
30442	8334	Sophia Mary Cross, 1890.	
30443	8335	Lady Gertrude, wife of Ernest Bruce Acland Lawford, 1867. *Winton, Oxted, Surrey.*	Great-granddaughter. Sister to No. 30436.
30444	8336	Constance Gertrude Lawford, 1894.	Great-great-grandchildren. Children of No. 30443.
30445	8337	Ernestine Teresa Wilhelmina Lawford, 1897.	
30446	8338	Adela Sophia Lawford, 1899.	
30447	8339	Lady Diana, wife of Harold Kenneth Allison, 1870.	Great-granddaughter. Youngest sister to No. 30436.
30448	8340	Wilfred Archibald Alexander, 1892. *Ballochmyle, Mauchline, Ayrshire.*	Great-great-grandchild. Son of No. 30447 by 1st husband, Sir Claud Alexander, 2nd Bart.
30449	8341	Edith Charlotte, wife of Captain Gilbert Spencer-Smith, *late* 85th Light Infantry. *Maidenstone Heath, near Bursledon, Southampton.*	Granddaughter. Daughter of Captain the Hon. Dudley Worsley Anderson-Pelham, 1812–1851.
30450	8342	Gilbert Seymour Worsley Spencer-Smith, 1894.	Great-grandchildren. Children of No. 30449.
30451	8343	Madeline Charlotte Spencer-Smith.	
30452	8344	Edith Frances Spencer-Smith.	
30453	8345	Grace Isabel Spencer-Smith.	
30454	8346	Mary Eleanor Spencer-Smith.	
30455	8347	Rachel Spencer-Smith.	
30456	8348	Frances Maude Spencer-Smith.	
30457	8349	Beatrice Evelyn Spencer-Smith.	
30458	8350	Octavia Spencer-Smith.	

615. Descendants of the Hon. Lucy Elizabeth Byng, 1766–1844, wife of Orlando, 1st Earl of Bradford, 1762–1825. (See Table XCVII.)

30459 -91	}	Same as Nos. 25684–25716.	Great-grandchildren, &c. Children of Orlando George Charles, 3rd Earl of Bradford, 1819–1898, and grandchildren of George Augustus, 2nd Earl of Bradford, 1789–1865.
30492 -503	}	Same as Nos. 27978–27989.	Great-grandchildren, &c. Sons of the Rev. and Hon. George Thomas Orlando Bridgeman, 1823–1895, 2nd son of the 2nd Earl.
30504	8351	William Clive Bridgeman, 1864. 13 *Mansfield Street, W.*	Great-grandson. Son of the Rev. and Hon. John Robert Orlando Bridgeman, 1831–1897.
30505	8352	Robert Clive Bridgeman, 1896.	Great-great-grandchildren. Children of No. 30504.
30506	8353	Geoffrey John Orlando Bridgeman, 1898.	
30507	8354	Robert George, 14th Baron Windsor [E.], 1857. 54 *Mount Street, W. Hewell Grange, Redditch.*	Great-grandson. Son of Lady Mary Selina Louisa Bridgeman (daughter of the 2nd Earl of Bradford), 1830–1889, and her husband, the Hon. Robert Windsor-Clive, M.P., 1824–1859.

30508	8355	Hon. Other Robert Windsor-Clive, 1884.	
30509	8356	Hon. Ivor Miles Windsor-Clive, 1889.	Great-great-grandchildren.
30510	8357	Hon. Archer Windsor-Clive, 1890.	Children of No. 30507.
30511	8358	Hon. Phyllis Windsor-Clive, 1886.	
30512	8359	Hon. Georgiana Harriet Charlotte Windsor-Clive, 1853.	
30513	8360	Hon. Henrietta Lucy Windsor-Clive, 1855.	Great-grandchildren. Sisters to No. 30507.
30514	8361	Hon. Mary Agnes, wife of John Knowsley Thornton, 1856. *Hildersham Hall, Cambridge.*	
30515	8362	Margery Gertrude Knowsley, 1896.	Great-great-grandchild. Child of No. 30514.
30516	8363	Ursula Judith Bridgeman, 1855.	Great-grandchildren. Children of the Rev. Edmund Wolryche Orlando Bridgeman, 1825–1897, and grandchildren of Vice-Admiral the Hon. Charles Orlando Bridgeman, 1791–1860.
30517	8364	Maud Bridgeman, 1857.	
30518	8365	Dorothy Bridgeman, 1861.	
30519	8366	Hon. Henry Charles Denison, Captain R.H.A., 1849. 36 *Charles Street, Mayfair, W.*	Great-grandchild. Son of Ursula Lucy Grace Bridgeman, 1823–1883 (daughter of Vice-Admiral the Hon. Charles Bridgeman, 1791–1860), who married 1st as 2nd wife, Albert, 1st Lord Londesborough, 1805–1860.
30520	8367	Edward Conyngham Denison, 1888.	Great-great-grandson. Son of No. 30519.
30521	8368	Hon. Conyngham Albert Denison, Commander R.N., 1851. *Halnaker, Chichester.*	Great-grandchild. Brother to No. 30519.
30522	8369	Conyngham Charles Denison, 1885.	Great-great-grandchildren. Children of No. 30521.
30523	8370	Gerald Evelyn Henry Denison, 1892.	
30524	8371	Beatrice Mildred Denison, 1887.	
30525	8372	Hon. Harold Albert Denison, *late* Lieutenant R.N., 1856. 30 *St. James' Square, S.W.*	Great-grandchild. Brother to No. 30519.
30526	8373	John Albert Lister Denison, 1901.	Great-great-grandchild. Child of No. 30525.
30527	8374	Gerald Otho FitzGerald, Captain, *late* 5th Battalion King's Royal Rifle Corps, 1862. 30 *St. James' Square, S.W.*	Great-grandchild. Son of Ursula Lucy Grace Bridgeman, 1823–1883 (*see above*), and her 2nd husband, the Right Hon. Lord Otho Augustus FitzGerald, P.C., M.P., 1827–1882.
30528	8375	Londesborough Granville Lawton Maud Dickinson, 1872.	Great-great-grandchildren. Children of the Hon. Ursula Elizabeth Denison (sister to No. 30519), 1848–1880, wife of the Rev. George Cockburn Dickinson.
30529	8376	Ernest Trevelyan Egerton Dickinson. 1874.	
30530	8377	Edgell Antonio Albert FitzGerald Dickinson, 1875.	
30531	8378	Edith Jane Katharine Christophina Ursula Dickinson.	
30532	8379	Eveline Haroldina Elizabeth Carnegie Dickinson.	
30533	8380	Hon. Albertina Agnes Mary, wife of Colonel Ivor John Caradoc Herbert, C.B., C.M.G., 1854. *Llanarth Court, Raglan.*	Great-grandchild. Sister to No. 30519.
30534	8381	Elydyr John Bernard Herbert, 1881.	Great-great-grandchildren. Children of No. 30533.
30535	8382	Florence Mary Ursula Herbert, 1879.	

30536	8383	Ina Blanche Georgie, wife of Lieut.-Col. Arthur Leopold Paget, 1864. *Highfield, Stratton, Cirencester.*	Great-grandchild. Sister to No. 30527.
30537	8384	Desmond Otho Paget, ⎫ twins, 1898.	Great-great-grandchildren.
30538	8385	Oswald Leopold Paget, ⎭	Children of No. 30536.
30539	8386	Cynthia Geraldine Ursula Paget, 1888.	
30540	8387	Emily Louisa Gertrude, widow of Lieut.-Col. Francis Beckford Ward, R.A., 1821–1876, 1826. 87 *Blenheim Crescent, Notting Hill, W.*	Granddaughter. Daughter of Vice-Admiral the Hon. Charles Orlando Bridgeman, 1791–1860.
30541	8388	Orlando Frank Montague Ward, 1868.	
30542	8389	Agnes Gertrude Ward, 1860.	
30543	8390	Edith Ursula Ward, 1861.	Great-grandchildren.
30544	8391	Cecily Emily Ward, 1863.	Children of No. 30540.
30545	8392	Serena Lucy, wife of the Rev. Francis George Ellerton, 1867. *Ellesmere Vicarage, Salop.*	
30546	8393	Margaret Ellerton, 1896.	Great-great-grandchildren.
30547	8394	Jacynth Ellerton, 1897.	Children of No. 30545.
30548	8395	Caroline Elizabeth Anne Agnes, widow of Sir Vincent Rowland Corbet, 3rd Bart., 1821–1891, 1833. *Kingsland House, Shrewsbury.*	Granddaughter. Sister to No. 30540.
30549	8396	Sir Walter Orlando Corbet, 4th Bart., 1856. *Acton Reynald, Shrewsbury.*	Great-grandson. Son of No. 30548.
30550	8397	Vincent Stewart Corbet, 1890.	Great-great-grandchildren.
30551	8398	Roland James Corbet, 1892.	Sons of No. 30549.
30552	8399	Gerald Vincent Corbet, 1868. *Forda, Brandiscorner, N. Devon.*	Great-grandchildren. Children of No. 30548.
30553	8400	Alice Nina, wife of George Fydell Rowley. *Priory Hill, St. Neots, Hants.*	
30554	8401	Owsley Vincent Fydell Rowley, 1885.	Great-great-grandchildren. Children of No. 30553.
30555	8402	George Richard Francis Rowley, 1889.	
30556	8403	Sybell Rachel, wife of Lieut.-Col. Edward Umfreville Blackett, R.A. *Wylam, Northumberland.*	Great-grandchild Child of No 30548.
30557	8404	Christopher John Walter Blackett, 1900.	Great-great-grandchildren. Children of No. 30556.
30558	8405	Frances Rachel Florence Blackett, 1897.	
30559	8406	Sybell Mary Blackett, 1899.	
30560	8407	Isabel Agnes, wife of Francis Edward Adams. *Moreton, Nettleham Road, Lincoln.*	Great-grandchildren. Children of No. 30548.
30561	8408	Beatrice Augusta Corbet.	
30562	8409	Judith Elizabeth, wife of the Rev. Henry Vernon Heber-Percy. *Hodnet Rectory, Market Drayton.*	
30563 –68	⎫⎭	Same as Nos. 21003–21008.	Great-great-grandchildren. Children of No. 30562.
30569	8410	Mabel Hermione Corbet.	Great-grandchildren. Children of No. 30548.
30570	8411	Constance Edith, Lady Sutton, wife of the Rev. Hubert Delaval Astley. *Benham Park, Newbury, Berks.*	
30571	8412	Sir Richard Vincent Sutton, 6th Bart., 1891.	Great-great-grandchild. Son of No. 30570 by 1st husband, Sir Richard Francis Sutton, 5th Bart., 1853–1891.

30572	8413	Philip Reginald Astley, 1896.	⎧ Great-great-grandchildren. Children of No. 30570 by 2nd husband.
30573	8414	Ruth Constance Astley, 1900.	
30574	8415	Gertrude Ursula Corbet, 1871.	⎧ Great-grandchild. Youngest daughter of No. 30548.
30575	8416	Charlotte Sobieski Isabel, Lady Cust, V.A., widow of Sir Leopold Cust, 2nd Bart., 1831–1878. 99 Onslow Square, S.W.	⎫ Granddaughter. Sister to No. 30540.
30576	8417	Sir Charles Leopold Cust, 3rd Bart., C.M.G., M.V.O., 1864. 90 Piccadilly, W.	⎫ Great-grandchildren. Children of No. 30575.
30577	8418	Leopold Peregrine Edward Cust, 1866.	
30578	8419	Aleen Isabel Cust.	
30579	8420	Ursula Cust.	
30580	8421	Katherine Selina, widow of Arthur Philip Lloyd, −1893, 1837. 86 Elm Park Gardens, S.W.	⎫ Granddaughter. Youngest sister to No. 30540.
30581	8422	Arthur Henry Orlando Lloyd, Captain (retired) Grenadier Guards, M.V.O., J.P.,1864. Leaton Knolls, near Shrewsbury.	⎫ Great-grandchild. Son of No. 30580.
30582	8423	John Arthur Lloyd, 1898.	⎫ Great-great-grandchildren. Children of No. 30581.
30583	8424	Gwynedd Margaret Lloyd.	
30584	8425	Gladys Isabel Lloyd.	⎫
30585	8426	Leila Bessie Clare Lloyd.	
30586	8427	Gwendoline Ursula, wife of Herbert George Ferguson-Davies. 12 Westgate Terrace, S.W.	Great-grandchildren. Daughters of No. 30580.
30587	8428	Kathleen Agatha, wife of Reginald Skipwith. 1 Culford Gardens, Chelsea, S.W.	
30588 –89	⎫	Same as Nos. 30320–30321.	⎧ Great-great-grandchildren. Children of No. 30587.
30590	8429	Nesta Margaret Lloyd.	⎧ Great-grandchild. Youngest daughter of No. 30580.
30591	8430	Lucy Selina Frances, wife of Albert, Count von Seinsheim [Bavaria], Chamberlain to the Prince Regent of Bavaria, 1847. 1, Amalien Strasse 91, Munich.	⎧ Great-grandchild. Daughter of Captain Francis Orlando Henry Bridgeman, 1819–1895, and granddaughter of Captain the Hon. Orlando Henry Bridgeman, 1794–1827.
		Children, if any, of No. 30591.	
30592	8431	Orlando Jack Charles Bridgeman, late Lieutenant 11th Hussars, 1823. 43 Coton Hill, Shrewsbury.	⎧ Grandson. Son of Captain the Hon. Orlando Henry Bridgeman,1794–1827.
30593	8432	Henry Orlando Bristowe, 1851.	⎧ Great-grandchildren. Children of Selina Bridgeman, 1825–1886, sister to No. 30592, and her husband, Sir Henry Fox Bristowe, Q.C., 1824–1893.
30594	8433	Leonard Hugh Bristowe, 1859.	
30595	8434	Alice Mary Bristowe, 1855.	
30596	8435	Georgina Emily Bristowe, 1858.	
30597	8436	Alfred Orlando Henry Bridgeman, 1855. Hinton, Abbey Road, Great Malvern.	⎧ Great-grandson. Son of Frederick Henry Orlando Bridgeman,1826–1878, and grandson of the Rev. and Hon. Henry Edmund Bridgeman, 1795–1872.

3 H

30598	8437	Greswolde Dudley Orlando Bridgeman, 1829.	⎫
30599	8438	Granville Henry Orlando Bridgeman, 1830.	
30600	8439	Arthur William Orlando Bridgeman, 1834. *Grosvenor.*	Grandchildren. Children of the Rev.
30601	8440	Edward Charles Orlando Bridgeman, 1840	and Hon. Henry
30602	8441	Caroline Louisa Sophia Georgiana, wife of William Joseph Kingsbury. *64 Burton Court, Lower Sloane Street, S.W.*	Edmund Bridgeman, 1795–1872. ⎭
30603	8442	Jack Bridgeman Kingsbury, 1900.	Great-great-grandchild. Child of Walter Bridgeman Kingsbury, 1864–1902.
30604	8443	Rev. William Evelyn Kingsbury, Curate of All Saints', Wigan, 1866. *Clergy House, Wigan.*	⎫
30605	8444	Gerald Francis Kingsbury, 1871. *Lythe House, East Meon, Hants.*	Great-grandchildren. Children of No.
30606	8445	Ethel Frances Emily, wife of the Rev. Roland George Matthew, Rector of Wigan. *The Hall, Wigan.*	30602.
30607	8446	Mary Eleanor Caroline Kingsbury.	⎭
30608	8447	Helen Gertrude Bridgeman, 1839.	Grandchild. Younger sister to No. 30598, &c.

616. Descendants of Major-General Lord George William Russell, G.C.B. (See Table XCVII.)

30609	8448	▽ Herbrand Arthur, 11th Duke of Bedford [E.], K.G., 1858. *15 Belgrave Square, S.W. Woburn Abbey, Bedfordshire.*	Grandson. Son of Francis Charles Hastings, 9th Duke of Bedford, 1819–1891.
30610	8449	▽ Hastings William Sackville, Marquis of Tavistock, 1888.	Great-grandson. Only child of No. 30609.
30611	8450	▽ Lady Ela Monica Sackville Russell, 1854. *51 Princes Gate, S.W.*	⎫
30612	8451	▽ Lady Ermyntrude Sackville, wife of the Right Hon. Sir Edward Baldwin Malet, P.C., G.C.B., G.C.M.G., 1856. *85 Eaton Square, S.W.*	Granddaughters. Sisters to No. 30609.
30613	8452	▽ Harold John Hastings Russell, Barrister-at-Law, 1868. *16 Beaufort Gardens, S.W.*	Grandson. Son of Lord Arthur John Edward Russell, M.P., 1825–1892.
30614		Same as No. 22369.	Great-granddaughter. Daughter to No. 30613.
30615	8453	▽ Claud Frederick William Russell, 3rd Secretary H.B.M.'s Diplomatic Service, 1871.	⎫
30616	8454	▽ Alwyne Byng Gilbert Russell, Lieutenant 3rd Battalion Grenadier Guards, 1875.	Grandchildren. Brothers and sisters to No.
30617	8455	▽ Conrad George Edward Russell, 1878.	30613.
30618	8456	▽ Flora Magdalene Isabel Russell, 1869.	
30619	8457	▽ Caroline Diana Rosalind Russell, 1874.	⎭
30620	8458	▽ Arthur Oliver Villiers, 2nd Lord Ampthill [U.K.], Governor of Madras, 1869. *Government House, Madras.*	Grandson. Son of Odo William Leopold, 1st Lord Ampthill, 1829–1884.
30621	8459	▽ Hon. John Hugo Russell, 1896.	⎫
30622	8460	▽ Hon. Guy Herbrand Edward Russell, 1898.	Great-grandchildren. Children of No.
30623	8461	▽ Hon. Edward Wriothesley Curzon Russell, 1901.	30620.

30624	8462	☐ Hon. Odo William Theophilus Villiers Russell, 2nd Secretary H.B.M.'s Diplomatic Service, 1870.
		19 *Stratford Place, W.*
		British Embassy, Vienna.
30625	8463	☐ Hon. Victor Alexander Frederick Villiers Russell, Lieutenant 3rd Battalion Bedfordshire Regiment, 1874.
		19 *Stratford Place, W.*
30626	8464	☐ Hon. Alexander Victor Frederick Villiers Russell, 1874, Major and Adjutant 3rd Battalion Grenadier Guards.
		19 *Stratford Place, W.*
30627	8465	☐ Hon. Constance Evelyn Villiers Russell, 1872.
30628	8466	☐ Hon. Augusta Louise Margaret Romola Villiers Russell, 1879.

Grandchildren. Brothers and sisters to No. 30620.

617. Descendants of John, 1st Earl Russell, K.G., 1792–1878. (See Table XCVII.)

30629	8467	John Francis Stanley, 2nd Earl Russell [U.K.], 1865.
		Ardsalla House, near Navan, Meath.
30630	8468	Hon. Bertrand Arthur William Russell, 1872.
		The Millhangar, Fernhurst, Haslemere.
30631	8469	Hon. George Gilbert William Russell, 1848.
30632	8470	Hon. Francis Albert Rollo Russell, 1849.
		Dunrozel, Haslemere.
30633	8471	Arthur John Godfrey Russell, 1886.
30634	8472	John Albert Russell, 1895.
30635	8473	Margaret Frances Russell, 1894.
30636	8474	Lady Georgiana Adelaide, wife of Archibald Peel, C.C., J.P., D.L., 1836.
		Westlea, Broxbourne, Herts.
30637	8475	Edward John Russell Peel, Captain R.A., 1869.
		White's.
30638	8476	Jonathan John Russell Peel, 2nd Lieutenant Royal Fusiliers, 1872.
30639	8477	Alfred Michael John Russell Peel, 1873.
		Salisbury, Mashonaland.
30640	8478	Fergus Lister Grosvenor John Russell Peel, Lieutenant 4th Battalion Bedfordshire Regiment, 1876.
30641	8479	Fanny Agatha Louisa, wife of Captain Hubert Lavie Butler, 1868.
30642	8480	Charles Hubert Archibald Butler, 1901.
30643	8481	Ethel Adelaide Georgiana Peel, 1875.
30644	8482	Grace Peel, 1878.
30645	8483	Henry Montagu Villiers, H.M.'s Consul in the Faroe Islands, 1863.
30646	8484	Cecil Montagu John Villiers, 1897.
30647	8485	George Dumba Villiers, 1900.

Grandchildren. Children of John, Viscount Amberley, M.P., 1842–1876.

Sons.

Grandchildren. Children of No. 30632.

Daughter.

Grandchildren. Children of No. 30636.

Great-grandchild. Son of No. 30641.

Grandchildren. Youngest daughters of No. 30636.

Grandson. Son of Lady Victoria Russell, 1838–1880, 1st wife of the Rev. Henry Montagu Villiers, of St. Paul's, Knightsbridge.

Great-grandchildren. Children of No. 30645.

30648	8486	John Russell Villiers, 1866. *49 Hans Place, S.W.*	} Grandson. Brother to No. 30645.
30649	8487	Arthur Henry Villiers, 1894.	} Great-grandchildren. Children of No. 30648.
30650	8488	William Earle Villiers, 1897.	
30651	8489	John Michael Villiers, 1899.	
30652	8490	Thomas Lister Villiers, 1869. *Dickoya, Ceylon.*	} Grandson. Brother to No. 30645.
30653	8491	Henry Lister Villiers, 1897.	{ Great-grandchild. Child of No. 30652.
30654	8492	Godfrey Robert Randell Villiers, 1877. *Dickoya, Ceylon.*	
30655	8493	Frances Adelaide, wife of Arthur Francis Walrond, 1862.	
30656	8494	Gwendolen Mary Villiers, 1864.	Grandchildren. Brother and sisters to No. 30645.
30657	8495	Margaret Evelyn Villiers, 1871.	
30658	8496	Dorothy, wife of the Rev. William Frederick Herbert Randolph, 1872. *Frome Selwood Vicarage.*	
30659	8497	Mabel Agatha Villiers, 1874.	
30660	8498	Katharine Helen Villiers, 1875.	
30661	8499	Lady Mary Agatha Russell, 1853. *Pembroke Lodge, Richmond, Surrey.*	} Younger daughter.

618. Descendants of the Hon. Isabella Elizabeth Byng, 1773–1830, wife of Thomas, 2nd Marquis of Bath, K.G., 1765–1837. (See Table XCVII.)

30662 -994	}	Same as Nos. 21654–21986.

619. Descendants, if any, of the Hon. William Cecil and the Hon. David Cecil, living 1643. (See Table XCVII.)

---

620. Descendants of Lady Barbara Ashley Cooper, 1788–1844, and her husband, William Francis, 1st Lord de Mauley, 1787–1855. (See Table XCVIII.)

30995 -1028	}	Same as Nos. 22517–22550.

621. Descendants of Cropley, 6th Earl of Shaftesbury, 1768–1851. (See Table XCVIII.)

| 31029 | 8500 | Anthony, 9th Earl of Shaftesbury [E.], 1869. *St. Giles' House, Salisbury. Belfast Castle, Belfast.* | { Great-grandchild. Son of Anthony, 8th Earl of Shaftesbury, 1831–1886, and grandson of Anthony, 7th Earl of Shaftesbury, K.G., 1801–1885. |
| 31030 -31 | } | Same as Nos. 22327–22328. | { Great-great-grandchildren. Children of No. 31029. |

31032	8501	Lady Margaret Emily, wife of Theophilus Basil Percy Levett, 1858. *Wychnor Park, co. Stafford.* *39 Wilton Crescent, S.W.*	Great-grandchildren. Elder sisters to No. 31029.
31033	8502	Evelyn Harriet, Lady Magheramorne [U.K.], 1865. *Magheramorne, co. Antrim.*	
31034	8503	Hon. Norah Evelyn M'Garet-Hogg, 1890.	Great-great-grandchild. Child of No. 31033.
31035	8504	Lady Mildred Georgiana, wife of the Hon. George Higgison Allsopp, M.P., 1867. *8 Hereford Gardens, S.W.*	Great-grandchild. 3rd sister to No. 31029.
31036	8505	Anthony Victor George Allsopp, 1899.	Great-great-grandchildren. Children of No. 31035.
31037	8506	Winifred Violet Allsopp, 1896.	
31038	8507	Susan Violet, Countess of Mar and Kellie [S.], 1868. *Alloa, Clackmannanshire.* *Kellie Castle, Fife.*	Great-grandchild. 4th sister to No. 31029.
31039	8508	John Francis Ashley, Lord Erskine, 1895.	Great-great-grandchildren. Sons of No. 31038.
31040	8509	Hon. Francis Walter Erskine, 1899.	
31041	8510	Lady Ethel Maud, wife of Captain Sir George John Scott Warrender, R.N., 7th Bart., 1870. *Bruntsfield House, Edinburgh.* *109 Gloucester Place, W.*	Great-grandchild. 6th sister to No. 31029.
31042	8511	Victor Alexander George Anthony Warrender, 1899.	Great-great-grandchildren. Children of No. 31041.
31043	8512	Violet Helen Marie Warrender, 1896.	
31044	8513	The Right Hon. (Anthony) Evelyn Melbourne Ashley - Cooper, P.C., 1836. *Broadlands, Romsay.*	Grandson. Eldest surviving son of Anthony, 7th Earl of Shaftesbury, K.G., 1801–1885.
31045	8514	Wilfred William Ashley-Cooper, Captain 3rd Battalion Hampshire Regiment, 1867.	Great-grandson. Son of No. 31044.
31046	8515	Edwina Annette Cynthia Ashley-Cooper, 1901.	Great-great-grandchild. Child of No. 31045.
31047	8516	Anthony Henry Evelyn Ashley-Cooper, 1894.	Great-grandchildren. Children of No. 31044.
31048	8517	Lilian Blanche Georgiana, wife of Major Hercules Arthur Pakenham, 1875.	
31049	8518	Hercules Dermot Wilfred Pakenham, 1901.	Great-great-grandchild. Child of No. 31048.
31050	8519	Hon. (Anthony) Lionel George Ashley, D.L., 1838. *Audley Mansions, South Audley Street, W.*	Grandchildren. Children of Anthony, 7th Earl of Shaftesbury, K.G., 1801–1885.
31051	8520	Hon. (Anthony) Cecil Ashley, D.L., 1849. *22 Halfmoon Street, W.*	
31052	8521	Victoria Elizabeth, Lady Templemore [U.K.], 1837. *11 Upper Grosvenor Street, W.*	
31053		Same as No. 27876.	Great-grandchild. Child of No. 31052.
31054	8522	Lady Edith Florence Ashley, 1847. *Audley Mansions, South Audley Street, W.*	Grandchild. Younger daughter of Anthony, 7th Earl of Shaftesbury, K.G., 1801–1885.
31055	8523	Margaret Jane Ashley, 1837.	Grandchildren. Children of Captain the Hon. (Anthony) Henry Ashley, M.P., 1807–1858.
31056	8524	Emily Frances, wife of Monsieur Henri de Satgé (3rd son of the 15th Viscount of Satgé de St. Jean, Chateau Castelnau, France), 1838. *Hartfield, Malvern Wells.*	

31057 -73	}	Same as Nos. 23495-23511.	Grandchildren, &c. Children of Lady Harriet Anne Ashley-Cooper, 1798-1868, and her husband, the Right Hon. Henry Thomas Lowry Corry, P.C., M.P., 1803-1873.

622. Descendants of Henry Charles Sturt, of Crichel, M.P., 1795-1866. (See Table XCVIII.)

31074 -99	}	Same as Nos. 20313-20338.

623. Descendants of Mary Ann Sturt, -1851, and her husband, the Rev. Frederick Ricketts, Rector of Eckington, Derby, -1843. (See Table XCVIII.)

31100	8525	Frederica Ricketts (living 1880).	Daughter.

624. Descendants, if any, of Lady Frances Ashley-Cooper, temp. 1750, wife of Francis Stonehouse, of Hungerford Park, Berks. (See Table XCVIII.)

625. Descendants of James Edward, 2nd Earl of Malmesbury, 1778-1841. (See Table XCVIII.)

31101	8526	James Edward, 5th Earl of Malmesbury [G.B.], 1872. *Heron Court, Christchurch, Hants.*	Great-grandchildren. Children of Edward James, 4th Earl of Malmesbury, 1842-1899, and grandchildren of Admiral the Hon. Sir Edward Alfred John Harris, R.N., K.C.B., 1808-1888.
31102	8527	Hon. Alexander Charles Harris, 1872. *Bachelors'.*	
31103	8528	Hon. Alfred Frederick William Harris, Lieutenant King's Royal Rifles, 1877. *Wellington.*	
31104	8529	Hon. John William Harris, Barrister Inner Temple, 1849. *East India United Service; National Liberal.*	Grandchildren. Children of Admiral the Hon. Sir Edward A. J. Harris. *See above.*
31105	8530	Lady Blanche Harriet Emma, widow of Captain Francis Henry Baillie, King's Royal Rifles, 1845-1879, 1850.	
31106	8531	Constance Ellen Baillie, 1878.	Great-grandchild. Child of No. 31105.
31107	8532	Dorothy Beatrice Rose Carew, 1881.	Great-grandchild. Daughter of Lady Rose Matilda Harris, 1852-1881, and her husband, Francis Henry Carew, 1852-1888, and granddaughter of the above-named Admiral the Hon. Sir Edward A. J. Harris.
31108	8533	Lady Florence Lucia, wife of Sir Charles Grant, K.C.S.I., 1854. *5 Marble Arch, W.*	Grandchild. Daughter of Admiral the Hon Sir Edward A. J. Harris. *See above.*

31109	8534	Allaster Edward George Grant, 1892.	{ Great-grandchild. Child of No. 31108.
31110	8535	Lady Alice Mary, wife of Colonel Henry Robert Eyre, *formerly* Coldstream Guards, 1857. 10 *Berkeley Square, W.*	{ Grandchild. Youngest daughter of Admiral the Hon. Sir Edward A. J. Harris. *See above.*

626. Descendants of the Rev. and Hon. Thomas Alfred Harris, Prebendary of York, 1782–1823. (See Table XCVIII.)

31111	8536	Charles Alfred Jameron, 1845.	{ Grandchild. Child of Louisa Cecilia Harris, 1820–1852, and her husband, M. Alfred Urbain Jameron, of Chatenay, near Tours.

627. Descendants of Lady Frances Harris, 1784–1847, wife of Lieut.-Gen. the Hon. Sir Galbraith Lowry Cole, G.C.B., 1772–1842. (See Table XCVIII.)

31112	8537	Arthur Willoughby George Lowry Cole, Major and Brevet-Colonel Royal Welsh Fusiliers, D.S.O., 1860.	
31113	8538	William John Lowry Cole, 1866.	Grandchildren. Children
31114	8539	Mary Frances Lowry Cole, 1856.	of Colonel Arthur Lowry
31115	8540	Florence Kate Lowry, wife of the Rev. Frank Henry Payne-Gallwey, 1857. *Chirk Vicarage, North Wales.*	Cole, C.B., 1817–1885.
31116	8541	Lowry Philip Payne-Gallwey, 1892.	
31117	8542	Philip Francis Payne-Gallwey, 1894.	Great-grandchildren. Chil-
31118	8543	Florence Mary Payne-Gallwey.	dren of No. 31115.
31119	8544	Beatrice Payne-Gallwey.	
31120	8545	Helen Isabel Payne-Gallwey.	
31121	8546	Maude Georgina Lowry Cole, 1859.	Grandchildren. Sisters of
31122	8547	Mabel Henrietta Lowry Cole, 1868.	Nos. 31112, &c.
31123	8548	Frances Maria Frederica Virginia Cole, 1824. 66 *Eaton Place, S.W.*	} Daughter.

628. Descendants, if any, of Lady Dorothy Ashley-Cooper, — 1749, and her husband, Edward Hooper, of Heron Court, Hants, and Boveridge, co. Dorset. (See Table XCVIII.)

629. Descendants of Edward, 2nd Earl of Powis, K.G., 1785–1848. (See Table XCIX.)

31124 –30	}	Same as Nos. 22472–22478.	{ Grandchildren, &c. Children, &c., of the Rt. Hon. Sir Percy Egerton Herbert, K.C.B., P.C., M.P., 1822–1876.
31131 –33	}	Same as Nos. 29403–29405.	{ Grandchildren. Children of the Very Rev. and Hon. George Herbert, Dean of Hereford, 1825–1894.

31134	8549	Edward William Herbert, C.B., Colonel, *late* Lieut.-Col. Commanding 4th Battalion King's Royal Rifle Corps, 1855. *Naval and Military ; Bachelors' ; Carlton.*	Grandson. Son of the Hon. Robert Charles Herbert, Barrister, 1827–1902.
31135	8550	Edward Robert Henry Herbert, 1889.	Great-grandchildren. Children of No. 31134.
31136	8551	Dorothy Marguerite Elizabeth Herbert, 1888.	
31137	8552	Phyllis Hedworth Camilla Herbert, 1894.	
31138	8553	Graham Cludde Herbert, Lieut.-Col. Commanding 3rd Battalion Royal Fusiliers (City of London Regiment), 1856. *Army and Navy ; Bachelors'.*	Grandchildren. Brothers and sisters of No. 31134.
31139	8554	Arthur Frederick Herbert, Lieutenant Royal Horse Artillery, King's Messenger, 1866. *22 Portman Street.*	
31140	8555	Florentia Caroline Herbert, 1858.	
31141	8556	Beatrice Mary, wife of George Henry Vaughan Jenkins, 1862. *Sydney, New South Wales.*	
31142	8557	Richard Charles Cluddie Jenkins, 1893.	Great-grandchildren. Children of No. 31141.
31143	8558	Victor George Herbert Jenkins, 1897.	
31144	8559	Annie Katherine Louisa Herbert, 1864.	Grandchild. Youngest sister of No. 31134.
31145	8560	Hon. William Henry Herbert, Major-General, *late* Colonel 4th West Indian Regiment, 1834. *Prestfelde, Shrewsbury.*	Youngest surviving son.
31146	8561	Henry James Herbert, 1882.	Grandchildren. Children of No. 31145.
31147	8562	Percy Mark Herbert, 1885.	
31148	8563	Lucy Edith Herbert, 1883.	
31149	8564	Alice Harriet Herbert, 1887.	
31150	8565	Lady Charlotte Elizabeth, widow of Hugh Montgomery, J.P., of Grey Abbey, co. Down, 1821–1894, 1821. *Grey Abbey, Newtonards, co. Down.*	Daughter.
31151	8566	William Edward Montgomery, Major-General, *late* Colonel 1st Battalion Scots Guards, 1847. *Grey Abbey, Newtonards, co. Down.*	Grandchildren. Children of No. 31150.
31152	8567	Robert Arthur Montgomery, C.B., Major-Gen. C.R.A., Southern District. *United Service.*	
31153	8568	Percy Hugh Seymour Montgomery, 1856. *Travellers' ; Junior Carlton.*	
31154	8569	Francis Henry Montgomery, 1857. *Junior Carlton.*	
31155	8570	George Fitzmaurice Montgomery, 1861.	
31156	8571	Lucy Florentia Montgomery.	
31157	8572	Edith Cecilia, wife of Colonel Henry Charles Geast Dugdale.	
31158	8573	Charles John Geast Dugdale, 1887.	Great-grandchild. Child of No. 31157.
31159	8574	Hugh Robert Edward Harrison, Lieutenant Grenadier Guards, 1875. *Guards'.*	Great-grandchildren. Children of Charlotte Henrietta Emily Montgomery, 18 – 19 , wife of Colonel Robert John Harrison, 18 –1894.
31160	8575	Cyril Price Harrison, 1880.	
31161	8576	Gwendolen Lucy Elizabeth Harrison, 1877.	
31162	8577	Evelyn Mary Montgomery.	Grandchild. 4th daughter of No. 31150.

The Blood Royal of Britain

630. Descendants of the Hon. Robert Henry Clive, of Oakly Park, Salop, M.P., 1789–1854. (See Table XCIX.)

31163 –71	}	Same as Nos. 30507–30515.	Grandchildren. Children of the Hon. Robert Windsor-Clive, M.P., 1824–1859.
31172	8578	Hon. George Herbert Windsor Windsor-Clive, J.P., D.L., late Lieut.-Col. Coldstream Guards, 1835. 12 *Stratford Place, W.*	} Son.
31173		Same as No. 20226.	Grandson. Son of No. 31172.
31174	8579	Edward Windsor Hussey, J.P., 1855. *Scotney Castle, Lamberhurst.*	Grandchildren. Children of the Hon. Henrietta Sarah Windsor-Clive, 1820–1899, wife of Edward Hussey, of Scotney Castle, Kent, 1807–1894.
31175	8580	William Clive Hussey, Major R.E., 1858. 113 *Park Street, Grosvenor Square, W.*	
31176		Same as No. 29404.	Great-grandchild. Son of No. 31175.
31177	8581	Arthur Herbert Hussey, Major R.A., 1863.	Grandchildren. Brothers and sisters to No. 31174, &c.
31178	8582	Henry Percy Hussey, 1865.	
31179	8583	Gertrude Anne Hussey, 1861.	
31180	8584	Mildred Harriet, wife of Sir Ralph Anstruther, 6th Bart., 1863. *Balcaskie, Pittenweem, Fife.*	
31181	8585	Robert Edward Anstruther, 1890.	Great-grandchildren. Children of No. 31180.
31182	8586	Margaret Christian Anstruther, 1887.	
31183	8587	Magdalen Janet Anstruther, 1889.	
31184	8588	Sarah Katherine Anstruther, 1894.	
31185	8589	Elizabeth Mildred Louisa Anstruther, 1896.	
31186	8590	Gertrude Mary Anstruther, 1900.	
31187	8591	Hon. Victoria Alexandrina, wife of the Rev. Edward ffarington Clayton, 1839. *The Rectory, Ludlow.*	} Daughter.
31188	8592	Edward Robert Clayton, Lieutenant Oxfordshire Light Infantry, 1877.	Grandchildren. Children of No. 31187.
31189	8593	Mildred Mary Clayton, 1876.	
31190	8594	Agnes Clayton, 1880.	

631. Descendants of Lady Henrietta Antonia Clive, 1786–1835, and her husband, Sir Watkin Williams Wynn, 5th Bart., M.P., 1772–1841. (See Table XCIX.)

31191 –221	}	Same as Nos. 24793–24823.

632. Descendants of William Henry Fellowes, M.P., of Ramsey Abbey, Hunts, 1769–1837. (See Table XCIX.)

31222	8595	William Henry, 2nd Baron De Ramsey [U.K.], 1848. *Ramsey Abbey, Hunts.* 3 *Belgrave Square, S.W.*	Grandson. Son of Edward, 1st Baron De Ramsey, 1809–1887.

433

3 I

31223	8596	Hon. Coulson Churchill Fellowes, Lieutenant 1st Life Guards, 1883.	Great-grandchildren. Children of No. 31222.
31224	8597	Hon. Reginald Ailwyn Fellowes, 1884.	
31225	8598	Hon. Alexandra Frances Anne Fellowes, 1880.	
31226	8599	Hon. Gladys Cecil Georgina Fellowes, 1885.	
31227	8600	Hon. Hermione Frances Caroline Fellowes, 1886.	
31228	8601	Hon. Sybil Inna Fellowes, 1888.	
31229	8602	Hon. Ailwyn Edward Fellowes, M.P., 1855. *Honingham Hall, Norwich.*	Grandson. Brother to No. 31222.
31230 –33		Same as Nos. 27931–27934.	Great-grandchildren. Children of No. 31229.
31234	8603	Hon. Inna, wife of Henry Laurence Whateley. *44 Eaton Square, S.W.*	Granddaughter. Sister to No. 31222.
31235	8604	Marion Emma, wife of Sir John Shelley, 9th Bart. *Shobrooke Park, Crediton.*	Granddaughter. Daughter of Richard Fellowes, *afterwards* Benyon, of Englefield, Berks, 1811–1897.
31236	8605	John Frederick Shelley, 1884.	Great-grandchildren. Children of No. 31235.
31237	8606	Richard Shelley, 1892.	
31238	8607	Elizabeth Marion Shelley.	
31239	8608	Constance May Shelley.	
31240	8609	Edith Gertrude, wife of Alfred Ernest Hoare. *51 Cadogan Gardens, S.W.*	Granddaughter. Sister to No. 31235.
31241	8610	Eustace Benyon Hoare, 1899.	Great-grandchildren. Children of No. 31240.
31242	8611	Reginald Alfred Hoare, 1900.	
31243	8612	Millicent Elizabeth Hoare, 1897.	
31244	8613	Julia, wife of Anthony Henry Wingfield, J.P. *18 Grosvenor Square, W.*	Granddaughter. Sister to No. 31235.
31245	8614	Anthony Edward Foulis Wingfield, 1892.	Great-grandchildren. Children of No. 31244.
31246	8615	Cecil Andrew Foulis Wingfield, 1895.	
31247	8616	James Herbert Benyon, *formerly* Fellowes, J.P., D.L., 1849. *Englefield House, near Reading.* *55 Pont Street, S.W.*	Grandson. Son of James Fellowes, of Kingston House, Dorchester, 1813–1889.
31248	8617	Henry Arthur Benyon.	Great-grandchildren. Children of No. 31247.
31249	8618	Gertrude, wife of the Rev. Francis E. Rooke. *Mortimer West End.*	
31250	8619	Henry Wallace Rooke, 1896.	Great-great-grandchildren. Children of No. 31249.
31251	8620	Marjorie Rooke.	
31252	8621	. . . . Benyon.	Great-grandchildren. Children of No. 31247.
31253	8622	. . . . Benyon.	
31254	8623	Malcolm Cosmo Bonsor, 1878.	Great-grandchildren. Children of Emily Gertrude Fellowes (sister to No. 31247), –1882, 1st wife of Henry Cosmo Orme Bonsor, M.P.
31255	8624	Reginald Bonsor, 1879.	
31256	8625	Robert Cecil Bonsor, 1880. *Kingswood Warren, Epsom, Surrey.*	
31257	8626	Arthur Charles Bonsor, 1882. *38 Belgrave Square, S.W.*	
31258	8627	Edith, wife of Henry Charles Thomas Hambro. *Milton Abbey, Dorset.*	
31259	8628	Valentine Hambro.	Great-great-grandchildren. Children of No. 31258.
31260	8629	Cecily Edith Hambro, 1899.	
31261	8630	Mary Emily, wife of Edward Hall Alderson. *25 Tite St., Chelsea.*	Great-grandchild. Sister to Nos. 31254, &c.
31262	8631	Pamela Vere Alderson, 1902.	Great-great-grandchild. Daughter of No. 31261.

| 31263 | 8632 | Georgina Charlotte, widow of Francis William Preston, 1851–1898. 16 *Montagu Square, S. W.* | Grandchild. Sister to No. 31247. |
| 31264 | 8633 | Violet Gertrude Alice Preston, 1894. | Great-grandchild. Daughter of No. 31263. |

633. Descendants, if any, of Vice-Admiral Edward Fellowes, of Little Gidding, Hants, 1772–18 . (See Table XCIX.)

634. Descendants of Newton, 4th Earl of Portsmouth, 1772–1854. (See Table XCIX.)

31265 –85	}	Same as Nos. 25058–25078.	Descendants of Isaac Newton, 5th Earl of Portsmouth, 1825–1891.
31286	8634	Nugent Chichester, Captain 7th Dragoons, 1827. *Calverleigh Court, Devon.*	Grandson. Son of the Lady Henrietta Caroline Fellowes, 1798–1880, wife of Joseph Chichester-Nagle, of Calverleigh, 1792–1880.
31287	8635	Joseph Chichester, Major Worcestershire Regiment, 1858.	
31288	8636	John Amyas Chichester, 1864.	
31289	8637	Philip Charles Chichester, 1865.	
31290	8638	Edward Chichester, 1866.	
31291	8639	Rev. Richard Chichester, 1867.	Great-grandchildren.
31292	8640	Walter Raleigh Chichester, Lieutenant Worcestershire Regiment, 1870.	Children of No. 31286.
31293	8641	Henrietta Chichester.	
31294	8642	Eveline Mary Chichester.	
31295	8643	Blanche Chichester.	
31296	8644	Lucy Chichester.	
31297	8645	Newton Charles Chichester, *late* Captain 7th Dragoons, 1828.	Grandson. Brother to No. 31286.
31298	8646	Frederick Newton Chichester, 1872.	Great-grandchildren. Children of No. 31297.
31299	8647	Cyril Ernest Chichester, 1873.	
31300	8648	Claude Oswald Chichester, 1876.	
31301	8649	Ivor Francis Chichester, 1876.	
31302	8650	Francis Sherard Chichester.	Grandchildren. Brother and sisters to No. 31286.
31303	8651	Urania Charlotte Chichester.	
31304	8652	Josephine, widow of Colonel Charles Lygon Cocks, D.L., 1821–1885. *Treverbyn-vean, Cornwall.*	
31305	8653	Josephine Una Cocks.	Great-grandchildren. Children of No. 31304.
31306	8654	Honoria Charlotte Cocks.	
31307 –31	}	Same as Nos. 25079–25103.	Daughters by 2nd wife, and their children.

635. Descendants, if any, of Lady Henrietta Dorothy Wallop, 1780–1862, wife of the Rev. John Comyns Churchill. (See Table XCIX.)

636. Descendants, if any, of Dorothy Herbert, 1709–1759, wife of John Harris, of Pickwell, co. Devon. (See Table XCIX.)

637. Descendants of the Rev. Folliott Herbert Walker Cornewall, D.D., successively Bishop of Bristol, Hereford, and Winchester, 1754–1831. (See Table XCIX.)

31332	8655	Henrietta, widow of the Hon. Spencer Lyttelton, 1818–1889. 11 *Eaton Terrace, S.W.*	Granddaughters. Daughters of Frederick Hamilton Cornewall, of Debury, 1791– .
31333	8656	Mary Fanny Cornewall.	
31334	8657	Herbert Somerset Hamilton Cornewall, 1826. *Haggard Road, Twickenham. Debury Hall, Salop.*	Grandson. Son of Herbert Cornewall, of Debury, 1794–1862.
31335	8658	Henry Folliott Hamilton Cornewall, 1864.	Great-grandchildren. Children of No. 31334.
31336	8659	Ada, wife of Andrew Soath.	
31337	8660	Charlotte Henrietta, wife of Dr. Walker. Children, if any, of No. 31337.	Grandchildren. Sisters to No. 31334.
31338	8661	Elizabeth Cornewall.	

638. Descendants, if any, of any brothers and sisters of Francis Herbert, M.P., Marlborough, 1696–17 . (See Table XCIX.)

639. Descendants, if any, of Mary Herbert (living ? 1710), wife 1st of William Nichols, and 2ndly of   Cæsar. (See Table XCIX.)

640. Descendants, if any, of the Hon. Alicia Herbert (living ? 1680), wife of John Buzzard, of Barby Manor, M.P. [? Paul Burrard.] (See Table XCIX.)

641. Descendants, if any, of Susan Napier (? 1719), wife of John Highlord, of Harrow, Frances Napier (? 1747), heiress of Luton Ho, Bedfordshire, or of Jane and Elizabeth Napier, living unmarried, 1741. (See Table C.)

642. Descendants, if any, of Katherine Courteen (sister of William Courteen, the great naturalist, 1642–1702), wife of Yongs. (See Table LXXXIII.)

643. Descendants, if any, of Charlotte Bowler, wife of Thomas Rishworth; of Elizabeth Bowler, wife of   Addy, living probably about 1740; of Frances Cutler, wife of Charles Wainwright; Helen Cutler; Penelope Cutler, wife of   ; Magdalen Cutler, wife of   Rotherford, of Worsborough; or of Grace Cutler, wife of Smith, of Hemsworth. (See Table CI.)

644. Descendants, if any, of Henry John Cutler, of Sidmouth, 1829–   ; Egerton Cutler, 1832–   ; Catherine Emma Cutler; Charles Cutler, of Calcutta, 1790–   ; Catherine Cutler; Elizabeth Cutler; and Eleanor Cutler; of George Henry Cutler, of Upton; Henry George Gervase Cutler; Frank Egerton Cutler; Fanny Annie Cutler; Eleanor Alice Cutler; Clara Sophia Cutler; Wingfield Cutler; Olive Cutler; Becket Cutler; Sarah Ellison Cutler,   –   , before 1838, wife of the Rev. Thomas Blackhall, Vicar of Tardebig, Worcester; Eleanor Cutler (? born about 1800), wife of the Rev. Robert Holdsworth, Vicar of Brixham; and of Katherine Cutler (born about 1730), wife of James Simms, of London, Merchant. (See Table CI.)

645. Descendants of Elizabeth Olive (? 1750), wife of Admiral Alexander Scott. (See Table CI.)

646. Descendants again, if any, of Henry John Cutler, of Sidmouth, 1829–   ; Egerton Cutler, 1832 –   ; Catherine Emma Cutler; Charles Cutler, of Calcutta, 1790–   ; Catherine Cutler; Elizabeth Cutler; and Eleanor Cutler. (See Table CI.)

647. Descendants, if any, of Anne Cutler, wife of Nathaniel Gall, of Chelsea, Merchant (? 1740); or of any sisters of Sir Egerton Cutler, 1678–   ; or of Magdalen Cutler, 1635–   , wife of the Rev. Henry Lewis; or Elizabeth Cutler, 1637–   , who married 1st as 2nd wife Sir Thomas Herbert, of Tintern, Bart., and 2ndly Henry Edmunds, of Worsborough. (See Table CI.)

648. Descendants of George Augustus Francis, 2nd Marquis of Hastings and 7th Earl of Loudoun, 1808–1844. (See Table CII.)

31339	8662	⛒ Charles Edward, 11th Earl of Loudoun [S.], 22nd Baron Botreaux, Hungerford, De Moleyns, and Hastings [E.], and 2nd Baron Donington [U.K.], 1855. *Loudoun Castle, Galston, N.B.*	Grandsons. Sons of Edith Maud, Countess of Loudoun (eldest daughter and co-heiress), 1833–1874, and her husband, Charles Frederic, Lord Donington, 1822–1895.
31340	8663	⛒ Hon. Paulyn Francis Cuthbert Rawdon-Hastings, *formerly* Abney-Hastings, 1856. *Towersey Manor, Thame, Oxford.*	

31341	8664	☐ Paulyn Charles James Reginald Rawdon-Hastings, 1889.	
31342	8665	☐ Edward Hugh Hastings Rawdon-Hastings, 1895.	Great-grandchildren. Children of No. 31340.
31343	8666	☐ Edith Maud Rawdon-Hastings, 1883.	
31344	8667	☐ Elizabeth Frances Rawdon-Hastings, 1884.	
31345	8668	☐ Flora Anne Rawdon-Hastings, 1885.	
31346	8669	☐ Isabel Jacqueline Rawdon-Hastings, 1887.	
31347	8670	☐ Hon. Gilbert Theophilus Clifton Clifton-Hastings-Campbell, *formerly* Abney-Hastings, 1859. *12 Hans Crescent, S.W.*	Grandson. Brother to Nos. 31339, &c.
31348	8671	☐ Margaret Selina Flora Maud Clifton-Hastings-Campbell, 1895.	Great-grandchildren. Children of No. 31347.
31349	8672	☐ Edith Winifred Lelgarde Clifton-Hastings-Campbell, 1897.	
31350	8673	☐ Irene Mary Egidia Clifton-Hastings-Campbell, 1898.	
31351	8674	☐ Rawdon George Grey, 24th Baron Grey de Ruthyn [E.], 1858. *Warton Hall, Lytham, Lancashire.*	Grandchildren. Children of Bertha Lelgarde, Lady Grey de Ruthyn (2nd daughter and co-heir), 1835–1887, and her husband, Augustus Wykeham Clifton.
31352	8675	☐ Hon. Cecil Talbot Clifton, 1862. *Northfields Ranche, Milner P.O., Montana, U.S.A.*	
31353	8676	☐ Hon. Ella Cecily Mary, wife of Lancelot George Butler-Bowdon, 1856. *Barlbro House, near Chesterfield.*	
31354	8677	John Lancelot Wykeham Butler-Bowdon, 1883.	Great-grandson. Son of No. 31353.
31355	8678	☐ Hon. Lelgarde Harry Florence, wife of Sir (Alan) Henry Bellingham, 4th Bart., 1870. *Bellingham Castle, Castle Bellingham, Louth.*	Granddaughter. Sister to Nos. 31351, &c.
31356	8679	☐ Count Hyacinth Edward Henry Charles Bodenham Lubienski, 1896.	Great-grandchildren. Children of Mary Evelyn Bertha Emily Kirwan, 1861–1902, wife of Count Louis Bodenham Lubienski, J.P., D.L., and grandchildren of the Lady Victoria Mary Louisa Rawdon-Hastings (3rd daughter and co-heir), 1837–1888, and her husband, John Forbes Stratford Kirwan, of Moyne, 1836–1892.
31357	8680	☐ Count Constantine Bodenham Lubienski, 1899 (twin).	*Rotherwas, Hereford; Bullingham Manor, Hereford.*
31358	8681	☐ Count Stanislaus Bodenham Lubienski, 1899 (twin).	
31359	8682	☐ May Flora Amy Kirwan, 1865. *49 Palace Court, Bayswater, W.*	Granddaughter. Daughter of the Lady Victoria Mary Louisa Rawdon-Hastings. *See above.*
31360	8683	☐ Frances Augusta Constance, Countess of [U.K.] and Baroness [G.B.] Romney, 1844. *4 Upper Belgrave Street, S.W.*	4th daughter and co-heir.
31361 –68	}	Same as Nos. 19825–19832.	Grandchildren, &c. Children of No. 31360.

649. Descendants of Lady Sophia Frederica Christiana Hastings, 1809–1859, wife of John, 2nd Marquis of Bute, K.T., 1793–1848. (See Table CII.)

31369 -72	}	Same as Nos. 28218–28221.	{ Grandchildren. Children of John Patrick, 3rd Marquis of Bute, K.T., 1847–1900.

650. Descendants of Lady Selina Constantia Hastings, 1810–1867, and her husband, Charles John Henry, –1879. (See Table CII.)

31373	8684	Mabel Henry.	
31374	8685	Agnes Henry.	} Daughters.
31375	8686	Eva Henry.	

651. Descendants of Elizabeth Anne Hastings, 1793–1874, wife of Major-General Lord George William Russell, G.C.B., 1790–1846. (See Table CII.)

31376 -95	}	Same as Nos. 30609–30628.

652. Descendants of George John, Viscount Forbes, 1785–1836. (See Table CII.)

31396 -400	}	Same as Nos. 23139–23143.	{ Grandchildren. Sons of George Arthur Hastings, 7th Earl of Granard, K.P., 1833–1889, by 2nd wife.
31401	8687	Lady Adelaide Jane Frances, widow of Lord Maurice FitzGerald, 1852–1901, 1860. *Johnstown Castle, co. Wexford.*	} Granddaughter. Daughter of George Arthur Hastings, 7th Earl of Granard, by 1st wife.
31402 -404	}	Same as Nos. 22303–22305.	{ Great-grandchildren. Children of No. 31401.
31405	8688	Lady Sophia Maria Elizabeth, wife of Sir Henry Christopher Grattan-Bellew, 3rd Bart., 1862. *Mount Bellew, co. Galway.*	} Granddaughter. Sister to No. 31401.
31406	8689	Herbert Michael Grattan-Bellew, 1886.	
31407	8690	Charlie Christopher Grattan-Bellew, 1887.	
31408	8691	William Arthur Grattan-Bellew, 1893.	} Great-grandchildren. Children of No. 31405.
31409	8692	Thomas Henry Grattan-Bellew, 1902.	
31410	8693	Helena Barbara Grattan-Bellew, 1889.	
31411	8694	Moira Jane Grattan-Bellew, 1891.	
31412	8695	Angela Mary Grattan-Bellew, 1894.	
31413 -14	}	Same as Nos. 23144–23145.	{ Granddaughters. Daughters of 7th Earl of Granard (*see above*), by 2nd wife.

31415	8696	George Francis Reginald Forbes, Captain 2nd Battalion Royal Irish Regiment, 1866.		
31416	8697	Ronald Ferdinande Forbes, 1879.	Grandchildren. Children of the Hon. William Francis Forbes, 1836–1899.	
31417	8698	Raymond Forbes, 1882.		
31418	8699	Angela Ida Evelyn Forbes, 1870.		
31419	8700	Flora Frances Forbes, 1877.		
31420	8701	Eva Adelaide Forbes, 1880.		

653. Descendants, if any, of Lady Charlotte Adelaide Constantia Rawdon, 1769–1834, wife of Hamilton FitzGerald. (See Table CII.)

---

654. Descendants of William Granville Hastings Medhurst, of Kippax Hall, York, 1789–1835. (See Table CIII.)

---

655. Descendants of the Rev. Charles Medhurst, afterwards Wheler, of Otterden Place, Kent, J.P., 1795–1877. (See Table CIII.)

31421	8702	Granville Charles Hastings Wheler, J.P., 1872. *Otterden Place, Kent.*	Grandchildren. Children of Charles Wheler Wheler, of Otterden Place, –1899.
31422	8703	George Bevil Hastings Wheler, 1874.	
31423	8704	Charles William Gilborne Hastings Wheler, 1880.	
31424	8705	Violet Grace Hastings Wheler, 1871.	
31425	8706	Anne Maria Wheler.	
31426	8707	Elizabeth Hastings, wife of Arthur Thomas Schreiber. *Becca Hall, Barwick-in-Elmet, Leeds.*	Elder daughters.
31427	8708	Evelyn Mary Bingham, wife of Captain Somerset Edward Deane Webb, York and Lancaster Regiment. *Hengeherst, Woodchurch, Kent.*	Grandchild. Daughter of No. 31426.
31428	8709	Hugh Molesworth St. Aubyn, *late* Captain 3rd Battalion Duke of Cornwall's Light Infantry, 1865. *Clowance, near Camborne, Cornwall.*	Grandchild. Son of Caroline Wheler, –1899, wife of the Rev. St. Aubyn Hender Molesworth St. Aubyn, of Clowance.
31429	8710	John Molesworth St. Aubyn, 1899.	Great-grandchildren. Children of No. 31428.
31430	8711	Guenevere May Molesworth St. Aubyn, 1895.	
31431	8712	Beville Molesworth St. Aubyn, 1871.	Grandchildren. Brother and sister to No. 31428.
31432	8713	Helen Flora, wife of the Rev. Charles Rowland Wynne de Cerjat. *Crowan Vicarage, Cornwall.*	
31433	8714	Charles Sigismund de Cerjat, 1895.	Great-grandchildren. Children of No. 31432.
31434	8715	Helen Dorothy de Cerjat, 1892.	
31435	8716	Anne Caroline, wife of Edward Harvey Williams. *Four-Burrow House, Scorrier, Cornwall.*	Grandchild. Younger sister to No. 31428.

656. Descendants, if any, of Catherine Sarah Anne Medhurst,   –
, wife (1831) of the Rev. Benjamin Edmondson, Vicar
of Collingham. (See Table CIII.)

657. Descendants of Thomas Loughnan Stuart-Menteth, Captain
16th Lancers, 1796–1854. (See Table CIII.)

31436	8717	Sir James Stuart-Menteth, *of Closeburn*, 3rd Bart., 1841. } Son. *Canandaigua, New York, U.S.A.*
31437	8718	Philadelphia Anna Stuart-Menteth. ⎱ Granddaughters. Daughters
31438	8719	Helen Isabel Stuart-Menteth. ⎰ of No. 31436.
31439	8720	Philadelphia, wife of Dr. Beard, 1834. Elder daughter. Children, if any, of No. 31440.
31440	8721	Alice Maria, wife of J. Tinley, 1853. Younger daughter. Children, if any, of No. 31441.

658. Descendants of Charles Granville Stuart-Menteth, of Entry
Hill House, Bath, 1800–1880. (See Table CIII.)

| 31441 | 8722 | Charles Granville Stuart-Menteth, J.P., 1828. } Son.
Rownhams Mount, near Southampton. |

659. Descendants of Colonel William Stuart - Menteth, Bengal
Army, 1805–1857. (See Table CIII.)

31442	8723	James Frederick Stuart-Menteth, Lieut.-Col. *late* 2nd ⎱ Son. Dragoon Guards, 1846. *Rownhams Mount, near Southampton.*
31443	8724	James Wallace Stuart-Menteth, 1871.
31444	8725	William Frederick Stuart-Menteth, 1874.
31445	8726	Walter Erskine Stuart-Menteth, 1877.
31446	8727	Arthur Hastings Stuart-Menteth, Lieutenant Grandchildren. unattached, 1882. Children of No. 31442.
31447	8728	Montagu Stuart-Menteth, 1893.
31448	8729	Lilian Frances Stuart-Menteth, 1884.
31449	8730	Margaret Alice Stuart-Menteth, 1889.
31450	8731	Katherine Olive Stuart-Menteth, 1890.
31451	8732	Alyson Mona Stuart-Menteth, 1895.
31452	8733	Ludivina, widow of Colonel Nembhard, –1856. Children, if any, of No. 31452.
31453	8734	Philadelphia Mary Grace, wife of Colonel Francis George ⎱ Daughters. Savage Curtis, C.M.G. [*Army and Navy*].
31454	8735	Helen Grace Stuart-Menteth Curtis. ⎰ Granddaughter. Daugh- ter of No. 31453.
31455	8736	Sarah Selina Hamilton, widow of Colonel Gerard Noel Money, C.B., –1895. Children, if any, of No. 31455. Daughters.
31456	8737	Harriet Rose Amy, wife of Colonel George Fletcher Ottley Boughey, C.S.I.

31457	8738	George Menteth Boughey, 1879.	
31458	8739	Amy Matilda, wife of William Arthur Briscoe.	Grandchildren.
31459	8740	Elizabeth Mabws, wife of Captain Duncan Darroch, 2nd Battalion Princess Louise's (Argyll and Sutherland Highlanders).	Children of No. 31456.
31460	8741	. . . . Darroch.	Great-granddaughter. Daughter of No. 31459.
31461	8742	Alice Annie Campbell, wife of Colonel Henry Doveton Hutchinson, I.S.C., *late* Director of Military Education in India.	Daughters.
31462	8743	Emily Edith Ada, wife of Captain James Edward Whiting, R.E.	

660. Descendants of the Rev. Francis Hastings Stuart-Menteth, Vicar of Thorpe Arch, Yorks, 1807–1875. (See Table CIII.)

31463	8744	Rosa Mary, widow of the Rev. George William Coopland, –1857.	Daughter.
31464	8745	Rev. George Bertram Philpot Coopland, 1857. *Honeybourne Vicarage, Worcestershire.*	Grandson. Only child of No. 31463.
31465	8746	Ludivina Sophia, wife of the Rev. D. H. Jackson. *The Vicarage, Thorpe Arch, Yorks.*	Daughters.
31466	8747	Catherine Maria, wife of the Rev. Thomas Hotchkin Vines. *Fiskerton Rectory, Lincoln.*	
31467	8748	Thomas Humfrey Vines, 1864.	Grandchildren. Children of No. 31466.
31468	8749	Walter Stuart Menteth Vines, 1867.	
31469	8750	Charles Granville Vines, 1873.	
31470	8751	Clement Erskine Vines, 1878.	

661. Descendants of Alexander Stuart-Menteth, 1809–1885. (See Table CIII.)

31471	8752	Patrick William Stuart-Menteth, 1845. *St. Jean de Luz, France.*	Sons.
31472	8753	Andrew Agnew Stuart-Menteth, *late* a Member of the House of Representatives, New Zealand, 1853. *Wellington, New Zealand.*	
31473	8754	Charles Bruce Stuart-Menteth, 1892.	Grandchildren. Children of No. 31472
31474	8755	. . . . Stuart-Menteth, 1893.	
31475	8756	Thomas Alexander Stuart-Menteth, 1901.	
31476	8757	Lois Elaine Stuart-Menteth, 1887.	
31477	8758	Valerie Harriet Stuart-Menteth, 1889.	
31478	8759	Jean Antoinette Stuart-Menteth, 1898.	

662. Descendants of the Rev. Granville Wheler Stuart-Menteth, Rector of Morcott, 1811–1887. (See Table CIII.)

31479	8760	Granville Thorold Stuart-Menteth, B.A., 1838. *Toftrees, East Molesey, Surrey.*	Son.
31480	8761	Charles Granville Stuart-Menteth, 1868.	Grandchildren. Children of No. 31479.
31481	8762	Rev. Edward Thorold Stuart-Menteth, 1871.	
31482	8763	Evelyn Ogilvy Stuart-Menteth, 1866.	
31483	8764	Mary Oliver Stuart-Menteth, 1875.	
31484	8765	Ludivina Granville Stuart-Menteth.	

663. Descendants, if any, of the brothers and sisters, if any, of Sir Charles Granville Stuart-Menteth, 1st Bart., 1769–1847. (See Table CIII.)

664. Descendants, if any, of Lady Margaret Hastings, 1700–1768, wife of the Rev. Benjamin Ingham, Rector of Aberford, 1712– . (See Table CII.)

665. Descendants, if any, of Lady Mary Hastings (? 1690), wife of Sir William Jolliffe, of Caverswell Castle, Stafford, Knight. (See Table CII.)

666. Descendants of James, Lord Glenlyon, 1782–1837. (See Table CIV.)

31485 –92	}	Same as Nos. 20946–20953.

667. Descendants of John Murray Drummond, of Megginch Castle, co. Perth, 1803–1889. (See Table CIV.)

31493	8766	Malcolm Drummond, J.P., D.L., *late* Captain Grenadier Guards, 1856. *Megginch Castle, Errol, co. Perth.*	} Son.
31494	8767	John Drummond, 1900.	
31495	8768	Jean Drummond.	Grandchildren. Children of No. 31493.
31496	8769	Victoria Alexandrina Frances Drummond.	
31497	8770	Frances Ada Drummond.	
31498	8771	Mary Drummond.	Daughter.

668. Descendants of Colonel Adam Augustus Drummond, 1806–1873. (See Table CIV.)

669. Descendants of Colonel Henry Maurice Drummond, of Seggieden, 1814–1896. (See Table CIV.)

31499	8772	James Adam Gordon Drummond-Hay, Major and Brevet-Lieut.-Col. Coldstream Guards, 1863. *Seggieden, Perth.*	
31500	8773	Henry Maurice Drummond-Hay, 1865.	Children.
31501	8774	Constance Margaret Jane Drummond-Hay.	
31502	8775	Alice Charlotte Drummond-Hay.	
31503	8776	Lucy Barbara Drummond-Hay.	
31504	8777	Edith Maude Drummond-Hay.	

670. Descendants of William Henry, 9th Viscount Strathallan, 1810-1886. (See Table CIV.)

31505	8778	William Huntley, 11th Viscount Strathallan [S.], 1871. *Machnay, Perthshire.*	
31506	8779	Hon. James Eric Drummond, Clerk in the Foreign Office, 1876.	Grandchildren. Children of James David, 10th Viscount Strathallan, 1839-1893.
31507	8780	Hon. Maurice Charles Andrew Drummond, Lieutenant Black Watch, 1877.	
31508	8781	Hon. Edmund Rupert Drummond, Midshipman R.N., 1884.	
31509	8782	Hon. Margaret Cecily Drummond, 1880.	
31510	8783	Hon. Sybil Frances Drummond, 1881.	
31511	8784	Hon. Robert Charles Drummond, *late* Captain Seaforth Highlanders, 1850. *Naval and Military.*	Children.
31512	8785	Hon. Amelia Anne, wife of Lieut.-Col. Charles Greenhill-Gardyne, *formerly* Coldstream Guards, 1836. *Finavon, Forfarshire.*	
31513	8786	Alan David Greenhill-Gardyne, Major Gordon Highlanders, 1868.	Grandchildren. Children of No. 31512.
31514	8787	Walter Greenhill-Gardyne, 1874.	
31515	8788	Mary Beatrice Greenhill-Gardyne, 1859.	
31516	8789	Helen Margaret Greenhill-Gardyne, 1860.	
31517	8790	Elizabeth Constance, wife of Lieut.-Col. Lionel Dudley Mackinnon (*formerly* 1st Battalion Coldstream Guards), 1861. *Dochgarroch, Inverness-shire.*	
31518	8791	Kenneth Mackinnon, 1881.	Great-grandchildren. Children of No. 31517.
31519	8792	Lionel Neil Alexander Mackinnon, 1884.	
31520	8793	Sheila Helen Mackinnon, 1886.	
31521	8794	Olive Mary Mackinnon, 1888.	
31522	8795	Agnes Hersey Greenhill-Gardyne, 1865.	Grandchildren. Younger daughters of No. 31512.
31523	8796	Emily Dora Greenhill-Gardyne, 1871.	
31524	8797	Alice Henrietta Greenhill-Gardyne, 1875.	
31525	8798	Hon. Hersey Annabella Drummond, 1846.	Younger daughters.
31526	8799	Hon. Frances Mary Drummond, sometime (1872-1901) Maid of Honour to Queen Victoria. *36 South Eaton Place, S.W.*	

671. Descendants of Admiral the Hon. Sir James Robert Drummond, G.C.B., 1812-1895. (See Table CIV.)

31527	8800	Laurence George Drummond, Major 3rd Battalion Scots Guards, and Military Secretary to Governor-General of Canada, 1861. *69 Cadogan Square, S.W.*	Son.
31528	8801	Lindsay Drummond, 1891.	Grandchildren. Children of No. 31527.
31529	8802	Stella Katherine Drummond, 1895.	
31530	8803	Lilias Anne Drummond, 1856.	Daughters.
31531	8804	Kate Gertrude Drummond, 1858.	
31532	8805	Mary Virginia Drummond, 1859.	

The Blood Royal of Britain

672. Descendants of the Hon. Sir Edmund Drummond, K.C.I.E., 1814-1895. (See Table CIV.)

31533	8806	Edmund Charles Drummond, Vice-Admiral R.N., 1841. *United Service.*	} Son.
31534	8807	John Edmund Drummond, Commander R.N., 1873.	} Grandchildren. Children of No. 31533.
31535	8808	Mary Drummond, 1877.	
31536	8809	Constance Dora Drummond, 1878.	
31537	8810	Francis Colebrooke Beresford-Drummond, *late* Captain 3rd Battalion Dorsetshire Regiment, 1846.	} 2nd son and daughters.
31538	8811	Julia Maria, wife of Horace Abel Cockerell, C.S.I., Secretary to Government of Bengal.	
31539	8812	Marianne Amelia Drummond, 1848. 36 *South Eaton Place, S.W.*	

31540	8813	Hon. Francis Charles Drummond, 1815. 58 *St George's Square, S.W.*	} Table CIV.

673. Descendants of the Hon. Robert Andrew John Drummond, I.C.S., 1820-1887. (See Table CIV.)

31541	8814	Malcolm Drummond, 1857.	} Sons.
31542	8815	Rev. Henry Murray Drummond, 1858. *The Rectory, Lonmay, Aberdeenshire.*	
31543	8816	Henry Murray Drummond, 1893.	} Grandchildren. Children of No. 31542.
31544	8817	Anna Maud Drummond, 1889.	
31545	8818	Olivia Margaret Murray Drummond, 1891.	
31546	8819	Walter John Drummond, 1861.	} Children.
31547	8820	Robert Hugh Drummond, 1862.	
31548	8821	Herbert Charles Drummond, 1864.	
31549	8822	Arthur David Drummond, 1865.	
31550	8823	Rev. Ernest George Drummond, 1868. *Edmondsham Rectory, Dorset.*	
31551	8824	Anna Euphemia Drummond, 1859.	

674. Descendants of the Hon. Marianne Jane Drummond, 1811-1876, and her husband, George Drummond-Græme, of Inchbrackie and Aberuthven, co. Perth, -1854. (See Table CIV.)

31552	8825	Patrick James Frederick Græme, *late* 79th Highlanders, 1849. *Lake Dauphin, Manitoba, Canada.*	} Son and daughter.
31553	8826	Amelia Anne Margaret, widow of Colonel Arwed Giersberg, of the German Army, -1899.	
31554	8827	Albert George Fergus Giersberg, 1875.	} Grandchildren. Children of No. 31553.
31555	8828	Perceval James Amelius Græme Giersberg, 1884.	
31556	8829	Marianne Jane Constance, wife of Laurence Ayscough Clarke, 1877.	
31557	8830	Enid Giersberg, 1880.	
31558	8831	Beatrice Marianne Jane Græme, Lady Superintendent Nurses' Home, Perth, 1851.	} Daughter.

The Blood Royal of Britain

675. Descendants of Lady Elizabeth Murray, 1787–1846, and her husband, General Sir Evan John Murray, afterwards MacGregor, K.C.B., G.C.H., 2nd Bart., 1785–1841. (See Table CIV.)

31559	8832	Sir Malcolm MacGregor, 5th Bart., Chief of Clan Gregor, 1873. *Edinchip, Lochearnhead, Perthshire.*	Great-grandson. Son of Rear-Admiral Sir Malcolm MacGregor, 4th Bart., 1834–1879, and grandson of Sir John Atholl Bannatyne Mac-Gregor, 3rd Bart., 1810–1851.
31560	8833	Alexander Ronald MacGregor, 1878.	
31561	8834	Malvina Charlotte, wife of the Hon. Granville William Richard Somerset, 1865. 5 *Tile Street, Chelsea, S.W.*	
31562	8835	Richard Granville Somerset, 1894.	Great-great-grandson. Son of No. 31561.
31563	8836	Margaret Helen Mary, wife of the Hon. Alan David Murray, 1867. *Moneydie House, Redgorton, Perth.*	Great-granddaughter. Sister to No. 31559.
31564	8837	Mungo David Malcolm Murray, 1899.	Great-great-grandchild. Child of No. 31563.
31565	8838	Maryel Alpina MacGregor, 1875.	Great-granddaughter. Sister to No. 31559.
31566	8839	Atholl MacGregor, *late* British Resident at Travancore, 1836. *Ard Choille, Perth.*	Grandson. Son of Sir John A. B. MacGregor, 3rd Bart., 1810–1851.
31567	8840	John Atholl MacGregor, 1880.	Great-grandchildren. Children of No 31566.
31568	8841	Robert Menzies MacGregor, 1882.	
31569	8842	Evan Malcolm MacGregor, 1883.	
31570	8843	Morna MacGregor, 1887.	
31571	8844	Sir Evan MacGregor, K.C.B., Permanent Secretary to the Admiralty, 1842. 3 *Egerton Place, S.W.*	Grandson. Next surviving brother to No. 31566.
31572	8845	Eva Mary MacGregor, 1885.	Great-grandchild. Child of No. 31571.
31573	8846	Emily Louisa, Viscountess Stormont, 1838. 41 *Upper Grosvenor Street, W.*	Granddaughter. Eldest sister of No. 31566.
31574	8847	William David, 5th Earl of Mansfield and Mansfield [G.B.], 10th Viscount Stormont [S.], 1860. 6 *St James' Place, S.W.*	Great-grandchildren. Children of No. 31573.
31575	8848	Hon. Alan David Murray, 1864. *Moneydie House, Redgorton, Perthshire.*	
31576		Same as No. 31564.	Great-great-grandchild. Child of No. 31575.
31577	8849	Hon. Alexander David Murray, Captain 3rd Battalion Black Watch, 1871. *Scones, Lethendy, Perthshire.*	Great-grandchildren. Children of No. 31573.
31578	8850	Lady Marjory Louisa, wife of Sir Kenneth John Mackenzie, 7th Bart., 1862. 10 *Moray Place, Edinburgh.*	
31579	8851	Hector David Mackenzie, 1893.	Great-great-grandchildren. Children of No. 31578.
31580	8852	Roderick Ian Mackenzie, 1895.	
31581	8853	Marjory Kythé Mackenzie, 1892.	
31582	8854	Lady Mabel Emily Murray, 1866.	Great-grandchild. Younger daughter of No. 31573.
31583	8855	Mary Elizabeth, wife of John Charles Thynne, 1848. 17B *Great Cumberland Place, W.*	Granddaughter. Younger sister of No. 31566.

31584 –88	}	Same as Nos. 21701–21705.	{ Great-grandchildren. Children of No. 31583.
31589	8856	Roderick Dhu Glenlyon Hamilton Burgoyne, Captain *late* 93rd Highlanders, 1837. *Kinghorn, Fife.*	Grandson. Son of Jane Anna Maria Macgregor, 1812–1880, and her 1st husband, John James Hamilton Burgoyne, 93rd Highlanders, 18 –18 .
31590	8857	Roderick Murrie Burgoyne, Captain Royal Scots Fusiliers, 1875.	Great-grandchildren. Children of No. 31589.
31591	8858	Margaret Emilia, wife of Frederick Wilfred Brunner, Captain R.E.	
31592	8859	Ernest Francis Evan Burgoyne, 1850.	
31593	8860	Isabella Abercorn, wife of Michael Le Renord, Chevalier of the Legion of Honour, 1841. *St. Briene, France.*	Grandchildren. Brother and sister of No. 31589.
31594	8861	. . . . Le Renord.	Great-grandchildren.
31595	8862	. . . . Le Renord.	Children of No.
31596	8863	. . . . Le Renord.	31593.
31597	8864	Arthur Maurice Cecil Blake, 1842. 80 *Guildhall Street, Bury St. Edmunds.*	Grandson. Son of Elizabeth Mary Anne Macgregor, 1816–1857, wife of Joseph Blake, of London, 18 – 18 .
31598	8865	Amelia Georgiana Murray MacGregor, 1829. 7 *Barossa Place, Perth.*	Daughter.

676. Descendants of the Right Rev. George Murray, Bishop of Sodor and Man (1814–1827), and of Rochester (1827–1860), 1784–1860. (See Table CV.)

31599	8866	▽ ▽ Sir George Herbert Murray, K.C.B., Secretary to the General Post Office, 1849. 50 *Grosvenor Gardens, S.W.*	Grandchild. Child of the Rev. George Edward Murray, 1818–1854.
31600	8867	▽ ▽ George Evelyn Pemberton Murray, 1880.	Great-grandchildren. Children of No. 31599.
31601	8868	▽ ▽ Irene Helen Murray, 1882.	
31602	8869	▽ ▽ Arthur Mordaunt Murray, Col. R.A., Assistant Commandant Royal Military Academy, Woolwich, 1852. *Woolwich.*	Grandchild. Brother to No. 31599.
31603	8870	▽ ▽ Arthur Stewart Pakington Murray, 1899.	Great-grandchildren. Children of No. 31602.
31604	8871	▽ ▽ Godfrey Pemberton Murray, 1901.	
31605	8872	▽ ▽ Helen Isabel Murray, 1896.	
31606	8873	▽ ▽ The Rev. Douglas Stuart Murray, 1853. *Blithfield Rectory, Rugeley, Staffordshire.*	Grandchild. Brother to No. 31599.
31607	8874	▽ ▽ Walter Murray, 1882.	Great-grandchildren. Children of No. 31606.
31608	8875	▽ ▽ George Murray, 1884.	
31609	8876	▽ ▽ Leonard Murray, 1896.	
31610	8877	▽ ▽ Edward Murray, 1899.	
31611	8878	▽ ▽ Emily Murray, 1886.	
31612	8879	▽ ▽ Mabel Murray, 1888.	
31613	8880	▽ ▽ Margaret Murray, 1894.	
31614	8881	▽ ▽ Alice Lilian, wife of the Rev. John Duncan, 1850. *Calne Vicarage, Wilts.*	Grandchild. Sister to No. 31599.

31615	8882	John Murray Duncan, 1884. ⎫	Great-grandchildren. Children of No. 31614.
31616	8883	Isabel Frances Duncan, 1872. ⎭	
31617	8884	☐ ☐ Marion Georgina Murray, 1854. *Highlands, Calne.*	Grandchild. Younger sister to No. 31599.
31618	8885	☐ ☐ Henry Edward Murray-Anderdon, J.P., 1848. *Henlade House, Taunton,* *27 Sloane Gardens, S.W.*	Grandson. Son of the Rev. Francis Henry Murray, 1820–1902.
31619	8886	☐ ☐ Robert Hay Murray, J.P., D.L., 1826. *Spinfield, Great Marlow, Bucks.*	Son.
31620	8887	☐ ☐ Robert Evelyn Hay Murray, 1851. *37 Elm Park Gardens, S.W.* *Hoe Farm House, Hascombe, Godalming.*	Grandson. Son of No. 31619.
31621	8888	☐ ☐ Eleanor Marjorie Hay Murray, 1880.	
31622	8889	☐ ☐ Augusta Muriel Hay Murray, 1882.	Great-grandchildren.
31623	8890	☐ ☐ Audrey Frances Hay Murray, 1884.	Children of No. 31620.
31624	8891	☐ ☐ Rhona Evelyn Hay Murray, 1888.	
31625	8892	☐ ☐ Mary Sancta Hay Murray, 1896.	
31626	8893	☐ ☐ Eleanor Augusta Hay, wife of Lionel Knight Rice [*Union Club*], 1860.	Grandchildren. Children of No. 31619.
31627	8894	☐ ☐ Edith Selina Hay, wife of Robert Leigh Pemberton, J.P. [*Army and Navy*], 1852.	
31628	8895	Robert Douglas Leigh Pemberton, 1896.	Great-grandchildren.
31629	8896	Nora Edith Pemberton, 1884.	Children of No. 31627.
31630	8897	Elsie Alice Pemberton, 1889.	
31631	8898	☐ ☐ Alice Lima Hay, wife of Edward Walter Archer, Chief Inspector of Fisheries for England, 1855.	Grandchild. 3rd daughter of No. 31619.
31632	8899	Hugh Edward Murray Archer, 1879.	
31633	8900	Harold Walter Archer, 1880.	Great-grandchildren.
31634	8901	Norman Archer, 1892.	Children of No. 31631.
31635	8902	Olive Eleanor Archer, 1882.	
31636	8903	Violet Ruth Archer, ⎱ twins, 1886.	
31637	8904	Esther Lima Archer, ⎰	
31638	8905	☐ ☐ Augusta Eleanor Hay, widow of Colonel Ormelie Campbell Hannay, –1901, 1857.	Grandchild. 4th daughter of No. 31619.
31639	8906	Robert Ormelie Fraser Hannay, 1883.	Great-grandchildren. Children of No. 31638.
31640	8907	☐ ☐ Mary Louisa Hay, wife of Arthur Egerton Leigh, J.P., 1859. *The Manor House, Sherborne, Dorset.*	Grandchild. 5th daughter of No. 31619.
31641		Same as No. 29922.	Great-grandchild. Child of No. 31640.
31642	8908	☐ ☐ Sir Herbert Harley Murray, K.C.B., *formerly* Governor of Newfoundland, 1829. *67 Eccleston Square, S.W.*	Son.
31643	8909	☐ ☐ Stewart Lygon Murray, Captain 1st Battalion Gordon Highlanders, 1863.	Grandson. Son of No. 31642.
31644	8910	☐ ☐ Elsie Dorothea Isabel Murray, 1897.	Great-granddaughter. Daughter of No. 31643.
31645	8911	☐ ☐ Gerald Otway Hay Murray, 1868.	
31646	8912	☐ ☐ Keith Norman Ward Murray, 1873.	Grandchildren.
31647	8913	☐ ☐ Mona Elizabeth Louise Murray, 1861.	Children of No. 31642.
31648	8914	☐ ☐ Maud Louise Rosalind Murray, 1864.	
31649	8915	☐ ☐ Isabel Salisbury Mabel Murray, 1871.	
31650	8916	☐ ☐ Rev. Frederick William Murray, Hon. Canon of Rochester, 1831. *Stone Rectory, Dartford.*	Son.

MARY QUEEN OF SCOTS.
1542-1587.
DRAWN BY FRANÇOIS CLOUET.

31651	8917	⋃ ⋃ Rev. Frederick Auriol Murray, 1865. *St. Peter's Vicarage, Rickmansworth.*	Grandchild. Child of No. 31650.
31652	8918	⋃ ⋃ Maurice Austin Murray, 1895.	Great-grandchildren. Children of No. 31651.
31653	8919	⋃ ⋃ George Ronald Auriol Murray, 1900.	
31654	8920	⋃ ⋃ Rev. Charles Hay Murray, 1869. *Firsby Rectory, Lincolnshire.*	
31655	8921	⋃ ⋃ Rev. Maurice William Murray, 1870. *Stone, Dartford, Kent.*	Grandchildren. Children of No. 31650.
31656	8922	⋃ ⋃ Cecil Austin Murray, 1872.	
31657	8923	⋃ ⋃ Mildred Sarah Maria Murray, 1874.	
31658	8924	⋃ ⋃ Geraldine Mary Murray, 1876.	
31659	8925	⋃ ⋃ Lilian Augusta, wife of Walter de Mérindol Malan, I.C.S. *Punjab.*	
31660	8926	John Charles, 4th Marquis [U.K.], and 5th Earl [G.B.], Camden, 1872. *Bayham Abbey, Lamberhurst.*	Great-grandson. Son of John Charles, 3rd Marquis Camden, 1840–1872, and grandson of George Charles, 2nd Marquis Camden, K.G., 1799–1866, and Harriet Murray, 1813–1854.
31661		Same as No. 27119.	Great-great-grandchild. Child of No. 31660.
31662	8927	Lady Clementine Frances Anne, wife of the Hon. Arthur Henry John Walsh, 1870. *Warfield Park, Bracknell, Berks.*	Great-granddaughter. Sister to No. 31660.
31663	8928	Lord George Murray Pratt, 1843. *Meadow Bank, Winkfield, Windsor.*	Grandchildren. Sons of George Charles, 2nd Marquis Camden, K.G., 1799–1866, and Harriet Murray,1813–1854.
31664	8929	Lord Charles Robert Pratt, *late* Colonel Oxfordshire Light Infantry, 1847. *Hilden Oaks, Tonbridge.*	
31665	8930	Cecil John Charles Pratt, ⎰ twins,	Great-grandchildren. Children of No. 31664.
31666	8931	Ronald Arthur Frederick Pratt,⎱ 1886.	
31667	8932	Sybyl Madeline Georgina Pratt, 1883.	
31668	8933	Lady Frances Sarah Harriet Pratt, 1836. *The Grove, Seal, Sevenoaks.*	
31669	8934	Lady Caroline Elizabeth Pratt, 1839.	
31670	8935	Lady Augusta Georgiana Pratt, 1844.	Grandchildren. Sisters to No. 31663.
31671	8936	Lady Eleanor Margaret Pratt, 1845.	
31672	8937	Lady Mary Eleanor Elizabeth Pratt, 1849.	
31673	8938	Lady Elizabeth Louisa Pratt, 1850.	
31674	8939	Lady Clara Isabella Pratt, 1852.	
31675	8940	Lady Theresa Sarah Pratt, 1853.	
31676	8941	⋃ ⋃ Caroline Sophia, Lady Mordaunt, 1814. 63 *Warwick Square, S.W.*	Daughter.
31677		Same as No. 19671.	Great-grandson. Son of Sir Charles Mordaunt, 10th Bart., 1836–1897, and grandson of No. 31676 by 1st husband, Sir John Mordaunt, 9th Bart., 1808–1845.
31678	8942	Violet Caroline, Marchioness of Bath [G.B.], Viscountess Weymouth [E.]. *Longleat, Warminster.*	Great-granddaughter. Daughter of Sir Charles Mordaunt, 10th Bart., 1836–1897 (by 1st wife), and granddaughter of No. 31676.
31679 –81		Same as Nos. 21655–21657.	Great-great-grandchildren. Children of No. 31678.
31682 –86		Same as Nos. 19672–19676.	Great-granddaughters. Daughters of Sir Charles Mordaunt, 10th Bart., 1836–1897, by 2nd wife.

31687	8943	John Murray Mordaunt, J.P., D.L., 1837. 66 *Eccleston Square, S.W.*	} Grandson. Son of No. 31676.
31688 -93	}	Same as Nos. 26311–26316.	{ Great-grandchildren. Children of No. 31687.
31694	8944	Rev. Osbert Mordaunt, 1842. *Hampton Lucy Rectory, Warwick.*	} Grandson. Son of No. 31676.
31695	8945	Caroline Mordaunt.	} Great-grandchildren. Children of No.
31696	8946	Bridget Mordaunt.	} 31694.
31697	8947	Mary Augusta, wife of the Rev. Humphrey Farran Hall. *Leasbrook, Dixton, Monmouth.*	
31698	8948	Alice, wife of the Rev. and Hon. Walter Berkeley Portman. *Corton Denham Rectory, Sherborne*	Grandchildren. Daughters of No. 31676.
31699	8949	Rev. Alan Berkeley Portman, 1872.	
31700	8950	Lionel Portman, 1873.	Great-grandchildren. Children of No.
31701	8951	Francis John Portman, 1878.	31698.
31702	8952	Ethel Portman, 1866.	
31703	8953	Eleanor, wife of John Frederick Clerk. *Harmer Green, Welwyn.*	Granddaughter. Elder daughter of No. 31676, by 2nd husband, Captain Gustavus Thomas Smith, –1875.
31704	8954	Aylmer Gustavus Clerk, 1888.	
31705	8955	Violet Clerk, 1886.	Great-grandchildren. Children of No. 31703.
31706	8956	Sybel Agnes Clerk, 1892.	
31707	8957	Constance, widow of Major Cooper, R.A., 1851–1890. 24 *Christ Church Road, Folkestone.*	Granddaughter. Youngest daughter of No. 31676, by 2nd husband. *See above.*
31708	8958	John Gustavus Cooper, 1889.	Great-grandchildren.
31709	8959	Gladys Eleanor Mary Cooper, 1883.	Children of No.
31710	8960	Geraldine Mary Cooper, 1887.	31707.
31711	8961	Herbert Perrott Murray, 3rd Lord Hampton [G.B.], 1848. *Waresley Court, Kidderminster.*	Grandson. Son of Augusta Murray, 1814–1848, and the Right Hon. Sir John Somerset Pakington, 1st Lord Hampton, 1799–1880.
31712	8962	Hon. Herbert Stuart Pakington, 1883.	
31713	8963	Hon. Hugh Charles Swinton Pakington, 1887.	
31714	8964	Hon. Humphrey Arthur Pakington, 1888.	
31715	8965	Hon. Mary Augusta Pakington, 1878.	Great-grandchildren.
31716	8966	Hon. Edith Frances Pakington, 1879.	Children of No.
31717	8967	Hon. Dorothy Alice Pakington, 1882.	31711.
31718	8968	Hon. Eleanor Gertrude Pakington, 1884.	
31719	8969	Hon. Hester Murray Pakington, 1893.	
31720	8970	Edward Roger Murray Pratt, J.P., Colonel *late* Norfolk Artillery, 1847. *Ryston Hall, near Downham, Norfolk.*	Grandson. Son of Mary Louisa Murray, 1823–1878, and her husband, the Rev. Jermyn Pratt, of Ryston, 1798–1867.
31721	8971	Edward Roger Pratt, 1882.	
31722	8972	Jermyn Harold Pratt, 1883.	Great-grandchildren. Children
31723	8973	Lionel Henry Pratt, 1889.	of No. 31720.
31724	8974	Dorothy Louisa Pratt, 1885.	
31725	8975	Ursula Frances Pratt, 1888.	

31726	8976	Walter Jermyn Murray Pratt, 1853.	
31727	8977	Reginald Henry Murray Pratt, 1854.	
31728	8978	Horace Reginald Pratt, 1888. } Great-grandchildren.	
31729	8979	Cecil Arden Pratt, 1889. } dren. Children of No. 31727.	
31730	8980	Ailwyn Murray Pratt, 1892.	
31731	8981	Gerald Henry Pratt, 1895.	

31726 | 8976 | Walter Jermyn Murray Pratt, 1853.
31727 | 8977 | Reginald Henry Murray Pratt, 1854.
31728 | 8978 | Horace Reginald Pratt, 1888. ⎫ Great-grandchil-
31729 | 8979 | Cecil Arden Pratt, 1889. ⎬ dren. Chil-
31730 | 8980 | Ailwyn Murray Pratt, 1892. ⎪ dren of No.
31731 | 8981 | Gerald Henry Pratt, 1895. ⎭ 31727.
31732 | 8982 | Blanche Eleanor Murray, wife of Captain James Boyle, H.B.M.'s Consul. *British Consulate, Copenhagen.*
31733 | 8983 | Henrietta Mary Murray, wife of Cecil Henry Spencer Percival.
31734 | 8984 | Alice Rosalinde Murray, wife of the Rev. Charles Francis Townley, of Fulbourne. *Christchurch Rectory, Wisbech.*

Grandchildren. Brothers and sisters to No. 31720.

31735–38 | } | Same as Nos. 29538–29541. ⎰ Great-grandchildren. Children ⎱ of No. 31734.

31739 | 8985 | George Edward Capel Cure, Major *late* Lancashire Fusiliers, 1853. *Blake Hall, Essex.* *23 Eaton Terrace, S.W.*
31740 | 8986 | Francis Capel Cure, 1854. *Badger Hall, Salop.*
31741 | 8987 | Herbert Capel Cure, Major Gloucester Regiment, D.S.O., 1859.
31742 | 8988 | Ernest Capel Cure, 1861.
31743 | 8989 | Adelaide Frederica, wife of Rowland John Beech, J.P., D.L. *The Shawe, near Cheadle, co. Stafford.* *Brandon Hall, Warwick.*

Grandchildren. Children of Sarah Maria Murray, 1825–1863, wife of Robert Capel Cure, of Blake Hall 1823–1878.

31744 | 8990 | Rowland Auriol James Beech, 1888.
31745 | 8991 | Douglas Charles Murray Beech, 1889.
31746 | 8992 | Christabel Emily Sarah Beech.
31747 | 8993 | Irene Frederica Beech.

Great-grandchildren. Children of No. 31743.

31748 | 8994 | Edward Augustus Murray Tufnell, 1855. *Porters, Boreham, Chelmsford.*

Grandson. Son of Eleanor Margaret Murray, 1829–1895, 2nd wife of John Jolliffe Tufnell, of Langleys, Essex, 1805–1894.

31749 | 8995 | Samuel Jolliffe Tufnell, 1893. ⎱ Great-grandchildren. Chil-
31750 | 8996 | Ruth Cecily Tufnell, 1891. ⎰ dren of No. 31748.
31751 | 8997 | George Murray Tufnell, Captain 1st Battalion Essex Regiment, 1868.
31752 | 8998 | Herbert Murray Tufnell, Captain 3rd Battalion Essex Regiment, 1872.

Grandchildren. Brothers to No. 31748.

31753 | 8999 | Barbara Evelyn Tufnell, 1894. ⎰ Great-grandchild. Daughter ⎱ of No. 31752.

31754 | 9000 | Maria Louisa, wife of the Hon. Edward Gerald Strutt. *Whitelands, Hatfield Peveril, Witham, Essex.*

Grandchild. Sister to No. 31748.

31755 | 9001 | Gerald Murray Strutt, Lieutenant Suffolk Imperial Yeomanry, 1880.
31756 | 9002 | John James Strutt, 1881.
31757 | 9003 | Edward Jolliffe Strutt, 1884.
31758 | 9004 | Emily Norah Strutt, 1879.
31759 | 9005 | Evelyn Mary Strutt, 1883.
31760 | 9006 | Clara Helena Strutt, 1888.

Great-grandchildren. Children of No. 31754.

31761 | 9007 | Frances Emily, wife of Francis Richard Round, ⎱ Grandchild. 2nd sis-
C.M.G. *Sutton Court, Surrey.* ⎰ ter to No. 31748.

31762	9008	Douglass Gray Round, 1882.	
31763	9009	George Jolliffe Round, 1884.	
31764	9010	Arthur John Maurice Round, ⎫ twins,	Great-grandchildren.
31765	9011	Auriol Francis Hay Round, ⎭ 1891.	Children of No.
31766	9012	James Murray Round, 1894.	31761.
31767	9013	Harold Cecil Round, 1896.	
31768	9014	Constance Round.	
31769	9015	Constance Helena, wife of Egerton John Glyn. *Newland Lodge, Ingatestone, Essex.*	Grandchild. 3rd sister to No. 31748.
31770		Same as No. 29601.	Great-grandchild. Son of No. 31769.
31771	9016	Caroline Margaret, wife of Bateman Hope. *Tofts, Little Baddow, Chelmsford.*	Grandchild. 4th sister to No. 31748.
31772	9017	Geoffrey Bateman Hope, 1893.	Great-grandchildren. Son
31773	9018	Irene Margaret Hope, 1891.	and daughters to No.
31774	9019	Sylva Eleanor Murray Hope, 1897.	31771.
31775	9020	Mabel Eleanor, widow of Captain Maurice Wrottesley Kirk, 1866–1900. *Hatfield Bury, Witham, Essex.*	Grandchild. 5th and youngest surviving sister to No. 31748.
31776	9021	Margaret Eleanor Kirk, 1899.	Great-grandchild. Daughter of No. 31775.

677. Descendants of the Rev. Edward Murray, Prebendary of St. Paul's and Vicar of Northolt, Middlesex, 1798–1852. (See Table CV.)

31777	9022	⛨ ⛨ Fane Wright Stapleton Murray, 1879.	
31778	9023	⛨ ⛨ Cecil de Grey Murray, 1880.	Grandchildren. Chil-
31779	9024	⛨ ⛨ Rupert Auriol Conant Murray, 1882.	dren of Charles Ed-
31780	9025	⛨ ⛨ Stracey Montagu Athole Murray, 1888.	ward Gostling Mur-
31781	9026	⛨ ⛨ Rosalind Emma, wife of Charles Edward Hungerford Atholl Colston, of *Roundway Park*, M.P., 1855. *54 Green Street, W.*	ray, of Whitton Park, Middlesex, 1825–1892.
31782	9027	Edward Murray Colston, 1880.	Great-grandson. Son of No. 31781
31783	9028	⛨ ⛨ Julia Ruperta, wife of Colonel Morgan (Samuel) Crofton, C.B., D.S.O., 1857. *Denton Court, Kent.*	Grandchild. Sister to No. 31777, &c.
31784	9029	Ione Willats, 1878.	Great-grandchildren. Children of No. 31783 by 1st husband,
31785	9030	Catherine Willats, 1880.	William Hale Willats, – 1893.
31786	9031	Eric Edward Wake Conant, 1879.	*Surfleet,*	Great-grandchildren. Children of Emily Murray (sister to No. 31777, &c.),
31787	9032	Charles Henry Conant, 1880.	*co. Lincoln.*	1859–1881, 1st wife of Captain Henry John Conant of Surfleet.
31788	9033	⛨ ⛨ Nina Murray, 1889.	Grandchildren. Sisters of
31789	9034	⛨ ⛨ Gwladys Murray, 1891.	Nos. 31777, &c.
31790	9035	Charles Edward Hungerford Atholl Colston, M.P., J.P., D.L. *Roundway Park, Devizes.* *54 Green Street, W.*	Grandson. Son of Louisa Ruperta Murray, 1824–1864, wife of Edward Colston, of Roundway Park, 1822–1864.

31791		Same as No. 31782. Great-grandson. Son of No. 31790.	
31792	9036	Amy Ruperta, wife of Sir Christopher William Baynes, 4th Bart.	Granddaughter. Sister to No. 31790.
31793	9037	William Edward Colston Baynes, LL.B., Barrister-at-Law, Inner Temple, 1876. *St. James'.*	
31794	9038	Ronald Christopher Baynes, 1878. *Wellington.*	Great-grandchildren. Children of No. 31792.
31795	9039	Christobel Ruperta Baynes.	
31796	9040	Dorothy Julia Baynes.	
31797	9041	Lilian Anne Colston.	Granddaughter. Younger sister to No. 31790.
31798	9042	Robert Murray Lawes, Captain Medway Division R.E. Militia, 1857. 19 *Queen Street, Mayfair, W.*	Grandson. Son of Emma Selina Murray, 1830–1896, and her husband, Major Robert Bartholomew Lawes, of Old Park, Dover, J.P., D.L.
31799	9043	Robert Lethbridge Murray Lawes, 1897.	Great-grandchildren. Children of No. 31798.
31800	9044	Muriel Evelyn Florence Murray Lawes, 1890.	
31801	9045	Evelyn Emma Murray, Lady Hamond-Græme, wife of Sir Graham Eden William Hamond-Græme, 4th Bart. 17 *Dorset Square, N.W.*	Granddaughter. Sister to No. 31798.
31802	9046	Egerton Hood Murray Hamond-Græme, 1877. *Brooks'.*	Great-grandchild. Son of No. 31801.
31803	9047	Marion Ruperta Murray, wife of Lieut.-Col. the Hon. Geoffrey Cecil Twisleton-Wykeham-Fiennes, Royal Scots Fusiliers. *Garlinge, Westgate.*	Granddaughter. Younger sister to No. 31798.
31804	9048	Geoffrey Rupert Cecil Twisleton-Wykeham-Fiennes, 1884.	Great-grandchildren. Children of No. 31803.
31805	9049	Ivo Murray Twisleton-Wykeham-Fiennes, 1885.	
31806	9050	Laurence John Evelyn Twisleton-Wykeham-Fiennes, 1890.	
31807	9051	Allen Rupert Ingelram Twisleton-Wykeham-Fiennes, 1897.	
31808	9052	Cecily Marion Violet Joan Twisleton-Wykeham-Fiennes, 1900.	

678. Descendants, if any, of Charlotte Sophia Murray, 1785–1866, and her husband, the Rev. Townshend Selwyn, Canon of Gloucester,   –1853. (See Table CV.)

---

679. Descendants of Lady Theresa Anna Maria Fox Strangways, 1814–1874, and her husband, Edward St. Vincent, 9th Lord, Digby, 1809–1889. (See Table CV.)

31809	9053	Edward Henry Trafalgar, 10th Baron Digby [I.], and 4th Baron Digby of Sherborne [G.B.], 1846. 39 *Belgrave Square, S.W.*	Eldest son.

31810	9054	Hon. Edward Kenelm Digby, 1894.	⎫
31811	9055	Hon. Lettice Theresa Digby, 1896.	Grandchildren. Children of No. 31809.
31812	9056	Hon. Geraldine Margot Digby, 1898.	
31813	9057	Hon. Venetia Jane Digby, 1900.	⎭
31814	9058	Hon. Everard Charles Digby, *late* Colonel Grenadier Guards, 1852. *Buckshaw House, Sherborne.*	2nd son.
31815	9059	Almarus Edward Henry Digby, 1889.	⎫ Grandchildren. Children of No. 31814.
31816	9060	Giles Stephen Digby, 1894.	
31817	9061	Theresa Emily Marjory Digby, 1888.	⎭
31818	9062	Hon. Gerald Fitzmaurice Digby, *late* Commander R.N., 1858. *Up Cerne Manor, Dorchester.*	3rd son and elder surviving daughter.
31819	9063	Hon. Victoria Alexandrina, wife of Richard Marker, 1840. *Combe, Honiton.*	
31820	9064	Raymond John Marker, Major Coldstream Guards, D.S.O., A.D.C. to Lord Kitchener, 1899–1901, 1867.	⎫ Grandchildren. Children of No. 31819.
31821	9065	Edward Richard Marker, 1872.	
31822	9066	Gertrude Margaret Marker.	⎭
31823	9067	Leonora Caroline, Lady Ashburton [U.K.], 1844. *16 Cadogan Square, S.W.*	Younger surviving daughter.
31824	9068	Francis Denzil Edward, 5th Lord Ashburton [U.K.], 1866. *The Grange, Alresford, Hants.*	Grandson. Son of No. 31823.
31825	9069	Hon. Alexander Francis St. Vincent Baring, 1898.	⎫ Great-grandchildren. Children of No. 31824.
31826	9070	Hon. Venetia Marjorie Mabel Baring, 1890.	
31827	9071	Hon. Aurea Vera Baring, 1891.	
31828	9072	Hon. Angela Mildred Baring, 1893.	
31829	9073	Hon. Violet Alma Madeline Baring, 1895.	⎭
31830	9074	Hon. Frederick Arthur Baring, Lieutenant Hampshire Imperial Yeomanry, 1867. *Candover House, Alresford, Hants.*	Grandchild. 2nd son of No. 31823.
31831	9075	Evelyn Claire Baring, 1891.	Great-grandchild. Child of No. 31830.
31832	9076	Hon. Alexander Henry Baring, 1869. *The Grange, Alresford.*	⎫ Grandchildren. Younger children of No. 31823.
31833	9077	Hon. Guy Victor Baring, Captain Coldstream Guards, 1873.	
31834	9078	Hon. Caryl Digby Baring, Lieutenant 2nd Battalion Coldstream Guards, 1880.	
31835	9079	Hon. Lilian Theresa Claire Baring, 1874.	⎭

680. Descendants of Louisa Anne Murray, 1790–1871, wife of Sir Robert Frankland Russell, 7th Bart., 1784–1849. (See Table CV.)

31836	9080	Thomas, 6th Lord Walsingham [G.B.], 1843. *Eaton House, 66A Eaton Square, S.W.* *Merton Hall, Thetford, Norfolk.*	Grandchild. Only child of Augusta Louisa Frankland, 1818–1844, 1st wife of Thomas, 5th Lord Walsingham, 1804–1870.
31837	9081	Emily Anne, Lady Payne-Frankland, widow of Sir William Payne-Gallwey, 2nd Bart., 1807–1881. *Thirkleby Park, Thirsk, Yorkshire.*	Daughter.
31838	9082	Sir Ralph William Payne-Gallwey, 3rd Bart., 1848. *Thirkleby Park, Thirsk, Yorkshire.*	Grandson. Son of No. 31837.

31839	9083	William Payne-Gallwey, Lieutenant Grenadier Guards, 1881.	Great-grandchildren. Children of No. 31838.
31840	9084	Margaret Emily Payne-Gallwey.	
31841	9085	Winifred Payne-Gallwey.	
31842	9086	Dorothy Payne-Gallwey.	
31843	9087	Geraldine Payne-Gallwey.	
31844	9088	Edwin John Payne-Gallwey, *late* Captain R.N., 1850. *Beacon Hill, Wyke Regis, Weymouth.*	Grandson. 2nd son of No. 31837.
31845	9089	John Payne-Gallwey, 1889.	Great-grandchildren. Children of No. 31844.
31846	9090	Lionel Payne-Gallwey, 1894.	
31847	9091	Maurice Hylton Frankland Payne-Gallwey, 1889.	Great-grandchildren. Children of Lionel Philip Payne-Gallwey, 1851–1891, 3rd son of No. 31837.
31848	9092	Kathleen Lucille Payne-Gallwey.	
31849	9093	Evelyn Mary Payne-Gallwey.	
31850	9094	Sybil Norah Payne-Gallwey.	
31851	9095	Cecily Olive Payne-Gallwey.	
31852	9096	Wyndham Harry Payne-Gallwey, 1855.	Grandson. 4th but 3rd surviving son of No. 31837.
31853	9097	Reginald Payne-Gallwey, 1889.	Great-grandchild. Son of No. 31852.
31854	9098	Bertha Louisa Payne-Gallwey.	Granddaughter. Only surviving daughter of No. 31837.
31855 –71	}	Same as Nos. 25186–25202.	Descendants of Julia Roberta Frankland, 1825–1892 (daughter), and her husband, Ralph Neville Grenville, M.P., 1817–1886.
31872	9099	Bertram Frankland Frankland-Russell-Astley, J.P., D.L., 1857. *Chequers Court, Bucks.* 21 *Eaton Place, S.W.*	Grandson. Son of Rosalind Alicia Frankland, 1828–1900, 2nd wife of Lieut.-Col. Francis L'Estrange Astley, 1810–1866.
31873 –74	}	Same as Nos. 27828–27829.	Great-grandchildren. Children of No. 31872.
31875	9100	Rev. Hubert Delaval Astley, 1860. *Benham Park, Newbury, Berks.*	Grandson. 2nd brother of No. 31872.
31876	9101	Philip Reginald Astley, 1896.	Great-grandchildren. Children of No. 31875.
31877	9102	Ruth Constance Astley, 1900.	
31878	9103	Reginald Basil Astley, 1862. *Acton Reynold, Shrewsbury.*	Grandson. 3rd brother to No. 31872.

681. Descendants of Vice-Admiral James Arthur Murray, 1799–1860. (See Table CIV.)

31879	9104	∪ ∪ George Delmé Murray, 1854. *Titchfield Abbey, co. Hants.* 12 *Anglesay Terrace, St. Leonards.*	Son.
31880	9105	∪ ∪ George Arthur Delmé Murray, 1879.	Grandchildren. Children of No. 31879.
31881	9106	∪ ∪ Reginald Murray, 1881.	
31882	9107	∪ ∪ William Murray, 1883.	
31883	9108	∪ ∪ Algernon Murray, 1887.	
31884	9109	∪ ∪ Julia Murray, 1882.	
31885	9110	Emily Margaret, wife of Colonel George Atkins, I.S.C., 1853.	Grandchild. Child of Harriet Coupland Murray, 1822–1893, wife of Harvey Winson Fellows.
31886	9111	George James Murray Atkins, 1874. *Carniyne.* *Chorleywood, Herts.*	Great-grandchildren. Children of No. 31885.
31887	9112	Mabel Atkins, 1875.	
31888	9113	Gladys Marguerite Murray Atkins, 1876.	

31889	9114	Caroline Peters Fellows. *Riverside, Rickmansworth.*	}	Grandchild. Sister to No. 31885.
31890	9115	James Murray Hamilton, 1871.		Grandchildren. Children
31891	9116	William John Rodney Hamilton, 1875.		of Julia Frances Delmé
31892	9117	Rosalind Maria Hamilton.		Murray, 1839–1897,
31893	9118	Lilian Louisa, wife of the Rev. Edmund Horace Fellowes, 1878. *The Cloisters, Windsor Castle.*		wife of Admiral Sir Richard Vesey Hamilton, G.C.B., *of The Elms, Chalfont St. Peter, Bucks.*
31894	9119	Horace Frederick Fellowes, 1899.	{	Great-grandchild. Son of No. 31893.
31895	9120	James Edward Murray Hanslow, 1874. *Melbourne.*		Grandchildren. Children of Mary
31896	9121	Arthur Eden Hanslow, 1876.		Anne Murray, 1842–1891, wife
31897	9122	May Delmé, wife of Holdsworth, 1873.		of Edward Eden Hanslow, *of Melbourne.*
31898	9123	Florence Hanslow, 1882.		
31899	9124	▽ ▽ Margaret Amelia, wife of Martin Seal, 1843. *17 Montserrat Road, Putney.*	}	3rd surviving daughter.

682. Descendants of Colonel Henry Murray, R.A., 1815–1864. (See Table CVI.)

31900	9125	▽ ▽ Rev. Richard Paget Murray, 1842. *Shapwick Vicarage, Blandford.*	}	Son.
31901	9126	▽ ▽ Henry James Stewart Murray, 1874.		
31902	9127	▽ ▽ Athole Evelyn Murray, 1881.		
31903	9128	▽ ▽ Arthur Hugh Murray, 1883.		
31904	9129	▽ ▽ Edward Douglas Murray, 1884.		Grandchildren. Children of No. 31900.
31905	9130	▽ ▽ Mona Blanche Murray, 1872.		
31906	9131	▽ ▽ Violet Constance Murray, 1885.		
31907	9132	▽ ▽ Ethel Mary Murray, 1886.		
31908	9133	▽ ▽ Muriel Gladys Angela Murray, 1889.		
31909	9134	▽ ▽ Henry Murray, Lieut.-Col. *late* Royal Munster Fusiliers, 1850. *43 Cromwell Houses, S.W.*		2nd son.
31910	9135	▽ ▽ Henry Francis Farquharson Murray, Lieutenant Black Watch, 1881.		Grandchildren. Children of No. 31909.
31911	9136	▽ ▽ Mona Anna Murray, 1884.		
31912	9137	▽ ▽ Edward Dudley Murray, 1854. *Otterburn, Walton, N.Z.*		3rd and 4th sons.
31913	9138	▽ ▽ Charles Nathaniel Murray, 1855. *Pyramid, Athenree, Bay of Plenty, N.Z.*		
31914	9139	▽ ▽ Athole Alma Emily Clare Murray, 1887.	}	Grandchildren. Children of No. 31913.
31915	9140	▽ ▽ Kathleen Stewart Murray, 1892.		
31916	9141	▽ ▽ Rev. Arthur Silver Murray, 1858. *Horningsham Vicarage, Warminster.*	}	5th son.
31917	9142	▽ ▽ Arthur Evelyn Francis Murray, 1888.		Grandchildren.
31918	9143	▽ ▽ Anne Evelyn Charlotte de la Trémouille Murray, 1895.		Children of No. 31916.
31919	9144	▽ ▽ Isabella Sophia Murray, 1845. *Convent of St. Mary of Nazareth, Finsbury, E.C.*		
31920	9145	▽ ▽ Elizabeth Emily Murray, 1847. *62 Oakley Street, Chelsea, S.W.*		Daughters.
31921	9146	▽ ▽ Mona Murray, 1852. *Leesen Strasse 16, Gotha.*		

683. Descendants of Charlotte Wilhelmina Murray, 1790–1835, wife 1st of William Scott, –1818, and 2ndly of Samuel Hibbert Ware, M.D., 1782–1848. (See Table CVI.)

31922	9147	. . . . Scott.	Great-great-grandchildren. Daughters of Douglas Murray Scott, 1860–1898, granddaughters of Henry Murray Scott, 1837–1898, and great-granddaughters of Archibald Hamilton Scott, 1812–1845.
31923	9148	. . . . Scott.	
31924	9149	. . . . Scott.	
31925	9150	. . . . Scott.	
31926	9151	Archibald Hamilton Scott, 1861. 102 *Quincey St., Brooklyn, New York.*	Great-grandchild. 2nd son of Henry Murray Scott, 1837–1898. *See above.*
31927	9152	Charles Pott, 1867.	Great-grandchildren. Children of Mona Murray Scott, 1842–1896, wife of Charles Pott, and grandchildren of Archibald Hamilton Scott, 1812–1845.
31928	9153	Annie Mona Pott, 1864. *Lachine, Montreal.*	
31929	9154	Jessie Angelique, widow of John Paterson, 1837–1898, 1845. *Kinburn, St. Andrews.*	Granddaughter. Daughter of Archibald Hamilton Scott, 1812–1845.
31930	9155	George Stephen Archibald Oliver, 1865. *Lachine, Montreal.*	Great-grandchild. Son of No. 31929 by 1st husband, Albert George Oliver.
31931	9156	Frederick Hall Oliver, 1896.	Great-great-grandchildren. Children of No. 31930.
31932	9157	George Murray Oliver, 1903.	
31933	9158	Dorothy Helena Oliver, 1894.	
31934	9159	Douglas Hamilton Oliver, 1867. *Superior, Nebraska, U.S.A.*	Great-grandson. Brother to No. 31930.
31935	9160	Percy Wheelock Oliver, 1892.	Great-great-grandchildren. Children of 31934.
31936	9161	Oran Oliver, 1893.	
31937	9162	Rose Ellen Scott. *Overton, Herbert Road, Bournemouth.*	Grandchild. Daughter of Major William Douglas Scott, 1818–1886.
31938	9163	Douglas Hibbert Ware.	Grandchildren. Children of the Rev. Richard Stewart Hibbert Ware.
31939	9164	William Hibbert Ware.	
31940	9165	Charlotte Hibbert Ware.	
31941	9166	Katherine Rose Hibbert Ware. *Southbank, Edinburgh.*	
31942	9167	Rev. George Hibbert Ware. *India.*	Grandchildren. Children of Captain Henry Hibbert Ware.
31943	9168	Jessie May Hibbert Ware.	
31944	9169	Caroline Hibbert Ware.	
31945	9170	Wilhelmina Hibbert Ware.	
31946	9171	Alice Hibbert Ware.	
31947	9172	Edith, wife of A. Hammond.	
31948	9173	Maud Hibbert Ware.	

684. Descendants of Amelia Jane Murray, 1800–1892, 2nd wife of General Sir John Oswald, of Dunnikier, Fife, G.C.B., G.C.M.G., 1771–1840. (See Table CVI.)

31949	9174	Rev. Henry Murray Oswald, 1832. *Great Hallingbury Rectory, Bishop Stortford.*	Children.
31950	9175	Elizabeth Jane Oswald, 1830. *Southbank, Edinburgh.*	

685. Descendants of John Murray-Aynsley, 1795–1870. (See Table CVII.)

31951	9176	☉ ☉ John Francis Murray-Aynsley, Commander R.N., 1866. *Hall Court, Boiley, Hants.*	Grandchildren. Children of the late Vice-Admiral Charles Murray-Aynsley, C.B., 1821–1901.
31952	9177	☉ ☉ Alicia Harriet, wife of the Rev. Alfred Evans Vinter, Principal of Bishop Stortford Diocesan Training College, 1864. *Diocesan Training College, Bishop Stortford.*	
31953	9178	Charles Murray Vinter, 1893.	Great-grandchildren. Children of No. 31952.
31954	9179	Augusta Murray Vinter, 1892.	
31955	9180	☉ ☉ Clara Adelaide, wife of the Rev. Samuel Martin Young, 1867. *St. Thomas Rectory, Lower Crumpsall, Manchester.*	Granddaughter. Daughter of Captain James Murray-Aynsley, 1823–1869.
31956	9181	☉ ☉ Dorothea Faith Murray Young.	Great-granddaughter. Daughter of No. 31955.
31957	9182	☉ ☉ Rev. John Cruger Murray-Aynsley, J.P., 1825. *Great Brampton, Herefordshire.*	Son.
31958	9183	☉ ☉ Charles Edward Murray-Aynsley, 1850. *Santa Coopa, Mercara, Coorg, India.*	Grandchildren. Children of Major-General George Herbert Murray-Aynsley, 1826–1887.
31959	9184	☉ ☉ John Percy Murray-Aynsley, 1853.	
31960	9185	☉ ☉ Emma, wife of Major Charles Bateman Prust, 60th Rifles.	
31961	9186	Robert Bateman Prust, 1875.	Great-grandchildren. Children of No. 31960.
31962	9187	Harriet Jane Prust.	
31963	9188	Ethel Georgiana Murray, wife of Captain Prise Kinnear Lewis, R.A.	
31964	9189	Prise Charles Murray Lewis, 1899.	Great-great-grandchild. Son of No. 31963.
31965	9190	Charles Maximilian Thomas Western, 1882.	Great-grandchildren. Children of Maud Murray (sister to No. 31958), 1860–1898, wife (1881) of Major C. M. T. Western, R.A.
31966	9191	Charles Edward Murray Western, 1885.	
31967	9192	Maud Harriet Atholl Western, 1886.	
31968	9193	Gilbert Murray Norton, 1889.	Great-grandchildren. Children of Alice Elizabeth Murray (sister to No. 31958), 1863–1896, wife (1882) of Major G. F. A. Norton, R.A.
31969	9194	Godfrey Oswald Norton, 1890.	
31970	9195	Mauddine Norton.	
31971	9196	Dorothy Norton.	
31972	9197	☉ ☉ Hugh Percy Murray-Aynsley, 1828. *Riverlaw, Christchurch, N.Z.*	2nd surviving son.
31973	9198	☉ ☉ John Henry Murray-Aynsley, M.R.C.S. (Eng.), and L.R.C.P. (Lond.), 1860. *Eketahunah, N.S.W.*	Grandchildren. Children of No. 31972.
31974	9199	☉ ☉ Charles Percy Murray-Aynsley, 1862.	
31975	9200	☉ ☉ Archibald Cruger Murray-Aynsley, 1864.	
31976	9201	☉ ☉ George Murray-Aynsley, 1865.	
31977	9202	☉ ☉ Agnes Athole Murray-Aynsley, 1863.	
31978	9203	☉ ☉ Emma Mary Murray-Aynsley, 1867.	
31979	9204	☉ ☉ Helen Elizabeth Murray-Aynsley, 1868.	

686. Descendants of Charlotte Murray-Aynsley, 1794–1827, 1st wife of General Sir John Oswald, of Dunnikier, Fife, G.C.B., G.C.M.G., 1771–1840. (See Table CVII.)

31980	9205	John Oswald, J.P., D.L., 1856. *Dunnikier, Kirkcaldy, Fife.*	Grandchildren. Children of Captain James Townsend Oswald, of Dunnikier, 1820-1893.
31981	9206	St. Clair Oswald, Lieut.-Col. 3rd Hussars, 1858.	
31982	9207	Clara, wife of the Rev. George Henry Egerton, Canon of Lichfield. *Myddle Rectory, Shropshire.*	
31983	9208	Arthur Oswald Egerton, 1890.	Great-grandchildren. Children of No. 31982.
31984	9209	Bridget Ellen Egerton, 1888.	
31985	9210	Charlotte Alice Oswald.	
31986	9211	Mary Oswald.	Grandchildren. Younger sisters to No. 31980.
31987	9212	Emily Oswald.	
31988	9213	Ellin Alexandra Oswald.	
31989	9214	Major-General Sir Henry Trotter, D.L., 1844. *Morton Hall, Edinburgh.* 38 *Cadogan Square, W.*	Grandson. Son of Mary Oswald, 1815-1851, wife of Richard Trotter, of Morton Hall, 1797-1874.
31990	9215	Algernon Richard Trotter, D.S.O., Captain *late* 2nd Life Guards, 1870.	Great-grandchildren. Children of No. 31989.
31991	9216	Gerald Frederic Trotter, D.S.O., Captain Grenadier Guards, 1871.	
31992	9217	Edward Henry Trotter, D.S.O., Captain *late* Grenadier Guards, 1872.	
31993	9218	Reginald Baird Trotter, Lieutenant Cameron Highlanders, 1874.	
31994	9219	Meta Trotter, 1868.	
31995	9220	Charlotte Atholl Mary, widow of Sir John Marjoribanks, 3rd Bart., of Lees, 1830-1884. *Lees, Coldstream, Berwick.*	Grandchildren. Sisters to No. 31989.
31996	9221	Margaret Catherine Trotter.	
31997	9222	Emily Frances, wife of Edward Murray Oakeley. *Bycliff, Sandgate.*	
31998	9223	Edward Richard Oakeley, 1887.	Great-grandchildren. Children of No. 31997.
31999	9224	Charlotte Mary Oakeley, 1889.	
32000	9225	David Murray Smythe, *late* Lieut.-Col. 3rd Battalion Royal Highlanders, 1850. *Methven Castle, Perth.*	Grandson. Son of Emily Oswald, 1816-1902, wife of William Smythe, of Methven Castle, J.P., D.L., 1803-1892.
32001		Same as No. 22231.	Great grandchild. Daughter of No. 32000.
32002	9226	Charles John Smythe, 1852. *Stratheam, Natal.*	Grandson. Brother of No. 32000.
32003	9227	David William Smythe, 1879, and others.	Great-grandchildren. Children of No. 32002.
32004	9228	Francis Henry Smythe, 1853.	Grandchildren. Brothers and sister of No. 32000.
32005	9229	William Frederick Smythe, 1859.	
32006	9230	Emily Beatrice Smythe.	
32007 -12	}	Same as Nos. 31493-31498.	Grandchildren. Children of Frances Jemima Oswald, 1818-1891, wife of John Murray Drummond, of Megginch Castle, 1803-1889.

687. Descendants of Atholl Keturah Murray-Aynsley, 1801–1844, and her husband, the Very Rev. Sir Herbert Oakeley, 3rd Bart., Dean of Bocking, Archdeacon of Colchester, 1791–1845. (See Table CVII.)

32013	9231	Sir Charles William Atholl Oakeley, 4th Bart., 1828. *The Oaks, Frant Road, Tunbridge Wells.*	} Son.
32014	9232	Charles John Oakeley, J.P., *late* Captain 4th Battalion Queen's Own Regiment, 1862. *Frittenden House, Staplehurst.*	} Grandson. Son of No. 32013.
32015	9233	Charles Richard Andrew Oakeley, 1900.	} Great-grandchildren. Children of No. 32014.
32016	9234	Ellen Beatrice Oakeley, 1891.	
32017	9235	Emily Charlotte Eileen Oakeley, 1896.	
32018	9236	Edward Francis Oakeley, Captain 1st South Lancashire Regiment, 1870. *Army and Navy ; Bath.*	} Grandson. 2nd son of No. 32013.
32019	9237	Edward Atholl Oakeley, 1900.	{ Great-grandson. Son of No. 32018.
32020	9238	Herbert William Oakeley, 1874. 18 *St. James' Place, S.W.*	} Grandson. 3rd son of No. 32013.
32021	9239	Clifford Charles William Morland Oakeley, 1897.	} Great-grandson. Son of No. 32020.
32022	9240	Sir Herbert Stanley Oakeley, M.A., Mus. Doc., Christ Church, Oxford, Dublin, St. Andrews, Edinburgh, Canterbury, and Adelaide, Emeritus Professor of Music in the University of Edinburgh, and Hon. Composer to H.M. in Scotland, LL.D., Aberdeen, Glasgow, and Edinburgh, &c., 1830. 58 *St. George's Square, S.W.*	} Sons.
32023	9241	Sir Henry Evelyn Oakeley, H.M. *late* Chief Inspector of Training Colleges, 1833. 97 *Warwick Road, S.W.*	
32024	9242	Alice Keturah, wife of Arthur Godfrey Roby, Barrister, 1864. 13 *Old Square, Lincoln's Inn, W.C.*	} Grandchildren. Children of No. 32023.
32025	9243	Hilda Diana Oakeley, Warden of the Royal Victoria College, McGill University, Montreal, 1867.	
32026	9244	Caroline Atholl, wife of David Arthur Fitzgerald Vesey, Barrister-at-Law. 8 *New Square, Lincoln's Inn, W.C.*	
32027	9245	Marion Adela Oakeley, 1875.	
32028	9246	Edward Murray Oakeley, *late* Master at Clifton College, 1840. *Bycliff, Sandgate, Kent.*	} 4th son.
32029 –30	}	Same as Nos. 31998–31999.	{ Grandchildren. Children of No. 32028.
32031	9247	Charlotte Mary Atholl, wife of the Hon. Francis Charles Drummond, 1828. 58 *St. George's Square, S.W.*	} Daughter.

688. Descendants of Charles William Martin, 1799–1861. (See Table CIV.)

32032	9248	George Edward Martin, 1833.	Son.
32033	9249	Annie Rosa, wife of F. Angel, 1861.	} Grandchild. Daughter of No. 32032.
32034	9250	Mary Emily Angel, 1901.	{ Great-grandchild. Daughter of No. 32033.

32035	9251	John James Martin, 1839.	Son.
32036	9252	George Frederick Martin, 1884.	⎫ Grandchildren.
32037	9253	Margaret E. Martin, 1878.	⎪
32038	9254	Eva L. M. Martin, 1879.	⎬ Children of
32039	9255	Kathleen M. Martin, 1886.	⎭ No. 32035.
32040	9256	Mary Catherine Martin, 1832.	⎫
32041	9257	Jane Sophia Martin, wife of the Rev. Phipps Onslow, 1834.	⎬ Daughters.
32042	9258	Harry Phipps Onslow, 1869. Grandson.	Son of No. 32041.
32043	9259	Arthur Phipps Onslow, 1899.	⎫ Great-grandchildren.
32044	9260	George Francis Onslow, 1901.	⎬ Children of No.
32045	9261	. . . . Onslow, 1902.	⎭ 32042.
32046	9262	Sarah Amelia Martin, widow of the Right Hon. Sir Richard P. Amphlett, −1883, 1836. *Latimers, Christchurch, Hants.*	⎬ Daughter.

689. Descendants of Charlotte Margaret Martin, 1788–1849, wife of John Edwards, of Ness Strange, co. Salop, 1773–1850. (See Table CIV.)

32047	9263	George Rowland Edwards, 1852. *The Hall, Ness Strange, near Shrewsbury.*	⎫ Grandchild. Son of Colonel ⎬ George Rowland Edwards, of ⎭ Ness Strange, 1810–1894.
32048	9264	Dorothy Esther Edwards, 1895.	⎧ Great-grandchild. Daughter of ⎨ Henry Charles Edwards, 1865– ⎩ 1896, brother of No. 32047.
32049	9265	Antoinette Charlotte, wife of Henry Ernest Boyes, 1848.	⎫
32050	9266	Catherine Edwards, 1849.	⎬ Grandchildren. Sisters of No.
32051	9267	Louisa Mary, wife of Commander Edward Henry Bayly, R.N., C.B., 1856.	⎭ 32047.
32052	9268	Cecil Charles Paget Bayly, 1885.	⎫ Great-grandchildren.
32053	9269	Frank Boscowen Bayly, 1891.	⎬ Children of No.
32054	9270	Dorothy Muriel Bayly, 1888.	⎪ 32051.
32055	9271	Norah May Bayly, 1895.	⎭
32056	9272	Eleanor Margaret Edwards, 1860.	⎫ Grandchildren.
32057	9273	Eliza Henriana Edwards, 1861.	⎬ Sisters of No.
32058	9274	Gertrude Helen, wife of the Rev. William Lightfoot Harrison, 1863.	⎭ 32047.
32059	9275	James Murray Rowland Harrison, 1894.	⎧ Great-grandchildren. ⎨ Children of No.
32060	9276	Gwynnedd Helen Lightfoot Harrison, 1896.	⎩ 32058.
32061	9277	Annie Elsie Florence, wife of the Rev. Arthur George Bainbridge West, 1867.	⎬ Grandchild. Sister to No. 32047.
32062	9278	Edward Miles Bainbridge West, 1899.	⎫ Great-grandchildren.
32063	9279	Gwendoline Dorothy Mona West, 1900.	⎬ Children of No.
32064	9280	Gwyneth Imogene Amy West, 1902.	⎭ 32061.
32065	9281	Mabel Constance, wife of Captain Edward Ross Morton, 1869.	⎬ Grandchild. Sister of No. 32047.
32066	9282	Boyce Edward Rowland Morton, 1901.	⎫ Great-grandchildren.
32067	9283	Mabel Helen Catherine Morton, 1895.	⎬ Children of No.
32068	9284	Joyce Ada Murray Morton, 1897.	⎭ 32065.
32069	9285	Grace Isabel Edwards, 1871. Grandchild.	Sister of No. 32047.
32070	9286	Georgiana, wife of John Naylor. *Leighton Hall, co. Montgomery.*	⎬ Daughter.
32071	9287	Christopher John Leyland, *formerly* Naylor, 1849. *Haggerston Castle, Beal.*	⎬ Grandson. Son of No. 32070.

32072	9288	Christopher Digby Leyland, 1892.	Great-grandchildren. Children of No. 32071.
32073	9289	Stanley Cuthbert Leyland, 1901.	
32074	9290	Hilda Georgiana, wife of Richard Vernon Cholmondeley, 1875.	
32075	9291	Hilda Cholmondeley, 1901.	Great-great-grandchildren. Children of No. 32074.
32076	9292	Victoria Millicent Cholmondeley, 1902.	
32077	9293	Dorothy Leyland, 1894.	Great-grandchildren. Children of No. 32071.
32078	9294	Joan Leyland, 1895.	
32079	9295	Angela Leyland, 1897.	
32080	9296	Rowland Edward Leyland Naylor, 1851.	Grandchildren. Sons of No. 32070.
32081	9297	John Naylor, 1856. *Leighton Hall, Welshpool, Montgomeryshire.*	
32082	9298	John Murray Naylor, 1888.	Great-grandchildren. Children of No. 32081.
32083	9299	Thomas Humphrey Naylor, 1890.	
32084	9300	Hugh Maxwell Naylor, } twins,	
32085	9301	Rowland Edmund Naylor, } 1894.	
32086 –88	}	Same as Nos. 31534–31536.	Great-grandchildren. Children of Dora Naylor, 1847–1878, wife of Admiral Edmund Drummond.
32089	9302	Margaret Naylor, 1848.	Grandchildren. Daughters of No. 32070.
32090	9303	Emily, wife of George Devereux Harrison, 1852. *Fronllwyd, co. Montgomery.*	
32091	9304	George Rowland Harrison, 1877.	Great-grandchildren. Children of No. 32090.
32092	9305	James Murray Robert Harrison, 1880.	
32093	9306	Henry Edward Harrison, 1882.	
32094	9307	Harriotte Emily Harrison, 1878.	
32095	9308	Edith Maud Harrison, 1879.	
32096	9309	Sybil Mary Harrison, 1891.	
32097	9310	Georgina Naylor, 1854.	Grandchildren. Daughters of No. 32070.
32098	9311	Frances Naylor, 1857.	
32099	9312	Eva, wife of Lieut.-Col. Alfred William Lambert Bayly, C.B., D.S.O., 1859. *Poona, India.*	
32100	9313	Eric Bayly, 1891.	Great-grandchild. Son of No. 32099.
32101	9314	Alice Maud, widow of John Urmson Hayes, 1863.	Grandchild. Youngest daughter of No. 32070.
32102	9315	Amelia Murray (Emily), widow of the Rev. George Richard Turner, 1828.	Daughter.
32103	9316	Rowlands Edwards Turner, 1863.	Grandchildren. Sons and daughters of No. 32102.
32104	9317	Gilbert Richard Turner, 1865.	
32105	9318	Amy, wife of Percy Raymond, 1860.	

690. Descendants of John, 4th Duke of Atholl, K.T., 1729–1774.
(See Table CIV.)

32106 –726	}	Same as Nos. 31485–32105.

691. Descendants of James Farquharson, of Invercauld, 1809–1862.
(See Table CIV.)

32727	9319	▽ Alexander Haldane Farquharson, of Invercauld, 1867. *40 Park Street, Grosvenor Square.*	Grandson. Son of James Ross Farquharson, of Invercauld, 1834–1888.

32728	9320	⛒ Myrtle Farquharson, 1897. ⎫	Great-grandchildren. Chil-
32729	9321	⛒ Sylvia Farquharson, 1899. ⎭	dren of No. 32727.
32730	9322	⛒ Louisa Elizabeth Farquharson. ⎫	Grandchildren. Sisters of
32731	9323	⛒ Elo Janet Catherine Farquharson. ⎭	No. 32727.
32732	9324	⛒ Janet Farquharson. ⎰	Grandchildren. Daughters of George Murray Farquharson,
32733	9325	⛒ Margaret Farquharson. ⎱	1835–1899.
32734	9326	⛒ Victor Alexander Farquharson, *late* Major Royal Scots, 1853. *Naval and Military.*	
32735	9327	⛒ Catherine, widow of Herbert Hutchings, −1898. *The Manor House, Sandford Orcas, co. Somerset.* 31 *Chester Street, S.W.*	Children.
32736	9328	⛒ Henrietta Dundas Farquharson.	
32737	9329	⛒ Janet Hamilton, widow of William Fenwick, −1895.	
32738	9330	Constance Louisa Hamilton Fenwick. ⎱	Grandchildren. Chil-
32739	9331	Evaline Frances Fenwick. ⎰	dren of No. 32737.
32740	9332	⛒ Amelia Farquharson.	Youngest daughter.

692. Descendants, if any, of Harriet Murray, wife 1st of Captain William Lindley, Westmorland Militia, divorced 1805, and 2ndly (1805) of John Francis Staveley, of York. (See Table CIV.)

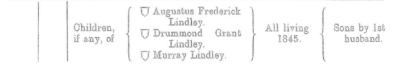

| | Children, if any, of | ⛒ Augustus Frederick Lindley. ⛒ Drummond Grant Lindley. ⛒ Murray Lindley. | All living 1845. | Sons by 1st husband. |

693. Descendants of George, 4th Earl of Aberdeen, K.G., K.T., 1784–1860. (See Table CVIII.)

32741	9333	John Campbell, 7th Earl of Aberdeen [S.], 4th Viscount Gordon [U.K.], P.C., 1847. *Haddo House, Aberdeen.* 58 *Grosvenor Square, W.*	Grandson. Son of George John James, 5th Earl of Aberdeen, 1816–1864.
32742	9334	George, Lord Haddo, 1879.	Great-grandchildren.
32743	9335	Hon. Dudley Gladstone Gordon, 1883.	Children of No.
32744	9336	Hon. Archibald Gordon, 1884.	32741.
32745	9337	Lady Marjorie Adeline Gordon, 1880.	
32746	9338	Mary, Lady Polwarth [S.], 1844. *Mertoun House, St. Boswells.*	Grandchild. Sister to No. 32741.
32747	9339	Walter George, Master of Polwarth, 1864. *Humbie House, Upper Keith, East Lothian.*	Great-grandchild. Child of No. 32746.
32748	9340	Walter Thomas Hepburne-Scott, 1890.	
32749	9341	Alexander Noel Hepburne-Scott, 1892.	Great-great-grand-
32750	9342	Patrick John Hepburne-Scott, 1899.	children. Chil-
32751	9343	Helen Victoria Hepburne-Scott, 1891.	dren of No.
32752	9344	Margaret Mary Hepburne-Scott, 1895.	32747.
32753	9345	Edith Christian Hepburne-Scott, 1891.	

32754	9346	Hon. Henry James Hepburne-Scott, 1866. *Whitefield Cottage, Carlisle.*	⎫
32755	9347	Hon. George Hepburne-Scott, 1871.	
32756	9348	Hon. Robert Hepburne-Scott, 1873.	
32757	9349	Hon. Charles Francis Hepburne-Scott, 1874.	Great-grandchildren.
32758	9350	Hon. Georgina Mary Hepburne-Scott, 1868.	Children of No.
32759	9351	Hon. Lilias Hepburne-Scott, 1875.	32746.
32760	9352	Hon. Mary Harriet Hepburne-Scott, 1877.	
32761	9353	Hon. Grisell Katherine Hepburne-Scott, 1879.	
32762	9354	Hon. Katherine Grace Hepburne-Scott, 1885.	⎭
32763	9355	Lady Harriet, wife of William Alexander Lindsay, K.C., Windsor Herald, 1849. *17 Cromwell Road, S.W.*	Grandchild. 2nd sister to No. 32741.
32764	9356	James Howard Lindsay, Barrister-at-Law, 1871.	⎫
32765	9357	Francis Howard Lindsay, Lieutenant 7th Middlesex Rifles (London Scottish), 1876.	Great-grandchildren.
32766	9358	John Colin Howard Lindsay, Lieutenant R.N., 1877.	Children of No. 32763.
32767	9359	David Howard Lindsay, 1882.	
32768	9360	Mary Haddo Lindsay, 1873.	
32769	9361	Margaret Louisa Lindsay, 1880.	⎭
32770	9362	Katherine Eliza, Lady Balfour of Burleigh [S.] *Kennet, Alloa.* *47 Cadogan Square, S.W.*	Grandchild. 3rd sister to No. 32741.
32771	9363	Robert, Master of Burleigh, Lieutenant 3rd Battalion (Princess Louise's) Argyll and Sutherland Highlanders, 1880.	⎫
32772	9364	Hon. George John Gordon Bruce, 1883.	Great-grandchildren.
32773	9365	Hon. Mary Bruce, 1877.	Children of No.
32774	9366	Hon. Jane Hamilton Bruce, 1879.	32770.
32775	9367	Hon. Victoria Alexandrina Katherine Bruce, 1898.	⎭
32776	9368	Alexander Hamilton-Gordon, Major and Brevet Lieut.-Col. R.A., D.A.Q.M.G., Aldershot, 1859.	Grandson. Son of General the Hon. Sir Alexander Hamilton Gordon, K.C.B., 1817–1890.
32777	9369	Alan Herschel Hamilton-Gordon, 1898.	Great-grandchildren. Chil-
32778	9370	Eileen Muriel Hamilton-Gordon, 1889.	dren of No. 32776.
32779	9371	Ernest Arthur Hamilton-Gordon, 1866.	
32780	9372	George Herschel Hamilton-Gordon, 1872.	
32781	9373	Victoria Alberta Alexandrina, wife of Victor Alexander Ernest Garth Marshall, 1854. *Monk Coniston, Ambleside.*	Grandchildren. Brothers and
32782	9374	Caroline Augusta, wife of Arthur John Lewis Gordon, C.M.G., 1856. *Ellon, Aberdeenshire.*	sisters to No. 32776.
32783	9375	Louisa Hamilton-Gordon, 1858.	
32784	9376	Kathleen Isabella Hamilton-Gordon, 1863.	
32785	9377	Douglas George Hamilton-Gordon, J.P., Captain 2nd Battalion (South) Middlesex Rifle Volunteers, 1852. *41 Tedworth Square, Chelsea.*	Grandson. Son of Rev. and Hon. Douglas Hamilton-Gordon, 1824–1901.
32786	9378	Douglas Walter Hamilton-Gordon, Lieutenant R.N., 1878.	⎫
32787	9379	Sholto Hamilton-Gordon, 1879.	Great-grandchildren.
32788	9380	Hugh Hamilton-Gordon, 1883.	Children of No.
32789	9381	Edith Hilda Hamilton-Gordon, 1881.	32785.
32790	9382	Rosamond Hamilton-Gordon, 1885.	⎭

32791	9383	George William Hamilton-Gordon, 1854.	⎫	
32792	9384	William Hugh Hamilton-Gordon, Clerk to the House of Lords, 1855. *Bywater House, Lymington, Hants.*	⎪	Grandchildren. Brothers and sisters of No. 32785.
32793	9385	Katherine Ellen Hamilton-Gordon.	⎬	
32794	9386	Ellen Louisa Hamilton-Gordon.	⎭	
32795	9387	Arthur, Lord Stanmore [U.K.], 1829. *The Red House, Ascot, Berks.*	⎫⎬⎭	Youngest son.
32796	9388	Hon. George Arthur Maurice Hamilton-Gordon, Capt. 3rd Battalion Gordon Highlanders, 1871.	⎫⎬	Grandchildren. Children of No. 32795.
32797	9389	Hon. Rachel Nevil Hamilton-Gordon, 1869.	⎭	

694. Descendants,[1] if any, of Lady Anne Gordon, –1821, wife of Edward Place, of Skelton Grange, York, –1842. (See Table CVIII.)

---

695. Descendants of the Rev. Joshua Thomas Horton, of Howroyde, Vicar of Ormskirk, Lancaster, 1791–1845. (See Table CVIII.)

32798	9390	Joshua Thomas Horton, 1860. *Howroyde, near Halifax.*	⎫	Grandchildren. Children of Joshua Thomas Horton, of Howroyde, 1836–1895.
32799	9391	William Theodore Horton, 1874.	⎬	
32800	9392	George Herbert Horton, 1877.	⎭	

696. Descendants of Lieut.-Col. George William Horton, of Halton Place, York, 1792–1877. (See Table CVIII.)

32801	9393	Rev. Le Gendre George Horton. *Wellow Vicarage, Bath.*	⎫⎬⎭	Grandchild. Child of the Rev. George William Horton, 1830–1886.
32802	9394	Le Gendre George William Horton, 1892.	⎫	Great-grandchildren. Children of No. 32801.
32803	9395	Frederick Henry Le Gendre Horton, 1894.	⎬	
32804	9396	Dorothy Mary Horton, 1893.	⎭	
32805	9397	Anne Frances, wife of the Rev. Atherton Gwillym Rawstorne. *Croston Rectory, Preston, Lancashire.*	⎫⎬⎭	Grandchild. Sister to No. 32801.
32806	9398	Richard Atherton Rawstorne.	⎫	Great-grandchildren. Children of No. 32805.
32807	9399	George Streynsham Rawstorne.	⎪	
32808	9400	Frances Marion Rawstorne.	⎬	
32809	9401	Jennett Rawstorne.	⎪	
32810	9402	Marjory Ella Rawstorne.	⎭	
32811	9403	Frances Laura Horton.		Daughter.

697. Descendants of Mary Horton, – , wife of Francis Beynon Hacket, of Moor Hall, Warwick, –1863. (See Table CVIII.)

32812	9404	George Algernon Beynon Disney Hacket, J.P., 1844. *Moor Hall, Sutton Coldfield, Warwick.*	⎫⎬⎭	Grandson. Son of Lieutenant John George Hacket, 91st Regiment, –1847.

---

[1] She is believed to have had a son and two daughters. One of the latter, a Mrs. Tireman, widow of a clergyman at Tintern, was living about 1850.

32813	9405	John Lisle Hacket, Captain Warwick-shire Regiment, 1869.	Great-grandson. Son of No. 32812.
32814	9406	John Eckford Hacket, 1893.	Great-great-grandchild. Son of No. 32813.
32815	9407	George Lisle Hacket, Lieutenant R.N., 1872.	
32816	9408	Charles Lisle Hacket, 1874.	
32817	9409	Andrew Lisle Hacket, 1877.	Great-grandchildren. Children of No. 32812.
32818	9410	Francis Lisle Hacket, 1883.	
32819	9411	Adela Mary, wife of Edward Kenneth Wilson. *Tranby Croft, Hull.*	
32820	9412	Charles Hacket	Grandchildren. Brother and sister to No. 32812.
32821	9413	Constance Helena Mary, wife of Captain Richard Newton Young, *late* R.A. Children, if any, of No. 32821.	
32822	9414	Frances Mary, wife of Captain Childers H. Thompson. *Bilbrough Hall, York.*	Daughter.
			Grandchildren. Children of No. 32822.
32823	9415	Katherine Alicia, wife of Colonel Bertie E. M. Gordon.	
32824	9416	Mary Hacket.	Daughters.
32825	9417	Charlotte Sarah Hacket.	
32826	9418	Richard Foulis Roundell, 1872. *Gledstone, near Skipton, co. York.*	Grandson. Son of Harriet Jane Hacket, −1895, wife of William Roundell, of Gledstone, 1817–1881.

698. Descendants of Charles, 5th Duke of Richmond and Lennox, K.G., 1791–1860. (See Table CIX.)

32827 −66	}	Same as Nos. 27763–27802.

699. Descendants of Lord John George Lennox, M.P., 1793–1873. (See Table CIX.)

32867	9419	George Montagu Lennox, Lieutenant I.S.C., 1874.	Grandchildren. Children of the late Major-General Augustus Frederick Francis Lennox, 1824–1883.
32868	9420	Algernon Lionel Lennox, 1876.	
32869	9421	Henry de Grey Lennox, 1879.	
32870	9422	Mabel Elizabeth, wife of the Rev. Frederick Alfred John Hervey, M.V.O., Canon of Norwich, 1860. *Sandringham Rectory, Norfolk.*	
32871	9423	Alexandra Leila Hervey, 1883.	Great-grandchild. Child of No. 32870.
32872	9424	Leila Ethel, wife of Alexander Donovan. *Carbrooke Hall, Watton, Norfolk.*	Grandchild. Sister to No. 32867, &c.
32873	9425	Alexander Maitland Donovan, 1892.	Great-grandchildren. Children of No. 32872.
32874	9426	Esmé Donovan, 1895.	
32875	9427	Gerald Wilbraham Stuart Lennox, Lieutenant 2nd Battalion Black Watch, 1862.	Grandchildren. Children of General Sir Wilbraham Oates Lennox, K.C.B., V.C., 1830–1897.
32876	9428	Cecil George Pelham Lennox, 1872. *Northumberland, Twickenham.*	
32877	9429	Claud Henry Maitland Lennox, *late* Lieutenant 2nd Battalion Northumberland Fusiliers, 1873.	
32878	9430	Cecilia Georgina Susan Lennox, 1875.	
32879	9431	John Maitland Lennox, Captain *late* R.M.L.I., 1833. *49 Claverton Terrace, St. George's Road, W.*	Son.

The Blood Royal of Britain

700. Descendants of Lord William Pitt Lennox, M.P., 1799–1881. (See Table CIX.)

32880	9432	William Robert Lennox, 1855.	Son.

701. Descendants of Lieut.-Col. the Lord Arthur Lennox, M.P., 1806–1864. (See Table CIX.)

32881	9433	Constance Charlotte Eliza, widow of Sir George Russell, 4th Bart., M.P., 1828–1898, 1839. *Swallowfield Park, Reading.*	Elder daughter.
32882	9434	Sir George Arthur Charles Russell, 5th Bart., 1868. *Swallowfield Park, Reading.*	Grandchildren. Children of No. 32881.
32883	9435	Arthur Edward Ian Montagu Russell, 1878.	
32884	9436	Marie Clotilde Russell.	
32885	9437	Ethel Lennox, 1844.	Younger daughter.

702. Descendants of the Lady Mary Lennox, 1790–1847, and her husband, Sir Charles Augustus Fitzroy, Governor of New South Wales, K.C.B., 1796–1858. (See Table CIX.)

32886	9438	Mary Jane, wife of Reginald Dykes Marshall, J.P., D.L., 1842. *Castlerigg Manor, Keswick.*	Granddaughter. Daughter of Mary Caroline Fitz-Roy, 1823–1895, wife of Admiral the Hon. Keith Stewart., C.B., 1814–1879.
32887	9439	FitzRoy Dykes Marshall, *late* Lieutenant 3rd Battalion Duke of Cornwall's L.I., 1869.	Great-grandchildren. Children of No. 32886.
32888	9440	Rosamund Stewart, wife of Robert Allen Lawther. 60 *Burton Court, Chelsea.*	
32889	9441	Mary Stewart Lawther, 1896.	Great-great-grandchildren. Children of No. 32888.
32890	9442	. . . . Lawther, 1902.	
32891	9443	Helen Blanche Dykes Marshall.	Great-grandchildren. Children of No. 32886.
32892	9444	Sybil Janet, wife of Major Herbert Alexander Chapman, R.A.	
32893	9445	Kyrle Arthur Stewart Chapman, 1895.	Great-great-grandchildren. Children of No. 32892.
32894	9446	Sybil Joyce Chapman, 1897.	
32895	9447	Ursula Wilhelmina, wife of Major Charles Vernon Hume, D.S.O., R.A.	Great-grandchild. Child of No. 32886.
32896	9448	Reginald Vernon Hume, 1898.	Great-great-grandchildren. Sons of No. 32895.
32897	9449	Gillian Hume, 1901.	
32898	9450	Cicely Mary Marshall.	Great-grandchildren. Children of No. 32886.
32899	9451	Evelyn Adela Marshall.	
32900	9452	Olive Edith, wife of Captain Robert H. Johnston-Steuart, R.N.	
32901	9453	Guy Stewart St. Aubyn, Captain and Brevet-Major King's Royal Rifle Corps, 1870. *Bachelors'.*	Great-grandson. Son of Edith Stewart (sister to No. 32886), –1875, 1st wife of Colonel Edward St. Aubyn.
32902	9454	Blanche Caroline, widow of Admiral Sir William Houston Stewart, G.C.B., 1822–1901, 1845. 51 *Hans Road, S.W.*	Granddaughter. Next surviving sister to No. 32886.
32903	9455	Blanche Nita Mary Stewart.	Great-granddaughter. Daughter of No. 32902.

32904	9456	Louisa Wilhelmina, widow of Kyrle Alfred Chapman, 1838–1891, 1847. *Shillingstone, Blandford.*	Granddaughter. 3rd surviving sister to No. 32886.
32905	9457	FitzRoy Keith Chapman, 1871. *White's.*	Great-grandchildren. Children of Ellinor Sydney Stewart, 1849–1901, wife of Spencer Chapman.
32906	9458	Sydney Katherine, wife of H. D. Peploe. *Garnston Castle, Hereford.*	
32907	9459	Daniel Spencer Peploe, 1891.	Great-great-grandchildren. Children of No. 32906.
32908	9460	Keith Peploe, 1893.	
32909	9461	Gerald Sydney Peploe.	
32910	9462	Hélène Adeline Blanche, wife of A. Glen Kidston.	Great-grandchild. Sister of No. 32905.
32911	9463	George Pearson Glen Kidston, 1899.	Great-great-grandchild. Child of No. 32910.
32912	9464	Ellinor Audrey Chapman.	Great-grandchild. Youngest sister of No. 32905.
32913	9465	John Harvey, 1875.	*Ickwell Bury, Biggleswade.*	Great-grandchildren. Children of Rosa Frances Stewart (sister to No. 32886), 1854–1880, wife of Captain John Edmund Audley Harvey, of Ickwell Bury.
32914	9466	Andalusia Beatrice Harvey.		
32915	9467	Marjory Rosa Bayly Harvey.		
32916	9468	Caroline Ethel Gertrude Stewart, 1860. *51 Hans Road, S.W.*	Granddaughters. 5th and 6th surviving sisters to No. 32886.
32917	9469	Mabel Augusta, wife of Gilbert Gordon Blane, *late* Scots Guards, 1862. *Foliejon Park, Windsor, Berks.*	
32918	9470	Malcolm Gilbert Stewart Blane, 1892.	Great-grandchildren. Children of No. 32917.
32919	9471	Miriam Ella Stewart Blane, 1889.	
32920	9472	Sylvia Stewart Blane, 1898.	
32921	9473	Hilda Eugenia, wife of Arthur Rhuvon Guest, 1868. *13 Cliveden Place, S.W.*	Granddaughter. Youngest sister to No. 32886.
32922	9474	Evan Rhuvon Guest, 1902.	Great-grandchild. Son of No. 32921.

703. Descendants of Lady Sarah Lennox, 1792–1873, and her husband, General Sir Peregrine Maitland, G.C.B., 1777–1854,
sometime (1843–1846) Governor and Commander-in-chief,
Cape of Good Hope. (See Table CIX.)

32923	9475	Horatio Arthur Lennox Maitland, Admiral R.N., 1834.	Younger, but only surviving son.
		Children of Sarah Maitland (daughter), 18 –18 , wife of General Thomas Bowes Forster, 18 –1870.	
		Children of Caroline Charlotte Maitland (daughter), 18 –18 , wife of John George Turnbull, Acct.-Gen., Madras, 18 –1872.	
32924	9476	Sir Thomas Wilmot Peregrine Blome-field, 4th Bart., 1848. 6 *The Grange, Wimbledon Common, S.W.*	Grandson. Son of Georgina Louisa Maitland, 18 – 1852, 1st wife of the Rev. Sir Thomas Eardley Wil-mot Blomefield, 3rd Bart., –1872.
32925	9477	Thomas Charles Alfred Blomefield, Lieutenant R.N., 1875.	Great-grandchildren. Children of No. 32924.
32926	9478	Nigel Napier Blomefield, 1877.	
32927	9479	Wilmot Blomefield, 1878.	
32928	9480	Lilias Marow Blomefield.	
32929	9481	Nancy Blomefield.	

32930	9482	Caroline Sarah Blomefield.	Granddaughters. Sisters to No. 32924.
32931	9483	Louisa Charlotte Emily, wife of Captain Theodosius Stuart Russell, D.L., Chief Constable of the West Riding of York. *St. John's, Wakefield.*	
32932	9484	Edmund Stuart Eardley Wilmot Russell, Captain R.F.A., Gunnery Instructor at School of Gunnery, Shoeburyness, 1869.	Great-grandchildren. Children of No. 32931.
32933	9485	Charles Lennox Somerville Russell, Foreign Under-Secretary to Government of India, 1872.	
32934	9486	Wilmot Peregrine Maitland Russell, Senior Consular Assistant, Hankow, 1874.	
32935	9487	Archibald George Blomefield Russell, 1879.	
32936	9488	Somerville Peregrine Brownlow Russell, R.N., 1883.	
32937	9489	Georgina Louisa Margaret, wife of the Rev. Henry Sinclair Brooke. *Pembury Vicarage, Tunbridge Wells.*	
32938	9490	Margaret Caroline Sarah Russell.	
32939	9491	Georgina Salome, wife of Loftus Henry Martin, *late* 69th Regiment. 23 *Albemarle Crescent, Scarborough.*	Granddaughter. Youngest sister to No. 32924.
32940	9492	Loftus Wilmot Martin, 1871.	Great-grandchildren. Children of No. 32939.
32941	9493	Frank Henry Eardley Martin, 1872.	
32942 –63		Same as Nos. 20166–20186.	Grandchildren, &c. Children of Emily Sophia Maitland, –1891, wife of Admiral Lord Frederic Herbert Kerr, 1818–1896.
32964	9494	Charles Ernest Maitland Desborough, Malay F. S. Civil Service, 1865.	Grandson. Son of Eliza Mary Maitland, 1832–18 , wife of Major-Gen. John Desborough, C.B., of Cross House, Northam, N. Devon, 1824.
32965	9495	John Noel Campbell Desborough, 1898.	Great-grandchildren. Children of No. 32964.
32966	9496	Joyce Ethel Maitland Desborough.	
32967	9497	Arthur Peregrine Henry Desborough, Captain *late* R.A., Inspector of Explosives, Home Office, 1868. 35 *Cheyne Court, Chelsea, S.W.*	Grandchildren. Brothers and sisters to No. 32964.
32968	9498	John Bertie Desborough, 1874.	
32969	9499	Leila Sarah Maitland Desborough.	
32970	9500	Henrietta Margaret Desborough.	
32971	9501	Emily Mary, wife of Commander Morgan Singer, R.N.	
32972	9502	Joan Frances Lennox Morgan Singer.	Great-grandchild. Daughter of No. 32971.
32973	9503	Madeline Annie Desborough.	Granddaughter. Youngest sister to No. 32964.

704. Descendants of the Lady Georgiana Lennox, 1795–1891, and her husband, William, 23rd Lord de Ros, 1797–1874. (See Table CIX.)

32974 –78		Same as Nos. 23286–23290.

705. Descendants of the Lady Jane Lennox, 1798–1861, and her husband, Lawrence Peel, of Kemptown, Brighton, 1801–1888. (See Table CIX.)

32979 –90	}	Same as Nos. 27894–27905. } Grandchildren, &c. Children, &c., of Sir Charles Lennox Peel, G.C.B., 1823–1899.	
32991	9504	Cecil Lennox Peel, Lieut.-Col. *late* Scots Guards, 1830. *Easthampstead Cottage, Wokingham.*	} Son.
32992	9505	Alice Jane Lennox Peel.	} Grandchildren.
32993	9506	Cecil Hester Lennox, wife of Leicester Morgan Reed. 61 *Harrington Gardens, S.W.*	Children of No. 32991.
32994	9507	Christian William Laurence Peel Reed, 1902.	{ Great-grandchildren.
32995	9508	Cyllene Mary Peel Reed, 1899.	Children of No. 32993.
32996	9509	Constance Augusta Lennox, wife of Colonel George Grant Gordon, C.V.O., C.B. *Oakhurst, Hampstead Heath, N.W.*	} Daughter.
32997	9510	Laurence George Frank Gordon, D.S.O., Major R.F.A. *Caledonian.*	} Grandson. Son of No. 32996.
32998	9511	Thelma Esme Florence Gordon, 1900.	} Great-grandchild. Daughter of No. 32997.
32999	9512	Christian Frederic Gordon, 1866.	Grandson. Son of No. 32996.
33000	9513	Cecily Margaret Gordon, 1899.	{ Great-grandchild. Daughter of No. 32999.
33001	9514	Helena Jane, wife of the Rev. William Henry Stone, 1870. *St. Mary's Vicarage, Kilburn, N.W.*	} Granddaughter. Daughter of No. 32996.
33002	9515	Thora Guinevere Stone, 1896.	} Great-granddaughters. Daughters of No. 33001.
33003	9516	Esther Mary Stone, 1897.	

706. Descendants of Lady Charlotte Lennox, 1804–1833, 1st wife of Maurice Frederick, 1st Lord Fitzhardinge, G.C.B., 1788–1867. (See Table CIX.)

33004	9517	Charles Paget Fitzhardinge, 3rd Lord Fitzhardinge [U.K.], 1830. *Berkeley Castle, Gloucester.*	} Children.
33005	9518	Frederica Charlotte Fitzhardinge, Lady Gifford [U.K.], 1825. *Hampton Court Palace.*	
33006	9519	Edric Frederick, 3rd Baron Gifford [U.K.], V.C., 1849. *Old Park, Chichester.*	Grandchildren.
33007	9520	Hon. Edgar Berkeley Gifford, 1857. *Bourne Stream, Wotton-under-Edge, Gloucester.*	Children of No. 33005.
33008	9521	Hon. Maurice Raymond Gifford, C.M.G., 1859. *Boothby Hall, Grantham.*	
33009	9522	Charles Maurice Elton Gifford, 1899.	} Great-grandchildren. Children of No. 33008.
33010	9523	Diana Frederica Gifford, 1901.	
33011	9524	Hon. Eva, wife of Major-General Sir Henry Trotter, K.C.V.O., Commanding Home District, 1846. *Morton Hall, Edinburgh.* 33 *Cadogan Square, S.W.*	Grandchild. Eldest daughter of No. 33005.
33012 –16	}	Same as Nos. 31990–31994.	{ Great-grandchildren. Children of No. 33011.

33017	9525	Hon. Harriet Ella, widow of Lieut.-Col. the Hon. Archibald Charles Henry Douglas-Pennant, 1837–1884, 1847. *Lillingstone Dayrell, Buckingham.* — Granddaughter. 2nd daughter of No. 33005.
33018	9526	Frank Douglas-Pennant, Captain the King's Royal Rifle Corps, 1865. — Great-grandson. Son of No. 33017.
33019	9527	Cyril Eustace Douglas-Pennant, 1894. — Great-great-grandchildren. Children of No. 33018.
33020	9528	Bridget Violet Douglas-Pennant, 1899.
33021	9529	Eileen Maud Douglas-Pennant, 1901.
33022	9530	Claud Douglas-Pennant, Barrister-at-Law, 1867. *2 Mitre Court Buildings, Temple, E.C.*
33023	9531	Algernon Douglas-Pennant, 1872. — Great-grandchildren. Children of No. 33017.
33024	9532	Archibald Douglas-Pennant, Lieutenant 3rd Battalion Royal Scots, 1881.
33025	9533	Muriel, wife of the Hon. Edward Algernon FitzRoy, M.P., 1869. *Fox Hill, West Haddon, Rugby.*
33026	9534	Robert Oliver FitzRoy, 1893. — Great-great-grandchildren. Children of No. 33025.
33027	9535	Michael Algernon Fitz-Roy, 1895.
33028	9536	John Maurice FitzRoy, 1897.
33029	9537	Nancy Jean FitzRoy, 1894.
33030	9538	Rachel, wife of the Hon. Gilbert Vanden-Bempde-Johnstone, 1874. *Wilton Crescent, S.W.* — Great-grandchild. Child of No. 33017.
33031	9539	Mark Vanden-Bempde-Johnstone, 1900. — Great-great-grandchildren. Children of No. 33030.
33032	9540	Hon. Emily, wife of Robert Thomas Napier Speir, 1847. *Culdees Castle, Perthshire.* — Granddaughter. 3rd daughter of No. 33005.
33033	9541	Guy Thomas Speir, 1875. Great-grandson. Son of No. 33032.
33034	9542	Bertha Marjorie Speir, 1899. — Great-great-grandchildren. Children of No. 33033.
33035	9543	Joan Mary Elspeth Speir, 1900.
33036	9544	Kenneth Robert Speir, Imperial Yeomanry, 1877.
33037	9545	Malcolm Scott Speir, 1887. — Great-grandchildren. Children of No. 33032.
33038	9546	Ronald Fitzhardinge Speir, 1888.
33039	9547	Gwendolen Mary Speir, 1870.
33040	9548	Marjorie Gifford, wife of Anthony White, 1879. *12 Chesham Place, S.W.*
33041	9549	Christopher Anthony White, 1900. — Great-great-grandchild. Son of No. 33040.
33042	9550	Hon. Evelyn Mary, wife of Thomas Arthur Fitzhardinge Kingscote, 1850. *The Abbey, Cirencester. St. James' Palace, S.W.* — Granddaughter. 4th daughter of No. 33005.
33043	9551	Edric Thomas Kingscote, 1885. — Great-grandchildren. Children of No. 33042.
33044	9552	Maurice Kingscote, 1887.
33045	9553	Hon. Eleanore, wife of Lieut.-Col. Edward M. Dansey, *late* 1st Life Guards, 1852. *Cams Hall, Fareham, Hants.* — Granddaughter. 5th daughter of No. 33005.
33046	9554	Claude Edward Marjoribank Dansey, 1876. — Great-grandchildren. Children of No. 33045.
33047	9555	Henry William Dansey, 1881.
33048	9556	Reginald Charles Dansey, 1882.
33049	9557	George Francis Dansey, 1884.
33050	9558	Miriam Eleanore Dansey, 1874.
33051	9559	Madeline Edith Dansey, 1878.
33052	9560	May Cecily Dansey, 1880.
33053	9561	Margaret Dansey, 1885.
33054	9562	Monica Dansey, 1890.

33055	9563	Hon. Elspeth Fitzhardinge, wife of Lt.-Col. Francis John Paul Butler, *late* 18th Hussars, 1855. *Wyck Hill, Wick Ressington, Stow-on-the-Wold.*	Granddaughter. 6th daughter of No. 33005.
33056	9564	John Fitzhardinge Paul Butler, 1888.	Great-grandchildren.
33057	5565	Muriel Butler, 1878.	Children of No.
33058	9566	Kathleen Louisa Butler, 1881.	33055.
33059	9567	Hon. Edith Charlotte Gifford, 1863. *Hampton Court Palace.*	Granddaughter. 7th daughter of No. 33005.
33060	9568	Hon. Fenella Fitzhardinge, widow of Lieut.-Col. Henry Armytage, 1828–1901, 1832. *47 Warwick Square, S.W.*	Younger daughter.
33061	9569	Percy Armytage, M.V.O., 1853. *28 Hans Place, S.W.*	Grandchildren
33062	9570	Maud Charlotte Armytage.	Children of
33063	9571	Constance, wife of Joseph Critchley Martin, 1859. *Narborough Hall, Swaffham.*	No. 33060.
33064	9572	Edith, wife of Philip Graham.	Great-grandchild. Child of No. 33063.
33065	9573	Alice Armytage. Grandchild. Youngest daughter of No. 33060.	

707. Descendants of Admiral Sir John Gordon Sinclair, 8th Bart., 1790–1863. (See Table CIX.)

33066	9574	Madelina, Hon. Mrs. Dudley Anderson-Pelham-Sinclair, widow of Captain the Hon. Dudley Worsley Anderson-Pelham, R.N., 1812–1851. *Murkle, Caithness. St Lawrence, Ventnor, I.W.*	Daughter.
33067 –76	}	Same as Nos. 30449–30458. {	Granddaughter, &c. &c., of No. 33066. Daughter,
33077	9575	Susan Hay, Lady Lennox, widow of General Sir Wilbraham Oates Lennox, K.C.B., V.C., 1830–1897. *East Pallant House, Chichester.*	Younger daughter.
33078 –80	}	Same as Nos. 32876–32878. {	Grandchildren. Children of No. 33077.

708. Descendants, if any, of Lady Magdalen Gordon, –1847, and her 2nd husband, Charles Fysche Palmer, of Luckley Park, Bedfordshire, M.P. (See Table CIX.)

709. Descendants of George, 6th Duke of Manchester, 1799–1855. (See Table CX.)

33081	9576	William Angus Drogo, 9th Duke [G.B.], and 12th Earl [E.] of Manchester, 1877. *Kimbolton Castle, St. Neots.*	Great-grandson. Son of George Victor Drogo, 8th Duke of Manchester, 1853–1892, and grandson of William Drogo, 7th Duke of Manchester, K.P., 1823–1890.
33082	9577	. . . . . . Viscount Mandeville, 1902.	Great-great-grandchildren
33083	9578	Lady Mary Alice Montagu, 1901.	Children of No. 33081.

33084	9579	Lord Charles William Augustus Montagu, *late* Lieutenant North Somerset Yeomanry Cavalry, 1860. 22 *Austin Friars, E.C.*	Grandchildren. Children of 7th Duke of Manchester. *See above.*
33085	9580	Mary Louisa Elizabeth, Duchess of Hamilton [S.] and Brandon [G.B.], 1854. *Upper Hall, Ledbury.*	
33086	9581	Lady Mary Louise Hamilton, 1884. *Easton Park, Wickham Market.*	Great-grandchild. Daughter of No. 33085.
33087	9582	Louisa Augusta Beatrice, Countess of Gosford [I.], Baroness Worlingham [U.K.], 1856. *Gosford Castle, co. Armagh.* 22 *Mansfield Street, Portland Place, W.*	Grandchild. Sister to Nos. 33085, &c.
33088	9583	Archibald Charles Montagu Brabazon, Viscount Acheson, 1877.	
33089	9584	Hon. Patrick Charles George Cavendish Acheson, Midshipman R.N., H.M.S. *Renown*, 1883.	Great-grandchildren. Children of No. 33087.
33090	9585	Lady Alexandra Louise Elizabeth Acheson, 1878.	
33091	9586	Lady Mary Acheson, 1881.	
33092	9587	Lady Theodosia Louisa Augusta Acheson, 1882.	
33093	9588	Alice Maude Olivia, Lady Stanley, 1862. 36 *Great Cumberland Place, W.*	Grandchild. Youngest sister to No. 33085.
33094	9589	Hon. Edward Montagu Cavendish Stanley, 1894.	Great-grandchildren. Children of No. 33093.
33095	9590	Hon. Oliver Frederick George Stanley, 1896.	
33096	9591	Hon. Victoria Alice Louise Stanley, 1892.	
33097	9592	Robert Acheson Cromie Montagu, 1854. *Cromore, Portstewart.*	Grandson. Son of the Right Hon. Lord Robert Montagu, P.C., 1825-1902.
33098	9593	John Michael Cromie Montagu, 1881.	Great-grandchildren. Children of No. 33097.
33099	9594	George Frederick Montagu, R.N., 1883.	
33100	9595	Cuthbert Francis Montagu, 1884.	
33101	9596	Austin Robert Montagu, 1885.	
33102	9597	Walter Philip Montagu, 1886.	
33103	9598	Gilbert Paul Montagu, 1887.	
33104	9599	Alexander Cyril Montagu, 1890.	
33105	9600	Mary Emily Winifred Montagu, 1892.	
33106	9601	Monthermer Stanley Hume Montagu, 1868.	Grandchildren. Brothers and sister of No. 33097.
33107	9602	Henry Bernard Montagu, Lieutenant R.N., 1872.	
33108	9603	St. John Edward Montagu, Captain Northumberland Fusiliers, 1878.	
33109	9604	Oliver Millicent, widow of Henry Lyons, 1828-1885, 1850. 2 *Ovington Gardens, S.W.*	
33110	9605	James Denis Lyons, 1877. *Croome House, co. Limerick.*	Great-grandchildren. Children of No. 33109.
33111	9606	Henry Montagu Lyons, 1882.	
33112	9607	John Cromie Lyons, 1883.	
33113	9608	Mary Eleanor Lyons.	
33114	9609	Oliver Millicent Lyons.	
33115	9610	Ethel Lyons.	
33116	9611	Ellen Mary Elizabeth Montagu, 1853.	Grandchildren. Sisters of No. 33097.
33117	9612	Elizabeth Catherine Mary Montagu, 1863.	
33118	9613	Millicent, wife of Walter Lionel Fenwick, J.P., 1865. *Wetham Hall, Bourne, Lincolnshire.*	

33119	9614	Keld Robert George Fenwick, 1892.	Great-grandchildren. Children of No. 33118.
33120	9615	Anthony Lionel Fenwick, 1893.	
33121	9616	Montagu John Fenwick, 1896.	
33122	9617	Olivia, Countess of Tankerville [G.B.], Baroness Ossulston [E.], 1830. *The Welkin, Lindfield, Sussex.*	Elder surviving daughter.
33123	9618	George Montagu, 7th Earl of Tankerville [G.B.], 8th Baron Ossulston [E.], 1852. *Chillingham Castle, Belford.* *Thornington House, Cornhill-on-Tweed.*	Grandson. Son of No. 33122.
33124	9619	Charles Augustus Ker, Lord Ossulston, 1897.	Great-grandchild. Child of No. 33123.
33125	9620	Lady Corisande Olivia Bennet, 1855.	Granddaughter. Daughter of No. 33122.
33126	9621	Arthur George Maule, 14th Earl of Dalhousie [S.], and 3rd Baron Ramsay [U.K.], 1878. *Dalhousie Castle, Bonnyrigg, Mid-Lothian.*	Great-grandchildren. Children of the Lady Ida Louise Bennet, —1887 (daughter of No. 33122), and her husband, John William, 13th Earl of Dalhousie, K.T., 1847–1887.
33127	9622	Hon. Patrick William Maule Ramsay, 1879.	
33128	9623	Hon. Alexander Robert Maule Ramsay, R.N., 1881.	
33129	9624	Hon. Ronald Edward Maule Ramsay, twins,	
33130	9625	Hon. Charles Fox Maule Ramsay, 1885.	
33131	9626	Sydney Charlotte, Countess of [S.], and Baroness [U.K.] Kintore, 1851. *Keith Hall, Inverurie.* *7 Cadogan Square, S.W.*	Younger surviving daughter.
33132	9627	Arthur George, Lord Falconer, 1879.	Grandchildren. Children of No. 33131.
33133	9628	Lady Ethel Sydney Keith-Falconer, 1874.	
33134	9629	Lady Hilda Madeline Keith-Falconer, 1875.	

710. Descendants of Lord William Francis Montagu, 1800–1842. (See Table CX.)

33135	9630	Emily, widow of John Cromie, —1875, 1832. *Cromore, Port Stewart, Londonderry.*	Daughter.
33136	9631	Owen Llewelyn Mansel, 1864.	
33137	9632	William Du Pre Mansel, *formerly* Lieutenant 4th Battalion King's Own Regiment, now Sub-Inspector Basutoland Police, 1869.	Grandchildren. Children of Louisa Catherine Montagu, 1835–1901, and her husband, the Rev. Owen Luttrell Mansel, 1827–1900.
33138	9633	Charles Pleydell Mansel, Lieutenant R.N., 1873.	
33139	9634	James Morton Mansel, 1876.	
33140	9635	Katherine Louisa Mansel.	
33141	9636	Emily Magdalene Mansel.	
33142	9637	Winifred Emma Mansel.	
33143	9638	Theresa Mary, wife of Algar Labouchere Thorold. *Skidbrooke, St. Mary Church, Torquay.*	
33144	9639	Anthony Herbert Gerald Thorold, 1896.	Great-grandchildren. Children of No. 33143.
33145	9640	Frances John Anselm Thorold, 1901.	
33146	9641	Wilhelmina Benedicta Mary Du Pre Thorold, 1895.	
33147	9642	Mary Catherine Ann Thorold, 1899.	

711. Descendants of Lady Elizabeth Montagu, 1795–1857, wife of Major-General Thomas Steele, –1847. (See Table CX.)

33148	9643	. . . . Steele, 1875. { Grandson. Son of General Sir Thomas Montagu Steele, K.C.B., 1820–

712. Descendants of Lady Susan Montagu, 1797–1870, and her husband, George, 8th Marquis of Tweeddale, K.T., 1787–1876. (See Table CX.)

33149	9644	William Montagu, 10th Marquis of Tweeddale [S.], 1st Baron Tweeddale of Yester [U.K.], K.T., 1826. *Yester House, Haddingtonshire.* 6 *Hill Street, Berkeley Square, W.* } Son.
33150	9645	William George Montagu, Earl of Gifford, 1884.
33151	9646	Lord Arthur Vincent Hay, 1886. } Grandchildren.
33152	9647	Lord Edward Douglas John Hay, 1888. Children of
33153	9648	Lady Susan Elizabeth Clementine, wife of Walter Waring, 1st Life Guards, 1879. No. 33149.
33154	9649	Lord John Hay, Admiral of the Fleet, G.C.B., 1827. *Fulmer Place, Slough.* } Son.
33155	9650	John Arthur Lambert Hay, Lieutenant R.N., 1877. } Grandchildren.
33156	9651	Thomas William Hay, 1882. Children of
33157	9652	Minnie Christina Brenda Hay, 1880. No. 33154.
33158	9653	Lord Charles Edward Hay, *late* Captain 2nd Foot, 1833. } Sons.
33159	9654	Lord Frederick Hay, *late* Bengal C.S., 1835.
33160	9655	Charles Fergusson, Major and Brevet-Colonel Grenadier Guards, D.S.O., 1865. 80 *Cornwall Gardens, S.W.*
33161	9656	James Andrew Fergusson, Commander R.N., 1871.
33162	9657	Susan Georgiana, wife of John George Baird, M.P. 89 *Eaton Square, S.W.*

Great-grandchildren. Children of Lady Edith Christian Ramsay, 1839–1871, 1st wife of the Right Hon. Sir James Fergusson, Bart., P.C., M.P., and grandchildren of Lady Susan Georgiana Hay, 1818–1853, wife of James Andrew, 10th Earl and 1st Marquis of Dalhousie, K.T., 1812–1860.

33163	9658	Edith Christian Baird, 1893. } Great-great-grandchildren.
33164	9659	Janet Mary Baird, 1895. Children of No. 33162.
33165	9660	George Simon Arthur Watson-Taylor, *late* Captain Wilts Yeomanry, J.P., D.L., 1850. *Erlestoke Park, Devizes.*
33166	9661	Arthur Wellesley Watson-Taylor, 1853.
33167	9662	Arthur Simon Watson-Taylor, 1884.
33168	9663	Harry Gerald Watson-Taylor, 1885.
33169	9664	Alfred Cyril Watson-Taylor, 1886.
33170	9665	Felix John Watson-Taylor, 1887.
33171	9666	Eric George Watson-Taylor, 1896.
33172	9667	John Arthur Watson-Taylor, J.P., Wilts, 1857.
33173	9668	William Arthur Watson-Taylor, 1859.
33174	9669	Anna Louisa, wife of the Hon. Alan de Tatton Egerton, M.P. 9 *Seamore Place, Mayfair, W.*

Grandchildren. Children of Lady Hannah Charlotte Hay, 1818–1887, wife of Simon Watson-Taylor, of Erlestoke Park.

Great-grandchildren. Children of No. 33166.

Grandchildren. Brothers and sister to No. 33165, &c.

33175		Same as No. 29281. Great-grandchild.	Son of No. 33174.
33176	9670	Susan Georgiana Montagu Frances Watson-Taylor.	Grandchildren. Sisters to Nos. 33165, &c.
33177	9671	Charlotte Isabella Joanna, widow of William Richard Winch. *Childown, Chertsey.*	
33178	9672	Arthur Winch, 1879.	Great-grandchildren. Children of No. 33177.
33179	9673	Henry Louis William Winch, 1882.	
33180	9674	Charlotte Isabella Mary Emma Winch, 1875.	
33181	9675	Aimée Constance Winch, 1878.	
33182	9676	Mary Elizabeth, wife of Lieut.-Col. Robert William Blackwood. *Cedars, Long Cross, Chertsey.*	Grandchild. 4th sister to Nos. 33165, &c.
33183	9677	Robert Montagu Blackwood, 2nd Lieutenant 2nd Battalion Derbyshire Regiment, 1881.	Great-grandchildren. Children of No. 33182.
33184	9678	Hans Frederick Blackwood, 1887.	
33185	9679	Elizabeth Mary Blackwood.	
33186	9680	Violet Emily, wife of Charles Augustus Verner. *War Coppice, near Caterham.*	Grandchild. 5th sister to No. 33165.
33187	9681	Guy William Hay Verner, 1880.	Great-grandchildren. Children of No. 33186.
33188	9682	Roland Charles Verner, 1885.	
33189	9683	Charles George Verner, 1893.	
33190	9684	Amélie Ella Violet Verner.	
33191	9685	Rose Verner.	
33192	9686	Violet Beatrice Verner.	
33193	9687	Rose Edith, widow of Robert Frederick Ward, 1846–1891. *4 Eaton Square.*	Grandchild. 6th sister to No. 33165.
33194	9688	Hamilton Frederick Ward, Lieutenant Irish Guards, 1880.	Great-grandchildren. Children of No. 33193.
33195	9689	Mabel Hariot Julia Ward, 1882.	
33196	9690	Victoria Watson-Taylor. Grandchild.	7th sister to No. 33165.
33197	9691	Robert George Wardlaw-Ramsay, J.P., D.L., Lieut.-Col. 6th Volunteer Battalion Royal Scots, 1852. *Whitehill, Rosewell, co. Edinburgh.*	Grandson. Son of Lady Louisa Jane Hay, 1819–1882, wife of Robert Balfour Wardlaw-Ramsay, of Whitehill, 1815–1882.
33198	9692	Arthur Balcarres Wardlaw-Ramsay, 1887.	Great-grandchildren. Children of No. 33197.
33199	9693	David Wardlaw-Ramsay, 1890.	
33200	9694	Ernest Wardlaw-Ramsay, 1892.	
33201	9695	Louisa Mary Wardlaw-Ramsay.	
33202	9696	Erica Violet Wardlaw-Ramsay.	
33203	9697	Susan Georgiana, wife of the Rev. Frederic Abel Leslie-Melville. *Welbourn Rectory, Lincoln.*	Grandchild. Sister to No. 33197.
33204	9698	Ruthven Wardlaw Leslie-Melville, 1879.	Great-grandchildren. Children of No. 33203.
33205	9699	Henry William Leslie-Melville, 1881.	
33206	9700	Malcolm Alexander Leslie-Melville, 1882.	
33207	9701	Annie Louisa Leslie-Melville, 1871.	
33208	9702	Lucy Mabel Leslie-Melville, 1873.	
33209	9703	Eleanor Leslie-Melville, 1875.	
33210	9704	Louisa Jane, wife of the Rev. Henry Venn. *Walmer Vicarage, Kent.*	Grandchild. 2nd sister to No. 33197.
33211	9705	Arthur Denis Venn, 1880. Great-grandchildren.	Children of No. 33210.
33212	9706	Lindsay Richard Venn, 1883.	
33213	9707	Elizabeth Caroline Wardlaw-Ramsay.	Grandchildren. Younger sisters to No. 33197.
33214	9708	May Alice Wardlaw-Ramsay.	
33215	9709	Edith Mary Wardlaw-Ramsay.	
33216	9710	Mabel Frances, widow of Robert Henry Duncan Fergusson.	

33217	9711	Robert Arthur Fergusson, 1878. ⎫ Great-grandchildren. Children	
33218	9712	Irene Hilda Fergusson. ⎭ of No. 33216.	

33219	9713	Emily Alexina, wife of Major James ⎫ Grandchild. Youngest
		    Otway Graham Toler, Highland ⎬ sister to No. 33197.
		    Light Infantry. ⎭	

33220	9714	Elizabeth, Duchess of Wellington [U.K.], of Ciudad
		    Rodrigo [Spain], and of Vittoria [Portugal],
		    Princess of Waterloo [Netherlands], Countess
		    of Mornington [I.], 1820.
		    Bearhill Park, Walton-on-Thames.	

33221	9715	Lady Jane, wife of Lieut.-Gen. Sir Richard Chambre
		    Hayes Taylor, K.C.B., 1830.
		    16 *Eaton Place, W.*
		    Dowestown, Navan, co. Meath.
			Daughters.

33222	9716	Richard Edward Montagu Taylor, 1871. ⎫	
33223	9717	Constance Mary Jane Taylor, 1864. ⎪ Grandchildren. Children	
33224	9718	Millicent Lilla Harriet Taylor, 1866. ⎬ of No. 33221.	
33225	9719	Evelyn Beatrice Charlotte Taylor, 1867. ⎪	
33226	9720	Florence Virginia Mathilde Taylor, 1869. ⎭	
33227	9721	Lady Julia Hay, 1831. ⎫	

33228	9722	Lady Emily, widow of the Right Hon. Sir Robert Peel, ⎪
		    3rd Bart., P.C., G.C.B., 1822–1895, 1836. ⎬ Daughters.
		    12 *Stratton Street, W.* ⎪
		    Villa Lammermoor, Geneva. ⎭	

33229	9723	Sir Robert Peel, 4th Bart., 1867. Grandson. Son of No. 33228.	
33230	9724	Robert Peel, 1898. Great-grandson. Son of No. 33229.	
33231	9725	Victoria Alexandrina Julia, wife of Daniel F. P. ⎫ Granddaughters. Barton. ⎬ Daughters of	
33232	9726	Evelyn Emily, wife of Ronald Macleay. ⎪ No. 33228.	
33233	9727	Agnes Helen, wife of Daniel von der Heydt. ⎭	
33234	9728	Alexandrina von der Heydt, ⎰ Great-granddaughter. Daughter of 1895. ⎱ No. 33233.	

33235	9729	Gwendoline, wife of Victor von Müller, ⎫ Granddaughter. Youngest
		    Lieutenant Prussian Guard Field ⎬ daughter of No. 33228.
		    Artillery. *Potsdam, Germany.* ⎭	

33236	9730	Hans Joachim von Müller, 1897. ⎫ Great-grandchildren. Son	
33237	9731	Gwendoline Victoria von Müller, 1899. ⎭ and daughter of No. 33235.	

713. Descendants of Lady Georgiana Frederica Montagu, 1803–1892, 2nd wife of Evan Baillie, of Dochfour, 1798–1883. (See Table CX.)

33238	9732	James Evan Bruce Baillie, of Dochfour, ⎫ Grandson. Son of Evan
		    M.P., 1859. ⎬ Peter Montagu Baillie,
		    71 *South Audley Street, W.* ⎭ 1824–1874.	

33239	9733	George Evan Michael Baillie, 1894. ⎫ Great-grandchildren. Chil-	
33240	9734	Arthur Malcolm Augustus Baillie, 1896. ⎬ dren of No. 33238.	
33241	9735	Victoria Frances Maud Baillie, 1899. ⎭	
33242	9736	Augustus Charles Baillie, *late* Lieut.-Col. R.H.A., ⎫ Grandchildren. 1861. ⎬ Brothers to	
33243	9737	Rev. Albert Victor Baillie, 1864. ⎭ No. 33238. *The Rectory, Rugby.*	
33244	9738	Alexander Gustavus Baillie, 1901. ⎰ Great-grandchildren. Children ⎱ of No. 33243.	

33245	9739	Hon. Victoria Matilda Susan, wife of Captain ⎫ Grandchild. Sister
		    Alaric Frederick Grant, R.N. ⎬ to No. 33238.
		    Ballindarnoch, co. Inverness. ⎭	

33246	9740	Granville Hugh Baillie, 1873. 18 *Pelham Place, S.W.*	Grandson. Son of William Montagu Baillie, J.P., 1827–1902.
33247	9741	Hilda Ina Baillie, 1899.	Great-grandchild. Daughter of No. 33246.
33248	9742	Isabella Georgiana Baillie. *Rotherhurst,*	Grandchildren. Sisters of No. 33246.
33249	9743	Caroline Mary Baillie. *Burwash.*	
33250	9744	Eva Baillie.	
33251	9745	Caroline Eliza Montague, Baroness Wynford [U.K.]. 5 *Lowndes Square, S.W.*	
33252	9746	Georgiana Mary, wife of Colonel the Hon. Sir William James Colville, K.C.V.O., C.B. 47 *Chester Square, S.W.*	Daughters.
33253	9747	Arthur Edward William Colville, Lieut.-Col. Rifle Brigade, 1857.	Grandson. Son of No. 33252.
33254	9748	Robert Alfred Colville, 1888.	Great-grandchild. Child of No. 33253.
33255	9749	Mary Catherine, wife of the Right Hon. Sir John Winfield-Bonser, P.C., Chief Justice of Ceylon.	Granddaughter. Daughter of No. 33252.
33256	9750	Mary Emily, wife of Francis Henry Beaumont. *Buckland Court, Reigate.*	3rd daughter.
33257	9751	Francis Montagu Beaumont, Major King's Royal Rifles, 1857.	
33258	9752	Spencer William Montagu Beaumont, Lieutenant R.N., 1864.	Grandchildren. Children of No. 33256.
33259	9753	Beatrice Caroline, wife of Col. Percival Scrope Marling, V.C., C.B., 18th Hussars. *Sedbury Park, Chepstow.*	
33260	9754	Mary Georgiana, wife of Henry Claude Fuller. *The Rookery, Dorking.*	
33261	9755	Arthur Loraine Claude Fuller, 1890.	
33262	9756	Beatrice Victoria Fuller, 1885.	
33263	9757	Mary Irene Georgina Fuller, 1886.	Great-grandchildren. Children of No. 33260.
33264	9758	Violet Ada Fuller, 1888.	
33265	9759	Ruby Hilda Catherine Fuller, 1893.	
33266	9760	Coralie Isabella Madeline Fuller, 1895.	
33267	9761	Evelyn Frances Fuller, 1898.	
33268	9762	Hilda Auguste Katherine, wife of Robert Massy Dawson Sanders. *Charleville Park, Charleville, Cork.*	Grandchild. Younger daughter of No. 33256.
33269	9763	Charles Craven Sanders, 1899.	Great-grandchildren. Children of No. 33268.
33270	9764	Terence Robert Beaumont Sanders, 1901.	

714. Descendants of Lady Caroline Catherine Montagu, 1804–1892, wife of John Hales Calcraft, of Rempstone Hall, M.P., 1796–1880. (See Table CX.)

33271	9765	Guy Marston, Lt. R.N.	Grandchildren. Children of Katharine Calcraft, 18 –1879, wife of the Rev. Charles Marston, –1876.
33272	9766	Caroline Marston.	
33273	9767	Catherine Marston.	
33274	9768	Georgiana Emily, wife of Dudley Henry Ryder, J.P., *late* Captain 5th Herts Rifle Volunteers. *Westbrook Hay, Hemel Hempstead.*	Daughter.
33275	9769	Dudley Granville Richard Ryder, J.P., Lt.-Col. *late* 3rd Battalion King's Royal Rifle Corps, 1858. *Old Fishery House, Boxmoor, Herts.*	Grandsons. Sons of No. 33274.
33276	9770	Cyril John Ryder, Captain *late* King's Royal Rifle Corps, 1863. *Naval and Military.*	

33277	9771	Dudley Claud Douglas Ryder, 1901. ⎫	Great-grandchildren. Children of No. 33276.
33278	9772	Iris Katharine Ryder, 1899. ⎭	
33279	9773	William Henry Ryder, *late* R.N., 1865. *Perth House, Leighton Buzzard.*	Grandchild. 3rd son of No. 33274.
33280	9774	Dudley William Ryder, 1893 ⎰	Great-grandchild. Son of No. 33279.
33281	9775	Cosmo Alan Cuthbert Ryder, 1870.	Grandchildren. 4th surviving son and daughters of No. 33274.
33282	9776	Katharine Susan Ryder, 1860.	
33283	9777	Evelyn Georgiana Ryder, 1862.	
33284	9778	Caroline Katharine, wife of Robert Armitage. *Farnley Hall, Leeds.*	
33285	9779	Robert William Armitage, 1900.	Great-grandchildren. Children of No. 33284.
33286	9780	Evelyn Caroline Armitage, 1891.	
33287	9781	Georgiana Emily Armitage, 1895.	
33288	9782	Margaret Katharine Armitage, 1897.	
33289	9783	Hon. Granville George Waldegrave, 1859. *4 Park Square West, Regent's Park, N.W.*	Grandchildren. Children of Susan Charlotte Calcraft, -1892, wife of Granville Augustus William, 3rd Baron Radstock.
33290	9784	Hon. Montagu Waldegrave, 1867. *Peshawur, India.*	
33291	9785	Esther Constance Waldegrave, 1900. ⎰	Great-grandchild. Child of No. 33290.
33292	9786	Hon. Edith Caroline, wife of Alister Gilian Fraser, 1862. *13B Harley House, Regent's Park.*	Grandchildren. Sisters to No. 33289, &c.
33293	9787	Hon. Mabel Waldegrave, 1863.	
33294	9788	Hon. Constance Waldegrave, 1865.	
33295	9789	Hon. Mary, wife of Edwyn Robert Bevan, 1871. *Banwell Abbey, Somerset.*	
33296	9790	Christina Elizabeth Frances Bevan, 1897.	Great-grandchildren. Children of No. 33295.
33297	9791	Anne Cornelia Favell Bevan, 1899.	

715. Descendants of Lady Jane Cornwallis, 1798-1856, and her husband, Richard, 3rd Lord Braybrooke, 1783-1858. (See Table CXI.)

33298 -326	⎰	Same as Nos. 25157-25185.

716. Descendants of Lady Jemima Cornwallis, 1803-1856, and her husband, Edward Granville, 3rd Earl of St. Germans, 1798-1877. (See Table CXI.)

33327	9792	Henry Cornwallis, 5th Earl of St. Germans [U.K.], 6th Baron Eliot [G.B.], 1835. *Port Eliot, St. Germans, Cornwall.* 13 *Grosvenor Gardens, S.W.*	Son.
33328	9793	Edward Henry John Cornwallis, Lord Eliot, 1885.	Grandchildren. Children of No. 33327.
33329	9794	Hon. John Granville Cornwallis Eliot, 1890.	
33330	9795	Granville John Eliot, 1867.	Grandchildren. Children of Colonel the Hon. Charles George Cornwallis Eliot, C.V.O., 1839-1901.
33331	9796	Montague Charles Eliot, Gentleman Usher to the King, 1870.	
33332	9797	Christian Edward Cornwallis Eliot, 1872. 114 *Sloane Street, S.W.*	

33333		Same as No. 26234. }	Great-grandchild. Child of No. 33332.
33334	9798	Arthur Ernest Henry Eliot, Lieutenant Kitchener's Horse, 1874.	Grandchildren. Brothers
33335	9799	Edward Granville Eliot, 1878.	and sisters of No.
33336	9800	Blanche Elizabeth Eliot, 1866.	33330.
33337	9801	Evelyn Radigund Eliot, 1869.	
33338	9802	Louisa Susan Cornwallis, Countess of Bessborough [I.], Baroness Ponsonby [G.B.] and Duncannon [U.K.], 1825. 38 *Eccleston Square, W. Bessborough, Piltown, co. Kilkenny.*	Daughter.
33339 –66	}	Same as Nos. 22402–22429.	Grandchildren, &c. Children of No. 33338.

717. Descendants of Lady Mary Cornwallis, 1804–1872, wife of Charles Ross, M.P., 1799–1860. (See Table CXI.)

33367	9803	Alexander George Gordon Ross, 1866.	Grandson. Son of Alexander Henry Ross, M.P., 1829–1888.
33368	9804	Louisa Isabella, widow of James Whatman, M.P., J.P., D.L. *Vinters', near Maidstone, Kent.*	Elder daughter.
33369	9805	Mary Eliza Cornwallis, wife of Captain Arthur George Dugdale, R.A., J.P. *Manor House, Fifehead Neville, Sturminster Newton.*	Grandchildren. Daughters of No. 33368.
33370	9806	Ellen Philippa Louisa, wife of Blakeney Persoe Trousdell, *late of Aughrim Park, co. Galway.*	
33371	9807	Hugh Cornwallis Trousdell.	
33372	9808	Charles Francis Trousdell.	
33373	9809	John Ponsonby Trousdell.	
33374	9810	Maurice George Trousdell.	Great-grandchildren.
33375	9811	Alexander James Trousdell.	Children of No.
33376	9812	Edith Ellen Trousdell.	33370.
33377	9813	Evelyn Louisa Trousdell.	
33378	9814	Catherine Ellen Trousdell.	
33379	9815	Philippa Trousdell.	
33380	9816	Florence Emma Jemima Whatman.	Grandchildren. Younger daughters of No.
33381	9817	Louisa Elizabeth Whatman.	33368.
33382	9818	Mary Jemima Ross.	Younger daughter.

718. Descendants of Lady Georgiana Gordon, 1781–1853, 2nd wife of John, 6th Duke of Bedford, K.G., 1766–1839. (See Table CIX.)

33383 –84	}	Same as Nos. 27603–27604.	Grandchildren. Children of the Rev. Lord Wriothesley Russell, Canon of Windsor, 1804–1886.
33385	9819	Rev. Henry Charles Russell, 1842. *Wollaton Rectory, Notts.*	Grandchild. Son of Lieut.-Col. the Lord Charles James Fox Russell, M.P., 1807–1894.

33386	9820	James Cosmo Russell, Lieutenant 9th Bengal Lancers, 1876.	⎫ Great-grandchildren. Children of No. 33385.
33387	9821	Thomas Wentworth Russell, 1879. *Cairo.*	
33388	9822	Leila Elizma, wife of Frank Evelyn Seely, J.P., 1876. *Calverton Hall, Nottingham.*	
33389	9823	Frank James Wriothesley Seely, 1901.	⎫ Great-great-grandchildren Children of No. 33388.
33390	9824	William Evelyn Seely, 1902.	
33391	9825	Leila Emily Seely, 1900.	
33392	9826	Marjory Violet Russell, 1881.	⎫ Great-grandchildren. Children of No. 33385.
33393	9827	Olive Isabel Russell, 1882.	
33394	9828	Sheila Russell, 1886.	
33395	9829	George William Erskine Russell, D.L., LL.D., 1853. 18 *Wilton Street, S.W.*	⎫ Grandchildren. Brother and sister to No. 33385.
33396	9830	Clarissa Elizabeth, wife of Major George Smijth-Windham, 1837. *Bembridge, Isle of Wight.*	
33397	9831	Charles Joseph Windham, Captain I.S.C., Political Assistant in Foreign Department of India, 1867.	⎫ Great-grandson. Son of No. 33396.
33398	9832	Ashe Wadham George Windham, 1894.	⎫ Great-great-grandchildren, Children of No. 33397.
33399	9833	John Bayntun Russell Windham, 1897.	
33400	9834	Walter George Windham, Lieutenant Royal Indian Marine, 1868.	⎫ Great-grandchildren. Children of No. 33396.
33401	9835	Claude Seymour Windham, 1869.	
33402	9836	Edward John Windham, 1871.	
33403	9837	James Ashe Windham, ⎱ twins, 1873.	
33404	9838	Henry Stewart Windham, ⎰	
33405	9839	Arthur Russell Windham, 1874.	
33406	9840	Evelyn Windham.	
33407	9841	Cosmo Bevan, D.L., 1863. *Widmore Court, Bromley, Kent.*	⎧ Great-grandson. Son of Elizabeth Marianne Russell (sister to No. 33385), 1820–1863, 1st wife of Francis Augustus Bevan, of Trent Park, Herts.
33408	9842	Desmond Russell Bevan, 1892.	⎰ Great-great-grandchild. Son of No. 33407.
33409	9843	General the Lord Alexander George Russell, C.B., 1821. *Uckfield House, Uckfield.*	⎱ Son.
33410	9844	Alexander Gordon Russell, *late* Lieutenant 2nd Battalion Rifle Brigade, 1854.	⎱ Grandchild. Son of No. 33409.
33411	9845	Ella Maude Emily Russell, 1886.	⎰ Great-grandchild. Child of No. 33410.
33412	9846	Leonard George Russell, *late* Captain 2nd Battalion Rifle Brigade, 1858.	⎱ Grandchild. 2nd son of No. 33409.
33413	9847	Leonard Cosmo Bolles Russell, 1895.	⎱ Great-grandchildren. Children of No. 33412.
33414	9848	Violet Agnes Mary Russell, 1891.	
33415	9849	Louisa Jane, Duchess [I.], Marchioness [G.B.], and Countess [S.] of Abercorn, Duchess of Châtellerault [France], V.A., 1812. *Coates Castle, Sussex.*	⎧ Grandchildren. Sons of Lady Georgiana Elizabeth Russell, 1810–1867, wife of Charles Romilly, Barrister-at-Law, 1808–1887. ⎱ Daughter.
33416	9850	James, 2nd Duke [I.], 3rd Marquis [G.B.], and 11th Earl [S.] of Abercorn, 15th Duke of Châtellerault [France], K.G., Heir Male of the House of Hamilton, 1838. *Baron's Court, Newton Stewart.* 61 *Green Street, W.*	⎱ Grandson. Son of No. 33415.
33417 –25	⎱	Same as Nos. 30163–30171.	⎰ Great-grandchildren, &c. Children of No. 33416.

33426	9851	Lord Claud John Hamilton, 1843. 4 *Hans Mansions, S.W.*	Grandson. 2nd son of No. 33415.
33427	9852	Gilbert Claud Hamilton, Lieutenant Grenadier Guards, 1879.	Great-grandchildren. Children of No. 33426.
33428	9853	Ida Hamilton, 1883.	
33429	9854	Right Hon. Lord George Hamilton, P.C., M.P., 1845. 17 *Montagu Street, W.*	Grandson. 3rd son of No. 33415.
33430 -32		Same as Nos. 21931-21933.	Great-grandchildren. Children of No. 33429.
33433	9855	Lord Frederick Spencer Hamilton, 1856. 13 *Great College Street, Westminster, S.W.*	Grandchildren. 4th and 5th sons of No. 33415.
33434	9856	Lord Ernest William Hamilton, 1858. *Shantock Hall, Bovingdon, Herts.*	
33435	9857	Guy Ernest Frederic Hamilton, 1894.	Great-grandchildren. Children of No. 33434.
33436	9858	John George Hamilton, 1900.	
33437	9859	Mary Brenda Hamilton, 1897.	
33438	9860	Jean Barbara Hamilton, 1898.	
33439	9861	Harriet Georgina Louisa, Countess of Lichfield [U.K.], 1834. 18 *Manchester Square, W.*	Granddaughter. Eldest daughter of No 33415.
33440	9862	Thomas Francis, 3rd Earl of Lichfield [U.K.], 1856. *Shugborough Hall, Stafford.* 38 *Great Cumberland Place, W.*	Great-grandchild. Son of No. 33439.
33441	9863	Thomas Edward Viscount Anson, 1883.	Great-great-grandchildren. Children of No. 33440.
33442	9864	Hon. Arthur Augustus Anson, 1887.	
33443	9865	Hon. Rupert Anson, 1889.	
33444	9866	Lady Bertha, wife of the Hon. Thomas Henry Frederick Egerton, 1879. 6 *Granville Place, Portman Square.*	
33445	9867	Lady Mabel Anson, 1882.	
33446	9868	Lady Violet Anson, 1886.	
33447	9869	Hon. George Augustus Anson, D.L., Chief Constable of Staffordshire, 1857. *Stafford.*	Great-grandchild. 2nd son of No. 33439.
33448	9870	John George Anson, 1886.	Great-great-grandchildren. Children of No. 33447.
33449	9871	Claud Ronald Anson, 1895.	
33450	9872	Barbara Grace Anson, 1889.	
33451	9873	Hon. Henry James Anson, Major 2nd Battalion Highland Light Infantry, 1858. *Army and Navy.*	Great-grandchildren. 3rd and 4th sons of No. 33439.
33452	9874	Hon. Frederic William Anson, J.P., 1862. *Cell Barnes, near St. Albans.*	
33453 -57		Same as Nos. 25860-25864.	Great-great-grandchildren. Children of No. 33452.
33458	9875	Hon. Claud Anson, 1864.	Great-grandchildren. Younger sons and eldest daughter of No. 33439.
33459	9876	Hon. Francis Anson, 1867.	
33460	9877	Hon. William Anson, 1872.	
33461	9878	Hon. Alfred Anson, 1876.	
33462	9879	Lady Florence Beatrice, wife of Lieut.-Col. Henry Streatfeild, Grenadier Guards, Private Secretary to the Commander-in-Chief, 1860. 81 *Gloucester Place, Portman Square, W.*	
33463	9880	Henry Sidney Streatfeild.	Great-great-grandson. Son of No. 33462.

33464	9881	Lady Beatrice, wife of Captain Richard Hamilton Rawson, *of Woodhurst, Sussex,* J.P., D.L., *late* 1st Life Guards, 1865. 116 *Park Street, W.*	Great-grandchild. 2nd daughter of No. 33439.
33465	9882	Richard Geoffrey Hamilton Rawson, 1896.	Great-great-grandchildren. Children of No. 33464.
33466	9883	Beatrice Violet Rawson, 1892.	
33467	9884	Dorothy Etta Rawson, 1899.	
33468	9885	Lady Mary Maud, wife of the Hon. Edward Alan Dudley Ryder, 1869. *Oakfield, Crawley, Sussex.*	Great-grandchild. 3rd daughter of No. 33439.
33469	9886	Henry Dudley Ryder, 1894.	Great-great-grandchildren. Children of No. 33468.
33470	9887	Evelyn Maud Ryder, 1897.	
33471	9888	Katherine Ryder, 1899.	
33472	9889	Lady Edith, wife of Captain the Hon. Lionel Fortescue King-Noel, 1870. *Horsley Towers, Leatherhead.*	Great-grandchild. 4th daughter of No. 33439.
33473 -75		Same as Nos. 25023-25025.	Great-great-grandchildren. Children of No. 33472.
33476 -505		Same as Nos. 27605-27634.	Great-grandchildren, &c. Children of Lady Beatrix Frances Hamilton, 1835-1871 (2nd daughter of No. 33415), and her husband, George Frederick D'Arcy, 2nd Earl of Durham, 1828-1879.
33506	9890	Louisa Jane, Duchess of Buccleuch and Queensberry [S.], Countess of Doncaster [E.], V.A., 1836. *Dalkeith House, Dalkeith.* *Montagu House, Whitehall, S.W.*	Granddaughter. 3rd but 2nd surviving daughter of No. 33415.
33507 -20		Same as Nos. 19725-19738.	Great-grandchildren, &c. Children of No. 33506.
33521	9891	Piers Alexander Hamilton, Viscount Valletort, 1865. *Marlborough ; Bachelors'.*	Great-grandchildren. Children of the Lady Katherine Elizabeth Hamilton, (4th daughter of No. 33415), 1840-1874, wife of William Henry, 4th Earl of Mount Edgecumbe, P.C.
33522	9892	Lady Victoria Frederica Caroline, wife of Lord Algernon Malcolm Arthur Percy, 1859. *Guy's Cliffe, Warwick.*	
33523 -24		Same as Nos. 20966-20967.	Great-great-grandchildren. Children of No. 33522.
33525	9893	Lady Albertha Louisa Florence, wife of Henry Yarde Buller Lopes, J.P., D.L., 1861. 45 *Lennox Gardens, S.W. Roborough House, Roborough, Devon.*	Great-grandchild. Sister of No. 33521.
33526	9894	Katherine Frederica Albertha Lopes, 1892.	Great-great-grandchildren. Children of No. 33525.
33527	9895	Bertha Louisa Victoria Lopes, 1895.	
33528	9896	Margaret Beatrice Lopes, 1898.	
33529	9897	Constance Elizabeth Lopes, 1901.	
33530	9898	Lady Edith Hilaria, wife of Major the Hon. John Townshend St. Aubyn, 1st Battalion Grenadier Guards, 1862. 53 *Cadogan Place, S.W.*	Great-grandchild. Youngest sister of No. 33521.
33531	9899	Marjorie Katharine Elizabeth Alexandra St. Aubyn, 1893.	Great-great-grandchildren. Children of No. 33530.
33532	9900	Hilaria Lily St. Aubyn, 1894.	

33533	9901	Georgiana Susan, Countess of Winterton [I.], 1841. *Shillinglee Park, Petworth.*	Granddaughter. 5th but 3rd surviving daughter of No. 33415.
33534	9902	Edward, Viscount Turnour, 1883.	Great-grandchild. Child of No. 33533.
33535	9903	Albertha Frances Anne, Marchioness of Blandford, 1847. 49 *Charles Street, Berkeley Square,* W.	Granddaughter. 6th but 4th surviving daughter of No. 33415.
33536	9904	Charles Richard John, 9th Duke of Marlborough [E.], Prince of Mindelheim [H.R.E.], K.G., P.C., 1871. *Blenheim Palace, Woodstock. Warwick House, Stableyard, St. James' Palace, S.W.*	Great-grandson. Son of No. 33535.
33537	9905	John Albert Edward William, Marquis of Blandford, 1897.	Great-great-grandchildren. Children of No. 33536.
33538	9906	Lord Ivor Charles Spencer Churchill, 1898.	
33539	9907	Lady Frances Louisa, wife of Sir Robert Gresley, 11th Bart., 1870. *Drakelowe Park, Burton-on-Trent.*	Great-granddaughter. Daughter of No. 33535.
33540	9908	Nigel Gresley, 1894.	Great-great-grandchildren. Children of No. 33539.
33541	9909	Lawrence Gresley, 1896.	
33542	9910	Lady Lilian Maud, wife of Cecil Alfred Grenfell, 1873. 4 *Great Cumberland Place,* W.	Great-granddaughter. 2nd daughter of No. 33535.
33543	9911	Iris Consuelo Grenfell, 1900.	Great-great-grandchildren. Children of No. 33542.
33544	9912	Daphne Mary Grenfell, 1901.	
33545	9913	Lady Norah Beatrice Henriette Spencer-Churchill, 1875.	Great-granddaughter. Youngest daughter of No. 33535.
33546	9914	Maud Evelyn, Marchioness of Lansdowne [G.B], Countess of Kerry and Shelburne [I.], Baroness Nairne [S.], V.A., C.I., 1850. *Lansdowne House, Berkeley Square,* W.	Granddaughter. 7th but 5th surviving daughter of No. 33415.
33547	9915	♉ Henry William Edmund, Earl of Kerry, D.S.O., 1872.	Great-grandchildren. Children of No. 33546.
33548	9916	♉ Lord Charles George Francis FitzMaurice, Captain 1st Dragoons, A.D.C. to Field-Marshal Lord Roberts, 1874.	
33549	9917	♉ Lady Evelyn Emily Mary, wife of Victor Christian William Cavendish, M.P., 1870. 37 *Park Lane,* W.	
33550 –53		Same as Nos. 22202–22205.	Great-great-grandchildren. Children of No. 33549.
33554	9918	♉ Beatrix Frances, Marchioness of Waterford [I.], Baroness Tyrone [G.B.], 1877. *Curraghmore, Portlaw, co. Waterford.*	Great-grandchild. Younger daughter of No. 33546.
33555 –58		Same as Nos. 20284–20287.	Great-great-grandchildren. Children of No. 33554.
33559	9919	James Francis Butler, 1857.	Grandchildren. Children of the Lady Rachel Evelyn Russell, 1826–1898, wife of Lord James Wandesford Butler, 1815–1893.
33560	9920	Julian George Butler, 1864.	
33561	9921	Grace Louisa Butler, 1858.	

719. Descendants of Field-Marshal Sir Alexander Woodford, G.C.B., 1782–1870. (See Table CXII.)

33562 -64	}	Same as Nos. 25976–25978. Other issue, if any.	{ Grandchildren, &c. Children of Charlotte Sophia Agnes Woodford, -1866, wife of Lieutenant-Colonel Francis William Newdigate, 1822–1893.

720. Descendants, if any, of Major-General Sir John Woodford, K.C.B., 1785–1879. (See Table CXII.)

721. Descendants of General John Drummond, 1793–1874. (See Table CXII.)

33565	9922	Georgiana Matilda, wife of George Onslow Deane, J.P. *Boyce Court, Gloucestershire.*	} Only daughter.
33566	9923	Horace Drummond Deane, J.P., 1854. *Junior Carlton.*	} Grandson. Son of No. 33565.
33567	9924	John Drummond Deane, 1885.	Great-grandchildren.
33568	9925	Mary Bertha Deane.	Son and daughters
33569	9926	Violet Deane.	of No. 33566.
33570	9927	Charles Hope Deane, 1858.	Grandchildren. Children
33571	9928	George FitzGerald Deane, 1861. *Junior Carlton.*	of No. 33565.
33572	9929	Malcolm Richard Boyce Deane, 1899.	Great-grandchild. Son of No. 33571.
33573	9930	Denis Onslow Dighton, 1893.	{ Great-grandchild. Son of Georgiana Louisa Deane, -1897 (daughter of No. 33565), wife of Stanley Moore Dighton.
33574	9931	Mary, wife of Archibald Thomas Mackenzie.	Grandchild. Daughter of No. 33565.
33575	9932	Ronald Archibald Mackenzie, 1902.	Great-grandchildren.
33576	9933	Rosalie Mackenzie.	Children of No.
33577	9934	Frances Georgiana Mackenzie.	33574.
33578	9935	Ethelred Lucy Deane.	Grandchildren. Children of
33579	9936	Augusta Evelyn Deane.	No. 33565.

722. Descendants of Susan Drummond, -1813, 1st wife of George Moore, of Appleby Parva Hall, Leicester, - 1827. (See Table CXII.)

33580	9937	George John Moore, J.P., D.L., 1842. *Appleby Hall, near Atherstone.*	{ Grandson. Son of George Moore, of Appleby, 1811–1871.
33581	9938	Charles Louis George Moore, 1876.	Great-grandchildren.
33582	9939	Gerald Henry Moore, 1877.	Children of No.
33583	9940	Launcelot Geoffrey Moore, 1886.	33580.
33584	9941	Elsie Louise Moore, 1889.	
33585	9942	Rev. Charles Thomas Moore. *Appleby Rectory, near Atherstone.*	} Grandson. Brother to No. 33580.

33586	9943	Charles Frederick Kirkstead Moore.	Great-grandchildren.
33587	9944	George Augustus William Moore.	Children of No.
33588	9945	Aubrey Gordon de Appleby Moore.	33585.
33589	9946	Sylvia Mary Moore.	
33590	9947	Clara Elizabeth, wife of Vaughan Hanning	Granddaughter.
		Vaughan-Lee, M.P.	Eldest sister
		Dillington Park, Ilminster.	to No. 33580.
33591	9948	Arthur Vaughan Hanning Vaughan-Lee,	
		J.P., Major Royal Horse Guards,	
		1862.	Great-grandchildren.
		Dillington Park, Ilminster.	Children of No.
33592	9949	John Edwards Vaughan, *late* Lieutenant	33590.
		Royal Scots Fusiliers, 1863.	
		Rheola, near Neath, Glamorgan.	
33593	9950	Doris Elizabeth Vaughan.	Great-great-grandchildren.
33594	9951	Marjorie Ethel Mary Vaughan.	Children of No. 33592.
33595	9952	Charles Lionel Vaughan-Lee, Lieutenant	
		R.N., 1867.	
33596	9953	Alec George Vaughan-Lee, 1868.	
		9 Clarence Lawn, Dover.	
33597	9954	Jessy Isabel, wife of Walter Boden, J.P.,	Great-grandchildren.
		Lieut.-Col. Derbyshire Yeomanry.	Children of No.
		Abbots Hill, co. Derby.	33590.
33598	9955	Katherine Mary Vaughan-Lee.	
33599	9956	Caroline Christine, wife of R. H. Ratcliff.	
		Stanford Hall, Loughboro'.	
33600	9957	Alice Clara Vaughan-Lee.	
33601	9958	Susan, wife of Walter Mainwaring Coyney.	Granddaughter. 2nd
		Weston Coyney, co. Stafford.	sister to No. 33580.
			Great-grandchildren.
			Children of No.
			33601.
33602	9959	Rosamond Moore.	Granddaughters. Younger
33603	9960	Katherine, wife of Wriothesley	sisters to No. 33580.
		Wingfield.	
			Great-grandson. Son of Charles
			Shuttleworth Holden, 1838–
33604	9961	Edward Charles Shuttleworth	1872, and grandson of Susan
		Holden, Major Derby-	Drummond Moore, 1813–1882,
		shire Yeomanry Cavalry,	and her husband, Edward An-
		J.P., D.S.O., 1865.	thony Holden, of Aston, 1805–
			1877.
			Grandson. Son of Susan
33605	9962	Rev. James Shuttleworth Holden,	Drummond Moore, 1813–
		1843.	1882, and her husband,
		Aston-on-Trent Rectory.	Edward Anthony Holden,
			of Aston, 1805–1877.
33606	9963	Edward James Shuttleworth Holden,	
		1878.	
33607	9964	Robert Shuttleworth Holden.	
33608	9965	Alexander Shuttleworth Holden.	
33609	9966	Geoffrey Shuttleworth Holden.	
33610	9967	Ughtred Shuttleworth Holden.	Great-grandchildren.
33611	9968	Wilfred Shuttleworth Holden.	Children of No.
33612	9969	Clare, wife of G. W. Vaughan.	33605.
		Broom Hall, Oswestry.	
33613	9970	Rosamond Shuttleworth Holden.	
33614	9971	Emmadonna Shuttleworth Holden.	
33615	9972	Theresa Shuttleworth Holden.	
33616	9973	Susan Shuttleworth Holden.	

33617	9974	Rev. John Shuttleworth Holden, 1847. *Lackford Manor, Suffolk.*	Grandson. Brother to No. 33605.
33618	9975	Cecil James Shuttleworth Holden, 1878.	
33619	9976	Arthur Shuttleworth Holden, 1880.	Great-grandchildren.
33620	9977	Hugh Shuttleworth Holden, 1881.	Children of No.
33621	9978	Ruth Alice Shuttleworth Holden, 1882.	33617.
33622	9979	Margaret Louisa Shuttleworth Holden, 1885.	
33623	9980	Francis Shuttleworth Rendall, *formerly* Holden, 1852. *Brigmerston House, Wilts.*	Grandson. Brother to No. 33605.
33624	9981	Francis Holden Shuttleworth Rendall, 1879.	
33625	9982	John Charles Shuttleworth Rendall, 1882.	Great-grandchildren.
33626	9983	Samuel Shuttleworth Rendall, 1883.	Children of No.
33627	9984	Thomas Shuttleworth Rendall, 1886.	33623.
33628	9985	Rachel Dorothy Shuttleworth Rendall, 1878.	
33629	9986	Marjory Shuttleworth Rendall, 1891.	
33630	9987	Anne Shuttleworth, wife of Horace Devas. *Spondon Hall, co. Derby.*	Grandchild. Eldest sister to No. 33605.
33631	9988	Edward Thomas Holden Devas, J.P., 1859.	Great-grandchild. Son of No. 33630.
33632	9989	Mary Shuttleworth, wife of Henry Boden, J.P., D.L., *The Friary, Derby.*	Granddaughter. 2nd sister to No. 33605.
33633	9990	Henry Walter Degge Shuttleworth Boden, J.P., 1867. *Hillmore, Somerset.*	
33634	9991	Anthony Drummond Boden, Lieutenant Rifle Brigade, 1872.	Great-grandchildren.
33635	9992	Reginald Sam Boden, 1872. *Westbury Cottage, Sherborne, Dorset.*	Children of No. 33632.
33636	9993	John Wadham Boden, 1883.	
33637	9994	Cherrie Evelyn, wife of Cecil Herbert Stepney, King's Royal Rifles.	
33638	9995	Rosamond Shuttleworth, wife of the Rev. Degge Wilmot Sitwell. *The Manor House, Leamington Hastings, Warwick.*	Granddaughter. 3rd sister to No. 33605.
33639	9996	Hervey Wheler Sitwell, 1865.	Great-grandson. Son of No. 33638.
33640	9997	Hervey Degge Sitwell, 1896.	Great-great-grandchildren.
33641	9998	George Charles Sitwell, 1898.	Sons of No. 33639.
33642	9999	William Sacheverell Sitwell, 1870.	
33643	10000	John Knightley Sitwell, 1874.	
33644	10001	Richard Degge Sitwell, 1877.	
33645	10002	Arthur Trevor Sitwell, 1878.	Great-grandchildren.
33646	10003	Ralph Sacheverell Sitwell, 1883.	Children of No. 33638.
33647	10004	Edward Holden Sitwell,	
33648	10005	Henry Shuttleworth Sitwell, } twins, 1887.	
33649	10006	Eleanor Wilmot, wife of Henry Edward Donald, 1867.	
			Great-great-grandchildren. Children of No. 33649.
33650	10007	Susan Charlotte Sitwell, 1869.	Great-grandchildren. Children of No. 33638.
33651	10008	Dorothea Mary, wife of John Lea, 1873.	
33652	10009	Robert Simcox Lea, 1897.	Great-great-grandchildren.
33653	10010	Eleanor Catherine Lea, 1899.	Children of No. 33651.
33654	10011	Harriet Wilmot Sitwell, 1880.	Great-granddaughter. Youngest daughter of No. 33638.
33655	10012	Emma Shuttleworth Holden.	Granddaughters. Younger sisters to No. 33605.
33656	10013	Caroline Shuttleworth, wife of the Rev. Charles Lovett Cameron.	

723. Descendants of Sir Charles Hugh Lowther, 3rd Bart., 1803–1894. (See Table CXII.)

33657	10014	Sir Charles Bingham Lowther, 4th Bart., 1880. *Swillington House, Leeds.*	
33658	10015	John George Lowther, 1885.	Grandchildren. Children of George William Lowther, 1837–1890.
33659	10016	Henrietta Isabella, wife of Captain Robert Lambert, D.S.O., Adjutant 8th Hussars, 1873. 1 *Sloane Gardens, S.W.*	
33660	10017	Alice Winsome Lambert.	Great-grandchild. Daughter of No. 33659.
33661	10018	Elizabeth Ida Lowther, 1875.	
33662	10019	Helen Katherine, wife of Hugh Douglas Blackett, 1876. *Matfen Hall, Newcastle-on-Tyne.*	Grandchildren. Sisters of No. 33657.
33663	10020	Emma Alice Lowther, 1878.	
33664	10021	Right Hon. James Lowther, P.C., M.P., 1840. 59 *Grosvenor Street, W.*	Son.
33665	10022	Frances Elizabeth, widow of William Gerard Lysley, 1831–1887. *Pewsham, Chippenham, Wilts.*	Daughter.
33666	10023	William Lowther Lysley, 1875. *Pewsham, Chippenham.*	Grandchildren. Children of No. 33665.
33667	10024	Isabella Gertrude, wife of the Rev. John H. Heigham, 1868.	

724. Descendants of Lady Mary Fane, 1774–1855, and her husband, George Fludyer, of Ayston, Rutland, M.P., 1761–1837. (See Table CXII.)

33668	10025	Sir Arthur John Fludyer, 5th Bart., 1844. *Ayston Hall, Uppingham, Rutland.*	
33669	10026	Henry Fludyer, Colonel commanding Scots Guards, C.V.O., 1847. 8 *William Street, Lowndes Square.*	Grandchildren. Children of the Rev. Sir John Henry Fludyer, 4th Bart., 1803–1896.
33670	10027	Katherine, wife of Henry Randolph Finch. *The Croft, Manton, Rutland.*	
33671	10028	James Finch, 1875.	
33672	10029	Vere Finch, 1879.	Great-grandchildren. Children of No. 33670.
33673	10030	Elsie Katharine Finch.	
33674	10031	Hon. Katherine Elizabeth Onslow, 1853.	Great-grandchildren. Children of Arthur George, Viscount Cranley, 1820–1856, and grandchildren of Arthur George, 3rd Earl of Onslow, 1777–1870, by his wife, Mary Fludyer, 1793–1830.
33675	10032	Hon. Emily Marian Onslow, 1856.	
33676 –77	}	Same as Nos. 33674–33675.	Great-grandchildren. Children of Arthur George, Viscount Cranley, 1820–1856, by his wife, Lady Katherine Anne Cust, 1822–1885, daughter of Caroline Fludyer, 1794–1824, wife of John, 1st Earl Brownlow, 1779–1858.

The Blood Royal of Britain

725. Descendants, if any, of Lady Catherine Gordon, 1751–1797, wife of Thomas Brooker, an officer in the army. (See Table CIX.)

726. Descendants of Alexander Edward, 6th Earl of Dunmore, 1804–1845. (See Table CXIII.)

33678	10033	⛨ Charles Adolphus, 7th Earl of [S.], and 3rd Baron Dunmore [U.K.], 1841. *Isle of Harris, Inverness-shire.* 61 *Great Cumberland Place, W.*	Son.
33679	10034	⛨ Alexander Edward, Viscount Fincastle, V.C., Captain 16th Lancers, A.D.C. to Lieutenant-General commanding Curragh District, 1871.	Grandchildren. Children of No. 33678.
33680	10035	⛨ Lady Evelyn, wife of John Depuis Cobbold, D.L., 1867. *Holy Wells, Ipswich.*	
33681	10036	John Murray Cobbold, 1897.	Great-grandchildren. Children of No. 33680.
33682	10037	Winifred Cobbold, 1892.	
33683	10038	Pamela Cobbold, 1900.	
33684	10039	⛨ Lady Muriel, wife of Lieutenant-Colonel Harold Gore-Browne, 2nd Battalion King's Royal Rifle Corps, 1869.	Grandchildren. Children of No. 33678.
33685	10040	⛨ Lady Grace, wife of William James Barry, 1873. *Witchingham Hall, Norwich.*	
33686	10041	Gerald Barry, 1896.	Great-grandchildren. Children of No. 33685.
33687	10042	Herbert Wyndham Barry, 1898.	
33688	10043	⛨ Lady Victoria Alexandrina Murray, 1877.	Grandchildren. Younger daughters of No. 33678.
33689	10044	⛨ Lady Mildred Murray, 1878.	
33690	10045	⛨ Susan Catherine Mary, Countess of Southesk [S.], Baroness Balinhard [U.K.], 1837. *Kinnaird Castle, Brechin.*	Daughter.
33691	10046	Hon. Lancelot Douglas Carnegie, M.V.O., 1861. *British Embassy, Berlin.*	Grandchild. Son of No. 33690.
33692	10047	Mariota Susan Carnegie, 1892.	Great-grandchild. Child of No. 33691.
33693	10048	Hon. Robert Francis Carnegie, Captain and Brevet-Major Gordon Highlanders, 1869. *Naval and Military.*	Grandchildren. Children of No. 33690.
33694	10049	Lady Dora Susan, wife of Ernest de Rodakowski, Lieutenant 1st Regiment Austrian Lancers, 1863. 28 *Frognal Lane, Hampstead, N.W.*	
33695	10050	Raymond Juzio Paul de Rodakowski, 1895.	Great-grandchildren. Children of No. 33694.
33696	10051	Susan Ottilia de Rodakowski, 1897.	
33697	10052	Lady Helena Mariota Carnegie, 1865.	Grandchildren. Younger daughters of No. 33690.
33698	10053	Lady Katharine Agnes Blanche, wife of Courtenay Charles Evan Morgan, 1867. *Ashford Court, Ludlow.*	
33699	10054	Evan Frederic Morgan, 1893.	Great-grandchildren. Children of No. 33698.
33700	10055	Gwyneth Erica Morgan, 1895.	
33701	10056	⛨ Constance Euphemia Woronzow, Baroness Elphinstone [S. & U.K.], 1838. *Carberry Tower, Musselburgh, N.B.*	2nd daughter.

33702	10057	Sidney Herbert, 16th Baron [S.], and 2nd Baron [U.K.] Elphinstone, 1869. *Carberry Tower, Musselburgh.*	}	Grandchildren.
33703	10058	Hon. Mountstuart William Elphinstone, 1871.	}	Children of No. 33701.
33704	10059	Hon. Lilian Elphinstone, 1867.		
33705	10060	⋃ Lady Alexandrina Victoria, widow of the Rev. Henry Cunliffe, 1826–1894, 1845. *Ellesborough Rectory, Butler's Cross, Bucks.*	}	Youngest daughter.

727. Descendants of the Hon. Sir Charles Augustus Murray, K.C.B., P.C., 1806–1895. (See Table CXIII.)

33706	10061	⋃ Charles James Murray, M.P., *of Loch Carron*, 1851. 41 *Belgrave Square, W.*	} Son.	
33707 -8	}	⋃ Same as Nos. 21310–21311.	{ Grandchildren. of No. 33706.	Children

728. Descendants of Lieut.-Col. the Hon. Alexander Murray, 1764–1842. (See Table CXIII.)

33709	10062	⋃ Augustus Charles Murray, Commander R.N., 1815.	Son.
33710	10063	⋃ Reginald Augustus Frederick Murray, 1846.	Grandchildren. Children of Captain Virginius Murray, 1817–1861.
33711	10064	⋃ George Sam Murray, 1850.	
33712	10065	⋃ Arthur Charles Murray, 1852.	
33713	10066	⋃ Henry Alexander Murray, 1857.	
33714	10067	⋃ Virginia Murray, 1890. Great-grandchild. Child of No. 33713.	
33715	10068	⋃ Charles Stewart Murray, C.I.E., B.C.S., 1858.	Grandson. Son of Brigadier-General Alexander Henry Murray, 1829–1885.
33716	10069	⋃ . . . . Murray, 1892. Great-grandson. Son of No. 33715.	
33717	10070	⋃ Cyril Francis Tyrrell Murray, Captain I.S.C., 1863.	Grandson. Brother to No. 33715.
33718	10071	⋃ Cyril Alexander George Octavius Murray, 1887.	Great-grandson. Son of No. 33717.
33719	10072	⋃ Malcolm Donald Murray, Captain Seaforth Highlanders, 1867.	Grandson. Youngest brother to No. 33715.
33720	10073	Félecie, Princess of Montléart, widow of Jules Max Thibaut, Fürst von Montléart [Austria], Principe di Montléart [Sardinia], and Marquis de Montléart [France], 1787–1865, 1836. *Paris:* 188 *boulevard Haussmann.*	Granddaughters. Daughters of Augusta Murray, 1814–1877, and her husband, Prince Louis Stanislaus de La Tremouille, 1768–1837.
33721	10074	Louise Marie, Princess of Torremuzza, wife of Gabriel Laurent Charles, Prince of Torremuzza [Sicily], 1836. *Palermo, Sicily.*	
33722	10075	⋃ Susan Emma, widow of the Rev. John Glover, M.A., Vicar of Brading, I.W., –1884, 1835.	} Daughter.

729. Descendants of the Hon. Leveson Grenville Keith Murray, M.C.S., 1770–1835. (See Table CXIII.)

33723	10076	⋃ Jack George Murray, 1853.	}	Grandchildren. Children of Rear-Admiral Jack Henry Murray, R.N., 1810–1881.
33724	10077	⋃ Emily Neil, wife of Arthur Edward Baird, 1846.	}	

33725	10078	Francis Charles Baird, 1868.	⎫ Great-grandchildren.
33726	10079	Dorothea Baird, 1872.	⎬ Children of No.
33727	10080	Una Estarra Georgina Baird, 1870.	⎭ 33724.
33728	10081	▽ Frances Balfour Murray, 1856.	Grandchild. Youngest sister to No. 33723.
33729	10082	▽ Hamilton George Dunmore Murray, 1841.	⎫ Grandchildren. Chil-
33730	10083	▽ Leveson Granville Keith Murray, 1843.	⎬ dren of Lieut.-Col.
33731	10084	▽ Susan Augusta, wife of Havillard le Mesurier, 1854.	⎭ Samuel Hood Mur-ray, 1814–1867.
33732	10085	. . . . le Mesurier, 1879.	⎫ Great-grandchildren. Son and
33733	10086	. . . . le Mesurier.	⎭ daughter of No. 33731.

Descendants, if any, of Jane Wemyss Murray (daughter), wife 1st (1824) of Major Charles Hay Campbell, E.I.C.S., 1807–1832, by whom she had two sons and three daughters, and 2ndly (1836) of Lieut.-Col. Christopher Simpson Maling, Bengal N.I.

Descendants, if any, of Augusta Murray, 1809–1833 (daughter), wife (1824) of John Gunn Collins, of Belmont, King's County, Captain 13th Light Dragoons, by whom she had two sons and two daughters.

---

730. Descendants, if any, of Lady Susan Murray,   –1826, by her 2nd husband, John Drew, or her 3rd husband, the Rev. Archibald Edward Douglas, of Carnalley and Outreagh, Rector of Drungoon, Ireland.   (See Table CXIII.)

---

731. Descendants, if any, of the Right Hon. Sir William Drummond, of Logie Almond, P.C., M.P.   (See Table CXIII.)

---

732. Descendants, if any, of Catherine Stewart,   –18 , wife (1833) of M. des Ondes.   (See Table CXIII.)

---

733. Descendants, if any, of Louisa Drummond, wife (1797) 1st of Lieutenant Cecil Windsor Forrester, and 2ndly (1805) of Robert Stewart, of Alderstone, Haddington.   (See Table CXIII.)

---

734. Descendants, if any, of Lady Elizabeth Murray, wife of the Rev. John Murray, Dean of Killaloe,   –1790.   (See Table CXIII.)

---

735. Descendants of Edward Geoffrey, 14th Earl of Derby, K.G., 1799–1869.   (See Table CXIV.)

| 33734 | 10087 | Frederick Arthur, 16th Earl of Derby [E.], 3rd Lord Stanley [U.K.], K.G., P.C., G.C.B., 1841. *Knowsley, Prescot. Derby House, 33 St. James' Square, S.W.* | ⎬ Son. |

33735	10088	Edward George Villiers, Lord Stanley, C.B., M.P., 1865. 36 Great Cumberland Place, W.	Grandson. Son of No. 33734.
33736 -38	}	Same as Nos. 33094–33096.	Great-grandchildren. Children of No. 33735.
33739	10089	Hon. Victor Albert Stanley, Commander R.N., 1867.	Grandson. 2nd son of No. 33734.
33740	10090	Violet Alice Stanley, 1897.	Great-grandchild. Daughter of No. 33739.
33741	10091	Hon. Arthur Stanley, M.P., 1869. 33 St. James' Square, S.W.	
33742	10092	Hon. Ferdinand Charles Stanley, D.S.O., Captain Grenadier Guards, 1871.	
33743	10093	Hon. George Frederick Stanley, Captain R.H.A., 1872.	
33744	10094	Hon. Algernon Francis Stanley, Lieutenant 1st Life Guards, 1874.	Grandchildren. Children of No. 33734.
33745	10095	Hon. Frederick William Stanley, Lieutenant 10th Hussars, 1878.	
33746	10096	Lady Isobel Constance Mary, wife of Captain the Hon. John Francis Gathorne-Hardy, Grenadier Guards, 1875. 2 Cadogan Square, S.W.	
33747	10097	Lady Emma Charlotte, widow of the Hon. Sir Wellington Patrick Manvers Chetwynd-Talbot, K.C.B., 1817–1898, 1835. Glenhurst, Esher. 15 Cromwell Road, S.W.	Daughter.
33748	10098	Frederick Gilbert Chetwynd-Talbot, D.S.O., Captain Rifle Brigade, 1868. Glenhurst, Esher, Surrey.	
33749	10099	Walter Stanley Chetwynd-Talbot, B.C.S., 1869.	
33750	10100	Henry Arthur Chetwynd-Talbot, 1872.	Grandchildren. Children of No. 33747.
33751	10101	Gilbert Edward Chetwynd-Talbot, Lieutenant 4th Battalion South Staffordshire Regiment, 1876.	
33752	10102	Cecil Emma, wife of William Seymour Eastwood, of 20 Old Square, Lincoln's Inn, W.C., 1864. Esher Lodge, Esher, Surrey.	
33753	10103	John Patrick Basil Eastwood, 1889.	Great-grandchildren. Children of No. 33752.
33754	10104	Charles Seymour Eastwood, 1893.	
33755	10105	Cecil Mary Eastwood, 1887.	
33756	10106	Gerald Arthur Eastwood, 1897.	
33757	10107	Edith Constance Louisa, wife of William Arthur Wigram, 1865. Madras. Hersham House, near Walton-on-Thames.	Granddaughter. 2nd daughter of No. 33747.
33758	10108	Charles Knox Wigram, 1889.	Great-grandchildren. Children of No. 33757.
33759	10109	Ivy Margaret Wigram, 1890.	
33760	10110	Helen Ivory Chetwynd-Talbot, 1880.	Granddaughter. Youngest daughter of No. 33747.

736. Descendants of the Hon. Henry Thomas Stanley, M.P., 1803–1875. (See Table CXIV.)

33761	10111	Edward Henry Stanley, 1838.	Son.
33762	10112	Charles Harry Stanley, 1863.	Grandchildren. Children of Captain Charles Geoffrey Stanley, 1839–1877.
33763	10113	Henry Edmund Stanley, 1868.	
33764	10114	Mary Kathleen Fanny, wife of Francis Horatio Lloyd, 1871.	

The Blood Royal of Britain

737. Descendants of Colonel the Hon. Charles James Fox Stanley, 1808-1884. (See Table CXIV.)

33765	10115	Charles Edward Henry Stanley, *late* Lieut.-Col. Grenadier Guards, 1843.	} Son.
33766	10116	Charles Douglas Stanley, 1878.	
33767	10117	Phipps Edward Stanley, 1881.	
33768	10118	John William Stanley, 1886.	Grandchildren. Children of No. 33765.
33769	10119	Frances Ellinor Stanley, 1882.	
33770	10120	Alice Margaret Stanley, 1884.	
33771	10121	Rev. Edmund Phipps Stanley, 1855. *Wootton Courtenay Rectory, Dunster.*	} 2nd surviving son.
33772	10122	Edmund Stewart Stanley, 1891. Grandson.	Son of No. 33771.
33773	10123	Evelyn Emma Stanley, 1840.	
33774	10124	Margaret Alice Stanley, 1844.	
33775	10125	Mary Louisa Stanley, 1846.	Daughters.
33776	10126	Constance Emily Stanley, 1853.	

738. Descendants of Lady Charlotte Elizabeth Stanley, 1801-1853, wife of Edward Penrhyn, formerly Leycester, J.P., D.L., 1795-1861. (See Table CXIV.)

33777	10127	Edward Hugh Leycester-Penrhyn, J.P., D.L., 1827. *The Cedars, East Sheen, Surrey.*	} Son.
33778	10128	Arthur Leycester-Penrhyn, Barrister-at-Law, 1866.	
33779	10129	George Leycester-Penrhyn, 1871.	
33780	10130	Charlotte Georgina Leycester-Penrhyn.	Grandchildren.
33781	10131	Constance Vere Leycester-Penrhyn.	Children of No. 33777.
33782	10132	Agnes Eleanor, wife of the Rev. Phipps John Hornby. *St. Michael's-on-Wyre Vicarage, Lancashire.*	
33783	10133	Amy Gertrude, wife of Major Arthur Harvey Hopwood.	
33784	10134	Robert Harvey Hopwood, 1890. { Great-grandchild. Son of No. 33783.	
33785	10135	Maud Lina, wife of Edward G. Waddilove. } Grandchildren. Chil-	
33786	10136	Cecil Mary Leycester-Penrhyn. dren of No. 33777.	
33787	10137	Rev. Oswald Henry Leycester-Penrhyn, Hon. Canon of Liverpool. *Winwick Rectory, Lancashire.*	} 2nd son.
33788	10138	Charles Windham Leycester-Penrhyn, 1873.	
33789	10139	Ethel Frances Leycester-Penrhyn.	Grandchildren. Children of No. 33787.
33790	10140	Mary Charlotte Leycester-Penrhyn.	
33791	10141	Elizabeth Gertrude Leycester-Penrhyn.	
33792	10142	Mary Charlotte Leycester, widow of Morgan Yeatman, of *Shawfield, Bromley, Kent,* and of *Richmond,* 1824-1889, 1824. *Cliefden, Eltham, Kent.*	Elder daughter.
33793	10143	Morgan Edward Yeatman, 1851. Grandchild.	Son of No. 33792.
33794	10144	Morgan John Yeatman, 1895. } Great-grandchildren. Children	
33795	10145	Ellinor Mary Yeatman, 1890. of No. 33793.	
33796	10146	Harry Oswald Yeatman, 1856. { Grandchild. 2nd son of No. 33792.	
33797	10147	Harry Morgan Yeatman, 1895.	
33798	10148	Robert Julian Yeatman, 1897.	Great-grandchildren. Chil-
33799	10149	Edith Benedicta Mary Yeatman, 1898.	dren of No. 33796.
33800	10150	Frances Alice Yeatman, 1900.	

33801	10151	Arthur William Yeatman, 1862.	⎫
33802	10152	Frank Pym Stanley Yeatman, 1869.	Grandchildren.
33803	10153	Ellinor Mary Yeatman, 1852.	Children of
33804	10154	Lucy Emma Yeatman, 1854.	No. 33792.
33805	10155	Florence Charlotte, wife of Charles E. Squire, 1855.	⎭
33806	10156	Edward Arnold Squire, 1892.	⎫
33807	10157	Stanley Charles Squire, 1893.	Great-grandchildren. Children
33808	10158	Giles Frederick Squire, 1894.	of No. 33805.
33809	10159	Cecily Beatrice Squire, 1896.	⎭
33810	10160	Edith Vere Yeatman, 1864.	Grandchild. Daughter of No. 33792.
33811	10161	Emma Catherine Leycester-Penrhyn.	Younger daughter.

739. Descendants of Lady Ellinor Mary Stanley, 1807–1887, wife of the Rev. Frank George Gregge-Hopwood, Canon of Chester, Rector of Linwick, 1810–1890. (See Table CXIV.)

33812	10162	Rev. Frank Edward Hopwood, 1843.	Son.
33813	10163	Frank Colvin Hopwood, 1874.	⎫
33814	10164	Geoffrey Hopwood, 1877.	
33815	10165	Harvey Hopwood, 1884.	Grandchildren. Children of
33816	10166	Ellinor Muriel Hopwood, 1876.	No. 33812.
33817	10167	Mary Helen Hopwood, 1879.	
33818	10168	Edith Vere Hopwood, 1881.	
33819	10169	Evelyn Hopwood, 1882.	⎭
33820	10170	Major Arthur Harvey Hopwood, 1845.	2nd son.
33821		Same as No. 33784.	Grandchild. Son of No. 33820.
33822	10171	Charles Augustus Harvey Hopwood, 1847.	⎫
33823	10172	Susan Harvey Hopwood, 1838.	Children.
33824	10173	Cecilia Catherine, wife of John Lionel Darby, Dean of Chester, 1839. *The Deanery, Chester.*	⎭
33825	10174	Lionel Frank Christopher Darby, 1873.	⎫
33826	10175	Arthur John Lovett Darby, 1875.	Grandchildren. Children of No. 33824.
33827	10176	Edward Henry d'Esterre Darby, 1880.	
33828	10177	Mary Cecilia Darby, 1872.	
33829	10178	Constance Ellinor Katharine Darby, 1882.	⎭

740. Descendants of Edmund George Hornby, of Dalton Hall, Westmorland, M.P., 1799–1865. (See Table CXIV.)

33830	10179	Edmund Geoffrey Stanley Hornby, J.P., D.L., Major 3rd Battalion Royal Lancaster Regiment, 1839. *Dalton Hall, near Burton, Westmorland.*	⎫
33831	10180	Lucy Francesca, wife of Charles Samuel Bagot, Barrister-at-Law, Commissioner in Lunacy. *East Sheen, S.W.*	Children.
33832	10181	Ellinor Georgiana Katharine, wife of the Rev. Henry Arbuthnot Feilden. *Kirkby Stephen Vicarage, Westmorland.*	
33833	10182	Helen Arbuthnot, wife of Colonel Henry Paul Mason. *Eden Place, Kirkby Stephen.*	Grandchild. Child of No. 33832.
33834	10183	Randle Paul Feilden Mason.	Great-grandchildren. Children of No. 33833.
33835	10184	Marcia Helen Arbuthnot Mason.	
33836	10185	Katharine Maud Feilden.	Grandchild. Child of No. 33832.

33837	10186	Charlotte Louisa Jane, wife of the Rev. Oswald Henry Leycester Penrhyn. *Winwick Rectory, Lancashire.*	4th daughter.
33838 -41	}	Same as Nos. 33788–33791.	Grandchildren. Children of No. 33837.
33842	10187	Victoria Susan, wife of the Rev. Charles James Satterthwaite. *Disley Vicarage, co. Chester.*	5th daughter.
33843	10188	Rev. Edmund James Satterthwaite.	
33844	10189	Charles Geoffrey Satterthwaite.	Grandchildren. Children of No. 33842.
33845	10190	Gertrude Mary Charlotte, wife of John Satterthwaite.	
33846	10191	Frank Satterthwaite.	
33847	10192	Maud Satterthwaite.	Great-grandchildren. Children of No. 33845.
33848	10193	Lettice Satterthwaite.	
33849	10194	Beatrice Satterthwaite.	
33850	10195	Gertrude Mary Augusta Hornby.	Youngest daughter.

741. Descendants of Edward Henry Cole, of Stoke Lyne, –1852. (See Table CXIV.)

33851	10196	Lilian Mary Olivia, wife of C. E. Pine-Coffin.	Granddaughter. Only child of Edward Campbell Stuart Cole, J.P., D.L., 1831–1901.
33852	10197	Norma Pine-Coffin, 1886.	Great-grandchild. Only daughter of No. 33851.
33853	10198	Lionel Beauchamp Cole, *late* Lieutenant 11th Hussars, 1842.	
33854	10199	Augusta Catherine Cole.	
33855	10200	Fanny Caroline Cole.	Children.
33856	10201	Sophy Mowbray Cole.	
33857	10202	Emily Mary, widow of Somerset Bassett Saunderson, *late* 11th Hussars, 1834–1892.	
33858 -61	}	Same as Nos. 23387–23390.	Grandchildren. Children of No. 33857.
33862	10203	Mary Elizabeth, wife of Captain the Hon. Richard Bingham, R.N. *8 Denmark Terrace, Brighton.*	Youngest daughter.
33863 -64	}	Same as Nos. 20412–20413.	Grandchildren. Children of No. 33862.

742. Descendants of George Beauchamp Cole, of Twickenham, D.L., 1807–1881. (See Table CXIV.)

33865	10204	Henry Ean Cole.	Sons.
33866	10205	George Ralph FitzRoy Cole. *98 Gloucester Place, Portman Square, W.*	
33867 -69	}	Same as Nos. 21397–21399.	Grandchildren. Children of No. 33866.
33870	10206	Charles Shirley Cole.	
33871	10207	Julia Mary Henrietta Cole. *89 Lexham Gardens, S.W.*	Children.
33872	10208	Emily Katherine, wife of George Dixon, J.P., D.L. *Astle Hall, Chelford, Chester.*	

33873	10209	John Baskervyle-Glegg, *late* Lieutenant Earl of Chester's Yeomanry Cavalry, 1876. *Withington Hall, Chelford, Cheshire. Gayton Hall, Neston.*	Grandchild. Son of No. 33872 by 1st husband, John Baskervyle-Glegg, of Old Withington Hall, –1877.
33874		Same as No. 26478.	Grandchild. Son of No. 33872 by 2nd husband.
33875	10210	Mary Cecily Baskervyle-Glegg.	Grandchildren. Daughters of
33876	10211	Emily Idonea Baskervyle-Glegg.	No. 33872 by 1st husband.
33877		Same as No. 26479.	Grandchild. Daughter of No. 33872 by 2nd husband.
33878	10212	Sophy Edith Hamilton, wife of Colonel Charles Parker Ridley.	3rd daughter.
33879	10213	Iris Brooke Ridley.	Grandchild. Child of No. 33878.
33880	10214	Mary Brenda Madeline, wife of Colonel Edward Robert Gregge-Hopwood, J.P. *Hopwood Hall, co. Lancashire.*	Youngest daughter.
33881	10215	Edward Byng George Gregge-Hopwood, 1880.	
33882	10216	Gerald Robert Gregge-Hopwood, 1885.	Grandchildren.
33883	10217	Judith, wife of William Henry von Schröder, J.P., *late* 9th Lancers. *The Cottage, Nantwich, Cheshire.*	Children of No. 33880.
33884	10218	John Henry William Charles von Schröder, 1900.	Great-grandchildren. Children of No.
33885	10219	Margery von Schröder, 1897.	33883.
33886	10220	Brenda Cecilia Gregge-Hopwood.	Grandchild. Younger daughter of No. 33880.

743. Descendants of the Hon. Eldred Mowbray Cole, Auditor-General of Cape Colony, –18 . (See Table CXIV.)

33887	10221	Henrietta, widow of Murdoch M. Tait, M.L.A. *Rondebosch, Cape Town.*	Eldest daughter and eventual co-heir.
33888	10222	Murdoch Morison Tait.	Great-grandchildren. Children of Murdoch Tait, 18 –18 , and grandchildren of No. 33887.
33889	10223	Helen Tait.	
33890	10224	Stella Tait.	
33891	10225	Robert Tait.	
33892	10226	Helen, wife of Sir Henry Hubert Juta, *late* Attorney-General of Cape Colony, and Speaker of the Legislative Assembly. *Mon Désir, Kenilworth, near Cape Town.*	Grandchild. Eldest daughter of No. 33887.
33893	10227	John Juta.	
33894	10228	Irene Juta.	
33895	10229	Helen Juta.	Great-grandchildren. Children of No. 33892.
33896	10230	Brenda Juta.	
33897	10231	Louisa Juta.	
33898	10232	Henrietta, wife of W. M. Bisset. *Kenilworth, near Cape Town.*	Grandchild. 2nd daughter of No. 33887.
33899	10233	Islay Bisset.	Great-grandchildren. Children of No. 33898.
33900	10234	Gwendoline Bisset.	
33901	10235	Helen Bisset.	
33902	10236	Violet, wife of Harry Stamper.	Grandchild. 3rd daughter of No. 33887.
33903	10237	William Stamper.	Great-grandchildren. Children of No. 33902.
33904	10238	Robert Stamper.	
33905	10239	Violet Stamper.	

33906	10240	Evelyn Blanche, wife of Otto E. Rathfelder. *Belle Ombre, Constantia.*	{ Grandchild. 4th daughter of No. 33887.
33907	10241	Helen, wife of Colonel Frederick Travers.	} Daughters and co-heirs.
33908	10242	Emily Cole.	
33909	10243	Edith, wife of [——] Ross.	
33910	10244	Maud Ross, wife of [——] Hodgson.	{ Grandchild. Daughter of No. 33909.
33911	10245	. . . . Hodgson.	Great-grandchildren.
33912	10246	. . . . Hodgson.	Children of No.
33913	10247	. . . . Hodgson.	33910.
33914	10248	Islay Whalley, wife of Everson Devenish.	{ Youngest daughter and co-heir.

744. Descendant of Elizabeth Cole, — , wife of Frederick
    Lee. (See Table CXIV.)

33915	10249	Augusta, widow of Vivian Webber.	Daughter.

745. Descendants of Catherine Isabella Cole, — , wife of
    Walter Frederick Campbell of Islay, M.P. (See Table
    CXIV.)

746. Descendants, if any, of Susan Janet Emilia Forbes, 1746– .
    (See Table CXIV.)

747. Descendants of Randolph, 9th Earl of Galloway, 1800–1873.
    (See Table CXV.)

33916	10250	Randolph Henry, 11th Earl of Galloway [S.], 5th Lord Stewart of Garlies [U.K.], 1836. *Galloway House, Garliestown. 74 Eccleston Square, S.W.*	} Eldest surviving son.
33917	10251	Randolph Algernon Ronald, Lord Garlies, 1892.	} Grandchildren. Children of No. 33916.
33918	10252	Hon. Keith Anthony Stewart, 1894.	
33919	10253	Walter Robert Stewart, 1888.	{ Grandchildren. Children of Major-General the Hon. Alexander Stewart, 1838–1896.
33920	10254	Adine Blanche Stewart, 1887.	
33921	10255	Hon. Walter John Stewart, Colonel, *formerly* commanding 12th Lancers, 1849. *155 Sloane Street, S.W.*	} Younger sons.
33922	10256	Hon. FitzRoy Somerset Keith Stewart, 1855. *10 Egerton Gardens, S.W.*	
33923	10257	Lilian Blanche Mary Stewart, 1889.	} Grandchildren. Children of No. 33922.
33924	10258	Vera Jane Estelle Stewart, 1893.	

3 R

33925	10259	Lady Helen Blanche, wife of Walter Clifford Meller, Count d'Ereso [H.R.E.], Knight Commander of the Order of the Holy Sepulchre, &c. &c., 1834. 20 *Cheyne Walk, S.W.*	Eldest daughter.
33926 –33	}	Same as Nos. 21532–21539.	Grandchildren, &c. Children, &c., of the Lady Emma Georgina Stewart, 1840–1869, and her husband, Wilbraham Frederic, 2nd Lord Tollemache.
33934	10260	Lady Mary Louisa, widow of Charles Edward Stephen Cooke, J.P., 1829–1895, 1842. 38 *Cadogan Square, S.W.*	2nd surviving daughter.
33935 33936	10261 10262	Blanche Frances Spedding, 1884. Mildred Emma Spedding, 1885.	Grandchildren. Children of the Lady Jane Charlotte Stewart, 1846–1897, and her husband, Henry Anthony Spedding, of Mirehouse, Cumberland, –1887.
33937	10263	Lady Emily Octavia, widow of the Hon. Francis Algernon James Chichester, 1829–1885, 1847. 9 *Ralston Street, Chelsea, S.W.*	3rd surviving daughter.
33938 –46	}	Same as Nos. 27884 and 27886–27893.	Grandchildren, &c. Children, &c., of No. 33937.
33947	10264	Lady Henrietta Caroline, wife of Algernon Turnor, C.B., 1850. *Goadby Hall, Melton Mowbray.*	4th surviving daughter.
33948 33949 33950 33951 33952	10265 10266 10267 10268 10269	Herbert Broke Turnor, 1885. Christopher Randolph Turnor, 1886. Marjorie Caroline Isabel Turnor, 1883. Algitha Blanche Turnor, 1884. Verena Henrietta Turnor, 1890.	Grandchildren. Children of No. 33947.
33953	10270	Lady Isabel Maud Stewart, 1852. 155 *Sloane Street, S.W.*	Youngest surviving daughter.

748. Descendants of Admiral the Hon. Keith Stewart, C.B., 1814-1879. (See Table CXV.)

33954 –90	}	Same as Nos. 32886–32922.

749. Descendants of John Winston, 7th Duke of Marlborough, K.G., 1822-1883. (See Table CXV.)

33991 –4000	}	Same as Nos. 33536–33545.	Descendants of George Charles, 8th Duke of Marlborough, 1844–1892.
34001	10271	Winston Leonard Spencer-Churchill, M.P., 1874. 105 *Mount Street, S.W.*	Grandchildren. Children of the Right Hon. Lord Randolph Henry Spencer-Churchill, P.C., M.P., 1849–1895.
34002	10272	John Strange Spencer-Churchill, 1880. 35A *Great Cumberland Place.*	
34003	10273	Cornelia Henrietta Maria, Baroness Wimborne [U.K.], 1847. *Canford Manor, Wimborne.* 22 *Arlington Street, W.*	Eldest daughter.

34004	10274	Hon. Ivor Churchill Guest, M.P., Lieutenant Dorset Yeomanry Cavalry, 1873.	
34005	10275	Hon. Christian Henry Charles Guest, Captain 1st Dragoons, 1874.	
34006	10276	Hon. Frederick Edward Guest, Lieutenant 1st Life Guards, 1875.	Grandchildren. Children of No. 34003.
34007	10277	Hon. Lionel George William Guest, 1880.	
34008	10278	Hon. Oscar Montagu Guest, 1888.	
34009	10279	Hon. Frances Charlotte, wife of the Hon. Frederic John Napier Thesiger, 1869. *46 Eaton Place, S.W.*	
34010	10280	Frederic Ivor Thesiger, 1896.	
34011	10281	Joan Frances Vera Thesiger, 1895.	Great-grandchildren. Children of No. 34009.
34012	10282	Anne Molyneux Thesiger, 1898.	
34013	10283	Bridget Mary Thesiger, 1900.	
34014	10284	Corisande Evelyn Vere, Baroness Rodney [G.B.], 1870. *Felthorpe, Norwich.*	Grandchild. 2nd daughter of No. 34003.
34015	10285	Hon. George Bridges Harley Guest Rodney, 1891.	Great-grandchildren. Children of No. 34014.
34016	10286	Hon. James Henry Bertie Rodney, 1893.	
34017	10287	Hon. Francis William Rodney, 1896.	
34018	10288	Hon. Elaine Augusta, wife of the Rev. Ernest Amherst Villiers, 1871. *Brandiston Rectory.*	Grandchildren. Younger daughters of No. 34003.
34019	10289	Hon. Rosamond Cornelia Gladys, wife of the Hon. Matthew White Ridley, M.P., 1877. *36 Portland Place, W.*	
34020	10290	Matthew White Ridley, 1902.	Great-grandchildren. Children of No. 34019.
34021	10291	Gladys Marjorie Ridley, 1900.	
34022	10292	Rosamond Jane Frances, Baroness De Ramsey [U.K.], 1851. *3 Belgrave Square, S.W.*	2nd daughter.
34023 –28		Same as Nos. 31223–31228.	Grandchildren. Children of No. 34022.
34029	10293	Fanny Octavia Louisa, Lady Tweedmouth [U.K.], 1853. *Guisachan, Beauly. Brook House, Park Lane, W.*	3rd daughter.
34030	10294	Hon. Dudley Churchill Marjoribanks, D.S.O., Lieutenant Royal Horse Guards, 1874. *Brook House, Park Lane, W.*	Grandson. Only child of No. 34029.
34031	10295	Moyra Marjoribanks, 1902. Great-grandchild. Child of No. 34030.	
34032	10296	Anne Emily, Duchess of Roxburghe [S.], Countess Innes [U.K.], V.A., 1854. *Broxmouth Park, Dunbar.*	4th daughter.
34033	10297	Henry John, 8th Duke of Roxburghe [S.], 3rd Earl Innes [U.K.], 1876. *Floors Castle, Kelso, Roxburghshire.*	
34034	10298	Lord Alastair Robert Innes-Ker, Lieutenant 1st Dragoons, 1880.	Grandchildren. Children of No. 34032.
34035	10299	Lord Robert Edward Innes-Ker, 1885.	
34036	10300	Lady Margaret Frances Susan, widow of Major James Alexander Orr-Ewing, 1857–1900, 1875. *9 Hill Street, Berkeley Square, W.*	
34037	10301	Milicent Lilian Elizabeth Orr-Ewing, 1899.	Great-grandchild. Child of No. 34036.
34038	10302	Lady Victoria Alexandrina, wife of Captain Charles Hyde Villiers, Royal Horse Guards, 1877.	Grandchild. Daughter of No. 34032.

34039	10303	Charles William Dudley Villiers, 1902.	}	Great-grandchild. Child of No. 34038.
34040	10304	Lady Isabel Innes-Ker, 1879.	}	Grandchildren. Daughters
34041	10305	Lady Evelyn Annie Innes-Ker, 1882.		of No. 34032.
34042	10306	Georgiana Elizabeth, Countess Howe [U.K.], Baroness Curzon and Howe [G.B.], 1860. 20 *Curzon Street, W.*	}	5th daughter.
34043		Same as No. 20241.	Grandchild.	Child of No. 34042.
34044	10307	Lady Sarah Isabel Augusta, wife of Captain Gordon Chesney Wilson, M.V.O., Royal Horse Guards, 1865. *Brooksby Hall, Leicester.*	}	6th daughter.
34045	10308	Randolph Gordon Wilson, 1893.	}	Grandchildren. Chil-
34046	10309	Alan Spencer Wilson, 1894.		dren of No. 34044.

750. Descendants of Lord Alfred Spencer-Churchill, M.P., 1824–1893. (See Table CXV.)

34047	10310	Jane, wife of Sir Francis Salway Winnington, Bart., 1858. *Stanford Court, Worcester.*	}	Daughter.
34048	10311	Francis Salway Winnington, Lieutenant 3rd Battalion Coldstream Guards, 1881.		
34049	10312	Charles Alfred Edward Winnington, 1882.		Grandchildren.
34050	10313	John Winston Foley Winnington, 1883.	}	Children of
34051	10314	Frances Jane, wife of Andrew Mansel Talbot Fletcher, Lieutenant 2nd Life Guards.		No. 34047.
34052	10315	Iris Harriet Helena Winnington.		
34053	10316	Olivia, wife of Lieut.-Col. Arthur Edward William Colville, C.B., 1st Battalion Rifle Brigade, 1859. 47 *Chester Square, S.W.*	}	2nd daughter.
34054	10317	Robert Alfred Colville, 1888.	Grandchild.	Child of No. 34053.
34055	10318	Adeline, wife of Lieut.-Col. William Hugh Williams, C.M.G., R.A. 33 *Chesham Street, S.W.*	}	Younger daughters.
34056	10319	Violet, wife of Major Charles FitzClarence, V.C., Irish Guards, 1864.		
34057	10320	Edward Charles FitzClarence, 1899.	{	Grandchild. Child of No. 34056.

751. Descendants of Lady Louisa Spencer-Churchill, 1821–1882, and her husband, the Hon. Robert Charles Henry Spencer, 1817–1881. (See Table CXV.)

34058 –66	}	Same as Nos. 26747–26755.

752. Descendants of Lady Louisa Stewart, 1804–1889, and her husband, William, 2nd Lord Feversham, 1798–1867. (See Table CXV.)

34067	10321	William Ernest, 1st Earl of Feversham [U.K.], 1829. *Duncombe Park, Helmsley.*	}	Son.

34068	10322	Charles William Reginald, Viscount Helmsley, 1879.	Great-grandchildren. Children of William Reginald, Viscount Helmsley, M.P., 1852–1881.
34069	10323	Hon. Mabel Theresa, wife of William Gervase Beckett, 1877. 1 *Hyde Park Place, W.*	
34070	10324	Marion Beckett, 1896.	Great-great-grandchildren. Children of No. 34069.
34071	10325	Cynthia Maud Beckett, 1900.	
34072	10326	Hon. Hubert Ernest Valentine Duncombe, D.S.O., 1862. 19 *Belgrave Square, S.W.*	Grandson. Son of No. 34067.
34073–75	}	Same as Nos. 22300–22302.	Great-grandchildren. Children of Lady Hermione Wilhelmina Duncombe, –1895, wife of Gerald, 5th Duke of Leinster, 1851–1893.
34076	10327	Lady Helen Venetia, wife of Sir Edgar Vincent, K.C.M.G., M.P., 1866. 3 *Buckingham Gate, S.W.*	Granddaughters. Daughters of No. 34067.
34077	10328	Lady Mabel Cynthia, wife of Sir Richard James Graham, 4th Bart., of Netherby, 1869. *Netherby, Longtown, Cumberland.*	
34078	10329	Frederick Fergus Graham, 1893.	Great-grandchildren. Children of No. 34077.
34079	10330	Richard Preston Graham, 1896.	
34080	10331	Lady Ulrica Duncombe, 1875.	Granddaughter. Younger daughter of No. 34067.
34081	10332	Charles William Ernest Duncombe, Captain Yorkshire Yeomanry Cavalry, 1862.	Grandchildren. Children of the Hon. Cecil Duncombe, 1832–1902.
34082	10333	Eleanor Rachel Duncombe, 1860.	
34083	10334	Violet Helen, wife of William Herbert St. Quinton, 1864. *Scampston·Hall, York.*	
34084	10335	Emily Catherine Louisa Duncombe, 1866.	
34085	10336	Albert William Parsons, 1850.	Grandchildren. Children of Lady Jane Duncombe, 1824–1894, 2nd wife of the Hon. Lawrence Parsons, 1805–1894.
34086	10337	Randolph Cecil Parsons, 1852.	
34087	10338	Louisa Alice, wife of Colonel John Fielden Brocklehurst, C.B., M.V.O., R.H.G., 1851. *Ranksborough, Oakham, Rutland.*	
34088	10339	Florence Helen Isabella, wife of 'Colonel Frederick Henry Harford, *late* Scots Guards. *Down Place, Windsor.*	
34089–102	}	Same as Nos. 26688–26701.	Grandchildren. Children of the Hon. Gertrude Duncombe, 1827, wife of Francis Horatio Fitzroy, 1823–1900.
34103	10340	Lieut.-Col. Ernest William Beckett, M.P., 1856. *Kirkstall Grange, near Leeds.* 17· *Stratton Street, W.*	Grandchild. Son of the Hon. Helen Duncombe, –1896, and her husband, William Beckett, of Meanwood Park, Leeds, M.P., 1826–1890.
34104	10341	Ralph William Ernest Beckett, 1891.	Great-grandchild. Son of No. 34103.
34105	10342	William Gervase Beckett, *late* Captain Yorkshire Hussars, 1816. 1 *Hyde Park Place, W.*	Grandson. Brother of No. 34103.
34106–107	}	Same as Nos. 34070–34071.	Great-grandchildren. Children of No. 34105.
34108	10343	Rupert Evelyn Beckett, Captain Yorkshire Hussars, I.Y., 1870. *The Lodge, Doncaster.*	Grandson. Brother of No. 34103.

34109 -111	}	Same as Nos. 27748-27750.	{ Great-grandchildren. Children of No. 34108.
34112	10344	Helen Louisa Beckett.	}
34113	10345	Adeline Gertrude, wife of the Right Hon. Sir Frederick George Milner, P.C., M.P., 7th Bart. 11 *Hereford Gardens, W.*	Grandchildren. Sisters to No. 34103.
34114	10346	William Frederick Victor Mordaunt Milner, 1893.	} Great-grandchildren. Children of No. 34113.
34115	10347	Violet Helen Milner.	
34116	10348	Doreen Maud Milner.	
34117	10349	Dorothy Violet Chandos-Pole. *Radbourne Hall, co. Derby.*	{ Great-grandchild. Daughter of Violet Katherine Beckett, -1883, 1st wife of Reginald Walkelyne Chandos-Pole, of Radbourne Hall.
34118	10350	Maud Augusta, wife of Lord Henry Nevill. *Eridye Castle, Frant.*	} Grandchild. Youngest sister to No. 34103.
34119 -121	}	Same as Nos. 27118-27120.	{ Great-grandchildren. Children of No. 34118.

753. Descendants of Captain Horatio Stewart, 1806–1835. (See Table CXV.)

34122	10351	Horatio Granville Murray-Stewart, J.P., D.L. *Cally, Gatehouse, Kirkcudbrightshire.*	} Son.

754. Descendants of Louisa Stewart, 1810–1872, and her husband, David Baillie, of Hill Park, Westerham, Kent, 1785–1861. (See Table CXV.)

34123	10352	James William Baillie, Colonel Leicestershire I.Y., *late* Royal Horse Guards, 1832. *Ilston Grange, Leicester.*	} Son.
34124	10353	Frederick David Baillie, *late* Major 4th Hussars, 1862.	} Grandchildren. Children of No. 34123.
34125	10354	Henry Thomas James Baillie, 1866.	
34126	10355	Violet Maud Mary, wife of Robert Andrew Falkner.	
34127	10356	William Henry Baillie.	} Younger sons.
34128	10357	Alexander Horatio Baillie.	
34129	10358	Arthur Charles Wombwell, *late* Coldstream Guards. *The Firs, Newbury.*	} Grandson, Son of Frances Baillie, 1830-1876, wife of Charles Orby Wombwell, 1813-1898.
34130	10359	Henry Revell Reynolds, 1856. *7 The Boltons, S.W.*	{ Grandchildren. Children of Jane Katherine Baillie, 1835-1875, and her husband, the Rev. Henry Revell Reynolds, Vicar of Markham Clinton, 1829-1896.
34131	10360	Evan Knatchbull Revell Reynolds, 1858. *Fyfield Rectory, Hants.*	
34132	10361	Henry Robert Reynolds, 1889.	} Great-grandchildren. Children of No. 34131.
34133	10362	Dorothy Margaret Reynolds, 1888.	
34134	10363	Sylvia Rachel Reynolds, 1891.	
34135	10364	Phyllis Janet Reynolds, 1895.	
34136	10365	Louis Baillie Reynolds, 1860. *32 Aldridge Road Villas, W.*	} Grandchild. Brother to Nos. 34130, &c.
34137	10366	Eustace Baillie Reynolds, 1893.	} Great-grandchildren. Children of No. 34136.
34138	10367	Paul Kenneth Baillie Reynolds, 1896.	
34139	10368	Donald Hugh Baillie Reynolds, 1900.	

34140	10369	Sydney Hugh Reynolds, 1867.	
34141	10370	Kenneth Lindsay Reynolds, 1870.	Grandchildren. Brothers
34142	10371	Dora Emily Vernon, wife of Ralph Iliffe Simey, 1872.	and sisters to No. 34130, &c.
34143	10372	Elsie Louisa Reynolds, 1874.	

755. Descendants of the Hon. Montgomery Granville John Stewart, of Castramont, N.B., 1780–1860. (See Table CXV.)

34144	10373	Herbert Galloway Stewart, 1866.	
34145	10374	Percy Marlborough Stewart, 1871. *The Elms, Pocklington, Yorks.*	
34146	10375	Horatio George Willoughby Stewart, 1877.	Grandchildren. Children of the Rev. James
34147	10376	Arthur Alexander Melville Stewart, 1879.	Stewart, Rector of Little Stukeley, near Hunting-
34148	10377	Isabel Mary Josephine, wife of Gordon Allan, 1868.	ton, 1819–1895.
34149	10378	Eva Katharine Graham Stewart, 1873.	
34150	10379	Olivia Margaret Agneta Stewart, 1877.	
34151	10380	Charles Stewart Montgomerie Lockart, 1842.	Grandchildren. Children of Anne Stewart, 1802– 1878, and her husband,
34152	10381	Alan Charles Stewart Lockart, 1846.	the Rev. Samuel John
34153	10382	Catherine Lockart.	Ingram Lockhart, Vicar
34154	10383	Anne Lockart.	of Hurstbourne, Hants.
			Grandchildren. Children of Susan Stewart, 1803– 1839, and her husband, the Rev. E. Willoughby Sewell.
			Grandchild. Child of Sophia Stewart, 1810–
34155		Same as No. 34122.	1888, and her husband, Captain Horatio Stewart, 1806–1835.
			Grandchild. Son of Caroline
34156	10384	Sir John Robert Heron-Maxwell, 7th Bart., *of Springkell,* 1836. 9 *Wilbraham Place, S.W.*	Stewart, 1813–1896, and her husband, Sir John Heron-Maxwell, 6th Bart., 1808–1885.
34157	10385	Ivor Walter Heron-Maxwell, 1871.	Great-grandchildren.
34158	10386	Maud Lucia Heron, wife of William Marshall Cazalet, J.P., D.L. 19 *Grosvenor Square, W.*	Children of No. 34156.
34159	10387	Edward Cazalet, 1894.	Great-great-grandchildren.
34160	10388	Victor Alexander Cazalet, 1896.	Children of No. 34158.
34161	10389	Thelma Cazalet, 1899.	
34162	10390	Gwendoline Heron, wife of Richard Bayley Chenevix Trench. *Lime Grove, Bangor, North Wales.*	Great-grandchild. 2nd daughter of No. 34156.
34163	10391	Hugo Trench, 1890.	
34164	10392	Eric Trench, } twins, 1892.	Great-great-grandchildren.
34165	10393	Ivor Trench, }	Children of No. 34162.
34166	10394	Lionel Chenevix Trench, 1901.	
34167	10395	Kathleen Edith Heron-Maxwell.	Great-granddaughters. Younger
34168	10396	Muriel Heron-Maxwell.	daughters of No. 34156.

34169	10397	Robert Charles Heron-Maxwell, Barrister, 1848. 93 St. George's Road, S.W.	
34170	10398	Arthur Wellington Heron-Maxwell, 1852. Conservative.	Grandchildren.
34171	10399	Spencer Horatio Walpole Heron-Maxwell, 1855.	Brothers and
34172	10400	Caroline Mary Heron-Maxwell.	sisters of No.
34173	10401	Mary Katherine Dundonald Heron-Maxwell.	34156.
34174	10402	Louisa Susan Marlborough Heron, widow of Sir James Robert Walker, 2nd Bart., 1829–1899. 13 Cadogan Gardens, S.W.	
34175	10403	Sir Robert James Milo Walker, 4th Bart., 1890. Sand Hutton, York.	Great-great-grandchildren. Children of Sir James
34176	10404	John Percy Ernest Walker, 1891.	Heron Walker, 3rd Bart.,
34177	10405	Ronald Heron Walker, 1896.	1865–1900, son of No.
34178	10406	Patrick Bruce Walker, 1898.	34174.
34179	10407	Cecily Etha Mary Walker.	
34180	10408	Rev. Reginald Edmund Walker, 1866. Frant Rectory, Tunbridge Wells.	Great-grandson. 2nd son of No. 34174.
34181	10409	Francis Hugh Seymour Walker, 1897.	
34182	10410	Lionel Reginald Walker, 1898.	Great-great-grandchildren. Children of No. 34180.
34183	10411	Margaret Edith Mary Walker, 1901.	
34184	10412	Harold Maxwell Walker, Captain 1st Life Guards, 1869.	
34185	10413	Francis Henry Walker, 1870.	Great-grandchildren. Younger sons and
34186	10414	Ernest Robert Walker, 1872. Shenleybury House, Shenley, Herts.	eldest daughter of No. 34174.
34187	10415	Mary Louisa, wife of Lieutenant-Colonel Edgar Allan Lambart, R.F.A. [Naval and Military].	
34188	10416	Julian Harold Legge Lambart, 1893.	Great-great-grandchild. Child of No. 34187.
34189	10417	Mildred Caroline, wife of Arthur Herbert Kerr. 2 Driffield Terrace, York.	Great-grandchild. 2nd daughter of No. 34174.
34190 –92	}	Same as Nos. 20167–20169.	Great-great-grandchildren. Children of No. 34189.
34193	10418	Beatrix Jane Frances, wife of the Rev. William Geoffrey Pennyman. 100 Oakley Street, Chelsea.	Great-grandchildren. Younger daughters
34194	10419	Olive Cecil, wife of Captain Seymour Campbell Johnstone, King's Own Scottish Borderers.	of No. 34174.
34195	10420	Conway Bruce Campbell Johnstone, 1898.	Great-great-grandchild. Child of No. 34194.
34196	10421	Edith Elphinstone Heron, widow of the Rev. George Napier.	Grandchildren. Younger sis-
34197	10422	Beatrice Ethel Heron-Maxwell, Lady-in-Waiting to H.R.H. the Duchess of Albany.	ters to No. 34156.
34198	10423	Jane, widow of the Rev. James Lawson, –1872, 1815. 29 Brockman Road, Folkestone.	Daughter.

756. Descendants of the Rev. Edward Stewart, 1808–1875. (See Table CXVI.)

34199	10424	Geoffrey Stewart, Lieutenant 2nd Battalion Coldstream Guards, 1878.	Grandson. Son of Major-General Sir Herbert Stewart, K.C.B., 1843–1885.

EDWARD THE FOURTH, KING OF ENGLAND AND FRANCE,
LORD OF IRELAND.

THE COMMON ANCESTOR OF NOS. 1–36735.

From the Picture by an unknown artist in the National Portrait Gallery.

34200	10425	Winifred, Lady Robinson, widow of Sir John Blencowe Robinson, 8th Bart., 1830–1877, 1839. *St. David's, Kingsthorpe, Northampton.*	⎫ ⎬ Daughters.
34201	10426	Katherine Elizabeth, widow of Henry Herbert, 1818–1898, 1842. *Dublin.*	⎭
34202	10427	Arthur Stewart Herbert, 1866. *Cohirnane, co. Killarney.*	Grandchild. Son of No. 34201.
34203		Same as No. 23320. Great-grandchild.	Child of No. 34202.
34204	10428	Kathleen Olive, wife of Herbert Everett.	⎫ Grandchildren. Children of No. 34201.
34205	10429	Violet Ina Jane Herbert.	⎬
34206	10430	Gwendoline Egerton Herbert.	⎭
34207	10431	Louisa Winifred, wife of Alexander Augustus Berens, 1848. *Castlemead, Windsor.*	3rd surviving daughter.
34208	10432	Blanche Mabel Berens.	⎫ Grandchildren. Children of No. 34207.
34209	10433	Olivia Elizabeth, Countess Cairns [U.K.]. *Paultons, Romsey, Hants.*	⎬
34210	10434	Lady Louise Rosemary Kathleen Virginia Cairns, 1899.	Great-grandchild. Only child of No. 34209 by 1st husband, Arthur William, 2nd Earl Cairns, 1861–1890.
34211		Same as No. 28944.	Great-grandchild. Only child of No. 34209 by 2nd husband, Roger Cyril Hans Sloane Stanley.
34212	10435	Florence Winifred, Lady Ross. *Castlemead, Windsor.*	Grandchild. Child of No. 34207.
34213	10436	Augusta Frances Harriet, widow of the Rev. Henry Everett, Rector of Dorchester, 18 – 1896, 1850. *105 Charlotte Street, Fitzroy Square, W.*	4th surviving daughter.
34214	10437	Herbert Everett, 1876. Grandchild.	Son of No. 34213.
34215	10438	Jane, wife of Arthur Frederick Tyrwhitt-Drake, 1854. *Dogdean, Salisbury.*	5th surviving daughter.
34216	10439	Dorothy Tyrwhitt-Drake, 1874.	Grandchild. Daughter of No. 34215.

757. Descendants of Algernon Stewart, 1811–1875. (See Table CXVI.)

34217	10440	Charles Edward Stewart, C.B., C.M.G., C.I.E., *late* Colonel I.S.C., 1836. *51 Redcliffe Square, S.W.*	Elder son.
34218	10441	Algernon Bingham Anstruther Stewart, D.S.O., Captain 2nd Battalion Seaforth Highlanders, 1869.	Grandsons. Sons of No. 34217.
34219	10442	Philip Charteris Anstruther Stewart, M.E., 1874.	
34220	10443	Algernon Augustus Stewart, Major-General, *late* Colonel R.A., 1839. *United Service.*	Younger son.
34221	10444	Leopold Charles Stewart, 1868. *Isthmian.*	⎫ Grandchildren. Children of No. 34220.
34222	10445	Charlotte Susan Stewart, 1865.	⎬
34223	10446	Eleanor Sophia Anne Stewart, 1870.	⎬
34224	10447	Albinia Frances Adelaide Stewart, 1879.	⎭

758. Descendants of Arthur Stewart, 1813–1879. (See Table CXVI.)

| 34225 –42 | } | Same as Nos. 26855–26872. |

759. Descendants of Jane Frances Clinton Stewart, 1817–1897, 3rd wife of George, 6th Duke of Marlborough, 1793–1857. (See Table CXVI.)

34243	10448	Lord Edward Spencer-Churchill, 1853. *28 Grosvenor Street, W.*	Son.
34244	10449	Edward George Spencer-Churchill, Lieutenant Grenadier Guards, 1876.	Grandchildren. Children of No. 34243.
34245	10450	Augusta Ruby, wife of Captain the Hon. Allen Benjamin Bathurst, 1877.	
34246	10451	Agnes Beryl Spencer-Churchill, 1881.	

760. Descendants of the Hon. James Henry Keith Stewart, C.B., 1783–1836. (See Table CXV.)

34247 –55	}	Same as Nos. 26846–26854.

761. Descendants of the Right Hon. Sir James Robert George Graham, of Netherby, 2nd Bart., P.C., G.C.B., 1791–1861. (See Table CXVII.)

34256	10452	Sir Richard James Graham, 4th Bart., J.P., D.L., 1859. *Netherby, Cumberland.*	Grandson. Son of Sir Frederick Ulric Graham, 3rd Bart., 1820–1888.
34257 –58	}	Same as Nos. 34078–34079.	Great-grandchildren. Children of No. 34256.
34259	10453	Hugh Graham, 1860. *Bucknell Manor, Bicester.*	Grandson. Brother to No. 34256.
34260	10454	Sybil Hattie Hermione Graham, 1893.	Great-granddaughters. Daughters of No. 34259.
34261	10455	Muriel Mary Graham, 1895.	
34262	10456	James Reginald Graham, 1864. *Scaurbank, Longtown, Cumberland.*	Grandson. Youngest brother to No. 34256.
34263	10457	Iris Enid Florence Graham, 1892.	Great-granddaughter. Daughter of No. 34262.
34264	10458	Margaret Frances, Countess of Verulam [U.K.], Viscountess Grimston [I.], Baroness Forrester [S.], Baroness Verulam [G.B.]. *Gorhambury, St. Albans.*	Granddaughter. Eldest sister to No. 34256.
34265	10459	James Walter, Viscount Grimston, 1880.	Great-grandchildren. Children of No. 34264.
34266	10460	Lady Helen Grimston, 1879.	
34267	10461	Lady Hermione Grimston, 1881.	
34268	10462	Lady Aline Grimston, 1883.	
34269	10463	Lady Elizabeth Grimston, 1885.	
34270	10464	Lady Sybil Grimston, 1887.	
34271	10465	Lady Vera Grimston, 1890.	
34272	10466	Violet Hermione, Duchess of Montrose [S.], Countess Graham [G.B.]. *Buchanan Castle, near Glasgow.*	Granddaughter. 2nd sister to No. 34256.

34273	10467	James, Marquis of Graham, 1878.	Great-grandchildren. Children of No. 34272.
34274	10468	Lord Douglas Malise Graham, 1883.	
34275	10469	Lord Alastair Mungo Graham, 1886.	
34276	10470	Lady Helen Violet Graham, 1879.	
34277	10471	Lady Hermione Emily Graham, 1882.	
34278 –80	}	Same as Nos. 26008–26010.	Great-grandchildren. Children of Sybil Marcia Graham, –1887 (3rd sister to No. 34256), and her husband, Robert Offley Ashburton, 2nd Lord Houghton, afterwards Earl of Crewe.
34281	10472	Hilda Georgiana, wife of George Denison Faber, M.P. 14 *Grosvenor Square, W.*	Granddaughter. 5th but 3rd surviving sister to No. 34256.
34282	10473	Arthur Malise Graham, 1865.	Grandchildren. Children of the Rev. Malise Reginald Graham, 1833–1895.
34283	10474	Reginald Graham, 1867. 2 *Park Mansions, Albert Gate, S.W.*	
34284	10475	Ernest Reginald Graham, 1893.	Great-grandchild. Child of No. 34283.
34285	10476	Rev. Ivor Charles Graham, 1868.	*Arthuret Rectory, Longtown, Cumberland.*	Grandchildren. Younger brother and sisters of No. 34282.
34286	10477	Sophia Augusta Graham,	
34287	10478	Maud Agnes Graham,	
34288	10479	Mabel Violet, Countess of Feversham [U.K.]. *Duncombe Park, Helmsley, near York.*	Elder surviving daughter.
34289 –301	}	Same as Nos. 34068–34080.	Grandchildren. Children of No. 34288.
34302	10480	Helen, widow of Lieut.-Gen. Charles Baring, 1829–1890. 31 *Adelaide Crescent, Brighton.*	Younger surviving daughter.
34303 –06	}	Same as Nos. 20383–20386.	Grandchildren, &c. Children, &c., of No. 34302.

762. Descendants of Major George Graham, Registrar-General of Births, Marriages, and Deaths, 1801–1888. (See Table CXVII.)

34307	10481	Richard John Cuninghame, 1871.	Grandchild. Child of Emily Graham, 1837–1887, wife of Captain John William Herbert Cuninghame, of Lainshaw, Ayr, 2nd Life Guards.
34308	10482	Florence Inger Maria, wife of Graham Hutchison. *Balmaghie, Castle Douglas, Kirkcudbright.*	Daughter.
34309	10483	Craufuird George Graham Hutchison, Captain 21st Lancers, 1874.	Grandchildren. Children of No. 34308.
34310	10484	Inger Margaretta Hutchison.	

763. Descendants of Elizabeth Anne Graham, 1792–1874, wife of the Rev. William James Darley Waddilove, 1786–1859. (See Table CXVII.)

34311	10485	George Hope Waddilove, *of Woodhorne, J.P.,* 1865. *Brunton House, Wall-on-. Tyne.*	Grandson. Son of Major George Marmaduke Darley Waddilove, of Woodhorne, 1823–1887.

34312	10486	Charles John Darley Waddilove, 1882.	
34313	10487	George Edward Darley Waddilove, 1885.	Grandchildren. Children of Admiral Charles Ludovic Darley Waddilove, 1828–1896.
34314	10488	Christopher Darley Waddilove, 1888.	
34315	10489	Katharine Alice Waddilove.	
34316	10490	Emily Hope Waddilove.	
34317	10491	Elinor Mary Waddilove.	
34318	10492	Mary Caroline Waddilove.	
34319	10493	Charles Lister Oxley, Vice-Admiral R.N., J.P. *The Hall, Ripon.*	Grandson. Son of Georgiana Maria Waddilove, 1822–1864, wife of Charles Christopher Oxley, of Ripon, J.P.
34320	10494	Charles Oxley, 1880.	
34321	10495	Christopher Oxley.	
34322	10496	Agnes Oxley.	Great-grandchildren. Children of No. 34319.
34323	10497	Violet Oxley.	
34324	10498	Margaret Oxley.	
34325	10499	Rose Oxley.	
34326	10500	Dorothy Oxley.	
34327	10501	Rev. William Henry Oxley, M.A. *Petersham Vicarage, Surrey.*	Grandson. Brother to No. 34319.
34328	10502	Selwyn Amor Nathaniel Oxley, 1890.	Great-grandchild. Son of No. 34327.
34329	10503	Charlotte Elizabeth, widow of the Rev. William Boycott, –1889.	Granddaughter. Elder sister to No. 34319.
34330	10504	Alfred Edmund Cunningham Boycott.	Great-grandchildren. Children of No. 34329.
34331	10505	Georgiana Maria Boycott.	
34332	10506	Susan, wife of the Rev. George Edward Oscar Watts. *Kensworth Vicarage, Herts.*	Granddaughter. Younger sister to No. 34319.
34333	10507	Francis George Foulis Watts.	Great-grandchildren. Children of No. 34332.
34334	10508	Rev. Charles Christopher Watts. *Wood Green.*	
34335	10509	Alfred Bernard Watts, Lieutenant R.N.	
34336	10510	Mary Grace Watts.	
34337	10511	Gertrude Mary Oxley. *6 Daniel Street, Bath.*	Granddaughter. Youngest sister to No. 34319.
34338	10512	Charlotte Jemima Waddilove.	Daughter.

764. Descendants of Caroline Graham, 1793–1870, and her husband, Sir Wilfrid Lawson, 1st Bart., 1795–1867. (See Table CXVII.)

34339	10513	Sir Wilfrid Lawson, 2nd Bart., M.P., 1829. *Brayton, Cumberland.*	Elder son.
34340	10514	Wilfrid Lawson, D.L., 1862. *Isel Hall, Cockermouth.*	Grandchildren. Children of No. 34339.
34341	10515	Arthur Lawson, 1866.	
34342	10516	Mordaunt Lawson, 1868.	
34343	10517	Hilton Lawson, 1895.	Great-grandchildren. Children of No. 34342.
34344	10518	Peter Lawson, 1898.	
34345	10519	Godfrey Lawson, 1880.	Grandchildren. Youngest son and eldest daughter of No. 34339.
34346	10520	Ellen, Hon. Mrs. Arthur Holland-Hibbert, wife of the Hon. Arthur Henry Holland-Hibbert. *Munden, Watford.*	

34347	10521	Thurstan Holland-Hibbert, 1888.	Great-grandchildren. Children of No. 34346.
34348	10522	Wilfrid Holland-Hibbert, 1893.	
34349	10523	Elsie Holland-Hibbert, 1886.	
34350	10524	Mabel, wife of Alan Delancy Curwen. *Workington Hall, Cumberland.*	Grandchild. 2nd daughter of No. 34339.
34351	10525	Alan Henry Curwen, 1899.	Great-grandchildren. Children of No. 34350.
34352	10526	Isabel Mary Curwen, 1897.	
34353	10527	Lucy, wife of Edmund Heathcote Thruston, J.P., D.L. *Pennal Town, Merioneth.*	Grandchild. 3rd daughter of No. 34339.
34354	10528	Margaret Thruston, 1897.	Great-grandchildren. Children of No. 34353.
34355	10529	Hoima Joan Thruston, 1901.	
34356	10530	Josephine Lawson.	Grandchild. Youngest daughter of No. 34339.
34357	10531	William Lawson, 1836.	Children.
34358	10532	Elizabeth Lawson.	
34359	10533	Catherine, widow of John Hampden Fordham, -1885. *9 Phillimore Gardens, W.*	
34360	10534	Alfred Russell Fordham, 1873.	Grandchildren. Children of No. 34359.
34361	10535	Edward Wilfrid Fordham, 1874.	
34362	10536	John Gurney Fordham, 1877.	

765. Descendants of Harriet Anne Graham, 1799–1836, 1st wife of Captain Frederick Madan, E.I.C.S., 1797–1863. (See Table CXVII.)

34363 -83	}	Same as Nos. 26812–26832.

766. Descendants of Charlotte Graham, –1873, and her husband, Sir George Musgrave, 10th Bart., of Edenhall, 1799–1872. (See Table CXVII.)

34384	10537	Sir Richard George Musgrave, 12th Bart.,1872. *17 Charles Street, Berkeley Square, S.W. Edenhall, Langwathby, Cumberland.*	Grandson. Son of Sir Richard Courtenay Musgrave, 11th Bart., 1838–1881.
34385	10538	Nigel Courtenay Musgrave, 1896.	Great-grandchildren. Children of No. 34384.
34386	10539	Christopher Musgrave, 1899.	
34387	10540	Philip Richard Musgrave, *late* Lieutenant 3rd Battalion Royal Sussex Regiment, 1873. *Bachelors'.*	Grandchildren. Brothers and sisters of No. 34384.
34388	10541	Thomas Charles Musgrave, 1875. *17 Clifford Street, W.*	
34389	10542	Dorothy Anne, wife of Henry Francis Compton. *Minstead Manor, Lyndhurst. Hants.*	
34390	10543	Henry Compton.	Great-grandchildren. Children of No. 34389.
34391	10544	Phyllis Compton.	
34392	10545	Daphne Compton.	
34393	10546	Zoe Caroline, wife of Alexander Haldane Farquharson, *of Invercauld.* *40 Park Street, Grosvenor Square, W.*	Grandchild. Sister to No. 34384.
34394 -95	}	Same as Nos. 32728–32729.	Great-grandchildren. Children of No. 34393.
34396	10547	Caroline, widow of William Stanley, *of Dalegarth and Ponsonby Hall, co. Cumberland,* 1829–1881.	Daughter.

34397	10548	William Stanley, D.L., 1861. *Ponsonby Hall, near Whitehaven.*	} Grandchildren. Children of
34398	10549	Philip Stanley, 1870.	No. 34396.
34399	10550	Caroline Lowry.	{ Great-grandchild. Daughter of Charlotte Stanley, –1895, and her husband, J. H. Lowry.
34400	10551	Margaret, wife of the Rev. H. T. G. Alington.	} Grandchild. Daughter of No. 34396.
34401	10552	Noel Stanley Alington, 1898.	} Great-grandchildren. Children
34402	10553	Ursula Margaret Alington, 1900.	of No. 34400.
34403	10554	Lucy Mildred Stanley.	} Grandchildren. Children
34404	10555	Constance Madeline Stanley.	of No. 34396.
34405	10556	Caroline Augusta Stanley.	
34406 –11	}	Same as Nos. 34282–34287.	{ Grandchildren. Children of Agnes Musgrave, –1901, wife of the Rev. Malaise Reginald Graham, 1833–1895.
34412	10557	Sophia, wife of Samuel Steuart Gladstone. *19 Lennox Gardens, S.W.*	} Younger daughter.
34413	10558	Hugh Steuart Gladstone, 1877.	} Grandchildren.
34414	10559	Winifrid Steuart, wife of Sydney R. Fothergill. *Lowbridge House, Kendal, Westmorland.*	Children of No. 34412.
34415	10560	Richard Fothergill, 1901.	} Great-grandchildren. Chil-
34416	10561	Mildred Helen Sophia Fothergill, 1898.	dren of No. 34414.

767. Descendants of George, 6th Duke of Marlborough, 1793–1857. (See Table CXVIII.)

34417 –83	}	Same as Nos. 33991–34057.	{ Sons (by 1st wife) and their children.
34484 –87	}	Same as Nos. 34243–34246.	{ Son (by 3rd wife) and his children.
34488 –96	}	Same as Nos. 34058–34066.	{ Children of daughter (by 1st wife).
34497 –99	}	Same as Nos. 31660–31662.	{ Grandchildren. Children of the Lady Clementine Augusta Spencer-Churchill (daughter by 2nd wife), 1848–1886, and her 1st husband, John Charles, 3rd Marquis Camden, 1840–1872.
34500	10562	Evelyn Frances Henrietta Green.	{ Grandchild. Child of the above-named Lady Clementine Augusta Spencer-Churchill, by her 2nd husband, Captain Philip Green, 9th Lancers.

768. Descendants of Lord Charles Spencer-Churchill, 1794–1840. (See Table CXVIII.)

34501	10563	John Kemyss George Thomas Spencer-Churchill, Colonial Secretary of the Bahamas, 1835. *Nassau, Bahamas.*	} Son.

34502	10564	John Eyre Nelson, 1858.	*Landford House, near Salisbury.*	Grandchildren. Children of the late Susan Spencer-Churchill, 1831–1898, and her husband, the Rev. and Hon. John Horatio Nelson, 1825.
34503	10565	Horatio Spencer Nelson, 1860.		
34504	10566	Lucy Caroline, wife of the Rev. John Fletcher Dixon-Stewart, 1833. *Stanton St. Bernard Rectory, Marlborough.*		Daughter.

769. Descendants of Arthur, 1st Lord Templemore, 1797–1837. (See Table CXV.)

34505 -42	}	Same as Nos. 27871–27908.

770. Descendants of Elizabeth Chichester, 1798–1882, and her husband, William, 1st Lord Bateman, 1780–1845. (See Table CXV.)

34543	10567	William Spencer, 3rd Baron Bateman [U.K.], 1856. *Shobdon Court, Shobdon, Hereford.*	Grandchildren. Children of William Bateman, 2nd Baron Bateman, 1826–1901.
34544	10568	Hon. Edward Reginald Bateman-Hanbury, *late* Major 4th Battalion Rifle Brigade, J.P., D.L., 1859. *Boodle's; Naval and Military; Pratt's.*	
34545	10569	Hon. Walter Bateman-Hanbury, D.L., 1862. *Piccadilly.*	
34546	10570	Hon. Charles Stanhope Melville Bateman-Hanbury, D.L., 1877. *Breckles Hall, Norfolk.*	
34547	10571	Hon. Maud Frances, wife of the Rev. and Hon. Archibald Parker, 1855. *Abbotsford, Wymondham, Norfolk.*	
34548	10572	Charles Edward Parker, 1890.	Great-grandchildren. Children of No. 34547.
34549	10573	Frederic Archibald Parker, 1894.	
34550	10574	Violet Maud Parker, 1892.	
34551	10575	Evelyn Sylvia Parker, 1897.	
34552	10576	Hon. Evelyn Augusta, wife of Robert John Foster, J.P., D.L., 1858. *Harrowins, Queensbury, Yorkshire. Stockeld Park, Wetherby, Yorkshire.*	Grandchild. 2nd daughter of William, 2nd Baron Bateman, 1826–1901.
34553	10577	Gerald Robert Foster, 1885.	Great-grandchildren. Children of No. 34552.
34554	10578	Cecil Geoffrey Foster, 1892.	
34555	10579	William Edward Foster, 1895.	
34556	10580	Agnes Evelyn Foster, 1887.	
34557	10581	Hon. Gertrude Emily, wife of John Wood, J.P., D.L., 1860. *Hengrave Hall, Bury St. Edmunds. Whitfield, Derbyshire.*	Grandchild. 3rd daughter of William, 2nd Baron Bateman, 1826–1901.
34558	10582	Edmund Walter Hanbury Wood, 1898.	Great-grandchild. Child of No. 34557.

34559	10583	Hon. Agnes Rosamond Bateman-Hanbury, 1866.	⎫ Grandchildren.
34560	10584	Hon. Margaret Cecilia Bateman-Hanbury, 1870.	⎪ Younger sisters of No. 34557.
34561	10585	Hon. Rachel Anne Selina Decima, wife of S. Hill Wood, 1875. *Moorfield, Glossop, Derbyshire.*	⎬
34562	10586	Basil Samuel Hill Wood, 1900.	⎰ Great-grandchild. Child of No. 34561.

771. Descendants of Lady Elizabeth Euphemia Stewart, 1771–1855, wife of William Phillips Inge, of Thorpe, 1773–1838. (See Table CXV.)

34563 –68	⎬	Same as Nos. 26794–26799.

772. Descendants of Edward, 2nd Lord Crofton, 1806–1869. (See Table CXIX.)

34569 –85	⎬	Same as Nos. 27854–27870.

773. Descendants of the Hon. Susannah Anne Crofton, 1802–1894, and her husband, St. George Francis Caulfeild, of Donamon Castle, co. Roscommon, 1806–1896. (See Table CXIX.)

34586	10587	Algernon Thomas St. George Caulfeild, 1869. *Donamon Castle, Roscommon.*	⎫ Grandson. Son of Captain St. George Francis Robert Caulfeild, 1831–1875.
34587	10588	Alfred Henry Caulfeild, 1834.	⎫
34588	10589	Emily Susan, Countess of Lonsdale [U.K.], Viscountess Lowther [G.B.], 1832. *Cottesmore Hall, Oakham.*	⎬ Children.
34589	10590	Lady Gladys Mary Juliet Lowther, 1881. *Coombe Court, Kingston Hill, Surrey.*	⎰ Great-grandchild. Daughter of St. George Henry, 4th Earl of Lonsdale, 1855–1882, and granddaughter of No. 34588.
34590	10591	Hugh Cecil, 5th Earl of Lonsdale [U.K.], and 6th Viscount Lowther [G.B.], 1857. *Lowther Castle, Penrith, Westmorland.* 14 and 15 Carlton House Crescent, S.W.	⎫ Grandchildren. Children of No. 34588.
34591	10592	Hon. Lancelot Edward Lowther, J.P., D.L., 1867. *Asfordby Hall, Melton Mowbray.*	⎰
34592	10593	Anthony Edward Lowther, 1896.	⎫ Great-grandchildren. Children of No. 34591.
34593	10594	Barbara Lowther, 1890.	⎬
34594	10595	Marjorie Lowther, 1895.	⎰
34595	10596	Lady Sybil Emily, widow of Major-General George Williams Knox, C.B., 1894, 1862. *Barrow House, Oakham.*	– ⎬ Grandchild. Elder daughter of No. 34588.
34596	10597	Henry Thomas Knox, 1887.	⎫ Great-grandchildren. Children of No. 34595.
34597	10598	Louisa Eileen Knox, 1891.	⎰
34598	10599	Verena Maud, Viscountess Churchill [U.K.], V.A., 1865. *Rolleston, Leicester.*	⎬ Grandchild. Younger daughter of No. 34588.
34599 –601	⎬	Same as Nos. 26704–26706.	⎰ Great-grandchildren. Children of No. 34598.

774. Descendants of the Hon. Charlotte Crofton, 1803–1839, 2nd wife of Gibbs Crawfurd Antrobus, of Eaton Hall, co. Chester, 1794–1861. (See Table CXIX.)

34602	10600	Charles Antrobus, 1836. *Holly Bank, Scholar Green, Stoke-on-Trent.*	⎫
34603	10601	Susan Emily Antrobus.	⎬ Children.
34604	10602	Anna Maria, wife of the Rev. Francis Richard Bryans. *Clevelands, Babbacombe, Torquay.*	⎭
34605	10603	Edith Ama Bryans.	⎱ Grandchildren. Children of No. 34604.
34606	10604	Bessie Bryans.	⎰

775. Descendants of the Hon. Frances Crofton, 1805–1881, and her husband, Daniel Tighe, of Rossana, co. Wicklow, 1796–1874. (See Table CXIX.)

34607 –08	}	Same as Nos. 22507–22508.	⎰ Grandson, &c. Son of Lieut.-Col. Frederick Edward Bunbury-Tighe, of Woodstock, 1826–1891.
34609	10605	James Stuart Tighe, Lieut.-Col. *late* 8th Madras Cavalry, J.P., D.L., 1831. *Rossana, co. Wicklow.*	⎱ Son.
34610	10606	Walter Stuart Tighe, 1861.	⎱ Grandchildren. Sons of No. 34609.
34611	10607	Wilfred Tighe, 1868.	⎰
34612	10608	Daniel Frederick Charles Tighe, 1899.	⎱ Great-grandchildren. Children of No. 34611.
34613	10609	Norah Una Tighe, 1902.	⎰
34614	10610	Louisa Tighe, ⎱ 1859.	⎫
34615	10611	Flora Tighe, ⎰	⎬ Grandchildren. Children of No. 34609.
34616	10612	Ana Emily Tighe, 1864.	
34617	10613	Maud May Tighe, 1866.	⎭
34618	10614	Frances Marianne, widow of the Hon. Frederick Arthur Henry Chichester, 1824–1863. *73 Cadogan Place, S.W.*	⎱ Eldest surviving daughter.
34619 –25	}	Same as Nos. 27877–27883.	⎰ Grandchildren. Children of No. 34618.
34626	10615	Louisa Elizabeth Tighe.	2nd surviving daughter.
34627 –32	}	Same as Nos. 27855–27860.	⎰ Grandchildren. Children of Theresa Augusta Tighe, 1833–1867, wife of the Hon. Charles St. George Crofton, R.N., 1836–1895.
34633	10616	Susan Diana Tighe.	Younger daughter.

776. Descendant of the Hon. Sophia Crofton, 1811–1884, wife of Eyre Evans, of Ash Hill Towers, Limerick, 1806–1852. (See Table CXIX.)

34634	10617	Sophia Helen Augusta, wife of William Panton Forbes. *Yardley Chase, Jamaica.*	⎱ Daughter.

777. Descendants of the Hon. Frederica Crofton, 1816–1881, wife of the Rev. Hubert McLaughlin, M.A., Prebendary of Hereford, Rector of Benford, Salop, –1883. (See Table CXIX.)

34635	10618	Randolph Humphrey McLaughlin-Berens. *Sidcup, Kent.*	Children.
34636	10619	William George McLaughlin.	

778. Descendants of Sophia Bligh, 1807–1846, 1st wife of Henry William, 3rd Lord Congleton, 1809–1896. (See Table CXV.)

34637	10620	Henry, 4th Baron Congleton [U.K.], 1839. *Rathleague, Queen's Co.* *28 Green Street, W.*	Son.
34638	10621	Hon. Henry Bligh Fortescue Parnell, 1890.	
34639	10622	Hon. John Brooke Molesworth Parnell, 1892.	Grandchildren. Children of No. 34637.
34640	10623	Hon. William Alastair Damer Parnell, 1894.	
34641	10624	Hon. Agnes Caroline Sophia Parnell, 1889.	
34642	10625	Hon. Arthur Parnell, Colonel *late* R.E., 1841. *97 Oakley Street, Chelsea, S.W.*	2nd son.
34643	10626	Arthur Reginald Bligh Parnell, 1871.	Grandchildren. Children of No. 34642.
34644	10627	Bertram Damer Parnell, 1876.	
34645	10628	Desmond Damer Parnell, 1900.	Great-grandchildren. Children of No. 34644.
34646	10629	Nancy Stewart Parnell, 1901.	
34647	10630	Harold Stewart Parnell, 1880.	
34648	10631	Geoffrey Brooke Parnell, 1882.	
34649	10632	Winifred Mary Parnell, 1869.	
34650	10633	Edith Caroline, wife of the Rev. William Thomas Farmiloe, Rector of St. Peter's, Great Windmill Street, W., 1870. *124 Ashley Gardens, S.W.*	Grandchildren Children of No. 34642.
34651	10634	Gwendolen Muriel Parnell, 1877.	
34652	10635	Yseulte Geraldine Parnell, 1886.	
34653	10636	Hon. Emma Sophia, widow of the Rev. George Booth Perry-Ayscough, –1885, 1842. *24 St. John's Church Road, Folkestone.*	Daughter.
34654	10637	Lionel Bligh Perry-Ayscough, 1868.	
34655	10638	Stewart Ayscough Perry-Ayscough, Lieutenant R.N., 1871.	
34656	10639	Henry George Charles Perry-Ayscough, Lieutenant 3rd Battalion Royal Munster Fusiliers, 1875.	Grandchildren. Children of No. 34653.
34657	10640	Violet Frances Mary, wife of Charles Harter.	
34658	10641	Ethel Sophia, widow of the Rev. Herbert Ramus, Rector of Playden, Sussex, –1895.	
34659	10642	Augusta Catherine Alice Perry-Ayscough.	
34660	10643	Caroline Margaret Lucy, wife of Cecil Firmin Lillie, M.D.	

779. Descendants of the Right Hon. James Alexander Stewart, afterwards Stewart-Mackenzie, of Glasserton, 1784–1843. (See Table CXV.)

34661	10644	James Alexander Francis Humberston Stewart-Mackenzie, *late* Colonel Commanding 9th Lancers, J.P., D.L., 1847. *4 Upper Grosvenor Street, W. Brahan, Conon Bridge, N.B.*	
34662	10645	Susan Mary Elizabeth, Lady Jeune, wife of the Right Hon. Sir Francis Henry Jeune, P.C., K.C.B., President of the Probate, Divorce and Admiralty Division of the High Court of Judicature. *79 Harley Street, W.*	Grandchildren. Children of Keith William Stewart-Mackenzie, 1818–1881.
34663	10646	Christian Francis Seaforth Jeune, 1882.	Great-grandchild. Son of No. 34662 by 2nd husband, Sir Francis Jeune.
34664	10647	Madeline Cecilia Carlyle Stanley, 1876.	Great-grandchildren. Children of No. 34662 by 1st husband, Lieut.-Col. the Hon. John Constantine Stanley, 1837–1878.
34665	10648	Osma Mary Dorothea, wife of Augustus Henry Eden Allhusen, M.P., J.P., D.L. *Stoke Court, Stoke Poges, Bucks.*	
34666	10649	Henry Christian Stanley Allhusen, 1899.	Great-great-grandchildren. Children of No. 34665.
34667	10650	Helena Madeleine Mary Allhusen, 1897.	
34668	10651	Julia Charlotte Sophia, Marchioness of Tweeddale [S.], 1846. *4 Chelsea Embankment, S.W.*	Grandchildren. Sisters to No. 34661.
34669	10652	Florence Meira Zelia, wife of Hugh St. John Clarke, 1872. *The White House, New Malden, Surrey.*	
34670	10653	Seaforth St. John Clarke, 1898.	Great-grandchildren. Children of No. 34669.
34671	10654	Moulie Seaforth St. John Clarke, 1900.	
34672	10655	Mary Frances, widow of the Hon. Philip Anstruther, –1863, 1819.	Daughter.
34673	10656	Mary Florence, Marchioness of Northampton [U.K.], Countess of Northampton [E.], 1860. *51 Lennox Gardens, S.W. Castle Ashby, Northampton.*	Granddaughter. Daughter of Louisa Caroline Stewart-Mackenzie, 1827–1902, 2nd wife of William, 2nd Baron Ashburton, 1799–1864.
34674	10657	William Bingham, Earl Compton, 1885.	Great-grandchildren. Children of No. 34673.
34675	10658	Lord Spencer Douglas Compton, 1893.	
34676	10659	Lady Margaret Louisa Lizzie Compton, 1886.	

780. Descendants of Leveson Douglas Stewart, 1786–1819. (See Table CXV.)

34677	10660	John Stewart, *late* Lieutenant 3rd Battalion Seaforth Highlanders, 1869. *Sutton, Ceylon.*	Great-grandchildren. Children of John Leveson Douglas Stewart, 1842–1887, and grandchildren of John Stewart, 1813–1867.
34678	10661	Grace Hamilton, wife of Edwin Arthur Russell Benham, 1871. *Colombo, Ceylon.*	

34679	10662	Leveson Douglas Stewart, 1844.	
34680	10663	Thomas Currie Stewart, 1846.	
34681	10664	Keith Stewart, 1851.	
34682	10665	James Dalrymple Hay Stewart, 1853. 34 *Minto Street, Edinburgh*.	Grandchildren. Children of George Stewart, 1814–1893.
34683	10666	Cleminta Ross Stewart.	
34684	10667	Elizabeth Stewart.	
34685	10668	Isabella Lydia Stewart.	
34686	10669	Leveson Douglas Stewart, 1850. 167 *Withington Road, Whalley Range, Manchester*.	
34687	10670	James Dalrymple Hay Stewart, W.S., 1862. 34 *Minto Street, Edinburgh*.	Grandchildren. Children of James Stewart, 1816–1895.
34688	10671	Ann Stewart.	
34689	10672	Elizabeth Grace, wife of James Dalrymple Hay Stewart.	
34690	10673	Elizabeth Charles.	Grandchildren. Children of Susan Stewart, – , wife of the Rev. George Charles, Minister of the Free Church, Stranraer, N.B.
34691	10674	Susan Charles.	

781. Descendants of Granville, 1st Earl Granville, 1773–1846. (See Table CXX.)

34692 –726	}	Same as Nos. 22366–22400.

782. Descendants of Edward Granville, 3rd Earl of St. Germans, 1798–1877. (See Table CXX.)

34727 –66	}	Same as Nos. 33327–33366.

783. Descendants of the Lady Susan Caroline Eliot, 1801–1835, and her husband, Henry, 4th Earl Beauchamp, 1784–1863. (See Table CXX.)

34767	10675	William, 7th Earl Beauchamp [U.K.], K.C.M.G., 1872. *Madresfield Court, Malvern Link*.	Grandchildren. Children of Frederick, 6th Earl Beauchamp, P.C., 1830–1891.
34768	10676	Hon. Robert Lygon, 1879. *Guards'; Bachelors'; Pratt's*.	
34769	10677	Hon. Henry Lygon, 1884.	
34770	10678	Lady Mary Lygon, Lady-in-Waiting to H.R.H. the Princess of Wales, 1869.	
34771	10679	Lady Susan, wife of Major Robert Gordon Gordon-Gilmour, D.S.O., D.L., 2nd Battalion Grenadier Guards, 1870.	
34772	10680	John Gordon-Gilmour, 1899.	Great-grandchildren. Children of No. 34771.
34773	10681	Mary Gordon-Gilmour, 1890.	
34774	10682	Margaret Gordon-Gilmour, 1892.	
34775	10683	Grizel Gordon-Gilmour, 1894.	
34776	10684	Margaret, Baroness Ampthill [U.K.], C.I., 1874. *Government House, Madras*.	Granddaughter. Sister to Nos. 34771, &c.

34777 -79	}	Same as Nos. 30621-30623.	{	Great-grandchildren. Children of No. 34776.
34780	10685	Lady Agnes Lygon, 1880.	⎫	Granddaughters. Sisters
34781	10686	Lady Maud Lygon, 1882.	⎬	to Nos. 34771, &c.
34782	10687	George Fitzroy Henry, 3rd Lord Raglan [U.K.], 1857. 27 *Half Moon Street, W. Cefntilla Court, Usk, Monmouthshire.*	⎫	Grandson. Son of the Lady Georgiana Lygon, 1832-1865, 1st wife of Richard Henry Fitzroy, 2nd Lord Raglan, 1817-1884.
34783 -88	}	Same as Nos. 22418-22423.	{	Great-grandchildren. Children of No. 34782.
34789	10688	Hon. Arthur Charles Edward Somerset, 1859. 19 *Bolton Street, Piccadilly.*	⎬	Grandson. Brother to No. 34782.
34790	10689	Norman Arthur Henry Somerset, 1894.	⎬	Great-grandson. Son of No. 34789.
34791	10690	Hon. Granville William Richard Somerset, 1862. 30 *Milner Street, Cadogan Square, S.W.*	}	Grandson. Brother to No. 34782.
34792	10691	Richard Granville Somerset, 1894.	{	Great-grandson. Son of No. 34791.

784. Descendants of the Lady Charlotte Sophia Eliot, 1802–1839, and her husband, the Rev. George Martin, Canon of Exeter and Chancellor of the Diocese, –1860. (See Table CXX.)

785. Descendants of Henry, 7th Duke of Beaufort, K.G., 1792–1853. (See Table CXX.)

34793 -808	}	Same as Nos. 20274-20289.	{	Children, &c., of Henry Charles FitzRoy, 8th Duke of Beaufort, K.G., P.C., 1824-1899.
		Descendants, if any, of Lady Charlotte Augusta Frederica Somerset (daughter), 1816-1850, and her husband, Baron Neuman, Austrian Ambassador to the Court of St. James, –1851.		
34809	10692	Sir Gerald William Henry Codrington, 1st Bart., 1850. *Dodington Park, co. Gloucester.*	⎧	Grandson. Son of the Lady Georgiana Charlotte Anne Somerset, V.A., 1817-1884, and her husband, Christopher William Codrington, M.P., Dodington Park, 1805-1864.
34810	10693	Christopher Gerald William Henry Codrington, 1894.	⎫	Great-grandchildren. Children of No. 34809.
34811	10694	Edith Georgiana Veronica Codrington, 1888.	⎬	
34812	10695	George John Granville Christopher Codrington, Captain and Hon. Major Gloucestershire Yeomanry Cavalry, 1855. *Sand's Court, Chippenham.*	⎫	Grandchildren. Brothers and sisters of No. 34809.
34813	10696	Alice Emily Georgiana Olivia, Lady Vavasour, wife of Sir Henry Mervin Vavasour, 3rd Bart. 11 *Stanhope Gardens, S.W.*		
34814	10697	Florance Adelaide Augusta Codrington.		
34815	10698	Evelyn Anna Blanche Codrington.		

34816	10699	Hon. Agnes Blanche Marie, wife of Herbert von Hindenburg, 3rd Secretary of the German Embassy at Rome, 1873. *64 Seymour Street, Portman Square, W.*	Great-grandchild. Daughter of George Robert, Viscount Dupplin, 1849–1886, and granddaughter of the Lady Emily Blanche Charlotte Somerset, 1828–1895, and her husband, George, 11th Earl of Kinnoull, 1827–1897.
34817	10700	Archibald Fitzroy George, 12th Earl of Kinnoull [S.], 6th Baron Hay [G.B.], 1855. *6 West Chapel Street, Mayfair, W. Dupplin Castle, Perth.*	Grandson. Son of the Lady Emily Blanche Charlotte Somerset, 1828–1895, and her husband, George, 11th Earl of Kinnoull, 1827–1897.
34818	10701	Edmund Alfred Rollo George, Viscount Dupplin, 1879. *18 Denmark Terrace, Brighton.*	Great-grandson. Son of No. 34817.
34819	10702	Hon. George Harley Hay.	Great-great-grandson. Son of No. 34818.
34820	10703	Hon. Alastair George Hay, 1861.	Grandson. Brother to No. 34817.
34821	10704	Auriol Camilla Sharlie Blanche Hay, 1893.	Great-grandchild. Daughter of No. 34820.
34822	10705	Hon. Claude George Hay, M.P., 1862. *5 Connaught Square, W.*	
34823	10706	Lady Constance Blanche Louisa, widow of Walter Henry Hadow, – 1898, 1851. *72 Cambridge Terrace, Hyde Park, W.*	Grandchildren. Brother and sister to No. 34817.
34824	10707	Ronald Walter Hadow, Lieutenant Black Watch, 1883.	Great-grandchildren. Children of No. 34823.
34825	10708	Alastair Patrick Hadow, 1885.	
34826	10709	Gladys Edith Muriel Hadow, 1882.	
34827	10710	Lady Muriel Henrietta Constance, wife of Count Alexander Munster, 1863. *2 Chandos Street, Cavendish Square, W.*	Grandchild. Younger sister to No. 34817.
34828	10711	Count Frederick George Constantine Hervey Ernest Alexander Munster, 1891.	Great-grandchild. Son of No. 34827.
34829	10712	Edith Rose Alma, wife of Charles King Francis, Barrister-at-Law.	Grandchildren. Children of the Lady Rose Caroline Mary Somerset, 1829–1885, wife of Francis Frederick Lovell, of Hinchelsea, co. Southampton, J.P., 1821.
34830	10713	Maud Rosalind Lovell.	
34831	10714	Rosalind Ida, wife of Captain Peter Audley David Arthur Lovell, J.P., D.L., *late* Coldstream Guards. *Cole Park, near Malmesbury.*	
34832	10715	Helen Rose Lovell.	
34833	10716	Lady Geraldine Harriet Anne Somerset, V.A., 1832. *8 Upper Brook Street, W.*	
34834	10717	Katherine Emily Mary, Baroness Ormathwaite, [U.K.], 1834. *Ormathwaite, Keswick, Cumberland.*	Daughters.
34835 –43		Same as Nos. 26197–26205.	Grandchildren. Children of No. 34834.
34844	10718	Edith Frances Wilhelmine, Countess of Londesborough [U.K.], 1838. *17 Norfolk Street, Park Lane, W.*	Youngest daughter.

34845	10719	William Francis Henry, 2nd Earl of Londesborough [U.K.], 1864. *Londesborough, Market Weighton.*	Grandson. Son of No. 34844.
34846 -48	}	Same as Nos. 20296-20298.	Great-grandchildren. Children of No. 34845.
34849	10720	Lady Edith Henrietta Sybil, wife of Sir Gerald William Henry Codrington, 1st Bart., 1866. *Dodington Park, Chipping Sodbury, Gloucestershire.*	Granddaughter. Eldest daughter of No. 34844.
34850 -51	}	Same as Nos. 34809-34810.	Great-grandchildren. Children of No. 34849.
34852	10721	John Francis Chaloner Ogle, 1898.	Great-grandchild. Child of Lady Lilian Katharine Selina Denison, 1867-1899, and her husband, Newton Charles Ogle, of Kirkley, and grandchild of No. 34844.
34853	10722	Lady Ida Emily Augusta, wife of Sir George Reresby Sitwell, 4th Bart., 1869. *Renishaw Hall, Chesterfield, Derbyshire.*	Granddaughter. Daughter of No. 34844.
34854	10723	Francis Osbert Sacheverell Sitwell, 1892.	Great-grandchildren. Children of No. 34853.
34855	10724	Sacheverell Sitwell, 1897	
34856	10725	Edith Louisa Sitwell, 1887.	
34857	10726	Lady Mildred Adelaide Cecilia Denison, 1872.	Granddaughter. Youngest daughter of No. 34844.

786. Descendants of the Right Hon. Lord Granville Charles Henry Somerset, P.C., M.P., 1792-1848. (See Table CXX.)

34858	10727	Raglan George Henry Somerset, 1831. 2 *Morpeth Terrace, S.W.*	Children.
34859	10728	Emily Catherine Ann, wife of Henry Ayshford Sanford, *late* Colonel 3rd Battalion Oxfordshire L.I., *of Waltham House, Essex*, 1826. 55 *Ennismore Gardens, S.W.*	
34860	10729	Granville Roland Francis Smith, Captain Coldstream Guards, 1860. *Duffield Hall, Derby.* 131 *Queen's Gate, S.W.*	Grandson. Son of Constance Henrietta Sophia Louisa Somerset, 1827-1893, wife of Rowland Smith, of Duffield Hall.
34861	10730	Granville Keith-Falconer Smith, 1886.	Great-grandchildren. Children of No. 34860.
34862	10731	Roland Audley Smith, 1887.	
34863	10732	Arthur Francis Smith, 1890.	
34864	10733	Geoffrey Leveson Ian Smith, 1893.	
34865	10734	Constance Eugenia, wife of the Rev. Algernon Charles Dudley Ryder, 1858. *Mansfield Rectory, Sussex.*	Granddaughter. Elder sister to No. 34860.
34866	10735	Algernon Frederick Roland Dudley Ryder, 1891.	Great-grandchildren. Children of No. 34865.
34867	10736	Hugh Granville Leveson Dudley Ryder, 1900.	
34868	10737	Mary Constance Eugenia Ryder, 1890.	
34869	10738	Cecily Blanche Dorothy Ryder, 1893.	
34870	10739	Philippa Constance Marian Ryder, 1895.	
34871	10740	Joan Florence Helena Ryder, 1897.	
34872	10741	Dorothy Evelyn Frances Ryder, 1900.	
34873	10742	Constance Emily Smith, 1874.	Granddaughter. Younger sister to No. 34860.

The Blood Royal of Britain

787. Descendants of Lady Charlotte Sophia Somerset, 1795–1865, and her husband, Frederick, 4th Lord Calthorpe, 1790–1868. (See Table CXX.)

34874	10743	Augustus Cholmondeley, 6th Baron Calthorpe [G.B.], 1829. 38 *Grosvenor Square, W.* *Elvetham Park, Winchfield.*	Elder surviving son.
34875 –79	}	Same as Nos. 21785–21789. {	Grandchildren. Children of No. 34874.
34880	10744	Hon. Somerset John Gough-Calthorpe, Lieutenant-General, 1831. 16 *Queen's Gate Place, S.W.*	Younger surviving son.
34881	10745	Somerset Frederick Gough-Calthorpe, late Captain 5th Battalion Royal Fusiliers, 1862. *The Bungalow, Hassocks.*	Grandson. Son of No. 34880.
34882	10746	Frederick Somerset Gough-Calthorpe, 1892.	Great-grandchild. Child of No. 34881.
34883	10747	Somerset Arthur Gough - Calthorpe, Captain R.N., 1864.	
34884	10748	Leila Mabel Gough-Calthorpe, 1868.	Grandchildren. Children of No. 34880.
34885	10749	Leila Evelyn, wife of Cecil Grosvenor Wilson.	
34886	10750	George Francis Addison Cresswell, 1852.	Grandchildren. Children of the Hon. Charlotte Georgiana Frances Gough-Calthorpe, 1824–1870, wife of Francis Joseph Cresswell, – 1882.
34887	10751	Cresswill Augustus Cresswell, 1856.	
34888	10752	Charlotte Rachel Frederica, wife of Vice-Admiral Sir Gerard Henry Uctred Noel, R.N., K.C.B., K.G.M.C. 16 *Cheyne Gardens, Chelsea, S.W.*	
34889	10753	Francis Arthur Gerard Noel, 1880.	Great-grandchildren. Children of No. 34888.
34890	10754	Charlotte Ida Frederica Noel, 1878.	
34891	10755	Constance Ida Diana Noel, 1879.	
34892	10756	Edith Frances Louisa, wife of Charles Edward Thornycroft, J.P. *Thornycroft Hall, Cheshire.*	Granddaughter. Younger sister to No. 34886, &c.
34893	10757	Charles Mytton Thornycroft, 1879.	Great-grandchildren. Children of No. 34892.
34894	10758	Francis John Mytton Thornycroft, 1886.	
34895	10759	Muriel Blanche, wife of John Black Atkins.	
34896	10760	Ruth Edith Sophia Thornycroft.	
34897	10761	Gwendolin Agnes Thornycroft.	
34898	10762	Frederica Frances Thornycroft.	
34899	10763	Granville Cholmondeley Feilden, D.S.O., Major Seaforth Highlanders, 1863.	Grandson. Elder son of the Hon. Frances Blanche Anne Gough-Calthorpe, 1828–1899, wife of the Rev. John Robert Feilden, 1827–1891.
34900	10764	Granville John Henry Feilden, 1895.	Great-grandchildren. Children of No. 34899.
34901	10765	Frances Blanche Mary Feilden, 1896.	
34902	10766	Dorothy Elliot Robina Feilden, 1899.	
34903	10767	Edith Millicent Noel Cholmondeley Feilden, 1901.	
34904	10768	Algernon Basil Feilden, 1865.	Grandchildren. Brother and sister to No. 34899.
34905	10769	Blanche, wife of John Robin Grey.	
34906 –16	}	Same as Nos. 34047–34057.	Grandchildren. Children of the Hon. Harriet Gough-Calthorpe, 1832–1901, wife of Lord Alfred Spencer-Churchill, 1824–1893.

788. Descendants of Lady Elizabeth Susan Somerset, 1798–1876, and her 2nd husband, Major-General James Orde, – 1850. (See Table CXX.)

34917	10770	Charles Somerville Orde, J.P., 1858. *Hopton House, Great Yarmouth.*	Grandson. Son of James Henry Orde, of Hopton House, 1830–1880.
34918	10771	Myrtle Evelyn Orde, 1890. }	Great-grandchildren. Children
34919	10772	Iris Rosalind Orde, 1892. }	of No. 34917.
34920	10773	Lancelot Francis Orde, 1859. *Foxburrow, Gunton, near Lowestoft.*	Grandson. Brother to No. 34917.
34921	10774	Ronald Orde. }	Great-grandchildren. Children
34922	10775	Violet Elizabeth Orde. }	of No. 34920.
34923	10776	Julian Walter Orde, 1861. *Inwood Barn, Tongham, Surrey.*	Grandson. Brother to No. 34917.
34924	10777	Michael Amyas Julian Orde, 1887.	
34925	10778	Cuthbert Julian Orde, 1888.	Great-grandchildren. Children of No. 34923.
34926	10779	Herbert Walter Julian Orde, 1889.	
34927	10780	Elizabeth Susan Orde.	
34928	10781	Mary Margaret Orde.	
34929	10782	Evelyn Alice, wife of Edwin Lancelot Orde.	
		Children of No. 34929.	
34930	10783	Sybil Margaret, wife of the Rev. Wilmot Eardley Carr.	
34931	10784	Margaret Louisa, wife of Major Cecil William Battine, 15th Hussars.	Grandchildren. Sisters to No. 34917.
34932	10785	Olive Elizabeth Emily, wife of Robert Basil Hoare. *Earsdon, Newcastle-on-Tyne.*	
		Children of No. 34932.	
34933	10786	Charlotte Elizabeth, wife of Major William Lloyd-Browne, 5th Royal Irish Lancers.	Daughter.
34934	10786a	Christian Cator, Lieutenant Oxford Light Infantry, 1874.	Grandchild. Son of Isabel Anne Orde, –1874, wife of the Rev. William Cator.

789. Descendants of Lady Georgiana Augusta Somerset, 1800–1865, and her husband, the Hon. Granville Dudley Ryder, 1799–1879. (See Table CXX.)

34935	10787	Dudley Henry Ryder, J.P., 1830. *Westbrook Hay, Hemel Hempstead.*	Only son.
34936 –49	}	Same as Nos. 33275–33288.	Grandchildren. Children of No. 34935.

790. Descendants of Lady Louisa Elizabeth Somerset, –1892, 2nd wife of George Finch, of Burley-on-the-Hill, –1870. (See Table CXX.)

34950	10788	George Henry Finch, M.P., 1835. *Burley-on-the-Hill, Oakham.*	Son.

34951		Same as No. 21798.
34952	10789	Somerset Alfred George Finch, Lieutenant 4th Battalion King's Royal Rifle Corps.
34953	10790	Wilfrid Henry Montgomery Finch.
34954 –55	}	Same as Nos. 21799–21800.
34956	10791	Edith Sybil Mary, wife of Laurence Currie.
34957	10792	Margaret Georgiana Finch.
34958	10793	Essex Finch.
34959	10794	Jasmine Cecilia Finch.
34960	10795	Verona Cecil Finch.
34961	10796	Hendry Randolph Finch.
34962	10797	Louisa Finch.

Grandchildren. Children of No. 34950.

Children.

Children, if any, of Charlotte Elizabeth Finch, wife of the Rev. George Waller.

791. Descendants of Lady Isabella Anne Somerset, 1808–1831, 1st wife of Colonel Thomas Henry Kingscote, of Kingscote, J.P., 1799–1861. (See Table CXX.)

34963	10798	Sir Robert Nigel Fitzhardinge Kingscote, Lieutenant-Colonel *late* Scots Guards, G.C.V.O., K.C.B. *Kingscote Park, co. Gloucester.* 19 *South Audley Street, W.*
34964 –69	}	Same as Nos. 20307–20312.
34970	10799	Isabella Charlotte Louisa, widow of Captain James Martin, *of Bloomfield, co. Sligo,* 1816–1860.

Son.

Grandchildren. Children of No. 34963.

Daughter.

792. Descendants of Lady Hariet Blanche Somerset, 1811–1885, and her husband, Randolph, 9th Earl of Galloway, 1800–1873. (See Table CXX.)

34971 –5008	}	Same as Nos. 33916–33953.
35009	10800	Lady Mary Octavia, widow of Sir Walter Rockcliffe Farquhar, 3rd Bart., 1810–1900, 1814.

Table CXX.

793. Descendants of No. 35009.

35010	10801	Sir Henry Thomas Farquhar, 4th Bart., 1838. 30 *Lennox Gardens, S.W. Gilmilnscroft, Mauchline, Ayr.*
35011	10802	Francis Douglas Farquhar, D.S.O., Captain Coldstream Guards, 1874. *White's; Guards'.*
35012	10803	Gertrude Farquhar, 1863.
35013	10804	Katharine, wife of Almeric William FitzRoy, C.V.O. 55 *Lower Belgrave Street, S.W.*
35014 –15	}	Same as Nos. 26689–26690.
35016	}	Same as No. 20552.

Son.

Grandchildren. Children of No. 35010.

Great-grandchildren. Children of No. 35013.

Grandson. Son of Walter Randolph Farquhar, 1842–1901.

35017	10805	Granville Frederick Richard Farquhar, 1849.	} 2nd surviving son.
		24 Park Street, Grosvenor Square, W.	
35018	10806	Edward Henry Granville Farquhar, 1896.	Grandchildren.
35019	10807	Guy William John Farquhar, 1899.	Children of
35020	10808	Diana Mary Farquhar, 1901.	No. 35017.
35021	10809	Fitzroy James Wilberforce Farquhar, 1858.	} 3rd surviving son.
		Naval and Military.	
35022	10810	Arthur Ronald Farquhar, 1888.	} Grandchildren. Children
35023	10811	Gladys Mary Farquhar.	of No. 35021.
35024	10812	Mary Blanche, Baroness Raglan [U.K.].	} Eldest daughter.
		4 Eaton Terrace, S.W.	
35025	10813	Hon. Violet Elizabeth Katharine, wife of Captain Wilfrid Robert Abel Smith, Grenadier Guards.	} Grandchild. Daughter of No. 35024.
35026 –29	}	Same as Nos. 31045–31046, and 31048–31049.	{ Grandchildren. Children of Sybella Charlotte Farquhar, –1886, 1st wife of the Rt. Hon. A. E. M. Ashley Cooper, P.C., M.P.
35030	10814	Charlotte Louisa Farquhar.	} Daughters.
35031	10815	Harriet Blanche Elizabeth, wife of Lieut.-Col. the Hon. George Aubrey Vere Bertie. Maresfield, East Cowes, I.W.	
35032	10816	Claude Peregrine Bertie, 1890.	} Grandchildren. Children of No. 35031.
35033	10817	Vere Mary Bertie, 1886.	
35034	10818	Margaret Adine Bertie, 1888.	
35035	10819	Caroline Emily Horatia Farquhar.	Youngest daughter.

794. Descendants of Dudley, 2nd Earl of Harrowby, K.G., 1798–1882. (See Table CXXI.)

35036	10820	John Herbert Dudley, 5th Earl of [U.K.], and 6th Baron Harrowby [G.B.], 1864. Sandon Hall, Stafford.	} Son.
35037	10821	Dudley, Viscount Sandon, 1892.	} Grandchildren. Children of No. 35036.
35038	10822	Lady Frances Ryder, 1888.	
35039	10823	Hon. Archibald Dudley Ryder, late Lieutenant Bedfordshire Regiment, 1867. 147 Victoria Street, S.W.	} 2nd son.
35040	10824	Archibald Stuart Dudley Ryder, 1899.	} Grandchildren. Children of No. 35039.
35041	10825	Victoria Ryder, 1901.	
35042	10826	Hon. Edward Alan Dudley Ryder, 1869. Oakfield, Crawley, Sussex.	} 3rd son.
35043 –45	}	Same as Nos. 33469–33471.	{ Grandchildren. Children of No. 35042.
35046	10827	Hon. Robert Nathaniel Dudley Ryder, Lieutenant 8th Hussars, 1882.	} Children.
35047	10828	Lady Margaret Susan Ryder, 1860.	
35048	10829	Lady Angela Mary Alice, wife of Colin Frederick Campbell, 1863. Everlands, Sevenoaks.	
35049	10830	Lady Constance Susan Euphemia Ryder, 1871.	
35050	10831	Lady Adelaide Audrey, wife of Major the Hon. Henry Anson, 1875.	

795. Descendants of Captain the Hon. Granville Dudley Ryder, R.N., 1799–1879. (See Table CXXI.)

| 35051 –65 | } | Same as Nos. 34935–34949. |

796. Descendants of the Hon. Frederick Dudley Ryder, 1806–1882. (See Table CXXI.)

35066	10832	John Edward Dudley Ryder, 1844. 9 *King Street, St. James's, S.W.*		Sons.
35067	10833	Rev. Algernon Charles Dudley Ryder, 1847. *Maresfield Rectory, Uckfield.*		
35068 -74	}	Same as Nos. 34866–34872.	Grandchildren. of No. 35067.	Children
35075	10834	Lionel George Dudley Ryder, 1849. 101 *Cadogan Gardens, S.W.*		Younger sons.
35076	10835	Stewart Leveson Dudley Ryder, 1850. *Rosewood, Ascot.*		
35077	10836	Aubrey Leveson Dudley Ryder, 1891.	Grandchildren. of No. 35076.	Children
35078	10837	Evelyn Margaret Ryder, 1884.		
35079	10838	Susan Marjorie Ryder, 1886.		
35080	10839	Lilian Beatrice Ryder, 1887.		
35081	10840	Marian Frances Georgiana, widow of the Rev. Arthur Brooking, –1890, 1840. *West Hill House, Frome.*		Eldest daughter.
35082	10841	Hugh Cecil Arthur Brooking, Captain South African Constabulary, 1870.	Grandchildren. Children of No. 35081.	
35083	10842	Blanche Mabel Marion Brooking, 1868.		
35084	10843	Alice Claude Florence Brooking, 1877.		
35085	10844	Beatrice Mary Frederica, widow of the Rev. Arthur Henry Delmé-Radcliffe, 1850–1896, 1852. 4 *Stanhope Gardens, S.W.*		2nd daughter.
35086	10845	Ralph Hubert John Delmé-Radcliffe, 1877.	Grandchildren. Children of No. 35085.	
35087	10846	Arthur Frederick Delmé-Radcliffe, 1880.		
35088	10847	Beatrice Alice Delmé-Radcliffe, 1875.		
35089	10848	Evelyn Penelope Delmé-Radcliffe, 1883.		
35090	10849	Frederica Constance Dorothy, widow of Captain Augustus Richard Davies (22nd Foot), –1878, 1854.		Daughter.
35091	10850	Clare, wife of Ernest Pease. 36 *Montagu Square, W.*	Granddaughter. of No. 35090.	Daughter
35092	10851	Helena Augusta Cockayne Ryder, 1855. *Hitchin, Herts.*		Daughter.

797. Descendants of the Lady Susan Ryder, 1796–1827, and her husband, Hugh, 2nd Earl Fortescue, K.G., 1783–1861. (See Table CXXL.)

35093 -119	}	Same as Nos. 24956–24982.

798. Descendants of the Lady Mary Ryder, 1801–1900, and her husband, Admiral Edward Saurin, R.N.,   –1878. (See Table CXXI.)

799. Descendants of the Lady Georgiana Elizabeth Ryder, 1804–1884, and her husband, John, 2nd Lord Wharncliffe, 1801–1855. (See Table CXXI.)

35120	10852	Francis John, 2nd Earl of Wharncliffe [U.K.], 1855. *Wortley Hall, Sheffield.*	Grandson. Son of the Hon. Francis Dudley Montagu-Stuart - Wortley, 1829–1893.
35121	10853	Archibald Ralph, Viscount Carlton, 1892.	
35122	10854	Hon. Edward Thomas Montagu-Stuart-Wortley, 1900.	
35123	10855	Lady Mary Violet Montagu-Stuart-Wortley, 1891.	Great-grandchildren. Children of No.
35124	10856	Lady Ellen Rachel Montagu-Stuart-Wortley, 1894.	35120.
35125	10857	Lady Joan Margaret Montagu-Stuart-Wortley, 1895.	
35126	10858	Hon. Edward James Montagu-Stuart-Wortley, C.M.G., D.S.O., Lieut.-Col. (h.p.), and Military Attaché at Paris, 1857. *British Embassy, Paris.* *31 Bruton Street, W.*	Grandson. Brother to No. 35120.
35127	10859	Nicholas Rothesay Montagu-Stuart-Wortley, 1892.	
35128	10860	Louise Violet Beatrice Montagu-Stuart-Wortley, 1893.	Great-grandchildren. Children of No. 35126.
35129	10861	Elizabeth Valetta Montagu-Stuart-Wortley, 1896.	
35130	10862	Hon. Ralph Granville Montagu-Stuart-Wortley, 1864. *65 West 85th Street, New York.*	Grandson. Brother to No. 35120.
35131	10863	Ralph Montagu-Stuart-Wortley, 1897.	Great-grandson. Son of No. 35130.
35132	10864	Hon. Alan Richard Montagu-Stuart-Wortley, D.S.O., Captain King's Royal Rifle Corps, 1868. *Naval and Military.*	Grandson. Brother to No. 35120.
35133	10865	Marjorie Susan Montagu-Stuart-Wortley, 1901.	Great-grandchild. Daughter of No. 35132.
35134	10866	Lady Mary Susan, wife of Sir George Everard Arthur Cayley, 9th Baronet, 1861. *High Hall, Brompton, R.S.O., Yorkshire.*	Granddaughter. Sister to No. 35120.
35135	10867	Francis Digby Edward Cayley, 1894.	
35136	10868	Kenelm Henry Ernest Cayley, 1896.	Great-grandchildren.
35137	10869	Dorothy Frances Cayley, 1888.	Children of No.
35138	10870	Margaret Renée Cayley, 1892.	35134.
35139	10871	Anne Letitia Mary Cayley, 1899.	
35140	10872	Cecily Susan, Baroness Montagu of Beaulieu [U.K.], 1835. *Palace House, Beaulieu, Hants.* *3 Tilney Street, W.*	Daughter.
35141 -48	}	Same as Nos. 19740–19747.	Grandchildren, &c. Children of No. 35140.

800. Descendants of Lady Harriet Charlotte Sophia Ryder, 1811–1899, and her husband, the Rev. Lord Charles Amelius Hervey, D.D., 1814–1880. (See Table CXXI.)

35149	10873	Dudley Francis Amelius Hervey, C.M.G., 1849. *Westfields, Aldeburgh-on-Sea, Suffolk.*	} Son.
35150	10874	Dudley Edward Francis Cyril Hervey, 1895.	} Grandchildren. Children of No. 35149.
35151	10875	Griselda Harriet Violet Finetta Georgiana Hervey, 1901.	
35152	10876	William George Edward Hervey, Vice-Consul, Ostend, 1850. *British Vice-Consulate, Ostend.*	} 2nd son.
35153	10877	Charles Granville Hervey, 1888.	} Grandchildren. Children of No. 35152.
35154	10878	Venetia Harriet Lepel Hervey, 1887.	
35155	10879	Osyth Christina Frederica Hervey, 1897.	
35156	10880	Susan Elizabeth Hervey, 1840.	} Daughters.
35157	10881	Louisa Frederica, Lady Graham, widow of Sir Cyril Clarke Graham, C.M.G., 5th and last Baronet, 1834–1895, 1842. *8 Cheyne Walk, Chelsea, S.W.*	
35158	10882	Violet Evelyn Cecilia, wife of William Montagu Harrison, now Graham Harrison, Barrister-at-Law. *36 Sloane Gardens, S.W.*	} Granddaughter. Elder daughter of No. 35157.
35159	10883	Evelyn Cyril Arthur Graham Harrison, 1901.	} Great-grandchildren. Children of No. 35158.
35160	10884	Frederica Montagu Cecilia Graham Harrison.	
35161	10885	Beatriz Margaret Irene Graham.	} Granddaughter. Younger daughter of No. 35157.
35162	10886	Edith Marian, wife of William Forbes, J.P., D.L., 1845. *Callendar House, Falkirk.*	} 3rd daughter.
35163	10887	Charles William Forbes, Lieutenant Glasgow Yeomanry Cavalry, 1871. *Ninewells House, Berwickshire.*	} Grandchild. Son of No. 35162.
35164	10888	William Dudley Henry Charles Forbes, 1902.	} Great-grandchildren. Children of No. 35163.
35165	10889	Marion Edith Georgiana Forbes, 1898.	
35166	10890	Margaret Lilian May Forbes, 1900.	
35167	10891	Agnes Marjorie Katharine Forbes, 1901.	
35168	10892	Edith Harriet Forbes, 1876.	} Grandchildren. Children of No. 35162.
35169	10893	Lilian Mary Forbes, 1878.	
35170	10894	Marjory Katharine Forbes, 1884.	
35171	10895	Dorothy Louisa Forbes, 1886.	
35172 –73	}	Same as Nos. 25051–25052.	} Grandchildren. Children of Isabella Sophia Hervey, 1847–1894, wife of Cyril Locke Calliphronas Locke.

801. Descendants of Lady Louisa Ryder, 1813–1899, wife of the Hon. George Matthew Fortescue, M.P., 1791–1877. (See Table CXXI.)

35174 –95	}	Same as Nos. 24983–25004.

802. Descendants of Charles, 10th Marquis of Huntly, 1792–1863.
(See Table CXXII.)

35196	10896	Charles, 11th Marquis of Huntly [S.], 3rd Baron Meldrum, of Morven [U.K.], P.C., 1847. *Aboyne Castle, Aberdeenshire.*	Elder son.
35197	10897	Beatrice Mary, wife of Francis Henry Meade, 1875. *Nates House, Medmenham, Great Marlow, Bucks.*	Granddaughter. Daughter of Lord Esme Stuart Gordon, 1853–1900.
35198	10898	Robert Sidney Stuart Meade, 1901.	Great-grandchildren. Children of No. 35197.
35199	10899	Lord Granville Armyne Gordon, 1856. 28 *Charles Street, Berkeley Square, W.*	Youngest surviving son.
35200	10900	Granville Cecil Douglas Gordon, 2nd Lieutenant Scots Guards, 1883.	Grandchildren. Children of No. 35199.
35201	10901	Armyne Evelyn Gordon, 1879.	
35202	10902	Lady Mary Katherine, wife of Edmund Turnor. *Panton Hall, Wragby. Stoke Rochford, Grantham.*	Eldest daughter.
35203	10903	Evelyn Elizabeth, Countess of Ancaster [U.K.], Baroness Willoughby de Eresby [E.], 1846. 12 *Belgrave Square, S.W. Normanton Park, Stamford.*	2nd daughter.
35204 –16		Same as Nos. 21515–21527.	Grandchildren. Children of No. 35203.
35217	10904	Grace Cicelie, Countess of Lonsdale [U.K.], Viscountess Lowther [G.B.], 1854. *Lowther Castle, Penrith.* 14 *Carlton House Terrace, S.W.*	3rd and 4th daughters.
35218	10905	Lady Margaret Ethel, wife of the Hon. George Ralph Charles Ormsby-Gore, M.P., 1858. *The Lodge, Malpas, Cheshire.*	
35219	10906	William George Arthur Ormsby-Gore, 1885.	Grandson. Son of No. 35218.
35220	10907	Lady Elena Mary, wife of Major George Lamplugh Wickham, *late* Royal Horse Guards, 1861.	5th daughter.
35221	10908	John Lamplugh Wickham, 1886.	Grandson. Son of No. 35220.
35222	10909	Lady Ethelreda Caroline, wife of Major Henry Wickham, *late* Scots Guards, 1864. *Barnwell Castle, Oundle.*	6th surviving daughter.
35223	10910	Mary Ethel Wickham, 1885.	Grandchildren. Children of No. 35222.
35224	10911	Alice Joan Wickham, 1888.	

803. Descendants of Lord Henry Gordon, H.E.I.C.S., 1802–1865.
(See Table CXXII.)

35225	10912	Henry Edward FitzClarence, 1853. 41 *Ovington Square, S.W.*	Grandchild. Son of Sarah Elizabeth Catherine Gordon, 1827–1901, and her husband, the Rev. Lord Augustus FitzClarence, 1805–1854.
35226	10913	Augustus Arthur Cornwallis FitzClarence, Lieutenant Royal Fusiliers, 1880.	Great-grandchildren. Children of No. 35225.
35227	10914	Cynthia Adela Victoria FitzClarence, 1887.	

35228	10915	Thomas Clarence Edward Goff, *of Oakport*, J.P., 1867. *Conyngham Hall, Knaresborough.*	Great-grandchildren. Children of Dorothea Fitz-Clarence, 1845-1870 (sister to No. 35225), and her husband, Captain Thomas William Goff, of Oakport, M.P., 1829-1876.
35229 -30	}	Same as Nos. 21524-21525. { Great-great-grandchildren. Children of No. 35228.	
35231	10916	Ethel Anne, wife of Henry de Courcy Agnew.	
35232	10917	Dorothea Alma Agnew. } . Great-great-grandchildren.	
35233	10918	Hazel Louisa Agnew. } Daughters of No. 35231.	
35234	10919	Muriel Helen Goff. Great-grandchild. Sister to No 35228.	
35235	10920	Eva FitzClarence, } twins, 1847. { Grandchildren. Sisters to	
35236	10921	Beatrix FitzClarence, } No. 35225.	
35237	10922	Hon. Louisa Frances Charlotte, widow of the Hon. } Daughter. Ashley George John Ponsonby, 1831-1898, } 1829.	
35238 -41	}	Same as Nos. 22539-22542. { Grandchildren. Children of No. 35237.	
35242	10923	Wilhelmina Gertrude Maria Gordon, } twins, 1844. { The Colonnade, Hampton Court Palace. } Daughters.	
35243	10924	Millicent Theresa Gordon,	
35244	10925	Pyers George Joseph Mostyn, 1893.	Great-grandchildren. Children of Augusta Mary Gerardine Walmesley, -1893, wife of George Trevor Basil Mostyn, and grandchildren of Augusta Gordon, 1849-1881, and her 1st husband, Captain William Gerard Walmesley, of Westwood House, 1841-1877.
35245	10926	Geraldine Mary Frances Mostyn.	

804. Descendants of Lord Cecil James Gordon-Moore, 1806-1878. (See Table CXXII.)

35246	10927	Cecil Crosbie Gordon-Moore, 1850.	
35247	10928	Arthur Henry Wyndham Gordon, 1853.	Children.
35248	10929	Hubert George Gordon-Moore, 1858.	
35249	10930	Catherine Augusta, widow of Oriel Farnell Walton, -1886, 1842.	
35250	10931	Harold Arthur Gordon Walton, 1886.	
35251	10932	Ethel Gordon, wife of Commander Frederick Mortimer Barwick, Royal Indian Marines, 1869.	Grandchildren. Children of No. 35249.
35252	10933	Winifrid Mary Gordon Walton, 1878.	
35253	10934	Constance Emily Gordon, wife of Douglas Brooking Sanders.	
35254	10935	Emily, widow of Charles Robert Besley, - 1896, 1843. *15 Palmeira Avenue, Hove.*	2nd daughter.
35255	10936	Robert William Edward Gordon Besley, 1878.	Grandchildren. Children of No. 35254.
35256	10937	Cecily Evelyn Gordon, wife of Henry Royston Parker. *Rothbury, Wynondham, Norfolk.*	
35257	10938	Henry Gordon Parker, 1897.	Great-grandchildren. Children of No. 35256.
35258	10939	Arthur Royston Parker, 1902.	
35259	10940	Hetty Mary Evelyn Parker, 1893.	

35260	10941	Lilias Emily Gordon, wife of Arthur Cecil Herbert Nickisson. 33 *Brunswick Gardens, Kensington, W.*	Grandchildren. Children of No. 35254.
35261	10942	Sybil Augusta Gordon Besley.	
35262	10943	Muriel Edith Gordon Besley.	
35263	10944	Edith, wife of Oscar Felix Henry Cornille, 1844.	3rd daughter.
35264	10945	Gabrielle Marguerite Cornille, 1881.	Grandchild. Child of No. 35263.
35265	10946	Esmé Gordon Milward, 1873.	Grandchildren. Children of Agnes Cecil Gordon-Moore, 1846–1902, and her 1st husband, James Milward, – 1879.
35266	10947	Margaret Gordon Milward, 1879.	
35267	10948	Adela Crosbie Gordon-Moore, 1847.	Younger daughters.
35268	10949	Evelyn Gordon-Moore, 1849.	
35269	10950	Philippa Jane, wife of Thomas Dunn, 1851.	
35270	10951	. . . . Dunn.	Grandchild. Daughter of No. 35269.

805. Descendants of Lieut.-Col. the Lord Francis Arthur Gordon, 1st Life Guards, 1808–1857. (See Table CXXII.)

35271	10952	George Grant Gordon, C.V.O., C.B., *late* Lieut.-Col. Scots Guards. *Oakhurst, Hampstead Heath, N.W.*	Son.
35272 -78	}	Same as Nos. 32997–33003. { Grandchildren, &c. of No. 35271.	Children, &c.,
35279	10953	Francis Frederick Gordon, *late* Clerk in the Admiralty, 1839. 90 *Queen's Gate, S.W.*	2nd son.
35280	10954	Francis Lewis Rawson Gordon, *late* Lieutenant 2nd Battalion Gordon Highlanders, 1878.	Grandchildren. Children of No. 35279.
35281	10955	Isabel Constance Helen Gordon, 1880.	
35282	10956	Nita Florence Gordon, 1882.	
35283	10957	Catherine Gordon, 1837. 10 *South Eaton Place, S.W.*	Daughter.

806. Descendants of Lady Susan Catherine Gordon, 1792–1866, and her husband, Charles Compton, 1st Lord Chesham, 1796–1863. (See Table CXXII.)

| 35284 -317 | } | Same as Nos. 22976–23009. | |

807. Descendants of Lady Mary Gordon, 1797–1825, 1st wife of Frederick Charles William Seymour, 1797–1856. (See Table CXXII.)

| 35318 | 10958 | Conway Frederick Charles Seymour, Gentleman Usher of the Privy Chamber, *late* Captain 85th Regiment, 1823. | Son. |

808. Descendants of Margaret Mina Elizabeth Beckford, 1784–1818, 1st wife of Lieutenant-General James Orde, –1850. (See Table CXXII.)

| 35319 | 10959 | Margaret Juliana Maria Orde.[1] | } | Daughters. |
| 35320 | 10960 | Susan Jemima Frances Orde.[1] | | |

809. Descendants of William Alexander Anthony Archibald, 11th Duke of Hamilton and 8th Duke of Brandon, 1811–1863. (See Table CXXII.)

35321		Same as No. 33086.	{ Granddaughter. Daughter of William Alexander Louis Stephen, 12th Duke of Hamilton, 9th Duke of Brandon, 1845–1895.
35322	10961	Lady Mary Victoria, wife of Count Tassils Festétics, 1850. *Eashtam Park, Brandon, Suffolk. Vienna; 8 Löwelstrasse.*	} Daughter.
35323	10962	Louis Honoré Charles Antoine, Hereditary Prince of Monaco, 1870. *The Palace, Monaco.*	{ Grandson. Son of No. 35322 by 1st husband, Albert, Prince of Monaco.

810. Descendants of Lady Susan Harriet Catherine Hamilton, 1814–1889, wife 1st of Henry, Earl of Lincoln (afterwards 5th Duke of Newcastle, K.G.), 1811–1879. (See Table CXXII.)

35324	10963	Henry Pelham Archibald Douglas, 7th Duke of Newcastle [G.B.], 14th Earl of Lincoln [E.], 1864. *Clumber, Worksop, Notts.* 11 *Hill Street, Berkeley Square, W.*	Grandchildren. Children of Henry Pelham Alexander, 6th Duke of Newcastle, 1834–1879.
35325	10964	Lord Henry Francis Hope Pelham-Clinton-Hope, 1866. *Castle Blayney, Ireland.*	
35326	10965	Lady Beatrice Adeline, wife of Cecil Edmund Lister-Kaye, 1862. *Denby Grange, Wakefield.*	
35327 –30	}	Same as Nos. 26331–26334.	{ Great-grandchildren. Children of No. 35326.
35331	10966	Emily Augusta Mary, Duchess of Avigliano, wife of Prince Alfonso Doria Pamphilj-Landj, Duke of Avigliano [Italy], 1863. *Palazzo Doria, Rome.*	} Grandchild. Sister to No. 35324.
35332	10967	Prince Filippo Doria Pamphilj-Landj, 1886.	} Great-grandchildren. Children of No. 35331.
35333	10968	Princess Orietta Doria Pamphilj-Landj, 1887.	
35334	10969	Lady Florence Josephine Pelham-Clinton, 1868.	} Grandchild. Youngest sister to No. 35324.

[1] If alive.

35335	10970	Lord Edward William Pelham-Clinton, G.C.V.O., K.C.B., 1836. 81 *Eccleston Square, S.W.*	Son.
35336	10971	Francis Adolphus Vane-Tempest, *late* Lieutenant 4th Battalion Durham Light Infantry, 1863.	Grandchild. Child of the Lady Susan Pelham Clinton, 1839–1875, and her husband, Lord Adolphus F. C. W. Vane-Tempest, 1825–1864.

811. Descendants of Alexander, 10th Duke of Hamilton, 7th Duke of Brandon, K.G., 1767–1852. (See Table CXXIII.)

35337 -52	}	Same as Nos. 35321–35336.

812. Descendants of Edward Adolphus, 12th Duke of Somerset, K.G., 1804–1885. (See Table CXXIII.)

35353	10972	Lady Jane Hermione, widow of Sir Frederick Ulric Graham, 3rd Bart., 1820–1888. 32 *Pont Street, S.W.*	Daughter.
35354 -79	}	Same as Nos. 34256–34281. { Grandchildren, &c. of No. 35353.	Children, &c.
35380	10973	Lady Ulrica Frederica Jane, wife of the Right Hon. Lord Henry Frederick Thynne, P.C., 1833. 30 *Grosvenor Gardens, S.W.*	2nd daughter.
35381 -88	}	Same as Nos. 21663–21670.	Grandchildren. Children of No. 35380.
35389	10974	Lady Helen Guendolen, wife of Sir John William Ramsden, 5th Bart., 1846. *Byram, Ferrybridge.*	3rd daughter.
35390	10975	John Frecheville Ramsden, D.L., 1877.	Grandchild. Child of No. 35389.
35391	10976	John St. Maur Ramsden, 1902.	Great-grandson. Son of No. 35390.
35392	10977	Hermione Charlotte Ramsden, 1867.	Grandchildren. Children of No. 35389.
35393	10978	Rosamund Isabel Ramsden, 1872.	

813. Descendants of Algernon Percy Banks, 14th Duke of Somerset, 1813–1894. (See Table CXXIII.)

35394	10979	Algernon, 15th Duke of Somerset [E.], 1846. *Maiden Bradley House, Bath.*	Sons.
35395	10980	Lord Percy St. Maur, 1847. 28 *Berkeley Square, W.*	
35396	10981	Helen Violet St. Maur, 1900.	Granddaughters. Daughters of No. 35395.
35397	10982	. . . . St. Maur, 1902.	
35398	10983	Lord Ernest St. Maur, 1847.	Younger sons.
35399	10984	Lord Edward St. Maur, 1849. *Brynglas Hall, Llanfair, Welshpool.*	

814. Descendants of Lady Charlotte Jane Seymour, 1803–1889, 2nd wife of William Blount, of Orleton, Hereford, M.P., 1799–1885. (See Table CXXIII.)

35400	10985	Archibald Henry Blount, 1840. *Orleton, Ludlow, Hereford.* *Orche Hill, Chalfont, Bucks.*	Sons.
35401	10986	Oscar Henry Blount, 1841. *The Hut, Windsor.*	
35402	10987	Mary Frances Charlotte Blount.	Grandchild. Daughter of No. 35401.
35403	10988	Constance Blount.	Daughter.

815. Descendants of Lady Anna Maria Jane Seymour, 1807–1873, 1st wife of William Tollemache, 1810–1886. (See Table CXXIII.)

35404 –10	}	Same as Nos. 21507–21513.

816. Descendants of Lady Susan Hamilton, 1774–1846, wife of George, 5th Earl of Dunmore, 1762–1856. (See Table CXXIII.)

35411 –41	}	Same as Nos. 33678–33708.

817. Descendants of Lady Charlotte Stewart, –1818, wife of John, 4th Earl of Dunmore, –1809. (See Table CXV.)

35442 –97	}	Same as Nos. 33678–33733.

818. Descendants of James Farquharson, of Invercauld, –1806. (See Table CIV.)

35498 –511	}	Same as Nos. 32727–32740.

819. Descendants of Margaret, Baroness Nairne and Keith, 1788–1867, and her husband, Augustus Charles Joseph, Count of Flahault de la Billardrie, sometime Ambassador of France at the Court of St. James', 1785–1870. (See Table CXXIV.)

35512	10989	▽ Henry Charles Keith Petty, 5th Marquis of Lansdowne [G.B.], 6th Earl of Kerry [I.], and Shelburne [I.], and 9th Baron Nairne [S.], K.G., P.C., 1845. *Lansdowne House, Berkeley Square, W. Bowood Park, Calne, Wilts.*	Grandson. Son of Emily Jane, Lady Nairne, 1819–1895, and her husband, Henry, 4th Marquis of Lansdowne, K.G., 1816–1866.

35513 -24	}	Same as Nos. 33547–33558.	Greatgrandchildren. Children of No. 35512.
35525	10990	⋃ Lord Edmund George Petty Fitzmaurice, M.P., 1846. *Leigh House, Bradford, Wilts.*	Grandchildren. Brother and sister to No. 35512.
35526	10991	⋃ Lady Emily Louisa Anne, wife of Colonel the Hon. Everard Charles Digby, 1855. 51 *Green Street, Park Lane, W.*	
35527 -29	}	Same as Nos. 31815–31817.	Great-grandchildren. Children of No. 35526.
35530	10992	⋃ Georgiana Gabrielle, Marchioness of La Valette [France]. 22 *Grosvenor Square, W.*	Daughter.

820. Descendants, if any, of the three sisters of Jane Mercer, Lady Keith,   –1789. (See Table CXXIV.)

821. Descendants, if any, of the brother of Colonel William Mercer, of Aldie,   –1790. (See Table CXXIV.)

822. Descendants, if any, of Margaret Mercer, wife of James Robertson, of Lude,   –1803. (See Table CXXIV.)

823. Descendants, if any, of Margaret Haldane, wife (1803) of General William Robertson, of Lude,   –1820. (See Table CXXV.)

824. Descendants of James Andrew John Lawrence Charles, 8th Viscount Strathallan, 1767–1851. (See Table CXXV.)

35531 -84	}	Same as Nos. 31505–31558.

825. Descendants of Andrew Robert Drummond, of Cadlands, 1794–1865. (See Table CXXV.)

35585 -680	}	Same as Nos. 25363–25458.

826. Descendants of Lieut.-Col. William Charles Drummond, 10th Hussars, 1796–1881. (See Table CXXV.)

35681	10993	Major William Charles Drummond, late 95th Foot, 1837.	Son.
35682	10994	Angela Nora Edith Humphrays, wife of John Arthur Levett, 1870. *Hollywood, The Glebe, Blackheath, S.E.*	Granddaughter. Daughter of No. 35681.

35683	10995	John Upton Humphrays Levett, 1888.	
35684	10996	Arthur Drummond Cookes Levett, 1893.	
35685	10997	Rowland Denham Griffith Levett, 1894.	Great-grandchildren.
35686	10998	Theodore Angelo Roderick Levett, 1897.	Children of No.
35687	10999	Donovan Rupert Horace Levett, 1900.	35682.
35688	11000	Violet Angela Theodora Levett, 1902.	

827. Descendants of Mary Drummond, 1793–1873, and her husband, the Right Rev. Francis Fulford, D.D., Bishop of Montreal, 1803–1868. (See Table CXXV.)

35689	11001	Francis Drummond Fulford, J.P., D.L., 1831. *Great Fulford, Dunsford, near Exeter.*	Son.
35690	11002	Francis Algernon Fulford, J.P., Inspector of the Board of Agriculture, 1861. *Great Fulford, Dunsford, near Exeter.*	Grandson. Son of No. 35689.
35691 –92		Same as Nos. 25373–25374.	Great-grandchildren. Children of No. 35690.
35693	11003	Robert Philip Perceval Fulford, 1863.	
35694	11004	Charles Holland Fulford, 1878.	
35695	11005	Evelyn Mary Fulford.	Grandchildren.
35696	11006	Beatrice Mary Fulford.	Children of
35697	11007	Maud Mary, wife of Reginald Martyn.	No. 35689.
35698	11008	Ethel Mary Fulford.	
35699	11009	Alice Mary, widow of the Rev. Henry Martin Lower, *late* Archdeacon of Newfoundland and Labrador, –1900.	Daughter.
35700	11010	Henry Lower, M.A., 1862.	Grandchildren. Children
35701	11011	Mary Lower.	of No. 35699.

828. Descendants of Catherine Isabel Drummond, –1870, and her husband, the Rev. Henry Perceval, Rector of Elmley Lovett, co. Worcester, 1799–1885. (See Table CXXV.)

35702	11012	Rev. Ascelin Spencer Perceval, 1855.	Grandchildren. Children
35703	11013	Amy Perceval.	of Henry Spencer Perce-
35704	11014	Lilian Perceval.	val, 1827–1876.
35705	11015	Catherine Mary Perceval.	Daughter.

829. Descendants of Charles Drummond, 1790–1858. (See Table CXXV.)

35706	11016	Charles Drummond, of Messrs. Drummond, Bankers. 6 *Great Cumberland Place*, W.	Grandchild. Son of Robert Drummond, 1822–1881.
35707	11017	Robert Charles Crosbie Drummond, 1896.	Great-grandchildren. Children of No.
35708	11018	Angela Cecilia Mary Drummond, 1893.	35706.
35709	11019	Wingfield Fraser Drummond, 1861. *Union.*	
35710	11020	Kenneth Mackenzie Drummond, Captain 2nd Battalion Prince of Wales' Leinster Regiment, 1862. *Army and Navy.*	Grandchildren. Brothers and sister to No. 35706.
35711	11021	Sybil Drummond, 1858.	

35712	11022	Lister Maurice Drummond, Barrister Inner Temple, 1856.
		3 *Essex Court, Temple, E.C.*
35713	11023	May Theresa Ella, wife of Basil Champneys, 1858.
		Hall Oak, Frognal, Hampstead, N.W.
35714	11024	Amian Lister Champneys, 1879.
35715	11025	Michael Weldon Champneys, 1884.
35716	11026	Cicely Marion Champneys, 1881.
35717	11027	Adelaide Mary Champneys, 1888.
35718	11028	Miriam Frances Lilian, wife of George John Barry Hayter, 1860.
		30 *Bramham Gardens, S.W.*
35719	11029	Ivy Christabel Adelaide Tuke Hayter, 1895.
35720	11030	Monica Catherine Annie Louise Drummond, 1868.
35721	11031	Berkeley Walter Drummond, Lieutenant R.N., 1866. *Constitutional.*
35722	11032	Henry Walter Drummond, 1867.
		Falcon Lodge, Putney.
35723	11033	Mabel Mary, wife of Vesey George Mackenzie Holt, 1854.
		Mount Mascal, Bexley.
35724	11034	Martin Drummond Vesey Holt, 1881.
35725	11035	Reginald Vesey Holt, R.N., 1884.
35726	11036	Felton Vesey Holt, 1886.
35727	11037	Alwyn Vesey Holt, 1887.
35728	11038	Edric Vesey Holt, 1889.
35729	11039	Geoffrey Vesey Holt, 1897.
35730	11040	Marjorie Vesey Holt, 1882.
35731	11041	Violet Catherine Drummond, 1862.
35732	11042	Dulcibella Frances Drummond, 1865.
35733	11043	Mary Selina, wife of Algernon Henry Peter Strickland, 1869.
		22 *Lower Sloane Street, S.W.*
35734	11044	Algernon Walter Strickland, 1891.
35735	11045	Barbara Mary Strickland, 1895.
35736	11046	Edmund Traherne Drummond, 1864.
		Fairfield, Woodford Wells, Essex.
35737	11047	Edith Charlotte Drummond, 1893.
35738	11048	Isabel Hilda Drummond, 1896.
35739	11049	Gerald Morton Drummond, 1866.
		Cleveland Road, South Woodford, Essex.
35740	11050	Edward Morton Drummond, 1898.
35741	11051	Caroline Dulcibella Drummond, 1865.
35742	11052	Maud Margaret Frances Drummond, 1870.

Grandchildren. Children of Maurice Drummond, C.B., 1825–1891.

Great-grandchildren. Children of No. 35713.

Grandchild. Sister to No. 35712.

Great-grandchild. Daughter of No. 35718.

Grandchild. Younger sister to No. 35712, &c.

Grandchildren. Children of the late Walter Drummond, 1830–1893.

Great-grandchildren. Children of No. 35723.

Grandchildren. Sisters to No. 35721.

Great-grandchildren. Children of No. 35733.

Grandchild. Son of the late Rev. Morton Drummond, 1832–1898.

Great-grandchildren. Children of No. 35736.

Grandson. Brother of No. 35736.

Great-grandson. Son of No. 35739.

Granddaughters. Sisters to No. 35736.

Children, if any, of Mary Dulcibella, –1874 (daughter), wife (1850) of Richard Wellesley, –1861.

830. Descendants of the Rev. Arthur Drummond, Rector of Charlton, 1797–1862. (See Table CXXV.)

35743	11053	Charles Spencer Drummond, 1834. 20 *Grosvenor Street, Toronto, Ontario, Canada.*	Son.

35744	11054	Lilias Charlotte Drummond, 1864.	⎫
35745	11055	Catherine Georgiana Drummond, 1866.	Grandchildren.
35746	11056	Gertrude Emily, wife of Walter Wilson Nation, Manager of the Dominion Bank, 1867. *Toronto, Canada.*	Daughters of No. 35743.
35747	11057	Rev. Canon Arthur Hislop Drummond, 1843. *All Saints' Vicarage, Boyne Hill, Maidenhead.*	} 2nd son.
35748	11058	Arthur Berkeley Drummond, Captain I.S.C., 1869.	Grandson. Son of No. 35747.
35749	11059	Nigel Fenton Drummond, 1895.	Great-grandchildren. Chil-
35750	11060	Eric Arthur Drummond, 1900.	dren of No. 35748.
35751	11061	Malcolm Cyril Drummond, 1880.	Grandchild. 2nd son of No. 35747.
			Grandchildren. Children of Frances Emily Cadogan Drummond, 1836– , wife of General Edmund Henry Cox, 1828–1893.
35752	11062	Lilias Maria Drummond, 1837.	⎫
35753	11063	Julia, wife of Francis Adams, 1838. *Cotswold Grange, Cheltenham.*	Daughters.
35754	11064	Francis Adams, Lieutenant 3rd Madras Lancers, 1874. *Cavalry.*	Grandchildren.
35755	11065	May Frances Drummond, wife of Major Oswald James Daniell, 1872. *Little Berkhampstead, Herts.*	Children of No. 35753.
35756	11066	Dorothy Frances Daniell, 1899.	Great-grandchild. Child of No. 35755.
35757	11067	Isabel Maria Adams, 1876.	*Llyfnant, Cheltenham.*	Grandchildren.
35758	11068	Mary Georgina Shute, wife of F. Hugh Ripley, 1879.		Children of No. 35753.
35759	11069	Catherine Georgina Drummond, 1845.	Youngest daughter.

831. Descendants of Henry Andrew Drummond, Captain H.E.I.C.M.S., 1791–186 . (See Table CXXV.)

35760	11070	Barbara Catherine Drummond, 1824.	⎫
35761	11071	Henrietta, widow of Frederick Le Gros Clark, F.R.S., 1811–1892, 1826. *St. Clére, Bradbourn, Park Road, Sevenoaks.*	Daughters.
35762	11072	Rev. Edward Travers Clark, 1864. *Newnham-on-Severn Vicarage, Gloucester.*	Grandchild. Child of No. 35761.
35763	11073	Frederick Le Gros Clark, 1892.	⎫ Great-grandchildren.
35764	11074	Cyril Drummond Le Gros Clark, 1894.	Children of No. 35762.
35765	11075	Wilfrid Edward Le Gros Clark, 1895.	
35766	11076	Edith Elsie Le Gros Clark, 1897.	
35767	11077	Mary Edith Clark, 1859.	Grandchild. Daughter of No. 35761.

832. Descendants, if any, of Catherine Drummond, – , and her husband, the Rev. George Randolph, – (See Table CXXV.)

833. Descendants of Lieut.-Col. Charles Towneley, of Towneley, 1803–1876. (See Table CXXV.)

35768 -75	}	Same as Nos. 28984–28986 and Nos. 28989–28993.	Grandson. Son of Caroline Theresa Towneley, – 1873, 1st wife of Montagu Arthur, 7th Earl of Abingdon.
35776		Same as No. 27785.	Grandchild. Son of Emily Frances Towneley, –1892, wife of Lord Alexander Gordon Lennox, 1825–1892.
35777	11078	Alice Mary, Baroness O'Hagan [U.K.]. 2 *Upper Belgrave Street, S.W.*	Daughter.
35778	11079	Maurice Herbert Ignatius Towneley, 3rd Baron O'Hagan [U.K.], 1882. *Pyrgo Park, Havering-atte-Bower.*	Grandchildren. Children of No. 35777.
35779	11080	Hon. Kathleen Mary, wife of the Rev. Leopold de Beaumont Klein, D.Sc., 1876.	
35780	11081	Hon. Caroline Mary O'Hagan, 1879.	

834. Descendants of Lieut.-Col. John Towneley, of Towneley, M.P., 1806–1878. (See Table CXXV.)

35781	11082	Theresa Harriet, wife of Captain John de la Cour.	
35782	11083	Lucy Evelyn, wife of John Murray, *of Touchadam and Polmaise Castle, co. Stirling.* 15 *Eaton Square, S.W.*	Daughters.
35783	11084	Mary Elizabeth Towneley, a nun. *Namur.*	
35784	11085	Mabel Anne, Baroness Clifford of Chudleigh [E.]. *Ugbrooke Park, Chudleigh.*	

835. Descendants of Frances Towneley, 1801–1880, wife of Thomas, 3rd Baron Camoys, 1797–1881. (See Table CXXV.)

35785	11086	Ralph Francis Julian, 6th Baron Camoys [E.], 1884. *Stonor Park, near Henley-on-Thames.*	Great-grandchildren. Children of Francis Robert, 4th Baron Camoys, 1856–1897, and grandchildren of the Hon. Francis Stonor, 1829–1881.
35786	11087	Hon. Edward Maurice Stonor, 1885.	
35787	11088	Hon. Hugo Robert William Stonor, 1887.	
35788	11089	Hon. Howard Carew Stonor, 1893.	
35789	11090	Hon. Henry Julian Stonor, M.V.O., 1859. 105 *Mount Street, W.*	Grandchildren. Children of the Hon. Francis Stonor, 1829–1881.
35790	11091	Hon. Edward Alexander Stonor, Clerk in the House of Lords, 1867. 27 *Montagu Square, W.*	
35791	11092	Francis Edward Stonor, 1900. Great-grandchild. Son of No. 35790.	
35792	11093	Julia Caroline, Marchioness of Hautpoul [France], 1861. 14 *Montagu Square, W.*	Grandchild. Daughter of the Hon. Francis Stonor, 1829–1881.
35793	11094	Monsignor the Most Rev. the Hon. Edmund Stonor, a Canon of St. John Lateran, Rome, Archbishop of Trebizond, 1831. 27 *Via Sistina, Rome.*	Children.
35794	11095	Hon. Catherine Frances Stonor, 1823. 41 *Green Street, Grosvenor Square, W.*	

35795	11096	Francis Somerled Silvertop, 1883. *Minster Acres, Riding-Mill-on-Tyne.*	Great-grandchildren. Children of Henry Thomas Silvertop, of Minster Acres, 1853–1893, and grandchildren of the Hon. Eliza Stonor, 1830–1860, wife of Henry Charles Silvertop, *formerly* Englefield, 1826–1887.
35796	11097	William Alexander Silvertop, 1884. *Lartington Hall, Yorks.*	
35797	11098	Charles Randal Silvertop, 1889.	
35798	11099	Margaret Mary Silvertop, 1886.	
35799	11100	Elise Mary Silvertop	
35800	11101	Rev. George Edward Silvertop, 1856.	Grandchildren. Children of the Hon. Eliza Stonor, 1830–1860, wife of Henry Charles Silvertop, *formerly* Englefield, 1826–1887.
35801	11102	Agnes Mary Silvertop, a nun.	
35802	11103	Hon. Maria, widow of Sir Charles Frederick Smythe, 7th Bart., 1819–1897, 1832. *Leamington.*	2nd surviving daughter.
35803	11104	Mary Frances, wife of Oscar Henry Blount, 1856. *The Hut, Windsor.*	Granddaughter. Daughter of No. 35802.
35804		Same as No. 35402. Great-grandchild.	Daughter of No. 35803.
35805	11105	Harriet, Viscountess Clifden [I.], Baroness Mendip [G.B.], 1836. 41 *Green Street, W.*	2nd surviving daughter.
35806 –11	}	Same as Nos. 22217–22222.	Grandchildren, &c. Children of No. 35805.
35812	11106	Major George Pereira, D.S.O., 1865. 5 *Hereford Gardens.*	Grandchildren. Children of the Hon. Margaret Ann Stonor, 1839–1894, wife of Edward Pereira, 1816–1872.
35813	11107	Rev. Edward Pereira, 1866.	
35814	11108	Captain Cecil Pereira, 1869.	
35815	11109	Evelyn, wife of F. O. Denham Parker, 1863. 5 *Hereford Gardens.*	

836. Descendants of Henry Drummond, of Albury Park, M.P., 1786–1860. (See Table CXXV.)

35816 –29	}	Same as Nos. 20954–20967.	Grandchildren, &c. Children, &c., of Louisa Drummond, 1813–1890, wife of Algernon George, 6th Duke of Northumberland, K.G., 1810–1899.

837. Descendants of the Rev. Spencer Rodney Drummond, 1790–1882. (See Table CXXV.)

35830	11110	Laura Louisa Lilia Vernon.	Granddaughter. Daughter of Caroline Anne Drummond, 1820–1883, wife of the Rev. Henry John Vernon, Vicar of Eckington, Worcester.

838. Descendants of Elizabeth Drummond, 1788–1848, 2nd wife of John Portal, of Freefolk and Laverstoke, Hants, 1764–1848. (See Table CXXV.)

35831	11111	Melville Portal, J.P., D.L., 1819. *Laverstoke House, near Overton, Hants.*	Son.

35832	11112	Alaric William John Portal, Lieutenant R.N., 1861.	Grandchildren. Children of No. 35831.
35833	11113	Adela Harriet, wife of Colonel Alfred Edward Codrington, Coldstream Guards. 110 *Eaton Square, S.W.*	
35834	11114	Geoffrey Ronald Codrington, 1888.	Great-grandchildren. Children of No. 35833.
35835	11115	William Melville Codrington, 1892.	
35836	11116	John Alfred Codrington, 1898.	
35837	11117	Mary Adela Codrington.	
35838	11118	Ethel Mary Portal.	Grandchildren. Younger daughters of No. 35831.
35839	11119	Katherine Charlotte, wife of Francis Walter Montagu-Douglas Scott. *Redbourn House, St. Albans.*	
35840	11120	Evelyn Adela Portal.	Granddaughter. Daughter of Lieut.-Col. Robert Portal, of Ashe Park, 1820–1888.
35841	11121	Sir Wyndham Spencer Portal, 1st Bart., J.P., D.L., 1822. *Malshanger, Basingstoke.*	2nd surviving son.
35842	11122	William Wyndham Portal, J.P. *Southington House, Overton.*	Grandson. Son of No. 35841.
35843	11123	Wyndham Raymond Portal, 1885.	Great-grandchildren. Children of No. 35842.
35844	11124	Robert St. Leger Portal, 1892.	
35845	11125	Margery Portal, 1881.	
35846	11126	Mary Florence Portal, 1884.	
35847	11127	Spencer John Portal, 1864. *Bere Hill, Whitchurch, Hants.*	Grandson. 2nd son of No. 35841.
35848	11128	Oldric Spencer Portal, 1893.	Great-grandchildren. Children of No. 35847.
35849	11129	Raymond Spencer Portal, 1897.	
35850	11130	Constance Spencer Portal, 1891.	
35851	11131	Bertram Percy Portal, Major 17th Lancers, 1866.	Grandchild. Son of No. 35841.
35852		Same as No. 20978.	Great-grandchild. Son of No. 35851.
35853	11132	Constance Mary, widow of William Howley Kingsmill, *of Sydmonton Court,* 1838–1894. *Sydmonton Court, Newbury.*	Grandchild. Daughter of No. 35841.
35854	11133	Andrew de Portal Kingsmill, Grenadier Guards, 1881. *Sydmonton Court, Newbury.*	Great-grandchildren. Children of No. 35853.
35855	11134	Dorothy Constance Kingsmill.	
35856	11135	Bridget Mary Kingsmill.	
35857	11136	Constance Anne Kingsmill.	
35858	11137	Eleanor Jane, widow of Chaloner William Chute, *of The Vyne, Hants,* 1838–1892. *The Vyne, Basingstoke.*	Grandchild. 2nd daughter of No. 35841.
35859	11138	Charles Lennard Chute, 1879. *The Vyne, Basingstoke.*	Great-grandchildren. Children of No. 35858.
35860	11139	John Chaloner Chute, 1881.	
35861	11140	Anthony William Chute, 1884.	
35862	11141	Rachel Eleanor Chute.	
35863	11142	Mary Adelaide, Baroness Addington [U.K.]. 24 *Prince's Gate, S.W.* *Addington Manor, Winslow, Bucks.*	Grandchild. 3rd daughter of No. 35841.
35864	11143	Hon. John Gellibrand Hubbard, 1883.	Great-grandchildren. Children of No. 35863.
35865	11144	Hon. Raymond Egerton Hubbard, 1884.	
35866	11145	Hon. Francis Spencer Hubbard, 1888.	
35867	11146	Hon. Winifred Mary Hubbard, 1881.	
35868	11147	Hon. Ruth Mary Hubbard, 1896.	

35869	11148	Eveline Maud, wife of the Hon. Evelyn Hubbard, M.P. *The Rookery, Down, Kent.*	Grandchild. Youngest daughter of No. 35841.
35870	11149	Harold Evelyn Hubbard, 1883.	Great-grandchildren.
35871	11150	Eric Wyndham Hubbard, 1885.	Children of No.
35872	11151	Bertram John Hubbard, 1895.	35869.
35873	11152	Maurice Raymond Portal, 1870.	Grandchildren. Children of
35874	11153	Helen Violet Portal.	the Rev. George Raymond
35875	11154	Helen Margaret Portal.	Portal, 1827–1889.
35876	11155	Montagu George Knight, J.P., D.L., 1844. *Chawton House, Alton, co. Hants.*	Grandchildren. Children of Adela Portal, –1870, 2nd wife of Edward Knight, of Godmersham Park and Chawton House, 1794–1879.
35877	11156	Rev. Charles Edward Knight, 1846. *Chawton Rectory, Alton.*	
35878	11157	Lionel Charles Edward Knight, Lieutenant East Kent Regiment, 1872.	
35879	11158	Henry Lewkenor Knight, Lieutenant Royal Irish Fusiliers, 1874.	Great-grandchildren. Children of No. 35877.
35880	11159	William John Knight, 1875.	
35881	11160	George Brook Knight, 1877.	
35882	11161	Richard Brodnax Knight, 1880.	
35883	11162	Major Evelyn Ridley Bradford, 1869.	Great-grandchildren. Children of Elizabeth Adela Knight (sister to No. 35876), –1896, 1st wife of Colonel Sir Edward Ridley Colborne Bradford, G.C.B., K.C.S.I., Chief Commissioner of Police.
35884	11163	Edward Austin Bradford, 1879.	
35885	11164	Beryl Adela Bradford, 1875.	
35886	11165	Adela Louisa Cassandra, widow of Herbert Carey Hardy, 1848–1888.	Grandchild. Sister to No. 35876.
35887	11166	Guy Charles Hardy, 1873. *Danehurst, Uckfield, Sussex.*	Great-grandchild. Son of No. 35886.
35888	11167	Herbert Ronald Hardy, 1900.	Great-great-grandchild. Son of No. 35887.
35889	11168	Ronald Montague Hardy, 1882.	
35890	11169	Adela Gertrude Catherine, wife of Arthur H. Wood.	
35891	11170	Marion Ethel Hardy.	Great-grandchildren. Children of No. 35886.
35892	11171	Margaret Louisa Hardy.	
35893	11172	Annie Kathleen Hardy.	
35894	11173	Norah Cassandra Hardy.	
35895	11174	Louisa Carey Hardy.	
35896	11175	Adela Mary Margaretta, wife of Major Charles Augustus Rice, R.E.	Granddaughter. Sister to No. 35876.
35897	11176	Helen Elizabeth Rice.	Great-grandchildren. Children of No. 35896.
35898	11177	Mary Adela Morland Rice.	
35899	11178	Ernestine Cecil Rice.	
35900	11179	Helen Adela, wife of the Rev. Fowler Babington Blogg. *Great Mongesham Rectory, Deal.*	Granddaughter. Sister to No. 35876.
35901	11180	Edward Basil Blogg, 1887.	
35902	11181	Hugh Babington Blogg, 1889.	Great-grandchildren. Children of No. 35900.
35903	11182	Claude Henry Blogg, 1890.	
35904	11183	Winifred Louisa Blogg, 1882.	
35905	11184	Helen Mabel Adela Blogg, 1885.	
35906	11185	Marjorie Blogg, 1892.	
35907	11186	Ethel Adela, wife of the Rev. Edward Worsley. *Evenley Vicarage, Brackley.*	Granddaughter. Youngest sister to No. 35876.

35908	11187	Harold Montagu Worsley, 1881.	
35909	11188	Arthur Edward Worsley, 1882.	
35910	11189	Herbert Henry Knight Worsley, 1885.	Great-grandchildren.
35911	11190	Robert Lewkenor Worsley, 1893.	Children of No.
35912	11191	Charles Edward Austin Worsley, 1902.	35907.
35913	11192	Madeline Ethel Worsley, 1887.	
35914	11193	Helen Margaret Joan Worsley, 1889.	
35915	11194	Katharine Mary Worsley, 1891.	
35916	11195	Lilias Elizabeth Dundas.	Granddaughter. Daughter of Jane Eliza Portal, –1900, wife of Major Thomas Dundas, 1825.

839. Descendants of Margaret Oliphant, 1799–1839, wife of Thomas Kington, of Charlton House, Somerset, 1797–1857. (See Table CXXVI.)

35917	11196	Philip Laurence Kington-Blair-Oliphant, Captain Rifle Brigade, 1867. *Gask, co. Perth. Ardblair Castle, Perthshire.*	Grandchildren. Children of Philip Oliphant Kington-Blair-Oliphant, of Ardblair, 1832–1892.
35918	11197	Emily Caroline Kington-Blair-Oliphant.	
35919	11198	Margaret Ethel, wife of James Maxtone-Graham. *Cultoquhey, Crieff.*	
35920	11199	Anthony James Oliphant Maxtone-Graham.	Great-grandchildren. Children of No. 35919.
35921	11200	Ysenda Mabel Maxtone-Graham, 1893.	
35922	11201	Rachel Caroline Maxtone-Graham, 1897.	
35923	11202	Lilian, wife of William Saxon Gregson-Ellis. *Plas Clough, co. Denbigh.*	Grandchild. Younger sister to No. 35917.
35924	11203	Philip George Saxon Gregson-Ellis, 1898.	Great-grandchildren. Children of No. 35923.
35925	11204	Mary Henrietta Christian Gregson-Ellis, 1900.	
35926	11205	Lilian Nairne Gregson-Ellis, 1901.	
35927	11206	William Miles Nairn Kington, Lieut.-Col. *late* 4th Hussars. *Charlton House, Wraxall, Somerset.*	Son.
35928	11207	William Miles Kington, Lieutenant Royal Welsh Fusiliers, 1876.	Grandchildren. Children of No. 35927.
35929	11208	Hugh Beresford Kington.	
35930	11209	Philip Urmston Kington, 1892.	
35931	11210	Stewart Brabazon Kington, 1896.	
35932	11211	Norah Skye Kington.	
35933	11212	Kathleen Frances, wife of the Ven. Arthur Evan David, Archdeacon of Brisbane. *Brisbane, Queensland.*	
35934	11213	Phyllis Nairn Kington.	
35935	11214	Gertrude Joan Kington.	
35936	11215	Marjorie Oliphant Kington.	
35937	11216	Joyce Adelaide Kington.	
35938	11217	William Kington Fyffe.	Grandchildren. Children of Caroline Margaret Kington, 1837–1897, wife of Dr. Fyffe.
35939	11218	Bertram Oliphant Fyffe.	
35940	11219	Rollestone Fyffe.	
35941	11220	Bruce Fyffe.	
35942	11221	Marion Annie Fyffe.	
35943	11222	Margaret Caroline Fyffe.	

840. Descendants of Marjory Ann Mary Oliphant, 1762–   , wife of Dr. Alexander Steuart, of Bonskeid, representative of Steuart of Garth. (See Table CXXVI.)

---

841. Descendants of Margaret Henrietta Maria Janet Steuart,   –
1857, wife of Major Horace Durrant, Bengal Cavalry,   –
. (See Table CXXVI.)

| 35944 | 11223 | John Nairne Durrant Steuart, 12th Laird of Dalguise,   –1883. *Dalguise, co. Perth.* | { Grandchild. Son of Charles Horace Durrant Steuart, 11th Laird of Dalguise, 1855–1890. |

842. Descendants of Amelia Helen Steuart, 1838–1869, wife of Sir Robert Tempest Tempest, *formerly* Ricketts, 3rd Bart., 1836–1901. (See Table CXXVI.)

| 35945 | 11224 | Sir Tristram Tempest Tempest, 4th Bart., 1865. *Tong Hall, Drighlington.* | } Children. |
| 35946 | 11225 | Henrietta Frances May, wife of John Hicks Graves. *Bradenham House, High Wycombe.* | |

843. Descendants, if any, of Margaret Oliphant, 17 –17 , wife of Peter Graham, of Inchbraikie. (See Table CXXVI.)

---

844. Descendants, if any, of [Sir] Alexander John William Oliphant Macgregor Drummond [3rd Baronet], of Balkaldie, 1758–1794. (See Table CXXVI.)

---

845. Descendants of Hon. Catherine Nairne,   –   , wife of William, 3rd Earl of Dunmore, 1687–1756. (See Table CXXIV.)

| 35947 –6002 | } | Same as Nos. 33678–33733. |

846. Descendants of Margaret Robertson, 1739/40–1774, wife of Laurence Oliphant, of Gask, 1724–1792. (See Table CXXIV.)

| 36003 –33 | } | Same as Nos. 35917–35946. |

847. Descendants, if any, of James Robertson, of Lude,   –1803. (See Table CXXIV.)

848. Descendants, if any, of Robert Henry Robertson, of Tully-betton, alive 1850. (See Table CXXIV.)

---

849. Descendants of Margaret Robertson,   —   , wife of Stewart Menzies, of Culdares. (See Table CXXIV.)

---

850. Descendants, if any, of the Hon. Louisa Nairne,   —1782, wife of David Graham, of Orchil. (See Table CXXIV.)

---

851. Descendants,[1] if any, of Lord Edward Murray, Captain Royal Scots,   —1739. (See Table CIV.)

---

852. Descendants, if any, of Lady Charlotte Murray,   —1735, wife (1690) of Thomas Cooper. (See Table CIV.)

---

853. Descendants of Norman MacLeod of that Ilk, 22nd Chief, 1812–1895. (See Table CXXVII.)

36034	11226	Norman Magnus MacLeod, 23rd Chief, C.M.G., *late* Captain 74th Highlanders, J.P., D.L., 1839. *Dunvegan Castle, Isle of Skye, N.B.*	Son.
36035	11227	Emily Pauline MacLeod, 1882. Grandchildren. Children	
36036	11228	Margaret Louisa MacLeod, 1884. of No. 36034.	
36037	11229	Reginald MacLeod, C.B., Under Secretary of State for Scotland, 1847. 50 *Draycott Place, S.W.*	2nd son.
36038	11230	Flora Louisa Cecilia, wife of Hubert Walter, 1878. 11 *Devonshire Terrace, Lancaster Gate, S.W.*	Grandchildren.
36039	11231	Alice Walter, 1902. { Great-grandchild. Child of No. 36038.	Children of No. 36037.
36040	11232	Olive Susan Miranda MacLeod, 1880.	
36041	11233	Rev. Roderic Charles MacLeod, J.P., 1852. *Mitford Vicarage, Morpeth.*	3rd son.
36042	11234	Ian Breac MacLeod, 1893.	Grandchildren. Chil-
36043	11235	Brenda Katherine MacLeod, 1887.	dren of No. 36041.
36044	11236	Eila St. John MacLeod, 1891.	
36045	11237	Louisa Cecilia, wife of John Moyer Heathcote, J.P., D.L. *Conington Castle, Peterborough, Hunts.*	Daughter.
36046	11238	John Norman Heathcote, 1863.	Grandchildren. Children
36047	11239	Arthur Ridley Heathcote, 1877.	of No. 36045.
36048	11240	Evelyn May Heathcote.	

---

[1] Would be entitled to quarter the royal arms.

854. Descendants of Anne Eliza MacLeod, 1813–1843, 1st wife of Lieut.-Col. James Ogilvy Fairlie, of Coodham, J.P., 1809–1870. (See Table CXXVII.)

36049	11241	Henry James Fairlie, Commander R.N., 1841.	Son.
36050	11242	James Gordon Fairlie, Lieutenant North Lancashire Regiment, 1877.	Grandchildren. Children of No. 36049.
36051	11243	Græme Ogilvy Fairlie, 1897.	
36052	11244	Dorothy Frances Fairlie.	
36053	11245	Isabella Catherine, widow of Archibald James Campbell, –1885.	Daughter.
36054	11246	Alastair Magnus Campbell, 1868. *Auchindarroch.*	
36055	11247	Archibald Campbell, 1878.	Grandchildren. Children of No. 36053.
36056	11248	Roma Constance, wife of the Rev. Dugald Macfarlane, 1870.	
36057	11249	Zella Muriel Mary Campbell, 1880.	

855. Descendants of Henrietta Maria MacLeod, 1817–1877, wife of John Campbell, of Glensaddell, Argyll, 1796–18 . (See Table CXXVII.)

856. Descendants of Mary Lowther MacLeod, 1819–1884, wife of Robert Ferguson, M.D., 1799– . (See Table CXXVII.)

36058	11250	Ronald Ferguson, a Clerk in the Treasury.	Son.
36059	11251	Torquil Ferguson.	
36060	11252	Roma Ferguson.	Grandchildren. Children of No. 36058.
36061	11253	Rachel Ferguson.	
36062	11254	Harold S. Ferguson. *Travancore, India.*	3rd son.
36063	11255	Robert Hamilton Ferguson, 1888.	Grandchildren. Children of No. 36062.
36064	11256	Stuart Frederick Maxwell Ferguson, 1889.	
36065	11257	Adam Ferguson, 1891.	
36066	11258	Mary Roma, wife of Colonel Cecil Farrant. *Malta.*	Elder daughter.
36067	11259	Harry Farrant.	
36068	11260	Cecily Farrant.	Grandchildren. Children of No. 36066.
36069	11261	Melvil Farrant.	
36070	11262	Marion Ferguson.	Younger daughter.

857. Descendants of Emelia Anne MacLeod, 18 –18 , 1st wife of Sir John Pringle, 5th Bart., 1784–1869. (See Table CXXVII.)

36071	11263	Emily Eliza Steele, Lady Cathcart, wife of Sir Reginald Archibald Edward Cathcart, 6th Bart. *Killochan Castle, Ayrshire, N.B. Titness Park, Sunninghill, Berks.*	Grandchild. Daughter of John Robert Pringle, Madras C.S., 1820–1847.
36072	11264	Katherine Margaret Swinton, 1846.	Granddaughter. Daughter of Katherine Pringle, –1846, and her husband, Archibald Swinton, Advocate.

36073	11265	John Pringle St. Clair, 1862.	⎧ Grandchildren. Children of
36074	11266	Susan Eva, wife of Henry Edward	⎪ Anne Crauford Pringle,
		Cousans, 1859.	⎨ 1821–1899, 2nd wife of the
		The Greenstones, Lincoln.	⎪ Hon. Charles St. Clair,
			⎩ 1811–1863.

858. Descendants of Anne Eliza MacLeod, 1797–1889, and her husband, Spencer Perceval, of Elm Grove, Ealing, M.P., 1795–1859. (See Table CXXVII.)

36075	11267	Louisa Perceval, 1827.	Daughter.
36076	11268	Alexander Perceval Matheson, Member of the Senate, Australia, 1861. *Perth, West Australia. Bachelors'.*	⎧ Grandson. Son of Eleanor ⎪ Irving Perceval, – ⎨ 1879, 3rd wife of Sir ⎪ Alexander Matheson, ⎩ 1st Bart., M.P., 1805–1886.
36077	11269	Ian Kenneth Matheson, 1893.	⎫
36078	11270	Alexander Perceval Matheson, 1895.	⎪
36079	11271	Roderick Kyrle Matheson, 1897.	⎬ Great-grandchildren. Chil-
36080	11272	Margaret Anna Matheson.	⎪ dren of No. 36076.
36081	11273	Norah Matheson.	⎪
36082	11274	Muriel Helen Matheson.	⎪
36083	11275	Eleanor Matheson.	⎭
36084	11276	Roderick Mackenzie Chisholm Matheson, 1861. 13 *Holmbush Road, Putney.*	⎫ Grandson. Brother ⎬ to No. 36076.
36085	11277	Ethel Ivy Flora Matheson, 1886.	⎰ Great-grandchild. Daughter ⎱ of No. 36084.
36086	11278	Torquhil George Matheson, Captain Coldstream Guards, 1871. 3 *Sloane Court, S.W.*	⎫ Grandson. Brother ⎬ to No. 36076, &c.
36087	11279	Hon. Grace Mary Eleanor Mostyn, 1887.	⎧ Great-grandchildren. Daugh- ⎪ ters of Eleanor Margaret ⎪ Matheson, 1863–1896 (sis-
36088	11280	Hon. Gladys Flora Mostyn, 1889.	⎨ ter to No. 36076), and her
36089	11281	Hon. Dorothy Alice Mostyn, 1893.	⎪ husband, Hubert George ⎪ Charles, 7th Lord Vaux of ⎩ Harrowden.
36090	11282	Anna Elizabeth Matheson.	⎫ Grandchildren.
36091	11283	Flora, Lady Pauncefort-Duncombe, widow of Sir Philip Henry Pauncefort-Duncombe, 2nd Bart., 1849–1895. *Brickhill Manor, near Bletchley.*	⎬ Sisters to ⎭ No. 36076.
36092	11284	Sir Everard Philip Digby Pauncefort-Duncombe, 3rd Bart., 1885. *Brickhill Manor, near Bletchley.*	⎫ Great-grandchil- ⎬ dren. Children
36093	11285	Constance Flora Eleanor Pauncefort-Duncombe, 1884.	⎭ of No. 36091.
36094	11286	Edward Howard Marsh, 1872. 30 *Bruton Street, W.*	⎫ Grandchildren. Chil- ⎪ dren of Jane Perce-
36095	11287	Margaret Helen, wife of Major F. B. Maurice, 1874. *Donnington, Camberley.*	⎬ val, –1896, wife ⎪ of Howard Marsh, of ⎭ Furnival's Inn.
36096	11288	Frederick Michael Perceval Maurice.	⎫ Great-grandchildren. Chil-
36097	11289	Helen Annie Maurice.	⎬ dren of No. 36095.

859. Descendants of Penelope MacKinnon, wife of A. MacKinnon, of Naples and Buenos Ayres. (See Table CXXVII.)

36098	11290	Susan Margaret, Duchess of Somerset [E.] *Maiden Bradley, Bath.* Other descendants, if any.	}	Granddaughter. Younger daughter of Charles MacKinnon.

860. Descendants of Mary MacLeod, – , wife of Captain Ramsay, R.N. (See Table CXXVII.)

861. Descendants, if any, of Emilia MacLeod, – , wife of Captain Gustavus Moore, of Saltston, Ireland. (See Table CXXVII.)

862. Descendants of Sir John Pringle, 5th Bart., 1784-1869. (See Table CXXVIII.)

36099 -102	}	Same as Nos. 36071-36074.	{	Descendants by 1st wife.
36103	11291	Mary Gavin, widow of the Hon. Robert Baillie Hamilton, M.P., 1828-1891. *Langton, Duns.*	}	Daughters by 2nd wife.
36104	11292	Magdalen Breadalbane, Lady Harvey, widow of Sir Robert Bateson Harvey, 1st Bart., 1825-1887. *19 Maresfield Gardens, N.W.*		

863. Descendants of Sir Norman Pringle, 6th Bart., 1787-1870. (See Table CXXVIII.)

36105	11293	Sir Norman Robert Pringle, 8th Bart., 1871. *99 Belgrave Road, S.W.*	}	Grandchildren. Children of Sir Norman William Drummond Pringle, 7th Bart., 1836-1897.
36106	11294	Magdalen Valerie Pringle.		
36107	11295	Violet Louisa Maria Pringle.		
36108	11296	Harriet Elizabeth Anne Pringle.	}	Daughters.
36109	11297	Emilia Margaret Pringle.		

864. Descendants, if any, of Eliza Pringle, –1865, wife of Archibald Todd, of Drygrange. (See Table CXXVIII.)

865. Descendants of George, 10th Earl of Haddington, 1802-1870. (See Table CXXVIII.)

36110	11298	George, 11th Earl of Haddington [S.], K.T., 1827. *Tyninghame House, Prestonkirk, Haddington.*	}	Son.
36111	11299	George, Lord Binning, M.V.O., 1856. *Mellerstain House, near Kelso.*	}	Grandson. Son of No. 36110.

36112	11300	Hon. George Baillie-Hamilton, 1894.	
36113	11301	Hon. Charles William Baillie-Hamilton, 1900.	Great-grandchildren. Children of No. 36111.
36114	11302	Hon. Helen Baillie-Hamilton, 1893.	

36115	11303	Hon. Henry Robert Baillie-Hamilton, 1862. Guards'; Wellington; New.	Grandchildren. Children of No. 36110.
36116	11304	Lady Ruth Baillie-Hamilton, 1855.	
36117	11305	Lady Grisell Baillie-Hamilton, 1861.	
36118	11306	Lady Cecily Baillie-Hamilton, 1868.	

36119	11307	Helen Georgina Baillie-Hamilton, 1874.	Grandchildren. Children of Commander the Hon. Henry Baillie - Hamilton, R.N., 1832–1895.
36120	11308	Amabel Georgina Baillie-Hamilton, 1876.	
36121	11309	Katherine Ada Georgina Baillie-Hamilton, 1879.	
36122	11310	Gena Mary Baillie-Hamilton, 1882.	
36123	11311	Margaret Ellinor Georgina Baillie-Hamilton, 1885.	

36124	11312	Rev. the Hon. Arthur Charles Baillie-Hamilton, J.P., 1838. Burley Lodge, Ringwood, Hants.	Younger surviving son.

36125	11313	Margaret Baillie-Hamilton, 1868.	Grandchild. Child of No. 36124.

36126	11314	Lady Mary, wife of the Rev. the Hon. Henry Douglas, 1825. St. Paul's, Worcester.	Daughter.

36127	11315	Mary Douglas, 1857.	Grandchild. Daughter of No. 36126.

36128	11316	Lady Frances Baillie-Hamilton, 1829.	Daughters.
36129	11317	Lady Georgina Sophia, wife of Sir Harry Foley Vernon, 1st Bart., 1839. Hanbury Hall, Droitwich.	

36130	11318	Bowater George Hamilton Vernon, Lieutenant Worcestershire Yeomanry Cavalry, 1865.	Grandchildren. Children of No. 36129.
36131	11319	Auda Lætitia Vernon, 1862.	

866. Descendants of the Hon. Charles Baillie, Lord Jerviswood, M.P., 1804–1879. (See Table CXXVIII.)

36132	11320	Alice Baillie, 1839.	Dryburgh House, St. Boswells.	Daughters.
36133	11321	Maria Theresa Baillie, 1846.		

867. Descendants of the Rev. and Hon. John Baillie, Canon of York, 1810–1888. (See Table CXXVIII.)

36134	11322	Hugh John Baillie, 1838.	Eldest son.
			Grandchildren. Children of No. 36134.
36135	11323	Rev. George Thomas Baillie. St. Matthew's Church, Upper Clapton, N.E.	2nd son.

36136	11324	Richard George Baillie, 1869.	
36137	11325	John Gordon Baillie, 1872.	
36138	11326	Robert Baillie, 1878.	
36139	11327	Charles Jerviswoode Baillie, 1882.	
36140	11328	Thomas Claude Noel Baillie, 1885.	Grandchildren. Children of No. 36135.
36141	11329	Cecilia Mary Baillie, 1871.	
36142	11330	Katherine Grisell Baillie, 1874.	
36143	11331	Edith Georgiana Baillie, 1875.	
36144	11332	Ellen Ruth Gertrude Baillie, 1877.	
36145	11333	Rachel Baillie, 1880.	
36146	11334	Beatrice Louisa Baillie, 1884.	
36147	11335	John Cecil Yorke, J.P., Captain Yorkshire Militia Artillery, 1867. *Halton Place, Hellifield, Yorks.*	Grandchildren. Children of Augusta Margaret Baillie, 1840–1879, 1st wife of Thomas Edward Yorke, of Bewerley Hall.
36148	11336	Henry Reay Yorke, Lieutenant Royal Munster Fusiliers, 1875.	
36149	11337	Mary Augusta Yorke.	
36150	11338	Helena Margaret, wife of Arthur Bailey. *Wramplingham Hall, Wymondham.*	
36151	11339	Anthony Yorke Bailey.	Great-grandchild. Child of No. 36150.
36152	11340	Louisa Caroline, wife of the Rev. Arthur Herbert Watson. *Ovingham-on-Tyne Rectory.*	Grandchildren. Sisters of Nos. 36147, &c.
36153	11341	Katherine Elizabeth Yorke.	
36154	11342	Ethel Lilian Yorke.	
36155	11343	Mary Georgina, wife of the Rev. Walter ffolliott Scott, 1844. *St. Andrews', Dunmore Park, Stirlingshire.*	Daughters.
36156	11344	Cecilia Clementina, wife of Henry Clements Barstow, B.C.S. *Hazelbush, York.*	
36157	11345	John Baillie Barstow, 1872.	
36158	11346	George Lewis Barstow, 1874.	
36159	11347	Henry Barstow, 1876.	Grandchildren. Children of No. 36156.
36160	11348	Walter Agar Thomas Barstow, 1886.	
36161	11349	Cecilia Mary Barstow, 1875.	
36162	11350	Beatrice Anne Barstow, 1883.	
36163	11351	Katherine Grisell Baillie, 1854.	Youngest daughter.

868. Descendants of the Lady Mary Baillie,   –1900, and her husband, George John James, 5th Earl of Aberdeen, 1816–1864.   (See Table CXXVIII.)

36164 –99	}	Same as Nos. 32741–32775.

869. Descendants of the Lady Georgina Baillie, 1816–1859, and her husband, Henry Francis, 7th Baron Polwarth, 1800–1867. (See Table CXXVIII.)

36200	11352	Walter Hugh, 8th Baron Polwarth [S.], 1838. *Mertoun House, St. Boswells, N.B.*	Eldest son.

36201 -16	}	Same as Nos. 32747–32762.	{ Grandchildren. Children, &c., of No. 36200.
36217	11353	Hon. Henry Robert Hepburne Scott, 1847. *Knipton Lodge, Grantham.*	} 2nd son.
36218 -21	}	Same as Nos. 19914–19917.	{ Grandchildren. Children of No. 36217.
36222	11354	Hon. Harriet Frances, widow of the Hon. Henry Baillie-Hamilton, 1832–1895, 1845. *Lennel House, Coldstream, N.B.*	} Daughter.
36223 -27	}	Same as Nos. 36119–36123.	{ Grandchildren. Children of No. 36222.

870. Descendants of Lady Katherine Charlotte Baillie, 1819–1894, and her husband, Bertram, 4th Earl of Ashburnham, 1797–1878. (See Table CXXVIII.)

| 36228 -39 | } | Same as Nos. 21141–21152. |

871. Descendants of Norman Shairp, of Houstoun, co. Linlithgow, 1779–1864. (See Table CXXVII.)

36240	11355	John Campbell Shairp, J.P., 1858. *Houstoun House, Uphall, co. Linlithgow.*	} Grandson. Son of Professor John Campbell Shairp, 1819–1885.
36241	11356	Norman Shairp, 1891.	} Great-grandchildren. Children of No. 36240.
36242	11357	John Walter Shairp, 1894.	
36243	11358	Christian Helen Shairp.	
36244	11359	Norman Houston Leckie, Major *late* Royal West Kent Regiment. *6 Grosvenor Street, Edinburgh.*	{ Grandchildren. Children of Elizabeth Bining Shairp, –1887, wife of Captain Charles T. Leckie, R.N., –1867.
36245	11360	Mary Alice Leckie.	
36246	11361	Grace Shairp.	Daughter.

872. Descendants of Anne MacLeod Shairp, 1785–1871, wife of Commander Thomas Innes, R.N., 1769–1844. (See Table CXXVII.)

36247	11362	Frederick Norman Innes Taylor, Major *late* 10th Foot, 1846. *Lincoln Lodge, Guildford.*	} Grandchildren. Children of Christiana Emma Elizabeth Innes, 1812–1887, wife of Bunbury Taylor, 1815–1883.
36248	11363	Harriet Emma Ballantine Taylor, 1843.	
36249	11364	Alice Mary Innes, widow of Arnold Hill Thompson, 1848.	
36250	11365	Evelyn Maud Innes Thompson.	{ Great-grandchild. Daughter of No. 36249.

873. Descendants of Christian Shairp, –1866, wife of William Mitchell-Innes, of Parsons Green, Whitehall, and Ayton, J.P., D.L., –1860. (See Table CXXVII.)

36251	11366	Alexander Harold Mitchell-Innes, J.P., 1870. *Whitehall, Chirnside, Berwick.*	
36252	11367	William Mitchell-Innes, 1901. { Great-great-grandchild. Child of No. 36251.	Great-grandchildren. Children of Captain William Mitchell-Innes, 1841–1879, and grandchildren of Captain Alexander Mitchell-Innes, of Whitehall, 1811–1886.
36253	11368	Inez Mary, wife of Captain John Alexander Miller.	
36254	11369	Charlotte Agnes, wife of Malcolm Wadham.	
36255	11370	Constance Ethel, wife of Lieut.-Col. Sir Henry Grey Dixon, K.C.B. *Berrywell, Duns, N.B.*	
36256		Same as No. 26482. { Great-great-grandchild. Son of No. 36255.	
36257	11371	Charles Lauder Mitchell-Innes, 1842.	Grandchild. Son of Captain Alexander Mitchell-Innes, of Whitehall, 1811–1886.
36258	11372	Norman William Ferdinand Mitchell-Innes, 1873.	Great-grandchildren. Children of Captain Ferdinand Henry Mitchell-Innes, 1847–1882, brother to No. 36251.
36259	11373	Eleanor Fanny Mitchell-Innes.	
36260	11374	Rev. Reginald John Simpson Mitchell-Innes, 1848.	
36261	11375	Arthur Vine Mitchell-Innes, 1853.	
36262	11376	James Edward Mitchell-Innes, 1854.	Grandchildren. Brothers and sister to No. 36251.
36263	11377	Thomas Alexander Mitchell-Innes, 1857.	
36264	11378	Gilbert Plantagenet Mitchell-Innes, 1863.	
36265	11379	Alfred Mitchell-Innes, 1864.	
36266	11380	Mary Blanche, widow of Robert Ambrose Morritt, J.P., D.L., 1816–1890. *Rokeby Park, Barnard Castle.*	
36267	11381	Henry Edward Morritt, 1880. *Rokeby Park, Barnard Castle.*	Great-grandchildren. Children of No. 36266.
36268	11382	Charlotte Greta Morritt, 1872.	
36269	11383	Florence Catherine Morritt, 1876.	
36270	11384	Hilda Mary Morritt, 1881.	
36271	11385	Linda Beatrice Morritt, 1886.	
36272	11386	Christian, wife of William Ramsay-L'Amy, of Dunkenny, J.P. *24 Cranley Gardens, S.W.*	Grandchild. 2nd sister to No. 36251.
36273	11387	Mary Winifrid Ramsay-L'Amy.	Great-grandchildren. Children of No. 36272.
36274	11388	Mabel Christian Ramsay-L'Amy.	
36275	11389	Sybil Fanny Ramsay-L'Amy.	
36276	11390	Frances Isobel, wife of James Alexander Ross-Hume, of Ninewells, J.P., D.L. *Golden Farm, Cirencester.*	Grandchild. Youngest sister to No. 36251.
36277	11391	Alexander Ross-Hume, 1884.	Great-grandchildren. Children of No. 36276.
36278	11392	Percy Gilbert Ross-Hume, 1888.	
36279	11393	Katherine Ross-Hume.	
36280	11394	Dorothy Ross-Hume.	

36281	11395	David Murray Anderson, Captain *late* 8th Hussars, 1867.	Great - grandchildren. Children of Christina Mitchell-Innes,
		Bourhouse, Dunbar.	1843–1902, wife of
36282	11396	Robert Warren Hastings Anderson, Major Highland Light Infantry, 1875.	J. W. Hastings Anderson, and grand-
36283	11397	Charlotte Elinor Anderson, 1870.	children of Thomas
36284	11398	Katharine Julia, wife of Alexander Harold Mitchell-Innes, J.P., 1872.	Shairp Mitchell-
		Whitehall, Chirnside.	Innes, 1813–18 .

36285 — Same as No. 36252.   Great-great-grandchild. Son of No. 36284.

36286 | 11399 | Isabella Mitchell-Innes, 1846. { Grandchild. Daughter of Thomas S. Mitchell-Innes.

36287	11400	Edwin Mitchell-Innes, 1846.	
36288	11401	Simpson Mitchell-Innes, 1850.	
36289	11402	George Simpson Mitchell-Innes, 1874.	Great-grandchildren. Chil-
36290	11403	Marie Louise, wife of Dr. John Rouillard,1875.	dren of No. 36288.
36291	11404	James Mitchell-Innes, Major *late* Highland Light Infantry, 1852	
36292	11405	Walter Mitchell-Innes, 1854.	
36293	11406	Norman Gilbert Mitchell-Innes, 1859.	Grandchildren. Chil-
36294	11407	Frederick Mitchell-Innes, 1862.	dren of George
36295	11408	Mary Lillias, wife of the Hon. James William Moncreiff, W.S., 1848.	Mitchell-Innes, of Bangour, J.P.,
		6 Ainslie Place, Edinburgh.	D.L., 1818–1886.
36296	11409	James Frederick Moncreiff, 1872.	
36297	11410	George Moncreiff, 1874.	Great-grandchil-
36298	11411	Henry Wellwood Moncreiff, 1876.	dren. Chil-
36299	11412	Edwin Robert Moncreiff, 1877.	dren of No. 36295.
36300	11413	William Francis Moncreiff, 1882.	
36301	11414	Christian Shairp Mitchell-Innes, 1858.	
36302	11415	. . . . Mitchell-Innes, 1902.	Great-grandchildren. Children of William Gilbert Mitchell-Innes, 1855– , and
36303	11416	. . . . Mitchell-Innes, 1900.	grandchildren of Gilbert Mitchell-Innes, 1823-1900.
36304	11417	Archibald Campbell Mitchell-Innes, 1860.	
36305	11418	Ernest Mitchell-Innes, 1862.	
36306	11419	Edward Alfred Mitchell-Innes, 1863.	
36307	11420	Gilbert Robert Mitchell-Innes, 1895.	
36308	11421	Josephine Mitchell-Innes, 1894.	Great-grandchil-
36309	11422	Norma Mitchell - Innes, 1896.	dren. Chil- dren of No.
36310	11423	Rhoda Frederic Mitchell-Innes, 1900.	36306.	Grandchildren. Children of Gilbert Mitchell-Innes, 1823–1900.
36311	11424	Elizabeth Mitchell-Innes, 1901.	
36312	11425	Cecil Mitchell-Innes, 1866.	
36313	11426	Norman James Mitchell-Innes, 1892.	Great-grandchil- dren. Chil-
36314	11427	Joan Antoinette Cecil Mitchell-Innes, 1898.	dren of No. 36312.
36315	11428	Norman MacLeod Mitchell-Innes, 1867.	
36316	11429	Robert Gordon Mitchell-Innes, 1870.	

		Children (2 sons and 3 daughters) of Norma Mitchell-Innes, 1853–1897, wife of Edward Cecil Daniell.	
36317	11430	William Ramsay L'Amy, of Dunkenny, J.P., 1850. 24 Cranley Gardens, S.W.	Grandson. Son of Mary Rich MacLeod Mitchell - Innes, –1875, 1st wife of John Ramsay - L'Amy of Dunkenny, 1813–1892.
36318 –20	}	Same as Nos. 36273–36275.	Great-grandchildren. Children of No. 36317.
36321	11431	Rev. John Alexander Ramsay L'Amy, 1852.	
36322	11432	Simpson MacLeod Ramsay L'Amy, 1860.	Grandchildren. Brothers and sister to No. 36317.
36323	11433	Mary Williamina Ramsay L'Amy.	

874. Descendants of James Scrymscoure Fothringham, of Pourie, 1785–1837. (See Table CXXIX.)

36324	11434	Walter Thomas James Scrymscoure Steuart-Fothringham, of Pourie and Grandtully, J.P., D.L., 1862. Fothringham, co. Forfar.	Grandchildren. Children of Captain Thomas Frederick Scrymscoure Fothringham, of Pourie, 1836–1864.
36325	11435	Marion Charlotte Susan, wife of Lionel Benson.	
		Children, if any, of the four daughters of the above-named J. S. Fothringham, of Pourie.	

875. Descendants, if any, of the four younger brothers and three sisters of James Scrymscoure Fothringham, of Pourie, 1785–1837. (See Table CXXIX.)

876. Descendants, if any, of the Hon. Hugh Mackenzie, an officer in the Dutch service, who d. s. p. m. (See Table CXXVII.)

877. Descendants of Archibald James Lamont, of Lamont, J.P., D.L., 1818–1862. (See Table CXXX.)

36326	11436	John Henry Lamont, of Lamont, J.P., D.L., Major late 9th Lancers, 1854. Golfstone, Westward Ho, Devon.	Children.
36327	11437	Adelaide Augusta Lamont.	
36328	11438	Evelyn Lamont.	
36329	11439	Marion Alice, wife of William Thomas Charlewood.	

878. Descendants, if any, of Amelia Helen Lamont   –1840, wife of James G. Davidson. (See Table CXXX.)

879. Descendants, if any, of any younger sons or any daughters, or brothers and sisters, of John Lamont, of Lamont, temp. 1800. (See Table CXXX.)

ELIZABETH OF YORK, DAUGHTER OF KING EDWARD IV., AND
QUEEN CONSORT OF KING HENRY VII.

THE COMMON ANCESTRESS OF NOS. 1–36735.

From the Picture by an unknown artist in the National Portrait Gallery.

880. Descendants of Sir William Keith Murray, 7th Bart. of Ochtertyre, 1801–1861. (See Table CXXXI.)

36330	11440	Sir Patrick Keith Murray, 8th Bart., 1835. Ochtertyre, Crieff, Perthshire.	Son.
36331	11441	William Keith Murray, Captain 3rd Battalion Black Watch, 1872.	
36332	11442	George Keith Murray, 1873.	Grandchildren. Children of No. 36330.
36333	11443	Patrick Keith Murray, 1878.	
36334	11444	John Keith Murray, 1881.	
36335	11445	Ione Keith Murray, 1877.	
36336	11446	Alexander Keith Murray, 1843.	2nd son.
36337	11447	Alastair William Murray, 1894. Grandson. Son of No. 36336.	
36338	11448	Henry Arthur Murray, Lieutenant (retired) R.N., 1846. Comrie, Perthshire.	3rd son.
36339	11449	Harry Edmund Colquhoun Murray, 1873.	Grandchildren. Children of No. 36338.
36340	11450	Caroline Mary Murray.	
36341	11451	David Keith Murray, 1849. Kindoli, Crieff, Scotland.	4th and 5th surviving sons.
36342	11452	Archibald Lamont Keith Murray, 1852. Bideford, North Devon.	
36343	11453	Archie Murray, 1886.	
36344	11454	Walter Herbert Murray, 1889.	
36345	11455	David Murray, 1900.	
36346	11456	Georgina Mary Murray, 1887.	Grandchildren. Children of No. 36342.
36347	11457	Adelaide Murray, 1891.	
36348	11458	Millicent Ethel Murray, 1893.	
36349	11459	Maud Louisa Murray, 1896.	
36350	11460	Jeanie Helen Murray, 1898.	
36351	11461	Mary Anne Charlotte Keith, widow of the Rev. Canon Edmund William Kissack, –1901, 1851. Tighvonie, Crieff.	Daughter.

881. Descendants of John Murray, afterwards Murray-Gartshore, of Ravelston, Edinburgh, 1804–1884. (See Table CXXXI.)

36352	11462	Mary Murray-Gartshore. Ravelston, Blackhall, Midlothian.	Only surviving child.

882. Descendants of the late Henry Dundas Murray, Stipendiary Magistrate at Gwaler, South Australia, 1818–1882. (See Table CXXXI.)

36353	11463	William Tullibardine Murray, 1853. New Zealand.	Son.
36354	11464	Henry Lamont Murray, 1891.	Grandchildren. Children of No. 36353.
36355	11465	Yolande Murray, 1887.	
36356	11466	Mary Isabella, wife of Robert Kinloch, W.S. Perth.	Daughter.
36357	11467	Alasdair Ian Kinloch, 1889.	Grandchildren. Children of No. 36356.
36358	11468	Adrian Moray Campbell Kinloch, 1889.	
36359	11469	Muriel Augusta Kinloch, 1885.	

883. Descendants of Georgina Murray, 1805–1877, wife of Anthony Murray, of Dollerie, co. Perth, 1802–1884. (See Table CXXXI.)

36360	11470	Anthony George Murray, J.P., 1830. *Dollerie, Crieff, co. Perth.* } Son.	
36361	11471	Anthony Hugh Murray, 1888. Grandson. Son of No. 36360.	
36362	11472	Mary Anne Murray.	
36363	11473	Georgina Helen, widow of Thomas Walton Campbell, *of Walton Park, Kirkcudbright,* –1893.	Daughters.
36364	11474	Augusta Campbell Murray.	
36365	11475	Charlotte Joanna, widow of Colonel Robert Stewart, *of Ardvorlich,* 1829–1882.	
36366	11476	Charlotte Stewart. } Granddaughter. Daughter *Ardvorlich, Lochearnhead, Perth.* of No. 36365.	
36367 –68	}	Same as Nos. 36331–36332. { Grandchildren. Children of Frances Amelia Jemima Murray, 1843–1874, 1st wife of Sir Patrick Keith Murray, 8th Bart.	
36369	11477	Isabella Louisa, widow of Captain J. G. Reddie, R.N. *Redhouse, co. Fife.* } Daughter	
36370	11478	John Murray Reddie, Captain Worcester Regiment, 1872.	Grandchildren. Children of No. 36369.
36371	11479	Anthony Julian Reddie, Captain South Wales Borderers, 1873.	
36372	11480	Wilhelmina, wife of John Stephens Blackett, C.E. *Inverard, Aberfoyle, N.B.* } Youngest daughter.	
36373	11481	John Patrick Murray Blackett, 1868. } Grandchildren. Children of No. 36372.	
36374	11482	Frances Charlotte Isabella Blackett, 1870.	

884. Descendants of Charlotte Elizabeth Murray, 1806–1892, and her husband, the Rev. Arthur Isham, Rector of Weston Turville, Bucks, 1809–1892. (See Table CXXXI.)

36375	11483	Vere Arthur Richard Isham, 1889.	*The Elms, Hillmorton, Rugby.*	Grandchildren. Children of Arthur Charles Isham, 1847–1897.
36376	11484	Henry Euseby Murray Isham, 1895.		
36377	11485	Dorothy Evelyn Vere Isham, 1888.		
36378	11486	Elizabeth Mary Victoria Isham, 1891.		
36379	11487	Anna Isham.		Daughter.

885. Descendants of Anthony Murray, of Dollerie, 1802–1884. (See Table CXXXI.)

36380 –94	}	Same as Nos. 36360–36374.

886. Descendants of Alexander Murray, C.M.G., Director of the Geological Survey of Newfoundland, 1811– . (See Table CXXXI.)

36395	11488	Anthony Hepburn Murray, Major-General *late* R.A., 1840. *The Pines, Camberley, Surrey.*	} Son.
36396	11489	Alexander Radcliffe Hepburn Murray, 1872.	} Grandchildren. Children of No. 36395.
36397	11490	Minnie Murray, 1873.	
36398	11491	Nellie Violet Murray, 1876.	
36399	11492	William Edmund Logan Murray, 1872.	
36400	11493	Alexander Græme Murray, 1876.	
36401	11494	Helen, wife of Bernard Fabricotti.	} Children.
36402	11495	. . . . Murray.	
36403	11496	Georgina Isabella Mary Logan Murray, 1869.	
36404	11497	Frances Augusta Murray, 1870.	
36405	11498	Alice Oliphant Murray, 1874.	

887. Descendants,[1] if any, of Joan Murray, wife (1769) of Colonel John Churchill. (See Table CXXXI.)

888. Descendants of Amelia Murray, wife (1731) of John Murray, of Lintrose. (See Table CXXXI.)

889. Descendants of Sir David Moncreiffe, 6th Bart., 1788–1830. (See Table CXXXII.)

36406	11499	Sir Robert Drummond Moncreiffe, 8th Bart., 1856. *Moncreiffe House, Bridge of Earn, Perthshire.* 16 *Hertfort Street, Mayfair.*	} Grandchild. Eldest son of Sir Thomas Moncreiffe, 7th Bart., 1822–1879.
36407	11500	John Robert Grey Moncreiffe, 1884.	Great-grandchildren. Children of Thomas George Harry Moncreiffe, 1860–1887, brother of No. 36406.
36408	11501	Thomas Gerald Auckland Moncreiffe, 1886.	
36409	11502	William Moncreiffe, 1863. *Moncreiffe House, Bridge of Earn, N.B.*	} Grandchildren. Brothers to No. 36406.
36410	11503	Ronald Moncreiffe, Captain Worcestershire Yeomanry Cavalry, 1864. *Turf; Marlborough; Bachelors'.*	
36411	11504	Malcolm Moncreiffe, 1866. *Bachelors'.*	
36412	11505	John Alexander Moncreiffe, 1871.	
36413 –18	}	Same as Nos. 20947–20952.	Great-grandchildren. Children of Louisa Moncreiffe, –1902, wife of John James, 8th Duke of Atholl, K.T.
36419	11506	Helen, Lady Forbes, widow of Sir Charles John Forbes, 4th Bart. of Newe, 1843–1884. 5 *St. George's Sqaure, S.W.*	} Granddaughter. Sister to No. 36406.

[1] They had one son, Charles Churchill, who married an Arab lady, by whom he had two daughters, who cannot now be traced.

36420	11507	Sir Charles Stewart Forbes, 5th Bart., 1867. *28 Queen's Gate Terrace, S.W.*	} Great-grandchild. Son of No. 36419.
36421	11508	John Stewart Forbes, 1901.	} Great-great-grandchildren. Children of No. 36420.
36422	11509	Evelyn Marjorie Forbes, 1892.	
36423	11510	Katherine Manuella Bettine Forbes, 1897.	
36424	11511	Bridget Roberta Forbes, 1899.	
36425	11512	Evelyn Elizabeth, wife of William James. *West Dean Park, Chichester.* *14 Great Stanhope Street, S.W.*	} Great-grandchildren. Daughters of No. 36419.
36426	11513	Helen Blanche, wife of John Blundell Leigh, D.L. *29 St James' Place, S.W.*	
36427	11514	Mabel Susan, Baroness St. Oswald [U.K.]. *11 Grosvenor Gardens, S.W.*	
36428	11515	Hon. Rowland George Winn, 1893.	} Great-great-grandchildren. Children of No. 36427.
36429	11516	Hon. Charles John Frederick Winn, 1896.	
36430	11517	Hon. Reginald Henry Winn, 1899.	
36431	11518	Hon. Edith Victoria Blanche Winn, 1895.	
36432	11519	Georgiana Elizabeth, Countess of Dudley [U.K.], Baroness Ward [E.]. *Pembroke Lodge, Richmond, Surrey.*	} Granddaughter. Sister to No. 36406.
36433 -44	}	Same as Nos. 26873–26884.	{ Great-grandchildren. Children of No. 36432.
36445	11520	Harriet Sarah, Lady Mordaunt.	{ Granddaughter. Sister to No. 36406, &c.
36446 -49	}	Same as Nos. 31678–31681.	{ Great-granddaughter, &c. Daughter, &c., of No. 36445.
36450	11521	Blanche, wife of Charles Archibald Murray. *Taymount, Stanley, Perthshire.* *4c Bickenhall Mansions, Gloucester Place, W.*	} Granddaughter. Sister to No. 36406.
36451	11522	Charles John Murray, 1881.	} Great-grandchildren. Children of No. 36450.
36452	11523	Gertrude Blanche Murray.	
36453	11524	Edith Lilian Murray.	
36454	11525	Frances Rose, Lady Muir-Mackenzie, wife of Sir Alexander Muir-Mackenzie, 3rd Bart. of Delvine. *Delvine, Dunkeld.*	} Granddaughter. Sister to No. 36406.
36455	11526	Gerald Archibald Arbuthnot, 1872. *Hollingbourne Manor, near Maidstone.*	{ Great-grandson. Son of Selina Moncreiffe, –1877 (sister to No. 36406), 2nd wife of General William Arbuthnot, C.B., 1838–1893.
36456	11527	Frances Gertrude Arbuthnot.	} Great-great-grandchildren. Children of No. 36455.
36457	11528	Cynthia Isabella Theresa Arbuthnot.	
36458	11529	Dorothea Helen Mary Arbuthnot.	
36459	11530	Mary Catherine, wife of Sir Basil Templer Graham-Montgomery, 4th Bart. *Stobo Castle, Peeblesshire.*	} Granddaughter. Sister to No. 36406.
36460	11531	Walter Basil Graham-Montgomery, 1881.	{ Great-grandchildren. Children of No. 36459.
36461	11532	Lena Graham-Montgomery.	
36462	11533	William Eneas Moncreiffe, 1825.	Son.
36463	11534	Charles Henry Wright, J.P., 1851. *Halston Hall, Oswestry.* (And others.)	{ Grandchildren. Children of Helen Moncreiffe, – 1874, wife of Captain Edmund Wright, of Halston Hall, Salop, J.P.
36464	11535	Elizabeth Moncreiffe.	Daughter.

890. Descendants of Georgina Moncreiffe, 1790–1842, 1st wife of
George Augustus, 2nd Earl of Bradford, 1789–1865. (See
Table CXXXII.)

36465 –521	}	Same as Nos. 30459–30515.

891. Descendants of Robert Graham, 14th of Fintry, 1816–1887.
(See Table CXXXIII.)

36522	11536	John James Graham, 15th of Fintry, 1847. *Newlands, Cape Town, South Africa.*	} Son.
36523	11537	Robert Graham, Younger of Fintry, 1877.	
36524	11538	James Mackay Graham, 1879.	
36525	11539	Malise Patrick Graham, 1885.	Grandchildren.
36526	11540	Cosmo Murray Graham, 1887.	Children of
36527	11541	Ronald David Graham, 1892.	No. 36522.
36528	11542	Ethel Jane Graham.	
36529	11543	Marion Kinloch Graham.	
36530	11544	Elysoun Douglas Graham.	Grandchild. Daughter of Robert Dundas Graham, –1894.
36531	11545	Francis George Cathcart Graham.	2nd surviving son.
36532	11546	Kenneth Graham.	Grandchildren. Children
36533	11547	Dorothy Graham.	of No. 36531.
36534	11548	Thomas Lyndoch Graham, Barrister-at-Law of the Inner Temple, and Advocate at the Cape.	3rd surviving son.
36535	11549	. . . . Graham.	Grandchildren. Sons
36536	11550	. . . . Graham.	and daughter of
36537	11551	. . . . Graham.	No. 36534.
36538	11552	Malcolm David Graham, Captain Northants Regiment, 1865.	4th surviving son.
36539	11553	John Alexander Graham, 1898.	Grandson. Son of No. 36538.
36540	11554	Mary Cathcart, wife of Hercules Tennant, Barristerat-Law, J.P. *Buona Vista, Wynberg, Cape Colony.*	
36541	11555	Jane Leith Hay, wife of Major Alexander Wilson, Argyll and Sutherland Highlanders.	
36542	11556	Roberta, widow of Lieutenant Edward Chamley Turner, –1892.	
36543	11557	Helen Lilias, wife of Captain Andrew Aytoun, Argyll and Sutherland Highlanders.	Daughters.
36544	11558	Margaret Elizabeth Keay, wife of Captain T. A. Scott, Argyll and Sutherland Highlanders.	
36545	11559	Caroline Isabella, wife of Captain H. L. Orde, East Yorks. Regiment.	
36546	11560	Albinia Helen Graham.	

892. Descendants, if any, of Isabella Graham,   –   , wife of
Sebastian Vaurenen, of High Constantia, Cape of Good
Hope,   –   . (See Table CXXXIII.)

893. Descendants of Anne Brodrick, wife of the Rev. William Pennefather, Rector of Callan, Ossory, 1811–1870. (See Table CXXXIII.)

36547	11561	Edward Graham Pennefather, Lieut.-Col. Inniskilling Dragoons, 1850.	
36548	11562	Mary Alice Pennefather.	
36549	11563	Margaret Susan Pennefather.	Children.
36550	11564	Florence Anne Pennefather.	
36551	11565	Ellen Isabella Pennefather.	
36552	11566	Agnes Elizabeth Pennefather.	

894. Descendants of Mary Elizabeth Brodrick, –1864, 1st wife of the Right Rev. Edmund Hobhouse, D.D., Bishop of Nelson, in New Zealand, 1817– . (See Table CXXXIII.)

36553	11567	Edmund Hobhouse, 1860.	Wells, Somerset.	Children.
36554	11568	Walter Hobhouse, 1862.		

895. Descendants of Helen Christian Graham, 1790–1871, wife of the Hon. Henry Cloete, LL.D., 1790–1870. (See Table CXXXIII.)

36555	11569	Peter Voltelyn Cloete, 1844.	
36556	11570	Henry Graham Cloete, 1845.	
36557	11571	William Brodrick Cloete, M.A., Captain West Somerset Imperial Yeomanry, Hare Park, Bottisham, Cambs.	Grandchildren. Children of Peter Lawrence Graham Cloete, 1817–1871.
36558	11572	Alexander Josias Cloete, 1855.	
36559	11573	Helen Elizabeth Cloete, 1856.	
36560	11574	Montrose Seeraas Cloete, 1860.	
36561	11575	Celine Euphemia Cloete, 1862.	
36562	11576	William James Dundas Cloete, 1823. Children of General Henry Daniel Cloete, 1829–1895 (son).	Son.
36563	11577	Charlotte Sophia, wife of General Woodbine Parish, 1828.	Daughter.
		Children of Helen Gehardine Cloete, 1832–1879 (daughter), wife of General Coreyra Romer, R.A.	
		Children of Anne Caroline Graham Cloete, 1836–1879 (daughter), wife of General Joshua Smith, R.E.	

896. Descendants of Graham Bower, of Kincaldrum, 17 –1844. (See Table CXXXIII.)

36564	11578	Sir Graham John Bower, Captain R.N., K.C.M.G., 1848. Reduit, Mauritius.	Grandson. Son of Admiral James P. Bower, 18 – 18 .
36565	11579	James Graham Bower, 1884.	Great-grandchildren. Children of No. 36564.
36566	11580	John Graham Bower, 1886.	
36567	11581	Maud Mary Bower.	
36568	11582	Hamilton St. Clair Bower, Lieut.-Col. Pekin.	Grandson. Brother to No. 36564.

36569	11583	Mary Hamilton Bower. }	Great-grandchildren. Daughters
36570	11584	Jean Ainslie Bower. }	of No. 36568.
36571	11585	John Alexander Bower, M.B.C.M.	{ Grandson. Brother to { No. 36564.
36572	11586	John Bower. }	Great-grandchildren. Children
36573	11587	Marjorie Bower. }	of No. 36571.
36574	11588	Barbara St. Clair, wife of the Rev. James } Farquhar.	Grandchild. Sister } to No. 36564.
36575	11589	Barbara Farquhar. }	
36576	11590	Margaret Farquhar. }	Great-grandchildren. Children
36577	11591	Elsie Farquhar. }	of No. 36574.
36578	11592	Jean Farquhar. }	
36579	11593	Emily St. Clair Bower. } *North Berwick.*	Grandchild. Younger sister } to No. 36564.
36580	11594	John Bower, Lieut.-Col. *late* Indian Army, 1809. *Steedwell Lodge, Droxford, Hants.*	3rd but only sur-} viving son.
36581	11595	Francis Walter Balfour, J.P., D.L., Major *late* Rifle Brigade, 1830. *Fernie Castle, Collessie.*	{ Grandson. Son of Margaret { Georgina Bower, 18 – { 1853, wife of Francis { Balfour of Fernie Castle, { –1854.
36582	11596	Francis Balfour, J.P., 1867. *Kindrogan, Perth.*	Great-grandchildren. Chil-} dren of No. 36581.
36583	11597	William Keir Balfour, 1869.	
36584	11598	. . . . Balfour.	{ Great-grandchildren. Son and daughter { of Lieutenant James Bower Balfour, { R.N., 1832–1864, brother to No. 36581.
36585	11599	. . . . Balfour.	

897. Descendants of Margaret St. Clair Bower, 17 –18 , wife of Patrick Carnegy, of Lour, 1757–1819. (See Table CXXXIII.)

36586	11600	Patrick Alexander Watson Carnegy, J.P., D.L., *late* Captain 15th Hussars, 1836. *Lour, Forfar.*	Grandson. Son of Patrick } Watson Carnegy, of Lour, } 1791–1838.
36587	11601	Isabella Eliza Butter, wife of Francis Edward Joseph. *Sydney, New South Wales.*	Great-grandchild. Daughter of Pat-} rick Carnegy, C.I.E., I.C.S., 1825–} 1886, and granddaughter of Major-} General Alexander Carnegy, C.B., } 1793–1862.
36588	11602	Charles Gilbert Carnegy, Captain I.S.C., 1864.	{ Great-grandchild. Son of General { Alexander Carnegy,C.B.,1829–18 , { and grandson of Major-General Alex-} ander Carnegy, C.B., 1793–1862.
36589	11603	Patrick Charles Alexander Car-} negy, 1896.	Great-great-grandchild. Son } of No. 36588.
36590	11604	Rev. Frederick Carnegy, 1865. *Eardisley, Hereford.*	Great-grandchildren. } Brothers to No. } 36588.
36591	11605	Harry George Carnegy, Captain I.S.C.	
36592	11606	Frederick Alexander Carnegy, 1895. }	Great-great-grandchildren.
36593	11607	Eileen Augusta Carnegy. }	Children of No. 36591.
36594	11608	Augusta Ker, wife of James F. T. } Hathornthwaite, M.A.	Great-grandchild. Sister to } No. 36588.

36595	11609	Mary Ann, widow of Major-General John Richardson Auldjo, –1879.	Granddaughters. Daughters of Major-General Alexander Carnegy, C.B., 1793–1862.
36596	11610	Georgina, widow of Major Edward Robert Bigsby Barnes, 35th Regiment, –1880.	
36597	11611	Isabella, widow of James Wilkie, –1871.	
36598	11612	Patrick Adrian Carnegy (if alive), 1818.	Grandson. Son of James Carnegy, 1794–1821.
36599	11613	Charles William Carnegy, 1839.	Grandsons. Children of Charles Carnegy, E.I.C. (Naval Service), 1808–1874.
36600	11614	Alexander St. Clair Bower Carnegy, 1846.	
36601	11615	Patrick Lewis St. Clair Carnegy, 1875.	Great-grandchildren. Children of No. 36600.
36602	11616	Elizabeth Mary Carnegy.	
36603	11617	James Souter Carnegy, 1847.	Grandchildren. Brothers and sisters to No. 36599.
36604	11618	Robert Bower Carnegy, 1849.	
36605	11619	Margaret Ann Ogilvy Carnegy.	
36606	11620	Alison Anne Carnegy.	
36607	11621	Wilhelmina Sophia Carnegy.	
36608	11622	Mary Augusta Hamilton Carnegy.	
		Children, if any, of Ann Carnegy (daughter), Souter.	–1870, wife of James
		Children of Helen Carnegy (daughter), Lieut.-Col. James Gardner.	–1832, wife (1832) of

898. Descendants of Ellen Fletcher Bower, –1847, wife of Anthony Murray, of Dollerie, –1838. (See Table CXXXIII.)

36609 –34	}	Same as Nos. 36380–36405.

899. Descendants of Catherine Bower, –18 , wife of Hogg. (See Table CXXXIII.)

36635	11623	Emily Hogg.	Daughters.
36636	11624	Augusta Hogg.	
36637	11625	Lydia, wife of Major Twining.	

900. Descendants of William Douglas, of Brigton, 1803–1869. (See Table CXXXIV.)

36638	11626	William Charles Douglas, D.S.O., J.P., Lieut.-Col. 3rd 'Battalion Cameronians (Scottish Rifles), Commissioner of Supply, 1862. *Brigton, Douglastown, near Forfar.*	Elder son.
36639	11627	Marion Ellen Douglas, 1893.	Grandchildren. Children of No. 36638.
36640	11628	Jeannette Elizabeth Edith Grizel Douglas, 1894.	
36641	11629	Margaret Euphram Duguid Douglas, 1898.	
36642	11630	Marjorie Alison Hutchison Douglas, 1899.	
36643	11631	Robert John Douglas, 1864.	Younger son and only daughter.
36644	11632	Mary Ellen, wife of Joseph Irvin, 1866.	
36645	11633	Ardern Douglas Irvin, 1889.	Grandchildren. Children of No. 36644.
36646	11634	Muiri Douglas Irvin, 1892.	

901. Descendants of Major Archibald Murray Douglas, 1790–18 . (See Table CXXXIV.)

36647	11635	Mary, widow of Captain James Cox, 92nd Highlanders, 1818. *Highcliffe, Lympstone.*	Only surviving child.
36648	11636	Mary Wedderburn, wife of Dr. Watt Black. 15 *Clarges Street, Piccadilly, W.*	Granddaughter. Eldest daughter of No. 36647.
36649	11637	Evelyn Mary Watt Black, 1870.	Great-grandchildren. Children of No. 36648.
36650	11638	Merriel Douglas Watt Black, 1877.	
36651	11639	Archibald Evans, R.A., 1879.	*Cantref Rectory, Brecon.*
36652	11640	Christopher Douglas Evans, 23rd Fusiliers, 1881.	Great-grandchildren. Children of Elizabeth Douglas Cox, 1849 – 1894, 2nd daughter of No. 36647, and her husband, the Rev. John T. Evans, of Cantref.
36653	11641	Mary Dorothea Evans, 1875.	
36654	11642	Eleanor Nesté Evans, 1878.	
36655	11643	Emily Margaret, wife of David Evans. *Ffrwdgrech, Brecon.*	Grandchild. 3rd daughter of No. 36647.
36656	11644	John D. Douglas Evans, 1881.	Great-grandchildren. Children of No. 36655.
36657	11645	J. W. Douglas Evans, 1884.	
36658	11646	H. K. Douglas Evans, 1886.	
36659	11647	Mary Violet Douglas Evans, 1878.	
36660	11648	Mabel Jane Evans, 1880.	
36661	11649	Amy Margaret Evans, 1883.	
36662	11650	Ida Guinevere Evans, 1887.	
36663	11651	Phœbe Evans, 1891.	
36664	11652	Jane Fanny Cox.	*Highcliffe, Lympstone, near Exeter.*
36665	11653	Anne Wedderburn Cox.	Granddaughters. 4th, 5th, and 6th daughters of No. 36647.
36666	11654	Elise, wife of Anthony Miers. *Gilston Talybout - on - Usk, South Wales.*	
36667	11655	J. Hanmer Miers, 1st Dragoon Guards, 1882.	Great-grandchildren. Children of No. 36666.
36668	11656	Mary Gertrude Miers, 1889.	
36669	11657	James Harries, 1890.	Great-grandchildren. Children of Louisa Rose Cox, 1858–1886, 7th daughter of No. 36647, wife of Gilbert Harries,
36670	11658	Ruby Harries, 1877.	
36671	11659	Elsie Mary Harries, 1888.	
36672	11660	Mary G. Rose Harries, 1892.	
36673	11661	Gertrude, wife of Captain E. J. Crowther, R.M.L.J.	Granddaughter. 8th daughter of No. 36647.
36674	11662	Douglas W. Gertrude Crowther, 1897.	Great-granddaughter. Child of No. 36673.

902. Descendants of Major William Hunter, of Burnside, Forfarshire, 1797–18 . (See Table CXXXIV.)

36675	11663	William George Hunter, of Burnside, Captain in the Army, 1847. *Huningham, Leamington.*	Grandson. Son of David Hunter, of Burnside, 1822–1847.

36676	11664	George Graham Guthrie Hunter.	
36677	11665	Charles Gawen Hunter.	
36678	11666	William Archibald Hunter.	
36679	11667	Robert Bruce Hunter.	
36680	11668	Mary Douglas Hunter.	Great-grandchildren. Children of No. 36675.
36681	11669	Kathleen Wemyss Hunter.	
36682	11670	Barbara Gordon Hunter.	
36683	11671	Joyce Allison Hunter.	
36684	11672	Lilian Murray Hunter.	
36685	11673	Helen Fraser Hunter.	
36686	11674	Carsina Gordon Gray. *Carse Gray House, co. Forfar.*	Great-granddaughter. Daughter of Charles William Gray, 1851–1884, and granddaughter of Captain William Hunter, *afterwards* Gray of Carse Gray, –1881.
36687	11675	Francis Hunter.	
36688	11676	Walter Gordon Hunter, Captain *late* 65th Regiment.	Grandchildren. Children of Captain William Hunter, *afterwards* Gray. (*See above.*)
36689	11677	William Maude Ramsay Hunter.	
36690	11678	Carsina, wife of Captain Legay, of the French Army.	
36691	11679	Mary, wife of H. Harrison.	
36692	11680	John Hunter.	
36693	11681	Mary, wife of Colonel E. Townshend.	Son and daughter.
36694	11682	William Townshend.	Grandson. Son of No. 36693.
36695	11683	Marton Townshend.	Great-grandchildren. Children of No. 36694.
36696	11684	Darcy Townshend.	
36697	11685	Hugh Townshend.	
36698	11686	John Farrington.	Grandchildren. Children of Margaret Douglas Hunter, 18 –18 , wife of Colonel Olaus Farrington.
36699	11687	Douglas Farrington.	

903. Descendants of Margaret Hunter, –18 , wife of Kirwan, –18 . (See Table CXXXIV.)

36700	11688	Margaret Kirwan.	Children.
36701	11689	Mattie, wife of Major Forbes Robertson.	

904. Descendants of John Guthrie, of Guthrie, D.L., 1805–1877. (See Table CXXXIV.)

36702	11690	John Douglas Maude Guthrie, Lord of the Barony of Guthrie, Captain *late* 19th Hussars, 1856. *Guthrie Castle, Guthrie, co. Forfar.*	Son.
36703	11691	John Neil Guthrie, 1885.	
36704	11692	Ivan Douglas Guthrie, 1886.	
36705	11693	Rupert Victor Davidson Guthrie, 1887.	Grandchildren. Children of No. 36702.
36706	11694	Duncan Nigel Guthrie, 1891.	
36707	11695	Maurice Guthrie, 1894.	
36708	11696	Mary Viola Guthrie.	
36709	11697	Harriet Maude, wife of Captain Arthur W. M'Kinstry, Leicester Regiment. 49 *Waverley Road, Southsea.*	Eldest daughter.

36710	11698	Alexander M'Kinstrey, 1883.
36711	11699	Arthur M'Kinstrey, 1884.
36712	11700	Ronald M'Kinstrey, 1892.
36713	11701	Maud M'Kinstrey.
36714	11702	Jean M'Kinstrey.
36715	11703	Edith Douglas Guthrie.
36716	11704	Mary Berthia, wife of Col. Duncan M'Neill, Madras Staff Corps. *The Corran, Larne, co. Antrim.*
36717	11705	John Guthrie M'Neill, 1878.
36718	11706	Malcolm Douglas M'Neill, 1886.
36719	11707	Lucy Edith M'Neill.

Grandchildren. Children of No. 36709.

Younger daughters.

Grandchildren. Children of No. 36716.

905. Descendants of Elizabeth Jane Guthrie, 1790–1839, wife of Thomas Mylne, of Mylnefield, 1785–1836. (See Table CXXXIV.)

36720	11708	General William Charles Robert Mylne, 1827. *Stangrove Park, Eden Bridge, Kent.*
36721	11709	William Hansbrow Mylne, 1861.
36722	11710	Arbuthnot Mackenzie Mylne, 1866.
36723	11711	Elizabeth Douglas Mylne, 1859.
36724	11712	Graham Ernest Mylne, 1866.
36725	11713	Thomas Herbert Mylne, 1869.
36726	11714	Anne Douglas Mylne, 1862.
36727	11715	Ethel Maude, wife of William Ogilvie, 1864. *Tulgilbae, New South Wales.*
36728	11716	Helena Mylne, 1871.
36729	11717	Nina Beatrice Mylne, 1873.

Son.

Grandchildren. Children of No. 36720.

Grandchildren. Children of Graham Mylne, 1834–1876.

906. Descendants of Helen Douglas Guthrie, 1814–1898, wife of John de Havilland Utermarck, The Bailiff of Guernsey, 1819–1884. (See Table CXXXIV.)

36730	11718	Reginald John Guthrie Utermarck, Major in the Army, 1856. *Vimiera, Guernsey.*
36731	11719	Ann Douglas, wife of James Forbes Chisholm-Batten, Lieut.-Col., *late* Captain 34th Regiment, 1851. *Kirkhill, co. Inverness.* *Thornfalcon, near Taunton.*
36732	11720	James Utermarck Chisholm-Batten, 1884.
36733	11721	Edmund Rodolphe Chisholm-Batten, 1887.
36734	11722	John de Havilland Chisholm-Batten, 1889.
36735	11723	Helen Douglas Guthrie Utermarck, 1853. *Guernsey.*

Children.

Grandchildren. Children of No. 36731.

Younger daughter.

907. Descendants,[1] if any, of Clinton Stanley (baptized at Chelsea, September 19), 1654– . (See Table CIV.)

---

[1] Would be entitled to quarter the royal arms.

CORRIGENDA AND ADDENDA

TABLE LIX.—In the *Complete Peerage*, under "Carhampton," vol. ii. p. 147, is the following footnote: "In a Tasmanian newspaper is notice of the death, on February 23, 1886, in his 65th year, 'At his residence, Somerset Cottage, Bellerive, [of] Edward Hungerford [Luttrell], eldest son of the late Edgar Luttrell, of H.M.'s Customs, and grandson of the late Edward Luttrell, late Surgeon-General of Tasmania, and EARL of CARHAMPTON.'" *Ex inform.* Justice Browne, Lord's Place, Hobart, Tasmania, who adds, "Mr. E H. Luttrell has been my tenant for many years; his grandfather, Dr. Luttrell, having the bar sinister, could not claim the Earldom, though it was always known that he was an offshoot of the family."

The use of "Hungerford" as a Christian name rather suggests that he more probably belonged to this branch of the family.

TABLE LXXIII.—Insert among children of Sir John Wrottesley, 4th Bart.,

Frances Wrottesley = Heigham Bendish of
         | East Ham, Essex.
         ?

TABLE LXXVIII.—Insert as eldest son of Frances Ward and Robert Pigott, "Robert Pigott of Chetwynd." He died 1770, leaving by his wife Anne Piers, two sons, (1) Robert Pigott of Chetwynd, who sold Chetwynd and died abroad, 1794, having had a son who *d. v. p.* ; (2) Rev. William Pigott of Edgmond, who, by his wife, Arabella Mytton, was grandfather of the Rev. George William Corbet, formerly Pigott, now of Sundorne Castle. See *Burke's Extinct Peerage.*

60–75, for "20–35" read "20–34."

TABLE LXXXI.—Frances Noel *m.* 2ndly (1690) Ralph Sneyd of Bradwell, 1660–1 , and had further issue : (1) Ralph Sneyd of Keele, &c., M.P., 1692–1733, ancestor of the present Ralph Sneyd of Keele, J.P. ; and (2) Honora Sneyd, wife of Sir Eusebius Buswell, Bart.

6051 has a son, Prince Alexander Edward Christian Frederick of Denmark, born 1903.

19616 has a son and heir, Edward Arthur Henry, Lord Silchester, 1902.

19824 should read, "Charles, 4th Earl of [U.K.] and 6th Baron [G.B.] Romney, 1841.'

21815 should now read, "Charles Henry Chandos, 6th Baron Henniker [I.], 3rd Baron Hartismere [U.K.], 1872."

22325 has a daughter, Lady Ursula Mary Olivia Grosvenor, 1902.

22338–22339 should read, "Son and eldest daughter."

After No. 23009 insert as under :—

268a. Descendants of Lady Anne Cavendish, 1787–1871, and her husband, Lord Charles FitzRoy, P.C., 1791–1865. (See Table XLI.)

23009ᵃ	3928ᵃ	Harold Charles Cavendish FitzRoy, 1870. *Woodlawn, Northwood, Middlesex.*	} Grandson. Son of Major Cavendish Charles Fitz-Roy, 1833–1894.
23009ᵇ	3928ᵇ	Charles Cavendish FitzRoy, 1900.	} Great-grandchildren. Chil-
23009ᶜ	3928ᶜ	Mary Georgina Anne FitzRoy, 1897.	dren of No. 23009a.

23009ᵈ	3928ᵈ	Anne Isobel, widow of Arthur Charles Hecht, –1901, 1861. 23 *Brandreth Road, Upper Tooting, S. W.*	Grandchild. Sister to No. 23009a.
23009ᵉ	3928ᵉ	Charles FitzRoy Hecht, 1895.	Great-grandchild. Son of No. 23009d.
23009ᶠ	3928ᶠ	Elizabeth Mary, widow of Henry Lee Steere, –1899, 1826. *The Cottage, Ockley, Surrey.*	Elder daughter.
23009ᵍ	3928ᵍ	Henry Charles Lee Steere, 1859. Grandson.	Son of No. 23009f.
23009ʰ	3928ʰ	John Henry Gordon Lee Steere, 1895.	Great-grandchild. Son of No. 23009g.
23009ⁱ	3928ⁱ	Maria Georgina Anne FitzRoy, 1829. *St. George's Bank, East Moulsey.*	Younger daughter.

23116 died 1902.

23117, read " Sir Henry Edward Paston-Bedingfeld, 8th Bart., &c."

23301, for " Stuart " read " Sturt."

After 25986 insert " Frances Amy Newdigate, youngest sister of Nos. 25979–25986."

26322–26327, read " Same as Nos. 25835–25840."

Section 458.—The following probably relate to this line, " Her Excellency the Baroness Keetzleben, a daughter."—*Hibernian Magazine*, December 1782. " 10th October, Lieut.-Col. William (Baron) Keetzleben, at Berhampore, Madras."—*West India List, Deaths,* 1845.

Section 459.—Harriet Wrottesley and General William Gardiner had a son, Charles, sometime on his father's staff in America, and (1810) aide-de-camp to the Duke of Richmond, Lord-Lieutenant of Ireland, and at least two daughters, the second of whom, Harriet Gardiner, *m.* 1805 Dr. Robert Patrick of Trearne, and had issue : (1) John Shedden Patrick, 1807–1844, father of the present William Ralston Patrick of Trearne, J.P.; (2) William Charles Richard Patrick, grandfather of the present Mrs. Eleanora Agnes Kennedy-Cochran-Patrick of Woodside.

29274–29279, omit names and read " Same as Nos. 21100–21105."

P. 447, line 14, for " Briene " read " Brieuc."

31593–31597, for " Renord " read " Renard," and add Christian names as follows : " Henry Ernest Aime Joseph, Michael Leon Felix, and Jane Gabrielle Amelia."

34151–34154, for " Lockart " read " Lockhart."

INDEX OF NAMES

Compound surnames are indexed under the first name. Those persons having two asterisks (**) before their names have Double the number of descents to those shown in the Index. The exact number of those other descents can be ascertained by adding 9786 to each of the numbers given. These duplicate descents are through the marriage of Mary Queen of Scots with Darnley.

567

Index

Index

Index

Index

Jndex

Jndex

Index

596

Index

Index

Index

Jndex

Index

620

THE END